Dictionary of Literary Biography

1 *The American Renaissance in New England,* edited by Joel Myerson (1978)

2 *American Novelists Since World War II,* edited by Jeffrey Helterman and Richard Layman (1978)

3 *Antebellum Writers in New York and the South,* edited by Joel Myerson (1979)

4 *American Writers in Paris, 1920–1939,* edited by Karen Lane Rood (1980)

5 *American Poets Since World War II,* 2 parts, edited by Donald J. Greiner (1980)

6 *American Novelists Since World War II, Second Series,* edited by James E. Kibler Jr. (1980)

7 *Twentieth-Century American Dramatists,* 2 parts, edited by John MacNicholas (1981)

8 *Twentieth-Century American Science-Fiction Writers,* 2 parts, edited by David Cowart and Thomas L. Wymer (1981)

9 *American Novelists, 1910–1945,* 3 parts, edited by James J. Martine (1981)

10 *Modern British Dramatists, 1900–1945,* 2 parts, edited by Stanley Weintraub (1982)

11 *American Humorists, 1800–1950,* 2 parts, edited by Stanley Trachtenberg (1982)

12 *American Realists and Naturalists,* edited by Donald Pizer and Earl N. Harbert (1982)

13 *British Dramatists Since World War II,* 2 parts, edited by Stanley Weintraub (1982)

14 *British Novelists Since 1960,* 2 parts, edited by Jay L. Halio (1983)

15 *British Novelists, 1930–1959,* 2 parts, edited by Bernard Oldsey (1983)

16 *The Beats: Literary Bohemians in Postwar America,* 2 parts, edited by Ann Charters (1983)

17 *Twentieth-Century American Historians,* edited by Clyde N. Wilson (1983)

18 *Victorian Novelists After 1885,* edited by Ira B. Nadel and William E. Fredeman (1983)

19 *British Poets, 1880–1914,* edited by Donald E. Stanford (1983)

20 *British Poets, 1914–1945,* edited by Donald E. Stanford (1983)

21 *Victorian Novelists Before 1885,* edited by Ira B. Nadel and William E. Fredeman (1983)

22 *American Writers for Children, 1900–1960,* edited by John Cech (1983)

23 *American Newspaper Journalists, 1873–1900,* edited by Perry J. Ashley (1983)

24 *American Colonial Writers, 1606–1734,* edited by Emory Elliott (1984)

25 *American Newspaper Journalists, 1901–1925,* edited by Perry J. Ashley (1984)

26 *American Screenwriters,* edited by Robert E. Morsberger, Stephen O. Lesser, and Randall Clark (1984)

27 *Poets of Great Britain and Ireland, 1945–1960,* edited by Vincent B. Sherry Jr. (1984)

28 *Twentieth-Century American-Jewish Fiction Writers,* edited by Daniel Walden (1984)

29 *American Newspaper Journalists, 1926–1950,* edited by Perry J. Ashley (1984)

30 *American Historians, 1607–1865,* edited by Clyde N. Wilson (1984)

31 *American Colonial Writers, 1735–1781,* edited by Emory Elliott (1984)

32 *Victorian Poets Before 1850,* edited by William E. Fredeman and Ira B. Nadel (1984)

33 *Afro-American Fiction Writers After 1955,* edited by Thadious M. Davis and Trudier Harris (1984)

34 *British Novelists, 1890–1929: Traditionalists,* edited by Thomas F. Staley (1985)

35 *Victorian Poets After 1850,* edited by William E. Fredeman and Ira B. Nadel (1985)

36 *British Novelists, 1890–1929: Modernists,* edited by Thomas F. Staley (1985)

37 *American Writers of the Early Republic,* edited by Emory Elliott (1985)

38 *Afro-American Writers After 1955: Dramatists and Prose Writers,* edited by Thadious M. Davis and Trudier Harris (1985)

39 *British Novelists, 1660–1800,* 2 parts, edited by Martin C. Battestin (1985)

40 *Poets of Great Britain and Ireland Since 1960,* 2 parts, edited by Vincent B. Sherry Jr. (1985)

41 *Afro-American Poets Since 1955,* edited by Trudier Harris and Thadious M. Davis (1985)

42 *American Writers for Children Before 1900,* edited by Glenn E. Estes (1985)

43 *American Newspaper Journalists, 1690–1872,* edited by Perry J. Ashley (1986)

44 *American Screenwriters, Second Series,* edited by Randall Clark, Robert E. Morsberger, and Stephen O. Lesser (1986)

45 *American Poets, 1880–1945, First Series,* edited by Peter Quartermain (1986)

46 *American Literary Publishing Houses, 1900–1980: Trade and Paperback,* edited by Peter Dzwonkoski (1986)

47 *American Historians, 1866–1912,* edited by Clyde N. Wilson (1986)

48 *American Poets, 1880–1945, Second Series,* edited by Peter Quartermain (1986)

49 *American Literary Publishing Houses, 1638–1899,* 2 parts, edited by Peter Dzwonkoski (1986)

50 *Afro-American Writers Before the Harlem Renaissance,* edited by Trudier Harris (1986)

51 *Afro-American Writers from the Harlem Renaissance to 1940,* edited by Trudier Harris (1987)

52 *American Writers for Children Since 1960: Fiction,* edited by Glenn E. Estes (1986)

53 *Canadian Writers Since 1960, First Series,* edited by W. H. New (1986)

54 *American Poets, 1880–1945, Third Series,* 2 parts, edited by Peter Quartermain (1987)

55 *Victorian Prose Writers Before 1867,* edited by William B. Thesing (1987)

56 *German Fiction Writers, 1914–1945,* edited by James Hardin (1987)

57 *Victorian Prose Writers After 1867,* edited by William B. Thesing (1987)

58 *Jacobean and Caroline Dramatists,* edited by Fredson Bowers (1987)

59 *American Literary Critics and Scholars, 1800–1850,* edited by John W. Rathbun and Monica M. Grecu (1987)

60 *Canadian Writers Since 1960, Second Series,* edited by W. H. New (1987)

61 *American Writers for Children Since 1960: Poets, Illustrators, and Nonfiction Authors,* edited by Glenn E. Estes (1987)

62 *Elizabethan Dramatists,* edited by Fredson Bowers (1987)

63 *Modern American Critics, 1920–1955,* edited by Gregory S. Jay (1988)

64 *American Literary Critics and Scholars, 1850–1880,* edited by John W. Rathbun and Monica M. Grecu (1988)

65 *French Novelists, 1900–1930,* edited by Catharine Savage Brosman (1988)

66 *German Fiction Writers, 1885–1913,* 2 parts, edited by James Hardin (1988)

67 *Modern American Critics Since 1955,* edited by Gregory S. Jay (1988)

68 *Canadian Writers, 1920–1959, First Series,* edited by W. H. New (1988)

69 *Contemporary German Fiction Writers, First Series,* edited by Wolfgang D. Elfe and James Hardin (1988)

70 *British Mystery Writers, 1860–1919,* edited by Bernard Benstock and Thomas F. Staley (1988)

71 *American Literary Critics and Scholars, 1880–1900*, edited by John W. Rathbun and Monica M. Grecu (1988)

72 *French Novelists, 1930–1960*, edited by Catharine Savage Brosman (1988)

73 *American Magazine Journalists, 1741–1850*, edited by Sam G. Riley (1988)

74 *American Short-Story Writers Before 1880*, edited by Bobby Ellen Kimbel, with the assistance of William E. Grant (1988)

75 *Contemporary German Fiction Writers, Second Series*, edited by Wolfgang D. Elfe and James Hardin (1988)

76 *Afro-American Writers, 1940–1955*, edited by Trudier Harris (1988)

77 *British Mystery Writers, 1920–1939*, edited by Bernard Benstock and Thomas F. Staley (1988)

78 *American Short-Story Writers, 1880–1910*, edited by Bobby Ellen Kimbel, with the assistance of William E. Grant (1988)

79 *American Magazine Journalists, 1850–1900*, edited by Sam G. Riley (1988)

80 *Restoration and Eighteenth-Century Dramatists, First Series*, edited by Paula R. Backscheider (1989)

81 *Austrian Fiction Writers, 1875–1913*, edited by James Hardin and Donald G. Daviau (1989)

82 *Chicano Writers, First Series*, edited by Francisco A. Lomelí and Carl R. Shirley (1989)

83 *French Novelists Since 1960*, edited by Catharine Savage Brosman (1989)

84 *Restoration and Eighteenth-Century Dramatists, Second Series*, edited by Paula R. Backscheider (1989)

85 *Austrian Fiction Writers After 1914*, edited by James Hardin and Donald G. Daviau (1989)

86 *American Short-Story Writers, 1910–1945, First Series*, edited by Bobby Ellen Kimbel (1989)

87 *British Mystery and Thriller Writers Since 1940, First Series*, edited by Bernard Benstock and Thomas F. Staley (1989)

88 *Canadian Writers, 1920–1959, Second Series*, edited by W. H. New (1989)

89 *Restoration and Eighteenth-Century Dramatists, Third Series*, edited by Paula R. Backscheider (1989)

90 *German Writers in the Age of Goethe, 1789–1832*, edited by James Hardin and Christoph E. Schweitzer (1989)

91 *American Magazine Journalists, 1900–1960, First Series*, edited by Sam G. Riley (1990)

92 *Canadian Writers, 1890–1920*, edited by W. H. New (1990)

93 *British Romantic Poets, 1789–1832, First Series*, edited by John R. Greenfield (1990)

94 *German Writers in the Age of Goethe: Sturm und Drang to Classicism*, edited by James Hardin and Christoph E. Schweitzer (1990)

95 *Eighteenth-Century British Poets, First Series*, edited by John Sitter (1990)

96 *British Romantic Poets, 1789–1832, Second Series*, edited by John R. Greenfield (1990)

97 *German Writers from the Enlightenment to Sturm und Drang, 1720–1764*, edited by James Hardin and Christoph E. Schweitzer (1990)

98 *Modern British Essayists, First Series*, edited by Robert Beum (1990)

99 *Canadian Writers Before 1890*, edited by W. H. New (1990)

100 *Modern British Essayists, Second Series*, edited by Robert Beum (1990)

101 *British Prose Writers, 1660–1800, First Series*, edited by Donald T. Siebert (1991)

102 *American Short-Story Writers, 1910–1945, Second Series*, edited by Bobby Ellen Kimbel (1991)

103 *American Literary Biographers, First Series*, edited by Steven Serafin (1991)

104 *British Prose Writers, 1660–1800, Second Series*, edited by Donald T. Siebert (1991)

105 *American Poets Since World War II, Second Series*, edited by R. S. Gwynn (1991)

106 *British Literary Publishing Houses, 1820–1880*, edited by Patricia J. Anderson and Jonathan Rose (1991)

107 *British Romantic Prose Writers, 1789–1832, First Series*, edited by John R. Greenfield (1991)

108 *Twentieth-Century Spanish Poets, First Series*, edited by Michael L. Perna (1991)

109 *Eighteenth-Century British Poets, Second Series*, edited by John Sitter (1991)

110 *British Romantic Prose Writers, 1789–1832, Second Series*, edited by John R. Greenfield (1991)

111 *American Literary Biographers, Second Series*, edited by Steven Serafin (1991)

112 *British Literary Publishing Houses, 1881–1965*, edited by Jonathan Rose and Patricia J. Anderson (1991)

113 *Modern Latin-American Fiction Writers, First Series*, edited by William Luis (1992)

114 *Twentieth-Century Italian Poets, First Series*, edited by Giovanna Wedel De Stasio, Glauco Cambon, and Antonio Illiano (1992)

115 *Medieval Philosophers*, edited by Jeremiah Hackett (1992)

116 *British Romantic Novelists, 1789–1832*, edited by Bradford K. Mudge (1992)

117 *Twentieth-Century Caribbean and Black African Writers, First Series*, edited by Bernth Lindfors and Reinhard Sander (1992)

118 *Twentieth-Century German Dramatists, 1889–1918*, edited by Wolfgang D. Elfe and James Hardin (1992)

119 *Nineteenth-Century French Fiction Writers: Romanticism and Realism, 1800–1860*, edited by Catharine Savage Brosman (1992)

120 *American Poets Since World War II, Third Series*, edited by R. S. Gwynn (1992)

121 *Seventeenth-Century British Nondramatic Poets, First Series*, edited by M. Thomas Hester (1992)

122 *Chicano Writers, Second Series*, edited by Francisco A. Lomelí and Carl R. Shirley (1992)

123 *Nineteenth-Century French Fiction Writers: Naturalism and Beyond, 1860–1900*, edited by Catharine Savage Brosman (1992)

124 *Twentieth-Century German Dramatists, 1919–1992*, edited by Wolfgang D. Elfe and James Hardin (1992)

125 *Twentieth-Century Caribbean and Black African Writers, Second Series*, edited by Bernth Lindfors and Reinhard Sander (1993)

126 *Seventeenth-Century British Nondramatic Poets, Second Series*, edited by M. Thomas Hester (1993)

127 *American Newspaper Publishers, 1950–1990*, edited by Perry J. Ashley (1993)

128 *Twentieth-Century Italian Poets, Second Series*, edited by Giovanna Wedel De Stasio, Glauco Cambon, and Antonio Illiano (1993)

129 *Nineteenth-Century German Writers, 1841–1900*, edited by James Hardin and Siegfried Mews (1993)

130 *American Short-Story Writers Since World War II*, edited by Patrick Meanor (1993)

131 *Seventeenth-Century British Nondramatic Poets, Third Series*, edited by M. Thomas Hester (1993)

132 *Sixteenth-Century British Nondramatic Writers, First Series*, edited by David A. Richardson (1993)

133 *Nineteenth-Century German Writers to 1840*, edited by James Hardin and Siegfried Mews (1993)

134 *Twentieth-Century Spanish Poets, Second Series*, edited by Jerry Phillips Winfield (1994)

135 *British Short-Fiction Writers, 1880–1914: The Realist Tradition*, edited by William B. Thesing (1994)

136 *Sixteenth-Century British Nondramatic Writers, Second Series*, edited by David A. Richardson (1994)

137 *American Magazine Journalists, 1900–1960, Second Series*, edited by Sam G. Riley (1994)

138 *German Writers and Works of the High Middle Ages: 1170–1280*, edited by James Hardin and Will Hasty (1994)

139 *British Short-Fiction Writers, 1945–1980*, edited by Dean Baldwin (1994)

140 *American Book-Collectors and Bibliographers, First Series,* edited by Joseph Rosenblum (1994)

141 *British Children's Writers, 1880–1914,* edited by Laura M. Zaidman (1994)

142 *Eighteenth-Century British Literary Biographers,* edited by Steven Serafin (1994)

143 *American Novelists Since World War II, Third Series,* edited by James R. Giles and Wanda H. Giles (1994)

144 *Nineteenth-Century British Literary Biographers,* edited by Steven Serafin (1994)

145 *Modern Latin-American Fiction Writers, Second Series,* edited by William Luis and Ann González (1994)

146 *Old and Middle English Literature,* edited by Jeffrey Helterman and Jerome Mitchell (1994)

147 *South Slavic Writers Before World War II,* edited by Vasa D. Mihailovich (1994)

148 *German Writers and Works of the Early Middle Ages: 800–1170,* edited by Will Hasty and James Hardin (1994)

149 *Late Nineteenth- and Early Twentieth-Century British Literary Biographers,* edited by Steven Serafin (1995)

150 *Early Modern Russian Writers, Late Seventeenth and Eighteenth Centuries,* edited by Marcus C. Levitt (1995)

151 *British Prose Writers of the Early Seventeenth Century,* edited by Clayton D. Lein (1995)

152 *American Novelists Since World War II, Fourth Series,* edited by James R. Giles and Wanda H. Giles (1995)

153 *Late-Victorian and Edwardian British Novelists, First Series,* edited by George M. Johnson (1995)

154 *The British Literary Book Trade, 1700–1820,* edited by James K. Bracken and Joel Silver (1995)

155 *Twentieth-Century British Literary Biographers,* edited by Steven Serafin (1995)

156 *British Short-Fiction Writers, 1880–1914: The Romantic Tradition,* edited by William F. Naufftus (1995)

157 *Twentieth-Century Caribbean and Black African Writers, Third Series,* edited by Bernth Lindfors and Reinhard Sander (1995)

158 *British Reform Writers, 1789–1832,* edited by Gary Kelly and Edd Applegate (1995)

159 *British Short-Fiction Writers, 1800–1880,* edited by John R. Greenfield (1996)

160 *British Children's Writers, 1914–1960,* edited by Donald R. Hettinga and Gary D. Schmidt (1996)

161 *British Children's Writers Since 1960, First Series,* edited by Caroline Hunt (1996)

162 *British Short-Fiction Writers, 1915–1945,* edited by John H. Rogers (1996)

163 *British Children's Writers, 1800–1880,* edited by Meena Khorana (1996)

164 *German Baroque Writers, 1580–1660,* edited by James Hardin (1996)

165 *American Poets Since World War II, Fourth Series,* edited by Joseph Conte (1996)

166 *British Travel Writers, 1837–1875,* edited by Barbara Brothers and Julia Gergits (1996)

167 *Sixteenth-Century British Nondramatic Writers, Third Series,* edited by David A. Richardson (1996)

168 *German Baroque Writers, 1661–1730,* edited by James Hardin (1996)

169 *American Poets Since World War II, Fifth Series,* edited by Joseph Conte (1996)

170 *The British Literary Book Trade, 1475–1700,* edited by James K. Bracken and Joel Silver (1996)

171 *Twentieth-Century American Sportswriters,* edited by Richard Orodenker (1996)

172 *Sixteenth-Century British Nondramatic Writers, Fourth Series,* edited by David A. Richardson (1996)

173 *American Novelists Since World War II, Fifth Series,* edited by James R. Giles and Wanda H. Giles (1996)

174 *British Travel Writers, 1876–1909,* edited by Barbara Brothers and Julia Gergits (1997)

175 *Native American Writers of the United States,* edited by Kenneth M. Roemer (1997)

176 *Ancient Greek Authors,* edited by Ward W. Briggs (1997)

177 *Italian Novelists Since World War II, 1945–1965,* edited by Augustus Pallotta (1997)

178 *British Fantasy and Science-Fiction Writers Before World War I,* edited by Darren Harris-Fain (1997)

179 *German Writers of the Renaissance and Reformation, 1280–1580,* edited by James Hardin and Max Reinhart (1997)

180 *Japanese Fiction Writers, 1868–1945,* edited by Van C. Gessel (1997)

181 *South Slavic Writers Since World War II,* edited by Vasa D. Mihailovich (1997)

182 *Japanese Fiction Writers Since World War II,* edited by Van C. Gessel (1997)

183 *American Travel Writers, 1776–1864,* edited by James J. Schramer and Donald Ross (1997)

184 *Nineteenth-Century British Book-Collectors and Bibliographers,* edited by William Baker and Kenneth Womack (1997)

185 *American Literary Journalists, 1945–1995, First Series,* edited by Arthur J. Kaul (1998)

186 *Nineteenth-Century American Western Writers,* edited by Robert L. Gale (1998)

187 *American Book Collectors and Bibliographers, Second Series,* edited by Joseph Rosenblum (1998)

188 *American Book and Magazine Illustrators to 1920,* edited by Steven E. Smith, Catherine A. Hastedt, and Donald H. Dyal (1998)

189 *American Travel Writers, 1850–1915,* edited by Donald Ross and James J. Schramer (1998)

190 *British Reform Writers, 1832–1914,* edited by Gary Kelly and Edd Applegate (1998)

191 *British Novelists Between the Wars,* edited by George M. Johnson (1998)

192 *French Dramatists, 1789–1914,* edited by Barbara T. Cooper (1998)

193 *American Poets Since World War II, Sixth Series,* edited by Joseph Conte (1998)

194 *British Novelists Since 1960, Second Series,* edited by Merritt Moseley (1998)

195 *British Travel Writers, 1910–1939,* edited by Barbara Brothers and Julia Gergits (1998)

196 *Italian Novelists Since World War II, 1965–1995,* edited by Augustus Pallotta (1999)

197 *Late-Victorian and Edwardian British Novelists, Second Series,* edited by George M. Johnson (1999)

198 *Russian Literature in the Age of Pushkin and Gogol: Prose,* edited by Christine A. Rydel (1999)

199 *Victorian Women Poets,* edited by William B. Thesing (1999)

200 *American Women Prose Writers to 1820,* edited by Carla J. Mulford, with Angela Vietto and Amy E. Winans (1999)

201 *Twentieth-Century British Book Collectors and Bibliographers,* edited by William Baker and Kenneth Womack (1999)

202 *Nineteenth-Century American Fiction Writers,* edited by Kent P. Ljungquist (1999)

203 *Medieval Japanese Writers,* edited by Steven D. Carter (1999)

204 *British Travel Writers, 1940–1997,* edited by Barbara Brothers and Julia M. Gergits (1999)

205 *Russian Literature in the Age of Pushkin and Gogol: Poetry and Drama,* edited by Christine A. Rydel (1999)

206 *Twentieth-Century American Western Writers, First Series,* edited by Richard H. Cracroft (1999)

207 *British Novelists Since 1960, Third Series,* edited by Merritt Moseley (1999)

208 *Literature of the French and Occitan Middle Ages: Eleventh to Fifteenth Centuries,* edited by Deborah Sinnreich-Levi and Ian S. Laurie (1999)

209 *Chicano Writers, Third Series,* edited by Francisco A. Lomelí and Carl R. Shirley (1999)

210 *Ernest Hemingway: A Documentary Volume,* edited by Robert W. Trogdon (1999)

211 *Ancient Roman Writers,* edited by Ward W. Briggs (1999)

212 *Twentieth-Century American Western Writers, Second Series*, edited by Richard H. Cracroft (1999)

213 *Pre-Nineteenth-Century British Book Collectors and Bibliographers*, edited by William Baker and Kenneth Womack (1999)

214 *Twentieth-Century Danish Writers*, edited by Marianne Stecher-Hansen (1999)

215 *Twentieth-Century Eastern European Writers, First Series*, edited by Steven Serafin (1999)

216 *British Poets of the Great War: Brooke, Rosenberg, Thomas. A Documentary Volume*, edited by Patrick Quinn (2000)

217 *Nineteenth-Century French Poets*, edited by Robert Beum (2000)

218 *American Short-Story Writers Since World War II, Second Series*, edited by Patrick Meanor and Gwen Crane (2000)

219 *F. Scott Fitzgerald's The Great Gatsby: A Documentary Volume*, edited by Matthew J. Bruccoli (2000)

220 *Twentieth-Century Eastern European Writers, Second Series*, edited by Steven Serafin (2000)

221 *American Women Prose Writers, 1870–1920*, edited by Sharon M. Harris, with the assistance of Heidi L. M. Jacobs and Jennifer Putzi (2000)

222 *H. L. Mencken: A Documentary Volume*, edited by Richard J. Schrader (2000)

223 *The American Renaissance in New England, Second Series*, edited by Wesley T. Mott (2000)

224 *Walt Whitman: A Documentary Volume*, edited by Joel Myerson (2000)

225 *South African Writers*, edited by Paul A. Scanlon (2000)

226 *American Hard-Boiled Crime Writers*, edited by George Parker Anderson and Julie B. Anderson (2000)

227 *American Novelists Since World War II, Sixth Series*, edited by James R. Giles and Wanda H. Giles (2000)

228 *Twentieth-Century American Dramatists, Second Series*, edited by Christopher J. Wheatley (2000)

229 *Thomas Wolfe: A Documentary Volume*, edited by Ted Mitchell (2001)

230 *Australian Literature, 1788–1914*, edited by Selina Samuels (2001)

231 *British Novelists Since 1960, Fourth Series*, edited by Merritt Moseley (2001)

232 *Twentieth-Century Eastern European Writers, Third Series*, edited by Steven Serafin (2001)

233 *British and Irish Dramatists Since World War II, Second Series*, edited by John Bull (2001)

234 *American Short-Story Writers Since World War II, Third Series*, edited by Patrick Meanor and Richard E. Lee (2001)

235 *The American Renaissance in New England, Third Series*, edited by Wesley T. Mott (2001)

236 *British Rhetoricians and Logicians, 1500–1660*, edited by Edward A. Malone (2001)

237 *The Beats: A Documentary Volume*, edited by Matt Theado (2001)

238 *Russian Novelists in the Age of Tolstoy and Dostoevsky*, edited by J. Alexander Ogden and Judith E. Kalb (2001)

239 *American Women Prose Writers: 1820–1870*, edited by Amy E. Hudock and Katharine Rodier (2001)

240 *Late Nineteenth- and Early Twentieth-Century British Women Poets*, edited by William B. Thesing (2001)

241 *American Sportswriters and Writers on Sport*, edited by Richard Orodenker (2001)

242 *Twentieth-Century European Cultural Theorists, First Series*, edited by Paul Hansom (2001)

243 *The American Renaissance in New England, Fourth Series*, edited by Wesley T. Mott (2001)

244 *American Short-Story Writers Since World War II, Fourth Series*, edited by Patrick Meanor and Joseph McNicholas (2001)

245 *British and Irish Dramatists Since World War II, Third Series*, edited by John Bull (2001)

246 *Twentieth-Century American Cultural Theorists*, edited by Paul Hansom (2001)

247 *James Joyce: A Documentary Volume*, edited by A. Nicholas Fargnoli (2001)

248 *Antebellum Writers in the South, Second Series*, edited by Kent Ljungquist (2001)

249 *Twentieth-Century American Dramatists, Third Series*, edited by Christopher Wheatley (2002)

250 *Antebellum Writers in New York, Second Series*, edited by Kent Ljungquist (2002)

251 *Canadian Fantasy and Science-Fiction Writers*, edited by Douglas Ivison (2002)

252 *British Philosophers, 1500–1799*, edited by Philip B. Dematteis and Peter S. Fosl (2002)

253 *Raymond Chandler: A Documentary Volume*, edited by Robert Moss (2002)

254 *The House of Putnam, 1837–1872: A Documentary Volume*, edited by Ezra Greenspan (2002)

255 *British Fantasy and Science-Fiction Writers, 1918–1960*, edited by Darren Harris-Fain (2002)

256 *Twentieth-Century American Western Writers, Third Series*, edited by Richard H. Cracroft (2002)

257 *Twentieth-Century Swedish Writers After World War II*, edited by Ann-Charlotte Gavel Adams (2002)

258 *Modern French Poets*, edited by Jean-François Leroux (2002)

259 *Twentieth-Century Swedish Writers Before World War II*, edited by Ann-Charlotte Gavel Adams (2002)

260 *Australian Writers, 1915–1950*, edited by Selina Samuels (2002)

261 *British Fantasy and Science-Fiction Writers Since 1960*, edited by Darren Harris-Fain (2002)

262 *British Philosophers, 1800–2000*, edited by Peter S. Fosl and Leemon B. McHenry (2002)

263 *William Shakespeare: A Documentary Volume*, edited by Catherine Loomis (2002)

264 *Italian Prose Writers, 1900–1945*, edited by Luca Somigli and Rocco Capozzi (2002)

265 *American Song Lyricists, 1920–1960*, edited by Philip Furia (2002)

266 *Twentieth-Century American Dramatists, Fourth Series*, edited by Christopher J. Wheatley (2002)

267 *Twenty-First-Century British and Irish Novelists*, edited by Michael R. Molino (2002)

268 *Seventeenth-Century French Writers*, edited by Françoise Jaouën (2002)

269 *Nathaniel Hawthorne: A Documentary Volume*, edited by Benjamin Franklin V (2002)

270 *American Philosophers Before 1950*, edited by Philip B. Dematteis and Leemon B. McHenry (2002)

271 *British and Irish Novelists Since 1960*, edited by Merritt Moseley (2002)

272 *Russian Prose Writers Between the World Wars*, edited by Christine Rydel (2003)

273 *F. Scott Fitzgerald's Tender Is the Night: A Documentary Volume*, edited by Matthew J. Bruccoli and George Parker Anderson (2003)

274 *John Dos Passos's U.S.A.: A Documentary Volume*, edited by Donald Pizer (2003)

275 *Twentieth-Century American Nature Writers: Prose*, edited by Roger Thompson and J. Scott Bryson (2003)

276 *British Mystery and Thriller Writers Since 1960*, edited by Gina Macdonald (2003)

277 *Russian Literature in the Age of Realism*, edited by Alyssa Dinega Gillespie (2003)

278 *American Novelists Since World War II, Seventh Series*, edited by James R. Giles and Wanda H. Giles (2003)

279 *American Philosophers, 1950–2000*, edited by Philip B. Dematteis and Leemon B. McHenry (2003)

280 *Dashiell Hammett's The Maltese Falcon: A Documentary Volume*, edited by Richard Layman (2003)

281 *British Rhetoricians and Logicians, 1500–1660, Second Series*, edited by Edward A. Malone (2003)

282 *New Formalist Poets*, edited by Jonathan N. Barron and Bruce Meyer (2003)

283 *Modern Spanish American Poets, First Series*, edited by María A. Salgado (2003)

284 *The House of Holt, 1866–1946: A Documentary Volume*, edited by Ellen D. Gilbert (2003)

285 *Russian Writers Since 1980,* edited by Marina Balina and Mark Lipoyvetsky (2004)

286 *Castilian Writers, 1400–1500,* edited by Frank A. Domínguez and George D. Greenia (2004)

287 *Portuguese Writers,* edited by Monica Rector and Fred M. Clark (2004)

288 *The House of Boni & Liveright, 1917–1933: A Documentary Volume,* edited by Charles Egleston (2004)

289 *Australian Writers, 1950–1975,* edited by Selina Samuels (2004)

290 *Modern Spanish American Poets, Second Series,* edited by María A. Salgado (2004)

291 *The Hoosier House: Bobbs-Merrill and Its Predecessors, 1850–1985: A Documentary Volume,* edited by Richard J. Schrader (2004)

292 *Twenty-First-Century American Novelists,* edited by Lisa Abney and Suzanne Disheroon-Green (2004)

293 *Icelandic Writers,* edited by Patrick J. Stevens (2004)

294 *James Gould Cozzens: A Documentary Volume,* edited by Matthew J. Bruccoli (2004)

295 *Russian Writers of the Silver Age, 1890–1925,* edited by Judith E. Kalb and J. Alexander Ogden with the collaboration of I. G. Vishnevetsky (2004)

296 *Twentieth-Century European Cultural Theorists, Second Series,* edited by Paul Hansom (2004)

297 *Twentieth-Century Norwegian Writers,* edited by Tanya Thresher (2004)

298 *Henry David Thoreau: A Documentary Volume,* edited by Richard J. Schneider (2004)

299 *Holocaust Novelists,* edited by Efraim Sicher (2004)

300 *Danish Writers from the Reformation to Decadence, 1550–1900,* edited by Marianne Stecher-Hansen (2004)

301 *Gustave Flaubert: A Documentary Volume,* edited by Éric Le Calvez (2004)

302 *Russian Prose Writers After World War II,* edited by Christine Rydel (2004)

303 *American Radical and Reform Writers, First Series,* edited by Steven Rosendale (2005)

304 *Bram Stoker's* Dracula: *A Documentary Volume,* edited by Elizabeth Miller (2005)

305 *Latin American Dramatists, First Series,* edited by Adam Versényi (2005)

306 *American Mystery and Detective Writers,* edited by George Parker Anderson (2005)

307 *Brazilian Writers,* edited by Monica Rector and Fred M. Clark (2005)

308 *Ernest Hemingway's* A Farewell to Arms: *A Documentary Volume,* edited by Charles Oliver (2005)

309 *John Steinbeck: A Documentary Volume,* edited by Luchen Li (2005)

310 *British and Irish Dramatists Since World War II, Fourth Series,* edited by John Bull (2005)

311 *Arabic Literary Culture, 500–925,* edited by Michael Cooperson and Shawkat M. Toorawa (2005)

312 *Asian American Writers,* edited by Deborah L. Madsen (2005)

313 *Writers of the French Enlightenment, I,* edited by Samia I. Spencer (2005)

314 *Writers of the French Enlightenment, II,* edited by Samia I. Spencer (2005)

315 *Langston Hughes: A Documentary Volume,* edited by Christopher C. De Santis (2005)

316 *American Prose Writers of World War I: A Documentary Volume,* edited by Steven Trout (2005)

317 *Twentieth-Century Russian Émigré Writers,* edited by Maria Rubins (2005)

318 *Sixteenth-Century Spanish Writers,* edited by Gregory B. Kaplan (2006)

319 *British and Irish Short-Fiction Writers 1945–2000,* edited by Cheryl Alexander Malcolm and David Malcolm (2006)

Dictionary of Literary Biography Documentary Series

1 *Sherwood Anderson, Willa Cather, John Dos Passos, Theodore Dreiser, F. Scott Fitzgerald, Ernest Hemingway, Sinclair Lewis,* edited by Margaret A. Van Antwerp (1982)

2 *James Gould Cozzens, James T. Farrell, William Faulkner, John O'Hara, John Steinbeck, Thomas Wolfe, Richard Wright,* edited by Margaret A. Van Antwerp (1982)

3 *Saul Bellow, Jack Kerouac, Norman Mailer, Vladimir Nabokov, John Updike, Kurt Vonnegut,* edited by Mary Bruccoli (1983)

4 *Tennessee Williams,* edited by Margaret A. Van Antwerp and Sally Johns (1984)

5 *American Transcendentalists,* edited by Joel Myerson (1988)

6 *Hardboiled Mystery Writers: Raymond Chandler, Dashiell Hammett, Ross Macdonald,* edited by Matthew J. Bruccoli and Richard Layman (1989)

7 *Modern American Poets: James Dickey, Robert Frost, Marianne Moore,* edited by Karen L. Rood (1989)

8 *The Black Aesthetic Movement,* edited by Jeffrey Louis Decker (1991)

9 *American Writers of the Vietnam War: W. D. Ehrhart, Larry Heinemann, Tim O'Brien, Walter McDonald, John M. Del Vecchio,* edited by Ronald Baughman (1991)

10 *The Bloomsbury Group,* edited by Edward L. Bishop (1992)

11 *American Proletarian Culture: The Twenties and The Thirties,* edited by Jon Christian Suggs (1993)

12 *Southern Women Writers: Flannery O'Connor, Katherine Anne Porter, Eudora Welty,* edited by Mary Ann Wimsatt and Karen L. Rood (1994)

13 *The House of Scribner, 1846–1904,* edited by John Delaney (1996)

14 *Four Women Writers for Children, 1868–1918,* edited by Caroline C. Hunt (1996)

15 *American Expatriate Writers: Paris in the Twenties,* edited by Matthew J. Bruccoli and Robert W. Trogdon (1997)

16 *The House of Scribner, 1905–1930,* edited by John Delaney (1997)

17 *The House of Scribner, 1931–1984,* edited by John Delaney (1998)

18 *British Poets of The Great War: Sassoon, Graves, Owen,* edited by Patrick Quinn (1999)

19 *James Dickey,* edited by Judith S. Baughman (1999)

See also DLB 210, 216, 219, 222, 224, 229, 237, 247, 253, 254, 263, 269, 273, 274, 280, 284, 288, 291, 294, 298, 301, 304, 308, 309, 315, 316

Dictionary of Literary Biography Yearbooks

1980 edited by Karen L. Rood, Jean W. Ross, and Richard Ziegfeld (1981)

1981 edited by Karen L. Rood, Jean W. Ross, and Richard Ziegfeld (1982)

1982 edited by Richard Ziegfeld; associate editors: Jean W. Ross and Lynne C. Zeigler (1983)

1983 edited by Mary Bruccoli and Jean W. Ross; associate editor Richard Ziegfeld (1984)

1984 edited by Jean W. Ross (1985)

1985 edited by Jean W. Ross (1986)

1986 edited by J. M. Brook (1987)

1987 edited by J. M. Brook (1988)

1988 edited by J. M. Brook (1989)

1989 edited by J. M. Brook (1990)

1990 edited by James W. Hipp (1991)

1991 edited by James W. Hipp (1992)

1992 edited by James W. Hipp (1993)

1993 edited by James W. Hipp, contributing editor George Garrett (1994)

1994 edited by James W. Hipp, contributing editor George Garrett (1995)

1995 edited by James W. Hipp, contributing editor George Garrett (1996)

1996 edited by Samuel W. Bruce and L. Kay Webster, contributing editor George Garrett (1997)

1997 edited by Matthew J. Bruccoli and George Garrett, with the assistance of L. Kay Webster (1998)

1998 edited by Matthew J. Bruccoli, contributing editor George Garrett, with the assistance of D. W. Thomas (1999)

1999 edited by Matthew J. Bruccoli, contributing editor George Garrett, with the assistance of D. W. Thomas (2000)

2000 edited by Matthew J. Bruccoli, contributing editor George Garrett, with the assistance of George Parker Anderson (2001)

2001 edited by Matthew J. Bruccoli, contributing editor George Garrett, with the assistance of George Parker Anderson (2002)

2002 edited by Matthew J. Bruccoli and George Garrett; George Parker Anderson, Assistant Editor (2003)

Concise Series

Concise Dictionary of American Literary Biography, 7 volumes (1988–1999): *The New Consciousness, 1941–1968; Colonization to the American Renaissance, 1640–1865; Realism, Naturalism, and Local Color, 1865–1917; The Twenties, 1917–1929; The Age of Maturity, 1929–1941; Broadening Views, 1968–1988; Supplement: Modern Writers, 1900–1998.*

Concise Dictionary of British Literary Biography, 8 volumes (1991–1992): *Writers of the Middle Ages and Renaissance Before 1660; Writers of the Restoration and Eighteenth Century, 1660–1789; Writers of the Romantic Period, 1789–1832; Victorian Writers, 1832–1890; Late-Victorian and Edwardian Writers, 1890–1914; Modern Writers, 1914–1945; Writers After World War II, 1945–1960; Contemporary Writers, 1960 to Present.*

Concise Dictionary of World Literary Biography, 4 volumes (1999–2000): *Ancient Greek and Roman Writers; German Writers; African, Caribbean, and Latin American Writers; South Slavic and Eastern European Writers.*

Dictionary of Literary Biography® • Volume Three Hundred Nineteen

British and Irish Short-Fiction Writers, 1945–2000

Dictionary of Literary Biography® • Volume Three Hundred Nineteen

British and Irish Short-Fiction Writers, 1945–2000

Edited by
Cheryl Alexander Malcolm
University of Gdańsk
and
David Malcolm
University of Gdańsk

A Bruccoli Clark Layman Book

THOMSON
GALE

ST. PHILIP'S COLLEGE LIBRARY

Detroit • New York • San Francisco • San Diego • New Haven, Conn. • Waterville, Maine • London • Munich

PR
829
.B67
2006

Dictionary of Literary Biography
Volume 319: British and Irish Short-Fiction Writers, 1945–2000
Cheryl Alexander Malcolm and David Malcolm

Editorial Directors
Matthew J. Bruccoli and Richard Layman

© 2006 Thomson Gale, a part of The Thomson Corporation.

Thomson and Star Logo are trademarks and Gale is a registered trademark used herein under license.

For more information, contact
Thomson Gale
27500 Drake Rd.
Farmington Hills, MI 48331-3535
Or you can visit our Internet site at
http://www.gale.com

ALL RIGHTS RESERVED
No part of this work covered by the copyright hereon may be reproduced or used in any form or by any means—graphic, electronic, or mechanical, including photocopying, recording, taping, Web distribution, or information storage retrieval systems—without the written permission of the publisher.

For permission to use material from this product, submit your request via Web at http://www.gale-edit.com/permissions, or you may download our Permissions Request form and submit your request by fax or mail to:

Permissions Department
Thomson Gale
27500 Drake Rd.
Farmington Hills, MI 48331-3535
Permissions Hotline:
248-699-8006 or 800-877-4253, ext. 8006
Fax: 248-699-8074 or 800-762-4058

While every effort has been made to ensure the reliability of the information presented in this publication, Thomson Gale does not guarantee the accuracy of the data contained herein. Thomson Gale accepts no payment for listing; and inclusion in the publication of any organization, agency, institution, publication, service, or individual does not imply endorsement of the editors or publisher. Errors brought to the attention of the publisher and verified to the satisfaction of the publisher will be corrected in future editions.

LIBRARY OF CONGRESS CATALOGING-IN-PUBLICATION DATA

British and Irish short-fiction writers, 1945–2000 / edited by Cheryl Alexander Malcolm and David Malcolm.
    p. cm. — (Dictionary of literary biography ; v. 319)
"A Bruccoli Clark Layman book."
Includes bibliographical references and index.
    ISBN 0-7876-8137-7 (alk. paper)
    1. Short stories, English—Bio-bibliography—Dictionaries. 2. Short stories, English—Irish authors—Bio-bibliography—Dictionaries. 3. Authors, English—20th century—Biography—Dictionaries. 4. Authors, Irish—20th century—Biography—Dictionaries. 5. Short stories, English—Irish authors—Dictionaries. 6. Short stories, English—Dictionaries. I. Malcolm, Cheryl Alexander. II. Malcom, David, 1952– III. Series.
    PR829.B67 2005
    823'.01090914—dc22
                                            2005020360

Printed in the United States of America
10 9 8 7 6 5 4 3 2 1

Contents

Plan of the Series xiii
Introduction xv

J. G. Ballard (1930–) 3
Andrzej Gasiorek

Mary Beckett (1926–) .12
Bridget Matthews-Kane

Samuel Beckett (1906–1989) 17
Shawn O'Hare

John Berger (1926–) 25
Ralf Hertel

Maeve Binchy (1940–) 34
Jude R. Meche

A. S. Byatt (1936–) 39
Sabine Coelsch-Foisner

Angela Carter (1940–1992) 48
Rosina Neginsky

Evelyn Conlon (1952–) 56
Irene Gilsenan Nordin

Mary Dorcey (1950–) 63
Moira E. Casey

Ronald Frame (1953–) 68
Brett Josef Grubisic

Brian Friel (1929–) 73
G. H. Timmermans

Janice Galloway (1956–) 80
Pilar Sánchez Calle

Anthony Glavin (1946–) 85
Pradyumna S. Chauhan

Alasdair Gray (1934–) 90
Gavin Miller

Jack Harte (1944–) 99
Pietra Palazzolo

Desmond Hogan (1951–) 105
Robert Ellis Hosmer Jr.

Dan Jacobson (1929–) 112
Janine Utell

Gabriel Josipovici (1940–) 121
Günther Jarfe

James Kelman (1946–) 128
Graeme Macdonald

Benedict Kiely (1919–) 137
Christopher Thomas Cairney

James Lasdun (1958–) 146
David Malcolm

Mary Lavin (1912–1996) 151
Greg C. Winston

Toby Litt (1968–) 165
David Malcolm

Shena Mackay (1944–) 171
Amy Lee

John MacKenna (1952–) 178
Lucy Collins

Julian Maclaren-Ross (James McLaren Ross)
(1912–1964) 183
Paul Willetts

Bryan MacMahon (1909–1998) 189
Mary Burke

E. A. Markham (1939–) 197
Greg C. Winston

Adam Mars-Jones (1954–) 206
Brett Josef Grubisic

Aidan Mathews (1956–) 211
Patrick Lonergan

Ian McEwan (1948–) 216
James M. Lang

John McGahern (1934-) 222
   David Malcolm

Naomi Mitchison (1897-1999) 235
   Moira Burgess

Michael Moorcock (1939-) 245
   Mitchell R. Lewis

Val Mulkerns (1925-) 257
   Marti D. Lee

Éilís Ní Dhuibhne (1954-) 263
   Christopher Thomas Cairney

Edna O'Brien (1930-) 270
   Robert Ellis Hosmer Jr.

Máirtín Ó Cadhain (1905-1970) 280
   Pádraigín Riggs

Julia O'Faolain (1932-) 289
   Peter Clandfield

Ben Okri (1959-) 298
   Wolfgang Görtschacher

Frederic Raphael (1931-) 304
   Mike W. Malm

Kate Roberts (1891-1985) 310
   Harri Pritchard Jones

Dilys Rose (1954-) 322
   Peter Clandfield

Clive Sinclair (1948-) 329
   Cheryl Alexander Malcolm

Iain Crichton Smith (Iain Mac A'Ghobhainn)
(1928-1998) 335
   Fiona Wilson

Denton Welch (1915-1948) 345
   Jed Mayer

Fay Weldon (1931-) 350
   Michael Meyer

Arnold Wesker (1932-) 360
   Kevin De Ornellas

Checklist of Further Readings 369
Contributors 371
Cumulative Index 375

Plan of the Series

> ... *Almost the most prodigious asset of a country, and perhaps its most precious possession, is its native literary product—when that product is fine and noble and enduring.*
>
> Mark Twain*

The advisory board, the editors, and the publisher of the *Dictionary of Literary Biography* are joined in endorsing Mark Twain's declaration. The literature of a nation provides an inexhaustible resource of permanent worth. Our purpose is to make literature and its creators better understood and more accessible to students and the reading public, while satisfying the needs of teachers and researchers.

To meet these requirements, *literary biography* has been construed in terms of the author's achievement. The most important thing about a writer is his writing. Accordingly, the entries in *DLB* are career biographies, tracing the development of the author's canon and the evolution of his reputation.

The purpose of *DLB* is not only to provide reliable information in a usable format but also to place the figures in the larger perspective of literary history and to offer appraisals of their accomplishments by qualified scholars.

The publication plan for *DLB* resulted from two years of preparation. The project was proposed to Bruccoli Clark by Frederick G. Ruffner, president of the Gale Research Company, in November 1975. After specimen entries were prepared and typeset, an advisory board was formed to refine the entry format and develop the series rationale. In meetings held during 1976, the publisher, series editors, and advisory board approved the scheme for a comprehensive biographical dictionary of persons who contributed to literature. Editorial work on the first volume began in January 1977, and it was published in 1978. In order to make *DLB* more than a dictionary and to compile volumes that individually have claim to status as literary history, it was decided to organize volumes by topic, period, or genre. Each of these freestanding volumes provides a biographical-bibliographical guide and overview for a particular area of literature. We are convinced that this organization—as opposed to a single alphabet method—constitutes a valuable innovation in the presentation of reference material. The volume plan necessarily requires many decisions for the placement and treatment of authors. Certain figures will be included in separate volumes, but with different entries emphasizing the aspect of his career appropriate to each volume. Ernest Hemingway, for example, is represented in *American Writers in Paris, 1920–1939* by an entry focusing on his expatriate apprenticeship; he is also in *American Novelists, 1910–1945* with an entry surveying his entire career, as well as in *American Short-Story Writers, 1910–1945, Second Series* with an entry concentrating on his short fiction. Each volume includes a cumulative index of the subject authors and articles.

Between 1981 and 2002 the series was augmented and updated by the *DLB Yearbooks*. There have also been nineteen *DLB Documentary Series* volumes, which provide illustrations, facsimiles, and biographical and critical source materials for figures, works, or groups judged to have particular interest for students. In 1999 the *Documentary Series* was incorporated into the *DLB* volume numbering system beginning with *DLB 210: Ernest Hemingway*.

We define literature as the *intellectual commerce of a nation*: not merely as belles lettres but as that ample and complex process by which ideas are generated, shaped, and transmitted. *DLB* entries are not limited to "creative writers" but extend to other figures who in their time and in their way influenced the mind of a people. Thus the series encompasses historians, journalists, publishers, book collectors, and screenwriters. By this means readers of *DLB* may be aided to perceive literature not as cult scripture in the keeping of intellectual high priests but firmly positioned at the center of a nation's life.

DLB includes the major writers appropriate to each volume and those standing in the ranks behind them. Scholarly and critical counsel has been sought in deciding which minor figures to include and how full their entries should be. Wherever possible, useful refer-

---

*From an unpublished section of Mark Twain's autobiography, copyright by the Mark Twain Company

Plan of the Series

ences are made to figures who do not warrant separate entries.

Each *DLB* volume has an expert volume editor responsible for planning the volume, selecting the figures for inclusion, and assigning the entries. Volume editors are also responsible for preparing, where appropriate, appendices surveying the major periodicals and literary and intellectual movements for their volumes, as well as lists of further readings. Work on the series as a whole is coordinated at the Bruccoli Clark Layman editorial center in Columbia, South Carolina, where the editorial staff is responsible for accuracy and utility of the published volumes.

One feature that distinguishes *DLB* is the illustration policy—its concern with the iconography of literature. Just as an author is influenced by his surroundings, so is the reader's understanding of the author enhanced by a knowledge of his environment. Therefore *DLB* volumes include not only drawings, paintings, and photographs of authors, often depicting them at various stages in their careers, but also illustrations of their families and places where they lived. Title pages are regularly reproduced in facsimile along with dust jackets for modern authors. The dust jackets are a special feature of *DLB* because they often document better than anything else the way in which an author's work was perceived in its own time. Specimens of the writers' manuscripts and letters are included when feasible.

Samuel Johnson rightly decreed that "The chief glory of every people arises from its authors." The purpose of the *Dictionary of Literary Biography* is to compile literary history in the surest way available to us—by accurate and comprehensive treatment of the lives and work of those who contributed to it.

The DLB Advisory Board

Introduction

Scholars have difficulty providing a clear definition of the short story. The question of how long or short a short story can be, the issue of whether short stories tend to have particular kinds of subject matter, and whether they focus on particular kinds of characters vex those who reflect on it in general terms. The length of the short story has important implications both for the kind of story material it can deal with and for the detail in which it can deal with characters. Story material must be less complex and extensive than that of the novel; characters cannot be developed as they can be in novels. Yet, the relative concision of the short story does not preclude a wider suggestiveness, either social or existential. Indeed, elliptical suggestiveness has often been taken to be characteristic of most short stories. The limited focus of the short story—it does not offer an overview of an entire society, as the novel does—means that it is particularly likely to give voice to the experience of the marginalized, the outcast, and the highly subjective vision of figures permanently or temporarily on the fringes of society.

Contrary to popular usage, the short story is not a genre, at least not if that term is used to describe detective fiction or the sonnet. The short story is best thought of as a category of text (blurring at the margins with the novel, but in most cases readily identifiable) that comprises a wide range of stories that belong to different well-established genres of prose fiction—for example, science fiction, the detective story, psychological fiction, gothic fiction, the beast fable, or the literary folktale. This volume attempts to avoid some of the problems of definition by having "short fiction" in the title, rather than "short story," as this designation permits discussion of texts at the boundaries of the category.

However one defines the short story or short fiction, in Britain it has earned little prestige or critical attention. Nonetheless, since the 1940s, writers and critics have prophesied a great future for the short story or a revival of its fortunes. H. E. Bates, for example, predicted the former in 1941 (only to retract his prophecy in 1965), and Clare Hanson, the latter in 1985, as did Malcolm Bradbury (with some qualification) in 1987. Alongside these are counterclaims that the short story is sorely neglected in Britain and headed for extinction. Hilary Corke argued in 1965 that short fiction is "dying," while J. G. Ballard dismissed Hanson's claim out of hand in 1993: "She must be mad."

The low status of the short story among British writers, critics, and publishers (since 1945, and before) is attested to by a long line of witnesses. For example, Ivan Reid in his monograph *The Short Story* (1977) argues that short fiction carries negative associations of slickness and triviality in Britain. Birgit Moosmüller confirms this assessment, as does Alan Coren. "What overtones of dilettantism, of superfluous also-running that title [of short-story writer] carries in England" (*Punch,* 26 August 1964). This view is confirmed by critics Thomas A. Gullason and Charles E. May, and major writers Graham Greene and V. S. Pritchett have also stressed a British disdain for the short story. Although the journals *Studies in Short Fiction* (from the 1960s) and *Journal of the Short Story in English* (from the 1980s) have attempted to correct this neglect (neither is published in the United Kingdom), and both concentrate heavily on United States and Irish, rather than British, short fiction, major critical studies of the short story—such as those of Dominic Head, John Bayley, and Hanson—are exceptions to the general critical disdain of British short fiction. One of the best and most thorough studies is not even written in English, but in German by German scholar Moosmüller. The low status and slow development of the short story in Britain in comparison to that in the United States has long been the subject of critical consideration. Dean Baldwin has written frequently and tellingly on this matter. The title of one of his essays, "The Tardy Development of the British Short Story," says it all.

The situation in the Irish Republic is different. Declan Kiberd contrasts the low regard that the British have for the short story with the high regard that the Irish lavish on it. "For the past eighty years," he wrote in *The Irish Short Story* (1979), "the short story [in Ireland] has been the most popular of all literary forms with readers." While Irish writers such as Mary Lavin, Frank O'Connor, William Trevor, and John McGahern are taken seriously as writers of short stories, as well as of novels, and have been given a chance to develop their oeuvre of short fiction (sometimes, paradoxically, by a British publisher), that is not the case with their British contemporaries (with the exception of Pritchett).

Institutions, as well as cultural attitudes, play an important role in this matter. The anti-short-story bias of British publishing since 1945 (and before) is a matter of record. Bates attributes the failure of his 1941 prophecy to the lack of publishing outlets for short fiction in Britain. Pritchett blames the lack of literary journals in which to publish short stories. There is a scholarly consensus that in the 1950s and 1960s only established authors could place their short stories, and that few literary journals or anthologies in the United Kingdom were interested in short fiction. Some important anthologies of short stories were published, such as *Pick of the Year's Short Stories* (1949–1965); *Winter's Tales* (from 1954); *New Stories* and *Scottish Short Stories* (both in the 1970s); *Penguin Modern Stories* (1969–1972); and *Best Short Stories* (from 1986). In addition, Walter Evans notes that in the 1970s, *London Magazine* and *Critical Quarterly* published short fiction, and Moosmüller pointed to *Granta, Cosmopolitan, Woman's Own,* and *Woman's Journal* as providing a forum in the 1980s and 1990s for short stories of serious quality, while Barry Menikoff argued that postwar British short-story writers found a place for their work in *The New Yorker*. This small number of magazines, however, does not indicate a thriving domestic publishing environment for short fiction. Instead, British writers are pressured not to write short stories. Doris Lessing is not alone in blaming British publishers for this situation. Many writers agree: Anthony Burgess (who points to a "lack of commercial underpinning" [*Journal of the Short Story in English,* January, 1984]), Pritchett ("It is very difficult to find anyone to publish a short story" [*Journal of the Short Story in English,* Spring 1986]), Micheline Wandor ("I don't think publishers are any more generous to short stories than they ever were" [*Die experimentelle englische Kurzgeschicte der Gagenwart,* 1993]), and Sarah Maitland ("There is practically no serious literary periodical access, and unless you write novels practically no book publishing" [*Die experimentelle englische Kurzgeschicte der Gagenwart,* 1993]). Highly acclaimed novelist Graham Swift records that his collection of short stories *Learning to Swim and Other Stories* (1982) was published only after he had brought out two successful novels (although the stories were in many cases older than the second novel). He sees his case as typical. His publishers were not supportive of his work in the shorter form. Critic Valerie Shaw in *The Short Story: A Critical Introduction* (1983) wrote that "the trap" described by Katherine Anne Porter, the pressure from publishers on a short-story writer to pull him/herself together and write a novel, is still in operation in postwar British publishing.

The situation in Ireland is different. Richard F. Peterson's observation in *Studies in Short Fiction* (Winter 1981) that "the short story is the literary form most closely associated with the Irish imagination" may well have something to do with the many outlets for new short fiction in the Irish Republic that have appeared since World War II. James F. Kilroy indicates that some of the periodicals have supported the development of the Irish short story—*The Bell* (1940–1954), edited by Sean O'Faolain until 1946; *Dublin Magazine* (1923–1958), edited by Seumas O'Sullivan; and *Irish Writing* (1946–1957), edited by Marcus. Maurice Harmon notes that, in April 1968, the major Irish newspaper *The Irish Press* (Dublin) started to devote a page every week to Irish writing (short stories, parts of novels, and some poems). Harmon considers that Tim Pat Coogan, editor of *The Irish Press,* and Marcus, its literary editor, "changed the conditions within which the young writer works." Younger writers were given opportunities to publish, and several anthologies of short fiction came out in the 1970s based on stories first published in *The Irish Press*. In 1987 Benedict Kiely attributed the strength of the short story in Ireland to this publishing venture, a view advanced also by Robert Hogan in 1984. Only in respect to state censorship of literature (under which such writers as John McGahern, Kiely, and Edna O'Brien suffered) may writers of short fiction in the Irish Republic be said to have had a harder time than their British counterparts.

That the situation is not the same for British and Irish short-story writers should not be a surprise. The United Kingdom of Great Britain and Northern Ireland and the Irish Republic are two separate nation-states (and have been so effectively since 1922). Although linked by a common past and geographical proximity, they have radically different institutions and histories of postwar social and economic development. The Irish Republic has a tiny population in comparison to that of the United Kingdom (3.5 million as opposed to almost 60 million) and has played and still plays a different role in world economic, political, and military affairs from that of its larger and much wealthier neighbor.

Two major aspects of the post–World War II history of the United Kingdom were its withdrawal from its imperial possessions (although the post-1968 "Troubles" in Northern Ireland, which provide subject matter for Mary Beckett's short fiction, are an enduring consequence of British imperial expansion) and its increasing orientation toward continental Europe. It became a member of the European Community in 1973. However, a major legacy of the British Empire that has shaped post–World War II Britain is emigration from former colonial possessions. Immigration was nothing new to Britain. Large numbers of Irish immigrants had been arriving in mainland Britain for more than a century by 1945 and continued to do so throughout the 1950s and 1960s. Substantial waves of Jewish immigration to Britain from Central Europe occurred during the late 1880s and the 1890s. But when the ship the *Empire Windrush* docked at Tilbury in London on 22 June 1948, and almost five hundred Jamaican men came ashore, a new chapter of British domestic history opened. They were followed by hundreds of thousands of immigrants from the Caribbean and the Indian subcontinent. Now almost 7 percent of the U.K. population is foreign born or of foreign descent. The world of immigrants to Britain from the Caribbean is the focus of short fiction by Markham, while Irish economic migrants to the United Kingdom are the subjects of short stories by McGahern. Ben Okri's short fiction, published in Britain, but with its eyes turned toward Africa, is a sign of these changing times, while Jewish immigrants to Britain, such as Dan Jacobson and Gabriel Josipovici, have enormously enriched the range of short fiction written in the United Kingdom.

Britain has changed in other ways, too. The culture of post–World War II Britain was much less deferential and much more egalitarian than it had been before 1939. On the back of considerable prosperity in the 1950s, substantial changes in people's behavior and outlook took place. Young people began to dress quite differently from their elders in the late 1950s and 1960s and to listen to different music. A much greater degree of personal mobility occurred; for example, a huge increase in car ownership occurred from the 1960s onward. Traditional sexual mores seemed to collapse. Adam Mars-Jones's short stories of homosexual experience and Ian McEwan's fictional treatments of sadism and sexual deviance are clearly responses to a culture of greater sexual freedom. Shena Mackay writes of disaffected youth in a rapidly changing social world. Education, too, became much more egalitarian. Many more teenagers stay at school and leave school with exam qualifications than in 1945. Many more of them can go to a university (many more universities existed in Britain in 2000 than in 1980, let alone than in 1945). Feminism shook patriarchal attitudes and opened up paths in education and work for many women. Angela Carter and Fay Weldon both respond to and help to promote changes in women's roles and status within British society. The developments indicated above are all similar to the kinds of changes that transformed the face of Western Europe and North America in a comparable period. Some distinctively British aspects of these changes, however, have been a marked trade-union militancy from the 1960s through the 1980s (reflected in the short stories of Arnold Wesker) and a complete erosion of traditional religious faith and church attendance in the United Kingdom. Figures from 1994 suggest that 24 percent of the population is nonreligious and that there are as many Muslims (2 percent) as Methodists in Britain; these figures also clearly show that considerably more practicing Catholics than Anglicans live in the United Kingdom, and they also reveal a substantial breakdown of the traditional model of the family, resulting in many single-parent families and widespread divorce. McEwan's, Carter's, and Weldon's fiction also touch on the breakdown of traditional family structures. Other examples of the shifting and nondeferential nature of British culture and society include the wildfire spread of Estuarine English (a southeast English working-class phonology and vocabulary) throughout the middle and upper classes of the United Kingdom in the 1990s and the more widespread appearance of broadcasters with regional (and working-class) accents on radio and television. The fashionableness of contemporary Scottish short fiction, with its marked regional and nonmetropolitan concerns and voice, parallels this linguistic egalitarianism. The public scrutiny and criticism of the monarchy and the various scandals in which the House of Windsor has been involved since the 1970s have destabilized the position of the British royal family within the country. Even when British short fiction does not directly touch on such disruptive trends, its whole ethos is nondeferential as it probes and dismisses traditional, pre-1945 hierarchies and values.

The movement toward devolution of political power to Scotland and Wales can also be seen in this context of shifting loyalties. The Scots (at approximately five million, the second-largest national group within the United Kingdom) have been particularly conscious of their claims to historical nationhood for almost a thousand years. These claims were assuaged by the prominent role that they played in the British Empire. Once the Empire began to dissolve after 1945, they were bound to reconsider the benefits of the Act of Union of 1707. Increasingly they did so, especially in the 1970s. By the 1980s, in any case, the political culture of Scotland, much more socially egalitarian and interventionist than that of England, was radically at odds with that of Westminster. By 1997 Scotland had no Conservative M.P.s (members of parliament) and Wales had none either. In referenda in 1998, the people of Scotland and Wales both voted for substantial degrees of autonomy within the United Kingdom. The Scots won the most. In 1999 the first Scottish Parliament (with tax-gathering powers) since 1707 met in Edinburgh. Whether this concession is a shrewd move by the London government or the beginning of the breakup of the United Kingdom remains to be seen. In any case, the aggressive Scottishness of short-story writers such as Alasdair Gray and James Kelman demonstrates a Scottish literary self-assertion that parallels the political one. In addition, the high status of writers from the traditionally ignored Scottish Gaelic and Welsh language communities of Britain (Iain Crichton Smith and Kate Roberts) indicates a recognition by the literary world of the importance of regional, often (in the past) marginalized, cultures.

Social class has long been seen as an aspect of British society that pervades many different levels of people's lives, from birth to death, and the British are said to be extraordinarily class-conscious. Whether this awareness is substantially different from the role that social class plays in other societies is open to dispute. Certainly, British fiction has long been fascinated by the prejudices and subtle gradations of class behavior and identification. John Berger's short fiction is deeply committed to exposing and attacking the inequities of European class structure in general, while Wesker's focuses on British social antagonisms. James Lasdun, Frederic Raphael, and McEwan all dissect the complexities of social-class relations. Wealth, educational privilege, language, professional success, living conditions, and health can all be seen as related to social class in the United Kingdom. Yet, examples of mobility also exist. The four British prime ministers of the 1970s and 1980s came from lower-middle-class backgrounds. Stockbrokers in the city of London no longer all speak with cut-glass accents. This mobility is echoed in the lack of traditional deference shown by many British short-story writers since the end of World War II. Regional distinctions within the United Kingdom, however, remain extremely strong and are partly related to social class. Within England itself, Northerners and Southerners dislike and distrust each other to a substantial extent. But regional cultures can be lionized in the metropolis, as they were in the 1960s when music and poetry from Liverpool was widely feted, or as working-class/lumpen-proletariat Scottish writing (for example, by Kelman) has been celebrated in the 1990s.

Since 1945 the history of the Irish Free State, and from 1949 of the Irish Republic, has been quite different. The Irish Free State was neutral during World War II, and despite the fact that some 50,000 citizens of the new state served in Allied armed forces against Germany, Prime Minister Eamon de Valera paid his respects in May 1945 at the German embassy in Dublin on receiving the news of Adolf Hitler's death. Commentators point to the deep introversion and isolation of Ireland during the World War II years, a position reflected in its refusal to join NATO in 1949. That year also saw the breaking of the last formal links between the southern part of Ireland and the United Kingdom. The government of the Irish Free State declared the existence of the Irish Republic and withdrew from the British Commonwealth. But political independence was not matched by economic success. Ireland in the late 1940s and 1950s was an extremely poor country, marked by lack of industrial investment, by rural conservatism, and by high figures for emigration (almost 120,000 persons between 1946 and 1951, almost 1.5 percent of the population between 1956 and 1961). Social services were at a much lower level than in Britain and Northern Ireland, and death from tuberculosis was rife until the early 1950s. This restricted and deeply provincial world provides the subject matter for short stories by Lavin, O'Brien, and McGahern.

Since the late 1950s, the situation has altered beyond recognition. A much more open economic policy, aimed at attracting foreign investment, had already raised living standards in the 1960s, but the accession of Ireland to the European Common Market in 1973 has utterly transformed the country. Ireland now exports much more to the other countries of the European Union than it does to Britain. In the mid 1990s almost 30 percent of Irish exports were in the field of electronics, and around one hundred thousand Irish jobs were connected with electronics, pharmaceuticals, engineering, and computer-software production. The European Union has poured money into Ireland, money spent in restructuring agriculture, retraining the workforce, and building roads. In 1973 Irish per capita Gross Domestic Product (GDP) stood at 58 percent of the European Community average; by 1996, it was reckoned to be almost 87 percent of the European Union average. Credible statistics indicate that Irish GDP per capita is now higher than that in the United Kingdom. The transformation of the country has provided material for Irish short-story writers such as Mary Dorcey, Val Mulkerns, Julia O'Faolain, Aidan Mathews, and McGahern.

In 2000 the Irish Republic was a country in which 40 percent of the population was under twenty-five and much of it highly educated. Emigration from mainland Britain and elsewhere to Ireland, and not emigration from Ireland to other countries, is now a phenomenon that the Irish people have to face. Dublin is a cosmopolitan city with a vast suburban sprawl. The role of the Catholic Church is increasingly questioned within the Irish Republic, as are traditional pillars of the Irish Constitution and Irish society, such as the virtual ban on abortion. Eilís Ní Dhuibhne, O'Brien, Dorcey, and Mulkerns all address the changing position of Irish women within these substantial social and cultural shifts. McGahern's ambitious short story "The Country Funeral" centers on the opposition of a traditional rural way of life and a modern urban, even cosmopolitan, one, and attempts to sum up their moral and historical relationship. One tradition is undeniably crumbling within the Irish Republic. Despite strong attempts to maintain Irish as a living language (and despite the work of such writers as Ní Dhuibhne in Irish), the number of native speakers of the language is small and its use among the rest of the population limited. However, one institution from the past that has survived and that directly affects literature (and has affected it throughout the postwar period) is censorship. The Irish Censorship Board has been in operation since 1930 and, despite legislative emendations in 1946, 1967, and 1979, continues to censor printed and movie materials. Between 1960 and 1965, a period considered to be relatively liberal in comparison to the 1950s, approximately 1,900 books were banned by the board. Works banned by the board during its existence include those by Marcel Proust, Vladimir Nabokov, Raymond Chandler, John Steinbeck, Thomas Mann, and a host of Irish writers—including Samuel Beckett, James Joyce, Brendan Behan, Brian Moore, Sean O'Faolain, and those listed earlier.

The short fiction of Britain and Ireland between 1945 and 2000 frequently refers to and participates in the kinds of social, political, and economic changes mentioned above. One can note the emergence of important new voices in these years. Working-class and lower-class writing has striking representatives. The legacy of an English working-class writer such as Alan Sillitoe has been strong, although much urban and working-class short fiction in these years comes from Scotland, where its concerns inevitably merge with those of national identity. There is a vibrant school of urban lower-class Scottish writing represented by Gray and Kelman. Their use of working-class Scottish dialect is uncompromising, and their bleak and often savage story materials tell of poverty and alienation. In different contexts, Berger's and McGahern's stories center on the urban and rural poor and present unsentimental accounts of their lives.

Women's voices have an importance in British and Irish short fiction. Hermione Lee has suggested in *The Secret Self: Short Stories by Women* (1985) that the short story, in its limited perspective, its openness to subjective expression, and its shortness (women writers are "likely to be interrupted"), may be a particularly appropriate kind of writing for women "as they emerge from a long history of obscurity and silence." Indeed, in 1986 Angela Carter—herself a major feminist short-fiction writer—edited an influential short-story anthology titled *Wayward Girls and Wicked Women*. Women writers such as A. S. Byatt, Carter, Janice Galloway, Mackay, Lessing, Naomi Mitchison, Dilys Rose, and Weldon play a vital role in the development of the postwar British short story, and their voices often rail against and devastate patriarchal practices. In the Irish Republic, too, women writers such as Evelyn Conlon, Dorcey, Lavin, Mulkerns, Ní Dhuibhne, and O'Brien have tackled the conservatism of Irish society and culture in telling ways, sometimes paying a substantial price (in terms of social criticism) for doing so.

Short fiction in languages other than English also plays a significant role in the postwar British and Irish literary world. Roberts, who wrote in Welsh, is clearly a major European writer, while a substantial body of Irish-language short fiction has been written, and Ian Crichton Smith (Iain Mac A'Ghobhain) speaks for a Scottish Gaelic culture, albeit one that faces certain extinction. But some of the most important new voices in British short fiction from the 1950s and 1960s have been those of writers who were immigrants themselves or the children of immigrants to the United Kingdom. Salman Rushdie's and V. S. Naipaul's work is significant in this area, but Okri and Markham are important extraterritorial voices, too, addressing the experiences of millions of black and Asian citizens of the United Kingdom. Although British writers of Caribbean or Indian subcontinent origin have not published many short stories—the pressure by British publishers to publish novels instead certainly plays a role in this matter—a significant body of black and Asian British short writing does exist.

The Irish contribution to short fiction in English, for reasons suggested above, is second to none. The list of major Irish writers who have devoted themselves to the short story is impressive and includes Samuel Beckett, Lavin, McGahern, O'Brien, and Julia O'Faolain. Like much Irish short fiction of the period, many of these authors' stories are accounts of conflict with authority, of repressive communities, and of severely patriarchal structures. Most of these conflicts end in blighted hope, failure, or flight. In this matter they are following a long tradition of socially critical and antagonistic Irish short fiction that dates from before the expulsion of the British in 1922.

Most short stories in Britain and Ireland between 1945 and 2000 are traditional in subject matter and in technique. An important science-fiction inheritance can be seen in the stories of Iain Banks, Ballard, and Michael Moorcock, but most short fiction remains rooted in the social-psychological conventions that it draws from prewar practitioners and, indeed, from the European nineteenth-century origins of the short story. An individual's psychological development, or an individual's state of mind, often carrying resonances beyond the particular character's situation within a realistically presented social world is the norm. (Clearly, the works of some authors deviate from this standard—for example, in Carter's and Byatt's reworked folktales with their motifs of magic and the supernatural—but these are limited in number.) Even short stories with an obviously highly shocking and challenging subject matter (for example, McEwan's stories of incest, child abuse, and mutilation, and Mars-Jones's accounts of AIDS sufferers) are traditional in narration and narrative strategy. Linear narratives and unified and largely trustworthy narrators predominate. Samuel Beckett is a major exception to this conservatism, but Moosmüller points to Gabriel Josipovici, Christine Brooke-Rose, and Mars-Jones (sometimes) as the only persistent experimenters in British short fiction. Their deviations from traditional linear narrative, their drawing attention to the textual substance of their stories, and their clearly metafictional interests (their stories are often about the problems of writing stories or of fiction in general) form an unusual strand in post–World War II British short fiction.

British short fiction may have met with critical disdain in the postwar period, and writers may constantly have been encouraged to write novels instead of short stories, but in the second half of the twentieth century many writers chose to ignore those pressures and have produced a substantial body of work. The Irish have been altogether luckier in the opportunities they have for publishing short fiction, and, accordingly, their contribution to the short story in English has been enormous. This situation is unlikely to change in the near future.

—*Cheryl Alexander Malcolm*
—*David Malcolm*

Acknowledgments

This book was produced by Bruccoli Clark Layman, Inc. Penelope M. Hope was the in-house editor. She was assisted by R. Bland Lawson and Charles Brower.

Production manager is Philip B. Dematteis.

Administrative support was provided by Carol A. Cheschi.

Accountant is Ann-Marie Holland.

Copyediting supervisor is Sally R. Evans. The copyediting staff includes Phyllis A. Avant, Caryl Brown, Melissa D. Hinton, Philip I. Jones, Rebecca Mayo, Nadirah Rahimah Shabazz, and Nancy E. Smith.

Pipeline manager is James F. Tidd Jr.

Editorial associates are Crystal Gleim, Elizabeth Leverton, and Timothy C. Simmons.

In-house vetter is Catherine M. Polit.

Permissions editor is Amber L. Coker.

Layout and graphics supervisor is Janet E. Hill. The graphics staff includes Zoe R. Cook and Sydney E. Hammock.

Office manager is Kathy Lawler Merlette.

Photography editor is Mark J. McEwan. Photography assistant is Dickson Monk.

Digital photographic copy work was performed by Joseph M. Bruccoli.

Systems manager is Donald Kevin Starling.

Typesetting supervisor is Kathleen M. Flanagan. The typesetting staff includes Patricia Marie Flanagan and Pamela D. Norton.

Library research was facilitated by the following librarians at the Thomas Cooper Library of the University of South Carolina: Elizabeth Suddeth and the rare-book department; Jo Cottingham, interlibrary loan department; circulation department head Tucker Taylor; reference department head Virginia W. Weathers; reference department staff Laurel Baker, Marilee Birchfield, Kate Boyd, Paul Cammarata, Joshua Garris, Gary Geer, Tom Marcil, Rose Marshall, and Sharon Verba; interlibrary loan department head Marna Hostetler; and interlibrary loan staff Bill Fetty and Nelson Rivera.

Dictionary of Literary Biography® • Volume Three Hundred Nineteen

British and Irish Short-Fiction Writers, 1945–2000

Dictionary of Literary Biography

J. G. Ballard
(15 November 1930 -)

Andrzej Gasiorek
University of Birmingham

See also the Ballard entries in *DLB 14: British Novelists Since 1960; DLB 207: British Novelists Since 1960, Third Series;* and *DLB 261: British Fantasy and Science-Fiction Writers Since 1960.*

BOOKS: *The Wind from Nowhere* (New York: Berkley, 1962; Harmondsworth, U.K.: Penguin, 1967);
The Voices of Time and Other Stories (New York: Berkley, 1962; London: Gollancz, 1962; revised edition, London: Orion, 1974);
Billenium (New York: Berkley, 1962);
The Drowned World (New York: Berkley, 1962; London: Gollancz, 1963);
The Four-Dimensional Nightmare (London: Gollancz, 1963; revised, 1974);
Passport to Eternity (New York: Berkley, 1963);
The Terminal Beach (London: Gollancz, 1964; New York: Berkley, 1964);
The Burning World (New York: Berkley, 1964); expanded as *The Drought* (London: Cape, 1965);
The Crystal World (New York: Farrar, Straus & Giroux, 1966; London: Cape, 1966);
The Assassination Weapon (London: Compact, 1966);
The Impossible Man and Other Stories (New York: Berkley, 1966);
The Day of Forever (London: Panther, 1967);
The Disaster Area (London: Cape, 1967; New York: Paladin, 1992);
The Overloaded Man (London: Panther, 1967); revised as *The Venus Hunters* (London: Granada, 1980);
Why I Want to Fuck Ronald Reagan (Brighton, U.K.: Unicorn Bookshop, 1968);
The Atrocity Exhibition (London: Cape, 1970); republished as *Love and Napalm: Export USA* (New York: Grove, 1972); revised, expanded, and annotated as *The Atrocity Exhibition* (San Francisco: RE/Search, 1990; London: Flamingo, 1993);

J. G. Ballard (photograph by Mark Gerson; from David Pringle and James Goddard, eds., J. G. Ballard: The First Twenty Years, *1976; Thomas Cooper Library, University of South Carolina)*

Chronopolis and Other Stories (New York: Putnam, 1971);
Vermilion Sands (New York: Berkley, 1971; London: Cape, 1973);
Crash (London: Cape, 1973; New York: Farrar, Straus & Giroux, 1973);

Concrete Island (London: Cape, 1974; New York: Farrar, Straus & Giroux, 1974);

High-Rise (London: Cape, 1975; New York: Holt, Rinehart & Winston, 1977);

Low-Flying Aircraft and Other Stories (London: Cape, 1976);

The Unlimited Dream Company (New York: Holt, Rinehart & Winston, 1979; London: Cape, 1979);

Hello America (London: Cape, 1981; New York: Carroll & Graf, 1988);

News from the Sun (London: Interzone, 1982);

Myths of the Near Future (London: Cape, 1982);

Empire of the Sun (London: Gollancz, 1984; New York: Simon & Schuster, 1984);

The Day of Creation (London: Gollancz, 1987; New York: Farrar, Straus & Giroux, 1988);

Memories of the Space Age (Sauk City, Wis.: Arkham House, 1988);

Running Wild (London: Century Hutchinson, 1988; New York: Farrar, Straus & Giroux, 1989);

War Fever (London: Collins, 1990; New York: Farrar, Straus & Giroux, 1991);

The Kindness of Women (London: HarperCollins, 1991; New York: Farrar, Straus & Giroux, 1991);

Rushing to Paradise (London: Flamingo, 1994; New York: Picador, 1995);

A User's Guide to the Millennium: Essays and Reviews (London: HarperCollins, 1996; New York: Picador USA, 1996);

Cocaine Nights (London: Flamingo, 1996; Washington, D.C.: Counterpoint, 1998);

Super-Cannes (London: Flamingo, 2000; New York: Picador, 2001);

Millennium People (London: Flamingo, 2003).

Collections: *The Best of J. G. Ballard* (London: Futura, 1977);

The Best Short Stories of J. G. Ballard (New York: Holt, Rinehart & Winston, 1978);

The Complete Short Stories (London: Flamingo, 2001);

Quotes, edited by Vivian Vale (San Francisco: RE/Search, 2005).

OTHER: David Larkin, ed., *Dali,* introduction by Ballard (New York: Ballantine, 1974);

Aldous Huxley, *The Doors of Perception; and Heaven and Hell,* foreword by Ballard (London: Flamingo, 1994).

SELECTED PERIODICAL PUBLICATIONS—UNCOLLECTED: "The Dying Fall," *Interzone,* 106 (April 1996);

"The Secret Autobiography of J. G. B******," *Interzone,* 106 (April 1996).

J. G. Ballard is difficult to categorize as a writer. His early work had an immediate impact on the science-fiction scene: he was heralded as one of the leading lights of the New Wave school of British science-fiction writers associated with *New Worlds,* the path-breaking magazine edited from 1964 by Michael Moorcock. Ballard published his first short story in 1956, and in the decade that followed wrote approximately fifty more stories, most of which boldly and inventively expanded the boundaries of science fiction. This frenetic pace gradually slowed down thereafter, partly because the writer began to focus more on the novel as a form. *The Wind from Nowhere,* his first full-length fiction, was published in 1962 and was quickly followed by the highly acclaimed *The Drowned World* (1962), *The Burning World* (1964), and *The Crystal World* (1966). Thus, Ballard was, from the early 1960s, publishing short stories and novels in tandem, but the latter began to predominate after 1970. Whereas he published his first fifty short stories in just ten years, another three decades were required for him to double this number. By the early 1990s he had almost stopped working in the short-story format.

The gradual move away from the short story represents one aspect of the trajectory of Ballard's career. His development as a writer has also been marked by his concern with themes that he seeks to explore in genres other than science fiction. Ballard's desire to engage directly with contemporary social existence helps to explain the shift from science fiction to avant-garde works such as *The Atrocity Exhibition* (1970) and *Crash* (1973); to dystopian evocations of urban life in *Concrete Island* (1974), *High-Rise* (1975), and *Running Wild* (1988); and to novels such as *Cocaine Nights* (1996), *Super-Cannes* (2000), and *Millennium People* (2003). Parallel to these works Ballard also created haunting visions of global regeneration in *The Unlimited Dream Company* (1979) and *The Day of Creation* (1987). In addition to these novels, Ballard wrote the much lauded *Empire of the Sun* (1984), a fictionalized but broadly autobiographical account of his experiences during World War II, and he followed this work with *The Kindness of Women* (1991), which concentrates on his life after his internment in a Japanese prisoner-of-war (POW) camp and offers a depiction of the postwar cultural milieu in England.

James Graham Ballard was born in Shanghai on 15 November 1930 to James and Edna Ballard, and with his younger sister he was raised in Shanghai until 1942. His father was the president of a company in Shanghai. After the attack on Pearl Harbor in 1941, the Ballard family was interned by the Japanese in a POW camp at Lunghua. Ballard recalled the experiences he underwent there in *Empire of the Sun.* In 1946 Ballard moved with his mother and sister to England (the country of his citizenship), while his father remained in

China until 1950. Ballard was initially unable to adjust to England, which he thought of as a strange, parochial place that had largely been untouched by the violence he had witnessed during the war. After attending the Leys School in Cambridge, he chose to study medicine, but he lasted for only two years at King's College, Cambridge, before switching to English, which he studied at London University for just one year. Beginning in 1953, he spent one year with the Royal Air Force in Moose Jaw, Saskatchewan, where he first came across American science fiction. Ballard married Helen Mary Matthews in 1955, and she gave birth to a son (James Christopher) soon after. During this time Ballard started publishing his short stories, the first of which, "Prima Belladonna," appeared in December 1956 in the influential *Science Fantasy* magazine. Through his links with *Science Fantasy,* Ballard was able to secure the position of assistant editor to the science journal *Chemistry and Industry,* and much of what he read in his capacity as an editor provided him with material for his early stories.

From the outset Ballard disdained the escapist dimension of science-fiction writing; he was concerned rather with using the genre as a way of exploring the hidden implications of the present. He writes in his introduction to *The Complete Short Stories* (2001) that he "was interested in the real future" that he "could see approaching, and less in the invented future that science fiction preferred." To critics' objections that Vermilion Sands—the strange, self-contained desert resort in which several of his early stories are set—is an unrealistic depiction of how the future would look, Ballard responds in the same introduction that they have misconceived the nature of his literary enterprise, since the resort "isn't set in the future at all, but in a kind of visionary present." He goes on to suggest that this attempt to extrapolate an imaginatively coherent future from contemporary life fits all his stories "and almost everything else I have written."

Some of Ballard's earliest stories, such as "Prima Belladonna" and "Venus Smiles" (June 1957), both published in *Science Fantasy* magazine, are set in Vermilion Sands, and they conjure up a dreamy, evocative landscape that is as much a state of mind as a habitable place. The resort is peopled by characters living out a limbo-like existence, while the mundane realities of their everyday lives are disturbed by exotic women, seen by David Pringle as exemplars of Carl Gustav Jung's concept of the anima. In "Prima Belladonna" the mysterious Jane Ciracylides exudes a potent glamour and sexuality from the moment of her arrival. Although she entrances the male characters in the concept of the story, she is principally interested in the narrator's singing plants, especially his prize possession, a rare orchid.

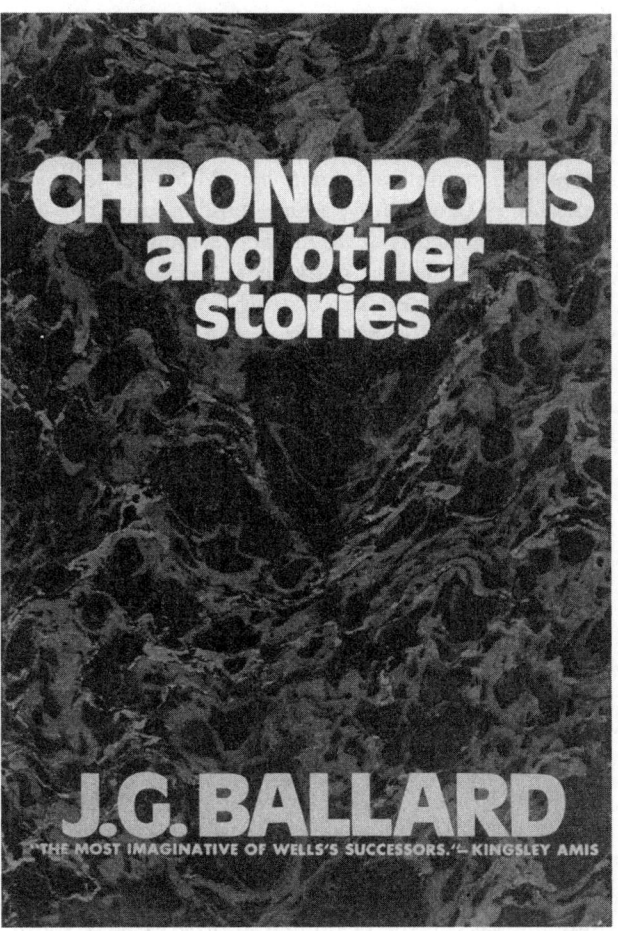

Dust jacket for Ballard's 1971 collection of science-fiction stories. The title refers to a society in which clocks have been outlawed (Richland County Public Library).

The story ends when plant and woman consummate their passion in an ecstasy that leaves Jane's fate uncertain. "Venus Smiles" explores transfiguring female power in a different way. Lorraine Drexel, a famous sculptor, is commissioned to make a sonic sculpture for the central square of Vermilion Sands, but her jagged metal construction is universally deplored. When the statue is destroyed and melted down, the metal is recycled for industrial use and turns up in the girders of new buildings, which start to hum and vibrate just as Drexel had intended her sculpture to do. The narrator of the story is struck by the beauty of the "strange abstracted music" and is elated at the prospect of a world transformed by song.

Other stories—such as "Escapement" (December 1956), "The Concentration City," first published as "Build-up" (January 1957), and "Manhole 69" (November 1957), all published in *New Worlds*—deal with themes of alienation and entrapment. In these stories Ballard tries to picture how the future might look if key features of contemporary life were to be taken to their logical end. They deal with problems such as urban sprawl, overpopulation, environmental despoliation, the contraction of living space, and the power of science to dominate human life. More generally, the question of temporality, a long-standing preoccupation, figures prominently. Two literary techniques frequently employed by Ballard mark these tales: they open in medias res, the narration starting from a point halfway into the chronological order of events and then track back to the beginning, a strategy that plunges the reader straight into the story; and they adopt a viewpoint that treats the central protagonist (often the narrator) as though he were deranged, while the world against which he is struggling is calmly accepted as normal and beneficent. This latter technique forces readers to question their habitual acceptance of social reality by playing on the discrepancy between "official" and "subversive" accounts of it and by emphasizing the power of dominant groups to impose their views of the world on ordinary people. An atmosphere of paranoia pervades many of these early stories, which are preoccupied with conspiracies against the questioning citizen.

"Escapement" is an example of Ballard's abiding concern with the question of time. The tale depicts a time loop in which events are repeated every fifteen minutes or so. The first-person narrator gradually realizes that the program he and his wife are watching is jumping back to the beginning in progressively shorter intervals of time, trapping him in a recursive temporal schema. His identity splits in two. One of his selves remains locked in the time loop, while the other observes what is happening but is powerless to alter events; his desperate attempts to tell his wife what is occurring meet with failure as the time available to him before the return to the beginning of the loop keeps running out. When the gap becomes infinitesimal, he is catapulted back into real time, but now the process has transferred itself to his wife. The story touches on the theme of entrapment in temporality and points to the inescapability of repetition in life, thereby hinting at the deadening effect of habit and routine.

These concerns are explored further in "The Concentration City," which focuses on a dream of escape from an all-enveloping urban space. Ballard imagines the city as an industrial hive inhabited by vast numbers of people and as an infinitely extended terrain. The notion of "non-functional" space, which serves no purpose but simply exists, is regarded as an absurdity. The central protagonist dreams of building a flying machine that will enable him to escape this technological anthill, but his attempt to discover the city limits ends in failure. Sent to see a psychiatrist because the search for free space is as ridiculous as the desire to escape time, he is told that egress from the city is impossible. A twist in the story, however, exposes this bureaucratic falsehood as a means of social control. The would-be escapee realizes that time has in fact been turned back when he spots that the date on the calendar is the same as when he embarked on his journey three weeks earlier, an occurrence suggesting that if time can be reversed then it might indeed be possible to escape urban space. "Manhole 69," in turn, depicts a scientist who strives to do away with the need for sleep in the belief that the ability to remain fully conscious at all times represents an evolutionary leap forward. In a critique of Enlightenment aspirations, Ballard presents this figure as making an assault on the unconscious and on the necessary archetypal race memories located there. The result of the experiment conducted on three human guinea pigs is their withdrawal into states of catatonia, which is presented as the consequence of their being forced to live without the possibility of any release from the burden of consciousness.

The theme of transformation is developed in two stories published in *New Worlds,* "The Waiting Grounds" (November 1959), in which the planet Murak stands revealed as the site on which the renewal of the cosmos will begin, and "The Voices of Time" (October 1960), with its poetic closing lines. "Studio 5, the Stars" (February 1961), published in *Science Fantasy,* describes how another beautiful woman weaves her magic, this time restoring genuine creativity to a group of poets whose works have hitherto been written by machines. "Chronopolis," published in *New Worlds* (June 1960), returns to the temporal theme, envisaging a world in which clock time has been outlawed. Its central figure is besotted by the precision and structure that clocks impose on life, and he escapes to the heart of a deserted city in order to try to start the clocks again, despite having been warned that time has been used in the past to regulate and mechanize human life. After he has been caught and sentenced to prison, he becomes aware of the incessant ticking of the clock on his wall, a reversal that hints at the tyranny of time. "Billenium," published in *New Worlds* (November 1961), describes a city so overpopulated that people are forced to live in four square meters of space. Space is so scarce that gridlock on the streets is caused not by cars but by people, who find themselves woven together for hours before they can be disentangled from one another. Two characters find a large hidden room but cannot resist sharing their secret; before long, two girlfriends and their parents have moved in, and the room is progressively subdivided until each individual's living space has been reduced to four square meters. The reader is left to wonder if the decision to share the room was an act of altruism or a sign that people have adapted to living in such close proximity to one another that they cannot cope with so much space. The desire to escape from personal identity and indeed from the world itself also figures in "The Overloaded Man," published in *New Worlds* (July 1961), in which the main character, finding coping with constant stimuli difficult, progressively blots out everything external to himself in a search for "an absolute continuum of existence uncontaminated by material excrescences."

"Thirteen to Centaurus," first published in *Amazing Stories* (April 1962), develops the theme of the scientist-experimenter in its depiction of a fake space mission to the planet Centaurus, which has been devised for the sole purpose of studying the reactions of the astronauts with a view to future space probes. A gifted boy on the spacecraft has seen through the subterfuge, and the story traces a reverse logic in which the reader learns that the astronauts have probably been in on the secret for some time and that Abel may be conducting an experiment of his own, studying the scientists no less than they are studying him. Another view of the significance of the space program is provided by "The Cage of Sand," a moving story from *New Worlds* (June 1962), which describes the efforts of three characters to keep faith with the dream of space travel in the aftermath of the failure to colonize Mars. In an attempt to stabilize the earth's core, the authorities have deposited huge amounts of Martian sand in the Atlantic Ocean and Caspian Sea, an act that has had disastrous ecological consequences. The contaminated terrain has been cordoned off and its inhabitants ordered to evacuate the area. Three isolated figures have chosen to remain in the area, however, each seeking to atone for some personal sense of failure by staying loyal to the dead astronauts whose abortive missions to Mars have left them orbiting space in the satellites that have become their coffins. This haunting tale evokes the human longing to free the spirit by extending the bounds of the conceivable; despite the failure of the attempt to colonize Mars, the protagonists continue to exult in the imaginative promise offered by space travel.

Ballard's stories of the 1960s explore a wide range of disparate themes. "The Subliminal Man," published in *New Worlds* (January 1963), offers an early view of anxieties about subliminal advertising techniques, which insidiously coerce individuals to purchase unnecessary products. The story portrays a world entirely driven by consumerism, and this world is blithely accepted by everybody except a maverick figure who is derided as a madman when really he is the only person to understand what is happening. "The Venus Hunters," originally published as "The Encounter" in *Amazing Stories* (June 1963), suggests that a Venusian

Front cover of the 1978 U.S. paperback, which includes early Ballard stories involving conspiracies against questioning citizens (Richland County Public Library)

spacecraft may have visited Earth. While most of the characters in the story mock this claim as nothing more than a fantasy dredged from the unconscious, a skeptical scientist witnesses a second Venusian landing and realizes that the claim is true. His attempts to persuade others meet with failure, though, and his career as an active research scientist is destroyed as a result of his loss of credibility.

Ballard was extraordinarily prolific during the late 1950s and early 1960s. He was now supporting a family with three children—two daughters, Fay and Beatrice, had followed the birth of James Christopher. Ballard's wife died unexpectedly from pneumonia in 1964, leaving him to bring up the three children on his own. Needing to provide for the family financially, he continued to produce stories and novels at an impressive rate. "Time of Passage" (February 1964), published in *Science Fantasy*, is an unsettling but strangely poetic tale that narrates a character's life story backward from the moment of his death to his birth. "The Terminal Beach," published in *New Worlds* (March 1964), offers a glimpse into the preoccupations that inform *The Atrocity Exhibition*. A former military pilot named Traven maroons himself on Eniwetok Island in an attempt to make sense of a series of seemingly unconnected events: the death of his wife and son, the meaning of the atomic-bomb tests, and the "cryptic alphabets" of the island landscape, with its derelict bunkers, blockhouses, and surveillance towers. Obsessed with death, Traven sees the period in which he is living as an interregnum before the onset of a third world war, the advent of which he believes can be predicted by decoding the language of the island, which he sees as "a fossil of time future."

The issue of personal identity is central to most of Ballard's stories, which explore the ways in which human beings might need to change in order to welcome a new reality, not just to cope with it. Inasmuch as many of them are cautionary tales warning of the dangers confronting a race in thrall to the wonders of technology, they also suggest that these dangers must be faced if they are to be overcome. In a 1976 interview, Ballard speculated that humans' "talent for the perverse, the violent, and the obscene, may be a good thing" and that humankind might have to pass through a disintegrative phase in order to move beyond "the equation, sex times technology equals the future." Many of Ballard's protagonists are thus questing figures who struggle against an alienated world or confront catastrophic events in an attempt to understand the logic of their situation and to meet the challenge it represents. Ballard sees this commitment to the quest as a form of optimism, and he suggested in a 1982 interview with Catherine Bresson that his is "a fiction of psychic fulfillment" that enables his protagonists gradually to learn "the truth about themselves." Ballard's stories thus focus as much on inner space—the response of the mind to far-reaching change—as on external events. The haunting, detritus-ridden lunar landscapes that feature in so much of his work function as portals to the unconscious, just as they do in the Surrealist paintings Ballard admires; the voyages upon which his characters embark represent attempts to synthesize the conscious and unconscious parts of the mind.

In the late 1960s and early 1970s Ballard's exploration of identity became more experimental. During this period he was overtly concerned with changes in the contemporary political and cultural landscape, a preoccupation that took him beyond science fiction. Although he continued to produce stories recognizable as science fiction, this shift lost him some of his former devotees, who were critical of the direction he was taking. Stories such as "The Assassination of John Fitzgerald Kennedy Considered as a Downhill Motor Race,"

published in *Ambit* (Spring 1966), and "Why I Want to Fuck Ronald Reagan" (*The Magazine of Poetry*, 1968), both of which are included in *The Atrocity Exhibition*, shocked many readers and critics by their irreverent approach to politics and their avant-garde conception of narrative structure. The former story, which was influenced by Alfred Jarry's "The Crucifixion Considered as an Uphill Bicycle Race" (1911), offers an alternative to the conventional view of what occurred in Dealey Plaza; it exposes the farcical nature of subsequent events and suggests that Vice President Lyndon Johnson may have been involved in Kennedy's death. The Reagan story, in turn, which focuses on Reagan's subliminal sexual appeal to voters, draws attention to the role played by television in contemporary politics, concentrating on the discrepancy between the public image of the then-governor of California and his policies. Ballard's calculatedly obscene story suggests that its shocking title and its sexualization of Reagan are as nothing compared with the real obscenity at work in contemporary culture—the treatment of politics as a form of advertising. This powerful story effects an assault on the culture of celebrity explored by Ballard in *The Atrocity Exhibition*, an experimental work that is equally concerned with psychosis, paranoia, apocalyptic violence, sexuality, and the influence of the communications industries.

"The Comsat Angels," published in *Worlds of If* (December 1968), pursues the link between technology and politics; Ballard imagines a situation in which a group of supremely intelligent child prodigies band together in a conspiracy to take over the world. "The Killing Ground," published in *New Worlds* (March 1969), critiques American imperialism in Vietnam by shifting the action to Britain, where a united peasantry opposes all attempts at pacification, a subject Ballard explores again in "Theatre of War," published in *Bananas* (Winter 1977). Meanwhile, the novel *Crash* pursues the union of sex and technology to a shocking conclusion by presenting the car crash as the symbol of a deviant contemporary logic. The dark and violent works from this period divided Ballard's critics. Whereas some of them objected to what they saw as a quietist acceptance of dehumanization and nihilism, others praised Ballard as a perceptive diagnostician of a posthumanist, narcissistic world and applauded his imaginative deployment of the collage technique to depict a fragmented reality.

Ballard's interest in the impact of the mass media and telecommunications industries on everyday life is a marked feature of his writing in the 1970s. "The Greatest Television Show on Earth," first published in *Ambit* (Winter 1972/1973), is a witty but serious exploration of the ways in which television has come to dominate late-twentieth-century life. The story is predicated on the possibility of time travel, which is exploited by television companies that travel back in time to film key historical events. When these events turn out to be insufficiently grandiose in scale and drama, the television companies start to employ actors and extras in order to make them more spectacular, before eventually changing history itself in order to boost ratings. The story shows how deeply television has colonized the imagination and exposes the extent to which its commercial imperatives drive it to falsify the past. A different aspect of the mediated image is at issue in "The 60 Minute Zoom" (Summer 1976) and "Motel Architecture" (Autumn 1978), both published in *Bananas*. The first of these stories focuses on the voyeuristic logic of the camera lens and its etiolation of the emotions. A man secretly films his wife's sexual infidelities, seeing her behavior as a series of stylized, abstract acts, which he relentlessly aestheticizes. His detachment from the reality of what he is filming and what it means to him personally is so complete that he absentmindedly kills his wife and then reruns the film of the killing in the serene conviction that he is thereby rediscovering the intimacies of his marriage. The story explores the damaging effects on subjectivity of a mediated social realm, focusing on its reduction of identity to a series of fantasized roles that detach the self from the external world. In "Motel Architecture" this desolation of identity is so unbearable that its narrator, who has spent years watching the murder scene in Alfred Hitchcock's motion picture *Psycho* (1960), is unable to stand what he has become and chooses to end his life. The stylization of human behavior that figures so prominently in Ballard's stories and novels is shown in these stories to be a parodic reflection of a cinematic imagery that distances subjects from both themselves and others, leading them to treat life as nothing but a huge, inconsequential fiction.

In the late 1970s, Ballard extended his range further still. By now an established and critically lauded writer, he continued to produce groundbreaking novels and innovative short stories. "The Smile," for example, published in *Bananas* (Autumn/Winter 1976), considers a man's obsession with a life-like mannequin that turns out to have been a real woman who has been embalmed by a taxidermist, while, in complete contrast to this tale, "The Dead Time," published in *Bananas* (Spring 1977), is Ballard's first attempt to write about his wartime internment in Lunghua Camp. From "The Dead Time" grew the award-winning novel *Empire of the Sun*, which was widely praised by critics, many of whom found this accessible novel more to their taste than Ballard's diverse explorations of narrative technique and his fascination with seemingly bizarre topics. "The Index," which like the previous two stories was published in *Bananas* (Summer 1977), is an experimental work that consists of an index to an autobiography and an editor's note explaining that nothing remains of this planned work by "one of the most remarkable figures of the 20th century," except for the index itself. Nothing seems to be known about this secretive figure's existence, the meaning of which can only be glimpsed in the brief headings of the index. Yet, its alphabetical entries permit the reader to reconstruct the life of a talismanic figure who seems to have been involved in the most significant events of the twentieth century. The piecing together of his life thus amounts to a reconstruction of the history of the last hundred years, but the structure of "The Index" also points to the different ways in which the story of a life can be told. It suggests that the traditional chronology of biographical accounts endows the history of a life with a comforting but false unity, which the elliptical index resolutely refuses to verify, thereby calling into question the factual basis upon which both history and biography are allegedly predicated. "The Intensive Care Unit," published in *Ambit* (Summer 1977), dramatizes the consequences of a social existence in which human beings never interact with each other physically but instead conduct their emotionless relationships by way of television screens. The first-person narrator makes the mistake of trying to meet his wife in the flesh, only to find that reality cannot live up to the expectations induced in him by the images of her to which he has grown accustomed. When he persists in trying to bring his wife and children together, the contact between the family members proves disastrous, and a scene of murderous violence ensues.

The relatively few short stories that Ballard produced in the 1980s and 1990s suggest that he was devoting more attention to his novels. "News from the Sun," published in *Ambit* (Autumn 1981), and "Memories of the Space Age" (1982), published in *Interzone*, both return to the theme of time and to the metaphysical significance of the now-abandoned space program. The first of these two stories takes place in the desert around Las Vegas, where a group of characters for whom time is coming to a halt tries to make sense of the implications of the space program. Speculating that space travel may have foreshadowed the possibility that the human race could escape temporality, the protagonist of the tale welcomes his entry into a cosmic present that will last for eternity, uniting him with the sun. In "Memories of the Space Age" the murder in space of an astronaut has destroyed the dream of exploring the cosmos. The story suggests that space travel is just the first stage of a more absolute flight altogether, an escape from temporality, which may represent an evolutionary step forward. Similar preoccupations inform "Myths of the Near Future," published in *Fantasy and Science Fiction* (October 1982), a story that further explores the visionary dimension of space travel.

Front cover for the 2002 London paperback edition (Thomas Cooper Library, University of South Carolina)

A different set of concerns lies behind the novella *Running Wild*. This chilling exercise in psychological notation depicts the grotesque consequences of a supposedly enlightened approach to family life. A massacre has taken place on a luxury housing estate: all the parents have been murdered, and the children have disappeared. The narrator, Dr. Greville, brought in to see if he can shed any light on what has happened, eventually grasps that the children have murdered their parents, but he also sees that the estate is a housing scheme designed to render its inhabitants visible at all times. The exposure of daily life to the eye of the security camera thus mirrors the parents' overly zealous approach to child rearing. Greville concludes that this overregulation of their lives has produced in the children a "schizophrenic detachment from reality" that has led them to embrace madness as a revolt against their entrapment "within a perfect universe" from which all traces of pleasure have been expunged. The novella thus mounts a critique of fantasies of order and control, suggesting that fetishes based on rationalism have destroyed the children's emotional lives and shattered their sense of moral value. A similar concern with an overly rational regulation of life also appears in "Love in a Colder Climate," published in *Interview* (January 1989), a story in which sex has become a compulsory social duty because the birth rate has collapsed. Like the narrator of Evgenii Zamiatin's *We* (1924), the central protagonist rebels by falling in love with a woman through whom he discovers "a wealth of emotion and affection" that makes him "envy all earlier generations."

The stories Ballard wrote in the late 1980s and early 1990s develop several of the themes that feature in his earliest work. In "The Enormous Space," published in *Interzone* (July/August 1989), a man shuts himself off from external reality in an attempt to enter a world more real than the "small illusory world" of everyday, routine-filled life. "The Largest Theme Park in the World" (*The Guardian*, 7 July 1989) subverts stereotypes about bohemian beach communities. In a newly federated Europe, a leisure society emerges in which groups of latter-day beatniks colonize the beaches of the Mediterranean. As they gain in strength and confidence, they develop a cult of bodily perfection and start to resemble the fascists of old, eventually creating "a nationalistic and authoritarian creed" as a counterpart to "the first totalitarian system based on leisure." The two-page "A Guide to Virtual Death" (*Interzone* [February 1992]) foretells the extinction of intelligent life on Earth through a simple conceit. It provides a twenty-four-hour television schedule filled with banal and dehumanizing programs concerned with violence, pornography, pseudoscience, and news items that deal only with disasters of one kind or another. The last tale in *The Complete Short Stories,* "Report from an Obscure Planet," first published in *Leonardo* (April 1992), neatly complements "A Guide to Virtual Death." The obscure planet is Earth, and the report offered by a visiting species suggests that the demise of its inhabitants may be traced back to their decision willingly to embrace a virtual realm in which "the imitation of reality was more convincing than the original." The slightly puzzled reporter then speculates that this decision perhaps led the inhabitants of the planet to see themselves and their world as "mere illusions by comparison with the electronically generated amusement park where they preferred to play," an existential choice that ultimately led to their extinction when "the computers of this planet, having welcomed the population into this cave of illusion, then made a desperate decision and entombed them magnetically."

Since publishing his first story in 1956, Ballard has contributed in inventive ways not only to the science-fiction tradition but also more generally to the short story. He has written on the most-pressing issues facing the late twentieth century, exposing the covert logics at work in a technologized information society and investigating their effects on human subjectivity. He has thus proved himself an important analyst of the age while simultaneously provoking a good deal of critical controversy. His multiple themes and his willingness to write in a wide variety of styles and genres make his work difficult to categorize, but his significance is no longer in dispute. Michel Delville, in his *J. G. Ballard* (1998), claims that Ballard's "fiction seeks to challenge nothing less than the psychic and material parameters" by which humans attempt to regulate their everyday lives. Since Ballard itemizes the negative features of the contemporary landscape, he has also tried to imagine how it might be transformed. Glimpses of a utopian alternative are offered in the metamorphic fictions he has written throughout his career. In his introduction to *Myths of the Near Future* (1982), for example, Ballard describes himself as a romantic who still believes that the "sense of the future remains intact, a submerged realm of hopes and dreams that lies below the surface of our minds, ready to wake again as one millennium closes and the next begins." Ballard thus suggests that the voyage into the depths of the untapped psyche is perhaps "the last journey waiting for all of us," a journey that will provide entry to "the inward passage to our truer and richer selves."

J. G. Ballard's excavations of the modern psyche in its manifold responses to the uncertainties of late-twentieth-century social life have gained him a considerable critical reputation, and he is widely regarded as one of the most significant chroniclers of an ambiguous and threatening age. He has been influential in the field of science fiction, has been a major spokesperson for the continuing vitality and relevance of the Surrealist legacy, and has produced groundbreaking apocalyptic fictions. At once a visionary and analytical writer, Ballard has tapped into the darkest sources of the mind in an attempt to lay bare the inner logics that inform the far-reaching processes of social, economic, political, and scientific change. Ballard is now widely recognized as a major postmodern writer whose unsettling mythologies of a future world, just visible over the horizon, make him a key postwar British novelist and short-story writer.

Interviews:

James Goddard and David Pringle, *J. G. Ballard: The First Twenty Years* (Hayes, U.K.: Bran's Head, 1976), pp. 8–35;

Alan Burns and Charles Sugnet, eds., *The Imagination on Trial: British and American Writers Discuss Their Working Methods* (London & New York: Allison & Busby, 1981), pp. 14–30;

Catherine Bresson, "J. G. Ballard at Home," *S.F. Fantastique: Métaphores,* 7 (1982): 5–29;

David Pringle, "From Shanghai to Shepperton," *Foundation: The Review of Science Fiction,* 24 (1982): 5–23;

Thomas Frick, "The Art of Fiction: J. G. Ballard," *Paris Review,* 94 (1984): 132–160;

Andrea Juno and Vivian Vale, "Interview with J. G. Ballard," in *RE/Search 8/9: J. G. Ballard,* edited by Juno and Vale (San Francisco: RE/Search, 1984), pp. 6–35;

Graeme Revell, "Interview with J. G. Ballard," in *RE/Search 8/9: J. G. Ballard,* pp. 42–52;

Will Self, "Conversations: J. G. Ballard," in his *Junk Mail* (London: Penguin, 1996), pp. 329–371;

Jason Cowley, "Portrait: J. G. Ballard," *Prospect* (August/September 1998).

Bibliographies:

James Goddard, *J. G. Ballard: A Bibliography* (Lymington, U.K.: Cypher Press, 1970);

David Pringle, *J. G. Ballard: A Primary and Secondary Bibliography* (Boston: G. K. Hall, 1984).

References:

Jean Baudrillard, "Ballard's *Crash,*" *Science Fiction Studies,* 55 (November 1991): 309–313;

Peter Brigg, *J. G. Ballard* (Mercer Island, Wash.: Starmont House, 1985);

Michel Delville, *J. G. Ballard* (Plymouth, U.K.: Northcote House, 1998);

Dennis Foster, "J. G. Ballard's Empire of the Senses: Perversion and the Failure of Authority," *PMLA,* 108 (May 1993): 519–532;

Colin Greenland, *The Entropy Exhibition: Michael Moorcock and the British "New Wave" in Science Fiction* (London: Routledge & Kegan Paul, 1983);

Roger Luckhurst, *"The Angle between Two Walls": The Fiction of J. G. Ballard* (New York: St. Martin's Press, 1997);

David Pringle, *Earth Is the Alien Planet: J. G. Ballard's Four-Dimensional Nightmare* (San Bernardino, Cal.: Borgo Press, 1979);

Pringle and James Goddard, eds., *J. G. Ballard: The First Twenty Years* (Hayes, U.K.: Bran's Head, 1976);

Gregory Stephenson, *Out of the Night and into the Dream: A Thematic Study of the Fiction of J. G. Ballard* (Westport, Conn.: Greenwood Press, 1991);

Vivian Vale and Andrea Juno, eds., *RE/Search 8/9: J. G. Ballard* (San Francisco: RE/Search, 1984).

Mary Beckett
(28 January 1926 –)

Bridget Matthews-Kane
University of Massachusetts, Amherst

BOOKS: *A Belfast Woman and Other Stories* (Dublin: Poolbeg, 1980; New York: Morrow, 1989);
Give Them Stones (Dublin: Poolbeg, 1987; New York: Beech Tree, 1987);
Orla Was Six (Dublin: Poolbeg, 1989);
A Literary Woman (London: Bloomsbury, 1990);
Orla at School (Dublin: Poolbeg, 1991);
A Family Tree (Dublin: Poolbeg, 1992);
Hannah or Pink Balloons (Dublin: Poolbeg, 1995).

PRODUCED SCRIPTS: "The Excursion," radio, BBC Northern Ireland, 25 October 1949;
"Someone to Play With," radio, BBC Northern Ireland, 18 March 1950; *Morning Story,* BBC, 2 November 1953;
"The Green Shirt," radio, BBC Northern Ireland, 7 June 1950;
"Education," radio, BBC Northern Ireland, 23 May 1951;
"Afternoon Team," radio, BBC Northern Ireland, 30 August 1951;
"The Pilgrimage," radio, BBC Northern Ireland, 9 April 1954;
"Give Them Stones," radio, *Booktime,* Radio Telefís Éireann, 9 November–4 December 1987; 10 October–4 November 1988.

TRANSLATION: Peadar O Doirnin, "Séamus Mac Murray," *Rann,* no. 20 (June 1953).

SELECTED PERIODICAL PUBLICATIONS–
UNCOLLECTED: "The Young Writer," *Bell,* 17 (October 1951): 18–20;
"Pilgrimage," *Bell,* 17 (January 1952): 13–20;
"Millstones," *Bell,* 19 (February 1954): 48–52;
"Three Dreams Cross," *Irish Writing,* 27 (June 1954): 34–39;
"The Weaker Sex," *Threshold,* 2 (Spring 1958): 6–11.

Mary Beckett (from the dust jacket for Give Them Stones, *1987; Richland County Public Library)*

Mary Beckett's reputation rests on her truthful portraits of the lives of women, particularly her groundbreaking work giving voice to Catholic women from Northern Ireland. Her talent for rendering faithful, unsentimental pictures of these women's lives added a new voice to Irish literature at the time of their initial publication. The deftness of her characterizations and her ability to crystallize a life into a moment propel her short stories. While the politics of Northern Ireland sometimes serves as a backdrop to her work, it often appears not so much in bombs and explosions as in the small details of women's lives.

Beckett was born in Belfast on 28 January 1926. Her parents, Sean Beckett, a principal teacher, and Catherine (Bryson) Beckett, a homemaker, had four children, two boys and two girls. While her father worked at a boy's school in a poor neighborhood, her family lived in a more prosperous section of Belfast. The family's Catholic and Nationalist background, however, separated them from their Protestant and Unionist neighbors. This difference, coupled with her father's socialist leanings, made Beckett particularly attuned to the social dynamics in Northern Ireland. While Belfast society had distinctive expectations for men and women, Beckett's neighborhood was filled with strong women who served as positive role models for the young writer.

Beckett received her education at St. Columban's National School and St. Dominic's High School. Coming from a family of educators, she continued her studies at St. Mary's Training College and upon graduating at age nineteen taught at Holy Cross primary school in Ardoyne, Belfast. She worked there for the next eleven years (1945–1956) and taught students of all ages, from four to fourteen, sometimes in large classes. The school served students from a Catholic, working-class area, and the parents and children often told Beckett their tales of hardship and deprivation, which she used as the basis for some of her first writings. The invisibility of Catholics in English and American literature further spurred Beckett to write. One of the few Catholic writers she read, Michael McLaverty, another teacher from Belfast, inspired her to try crafting her own short stories in the evening after teaching. When in 1949 she heard about a BBC short-story competition being held in Northern Ireland, she entered her story "The Excursion," which won first prize. In the tale, Mrs. Teggart, a stifled housewife from the Belfast countryside, wishes to participate in a group trip to Dublin. Prevented from traveling by her reticence and her husband's uncharacteristic desire to travel, she stays behind and fantasizes how this break in her husband's routine will also break the dull monotony of their marriage. Enraged to find upon his return that he spent the day drinking in a pub, the frustrated woman stops imagining her revitalized life and instead imagines his death as she briefly considers pushing his inebriated body into the fire. The quiet desperation and trapped circumstances of the main character introduce themes that persist throughout Beckett's literary career.

After Beckett's initial success with "The Excursion," more of her stories were broadcast on the Northern Ireland Home Service of the BBC, a medium that made her attuned to the oral qualities of her work. She also published short stories in the influential Irish publications of the day: the literary journal *Threshold* (Belfast), the liberal literary monthly *The Bell* (Dublin), and David Marcus's literary quarterly *Irish Writing* (Cork). Her stories, set in and around Belfast, portray a world in which even the blessings of life can be tainted, leaving the characters in an ambivalent and compromised state. In "A Farm of Land," published in *The Bell* in July 1951, Susan Lavery sells the family farm. Her neighbors disapprove of how quickly she abandons the rich fields that were her parents' pride, but Susan knows the farm was bought at far too high a price: years of backbreaking frugality, the early deaths of her brothers, and the sacrifice of her education. "Flags and Emblems," from the Autumn 1955 issue of *Irish Writing,* portrays a moment in a Belfast "mixed marriage." Rachel, a Protestant Unionist, impulsively thrusts a small Union Jack into her young son's hand after a tiff with her husband, Fergus. The public sight of the father, a Catholic Nationalist, standing with his young son waving the British flag sets him up to be completely ostracized by his community. Only after, does the wife realize the gravity of her action, but the love between the two redeems the quiet tragedy that has unfolded. In "Ruth," from the first issue of *Threshold* (February 1957), Rose Killen regretfully realizes how her unquestioning acceptance of the cultural norm of silence and reserve has intensified her family's troubles. As she tells two nosy neighbors: "Why do we not talk about things? Because that's another risk. It's giving a wee bit of yourself, nearly like loving. It's safer saying nothing, give nothing, love nothing. . . . That's the way I've lived my life, and I've lost my child and my grandchild." Beckett's careful rendering of conversation colored by hints and innuendos subtly echoes the themes of the story.

During the mid 1950s, Beckett traveled to Inishmore, one of the Aran Islands off the west coast of Ireland, and met another vacationer, Peter Gaffey, a civil servant from Dublin. Beckett teases that he was initially attracted to her because she was a writer. After a correspondence, they married in 1956. She moved to Dublin, and they started a family, which after the death of her first child in infancy eventually grew to include two daughters, Anne and Veronica, and three sons, Michael, Gerard, and John. Her writing stopped. While the pressure of raising a family became an impediment, the closing of the small literary magazines she wrote for and her dislocation from Belfast, the setting she knew so intimately, also hindered her creativity.

During the intervening years, life in the north of Ireland changed. After the start of the Troubles in 1968 marked a new escalation to the conflict, Belfast, never an easy place for a Catholic to live in, became

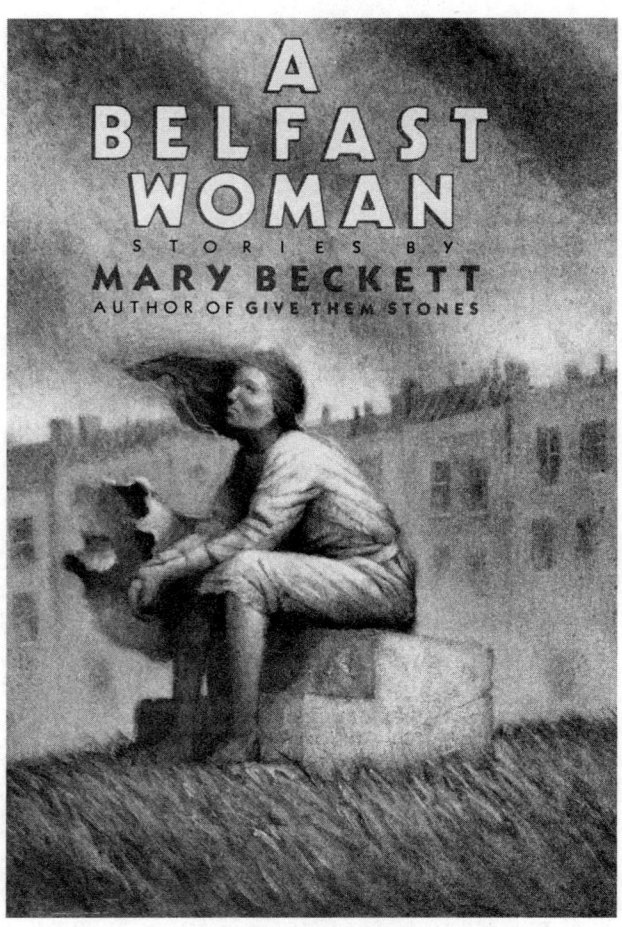

Dust jacket for Beckett's first short-story collection. Some stories deal with the "Troubles," while others deal with common problems, such as distant husbands and illegitimate babies (Richland County Public Library).

even more difficult. Living in the comfortable Dublin suburb of Templeogue, Beckett found her middle-class neighbors did not understand the situation in the North, a realization that motivated her to attempt an explanation. At the same time, an editor who was familiar with her earlier works encouraged her to start writing again. She published a new story, "A Belfast Woman," in the literary section of the *Irish Press* (10 March 1979). In the tale, Mary Harrison, a Catholic whose life is punctuated by terror, reminisces about her years in Belfast. The continuing violence in her life demonstrates that the Troubles is not a new problem but rather a continuance of old grievances. The home of Mary's parents was burned down in 1921, and when they were threatened with the same again in 1935, they moved. Her son Liam is burned out in 1972, but when Mary is threatened as an elderly lady, she takes a stand. Her resolution to stay makes the reader hopeful that the cycle of violence can stop. The ending of the story, which reveals that the beautiful sunsets of Belfast are caused by smog, underscores this optimistic message. As a traveling salesman comments, " . . . if the dirt and dust and smoke and pollution of Belfast just with the help of the sun can make a sky like that, then there's hope for all of us."

The success of "A Belfast Woman" eventually led Poolbeg Press to publish a collection with the same title in 1980. While *A Belfast Woman* includes a new story, "Failing Years," most of the eleven stories are reprints of her earlier publications: "Theresa," "A Farm of Land," "Saints and Scholars," and "The Balancing of the Clouds" from *The Bell* (May 1951, July 1951, March 1953, and November 1954 respectively); "Flags and Emblems" from *Irish Writing* (Autumn 1955); "Ruth" from *Threshold* (February 1957); and "The Excursion" from the BBC competition. The stories deal with women's lives and the ways the world tramples them and their aspirations. Some tales deal directly with the Troubles, while others deal with more-common female dilemmas: aloof husbands, lost loves, distant children, illegitimate babies, and spiteful mothers-in-law. The melancholy stories all plumb the pain of these women's lives, but Beckett's understated and unsentimental prose turns their grief into beauty. Critics commented on the spare, subtle, and simple (but not simplistic) power of her writing; Gregory Schirmer, for example, observed in his review for the *Washington Post* (19 February 1989) that the stories "demonstrate an admirable ability to get to the emotional center of a given situation." Beckett demonstrates this skill in "The Master and the Bombs," a story she wrote in the 1960s. In this tale a schoolteacher is charged with storing munitions for the Irish Republican Army (IRA) in a coal shed. The narrator vehemently insists her husband is innocent of all charges, and whether this claim is denial or the truth, her husband can use the allegations as a convenient escape from the drudgery of his work and the staleness of his marriage. The narrator's revelations expose that she, too, has sought an escape from the stagnation of her loveless marriage and life in Northern Ireland, except her route has been the bearing and raising of children. The final story of the collection, "Failing Years," nicely balances the opening story, "The Excursion." In this story, an elderly woman named Nora desires to travel from Dublin to Belfast, the city of her childhood. Nora attempts the journey as a way of recapturing the security and warmth of her youth and escaping the trapped life she now has with her caretaker daughter, Una. Bombs on the railway line, however, have made the journey difficult, and the weak and forgetful woman ends up back home, confronted by her worried daughter. The story portrays how violence prevents Northerners from separating themselves from their history or recapturing the snatches of safety and security they experienced in the past.

In 1987 Beckett followed up her first collection with the publication of *Give Them Stones,* for which she won an Arts Award from the Dublin *Sunday Tribune.* This realistic novel, which took Beckett four years to write, portrays the life of the narrator, Martha Murtagh, a stoic working-class Catholic from Belfast. Martha's plainspoken and sometimes dreary voice relates her experiences from her childhood in the 1930s to her middle age. Beckett explores the connections between nationalism, feminism, and socialism and demonstrates, as Donna Perry stated in a 1993 interview with Beckett, "one woman's radicalization, . . . one woman's coming to political consciousness." Martha's problems, from asking her husband for cash to having her house burned down for refusing to pay the IRA protection money, demonstrate both the small indignities and the larger injustices that women, especially poor Catholic women, face in the North. Evenhanded in her portrayal of the Troubles, Beckett depicts both the pettiness of the IRA and the humanity of the British soldiers.

Beckett's next collection of short stories, *A Literary Woman* (1990), marks a break from her previous work; these tales are set in a middle-class Dublin suburb. The ten stories, which involve families, again depict the disappointments and failings in the lives of their female protagonists. An anonymous letter writer, who speculates on the shortcomings of her neighbors and then mails spiteful accusations to them, unifies the collection; in each piece the reader watches the repercussions the letter has set in motion. Only in the penultimate story, "A Literary Woman," does the reader learn the identity of the malicious mischief maker and hear her own sad tale. This ironically titled story shows the readers the potential destruction possible in the art of fiction. Beckett further emphasizes the power of writing with the story "Under Control," an epistle from one sister to another. In it a woman gives vent to feelings of annoyance with her oldest daughter. As the letter progresses, the reader learns that this daughter had an illegitimate child, whom the grandmother is now raising as her own. The story is most effective in its use of its unreliable narrator, who inadvertently displays her domineering and controlling nature.

As in her earlier collection, Beckett's strength lies in the subtle conveyance of her characters' dilemmas. Like many other critics, Miranda Seymour, in her review in *The Sunday Times* (22 April 1990), observed that the "unusual quality of Beckett's writing lies in the sharpness of her discretely conveyed perceptions. Nothing is stated directly; everything is suggested by artful juxtaposition or the unexpected twist of the sentence." In her stories Beckett balances the pain and anguish in her characters' lives with the beauty of her writing and her compassion toward her characters' shortcomings. Patricia Coughlan, in her essay "Special Pleading?" (1991), argues that in the collection Beckett qualifies her endorsement of women's liberation. While in "Sudden Infant Death" and the often-anthologized "Heaven" she shows the hollowness and loss of self that can occur in women who too strictly follow the dictates of traditional gender roles, in "Inheritance" and "The Cypress Trees" she shows the shallowness and selfishness that can occur in women who too strictly cleave to the newer dictates of feminism.

Besides her novel and short stories, Beckett has also written several children's novels based on her own experiences as a girl and as the mother and teacher of girls. The settings of *Orla Was Six* (1989), *Orla at School* (1991), and *A Family Tree* (1992) mark a return to her native city, Belfast. Her 1995 children's novel, *Hannah or Pink Balloons,* received the 1995 Bistro Merit Award, which recognizes excellence in Irish children's literature.

"I always write about trouble," Beckett acknowledged in her 1995 interview with Megan Sullivan. While this predilection causes a distinctive cynicism and sadness to permeate her stories, her tales never sink into hopelessness, as they ultimately show the strength and resilience in the women she portrays. The beauty and the balance of her writing also lift the mood of the unsentimental tales. Beckett's other forte is her ability to condense a whole life into an anecdote or a whole character into a gesture. The examples of Frank O'Connor and Sean O'Faolain helped shape her writing, but her greatest influence was McLaverty. Like him, she can portray even disturbing characters sympathetically and intersperse her tales with lovely physical details.

Explaining to Sullivan why her texts focus on the lives of women, Beckett says, "I couldn't–wouldn't–know what goes on in a man's head. If I am being honest, I have to write about women." Her focus on the routine details that can make up women's lives leads some critics to pigeonhole her as a domestic writer. Male journalists in particular tend to characterize Mary Beckett as a homemaker who writes, while feminist scholars tend to view her as a writer who articulates truths about nationalism, gender, and class through her portraits of families and relationships.

Beckett herself reflected in the interview with Perry on the stereotyping of her work:

> *Give Them Stones,* got a lot of attention in the Irish papers because it's political. I wrote *A Literary Woman,* but it's about families, so they sent these people to interview me in my house, but they don't give it any kind of a literary review. If you're a woman writing about something, presumably, outside the home and outside woman's concerns, you'll get the attention. But if it's just about a woman's world, the papers just aren't going to bother.

Sullivan commented that even the more overtly political acts in Beckett's texts become characterized as minor events because of their connection to the home and family. The further conflation of the two occurs because Beckett, growing up Catholic and Nationalist in Protestant, Unionist Belfast, came to know that these small, yet essential, particulars of a person's world, from her place of worship to her name, the street she lives on, and her occupation, are inherently and even explicitly political. Because of this link, Beckett's writing shows a world in which small details can stand for larger issues and small deeds can represent larger acts of defiance. Her fiction illuminates the artificial divide between the private and the public, the personal and the political.

Interviews:

"Mary Beckett," in *Backtalk: Women Writers Speak Out,* edited by Donna Perry (New Brunswick, N.J.: Rutgers University Press, 1993), pp. 63–82;

Megan Sullivan, "Mary Beckett: An Interview," *Irish Literary Supplement,* 14 (Fall 1995): 10–12.

References:

Patricia Coughlan, "Special Pleading?" *Irish Review,* no. 10 (Spring 1991): 127–131;

Ann Owens Weekes, *Unveiling Treasures: The Attic Guide to the Published Works of Irish Women Literary Writers* (Dublin: Attic, 1993), pp. 29–31.

Samuel Beckett
(13 April 1906 – 22 December 1989)

Shawn O'Hare
Carson-Newman College

See also the Beckett entries in *DLB 13: British Dramatists Since World War II; DLB 15: British Novelists, 1930–1959; DLB 233: British and Irish Dramatists Since World War II, Second Series;* and *DLB Yearbook: 1990.*

BOOKS: *Whoroscope* (Paris: Hours Press, 1930);
Proust (London: Chatto & Windus, 1931; New York: Grove, 1957);
More Pricks Than Kicks (London: Chatto & Windus, 1934; New York: Grove, 1972);
Echo's Bones and Other Precipitates (Paris: Europa Press, 1935);
Murphy (London: Routledge, 1938; New York: Grove, 1957); translated into French by Beckett under the same title (Paris: Bordas, 1947);
Molloy (Paris: Minuit, 1951); translated by Beckett and Patrick Bowles under the same title (Paris: Olympia, 1955; New York: Grove, 1955; London: Calder & Boyars, 1966);
Malone muert (Paris: Minuit, 1951); translated by Beckett as *Malone Dies* (New York: Grove, 1956; London: Calder, 1958);
En attendant Godot (Paris: Minuit, 1952); translated by Beckett as *Waiting for Godot* (New York: Grove, 1954; London: Faber & Faber, 1956);
L'Innommable (Paris: Minuit, 1953); translated by Beckett as *The Unnamable* (New York: Grove, 1958; London: Calder, 1975);
Watt (Paris: Olympia Press, 1953; New York: Grove, 1959; London: Calder, 1963); translated into French by Beckett, Ludovic Janvier, and Agnès Janvier under the same title (Paris: Minuit, 1968);
Nouvelles et textes pour rien (Paris: Minuit, 1955); translated by Beckett as *Stories and Texts for Nothing* (New York: Grove, 1967);
All That Fall (London: Faber & Faber, 1957; New York: Grove, 1957); translated by Beckett and Robert Pinget as *Tous ceux qui tombent* (Paris: Minuit, 1957);
Fin de partie, suivi de Acte sans paroles (Paris: Minuit, 1957); translated by Beckett as *Endgame, A Play in One Act, Followed by Act without Words, a Mime for One Player* (London: Faber & Faber, 1958; New York: Grove, 1958);
From an Abandoned Work (London: Faber & Faber, 1958); translated into French by Beckett, Ludovic Janvier, and Agnès Janvier as *D'un ouvrage abandonné* (Paris: Minuit, 1967);
Molloy, Malone Dies (1959), *and The Unnamable: Three Novels* (New York: Grove, 1959; London: Calder, 1959; Paris: Olympia, 1959);
Krapp's Last Tape and Embers (London: Faber & Faber, 1959); translated into French by Beckett and

Samuel Beckett (photograph by Jerry Bauer; from Mercier and Camier, *1974; Richland County Public Library)*

Pierre Leyris as *La Dernière bande, suivi de Cendres* (Paris: Minuit, 1960);

Krapp's Last Tape and Other Dramatic Pieces (New York: Grove, 1960)–comprises *Krapp's Last Tape, All That Fall, Embers, Act without Words I,* and *Act without Words II;*

Comment c'est (Paris: Minuit, 1961); translated by Beckett as *How It Is* (New York: Grove, 1964; London: Calder, 1964);

Poems in English (London: Calder & Boyars, 1961; New York: Grove, 1963);

Happy Days (New York: Grove, 1961; London: Faber & Faber, 1962); translated into French by Beckett as *Oh les beaux jours* (Paris: Minuit, 1963);

Play and Two Short Pieces for Radio (London: Faber & Faber, 1964)–comprises *Play, Words and Music,* and *Cascando;*

Comédie et actes divers (Paris: Minuit, 1966);

Eh Joe and Other Writings (London: Faber & Faber, 1967; New York: Grove, 1969)–comprises *Eh Joe, Act without Words II,* and *Film;*

Têtes-mortes, translated from English by Beckett, Ludovic Janvier, and Agnès Janvier (Paris: Minuit, 1967)–comprises *D'un ouvrage abandonné, Assez, Imagination morte imaginez,* and *Bing;*

No's Knife: Collected Shorter Prose 1945–1966 (London: Calder & Boyars, 1967);

Cascando and Other Short Dramatic Pieces (New York: Grove, 1968?)–comprises *Cascando, Words and Music, Eh Joe, Play,* and *Come and Go;*

Poèmes (Paris: Minuit, 1968);

Film (New York: Grove, 1969; London: Faber & Faber, 1972);

Sans (Paris: Minuit, 1969); translated by Beckett as *Lessness* (London: Calder & Boyars, 1970);

Le Dépeupleur (Paris: Minuit, 1970); translated by Beckett as *The Lost Ones* (London: Calder & Boyars, 1972; New York: Grove, 1972);

Mercier et Camier (Paris: Minuit, 1970); translated by Beckett as *Mercier and Camier* (London: Calder & Boyars, 1974; New York: Grove, 1975);

Premier amour (Paris: Minuit, 1970); translated by Beckett as *First Love* (London: Calder & Boyars, 1973);

Breath and Other Short Plays (London: Faber & Faber, 1972)–comprises *Breath, Come and Go, Act without Words I, Act without Words II,* and *From an Abandoned Work;*

Not I (London: Faber & Faber, 1973); translated into French by Beckett as *Pas moi* (Paris: Minuit, 1975);

Au loin un oiseau (New York: Double Elephant Press, 1973);

First Love and Other Shorts (New York: Grove, 1974)–comprises *First Love, From an Abandoned Work, Enough, Imagination Dead Imagine, Ping, Not I,* and *Breath;*

Still (Milan: M'Arte Edizione, 1974);

All Strange Away (New York: Gotham Book Mart, 1976; London: Calder, 1979);

Ends and Odds (New York: Grove; 1976; London: Faber & Faber, 1977);

Footfalls (London: Faber & Faber, 1976);

Pour finir encore et autres foirades (Paris: Minuit, 1976); translated by Beckett as *For to End Yet Again and Other Fizzles* (London: Calder, 1976); also published as *Fizzles* (New York: Grove, 1976);

Still (London: Calder & Boyars, 1976)–comprises "Still" and other stories translated from French by Beckett;

That Time (New York: Faber & Faber, 1976);

Collected Poems in English and French (London: Calder, 1977);

Poèmes (Paris: Minuit, 1978);

Company (London: Calder, 1979; New York: Grove, 1980);

Mal vu mal dit (Paris: Minuit, 1981); translated by Beckett as *Ill Seen Ill Said* (New York: Grove, 1981; London: Calder, 1982);

Rockaby and Other Short Pieces (New York: Grove, 1981)–comprises *Rockaby, Ohio Impromptu, All Strange Away, A Piece of Monologue,* and *But the Clouds;*

Three Occasional Pieces (London: Faber & Faber, 1982);

Catastrophe et autres dramaticules (Paris: Minuit, 1982);

Ohio Impromptu, Catastrophe, What Where (New York: Grove, 1983);

Worstward Ho (London: Calder, 1983; New York: Grove, 1983);

Disjecta: Miscellaneous Writings and a Dramatic Fragment, edited by Ruby Cohn (London: Calder, 1983; New York: Grove, 1984);

Catastrophe (London: Faber & Faber, 1984);

Collected Shorter Plays (London: Faber & Faber, 1984; New York: Grove, 1984);

Collected Poems 1930–1978 (London: Calder, 1984);

Stirrings Still, illustrations by Louis Le Brocquy (London: Calder, 1988; New York: Blue Moon, 1988);

Collected Shorter Prose 1945–1980 (London: Calder, 1988);

Comment dire (Paris: Minuit, 1989);

Nohow On (London: Calder, 1989; New York: Grove, 1995 [i.e., 1996])–comprises *Company, Ill Seen Ill Said,* and *Worstward Ho;*

As the Story Was Told: Uncollected and Late Prose (London: Calder, 1990);

Dream of Fair to Middling Women, edited by Eoin O'Brien and Edith Fournier (Dublin: Black Cat Press,

1992; Paris: Calder / New York: Riverrun, 1992);
Eleuthéria (Paris: Minuit, 1995); translated from French by Michael Brodsky (New York: Foxrock, 1995); translated from French by Barbara Wright (London: Faber & Faber, 1996);
Samuel Beckett: The Complete Short Prose, 1929–1989, edited, with an introduction, by S. E. Gontarski (New York: Grove, 1995).

PLAY PRODUCTIONS: *Le Kid,* by Beckett and Georges Pelorson, Dublin, Peacock Theatre, February 1931;
En attendant Godot, Paris, Théâtre de Babylone, 5 January 1953; produced as *Waiting for Godot,* London, Arts Theatre Club, 3 August 1955; transferred to the Criterion Theatre, 12 September 1955; Miami, Coconut Grove Playhouse, 3 January 1956; New York, John Golden Theatre, 19 April 1956;
Fin de partie and *Acte sans paroles (I),* London, Royal Court Theatre, 3 April 1957; Paris, Studio des Champs-Elysées, 26 April 1957; translated by Beckett as *Endgame* and *Act without Words I,* New York, Cherry Lane Theatre, 28 January 1958; London, Royal Court Theatre, 28 October 1958;
Krapp's Last Tape, London, Royal Court Theatre, 28 October 1958 [produced with *Endgame*]; New York, Provincetown Playhouse, 14 January 1960; translated into French by Beckett as *La Dernière bande,* Paris, Théâtre Récamier, 22 March 1960;
Act without Words II, London, Institute of Contemporary Arts, 25 January 1960; Milwaukee, University of Wisconsin, 10 July 1962;
Happy Days, New York, Cherry Lane Theatre, 17 September 1961; London, Royal Court Theatre, 1 November 1962; translated into French by Beckett as *Oh les beaux jours,* Venice, Teatro del Ridotto, 28 September 1963; Paris, Odéon-Théâtre de France, 15 November 1963;
Spiel, translated into German by Elmar Tophoven and Erika Tophoven, Ulm-Donau, Germany, Ulmer Theater, 14 June 1963; original English version produced as *Play,* New York, Cherry Lane Theatre, 4 January 1964; London, Old Vic Theatre, 7 April 1964; translated into French by Beckett as *Comédie,* Paris, Pavillon de Marsan, 11 June 1964;
Kommen und Gehen, translated into German by Elmar Tophoven and Erika Tophoven, Berlin, Schiller-Theater Werkstatt, 14 January 1966; translated into French by Beckett as *Va et vient,* Paris, Odéon-Théâtre de France, 28 February 1966; original English version produced as *Come and Go,* Dublin, Peacock Theatre, 28 February 1968; London, Royal Festival Hall, 9 December 1968; Milwaukee, University of Wisconsin, Performing Arts Center, 23 November 1970;
Breath, New York, Eden Theatre, 17 June 1969 [as part of *Oh! Calcutta!*]; Oxford, Oxford Playhouse, 8 March 1970;
Not I, New York, Lincoln Center, 22 November 1972; London, Royal Court Theatre, 16 January 1973; translated into French by Beckett as *Pas moi,* Paris, Théâtre d'Orsay, 3 April 1975;
The Lost Ones, New York, Theatre for the New City, 7 April 1975;
That Time and *Footfalls,* London, Royal Court Theatre, 20 May 1976; Washington, D.C., Arena Stage, 3 December 1976; *Footfalls* translated into French by Beckett as *Pas,* Paris, Théâtre d'Orsay, 11 April 1978;
A Piece of Monologue, New York, La Mama Experimental Theatre Club, 14 December 1979;
Texts for Nothing, New York, Public Theatre, 24 February 1981;
Rockaby, Buffalo, State University of New York at Buffalo, 8 April 1981; London, Cottesloe Theatre (National Theatre), 9 December 1982; translated into French by Beckett as *Berceuse,* Paris, Centre Georges Pompidou, 14 October 1981;
Ohio Impromptu, Columbus, Ohio State University, 9 May 1981; Nottingham, University of Nottingham Dramatic Society, 22 June 1984; first professional production, Edinburgh, Edinburgh Festival, 13 August 1984; translated into French by Beckett as *Impromptu d'Ohio,* Paris, Théâtre du Rond-Point, 15 September 1983;
Catastrophe, Avignon, Avignon Festival, 21 July 1982; English version produced with *What Where,* New York, Harold Clurman Theatre, 15 June 1983; Edinburgh, Edinburgh Festival, 13 August 1984; *What Where* translated into French by Beckett as *Quoi où,* Paris, Théâtre du Rond-Point, April 1986.

PRODUCED SCRIPTS: *All That Fall,* radio, BBC Third Programme, 13 January 1957;
Embers, radio, BBC Third Programme, 24 June 1959;
Words and Music, radio, BBC Third Programme, 13 November 1962;
Cascando, radio, RTF-France Culture, 13 October 1963; English version, BBC Third Programme, 6 October 1964;
Film, motion picture, Evergreen, 1965;

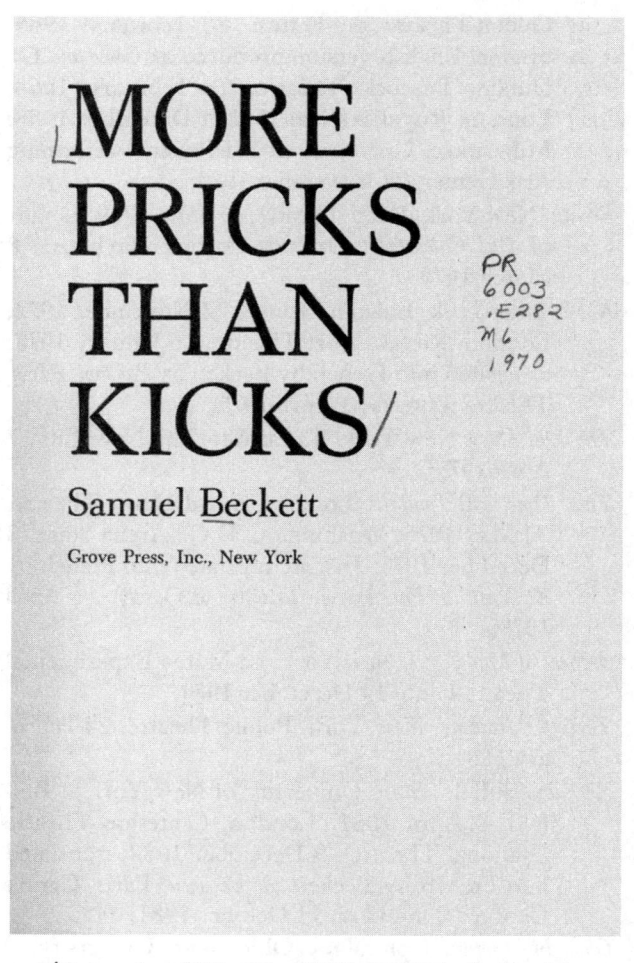

Title page for a 1970 edition of Beckett's 1934 collection of short stories that follow a single protagonist from his early student days until his death (Thomas Cooper Library, University of South Carolina)

Eh, Joe, television, Süddeutscher Rundfunk, 13 April 1966; original English version, BBC 2, 4 July 1966;

Rough for Radio II, radio, BBC Radio 3, 13 April 1976;

Ghost Trio, . . .but the clouds. . . , and *Shades [Not I],* television, BBC 2, 17 April 1977;

Quadrat 1 + 2, television, Süddeutscher Rundfunk, 8 October 1981; English version broadcast as *Quad,* BBC 2, 16 December 1982;

Nacht und Träume, television, Süddeutscher Rundfunk, 19 May 1983;

Was wo [What Where], television, Süddeutscher Rundfunk, 13 April 1986.

TRANSLATIONS: *Anthology of Mexican Poetry,* translated by Beckett, compiled by Octavio Paz (Bloomington: Indiana University Press, 1958);

Arthur Rimbaud, *Drunken Boat,* translated by Beckett (Reading, U.K.: Whiteknights Press, 1976).

Samuel Beckett, winner of the Nobel Prize in literature in 1969, is one of the most important writers of the twentieth century. His standing rests primarily on his work as a playwright—which includes *Waiting for Godot* (published in 1952 as *En attendant Godot*), *Endgame* (1958; performed as *Fin de partie,* 1957), and *Happy Days* (1961)—and as a novelist, notably with *Murphy* (1938), *Molloy* (1951; translated into English as *Molloy,* 1955), *Malone muert* (1951; translated as *Malone Dies,* 1956), and *The Unnamable* (published as *L'Innommable,* 1953; translated, 1958). Beckett, however, is also highly regarded for his short prose, which often served as an impetus for his longer writings.

Samuel Barclay Beckett was born on 13 April 1906 in Foxrock, County Dublin, Ireland. He was the second son of William and May Roe Beckett. The family was Protestant, and the Becketts enjoyed a comfortable upper-middle-class life. In October 1923 Beckett enrolled in Trinity College, Dublin, where he distinguished himself as a student and scholar in French and Italian. In 1927 he graduated with a B.A. in Modern Languages. From 1928 to 1930 he worked in Paris as a *lecteur* at the Ecole Normale Supérieure.

During his time in Paris, Beckett made friends with Irish novelist James Joyce, who undoubtedly had a major influence on Beckett's writing. In 1929 Beckett's first published short story, "Assumption," appeared in *transition* magazine (nos. 16–17). "Assumption" begins with a sentence that has become classically Beckettian: "He could have shouted and could not." Thus, in the first line of his first published short story, Beckett expresses his lifelong obsession with paradox. "Assumption" is in the modern tradition, densely written and packed with analogies. It is the story of an unnamed writer who struggles with his art and his role as an artist.

For the fall 1930 term, Beckett returned to Dublin and accepted the position of Lecturer in French at Trinity College Dublin, where he was also pursuing an M.A. degree. When he received his degree in December 1931, Beckett resigned his position and left for the Continent; he never again made Ireland his primary home. During the summer of 1932 Beckett worked on a novel, *Dream of Fair to Middling Women,* which was not published until 1992, three years after his death. Beckett's second published short story appeared in March 1932 in *transition,* the same journal as his first story. "Sedendo et Quiescendo" was, like two future short stories, a section culled from *Dream of Fair to Middling Women.* "Sedendo et Quiescendo" is a frantic, stream-of-consciousness narrative of a taxicab ride taken by Belacqua Shuah and the Smeraldina. Beckett's third published story, "Text," first appeared in poem form in *New Review* (Winter 1931–1932) and then in prose form in

New Review 2 (April 1932). "Text," also a segment from *Dream of Fair to Middling Women,* is a one-sentence, one-paragraph contemplation by a narrator who is preparing to "grow into the earth mother of whom clapdish and foreshop."

The fourth short story Beckett published was "A Case in a Thousand," which appeared in the August 1934 issue of *The Bookman.* Compared to his first three published stories, "A Case in a Thousand" was the most traditional and accessible to date. Also in 1934, Beckett's first book-length work of fiction was published: *More Pricks Than Kicks,* a collection of stories that can also function as a novel. In fact, the central figure in the ten-story collection is Belacqua Shuah, who was also the main character in *Dream of Fair to Middling Women.* *More Pricks Than Kicks*—the title comes from Acts 26:14, when Jesus tells Paul (then called Saul), "it is hard for thee to kick against the pricks"—traces the life of Belacqua from his early days as a student to his burial. *More Pricks Than Kicks* serves as an introduction to Beckett's dark and often absurd and bizarre sense of humor, a trait that eventually was called Beckettian. The opening story in *More Pricks Than Kicks* is "Dante and the Lobster," and it is probably Beckett's single best-known story, a tale of loss and futility. Another well-known story is "A Wet Night," a parody of Joyce's story "The Dead."

After *More Pricks Than Kicks,* Beckett went more than a decade before writing another short story, and another decade passed after that until one was published. From 1933 to 1935, Beckett lived in London. He spent much of 1936 and 1937 traveling around Germany; that wandering journey was followed by a short stay at his family home in Ireland. Finally, in October 1937 he settled in Paris, and France remained his home for the rest of his life. The late 1930s and the 1940s were eventful for Beckett. In 1938 he was stabbed in a Paris street; during World War II he was active in the French Resistance. In 1946 Beckett wrote, in French, three short stories—"The End," "The Expelled," and "The Calmative"—which were not published until 1955, in *Nouvelles et textes pour rien* (translated as *Stories and Texts for Nothing,* 1967). He also wrote *First Love,* although it did not appear in print until 1973.

The last years of the 1940s, often called "the siege in the room," were one of the most creative and productive periods in Beckett's career. During that time he wrote, in French, the trilogy of novels *Molloy, Malone muert,* and *L'Innommable,* as well as two plays: *Eleuthéria* (published posthumously in 1995) and *Waiting for Godot.*

In 1955, *Nouvelles et textes pour rien* appeared. The four stories in the collection that Beckett wrote in 1946—"First Love," "The End," "The Expelled," and "The Calmative"—represent his new commitment to write in his adopted tongue, French. The works share some characteristics, including unnamed first-person narrators, though most notably each of the stories from this era deals with the main characters' being forced out of their domiciles. The thirteen stories that make up the rest of *Nouvelles et textes pour rien* serve as Beckett's entrance into literary postmodernism. S. E. Gontarski argues that the other stories are a "major leap" from the four pieces written in 1946. Each story has an unnamed narrator, and the themes that are typical of Beckett's work, particularly his short fiction, are dominant: loneliness, isolation, and alienation.

In 1956 Beckett returned to his native language and wrote what came to be known as *From an Abandoned Work* (1958), a first-person story narrated by an elderly man as he reflects on three days from his youth. Although the ten-page story is one long paragraph, the linear narrative makes it more accessible than the stories from *Texts for Nothing.* The three-page, one-sentence story "The Image" (originally composed in French as "L'Image," and published in *X: A Quarterly Review* in November 1959 and later translated by Beckett's friend Edith Fournier) was also written in 1956. It is, as the title suggests, a series of images; without punctuation and capital letters (with the exception of "I" and proper names), the piece is a challenging read. The key image in the story is a tongue in a mouth.

Although at the end of the 1950s Beckett's emphasis shifted back to drama, between 1963 and 1964, his short fiction took another turn with "All Strange Away," published in 1976. This story is more concerned with the situation than the actions of the characters. The story "Imagination Dead Imagine" was written in 1965 and first published in the 7 November 1965 issue of the *Sunday Times.* The story shares some similarities with "All Strange Away," most notably that the characters are trapped in a rotunda. The clinical description of the characters and their condition is the most haunting aspect of the story as Beckett depersonalizes them and their "human" experience. Also written in 1965 (though not published until 1974, in *First Love and Other Shorts*) was "Enough," though it is different from its two predecessors. "Enough" is a much more straightforward narrative, about a woman who takes care of an older man. The simplicity of the story, however, has caused some critics to seek other possible interpretations, and some have suggested that the woman character could be another man or even a hermaphrodite.

The experimental nature of Beckett's short fiction returns in the story *Ping* (*Bing,* in the original French), written in 1966 and published in February 1967 in *Encounter* (volume 28, no. 2). Gontarski cites David Lodge's comment that *Ping* "is the rendering of the con-

Title page for the British edition of Beckett's 1976 collection of stories on the themes of entrapment and hopelessness (Thomas Cooper Library, University of South Carolina)

sciousness of a person confined in a small, bare, white room, a person who is evidently under extreme duress, and probably at the last gasp of life." *Ping* has attracted much scholarly attention, as Beckett made available the various drafts of the work; in fact, it is undoubtedly one of Beckett's most closely examined works.

The story *Lessness,* written in 1969 and published in *The Evergreen Review* in July 1970, is also a highly experimental piece. This tale, however, has a mathematical twist: it has twenty-four paragraphs and is divided into two twelve-paragraph halves. There are sixty different sentences, each used twice. In *Lessness,* Beckett once again explores quietness, loneliness, and isolation, reducing those feelings to a less-than-minimal state. In 1969 Beckett was awarded the Nobel Prize in literature, although he did not attend the ceremony in Stockholm, Sweden.

The Lost Ones was published in 1972. Like "All Strange Away" and "Imagination Dead Imagine," "The Lost Ones" is a story about characters who are physically trapped in an "Abode where lost bodies roam each searching for its lost one." Beckett's commitment to narrative experimentation in short fiction continued in 1976 with the publication of eight stories—published in the United States as *Fizzles,* in the United Kingdom as *For to End Yet Again and Other Fizzles,* and in France as *Pour finir encore et autres foirades.* In each version of the book, the order of the stories is changed. "Fizzles 1" is representative of the collection. It is the story of a character who appears to be in a prison. Told in the third person (the rest of the stories are in the first person), "Fizzles 1" traces the movement of a character as he walks around bent over, eyes looking at the ground. He inevitably runs into walls and bloodies his face. As well as meandering aimlessly, the character is forced to breathe air that is repulsive. Entrapment and hopelessness dominate this text and all the "Fizzles" stories.

"As the Story Was Told" appeared in the *Chicago Review* in 1982, though Beckett wrote it in August 1973. This brief story is told by a first-person narrator who describes a "tent" where "sessions" take place, though neither the speaker nor the reader knows exactly what those sessions involve. Some critics suggest that Beckett is "deconstructing" his writing when the narrator receives a "sheet of writing" that he promptly rips into four pieces and returns to a "waiting hand." Two other late and brief pieces, "The Cliff" and "neither," are close to poetry. "The Cliff," translated from the French by Fournier, is an imagistic description of a sea cliff; "neither" was first published in the *Journal of Beckett Studies* (volume 4) in the Spring 1979 issue with line breaks that made it look like a poem. However, when Beckett's *Collected Poems 1930–1978* (1984) was about to be published, he told the publisher, John Calder, that "neither" was prose, not poetry.

Beckett's final pieces of short fiction—the three stories that compose *Stirrings Still* (1988)—were written in honor of Barney Rosset, Beckett's longtime American publisher. The three stories of *Stirrings Still* are similar, and, in fact, they are examples of Beckett's use of repetition, most evident in the plays *Waiting for Godot* and *Ohio Impromptu* (1981). The opening line of "Stirrings Still 1" is "One night as he sat at his table head on hands he saw himself rise and go." The protagonist then thinks about how he used to look at the sky through a window, and the Beckettian theme of loneliness and isolation is once again evident. In "Stirrings Still 2," the same character (presumably) is still sitting and thinking, and again the ticking clock and the cries from outside surround him. In the end, in "Stirrings Still 3," after describing the "hubbub in his mind," the narrator concludes, "No matter how no matter where. Time and grief and self so-called. Oh to end all." Thus,

Samuel Beckett's work as a short-story writer—which spans fifty-nine years—comes to an end. The following year, on 22 December 1989, Beckett died, and although he is regarded most highly for his plays and novels, his short fiction is of great importance and often served as a gateway to his longer works. His short fiction solidifies his reputation as one of the most important artists of the twentieth century.

Biographies:

Deirdre Bair, *Samuel Beckett: A Biography* (London: Cape, 1978);

James Knowlson, *Damned to Fame: The Life of Samuel Beckett* (New York: Simon & Schuster, 1996);

Anthony Cronin, *The Last Modernist* (New York: Harper Collins, 1997).

References:

Morris Beja, S. E. Gontarski, and Pierre Astier, eds., *Samuel Beckett: Humanistic Perspectives* (Columbus: Ohio State University Press, 1983);

Linda Ben-Zvi, *Samuel Beckett* (Boston: Twayne, 1986);

Ben-Zvi, ed., *Women in Beckett: Performance and Critical Perspectives* (Urbana: University of Illinois Press, 1990);

Enoch Brater, ed., *Beckett at 80: Beckett in Context* (Oxford: Oxford University Press, 1986);

Mary Bryden, *Women in Samuel Beckett's Prose and Drama* (London: Macmillan, 1993);

Lance St. John Butler and Robin J. Davis, eds., *"Make Sense Who May": Essays on Samuel Beckett's Later Work* (Gerrards Cross, U.K.: Colin Smythe, 1989);

Butler and Davis, eds., *Rethinking Beckett: A Collection of Critical Essays* (London: Macmillan, 1990);

John Calder, ed., *Beckett at Sixty: A Festschrift* (London: Calder & Boyars, 1967);

Robert Cochran, *Samuel Beckett: A Study of the Short Fiction* (Boston: Twayne, 1992);

Ruby Cohn, *Back to Beckett* (Princeton: Princeton University Press, 1973);

Cohn, *The Comic Gamut* (New Brunswick, N.J.: Rutgers University Press, 1962);

Cohn, ed., *Samuel Beckett: A Collection of Criticism* (New York: McGraw-Hill, 1962);

Paul Davies, *The Ideal Real: Beckett's Fiction and Imagination* (London: Associated University Presses, 1994);

Martin Esslin, ed., *Samuel Beckett: A Collection of Critical Essays* (Englewood Cliffs, N.J.: Prentice-Hall, 1965);

Raymond Federman, *Journey to Chaos: Samuel Beckett's Early Fiction* (Berkeley: University of California Press, 1965);

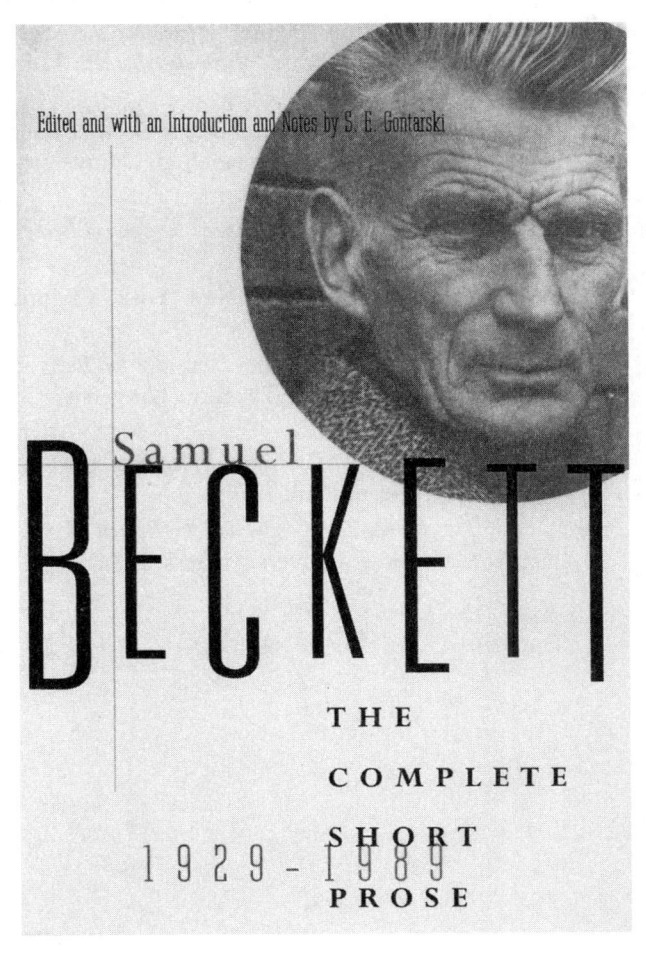

Dust jacket for the Beckett collection published in 1995, six years after his death (Richland County Public Library)

Federman and John Fletcher, *Samuel Beckett: His Works and His Critics* (Berkeley: University of California Press, 1970);

Peter Gidal, *Understanding Beckett* (London: Macmillan, 1986);

S. E. Gontarski, ed., *The Beckett Studies Reader* (Gainesville: University Press of Florida, 1993);

Gontarski, ed., *On Beckett: Essays and Criticism* (New York: Grove, 1986);

Lawrence Graver and Federman, eds., *Samuel Beckett: The Critical Heritage* (London: Routledge & Kegan Paul, 1979);

John P. Harrington, *The Irish Beckett* (Syracuse, N.Y.: Syracuse University Press, 1991);

Hugh Kenner, *A Reader's Guide to Samuel Beckett* (London: Thames & Hudson, 1973);

Kenner, *Samuel Beckett: A Critical Study* (Berkeley: University of California Press, 1968);

James Knowlson and John Pilling, *Frescoes of the Skull: The Recent Prose and Drama of Samuel Beckett* (London: Calder, 1979);

Carla Locatelli, *Unwording the Word: Samuel Beckett's Prose Works after the Nobel Prize* (Philadelphia: University of Pennsylvania Press, 1990);

Patrick A. McCarthy, ed., *Critical Essays on Samuel Beckett* (Boston: G. K. Hall, 1986);

Vivian Mercier, *Beckett / Beckett* (New York: Oxford University Press, 1977);

P. J. Murphy, *Reconstructing Beckett: Language for Being in Samuel Beckett's Fiction* (Toronto: University of Toronto Press, 1990);

John Pilling, *Samuel Beckett* (London, Henley & Boston: Routledge & Kegan Paul, 1976);

Pilling, ed., *The Cambridge Companion to Beckett* (Cambridge: Cambridge University Press, 1994);

Rubin Rabinovitz, *The Development of Samuel Beckett's Fiction* (Urbana: University of Illinois Press, 1984);

William York Tindall, *Samuel Beckett* (New York: Columbia University Press, 1964).

Papers:

The major collections of Samuel Beckett's papers are held at the Beckett International Foundation, University of Reading; Harry Ransom Humanities Research Center, University of Texas at Austin; and Trinity College Dublin. Other collections are housed at John J. Burns Library, Boston College; Baker-Berry Library, Dartmouth College; The Lilly Library, Indiana University; Institut des Mémoires de l'Edition Contemporaine, Paris; Ohio State University Libraries, Columbus; Princeton University Library; Syracuse University, New York; University of Washington, St. Louis, Missouri; and the Beinecke Library, Yale University.

John Berger

(5 November 1926 –   )

Ralf Hertel
Free University Berlin

See also the Berger entries in *DLB 14: British Novelists Since 1960* and *DLB 207: British Novelists Since 1960, Third Series.*

BOOKS: *Renato Guttuso,* translated from the original English manuscript by Wolfgang Martini (Dresden: Verlag der Kunst, 1957);
A Painter of Our Time (London: Secker & Warburg, 1958; New York: Simon & Schuster, 1959);
Permanent Red: Essays in Seeing (London: Methuen, 1960); republished as *Toward Reality: Essays in Seeing* (New York: Knopf, 1962);
The Foot of Clive (London: Methuen, 1962);
Corker's Freedom (London: Methuen, 1964; New York: Pantheon, 1993);
The Success and Failure of Picasso (Harmondsworth, U.K.: Penguin, 1965; New York: Pantheon, 1980);
A Fortunate Man: The Story of a Country Doctor, photographs by Jean Mohr, text by Berger (London: Allen Lane, 1967; New York: Holt, Rinehart & Winston, 1967);
Art and Revolution: Ernst Neizvestny and the Role of the Artist in the U.S.S.R. (London: Weidenfeld & Nicolson, 1969; New York: Pantheon, 1969);
The Moment of Cubism and Other Essays (London: Weidenfeld & Nicolson, 1969; New York: Pantheon, 1969);
The Look of Things: Selected Essays and Articles, edited by Nikos Stangos (Harmondsworth, U.K.: Penguin, 1971; New York: Viking, 1972);
Ways of Seeing, by Berger and others (London: British Broadcasting Corporation / Harmondsworth, U.K.: Penguin, 1972; New York: Viking, 1973);
G (London: Weidenfeld & Nicolson, 1972; New York: Viking, 1972);
A Seventh Man: A Book of Images and Words about the Experience of Migrant Workers in Europe, photographs by Mohr, text by Berger (Harmondsworth, U.K. & Baltimore: Penguin, 1975);
Pig Earth (London: Writers and Readers, 1979; New York: Pantheon, 1979);

John Berger (photograph © H. Cartier-Bresson/Magnum Photos; from Photocopies, *1996; Richland County Public Library)*

About Looking (London: Writers and Readers, 1980; New York: Pantheon, 1980);
Another Way of Telling, by Berger and Mohr (London: Writers and Readers, 1982; New York: Pantheon, 1982);
And Our Faces, My Heart, Brief as Photos (London: Writers and Readers, 1984; New York: Pantheon, 1984);

Question de Géographie, by Berger and Nella Bielski (Marseille: Laffitte, 1984); translated as *A Question of Geography* (London: Faber & Faber, 1987);

The White Bird: Writings by John Berger, edited, with an introduction, by Lloyd Spencer (London: Chatto & Windus, 1985); republished as *The Sense of Sight* (New York: Pantheon, 1985);

Once in Europa (New York: Pantheon, 1987; London: Granta, 1989);

Goya's Last Portrait: The Painter Played Today, by Berger and Bielski (London: Faber & Faber, 1989);

Lilac and Flag: An Old Wives' Tale of a City (New York: Pantheon, 1990; Cambridge: Penguin/Granta, 1991);

Keeping a Rendezvous (New York: Pantheon, 1991; London: Granta, 1992);

Pages of the Wound: Poems, Drawings, Photographs, 1956–1994 (London: Circle, 1994);

To the Wedding (London: Bloomsbury, 1995; New York: Pantheon, 1995);

Mann und Frau, unter einem Pflaumenbaum stehend, German translation by Jörg Trobitius (Munich: Hanser, 1995); enlarged as *Photocopies* (New York: Pantheon, 1996; London: Bloomsbury, 1997);

Titian: Nymph and Shepherd, by Berger and Katya Berger (Munich & New York: Prestel, 1996);

Isabelle: A Story in Shots (London & Chester Springs, Pa.: Arcadia, 1996);

King: A Street Story (London: Bloomsbury, 1999; New York: Pantheon, 1999);

The Shape of a Pocket (London: Bloomsbury, 2001; New York: Pantheon, 2001).

Editions and Collections: *Into Their Labours* (New York: Pantheon, 1991; London: Granta, 1992)—comprises *Pig Earth, Once in Europa,* and *Lilac and Flag;*

Once in Europa, photographs by Patricia Macdonald and Angus Macdonald (London: Bloomsbury, 2000);

Selected Essays, edited by Geoff Dyer (London: Bloomsbury, 2001; New York: Pantheon, 2001).

PRODUCED SCRIPTS: *La Salamandre,* by Berger and Alain Tanner, motion picture, Citel Films, 1971;

Ways of Seeing, by Berger, Sven Blomberg, Chris Fox, Michael Dibb, and Richard Hollis, television, BBC, 1972;

Le milieu du monde, by Berger and Tanner, motion picture, Citel Films, 1973;

Jonas qui aura 25 ans en l'an 2000, by Berger and Tanner, motion picture, Action Films and Citel Films, 1976;

Play Me Something, by Berger and Tim Neat, motion picture, British Film Institute, 1989.

OTHER: Euan Duff, *How We Are: A Book of Photographs in Six Sections,* introduction by Berger (London: Allen Lane, 1971);

Howard Daniel, *Encyclopaedia of Themes and Subjects in Painting,* introduction by Berger (London: Thames & Hudson, 1971);

Lee Baxandall, ed., *Radical Perspectives in the Arts* (Harmondsworth, U.K.: Penguin, 1972)—includes contribution by Berger;

Alinari: Photographers of Florence, 1852–1920, edited by Filippo Zeri, introduction by Berger (London: Idea, 1978);

Nick Waplington, *Living Room* (Manchester, U.K.: Cornerhouse, 1991; New York: Aperture, 1991)—includes essay by Berger;

Albrecht Dürer, *Albrecht Dürer: Watercolours and Drawings* (Cologne & New York: Taschen, 1994)—includes essay by Berger;

Juan Muñoz, ed., *Silence Please! Stories after the Works of Juan Muñoz* (Zurich & New York: Scalo Books, 1996)—includes contribution by Berger;

Wet Rocks Seen from Above: Paintings by Christoph Hansli, texts by Berger (Zurich: Memory/Cage, 1996);

Timothy O'Grady, *I Could Read the Sky,* introduction by Berger (London: Harvill, 1997);

Martine Franck, *One Day to the Next,* foreword by Berger and Franck (London: Thames & Hudson, 1998; New York: Aperture, 1998);

Jean Mohr, *At the Edge of the World,* introduction by Berger (London: Reaktion, 1999);

Fiona Tan, *Scenario* (Amsterdam: Vandenberg & Wallroth, 2000)—includes a correspondence between Berger and Tan;

Nearly Invisible, photographs by Moyra Peralta, texts by Berger and Alan Bennett (London: Inside Eye, 2001);

Arturo Di Stefano, *Arturo Di Stefano,* contributions by Berger, Michael Hofmann, and Christopher Lloyd (London: Merrell, 2001);

"A Certain Tradition of Heat: Some Notes Played for Tony," in *Anthony Fry* (New York: Umbrage, 2001).

TRANSLATIONS: Bertolt Brecht, *Poems on the Theatre,* translated by Berger and Anna Bostock (Lowestoft, U.K.: Scorpion, 1961);

Brecht, *Helene Weigel, Actress,* photographs by Gerda Goedhart, edited by Wolfgang Pintzka, translated by Berger and Bostock (Leipzig: VEB, 1961);

Aimé Césaire, *Return to My Native Land,* translated by Berger and Bostock (Baltimore: Penguin, 1969);

Nella Bielski, *Oranges for the Son of Alexander Levy,* translated by Berger and Lisa Appignanesi (London: Writers and Readers, 1982).

John Berger originally wanted to become a painter. Yet, in his late twenties he gave up painting "not because I thought I had no talent, but because painting pictures in the early '50s seemed a not direct enough way to try to stop the world's annihilation by nuclear war. The printed word was a little more effective." This decision shows that from the beginning Berger regarded writing as a political instrument. His political commitment not only started his career, though; it also made him highly unpopular with the literary circles of postwar Britain. He has remained an outsider despite winning the Booker Prize in 1972 for his novel *G* (1972). Berger has always opposed the separation of the work of art from the intention of its author, since he does not believe in an autonomous character of art. To gain an insight into the formation of his political ideology before approaching his literary work is, therefore, crucial.

John Peter Berger was born in Stoke Newington, London, on 5 November 1926. His father, S. J. D. Berger, like several of his ancestors, served as an officer in the British army before taking charge of a financial advisory institute in London. Because of the economic growth of the financial sector, this job provided the Berger family with a limited yet steady income in the difficult years between the two world wars. Berger's mother, Miriam Branson Berger, came from a working-class family. She opened a coffee shop outside London in order to add to the family's income and to help finance John's education.

He was sent to St. Edward's in Oxford, an Anglo-Irish public school. In retrospect he remembered it as a brutal institute aimed at producing minor colonial administrators and army officers. Berger himself did not show any military ambitions; instead, he began writing poetry and drawing. At the age of sixteen he decided–against his parents' wishes–to leave St. Edward's, where he had felt like a prisoner. By that time he had already read widely of anarchist writers such as Russian author Peter Alekseyevich Kropotkin. Despite Berger's excellent marks, he did not pursue an academic career but decided instead to return to London and become a painter. His parents attempted to make him change his decision by refusing him the right to stay in their house. Berger, however, obtained a small scholarship and was thus able to matriculate at the Central School of Arts and Crafts in London. While there he first came into contact with the Marxist ideas that eventually became the foundation of his ideology. His studies came to an abrupt end, though, when he had to join the army in 1944. Because of his family background he was expected to take a commission, but he refused. Instead, he served the next two years, first as a common soldier and then as a military instructor in Northern Ireland. He was brought into contact with working-class men and provided with insights into their lives and their particular problems. This experience proved crucial for the awakening of his social awareness, which influenced his subsequent work. His military service also sparked a keen interest in Ireland, and after the war he traveled back to Ireland several times, where he was in contact with painter Jack Yeats, brother of poet William Butler Yeats.

A grant from the army enabled Berger to continue his studies at the Chelsea School of Arts after the war. While at the school, he became closely involved with the Communist Party, although he did not join. He did, however, speak on their platforms and publish in their magazines on several occasions. His own art was close in style to that of social realism: he painted construction-site workers, sportsmen,

Front cover for the 1977 paperback reprint of Berger's 1972 book in which he tells stories to explain works of art (Richland County Public Library)

and fishermen and spent several months in a foundry clocking in and out with the workers, sketching systematically. In his Marxist convictions he was greatly influenced by Hungarian-born art historian Frederik Antal, who had immigrated to Britain in 1933. In general, Berger felt at home with the London immigrants, and many of his friends from the 1950s were of Central or Eastern European background. Exile and emigration later became crucial themes not only of his writings but also of his own biography.

His international attitude, as well as his Marxist convictions and his painterly style, singled him out in a postwar Britain that was characterized by increasing conservatism, nationalism, and the Cold War. After the Soviet blockade of Berlin in 1948, the Korean War of 1950–1953, and the Soviet invasion of Hungary, the general attitude in Britain was clearly anti-Soviet and anti-Communist. Berger, who openly supported Communism, inevitably made himself many well-known enemies, such as critics Stephen Spender and Herbert Read. Patrick Heron, an art critic against whom Berger fervently defended social realism in a debate in *The New Statesman,* rebuked him for dragging politics into the realm of art, a charge that Berger denied:

> All my life I have been passionately concerned with painting. Besides practising as a painter, I have tried to think about and *for* art. But I have tried to think beyond the painter's brush; and, as a consequence, it has been my concern for art which has largely led to my general political and social convictions. Far from my dragging politics into art, art has dragged me into politics.

Controversial though it was, Berger's voice became more and more prominent. Starting with weekly twenty-minute radio talks on European masterpieces for the BBC West African Service, he soon became a regular and well-known contributor to *The New Statesman,* British newspapers such as *The Sunday Times* and *The Observer,* and also to *The Daily Worker* and *Marxism Today.* He was repeatedly invited to appear on the television show *Monitor,* and in 1972 he produced his own highly popular television series on art, *Ways of Seeing.* By the late 1950s he had already established himself as a highly controversial art critic who openly propagated Communist views and refused to consider art as separated from the modes of its production:

> Whenever I look at a work of art as a critic, I try—Ariadne like for the path is by no means a straight one—to follow up the threads connecting it to the early Renaissance, Pablo Picasso, the Five Year Plan of Asia, the man-eating hypocrisy and sentimentality of our establishment, and to an eventual socialist revolution in this country. And if the aesthetes jump at this confession to say that it proves that I am a political propagandist, I am proud of it. But my heart and eye have remained those of a painter.

Yet, no matter how fervently he fought his cause, art history seemed to follow a different course. Soon he felt that he was the only propagator of social realism in Britain and was confronted with the triumph of abstract art, above all from the United States. The reviews he wrote became more and more often unfavorable and showed a growing disillusionment with the London art world that he felt "was dominated by people who knew nothing about art at all."

In the late 1950s Berger left Britain to live in various European locations before settling in a small mountain village in the French Alps in the early 1970s. By then he had already published, among other texts, several collections of art criticism—*Permanent Red: Essays in Seeing* (1960), *The Success and Failure of Picasso* (1965), *The Moment of Cubism and Other Essays* (1969), and *Art and Revolution: Ernst Neizvestny and the Role of the Artist in the U.S.S.R.* (1969)—and four novels—*A Painter of Our Time* (1958), *The Foot of Clive* (1962), *Corker's Freedom* (1964), and *G*. The border between fiction and criticism frequently becomes permeable in these early writings. *A Painter of Our Time,* for instance, clearly draws on Berger's experience as a painter, while much of his art criticism borders on storytelling. In these essays the focus is usually not exclusively on a painting; instead, the reader learns much about the peculiar moment when Berger went to look at the painting, about other visitors, the atmosphere of the building in which the painting was displayed, and about the painter's individual biography. Berger does not treat the painting as a timeless and self-contained work of art, but as a product intimately linked not only with the artist's life but also with the particular situation in which it is perceived. The painting is, for Berger, an expression of a creative process on the part of the artist and, at the same time, a stimulus for free associations in the onlooker, who in his imagination creates his own personal version of the painting.

According to this conviction, merely to describe in a formalist way what paintings depict would be inappropriate. Instead, Berger attempts to narrate the creative process of the artist as well as that of the onlooker interpreting it. He explains, for instance, Paul Gaugin's style of painting with his peculiar biography of a man on the run ("Gaugin's Crime" in *Permanent Red*) and analyzes how the death of an artist changes the way the world looks at the works he produced (the sculptures of "Alberto Giacometti" in *The*

Moment of Cubism). In "Between Two Colmars" from *About Looking* (1980), he describes how his impressions of Matthias Grünewald's altarpiece change with his own biography: first coming across it in 1963, he was full of fury with the injustice of capitalist society and saw "bleakness" in it, convinced that Grünewald regarded disease as "the condition of life." Seeing the piece again ten years later when he was disillusioned by the events of 1968, he discovered a bond between the artist and the diseased in the same altarpiece. To show how biographical knowledge changes ways of perceiving art, a reproduction of a painting by Vincent Van Gogh in the book *Ways of Seeing* (1972) is followed by information that it was the last painting done before the artist's suicide. Instead of meticulously describing the content of a painting, he tells stories that shed on them a subjective, yet often revealing, light. In this way, Berger's essays on art frequently cross the borders of genres. As he explains, "even when I was writing on art, it was really a way of telling stories."

While Berger's early publications, including his first novel, were still much indebted to his experience as a painter and his intimate knowledge of the London art world, the focus of his literary work changed significantly with his move to the French Alps. Living in a small rural community, he began to explore the rural world in his fiction. *Pig Earth* (1979), the first part of a trilogy of short-story collections titled *Into Their Labours* (1991) and intended to document living conditions in the community, tells unpretentious stories of everyday life in the mountains. In 1987 the second part, *Once in Europa,* was published. It describes the hardships of everyday lives in the mountains; yet, it also analyzes the advent of industrialism and contrasts farming life with the life of factory workers. Berger finally completed the project in 1990 with *Lilac and Flag: An Old Wives' Tale of a City*. While the first two collections are set in the mountains, this last collection follows the inhabitants into the cities.

In a time of rapid economic growth in the industrial and financial sectors and increasing globalization, Berger's deliberate recourse to rural life appeared irritatingly anachronistic even to Marxist critics such as Terry Eagleton. Berger does not, however, simply propagate a general return to nature. He is aware that the agricultural form of life is about to end. He does, however, consider it a third way of existence, with elements worth preserving beyond the dualism of capitalist life with its unfair distribution of goods and exploitation, on the one hand, and the form of Communism practiced—unsuccessfully in his view—in the Soviet Union, on the other. Given these two options, he thought rural life was a more humane form of

Dust jacket for the second volume (1987) of Berger's trilogy of story collections in which he contrasts everyday life in a mountain community with that of a factory worker in the city (Richland County Public Library)

existence. Still largely autonomous, independent of mass production, and not yet under the spell of alienation, rural life forms an alternative—although one that is on the brink of vanishing. Consequently, preserving it is even more important, if only in the form of literature. As he remarks in the essay "The Ideal Palace" from *Keeping a Rendezvous* (1991), "the peasant's soul is as unfamiliar or unknown to most urban people as is his physical endurance and the material conditions of his labour." While writing about rural life, however, or rather, precisely by writing about it, Berger remains an outsider. He contributes to the life of the rural community, though, by giving it a voice and preserving its worries and hopes in literature.

The harshness of rural living is rendered in a realistic prose style that spares the reader none of the cruelty of mountain life. Berger writes about the slaughter of a cow, the birth of a calf, the mating of goats, the repair of a water pipe, and the advent of tractors in the village. Yet, to dismiss this style as social realism does injustice to the texts. The multitude of realistic descriptions always leaves space for the poetic—in fact, the stories alternate with poems—and even the mysterious. In the longest story in *Pig Earth,* "The Three Lives of Lucy Cabrol," for example, the protagonist is a picaresque woman who grows only to half a normal woman's size and is known as "the *cocadrille*" among the villagers: "A *cocadrille* comes from a cock's egg hatched in a dung heap. As soon as it comes out of its egg, it makes its way to the most unlikely place. If it is seen by somebody it has not seen, it dies. Otherwise, it can defend itself and kill anything it chooses, except the weasel. The poison, with which it kills, comes from its eyes and travels along its gaze." From early on, the woman disappears suddenly for days and frightens the villagers with her intense stare until one day she is sent to live in a remote hut. In the course of many years she grows into an old, witch-like figure, picking mushrooms and berries to sell at the market, slowly but steadily accumulating an almost legendary wealth. With her grotesque appearance and mysterious qualities, Lucy becomes an enigmatic figure not unlike those found in the magic-realist writings of German author Günter Grass or Colombian novelist Gabriel García Márquez. In stories similar to this one, material existence in rural communities is conveyed in the manner of folktale and myth.

Oral storytelling, too, plays an important role—in fact, most of what the narrator tells about Lucy is based on hearsay, since he has only recently returned from a long trip to Argentina. The oral tale is not only important in the development of this particular story, but also informs Berger's own prose. Writing about a form of life that is largely without literary documents and therefore without a record of its own history and that relies on the tradition of oral storytelling to preserve its identity, Berger emulates the style of the oral tale in his texts. Deliberately simple in structure, the stories in *Into Their Labours* are written in short, sometimes repetitious, sentences that lack all the qualities of an elaborate, literary style.

This style imbues the stories with a direct and sensuous quality. In place of abstract considerations, they include images of concrete objects and similes that refer to sensuous experiences: "The ceiling was smoked dark brown like the hide of a ham" or "the Milky Way was folded into the sky like ranunculi bordering the stream are folded into the hill beside the abandoned Cabrol chalet." Thus, Berger turns descriptions that might otherwise remain abstract into almost tangible pictures.

Diverse as the individual stories of the trilogy are, they share common motifs. Existential moments of life recur: procreation, disease, and death. Many of the stories reveal a cyclic concept of time: spans of time are not measured in months or years but according to seasons or events in the village (for instance, before and after Lucy's death). Time is not an abstract measurement but a lived experience—a day starts not at six o'clock but when the cows have to be milked. Thus, time appears more natural than mechanical. Furthermore, by measuring the flow of time according to the seasons or the needs of their animals, the characters in the villages appear organically connected to the nature surrounding them, unlike those villagers who leave for the cities. In Berger's prose, male protagonists most often emigrate from the villages, while the females stay. Yet, tellingly, women are frequently depicted as stronger and more in touch with nature: they raise children in the absence of fathers and, like Lucy, know the secret places where certain plants grow. For Berger, the typical villager has the face of a woman, while men are disempowered when they lose touch with nature.

> . . . in the village, it is you who do everything, and the way you do it gives you a certain authority. There are accidents and many things are beyond your control, but it is you who have to deal with the consequences of these. When you arrive in the city, where so much is happening and so much is being done and shifted, you realize with astonishment that nothing is in your control. It is like being a bee against the window pane.

Berger imitates this interrelatedness of the peasant experience in the structure of his trilogy: even though the various stories deal with different aspects of rural life, they are all related to each other through setting and tone. Sometimes intertextual references explicitly link several stories: a grandfather mentioned in *Lilac and Flag,* who left behind a shoe made from a single block of wood, refers to a story about a similarly shaped shoe in *Pig Earth;* Michael, who loses both his legs in *Once in Europa,* returns in *Lilac and Flag;* and even Lucy Cabrol from *Pig Earth* makes an appearance in *Once in Europa.* Just as the characters understand themselves as parts of a community, Berger's stories can be understood to be part of a greater unity or narrative community.

Furthermore, Berger's stories are characterized by an openness of form. They are associative in a way that reminds one of photography or motion pictures. He frequently presents nothing more than a literary snapshot of a crucial moment in a character's life, one that is devoid of a past or future. His narrative stance is that of a writer recording what he sees

Dust jacket for Berger's 1996 short-story collection (first published in German in 1995) comprising brief descriptions of the lives of people he has known (Richland County Public Library)

rather than inventing intricate stories. No conspiracy exists between the narrator and the reader; no ironic wink is exchanged based on some knowledge that they share and of which the characters in the stories are ignorant. Instead, Berger's narrators are face to face with the characters in their stories—they share the peasant experience rather than evaluate it. In Berger's own words: "The art of the short story is so to place the moment in the life or lives of which it is part, that it becomes impossible to judge it from the outside." Berger does not judge the figures he writes about, and many of his stories are characterized by a lack of closure. Aware that narrating their lives exhaustively would mean reducing them to the logic of one master narrative, he leaves space for many possible endings and refuses to bring his stories to final solutions. In this regard, his prose style once more imitates the rural life of his characters: "Inevitability on one hand, initiative on the other. Peasants can live with contradictions without always trying to resolve them. Under certain circumstances this gives them a special kind of endurance."

Berger's subsequent short fiction is in many regards similar to *Into Their Labours*. Both *And Our Faces, My Heart, Brief as Photos* (1984) and *Keeping a Rendezvous* demonstrate the same interest as the trilogy in existential human situations such as displacement or approaching death. The scope of topics goes beyond rural life, though, and Berger speaks in rapid alternation of workers in Turkey, his own infancy, Michelangelo da Caravaggio and Van Gogh, and the feeling of emptiness after having posted a parcel (in *And Our Faces, My Heart, Brief as Photos*); and the behavior of apes in a zoo, Picasso's sexuality, and the self-built palace of the French peasant writer Ferdinand Cheval (in *Keeping a Rendezvous*). The structure of the collections—especially of *And Our Faces, My Heart, Brief as Photos*—corresponds to this willful incoherence of themes. Berger chooses an open, experimental form of prose that is difficult to classify. As in *Into Their*

Labours, he intersperses stories with poems; yet, both later collections are freer and at the same time more fragmentary in form. In fact, neither volume is a collection of short stories in the strict sense but unites a rather disparate diversity of genres such as diary entries, art criticism, essays, and documentary records. Many of Berger's texts are extremely short and again resemble literary snapshots. This resemblance is no coincidence, for Berger regards himself as both a writer and a painter, and his desire to link text and image is shown strongly in these publications, in which he experiments with visual matter (such as drawings and photographs) that somehow control interpretation of the texts.

The lack of closure in the individual stories he tells corresponds to the openness of the overall structure of the collections. In "Once upon a Time," from *And Our Faces, My Heart, Brief as Photos,* he speaks of various animals: a hare that distracts the attention of French customs officers, a white kitten that seems to disappear lying on a pile of white washing, a drake mating, and a solitary glowworm. His stories, however, repeatedly lack chronological development. Instead, he presents only momentary glimpses of these creatures. In "A Story for Aesop" (from *Keeping a Rendezvous*) the narrator gives an account of an encounter with a dog. The dog dislikes him and keeps barking at him. Only when the narrator sits down to tell the story of how he once helped another dog out of a trench does it stop, and when the narrator gets up to leave, the dog tugs him back to where he had been sitting as if he wants to hear another story. The story concludes, "You can make what you like of it. How much can dogs understand? The story becomes a story because we are not quite sure; because we remain skeptical either way." This uncertainty is characteristic of many of Berger's stories and novels. *To the Wedding* (1995), for instance, is about a wedding that might or might not have taken place. Berger's stories without endings, characterized by their quick succession of various topics, require an active reader, who has both to interrelate the disparate stories and to find endings to the individual fragments in order to give them some sense of coherence. In his early art criticism, Berger stresses the importance of the onlooker interpreting the painting. His short fiction, similarly, stresses the creativity of the act of reading by denying closure and by providing narrative gaps.

Photocopies (1996), originally published in German in 1995 as *Mann und Frau, unter einem Pflaumenbaum stehend,* is in many ways similar to the earlier collections. It consists of brief descriptions of mostly everyday life situations. Yet, it has a clearer thematic focus than *And Our Faces, My Heart, Brief as Photos* and *Keeping a Rendezvous:* it is about people Berger has met during his lifetime or people who have left a lasting impression on him. Thus, the protagonists of these stories are such people as a prisoner, a pregnant sixteen-year-old girl in the Irish countryside, a motorbike racer, a woman traveling from Sweden to France on a bicycle, a mountain dweller, and an old woman pushing her belongings in a trolley across Oxford Circus in London, but also the French philosopher Simone Weil and the Mexican revolutionary *subcomandante* Marcos. In Berger's imagination—and in his short-story collection—they form a unity of sometimes odd characters and outsiders that claim their right to exist. Berger's stories again resemble snapshots—in fact, the collection opens with a photograph of Berger and one of his visitors. The stories, seldom longer than two or three pages, attempt to portray the one moment that sheds a revealing light on the individual characters—hence, the title *Photocopies.* Like photographs in an album, these glimpses are intended to save those depicted from oblivion; they are documentaries of their existence. Many of the characters—for example, the beggars, the homeless, and the prisoners—belong to those social groups that are easily overlooked and forgotten in contemporary society. In Berger's stories they claim the right to be remembered and considered. Accordingly, he does not draw attention to himself as the narrator of these stories. The language is plain and sparse; no elaborate literary device deflects attention from those portrayed. Berger retreats behind the stories so that the people he writes about are the focus. His narrative stance is to bear witness: in many cases, he lends his voice to those who usually cannot make themselves heard or are silenced by a society that does not want to be confronted with its outcasts. Therefore, *Photocopies* demonstrates the same social impetus that characterized Berger's early writings, although the later stories are subtler and less propagandistic.

Berger's fiction clearly shows the author's social engagement. Although projects such as his photo book about migrant workers might demonstrate this engagement more directly, the desire to create social awareness in the reader has clearly left its imprint on the short stories, too: both theme and form of Berger's short fiction demonstrate this dedication. Many of his protagonists cross borders in one way or another: they are migrants, emigrants, exiles, or people marginalized by a society that tries to expel them from its field of vision. Berger, an immigrant to the French Alps, continually crosses borders of literary convention by turning into heroes those who are often regarded as losers or outcasts—a strategy that can also be observed in novels such as *To the Wedding* and *King: A Street Story* (1999), which center on AIDS victims or the homeless. Finally, on a different level, his short stories cross the frontiers of genres. Combining images with essayistic elements, poetry, elements of art criticism, diary entries, and letters, they defy classification. Furthermore, Berger's short fiction demonstrates an openness of form both in the arrangement of the stories within the various collections and within the structure of each individual story. It is associative and demanding, and it requires an active, participating reader. Rather than providing conclusions and ultimate answers, he demonstrates the complexity of life in his short fiction.

John Berger is one of the most pronounced voices of socially engaged literature, and *Ways of Seeing* has become a classic of art criticism. Yet, as a writer of fiction he is outside the British literary establishment. Not only did he withdraw from the British literary world by immigrating to France, but also the reception of his texts is sometimes still impeded by political aversions. While in the early stages of his literary career he was frequently reproached for being overly moralistic, and critic Herbert Read, an influential voice in the cultural establishment, even called "Bergerism" "a post-Marxian heresy," general opinion is slowly changing. Although Geoff Dyer's observation in his *Ways of Telling: The Work of John Berger* (1986) that "Berger's official standing as a writer is uncertain" and that "his exploration of different forms and media has denied him the kind of following a writer usually gains within a distinct category of work" still holds true, Berger is gaining recognition for his literary achievements. Less dogmatic and more humane than his early writings, his later work has been praised by writers as diverse as Susan Sontag, Michael Ondaatje, Angela Carter, and Allan Massie. For the British novelist Salman Rushdie, Berger is "a formidable protagonist in one of the most crucial battles of our age: the war over the nature of reality."

Letters:

I Send You This Cadmium Red–A Correspondence between John Berger and John Christie (Barcelona: ACTAR, 2000).

Interviews:

Theodor Shanin, "Can Peasant Society Survive?" *Listener*, 21 June 1979, pp. 647–848;

Nigel Gray, "John Berger," in his *Writers Talking* (London: Caliban, 1989).

References:

Geoff Dyer, *Ways of Telling: The Work of John Berger* (London & Dover, N.H.: Pluto, 1986);

Peter Fuller, *Seeing through Berger* (London: Claridge, 1988);

Joseph McMahon, "Marxists' Fictions: The Novels of John Berger," *Contemporary Literature*, 23, no. 2 (1982): 202–224;

Nikos Papastergiadis, *Modernity as Exile: The Stranger in John Berger's Writing* (Manchester, U.K. & New York: Manchester University Press, 1993);

Stefan Welz, *Ways of Seeing, Limits of Telling: Sehen und Erzählen in den Romanen John Bergers* (Eggingen: Isele, 1996).

Maeve Binchy
(28 May 1940 –   )

Jude R. Meche
Missouri Southern State University

BOOKS: *My First Book* (Dublin: Irish Times, 1970);

The Central Line: Stories of Big City Life (London: Quartet, 1978);

Deeply Regretted By (Dublin: Turoe, 1979);

Maeve's Diary: From Maeve Binchy's Column in the "Irish Times" (Dublin: Irish Times, 1979);

Victoria Line (London: Quartet / Swords, Ireland: Ward River Press, 1980);

Light a Penny Candle (London: Century, 1982; New York: Viking, 1983);

Dublin 4 (Swords, Ireland: Ward River Press, 1982);

London Transports (London: Century, 1983; New York: Dell, 1986)–comprises *The Central Line* and *Victoria Line;*

The Lilac Bus (Swords, Ireland: Ward River Press, 1984; New York: Delacorte, 1991);

Echoes (London: Century, 1985; New York: Viking, 1985);

Firefly Summer (London: Century, 1987; New York: Delacorte, 1988);

Silver Wedding (London: Century, 1988; New York: Delacorte, 1989);

Circle of Friends (London: Century, 1990; Franklin Center, Pa.: Franklin Library, 1990);

The Copper Beech (London: Orion, 1992; New York: Delacorte, 1992);

The Glass Lake (London: Orion, 1994; New York: Delacorte, 1995);

Dear Maeve (Dublin: Poolbeg, 1995);

This Year It Will Be Different and Other Stories: A Christmas Treasury (St Leonards, New South Wales: Allen & Unwin, 1995; New York: Delacorte, 1996);

Evening Class (London: Orion, 1996; New York: Delacorte, 1996);

The Return Journey and Other Stories (New York: Delacorte, 1998; London: Orion, 1999);

Aches and Pains (Toronto: McArthur, 1998; Dublin: Orion, 1999; New York: Delacorte, 2000);

Tara Road (London: Orion, 1998; New York: Delacorte, 1998);

Maeve Binchy (photograph © Liam White Photography; from the dust jacket for The Lilac Bus, *1991; Richland County Public Library)*

Scarlet Feather (London: Orion, 2000; New York: Dutton, 2001);

Quentins (London: Orion, 2002; New York: Dutton, 2002);

Healing Hands: People Remember Nurses, text by Binchy, photographs by Ann Henrick (Dublin: New Island, 2004);

Nights of Rain and Stars (London: Orion, 2004; New York: Dutton, 2004).

OTHER: *Irish Girls about Town: An Anthology of Irish Short Stories,* by Binchy, Marian Keyes, Cathy Kelly, and others (New York & London: Pocket Books, 2002).

In the late twentieth century, Maeve Binchy became one of the most popular living Irish authors, enjoying a wide readership, significant sales, and acclaim. Her works routinely appeared on *The New York Times* bestseller list, and *Tara Road* (1998) was selected as an Oprah Winfrey book-club selection. Binchy's novel *Circle of Friends* (1990) was adapted into a motion picture starring Chris O'Donnell and Minnie Driver. Binchy's success both abroad and in Ireland has led the popular writer to outsell what she calls "the greats of Irish literature," including Samuel Beckett, Brendan Behan, and Oscar Wilde. In an interview with Jana Siciliano for *Bookreporter.com* she distinguished between her success in book sales and the accomplishments of great Irish writers: "I was very pleased, obviously, to have outsold such great writers. But I'm not insane—I do realize that I am a popular writer who people buy to take on vacation. I'm an escapist kind of writer. . . . After all, if you were going on a long plane journey and you had a choice between one of my books and *Ulysses,* you'd probably opt for one of my books!"

Maeve Binchy was born in Dalkey, Ireland, on 28 May 1940, to William Binchy, a lawyer, and Maureen Binchy, a nurse. Maeve has a brother and two sisters. She recounts a happy childhood lived ten miles out of Dublin. She attended school at Holy Child Convent in Killiney, County Dublin. Binchy earned a degree in history at University College Dublin in 1960. She then taught French at a girls' school from 1961 until 1968. When Binchy took a trip to Israel in 1963, her parents had one of her letters published in the local newspaper. The letter led Binchy to a post as a writer for the *Irish Times,* although for a while she continued to teach. Extracts from her column for the *Irish Times* formed the basis of *My First Book* (1970).

Binchy's career as a twice-weekly columnist for the *Irish Times* took her to London, where she met Gordon Snell, a British Broadcasting Corporation (BBC) presenter who later became a children's writer. Binchy and Snell married on 29 January 1977 and settled in Dalkey. Binchy notes that she remains in close contact with her siblings and continues to write.

Binchy's first forays into fiction came in the form of short stories, which have since been collected in *The Central Line* (1978) and *Victoria Line* (1980). As the emphasis upon travel in the titles suggests, Binchy's stories are attempts to capture slices of life from throughout the city. Likewise, her emphasis is upon individuals isolated or estranged from their fellow Londoners. A representative story is "Holland Park," in which an unnamed female narrator experiences a revelation. The story begins as the narrator recounts a "perfect" couple she encountered on a vacation to Greece. This couple, Melissa and Malcolm, have become a running joke for the narrator and her friend Alice, and the couple's names are invoked whenever a person or situation appears "too perfect." When Melissa and Malcolm invite the narrator over for a reunion dinner party, she becomes distraught and jealous when Alice begins to bond with them. This jealousy mixes with horror when the narrator realizes that she and Alice have been mistaken for a lesbian couple by their hosts and the other dinner guests. Through this conflation of jealousy and sexual misidentification, however, Binchy's narrator discovers the depth of her feelings for her friend Alice.

Binchy's first novel, *Light a Penny Candle,* was published in 1982 and indicates that, as a fiction writer, Binchy had already discovered the themes and characteristics that have marked her subsequent literary output. *Light a Penny Candle* focuses on family and familial relations. In a largely epistolary form, it spans twenty years, beginning in 1940 and concluding in 1960. It centers on Elizabeth White and her Irish friend Aisling O'Connor who meet when Elizabeth's mother, Violet, sends Elizabeth to Kilgarret, Ireland, to live during the Blitz of World War II. While the novel is characterized by sentimentality, Binchy steers clear of idealistic endings for her characters. Her plots have a fidelity to real life, and her characters remain real people with real problems. Happy endings are only tentative, at best. *Light a Penny Candle* and Binchy's subsequent novels and short fiction focus predominantly on female characters who must navigate the demands of the modern world. In this world, relationships have the power both to sustain and cripple Binchy's protagonists.

In contrast to the short stories in which the intimate details of characters' lives unfold during episodes of travel, *Dublin 4* (1982) portrays characters during the course of everyday life. While divulging equal amounts of information about her protagonists and characters to those of her travel stories, this collection functions through a gradual teasing out of the crucial revelations that add context to Binchy's characters. The opening story in *Dublin 4,* "Dinner in Donnybrook," offers an example of this slow movement toward discovery as Binchy opts to leave the central character of the story, Carmel, a mystery until the ending. When Carmel begins the arrangements for a dinner party for a local artist, the reader is presented with the speculations of her friends and family over the woman's motives. The reader slowly realizes that most of her acquaintances view Carmel as a fragile and somewhat vulnerable woman. The reader also learns over time, however, that the guest of honor at this dinner party is a local artist with whom Carmel's husband is having an affair. The reader does not discover until the conclusion of the story that the purpose of the dinner party is to cause

Dust jacket for the 1991 first U.S. edition of Binchy's 1984 short-story collection, which comprises character sketches of seven people who travel every weekend from Dublin, where they work, to their hometown of Rathdoon (Richland County Public Library)

discomfort to her husband and his mistress and that Carmel is a competent and intelligent woman capable of guile.

In "Murmurs in Montrose," Binchy offers another slowly developing portrait of a protagonist. In this story she chronicles the events following Gerry's life after he completes his rehabilitation regimen for alcoholism. As is the case in "Dinner in Donnybrook," the story functions by maintaining suspense. As Gerry reshapes his life and attempts to restart his career as a professional photographer, his family waits to see if he will return to his previous life as an alcoholic.

The interdependency of people is Binchy's focus in her short fiction as well as in her novels. In the collection *The Lilac Bus* (1984) she offers character sketches of seven passengers who take a bus trip from Dublin to Rathdoon each weekend. The collection examines each character's concerns and preoccupations, weaving a network of interrelations between the passengers along the way. *The Lilac Bus* offers a portrait of the Irish that is both rural and cosmopolitan, both antiquated and modern. As these characters travel from the metropolis of Dublin every weekend toward their hometown of Rathdoon, Binchy offers an image of people who remain, at heart, more nostalgic and fearful of cosmopolitanism than they perhaps should be. These seven passengers carry such concerns as illicit affairs, closet homosexuality, and the trafficking of illegal drugs back home with them. The weekly trip home becomes, simultaneously, a nostalgic gesture and a futile effort at flight from the world that awaits them the following Monday. For some of these passengers, Binchy offers somewhat happy resolutions; for others, no clear-cut answer is in sight.

The transitory metaphor that Binchy offered in *The Lilac Bus* and through the place-name story titles of *The Central Line* and *Victoria Line* continues in her collection *The Return Journey and Other Stories* (1998). As with the previous collection, *The Return Journey and Other Stories* depicts protagonists caught in flux. The title story concerns movement back toward a point of origin. It is told in the form of a correspondence between a mother and daughter, Freda and Gina. The epistolary structure signifies a marked development for Binchy from an earlier epistolary story, "Chancery Lane," in *London Transports* (1983). While the earlier story concerns a flirtation between John and Jilly that develops into a romance and an eventual engagement, the letters exchanged in "The Return Journey" disclose a weightier subject. Freda, an American émigré from Ireland, has told her daughter little of her life prior to arriving in the United States; Gina, consequently, has embarked upon a trip to Ireland to discover for herself the details of her family origins. The letters that the two write back and forth are often terse and betray tensions between the two women. Their correspondence begins with frustration over how Gina should address her mother in print: neither "Freda" nor "Mother" seems wholly appropriate. The two also bicker because Freda fears that her daughter will hastily marry a man who is wrong for her, as Freda did. Tensions mount as Gina moves further into the landscape that was Freda's early life and as she nears the details of her mother's mistaken romance. Gina and Freda reach some small resolution, however, as Gina finds and meets her mother's nursemaid and family servant, Peggy. Reminded of Peggy, Freda realizes that her early life had moments of happiness amid the painful episodes that she has tried to forget, and she realizes that Gina will find similar joys in whatever path she chooses.

While "The Return Journey" offers an example of healing derived from a journey back to one's roots, many of the other stories in this collection do not. The flux brought about in anticipation of a journey leads to tensions between a man and wife as they search for a house sitter in "The Home Sitter." As Maura and James plan for their extended stay in the United States, they hire Allie to care for their home. Throughout their stay abroad, however, Maura develops a persistent fear of Allie and becomes preoccupied with the possibility that James might leave her for Allie. Likewise, travel reveals new, not entirely welcome, dimensions of people's personalities in "The Business Trip." In this story, Lena desires a closer relationship with Shay, a coworker. Prior to their business trip together, Lena has long admired Shay from afar, despite that she knows little about him. With the help of her friend Maggie, who has little trouble getting men's attention, she uses the business trip as an opportunity to get to know Shay and to gain his interest. Maggie helps Lena willingly, but she also warns Lena that "He will notice you, he will fancy you. Truthfully, but you may not fancy him." While Lena at first scoffs at her friend's warning, Maggie's prediction comes to pass. As Shay becomes enamored with Lena and the two get to know each other better, Lena discovers that Shay's charms are purely superficial. By the end of their business trip, Lena's interest in Shay has dissipated, and she moves on with her life.

In many cases throughout *The Return Journey and Other Stories,* intimacy seems to arise out of characters' homelessness. Stripped of the security and comfort of a home environment, characters form temporary but surprisingly intimate friendships during the course of their journeys. Lavender and Mary share such an intimacy on a ferry from Ireland to Liverpool in "The Crossing." Mary tells Lavender of the tensions between her and her in-laws, while Lavender confides to Mary that Lavender's daughter has found a husband with whom Lavender is uncomfortable. Approaching the difficulties between in-laws from both the parents' and child's perspectives, the two women offer advice and comfort to each other, making both feel more optimistic about their futures with their relations.

Binchy's *This Year It Will Be Different and Other Stories: A Christmas Treasury* (1995) reveals her protagonists' characters as they live through the tensions associated with the holidays. In "The Ten Snaps of Christmas," for example, Maura worries over her difficult daughter's emotional volatility. As the mother rests comfortably in her belief that her daughter Orla is the family's only problem, Orla proceeds to document her family's troubled life with her Christmas gift, a Polaroid camera. In ten photographs, she records her mother's difficulties keeping the turkey off the floor, her father's affair with the family's au pair, a family friend's theft of her host's silver, and her grandmother's alcoholism. Another of Binchy's Christmas stories, "A Typical Irish Christmas . . . ," recounts Ben's difficulties dealing with the holidays after the death of his wife, Ellen. In a bid to get out of holiday invitations proffered by sympathetic coworkers, Ben makes plans to visit Ireland for Christmas. As he arranges his trip, he meets Fionnula, a travel agent. During the course of his trip, he eases his own loneliness as he plays peacemaker between Fionnula and her estranged father. Though more heartwarming than "The Ten Snaps of Christmas," this story also offers a clearer view of characters by catching them in the midst of holiday stress.

Dust jacket for Binchy's 1998 collection of stories about people who form intimate friendships in the course of journeys (Richland County Public Library)

Despite her admission of her popular rather than literary status, Binchy's works offer a compelling insight into Ireland at the close of the twentieth century. Her characters dwell in a world made homogeneous by media saturation and easy transportation. Based solely upon her characterizations, the reader might as easily assume her Irish characters are American or English.

This sense of cultural homogenization in Binchy's works is heightened by the author's reliance upon the flux of travel as a means of gestating intimacies and forging meetings. Her story collections almost always include travel or movement; consequently, they resist static national characterizations.

The Irish landscape, though, functions in an ironically romantic way in many of Binchy's works. Since Matthew Arnold cited the supposedly inescapable "sentimentality" of the Celt, authors have capitalized upon assumptions about the Irish as a prototypically romantic people. For Binchy, however, the evocative terrain often serves as an ironic contrast to the characters in her novels and short stories. While the mention of Ireland brings with it connotations of romance, these expectations are typically dashed as Binchy's protagonists confront a modern world in which Orla's Polaroid snapshots replace the sentimental images of an Irish Christmas. Even at their best, Binchy's Irish characters—such as Lena and Shay from "The Business Trip"—have little or no time for romance or reveal a genuine ineptitude for romantic relationships.

While her preoccupation with themes of love and relationships has guaranteed her a popular audience, critical reception of Maeve Binchy's work has been less than enthusiastic. Her reliance upon conventional forms and Hollywood-style tricks and coincidences in her plots has led to a low critical estimation of her writing. Although Binchy has drawn attention from scholars exploring Irish pop culture or Irish women's writing, she will likely remain a predominantly popular phenomenon.

Interviews:

"Best-Selling Irish Author Maeve Binchy Discusses Her Career as a Novelist and Her New Book *The Glass Lake*," *Europe* (April 1995): 22;

"A Conversation with Maeve Binchy," *Writer*, 113 (1 February 2000): 14;

Jana Siciliano, "Maeve Binchy," *Bookreporter.com* <http://www.bookreporter.com/authors/au-binchy-maeve.asp>.

References:

"Feisty Maeve Binchy, Ireland's Favorite Storyteller, Heads for Greener Pastures," *People Weekly* (28 August 2000): 147;

Christine St. Peter, *Changing Ireland: Strategies in Contemporary Women's Fiction* (Basingstoke, U.K.: Macmillan / New York: St. Martin's Press, 2000).

A. S. Byatt
(24 August 1936 –)

Sabine Coelsch-Foisner
University of Salzburg

See also the Byatt entries in *DLB 14: British Novelists Since 1960* and *DLB 194: British Novelists Since 1960, Second Series.*

BOOKS: *Shadow of a Sun* (London: Chatto & Windus, 1964; New York: Harcourt, Brace & World, 1964);

Degrees of Freedom: The Novels of Iris Murdoch (London: Chatto & Windus, 1965; New York: Barnes & Noble, 1965); republished with additional material as *Degrees of Freedom: The Early Novels of Iris Murdoch* (London: Vintage, 1994);

The Game (London: Chatto & Windus, 1967; New York: Scribners, 1968);

Wordsworth and Coleridge in Their Time (London: Thomas Nelson, 1970; New York: Crane, Russak, 1973); republished as *Unruly Times: Wordsworth and Coleridge in Their Time* (London: Hogarth, 1989);

Iris Murdoch, Writers and Their Work Series, no. 251 (Harlow: Longman in association with the British Council, 1976);

Iris Murdoch: The Black Prince, Notes on Literature, no. 170 (London: The British Council, 1977);

The Virgin in the Garden (London: Chatto & Windus, 1978; New York: Knopf, 1979);

Still Life (London: Chatto & Windus, 1985; New York: Scribners, 1985);

Sugar and Other Stories (London: Chatto & Windus, 1987; New York: Scribners, 1987);

Possession: A Romance (London: Chatto & Windus, 1990; New York: Random House, 1990);

Angels and Insects: Two Novellas (London: Chatto & Windus, 1992; New York: Random House, 1993);

The Matisse Stories (London: Chatto & Windus, 1993; New York: Random House, 1995);

The Djinn in the Nightingale's Eye: Five Fairy Stories (London: Chatto & Windus, 1994; New York: Random House, 1997);

Imagining Characters: Six Conversations about Women Writers, by Byatt and Ignês Sodré, edited by Rebecca

A. S. Byatt (photograph © Tara Heinemann 1986; from the dust jacket for Sugar and Other Stories, *1987; Richland County Public Library)*

Swift (London: Chatto & Windus, 1995; New York: Vintage, 1997);

Babel Tower (London: Chatto & Windus, 1996; New York: Random House, 1996);

Elementals: Stories of Fire and Ice (London: Chatto & Windus, 1998; New York: Random House, 1999);

The Biographer's Tale (London: Chatto & Windus, 2000; New York: Knopf, 2001);

The Bird Hand Book, text by Byatt, photographs by Victor Schrager (New York: Graphis, 2001);

Portraits in Fiction (London: Chatto & Windus, 2001);

A Whistling Woman (London: Chatto & Windus, 2002; New York: Knopf, 2003);

Little Black Book of Stories (London: Chatto & Windus, 2003; New York: Knopf, 2004).

Collections: *Passions of the Mind: Selected Writings* (London: Chatto & Windus, 1991; New York: Turtle Bay, 1992);

On Histories and Stories: Selected Essays (London: Chatto & Windus, 2000; Cambridge, Mass.: Harvard University Press, 2001).

OTHER: "The Lyric Structure of Tennyson's Maud," in *The Major Victorian Poets Reconsidered,* edited by Isobel Armstrong (London: Routledge & Kegan Paul, 1969), pp. 69–93;

Elizabeth Bowen, *The House in Paris,* introduction by Byatt (London: Penguin, 1976);

"People in Paper Houses: Attitudes to 'Realism' and 'Experiment' in English Postwar Fiction," in *The Contemporary English Novel,* edited by Malcolm Bradbury (London: Edward Arnold, 1979), pp. 19–41;

George Eliot, *The Mill on the Floss,* edited by Byatt and Nicholas Warren, with an introduction by Byatt (London: Penguin, 1979);

Grace Paley, *Enormous Changes at the Last Minute,* introduction by Byatt (London: Virago, 1979);

Willa Cather, *A Lost Lady,* introduction by Byatt (London: Virago, 1980);

Cather, *My Antonia,* introduction by Byatt (London: Virago, 1980);

Paley, *The Little Disturbances of Man,* introduction by Byatt (London: Virago, 1980);

Cather, *The Song of the Lark,* introduction by Byatt (London: Virago, 1989);

Cather, *Death Comes for the Archbishop,* introduction by Byatt (London: Virago, 1989);

Robert Browning, *Dramatic Monologues,* edited by Byatt (London: Folio Society, 1990);

George Eliot: Selected Essays, Poems and Other Writings, edited by Byatt and Warren (Harmondsworth, U.K.: Penguin, 1990);

Marie-Catherine Le Jumel de Barneville, comtesse d'Aulnoy, "The Great Green Worm," translated by Byatt, in *Wonder Tales: Six Stories of Enchantment,* edited by Marina Warner (London: Chatto & Windus, 1994), pp. 189–229;

"A New Body of Writing: Darwin and Recent British Fiction," in *New Writing 4,* edited by Byatt and Alan Hollinghurst (London: Vintage in association with the British Council, 1995), pp. 439–448;

New Writing 6, edited by Byatt and Peter Porter (London: Vintage in association with the British Council, 1997);

The Oxford Book of English Short Stories, edited by Byatt (Oxford & New York: Oxford University Press, 1998).

SELECTED PERIODICAL PUBLICATIONS–
UNCOLLECTED: "The Obsession with Amorphous Mankind," *Encounter,* 27, no. 9 (September 1966): 63–69;

"The Battle between Real People and Images," *Encounter,* 28, no. 2 (February 1967): 71–78;

"Wallace Stevens: Criticism, Repetition, and Creativity," *American Studies,* 12, no. 3 (1978): 369–375;

"Reading, Writing, Studying: Some Questions about Changing Conditions for Writers and Readers," *Critical Quarterly,* 35, no. 4 (Winter 1993): 3–7.

A best-selling novelist, short-story writer, distinguished critic, and winner of many prestigious awards and prizes, A. S. Byatt enjoys a high profile in the media and in public life in general. Her fifth novel, *Possession: A Romance* (1990), catapulted her to the forefront of contemporary British writers and prompted a surge in critical studies about her work and a mass of interviews with her both in academic journals and in popular magazines. Byatt's short stories are of crucial interest in connection with her overall work and with regard to postmodernist developments of the genre. While foregrounding such aspects as the literary quality of a text, the interplay of fact and fiction, the incompleteness and fluidity of life, and a sense that the past constructs the present, Byatt also has a great respect for "just what is there," as she explained in an interview with Juliet Dusinberre included in the collection *Women Writers Talking* (1983). A major concern in all her fiction is the individual's experience of what it is to be alive. For Byatt, this experience is inseparable from the world of language and the sensuousness of words. As she said in the interview with Dusinberre, "When I read I inhabit a world which is more real than the world in which I live, or perhaps I should say that I am more alive in it. It is a language world."

Antonia Susan Drabble was born on 24 August 1936 in Sheffield, England, the eldest daughter of John Frederick Drabble, a courtroom lawyer, and Kathleen Marie (née Bloor), a schoolteacher. Antonia is the sister of Margaret Drabble and was educated at Sheffield High School and the Mount School, York, a Quaker foundation. Antonia took a B.A. (first-class honors) from Newnham College, Cambridge, and pursued postgraduate study at Bryn Mawr College in Pennsylvania (1957–1958) and Somerville College, Oxford (1958–1959). On 4 July 1959 she married Ian Charles Rayner Byatt, with whom she had two children, Charles and Antonia. (Charles died in a car accident in

1972). The marriage was dissolved in 1969. From 1962 to 1971, she taught in the Extra-Mural Department of London University and at the Central School of Art and Design, London, from 1965 to 1969. She also published her first two novels, *Shadow of a Sun* (1964) and *The Game* (1967), as well as her first study on Iris Murdoch, *Degrees of Freedom* (1965). In 1969 Byatt married Peter John Duffy, with whom she has two daughters, Isabel and Miranda.

The 1970s were a fruitful decade for Byatt in terms of academic work. In 1970 she published the study *Wordsworth and Coleridge in Their Time,* which was followed by her second monograph on Murdoch, published in 1976. In 1972 she was appointed a full-time lecturer in English and American literature at University College London. She was appointed a Booker Prize judge for 1974 and a member of the BBC Social Effects of Television Advisory Group (1974–1977) as well as of the Board of Communications and Cultural Studies of the Council for National Academic Awards (1978–1984). After publishing her third novel, *The Virgin in the Garden* (1978), she edited, together with Nicholas Warren, George Eliot's *The Mill on the Floss* for Penguin Classics (1979).

In 1981 she was promoted to a senior lectureship. In 1983, when Byatt was elected fellow of the Royal Society of Literature, she retired from academic life to write full-time. In 1985 she published her fourth novel, *Still Life,* which won the PEN/Macmillan Silver Pen Award for fiction. She served on the Board of Creative and Performing Arts (1985–1987) as well as the Kingman Committee on the Teaching of English (1987–1988), and in 1990 she published *George Eliot: Selected Essays, Poems and Other Writings*.

Byatt's career as a novelist reached a turning point in 1990. The publication of *Possession: A Romance* brought her international fame. She was appointed a Commander of the British Empire (CBE) in addition to winning the *Irish Times*/Aer Lingus International Fiction Prize, the Eurasian Regional Award of the Commonwealth Writers Prize, and, most important of all, the Booker Prize for Fiction. By December 1995 *Possession* had been translated into sixteen languages, and its phenomenal success has often been compared to that of Umberto Eco's *The Name of the Rose* (1980) or Salmon Rushdie's *Midnight's Children* (1981). The publication of *Possession* also led to a reappraisal of Byatt's earlier work, a compilation of which was published in *Passions of the Mind: Selected Writings* (1991). This selection of earlier writings includes reviews and essays on Robert Browning, Eliot, Vincent Van Gogh, Willa Cather, Elizabeth Bowen, Sylvia Plath, Toni Morrison, Barbara Pym, and Monique Wittig. In the introduction to *Passions of the Mind,* Byatt explains a feature characteristic of her

Dust jacket for the U.S. edition of Byatt's 1987 collection of stories interlinked through similar themes and characters (Richland County Public Library)

whole writing career—the link between creative and academic work, the "encounter with other minds" and with the cultural past:

> Novelists sometimes claim that their fiction is a quite separate thing from their other written work. Iris Murdoch likes to separate her philosophy from her novels; David Lodge says that his critical and narrative selves are a schizoid pair. I have never felt such a separation, nor wanted to make such claims. From my early childhood, reading and writing seemed to me to be points on a circle. Greedy reading made me want to write, as if this was the only adequate response to the pleasure and power of books.

Byatt's next novel, *Babel Tower* (1996), took six years to write and publish. In 1998 Byatt was awarded the Mythopoeic Fantasy Award for Adult Literature; in 1990 she was appointed a CBE, and in 1999 she was appointed a Dame Commander of the Order of the British Empire (DBE) for her work as a writer. In 2000 she published her seventh novel, *The Biographer's Tale,* and a year later, *Portraits in Fiction,* a monograph on instances of painting in novels, including works by Emile Zola, Marcel Proust, and Murdoch. Byatt had first explored this subject in a lecture held at the National Portrait Gallery, London, in 2000. In 2002 Byatt was awarded the Shakespeare Prize by the Alfred Toepfer Foundation, Hamburg, in recognition of her contribution to British culture. She holds several honorary doctorates, lives in London, and contributes regularly to journals and newspapers including *TLS: The Times Literary Supplement, The Independent,* and the *Sunday Times,* as well as to radio programs and the British Broadcasting Corporation (BBC).

Byatt took up writing short stories late in her life. In 1987 her first collection, *Sugar and Other Stories,* appeared, followed in 1992 by two connected novellas published under the title *Angels and Insects,* adapted and made into a motion picture by Samuel Goldwyn Co. (1995). Two more short-story collections followed, *The Matisse Stories* (1993) and *The Djinn in the Nightingale's Eye: Five Fairy Stories* (1994). In 1994 Byatt contributed "The Great Green Worm," a translation of Marie-Catherine Le Jumel de Barneville, comtesse d'Aulnoy's "Le Serpentin vert," to Marina Warner's *Wonder Tales: Six Stories of Enchantment,* and in 1998 her fourth collection of stories appeared: *Elementals: Stories of Fire and Ice.* Byatt considers the short story closer to the poem than the novel, with its condensed, symbolic force, its potential relationship with the marvelous, its concentration on images, and its capacity for turning "the reader into a reader of a reading," as she explained in an interview with Jean-Louis Chevalier in 1994. A novel—*Possession*—reflects Byatt's increasing interest in the short story, because it includes, in the work of the character Christabel LaMotte, "wonder tales," two of which were reprinted as separate stories in *The Djinn in the Nightingale's Eye:* "The Glass Coffin" and "Gode's Story." While Richard Todd, in his *A. S. Byatt* (1997), has argued that these stories read differently divorced from the context of the novel, Chevalier and Jane L. Campbell in her "'The Somehow May Be Thishow': Fact, Fiction, and Intertextuality in Antonia Byatt's 'Precipe-Encurled'" (1991) have stressed the experimental, intertextual quality of the stories themselves. The narrative strategies that operate in the larger narratives are microscopically present in the shorter forms, with which Byatt experimented so skillfully in the 1990s. Her preoccupation with various forms of short fiction is reflected in the terms she uses—"stories," "short stories," "fairy stories," "wonder tales"—both as subtitles and in metafictional comments.

A central characteristic of Byatt's handling of stories is the manner in which they are made to refer to their own status as texts and the ways in which different narrative expectations and multiple types of text—letters, diaries, journals, fairy tales—are merged. In this respect, Byatt's entire oeuvre, novels and story collections, abounds in intertextual references, metanarrative signposts, that is, in echoes of earlier works or works by other authors as well as in self-conscious allusions to the narrative. As one reads Byatt's fiction, one constantly recognizes characters (the academic, the professional storyteller, the woman writer, the painter or craftsman, siblings, daughters, children suspended between life and death, marginalized middle-aged women), their interest in art and literature, and their obsessions with words, with truthfulness, with the body, and with the past, as well as recurrent symbols and images, such as snakes, pools, paintings, and glass objects.

Sugar and Other Stories comprises eleven stories that are characteristically interlinked through motifs, themes, and similar characters. "Racine and the Tablecloth," "Rose-Coloured Teacups," "The July Ghost," and "The Next Room" deal with a parent-child relationship and the continuous life of the dead; "The Dried Witch" and "Loss of Face" explore a remote culture and are connected; "On the Day That E. M. Forster Died" and "The Changeling" portray the situation of women writers; "In the Air" echoes the unsolved mystery of "The July Ghost" and repeats the figure of the threatened woman from "The Dried Witch"; "Precipice-Encurled" and "Sugar" self-consciously refer to the writing process. Though more heterogeneous in terms of themes and topics than Byatt's later collections, *Sugar and Other Stories* combines three features characteristic of Byatt's short fiction: an obvious autobiographical focus, a fantastic quality, and—if one takes these stories in sequence—an increasingly self-reflexive and experimental element.

Critics have unanimously praised the way in which Byatt weaves intricate fictions out of small details and situations. Although many incidents in her early stories point to Byatt's own life, the emphasis is less on their autobiographical dimension than on how fantasy interacts with real life. Lived experience furnishes the raw data out of which the writer spins her tales. This idea is strengthened by the metaphor of confection used in the title story, "Sugar," which Byatt in an interview with Eleanor Wachtel in 1993 described as "autobiographical." "I select and confect," says the female narrator in the story, pointing to both the fabrication of the things said and the "long black shadows of the things left unsaid." "Sugar" is the story of a woman who embarks on a quest for her family history through a wealth of stories, tales, myths, and lies. Although motivated by a "wish to be exact," she is constantly made aware of the shaping quality of the human mind. Her mother, for example, proves a "breathless and breathtaking raconteur" who "lied floridly and beautifully." Throughout the story the protagonist's passion for truth and truthfulness is counterbalanced by currents undermining the possibility of approximating the real. In the end, her respect for evidence is defeated, and she reaches a conclusion typical of Byatt's own attitude to fiction: "The real thing, the true moment, is . . . inaccessible. . . . More things come back as I write; the gold-winged buttons on his jacket, forgotten between then and now. None of these words, none of these things recall him." The result is a "skeletal and discontinuous" account of the past, which begins to resemble a Victorian melodrama as truth and invention merge.

The idea that "the real is beyond form," as Dusinberre has emphasized, is indebted to Murdoch's concept of contingency: "what is random, accidental, merely factual . . . and not part of any formal plan or pattern," which Byatt quotes in *Degrees of Freedom*. Byatt refuses to give shape and finality to her characters and the conditions in which they find themselves. This impression of indeterminacy and openness enhances her "fantastic vein" (to use Todd's phrase), reflected either in a direct confrontation with the other world or in a self-conscious calling into doubt of the rationality, linearity, and causality of life, characteristic of her more experimental stories.

Influenced by the Chinese short stories of Shen Ts'ung-wen, "The Dried Witch" is a prime example of Byatt's effort to accommodate the strange in fiction. Set in an Asian peasant village, the story deals with the discrimination against postmenopausal women. In it, Byatt leads the reader into a remote and menacing world of magic potions, superstitions, and primitive rites. After A-Oa's four sons die, her husband is taken by the army and her brother-in-law disappears. A-Oa strives to give meaning to her life by becoming a jinx. The story ends with her execution by being dried in the sun, which is related from the point of view of her own consciousness until her mind is severed from her scorched body. The graphic description of A-Oa's death brings to completion the thematic fixation in the story on heat and dryness—drought, the drying out of bodily liquids (saliva, pus, blood, water, sweat, and milk), and dried herbs and animals:

> Her tongue, huge, a weightless boulder, cracking against her teeth. Heat ran down her spine and killed and fetched up the colourless scales and cushions of skin above the vertebrae, where it was thin, where it flaked back to expose raw wet flesh that dried, fast. A sound came in her ears, a hissing and squeaking, the contents of her skull writhing and shrinking like intestines in a frying pan. . . . On the third day, she was two. Her mind stood outside herself, looking down on the shrivelling flesh, with its blues and umbers, on the cracked face, the snarling mouth, the bared, dry-bone teeth. . . . The eddies of heat from the burning swirled out across the muddy ground and took her with them, away from the strapped and cracking thing, away.

In "Rose-Coloured Teacups" the supernatural constitutes the fiction that gives coherence to people's lives. It is a story of how imagined scenes interpenetrate with lived experience, how the present is fused with the past, and how the generations are linked by invisible and incomprehensible connections. In a reverie, Veronica tries to visualize her mother as a student waiting with friends in a college room to entertain a group of male students at a tea party. Her ability to imagine the scene stops at the point when the young men arrive. Focusing on the verb *seeing*, the story paradoxically points to the limits of vision and the borders of the visible world, such as the inaccurately perceived flowers on a tablecloth: "She mostly saw the flowers as roses, though many of them, looked at more closely, were hybrid or imaginary creations." Significantly, the story ends on a failure of vision: "She could never see any further: from there, it always began again, chairs, tablecloth, sunny window, rosy teacups, a safe place." Far from being a "safe place," life is shown to abound in gaps and ultimately eludes Veronica's full control, as Byatt argued in her essay "Reading, Writing, Studying: Some Questions about Changing Conditions for Writers and Readers" (*Critical Quarterly*, 1993): "and nothing is ever wholly to be understood."

In accordance with this dictum, Byatt's stories attach great importance to space and place, contrasting narrow, confined places (rooms, houses, and walled gardens) with phenomena that outgrow space (memories, illusions, and apparitions). The solid, visible, tangible world constantly points to realms that are the province of fantasy—hesitation, uncertainty, and ambivalence—and the province of experiment as far as narrative strategies are concerned.

"The July Ghost" is a prime example of how fantasy and technical experiment interact. An unnamed male academic takes lodgings with Imogen, whose son was killed in a car accident, and repeatedly beholds a boy in her garden. Suggestions of irrationality are made at the outset of the story that, though seemingly insignificant, have a disruptive effect on the process of reading: the academic occupies the "attics"; the landlady screams "hysterically" when her husband returns home and later explains to her new tenant that "The Common is an illusion of space" and that "no illusions are pleasant." These premonitions of something eerie crystallize into the figure of the boy—obviously the ghost of Imogen's dead son, who regularly

Dust jacket for the 1997 U.S. edition of Byatt's 1994 collection of short stories that characteristically combine an autobiographical focus, fantasy, and experiment in form (Richland County Public Library)

visits the lodger but remains invisible to his mother. At this point, the story abandons the path of realism in favor of fantasy. Faced with the mystery of the ghost's presence, which cannot securely be explained as a projection of Imogen's desperate longing to see her son again or as the male protagonist's intuition of her needs, both Imogen and her lodger can only accept that they are under the spell of "some undefined authority."

"The July Ghost" is a multilayered frame story that self-consciously draws the reader's attention to the level of storytelling (it is a ghost story within a realistic story told by the male protagonist to an American colleague at a party), the level of experience (the protagonist's perceptions), and the level of the uncanny, which calls even the possibility of representation into doubt (hence, in the version he tells his American interlocutor, the protagonist does not mention the ghost). Abounding in breaks and pauses, shifts of perspective, ambiguities, and leaps in time, the text challenges the reader's exegetic effort in a manner comparable to the male protagonist's pragmatic attempt at making sense of the ghost's presence. The end is open.

In *The Matisse Stories* a shift occurs from literary allusions, references, and quotations to visual references. The volume consists of three stories—"Medusa's Ankles," "Art Work," and "The Chinese Lobster"—each transporting a painting by Henri Matisse to a modern setting: a hairdresser's salon, a modern flat, and a Chinese restaurant, respectively. Byatt's irony becomes more poignant in these stories; her minute observations of everyday life become more piercing and uncompromising. Characteristically, the situations in which the female protagonists are depicted are domestic worlds, wholly devoid of excitement and romance and occasionally more real than reality.

"Medusa's Ankles" is set in a hairdresser's salon and exposes with shrewd irony the clashing worlds of youth and middle age, passion and routine, academia and the trivia of life. As Susannah regularly visits Lucian's salon, she sees it one day transformed from the pleasant "interior of a rosy cloud, all pinks and creams" matching the hues of Matisse's *Rosy Nude,* which first attracted her to it, into a high-tech salon in "battleship-grey and maroon," which she despises. Her own consciousness is divided between the inner image of her young body and the image of her plump, wrinkled face and her greying, lusterless hair reflected in the hairdresser's mirror. One day when Lucian forces on his client his usual stories about his wife with her fat ankles and his escapades with a young mistress, Susannah gets so distraught that she hurls a bottle of gel against a glass shelf and demolishes the whole salon. The mirror cracks, but the futility of Susannah's revolt against the degrading cult of female beauty, which makes her hate her aging body, is driven home with bitter irony. When she comes home, her husband compliments her on her new hairstyle: "You look lovely. It takes twenty years off you. You should have it done more often."

In "Art Work," Byatt sketches the life of an artistic family: the unsuccessful painter Robin Dennison and his talented and efficient wife, Debbie; their two children; and Mrs. Brown, their domestic help. Robin's "neo-realistic" paintings provide the visual subtext to the narrative: "He painted what he saw, metal surfaces, wooden surfaces, plaster surfaces, with hallucinatory skill and accuracy." Such is precisely Byatt's method of telling this story as she focuses on "*unprivileged* things" and "modern *vanitases,*" which are "about the *littleness* of our life." Matisse's painting *Le silence habité des maisons,* described at the beginning of the story, is related to the text as a contrast. Matisse's "extraordinary virility" is opposed to Robin's incompetence as a painter and breadwinner, and the silence is violently disturbed by the nerve-wracking noises in the Dennisons' house: the "churning hum of the washing-machine, a kind of splashy mechanical giggle, with a grinding note in it"; the "chuntering" of the dryer; the "cheery squitter of female presenters of children's TV"; the "circular rush and swish" of Jamie's electric trains; the "beating vibrations and exploding howls and ululations" of Natasha's record player; and the "roaring and wheezing noise" of the vacuum cleaner. By returning to the theme of art preying on life, central in Byatt's novel *The Game*, "Art Work" tells a story of failure with a final streak of optimism. Initially imitating Matisse, Robin fails to attract the gallery owners' attention but eventually develops a style of his own, while Mrs. Brown becomes a famous artist precisely by borrowing Robin's aesthetic credo, and Debbie starts writing fairy books, modeling her fairies' faces on Mrs. Brown and her successor, Mrs. Stimpson.

Gerda Himmelblau in "The Chinese Lobster" is another "solitary intellectual, nearing retirement" and, like her predecessors in *Sugar and Other Stories*, committed to accuracy and truthfulness. Set in a Chinese restaurant, the story presents conflicting views about Matisse's art and is held together by the image of a lobster in a glass case—an echo of Samuel Beckett's 1934 story "Dante and the Lobster," as Byatt explained in her interview with Chevalier in 1994, and a symbol of defeat and death-in-life. In fact, death is in the air when Himmelblau, dean of women students, and Professor Peregrine Diss, an enthusiastic admirer of Matisse, discuss a complaint filed against the latter by Peggi Nollett, an art student, on grounds of sexual harassment. Peggi, who suffers from anorexia, pursues an unconventional, feminist project of "*revising* or *reviewing* or *rearranging* Matisse." Disparaging Matisse's nudes as "one monstrous female corpse bursting with male aggression," her work constitutes an outrage to Diss's hedonist passion for the painter. Far from being a mere dispute about artistic likes and dislikes, the conversation triggers in Himmelblau painful memories of her best friend, who committed suicide, and, coupled with these, a tragic feeling that she "is next in line." What Matisse ultimately conveys to her is a sense of "quiet terror." "The Chinese Lobster" is representative of the whole volume: it pinpoints the reception of Matisse's art, the disparate and idiosyncratic views it elicits, and the damaging and mobilizing effect it has on its admirers and critics. Works of art are shown to be ambivalent, elusive, and affective. In this respect, Matisse's own oxymoronic dictum (as remembered by Diss) is characteristic of the multiple contradictions and tensions explored in all three Matisse stories: "black is the colour of light."

The format and layout of *The Matisse Stories* is maintained in *The Djinn in the Nightingale's Eye*, which includes "The Glass Coffin"; "Gode's Story"; "The Story of the Eldest Princess," originally commissioned for the 1992 Vintage collection *Caught in a Story: Contemporary Fairytales and Fables*, as a fairy tale of the writer's own life; "Dragon's Breath," which was "written for Sarajevo" out of a feeling of "something having gone wrong," as she explained in a later interview with Chevalier in 1999; and the title story, which runs to almost two hundred pages and thus far exceeds the scope of a conventional fairy story. Byatt's interest in the fantastic is given new expression in these stories. By calling them "fairy stories," she explicitly places them within a clearly defined generic tradition but subverts conventions of plot, character, atmosphere, and narrative technique. Of her four collections of stories, *The Djinn in the Nightingale's Eye* is the most consistently self-conscious volume: the stories are open and mysterious; they are stories within stories, about stories, or about storytelling. The fairy-tale element in them is reflected in both form and content.

Each of the five stories opens with the familiar phrase–"There was once . . ." or "Once upon a time . . ."– and ends on a happy vision, a reunion, an improvement of a person's or a people's state of affairs, or the restitution of previous happiness malevolently destroyed by an evil spirit. They include all the ingredients of fairy-tale literature: strange encounters, three wishes, an enchanted prince or princess, spells, adventures and marvelous places, a quest motif, mythical creatures, uncanny forces, and illogical happenings that drive the action forward. Incidents happen or things come into being without any plausible cause, and solutions are brought about by mere desires. "The Glass Coffin," in particular, draws on stock conventions of fairy-tale lore. A humble tailor loses his way in a thick wood, chances upon an old grey-haired man with an evil-looking but kindly dog, and in return for his work is presented three objects from which he may select one: a purse, a pot, and a glass key. He chooses the key and sets out on an adventurous quest, the object of which is unknown to him. The journey leads him to a sinister place with a magic, miniature castle in a glass dome and a glass coffin with a sleeping beauty. The tailor's key fits the coffin; the princess is brought back to life by the obligatory kiss; the castle is restored to normal size; and the princess's brother, who had been transformed into the dog, is freed. Everyone lives happily ever after.

Yet, Byatt's story is an adult fairy story, and the storyteller is an adult speaking to and about adults, ironically commenting on the tailor's actions and freely addressing the audience: "And you, my sagacious readers, will have perceived and understood that. . . ." The tailor, too, proves well versed in fairy tales and knows exactly how to behave in the story. He chooses the glass key because he prefers adventure to inexhaustible food and money; he kisses the sleeping beauty because it seems the proper thing to do in such a situation ("And he knew–it is always so, after all–that the true adventure was the release of this sleeper, who would then be his grateful bride"); and he slays the evil magician out of a sense of duty. While complying with a textual code familiar to him, he also brings into the story his adult consciousness. Thus, he doubts

Dust jacket for the 1999 U.S. edition of Byatt's 1998 story collection that deals with artists and the artistic process (Richland County Public Library)

whether he is a fit mate for the princess and in the end carries on his trade in the castle, because a true craftsman cannot accept fairy-tale idleness. Both this mingling of fairy-tale plot and grown-up perspective and the narrator's complicity with the reading audience have a disruptive effect on the story and highlight its artificiality.

The same effect is achieved in "Dragon's Breath," which, by treating natural phenomena in terms of myth lore, organically emerges as a story about the origin of tales, their communal function, and the necessity of myth and mystery in the lives of ordinary men. "The Story of the Eldest Princess" dismantles the reader's expectations by having the eldest princess reflect on her own role in the story. She is widely read and constantly measures the things happening to her in the course of her quest after the blue sky against the familiar canon of quest literature. In fact, her experience is largely the result of stories: "I know that story too," she remarks. Aware that she is "in a pattern" according to which she is bound to fail—the eldest princess is always imprisoned or turned into stone—she determines to leave this "inconvenient story" and sets out on a quest for the wise old woman, the supposed healer of all the ailing creatures she encounters on her way: an injured scorpion; a bleeding toad, who admonishes her not to believe in human stories of toads turning into handsome princes; and a giant cockroach entangled in cotton threads. Significantly, by telling their stories, the creatures are healed.

The last and longest story, "The Djinn in the Nightingale's Eye," deals with the experience of life in terms of stories of a narratologist (one who studies the structure of narratives). The setting is a conference in Turkey, and the protagonist, Gillian Perholt, is a middle-aged woman who feels pleasantly redundant in life, as her two children are grown up and her husband has run off with a younger woman. She shares the wisdom of Byatt's academic women and the discomforts and inhibitions they experience with respect to their declining bodies. The reality of academic life is mingled with Eastern myth lore. Occident and Orient meet in a succession of stories told in the course of the conference and recalled or alluded to in connection with a sightseeing and a shopping tour. The title is explained late in the story, when Gillian buys a bottle, a "nightingale's eye," and out of it comes a djinn, who grants her three wishes. Gillian is given back her youthful body, is made love to by the djinn, and is visited every now and then by him after she sets him free. By admitting the djinn into her life, Gillian, like all other protagonists in this volume, breaks out of a pattern prescribed for her by social and literary traditions. As in Byatt's earlier fantastic stories, fact and fantasy are treated as complementary modes in the constitution of a character's consciousness.

In *Elementals,* Byatt returns to familiar territory, dealing once more with visual art, artists, and the artistic process. Yet, in each of the six stories—"Crocodile Tears," "A Lamia in the Cévennes," "Cold," "Baglady," "Jael," and "Christ in the House of Martha and Mary"—this concern acquires a sterner philosophical note, alerting the reader to "that element in the visual which completely defeats language," as Byatt defined her interest in painting in an interview with Boyd Tonkin in 1999.

The subtitle of the volume, *Stories of Fire and Ice,* is evocative of a contrast that is both symbolic and existential or elemental. "Baglady" explores the contrast between individuality and anonymity. It is the story of a woman who, accompanying her husband to a professional meeting in the Orient, literally gets lost in a gigantic shopping mall. Significantly, the two longest stories in the volume, "Crocodile Tears" and "Cold," are structured along the contrast of heat and cold. In both stories art overcomes the gulf between South and North. In "Crocodile Tears," Patricia Nimmo, after the death of her husband, flees from London to the south of France, where she meets the Norwegian Nils Isaksen. Hoping to escape death, she finds herself surrounded by a long history of killing and bloodshed and, through a visit to the tombstones of the gladiators in the ethnological museum of Nîmes, acquires a new curiosity about life. In "Cold" the desert prince Sasan, a glassblower and craftsman, builds a crystal palace in the desert for his ice princess so that they can live together in happiness without either of them suffering from weather conditions ill suited to their temperamental inclinations. In "Christ in the House of Martha and Mary," art, too, achieves a kind of reconciliation. The sullen cook Dolores is freed from her anger and discontent by a naturalistic painting of her. Through this immortalization of her ugliness she learns to accept her low birth and uncomely features. Art is viewed less as a self-conscious act as it becomes a mode of existing.

With the exception of "Jael," in which the first-person narrator, a voracious reader, self-consciously examines the importance of the biblical story of Jael and Sisera for her own life, the concern with writing, language, and previous voices is no longer explicit in these stories. References to writers or mythical figures have become inseparably fused with the imaginative lives of the characters, as is shown in "A Lamia in the Cévennes." Mystery and myth are the source of Bernard Lycett-Kean's art and the touchstone of artistic ingenuity. Reminding the reader of the actor Charles Arrowby, in Murdoch's *The Sea, the Sea* (1978), who longs for solitude and retires to the seaside, Bernard retires to the Cévennes. A passionate swimmer like Arrowby, he has a pool built and dedicates all his art—once more in the fashion of Matisse—to painting the transparency of water, its changing shades of blue and grey against the sky, against the surrounding mountains, and against the movements of his body. One day Bernhard beholds a water snake (as does Arrowby), more beautiful and more terrifying than anything he has seen before: "a velvety-black . . . with long bars of crimson and peacock-eyed spots, gold, green, blue, mixed with silver moonshapes." The snake is a lamia, an enchanted woman who begs to be released by a kiss. Its hybridity combines symbolic, mythic, and narrative functions, signaling the sudden eruption of irrational forces while furnishing a Keatsian and Faustian subtext. The lamia is an ambivalent symbol of salvation and terror, because Bernard is at once inspired by her otherness and oppressed by her wish to become a woman. Yet, this mixture "of aesthetic frenzy and repulsion" is quintessential to his art. Thus, when the lamia is released by a friend of Bernard's and departs with the latter, Bernard's interest is soon aroused by another sublime creature: a "rather nondescript orange-brown butterfly."

The myth of the lamia relates to the many artificial worlds established in *Elementals* and, in a more general sense, expresses Byatt's rationale as a short-story writer. Not entirely set in a fantasy land, the hybrid snake is an organic image of Byatt's characteristic blending of the real and the imagined. It embodies what Byatt in a 1994 interview with Nicolas Tredell called "varieties of human experience," reflected in the characters' efforts to relate their inner worlds to the outer world by confronting existential challenges and by becoming aware of themselves as creators and objects of creation. They are both weavers of tales and trapped inside tales.

A. S. Byatt is one of the most ambitious writers of postmodern short stories. Her stories cover a wide range of subjects and are marked by great stylistic versatility and bold experimentation. The fascination of her stories lies in Byatt's great gift for creating and analyzing artificial worlds, for enchanting her readers with the pleasure and power of fiction. Through her imaginative wisdom and understanding of contemporary culture, Byatt's short stories significantly enrich the postmodern literary scene.

Interviews:

Juliet Dusinberre, "A. S. Byatt," in *Women Writers' Talking,* edited by Janet Todd (New York: Holmes & Meier, 1983), pp. 181–195;

Eleanor Wachtel, "A. S. Byatt," in her *Writers and Company* (Toronto & New York: Knopf, 1993), pp. 77–89;

Nicolas Tredell, "A. S. Byatt," in *Conversations with Critics* (Manchester: Carcanet / Riverdale-on-Hudson: Sheep Meadow, 1994), pp. 58–74;

Jean-Louis Chevalier, "Entretien avec A. S. Byatt," in *JSSE: Proceedings of the Conference on The English Short Story since 1946,* 22 (1994): 11–28;

Boyd Tonkin, "Antonia S. Byatt in Interview with Boyd Tonkin," *Anglistik,* 10, no. 2 (September 1999): 15–26;

Chevalier, "'Speaking of Sources': An Interview with A. S. Byatt," *Sources,* 7 (Autumn 1999): 6–28.

References:

Jane L. Campbell, "Confecting *Sugar:* Narrative Theory and Practice in A. S. Byatt's Short Stories," *Critique,* 38, no. 2 (Winter 1997): 105–122;

Campbell, "'The Somehow May Be Thishow': Fact, Fiction, and Intertextuality in Antonia Byatt's 'Precipice-Encurled,'" *Studies in Short Fiction,* 28, no. 2 (Spring 1991): 115–123;

Juliet Dusinberre, "Forms of Reality in A. S. Byatt's *The Virgin in the Garden,*" *Critique,* 24, no. 1 (1982): 55–62;

Richard Todd, *A. S. Byatt* (Plymouth, U.K.: Northcote House in association with the British Council, 1997).

Angela Carter
(7 May 1940 – 16 February 1992)

Rosina Neginsky
University of Illinois at Springfield

See also the Carter entries in *DLB 14: British Novelists Since 1960; DLB 207: British Novelists Since 1960, Third Series;* and *DLB 261: British Fantasy and Science-Fiction Writers Since 1960.*

BOOKS: *Shadow Dance* (London: Heinemann, 1966); republished as *Honeybuzzard* (New York: Simon & Schuster, 1967);
The Magic Toyshop (London: Heinemann, 1967; New York: Simon & Schuster, 1968);
Several Perceptions (London: Heinemann, 1968; New York: Simon & Schuster, 1968);
Heroes and Villains (London: Heinemann, 1968; New York: Simon & Schuster, 1969);
Love: A Novel (London: Rubert Hart-Davis, 1971; revised edition, London: Chatto & Windus, 1987; New York: Penguin, 1988);
The Infernal Desire Machines of Doctor Hoffman (London: Hart-Davis, 1972); reprinted as *The War of Dreams* (New York: Harcourt Brace Jovanovich, 1974);
Fireworks: Nine Profane Pieces (London: Quartet, 1974); republished as *Fireworks: Nine Stories in Various Disguises* (New York: Harper & Row, 1981); revised as *Fireworks* (London: Chatto & Windus, 1987);
The Passion of New Eve (London: Gollancz, 1977; New York: Harcourt Brace Jovanovich, 1977);
The Sadeian Woman: and the Ideology of Pornography (New York: Pantheon, 1978); republished as *The Sadeian Woman: An Exercise in Cultural History* (London: Virago, 1979);
The Bloody Chamber and Other Stories (London: Gollancz, 1979; New York: Harper & Row, 1980);
Nothing Sacred: Selected Writings (London: Virago, 1982);
Nights at the Circus (London: Chatto & Windus, 1984; New York: Viking, 1985);
Black Venus (London: Chatto & Windus/Hogarth, 1985); reprinted as *Saints and Strangers* (New York: Viking, 1987);
Come Unto These Yellow Sands (Newcastle upon Tyne: Bloodaxe Books, 1985);

Angela Carter (photograph by Miriam Berkley; from Burning Your Boats: Collected Short Stories, *1996; Richland County Public Library)*

Wise Children (London: Chatto & Windus, 1991; New York: Farrar, Straus & Giroux, 1992);
Expletives Deleted: Selected Writings (London: Chatto & Windus, 1992);
American Ghosts and Old World Wonders (London: Chatto & Windus, 1993).

Collections: *Burning Your Boats: Stories,* edited, with an introduction, by Salman Rushdie (London: Chatto & Windus, 1995); published as *Burning Your Boats: Collected Short Stories* (New York: Holt, 1996);
The Curious Room: Plays, Film Scripts, and an Opera, edited, with production notes, by Mark Bell, introduc-

tion by Susannah Clapp (London: Chatto & Windus, 1996);

Shaking a Leg: Journalism and Writings, edited by Jenny Uglow, with an introduction by Joan Smith (London: Chatto & Windus, 1997); published as *Shaking a Leg: Collected Writings* (New York: Penguin, 1998).

PRODUCED SCRIPTS: *The Company of Wolves,* motion picture, screenplay by Carter and Neil Jordan, ITC Entertainment, 1984;

The Magic Toyshop, television, Granada, 1989.

TRANSLATION: *The Fairy Tales of Charles Perrault* (London: Gollancz, 1977); republished as *Sleeping Beauty and Other Favourite Fairy Tales,* illustrated by Michael Foreman (New York: Schocken Books, 1984).

Angela Carter, who is mainly known as an author of novels, nonfiction essays, plays, and children's books, was also a short-story writer. During her short life she published three collections of short stories—*Fireworks: Nine Profane Pieces* (1974), *The Bloody Chamber and Other Stories* (1979), and *Black Venus* (1985). Two additional collections, *American Ghosts and Old World Wonders* (1993) and *Burning Your Boats* (1995), were published posthumously. Each of these collections bears the originality that has determined Carter's place among the most highly regarded end-of-the-twentieth-century British writers.

During Carter's life and after her death in 1992, literary critics tried to decide on the literary trend to which her works belong. Some perceive her as a writer of the Gothic; others associate her with Magic Realism. Her short stories, however, are distinctly postmodern.

Angela Carter was born Angela Olive Stalker on 7 May 1940 in Eastbourne, England. Her father, Hugh Alexander Stalker, originally came from Scotland. He worked as a journalist and was in his mid forties when Angela was born. Her mother, Olive (Farthing) Stalker, originally came from South Yorkshire. Because Eastbourne was located close to the English Channel, and therefore to the occupying German army stationed along the French coast during World War II, Carter's mother, brother, and grandmother moved back to South Yorkshire. Carter's memories of her war years are inseparable from those of her grandmother, who, as described in Alison Lee's *Angela Carter* (1997), "'talked broad Yorkshire,' 'hated tears and whining,' and reared her granddaughter as a 'tough, arrogant and pragmatic Yorkshire child.'"

After the war, the family moved to Balham, South London, where Carter went to school. The picture Carter paints of her family life in Lee's book is warm and affectionate, and her description of her childhood home emphasizes its dream-like atmosphere: "life passed at a languorous pace, everything was gently untidy, and none of the clocks ever told the right time." Carter was fond of her father, whom she describes (in *Angela Carter*) as "handsome, sentimental, and volatile." He liked cats and was suspicious of his daughter's boyfriends. The latter part of his life he lived in Scotland, where he moved after Carter's mother's death.

In 1960 Angela married Paul Carter. They moved to Bristol, where, in 1965, Angela Carter graduated from Bristol University with a degree in English literature. In 1966 she published her first novel, *Shadow Dance,* followed in 1967 by *The Magic Toyshop* and in 1968 by *Several Perceptions.* For *The Magic Toyshop* Carter received the Llewellen Rhys Memorial Prize, and for *Several Perceptions* she won the Somerset Maugham Award. In 1968 Carter separated from her husband and then divorced him in 1972. She used the money she received for her books to travel to Japan, "to experience life in a culture that is not Judeo-Christian." She lived and worked there for almost three years, from 1969 to 1972.

According to Carter's biographers Lorna Sage and Alison Lee, Carter had a difficult time after her return to England because she was not well known when she left, and she had to reestablish herself within the literary community and with a publisher. Her novel *The Infernal Desire Machines of Doctor Hoffman,* published in 1972 on her return from Japan, did not attract critical attention. Her later publications, however, were more successful.

In 1974 she published her first collection of short stories, *Fireworks,* which was partly inspired by her stay in Japan. In the afterword, Carter explains the connection between Japan and the structure of her short stories: "I started to write short pieces, when I was living in a room too small to write a novel in. So the size of my room modified what I did inside it and it was the same with the pieces themselves."

In "A Souvenir of Japan," the first story in the collection, Carter couples narrative experimentation with themes related to Japan. The main idea of "A Souvenir of Japan" is the "otherness" of Eastern and Western cultures, which, even in the best circumstances, would never understand each other. The fireworks that the children watch at the beginning of the story and that the narrator and her companion go to watch later in the story are a symbol of a culture of appearances in which people create illusions of life, of ways of thinking, and of being, and then try to convince themselves of their truth. Carter believes, nonetheless, that if the Japanese allowed themselves to question their culture, they

Dust jacket for the 1981 U.S. edition of Carter's 1974 collection dealing with illusion, which she wrote while living in Japan (Richland County Public Library)

would not be as convinced of their truth as they seem to be.

To convey this view, Carter uses a striking narrative device. Her narration is not one of a story that has a beginning, then culminates in an event, and then descends toward a conclusion. Her narrative, like the culture she examines, is illusory. She creates an illusion of intending to talk about one thing—a love story—whereas the real purpose of her narrative is neither a love story nor a story with a plot at all, but a desire to sketch an impressionistic picture of the memoirs written under the appearances of the story so that it would empower some of her impressions, especially her perception of the relationships between men and women and the way Japanese men perceive love.

The next story, "The Executioner's Beautiful Daughter," is an example of Carter's interest in extremes of human sexuality and in violence. The story is about incest, love, revenge, and hypocrisy. These themes periodically reappear in Carter's later collections. Of particular interest in this story is her narrative style, which she often uses in later short stories as well. She recounts the story in the present tense, as if it were happening in front of the reader's eyes: "Here, we are night in the uplands. . . . Our feet crunch upon dryly whispering shifting sawdust freshly scattered over impacted surfaces of years of sawdusts clotted, here and there. . . . There is no brightness in the air. . . . Time, suspended like the rain, begins again in silence, slowly." This way of narrating the story creates an impression of a photographic image that makes the story more real, more striking, and more powerful.

The story "The Loves of Lady Purple" is a story within a story. The frame of the story is a puppet show, given in different cities and countries by "the Asiatic professor." But the story itself is about a perverse, cruel prostitute who is also a vampire and who, as a punishment for her perversities, forfeits her vitality and is transformed into a puppet, used for presentations by the Asiatic professor, who worships her as a puppet because she is an embodiment of his art. The theme of the fusion between the artist and the object of his art interested Carter and appeared in her early short story "The Man Who Loved a Double Bass," published after her death in the collection *Burning Your Boats*.

The most interesting part of the story "The Loves of Lady Purple" is the transition between the frame story and the story itself, when the frame story becomes the part of the unreal illusory theatrical story. The puppet, the object of art, through love, power, and faith of the artist in his own art, returns to life to become once again what she had been, whereas the frame, the show, and the Asiatic professor cease to exist, overcome by the power of his creation, which in this case is a destructive evil. This theme has recurred in art and literature since the Renaissance. The relationships between the artist, art, and art's destructive power have fascinated artists, poets, and writers throughout the centuries. In this story Carter finds her own original way to introduce this theme.

"Flesh and the Mirror" is a meditation on being in love. "Flesh" in this case is associated with passion, whereas "mirror" is associated with an understanding of one's soul, its own inner reflection, and how that understanding might change one's life. Carter's statement is of a philosophical nature: a person often does not love the object of his love but rather the reflection in the mirror, which is often one's own reflection. The true object of love is often the mirror through which a person can see him- or herself: "In order to create the loved object . . . and to issue it with its certificate of authentication, as beloved, I had also to labor at the idea of myself in love. I watched myself closely for all the signs and, precisely upon cue, here they were! Longing, desire, self-abnegation, etc."

"Master," the next short story in the collection, seems to be built upon the motifs of either Gustave Flaubert's "La Légende de saint Julien l'Hospitalier" (1877, St. Julian, The Hospitaller) or simply the legend of Saint Julian, before Saint Julian repented and became a saint. Carter's story takes an image of Saint Julian as a basis, but to tell Saint Julian's legend is not her purpose. Her Saint Julian, a cruel hunter, dies at the hand of a woman whom he abused and eventually would have killed if events had unfolded differently. Carter treats the issue of the inverse relationships between a man and a woman, when the one who is the Master, in this case a man, becomes a victim, whereas his prey, a woman, becomes his Master and kills him: "His prey had shot the hunter." The story is filled with naturalistic elements of murder and images of brutal sexuality, which Carter employs to highlight the inequality and, to a degree, abusive animal perversity that can exist in the relationships between men and women.

The last two stories in the collection, "Reflections" and "Elegy for a Freelance," are a free exploration of some motifs of two famous novels. "Reflections" twists the theme of Charles Dickens's *Great Expectations* (1861). The reader finds in "Reflections" all of the main characters of *Great Expectations*–Estella (Anna in Carter's version), Pip (the narrator), and Miss Havisham (the androgyne). Although the frame story has its own story, different from *Great Expectations,* the spirit of "Reflections," the relationships that develop between three characters, the bond that exists between Anna and the androgyne, and even the notion of the androgyne and Miss Havisham, a self-made androgyne–are similar to central elements in *Great Expectations*.

"Reflections" is told as are many other of Carter's stories in this collection, without a strong cohesive element. The narrative wanders and creates an impression that where it will go or whether it will go somewhere is unclear. On the surface, things just happen, but on reflection the reader sees that the structure, characters, and plotting have been calculated and exposed in an effective way.

"Elegy for a Freelance" uses Fyodor Dostoevsky's *Crime and Punishment* (1866) almost without twisting, just by changing the frame story. Carter employs the major elements of *Crime and Punishment*: the experiment (the crime) and the punishment. In "Elegy for a Freelance," the remorse is not attributed to the murderer himself, but to his followers, who judge him and kill him for the crime he committed, the murder of an innocent person, who according to the murderer was guilty for being a useless parasite living his life without aim and purpose. Like Dostoevsky, Carter makes a point that a human who dares to determine who is useful and to decide on another human's hour of death must be punished.

"Elegy for a Freelance" has a structure that is more cohesive and characters and plotting that are more classical than does "Reflections." However, the brutalities and cruelties the reader has come to expect are present in this story as well.

In 1975 Carter began to write for *New Society*. Between 1976 and 1978 she worked as a fellow in creative writing at Sheffield University. In 1977 her translation of *The Fairy Tales of Charles Perrault* and a novel, *The Passion of New Eve,* were published. In 1979 she published her second collection of short stories, *The Bloody Chamber and Other Stories,* which won the Cheltenham Festival of Literature Award.

The Bloody Chamber and Other Stories is based on fairy tales, legends, and motifs from literary works or phenomena that interested Carter. The collection includes ten short stories. Two major themes are woven into the collection: the power of women and the "Beauty and the Beast" theme. As in other stories, Carter likes to upset preconceived and received ideas of how classic stories will unfold. Sometimes "the Beast" is the woman, and "the Beauty" is the man. The first story, "The Bloody Chamber," is a retelling of the fairy tale "Blue Beard," with many references to the Marquis de Sade and admixtures–sometimes inappropriate–of symbolist art and literature of the second part of the nineteenth century. The atmosphere of the story recalls the novel *Rebecca* (1938) by Daphne du Maurier. The story ends with a feminist twist. A mother, a woman–instead of a father and his sons as in "Blue Beard"–saves her daughter from the hands of her husband, the Blue Beard, who is also the unnamed personification of the Marquis de Sade. The Beauty and the Beast theme is reflected in a fairy-tale love affair between two unequals, the Beast/Marquis de Sade/Blue Beard, and the Beauty, who is unsuccessful in saving the Beast, but successful in saving herself.

The second story, "The Courtship of Mr Lyon," is based on the fairy tale "The Beauty and the Beast." As in the original story, "the Beauty" saves "the Beast." The third story, "The Tiger's Bride," can be also considered a version of "The Beauty and the Beast," but with a twist. If in "The Beauty and the Beast" the Beast, saved by his beloved, becomes human to reunite with the Beauty and to become her life companion, in "The Tiger's Bride" the Beauty becomes an animal to reunite with the Beast, the Tiger. The Beauty, when confronted with the choice of returning to a human state and to her father, who sent her to the Beast as payment for his gambling losses, chooses to stay with an animal, who is more noble and generous than the unworthy human. The woman is fearless, and she makes her own decision to stay with a Beast for life.

In the story "The Lady of the House of Love," the Beast is a young, beautiful girl who is also a vampire, and in this story, the Beauty is a young man with whom the young girl falls in love and through whose love she is saved from her eternal "bloody" life and unhappiness related to her nature, because of which she is forced to kill in order to survive, something that she hates to do.

"The Erl-King" appears to be based on the mythological character from Johann Wolfgang von Goethe's poem "Der Erlkönig" and possibly Franz Schubert's setting of it. In this story the Beauty and the Beast are not reconciled, and the Beauty chooses to kill the Erl-King in a scene inspired by Robert Browning's famous poem "Porphyria's Lover," in which a lover strangles his beloved with her own hair. Contrary to Browning's version however, the woman strangles her beloved, Erl-King, with her own hair.

The stories "The Werewolf" and "The Company of Wolves" are variations of Perrault's "Little Red Riding Hood," with a Carterian twist. "The Werewolf" has an ingredient of a vampire story in addition to some features of the story "Little Red Riding Hood" and implies that the grandmother herself is a wolf. "The Company of Wolves" sets the character of Little Red Riding Hood, or "the Beauty," in the form of a bestial predator, who not only overcomes the fear of the wolf who ate her grandmother and is ready to eat her, but who seduces him. In this story the Beauty and the Beast meet halfway. The Beast, or wolf, preserves his double nature, and the girl, the Beauty, remaining human, discovers the aspects of her animal nature that give her power over the Beast.

The last story in this collection, "Wolf-Alice," is inspired by vampire stories. The Beauty, a human girl, nursed and raised by wolves, and the Beast, the vampire Duke, unite, but in an unexpected way. At the moment of his death, the wounded Duke, cared for by Alice, sees his reflection in a mirror, signifying that he has been returned from the bestial undead state through the care of a woman. This story also has echoes of Richard Wagner's opera *Der Fliegende Holländer* (1841, The Flying Dutchman). This story has the same protagonist, Wolf-Alice, as the later story, "Peter and the Wolf," the wolf story that appears in the next collection, *Black Venus*.

In 1977 Carter settled with her life companion, Mark Pearce, in Clapham, South London. In 1978 she published a nonfictional work, *The Sadeian Woman: and the Ideology of Pornography,* republished the following year as *The Sadeian Woman: An Exercise in Cultural History* by the then fashionable Virago Press, on whose editorial board Carter served in 1977 and that exclusively published women's writing. Between 1980 and 1981 Carter worked as a visiting professor in the Writing Program at Brown University, in the United States. In 1982 her publisher, Carmen Callil, who previously worked for Virago Press, moved to Chatto and Windus, which then became Carter's publisher. In 1984 she published a novel, *Nights at the Circus,* for which she is best known, and that won the James Tait Black Memorial Prize. While writing this novel, she became pregnant, and in November 1983, when she was forty-three, she gave birth to her son, Alexander Pearce.

Despite the birth of her child, between 1984 and 1988 Carter led a nomadic life. For three years, 1984–1987, she taught part-time at the University of East Anglia. In 1984 she was also a writer in residence at the University of Adelaide, South Australia. A series of teaching appointments followed, in 1985 at the University of Texas at Austin; in 1986, at the Iowa Writers' Workshop in Iowa City; and in 1988, at the State University of New York at Albany.

The third collection of short stories, *Black Venus,* includes eight stories. They were all previously published in different literary magazines, series, or anthologies. "Black Venus" first appeared in 1980 in the series "Next Editions." "The Kiss" was originally published in 1977, in *Harper's and Queen*. "Ouverture and Incidental Music to a Midsummer Night's Dream" and "The Cabinet of Edgar Allan Poe" both first appeared in 1982, in *Interzone*. A version of "The Kitchen Child" was published in *Vogue* in 1979 and "Peter and the Wolf" in 1982, in *Firebird*. "Our Lady of the Massacre" was reprinted under a different title ("Captured by the Red Man"), in the anthology *The Saturday Night Reader* (1979).

The stories in this collection, like those in *Fireworks,* and unlike those in *The Bloody Chamber,* do not have one or two recurring themes. They are all different, although in them Carter experiments with a new technique, which is interwoven in most of the stories, most of which are character studies. They share many postmodern elements seen in the stories in *Fireworks,* but are narrated in more traditional ways.

The first story, "The Fall River Axe Murders," seems to be inspired by a children's song, which Carter uses as an epigraph:

> Lizzie Borden with an axe
> Gave her father forty whacks
> When she saw what she had done
> She gave her mother forty one.

The story relates a day in the life of Lizzie Borden, the daughter of a stingy, successful owner of a funeral parlor in New England. The story depicts the day when Borden kills her father and her hated stepmother. The blood of her parents is mixed with her own, because the murder is committed on a day of her menstruation. The story has a cohesiveness that keeps the attention of the reader, and its plot is clearly defined.

In the next collection of short stories, *American Ghosts and Old World Wonders,* Carter included one more short story about Lizzie Borden, "Lizzie's Tiger." The events of the story take place when Lizzie is only four years old. Both stories are character studies. Both seem to be in preparation for a novel that was never written.

Another striking character study and portrait is "Our Lady of the Massacre." The story is picaresque and tells of the "adventures" of an English prostitute sent to the New World to become a "new" person. The story has a negative view of "civilized" humanity as opposed to true humanity, in this case that of the Indians, who are "uncivilized" but live in harmony with their environment and have more compassion and humanity than those who came from the so-called civilized world. The theme of the story seems to be influenced by Daniel Defoe's novel *Moll Flanders* (1722).

"Black Venus" is a portrait of Jeanne Duval, the black lover of Charles Baudelaire. "The Cabinet of Edgar Allan Poe" is a literary picture with some unusual and dazzling interpretations of Poe's origins and life. "Peter and the Wolf" is an earlier episode in the life of Wolf-Alice, the protagonist of the short story by the same title in the collection *The Bloody Chamber,* and is the last Carter story inspired by fairy tales about wolves.

Carter's last novel, *Wise Children,* published in 1991, was her favorite. As Lee writes, "It is perhaps too easy to view the novel with hindsight as a swan song, dealing as it does with issues of personal history, public culture, birth, aging, and death." The novel appeared too near her death, however, to avoid such speculation. These concerns were not new to Carter's writing; rather, their appearance in her last novel gives them a poignancy. *Wise Children* is too raucous and too joyful for any sort of maudlin interpretation, and in that sense it provides an appropriate swan song. "A good writer," Carter wrote, "can make you believe time stands still," and *Wise Children* suggests that time is best spent with laughter and optimism.

In 1991 Carter was diagnosed with lung cancer. She died at her home on 16 February 1992. In 1993 her fourth collection of short stories, *American Ghosts and Old World Wonders,* was published, and in 1995, her last one, *Burning Your Boats,* appeared in print. In the introduction to the fourth collection, Susannah Clapp, Carter's literary executor, explains that Carter "left particular notes about two books she hoped would be published soon." One of these books was called *American Ghosts and Old*

Dust jacket for the 1996 U.S. edition of the 1995 posthumously published collection of Carter's four volumes of short stories (Richland County Public Library)

World Wonders and includes seven stories previously published in literary journals. The first short story, "Lizzie's Tiger," first appeared in 1991 in *Cosmopolitan* under the title "Mise-en-Scène for a Parricide" and was broadcast on Radio 3 in the United Kingdom. "John Ford's 'Tis Pity She's a Whore" appeared in 1988, in *Granta 25.* A version of "The Merchant of Shadows" was printed in 1989 in the *London Review of Books,* and "In Pantoland" was published in 1991 in *The Guardian.* "Ashputtle or The Mother's Ghost" was first published in 1987 in the *Virago Book of Ghost Stories,* and its shorter version appeared in 1991 in *Soho Square.* "Impressions: The Wrightsman Magdalene" was first published in 1992, in *FMR Magazine.*

After Carter's death some other uncollected works were discovered and considered for this book. But only two were included: "Gun for the Devil," "an unfinished draft for a screenplay, attached itself naturally by form and content to the more polished and punning 'John Ford's *'Tis Pity She's a Whore.*'" The collection includes stories related to the wonders of the New World, or the United States, and to the wonders of the Old World, or Europe. The book starts with the picaresque story "Lizzie's Tiger," which like its predecessor "The Fall River Axe Murders" takes place in New England. By telling the story and the "adventures" of a four-year-old girl, Lizzie, it paints a picture of a determined, manipulative, fearless, stubborn, but also still innocent, little girl. She sees a poster for the circus hanging on the fence of her father's house and is determined, despite all family objections, to go and see the tiger. The story is first set in Borden's house and then in the circus. It is written with much irony; its language is sharp and striking. Carter "plays" with points of view. Sometimes the story is told from Lizzie's point of view, and other times it is told from the point of view of a third-person narrator. Carter uses this device as a part of the character study, to emphasize through Lizzie's point of view, her way of seeing the world, and thus to give the reader a more forceful impression of Lizzie's personality.

The next two stories, "John Ford's *'Tis Pity She's a Whore*" and "Gun for the Devil," have complicated plots. "John Ford's *'Tis Pity She's a Whore,*" a story within a story, resembles a scenario for a motion picture by American director John Ford, which Carter claims is based on a tragedy by another John Ford, *'Tis Pity She's a Whore* (1633). In part, the idea of Carter's story is that human nature does not depend on location. The same events can take place anywhere. Consequently, the passions of "John Ford's *'Tis Pity She's a Whore*" are universal and can take place in Italy as well as in England or America. At the beginning of the story Carter claims in the introduction that America has a reputation of having a cold head and lack of harmony between the head and the heart: America's "central paradox resides in this: that the top half doesn't know what the bottom half is doing." She illustrates this point through the story. Although the subject of the story, the passion between a brother and a sister and how that feeling destroys them and those who come between them, is dramatic, Carter uses a narrational device that deliberately decreases its dramatic effect. At times, she almost mocks the passions in the story. She constantly emphasizes that it is only a story. She plays with names of the characters to stress that they can be taken from any kind of literary work of any period. Sometimes she starts her sentences with the word "Imagine . . ." to stress that it is only a story she is building. To highlight a dramatic situation, she uses repetitions and additions. For instance, to emphasize the beginning of the love affair between the brother and sister, Carter uses the Pre-Raphaelite image of the young girl's hair, the symbol of a fatal sexual attraction: "She [the young girl] washed her hair in a tub. She washed her long, yellow hair. She was fifteen. It was spring. She washed her hair. . . . She sat on the porch to dry her hair. . . . She combed out her wet hair in the mirror." Carter ends the story with a note that says that she only tries to imagine how the drama set in the Old World would turn out in the New World. Her narration ends with Johnny-Giovanni shooting pregnant Annie-Belle-Annabella, her husband, and himself. The note says that "The Old World John Ford made Giovanni cut out Annabella's heart and carry it on stage; the stage direction reads: *Enter Giovanni with a heart upon his dagger.* The New World John Ford would have no means of representing this scene on celluloid. . . ."

"Gun for the Devil" is based on the opera *Der Freischütz* (1821, The Free Marksman) by Karl Maria von Weber, which is based on a German legend. The essence of the story is Faustian; in it a man makes a pact with the Devil–"his soul for a magic bullet." In Carter's story, the man, by making a pact, becomes either a devil himself or devil's prey, when and if he uses the last bullet. By depicting this Old World story in the New World, Carter shows that location is unimportant.

Among the Old World Wonders are two particularly striking stories. One is "Ashputtle," a dark version of Cinderella, in which the mother mutilates her own daughters' feet so that one of the girls will be able to wear the crystal shoe and become the prince's wife. The other story is a sketch, "Impressions: The Wrightsman Magdalene," related to paintings depicting Mary Magdalene and the idea of penitence, associated with the last thirty years of Mary's life, painted and perceived differently by each painter. One of the questions pursued in the story is whether the painter may be disgusted with the idea of penitence. Carter's answer is yes. The child, born out of penitence, out of withdrawal from life and refusal of life, can only be death.

The last collection of stories, *Burning Your Boats,* includes all four collections, three short stories–"The Man Who Loved a Double Bass," "A Very, Very Great Lady and Her Son at Home," and "A Victorian Fable (with Glossary)" at the beginning, presented under the title "Early Works, 1962–6"–and three short stories at the end–"The Scarlet House," "The Snow Pavilion," and "The Quilt Maker," presented under the title "Uncollected Stories, 1970–81." "The Man Who Loved a Double Bass" is comparable to "The Loves of Lady Purple"; it concerns the relationship between the artist and the object of his art.

Before her death, Carter provided extensive directions on how to deal with her literary estate. Her main concerns were related to "her boys," her husband and her son–that her works would provide an income for them, that "any one of her fifteen books could be set to music or acted on ice."

After reading several volumes of Carter's short fiction, the informed reader is likely to have three responses. Carter is indebted to world literature, and she pays homage to it. She is also inclined toward the Gothic, naturalistic, and postmodern ways of viewing human nature—a focus on revealing human nature and the existential environment in which it must persist with eyes wide open. A third dimension is an exploration of narrative style, which often departs from that of the nineteenth century—introduction, development, and conclusion—to one in which character development, plot, and themes have a less teleological relationship.

Although Carter's short stories vary from one another in structure and narrative techniques, they have many similarities. The uniting elements of all Carter's stories are their postmodern flavor and several shared themes. Though all the stories have a clearly defined structure, just as with many postmodern works, they often create an impression of not having a plot. The narration starts with one thought and then in the middle it changes tack and takes the reader in a completely different and often unexpected direction.

Almost all Carter's stories include a motif from a classic literary work, a fairy tale, or a legend. Like many postmodern works, many of her stories deal with extreme cases of sexuality, and frequently, with its cruel and perverse sides. Her short stories also have elements of violence. Her purpose is not to describe the horror or to retell an already existing novel, or a legend, or a fairy tale, but to tell her own story so it will carry her own message. For this reason, especially in early collections, the structure of her stories preoccupies her more than the stories themselves. This characteristic is evident even in her first collection of short stories, *Fireworks*.

Angela Carter's experiments with narrative form and her use of fairy-tale and real-life characters may have been the reason, as Salman Rushdie writes in his introduction to *Burning Your Boats,* that she was "dismissed by many in her lifetime as a marginal, cultish figure, an exotic hothouse flower." Since her death, however, Carter has become, at British universities, one of the most studied of late-twentieth-century writers.

References:

Alison Lee, *Angela Carter,* Twayne's English Authors Series, no. 540 (New York: Twayne / London: Prentice Hall, 1997);

Lorna Sage, *Angela Carter* (Plymouth, U.K.: Northcote House, 1994);

Sage, *Women in the House of Fiction* (London: Macmillan, 1992).

Evelyn Conlon

(5 November 1952 –)

Irene Gilsenan Nordin
Dalarna University, Sweden

BOOKS: *My Head Is Opening* (Dublin: Attic, 1987);
Stars in the Daytime (Dublin: Attic, 1989; London: Women's Press, 1990);
Taking Scarlet as a Real Colour (Belfast: Blackstaff, 1993);
A Glassful of Letters (Belfast: Blackstaff, 1998);
Telling, New and Selected Stories (Belfast: Blackstaff, 2000);
Skin of Dreams (Dingle, Ireland: Brandon, 2003).

PLAY PRODUCTION: *Taking Scarlet as a Real Colour*, Edinburgh Theatre Festival, 1994.

OTHER: Mary Lavin, *Tales from Bective Bridge*, introduction by Conlon (Dublin: Town House, 1996);
An Cloigeann Is a Luach / What Worth the Head, in *The Limerick Anthology of Writing*, edited by Conlon (Limerick: Limerick County Council, 1998);
Cutting the Night in Two: Short Stories by Irish Women Writers, edited by Conlon and Hans-Christian Oeser (Dublin: New Island, 2001);
Later On: The Monaghan Bombing Memorial Anthology, edited by Conlon (Dingle, Ireland: Brandon, 2004).

Evelyn Conlon has been described, by Niall MacMonagle in "Telling Tales" (*Irish Times*, 20 May 2000), as "one of the spikiest and most distinctive voices in Irish fiction." In her novels and short stories she explores everyday life in contemporary Ireland. Her writing examines themes such as friendship, love, marriage, and familial relationships, as well as themes dealing with guilt, isolation, and homelessness. She gives voice especially to the experiences of women and explores female identity and the image of women in present-day Irish society, vividly describing their world from a woman's viewpoint. While her characters are usually concerned with the mundane activities of everyday existence, they are nevertheless highly complex individuals, striving to come to terms with the disillusionments of life at the same time as they search for some sense of meaning to their lives. Thus, while Conlon's characters thoughtfully, and often sar-

Evelyn Conlon (from the cover for Taking Scarlet as a Real Colour, *1993; Bruccoli Clark Layman Archives)*

donically, illustrate life's frustrations and ironies, they simultaneously expose the injustices and constrictions imposed on women in a male-dominated society. Gender issues and the status of Irish women, both within the home and in society generally—not least, women's roles in a traditional Catholic patriarchy—are important themes in her work. This aspect of her writing offers a strong socially critical testament.

Conlon was born on 5 November 1952 in Rockcorry, County Monaghan, in the Irish Republic. Her father, John, was a farmer, and her mother, Mary Ellen, was a midwife. Evelyn was educated at St. Louis

Convent Monaghan from 1965 to 1970, and in 1969 she won the European Schools Essay Competition. In 1970 Conlon began studies at University College Dublin, and in the same year she had her first short stories published as "New Irish Writing" in the *Irish Press*. She left the university after a year because she wanted to travel and in 1972 moved to Australia, where she held various jobs, including one with *The Geographic Encyclopaedia*. After traveling in Australia, Asia, and the Soviet Union, she returned to Ireland in 1975 and resumed her B.A. studies in 1976 at St. Patrick's College Maynooth. Conlon has two sons; her first was born in 1976, and she opened a day-care center at St. Patrick's College to look after him and other children. She had her second son in 1978, and she completed her Higher Diploma in Education in 1980. From 1980 to 1982 she taught English in Dublin, and from 1983 to 1987, when her first collection of short stories was published, she had short stories published in various newspapers and magazines—for example, the *Irish Press*, the *Irish Times Collection*, *North* magazine, and the *Sunday Tribune*—as well as having her short stories read on BBC Radio 4 and BBC World Service. During that time she also did extensive reviewing and broadcasting on radio and television, including reviews of each year's Booker Prize nominations. Conlon is a founding member of the Rape Crisis Center and is a regular commentator on the arts and a literary reviewer for newspapers, radio, and television. She lives in Dublin.

With the publication of her first collection of short stories, *My Head Is Opening* (1987), Conlon was hailed as an important new Irish writer, with an original and unmistakably fresh voice. The collection describes a woman's world, in which themes of isolation and loneliness are central. In this collection, as in Conlon's other works of fiction, many of the characters find themselves alienated from their own sense of self and from society while they grapple with ways to come to terms with their sense of frustration and homelessness. In the character of Louise, the protagonist from the title story of the collection, Conlon presents a disillusioned housewife and mother struggling to survive in a marriage that has long since lost its romantic appeal, while her husband is preoccupied with his own busy life of work and socializing. Louise has learned to eliminate certain human desires, such as an "obsessive need for adult company," and has long since left behind "the slight madness that hits new mothers who want and want and who remember themselves as they were before." She tries to alleviate her loneliness and unhappiness by turning to pills, but after a shocking encounter that brings her face to face with the strange figure of Daft Dan, a maniacal voice from the wilderness, and "her only soulmate," she suffers a total breakdown. Her recuperation comes with the gradual realization that the answer to her problem lies more in an honest confrontation with her own lost self than in any trite attempts of her husband to provide her with expensive therapy or "better" pills that will further dull her brain and increase her sense of alienation.

In her review of *My Head Is Opening*, in "Irish Women: Images and Voices" (*Irish Review 3*, 1987), Marion Tracey claimed that the book lacks "narrative control" and displays "too much personal anger," but she found Conlon's representations of the theme of alienated women "realistically daunting." Despite the empty, often disturbed, world that many of the characters in this collection inhabit, they also possess an ironic sense of humor that gives them a momentary release from their unhappiness. An example occurs in the story "In Reply to Florence" with the middle-aged Mona, whose marriage has settled into "compatibility" and who has come to realize that "happiness was a myth, that love was a transient trick." Mona nonetheless experiences some fleeting excitement while on vacation in Italy. After breaking her leg, Mona has to use crutches on the trip. But this mishap does not daunt her. She is, after all, used to inconvenience and pain, having survived "several miscarriages, one pouting serious child, a varicose veins operation and a collapsed uterus." The story ends with her lashing out with her crutch at Michelangelo's nude sculpture of David. This unexplained moment of madness results in her arrest. Like Mona, Conlon's other characters often react to the frustrations of life in bizarre and ironic ways at the same time that they show a fiery determination to survive somehow.

In 1988 Conlon was awarded the Arts Council Bursary in Literature, and her second work of fiction, a novel titled *Stars in the Daytime,* was published the following year. In 1990 the novel was republished by The Women's Press in Britain and also chosen as Selected Title for Book Fortnight. *Stars in the Daytime* tells the story of Rose, a young girl growing up in rural Ireland during the 1950s and 1960s. The novel is written in the style of a bildungsroman, tracing the difficulties and delights of the young protagonist as she makes her way into womanhood. This theme recurs in much of Conlon's short fiction, where the concern with female experience is a major preoccupation. The story begins with the description of the eight-year-old Rose, waiting at the farmyard gate for her father to come home with the horse and cart, so that she can help him lift out the "craymery can of skim milk," or the "bucket of pigs' mail." Rose is an only child, thoughtful and imaginative, "sometimes vague and restless," but mostly "happy enough with the predictability

Front cover for Conlon's first short-story collection, which introduced the theme of alienation in her fiction and which brought her attention as an important new Irish writer (Bruccoli Clark Layman Archives)

around her." *Stars in the Daytime* follows the gradual development of Rose, as she begins to question the confines of the world around her: the role of women, the role of the Catholic Church, and the parochial restraints of Irish rural life that unfold about her. The novel highlights Rose's growing awareness of the social restrictions on the women in her small world: from her early image of her grandmother as the center of power and importance—a woman who had produced more than a dozen children and more than forty-five grandchildren—grows the sad awareness of the restricted life that this seemingly strong woman lived. Rose comes to realize that her grandmother, too, is just one of the mass of Irish women "who had not one choice available to them about anything in their lives except perhaps the naming of their children." Her grandmother's life was one of acceptance, a role that she moved through with ease, carried out "partly through ignorance, partly from exhaustion." Rose vows that her life will be different: she will decide her own fate; she will make her own choices. But, as the story unfolds, it transpires that Rose, too, will suffer. In a desperate search for happiness and fulfillment, she leaves home and Ireland, to experience love, marriage, miscarriage, divorce, promiscuousness, and finally a return home, as a "once-married-now-not-married-pregnant woman." Throughout the novel the tortured relationship between mother and daughter is a central theme, the "clinging entity" that sums up the bond between them, which refuses "to give up the fight" even long after Rose has left home and become an adult. This troubled relationship is movingly described in the image of the mother "standing there hurt to the bone," while the daughter, in a strained attempt at communication, begrudgingly provides information about her new life away from home. It is given in the form of the "half truths," the "not saying," which opens up "tracts of distance between them much bigger than the real miles."

As in many of her narratives, such as "My Head Is Opening" and "In Reply to Florence," Conlon in *Stars in the Daytime* candidly and unsentimentally portrays the experiences of the protagonist—events that are not only physically and emotionally hurtful but that also gradually leave the character with a profound insight. Like the character Louise in "My Head Is Opening" or Mona in "In Reply to Florence," Rose, in the final lines of *Stars in the Daytime,* arrives at self-understanding. What her experiences have shown her is not the existence of some great truth about women's lives, some great truth that can be "stitched together with what was already there to make a whole truth," but rather the importance of all the "little" lives that go to make up the larger pattern, lives like those of her grandmother and, indeed, of her own mother. These lives are the ones that Conlon seeks to highlight in her short fiction, lives that have been forgotten in what she calls the "terrible forgetting that was done—the fingerwork, the words, the thoughts of dead women," histories that have passed and gone without testimony.

In 1990 Conlon was appointed Dublin City Libraries writer-in-residence, while Dublin was European City of Culture for the year (1990–1991), and the following year, 1992, she was appointed writer-in-residence in Kilkenny. In 1993 her second collection of short stories, *Taking Scarlet as a Real Colour,* was published, and during that year she was also appointed writer-in-residence in Cavan. *Taking Scarlet as a Real Colour* takes its title from the last story in the book, recounted in one long paragraph, in the first-person narrative of the protagonist. In this story, as in many others in the collection, Conlon once again deals with the theme of isolation. This alienation is evident in the protagonist's repeated assertion that somehow she is on the margin of things. If asked, for instance, where she was on the day John F. Kennedy was shot, a question that most people would readily be able to answer by giving an exact location, she answers "nowhere." Then, in a swift flow of language, typical of Conlon's rhythmic prose style, she proceeds to explain where "nowhere" actually is: "Unless you'd call walking with my sister up on a ditch down our road to the shop, carrying a flash lamp that you had to shake all the time to get the battery to connect to whatever it's supposed to connect with, the frozen grass and weeds cutting patterns on our mucky wellingtons, somewhere. Which I don't." The same character demonstrates her desire to be different when rather than going to see the Pope on his visit to Dublin, as most of Ireland's population does, she heads off to Cork, "because it was a pope-free zone." As in Conlon's previous work and in the collection generally, the title story of *Taking Scarlet as a Real Colour* gives voice to the untold, unrecorded lives of "ordinary" women. The story levels criticism at the absence of a woman's voice in literature and the misrepresentation of female experience by male writers: "I used to read books to find out but I'm afraid there was nothing in them." The story derides the constructed images of Irish womanhood made in the name of religion and the church: "The books made us saints, cheap, plastic saints with lack of love, or they called us scarlet, but they didn't see it as a real colour. No Irish book ever told me about love unless it was referring to carvings on church walls. . . ."

In her review of *Taking Scarlet as a Real Colour*, in "Where Anglo-Saxons Fear to Tread" (*Times*, 14 June 1993) Erica Wagner described Conlon as having "the rare ability to give her words an almost mythic overtone without ever sounding forced," and she called Conlon's writing "an articulation of a strong feminine sensibility that takes its place in the new tradition of Irish writing." The story from this collection "On the Inside of Cars" might be said to illustrate this sense of mythic overtone. The story recounts the mixed emotions of the protagonist, Chrissie, a divorced Irish mother of three, as she prepares her children to go away on a long weekend trip with their father–her former husband–to their paternal grandparents' in "Ingaland." Her former husband is not only English but "on top of that" is "a class up" from Chrissie. The story traces the inner thoughts of the protagonist as she fusses around helping her children get dressed, hoping to prove to both her former husband and former in-laws that "she could have children with polished shoes and matching clothes." The reader is given a description of Chrissie's contrasting emotions as she closely observes the faces of her children eating breakfast, "the older two trying, out of remarkable sensitivity, not to be too excited." As the punctual and meticulous father arrives and whisks them away in his "dust-free comfort" car, Chrissie waves goodbye to the children at the same time as she pulls away her "body and life" from the car, an apt metaphor for the dead relationship from which she has escaped. The story, which is narrated for the most part in the third person, is interlaced with interjections from the protagonist as the first-person speaker. This voice retraces the broken relationship with the former husband; addressing herself to an imaginary "*Sir*," she poignantly remarks on how "desperate" and "terrible" it is that, after all the "dazzlement" the relationship once held, "not even a nod of friendship" is left.

In 1994 Conlon conducted a workshop in the Irish Writers' Center at Washington State University, and the following year a workshop series at the Irish Writers' Center in Dublin. She also worked with Bosnian refugees on a writing project and compiled and edited their magazine *ZVONO*, published in June 1995. The same year she was awarded the Arts Council Bursary again and wrote commissioned educational video scripts for the Dublin City University Distance Education project, as well as being attached to The Open University as tutor for creative arts. In 1996 she was director of the Listowel Writers' Week Fiction Workshop, and gave readings at the Frankfurt Book Fair. In 1997 she was appointed writer-in-residence at Mishkenot Sh'ananim Writers' Center, in Jerusalem.

The following year, 1998, *A Glassful of Letters*, Conlon's second novel, was published to critical acclaim. This semiepistolary novel is set mainly in Dublin and New York, with every second chapter written in the form of a tightly interwoven series of letters sent between a group of friends. Through the linked contrasting stories of the everyday lives of these characters, Conlon traces a complex mesh of intellectual and emotional experiences. In a review of *A Glassful of Letters* in "Winners and losers in the game of life" (*Irish Times*, 18 April 1998), Ellen Beardsley claimed that this novel marks a "significant departure from the predominantly confessional tone of contemporary fiction" and saw this work as a champion of the individual, "the Everyman and the Everywoman." In exploring the exchanges between these diverse individuals, Conlon widens her scope of subject in this novel to include a more socially encompassing range of characters. Thus, the reader is introduced to Helena, with her "easy-going" husband Kevin–"pleasant-looking, with a few minor faults"–and their "beautiful" young son; their housewife neighbor, Connie, mother of

Front cover for Conlon's 1993 short-story collection, which deals with the lives of ordinary women who feel marginalized and alienated (Bruccoli Clark Layman Archives)

three children, "the greatest blessing that could be bestowed on a street," and her husband Desmond, who "loved no one but himself," and with whom she has a cold, unfulfilled relationship; Desmond's father, Bernard; and not least, Fergal, "our single-man, although technically he wasn't single at all," but an out-of-work architect, who, at the beginning of the story, has lost his job and so decides to rent out his house and go to work in New York.

The plot of *A Glassful of Letters* is built around Fergal's leaving for America and the need that both he and his friends have to keep in touch during his absence. The forthright correspondence between the characters gives a vivid account of life in contemporary Irish society, dealing with themes such as friendship, love, political engagement, and emigration, expressed in contrasting states of homelessness and home. A central overriding quality that Connie, the main character, displays is bravery, a quality possessed by those who rather than "mistakenly" think they are brave see their lives as having been "merely lived," and yet show "great courage" in their day-to-day living. The letters between the characters are held together by the narrative voice of Helena, whose job as an airline hostess allows her a certain authorial distance from the other, more troubled characters. She acts as an omniscient observer from her vantage point in the air, where "the mêlée of egos is suspended." Helena has chosen the occupation of airline hostess to help her carve out for herself "a small piece of fresh air" to keep her "sane." This life of "movement" and "coming and going" offers a sense of freedom, a state between the paralyzing certainty of knowing what the future holds for "every day at whatever time, for years to come," and the contrasting experience of emigrants, who "spend their lives being Irish rather than living a life." The epistolary style of *A Glassful of Letters* gives the narrative a sense of immediacy and intimacy and, as Conlon herself pointed out in a 2000 interview with Rebecca Pelan, calls for a wide range and depth in the development of the characters, since the writing of letters gives individual expression to the personality of the character. In her interview with Pelan, Conlon commented on the large number of letters she received from readers after the publication of *A Glassful of Letters*, which expressed appreciation of her use of the letter as a narrative device, since it is a means of personal communication that is rapidly disappearing. The interlinking stories not only reflect the changing patterns of life in present-day Ireland but also highlight the existential and moral choices that the individual characters are faced with. The people Fergal rents his house to when he is away turn out to be an assorted group of individuals: "one anarchist, one socialist, one feminist, or crossovers of all three." One of these tenants is friendly with a political prisoner, and gradually the other characters, with varying degrees of reluctance, are drawn into his humanitarian project, an experience that causes some of them to rethink their prejudices, as well as their political standpoints.

In 1999 Conlon was awarded the Artist Diane Wood Middlebrook Fellowship for residency in Djerassi Foundation, California, and was a visiting writer at the University of St. Thomas, St. Paul, Minnesota. She attended the Melbourne Writers' Festival, where she gave a reading and took part in a panel discussion. She also gave a workshop for the Victorian Writers' Center at Castlemaine, as well as readings in Brisbane and at the Sydney Spring Festival, Rozelle.

Conlon's next published work of fiction, *Telling, New and Selected Stories* (2000), includes nine new stories, together with ten of the best stories from her previously published works. In this collection Conlon, as in *A Glassful of Letters,* concerns herself with the broader spectrum of human experience and shows how the individual, both male and female, deals with the pressures and traumas of contemporary living. In the story "The Long Drop," Thomas McGurk, a public-relations man who relies on his communication skills in order to survive, suffers from a personal and professional crisis. McGurk used to have "that unfailingly dependent desire to master the next goal, to get the next most important job, to meet key people," but he now loses both his personal and professional self-confidence and finds himself in the debilitating position of being unable even to say "boo to a goose." In the first line of the story the trouble that is to come is foreshadowed in the picture of McGurk, who knew that people when they got older became more confident and were able to "tackle the small matters in life as if they were what they were." But now he begins to realize that he knows nothing for certain anymore. He is surrounded on the one side by a good-looking son, who acts as if he owns the world, and on the other side by an aging father, who hoards bits of useless information, "silly womanish things" that he would have told his wife if she were still alive and that he now repeats to his "personal vacuum," expecting to receive an intelligible response. The disintegrating mental state of the protagonist and his increasing sense of disorientation are movingly portrayed, from his watching his Irish accent in the café to avoid "confrontation," to his humorous, yet poignant response to a prospective client's request for a "space theme," which forces him to admit that "he couldn't cope with his own sitting room," much less come up with any clever idea to please a client. The character's self-deceit is revealed in his failure to come to grips with his own problems: "The tricks of happiness include explaining to strangers the politics of one's country to one's own satisfaction, leaving out the aggravating truths." Similarly, McGurk expresses a sense of homelessness in his attempts at defining an identity both in personal and political terms: "In hotels at night, in strange countries, you can draw maps to show the bar staff where you were born in relation to Dublin and the border. They won't know that you've got the shape of the country all wrong."

The collection not only illustrates Conlon's preoccupation with themes portraying inner private experience but also shows her interest in concerns of a more public and ethical nature, such as class issues and the injustices of society generally. In the title story of the collection, "Telling," an encounter between the private and the public is narrated in the voice of a female who attends a writing workshop given by an Irish male writer. This male writer, "one of the best," is giving the course for a group of "fledgling writers," all of whom are women, and the story explores the tensions between the male writer and the silent female listeners. The female speaker recounts the tale the male writer tells the women, a grim and tragic account of the fate of an abused wife who is finally shot dead by her husband as she tries to escape from him. It is a "true" story that the writer tells dispassionately and dismisses lightly, a story he does not "want" but which they can take and use, if they want. The female speaker, who believes that the male writer has little to teach her, since she is already on a hill that gives a "better view," concludes that the real story is not what the male writer tells, nor is it what the women think of it. Instead, the real story may be what the reader thinks of "what they thought of what he thought."

Conlon treats even as serious a subject as domestic violence with humor and irony. She typically portrays with wit characters who expose the double standards that confuse relationships between the sexes. Such a character is Bridie in "Park-Going Days," a story about an outing when the mothers take their "chairs and children," on one of the few "park-going days of sunshine," which are truly numbered in Ireland. This story appears in *Telling, New and Selected Stories,* and again in *Cutting the Night in Two: Short Stories by Irish Women Writers* (2001), edited by Conlon. Bridie in this story is one of the "ordinary" women to whom Conlon likes to give a voice. She is described as a woman with "the fat, the veins, the sighs" that are "the backbone of the country." This story presents a picture of womanhood that, according to the speaker, is not conjured up by male advertisers: "You'd never think it to see the corkscrew, frown-free pictures that poured from the ad men's anorexic fantasies."

The way in which characters speak in Conlon's short stories contributes to their seeming more real than idealized. Chain-smoking Molly in "Park-Going Days," for example, speaks with the humor, rhythm, and syntax of the working-class Irish. "I had meself burnt," she says, "Me lips, me skirts, me bras, me slips. One match would do me the whole day. Lit one off the other." By grounding speech in everyday realities, Conlon avoids sentimentalizing her characters. A mother in "Park-Going Days" calls to a child with a dirty face: "Look at the face of her. Come here to me until I give you a wipe. Disgracing me." This passage is followed by a description of the reciprocal shame experienced by the child, as the mother carries out the threatened wiping: "She dug the face cloth into the child's face, disgracing it in front of friends who hadn't noticed at all." The story contrasts the experiences of motherhood with those of the childless outsider, Rita, who overcomes her feeling of isolation and joins the women and the children in the park for one brief sunny afternoon. The story ends with Rita's moving out and new tenants moving in; life goes on, and the mothers continue "cleaning noses, swiping at bare legs," and "bending over babies in the way that causes bad backs," while outside the rain pours down.

In 2000 Conlon gave a fiction workshop in The Irish Writers' Centre in Dublin and a workshop for Eastern Washington State University. She also directed a workshop on Rathlin Island, off the north coast of Ireland, and was awarded the Arts Council Bursary for Literature for the third time. In 2001 she was elected to the Aosdána, the affiliation of Irish creative artists, in recognition of her work. In 2002 she began research for her next novel, *Skin of Dreams* (2003), and was awarded a residency in the Varuna Writers' Center in Australia.

Evelyn Conlon's work is important because she uses the rich Irish short-story tradition that reached its maturity in the work of James Joyce, Frank O'Connor, Elizabeth Bowen, and Sean O'Faolain, and—like more-contemporary short-story writers, such as Mary Lavin, William Trevor, and Bernard MacLaverty—she develops the genre. She responds to the changing concerns of the time by giving voice to woman's experience, as well as the social and political conditions of the day. In the short-story tradition, she suggests rather than states. Her tone is sharp and witty, and dialogue is cut to a minimum. Conlon's prose explores the disappointments and ironies of life. In revealing what lies below the surface of her characters' lives and the world they inhabit, she shows a concern with wider issues that are central to contemporary living, and thus her work gives expression to the everyday voice of human experience.

Interview:

Rebecca Pelan, "Interview with Evelyn Conlon," *Hecate,* 26, no. 1 (2000): 62–73.

Mary Dorcey
(1950 -)

Moira E. Casey
Miami University of Ohio at Middletown

BOOKS: *Kindling* (London: Onlywomen, 1982);
A Noise from the Woodshed (London: Onlywomen, 1989);
Moving into the Space Cleared by Our Mothers (Galway: Salmon, 1991);
The River that Carries Me (Galway: Salmon, 1995);
Biography of Desire (Dublin: Poolbeg, 1997);
Like Joy in Season, Like Sorrow (Cliffs of Moher, Ireland: Salmon, 2001).

OTHER: "The Fate of Aoife and the Children of Aobh," in *Mad and Bad Fairies: A Collection of Feminist Fairytales* (Dublin: Attic, 1987), pp. 5–14;
"Scarlet O'Hara," in *In and Out of Time,* edited by Patricia Duncker (London: Onlywomen, 1990);
"Extract from a Novel-in-Progress," in *New Irish Writing,* edited by Colm Tóibín (London: Bloomsbury, 1993), pp. 275–283.

Although the majority of Mary Dorcey's published works are collections of poetry, she is perhaps best known for her groundbreaking 1989 collection of short fiction, *A Noise from the Woodshed.* The stories in this collection explore frankly a variety of Irish women's sexual, marital, and social challenges. Several of these stories have been anthologized in collections of Irish short fiction. With the publication of *A Noise from the Woodshed,* Dorcey became one of the first contemporary Irish writers to write fiction that openly and successfully focuses on lesbian characters, and by doing so, Dorcey has influenced other Irish lesbian writers such as Emma Donoghue. An active feminist and a lesbian, Dorcey's sexuality and her personal political beliefs have always informed her art. Widely traveled, she has lived in France, the United States, England, and Japan; she, nevertheless, remains firmly committed to Ireland and to the causes that she espouses there.

Dorcey was born in Dublin in 1950, long before the start of the Irish feminist movement in the early 1970s. Although she characterizes the cultural climate in Ireland during her childhood as marked by censorship, sexual repression, and the general repression of ideas and information, she remembers her own family life as quite happy. With her three older brothers and her one sister, Dorcey spent much of her childhood swimming, bicycling, going to the movies, and participating in other such activities typical of a middle-class childhood. In an interview with Ide O'Carroll and Eoin Collins in *Lesbian and Gay Visions of Ireland* (1995) Dorcey described her childhood in County Dublin as one "of great freedom and variety" and her childhood self as "athletic, extroverted and gregarious." Her four great passions while growing up, she says, were books, movies, music, and sports, and she particularly enjoyed the physical experience of being in nature.

Creativity in the art of writing came naturally to Dorcey. She has said that she felt the desire to write early in her life and that as a young child she delighted in making up stories, songs, and poems. Dorcey also read avidly as a child, primarily nineteenth-century classics by Jane Austen, George Eliot, and Charlotte Brontë. When she was twelve, she began to read modern American and English literature, eventually including such writers as Sidonie Gabrielle Colette, Virginia Woolf, and Katherine Mansfield. In terms of Irish literary influences, she says that the only Irish women writers she knew of as a child were Edith Œnone Somerville, Martin Ross, Kate O'Brien, and Maria Edgeworth. Later, in her twenties, she began to read some of the classics of feminist politics, such as Simone de Beauvoir's *The Second Sex* (1953; translation of *Le deuxième sexe* [1949]), Kate Millett's *Sexual Politics* (1970), and Germaine Greer's *The Female Eunuch* (1970). These texts contributed to two important realizations—that women writers in Ireland were scarce and that Irish women needed to have their lives and passions validated by writers of their own sex and nationality. These insights later drove Dorcey's own artistic achievements.

When Dorcey was seven years old, her father died. For the family, the father's death meant a lack of financial security, as Dorcey's mother was left to raise five children on her own. For Dorcey, it meant having more freedom than she might have had with two parents. With her mother preoccupied with family finances, Dorcey was left to read and write all she wanted.

Dorcey was conscious of a difference between herself and others at a young age, and she resisted the socialization process that confined girls to narrow roles. However, she remained unaware of lesbian sexuality and did not recognize her own sexual orientation until she reached her late teens. When she did first hear about male and female homosexuality, she became curious, and she began to read about the life and works of Oscar Wilde and Colette.

In 1969, at the age of seventeen, Dorcey fell in love with a woman and thereby discovered her sexual preference, although she did not at the time define herself distinctly as "lesbian." Not long after, while living in Paris, Dorcey met a group of women whom she suspected were lesbians. Meeting these women caused her to realize that the open expression of lesbianism was an actual possibility and that leading a life as a lesbian did not necessarily mean living in poverty as a social outcast. These women supported each other and had created their own community independent of heterosexual men. Dorcey had to come to terms with the invisibility of her sexual orientation in Irish society and the simultaneous stigma attached to it. In her interview with O'Carroll and Collins, she commented on this realization: "The word 'homosexual' was not spoken or written in Ireland before the 1970s. The word 'gay' didn't exist. I had never heard of a bisexual. I had never seen or spoken to one." She concludes by asking, "So how did I manage to become one?"

With her new views of lesbianism and feminism, Dorcey returned to Ireland in 1972 and began to attend meetings of the Irish Women's Movement. When she and her girlfriend saw a poster at Trinity College advertising the first meeting of the Sexual Liberation Movement, they decided to attend. Five gay men, two bisexual women, and one lesbian attended the meeting. At this point, Dorcey and her girlfriend made the conscious choice to define themselves openly as lesbians. Dorcey has, however, recognized the complexities of her sexual orientation. In the interview with O'Carroll and Collins, she insisted that "I am a lesbian because I have loved women more than men. That is, I have loved women more deeply, more completely. . . . I think I was born bisexual and chose to become a lesbian when I fell in love with a lesbian." She later attended the first meeting of the Sexual Liberation Movement, a symposium on gay rights held in 1973 and attended by hundreds of people. Dorcey gradually became heavily involved with the Irish women's and gay and lesbian rights movements that evolved out of these early meetings. She began to give talks on sexuality and gay rights at various venues, including universities around Ireland.

Dorcey's first speech as an "out" lesbian occurred when she spoke on sexuality at Women's Week in University College Dublin. This speech was reported in *The Irish Times,* and Dorcey was thus publicly exposed as a lesbian. The press coverage created a scandal among those who knew Dorcey but had not yet discovered her sexual orientation. Dorcey, however, was so busy supporting women's and gay liberation movements that she barely noticed the horrified reactions of her mother and her friends and neighbors. She was cofounder of Irish Women United (a nationalist feminist group based in Dublin) and of the Irish Gay Rights Movement.

In the early 1970s, Dorcey began publishing poems in British journals. When Lilian Mohen from Onlywomen Press noticed Dorcey's poetry, she approached Dorcey and told her she would like to publish a collection of her works. The result was *Kindling,* Dorcey's first collection of poetry, published in London in 1982. Although the book was well received in London, the Irish press virtually ignored it.

In the mid 1980s, Dorcey went to live in Kerry, where she wrote the stories that make up her next published work. She followed *Kindling* with a book of those stories, *A Noise from the Woodshed,* which was also published by Onlywomen Press. This collection of short stories earned Dorcey the prestigious Rooney Prize for Literature in 1990. The award was significant for acknowledging Dorcey as an Irish writer, and not merely as a "woman writer" or "lesbian writer." This same year, Dorcey was awarded her first Arts Council bursary in literature (she was awarded a second bursary in 1995 and a third in 1999).

A Noise from the Woodshed, which remains Dorcey's sole collection of short fiction, is composed of nine short stories. All of the stories reflect the tensions in Ireland between the older values of the conservative and primarily Catholic state and the newer feminist theory and practices that Dorcey and her fellow activists sought to promote. The conservative Irish state officially preferred women in the domestic roles of wife and mother. (Not until the mid 1970s was the marriage bar, a law forbidding women to hold jobs once they had married, repealed). But the Irish feminist movement worked to liberate women from narrow options and the psychological and physical abuse that the domestic sphere held for many Irish women. Dorcey's lesbian fiction acknowledges the psychic and cultural pull of the domestic sphere while simultaneously addressing the often disruptive presence of lesbian sexual desire within that sphere.

Front cover for Dorcey's 1989 short-story collection, one of the first contemporary Irish volumes of short fiction to focus on lesbian characters (Thomas Cooper Library, University of South Carolina)

The title story in *A Noise from the Woodshed* reads more like a postmodern fable than an actual story, and in it Dorcey positions lesbian voices and lesbian sexual activity as powerful antidotes to patriarchal roles that either literally or metaphorically abuse the work of women. The story describes the relationship of one lesbian couple as they make a home together in a ramshackle country house. The house is depicted as a place of freedom, sharply contrasted with the suburban homes in which married, heterosexual women are imprisoned. At one point in the narrative, the couple hears noises coming from the woodshed; when they investigate, they discover more lesbians making love in the woodshed. The country house and its surroundings thus serve as a refuge for lesbian women.

The experimental form of this short story indicates Dorcey's need to distance herself from conventional modes of narrative in order to write about the sexually unconventional lives of Irish lesbians. (The rest of the stories in the collection return to a realist form.) "A Noise from the Woodshed," positioned first as the title story of the collection, initiates a polyvoiced discussion of lesbianism that many of the subsequent stories in the collection continue. "A Noise from the Woodshed" addresses the transitions that women make from their conventional domestic roles as Irish women—primarily as wives and mothers—to their lives as lesbians.

The stories that follow "A Noise from the Woodshed" build upon the themes established in the title story. In "The Husband," one of the most anthologized stories from the book, the narrative is made up of the thoughts of a man about to lose his wife to her female lover. This narrative focus allows Dorcey to expose a wide range of views of lesbianism. At one point, for example, the husband fantasizes about the two women.

He imagines having them both in his bed. At another point, he is disgusted and repelled by the sounds he hears them make when they are having sex—almost as if Dorcey were attempting to show what the "noise from the woodshed" might sound like to a heterosexual man. Later in the text, he feels assured that his wife cannot be satisfied by a woman, even as his wife prepares to leave him in favor of her lesbian lover.

Not all of Dorcey's stories focus on lesbian relationships. Yet, whether or not they focus on lesbianism, many of her stories address the struggle for Irish women to assert control over their lives in a society that privileges the needs and perspectives of men. In "A Country Dance," two women are threatened by the violent homophobia of a rural community when they dance together in public. In "Introducing Nessa," the protagonist's inability to reveal her lesbian relationship to her friends is sharply contrasted with her former husband's openly gay relationship. "A Sense of Humour" follows the emotions of an abused wife as she resolves to leave her husband and the restrictive confines of her hometown, and "Flowers for Easter" narrates the feelings of a young girl whose mother neglects her daughter while trying to cope with her husband's illness and death.

In regard to influences from Irish literature, Dorcey feels that no literary path exists for her to follow, particularly when it comes to Irish lesbian writing. The few Irish lesbian works that did exist were already out of print when Dorcey was a young woman. Only in the late 1970s and 1980s did lesbian literature begin to be more available in Ireland as feminist presses began to rediscover and republish this work. As a result of her lack of direct Irish artistic influences, Dorcey has said that she has had to forge her own sense of style and form for her particular needs. However, she does acknowledge the influence of some key modern and contemporary Irish writers, such as Wilde, George Bernard Shaw, Elizabeth Bowen, Mary Lavin, James Joyce, John McGahern, Edna O'Brien, Samuel Beckett, Jennifer Johnston, and Kate Cruise O'Brien. The writers whom she read between the ages of ten and twenty-five she says affected her the most, because, as she told Anne Owen Weekes in the *Irish Literary Supplement,* these were writers "who dealt with atmosphere and inner sensation rather than the world of action." Such writers included Woolf, Mansfield, Beckett, Colette, Albert Camus, Jean Genet, D. H. Lawrence, W. H. Auden, William Butler Yeats, Dylan Thomas, Sylvia Plath, and Anne Sexton.

Despite her own sense of a lack of a tradition for her writing, clearly Dorcey is contributing to an Irish lesbian tradition both in her writing and in her teaching. In an interview with BooksIrish.com, Donoghue named Dorcey as an inspiration: "One key moment I do remember . . . is coming across Mary Dorcey's poems in the UCD library, and thinking 'Irish! lesbian! and damn good!–so it can be done.'" Literary critics and scholars are beginning to recognize the importance of Dorcey's short fiction. In an attempt to trace the tradition of Irish lesbian writing, Weekes points to Dorcey's work as a major turning point in this tradition. In her study of Irish lesbian literature, "A Trackless Road: Irish Nationalisms and Lesbian Writing," Weekes describes *A Noise from the Woodshed* as having interrupted the thirty-year silence since the last work of Irish lesbian fiction (Cruise O'Brien's 1958 novel *As Music and Splendour*). Weekes also views the collection as a literary precursor to the legal decriminalization of homosexuality that occurred in Ireland in 1993: "In 1989 *A Noise from the Woodshed* burst triumphantly upon the scene, joyfully presenting the delight of lesbian love and heralding alternatives that the 1993 law would uphold."

The stories in *A Noise from the Woodshed* have been extensively anthologized. The title story was included in the 1999 *Vintage Book of International Lesbian Fiction,* edited by Naomi Horloch and Joan Nestle, and Dermot Bolger chose "The Husband" for his *Picador Book of Contemporary Irish Fiction* (1993). "A Country Dance" has proved even more popular: it was included in the 1985 anthology *Girls Next Door,* edited by Jen Bradshaw and Mary Hemming; the 1999 anthology *The Mammoth Book of Lesbian Short Stories,* edited by Donoghue; and Colm Tóibín's influential *Penguin Anthology of Irish Fiction,* also published in 1999. A further short story, "The Orphan," was anthologized in 1998 in *In Sunshine or in Shadow,* edited by Cruise O'Brien and Mary Maher. (The anthology also includes short stories by Maeve Binchy, Margaret Dolan, and Jennifer Johnston.)

Since the publication of *A Noise from the Woodshed* and the winning of the Rooney Prize, Dorcey has enjoyed the increased opportunities for writing and publishing that come with such acclaim. A novella titled "Scarlet O'Hara" was included in *In and Out of Time,* edited by Patricia Duncker in 1990. Dorcey published two more volumes of poetry, *Moving into the Space Cleared by Our Mothers* (1991) and *The River that Carries Me* (1995). Both collections were published by Salmon Publishing, a new press specifically aimed at providing an outlet for women writers in Ireland. Thus, even in her choice of publishers Dorcey remains a committed feminist. Irish Arts Council bursaries helped her to write her first and only novel, *Biography of Desire,* which was published in 1997, as well as a fourth book of poetry, *Like Joy in Season, Like Sorrow* (2001), also published by Salmon Publishing. She has contributed to such feminist journals as *Banshee* and *Wicca* and staged dramatizations of her poetry at the Project Arts Centre in Dublin. She has been involved with the Attic Press's project to produce collections of feminist fairy tales, her work appearing in volumes such as *Mad and Bad Fairies* (1987) and *Ride on, Rapunzel* (1992). Despite these successes, Dorcey has said that she feels that the Irish literary community has not been particularly supportive of her work. The academic community, however, has supported her work from the beginning. For example, Patricia Coughlan celebrates her work in the *Irish Review* (Spring 1991), as well as in Coughlan's chapter in the seminal collection on Irish literature and sexuality, *Sex, Nation and Dissent in Irish Writing* (1997). Here she favorably compares Dorcey to a more canonical Irish woman writer, Kate O'Brien, stating that both writers' exploit and extend "the conventions of lesbian erotic narratives."

As a result of this critical interest, Dorcey is frequently invited to read at universities, and all of the Irish universities include her writing in their courses. British and American universities also teach her work in Irish studies and women's studies courses, and many theses, dissertations, and critical articles have explored the artistic and cultural impact of her work. Dorcey is herself an active teacher. She has taught writing courses for the Liverpool lesbian and gay writers' group "Queer Scribes." Currently, Dorcey is a lecturer and research associate at Trinity College Dublin. In Trinity's Centre for Gender and Women's Studies, she works as a writer in residence leading creative-writing workshops and conducting seminars in contemporary English literature. Although Dorcey's output of short stories is slim, she remains an influential, much anthologized, and much admired writer in this form.

Interviews:

Ide O'Carroll and Eoin Collins, eds., "Mary Dorcey," in *Lesbian and Gay Visions of Ireland* (London: Cassell, 1995), pp. 25–44;

Anne Owen Weekes, "Real Lives–An Interview with Mary Dorcey," *Irish Literary Supplement* (Fall 2000): 18–19.

Reference:

Patricia Coughlan, "The Ear of the Other: Dissident Voices in Kate O'Brien's *As Music and Splendour* and Mary Dorcey's *A Noise from the Woodshed*," in *Sex, Nation and Dissent in Irish Writing,* edited by Eibhear Walshe (Cork: Cork University Press, 1997), pp. 202–220;

Anne Owen Weekes, "A Trackless Road: Irish Nationalisms and Lesbian Writing," in *Border Crossings: Irish Women Writers and National Identities,* edited by Kathryn Kirkpatrick (Tuscaloosa: University of Alabama Press, 2000), pp. 123–156.

Ronald Frame
(23 May 1953 –)

Brett Josef Grubisic
University of British Columbia

BOOKS: *Winter Journey* (London: Bodley Head, 1984; New York: Beaufort, 1984);
Watching Mrs Gordon and Other Stories (London: Bodley Head, 1985);
A Long Weekend with Marcel Proust: Seven Stories and a Novel (London: Bodley Head, 1986);
A Woman of Judah: A Novel and Fifteen Stories (London: Bodley Head, 1987; New York: Norton, 1989);
Paris: A Play for Television (London: Faber & Faber, 1987);
Sandmouth People (London: Bodley Head, 1987); republished as *Sandmouth* (New York: Knopf, 1988);
Penelope's Hat (London: Hodder & Stoughton, 1989; New York: Simon & Schuster, 1989);
Bluette (London: Hodder & Stoughton, 1990);
Underwood and After (London: Hodder & Stoughton, 1991);
Walking My Mistress in Deauville: A Novella and Nine Stories (London: Hodder & Stoughton, 1992);
The Sun on the Wall: Three Novels (London: Hodder & Stoughton, 1994);
The Lantern Bearers (London: Duckworth, 1999; Washington, D.C.: Counterpoint, 2001);
Permanent Violet (Edinburgh: Polygon, 2002);
Time in Carnbeg (Edinburgh: Polygon, 2004).

PRODUCED SCRIPTS: *Winter Journey,* radio, BBC, 17 November 1985;
Twister, radio, BBC, 3 April 1986;
Out of Time, television, BBC, 1987;
Rendezvous, radio, BBC, 27 April 1987;
Ghost City, motion picture, BBC, 1988;
Cara, radio, BBC, 24 January 1989;
Marina Bray, radio, BBC, 27 June 1989;
A Woman of Judah, radio, BBC, 16 August 1993;
The Lantern Bearers, radio, BBC, 17 February 1997;
The Hydro, radio, BBC, 30 April 1997;
Havisham, radio, BBC, 16 August 1999;
Pharos, radio, BBC, 6 June 2000;

Ronald Frame (from The Lantern Bearers, *1999; Richland County Public Library)*

Sunday at Sant' Agata, radio, BBC, 30 December 2001;
Greyfriars, radio, BBC, 31 August 2002.

A novelist and writer of short fiction, radio plays, and movie scripts, Ronald Frame has produced a body of work that despite its eclecticism remains focused on the importance (and unreliability) of memory, the fluidity (as well as duplicity) of identity, and the frequently destructive nature or consequences of marriages and romances. Often utilizing luxurious settings in the United Kingdom, continental Europe, and the Americas, his work exposes the tensions in the lives of middle-class characters who have profound investments in "maintaining appearances." Critics are widely divided about the ultimate merit of his work; some applaud his innovation, characterization, and inventiveness, while others fault his fiction for being overly contrived, precious, melodramatic, or mannered.

Born in Glasgow on 23 May 1953, Frame–who currently lives in Bearsden, a venerable satellite community of Glasgow–spoke in "A Conversation with Ronald Frame" (1999) of growing up comfortably with parents Alexander (an advertising agent) and Subel (Sutherland) Frame in "a leafy suburb" of Glasgow and attending "a private boys' day school, 850 years old." The author, who has rarely made himself available for interviews, published his first story when he was seventeen; he received an M.A. from the University of Glasgow in 1975 and a B.Litt. from Oxford in 1979. In the same 1999 interview, Frame lists his influences as the great European movie auteurs (Michaelangelo Antonioni, François Truffaut, Claude Chabrol, Ingmar Bergman, and Luchino Visconti), and points to Argentine Jorge Luis Borges, the early work of Mexican Carlos Fuentes, the "European" Vladimir Nabokov, and "American writers with European sensibilities" (Michael Cunningham, John Cheever, Susan Minot, and Harold Brodkey) as writers from whom he draws inspiration. Though commonly set in Scotland, his fiction has a broader geographic purview and ambience. In "A Conversation with Ronald Frame" he acknowledged his unusual aesthete's perspective: while class-bound yet more democratic than Britain, he noted, in "macho-obsessed Celtic cultures like the Scottish one, it's still thought very unusual, if not perverse, for a man to write sensually, even hedonistically." Scottish critic Douglas Dunn has labeled Frame a "hedonistic tragedian" on account of his customary mise-en-scène (detailed description of the physical setting) and disposition (crafting characters with financially secure lives that are riddled with deceit, anxiety, delusion, misery, and failure).

While Frame has spoken sparingly about himself and his writing, he has offered some explanations about his motivations and objectives. In "A Conversation with Ronald Frame," which coincided with the publication of *The Lantern Bearers* (1999), he explained, "In my fiction I resist having heroes and villains. I try to create rounded, three-dimensional, and necessarily inconsistent characters." He added, "When I read a book, a novel, I want to learn something about human nature which I didn't know or failed to appreciate at the outset (the Presbyterian still lodged inside me!)." Elsewhere, Frame outlines some key rationales for his work. In the foreword to his Samuel Beckett Prize and Television Industries Award–winning screenplay *Paris* (1987), Frame discloses that "as usual in my stories–even if the admission is presumptuous sounding–I wanted to locate the inner life, with all of its manifold contradictions." Moreover, he states that the work reflects his conviction that "we all live between rigorous, unmendable 'truth' and our chosen interpretations, our preferred, selective fictions." In the foreword he concludes with what amounts to a writer's summa: "I don't write to make political points, or to be circumstantially 'relevant' in the social sense. The best I can hope for, how I justify myself, is to try to induce an awareness of what merits our sympathy and understanding in lives that may appear utterly distinct and apart from our own."

Frame's first novel, *Winter Journey* (1984), joint winner of the inaugural Betty Trask Prize, recounts the childhood of Annoele Tomlinson, whose feckless if affluent and cultured parents–he an attaché with the British embassy, she most comfortable amidst the European beau monde–made her feel "like a parcel neither of them wanted to have a final claim on." In the present day, her parents having died in mysterious circumstances, the anchorless narrator anxiously examines her history–moving from Czechoslovakia to Austria to Germany to England in her parent's Jaguar in the early 1960s–in order to secure a clearer future for herself.

Winter Journey is notable for its sensuality and attention to the physical markers of well-heeled society. Its thematic focus on the recovery of the past, the vicissitudes of perception, the chasm between appearance and reality, and the fluidity of identity is developed further in Frame's first collection of short fiction, *Watching Mrs Gordon and Other Stories* (1985), published fifteen years after the appearance of his first story in 1970. While perceivable in *Winter Journey,* Frame's fascination with the nuances of class- and convention-bound society is emphasized in later work. Set in Canada, Italy, France, and the United Kingdom, the thirteen stories reflect Frame's characteristic themes. The title piece, "Excavations," "Piccadilly Peccadilloes," "Harlequinade," and "Secrets" describe ostensibly successful marriages whose routines and lack of material want belie their true alienation, profound unhappiness, and strata of deceit. The women in "Excavations" and "Piccadilly Peccadilloes," for instance, can barely cope with the cost of keeping up appearances. In the former, an elderly matron recalls that though she benefited from her privilege and position, her marriage was hollow–a front, in fact, for her status-obsessed homosexual husband; the anxious middle-aged woman in the latter endures her husband's alcoholic rages by shopping and assuming a cavalier public persona. Likewise, the male narrators in "Watching Mrs Gordon" and "Secrets" reflect on their marriages, remaining committed to the status and security they provide while being deeply discontented with the compromise that security requires.

Other stories are characteristic insofar as they feature narrators looking back at an enigmatic yet significant moment from their pasts. The narrator of "The Tree House" recalls his unpleasant involvement with two "evil" children in his affluent neighborhood. Set in Berkshire in 1962, "My Cousin from Des Moines" describes a conventional family whose "pattern of normality" is subtly but permanently altered by the arrival of a scandalous, freethinking divorcée aunt and her son from the United States.

Both "Palladian" and "Paris" examine characters who strive to change the unsatisfactory shape of their lives. In the former, a married woman decides to confront a man from her past. Yet, her startling realization about him (and herself) hastens a prompt return to the safe but confining comforts of middle-class community with her husband–to "their quiet, steady, anchored lives with no surprises allowed." The elderly Scottish women in the latter story build a friendship based on recalling their vibrant past lives. The memories are heavily embroidered, though, an apparent symptom of the unwillingness of each to accept the failure of her aspirations. Similarly, "Thicker Than Water" is written from two points of view and describes the tension that accompanies the annual vacation of Elspeth and her sister Florence.

Frame veers from strict realism in several pieces. "Endpiece" is a kind of ghost story set among the falling bombs and rolling fogs of wartime London. Likewise eerie and atmospheric, "Other" follows the thoughts of an anxious married man about to embark on an ill-starred tryst with a handsome and mysterious stranger. The antic "Tragedy" is an unexpectedly comic tale in which a retired and apparently delusional actor living in Canada recalls her fatal involvement with a Hollywood director in the late 1970s. Surveying the stories in *TLS: The Times Literary Supplement* (5 July 1985), Gerald Mangan took exception to Frame's "jarringly lame" sentences, "damagingly vague" visual sense, and "weakly dramatized" themes.

Frame's second collection of fiction was published a year later. *A Long Weekend with Marcel Proust: Seven Stories and a Novel* (1986) opens with an epigraph by Maxine Kumin–"We are, each of us, our own prisoners. We are locked up in our own story"–that foregrounds the imprisoning conditions in which the generally middle-class characters find themselves. In these stories, Frame further develops his vision of marriage and romance as contradictory relationships, fraught with misperceptions, compromises, tension, or deceit. The title story, "The Camelhair Jacket," and the story "The Blue Jug" anatomize such dynamics. Like the narrator of "A Long Weekend with Marcel Proust" (who, grateful to be completing her tense weekend in Normandy, concludes, "the more you read, the less there is in this spinning world you can be sure about"), the stories emphasize the fragility and, at times, futility of human interaction.

When not studying the disasters of erotic love, Frame attends to the failings of other endeavors. "Merlewood" uses the device of a retrospective narrator studying a photograph of a Scottish family's vacation (circa 1965) in order to illustrate how that ostensibly innocent time was in fact complicated by familial politics. "Incident at Le Lavandou" describes the life and death of Miss Simms, a Scottish woman who abandoned her restrictive birthplace in order to live freely in the Côte d'Azur. Like "Paris," "The Lunch Table" observes the friendship between two women whose twice-monthly luncheons are predicated on a "diversion from the facts"–the "facts" are unhappy marriages and fears about becoming old and insignificant. Dedicated to Alain Robbe-Grillet, "Fandango" is an appropriately self-conscious literary exercise that offers an account of a man's hurried flight from Mexico City.

In "A Conversation with Ronald Frame" the author remarks that he's "tired of clever-clever, self-referential 'literary' prose." *Prelude and Fugue* (made into a Channel Four movie called *Out of Time*) is, however, highly literary and formally experimental; it describes the fears and memories of a young woman during aerial bombing in wartime London.

Despite his "Conversation" statement that "150–200 pages is more than sufficient to tell a story," Frame's next novels recall the conventions of Victorian novel length. The 476-page *Sandmouth People* (1987) is set in a small resort town on the south coast of England in the mid 1950s. A record of one day in a town with a wide gallery of inhabitants, it runs the gamut from comedy to tragedy and paints an evocative portrait of "the new Britain."

Another story collection also appeared in 1987–*A Woman of Judah: A Novel and Fifteen Stories*. In the 179-page eponymous novel, a seventy-four-year-old retired judge recalls his youth in Wessex in the 1930s and his illicit involvement with the sensual and striking Mrs. Davies, whose narcissism and affinity for Hollywood glamour raises the ire of the townspeople.

Marital and relational discord, disgrace, and failure are the focal points of the subsequent fifteen stories. As she readies herself for an evening of socializing, the bitter and alcoholic widow of "Sundowners" recalls her diplomat husband's serial adultery. "The Second Marriage" describes an affluent couple living "on the right and proper side of cliché–just." Both the husband and the wife know the marriage was an impulsive mistake. "Rendezvous" counterpoints lovers' perspectives in order to anatomize a desultory long-term affair complicated by abortion, prostitution, and seeming blackmail. "Evacuee," set in 1957, offers the feverish reminiscence of a woman whose lifeless marriage keeps her awake at night; though she has acquired "social polish," she has not found it sufficient to satisfy her, and she seeks out adulterous means to pass the time. In "Water Boy" a married (and soon to be drowned) businessman contemplates leaving his comfortable life in a "desirable and expensive area" during a cruise on the Nile. In "Fruits de Mer" the narrator analyzes patrons at a restaurant in order to study their loneliness and relieve his own. "An Evening in Granada" and "The Ghost Cupboard" likewise chronicle the fallout from relationships run astray.

A Woman of Judah also highlights Frame's experimentation with form and genre, especially his affinity for the fantastic and unexplained. In "The Chinese Garden" the narrator attempts to solve the mysterious murder of a woman in the titular Parisian garden. Like the 1985 story "Tragedy," "Schwimmbad Mitternachts" is set in Hollywood and features a comically manic narrator whose obsession with fame and celebrities leads to misadventure. "Begun at Midnight" takes the shape of one-way "Correspondence of an Intimate Nature" and offers an account of a Victorian gentleman's erotic affection for another man. "Divertissement" is an account of the unwelcome revelations that result when guests at a rural Scottish hotel partake in The Mesmerising Dr Mesmer's mass hypnosis. "Fludde's Ark," set in a postapocalyptic England, circa 2017, describes the narrator's attempts to catalogue and preserve written artifacts at a time of exceptional uncertainty and chaos. "The Corner Table" and "Sur la Plage à Trouville" examine the distance between perception and actuality. While Anthony Sattin's review in *TLS* (11 December 1987) praised the ability of Frame's "earlier novels and short stories" to evoke atmosphere and character, he admitted to disappointment with the desultory tone of the "well conceived" works.

Critic Dunn noted the "astounding as well as remarkably extensive *Englishness*" of the 440-page *Penelope's Hat* (1989). From Borneo in 1926 to Cornwall in 1986, the novel captures the restless and event-filled life of Penelope Milne. Frame's subsequent novel, the sprawling 531-page *Bluette* (1990), describes another obsessive, self-absorbed, and wandering English protagonist, Catherine Hammond; it illuminates her experiences in the Canadian Rockies and Scottish Trossachs as well as ones in glamorous social scenes in mid-twentieth-century London and Hollywood. The reviewer for *TLS* (6 July 1990) assessed it as "a perplexing, sad development in a writer who began with some rewarding stories."

Dust jacket for the 1989 U.S. edition of Frame's 1987 collection of works, some of which are about marital and relational discord, disgrace, and failure (Richland County Public Library)

Half the length of *Bluette,* yet similarly concerned with unpeeling the strata of British society, *Underwood and After* (1991) opens with a sentence that points to one of Frame's thematic preoccupations: "Thirty years later, in 1986, I was revisited by the past." The economical novel features the reminiscences of Ralph, whose memories (recreating scenes from Cornwall, circa 1956) reveal involvement with an enigmatic and wealthy family and their "ghostly paradise of privilege," a manor named Underwood.

The following year, Frame published *Walking My Mistress in Deauville: A Novella and Nine Stories*. Introduced with an epigraph by Jean-Luc Godard—"Seeing Is Deceiving"—the 162-page novel is set on the south coast of England circa 1957 and traces the relationship between the narrator, Charles, who marries Marina, his "high-quality wife" because he was "tired of good sense and caution." Yet, like the enigmatic wife of "Watching Mrs Gordon," she appears to live a double life and becomes the object of her husband's scrutiny.

Frame's attentiveness to the limitations of relationships continues unabated in the stories that follow.

As usual, they are marked by attention to detail and an emphasis on the distance between appearance and reality, especially as that idea relates to the often duplicitous and illusory nature of marriage and romances. The seeming whimsy of the title piece—told by Rufus, a dachshund whose owner is unhappily entangled with a shifty underworld boss—is offset by its explication of a life that though immersed in well-appointed luxury is little other than a prison. "Mirror, Mirror" recounts a woman's sudden realization that her husband has used their weekend trips to antique shops to set up covert erotic encounters with men. As in "Rendezvous," Frame utilizes counterpoint to underscore the divergent perceptions of the disgruntled lovers in "The Siege." Similarly, "Oysters and Cigars" shifts between scenes of a mother and daughter on vacation and vignettes of the daughter beginning another affair. A mere two pages, "Drive" records the anxious stream of thoughts of an adulterous wife as she hastens to return home. Running fifty-four pages and set in a familiar genteel and moneyed society, "Table Talk" frequently shifts between narrators to reveal the complicated relationship between a mother and her daughter (and the licit and illicit romances both carry on). While they are retrospective narratives, "Crossing the Alps" and "Gregor's Garage" both focus on marriages that cause hardship and damage to the participants. When a character in "Table Talk" surveys her past and announces, "Man and woman, it isn't a game for amateurs," she could be speaking as well of the author's perspective.

Like "Paris," the brief "Privateers" depicts the daily routine of an elderly woman who, while unmarried, nonetheless lives immersed in deceptions and half-truths: she has become increasingly drawn to reveries about "her desirable, imagined past." Of the stories, Nicola Walker in *TLS* (6 August 1993) complained, "If Ronald Frame hadn't striven so hard for moral significance several of them might have been, if not inspirational, at least enjoyable."

Frame's most recent publications have been the novels *The Sun on the Wall: Three Novels* (1994), *The Lantern Bearers, Permanent Violet* (2002), and *Time in Carnbeg* (2004). *The Sun on the Wall* is composed of three novels. *I've Been Here Before,* set in 1955, is told by the son of Decca Blane, a briefly notorious British film star. Frame collapses the narrative point of view so that it simultaneously represents adult and child; as Merlin explains in pondering his mother's suicide, "the man is disposed to explain, the boy to describe." In the eponymous novel, the narrator, Hermione, becomes thoughtful upon the death of her father, an illustrious Oxford don. Though she's concerned with keeping up appearances following his death, her recollection reveals how his incestuous relationship with her effectively diminished the scope of her entire life. *The Broch* is divided into four parts and features multiple narrators (family members and servants) tied in various ways and at various times to a sprawling Edwardian manor outside of Glasgow.

Winner of the Saltire Society's Book of the Year, *The Lantern Bearers* is a coming-of-age story largely set in a Scottish seaside town in the early 1960s. Narrated by an ailing writer named Neil Pritchard (who has agreed to write a biography of Euan Bone, a composer who died in 1963), the novel depicts Pritchard's boyhood amorous friendship with Bone. Pritchard's recollection also exposes his guilty awareness that Bone's mysterious death resulted from a sex scandal his false accusation precipitated. Reminiscent of Frame's 1986 short story "The Blue Jug," *Permanent Violet* traces the tempestuous marriage and illustrious career of the recently deceased painter Colin Brogan, whose unreliable wife, Eilidh, reconstructs their life together in Scotland and France. Based on an acclaimed radio series and set in an imaginary small Scottish resort town, *Time in Carnbeg* recalls *Sandmouth People* insofar as it weaves in and out of the lives of the town's inhabitants and encompasses a broad spectrum of experience, from comedy to tragedy.

Though the settings of Ronald Frame's novels, novellas, and short fiction span great stretches of time and geography, overall the works are unified to a significant degree by consistent focal points. Anchored by a fascination with (and recording of) the physical markers, rituals, and minutiae of middle-class and affluent society, and frequently attentive to the nuance of troubled and decayed relationships (within families, between spouses), Frame's fiction strives—he claims in his foreword to *Paris*—to "induce an awareness of what merits our sympathy and understanding in lives that may appear utterly distinct and apart from our own." In doing so, his fiction anatomizes a society damaged by the developments of its history and characters stymied by their duplicitous and restless psyches. While indicating familiarity with postmodern narrating techniques, Frame's overall interest in the domestic lives of affluent Anglo-Saxons and middle-class aspirants places him much closer in theme to chroniclers like Marcel Proust and Anthony Powell than to contemporary postmodernists like Jeanette Winterson or Salman Rushdie.

Reference:

Douglas Dunn, "Divergent Scottishness: William Boyd, Allan Massie, Ronald Frame," in *The Scottish Novel Since the Seventies,* edited by Gavin Wallace and Randall Stevenson (Edinburgh: Edinburgh University Press, 1993), pp. 149–169.

Brian Friel
(9 or 10 January 1929 -   )

G. H. Timmermans
University of Macau

See also the Friel entry in *DLB 13: British Dramatists Since World War II.*

BOOKS: *The Saucer of Larks* (London: Gollancz, 1962; Garden City, N.Y.: Doubleday, 1962); revised and enlarged with stories from *The Gold in the Sea* as *The Saucer of Larks: Stories from Ireland* (London: Arrow, 1969);

Philadelphia, Here I Come! (London: Faber & Faber, 1965; New York: Noonday, 1965);

The Loves of Cass McGuire (New York: S. French, 1966; London: Faber & Faber, 1967);

The Gold in the Sea (London: Gollancz, 1966; Garden City, N.Y.: Doubleday, 1966);

Lovers: Winners & Losers (New York: Farrar, Straus & Giroux, 1968; London: Faber & Faber, 1968);

Crystal and Fox (London: Faber & Faber, 1970; Dublin: Gallery, 1984);

The Mundy Scheme (New York: S. French, 1970);

Crystal and Fox & The Mundy Scheme (New York: Farrar, Straus & Giroux, 1970);

The Gentle Island (London: Davis-Poynter, 1973 [i.e., 1974]);

The Freedom of the City (London: Faber & Faber, 1974; New York & London: S. French, 1979?);

The Enemy Within (Newark, Del.: Proscenium Press, 1975; Dublin: Gallery, 1979);

Living Quarters (London & Boston: Faber & Faber, 1978);

Volunteers (London & Boston: Faber & Faber, 1979; Oldcastle, Ireland: Gallery, 1989);

Selected Stories (Oldcastle, Ireland: Gallery, 1979); republished as *The Diviner: The Best Stories of Brian Friel,* with an introduction by Seamus Deane (Dublin: O'Brien / London: Allison & Busby, 1983; Old Greenwich, Conn.: Devin-Adair, 1983);

Faith Healer (London & Boston: Faber & Faber, 1980);

Aristocrats (New York & London: S. French, 1980);

Translations (London & Boston: Faber & Faber, 1981);

Anton Chekhov's Three Sisters (Dublin: Gallery, 1981);

The Communication Cord (London & Boston: Faber & Faber, 1983);

Brian Friel (from Selected Stories, *1994; Thomas Cooper Library, University of South Carolina)*

Selected Plays of Brian Friel (London: Faber & Faber, 1984; Washington, D.C.: Catholic University of America Press, 1986); republished as *Plays One* (London: Faber & Faber, 1996)—comprises *Philadelphia, Here I Come!, The Freedom of the City, Living Quarters, Aristocrats, Faith Healer,* and *Translations;*

Fathers and Sons (London: Faber & Faber, 1987; New York: S. French, 1987);

Making History (London & Boston: Faber & Faber, 1989);

Dancing at Lughnasa (London & Boston: Faber & Faber, 1990);

The London Vertigo (Oldcastle, Ireland: Gallery, 1990);

A Month in the Country (Oldcastle, Ireland: Gallery, 1992; New York: Dramatists Play Service, 1993);

Wonderful Tennessee (London & Boston: Faber & Faber, 1993);

Molly Sweeney (London & New York: Penguin, 1994);

Give Me Your Answer, Do! (Oldcastle, Ireland: Gallery, 1997; London: Penguin, 1997);

Uncle Vanya (Oldcastle, Ireland: Gallery, 1998; New York: Dramatists Play Service, 2000);

Brian Friel: Essays, Diaries, Interviews, 1964–1999, edited by Christopher Murray (London: Faber & Faber, 1999);

Plays Two (London: Faber & Faber, 1999)—comprises *Dancing at Lughnasa, Fathers and Sons, Making History, Wonderful Tennessee, Molly Sweeney;*

The Yalta Game (Oldcastle, Ireland: Gallery, 2001);

Three Plays After (London: Faber & Faber, 2002; Oldcastle, Ireland: Gallery, 2002)—comprises *The Yalta Game, The Bear,* and *Afterplay;*

Performances (Oldcastle, Ireland: Gallery, 2003);

The Home Place (London: Faber & Faber, 2005; Oldcastle, Ireland: Gallery, 2005).

PLAY PRODUCTIONS: *The Francophile,* Belfast, Group Theatre, 1960;

The Enemy Within, Dublin, Abbey Theatre, 1962;

The Blind Mice, Dublin, Eblana Theatre, 1963;

Philadelphia, Here I Come! Dublin, Gaeity Theatre, 1964;

The Loves of Cass Maguire, New York, Helen Hayes Theatre, 1966;

Lovers, Dublin, Gate Theatre, 1967;

Crystal and Fox, Dublin, Gaeity Theatre, 1968;

The Mundy Scheme, Dublin, Olympia Theatre, 1971;

The Freedom of the City, Dublin, Abbey Theatre, 1973;

Volunteers, Dublin, Abbey Theatre, 1975;

Living Quarters, Dublin, Abbey Theatre, 1977;

Aristocrats, Dublin, Abbey Theatre, 1979;

Faith Healer, New York, Longacre Theatre, 1979;

Translations, Derry, The Guildhall, 1980;

Three Sisters, Derry, The Guildhall, 1981;

The Communication Cord, Derry, The Guildhall, 1982;

Fathers and Sons, London, Lyttleton Theatre, 1987;

Making History, Derry, The Guildhall, 1988;

Dancing at Lughnasa, Dublin, Abbey Theatre, 1990;

The London Vertigo, Dublin, Andrews Lane Theatre, 1992;

Wonderful Tennessee, Dublin, Abbey Theatre, 1993;

Molly Sweeney, Dublin, Gate Theatre, 1995;

Give Me Your Answer, Do! Dublin, Abbey Theatre, 1997;

The Yalta Game, Dublin, Gate Theatre, 2001;

Afterplay, Dublin, Gate Theatre, 2002; London, Gielgud Theatre, 2002;

The Home Place, Dublin, Gate Theatre, 2005.

PRODUCED SCRIPTS: "The Good Old Days," BBC Radio, Northern Ireland Home Service, 2 May 1956;

"Red, Red Rose," BBC Radio, Northern Ireland Home Service, 5 April 1957;

"My True Kinsman," BBC Radio, Northern Ireland Home Service, 5 December 1957;

"The Fishing Lesson," BBC Radio, Northern Ireland Home Service, 18 July 1958;

"Segova, the Savage Turk," BBC Radio, Northern Ireland Home Service, 27 October 1960; BBC Radio Two, *Morning Story,* 27 August 1971;

"The Fawn Pup," BBC Radio, *Morning Story,* Light Programme, 5 December 1963; BBC Radio, Northern Ireland Home Service, 11 March 1964;

"The Saucer of Larks," BBC Radio, *Morning Story,* Light Programme, 5 March 1964;

"The Potato Gatherers," BBC Radio, *Morning Story,* Light Programme, 11 March 1965;

"My Own Kinsman," BBC Radio, *Morning Story,* Light Programme, 7 August 1965;

"The Queen of Troy Close," BBC Radio, *Morning Story,* Light Programme, 9 December 1965; BBC Radio, *Interval Talk,* Northern Ireland Home Service, 1 April 1966;

"The Skelper," BBC Radio Four, *Morning Story,* 27 November 1967;

"Among the Ruins," BBC Radio Two, *Morning Story,* 8 March 1968;

"Johnny and Nick," BBC Radio Two, *Morning Story,* 12 July 1968;

"Green Peas and Barley O," BBC Television Northern Ireland, *The Magic Sovereign,* 18 May 1979;

"The Giant," BBC Radio Four, *Morning Story,* 20 July 1990.

OTHER: "Extracts from a Sporadic Diary," in *The Writers: A Sense of Ireland,* edited by Andrew Carpenter and Peter Fallon (Dublin: O'Brien Press, 1980);

"American Welcome," in *Best Short Plays 1981,* edited by Stanley Richards (Radnor, Pa.: Chilton, 1981), pp. 112–114;

Charles McGlinchey, *The Last of the Name,* introduction by Friel (Belfast: Blackstaff, 1986);

Michael Herity, *Ordnance Survey Letters: Donegal,* preface by Friel (Dublin: Four Masters Press, 2000).

SELECTED PERIODICAL PUBLICATIONS—UNCOLLECTED: "For Export Only," *Commonweal,* 15 February 1957, pp. 509–510;

"The Lighter Side: The Afternoon of a Fawn Pup," *Irish Press,* 7 July 1962, p. 8;

"To the Wee Lake Beyond: A Journey with Brian Friel," *Irish Press,* 4 August 1962, pp. 17–22;

"Self-Portrait," *Aquarius,* no. 5 (1972): 56–61;

"Extracts from a Sporadic Diary," in *Ireland and the Arts,* edited by Tim Pat Coogan (London: Namara Press, 1983), pp. 39–43.

Brian Friel, one of the leading Irish dramatists of the late twentieth century, began his literary apprenticeship as an author of short stories, and his early success in this field allowed him the means to become a full-time writer. These stories, exploring the rituals and parochial ambitions of small-town Irish life, offer a view of a particular period and place in Ireland's history, and Friel further develops this world in his most successful dramatic works.

In both his stories and his plays Friel has created his own fictional landscape—later called Ballybeg, literally "small town" (from the Irish *Baile Beag*)—and that imaginative territory of his boyhood lies in the geographical borderlands between County Derry and County Tyrone in Northern Ireland and County Donegal in the Republic of Ireland. All of the area is part of the historical province of Ulster; Friel describes and analyzes this rural country and its people, seemingly indifferent to political division, in his stories. As a writer of short fiction, Friel is now relatively neglected, but the short stories are an important part of his literary development, and they also provide useful insights into a way of life before the resurgence of political violence in Northern Ireland and the Republic of Ireland's entry into the European Community.

Friel, writer and dramatist, was born Bernard Patrick Friel in Killyclogher, near Omagh, in County Tyrone, Northern Ireland, on 9 or 10 January 1929. His father, Patrick, was a primary-school principal from Derry, and his mother, Christina MacLoone, was a postmistress from Glenties in County Donegal. The family moved in 1939 to the Bogside area of Derry, where Friel's father became principal of the Long Tower School. Friel himself attended this school before going on to St. Columb's College, also in Derry, in 1941. After completing his secondary education in 1945, Friel went to the National Seminary, St. Patrick's College, at Maynooth. Two and a half years into his training he realized that he did not have a vocation for the priesthood, and on completing his B.A. in 1949 he moved instead to St. Joseph's Teacher Training College in Belfast. After qualifying in 1950, Friel returned to the Derry area and spent the next ten years as a teacher in various schools. (The figure of the schoolmaster is present in many of his stories and plays.) On 27 December 1954 he married Anne Morrison. They have four daughters and a son—Paddy, Mary, Judy, Sally, and David.

Friel was a member of the Nationalist Party in Derry and involved himself in the political activism of

Dust jacket for the U.S. edition of Friel's 1966 collection of thirteen stories that had previously been published in The New Yorker *or* The Saturday Evening Post *(Richland County Public Library)*

the 1950s and 1960s, the era of the Irish Civil Rights Movement, but he eventually resigned because of the gradual loss of clear direction among nationalist groups. The politics of this period are, however, wholly absent from his writing, and only in two plays, *The Freedom of the City* (produced 1973; published 1974) and *Volunteers* (produced 1975, published 1979), does he engage directly with the sectarian politics and violence that are so dominant a part of Irish political and literary history, especially of the Derry Bogside in which he grew up.

Friel first began to write short stories, a medium in which he soon found relative success, during his years as a schoolteacher. His first story, "The Child," was published in 1952 in *The Bell,* one of the leading Irish literary journals of its time (1940–1954). This story remains uncollected on Friel's own insistence, but Richard Pine has described it as a "seminal work from which flow all his insights into the question of love, language, and freedom." This story describes the disappointment of a child who hopes and prays against experience that his parents will stop their continual fighting. The disruption of the child's world when his drunken father overturns the domestic security established by the mother touches on home and the division between hope and reality, themes central to much of Friel's writing.

In 1956 Friel began a successful relationship with BBC Radio Northern Ireland Home Service, and his first radio story, "The Good Old Days," was broadcast on 2 May of that year. In 1959 Friel published in *The New Yorker* for the first time and was soon offered a contract of first refusal with this influential literary magazine. "The Skelper" appeared on 1 August, and Friel continued to publish in *The New Yorker* through 1965, when he became a full-time dramatist. In an interview with Graham Morison, Friel spoke about that relationship with *The New Yorker,* the influence on his writing of his editor, Roger Angell, and the crucial financial support that allowed him to develop as a writer. Friel also defended himself against the charge made by various critics that his stories are compromised by their *New Yorker* formula, but those stories have a wistful and occasionally sentimental quality that appeals to a foreign sense of idealized Irishness. This interview with Morison is the only published piece in which Friel spoke at length about his short stories; it emphasized his prose rather than his plays.

In addition to his stories, Friel also worked as a freelance journalist, and his articles in *Commonweal,* the *Irish Press, Holiday,* and *The Critic* often engage with the same territory as his stories. They provide important background information to the people and places in Friel's stories as well as autobiographical detail.

Throughout the late 1950s and early 1960s, Friel had stories broadcast on BBC Radio that had already appeared in *The New Yorker,* and stories they rejected were sometimes published in *The Saturday Evening Post.* One story, "The Visitation," was published in *The Kilkenny Magazine* (Autumn/Winter, 1961–1962) and, together with "The Child," remains uncollected.

In 1962 Friel published *The Saucer of Larks,* a collection of eighteen stories from *The New Yorker* and BBC Radio–"The Saucer of Larks," "Among the Ruins," "The Skelper," "The Fawn Pup," "Foundry House," "My True Kinsman," "The Potato Gatherers," "Kelly's Hall," "A Man's World," "Segova, the Savage Turk," "Aunt Maggie, the Strong One," "Johnny and Nick," "The Giant," "Ebb Tide," "Straight from His Colonial Success," "Mr Sing My Heart's Delight," "My Father and the Sergeant," and "Stories on the Verandah." A theme common to almost all the stories in this first collection is the importance of personal or private hope, and the human need to believe that things either are better or can only get better than the evidence allows. The triumph of hope over experience is a theme repeatedly explored in both Irish literature and Irish history, and for Friel this self-deception is also an essential aspect of what to be fully human means. He develops and explores this idea in many stories and later plays, most effectively in one of his greatest dramatic works, *Faith Healer* (1979).

"The Saucer of Larks" is a celebration of the Donegal countryside and of its natural beauty. The local police sergeant "had been twenty-six years in Donegal but there were times when its beauty still shocked him," and he briefly compromises his own authority to ask two Germans to disobey orders from their War Graves Commission and to leave the body of a young pilot buried in a remote rural spot. They refuse, and he is left humiliated and partly admiring of their efficiency and lack of sentimentality. In the end, his desire to leave the pilot at rest within that natural grave is what redeems him in the eyes of the reader.

In "Among the Ruins," the protagonist, Joe, takes his wife and two young children back to his childhood home in rural Donegal, in what becomes a nostalgic return to the world of lost youth. The story is interesting for its attempts at representing consciousness, as Joe recalls his childhood games with his sister; narrative experimentation is rare in Friel's prose writing, although he often employs bold innovations in his plays. A self-conscious use of Irish names evokes a sense of place, showing how geographical association is central to the stirring of memory and a sense of identity, and Friel develops this strategy in other stories and some of his finest plays: "Corradinna lay at the foot of Errigal mountain, a pyramid of granite that rose three thousand feet out of the black bog earth . . . with Meenalaragan and Pigeon Top . . . and Glenmakennif and Altanure. . . ." This listing of geographical place-names is perhaps a reference to the Gaelic tradition of *dinnseanchas* (place-name poems), invoked also by Friel's friend and contemporary, poet Seamus Heaney. In the end, Joe's attempt to recapture memories of childhood is disappointing, as he realizes that the "past is a mirage–a soft illusion into which one steps in order to escape the present." But as he watches his son on the drive back home, Joe experiences an epiphanic moment, realizing that the boy will retain memories of this day, and that they represent continuity between generations of fathers and sons, like a thread through family histories: "The past did have meaning. It was neither reality nor dreams. . . . It was simply continuance, life repeating itself and surviving."

"Foundry House," first published in *The New Yorker* (18 November 1961), is an early version of Friel's play *Aristocrats* (produced 1979; published 1980). Joe Brennan, the local "radio-and-television mechanic in the Music Shop," moves back into the gate lodge of a large country estate, the Foundry House, where his parents once lived. The house is the seat of the Hogans, "one of the best Catholic families in the North of Ireland," and his return is also a retreat into the mythology of his own childhood. When Joe visits the family, he finds only decline, decay, and the collapse of everything he remembered. But he tells his wife and children that it is "the same as ever. A great family. A grand family." Like his namesake in "Among the Ruins," Joe's self-definition derives from the memories of his childhood and thus the importance of sustaining this illusion of unchanging continuity.

Rural Ireland features as a repository for childhood memory in many of these stories, so that a form of Irish pastoral and its association with innocence offers a counterpoint to the urban Derry in which Friel himself grew up. None of Friel's stories has an urban setting, and they are peopled entirely by characters who maintain a slightly naive understanding of the world. No one is particularly evil, and deceptions and lies are perpetrated against the self, toward sustaining illusion, rather than against others.

In "The Potato Gatherers," one of Friel's most popular stories, he inverts his more usual concern with adult memories of childish reverie; the central characters are two boys who skip school to work harvesting potatoes. They do this work largely to support their parents but nonetheless are sustained in their labor by thoughts of how their wages will be spent, of buying "a scout knife with one of those leather scabbards" and "a pair of red silk socks." The appeal of this story derives from its deeply sympathetic portrayal of the rural poor, from the importance, again, of sustaining illusions, and from the place of dignity in the lives of all Friel's characters.

Friel's childhood has proved a rich source for his fiction, and two stories in particular, "Aunt Maggie, the Strong One" and "A Man's World," are also his most overtly autobiographical works, in which he revisits the rural Glenties home of his maternal aunts, even using their real names and incidents from their lives. These stories were also later extensively reused in *Dancing at Lughnasa* (1990), his greatest commercial success as a playwright and later adapted for cinema (1998) by Irish dramatist Frank McGuinness. This interest in personal mythologies of childhood is a recurring theme in many stories, in which the particularities of boyhood are often the focus. Friel has spoken at length of the validity of "how an autobiographical fact can be pure fiction and no less true or reliable for that." That gap between fact and fiction, and its frequent concomitant, hope and despair, and the absolute importance of self-respect and personal dignity, often established or maintained precisely through illusion and individual myth, is what all these stories, in one way or another, have in common.

Front cover for Friel's 1994 republication of stories he selected from The Saucer of Larks: Stories from Ireland *(Thomas Cooper Library, University of South Carolina)*

Friel's stories also impressed theater impresario Sir Tyrone Guthrie and led to an invitation in 1963 for Friel to visit the Guthrie Theatre in Minneapolis, Minnesota. The four months Friel spent observing Guthrie direct *Hamlet* and Anton Chekhov's *Three Sisters* had a profound effect on him and initiated the shift from short-story writer to full-time dramatist. To talk of Chekhov's influence on Friel has become a critical commonplace, but it can be traced to the time spent with Guthrie. The presence of Chekhov, however, is felt in the plays only, while the short stories are peculiarly Irish in origin and influence.

Friel followed his first collection of stories with *The Gold in the Sea* in 1966. This collection of thirteen stories either had previously been aired on BBC Radio or published in *The New Yorker* and *The Saturday Evening Post*. It includes "The Widowhood System," "The Illusionists," "The Queen of Troy Close," "The Death of a Scientific Humanist," "The Wee Lake Beyond," "The Highwayman and the Saint," "The Gold in the Sea," "The Barney Game," "The Diviner," "The Flower of Kiltymore," "Everything Neat and Tidy," "The First of My Sins," and "Ginger Hero."

In the title story, "The Gold in the Sea," a small-time fisherman, Con, in an endless retelling of folk memory, beguiles the narrator and two local men with tales of bullion lying off the coast. The two local men are thrilled by thoughts of salvaging the treasure, of visualizing their community as "sitting on a gold mine," even though Dutch salvage workers have already taken all the gold. At the end Con admits that he wants the men still to believe in the treasure because "they're young men . . . they never got much out of life."

"The Diviner" also appeals to a pastoral, or rural and unchanging, Ireland. In this story, a search for the body of a drowned man fails, so against the wishes of the local priest, the eponymous water diviner is summoned to help find the body. The diviner succeeds where the others failed, but by doing so, he unwittingly destroys the already despairing widow's sense of self. Her husband's body is dredged up from the lake, and empty whiskey bottles are found in his pockets. This disclosure is a final humiliation for her, and she breaks down, deprived of her small-town social standing, and so she grieves for the loss of a "foothold on respectability [that] had almost been established." The folk healer, rather than the priest, divines the true nature and fragility of human relationships, an idea revived in the play *Faith Healer*.

In "The Illusionists," a traveling conjurer, M. L'Estrange, makes his annual visit to a school and is entertained afterward by the headmaster and his family. The headmaster's son, the narrator of the story, is most enchanted by their visitor. He nurtures childish dreams of joining the magician and learning his tricks. But as the long evening draws on, his father and the conjurer quarrel in drunken anger, and the narrator realizes that his father, too, is an illusionist, sustained by false hope and petty ambition.

In these stories, the various misfits and outsiders—whether diviners, magicians, or traveling salesmen—offer a panoply of characters common in much Irish fiction. Friel draws on these types to investigate and analyze ideas central to his own imaginative world. They also offer a retreat into a rural idyll and a myth of an Ireland beyond sectarian politics; they appeal to a wholly idealized version of Irishness, and hence, in part, suggest that Friel was writing for a particular audience.

In his 1965 interview with Morison, Friel spoke of his disdain for some of that early fiction and said stories that "appeared in the collection *The Saucer of Larks* should never have gone into it. Many of them are not good at all." Thus, though Friel was no longer writing short stories, a further collection, of eleven stories from *The Saucer of Larks* and seven stories from *The Gold in the Sea*, was published in 1969, again under the title *The Saucer of Larks*, only with an added subtitle, "Stories from Ireland." This collection afforded Friel the opportunity to collect in a single volume those stories with which he was happy to be associated: "Among the Ruins," "The Death of a Scientific Humanist," "The Potato Gatherers," "The Diviner," "Mr Sing My Heart's Delight," "Foundry House," "The Fawn Pup," "Everything Neat and Tidy," "My True Kinsman," "The Widowhood System," "My Father and the Sergeant," "Ginger Hero," "Aunt Maggie, the Strong One," "The Saucer of Larks," "Straight from His Colonial Success," "The Illusionists," "The Skelper," and "The Gold in the Sea." Another volume, drawing only from this 1969 collection, was published as *Selected Stories* in 1979, and a new edition was published in 1994. The same selection was also published as *The Diviner* in 1983. This revival of interest in these stories derived largely from Friel's growing international reputation as a dramatist.

Friel's stories have been well received, and Walter Allen, a well-known critic of modern English prose, considers Friel "a natural story-writer [who] accepts his findings about life . . . and who transmits admirably the feel of ordinary life." Friel, however, is not considered a master of the form, and the consensus among critics is that all his stories tend toward sameness in idea and execution and are too derivative in style of other Irish writers—especially Frank O'Connor, Sean O'Faolain, and Liam O'Flaherty—to stand as works of great originality. Friel has expressed his indebtedness to O'Faolain on many occasions, and in a 1970 interview with Desmond Rushe, he has spoken also of his admiration for the short fiction of John Updike and V. S. Pritchett. Yet, Friel's stories have played an important part in his development as a major Irish dramatist.

These stories explore the hopes and ambitions of ordinary people in rural Ireland in a time resonant of Friel's youth. While none of the stories can be traced to a particular date, the details—traveling salesmen ("Mr Sing My Heart's Delight"), itinerant entertainers ("The Illusionist"), German war dead ("The Saucer of Larks")—all suggest their origin in the author's own memories from the 1930s, 1940s, and 1950s. Critical studies of Friel's work appear in ever increasing numbers, but most focus exclusively on the dramatic works or discuss the short fiction only as a prelude to themes and ideas in the later drama. Irish academic Seamus Deane, a friend of Friel with a similar background, provides a discussion of Friel's stories in an introduction to the 1983 edition of *The Diviner*. Similarly, John Cronin, in his 1993 article on Friel's fiction, offers an analysis of those stories for their own sake and is valuable for the specificity of its focus. Both critics emphasize the importance of place in Friel's fictional world, and Friel also acknowledges it.

Friel's double birthday, for which there are two birth certificates, and on both of which his name appears as Bernard Patrick Friel, has been used by both Friel himself and literary critics as a metaphor for the duality of the Irish writer's loyalties to the Ireland of his birth and a united Ireland of his literary imagination and political aspiration. In a 1982 interview with Fintan O'Toole, Friel spoke of this sense of displacement within his own country and the division of loyalty: "you can't deposit fealty to a situation that you don't believe in. Then you look south of the border and that enterprise is in so many ways distasteful. And yet both places are your home, so that you are an exile in your own home in some kind of sense." This sense of internal exile and the simultaneous need to belong, with the crucial idea of home and the various tensions arising between them, are recurring themes in much twentieth-century Irish literature and feature in most of Friel's stories and plays. Friel now lives in Greencastle in County Donegal, only a few miles across the border from Derry, where, in 1980, together with Irish actor Stephen Rea, he established the Field Day Theatre Company. Friel subsequently resigned from Field Day in 1994, but the company was committed to the promotion of a Fifth Province, a cultural and literary dimension transcending the four geographical and historical provinces of Ireland, and so an imaginative place without borders, to which Friel and others with similar beliefs could offer fealty.

Brian Friel has received many literary awards throughout his career as a writer, and in 1982 he was elected to Aosdána, a mark of esteem bestowed on Irish writers and artists. In 1987 he was appointed to the Irish Senate, the first writer to be honored in this way since William Butler Yeats, but as a "silent senator," he never took up the opportunity to speak in the Irish legislature.

Friel has said that his maternal grandmother and paternal grandfather were illiterate Irish-speaking peasants, and the short historical distance between them and his own international reputation as a writer in English is an idea that fascinates him and motivates his interest in language and the peculiarities of English as spoken in Ireland. People similar to his own grandparents, often unsophisticated, but defined by their geographical place and their language, populate the imaginative landscape of his short stories.

Interviews:

Peter Lennon, "Playwright of the Western World," *Guardian*, 8 October 1964, p. 8;

Graham Morison, "An Ulster Writer: Brian Friel," *Acorn*, 8 (Spring 1965): 4–15;

Desmond Rushe, "Kathleen Mavourneen, Here Comes Brian Friel," *Word* (February 1970): 12–15;

Paddy Agnew, "Talking to Ourselves," *Magill*, 4, no. 3 (December 1980): 59–61;

Fintan O'Toole, "The Man From God Knows Where," *In Dublin*, no. 165 (28 October 1982): 20–23;

Julie Kavanagh, "Friel at Last," *Vanity Fair* (October 1991): 48–53.

Bibliographies:

George O'Brien, *Brian Friel: A Reference Guide 1962–1992* (New York: G. K. Hall, 1995);

Paul Delaney, "Bibliography," in *Brian Friel in Conversation*, edited by Delaney (Ann Arbor: University of Michigan Press, 2000).

References:

Walter Allen, *The Short Story in English* (Oxford: Clarendon Press, 1981), p. 389;

John Cronin, "'Donging the Tower'–The Past Did Have Meaning: The Short Stories of Brian Friel," in *The Achievement of Brian Friel*, edited by Alan Peacock (Gerrards Cross, U.K.: Colin Smythe, 1993);

Paul Delaney, ed., *Brian Friel in Conversation* (Ann Arbor: University of Michigan Press, 2000);

Richard Pine, *Brian Friel and Ireland's Drama* (London: Routledge, 1990).

Janice Galloway
(2 December 1956 -   )

Pilar Sánchez Calle
University of Jaén, Spain

BOOKS: *The Trick Is to Keep Breathing* (Edinburgh: Polygon Press, 1989; Normal, Ill.: Dalkey Archive Press, 1994);

Blood (London: Secker & Warburg, 1991; New York: Random House, 1991);

A Parcel of Rogues, by Galloway and others (Stromness: Clocktower Press, 1992);

Foreign Parts (London: Cape, 1994; Normal, Ill.: Dalkey Archive Press, 1995);

Where You Find It (London: Cape, 1996; New York: Simon & Schuster, 2002);

Chute, translated by Jean-Michel Desprats (Paris: Editions Solaires Intempestifs, 1998, in French edition only);

House in the Woods: Five Contemporary German Sculptors [Thomas Schütte, Mariele Neudecker, Stephen Balkenhol, Wiebke Siem, Martin Honert], by Galloway and others (Glasgow: Third Eye Centre, 1998);

Clara (London: Cape, 2002; New York: Simon & Schuster, 2003).

OTHER: *The Day I Met the Queen Mother,* edited by Galloway and Hamish Whyte (Aberdeen: Aberdeen University Press, 1990);

Scream if You Want to Go Faster, edited by Galloway and Whyte (Aberdeen: Aberdeen University Press, 1991);

Pig Squealing, edited by Galloway and Whyte (Aberdeen: Aberdeen University Press, 1992);

Newspaper Children, fiction by Galloway to accompany David Finn's exhibition (Leeds: Leeds Art Gallery, 1992);

Meantime: Looking Forward to the Millennium, edited by Galloway (Edinburgh: Polygon in association with Women, 2000);

Anne Bevan: Pipelines, text by Galloway to accompany Ann Bevan's exhibition (Edinburgh: Fruitmarket Gallery, 2000);

Janice Galloway (from the dust jacket for Where You Find It, *2002; Richland County Public Library)*

Monster: An Opera in Two Acts, music by Sally Beamish, libretto by Galloway (Glasgow: Scottish Opera, 2002).

SELECTED PERIODICAL PUBLICATIONS—UNCOLLECTED: "Women and Namelessness—or Why There Are so Few Women Composers," *Edinburgh Review,* 92 (Summer 1994): 101–109;

"Different Oracles: Me and Alasdair Gray," *Review of Contemporary Fiction,* 15 (Summer 1995): 193–196;

"Bad Times," *Review of Contemporary Fiction,* 16 (Spring 1996): 39–43;

"Classical Music in One Easy Step," *Southfields,* 5 (1998): 39–44.

Janice Galloway's short stories, articles, and novels are part of the revival of fiction in the west of Scotland alongside the work of other Glasgow-based writers of the late twentieth century such as Alasdair Gray and James Kelman. Galloway's first novel, *The Trick Is to Keep Breathing* (1989), won the Mind/Allan Lane Book of the year award and the E. M. Forster Award, and her subsequent books had highly positive critical receptions. Galloway's works are now included on English literature reading lists, though still more often in courses devoted to women's or Scottish studies. Gender and Scottishness constitute two of Galloway's most significant concerns. Her formal experiments emphasize the physicality of the human body and of the literary text itself; however, Galloway's emphasis on the accessibility of fiction can be appreciated in her use of both high culture and pop culture in her texts, including social commentary, local language, and caustic humor.

Janice Galloway was born 2 December 1956 in Saltcoats, Scotland, the second daughter of James Galloway and Janet Clark McBride. Her mother belonged to a mining family and had worked as a domestic servant and carder in the cotton mills. Galloway's father was a bus driver. Their first child was stillborn, and their second, Nora, was born in 1938. Galloway remembers her mother saying that her birth, much later than those of the other children, had been a mistake. Galloway's parents separated when she was four, and her father died two years later. He had been an absent figure even before his death. Consequently, Galloway grew up with her much older sister and her mother. Her childhood was often difficult and painful, and although she liked school and was bright and attentive, her love of reading was not encouraged.

Galloway enrolled at Glasgow University to study music and English, but she was disappointed with the education she received there because she did not find the intellectual freedom she was looking for. Galloway became aware that few women and Scots were on her English literature syllabi. She also felt uncomfortable because of students' and faculty's feelings of inferiority as a result of their Scottishness and their accent, which was widely regarded as middle-class. By her third year, Galloway suffered a period of depression and took a leave of absence. She spent that year doing social work and then returned to the university in 1977, finishing her degree and taking an M.A. in philosophy and French in 1978. Galloway became a schoolteacher and worked for ten years at the same school. She left in 1989 to write full-time. During the 1990s Galloway served as a writer-in-residence at four Scottish prisons and became highly involved with the Scottish literary scene. She is an active contributor to the *Edinburgh Review* as well as an occasional contributor to the *New Statesman*. At various times she has been a music reviewer for Radios 3 and 4 and the *Glasgow Herald,* as well as classical-music correspondent for *Scotland on Sunday*. She has a son, James Alexander Galloway McNaught, and lives in Glasgow.

In a 1999 interview with Christie Leigh March, Galloway confessed, "I want to write as though having a female perspective is normal which is a damn sight harder than it sounds." She extended this idea of reprioritizing to making Scottish literature a normal perspective. Galloway's literary influences have to do with writers whose point in common is their writing from the margins. She cites Tom Leonard, Toni Morrison, Marguerite Duras, Machado de Assis, Jessie Kesson, Virginia Woolf, and Lewis Grassic Gibbon, but she refers to "aesthetic encounter, not acquisition."

Some literary critics have focused on Galloway's exploration of Scottishness and female identity, whereas others have analyzed her interest in the physicality of the body and have discussed her textual form as well. Other aspects of Galloway's writing that have aroused critical interest are the sense that Scottish culture is peripheral and that gender is as well. This link between gender, body, and nation is considered the core of Galloway's works, exemplified in concerns such as the subordination of women in society, the interaction between mind and body, the status of the Scottish people and language in Britain and the world, the significance of textual innovation, and the problematic nature of family relationships.

Before publishing her first novel, Galloway had already written some stories as a means of experimenting with fiction. This formal experimentation is present in her first work, *The Trick Is to Keep Breathing* (1989). Written largely as a first-person narration, with little dialogue, the novel tells the story of Joy Stone, a schoolteacher in her late twenties who suffers from depression after her lover drowned while they were on vacation together. As Douglas Gifford notes, some features of this novel, such as an immediate sense of the absurd and a keen eye for banal detail, together with a sense of horror, are shared by Galloway's collections of short stories.

In 1991 Galloway published her first collection of short stories, *Blood,* which was well received; some of the stories had appeared first in such periodicals as the *Edinburgh Review* and the *New Statesman*. More than developing a plotline, the pieces in this collection show female characters facing certain events—a girl's first period (in "Blood"), an encounter with hostile male types (in "Frostbite and Fearless"), the death of a neighbor (in "Breaking Through"), the discovery of

Dust jacket for the U.S. edition of Galloway's 1991 collection of stories about the emotional lives of women (Richland County Public Library)

sexuality (in "A Week with Uncle Felix")—and struggling in the middle of difficult relationships and hostile environments. Little happens in these stories in which what matters is the emotional impact of the situations on the characters. According to Mary McGlynn and Josiane Paccaud-Huguet, the stories challenge readers' traditional expectations of narrative gratification and sense of resolution, and the idea of fragmentation is used both as a motif and as a structuring principle.

In the title story, "Blood," Galloway uses a variety of images and ideas of blood to suggest the moods of a schoolgirl during the day she visits a dentist to have a tooth pulled, and her period starts. The girl is overwhelmed by guilt and shame. Her feminine body is a subject of both fear and embarrassment to her under her unsuccessful attempts to make it look clean.

The grotesque element can be appreciated in the stories titled "Scenes from the Life number 23: Paternal Advice," "Scenes from the Life number 29: Dianne," "Scenes from the Life number 26: The Community and the Senior Citizen," and "Scenes from the Life number 27: Living In," in which Galloway shocks the reader by challenging his/her narrative expectations with merely scenic presentation and the use of theme in the opening sentences of the stories. This technique makes readers feel they are entering a closed world from which they can only be alienated. Gifford thinks Galloway also handles west-of-Scotland macho humor effectively, parodying male attitudes. In "Scenes from the Life number 23: Paternal Advice," Sammy encourages Wee Sammy, his son, to jump into his arms, but when the boy does so, Sammy steps aside to let the boy fall onto the ground: "SAMMY: Let that be a lesson to you son. Trust nae cunt." Galloway makes use of black humor to suggest that human nature is not trustworthy.

"Two Fragments" includes a mixture of black humor and surrealism. In this story, the first-person narrator, a grown woman, becomes a little girl listening to her Mother's comic and dreadful tales about how her father lost his fingers by eating chips too quickly, and how her grandmother lost her eye after suffering an attack from the tomcat she was trying to boil to death. The black humor and surrealism cover the truth of two facts: the father lost his finger in the army, and the grandmother's eye was taken away by the explosion of impure coal.

"Frostbite" and "Fearless" have as protagonists girls having to deal with hostile male types. In the first story, a young girl on her way home from piano practice encounters "a man lumping up and over the top of the hill, flapping after the buses." She helps him, but his response toward her is hostile and portrays his underlying misogyny. Yet, the girl expresses her own anger at the end of the story, a reaction illustrating that the male discourse about "bastart women" does not have any power over her.

The young protagonist of "Fearless" is not afraid of Fearless, a man who "just appeared suddenly, shouting threats up the main streets" at people who have to avert their eyes. One day Fearless chooses the narrator's mother as his victim, but the girl looks back at him in anger and kicks him, exposing him for the bully he is. Galloway suggests that the narrator's victory is limited because, as Fearless limps away, the girl's mother upbraids her; yet, the story also presents a new generation of women who are not intimidated by misogyny: "The outrage is still strong, and I kick like a mule."

Galloway experiments with traditional supernatural elements, which lend shock value in "Breaking Through," in which a girl, Janet, lives with her mother next to the cemetery wall and to another flat occupied by an old woman, Bessie, and her cat, Blackie. On one visit, Blackie falls into the fire and burns. Janet does not do anything to rescue him, because "She had been taught to respect his privacy too well." A few days later the old lady walks into the fire herself, and the girl lifts the poker to help her die. Galloway suggests Janet's desire for the touch of death, first with the cat, then with the old lady.

In "Fair Ellen and the Wanderer Returned," the reader finds a kind of subverted ballad rewritten from the perspective of the female. Traditional situations appear in this subgenre—such as the man who is at the center of the woman's vision and life, and the man who goes away while the woman is supposed to wait for him. These clichés, however, are systematically questioned. For example, when her beloved returns from several years of being away, Ellen is a tired and dissapointed middle-aged woman. Her voice, "full of splinters," reveals the dullness of the waiting years and the unhappiness of a loveless marriage in the beloved's absence. Instead of accepting him with joy, as in the traditional tales, Ellen shows resentment.

The last and longest story, "A Week with Uncle Felix," is told from the point of view of a young girl who goes to spend a week with her dead father's brother. Senga, the protagonist, is an orphan who experiences loss as she is initiated into the knowledge of death and the discovery of sexuality, both of which entail the awareness of absence and sexual difference. Senga develops a sense of guilt about her body, and the idea that everything is her fault resounds in her mind, particularly when her uncle remarks, before he tries to abuse her, that she is going to be a "wanton little thing." Josiane Paccaud-Huguet suggests that the story's circular structure reinforces the lack of a conclusive answer to Senga's father's death and to the mysteries and pains of her discovery of sexuality.

Galloway's next book is the novel *Foreign Parts* (1994), which tells the story of two middle-aged social workers, Rona and Cassie, on vacation in France. Galloway explores in a humorous way the pressures of commercial tourism by presenting two characters with different ways of perceiving the holidays. Their different views lead to the emergence of repressed tensions between them. Toward the end of the novel, both friends move toward mutual understanding.

Where You Find It (1996), Galloway's most recent short-story collection, focuses on romantic relationships. They suggest the ambivalence of affection and the dimension of disturbance that powerful feelings always include. Galloway re-creates her characters' fragmented impressions and moments of realization, suggesting the elusiveness of love, human warmth, and happiness. The point of consciousness is usually the woman's, although Galloway shows a sympathy for both parties in male-female relations. Both men and women are presented in unattractive lights.

The main stories tell the reader about varieties of contemporary sexual and emotional relationships. They tell of couples in typical modern premarital live-in situations. Galloway observes the rites of passage of these mismatched couples, exploring the banality of their relationships, their failed attempts at communicating their intimate feelings, and the gaps even in closeness that characterize so many human connections. In the first story, "Valentine," the female narrator wishes to please an overly critical man. She rationalizes her boyfriend's inadequacies while she dismisses her own responses as indications of her weakness. "The Bridge" presents the conversation between Fiona, a young artist, and Charlie, a successful painter. Charlie seems to inhabit the world of art, despising what he calls "women's priorities." The fascination Fiona feels for Charlie slowly gives way to feelings of deception and anger after his careless remarks about everything that is important for Fiona: love, cultural identity, human connection, and life.

Stories such as "Waiting for Marilyn" and "Hope" exude anxiety, frustration, and disappointment. The first story gives a short account of a woman's sexual fantasies, while having her hair done, about her favorite hairdresser, Marilyn. The woman reveals her increasing mixture of pleasure and anxiety at being touched by Marilyn, as well as her careful look at Marilyn's sexy outfit. The most trivial occurrence is perceived by this woman as an exciting experience. Everything changes when she sees something glittering on Marilyn's hand, and it turns out to be an engagement ring. Suddenly the protagonist's fantasies seem like wasted thoughts, like an ironic but painful pastime; she thinks, "You can't work out why this is washing over you like iced water, whether you're jealous. Of whom." In "Hope" a man offers a snapshot of his domestic life, including a portrait of his wife that suggests his entrapment in a loveless marriage, his boredom, and his nausea. As usual in Galloway's fiction, emotions and feelings are evoked through the presence of objects and the physical description of the domestic environment. The atmosphere becomes more and more suffocating, but a coming change is suggested as the protagonist thinks, "Sooner or later I will have to open my eyes."

"After the Rains" and "Tourists from the South Arrive in the Independent State" touch upon the surreal and the odd. In the first story, rain has fallen for months, giving way to glorious sunlight and a rainbow while people start turning into flowers and fruits. This Gothic situation of unexpected transformations may be connected with the central theme of this collection: the

Dust jacket for the 2002 U.S. edition of Galloway's 1996 collection of short stories about romantic relationships (Richland County Public Library)

elusiveness of love and its frequent evolution into something unexpected and horrific. The second story parodies stereotypical ideas about Scottish hospitality by describing the arrival of a group of foreigners to an independent Scotland. Notions of a better postindependent state are mocked by the cold treatment the tourists receive. The response of the natives is not necessarily nicer or better than before.

Galloway also explores the realm of human experience beyond the possibility of love. In "Someone Had To," the angry voice of an adult man justifies the extreme punishment given to his young niece. According to him, she is insolent and proud and needs a lesson. First, he shuts her in a cupboard, but the girl starts whining and scratching the cupboard door. He then burns the girl with his cigarette. As the girl does not apologize, "the INSIDE OF HER black mouth open not saying a word just WATCHING while I DON'T TELL ME IT'S NORMAL FOR A CHILD NOT TO CRY OUT," the man overflows with irritation and hurt feelings at his failure to make his niece behave well. Finally, he introduces her into a bathtub full of boiling water. The last image is that of his niece's blue eyes: "Those big blue eyes still staring up like butter wouldn't melt."

Galloway departs from Scotland in her new novel *Clara,* published in 2002. The book is about Clara Schumann, a gifted musician and composer who subordinated her own career interests to her husband's and to motherhood. In McGlynn's words, Galloway combines her passion for music and her permanent interest in the historic marginalization of women in this work, the structure of which is inspired by a Schumann song cycle.

The multiplicity of voices, Galloway's vivid language, her fresh and ironic look at old and new themes concerning women's existences and contemporary urban life, and her formal experimentation have proved her artistry and her creative powers. Her books are demanding because little happens, a fact that challenges readers' expectations about fiction. Galloway, however, has always been interested in breaking linguistic hierarchies and in giving space to both popular culture and so-called high culture in her books. She enjoys a high popularity in Scotland and the United Kingdom, and her novels and short-story collections have received many awards.

Interview:

Christie Leigh March, "Interview with Janice Galloway," *Edinburgh Review,* 101 (Summer 1999): 85–98.

References:

Douglas Gifford, "Contemporary Fiction II: Seven Writers in Scotland," in *A History of Scottish Women's Writing,* edited by Gifford and Dorothy McMillan (Edinburgh: Edinburgh University Press, 1997), pp. 606–620;

Alison Lumsden, "Scottish Women's Short Stories: 'Repositories of Life Swiftly Apprehended,'" in *Contemporary Scottish Women Writers,* edited by Aileen Christianson and Lumsden (Edinburgh: Edinburgh University Press, 2000), pp. 156–169;

Mary McGlynn, "Janice Galloway," *Review of Contemporary Fiction,* 31 (Summer 2001): 7–40;

Josiane Paccaud-Huguet, "Breaking Through Cracked Mirrors. The Short Stories of Janice Galloway," *Etudes Ecossaises,* 2 (1993): 5–29.

Anthony Glavin
(28 August 1946 -   )

Pradyumna S. Chauhan
Arcadia University

BOOKS: *One for Sorrow and Other Stories* (Swords, Ireland: Poolbeg Press, 1980);
Nighthawk Alley (Dublin: New Island Books, 1997);
The Draughtsman and the Unicorn (Dublin: New Island Books, 1999).

OTHER: "Home(boy) Thoughts from Abroad," in *Playing the Field: Irish Writers on Sport,* edited by George O'Brien (Dublin: New Island Books, 2000), pp. 74–88;
"Treasure Island," in *Stories for Jamie,* edited by John Scally (Dublin: Blackwater Press, 2002), pp. 117–122.

SELECTED PERIODICAL PUBLICATIONS–UNCOLLECTED: "Happy Memories of the Other Cambridge," *Irish Times/Education and Living Supplement,* 14 October 1997, p. 12;
"The Stairway Behind the Stage," *Irish Times Magazine,* 17 March 2001, p. 82;
"An Irishman's Diary," *Irish Times,* 1 February 2003, p. 15;
"An Irishman's Diary," *Irish Times,* 14 April 2003, p. 15;
"An Irishman's Diary," *Irish Times,* 5 July 2003, p. 13;
"An Irishman's Diary," *Irish Times,* 11 August 2003, p. 15;
"An Irishman's Diary," *Irish Times,* 6 October 2003, p. 15;
"An Irishman's Diary," *Irish Times,* 8 November 2003, p. 19;
"An Irishman's Diary," *Irish Times,* 13 January 2004, p. 15;
"An Irishman's Diary," *Irish Times,* 20 October 2004, p. 14.

Anthony Glavin is a writer whose life and work bridge two countries, the United States and Ireland. Born in Boston, Massachusetts, Glavin's literary output—two well-received volumes of short stories and a novel (itself a development of one of his pieces of short fiction)—dates from his settling in the Irish Republic.

Anthony Glavin (courtesy of the author)

His work belongs to a development of the Anglo-Irish short story—the Irish American story—a narrative distinguished as much by its form as by its wit and content. Glavin's fiction is concerned with migrants and the displaced, with their psychological makeup and their outcast status, and with their hopes, struggles, and subterfuges. In this respect, his work achieves a resonance beyond its particular Irish American setting. His principal characters belong to the segment of modern humanity that, once exiled from home, never puts down roots anywhere, not even if it goes back home. Psychologically, these people are trapped in transitory states forever. In his transnational focus, Glavin is emblematic of the position of many writers in the late twentieth and early twenty-first centuries.

Anthony Glavin—story writer, novelist, and essayist—was born 28 August 1946, in Boston, Massachusetts. His father, Anthony G. Glavin, was a newspaperman and market researcher. His mother, Mary Alice (née McInerny) taught history at Sarah Lawrence College, Bronxville, New York, before her marriage; later, she worked as a research librarian. The Glavins and the McInernys had, according to the family legend, emigrated from Ireland during the period of the Irish Famine, around 1849—the former from County Kerry, the latter from County Clare. The Glavins, according to the family story, landed first in Canada, and the McInernys in Baltimore. For all his Irish ancestry deriving from distant Irish counties, Anthony Glavin grew up, as he says in his interview with Ciaran Carty of the *Tribune Magazine* (12 October 1997), "in a very typical greater Boston Irish American milieu." This milieu had consequences, for, as Colin Lacey writes, "Steeped in Irish literature and culture and suffused with Boston Irish politics, he grew up literate, Catholic, and staunchly Democratic."

Glavin went to an urban public school in the Greater Boston area—the Cambridge High and Latin School, Cambridge, Massachusetts. Located within a large working-class and African American population, the Cambridge school could at once boast of typical American diversity and a prestigious academic neighborhood. Although the school, as Glavin recounts in "Happy Memories of the Other Cambridge" (*Irish Times*, 14 October 1997), was "less than half a mile away from Harvard University, and MIT was close by, neither college had any involvement with the school." All the same, Cambridge High and Latin School was well known for its high academic record and "a particularly good English department which was full of unmarried women with Irish surnames." Glavin acknowledges, "I was taught by Higginses, O'Sullivans, Murphys, Conlons and Toomeys." Despite the predominance of Irish American teachers, he says that "at school, I read no Irish literature." His home, presided over by educated parents, was different. His mother had inherited the library of the South Bend, Indiana, Irish Women's Society when it closed. "And so from quite a young age I was aware of Ireland's literary heritage," Glavin recounts.

In the mid 1930s, the Glavin couple ran a weekly newspaper in Pawling, a small New York State town, before they moved on to Boston. The father then became publisher and the mother editor, "a division of labor which," says Glavin, "meant my mother got to photograph my father shaking the hand of Franklin Delano Roosevelt, when FDR visited the town on a presidential campaign stop." However, the mother, according to Glavin's account in *The Irish Times* (14 April 2003), had "neglected to check if there was any film in the camera!" Glavin had his own share of important political encounters during his years in Boston. In 1952, for example, when he was six, his mother took him to Boston "to see the Democratic presidential candidate, Adlai Stevenson, sweep by in a Cadillac." His elder sister Kathleen stated in later years that, at nine, she was allowed to sit on John F. Kennedy's lap when he was a congressman and their aunt Kate was a lobbyist in Washington, D.C.

Brought up in an active political atmosphere, young Glavin volunteered to work in the campaigns of several Democratic candidates for national offices including those of Edward Kennedy and Father Robert Drinan, an anti-Vietnam War Jesuit, who was successfully elected to Congress in 1970. As an activist, Glavin worked for George McGovern, who, according to "An Irishman's Diary" in *The Irish Times* (14 April 2003), was "one of the best presidents that America failed to elect." Glavin recalls, too, that when he was a student, as part of the "term-time job on the Harvard Buildings and Grounds Porter Crew, I cleaned the freshman dormitory bathroom of Al Gore and actor Tommy Lee in either Matthews or Weld Halls." "They were both a year behind me and," he reports in *The Irish Times* (14 October 1997), "at the time were just regular guys." From such associations, after earning a B.A. from Harvard (1968), he volunteered, as a member of the Peace Corps, to work in Costa Rica for two years. His love of the battle of political ideas has continued into his later years. In 2004, he crossed the Atlantic to work through the fall for Senator John Kerry's presidential campaign in Florida.

After completing his term with the Peace Corps, though, Glavin returned to the Cambridge High and Latin School to teach. During his service to the school and its community (1970–1974), he went on TV once, according to an interview in the *Tribune Magazine* (12 October 1997), to defend the rioting students of the school only to be "denounced as a commie." In 1976 he earned an M.A. in English from Boston College.

Although he kept returning to the Boston area, in 1974 Glavin decided to move to Ireland. "I wanted to chance my arm at writing," he says in an interview given to the *Cork Examiner* (25 October 1997), "and it was a choice between Ireland and Spain." The pull of home won out, for, as he says, "I had visited Donegal in 1967 and was struck by the beauty of the place. I had been well aware of Ireland—my mother was a keen reader of Irish literature and I grew up in a state o'chassis [i.e., of chaos], . . . so I went back to Donegal to try to write."

Glavin's literary career began with the publication of some chiseled and taut stories in the series "New Irish Writing" for *The Irish Press,* in *Best Irish Short Stories 3* (1978), and in the magazine *Irish Heritage*. Glavin's first book of stories, *One for Sorrow and Other Stories,* was published by Poolbeg Press in 1980 in Dublin, the place where he met Adrienne, his life partner. They have three children: a son (Neill) and two daughters (Caitrin and Aoife).

One for Sorrow and Other Stories, a collection of ten pieces, brings together a large cast of characters, from consultants to speculators, from the so-called saints and scholars to delusional figures trapped in fantasies of what never was. The stories, anchored in finely etched landscapes, whether of Ireland or Majorca, summon up a host of moving memories or an array of transient moods. Typical are the preoccupation and atmosphere of the first story, "Kinnakillew Sunday," which begins, "It was a spring evening at a rock quarry south of Boston when Liam finally laid hold of what had taken his uncle's life." In Ireland, Liam had never "seen a woman naked whom he had not bedded," and here he is treading water with Lisa, a new friend, obliged by her example to take off his clothes, noticing how "her breasts look no larger than [his] own." The new sensation of nakedness in public waters suddenly illuminates for Liam the cause of his uncle's drowning in the bay he had swum across hundreds of times. His father's explanation of years ago that the uncle perhaps did not want to "come in on the strand where there were people, with himself exposed" begins to make sense. That is why he was discovered dashed against the rocks. Thus enlightened, Liam sinks into Lisa's arms, "matching the movement of the water with Lisa's breathing." The moment of lovemaking reveals buried memories surfacing and the Irish rural life as lying exposed beside the liberated, and liberating, daughter of metropolitan Boston. Frequently, Glavin's unhurried narrative and modes of indirection end with a Joycean epiphany, and not the least because of his startling images. Cassie, in "Nettle Broth," has been enchanted by Declan, a reclusive jeweler, especially by his choice of words. The reader learns that "if it had been his language that first attracted her, she soon came to feel herself all filigree and arabesque beneath his touch." The imagery makes an imperceptible transition from the jeweler's art creating silver filigree or jeweled arabesque designs to his sensuous touch awakening sensations, all filigree and arabesque, inside Cassie.

Glavin's involvement with the Irish literary scene intensified in the 1980s. He had been contributing stories to the "New Irish Writing" page of the *Irish Press,*

Front cover for Glavin's 1980 collection of ten stories set in Ireland and Majorca (Bruccoli Clark Layman Archives)

and in 1985 he became the editor of the *Irish Press* page, still striving to make time for his own fictional writing. Soon he was appointed the literary editor of New Island Books, where Dermot Bolger, a colleague, suggested that he extend his short story "Transplants" into a novel. "Transplants" had been published in *Phoenix Irish Short Stories 1997*. Glavin followed Bolger's advice. That same year *Nighthawk Alley* was published, a novel interweaving lives of immigrants, exiles, and itinerant cast-offs, all caught in awkward relations, gingerly putting down roots in a new soil. The novel is full of horticultural images and gardening metaphors. Mickey McKenna, the garage-owner narrator, tries to persuade Fintan, a recent arrival and new "transplant" from Ireland, to take up gardening. "As if by putting in a few vegetables, he might also put down a few roots." As it turns out, Fintan never does; he has pushed his car off a cliff, thrown his clothes and a new bowling ball after it,

Front cover for Glavin's 1999 collection of minimalist postmodern stories about protagonists who are all, in some fashion, adrift in the modern world (Bruccoli Clark Layman Archives)

and moved on—his current address unknown. As the story comes to a close, McKenna delivers a homily about the basic immigrant existence: "I don't know you're ever anything but a transplant, away from home. And I know I carry Dublin inside me." If his characters are transplants abroad, they are aliens when back home, as if the ties once severed cannot ever be restored.

Whatever the gravitational pull of Dublin on the transplants, the focus of the novel is truly the geography of Boston. The ethos of neighborhoods from Harvard Square to Trowbridge Street, from Sheppard Street to Fenway Park, is carefully presented. Indeed, the spilling trash, the rusting cars lining the alleys, the smoky cafés, and the clanking diners preserve an era of the history of South Boston, where old acquaintances can recall their past mishaps, report the latest from "the land across the pond" (that is, Ireland), or just trade gossip about someone's loss or illness. Gradually, Glavin conjures up the communal life of the city of Boston, with its fairs and ballparks, its railway yards and its beaches.

Nighthawk Alley, superficially a narrative of the lives of the displaced—Irish, Italian, Jamaican, and Polish—most of them raised on the same diet of "potatoes, Church, and alcohol," is many things besides. It is an exhibition of the spiritual enigma of expatriates, who live "here" but dwell "there," unable to depart from their new environs and yet unable to escape the grip of their old homeland. To that extent, the novel is about the recent migrants in every part of the world, cast up, like Glavin's Irish characters, "somewhere in between." The unsentimental and impartial treatment of the modern phenomenon of migration of peoples opens up a new seam of human experience for contemporary fiction. No less clearly does the novel offer a critique of the contemporary cultural scene. By importing into the story a naive Irishman from home and a disillusioned black Vietnam veteran, Glavin offers a convincing commentary on contemporary American manners. Similar to Henry James, Glavin brings together representatives of two cultures for transvaluation, each group crosslighting the heritage of the other. The reader encounters remarks such as "that's what people do here—buy a nice house, but never stay home," or "people here spend a lifetime blaming their parents for what they did, or didn't, do. Instead of simply getting on with it." Allowing the newcomer the privilege of the outsider to comment on what is new, odd, or different, Glavin creates suitable space in the novel for a cultural critique. On the whole, despite passages of wit and irreverence, *Nighthawk Alley* is a grim tale of all those nighthawks, "trying to steady the nerve with cigarettes or coffee, or deaden it with alcohol . . . all uprooted or rootless transplants that somehow didn't take."

Although Glavin has finished another novel, tentatively called "Something to Write Home About," his latest publication to date is *The Draughtsman and the Unicorn* (1999), a collection of thirteen stories, all new except part 1 of "Of Saints, Scholars and Dogs," which, under the title "Of Saints and Scholars," had appeared in *One for Sorrow*. Wider in its psychological scope and bustling with characters departing for the United States or Nicaragua, or arriving from Germany or Ghana, this collection boasts well-crafted stories studded with symbolism. Though Ireland is still the locale of many stories, a wider world and its anxieties form the background.

In the title story, "The Draughtsman and the Unicorn," Nicholas, a draftsman from London, visits Glenmore in the company of Elke, "a German lass" with a kind of cone, her unicorn, atop her blonde head. A trained draftsman, Nick has given up the job in his father's architectural firm in London to try hang gliding in Ireland. While he goes around surveying the cliffs of Glenmore, Elke drifts closer to Timothy, their painter host, who is intrigued by her. On his first attempt at hang gliding the next day, Nick plunges four hundred feet to the rocks. He survives, suffering nothing worse than a broken arm and a damaged leg. Timothy is left thinking of Icarus, who had gone beyond the bounds of caution, and the unicorn, so vulnerable in a world bent on seeking instant gratification. The fleeting summer images and emotions are rendered in this work through famous artworks: Glenmore scenes "surface out of Brueghel," and a local "looks as if he walked straight out of [Van Gogh's] *The Potato Eaters*." Such images enhance the unreal, dream-like relations and expectations of Elke and Nicholas.

The protagonists of most of the stories in this collection are, like Nicholas, of *Luftmensch* lineage—"Men of air who operate without timetables, floating through life in irresponsible, solipsistic fashion." Without anchor anywhere, they are adrift, appearing and disappearing like Fintan in *Nighthawk Alley,* "more a once-off annual than a perennial." In "Salvage," Dinny Flynn of Mayo, Ireland, is "so utterly seduced by Massachusetts," its toy cars, and motor lanes, that he exchanges everything for the American Dream, only to end up with his auto, a Delta 88, "wrapped around a lamppost." The news is received by his friends far away, the "two Irish exiles in a Nicaraguan rain forest." They keep wondering what Dinny's German fiancée would see in Mayo, "seated in the wake house, shaking hands with an entire parish, puzzling at . . . the plates of cigarettes, trays of tea and sandwiches." Glavin in this story writes of a world out of key, an unstable universe where everything seems out of place, where all dreams are only temporary adjustments to reality, and where all acts are only matters of expediency.

In light of his fiction, short and long, Anthony Glavin emerges as a narrator of a postmodern humanity, the mobile and the unhoused. He resorts to flashbacks to reconstruct the past that his wandering characters are unable to exit. He discards linear narrative as well to indicate the absence of any rational structure from the lives of his floating characters. Yet, in the words of Mickey McKenna, the narrator of *Nighthawk Alley,* he is "happy just to have a ringside seat. Looking on and looking back," content to portray the scenes as he finds them, without embarrassment or embellishment. As Noel Hannan, reviewing *The Draughtsman and the Unicorn* for *Local Ireland* (16 December 2002), said, "Sentimentality is not something [Glavin] could be accused of." His emotions are as sparse as his style is minimalist.

Interviews:

Ciaran Carty, "From Boston Student Radical to New Irish Writer," *Tribune Magazine,* 12 October 1997, p. 17;

Colin Lacy, "The Long Way Home," *Cork Examiner,* 25 October 1997, p. 24;

Allegra Wong, "An Interview with Anthony Glavin," *Full Circle Journal* (Spring/Summer 2003): 5–16.

Alasdair Gray
(28 December 1934 -   )

Gavin Miller
University of Glasgow

See also the Alasdair Gray entries in *DLB 194: British Novelists Since 1960, Second Series* and *DLB 261: British Fantasy and Science-Fiction Writers Since 1960.*

BOOKS: *Dialogue,* Play of the Month, no. 3 (Kirknewton: Scottish Theatre, 1971);

The Comedy of the White Dog (Glasgow: Print Studio, 1979)—comprises "The Comedy of the White Dog" and "The Crank Who Made the Revolution";

Lanark: A Life in Four Books (Edinburgh: Canongate, 1981; New York: Harper & Row, 1981);

Unlikely Stories, Mostly (Edinburgh: Canongate, 1983; New York: Penguin, 1984; revised edition, Edinburgh: Canongate, 1997);

1982 Janine (London: Cape, 1984; New York: Viking, 1984);

Lean Tales, by Gray, James Kelman, and Agnes Owens (London: Cape, 1985);

The Fall of Kelvin Walker: A Fable of the Sixties (Edinburgh: Canongate, 1985; New York: George Braziller, 1986);

Alasdair Gray, Saltire Self-Portraits, no. 4 (Edinburgh: Saltire Society, 1988);

Old Negatives: Four Verse Sequences (London: Cape, 1989);

McGrotty and Ludmilla; or, The Harbinger Report (Glasgow: Dog and Bone, 1990);

Something Leather (London: Cape, 1990; New York: Random House, 1990);

Poor Things: Episodes from the Early Life of Archibald McCandless M.D. Scottish Public Health Officer (London: Bloomsbury, 1992; New York: Harcourt Brace Jovanovich, 1992);

Independence: Why Scots Should Rule Scotland (Edinburgh: Canongate, 1992); revised as *Why Scots Should Rule Scotland, 1997: A Carnaptious History of Britain from Roman Times Until Now* (Edinburgh: Canongate, 1997);

Ten Tales Tall and True: Social Realism, Sexual Comedy, Science Fiction and Satire (London: Bloomsbury, 1993; New York: Harcourt Brace Jovanovich, 1993);

Alasdair Gray (photograph by Renate von Mangoldt; Bruccoli Clark Layman Archives)

A History Maker (Edinburgh: Canongate, 1994; San Diego: Harcourt Brace, 1996);

Mavis Belfrage: A Romantic Novel with Five Shorter Tales (London: Bloomsbury, 1996)—comprises *Mavis Belfrage,* "A Night Off," "Mr. Goodchild," "Money," "Edison's Tractatus," and "The Shortest Tale";

Working Legs: A Two-Act Play for People without Them, Dog and Bone Playbook, no. 1 (Glasgow: Dog and Bone, 1997);

Sixteen Occasional Poems: 1990–2000 (Glasgow: Morag McAlpine, 2000);

A Short Survey of Classic Scottish Writing, Canongate Pocket Classics, no. 7 (Edinburgh: Canongate, 2001);

The Ends of Our Tethers: 13 Sorry Stories (Edinburgh: Canongate, 2003; New York: Canongate, 2003);

How We Should Rule Ourselves, by Gray and Adam Tomkins (Edinburgh: Canongate, 2005).

PLAY PRODUCTIONS: *Dialogue,* Edinburgh, Pool Lunch Hour Theatre, 1971;

Homeward Bound, Edinburgh, Pool Lunch Hour Theatre, 1971;

The Fall of Kelvin Walker, touring, Scottish Stage Company, 1972;

The Loss of the Golden Silence, Edinburgh, Pool Lunch Hour Theatre, 1973;

McGrotty and Ludmilla, Glasgow, Tron Theatre, 1975;

Tickly Mince, by Gray, Tom Leonard, and Liz Lochhead, Glasgow, Tron Theatre, and Edinburgh, The Pleasance, 1982;

The Pie of Damocles, by Gray, Lochhead, Leonard, and James Kelman, Glasgow, Tron Theatre, and Edinburgh, The Pleasance, 1983;

Working Legs: A Play for People without Them, Cumbernauld, Alpha Project, 1998.

PRODUCED SCRIPTS: "Under the Helmet," BBC Television, 1965;

"The Fall of Kelvin Walker," BBC 2 Television, 1968;

"Quiet People," BBC Radio Scotland, 1968;

"Dialogue," BBC Radio, 1969;

"Thomas Muir of Huntershill," BBC Radio Scotland, 1970;

"The Night Off," BBC Radio Scotland, 1971;

"Dialogue," Granada Television, 1972;

"Martin," television, Scottish BBC Schools, 1972;

"Agnes Belfrage/Cholchis/Triangles," Granada Television, 1972;

"Today and Yesterday," BBC Television, 1972;

"The Man Who Knew about Electricity," BBC Television, 1973;

"Honesty," Granada Television, 1974;

"The Loss of the Golden Silence," BBC Radio Scotland, 1974;

"The Harbinger Report," BBC Radio, 1975;

"McGrotty and Ludmilla," BBC Radio, 1975;

"Henry Prince," as Martin Green, Granada Television, 1976;

"The Gadfly," Granada Television, 1977;

"The Vital Witness," Scottish BBC Radio, 1979;

"Near the Driver," radio, West Deutsche Rundfunk, 1983;

"The Story of a Recluse," adapted from the story by Robert Louis Stevenson, BBC 2 Television, 1987.

RECORDINGS: *Some Unlikely Stories,* read by Gray, Canongate Audio, 1994;

Scenes from Alasdair Gray's Lanark, 2 volumes, read by Gray, Canongate Audio, 1995–1996–comprises volume 1, *Lanark and Rima* (1995), and volume 2 [untitled] (1996).

OTHER: Agnes Owens, *Gentlemen of the West,* postscript by Gray (Harmondsworth, U.K.: Penguin, 1986);

Pierre Lavalle: Paintings 1947–1975, essay by Gray (Glasgow: Lavalle Retrospective Group, 1990);

Jack Withers, *A Real Glasgow Archipelago,* introduction by Gray (Glendaruel: Argyll, 1993);

Ian McCulloch, *The Artist in His World: Prints 1986–1997,* descriptive poems by Gray (Glendaruel: Argyll, 1998);

The Books of Jonah, Micah and Nahum: Authorised King James Version, introduction by Gray (Edinburgh: Canongate, 1999);

What a State!: Is Devolution for Scotland the End of Britain? essays by Gray and Angus Calder (London: HarperCollins, 2000);

The Book of Prefaces: A Short History of Literate Thought by Great Writers of Four Nations from the 7th to the 20th Century, edited, with essays, by Gray (London & New York: Bloomsbury, 2000);

Thomas Carlyle, *Sartor Resartus,* introduction by Gray (Edinburgh: Canongate, 2002);

Alasdair Gray: Critical Appreciations and a Bibliography, autobiographical essay by Gray (Boston Spa: British Library, 2002).

SELECTED PERIODICAL PUBLICATIONS–UNCOLLECTED: "The History Maker," *Chapman* 50/51 (Summer/ Winter 1987): 128–131;

"Big Pockets with Buttoned Flaps," *New Writing,* 9 (2000): 10–14.

Like many novelists, Alasdair Gray has also produced a significant body of short fiction. His first published book was *The Comedy of the White Dog* (1979), a volume of two short stories, "The Comedy of the White Dog" and "The Crank Who Made the Revolution." These stories were republished in his first collection of short fiction, *Unlikely Stories, Mostly* (1983). Gray has since produced four further collections: *Lean Tales* (1985) with James Kelman and Agnes Owens, *Ten Tales*

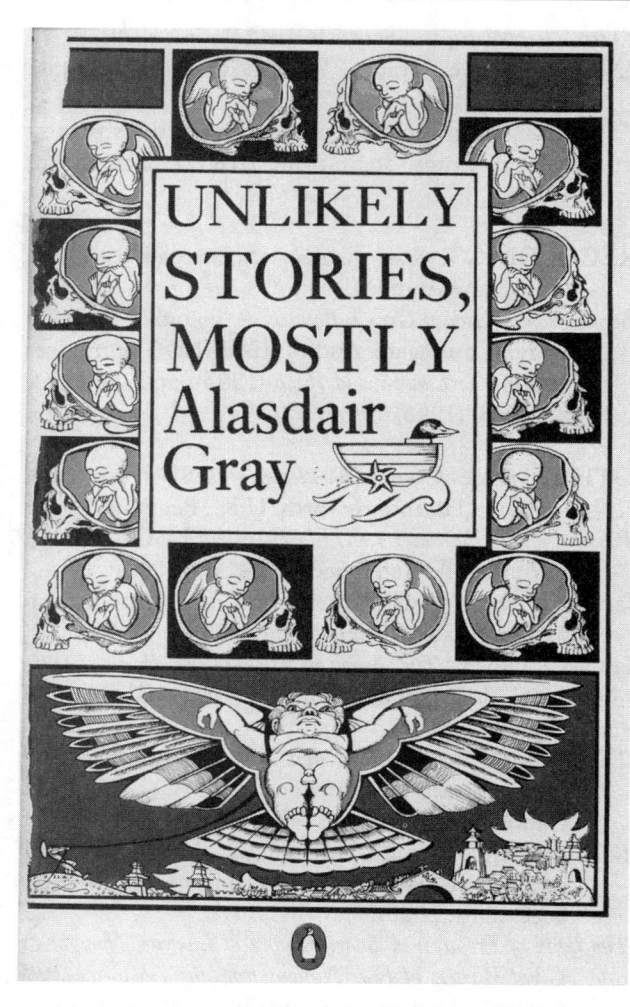

Front cover for the 1984 U.S. edition of Gray's first significant collection of short stories (1983), which reflects his artistic training in its varied typography and black-and-white illustrations (Thomas Cooper Library, University of South Carolina)

Tall and True: Social Realism, Sexual Comedy, Science Fiction and Satire (1993), and *Mavis Belfrage: A Romantic Novel With Five Shorter Tales* (1996), and *The Ends of Our Tethers: 13 Sorry Stories* (2003). Gray admits that he had no particular ambition to be a fiction writer. In a 1986 interview with novelist Kathy Acker, he stated, "I only meant to write one novel and one book of short stories." For much of his life, in addition, he was a visual artist, working in portraiture, book design, and murals. In her article "Art for the Early Days of a Better Nation" (2002), Elspeth King, former curator of the People's Palace museum in Glasgow, recalls Gray's announcement in 1977 that he was leaving his post as artist recorder: "This came as a shock and disappointment. It seemed to be a waste of his time and talent as an artist." This seemingly misdirected talent produced novels such as *Poor Things: Episodes from the Early Life of Archibald McCandless M.D. Scottish Public Health Officer* (1992); *1982 Janine* (1984); and, above all, his epic novel, *Lanark: A Life in Four Books* (1981). As Philip Hobsbaum notes in his essay "Arcadia and Apocalypse: The Garden of Eden and the Triumph of Death" (2002), Gray's short stories have been overshadowed by the impact of his longer fiction: "Compared with his novels, the various commentators have tended to ignore his stories. Yet, it is in these smaller forms that one finds his most exquisite craftsmanship." Gray's short stories, though, are sometimes marred by a tendency (also apparent in such novels as *Something Leather* [1990]) to reuse neglected or unpublished work from his early career. At their best, however, they fulfill Gray's long-standing ambition to commemorate artistically the world he has known. As he states in his textual self-portrait for the Saltire Society, *Alasdair Gray* (1988), his life experience is an important source of inspiration: "I tried to tell convincing stories by copying into them pieces of myself and people I knew, cutting, warping and joining the pieces in ways suggested by imagination and the example of other story-makers." Although *Lanark* is the clearest example of this creative process, Gray's short fiction also shows a significant biographical debt.

Alasdair James Gray was born in Glasgow, Scotland, on 28 December 1934. His father, Alexander, was a machine operator in a local factory; his mother, Amy (née Fleming), was a sales assistant in a clothes shop. The family moved to various locations during World War II. Gray, his sister, and his mother were first evacuated to the countryside, then later reunited with Alexander Gray at a hostel for munitions workers in Yorkshire, which he was managing. The family returned to Glasgow after the war, and Gray began his often unhappy progression through the Scottish educational system. In "Alasdair Gray's Personal Curriculum Vitae," published in *Alasdair Gray: Critical Appreciations and a Bibliography* (2002), Gray notes the psychosomatic impact of his schooling: "I consciously hated then (and still hate) the idea that anyone should suffer boredom and pain now in order to enjoy a better life later, but the ruling educational system was based on this, which may explain why I alternated between eczema and asthma attacks until my mid-twenties." Secondary school, however, did at least develop Gray's literary talents. He made frequent contributions to the school magazine and had stories published in *Collins Magazine for Boys and Girls*.

Gray's mother died in 1952 while he was still a teenager. He entered Glasgow School of Art in the same year, and in 1957, he graduated in design and mural painting. He subsequently received a traveling scholarship and embarked on an attempt to travel through Spain. The journey was cut short, however, by recurrent asthma attacks. His account of his travels was eventually published in *Lean Tales* as "A Report to the Trustees of the Bellahouston Travelling Scholarship." Gray worked as a teacher for a period in the early 1960s, married in 1961, and had a son, Andrew, in 1963; the marriage, to Danish nurse Inge Sørensen, ended in 1970.

For much of the 1960s and 1970s, Gray worked primarily as a painter, with occasional literary successes writing radio, television, and theater scripts. In 1972 he joined a creative-writing group run by Hobsbaum, a literature professor at Glasgow University. Through this group, Gray came into contact with other Glaswegian authors, such as Kelman and Tom Leonard. From 1977 to 1979, Gray was writer-in-residence at Glasgow University. In this period, Canongate agreed to publish *Lanark*. Its publication in 1981 allowed Gray to dedicate himself more to his literary endeavors.

Gray did not begin publishing much until he was in his forties; yet, much of his work was composed long before this period. This pattern is reflected in *Unlikely Stories, Mostly*, his first significant volume of short fiction, which was published in 1983. Like most of Gray's output, this volume shows the impact of his artistic training. The typography is varied and elaborate and is complemented with black-and-white illustrations. Most of the fiction in *Unlikely Stories, Mostly* appeared originally in various minor periodicals during the previous three decades. Indeed, the first story in the volume, "The Star," was one of those originally published while Gray was at high school. In this story, a boy discovers a fallen star in his back garden and takes it to school for comfort and reassurance. When challenged by a teacher, who mistakes it for a marble, the boy swallows the star and finds himself elevated into the heavens. The story mixes Glaswegian realism—the star has fallen "in the midden [refuse heap] on a decayed cabbage leaf"—with carefully described fantastic detail: "It was smooth and round, the size of a glass marble, and it shone with a light which made it seem to rest on a precious bit of green and yellow velvet." This mingling of mundane reality with fantasy reflects the state of Gray's mind for much of his youth. He recalls in the later short story "Mister Meikle—an Epilogue," from *Ten Tales Tall and True*, how "my addiction to fictional worlds was worse than normal, being magnified by my inability to enjoy much else." This obsession led Gray to a parallel life of "prehistoric monsters, Roman arenas, volcanos, cruel queens and life on other planets."

Gray's literary creations reflect his psychic transition from mundane reality to vividly conceived fantasy. Hobsbaum comments that in Gray's work, "fantastic and even apocalyptic circumstance is told in a circumstantial manner so as to render it credible." In "The Cause of Some Recent Changes," first published while he was at the Glasgow School of Art, Gray satirizes the listlessness of his fellow students. The fictional students find a focus, however, in tunneling to the center of the planet, where they discover that a steam engine, rather than gravity, drives the earth round the Sun. Unfortunately, their desire to improve this machine inadvertently shatters the earth into fragments. A similar misplaced ambition is found in the two stories "The Start of the Axletree" and "The End of the Axletree," in which an entire empire is founded on a project to build a tower to the sun. The builders discover, however, that the sky is a barrier "cool and silken smooth with an underlying softness and warmth." Their attempt to burn through the sky causes the tower to collapse and the monoglot empire to crumble.

The blend of fantastic content with a realist register is further apparent in "The Spread of Ian Nicol" and "The Comedy of the White Dog." Ian Nicol, a riveter by trade, finds himself reproducing, like an amoeba, by binary fission. The "White Dog," meanwhile, the narrator solemnly tells the reader, is a living archetype from Celtic myth. A woman betrothed to the white dog must surrender herself to it on the night before her wedding and on each anniversary of that night. This myth has unfortunate implications for Gordon, whose fiancée Nan must make this sacrifice. Indeed, anthropology seems to provide a fertile ground for Gray's literary imagination in *Unlikely Stories, Mostly*. "The Great Bear Cult" tells of a craze that sweeps 1930s Britain, in which men and women adopt the bear as their totemic animal and dress in bear suits. The mania dies down only when the prime minister proscribes the cult. Yet, for all this whimsical blend of reality and fantasy, the story makes a sobering comparison with fascism: "Bearhoards attack local labour party headquarters throughout South London. The police remain aloof until the riots are nearly over and most of the people they arrest are left-wing and furless." The anthropologist in "Prometheus" is also associated with the left wing—he admits to having supported the French National Front in the 1930s. The moral of his story, though, is as much personal as political. His habitual solitude and aloofness, like that of many of Gray's male protagonists, is destroyed by an accidental encounter with a woman.

Gray's move from the People's Palace Museum to the University of Glasgow in 1977 was, Hobsbaum suggests, the inspiration behind "Five Letters from an Eastern Empire": "This story was written immediately after Alasdair Gray at last became a senior member of

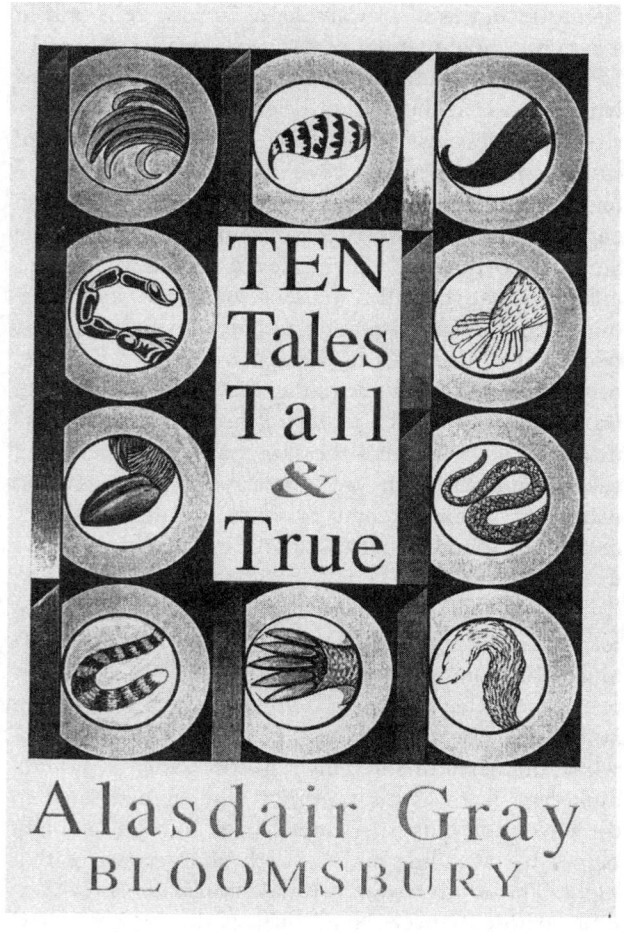

Dust jacket for Gray's 1993 collection, each story of which is accompanied by an illustration of an animal emblematic of the tale (G. Ross Roy Collection of Scottish Literature, Thomas Cooper Library, University of South Carolina)

a great university, its Fellow in Creative Writing." Hobsbaum implies that the appointment was a disenchanting experience for Gray: "Without interpreting 'Five Letters from an Eastern Empire' as a wholesale attack on university education, it is warrantable to suggest that the entry of the author into the system was not the intellectual paradise he might have hoped it would be." The protagonist of "Five Letters from an Eastern Empire," the imperial poet Bohu, is manipulated into writing what he thinks is a poetic outcry against the emperor's destruction of the old capital. The "Headmaster of modern and classical literature" closely reads Bohu's poem and applauds the way in which it "presents the destruction as a simple, stunning, inevitable fact"—this way, he concludes, is "how all governments should appear to the people who are not in them." He advises only one change: the title, "The Emperor's Injustice," should lose "the first syllable in the last word."

Overall, *Unlikely Stories, Mostly* is Gray's most successful collection of short fiction. In his review for *TLS: The Times Literary Supplement* (18 March 1983), Adam Mars-Jones concluded that although "some of the early stories, naturally enough, are lightweight . . . *Unlikely Stories, Mostly,* in spite of its unevenness, is an impressive, playful and beautiful book."

Lean Tales, on the other hand, is a curious addition to Gray's oeuvre of short fiction. Though Gray's work was highly publishable by the 1980s, his supply of work was exceeded by the demands of his publishers. As Gray remarks in the postscript to *Lean Tales* (referring to himself in the third person), "A director of a London publishing house asked him if he had enough stories to make another collection. Gray said no. There was a handful of stories he had intended to build into another collection, but found he could not, as he had no more ideas for prose fictions." Gray's stories were therefore collected, at his suggestion, with tales by two fellow Glaswegian writers. *Lean Tales* is largely a trailer for the talent of Owens and for Kelman, whom Gray had come to know in the 1970s from their membership in Hobsbaum's creative-writing group. The same publicizing function is also apparent in Gray's section within the volume. Three pieces—"Portrait of a Playwright," "Portrait of a Painter," and "A Small Thistle"—are advertisements for neglected Scottish artists. Gray's contribution to the volume is also expanded by the addition of some fragments and some prose poems. Although James Campbell in his review for *TLS* (10 May 1985) concluded that "the collection is a trove of invention and resourcefulness," he admitted that "my enthusiasm for the Glasgow school of writing . . . guttered ominously at the prospect of this book; scrapings, it seemed fair to assume." Gray's contribution, thought Campbell, was particularly slight, including "only three short stories—pretty thin ones at that."

Lean Tales, however, is of interest for the biographical insight that is supplied by "A Report to the Trustees of the Bellahouston Travelling Scholarship." After Gray graduated from the Glasgow School of Art, he was awarded the scholarship and intended to travel through Spain and France. The trip was a disaster: Gray was frequently disabled by asthma and "eventually spent two days in Spain and saw nothing of interest." He spent most of his time in the hospital, or in a hostel in Gibraltar. He found during this time that "my mind hovered above the person I had been in perfect safety, without affection but with great curiosity." In some way, the trip seems, despite its failures, to have given Gray a crucial insight into himself: "I was afraid of losing the habits by which I knew myself, so withdrew into asthma. My tour was spent in an effort to avoid the maturity gained from new experiences." He later represented this ordeal of painful growth fantastically in *Lanark,* when the protagonist ends up in a hospital after escaping the rigid "dragonhide" that encrusts his body. Indeed, an axiom of Gray's work is that humans are creatures of habit, who may yet be imprisoned by them. A human being, he writes in *Alasdair Gray,* is the result of "an always changing *when* and *where* pressing on a unique yet always ripening or rotting bundle of traits; traits joined by a painfully conscious need to both stay the same and grow different."

Gray's experience of imprisonment in habit also provides material for at least one piece in *Lean Tales.* "The Grumbler" is a story, clearly with some autobiographical import, of a man who toils in miserable obscurity until he receives money and success in middle age. Like the Gray of "A Report to the Trustees of the Bellahouston Travelling Scholarship," the "grumbler" is unable to benefit from his success: "Friends ask me what's wrong, but when I tell them I have everything I want they are unable to sympathise." The character, like Gray, clearly feels bound by habit: "I now turn everything into worry and boredom in order to feel like a decent human being. This must stop. I refuse to be the creature of my education, a creature of habit. I will change myself tomorrow. Yes, tomorrow. Tomorrow."

The remaining stories in *Lean Tales* show less biographical inspiration. "The Domino Game" is a geopolitical fable featuring a dispute over a small independent territory. "The Story of a Recluse," on the other hand, is Gray's attempt to complete Robert Louis Stevenson's unfinished tale. Gray's ending is quite unlike anything Stevenson would have written. The hero, instead of winning the hand of the beautiful damsel in distress, discovers that she has betrayed him—her loyalties are to her apparent captor rather than to the dull, unattractive man who has fastened onto her.

Some seven years separate *Lean Tales* from Gray's next collection of short fiction. During this time Gray was involved in a variety of activities. His achievements in the visual arts were celebrated by a retrospective exhibition in 1986. He continued to publish poetry and fiction, and worked on television and theater scripts. He also employed his book-design talents for Dog and Bone Press, a small, short-lived Glaswegian publishing house. In 1991, Gray married his second wife, Morag McAlpine. In 1992, he produced a superior work of long fiction, *Poor Things.* Elizabeth Young in *The Guardian* (3 September 1992) announced that "this new book is his most substantial since *Lanark*" and applauded it as "a bibliophile's paradise of postmodern precision." By 1993 the time was ripe for the arrival of *Ten Tales Tall and True,* which includes, in fact, twelve short stories, an epilogue, a prologue, and Gray's customary "Notes, Thanks, and Critic Fuel." Like many of Gray's books, the volume is lovingly designed and illustrated. Each tale, for example, is accompanied by an illustration of an animal emblematic of the story. On the frontispiece and title page, Gray provides a visual pun: he collects together illustrations of the "tails" of the animals that accompany the "tales" within the collection.

Ron Loewinshon in *The New York Times Book Review* (6 March 1994) saw these stories as continuing "one of Mr. Gray's persistent themes: our escapes almost always lead us only to another prison." As Gray himself confessed in his interview with Acker, writing functioned as such an illusory escape during the failure of his first marriage in the late 1960s: "I saw the domestic situation I was in and thought, 'I don't want to face this world, let's get back to the hellish one I'm imagining.'" Like Gray, the narrator of "Time Travel" in *Ten Tales Tall and True* uses imagination to escape his domestic reality. His attention is eventually drawn, though, to a letter congratulating him on his hundredth birthday. He is, he recalls, a lonely, widowed man who has seen no political change in his lifetime. He returns to meditating on a chair once owned by his wife, an item that provides an imaginative exit via its rich associations to his optimistic younger days. "The Trendelenburg Position" develops this motif in a satirical direction. A dentist suggests a technological solution for those who are unable imaginatively to escape their reality. He proposes a virtual-reality suit distributed by the state. The middle classes can use it for education and adventure; the lower classes to imagine that they live in material security.

The capacity to misuse imagination and make-believe is a frank concern for Gray. In "Fictional Exits," Gray imagines an artist imprisoned in a cell who draws a realistic door through which he makes his exit: in this way, he tells us, "new arts and sciences, new religions and nations are created." He contrasts this idea with the reality of Glasgow in 1990 through an anecdote of police corruption. A blind man is assaulted by police, who then cover up their actions by arbitrarily redefining their own words. They have been tape-recorded planning to "stitch-up" their victim; they later tell the court that this is special police slang for legitimate arrest. Their "fictional exit" abets, rather than opposes, oppression.

In the British general election of 1992, Gray published a pamphlet advocating Scottish independence. Much of *Ten Tales Tall and True* reflects this political biography. "In the fifties and sixties," states Gray in the 1997 revision of *Why Scots Should Rule Scotland,* "I took the future of British socialism for granted." But later he came to see Britain as "a garish Las Vegas glittering with adverts for strip shows and gambling." Lesley, the fictional author of "Internal Memorandum," seems to follow Gray's favored possibility for genuine freedom—that of Scottish autonomy. Lesley dreams of escaping his thralldom by buying out the business organization in which he works. The alternative, he suspects, is that it will be taken over by an English company.

"Near the Driver" shows the consequences of this increasing centralization and the corresponding loss of autonomy. No escape route is possible in a Scottish train controlled by a centralized computer system based in an English town. The passengers find themselves on a preordained collision course with another train. Their driver is powerless to stop his vehicle; his only function is to imprison the passengers securely in case they interfere with the smooth running of the system. The powerless characters in this story resemble the central character of "A New World," who gives everything he has to leave his oppressive reality for a new society. In this putative new world, with its "strong smell of fresh paint," he is led to an exit; but on the way he has mysteriously shrunk, and in this powerless, infantile condition he is unable to reach the doorknob.

"You," "Homeward Bound," and "Loss of the Golden Silence," notes Stephen Bernstein in *Alasdair Gray* (1999), "show sexual politics rivaling national ones at the center of Gray's attention." The college-lecturer protagonist of "Homeward Bound" entertains himself with eighteen-year-old students. The unnamed first-person narrator of "You" begins an affair with a middle-class Englishman—but the Cinderella story is cut short when he abruptly rejects her as she begins to encroach on his personal life. In "Loss of the Golden Silence," both parties attempt to remain mysterious to each other, until their relationship is threatened by the male's discovery that his mistress is secretly writing a thesis on the British epic.

Perhaps the most sympathetic escapee in *Ten Tales Tall and True* is the female protagonist of "Are You a Lesbian?" who is seeking refuge from a marriage in which she is no longer interested. She goes to a pub, not to drink or to start an affair, but to reread the religious texts that once gave her hope. Unlike the mean, humdrum voice of "The Marriage Feast," which characterizes Jesus as a 1960s guru, she seeks a genuine, hopeful meaning in religious imagination.

Ten Tales Tall and True ends with "Mister Meikle—an Epilogue," a reminiscence of the inspiration Gray found in his favorite secondary-school teacher. He confesses that his youthful "addiction to fictional worlds" was merely an escape route from his boredom with school: "My body put on an obedient, hypocritical act while my mind dodged out through imaginary doors." With Meikle's help, however, Gray's imagination was directed back toward his surroundings: the citizens of Glasgow began to seem "as interesting as any people in fiction." Without this education, Gray implies, his imagination would be little more than a God-given virtual-reality suit.

Gray's collection of short fiction, *Mavis Belfrage*, further displays this concern with the teaching profession. Although subtitled *A Romantic Novel with Five Shorter Tales,* the outside cover confesses that "this book should be called *Teachers: 6 Short Tales*" but is billed as a novel because "most readers prefer long stories to short." The rather slim size of the volume led John Sutherland to observe in his review for *TLS* (17 May 1996) that "*Mavis Belfrage* continues the curious diminuendo in Alasdair Gray's career since the monumental achievement of *Lanark*." The time lag between Gray's experience and his literary output is also especially marked: Gray left teaching in 1962, thirty-four years before the publication of this volume. The pieces themselves are rather anachronistic. The two longest, "Mavis Belfrage" and "A Night Off," are set in a nebulous period in the 1960s, and the next longest, "Mr Goodchild," could equally belong in the same time but for a few superficial details.

"Mavis Belfrage," a reworked television script from the 1970s, returns to a traditional Gray theme. As Gray admits in his novel *Something Leather,* "my stories described men who found life a task they never doubted until an unexpected collision opened their eyes and changed their habits. This collision was usually with a woman." True to form, Gray tells of the affair between Colin Kerr, a repressed college lecturer, and Mavis Belfrage, a former student and single mother. Eventually, after being betrayed and humiliated by Mavis, Colin abandons teaching and immigrates to Africa. This change in habits, however, is ambivalent. Colin divorces his African wife fourteen years later and suffers from a stomach ulcer psychosomatically linked to his rejection by Mavis.

"A Night Off" and "Mr Goodchild" (also both recycled scripts) use their unexpected collisions to direct men back toward the warmth of domestic relationships rather than adventure. The protagonist of "A Night Off," called simply "the teacher," encounters a self-aggrandizing photographer, whose shallow ambition contrasts with the neglected depth of feeling between "the teacher" and his wife, his child, and his half-forgotten grandparents. George Goodchild in "Mr Goodchild" has fled his son's home because it encroaches upon his self-sufficiency. Yet, his newfound isolation forces him to communicate with his son by a letter, in which he explicitly acknowledges the value of their relationship—a connection that he has unwittingly stifled with his didactic displays.

The volume ends with an anecdote on the use of corporal punishment in Scottish schools in 1972: the sanction itself, though, effectively died out in the ten to fifteen years before the publication of *Mavis Belfrage*. The schoolteacher, or "dominie," is a traditional motif in Scottish fiction and has been a subject for such writers as J. M. Barrie, Robin Jenkins, and Kelman. Gray's contribution to the genre, however, offers little in the way of contemporary engagement. The collection gives the impression of literary leftovers reheated and re-served late in the writer's career. Gray's tendency to recycle work had earlier led to an unfavorable reception for his novel *Something Leather*. Gerald Mangan in *TLS* (6 July 1990) concluded that it was a book whose "argument is as superficial and incoherent as its characters." This fault resulted primarily, Mangan observed, from Gray's propensity to recycle work: "very few chapters make any effort to conceal their unrelated origins as stories and plays." The same parsimonious attitude was of little benefit to *Mavis Belfrage*. Douglas Gifford in *The Scotsman* (11 May 1996) commented that without "the mingling of fantasy and social satire" found in Gray's earlier stories, "the net effect is of irresolute or even irrelevant tales, mostly."

In "Edison's Tractatus" from *Mavis Belfrage*, Gray reveals his indebtedness to Andrew Sykes, whose income as professor of sociology to Strathclyde University supplied Gray with patronage from "1961 to 1974." Gray was supported by the income from his appointment in 2001 to a chair in creative writing, which he shared with Leonard and Kelman, at the University of Glasgow. Appropriately, this post followed upon the scholarly anthologizing of *The Book of Prefaces* (2000). The volume is a collection of well-known literary prefaces with annotations by Gray and several collaborators. In the postscript, Gray pays homage again to teachers—the anthology is "a memorial to the kind of education British governments now think useless, especially for British working class children. But it has been my education, so I am bound to believe it one of the best in the world." By 2003 Gray, Leonard, and Kelman had resigned their positions at the University of Glasgow, as the weight of the work there had become too great.

Alasdair Gray's short fiction, like his novels, has been shaped by the trajectory of his career. His relatively late success as a writer and his early focus on visual art have created a curious time lag between composition and publication. Gray's short stories rarely have the modish impact of work by such contemporary

Dust jacket for Gray's 1996 collection of stories. The title story is called a novel, the author said, "because most readers prefer long stories to short" (G. Ross Roy Collection of Scottish Literature, Thomas Cooper Library, University of South Carolina).

Scottish authors as Irvine Welsh or Iain Banks. Gray's work will also generally be judged by the quality of his greatest achievements: *Lanark, 1982 Janine,* and *Poor Things*. These works fulfill Gray's ambition to address as broad an audience as possible. In a 1983 interview with Carol Anderson and Glenda Norquay, Gray revealed his intention to appeal to "an English-speaking tribe which extends to Capetown in the South, Bengal in the East, California in the West and George Mackay Brown in the North." Gray admitted, though, in an interview with Mark Axelrod in 1995, that he may fall short of this goal because of his own limitations as a writer: "If an American reader finds my Scottish references and idioms more confusing than the Wessex ones of Hardy and the Irish ones of Joyce, it is because I am an inferior writer, not because I write with a narrower audience in mind." Despite the variable quality of his work, however, Gray's place in the canon of modern short fiction is assured by his capacity to equal the ability of Thomas Hardy and James Joyce to appeal to a cosmopolitan audience with a locally based art. In her 1995 essay, "Different Oracles: Me and Alasdair Gray," Janice Galloway, a fellow Scottish writer, sums up Gray's ability to create universal art from his personal experience: "Alasdair Gray's was a voice that offered me something freeing. It wasn't distant or assumptive. It knew words, syntax, and places I also knew yet used them without any tang of apology. It took its own experience and culture as valid and central." Gray's best short fiction confirms his statement to Norquay and Anderson that "I'm essentially the same as other men, women and children, so if I am careful and talk honestly to myself they'll be able to hear me."

Interviews:
Carol Anderson and Glenda Norquay, "Interview with Alasdair Gray," *Cencrastus,* 13 (1983): 6–10;

Elizabeth C. Donaldson, "Alasdair Gray Talking with Elizabeth C. Donaldson," *Verse,* 1 (1984): 30–35;

Sean Figgis and Andrew McAllister, "Alasdair Gray: An Interview with Sean Figgis and Andrew McAllister, 6th February, 1988," *Bête Noire,* 5 (1988): 17–44;

Mark Axelrod, "An Epistolary Interview, Mostly with Alasdair Gray," *Review of Contemporary Fiction,* 15, no. 2 (1995): 106–115;

Kathy Acker, "Alasdair Gray Interviewed by Kathy Acker: 1986," in *Alasdair Gray: Critical Appreciations and a Bibliography,* edited by Phil Moores (Boston Spa: British Library, 2002), pp. 45–57.

Bibliography:
Alasdair Gray: Critical Appreciations and a Bibliography, edited by Phil Moores (Boston Spa: British Library, 2002).

References:
Stephen Bernstein, *Alasdair Gray* (Lewisburg, Pa.: Bucknell University Press, 1999);

Janice Galloway, "Different Oracles: Me and Alasdair Gray," *Review of Contemporary Fiction,* 15, no. 2 (1995): 193–196;

Philip Hobsbaum, "Arcadia and Apocalypse: The Garden of Eden and the Triumph of Death," in *Alasdair Gray: Critical Appreciations and a Bibliography,* edited by Phil Moores (Boston Spa: British Library, 2002), pp. 5–29;

Elspeth King, "Art for the Early Days of a Better Nation," in *Alasdair Gray: Critical Appreciations and a Bibliography,* edited by Moores (Boston Spa: British Library, 2002), pp. 93–121;

Anne Varty, "How the Laws of Fiction Lie: A Reading of Gray's Shorter Stories," in *The Arts of Alasdair Gray,* edited by Robert Crawford and Thom Nairn (Edinburgh: Edinburgh University, 1991), pp. 124–135.

Papers:
Collections of Alasdair Gray's manuscripts and other papers are held in the Mitchell Library, Glasgow; Glasgow University Library; and in the National Library of Scotland, Edinburgh.

Jack Harte
(1 September 1944 -   )

Pietra Palazzolo
University of Essex

BOOKS: *Poems of Alienation* (Dublin: Matrix, 1969);
The Land of Ire (Dublin: Matrix, 1972);
Murphy in the Underworld (Dublin: Glendale, 1986);
Homage (Dublin: Dedalus, 1992);
Birds & Other Tails (Dublin: Dedalus, 1996);
From Under Gogol's Nose: New & Selected Stories (Dublin: Scotus, 2004).

OTHER: "The Bleeding Stone of Knockaculleen," in *7 Stories,* edited by F. Mitchell (Dublin: Profile Press, 1975), pp. 53–61;
"In the Retirement Colony" and "The Thane of Cawdor Lives," in *Profiles 2,* edited by John F. Deane (Dublin: Profile Press, 1978), pp. 25–37;
"Murphy in the Underworld," in *EsTu: An Anthology of Contemporary Irish Writing,* various editors (Clondalkin, Ireland, 1981), pp. 10–17;
"His First Job," in *EsTu,* various editors (Clondalkin, Ireland, 1982), pp. 24–35;
"The Lesson," in *Achill Island,* edited by P. Lineen (Achill Island, Ireland: Lineen, 1991);
"Requiem for Johnny Murtagh," in *Goodbye and Hello,* edited by Clodagh Corcoran and Margot Tyrell (Ringwood, Australia & Harmondsworth, U.K.: Viking, 1992), pp. 131–143;
"Painter," in *Toward Harmony, A Celebration: for Tony O Malley,* edited by John F. Deane (Dublin: Dedalus, 1993), pp. 20–22;
"Bike," in *Water Baby,* edited by John Murray, Panurge Anthology, no. 23 (Brampton: Panurge, 1995), pp. 16–26;
"Requiem for Johnny Murtagh," in *New Galaxy 1,* edited by John Moriarty (Dublin: Mentor Publications, 1995), pp. 109–117;
"A Message to Sparta," in *Heinrich Böll Cottage on Achill Island,* edited by John McHugh (Achill Island, Ireland: Achill Heinrich Böll Committee, 1998), pp. 9–19.

Jack Harte (from Birds & Other Tails, *1996; Bruccoli Clark Layman Archives)*

TRANSLATION: Lyubomir Levchev, *And Here I Am,* Poetry Europe Series, no. 16 (Dublin: Dedalus, 2003).

SELECTED PERIODICAL PUBLICATIONS–
UNCOLLECTED: "The New Girl," *Anvil* (1971): 19–21;
"Ag Diugadh Poitin le Zorba Greagach" (Drinking Poteen with Zorba the Greek), *Inniu,* 14 March 1975;
"The New House, 1948," *Clondalkin Magazine* (1976): 14–21;

"The New House," *Reality* (November 1977): 28–32;

"The Journey of the Fourth Wise King," *Young Citizen* (January 1988): 10–12;

"Turfman," *Suburb* (February 2002): 30.

Jack Harte has been described as a "pioneering artificer" for his experiments with the story form. As Frank O'Carroll observed in a review of *Birds & Other Tails* (1996) for the December 1996 issue of *Astir*: "in exorcising the spirits of Tradition and by blending the magic of myth with realism Mr Harte has created a fiction that itself has more than a touch of magic about it." Harte's stories display a playfulness of style and genre that demonstrates the desire to push the story to its limits, so that it is on the borderline with the oral tradition (myth, folktale, and poetry) and written tradition (the critical essay and the metafictional narrative). With little interest in building up character or evoking a sense of linear time and place, Harte's short fiction defies definitions of the short story that prescribe a realistic approach. In contrast to other stories of epiphanies, such as Frank O'Connor's "Guests of the Nation," in which the protagonist finds himself moving through events toward a moment of sudden realization, Harte's writings dispense with plot devices and characterization, often starting with cryptic sentences that immediately demand the reader's attention. The ending is often without resolution, accompanied as it is with looming suggestions and nuances coaxing the reader's imagination.

Pondering the difficulty of labeling Harte's *Birds and Other Tails* and categorizing his versatility of style, Bill Maxwell, in the *Irish Independent* (5 October 1996), describes the stories of this second collection as "fables of our modern times"; he says of Harte, "he is like the old oral Gaelic storytellers who could improvise on any theme at will. He bends language to his needs like a sculptor moulding clay." Indeed, Harte links the short story with the oral tradition as he does in the Preface to *From Under Gogol's Nose*: "The modern short story is the closest continuation of the tradition of storytelling and belongs to the one genre with folktales, myths and legends . . . it is essentially an oral form, like the poem, which appeals to the mind's ear, rather than the mind's eye." His stories also display a significant variety of tone, which explores the subtle nuances of specific themes: comic, tragic, ironic, elegiac, satirical, and surreal. Love, for example, is shown in its many guises in Harte's stories: the need for companionship and the frailty of human bonds; the delusions of men chasing women in casual street encounters or in their memories of the past; and the tragic outcome of love bordering on fanaticism and madness. Harte never carries experimentation with the story form to extremes, however, as he stressed in an interview with Ciaran Carty, "Harte to Harte," published in the 25 May 1986 *Sunday Tribune*: "any technique used in writing should be to assist the reader rather than to throw obstacles in the way of communication."

Harte started his literary career as a poet with the publication of *Poems of Alienation* (1969) but soon converted to the short story, balancing his teaching duties with creative writing while publishing several English textbooks for schools. Before being collected, his stories were widely published in magazines and journals—for example, *Matrix Press, Reality, Ulster Tatler, Pacific Quarterly, Tracks, Sunday Independent,* the *Journal of Irish Literature,* and *Suburb Magazine*—in Ireland, and abroad in Britain, the United States, Australia, New Zealand, Finland, and Bulgaria. Many stories have also been anthologized in various textbooks and broadcast on RTE Radio (Irish public radio).

Jack Harte was born 1 September 1944 in Killeenduff, near Easkey, County Sligo. His mother's name was Lollie Foley, and his father, John Harte, was the blacksmith of the village; the forge was a constant source of excitement in Harte's childhood. When he was nine years old, his family moved to Lanesboro, County Longford, where his father worked for Bord-na-Móna, a company established in 1946 as a statutory body by the Turf Development Act for the development of Ireland's peat and bog resources. At the age of eighteen, he moved to Dublin, where he still lives. Harte married Celia de Freine, the poet and playwright, in 1972 and has five children: Lara (who is a novelist), Vanya, Fiachra, Aonghus, and Audrey. He attended primary schools at Killeenduff and Dromore West, County Sligo, and at Lanesboro. His secondary education was at Ballyleague, County Roscommon, and Roscommon town. After attending night lectures at University College Dublin, Harte earned a B.A. and a higher diploma in education. His first job was as a bog laborer with Bord-na-Móna. In Dublin, after a brief period working as an executive officer in the civil service, he took up teaching at Clondalkin Vocational School, County Dublin. Moving to Lucan Vocational School (later, Lucan Community College), he was principal from 1983 to 2000, the year in which he resigned to become a full-time writer.

Harte is also widely known for his achievements as an arts activist. In the mid 1970s he helped to set up the Profile Press, which published newly emerging writers such as John F. Deane, Padraig J. Daly, and Conleth O'Connor and encouraged such young artists as Henry Sharpe. Harte was also co-editor, together with Deane, of the literary magazine *Tracks* during 1982 and 1983. As principal of Lucan Community College, Harte contributed to the improvement of teaching conditions, focusing on the development of creative writing in schools. In 1985 he set up the Writers' Project at Lucan Vocational School, the first to bring creative writing into a pedagogical frame, and the following year he appointed Joe Jackson, the first writer-in-residence in Ireland. Harte's efforts to provide suitable structures and opportunities for writers reflect his emphasis on writing as a form of self-expression rather than as just a subject, as he stressed in the 25 May 1986 interview with Carty: "by bringing a writer into the school like this, writing ceases to be just a subject to be studied. It becomes a very practical thing to do as a living." While acknowledging the role of university education in underscoring the importance of writing—Trinity College, for example, still has its writer-in-residence—Harte's major concern was to broaden the scope of public access to literature. In a 26 May 1992 interview with Jackson in the *Irish Times,* "Fighting for Writers' Rights," Harte said that he sees "writing more as a form of activity which should be available to everyone." Harte is best known for his marked contribution to the development of writers' organizations. In January 1987 he founded the Irish Writers' Union while setting out to establish the Irish Writers' Centre, which officially opened at 19 Parnell Square in 1991. The project was the result of Harte's efforts to provide a vibrant center for writers and his negotiations in the late 1980s with Matt McNulty of Dublin Tourism, who in that period was in the process of setting up the Dublin Writers' Museum at 18 Parnell Square. Harte has also acted as judge of the Irish Schools Creative Writing Awards and the Listowel Writers' Week Short Story Competition. He has served on the International reading Panel for G.E.S., the French-sponsored European Creative Writing Project for young people. He has given creative-writing workshops throughout the country, including the Fiction Workshop at Listowel Writers' Week.

His first collection of stories, *Murphy in the Underworld* (1986), opens and ends in Hades. The stories, seventeen in all, break away from the traditional mold of social realism; they are sustained by inner consistency and a language that is refreshingly free from sentimentalism. As Deane wrote in the *Sunday Independent* (29 June 1986), the collection "opens up new and unexpected perspectives and gives the story form a refreshing impetus." The title story narrates Murphy's attempt to return to Earth for one November night, the brief stretch of time in which "the laws of eternity and infinity lapse" and souls are allowed to

Front cover for Harte's 1986 collection of short stories that begins and ends in Hades. Many of the stories concern people who fall prey to greed (Bruccoli Clark Layman Archives).

return to the world. His plan to visit his mother is hampered by an intricate Kafkaesque bureaucratic system that sends him from one office to another. The story ends with Murphy's ongoing search for his mother in the Lost Souls' Section, a throng of restless souls waiting to be registered and looking for their siblings. The collection ends in Hades with "Three for Oblivion," a story within a story narrated by the ferryman who takes the dead souls across the mythical river Lethe. Trying to remind his new passenger of the fare for the trip, the ferryman tells him the story of three Irishmen he once helped cross the river. The three men are first presented as different in character and political leaning, but their differences are layered with subtler nuances of human emotion, beyond political and social troubles. After taking their bright-colored ties (green, white, and orange) as a reasonable fare for the trip, the ferryman ponders on how totally indistinguishable they look: "they were far more similar to begin with than they would have been honest enough to admit."

In this first collection of stories the reader is at times confronted with harsh themes, as in "Come, Follow Me," which recounts the tragic fate of the people living in Bonaparte Lane after their lives are devastated by a sailor who beats them in cardplaying and then seduces them to the pleasures of an unethical attitude toward games. Some stories "capture a moment of meditation between this world and the next, at once pure symbolism and pure realism," as Paul Durcan notes in the *Cork Examiner* (1978) in relation to "In the Retirement Colony," a tale about an architect who finds the retirement colony he has been assigned to too constricting. He dies while trying to dig a tunnel underneath the wall that divides his colony from that of his relatives. The tragic ending is yoked with a surreal and symbolic element that endows the story with a subtle critique of man-made systems of order. One recurrent theme in Harte's stories is the way people fall prey to greed, as in "The Thane of Cawdor Lives" and "The Alchemist of Ballykillcash." While the former delves into the cruel heart of a civil servant who takes pleasure in keeping his inferiors at a distance and shows how he is betrayed by the only man he thought would not harm him, the latter story uses folktale elements to unveil the dangers of human greed. In the end, the Alchemist's "indomitable optimism" is recognized as his best quality, despite the King's belief in the former's ability to create gold and fund his war against the neighboring King of Tirawley. "The Land of Dwarfs" also relies on the incantatory tone of the folktale, in a story in which myth and everyday life interconnect. Fugitive dwarfs find shelter in a strange land and soon learn how to manipulate the people of the island, breeding them into their likeness. Children are submitted to a painful regime at school and are forced to wear "the sacred cast," an iron frame that twists their bones and hunches their backs. Only one youth by chance escapes this torture, but he is crucified when his subversive intent is discovered by the dwarfs. Though not well received and described as "fanciful construction" by Gerry Colgan in the *Irish Independent* (31 May 1986), the story subtly mixes different styles and points of view, as is often the case in Harte's fiction. "Queen B" is a witty story that involves the female reproductive cycle of a mythical insect, a queen B. Narrated in the third person, the story has Monday as a protagonist, the first and most important worker of the week to retire to the chamber of Queen B; he desperately tries to escape his fate, only to find himself still trapped in the same role.

Between his first and second collections of stories, Harte published *Homage* (1992), a work that, though labeled as a novel, is more akin to the short story or novella in design. The difficulty of categorizing *Homage* has engendered contrasting views and at times even harsh criticism, especially by those who insist upon viewing it as a novel. Considered as a further elaboration on the short story, *Homage* displays characteristics that have already been praised in Harte's short fiction: economy of style and internal consistency, which derive from his use of language and subtle handling of a theme that would otherwise border upon a sentimental tale of love longing. Three men–a poet, a sculptor, and a musician–spend the summer in a country cottage in the company of Shiofra, the girl whose heart each tries to win by means of his art. Each pays homage to the girl by producing an original work that suits his skills, though, as she muses toward the end of the book, homage is "no substitute for love": "their pieces were an alternative to communication. . . . By objectifying what they wanted to say, they were removing the need to say it. They were sublimating their loneliness, their passion, instead of expressing it." The ending shows all the characters open to new possibilities of expression and looking back at the cottage experience as a significant turning point in their lives.

Harte's second collection of stories, *Birds and Other Tails*–twenty tales in all–deploys a greater range of theme and generic experimentation than *Murphy in the Underworld;* it displays a significant cross-genre search for the possibility of the story in its use of elegy, folktale, critical writing, and poetry. "Birds," for example, incorporates structural elements of poetry–its rhythm and intensity. Graphically arranged in irregular lines, the story tells of Sweeney, a farmer whose delight is to listen to the continual chorus of the meadow birds, the cuckoo, and the corncrakes "from the five corners of his sixteen-acre field." Forced to turn his crop into silage by the harsh weather conditions, he drives at the field with a powerful Ferguson silage-maker, getting rid of bird nests and colonies. In desperation, he flees to the woods, singing like a bird, while only "the vulgar noise of the crows" breaks the silence and seems to applaud "the wisdom of his deed." "Birds" addresses environmental and social issues–the disappearance of rare birds such as the corncrake because of modern farming techniques and the waning of man's union with nature–but it does so in a way that is both fearless and refreshingly devoid of sentimentalism, a characteristic that pervades all his work. "Birds" is an elegy to a last desperate attempt to preserve the land and the beauty of a fascinating encounter with nature from the merciless pace of progress. The same theme is explored in "Audit," which narrates the possible taking over of the manager's firm by the auditors who have been sent to assess his work that year. They seem to take longer this time, intent in their work "like weasels sniffing out a likely quarry." The outcome of their restless work is undisclosed in the story, which ends with the manager's decision to resign rather than to go through humiliation and despair. The minimalist handling of such a crucial juncture for Ireland's economy veers to a symbolic flashback to the manager's uncles attuned to the colors and smells of the country when working on the farm but doomed to be replaced by "economic sleight-of-hand."

As the first collection does, this one displays a variety of tone, from the comic to the tragic and surreal. "Believers," for example, addresses compelling social issues by focusing on a poor family who squander all their savings on the Lotto, believing in imminent luck and dreaming about a plentiful, happy time. The family's strong belief in the power of the Lotto is rendered with unflinching accuracy in the ironic nuances of a dialogue between the head of the household and the priest. At times, passages of conventional narrative are pitched against one-word, Beckettian sentences that echo in the reader's mind with enduring intensity, as in "The Liberation of Martin Reilly" and "And What Is the Thunder." In the former story, the plan of an all too good-natured protagonist to avoid meeting people he knows once in heaven is doomed to failure by his inability to sin. The tone is ironic in its subtle handling of religious creeds and moral assumptions.

Harte's ability to combine absolute mundaneness with a sense of the absurd has equally puzzled and interested both commentators and reviewers, though the majority tend to think he is at his best in depicting gritty realism rather than when bordering on abstraction. Nevertheless, the stories in which Harte mixes these two contrasting senses of mundaneness and absurdity, such as "The Great Silence" and "Australia," are also the most compelling, as Cormac Deane states in *The Irish Times* (18 January 1997), "producing the grisly yet attractive atmosphere of a fairy tale." In "The Great Silence" Harte takes the short story as close as possible to the discursive essay but essentially keeps it a story. Taking the shape of a tale addressed to an absent interlocutor, Zee, the story provides an illustration of the "extreme fluctuations in the fortunes of writers"; it links the Irish crisis at the end of the sixth century with the Great Silence in recent

Dust jacket for Harte's second short-story collection (1996), which draws on various forms including elegy, folktale, critical writing, and poetry. The most important story, "Birds," deals with the disappearance of rare birds (Bruccoli Clark Layman Archives).

times. In its satire on the act of writing, "The Great Silence" offers a social comment on the conditions of writers in Ireland. "Australia" is about a middle-aged bachelor farmer, whose vivid dream of an alternative life in Australia gains a life of its own, which is rendered with surreal undertones. In a review of *Water Baby* (1995) for the *Northern Review* (December 1995–January 1996), David Whetstone described "Bike," one of Harte's most amusing stories, as "a beautifully crafted piece of eccentricity with shades of Flann O'Brien." A man offers his bike for sale, and a prospective buyer comes to test it, ecstatic to find the same brand of bike she used to ride in her youth. The woman leaves her baby and a girl with the man while she goes for a test ride and never comes back. Eventually, the owner succeeds in finding the woman, who is happily enjoying her freedom in a quarter of Dublin completely unknown to him, and in the end he decides not to intrude on the woman's dream to travel around the world by bike. "The House," described as a Kafkaesque story, narrates the vicissitudes of a retired civil servant who is haunted by his past. The story, like most of Harte's works, also displays elements that are typical of Nikolai Gogol's style, especially in its combination of realism and the absurd. Harte's *From Under Gogol's Nose* (2004) puts forward new ideas on the short story and includes a satire, "The State of the Irish Short Story," which is meant as a response to Frank O'Connor's (and Ivan Sergeevich Turgenev's) statement that "we all came out from under Gogol's 'Overcoat.'" He disputes Turgenev's and O'Connor's tracing of the history of the modern short story to Gogol's story "The Overcoat" by asking what came from under Gogol's surrealist story, "The Nose."

If Jack Harte's stories repudiate the social realism of Sean Faolain and O'Connor, they access reality through a different route, by the use of experimentation that, while breaking with tradition, is unyielding to the arbitrary fragmentation of aesthetic forms, and the evocation of mythical and fairy-tale atmospheres. Attention to the evanescent grounds of myth and folktale heightens, by contrast, the reader's appreciation of reality, fissured with a sense of human mortality.

Interviews:

Ciaran Carty, "Harte to Harte," *Sunday Tribune,* 25 May 1986, p. 18;

Joe Jackson, "Fighting for Writers' Rights," *Irish Times,* 26 May 1992, p. 11.

References:

Gerry Colgan, "Take Harte, for Jack's no Bore," *Irish Independent,* 31 May 1986, p. 9;

Cormac Deane, "When the Parts Are Greater than the Whole," *Irish Times,* 18 January 1997, p. 8;

Paul Durcan, "Cork Poet in Profiles (2)," *Cork Examiner,* 1978;

Robert Hogan, ed., *Dictionary of Irish Literature,* 2 volumes (London: Aldwych Press, 1996), I: 527;

Jack Harte <www.jackharte.com>;

Shawn MacMahon and Jo Donoghue, eds., *The Mercier Companion to Irish Literature* (Cork, Ireland: Mercier Press, 1998), p. 83;

Bill Maxwell, "Fables of Our Modern Times," *Irish Independent,* 5 October 1996, p. 11;

Robert Welch, *Oxford Concise Companion to Irish Literature* (Oxford & New York: Oxford University Press, 2000), p. 145.

Desmond Hogan

(10 December 1951 -   )

Robert Ellis Hosmer Jr.
Smith College

See the Hogan entry in *DLB 14: British Novelists Since 1960*.

BOOKS: *The Ikon Maker* (Dublin: Co-op Books, 1976; New York: George Braziller, 1979);

The Diamonds at the Bottom of the Sea and Other Stories (London: Hamilton, 1979; New York: George Braziller, 1980);

The Leaves on Grey (London: Hamilton, 1979; New York: George Braziller, 1980);

Children of Lir: Stories from Ireland (London: Hamilton, 1981; New York: George Braziller, 1981);

Stories: The Diamonds at the Bottom of the Sea, Children of Lir (London: Pan, 1982);

A Curious Street (London: Hamilton, 1984; New York: George Braziller, 1984);

A New Shirt (London: Hamilton, 1986);

The Mourning Thief and Other Stories (London & Boston: Faber & Faber, 1987);

Lebanon Lodge (London & Boston: Faber & Faber, 1988);

A Link with the River, with an introduction by Louise Erdrich (New York: Farrar, Straus & Giroux, 1989)—comprises *The Mourning Thief and Other Stories* and *Lebanon Lodge;*

The Edge of the City: A Scrapbook, 1976-1991 (Dublin: Lilliput, 1993; London & Boston: Faber & Faber, 1993);

Farewell to Prague (London & Boston: Faber & Faber, 1995).

PLAY PRODUCTIONS: *A Short Walk to the Sea,* Dublin, Peacock Theatre, October 1975;

Sanctified Distances, Dublin, Peacock Theatre, December 1976;

The Ikon Maker, Berkshire, U.K., Bracknell South Hill Park Arts Centre, September 1980.

PRODUCED SCRIPTS: *Jimmy,* radio, BBC Radio 3, August 1978;

The Mourning Thief, television, BBC, 1984.

Desmond Hogan (from the dust jacket for the U.S. edition of The Leaves on Grey, *1980; Richland County Public Library)*

OTHER: "Thoughts," in *Firebird I: Writing Today,* edited by T. J. Binding (Harmondsworth, U.K.: Penguin, 1982), pp. 131-140;

Kate O'Brien, *Without My Cloak,* introduction by Hogan (London: Virago, 1984);

O'Brien, *That Lady,* introduction by Hogan (London: Virago, 1985);

"Guy 'Micko' Delaney," in *Winter's Tales: New Series 4,* edited by Robin Baird Smith (London: Constable, 1988), pp. 161-186;

"The Airedale," in *The Oxford Book of Irish Short Stories,* edited by William Trevor (Oxford & New York: Oxford University Press, 1989), pp. 553-563;

"Afternoon," in *The Brandon Book of Irish Short Stories,* edited by Steve MacDonogh (Dingle, Ireland: Mount Eagle Press, 1998), pp. 237–254;

"The Bombs," in *The Anchor Book of New Irish Writing,* edited by John Somer and John J. Daly (New York: Anchor, 2000), pp. 44–55;

"Winter Swimmers," in *New Writing 11,* edited by Andrew O'Hagan and Tóibín (London: Picador, 2002), pp. 217–231.

The reputation of Desmond Hogan—sometime actor, playwright, and novelist—as a writer of short stories rests on three collections printed and reprinted within a relatively short time (1979–1989); with the addition of stories published elsewhere, Hogan's entire oeuvre of short fiction consists of approximately fifty stories. His work is marked by an enduring concern with identity and exile, both cultural and personal; corollary to that interest is a fascination with outsiders, marginalized figures, and those trapped and longing to escape. Sex and violence figure prominently in stories that are usually set in the late 1960s or the 1970s, decades of substantial change in Hogan's native Ireland. However, for all his concern with the modern world and its ways, Hogan remains a traditional, conservative writer in many of his attitudes and in his narrative strategies. He is not an innovator in literary terms. Rather, he is a writer of intensely lyrical, self-consciously autobiographical, and highly impressionistic pieces that seem remnants of an older, more romantic age. His high regard for traditional storytelling and the anecdote is symptomatic of this attitude. "The best stories," he told Robert McCrum, "are often told by uneducated people who've not been to university." Despite its conservatism, his work has been included in important anthologies of Irish short fiction. It has also been reviewed by major critics and writers such as Denis Donoghue, Louise Erdrich, Eva Hoffman, Joyce Carol Oates, and Julia O'Faolain, and although not all those who have commented on his work have done so with unmixed approval, influential voices such as Oates's speak highly of him. The literary prizes he has garnered in his brief career also suggest his stature as a novelist and short-story writer.

Born on 10 December 1951 in Ballinasloe, County Galway, Ireland, Hogan was one of five sons born to the owner of a drapery shop, William Hogan, and his wife, Christina (Connolly) Hogan. Ballinasloe is a town known for its annual horse fair and its connection with Irish gypsies. While living there, Hogan developed a love of swimming that he has maintained throughout his life and that forms a central image in one of his most celebrated stories, "Winter Swimmers." Local convent primary school and Roman Catholic secondary school prepared Hogan for study at University College Dublin, where he read English and philosophy. In 1968 Hogan visited Paris during the period of revolutionary student riots against the French government and capitalist system. A writer of plays and stories from an early age, Hogan won the Hennessy Literary Award in 1970. He was a successful university student, earning both a B.A. degree (1972) and an M.A. (1973). After a six-month hitchhiking tour of continental Europe, Hogan taught English in a vocational school while continuing to publish stories and working on what became his first novel, *The Ikon Maker* (1976).

From January 1975 until mid 1977 Hogan performed with a children's theater company and wrote plays of his own. Two, *A Short Walk to the Sea* and *Sanctified Distances,* were produced in the Peacock Theatre in Dublin in 1975 and 1976. In 1976 he was cofounder, along with celebrated writer and moviemaker Neil Jordan and Steve MacDonagh, of the Irish Writers' Cooperative, which published *The Ikon Maker* in that year. This novel deals with a mother's passion for her son and her unwilling recognition of his homosexuality. It has been praised widely; Colm Tóibín, for example, describes it as having been "an iconic book for anyone interested in writing" in his generation of novelists and short-story writers. Hogan won the Rooney Prize for his work in 1977. Travel to California, Egypt, and Greece preceded his settling in London and working as a substitute teacher. More literary success followed. For the publication of his first collection of stories, *The Diamonds at the Bottom of the Sea and Other Stories* (1979), Hogan was awarded the Llewelyn Rhys Memorial Prize in 1980.

The Diamonds at the Bottom of the Sea includes seventeen stories, some of which had already been published in such magazines and journals as the *Transatlantic Review, New Irish Review,* and *Stand* or broadcast on RTE (Irish public radio and television) or the BBC. Taken together, the collection is varied: some stories are tales of alienation, exile, and spiritual and artistic quest in which readers are asked to identify with the protagonists and their situations; others avoid a strong narrative line, employ a self-reflexive literary style, and present characters only in outline.

Many stories in the collection do not have plots of any complexity but are close to being anecdotes. Examples are "Blow Ball," a ghost story involving three children's experiences in the course of one summer; "Portrait of a Dancer," a tale of a romantic painter that touches on the subjects of love and suicide; and "Mothers of Children," a five-page story about two women finding their way through contemporary counterculture to attain discoveries about life. "A Vision of Dublin" has a substantial plot, however: twenty-two-year-old

Des, recently parted from Eleanor, meets twenty-five-year-old Tom in Rome and is attracted to him. No passionate or lasting relationship, however, results from this meeting. Tom has a woman from whom he is estranged back in Dublin (and a child as well). On his return to Dublin, Des sees Tom in a café but does not speak to him. Months later, by chance, he meets Tom's woman in a bar and learns that Tom has died of a drug overdose. "A Vision of Dublin" is a story driven by coincidence and marked by symbolism—from a visit to John Keats's grave in Rome to references to Richard Wagner's *Die Walküre* and the Beatles' "Yesterday." The story is further distinguished by the narrator's didactic observations, as in the last paragraph of the story: "To preserve myself, I had to walk out of shadows and romantic images. I had to give up a way of life, one such born in the streets of Dublin which led me to Tom, the casual acquaintance, the enigmatic stranger, the person destined to stand between you and what I couldn't help thinking that night was eternity."

In other stories, readers encounter unusual similes and metaphors: for example, the reader is told of a woman's face, "Instead it was calm—like the Book of Kells" ("Portrait of a Dancer"); in "Poltergeists" the city of Athlone is described as "a business town, lying in an obesity of river and houses"; in "The Birth of Laughter," the reader learns, "Europe was going to pieces but we traveled like patterns on wallpaper to Cairo"; in "Afternoon," "the sky dropped snow like penance." The intense and self-conscious literariness of Hogan's prose is also illustrated by intertextual allusions. No story demonstrates Hogan's prominent use of references to other texts better than "The Bombs." In fourteen pages, Hogan builds up allusions to Hermann Hesse, Rainer Maria Rilke, the Bible, Thomas Merton, Brother Antoninus, Jack Kerouac, Allen Ginsberg, Johann Sebastian Bach, Pyotr Ilich Tchaikovsky, Felix Mendelssohn, Giacomo Puccini, Gioacchino Rossini, Bob Dylan, Charlie Parker, Sandro Botticelli, and Jan Vermeer.

The Diamonds at the Bottom of the Sea presents stories that readers have found both poignant and haunting. Hogan displays a facility in depicting women's lives, whether from a first- or third-person perspective. In "The Last Time" he uses a first-person narrator, Maria Mulcahy, an orphan girl forcibly separated from her first love, Jamesy, eventually married to someone else and working in a London hotel. Hogan's refusal to follow a predictable plot pattern makes "The Last Time" a powerful tale of middle-aged nostalgia. In "Afternoon," ninety-one-year-old Eileen, tinker queen and mother of fifteen, lies dying, her head filled with fragments of variegated experience; Hogan's empathetic insight allows her to assume forceful humanity and narrative centrality. The same strategy of memory as narrative filter is employed in "The Birth of Laughter," a story divided into two loosely connected narratives, one set in the present and another in the past. Only five pages long, "Foils" carefully aligns the life stories of a lonely old woman and a lonely young boy; drawn to each other for a while, they drift apart only to be connected again by circumstances beyond their control.

Dust jacket for Hogan's 1981 collection of stories about Irish life and Celtic mythology (Richland County Public Library)

Hogan's second novel, an autobiographical text called *The Leaves on Grey,* also appeared in 1979. Its success encouraged Hogan to devote all his efforts to writing. In an article on Hogan in the *Observer* (14 November 2004), McCrum, Hogan's editor at Faber and Faber from 1986 to 1995, describes him in the early 1980s as being "as hot as they come: widely celebrated as the author of a short story collection *The Diamonds at the Bottom of the Sea* and, among literary circles in London and New York, beginning to be spoken of as a dazzling young Irish writer to watch." Living at this time in Catford in South London, Hogan counted the major British author Kazuo Ishiguro among his friends and was represented by one of the leading literary agencies in London, the Deborah Rogers agency. Most friends and acquaintances from this period comment on Hogan's eccentricity and single-minded concern with literature. A dramatic version of his novel *The Ikon Maker* was performed at the Bracknell South Hill Park Arts Centre in Berkshire in September 1980.

A second collection of short stories, *Children of Lir*, was published by the important British publisher Hamilton in 1981. *Children of Lir* combines a focus on the realities of Irish life with an interest in traditional Celtic mythology. The title refers to the Irish legend of the four children of Lir, transformed into swans by their jealous stepmother and sent into a long exile from which they return only to die. Hogan's collection includes twenty-five stories, all concerned with some sort of exile. In "The Mourning Thief" Hogan recounts the return of Liam Fogarthy from London to the bedside of his dying father in east Galway. Accompanied by his wife, Susan, and his lover, Gerard, Liam brings the burden of old griefs, unresolved conflicts, and frayed relationships to the household. Mr. Fogarthy, a retired policeman who had fought in the 1916 uprising, has had no use for his adolescent son's opposition to war and violence and has even less for his son's present occupation as a music teacher in a free school. Now the dying father dwells on the violence of 1916, the reflection prompted not only by his imminent death but also by the presence of his pacifist son. With restraint and psychological precision, Hogan crafts a story that becomes a meditation on the search for identity, both personal and political.

Exile and loss are the themes of other stories in the collection. In the first paragraph of "The Man from Korea," the narrator announces, "I will make my own version," and his story depicts the keen disappointment of a five-year-old boy at the departure of Karl, an American veteran of the Korean conflict, who has settled in an Irish village and befriended the child. Its central point is that Karl's departure is "the first hurt of my life," as the narrator tells the reader, and the text uses an older, wiser narrator, who is able to look back on the experience with a combination of sensitivity and satire. "A Fancy Dress Party" chronicles the last performance of a circus troupe and the humbling of its male protagonist, who later sleeps and dreams of "caravans headed West." "The Irish in Love" presents the festivities attendant to the ordination of young Gerald Hanratty, soon to be departing for missionary work in South Africa. Hogan's narrator gives the reader access to Father Hanratty's thoughts about his vocation, about what that vocation is likely to entail in the missions, and about how he hopes to reconcile his vocation with the reality of his own sexual needs in another place, where "different laws" prevail.

Two stories in *Children of Lir* again demonstrate a didactic tendency in Hogan's work. In "Protestant Boy," Hogan tells the story of two young men—Danny, a member of the Northern Irish Protestant elite, and the narrator, a middle-class youth from a Southern Irish Roman Catholic background. They meet as boys at summer camp, and the story of their intermittent friendship and occasional later encounters evolves against the backdrop of the renewed hostilities of the 1970s. Each comes to insight and maturity. In the last paragraphs, Hogan overtly interprets what has preceded by having his narrator assert, "I knew I could never again return to an ideology that made criminals of an entire race." "Teddyboys" is another tale of two boys (Jamesy and the narrator, Desmond). Their relationship, consisting only of the narrator's "exhausted and infatuated" observations of Jamesy, deals with death and guilt. It concludes by returning to the image of Our Lady of Fatima, used earlier in the text, to give the story a clear closure.

Other stories in the collection constantly return to the theme of exile. "The Sojourners" gives an account of a brother and his sister, just released from a mental hospital, who live together for a while in London before she returns home to Ireland, and he departs for work in southern Europe. Still other stories—for example, "Soho Gardens," "Memories of Swinging London," and "Cats"—present a world populated by wandering and displaced tinkers, lunatics, teddy boys, hippies, and gypsies. In "A Poet and an Englishman," a man and a woman move from Belfast to southern Ireland to escape the northern city's violence. The story depicts their attempt to understand and support each other. The title story, "The Children of Lir," is a traditional autobiographical story; Hogan's use of the "Children of Lir" folktale is a central metaphor, and the story is unified by images of swans drawn from the legend.

The 1980s were a productive and successful decade for Hogan. According to McCrum, Hogan was popular and celebrated in the London literary scene of those years. A short story titled "Thoughts" appeared in *Firebird I: Writing Today* (1982) and was placed among contributions by such important writers as Bernard MacLaverty, Angela Carter, Alasdair Gray, Salman Rushdie, Graham Swift, and William Trevor. "Thoughts" is the story of Grainne Dempsey, discontented daughter of wealth and privilege, educated at a French convent school and the Sorbonne, who has returned to Ireland after an unhappy love affair with a bisexual Austrian writer. In a small village, she teaches French, meets sixteen-year-old Eugene McMurrough, and shares her passionate love for literature with him. Their lives diverge: he leaves for Paris to study and she remains in Ireland. His place is taken by a rugby player who gets her pregnant, while she is replaced in Eugene's life by "a big fat French student who ate lollipops all the time." Eugene eventually returns to Ireland and to Grainne. In 1982, a collection of thirty of Hogan's short stories, all reprints from earlier volumes, appeared as *Stories: The Diamonds at the Bottom of the Sea, Children of Lir*.

In 1984 Hogan published *A Curious Street*, a complex novel set in seventeenth-century Europe, 1930s Dublin, and contemporary Belfast. He followed this work with the novel *A New Shirt* (1986) and *The Mourning Thief and Other Stories*, published in 1987, which reprints the entire contents of both *The Diamonds at the Bottom of the Sea* and *Children of Lir*. A short story, "Guy 'Micko' Delaney," appeared in *Winter's Tales: New Series 4* in 1988, one of fourteen stories in a collection by established writers (Francis King and Monica Furlong) and newer talents (Jeanette Winterson and David Leavitt). Hogan's story deals with Guy, son of the absent and mysterious "Micko" and a woman who, like so many female characters in Hogan's stories, descends into madness before dying and leaving eighteen-year-old Guy utterly on his own. Several years later, Guy leaves for South Africa by way of London; in a Cape Town jazz club he meets an acquaintance of his father who tells Guy he has a stepbrother in London. Encountering little but disdain from his stepbrother, Jonathan, Guy nevertheless settles in London. Intermittent meetings with Jonathan punctuate Guy's bleak existence as a carpet salesman. Guy reconstructs the story of his father's life and visits his grave. Interwoven with that story is Guy's own. "Guy 'Micko' Delaney" consists of a loose story line set against a familiar Hogan backdrop of nuns, priests, alcoholics, eccentrics, mad old women, mental patients, and flamboyant homosexuals. As the story ends, Hogan's narrator asks questions such as "Who are you?" and "What held you back?" in an overt attempt to focus the reader's attention on the point of the text.

Hogan published his third group of previously uncollected short stories, *Lebanon Lodge*, in 1988. *Lebanon Lodge* consists of thirteen stories. As in earlier volumes, outsiders and exiles figure prominently as protagonists. "Elysium" is the story of Mary, who deserts her husband, taking her three boys to London to begin a new life. Hogan's use of elements from social, political, and personal turmoil creates a context for the concluding revelation of the story. "The Tipperary Finale" is a complex piece of fiction dealing with both political and sexual violence; the story presents characters of mixed (Italian and Irish) ethnic backgrounds. "Players" is an account of cultural and social change seen through a company of theatrical players who come to an Irish village every year, and "Martyrs" is the story of Sister Honor, who leaves the relative comforts of convent-school teaching to die as an activist working with a Latin American religious community. These stories demonstrate Hogan's attempts to provide insight into psychologically complex characters. The same is true of "A Marriage in the Country," which deals with Magella, a pyromaniac and sometime patient in a mental hospital, and Boris, the orphan son of a Russian sailor and a Wexford prostitute, two outcasts who discover an intimacy and depth in marriage. This story represents one of the few texts in which Hogan has attempted to portray love between a man and a woman. In Magella he offers a portrait of a woman scarred by experience, who finds the lost worlds of youth in the embraces of a younger, foreign man; in Boris, Hogan presents an alienated man in search of another's love. "A Marriage in the Country" is a meditation on identity and the search for lost selves.

In "Ties," the narrator tells of his father, a tailor, and his assistant, Patsy Fogarthy, described as "our small-town Oscar Wilde," a local eccentric whose relationship with the narrator's father is set out in detail in the course of the story. Patsy ends up expelled from the village and a resident in a mental hospital, but not before he has wound a symbolic scarlet tie round the narrator's neck. "Miles" is the portrait of Rose, a woman who had abandoned her children in Ireland many years before to live in London and work as a chambermaid. Every year she goes on pilgrimage to the shrine of the Virgin Mary at Walsingham, Norfolk; each year her faith and hope lessen until the pilgrimage becomes nothing more than an excuse to drink and meet pathetic men. Drawn also to the shrine in the focal year of the story is an assortment of characters, including Miles, the son she left behind. The story is unusual in that it is a twenty-page text divided into thirty-seven short sections.

"The Vicar's Wife" concerns the marriage between Joly, a Roman Catholic beauty queen, and Colin, a Protestant vicar freshly graduated from Trinity College Dublin. Joly turns her back on her family and religion and marries Colin, only to discover terrible secrets that cause her to leave and drift for nearly twenty years before returning to him. The title story, "Lebanon Lodge," is a tale about Lucien Hoagman. His story, interwoven from strands of Jewish and Irish family history, is complex; descriptive detail provides a context within which the psychobiographical narrative of Hoagman acquires depth. Hogan's use of the physical presence and space of Lebanon Lodge not only is a metaphor but also a link to the tradition of the "big

Front cover for the 1989 paperback edition of Hogan's 1988 collection of stories, primarily about outsiders and exiles (Bruccoli Clark Layman Archives)

house" fiction practiced by two other Irish writers, Elizabeth Bowen and Molly Keane. Of the five remaining stories in *Lebanon Lodge,* "The Airedale" is an homage to Joyce; "Recovery" is marked by its use of symbolism; "Grief" is a brief character sketch; and the last story in the collection, "By the River," is a prose-poem.

McCrum writes of Hogan in the 1980s that despite his success, he was not a happy man. In addition, he lived a life of isolation, setting himself somewhat apart from London society. As McCrum recalls, "Hogan's answer to the philistine exuberance of Thatcher's Britain was a life of rare, even priestlike, simplicity. He lived on nothing. He never went to the doctor, preferring herbal remedies. He wrote in longhand or on a battered portable typewriter. His typescripts were xeroxed collages of cut-and-pasted paragraphs, lit up with startling and brilliant jewel-like images." In the late 1980s he taught briefly at the University of Alabama, finding the southern United States congenial. But he returned to Europe, first to London, and then traveled to Amsterdam, Berlin, and Prague. McCrum states that Hogan had fallen in love with a young man named Sammy, who was based in Berlin. In 1991, Hogan was awarded a DAAD (German Academic Exchange Service) grant to go to Berlin.

Hogan's most recent collection of short fiction to be published in the United States is a volume of reprints. *A Link with the River* (1989) gathers twenty-five stories, seven from *The Diamonds at the Bottom of the Sea,* thirteen from *Lebanon Lodge,* and five from *Children of Lir.* It has an introduction by Erdrich, and it made Hogan's work more accessible in the United States. It also elicited a substantial critical essay on Hogan's short fiction, written by Donoghue, "Making the Most of Dublin" (in the *New York Times Book Review,* 16 July 1989), in which Donoghue mixes praise and censure of the author's work. Hogan's travels in Europe led to two nonfiction books, *The Edge of the City: A Scrapbook, 1976–1991* (1993) and *Farewell to Prague* (1995), the latter a complex collage-like collection of notes and observations. In the on-line journal *The Richmond Review,* Adam Baron wrote that, in *Farewell to Prague,* Hogan's "prose style . . . aptly conveys the schizophrenia of a changing continent." Baron also called it "a beautiful, haunting elegy to lost love and friendship." McCrum speculates that at this time Hogan's companion Sammy died of AIDS and that Hogan himself was near to a nervous breakdown, obsessed with death and visiting the old Jewish cemeteries of European cities.

For several years Hogan appears to have distanced himself from friends and acquaintances, and to have done little writing. In 1995 he returned to Ireland, living a life of considerable poverty on the margins of established society, moving frequently from place to place. He associated at this time with Irish travelers (gypsies), listening to their stories, which, according to him, were "amazing." Irish publisher Anthony Farrell, however, kept in contact with Hogan and was able eventually to secure him an Irish Arts Council grant and to commit the Lilliput Press in Dublin to publish a new collection of Hogan's stories, as well as his earlier works. Hogan's return to the public and literary world was marked by a period of employment as a professor at the University of California in San Diego in 1997, where he particularly enjoyed teaching students who surfed. In addition, Tóibín published "Memories of Swinging London" in the influential *Penguin Anthology of Irish Fiction* (1999), where it stands beside works by the most outstanding Irish writers of the past three centuries, as well as that of Hogan's contemporaries.

"Winter Swimmers" also appeared in *New Writing 11* (2002), edited by Andrew O'Hagan and Tóibín. Loosely organized and full of typical Hogan preoccupations (adolescent sexuality, identity, homosexual activity) and a self-reflexive literary style, it covers territory familiar from Hogan's earlier work. "Winter Swimmers" is a first-person recollection that juxtaposes diverse fragments of experience, all of them somehow connected to the custom of winter swimming in an Irish tidal river. The experience serves as a touchstone for memory, enabling the narrator to describe some of his fellow swimmers, particularly "the youth with the primrose-flecked hair," for whom he has an obsessive concern. Hogan's prose is frequently descriptive ("the bog cotton blew like patriarchs' beards"), and his narrator revels in describing male objects of desire ("a boy on a Shetland pony, with copper-crenelled mid-sixties hair and ultramarine irises" and another with "liquid ebony hair, a fringe beard . . . [and] cherry-colored nipples"). In *TLS: The Times Literary Supplement* (12 April 2002), Oates singled out this story for praise. Of it she wrote, "described as a short story, Hogan's piece is essentially a daringly sustained prose poem that, instead of gathering to a climax at its conclusion, simply dissolves into jewel-like elements." "Winter Swimmers" is certainly a fragmentary text that eschews narrative in favor of description. Its conclusion is described by Oates as "elegiac."

Desmond Hogan's short stories foreground enduring concerns with identity and Ireland. His Ireland is the Ireland of political division, religious hostilities, and guerrilla violence, a place he knows well from his early years, though he made his home in London for a decade and has traveled widely in Europe and the United States. Within this context, his characters—men and women considerably distressed, alienated, and full of conflicts—seek, and most often fail, to find a place for themselves. Exile of one sort or another is inevitable. Though Britain and continental Europe may provide temporary respite, the pull of the mother country exerts itself with powerful, often fatal, force. The deep paradoxes inherent in the possibility, and yet the impossibility, of going home provide substance and tension to many of his stories.

When Hogan focuses primarily on one character, as in "Afternoon" or "The Irish in Love," his lyrical and fragmented style is a metaphor for personal, social, and national conflicts. His work has received high praise from some critics, such as Padraigin McGillicuddy in the *San Francisco Chronicle* (6 August 1989), who wrote, "Hogan's mastery of language and characterization rivals that of Flannery O'Connor and Anton Chekhov." Erdrich, in her preface to *A Link with the River,* insists that "In his hands, fiction becomes transformative. The stories . . . are acts that verge upon the sacramental." Yet, the tone of Hogan's short fiction, as Oates has noted, is also deeply melancholic, the landscape bleak and haunted, the opportunities for deliverance virtually nonexistent. In addition, some critics have pointed to an unevenness in the quality in his work—for example, Donoghue, who, in a review of *A Link with the River* in the *New York Times Book Review* of 16 July 1989, concludes, "Hogan's talent seems to me, like the Ireland he writes about, irregular, unreliable, often deplorable, but somehow distinctive." For many younger Irish writers, however, McCrum declares, Hogan is an exemplary writer, one devoted to his craft and unwilling to join in the consumerism of contemporary Ireland. Despite his absence from the literary scene in the early 1990s, his career has started up again, and the Lilliput Press in Dublin has announced that it will publish a partly new collection of short stories, *Winter Swimmers: New and Collected Stories,* in September 2005.

References

Theo D'Hean, "Desmond Hogan and Ireland's Postmodern Part," in *History and Violence in Anglo-Irish Literature,* edited by Joris Duytschaeuer and Geert Lernout (Amsterdam: Rodopi, 1988), pp. 79–84;

D'Hean, "Irish Regionalism, Magic Realism and Postmodernism," in *British Postmodern Fiction,* edited by D'Hean and Hans Bertens (Amsterdam & Atlanta: Rodopi, 1993), pp. 33–46;

Robert McCrum, "The Vanishing Man," *Observer* (14 November 2004) <http://observer.guardian.co.uk>.

Dan Jacobson
(7 March 1929 –   )

Janine Utell
Widener University

See also the Jacobson entries in *DLB 14: British Novelists Since 1960; DLB 207: British Novelists Since 1960, Third Series;* and *DLB 225: South African Writers.*

BOOKS: *The Trap* (London: Weidenfeld & Nicolson, 1955; New York: Harcourt, Brace, 1955);

A Dance in the Sun (London: Weidenfeld & Nicolson, 1956; New York: Harcourt, Brace, 1956);

No Further West: California Visited (London: Weidenfeld & Nicolson, 1957; New York: Macmillan, 1961);

The Price of Diamonds (London: Weidenfeld & Nicolson, 1957; New York: Knopf, 1958);

A Long Way from London (London: Weidenfeld & Nicolson, 1958); republished as *The Zulu and the Zeide* (Boston: Little, Brown, 1959);

The Evidence of Love (London: Weidenfeld & Nicolson, 1960; Boston: Little, Brown, 1960);

Time of Arrival and Other Essays (London: Weidenfeld & Nicolson, 1962);

Beggar My Neighbour: Short Stories (London: Weidenfeld & Nicolson, 1964);

The Beginners (London: Weidenfeld & Nicolson, 1966; New York: Macmillan, 1966);

Through the Wilderness and Other Stories (New York: Macmillan, 1968);

The Rape of Tamar (London: Weidenfeld & Nicolson, 1970; New York: Macmillan, 1970);

A Way of Life and Other Stories (London: Longman, 1971);

Inklings: Selected Stories (London: Weidenfeld & Nicolson, 1973);

The Wonder-Worker (London: Weidenfeld & Nicolson, 1973; Boston: Little, Brown, 1974);

The Confessions of Josef Baisz (London: Secker & Warburg, 1977; New York: Harper & Row, 1977);

The Story of Stories: The Chosen People and Its God (London: Secker & Warburg, 1982; New York: Harper & Row, 1982);

Time and Time Again: Autobiographies (London: Deutsch, 1985; Boston: Atlantic Monthly Press, 1985);

Her Story (London: Deutsch, 1987);

Dan Jacobson (from the dust jacket for Time and Time Again: Autobiographies, *1985; Richland County Public Library)*

Adult Pleasures: Essays on Writers and Readers (London: Deutsch, 1988);

Hidden in the Heart (London: Bloomsbury, 1991);

The God-Fearer (London: Bloomsbury, 1992; New York: Scribners, 1993);

The Electronic Elephant: A Southern African Journey (London: Hamilton, 1994);

Heshel's Kingdom (London: Hamilton, 1998; Evanston, Ill.: Northwestern University Press, 1999);
All for Love (London & New York: Hamilton, 2005).

OTHER: "Beggar My Neighbour," in *South African Writing Today,* edited by Anthony Sampson (London: Penguin, 1967), pp. 36–47;
Olive Schreiner, *The Story of an African Farm,* introduction by Jacobson (London & New York: Penguin, 1971);
"Beggar My Neighbour," in *South African Jewish Voices,* edited by Robert and Roberta Kalechofsky (Marblehead, Mass.: Micah, 1982), pp. 95–106;
Henk van Woerden, *The Assassin,* translated by Jacobson (London: Granta, 2000);
"The Zulu and the Zeide," in *Contemporary Jewish Writing in South Africa: An Anthology,* edited by Claudia Bathsheba Braude (Lincoln: University of Nebraska Press, 2001), pp. 31–44.

SELECTED PERIODICAL PUBLICATIONS–UNCOLLECTED: "Settling in England: Reflections of a South African Jew," *Commentary,* 29 (1960): 23–28;
"Return to South Africa," *Commentary,* 30 (1960): 6–16;
"My Jewish Childhood," *Commentary,* 110 (2000): 38–43.

Over the course of his career, Dan Jacobson has worked in many different genres and with many different subjects. In addition to his novels and short stories, he has published travel writings, essays on literature and religion, autobiography, and several books and articles on politics and history. He has won six major literary awards and has held teaching positions at Stanford University, Syracuse University, and University College London. Yet, outside the realm of those who read Jewish fiction, South African fiction, or postcolonial fiction, Jacobson remains overlooked, a fact he himself has acknowledged. This neglect may have occurred in part because he is difficult to categorize. He is a South African who has spent much of his life outside South Africa, a liberal who acknowledges his own prejudices, a Jewish writer who approaches his Judaism with the eye of a secular rationalist, and a cosmopolitan who questions ideas of exile and homeland.

Jacobson's short stories, which were written and published between 1953 and 1968, address many of these themes and issues. Although only the two earliest were written while Jacobson still lived in South Africa, most are set there and deal with the social and political tensions of that country in both public and private life; others, set in London, examine the postcolonial self and its relationship to the center or site of colonial power. They are characterized by a sense of fatalism and alienation; they explore how individuals fail to connect, reflecting the atmosphere of proto-apartheid South Africa (a society riven by racial and class conflict) in the decades when Jacobson was writing them.

Jacobson himself has described feeling a lack of connection to the land of his childhood, to the country he has adopted—indeed, to the audience for his works. Yet, he noted in a 1986 interview with Stephen Gray that the stories are what readers most often seem to remember and want to discuss with him. Although many critics praise the integrity and humanity of his vision, some critics, particularly those writing after the end of apartheid, censure Jacobson for what they view as his lack of political commitment, especially during the time of the composition and publication of his short stories.

Jacobson's parents were Eastern European Jews who arrived in South Africa as part of a wave of Jewish immigrants to that country around the turn of the century. At the time of Jacobson's youth, 130 Jewish families were living in Kimberley, where the family ultimately settled in the 1930s. (Approximately 150,000 Jews lived in the entire country.) His father, Michael, came from Latvia and his mother, Liebe Melamed, came from Lithuania; they moved to Johannesburg and married somewhat late in life. Dan was born in Johannesburg 7 March 1929, the youngest of three sons and a daughter. Michael Jacobson worked in a variety of trades: milk deliveryman, soldier, farmer, and editor. The family moved to Kimberley when Dan Jacobson was four, where Michael Jacobson ran a butter factory, Mills and Feeds, Ltd. Michael was also a Zionist and active in the Jewish community in Kimberley, serving on his synagogue committee, in the Zionist society, and in the Chamber of Commerce and the United Party, which governed South Africa until the Afrikaner Nationalist Party came to power in 1948. Liebe Jacobson was a quiet, melancholic woman who worked as a bookkeeper in the family butter factory. The family was middle-class and middlebrow, respectable among the other bourgeois whites, gripped by what Jacobson calls in *Time and Time Again* (1985) "their sedate preoccupation with their jobs, their gardens, their cars, their bowls and tennis clubs, their Sunday outings, their cousinage, their gossip about one another, their exact status in the quite elaborate social hierarchy they had arranged among themselves."

The Jacobsons' marriage was not a harmonious one. Michael Jacobson was a man of violent temper and great pride. He worried endlessly about his status in Kimberley, his wealth—which in later years was considerable—and the respect he believed it should bring him but always felt it did not. Liebe Jacobson, in contrast,

Title page for the retitled 1959 U.S. edition of Jacobson's 1958 collection of short stories, A Long Way from London, written after Jacobson moved to England from South Africa. The book won the Llewelyn Rhys Memorial Prize for 1959 (Thomas Cooper Library, University of South Carolina).

was unconcerned with status and class, content to work in the factory and read European novels. In addition to this clash of dissimilar personalities and values, the Jacobsons argued over the best way to raise their children in the Jewish faith and community. The Jewish community in Kimberley was small and close-knit, and Michael Jacobson was adamant that his children be part of it. He insisted that they go to synagogue and Hebrew lessons, and accused his wife of corrupting the children and undermining his authority when she rejected Jewish tradition and practice. At the same time, however, their shared immigrant experience and the tensions among the various groups in the society in which they lived brought them together.

Kimberley at the time was essentially a company town of the De Beers diamond company. It was hot, dry, and, during Jacobson's youth, perceived as economically inert. At the time of his parents' move there, the city was just emerging from a period of stagnation when the diamond mines had ceased to function. Prior to this moment of resurgence, Kimberley was a ghost town, isolated and forgotten. It stands in the middle of the veld, or grass field, a place portrayed in Jacobson's fiction as indifferent, silent, and empty.

Jacobson's stories move between the fatal openness, the existential blankness of the veld, and the stifling claustrophobia of town life. Kimberley, like other South African cities, was highly regimented and hierarchical. The Anglo-Boer War, lasting from 1899 to 1902, during which the separate Afrikaner states were defeated by the British and incorporated into the Union of South Africa, was still part of the collective historical memory. The English were dominant and remained at the top of the social ladder. The Afrikaner population was smaller than in other areas of the country, and they lived separately from the English, attending separate schools and living in different neighborhoods. The Coloureds, or those of "mixed race," lived in "locations," isolated from the whites. The blacks existed, or subsisted rather, at the bottom of the social ladder. Each group spoke its own language, had its own codes, and lived in suspicion of the others.

Because of the dominance of the English, Kimberley was a colonial town. Vestiges of the Victorian period were to be found in the architecture, the public spaces, and the monuments. The streets were named for English military heroes; the suburbs, for London neighborhoods. As a boy, Jacobson attended an "English" school, playing cricket and rugby and reading English literature. The permeation of his country by English influence and cultural dominance became important later in his fiction. He wrote in an article for *Commentary*, "Settling in England" (1960), "The 'Englishness' of the city as it appeared to me in my boyhood . . . may help the reader to understand how it was that in a hot tin-roofed mining town on the edge of the Karroo, I felt myself to be involved very deeply, and very early, with an idea of England." This involvement created in Jacobson from an early age the sense that the country in which he lived–the veld, the small houses with their *stoeps* (front porches), the Karroo, and the mines–was somehow unreal, that the England of his books and the Englishness after which his society grasped was reality.

While England felt far away, the events in Europe, despite their distance, felt too close. Jacobson's youth was marked by the Holocaust; although it does not overtly appear in any of his short stories, themselves inspired by so much of his youthful experience, the awareness of what was happening in Europe affected Jacobson's relationship to his family, to his Judaism, and to his country. For Jacobson, being Jewish at such a time meant one was international. One's fate was inextricably linked with that of the rest of the world; the individual was part of history.

In South Africa, the Zionist movement was important, and Jews felt a connection to England both because of their residence in a colonial country and because of British support for the establishment of a Jewish homeland in Palestine. Possibly because they already lived in a racially charged state, Jews in South Africa felt passionately about the Zionist cause. They themselves existed on a lower rung of the social ladder than other whites. As a result, perhaps slightly less racism toward blacks existed among Jews, a fact that Jacobson recalls and discusses with some ambivalence. He notes his own prejudices, yet acknowledges some affinity with the blacks of the country.

This awareness of racial divides became even more charged during Jacobson's boyhood with the rise of Nazi sympathies in South Africa, in the years leading up to and during World War II. He was confronted with anti-Semitism at school. Greyshirts, or Afrikaner Nazi sympathizers, took to the streets with pro-German propaganda. Jacobson recalled in an article called "My Jewish Childhood" (2000) that South African society was friendly enough to the kind of racist ideology the Nazis were preaching that, if the war had gone badly on the British side, the country would have become a dangerous place for Jews. This environment made Jacobson all the more conscious of his Judaism and the place Jews held in world affairs. Even though his upbringing was primarily secular, this consciousness permeated his South African fiction throughout the 1950s and 1960s.

After graduating from Kimberley Boys High School at the age of sixteen, Jacobson went to the University of Witwatersrand in Johannesburg, where he studied English for three years. Upon graduating in 1948, he traveled to Israel to work on a kibbutz for two years. In 1948 also, the Afrikaner Nationalist Party came to power and consolidated its policies of apartheid. The tightening of racist ideology in the late 1940s and 1950s created the social and political climate that came to inform Jacobson's South African fiction. This "first career," as Gray called it in his interview with Jacobson, covers those of Jacobson's books set in South Africa, dealing with the social and political issues of that country; this period includes the short stories collected in *A Long Way from London* (1958; republished as *The Zulu and the Zeide*, 1959) and *Beggar My Neighbour* (1964). These stories also appeared, with other previously uncollected stories, in a collection titled *Through the Wilderness and Other Stories* (published in the United States in 1968).

Jacobson made his first trip to London in 1950, at the age of twenty-one, with his brother. He wrote in "Settling in England": "I felt, I suppose, what every provincial or colonial feels when he comes for the first time to the center of things; and I felt too an unexpected gratitude both to the circumstances in my life which had made it possible for me to come to the center, and to the center itself for being as metropolitan, as orderly, rich, and various as it was." On this trip, encountering the center of his cultural universe, Jacobson felt the first stirring of ambition, of hope that he might do work of significance. The period was also one of isolation and loneliness as he attempted to survive in the city on his own once his brother left to return home; he did, however, meet his future wife, Margaret Pye, originally of Rhodesia (now Zimbabwe). He worked in an Orthodox Jewish boys' school for a term until he was asked to leave for "giving offense": he was tricked by the students into saying that he did not believe God created the universe. This first trip to England proved to be a moment when Jacobson had to come to terms with his own outsider status, as a colonial who wished to come to the center and as a Jew who was adamantly secular. As Paul Gready notes in "Dan Jacobson as Expatriate Writer" (1994), Jacobson is "caught between worlds, forever in the act of crossing over." He never quite seems to reconcile himself to being an outsider, claiming no real connection with either South Africa or England, rejecting a notion of "belonging."

Jacobson returned to South Africa in 1951, where he worked for several years as a journalist and then in the family butter factory. In this brief interlude before returning to England for good in 1954, he wrote his first two South Africa stories, "The Box" and "A Day in the Country," the only two actually written in South Africa. In the first story, a white boy keeps homing pigeons as a hobby. His relationship with the black houseboy, Jan, is casual, and the white boy takes no real notice of the servant's potterings. One day, Jan creates an elaborate box for the pigeons to live in, with walls and doors and a little bench. He is pleased with his handiwork, but his young master thinks the box is useless and dismantles it. When Jan confronts him, crying, "What have you done?" the boy realizes that the "Kaffir" has feelings; he has an inner emotional life, which before had been incomprehensible to the boy: "Somehow they weren't real emotions; my emotions; they were black emotions, different from my own. But now Jan had crossed the barrier. He was crying as I might cry. There was no difference between us at all. He was human, and he was crying." Simultaneously, however, the boy discovers he cannot reach across the gulf of their racial difference to comfort Jan. He cannot touch him or console him. In this story, Jacobson

Dust jacket for Jacobson's 1964 collection of short stories in which he explores the relationship between decency and liberal thinking (Bruccoli Clark Layman Archives)

addresses the ambivalence of the basically decent white person living in South African society. Within such a person a conflict exists, knowing that the way in which he lives is wrong and feeling guilt over it, yet unable to overcome his own prejudices and repulsion toward the other.

In "A Day in the Country," the other early work and one based on an autobiographical incident, Jacobson tells the story of a Jewish family driving in the veld on the way home from their farm when they see an Afrikaner family tormenting a black child. The Jews condemn the family silently and drive on. The Afrikaner family follows them and shouts an insult (it is implied in the story that they call out a derogatory term for Jews). The story culminates in a confrontation between the Jews and Afrikaners as each side believes it has been insulted. Neither group wants to resort to violence; neither wants to back down. As the characters argue, the narrator—one of the Jewish boys—realizes that the fight is unwinnable. There can be no satisfactory resolution, because all groups exist in mistrust of one another, and all groups believe they are right. There can be no peace, because there can be no connection and no reconciliation. Finally, the Afrikaner family admits that the "sport" they had been making of the black child was wrong, but the narrator sees that there was no victory: "We had all lost, so much, somewhere, farther back along that dusty road." The story examines the deep-rooted tensions in South African society and illustrates Jacobson's sense that no one who lives in such a society is innocent.

In February 1954 Jacobson married in Cape Town and moved to England permanently; he and his wife had three children—Simon Orde, Matthew Lindsay, and Jessica Liebe. Since his move to England, however, he has traveled to South Africa frequently, as well as throughout Africa, the United States, Israel, and Eastern Europe. During the 1950s and 1960s Jacobson composed his South Africa works. These works include the novellas *The Trap* (1955) and *A Dance in the Sun* (1956), which look at racial and family tensions; the novels *The Price of Diamonds* (1957), a study of corruption centered around illicit diamond buying; *The Evidence of Love* (1960); and *The Beginners* (1966), a multigenerational naturalistic novel about a South African Jewish family.

Jacobson has written about his decision to leave the country of his birth, noting in "Settling in England" that South Africa is "a miserable country to live in.... But what people do not usually realize is that this misery is only rarely dramatic and poignant: usually it is dull and dragging and wearisome, a sickness of discord and disaffection, of division and self-division, which has neither crisis nor abatement." In contrast, England, in his eyes, is a country of power, of freedom from authoritarian rule, of liberty and privacy. In "Return to South Africa" (1960), written after one of his early trips back after the move to England, he noted the poverty and political crises that were tearing the country apart. He also struggled with the impossibility of being a liberal, of attempting to foster political change without brute force in a country of violence and dangerous ideology. This conflict—this rejection of political force and of the seeking out of power—characterizes Jacobson's stories and forms the foundation for some of the harshest criticism of his work.

"The Box" and "A Day in the Country" appeared in the 1958 collection *A Long Way from London,* along with other stories composed after Jacobson moved to England. The collection won the Llewelyn Rhys Memorial Prize for 1959. In America, the collection, published as *The Zulu and the Zeide,* was praised for its "insight and sympathy" in *Booklist* (1 September 1959). Robert Gutwillig, in *Commonweal* (5 June 1959), noted that while occasionally the "material is not as impressive as his technique," Jacobson is "not only South Africa's best writer, which may or may not be an invidious distinction, but he is one of the best writers of short fiction anywhere."

Many of the stories have clear autobiographical roots. For example, "After the Riot," which examines the aftermath of a black riot in a small mining town, stems from Jacobson's experience in his father's factory. An ominous pall of violence hangs over the story as the day and night after the riot unfurl; this sense of violence on the brink of exploding is common to many of Jacobson's stories. Just as common, though, is the violence that never bursts out, but instead is defused, leaving only exhaustion and the feeling that the next time could be worse. "After the Riot" leaves the reader with the experience of violence unfulfilled, creating a sense of impotence, paralysis, and the unsettling sensation that another eruption may take place. The action of the story unfolds as trouble starts to brew at the factory. The patriarch of the family is summoned, and the sons follow. Up until the moment when the sons see the father's smiling face surrounded by armed police at the entrance of the factory, they—and the reader—expect the worst. The rest of the story is an explanation that no violence had taken place at the factory, only an incident of a black worker having a sexual tryst with a woman. In this moment of normality, of the simple fulfilling of human appetite and connection, a potentially dangerous situation is neutralized.

In "After the Riot," the reader is left with a dominant impression of the fear of the whites in the story. They live under siege, unable to do anything about the consequences of the ideological machine they have set into motion, the wrath of the oppressed they have incurred, and the undertow of violence that threatens to tear the society apart. Jacobson explores this problem in microcosm as well, looking into the intimacy of the domestic world and how it is poisoned by the violence that is endemic to South African society. "Stop Thief!" tells the story of a family ruled by a roughhousing patriarch who plays aggressive, sometimes cruel, games with his children. He chases the children, and simple games of hide-and-seek are represented as instances when the children are forced to submit to his will. Jacobson makes a profound connection between the wealth and power of the whites and the viciousness of their intimacies: "It was for their father's mock anger that they [the children] lived. The mother knew this and did not resent it: she believed that the insolence she loved in them had come from their father, and for her her husband's violence was profoundly confused with his wealth." Here the reader notes the problematic relationship between parent and child, husband and wife, corrupted by the society in which the family unit exists.

Finally, this outside world invades the home in the person of a burglar. When the burglar is caught in the kitchen, the son demands he be beaten: " 'Why don't you hit the burglar? You must hit the burglar.' He danced like a little demon in his light pajamas. 'Hit!' he screamed. 'Hit!'" The child is transformed by a desire for violence, and the family is never the same as the father sees that it is "from his hands in one night the violence in the family had passed." The desire for revenge, for brutality, is passed down from generation to generation, within families and within South African society.

"The Little Pet" explores the presence of violence in the domestic sphere in an even more visceral way. A mother and a father bring home a pregnant rabbit for their little son. The "little pet" of the title is ambiguous; it could be the innocuous little bunny, or it could be the son, who is treated as a toy by his overprotective, overly solicitous parents. After the rabbit gives birth, she eats her baby; when the parents discover the bloody mess, they want to get rid of her, to expel her from the home. The son insists the family keep the pet. The story concludes with the boy saying, "I'm not cross with you. I knew you didn't like your baby." The link between the intimacy of the family and the intimacy of birth and cruelty is profound. The boy himself senses that his parents reject him emotionally, and he feels an affinity with the brutality of his pet. At a young age, he recognizes that human relationships are founded on this visceral kind of brutality.

Jacobson uses his stories to explore the invasion of the individual's privacy by politics, as Richard Peck claims in his book *A Morbid Fascination* (1997); when the landscape itself is political, no escape from the political landscape is possible. The layout of the streets in quasi-Victorian Kimberley, the location of the "locations" where the Coloureds and poor whites lived, the veld and the mining fields abandoned by imperial capitalists—all of these elements have a political existence that infiltrates the private life of the individual. It infiltrates Jacobson's fiction, which is why to a certain extent he ultimately stopped writing about South Africa. He notes about his decision to move to England in "Settling in England" that the individual desires to live "unmolested" in his own home. Thus, he chose to make his home elsewhere, although in his South Africa fiction the domestic sphere is still invaded by politics.

The much-anthologized story "The Zulu and the Zeide," which was adapted as a musical in 1966 by Harold Rome, Howard da Silva, and Felix Leon, shows what happens when family and politics collide. In the text, Grossman is trying to care for his senile old father, who keeps running away. He hires a "Zulu" named Paulus, a black man, to watch over the "zeide," or

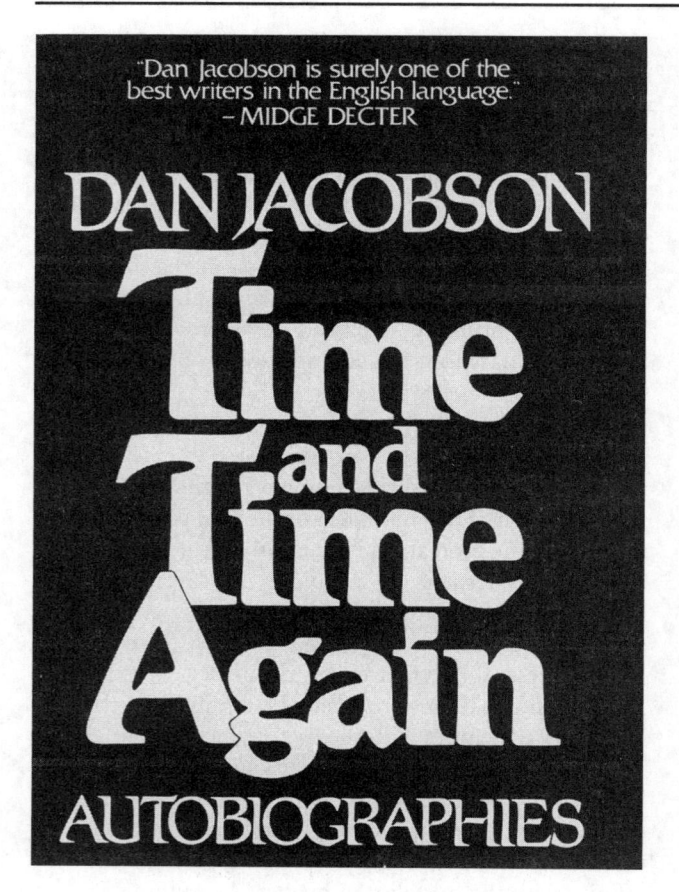

Dust jacket for the 1985 U.S. edition of Jacobson's recollections about the South African Jewish culture in which he grew up (Richland County Public Library)

grandfather. Grossman's resentment and prejudices emerge when the old man grows deeply attached to Paulus. As the old man comes to rely more on Paulus for his most intimate care–feeding, bathing, and clothing–he further rejects his son. The old man demands that his son leave the house and refuses to speak to him. The story illustrates the greatest fear of the whites: the black man taking over the home, supplanting the *baas,* or white superior. Paulus and old man Grossman live outside of language, neither being able to understand what the other is saying, since one speaks Zulu and one speaks Yiddish, but the connection is physical and intimate. This story speaks also to the traditional sympathy Jews in South Africa had for blacks as fellow outsiders. Yet, Grossman rejects this sympathy, exemplifying the deep ambivalence Jacobson displays in other works. He sends Paulus away without telling his father where Paulus has gone. In his great distress, the old man runs out into the street and is killed by a bicyclist. At the conclusion of the story, Grossman cries at learning that Paulus had been saving to bring his family from Zululand to Johannesburg, as his own father had saved to move his family. The connection with the Zulu proves too much for Grossman, as he realizes how his own connection with his father was severed.

While Jacobson never ended his connection with South Africa, he found himself unable to live there, a truth he considers in "A Long Way from London." A reviewer in *The New York Times* (31 May 1959) noted that the stories set in England do not quite reach the level of insight that those set in South Africa do; nevertheless, this story speaks to Jacobson's own ambivalence. In the story, Arthur Panter moves to London; yet, he feels the same ambivalence and lack of belonging he felt at home. He had "an intense distaste for the country of his birth: South Africa was colonial, tawdry, second-rate"; yet, in England, "he had priced it all, and knew that it wasn't worth the effort. True, there was nothing else. He could never go back. He would die in the desert airs of the Eastern Province; but all the same, England wasn't civilized enough." The imaginary homeland of England does not measure up to the reality of England Arthur finds when he gets there, but neither can he return to the margins, to South Africa, which is even less real to him.

Arthur has also left South Africa because he can no longer stand to be a "liberal." He has left to escape his own inevitable political fate: "In South Africa one had to be a 'liberal,' lest one find oneself among the supporters of the South African government, and supporters of the South African government were even more unspeakable than South African 'liberals.'" He sees his options as rejecting political action, or struggling for change, or falling into line with the Afrikaner nationalist ideology. So Arthur simply refuses to choose. Yet, when his mother arrives for a visit with a black man in tow and asks Arthur to permit the man to stay, Arthur refuses. His mother attempts to justify her son's behavior by saying he is treating the visitor as an "equal," but Arthur cannot help thinking he has made an inhuman choice, that he has carried his prejudices with him across continents, that he has never really left his place of origin. Arthur and his mother perpetuate the fiction that things are "different there," but the story leaves the reader with the idea that decency is the same anywhere, and if one rejects political action, the least one can do is to be decent.

This problematic relationship to decency and to liberal thinking continued to haunt Jacobson's fiction, including his second collection of stories, *Beggar My Neighbour*. Stories in this collection and those in the first were brought together in *Inklings* (1973). Reviewers criticized these stories for a "lack of large gestures" (as Sheila Roberts said in *Stand,* 1973), but Jacobson's purpose seems to be to show that large gestures in such a claustrophobic society are impossible. In "Another Day," when the black servant woman of a white family gets sick, it is the "liberal," decent thing to do to continue to pay her an allowance and to take her back to work even though clearly she will never be completely well again. This attempt to help the servant is a gesture toward humanity, even if it is not a gesture toward political change.

In the title story of the collection, "Beggar My Neighbour," a white child, Michael, gives bread to a black brother and sister he finds begging outside his school. He continues to give them bread, all the while becoming more impressed with what he sees as his generosity. He values his own gesture of magnanimity and humanity, thus denying the children their own humanity. He fantasizes about elaborate displays of gratitude on their part, never suspecting for a moment they may despise him: "Sometimes Michael wished that they were more demonstrative in their expressions of gratitude to him; he thought that they could, for instance, seize his hand and embrace it; or go down on their knees and weep, just once." When they continue to haunt him for bread, he loses patience and shuns them, exerting a capricious power over their needs. His fantasies become violent imaginations; he daydreams about ordering them around or having them shot. Jacobson in this story represents the dual sides of power: pride in one's own generosity and condescension toward the recipient, and scorn and anger at the neediness of the individual who has subjected him- or herself. Michael comes to hate the children, a sickness of his soul that manifests itself in a physical illness. While he is sick, he has horrible nightmares of raping the girl, murdering the boy. When he realizes what he has become, he finds them, reaches out to them, kisses them, and is grief-stricken to find that this moment of connection and reconciliation is a dream. He never sees the children again. In this story, Jacobson shows how gestures toward decency fail when the underlying human feeling does not exist.

In "Fresh Fields" Jacobson returns to the problem of finding a voice, of representing a reality that has gone unrepresented. In this work, a young South African writer seeks out an older, established poet, Frederick Traill, a fellow countryman who has settled in England. The young writer looks to Traill for guidance and is told by the old man, "Go home! Don't do what I did! Go home!" The poet continues, "When I came here I had my store with me, and I began unpacking it, and the more I unpacked the more there seemed to be. I felt free and happy, ready to work for a lifetime. All around me was this—all this, just what I had hankered for, out there in the veld. Until one day I found that there was no more work for me to do, the store was finished. . . . So now I'm dumb. Dumb, that's all." Traill is the postcolonial self who has been silenced by his journey to the center. His country of origin was his material, and leaving it has left him with nothing. After his conversation, the young author gets a letter from Traill asking to see some of his work. The young author soon realizes that Traill is plagiarizing from his work and publishing it. When confronted, Traill points out what the young man himself said: the work was inspired by Traill's writing. The young author's stories are ghosts of the older man's poetry, and the young man ultimately decides they belong to Traill. The young man is forced to confront the ghosts of his own heritage in South Africa and the imaginary homeland of England, where he believes his ambitions lie. He is caught between the past and future, belonging to neither, struggling for a voice.

This dilemma seems to echo what Jacobson went through in his own writing life once he decided to stop writing about South Africa. He went through something of a dry spell and then began his "second career" with *The Rape of Tamar* (1970). He also stopped writing short stories, which some critics believed were his best work. In his later works, Jacobson has composed texts that look more toward Jewish tradition for inspiration; for instance, in *The Rape of Tamar,* he retells the story of the rape by her half brother of King David's daughter. This novel is concerned with issues of power and narrative, as many of Jacobson's other later novels are. *The Wonder-Worker* (1973) is a tale of a boy who believes he has supernatural powers. *The Confessions of Josef Baisz* (1977) is a dystopian novel set in an imaginary totalitarian state. *Her Story* (1987) joins once again biblical themes and metafictional considerations as it tells of the discovery of a manuscript that relates the story of a woman whose son was one of the thieves at the Crucifixion. Jacobson's book *Heshel's Kingdom* (1998) mixes autobiography and Jewish concerns as it focuses on his grandfather, a rabbi in Lithuania. While another recent book, *The Electronic Elephant: A Southern African Journey* (1994), considers one of Jacobson's later trips to South Africa, the country has become peripheral to his fiction.

In his interview with Gray, Jacobson confessed to feeling relief at not having to write about South Africa, at not having the responsibility to discuss "THE SITUATION with a capital T and capital S, indeed the whole thing in capitals. So when I say that in the other writing I've done I have felt a sense of escape or release or irresponsibility, I don't mean that in any pejorative way. Far from it. To be free of those pressures was perhaps to be free to attend to other, internal needs which might otherwise never have been known to me."

Some criticism of Jacobson's works has condemned him for his lack of political engagement and for his moral ambivalence. In Christopher Heywood's book *Aspects of South African Literature* (1976), the author sees Jacobson as a key transitional figure who attempted to work through the difficult moral and ethical tensions of living in South Africa. More recently, Peck has criticized Jacobson's work for not espousing political engagement and commitment, for being too "depoliticized," and for putting forth the naive liberal belief that if whites could just be enlightened and appealed to on the level of moral decency, then the problems of South Africa would disappear. Jacobson found to write about the individual was difficult, when in the society he was focusing on, being an individual was an impossibility. A South African writer could write about only one thing; Jacobson felt the need to expand his own horizons and those of his fiction. In his novel *All for Love* (2005) he moved away from writing about his Jewish roots, crafting an historical romance set in the Austro-Hungarian empire just before World War I.

Although Dan Jacobson has not published any new short stories in three decades, they remain a significant aspect of his achievement. They depict a deeply moral universe and engage seriously with ethical struggle. They are notable for their spareness, their evocation of the ominous claustrophobia of a society in which personal relationships are poisoned by a dangerous political environment, and the desire to escape to a larger world, even if one will never fully belong to that world.

Interviews:

Ian Hamilton, "Interview with Dan Jacobson," *New Review*, 4 (1977): 25–29;

Stephen Gray, "In Conversation with Dan Jacobson," *Contrast*, 62 (1986): 30–41;

Hamilton, *Ian Hamilton in Conversation with Dan Jacobson* (London: Between the Lines, 2002);

Jacobson interviewed by Lewis Nkosi, London, Transcription Feature Service, n.d.

Bibliography:

Myra Yudelman, *Dan Jacobson: A Bibliography* (Johannesburg: University of Witwatersrand, Department of Bibliography, Librarianship, and Typography, 1967).

References:

Claudia Bathsheba Braude, introduction, in *Contemporary Jewish Writing in South Africa: An Anthology*, edited by Braude (Lincoln: University of Nebraska Press, 2001);

Paul Gready, "Dan Jacobson as Expatriate Writer: South Africa as Private Resource and Half-Code and the Literature of Multiple Exposure," *Research in African Literatures*, 25 (1994): 17–32;

Christopher Heywood, introduction, in *Aspects of South African Literature*, edited by Heywood (New York: Africana, 1976);

Marcia Leveson, *People of the Book: Images of the Jew in South African English Fiction, 1880–1992* (Johannesburg: Witwatersrand University Press, 2001);

Richard Peck, "Undermining the Liberal Tradition: Dan Jacobson, Phyllis Altman, and Mary Benson," in his *A Morbid Fascination: White Prose and Politics in Apartheid South Africa* (Westport, Conn.: Greenwood Press, 1997), pp. 109–120;

Sheila Roberts, "At a Distance: Dan Jacobson's South African Fiction," in *Perspectives on South African English Literature*, edited by Michael Chapman, Colin Gardner, and Es'kia Mshahlele (Parklands, South Africa: Donker, 1992), pp. 213–220;

Roberts, *Dan Jacobson* (Boston: Twayne, 1984).

Papers:

A collection of Dan Jacobson's papers may be found at the Harry Ransom Humanities Research Center, University of Texas at Austin. The Jacobson collection consists of typescripts, holograph manuscripts, notebooks, correspondence, proofs, and personal documents. Other relevant papers are housed in the John Lehmann and London Magazine collections at the HRHRC.

Gabriel Josipovici
(8 October 1940 –)

Günther Jarfe
University of Passau

See also the Josipovici entry in *DLB 14: British Novelists Since 1960, Part 2*.

BOOKS: *The Inventory* (London: Joseph, 1968);
Words: A Novel (London: Gollancz, 1971);
The World and the Book: A Study of Modern Fiction (London: Macmillan, 1971; Stanford: Stanford University Press, 1979);
Mobius the Stripper: Stories and Short Plays (London: Gollancz, 1974);
The Present: A Novel (London: Gollancz, 1975);
Four Stories (London: Menard, 1977);
The Lessons of Modernism, and Other Essays (London: Macmillan, 1977; Totowa, N.J.: Rowman & Littlefield, 1977);
Migrations (Hassocks: Harvester Press, 1977);
The Echo Chamber (Brighton: Harvester Press, 1980);
The Air We Breathe (Brighton: Harvester Press, 1981);
Vergil Dying (Windsor: SPAN/Windsor Arts Centre Press, 1981);
Writing and the Body, Northcliffe Lectures, 1981 (Brighton: Harvester Press, 1982; Princeton: Princeton University Press, 1982);
Conversations in Another Room: A Novel (London: Methuen, 1984);
Contre-Jour: A Triptych After Pierre Bonnard (Manchester: Carcanet, 1986);
In the Fertile Land (Manchester & New York: Carcanet, 1987);
The Book of God: A Response to the Bible (New Haven: Yale University Press, 1988);
The Big Glass (Manchester: Carcanet, 1991);
In a Hotel Garden (Manchester: Carcanet, 1993; New York: New Directions, 1995);
Moo Pak: A Novel (Manchester: Carcanet, 1994);
Touch (New Haven: Yale University Press, 1996);
Now (Manchester: Carcanet, 1998);
On Trust: Art and the Temptations of Suspicion (New Haven: Yale University Press, 1999);
A Life (London: London Magazine Editions/European Jewish Publication Society, 2001);

Gabriel Josipovici (photograph by Duncan Fraser; from the dust jacket for Contre-Jour: A Triptych After Pierre Bonnard, *1986; Richland County Public Library)*

Goldberg: Variations (Manchester: Carcanet, 2002).
Collections: *The Mirror of Criticism: Selected Reviews, 1977–1982* (Brighton: Harvester Press, 1983; Totowa, N.J.: Barnes & Noble, 1983);
Steps: Selected Fiction and Drama (Manchester: Carcanet, 1990);
Text and Voice: Essays, 1981–1991 (Manchester: Carcanet, 1992; New York: St. Martin's Press, 1992).

OTHER: Saul Bellow, *The Portable Saul Bellow,* edited by Edith Tarcov, introduction by Josipovici (New

York: Viking, 1974; Harmondsworth, U.K.: Penguin, 1977);

The Modern English Novel: The Reader, the Writer and the Work, edited by Josipovici (London: Open Books, 1976; New York: Barnes & Noble, 1976);

Maurice Blanchot, *The Sirens' Song: Selected Essays,* translated by Sacha Rabinovitch, edited, with an introduction, by Josipovici (Brighton: Harvester Press, 1982; Bloomington: Indiana University Press, 1982);

"Some Thoughts on the Libretto," in Paul Griffiths, *Igor Stravinsky: The Rake's Progress* (Cambridge & New York: Cambridge University Press, 1982), pp. 60–74;

"Eating Your Words: Dante as Modernist," in *On Modern Poetry: Essays Presented to Donald Davie,* edited by Vereen Bell and Laurence Lerner (Nashville: Vanderbilt University Press, 1988), pp. 103–118;

T. S. Eliot, *Quatre quatuors,* translated by Claude Vigée, commentary by Josipovici (London: Menard, 1991);

Aharon Appelfeld, *The Age of Wonders,* translated by Dalya Bilu, introduction by Josipovici (London: Quartet, 1993);

Franz Kafka, *Collected Stories,* translated by Willa and Edwin Muir, edited, with an introduction, by Josipovici (London: Everyman's Library, 1993; New York: Knopf, 1993);

Andrzej Jackowski, *Reveries of Dispossession: Paintings and Drawings, 1992–94,* introduction by Josipovici (London: Purdy Hicks Gallery, 1994);

Kafka, *The Collected Aphorisms,* translated by Malcolm Pasley, preface by Josipovici (London & New York: Penguin, 1994);

Appelfeld, *For Every Sin,* translated by Jeffrey M. Green, introduction by Josipovici (London: Quartet, 1995);

Samuel Beckett, *Molloy; Malone Dies; The Unnamable,* translated by Beckett, introduction by Josipovici (New York: Knopf, 1997);

"Kierkegaard and the Novel," in *Kierkegaard: A Critical Reader,* edited by Jonathan Rée and Jane Chamberlain (Oxford & Malden, Mass.: Blackwell, 1998), pp. 114–128;

Timothy Hyman, *Timothy Hyman: Recent Work,* text by Hyman and Josipovici (London: Austin/Desmond Fine Art, 2003);

Appelfeld, *Badenheim 1939,* translated by Bilu, introduction by Josipovici (London: Penguin, 2005).

SELECTED PERIODICAL PUBLICATIONS–UNCOLLECTED: "Writing, Reading, and the Study of Literature," *New Literary History,* 21 (Autumn 1989): 75–95;

"Egypt and After," *London Magazine,* 30 (October–November 1990): 38–65;

"Nice, 1943," *London Magazine,* 39 (August–September 1999): 84–88.

Since the late 1960s Gabriel Josipovici has published more than a dozen novels, four short-story collections, and many critical essays and reviews. He has also written plays and radio plays. Josipovici is prolific, versatile, and innovative but also rather idiosyncratic. This last quality may explain to some extent why he is still less well known than he might be. A certain reserve on the part of his readers and critics may also be attributed to his background and other biographical details. Josipovici is a truly cosmopolitan writer.

Gabriel David Josipovici was born on 8 October 1940 in Nice, France. His father, Jean Josipovici, was of Romanian-Jewish descent, and his mother, Sacha Rabinovitch, was of Russian-Jewish origin. The couple met in Cairo, where their respective families lived. They decided to go to France for their university studies, but Jean Josipovici soon separated from his wife. At the end of World War II she and her son, having survived Nazi persecution, returned to Cairo. Gabriel Josipovici was educated at Victoria College, Cairo, from 1950 to 1956; Cheltenham College, England, from 1956 to 1957; and St. Edmund Hall, Oxford University, from 1958 to 1961. He began his academic career as a lecturer at the University of Sussex in 1963. He was married that same year but separated from his wife soon afterward. In 1984 Josipovici became a professor of English at the University of Sussex and taught in the School of European Studies until 1998, when he retired to devote himself more fully to his creative work.

Josipovici first gained notice as a short-story writer. His reputation as the most consistent and radical of British postmodernist writers of short fiction rests on more than forty stories published since the early 1970s, not all of them collected. By 1990 he had published four collections comprising forty-one stories altogether. Some of the stories have been republished more than once, apparently because Josipovici considers them relevant and successful. The ten stories in *Steps: Selected Fiction and Drama* (1990) had all been included in the earlier volumes. The four collections gather together twenty-eight of his stories.

In approaching Josipovici's short fiction, one must first give up any notion of a traditional story line and any expectation of descriptive passages and character sketches. Most of his stories are uneventful. Although he chooses topics to which most people will relate–loneliness, old age, and death–they are usually treated in a way that frustrates expectations and prevents easy understanding.

Josipovici's first story collection, *Mobius the Stripper: Stories and Short Plays* (1974), was immediately recognized as a major contribution to the genre and won him instant fame and notoriety as an experimentalist. The prestigious Somerset Maugham Award in short fiction was conferred upon him in 1975 but was later taken away because he had not been born in England. *Mobius the Stripper* consists of nine stories that, although not all equally challenging, display an astonishing variety in formal qualities and themes but also a certain family likeness. Three stories in particular illuminate Josipovici's literary strategies and his antimimetic bias.

"Little Words" is a seemingly simple story about an old lady who has come from overseas to stay with her son's family. Her mind seems to be wandering, but neither her son nor her daughter-in-law concern themselves with her well-being. Most of the time her only companion is her granddaughter, a girl of seven who acts as a go-between. After a short while the old lady commits suicide by throwing herself out of a window, possibly helped by her grandchild. The story, told in a circuitous way, is made up of ten brief scenes consisting mainly of dialogue. What little plot there is has to be pieced together from what the characters say. Much guesswork is required since the scenes do not follow one another in any logical or chronological fashion. On one level "Little Words" is about a failure of communication between an old lady and her closest relatives. The dialogue reveals the son's and daughter-in-law's incredible callousness. Almost imperceptibly in the course of the story, however, the old lady reveals herself to be a storyteller, and her love of toffee is eclipsed by her love of words and stories. In the last scene, while speaking with the girl, she makes an enigmatic statement that gives the story a metafictional twist: "'I am no longer sure if I am an old lady or a little girl, or both, or neither, talking to myself, listening to the words, trying to tell a story that can never be told. And what's funny,' said the old lady, 'is that I will go on.'" Thus, a story about the frightening alienation of people from themselves and their relatives turns out also to be a statement about the ceaseless attempt "to tell a story that can never be told." The ending suggests an allegorical reading of the death of the old storyteller, who lives on through her words, as well as the difficulty of telling stories.

The title story of the collection, "Mobius the Stripper," employs an intriguing metafictional strategy. It consists of two stories, the first one printed on the upper half of the pages and told in the third person, the second one printed on the lower half of the pages and told in the first person. Each page is divided in the middle by a black line. While the first narrative deals with a fat man, Mobius, who earns his living by stripping in a club, the second one presents a would-be writer who is sitting in front of a blank page suffering from writer's block. Both Mobius and the writer claim that they are interested in getting at the truth. Mobius explains that his motive for stripping is metaphysical; he wants to get "To the centre of myself." The writer knows that once he has started to write, he will be given back his "lost self." Mobius is not totally unknown to the writer, whose girlfriend keeps telling him to go and see Mobius perform. Yet, the real connection between the two stories can be derived from the title, a pun on the geometrical concept of the Möbius strip, which implies that the two stories are to be read continuously, so that one can begin with either the first or the second narrative. If Mobius's story is read first, then the second narrative represents one of the voices that he keeps hearing. If the writer's narrative is read first, then Mobius's represents the story that the writer is at last able to put to paper.

Front cover for Josipovici's 1977 collection of metafictional stories that explore the possibilities and responsibilities of authorship (Amherst College Library)

"Mobius the Stripper" is more than just a game of presenting two story lines as a Möbius strip. It ingeniously deals with the postmodern writer's dilemma of how to write a story and what to write about. Both Mobius and the writer search for identity and truth and want to free themselves from the fetters that society or literary tradition have placed upon them. The more Mobius strips, however, the less he finds; there is nothing beneath all the layers. All that remains for him to do is to take his own life. The writer, who, after an epiphanic moment, seems finally able to fill the empty page in front of him, will have to write about this insight, namely, that the truth fails to materialize.

The most extreme instance of the frustration of readers' expectations in *Mobius the Stripper* is found in "The Reconstruction." The setting seems to be a police questioning. Somebody has been found in a subway passage and has apparently been taken to the police. The man is subjected to an endless interrogation: "Don't stop. Go on. Don't stop," the first speaker in the story repeatedly says. Since the man remembers almost nothing, the questioning is repetitive and leads nowhere. The title refers not only to the interrogator's effort to piece together the few fragments but also to the reader's futile attempts to make sense of the story. Stories such as "The Reconstruction" are probably responsible for Josipovici's reputation as an experimentalist—a term that unduly stresses the surface structure of the texts and has effectively kept his readership small. Thus, Christopher Burns, reviewing Josipovici's third story collection, *In the Fertile Land* (1987), in *The London Review of Books* (31 March 1988), counts him among "the generation of experimentalists loosely associated with the *nouveau roman*," calling his style "faintly antiseptic" and even advising readers "to take the work, like any medicine, in small doses."

Four Stories (1977) is a weighty contribution to the contemporary British short-story genre. In narrative presentation and topics these stories are quite different from each other, but they share a metafictional quality, a questioning of the writer's possibilities and responsibilities. "Contiguities" consists of forty short sections or scenes and resembles a screenplay in that there are cuts and gaps between the scenes. It is difficult to determine how many people are involved in the repetitive scenes and exchanges. The elaborate questioning acted out is reminiscent of the interrogation of K in Franz Kafka's novel *Der Prozeß* (1925; translated as *The Trial*, 1937). "Contiguities" is related to "The Reconstruction," with which it shares the situation of a questioning, as well as a certain number of sentences. The interrogator, for example, keeps repeating, "Go on. Don't stop. Go on." In this case, however, he is shown as someone obviously taken up with his daily routine: "When the alarm goes I stretch out my hand and silence it. Then I am awake." It is "you," however, who does not like to conform. It is "you" who likes to stay behind, "Lying on the bed" and having "the sense of many people hurrying about their tasks." It is "you" who lacks the words and confidence and can only stammer: "I don't– . . . I can't– . . ." "Contiguities" offers great resistance to a reading that makes sense of it. It seems clear, however, that "you" stands for the modern writer, not unlike the title character in Kafka's story "Ein Hungerkünstler" (1924; translated as "The Hunger-Artist," 1938), who has lost his audience and leads an existence seemingly cut off from society and without any assured meaning.

The second story in *Four Stories,* "Death of the Word," begins with the statement "Yesterday I talked to my father." For several pages the first-person narrator tries to remember the games he used to play with his father and tries to fathom the peculiar relationship between them that resulted from their playing ball together. After a while, certain passages begin to reappear, as if the narrator had lost the thread and was trying to take it up again. Then the situation of the writer sitting at his desk asserts itself, thus turning the memories of his father into mere fiction: "I remember nothing. . . . I sit at my desk and write: Yesterday I talked to my father . . . now it is clear to me that these so-called memories which have come to me in the wake of that initial sentence have had only one purpose: to oust my father from his pre-eminent position. . . ." But after getting rid of him, the narrator is at a loss as to how to continue: "I am only this sentence, hesitating, uncertain, with nowhere to go and nothing to say any more." "Death of the Word" is not only about the ambiguous relationship between fathers and sons, it is also about the writer's attitude toward those forces that have shaped him, on which his development depended and from which he has to emancipate himself. The story raises the question of how people are to live if they cut themselves off from tradition.

The third story, "Second Person Looking Out," concerns someone who is on his way to a peculiar house with seventeen rooms. Each room, a guide tells him, has three movable windows. Whenever someone has looked out through one of them, its position is changed. Consequently, no guest ever has the same view of the landscape from a window that he or anyone else has had. The path leading to the house is narrow and winding. Sometimes the house seems close; sometimes it is far removed. Before anyone can reach it, he has already seen many different aspects of it. When someone wants to leave the place, certain rules have to be strictly observed, almost as if one were looking for the way out of a maze. The story is told in an antilinear fashion. While still walking toward the house, the protagonist is suddenly shown to be inside drinking champagne; then he is outside again asking how far away it is. An additional source of confusion is that the story falls into three sections, which are told in the first person, third person, and second person, respectively. Although the story appears to be a metafictional game, it can also be read allegorically as Josipovici's version of Henry James's statement in the preface to *The Portrait of a Lady* (1881) that "The house of fiction has in short not one window, but a million." Read in this way, "Second Person Looking Out" poses, as Walter Evans has written, several fascinating questions: "What is it to be inside the house as opposed to out? When is one involved in a fiction, when not? What is the relationship between one outside the fiction (a reader?) looking in (at characters? at the narrative consciousness?) and between a 'second person looking out'?"

The fourth story, "He," seems to be a traditional narrative at first. The title refers to the protagonist, a young man who learns that his closest friend has committed suicide. The story reports his various attempts to come to terms with this shattering news and with his lack of understanding. When all the traditional means of coping with the fact of death fail him, the young man decides to go to a mountain hotel to compose an elegy for his friend, believing this to be the only way to restore his peace of mind. Here the story takes a metafictional turn, for, as it happens, the elegy does not come easily, either. The man ponders his problems; as he writes down his reflections, they turn into a meditation on how art can help one cope with and understand the meaning of death. Pain, anger, and mourning, though selfish emotions, must not be suppressed, he muses; they must be articulated. At the same time one must be aware that putting these feelings into words always implies a falsification. Yet, there is ultimately the hope that practicing his art helps to release in the artist a human potential that transcends the individual artist. If it does, the resulting work of art "can also make manifest that which it cannot express." This idea of a potential transcendence is, according to Werner Wolf in "'To understand our distance from understanding': Gabriel Josipovicis epistemologisch-metafiktionale Kurzgeschichten als Inszenierungen transzendenter Negativität" (1993, "To Understand Our Distance from Understanding": Gabriel Josipovici's Epistemological-Metafictional Short Stories as Stagings of a Transcendent Negativity), central to Josipovici's concept of art. With a statement in the last paragraph, "He stopped in the silence of the hotel room and looked up from his page," it becomes evident that the story is a sort of equivalent of the elegy the writer had planned to compose and that the title "He" also refers to the dead friend for whom the story is meant to be a memorial.

Dust jacket for Josipovici's third story collection, published in 1987, which prompted comparisons with the works of the French writers of the nouveau roman *(Richland County Public Library)*

In the Fertile Land, published in 1987, is a collection of eighteen stories, fifteen of which had not been collected before. (The remaining three were taken from *Four Stories* to give them a wider audience; only "Contiguities" was not republished.) What immediately strikes one is the variety of fictional devices used by Josipovici. There is something dialectical, though, that runs through all of his writing. The short title story provides an example. It opens, "We live in a fertile land. Here we have all we want. Beyond the borders, far away, lies the desert, where nothing grows." At the beginning the fertile land and the desert seem to be opposites, mutually exclusive of one another. The fertility is then exemplified by the flowering of speech in this land: "when we speak the words flow out in torrents, another aspect of the general fertility." This talkativeness is then contrasted with the silence prevailing in the desert. Suddenly it dawns on the speaker that the fertility may itself be a form of aridity: "Even as I talk though, the thought strikes me that perhaps I am actually in the desert already, that I have crossed over and not returned, and that what the desert is really like is this, a place where everyone talks but where no one speaks of what concerns him most." This story is prototypical of many of Josipovici's fictions. It does not tell a story so much as present a situation, which is then examined from different angles so as to reveal that whatever is stated about human achievements, emotions, or relationships, the reverse will also be true.

In "Steps" the protagonist has the conviction that "In the one life there are many lives. Alternate lives. Alternative lives." The story illuminates this view not by having people reflect upon and talk about this statement but by creating and mixing up different planes of reality and keeping the reader uninformed about which one represents everyday reality. The opening seems unambiguous enough: "He had been living in Paris for many years." The reader is told that after his wife's death the man had left England and moved to Paris. Then his daily routine as a translator and the flat where he lives are described: "To reach it you went through the dark narrow rue St. Julien and climbed a steep flight of steps. . . ." After a few paragraphs, though, it seems that his life in Paris has long been a thing of the past. There is a second wife and quite a bit of social life: "Friends who came to stay and neighbours who dropped in on them in their converted farmhouse in the Black Mountains, up above Abergavenny, were indeed often entertained to an evening of baroque music." Confused, the reader takes in a sentence such as "Going up and down steps lets the mind float free" without realizing that it may imply an important clue. Not until the last sentence—"With his soft grey hat pulled low over his eyes, he climbs the steps out of the rue St-Julien"—does a possible solution of the puzzle finally suggest itself to the reader: most of the story refers to one of those alternative lives that the man invented while climbing the steps on the way back to his flat. As often happens in Josipovici's writing, the last paragraph upsets the ontological status of the narrative and undermines any belief in a simple reality.

"Fuga" provides a good example of Josipovici's most mature antimimetic, self-reflexive writing but nevertheless presents situations that are of vital importance to the people concerned. A young man, a would-be painter, introduces a friend to his mother and sister, apparently in the hope that the friend will become a companion or even a husband for his sister. At the beginning everything seems to go well, but eventually the attempt at establishing a meaningful new relationship fails. The sister feels that her "body had turned to stone." Her brother also feels "it was the end of something the end of a hope." There is hardly any trace of a traditional story left in "Fuga." Dealing as it does with the inability of people to break away from existing conditions or to form new relationships, the story translates this thematic concern almost completely into structural terms by presenting the narrative as an uninterrupted sequence of three monologues (by the visitor, the sister, and the brother) offering different views of the same situation. The formal literary accomplishment of "Fuga"—the way each voice handles the same material but follows its own line—is a defeat to the human beings trying to overcome their loneliness. Their existence boils down to repetitiveness and boredom: "perhaps that is life the end of all hopes." As Wolf has shown in "Postmodernist Musicalization of Fiction III: Josipovici, 'Fuga'" (1999), the anonymity of the figures and the simplicity of the setting also allow for an allegorical reading. The failure to establish a relationship with an outside figure may be seen to indicate the impossibility of nourishing metaphysical hopes.

Josipovici's short stories share several features: they are mostly told through dialogue; narrative voice is reduced to a minimum; the idea of everyday reality is undermined; often it is doubtful whether something is real, imagined, or part of a dream; in many cases there is a self-referential quality drawing the reader's attention to the fictionality of the text; there is a tendency toward allegorization (through the use of anonymous figures and simple settings); events are not presented in a linear way; and expectations of coherence are frustrated. These same qualities identify Josipovici as a postmodernist. In "Postmodernist Musicalization of Fiction III: Josipovici, 'Fuga,'" Wolf writes, "These are concise, 'difficult,' metafictional and/or allegorical texts, which lack realistic detail and illusionist appeal . . . and frequently frustrate any search for a unified (referential) meaning." This approach to short fiction is not just Josipovici's whim, however. He is convinced that stories told in a traditional mode cannot do justice to the inconsistency and ambiguity of human behavior. It is the writer's task not to cater to his readers' laziness but to try to shake them up. In the essay "Egypt and After" (1990) Josipovici writes, "Only fiction, in the right hands, can awaken in us the sense of how little we know of ourselves and the world, and how intense is our desire to change that condition." To Bryan Cheyette, undeniably, with Josipovici, fiction is "in the right hands." In his review of *In the Fertile Land* in *TLS: The Times Literary Supplement* (13 May 1988) Cheyette reached the conclusion "that Josipovici is able to relate ordinary human concerns to some of the most important intellectual issues of the twentieth century. There are few writers in England of whom this can be said."

References:

Paddy Bostock, "Poststructuralism, Postmodernism and British Academic Attitudes: With Special Reference to David Lodge, Malcolm Bradbury and Gabriel Josipovici," dissertation, Polytechnic of North London, 1989;

Walter Evans, "The English Short Story in the Seventies," in *The English Short Story, 1945–1980: A Critical History,* edited by Dennis Vannatta (Boston: Twayne, 1985), pp. 120–172;

Monika Fludernik, *Echoes and Mirrorings: Gabriel Josipovici's Creative Oeuvre* (Frankfurt am Main & New York: Peter Lang, 2000);

James Hansford, "Making and Breaking: The Fiction of Gabriel Josipovici," *Prospice,* 17 (1985): 23–38;

Rüdiger Imhof, "Gabriel Josipovici," in *Der englische Roman der Gegenwart,* edited by Imhof and Annegret Maack (Tübingen: Francke, 1987), pp. 245–265;

Dominique Pernot, "Biblical, Modern, and Postmodern Winding and Unwinding in Gabriel Josipovici's Fiction," *Germanisch-Romanische Monatsschrift,* 49 (1999): 351–360;

Werner Wolf, "Postmodernist Musicalization of Fiction III: Josipovici, 'Fuga,'" in his *The Musicalization of Fiction: A Study in the Theory and History of Intermediality* (Amsterdam & Atlanta: Rodopi, 1999), pp. 217–228;

Wolf, "'To understand our distance from understanding': Gabriel Josipovicis epistemologisch-metafiktionale Kurzgeschichten als Inszenierungen transzendenter Negativität," in *Recent British Short Story Writing,* edited by Hans-Jürgen Diller (Heidelberg: Winter, 1993), pp. 131–152.

James Kelman
(9 June 1946 -   )

Graeme Macdonald
University of Warwick

See also the Kelman entry in *DLB 194: British Novelists Since 1960.*

BOOKS: *An Old Pub near the Angel and Other Stories* (Orono, Me.: Puckerbrush, 1973);
Three Glasgow Writers, by Kelman, Alex Hamilton, and Tom Leonard (Glasgow: Molendinar, 1975);
Short Tales from the Nightshift (Glasgow: Print Studio, 1978);
Not Not While the Giro and Other Stories (Edinburgh: Polygon, 1983; New York: Random House, 1997);
The Busconductor Hines (Edinburgh: Polygon, 1984);
A Chancer (Edinburgh: Polygon, 1985);
Lean Tales, by Kelman, Agnes Owens, and Alasdair Gray (London: Cape, 1985);
Greyhound for Breakfast (Edinburgh: Polygon, 1987; New York: Farrar Straus Giroux, 1988);
A Disaffection (London: Secker & Warburg, 1989; New York: Farrar Straus Giroux, 1989);
Fighting for Survival: The Steel Industry in Scotland (Glasgow: Clydeside Press, 1990);
The Burn (London: Secker & Warburg, 1991);
Hardie and Baird, and Other Plays (London: Secker & Warburg, 1991);
Some Recent Attacks: Essays Cultural and Political (Stirling & San Francisco: AK Press, 1992);
How Late it Was, How Late (London: Secker & Warburg, 1994; London & New York: Norton, 1995);
Busted Scotch: Selected Stories (New York: Norton, 1997);
The Good Times (London: Secker & Warburg, 1998; New York: Anchor, 1999);
Selected Stories (Edinburgh: Canongate, 2001);
Translated Accounts (London: Secker & Warburg, 2001; New York: Doubleday, 2001);
"And the Judges Said—" Essays (London: Secker & Warburg, 2002);
You Have to Be Careful in the Land of the Free (London: Hamilton, 2004; Orlando, Fla.: Harcourt, 2004);
Where I Was, James Kelman Series: Pocket Penguin, no. 19 (London: Penguin, 2005).

James Kelman (from the dust jacket for the U.S. edition of Greyhound for Breakfast, *1988; Richland County Public Library)*

RECORDING: *Seven Stories,* read by Kelman, Oakland, Cal. & Edinburgh, AK Press Audio, 1997.

OTHER: *The Renfrew Line,* edited by Kelman (Paisley: Renfrew District Libraries, 1979);
East End Anthology, edited, with an introduction, by Kelman (Glasgow: Clydeside Press, 1988);
George Elder Davie, *Scottish Enlightenment and Other Essays,* foreword by Kelman (Edinburgh: Polygon, 1991).

Neither a Scottish nor an English publisher commissioned James Kelman's first collection of stories. *An Old Pub near the Angel and Other Stories* (1973) was published in the United States, a country with a short-story tradition sympathetic to the issues and themes that animate Kelman's work and one with a less restrictive notion than that of the United Kingdom of what constitutes "appropriate" literary language. These thirteen stories were published in 1973 when Kelman was twenty-seven, five years after he began writing. They establish themes that have developed throughout his career. The opening story, "The Cards," which concerns a sacked bus conductor from a specific Glaswegian milieu, demonstrates a central feature of Kelman's work and his impetus to write—his determination to portray with detailed fidelity lives and locales that have traditionally been underrepresented in fiction in Britain. All Kelman's writing has been characterized by a provocative stance toward the conventional institution of English literature, in its dissemination and determination of subject matter and language. He has been a consistent critic of a tradition he believes based on cultural exclusion, one that has provided little scope for the values, experiences, and language of his own culture. He insists in his 1994 Booker Prize speech that his "culture has the right to exist and no-one has the authority to dismiss that right." Kelman has been described over the course of his career as a "Scottish" writer, a "working-class" writer, a "Glaswegian," even a "West of Scotland" writer, a "post-colonial" writer, an "existential" writer, and a "political" writer. All of these terms are applicable, and yet each neglects aspects of his output. A term that can consistently be applied to Kelman is that of radical writer, one who has always been concerned to question the terms on which literature is usually based. Central to his work is an argument concerning literary and linguistic freedom: one that asserts that literature is (or should be) a classless, universal phenomenon, made available to all and open to any subject.

That so many of Kelman's characters are working-class is a reflection of this argument and relates to his own experience. Born in Glasgow on 9 June 1946, the second of five brothers, Kelman spent his childhood in two working-class districts, Govan and Drumchapel. His father, like his grandfather, worked in his own business as a picture framer and gilder; his mother was a full-time parent and later a primary-school teacher. Despite a respect for education and reading instilled in his household, Kelman's experience of a 1950s Scottish educational system was negative, and he left school at fifteen. He has had an ambivalent attitude toward educational institutions ever since. He began an apprenticeship as a compositor and in 1963 left Scotland with the rest of his family for the United States, an abortive emigration that lasted three months. After his return to Scotland he worked for ten years in a variety of jobs—from factory work to bus conducting—in cities all over the United Kingdom, including London, where he began to write and where many of his early stories are set. While there, he met Marie Connors, a social worker, whom he married in 1969 and who returned with him to Glasgow in the early 1970s; they have two daughters.

In 1971 Kelman attended an open series of writing classes run by Professor Philip Hobsbaum of Glasgow University, which were influential in developing his work and in introducing him to some like-minded local writers. The encouragement he received from them bolstered his committed literary stance. In his essay "Elitism and English Literature, Speaking as a Writer," first published in *And the Judges Said,* Kelman writes of his early experiences as a writer. Encouraged to write from his own experience, he felt that characters from his kind of background were "confined to the margins" of fiction in English and never explored from within. He insists that he could find no models in an English literary tradition for what he wanted to write about, although he did find them in U.S. fiction and in translations of foreign-language literature, such as Russian. These non-British writings gave him "freedom" to "create stories based on things I knew about: snooker halls and betting shops and DSS [Social Security] offices" and to write about the people he knew best who lived in that world. In a 1985 interview with Duncan McLean for the *Edinburgh Review,* Kelman remarked that meeting with fellow Glaswegian writers helped him to discover "that I wasn't alone." Despite his usually hostile attitude toward educational institutions, Kelman at the age of twenty-eight began to study philosophy and literature at the University of Strathclyde, enrolling, by his own admission, to get access to grant money, since his unemployment benefit had ceased. However, he refused to take his final exams for reasons to do with the syllabus and the principles behind its teaching.

An Old Pub near the Angel establishes the main outlines of Kelman's created world, subject matter, and political and formal concerns. His culture is that of the west of Scotland, specifically working-class Glasgow, the city where he lives and where many of his stories are set. His work to date covers a thirty-year period of changing fortunes for the people of this region, brought about by the collapse of the traditional heavy-manufacturing industry. It examines the subsequent downgrading of lower-class people and their experience. However, Kelman has insisted that his Glasgow could be any comparable town in Britain. Often he does not write of a specific location, but rather of an unidentifiable place that is

Front cover for Kelman's 1983 collection of twenty-six metafictional short stories (Thomas Cooper Library, University of South Carolina)

more existential than geographic. In his introduction to the *East End Anthology* (1988), Kelman argues that "ninety per cent of the literature in Great Britain concerns people who never have to worry about money at all," and his work is generally concerned with the powerless of society. Many of his stories insist that they are recording and recovering "uninteresting" lives traditionally alien to mainstream or "serious" fiction.

The importance of Kelman's work to the body of literature with a working-class subject matter has been in formal advances and in his refusal to compromise a radical linguistic literary politics. Cairns Craig (and others, including Kelman himself) has written on this subject, noting Kelman's disruption of the hierarchical distinctions between narration and dialogue. A corollary of this commitment to using the language people use every day as both narrational discourse and dialogue has brought Kelman notoriety and also impassioned defenders, particularly because of his frequent use of taboo language. "Abject Misery," from his first volume of short stories, is an example of a story including such language. Kelman's work is committed to breaking the linguistic, social, and literary conventions that look down on working-class, provincial speech. The Glaswegian voice's ability to speak, narrate, and be heard without constraint is a significant feature of his stories, and one of his first, "He Knew Him Well," aptly opens with a man clearing his throat to enable himself to begin speaking. He then struggles to be heard above the other voices in a pub. Kelman's stories have always played with a variety of levels of linguistic formality. In *An Old Pub near the Angel,* "Nice to Be Nice," for example, is an early experiment with phonetic narration, which later modulates into other types of English, refusing to recognize a standard, dominant form. The title story of the volume, "An Old Pub near the Angel," concerns an unemployed Scottish drifter in London, a common character in the early stories. His narration is marked by shifts into an upper-class vernacular, parodying the "adventures of" school of literature, featuring upper-class heroes, values, and voices. Kelman has repeatedly attacked such literature as one that many people are brought up to expect as the standard in English (and Scottish) literature.

An Old Pub near the Angel was followed by other smaller, local-press collections, and ten years passed before Kelman's first major collection, *Not Not While the Giro and Other Stories* (1983), appeared. These twenty-six stories, published in Scotland by Polygon in 1983, with the help of a grant from the Scottish Arts Council, include stories from previous collections and new ones that consolidate already-present themes. These stories demonstrate Kelman's use of interior monologue and indirect free speech, blurring the distinction between character and narrator. They rely on the naturalistic observation of intricate, "minor" details; yet, these details are often subtly metaphorical. Kelman has professed his admiration for Anton Chekhov, and like the Russian author, he employs a strategy of showing rather than telling.

Recent criticism has recognized the degree of textual play in Kelman's work, and metafictional concerns in his stories force the reader to consider questions about meaning, relevance, and literary structure. "Acid," from *Not Not While the Giro,* is a good example of the way Kelman's stories challenge the reader to pay attention to narrated detail and to scrutinize the way it is presented. This apparently objective story of an industrial accident employs a textual arrangement that controls and expresses an appeal against unsafe industrial conditions. That the story (of a man falling into a vat of acid) seems unbelievable is the effect Kelman's writing seeks. It is an alien and inviting form of fiction that presents a challenge to certain traditional worldviews, demanding the reader's involvement in the (in)credible social world of the text.

The tribulations of the workplace, made up of a stark alternative–boredom or destitution–are central throughout Kelman's writing. He draws on his own working experiences, having worked at a variety of jobs as well as having spent periods on unemployment relief. In his stories, the menial, temporary nature of employment intensifies the feeling of its apparent arbitrariness, balanced with its necessity as a means of survival. For example, "The Bevel" begins in a noxious, claustrophobic tank, where harsh breathing conditions are a metaphor for a lack of articulate protest. In "The Chief Thing about this Game," a factory initiate relates "astonishing conditions"; the reader is both amazed and yet not surprised when lack of safety equipment leads to a fire. The stories in *Not Not While the Giro* usually resist authority through unpredictability and interpretive ambiguity, intending to provoke social and textual debate over their interpretation. Their indeterminate, inconclusive quality is consistent with lives that many characters are forced to live. Many have no plans and are left confronting unresolved difficulties at the ends of the stories. Such positions are evident in stories that signal the development of Kelman's skill, reminiscent of the works of Jorge Luis Borges or Nikolai Gogol, in finely balancing the line between the real and the grotesque or surreal, a technique intended to question the qualities of the material world that people take for granted. This technique often initiates a textual investigation into the procedures of storytelling. In "The Block," a block of "matter"–a dead man–lands at a milkman/artist's feet; how and why, the reader is not told. The subsequent police interrogation is presented through the milkman/artist's own existential self-questioning. The "matter" of the story is also questionable, as testimony and alibi. In other stories, seemingly bizarre events are made apparently plausible. "Roofsliding" reads like a short anthropological report of an odd practice common to the inhabitants of Glasgow tenements.

Many characters in the stories in *Not Not While the Giro* ask why they should work at a disagreeable job. Social responsibility is often the pressing answer, as is the unpleasant nature of unemployment. This question is the subject of the title story, placed, as is usual for Kelman, at the end of the collection. A man contemplates suicide while waiting for his unemployment check. The story is despairingly humorous and as absurd as it is tragic. It displays a Beckettian attention to the seemingly trivial details of everyday life, a recurrent feature of Kelman's work. The story dramatizes banality and ponders the imponderable. Its elliptical narrative engages with a life in some form of textual and social limbo–where "nothing" is exactly what a character has to think of–hence his absurd fantasies at the close.

Kelman's next collection was published in 1985, after two novels, *The Busconductor Hines* (1984) and *A Chancer* (1985), enhanced his growing reputation, although they also aroused considerable controversy among reviewers. *Lean Tales* was written in collaboration with two other Scottish writers, Alasdair Gray and Agnes Owens. Kelman met both writers in Hobsbaum's Glasgow writing group in the 1970s. A political and creative camaraderie has extended to the present day, with Kelman, Gray, and Tom Leonard (also a member of the group) incumbent since 2002 as joint professors of creative writing at the universities of Glasgow and Strathclyde.

The collaborative nature of *Lean Tales* is itself a challenge to the norms of British publishing, and, indeed, Gray's "Postscript" to *Lean Tales* is a polemic on the staid elements of mainstream British publishing that have ignored "difficult" writers such as Kelman. Kelman's section of *Lean Tales* establishes and consolidates lesser-known stories with new ones. The eighteen tales are lean in length, only two exceeding ten pages, most around two and a half. Their slightness embodies the random, seemingly marginal nature of characters' lean existences. Most of the stories are again concerned with the experience of vagrancy. They provide fleeting glances at insolvent lives lived from moment to moment. Unnamed characters relate "minor" details, consistently contemplating the point of living in their condition. Routine, deadening jobs are again rejected, a course that paradoxically leads to boredom as a result of a lack of money and of social isolation. This struggle for purpose, place, and identity becomes a deeper existential dilemma, especially as Kelman's work develops. In "The Same Is Here Again" another of Kelman's down-and-out Scots in London worries about his sanity in a series of fragmented statements. Similarly, the narrator of "The Paperbag" declares, "I was without funds, absolutely fucking without funds." He contemplates his usefulness, fails to establish any connection with others, and proceeds onward.

Some characters in the stories in *Lean Tales,* such as the itinerant narrator of "Are You Drinking Sir," are being monitored and interrogated–by whom the reader is left to guess. A sense of menace forces readers to investigate further the "drama" and context of such lives. The story also asks the reader to contemplate whether they should be suspicious of the narrator–as the police seem to be–simply for being unidentifiable, "foreign," and different. Identity and itinerancy are important in Kelman's writing, itself formally itinerant in its attempt to formalize fleeting, usually under-reported,

Dust jacket for the 1988 U.S. edition of Kelman's 1987 short-story collection, winner of the Cheltenham Literary Festival Prize (Richland County Public Library)

experience. Stories such as "Busted Scotch," "The Same Is Here Again," "The Glenchecked Effort," "Are You Drinking Sir?" "Old Holborn," and "A Nightboilerman's Notes" are set in alienating times and spaces. These alienating scenarios include working night shift in an isolated factory; morning drinking in murky pubs; wandering foreign city streets after midnight; working abroad; and rambling in an unknown countryside. Many protagonists—temporary workers, unemployed men, disaffected youths, vulnerable women, struggling pensioners, street hustlers, and solitary drinkers—are estranged economically, geographically, spatially, linguistically, psychologically, and socially. Identity—individual, familial, national—is negotiable and questionable. Social and mental insecurity is often the center of a Kelman story. Characters face painful, often precarious, predicaments, confronted by the sheer pressure of social and material forces and circumstances, and their own lack of resistance generates perpetual difficulty.

Greyhound for Breakfast, published in 1987, encapsulates these elements. Kelman's second major collection is considered the one that consolidated his position as one of the most important writers in contemporary Britain. It was awarded the prestigious Cheltenham Literary Festival Prize in 1987. Forty-seven stories, many of them fewer than two pages, demonstrate the convergence of Kelman's main influences: American realism and European existentialism. Tim Dooley notes in a review in *TLS: The Times Literary Supplement* (8 May 1987) that this collection "draws attention to two potentially conflicting tendencies—proletarian realism and experimental modernism—which James Kelman's fiction more typically attempts to resolve." In *Greyhound for Breakfast,* the characters are once again drawn from the margins of society. They are presented in short, fragmented, "unfinished" pieces—a technique that reinforces the notion that what is presented is just the surface of such lives. "A History" exemplifies this technique. The title is ironic, considering its narrator's opening insistence that "I had no history to consider. None whatsoever." Trapped in a remote place, this character seems to be exiled or imprisoned as much existentially as geographically. "The Failure" opens with a philosophical rumination on leaping into an abyss. The narrator ends stuck in a crevice that defies the imagination: "the sensation of the fall is indescribable." This story is about paralysis—of mind and/or body—and the ability to transcend it. Contemplative immobility is also central to "Of the Spirit," a monologue in which a man faced with another vague situation contemplates a decision.

Kelman has consistently sought to investigate and analyze linguistic hegemony wherever it appears, in the media or in institutional and personal settings. Many characters in the stories in this collection are faced with authoritative forms of language that challenge their linguistic and cultural autonomy. Their dilemma is exemplified in "In with the Doctor," in which a patient is faced with a hypocritical doctor seeking to display his cross-class credentials. In *Greyhound for Breakfast,* Kelman is also concerned with questions of narrational authority and power. Many stories lack the kind of helpful, authoritative narrator who is part of much traditional fiction. The reader is often left to work things out for him- or herself. This dilemma is apparent in the single paragraph stories that are a distinguishing feature of *Greyhound for Breakfast*. These "stories" have ambiguous meanings. They turn on enigma, inference, speculation, and insecurity, all formal and thematic concerns of Kelman's work as a whole. The meaning of these laconic fragments is not made clear. There is no explanation, as there is in so much traditional fiction, about events, characters, or settings. In "The Guy with the Crutch" a tramp who is an amputee trudges across wasteland; in "Cute Chick!" an infamous old lady roams Glasgow betting shops; in "Incident on a Windswept Beach" a man walks out of the sea wearing a boiler suit and casually lights a cigarette. The reader is invited to wonder what wider contexts these episodes have. Other stories subvert the authority of the official notice. "ONE SUCH PREPARATION," for example, is set entirely in capitals, as if its "message" is straightforward, but it is not. Others, such as "Leader from a Quality Newspaper," "Half an Hour Before He Died," "That Other," and "More Complaints from the American Correspondent" read as if they were sections clipped from newspaper columns, reported fragments without narrational explanation. They are meant to be oblique and obstructive, resisting the notionally "full" or "objective" explanation that a more traditional literary text might provide.

What is omitted or unsaid in these stories often becomes crucial to their political stance. In "Governor of the Situation," a local government leader professes open "disgust" at the urban poor and their environment. That policy implementation is dependent on such opinion is the point of this paragraph-length story, magnified by its insistence that it is the "final word" on the issue. In "This Man for Fuck Sake," people watch someone struggling in a gutter. The situation is unclear: "all we could do was watch his progress and infer." The challenge to become more involved is made evident with the last line, a plea and excuse: "how can you blame us? You can't fucking blame us." The subtext of this story is can the characters, and by extension the readers, do anything? Can they, indeed, be blamed? This last story asks how urban destitution is observed, and it is part of a general reconsideration by Kelman as to what is understood as contemporary literary "realism"—and the legitimacy of such a project in a society in which events seem incredible precisely *because* of their horrific reality. In a 1989 interview with Kirsty McNeill in *Chapman,* Kelman insisted, "I think the most ordinary person's life is fairly dramatic; all you've got to do is follow some people around and look at their existence for 24 hours, and it will be horror. It will just be horror. You don't need any beginning, middle and end at all. All you have to do is show this one day in maybe this person's life and it'll be horror."

The stories in this collection often present lives of people at the limits of understanding. Formlessness is a trope for the portrayal of lives close to dissolution. This lack of structure is elaborated in the longer stories of *Greyhound for Breakfast,* such as the opening of one, "Old Francis," in which an old tramp philosophizes about the contingent nature of his life. The sheer pressure of existence demands unwanted choices, compromised as he and other characters are by the search for money to survive. Many stories demonstrate such dramas of the mundane. In "The Band of Hope" the "casino" subculture of small-time Glaswegian gamblers is the context of an examination of thwarted camaraderie as people get by–relying on chance, singular scraps of luck, and the possibility of free sandwiches. Consistent, stable relations are hard to achieve. This theme recurs, particularly in stories dealing with those returning "home." In "Where but What" a man relates his difficulty in establishing a relationship with his wife, the "imprecise" syntax mirroring his inability to articulate his feelings. *Greyhound for Breakfast* also includes stories from women's perspectives, a significant development in Kelman's work. In "A Sunday Evening" a bored wife has fantasies her partner is unlikely either to discover or to think her capable of having. A similar elision of the border between reality and dream underlines the title story. Ronnie buys a greyhound intending to enter it in races; this simple gesture is fraught with risk, irresponsibility, and emotional tension. This story, like many Kelman stories, provides brief details of the character's social world and thus forces the reader to pay attention to slight details before he or she makes any judgments on characters' actions. Ronnie is unemployed; his son has recently left for undisclosed reasons; his wife does not know of the risky purchase of the dog. The purchase is a gamble, perhaps a final desperate one, perhaps an understandable one, nonetheless.

The deterministic relation between background and individual, social context and self, and state and subject is a powerful feature of *The Burn,* Kelman's next collection of stories (twenty-six), published two years after the novel *A Disaffection* (1989). In a profile on Kelman in *Books in Scotland,* Douglas Gifford notes the evolution of Kelman's work to a point at which its central emphasis is on the existential experience of its characters and observes an "unanswered question as to whether their protagonists are victims of a Scottish, deprived, post-war and grey environment and upbringing or whether the faults lie essentially in themselves."

The opening and closing stories encompass the central themes of a collection that is darker in tone than Kelman's earlier ones. Uncomfortable memories trigger ruminations on the possible pointlessness of life. The endeavor to articulate experience is common, as is a resolute, sometimes desperate, rage. In "Pictures" an embittered, nihilistic young man considers responding to a crying woman in the cinema. He does not help her, though; all he can do is hypothesize fictional scenarios about her. A withheld fact becomes a recollection and a

Front cover for the 1999 U.S. paperback edition of Kelman's 1998 short-story collection, which explores the balance between good times and bad (Bruccoli Clark Layman Archives)

confession: "when he was a boy he had once went with a man for money and it was a horror, a horror story. Except it was real." As in earlier collections, Kelman insists that such horrors are common in the lives of those alienated from British society. A recurrent theme is the difficulty of social/romantic/familial relationships and men's reliance on women. "A Walk in the Park" relates two adulterers' inability to be open about their problems. "That Thread," a two-page monologue, details a man's uncomfortable longing for an attractive woman. Barely informative fragments make "From the Window" a disturbing text in which vague and intense worry stems from hints about the inability of a father to live without his absent wife. The consideration of female subjectivity is a further distinguishing feature of *The Burn*. "A Decision" recounts the breakup of a relationship from both sides, giving full weight both to male and female points of view. In "Real Stories" a woman takes refuge in her imagination from the difficulties of her "real" life. The end is ambivalent, and such uncertainty is a feature of "Lassies Are Trained That Way," in which a man attempts to engage a younger woman in conversation in a pub. This story examines the limits and possibilities of genuine communication between people in a society in which people are often forced to distrust each other and in which the more powerless members have limits placed on their freedom.

Some stories in *The Burn* have a philosophical dimension. An existential questioning plagues characters who are racked by indecision, from which they seem unable to escape. Other stories mix peculiar events with the everyday. The longest story in Kelman's oeuvre, "A Situation," is one of the most intriguing, with echoes of Chekhov, Franz Kafka, and Gogol, in a narrative that mixes genres. A young salesman living in a shabby one-room apartment frets over his girlfriend's impending visit. The plot twists when an elderly couple, his neighbors, unexpectedly intervene. The fantastic pervades an incoherently coherent world where weird events are at times normal, even inevitable. The older man—a sinister, possibly devilish, character—forces the younger to listen to a rather sketchy confession of his involvement in a past event that embodies the themes of surveillance, paranoia, guilt, conscience, responsibility, suffering, faith, and doubt that run through this story and the collection.

An impulse toward discovery marks stories featuring those on the fringes of society. "Sarah Crosbie" reappears from the earlier 1978 collection, *Short Tales from the Nightshift*, as if to emphasize that her story and her situation remain unresolved. She is a dead woman "nobody knew," embroiled in odd events that catch the attention of a reporter. The apparent insignificance of the story tantalizes the reader. Powerlessness in the grip of authority is the theme of "Street-Sweeper," in which a council worker's plight is compromised by worries over being watched by superiors. He contemplates the corpse-like figure of a tramp, a reminder of his own proximity to such a fate. The nightmarish "Naval History" is about literature and authority. Former associates, possibly the police, accost a man in a bookstore. He appears to be a writer and is tormented for his art ("wee stories with a working-class theme"), his politics, and his past. The man resists the others' claims on him, stating: "it's realism I'm into as well if it makes any difference." In what is clearly an allegory about censorship and literary freedom, the protagonist is eventually escorted from the bookstore.

The indiscriminate manner of death and the enduring power of past events infuse the final two stories of *The Burn*. "Events in Yer Life" concerns a young man's return to Scotland for his mother's funeral, a journey that spurs a reconsideration of his life. This story is about the cynical loss of youthful ideals and an exploration of what constitutes maturity. Eventual resolution of the protagonist's problem is also important in the title story, "By the Burn." The title refers to the scar of an unhappy memory branded on the mind of the solitary protagonist. A father, caught in mud and rain in an indeterminate waste ground, finds himself facing the spot where his young daughter was accidentally buried alive. His struggle to maintain perspective is challenged when he has to cross a roaring burn (the Scots word for a small river). Like the memory, the burn seems unavoidable, an obstacle that needs to be confronted. Death brings a resolution of sorts, perhaps one that can be seen as a form of defiance.

Kelman's next collection, *The Good Times* (1998), did not appear until seven years later. He spent part of this time as an unpaid adviser working for the Clydeside Action on Asbestos group, and an essay on the refusal of corporations to accept culpability for their former employees' medical conditions appeared in a book of polemics, *Some Recent Attacks* (1992). The experience of the connection between physical, legal, and linguistic disempowerment was subsequently prominent in Kelman's controversial Booker Prize–winning novel, *How Late it Was, How Late* (1994). *The Good Times* was Kelman's first published new fiction after the prize-winning novel. (*Busted Scotch* was a selection for the U.S. market from previous volumes.) Many reviewers praised the collection. Gifford in *Books in Scotland* (Autumn 1998) declared Kelman "a writer at the top of his powers," uncompromising in the face of post–Booker Prize criticism, which had seen him as talentless, vulgar, naive, and boring. The twenty stories in this collection rework and broaden Kelman's usual themes. The title is misleading, however, since the book includes as many bad times as good. The balance is what these stories explore.

The collection opens on the same kind of wasteland territory *The Burn* closed in, a derelict site familiar throughout postindustrial Glasgow. In "Joe Laughed" a group of young friends play soccer in front of a closed factory in the shadow of a scrap yard. A young boy considers his life while venturing through dangerous, gutted buildings. His potential to transcend such surroundings through sports prowess is hinted at; yet, the dilapidated surroundings suggest the difficulty of his attaining future "success." The stories usually involve marginalized figures trying to make sense of their present situations and their pasts. "Gardens Go on Forever" is a comic story about the pain and distraction of having to work in a menial job when wanting to pursue other activities, such as reading literature. The narrator is simultaneously cursed and liberated by the power of art, thought to transport him from the arduous monotony of his situation, only to intensify his awareness of it. In "It Happened to Me Once" queuing for unemployment benefits initiates a full-blown contemplation of a wretched existence.

Such self-examinations are prevalent throughout *The Good Times*, often concerning one's "success" in life. In "I Was Asking a Question Too" a reader, who is also a writer, contemplates a novel "where the action stops and the writer starts discussing questions to do with life and death, existence." This story is about managing a literary life, a task that seems somehow to revel in and yet be "bamboozled" by the number of possible, even random, readings, statements, and "information" available to readers. Communicative estrangement ends this story and is part of the next, "Yeh, These Stages," in which a man who has lost his partner reflects on the drifting life this absence brings. Such isolation also animates "Oh My Darling," in which "a demonstrative person, a most untypical Scottish male," ponders the idea of a genuine relationship transcending self-centeredness. Similar worries concern the drinker waiting for his companion in "Every Fucking Time," the title expressing resigned rage toward a life of routine boredom. This story is similar to another pub-based story, "The Comfort," in which two drinking partners battle against a "carefree life going nowhere and doing nothing."

Many of the themes and motifs in *The Good Times*—time passing, absurd communication, and rumination about the meaning of life—converge in the longest story, "Comic Cuts," about four friends randomly conversing while waiting for a perpetually deferred pot of soup. Exuberance is shown in their verbal sparring. Their progressive inebriation and tendency to enter communicative cul-de-sacs give the story its "disjointed yet strangely coherent" drift, as one of the characters puts it. The story was broadcast in July 1998 as *The Art of the Big Bass Drum* on BBC Radio. It is emblematic of all the stories in *The Good Times*. The conversational riffs, register switches, non sequiturs, neologisms, unrelated and uncertain speakers, and trailing subjects constitute the material of Kelman's storytelling. Having the courage to reconcile oneself to one's situation is a strong feature in the closing stories. "Constellation," in which a young man strides towards a night encounter with a woman, is such an exploration of all "the things that go to make up yer life." The closing story returns to the deliberations begun in *An Old Pub near the Angel*. A man wakes from his nightmares and contemplates his being; his certain death; his relationship with another; his past; the slippage of his dreams and aspirations; and the "junk" he possesses. This story returns to the opening story, with the older man rethinking the limits of his younger ambitions. The closing line, in which he thinks he has gained some "genuine insight," is ambiguous: "but these are the good times."

James Kelman is one of the major short-story writers of contemporary Scottish literature. His is a fiction driven by a political insistence that the lives of the poor, oppressed, marginalized, and often inarticulate are worthy of attention and faithful representation, often in their own words. He is a writer who focuses with a rare forcefulness on the existential dilemmas of horrific living and working conditions, boredom, destitution, powerlessness, and loss. In an interview with McNeill in *Chapman*, Kelman claimed that "good art is usually dissent. I want to be involved in creating good art." His is a radical and unignorable voice in contemporary British fiction.

Interviews:

Duncan McLean, "Interview with James Kelman," *Edinburgh Review*, no. 71 (1985): 64–80;

Kathleen Jamie, "The Voice of the Oppressed; James Kelman," *Scotland on Sunday,* 19 February 1989, p. 25;

Kirsty McNeill, "Interview with James Kelman," *Chapman,* no. 57 (Summer 1989): 2–10;

Nicholas Roe, "Glasgow Kith: James Kelman Profile," *Guardian Saturday Review,* 2 June 2001, pp. 6–7.

References:

Ian Bell, "James Kelman," *New Welsh Review,* no. 3 (Autumn 1990): 18–22;

Cairns Craig, "Resisting Arrest: James Kelman," in *The Scottish Novel Since the Seventies,* edited by Gavin Wallace and Randall Stevenson (Edinburgh: Edinburgh University Press, 1993), pp. 99–114;

Douglas Gifford, "Discovering Lost Voices: Profile of James Kelman," *Books in Scotland,* no. 38 (Summer 1991): 1–6;

Ellen-Raïssa Jackson and Willy Maley, "Committing to Kelman: The Art of Integrity and the Politics of Dissent," *Edinburgh Review,* no. 108 (2001): 22–27;

Lee Spinks, "In Juxtaposition to Which: Narrative, System and Subjectivity in the Fiction of James Kelman," *Edinburgh Review,* no. 108 (2001): 85–105.

Papers:

A collection of James Kelman's manuscripts is at the Mitchell Library, Glasgow. Some letters, plays, and novels are in the National Library of Scotland, Edinburgh.

Benedict Kiely

(15 August 1919 -)

Christopher Thomas Cairney
Istanbul Dogus University

See also the Kiely entry in *DLB 15: British Novelists, 1930–1959*.

BOOKS: *Counties of Contention: A Study of the Origins and Implications of the Partition of Ireland* (Cork: Mercier, 1945);

Land without Stars (London: C. Johnson, 1946);

Poor Scholar: A Study of the Works and Days of William Carleton, 1794–1869 (London: Sheed & Ward, 1947; New York: Sheed & Ward, 1948);

In a Harbour Green (London: Cape, 1949; New York: Dutton, 1950);

Call for a Miracle (London: Cape, 1950; New York: Dutton, 1951);

Modern Irish Fiction: A Critique (Dublin: Golden Eagle, 1950);

Honey Seems Bitter (New York: Dutton, 1952; London: Methuen, 1954); republished as *The Evil Men Do (Honey Seems Bitter)* (New York: Dell, 1952);

The Cards of the Gambler: A Folktale (London: Methuen, 1953);

There Was an Ancient House (London: Methuen, 1955);

The Captain with the Whiskers (London: Methuen, 1960; New York: Criterion, 1961);

A Journey to the Seven Streams: Seventeen Stories (London: Methuen, 1963);

Dogs Enjoy the Morning (London: Gollancz, 1968);

A Ball of Malt and Madame Butterfly: A Dozen Stories (London: Gollancz, 1973);

Proxopera (London: Gollancz, 1977); republished as *Proxopera: A Tale of Modern Ireland* (Boston: Godine, 1986);

All the Way to Bantry Bay, and Other Irish Journeys (London: Gollancz, 1978);

A Cow in the House, and Nine Other Stories (London: Gollancz, 1978);

Nothing Happens in Carmincross (London: Gollancz, 1985; Boston: Godine, 1985);

A Letter to Peachtree and Nine Other Stories (London: Gollancz, 1987; Boston: Godine, 1988);

Drink to the Bird: A Memoir (London: Methuen, 1991);

Benedict Kiely (from the dust jacket for A Letter to Peachtree and Nine Other Stories, *1988; Bruccoli Clark Layman Archives)*

God's Own Country: Selected Short Stories, 1963–1993 (London: Minerva, 1993);

The Trout in the Turnhole (Dublin: Wolfhound Press, 1995);

The Waves Behind Us: A Memoir (New York: Methuen, 1999);

A Raid into Dark Corners and Other Essays (Cork: Cork University Press, 1999).

Collections: *The State of Ireland: A Novella and Seventeen Stories,* introduction by Thomas Flanagan (Boston: Godine, 1980; Harmondsworth, U.K. & New York: Penguin, 1982);

The Collected Stories of Benedict Kiely, introduction by Colum McCann (London: Methuen, 2001; Boston: Godine, 2003).

OTHER: Charles J. Kickham, *Sing a Song of Kickham: Songs of Charles J. Kickham,* edited by James Maher, introduction by Kiely (Dublin: J. Duffy, 1965);

"Ripeness Was Not All: John Barth's Giles Goat-Boy," in *The Sounder Few: Essays from the Hollins Critic,* edited by R. H. W. Dillard, George Garrett, and John Rees Moore (Athens: University of Georgia Press, 1971), pp. 195–210;

"That Old Triangle: A Memory of Brendan Behan," in *The Sounder Few,* pp. 85–99;

Liam C. Martin, *Liam C. Martin's Dublin Shopfronts & Street Scenes,* introduction by Kiely (Dublin: Cobblestone Press, 1974);

Flann O'Brien, *The Various Lives of Keats and Chapman; and, The Brother,* edited, with an introduction, by Kiely (London: Hart-Davis MacGibbon, 1976);

Paddy Tunney, *The Stone Fiddle: My Way to Traditional Song,* introduction by Kiely (Dublin: Dalton, 1979);

The Penguin Book of Irish Short Stories, edited by Kiely (London: Penguin, 1981);

Padraic Colum, *The Poet's Circuits: Collected Poems of Ireland,* second edition, preface by Kiely (Portlaoise: Dolmen Press, 1981);

Brendan Behan, *Borstal Boy,* afterword by Kiely (Boston: Godine, 1982);

Patrick Boyle, *The Port Wine Stain: Patrick Boyle's Best Stories,* introduction by Kiely (Dublin: O'Brien / London: Allison & Busby, 1983; Old Greenwich, Conn.: Devin-Adair, 1983);

Dublin, edited by Kiely (Oxford & New York: Oxford University Press, 1983);

William Butler Yeats, ed., *Fairy and Folk Tales of Ireland,* foreword by Kiely (New York: Macmillan, 1983);

Seumas O'Kelly, *The Weaver's Grave: Seumas O'Kelly's Masterpiece and a Selection of His Short Stories,* introduction by Kiely (Dublin: O'Brien / London: Allison & Busby, 1984);

The Aerofilms Book of Ireland from the Air, text by Kiely (London: Weidenfeld & Nicolson, 1985); republished as *Ireland from the Air* (New York: Crown, 1985);

"The Historical Novel," in *The Genius of Irish Prose,* edited by Augustine Martin (Dublin: Mercier, 1985), pp. 53–66;

Sean O'Faolain, *Bird Alone,* introduction by Kiely (Oxford & New York: Oxford University Press, 1985);

Ben Forkner, ed., *A New Book of Dubliners: Short Stories of Modern Dublin,* preface by Kiely (London: Minerva, 1989);

Michael J. Murphy, *My Man Jack: Bawdy Tales from Irish Folklore,* introduction by Kiely (Dingle: Brandon, 1989);

Yeats' Ireland: An Illustrated Anthology, edited by Kiely (London: Aurum Press, 1989); republished as *Yeats' Ireland: An Enchanted Vision* (New York: C. N. Potter, 1989);

John Jordan, *Collected Stories,* edited by Hugh McFadden, introduction by Kiely (Swords: Poolbeg, 1991);

William O'Kane, ed., *You Don't Say? The Tyrone Crystal Book of Ulster Dialect,* foreword by Kiely (Dungannon: Irish World, 1991);

William Carleton, *Fardorougha, the Miser; or, The Convicts of Lisnamona,* introduction by Kiely (Belfast: Appletree Press, 1992);

James Horan, *25 Views of Dublin,* commentary by Kiely (Dublin: Town House/Office of Public Works, 1994);

And as I Rode by Granard Moat, edited by Kiely (Dublin: Lilliput Press, 1996);

J. J. Barrett, *Not for Dedalus: A Collection of Poems,* introduction by Kiely (Bray: Dub Press, 1996);

Carleton, *William Carleton: The Autobiography,* edited, with a foreword, by Kiely (Belfast: White Row Press, 1996);

Michael Walsh, *Collected Poems,* introduction by Kiely (Dublin: P. Walsh, 1996);

Walsh, *Along My Father's Hills: A Miscellany,* foreword by Kiely (Dublin: P. Walsh, 1997);

Stephen Haddelsey, *Charles Lever: The Lost Victorian,* foreword by Kiely (Gerrards Cross, U.K.: C. Smythe, 2000);

Bill Doyle, *Images of Dublin: A Time Remembered,* introduction by Kiely (Dublin: Lilliput Press, 2001).

Benedict Kiely is a novelist, short-story writer, and essayist. He has also been active in the Dublin media scene since the 1950s as a popular radio voice and broadcast personality. Active in the Irish literary world for more than sixty years as a journalist and literary critic, he has written about all the famous figures of modern Irish literature, many of whom he has known personally. Throughout his career, which took him to Dublin and then to the United States, he has adhered tenaciously to a sense of locality, specifically for his native Ulster. Thus, it can be said that while in his career Kiely became a man of Dublin, in his fiction he has always remained a man of the North.

Benedict "Ben" Kiely was born on 15 August 1919 near Dromore, in County Tyrone, Northern Ireland, the son of Thomas Joseph Kiely and Sarah Alice

Gormley Kiely. Thomas Kiely had traveled the world as a soldier in the British army and was to have a lasting influence on his son's writing. After leaving the army, he met his future wife while she was working as a barmaid at Doyle's Hotel in Drumquin. In 1920 the Kielys moved to Omagh, where Ben grew up. His father was originally from Donegal, and during summer vacations the young Kiely spent time at an Irish college in the Donegal Gaeltacht (Irish-speaking region), where he polished his Irish-language skills and listened intently to the songs and stories that were later to appear in his fiction. After graduating from the Christian Brothers Grammar School in Omagh in 1936, Kiely worked in the town's post office for a year and then entered the Jesuit novitiate at Emo Park in Portarlington, sixty miles west of Dublin, with the intention of becoming a priest. A serious spinal ailment forced him out of the novitiate. After a year and a half as a patient at Cappagh Hospital in Finglas, County Dublin, he returned to Omagh and made preparations to enter University College, Dublin (UCD), a constituent college of the National University of Ireland. He graduated with a B.A. degree in history and letters (with honors) in 1943.

While at UCD, Kiely made key contacts with figures such as the writer and broadcaster Francis MacManus and Senan Moynihan, editor of *The Capuchin Annual*, which led him to a career in journalism. Two poems by Kiely, "Long After O'Neill" and "Journey in Ulster," were published in the 1943 issue of *The Capuchin Annual*. In 1944 Kiely married Maureen O'Connell, with whom he eventually had four children, Mary, Anne, John, and Emer. He also began work on an M.A. in history at UCD. He cut short his graduate work that same year to take a position at the *Irish Independent* as a columnist and editorialist, but not before finishing a political treatise, *Counties of Contention: A Study of the Origins and Implications of the Partition of Ireland*, published in 1945. During this period Kiely also contributed to *The Standard*, a Catholic weekly. These early writings were followed in 1946 by his first novel, *Land without Stars*, a story of two brothers and political violence set in Donegal and Tyrone. His essay "Orange Lily," on the Protestant Ulster author Shan F. Bullock, was published in the June 1947 issue of *The Irish Bookman*. Kiely revisited the subject of Bullock in a four-part 1972 article for *The Irish Times*.

In 1947 Kiely's study of the Irish writer William Carleton, *Poor Scholar: A Study of the Works and Days of William Carleton, 1794–1869*, was published. Reviewing the book at the time of its republication in 1997, Brian Fallon noted in *The Irish Times* (22 November 1997) that it "did a great deal to bring Carleton back into public notice." Pauline Ferrie wrote in the on-line journal *Book-*

Title page for Kiely's first collection, published in 1963, in which most of the stories feature an obtrusive, moralizing narrative voice (Davis Library, University of North Carolina at Chapel Hill)

View Ireland (August 1997) that "Kiely paints a picture of the idle scholar who disdained the priesthood and set off south from his native Tyrone to spend most of his life in Dublin." In his study Kiely calls Carleton "possibly the greatest writer of fiction that Ireland has given to the English language." He seems to have modeled his own career on that of Carleton, a point made by Daniel J. Casey and James M. Cahalan. Some commentators have suggested that, like Carleton, Kiely mostly seeks to avoid direct confrontation with political issues in his writing.

In his second novel, *In a Harbour Green* (1949), concerning a woman's seduction by one man and another man's devotion to her, Kiely contrasts the honesty and justice of country people with the hypocrisy and self-interest of townsfolk, especially predatory

Title page for Kiely's second short-story collection, which is characterized by a tone of nostalgia for earlier, simpler times in Irish society (Homer Babbidge Library, University of Connecticut)

shopkeepers. *Call for a Miracle* (1950), his next novel, was banned in Ireland by the Censorship Board for its sexual content. Kiely's study *Modern Irish Fiction: A Critique* (1950), covering the principal Irish novelists of the period 1900–1950, was well received and aided his career, for in 1951 he succeeded to the post of literary editor at *The Irish Press*. In 1952 he published another novel, *Honey Seems Bitter*. A Kafkaesque study of personal treachery and inconstancy during a murder trial in Dublin, it came out that same year in the United States as *The Evil Men Do (Honey Seems Bitter)*. *The Cards of the Gambler: A Folktale* (1953) is a novel built on a series of digressions loosely structured around the thread of an eighteenth-century Gaelic folktale.

In the novel *There Was an Ancient House* (1955) Kiely examines the decision by several male characters to enter a novitiate for a sequestered life, in preparation for eventually entering the priesthood. Like *The Cards of the Gambler,* however, it is a Catholic novel. Although it raises complaints about discipline and belief, it never seriously challenges the Catholic Church but remains an affirmation of traditional Irish religious life. In 1957 Kiely's essay "Canon Sheehan: The Reluctant Novelist" appeared in the magazine *Irish Writing,* and in 1960 he published *The Captain with the Whiskers,* a novel set in the North of Ireland that involves the ominous dissolution of the family of a tyrannical Protestant aristocrat.

Three years later Kiely's *A Journey to the Seven Streams: Seventeen Stories* (1963), his first collection of short fiction, was published. The stories are marked by the presence of an obtrusive and moralizing narrator, a device that may owe something to the oral tradition of Ireland and the "peasant" background of both Kiely and his model, Carleton. It certainly distinguishes the texts from the modern short-story tradition established in late-nineteenth-century Russia, France, and America. The first story in the collection is "The White Wild Bronco," first published in *The New Yorker*. There is irony here, but readers are asked to accept the worldview advanced by the writer: they are not left, as in the short fiction of James Joyce, to discover the meaning for themselves. Kiely does not focus on a particular incident or episode in a character's life. Rather, he delineates (as elsewhere in his fiction) a condition of dissatisfaction and melancholy and a kind of paralysis, though not the paralysis suggested by Joyce. In this case it is a rural and northern malaise, not a busy Dublin one.

Kiely focuses on depression and psychotic escape from oppressive circumstances. The reader learns, for instance, that one of the characters in "The White Wild Bronco," Cowboy Carson, is "the only man in our town who lived completely in the imagination." The key word is "completely," for most of the other characters seem to seek similar escape, although less successfully, from their own realities. The final paragraph of the story catalogues a depressing list of the numb and dreary outcomes in the characters' lives:

> By that time the old fusilier was dead, and buried by Doherty the undertaker; Attention Dale had been succeeded by a nephew who couldn't face the sun and sold the telescope; Mickey Fish was confined to a mental home for chasing young girls to ask them the time of evening; and arthritis prevented Pat Moses Gavigan from fishing pike or cutting blackthorns. And Isaac the fusilier's son realized that he would never be a German. He came like a bird as a paratrooper into Narvik, came out again alive, and possibly helped the three Americans who had listened to the Cowboy to storm the French shore. Until he was killed at the Rhine crossing he remained the best fighter our town ever had.

In contrast to most of the stories in *A Journey to the Seven Streams,* with their relatively formless nature and didactic thrust, "The House in Jail Square" is more tightly structured and shows some formal development: there is a clear beginning, middle, and end, and the characters are effective types. It is a story about growing up, describing a situation in which the truth is a concept more political than logical when its definition falls under the control of two women portrayed as domestic tyrants. Kiely often uses songs in dialogue, such as in the title story of the collection. In a review of *The Collected Stories of Benedict Kiely* (2001) Maurice Harmon, writing for *The Irish Times* (7 July 2001), described "A Journey to the Seven Streams" as "typical of one kind of Kiely story, a spate of description, conversation, one-liners, memories, characterization, a variety of voices and perceptions all held together by the central motif of the return." Such narrative mixing anticipates the technique used in Kiely's novel *Nothing Happens in Carmincross* (1985). Another technique in "A Journey to the Seven Streams" that anticipates *Nothing Happens in Carmincross* is Kiely's constant habit of "digression and return"; there is minimal plot development but frequent digressions that eventually return to some aspect of plot mentioned earlier in the story. Usually, instead of then developing action and moving forward, Kiely prepares the reader for yet another digression.

The world of *A Journey to the Seven Streams* is a dreamy one, and the reverie of the narrator is often more important than the action, especially in stories such as "The Enchanted Palace," "The Dogs in the Great Glen," and "The Shortest Way Home." Kiely introduces a strong sense of intertextual reference among his own works or at least recycles stock situations, often creating surprising links among his various novels and stories. For instance, an older man is described as "bald as a coot" in both "The House in Jail Square" and "Blackbird on a Bramble Bough." The situation in "Blackbird on a Bramble Bough" (first published in *The Irish Bookman* in 1946) of "a slippery, polished hallway" where a priest has "fallen and broken his hip" also figures in *There Was an Ancient House.* Soldiers are a common subject in the stories, reflecting the fact that Kiely's Omagh was a "garrison town" for British and American forces during World War II. In both "Soldier, Red Soldier" and "The Dogs in the Great Glen" a sergeant finds that he must apply for a transfer in order to escape disgrace.

The title story, "A Journey to the Seven Streams," seems autobiographical, possesses a great deal of local color, and, although it includes many smaller stories, has little overall plot. The story allows Kiely to reminisce about "good old days" that were better or purer than the present. This common literary theme appears in many of the stories in the collection, including "The Shortest Way Home," "The Dogs in the Great Glen," "Soldier, Red Soldier," "Homes on the Mountain," "Blackbird on a Bramble Bough," "The Wild Boy," "The Enchanted Palace," "The House in Jail Square," "The Pilgrims," "A View from the Treetop," "The Heroes in the Dark House," and "The White Wild Bronco." Kiely's usual way of concluding these stories of reminiscence is to make a catalogue at the end informing readers of the subsequent fate of his characters, which he typically does with a strong tone of pathos. The theme is usually the destructive passage of time; the stories are depressing and judgmental.

Other stories in *A Journey to the Seven Streams* concern women and would be considered misogynistic today. They are told from a boy's or a young man's perspective and include strong images of confusion and even urban alienation and danger, especially if the main character comes into the city from a village, or into the world of adults for the first time, without a guide. The stories in this category include "Rich and Rare Were the Gems She Wore," which first appeared in *Irish Writing;* "Mon Ami, Emile"; "The Bright Graves"; "The Pilgrims"; and "Ten Pretty Girls." These stories are not simple reminiscences but describe sorties into a dangerous, confusing, and changeable world.

In 1964 Kiely traveled to the United States, where he served for a year as writer-in-residence at Hollins College, in Roanoke, Virginia. The following year he became a professor of creative writing at the University of Oregon; he was then writer-in-residence at Emory University in Atlanta from 1966 until his return in 1968 to Ireland, where his family had remained throughout this period. While in America he wrote a popular column on American life and peculiarities for *The Irish Times.* He also continued to publish stories in *The New Yorker,* wrote reviews for *The New York Times Book Review,* and contributed to *The Kenyon Review* and *The Nation.* On his return to Ireland, Kiely brought out another novel, *Dogs Enjoy the Morning* (1968), which is, as Casey points out, "a departure in style, in mood, in technique." Generally considered Kiely's best novel, *Dogs Enjoy the Morning* is a satire, using subjects and contrasts recycled from his earlier novels: myth, folklore, religion, rebellion, and exile are all represented, while the author contrasts the Christian with the pagan, abstinence with sexuality, the rural with the urban, and old age with youth. Fallon, reviewing the novel in *The Irish Times* (22 June 1996) when it was republished in 1996, called it "oblique social satire," suggesting that "under a facade of quasi-rural realism, the book is anarchic and almost surreal" and that in this way *Dogs Enjoy the Morning* recalls *The Cards of the Gambler* and anticipates *Nothing Happens in Carmincross.*

Kiely's second short-story collection, *A Ball of Malt and Madame Butterfly: A Dozen Stories,* was published in 1973. This volume includes the story "Down Then by Derry," which had previously appeared in *The Dublin*

Dust jacket for Kiely's third short-story collection, published in 1978, which includes stories exploring the tensions between Catholics and Protestants in Northern Ireland (Bruccoli Clark Layman Archives)

Magazine in 1970. Another story from the collection, "A Room in Linden," had appeared the year before in *The New Yorker*. According to Harmon, "A Room in Linden" "tells of death in the midst of life." Another story, "Wild Rover No More," is based on Kiely's memories of his father and mother. Harmon finds it "packed with memorable figures, each forming a background to the central theme of eccentricity—misfits, half wits, half-saints—all rubbing shoulders," but behind all the "ravings" of the characters there exists some fatal or irrevocable tragedy that lies half hidden in the past.

In *A Ball of Malt and Madame Butterfly*, Kiely again provides stories that can be grouped in terms of theme and tone into two categories. Some of the stories deal with the past in a benign way, with frequent use of the past tense, while others handle the past in a manner that primarily employs the present tense and possesses a harder emotional tone, particularly one of uncertainty and confusion, although the narrator's outlook is conventionally moralizing rather than existentially doubtful. The more benign stories in the collection include "A Great God's Angel Standing," "Wild Rover No More," "A Bottle of Brown Sherry," "A Ball of Malt and Madame Butterfly," and "Down Then by Derry." They are reminiscences about earlier, less-confusing times and events. Sometimes a story is primarily positive in outlook, such as the title story, "A Ball of Malt and Madame Butterfly." Others are more sentimental, dominated by a sense of pathos and inevitable decay. Despite criticisms of Catholicism, the stories of this kind are firmly and unapologetically grounded in traditional Catholic morality.

The stories with a harsher outlook on life include "The Little Wrens and Robins," "A Room in Linden," "God's Own Country," "An Old Friend," "The Green Lanes," "The Weavers at the Mill," and "Maiden's Leap." The last is a tale of a rich, well-educated, but somewhat sheltered author and a jealous but insightful relative. The story provides the reader with surprises rather than the firm attitudes of Kiely's typical moralizing narrative. Surprise, however, is not reflected on a technical level, for "Maiden's Leap" has a clear beginning, middle, and end. These harsher stories describe situations of uncertainty and appear more modern, in contrast with those representing a safe "golden" world of the past.

Kiely edited and wrote the introduction for *The Various Lives of Keats and Chapman; and, The Brother*, a 1976 compilation of columns from *The Irish Times* by Flann O'Brien (pseudonym of Brian O'Nolan). That same year Kiely was elected to the Irish Academy of Letters and accepted an appointment at the University of Delaware, where he taught for a few months. In 1977 he published the novella *Proxopera*, the story of a group of awkward Irish Republican Army (IRA) insurgents who kidnap a family and try to force the father to carry out a bombing on their behalf. That year Kiely also became a founding member of Aosdána, an association of creative artists in Ireland established by the Arts Council. A nonfiction work, *All the Way to Bantry Bay, and Other Irish Journeys,* and *A Cow in the House, and Nine Other Stories* were both published in 1978. All but one of the stories in the collection represent the less-harsh variety of Kiely's stories: "Make Straight for the Shore," "There Are Meadows in Lanark," "Bluebell Meadow," "The Night We Rode with Sarsfield," "The Players and the Kings," "The Fairy Women of Lisbellaw," "Elm Valley Valerie," and the title story. The last story in the collection, however, is of the darker variety: "Near Bainbridge Town" is a tale of drunkenness set around 1960 but carefully justified for traditional Catholic readers by its sense of pathos and loss at the conclusion.

"Make Straight for the Shore" is scarcely a story but more a reminiscence, while "There Are Meadows in

Lanark" simultaneously depicts a boy's awakening sexuality and provides an appreciation of the Scots—a persistent theme in Kiely's fiction—in particular of the working-class Scots who once holidayed in large numbers in the North of Ireland. "Bluebell Meadow" is the most overtly political story in the collection, presenting Protestant bigotry as it affects a young couple, a Protestant boy and a Catholic girl, who are prevented or discouraged from seeing each other by an unlikely but politically motivated and self-appointed chaperone. "The Night We Rode with Sarsfield" is Kiely's account of a reconciliation between Catholic and Ulster Presbyterian cultures. The story is complex because it subtly avoids the easy division of characters into members of diametrically opposed ethnic camps. It opens with the reminiscence of a Catholic man about the time he moved with his family to Omagh as a boy, clearly an echo of Kiely's own biography. The man's father, failing to find a room in Omagh proper, is forced to look outside the town and finally obtains lodging for his family in the farmhouse of a Protestant couple, Willy and Jinny Norris, some miles out in the countryside. Living together brings a degree of understanding, respect, and friendship.

Kiely wrote the introduction for Paddy Tunney's song collection *The Stone Fiddle: My Way to Traditional Song* (1979) and the preface for the 1981 edition of Padraic Colum's *The Poet's Circuits: Collected Poems of Ireland*. That same year he edited *The Penguin Book of Irish Short Stories*. *The State of Ireland: A Novella and Seventeen Stories*, a collection of his stories selected from *A Journey to the Seven Streams*, *A Ball of Malt and Madame Butterfly*, and *A Cow in the House* that also includes *Proxopera* (the novella of the subtitle), was published in 1980. The volume, with an introduction by Thomas Flanagan, is now out of print.

The Penguin Book of Irish Short Stories opens with an adaptation by Isabella Augusta Persse, Lady Gregory, of a tale from *An Fhiannaíocht*, the ancient Irish story cycle of Finn and the Fianna. This surprising choice seems more a translation than an original short story, but Kiely exercised his prerogative as editor, bringing together well-known authors with less-familiar contemporary ones and including his own translation of a folktale, "The Cards of the Gambler," which he knew well since he used it as a loose structuring device for his novel of the same name. Kiely later edited *Dublin* (1983), a literary anthology, and wrote the foreword for the 1983 edition of *Fairy and Folk Tales of Ireland*, a combination of two collections of Irish folklore edited by William Butler Yeats that were first published together in 1973. (Yeats's collections originally appeared in 1888 and 1892.) In his foreword Kiely notes that Yeats sought "not for the meaning of any mystery but for what he had already determined to find . . . a world of the imagination . . . a world that fed on dreaming and not on the painted toy of grey truth." Kiely also wrote the introduction for *The Weaver's Grave: Seumas O'Kelly's Masterpiece and a Selection of His Short Stories* (1984). He next edited the 1985 edition of Sean O'Faolain's 1936 novel *Bird Alone* and contributed a chapter, titled "The Historical Novel," to *The Genius of Irish Prose* (1985), edited by Augustine Martin.

Kiely's novel *Nothing Happens in Carmincross*, published in 1985, deals with the violence of sectarian conflict in Ulster, although the plot centers on an aged, drunken, and divorced "professionally Irish" writer who returns from New York to Ireland and shows a passive willingness to have sex with as many women over forty as will have him. In *The New York Review of Books* (8 May 1985) Conor Cruise O'Brien described it as "a funny book, always skirting the edge of horror, and finally going over the edge." John Dunne, however, reviewing the novel in *Books Ireland* (May 1987), called it "one of the most overrated Irish books of recent years," noting Kiely's "special brand of galloping garrulity." He suggested that Kiely's "motley crew of rollicking Irish men and women" were conceived with "one eye on the transatlantic market." Dunne further suggested that the novel "carries so much allusive baggage that, less than halfway through, it collapses under the strain." "But," he added, "there is great stuff here."

The Aerofilms Book of Ireland from the Air (1985) is a photography collection for which Kiely supplied the text, providing historical, political, and literary anecdotes to accompany the photographs. His next book was *A Letter to Peachtree and Nine Other Stories* (1987), in which, as Donald P. Kaczvinsky pointed out in his May 1988 *Library Journal* review, "Kiely captures the Irish environment better than any contemporary writer. . . . Kiely captures both the beauty and bitterness of Irish life." Writing about one of the stories, "Mock Battle," in a review of *The Collected Stories of Benedict Kiely*, John Kenny in *TLS: The Times Literary Supplement* (20 June 2001) observed that "when dealing with Irish history . . . Kiely's stories can also be effectively quasi-historic," adding that Kiely's writing can be "hard edged and politically contentious." Kenny found "Through the Fields in Gloves," another story from *A Letter to Peachtree*, "quirkily threatening" but noted that generally in Kiely's stories the "psychotic malcontents and the agonized narrators we are familiar with in modern fiction are singularly absent."

The gentler stories in *A Letter to Peachtree* include "Eton Crop," which begins in sexual exploration and ends with a tone of sadness and regret; "Mock Battle"; "Your Left Foot Is Crazy"; "The Jeweller's Boy," another reminiscence of boyhood set in Northern Ireland, with comforting wisdom drawn from a past that is safely distanced; "A Walk in the Wheat," a story about the passage of time; and the title story of the collection. "Bloodless Byrne of a Monday," "The Python," "Second-

Dust jacket for the 1988 American edition of Kiely's 1987 short-story collection, which reviewers praised for its vivid portrayal of contemporary Irish life (Bruccoli Clark Layman Archives)

ary Top," and "Through the Fields in Gloves" are some of Kiely's harsher stories, dealing less with Ireland and more with disturbed psychological states. "Through the Fields in Gloves" concerns an impoverished working-class man who, out of frustrated compassion for his hopelessly obese wife and out of resentment, stalks "thin bitches" who are "dressed to the nines" and attacks them with paint.

The title story, "A Letter to Peachtree," is in the form of a letter written to a woman in America. As a letter it is not believable, for the "writer" disregards the letter format throughout much of the text and uses it as an excuse to tell a story. The narrative is structured around "a trip to the races" on a train, and after a series of comic and drunken misadventures, the writer tells the recipient of the letter, "Here I give you a genuine slice, or bottle, of old Ireland, as I ate, or drank, it." This statement may be intended as an epigraph, not just to "A Letter to Peach-

tree" but to all of Kiely's stories. The letter writer continues with a warning to modern Ireland: "There may yet be worse things than parish priests in store for the new Ireland."

In 1991 Kiely published the first of two autobiographical volumes, *Drink to the Bird: A Memoir*. Patricia Craig, reviewing the book in *TLS* (24 April 1992), noted Kiely's "celebratory cast of mind" and suggested that his "overblown approach" did not match the "too easy accessibility" of the memoir, calling attention to the "blurred edges" and an "ebullient Irishness designed to take us in." She wrote that Kiely "gives hardly anything away, neither his attitude towards his upbringing nor the reasons for his espousal and renunciation of the priesthood." In Craig's view, "Kiely's expansiveness is actually a way of being self-effacing . . . his book consists of anecdotes, local lore, facts, figments, snatches of verse, scenes of childhood and outbreaks of out-and-out nostalgia." For instance, he recalls that the Christian Brothers "never did him harm" but that they "instilled into their pupils a bias towards Irish nationalism . . . an old style nationalism [that] had nothing to do with blowing the legs off girls in coffee bars."

God's Own Country: Selected Short Stories, 1963–1993 was published in 1993. Like *The State of Ireland*, it is now out of print and has been superceded by *The Collected Stories of Benedict Kiely*. *God's Own Country* was followed in 1995 by *The Trout in the Turnhole,* Kiely's only children's book. He edited two 1996 volumes, *William Carleton: The Autobiography* and *And as I Rode by Granard Moat,* a collection of poetry and traditional songs. The latter is a kind of homage to the lyrics that are a common feature in many of Kiely's novels and stories. Reviewing *And as I Rode by Granard Moat* in *The Irish Times* (25 January 1997), John Boland pointed out several typical aspects of Kiely's art, including "his life-long fondness for digression." In his writing, Boland noted, "something is always putting Ben Kiely in mind of something else," an insightful comment about the author's associative rather than linear way of organizing narratives.

In 1996 Kiely was elected *saoi* (wise man) of Aosdána, the Irish artists' organization he helped found. The second volume of his autobiography, *The Waves Behind Us: A Memoir,* was published in 1999. That same year, to mark Kiely's eightieth birthday, Cork University Press published *A Raid into Dark Corners and Other Essays,* a collection of his essays and literary appreciations of various Irish authors. Most of the essays were originally published in *The Irish Times, The Hollins Critic,* and *The Kilkenny Magazine* from the 1940s to the 1970s. Some are political in focus, thus anticipating the political contentiousness one finds in some of Kiely's fiction, including *Proxopera* and *Nothing Happens in Carmincross*. In *The Waves Behind Us* Kiely traces his life from 1941 to 1999, including his career as a Dublin journalist and writer, and makes references to many of the figures he met in Dublin, especially other writers, such as Brendan Behan and Patrick Kavanagh.

In 2001 Methuen, a publishing house with which Kiely has had a long relationship, published *The Collected Stories of Benedict Kiely,* including the stories from *A Journey to the Seven Streams, A Ball of Malt and Madame Butterfly, A Cow in the House,* and *A Letter to Peachtree,* as well as *Proxopera.* In his introduction Colum McCann describes the novella as "undoubtedly one of the greatest anti-war books ever written." Bill Doyle's *Images of Dublin: A Time Remembered,* with an introduction by Kiely, was published that same year. After the death of his wife, Maureen, Kiely married Frances Daly in 2004.

Kiely's short fiction shows imagination and invention, and many of his characters are memorable, as are some of the situations. The stories mostly show a strong measure of affection for the Irish people, with an air of acceptance of the foibles and faults of less-than-perfect people and wounded individuals in decay. The only unforgivable fault for Kiely seems to be the lack of a sense of humor. In his review of *The Collected Stories of Benedict Kiely,* Harmon wrote, "Kiely's stories have the freedom of folk tales. . . . The hallmark of Kiely's stories is a copiousness of language, a variety of incident and an inclusive vision of humanity." According to Ferrie, reviewing the collection in *BookView Ireland* (May 2002), Kiely's stories "delight, provoke, amuse and induce contemplation" and also "explore his native place and the people who inhabit it." In his introduction McCann writes of Kiely's "deep, enduring and moving adoration for the landscape and the people of his country." Kenny suggested in his *TLS* review of the collection that "Kiely is unlikely to be remembered primarily for his novels," described as "variable," but rather for his short stories: "it is his copious . . . output in this genre that most contains the older, largely rural Irish world he knows best." Kenny observed, however, that "Kiely . . . can too readily be accused of engaging in outmoded soft-core Paddywhackery" by giving his readers too many stories with "sub-Robert Burns language" and a "parlor-armchair atmosphere" of "nostalgic idylls."

Benedict Kiely has had a long career as a writer, and his success is partly the result of an indefatigable application to his craft. His stories have been widely anthologized, appearing in such collections as *The Oxford Book of Travel Stories* (1996), *Irish Christmas Stories II* (1997), *The Penguin Book of Irish Fiction* (1999), *The New Picador Book of Contemporary Irish Fiction* (2000), and *The Derry Anthology* (2002). As Kenny observed in his review of *The Collected Stories of Benedict Kiely,* "Puckish above all else, Benedict Kiely is behind these stories chuckling volubly for very love of the world."

References:

James M. Cahalan, *The Irish Novel: A Critical History* (Boston: Twayne, 1988);

Daniel J. Casey, *Benedict Kiely* (Lewisburg, Pa.: Bucknell University Press / London: Associated University Presses, 1974).

Papers:

Benedict Kiely's papers are in the National Library of Ireland in Dublin.

James Lasdun
(8 June 1958 –)

David Malcolm
University of Gdańsk

BOOKS: *The Silver Age* (London: Cape, 1985); republished as *Delirium Eclipse and Other Stories* (New York: Harper & Row, 1985);

A Jump Start (London: Secker & Warburg, 1987; New York: Norton, 1988);

Three Evenings and Other Stories (London: Secker & Warburg, 1992; New York: Farrar, Straus & Giroux, 1992);

The Revenant (London: Cape, 1995); republished as *Woman Police Officer in Elevator* (New York: Norton, 1997);

Walking and Eating in Tuscany and Umbria, by Lasdun and Pia Davis (London & New York: Penguin, 1997);

The Siege and Other Stories (London: Vintage, 1999); republished as *Besieged* (New York: Norton, 2000);

Landscape with Chainsaw (London: Cape, 2001; New York: Norton, 2001);

The Horned Man (London: Cape, 2002; New York: Norton, 2002);

Seven Lies: A Novel (New York: Norton, 2005).

PRODUCED SCRIPTS: *Sunday,* motion picture, by Lasdun and Jonathan Nossiter, Goatwork Films, 1997;

Signs and Wonders, motion picture, by Lasdun and Nossiter, Ideefixe Productions/Industry Entertainment/Sunshine Amalgamedia/Goatwork Films, 2001.

OTHER: *After Ovid: New Metamorphoses,* edited by Lasdun and Michael Hofmann (London: Faber & Faber, 1994; New York: Farrar, Straus & Giroux, 1995);

Paul Bowles, *Stories,* introduction by Lasdun (Harmondsworth, U.K.: Penguin, 2000).

SELECTED PERIODICAL PUBLICATION–
UNCOLLECTED: "A Bourgeois Story," *Prospect* (April 2002): 54–58.

James Lasdun is a many-sided writer—poet, novelist, writer of screenplays, author of a travel book, and

James Lasdun (from the dust jacket for The Horned Man, *2002; Richland County Public Library)*

short-story writer. His life shows a similar multifaceted quality: born and brought up in England in an Anglo-Jewish family, he has lived since 1987 in the United States and is married to an American, Pia Davis. His work bridges the two continents and shows an awareness of the complexities of personal, political, and social affiliations and rejections. Although some critics have expressed reservations about his short fiction, his three collections of short stories have met with general approval. For example, Joyce Reiser Kornblatt in *The New York Times Book Review* (5 July 1992) called Lasdun's voice "erudite, disturbing, and inventive," while in *TLS: The Times Literary Supplement* (28 February 1992), Shena Mackay summed up his career at that point: "James Lasdun's collection of short stories *The Silver Age* (1985) gave notice that here was a real writer . . . this collection [*Three Evenings*] . . . , poetic and intelligent, consolidates his growing reputation." He has won important literary prizes for both his poetry and his short fiction; one short story, "The Siege," was made into a movie by Italian director Bernardo Bertolucci; and Lasdun's novel, *The Horned Man* (2002), has had considerable critical success.

James Lasdun was born on 8 June 1958 in London. He is the son of Denys Louis Lasdun and Susan Virginia (Bendit) Lasdun–the second of three children. Lasdun's mother is a writer and designer; his father is an important British architect. Sir Denys Lasdun was the architect for such major building projects as the University of East Anglia campus in Norwich, England (1962–1968) and the National Theatre in London (1967–1976). In a poem titled "American Mountain," from the collection *Landscape with Chainsaw* (2001), Lasdun appears to speak about himself and his attitude toward growing up in England. He writes that his family's upper-class "accents" set them off from the "masses," while "our looks and name / did the same for the upper classes." He later describes his family as "Anglophone Russian-German apostate Jews / mouthing Anglican hymns at church / till we renounced that too." Although Jewish characters and topics do not appear in Lasdun's fiction, many of the characters in his short stories and novels have to negotiate difficult social borders between acceptance and rejection. Nevertheless, Lasdun's early life in Britain took a successful path. He received a B.A. from Bristol University in 1979 with honors, and found work as a publisher's reader in London in 1980, a profession that he followed until 1986. During this period he was also the co-editor of the journal *Straight Lines* (1979–1984).

In 1985 Lasdun published his first collection of short stories, *The Silver Age*, which met with critical approval. Michael Hulse, writing in *Encounter* (September–October 1986) claimed that two of the stories, "Property" and "The Siege," "belong with the best short fiction I have seen in the 1980s." Hulse compared Lasdun's work with Ian McEwan's and summed up Lasdun as "a glittering, uncanny, oddly-angled writer, of considerable energy and imagination." Responses in the United States were similarly positive. Despite his reservations about unpleasant aspects of Lasdun's stories, William H. Pritchard in *The Hudson Review* (1987) called the collection "a handsomely unforgiving group of pieces," while the anonymous reviewer in *The Antioch Review* (1987) was confident that "Property" and "The Siege" "will doubtlessly be anthologized for years to come."

The Silver Age includes ten short stories of varying lengths. "Heart's Desire," "The Spoiling," and "The Siege" are more than twenty pages long, while "Snow" is only seven. They include first-person narrations ("Property," "Dead Labour," "Heart's Desire," and "Snow"), but the majority are written in the third person, usually with a restricted point of view. "England's Finest" and parts of "The Spoiling," exceptions in this respect, employ a third-person omniscient narrator. The overall title of the collection published in Britain, *The Silver Age,* suggests decadence and even corruption (since a silver age is inferior to a golden one). Most of the stories center on disturbing, often degrading, and usually unpleasant experiences that have lasting and unfortunate consequences (implied or presented) for the characters involved. Perhaps the only exception is "The Siege," in which Marietta's experience is disturbing and full of consequences, but not in itself unwholesome. Overall, the stories are full of classical echoes, role reversals, and motifs of excess (from the jewels in "Property," to the food in "The Spoiling," and the colored carpets in "Delirium Eclipse").

The collection opens with one of its most admired stories, "Property." The unnamed narrator tells the story of three days during a visit to his grandmother's Mayfair apartment. Although the language is not that of a young boy, the narrator restricts himself to the young protagonist's point of view, and the events are not interpreted by a more mature consciousness. The grandmother, who is a wealthy woman, receives items over three days from a former nurse or servant named Mary Prosser, who left her service many years before. These items, in restitution for faults committed in the past, open a "fissure" in the grandmother's mind and produce chaotic streams of memories. They act as mementos mori, and at the end of the story, the grandmother dies. "Property" is full of motifs of money and a surfeit of material goods, but it also includes reminders of death and transience–for example, the grandmother's thinning hair. The story is haunted by enigmas. What was the relationship between the grandmother and Mary Prosser, and why do Mary's actions affect the grandmother as they do? "Property" is, indeed, a rich and ambiguous text that has drawn critics' approval.

Dust jacket for the U.S. publication of Lasdun's 1985 short-story collection. Most of the stories are about unpleasant experiences that have lasting consequences (Richland County Public Library).

"The Bugle" presents another servant/companion, in this case Alice Cottle, a sinister woman, whom the protagonist David Pesketh finds once more in charge of his aging parents when he returns to England after spending three years abroad. Cottle controls her employers and achieves ascendancy over David. As in "Property," roles are reversed: the servant dominates the employer. The story also presents motifs of transience. Cottle is clearing out the Pesketh family home by burning the detritus of the past in the back garden, where David sees the embodiment of his defiance of Cottle's repression, a bugle, being destroyed. Reversal and transformation also mark the third story in the collection, "Dead Labour." In it, the unnamed narrator is seduced, literally and metaphorically, from his former austere and egalitarian political beliefs to a life of excess and self-indulgence, by the lovely but exploitative Phillipa. The story, which is also filled with motifs of transience, ends in a sinister and orgiastic carnival in which Phillipa abandons the narrator, and he is mocked by the people of the world he has sought to enter. In "England's Finest," too, Edward's transformation, at the hands of materialist and social-climbing parents, into a model English schoolboy and cruel, almost inhuman, future monster, is equally unsavory.

Attraction toward what is different from oneself is a central motif in the two stories that follow. In "Escapes," an African American professor in Paris attempts to seduce the blond Lena. When his pursuit comes to nothing, he finds himself trapped in the underworld of the Paris Metro, like a lost soul in Hades. The classical overtones of "Escapes" are echoed in "Heart's Desire," in which a socially displaced young man, Simon, feels himself irresistibly attracted to and painfully excluded from a god-like trio of social superiors. However, when the two male figures attempt to rape the beautiful Julia, Simon is able to save her. Perhaps, although the story is ambiguous at this point, he is also able to free himself from his attraction to his social superiors.

"Snow" and "The Spoiling" deal with children's encounters with the adult world. In "Snow" the narrator is the unknowing observer of his aunt's adultery, while in "The Spoiling" Marty, by accident, saves his mother from a marriage to the wicked Ronald when he reveals his future stepfather's true character. Both stories are marked by the motifs of physical excess—in both instances, of food—that are common in Lasdun's stories. "The Siege" is one of the most highly regarded of the stories in *The Silver Age*. Part political fable, part modern version of a classical story of a god's seduction of a mortal, it depicts the process by which the wealthy Mr. Kinsky wins over his servant Marietta to become his lover. He does so by selling all his valuable artifacts to pay for the release of her husband, who is held in the jail of an unnamed foreign dictatorship. Throughout his courting of Marietta, Mr. Kinsky behaves with great delicacy; however, the story demonstrates Marietta's impotence in the face of what she thinks of as "the treacherous magnanimity of the powerful." As often in Lasdun's work, the text ends ambiguously—with Marietta in Mr. Kinsky's bed and her husband arriving at the door of the house. If "The Siege" demonstrates a magnanimity of the rich and powerful (albeit an ambiguous one), "Delirium Excess" shows punishment for their hubris. Jackson, the male protagonist from whose point of view the story is told, is successful and has command of large sums of international-development money. On a trip to India with Clare, whom he wishes to charm and control, he falls ill; the international development project collapses; and Clare drifts out of his power. At the end of the story, he has become a ridiculous and humiliated figure.

Lasdun's skill as a short-story writer was recognized in 1986 when he won the Dylan Thomas Award for short fiction. His next published work, however, was his first collection of poetry, *A Jump Start,* which appeared in 1987. It was well received by critics; Simon Rae, for example, in *TLS* (20 November 1989), noted the "glittering brilliance" of Lasdun's verse. The collection echoes *The Silver Age* in its concern with transience, in its motifs of opulent excess, and in the poem "Hermaphropditus," one of the first of Lasdun's many engagements with the work of Ovid. In 1987 Lasdun took positions as instructor in creative writing at both Columbia University and Princeton University. In an interview with Kevin Connolly, Lasdun revealed that he decided to go to the United States for financial reasons, as teaching positions there made possible for him a life as a poet. Lasdun has had a successful academic career since his arrival in the United States. From 1988 to 1991 he was an instructor in creative writing at New York University, and in 1991 he was appointed instructor in creative writing at Bennington College in Vermont, a position he still holds. In 1989 he was the recipient of a Guggenheim Fellowship for poetry.

Lasdun's next work was a collection of short stories, published in 1992 under the title *Three Evenings and Other Stories.* United States critics were more hesitant in their responses to this collection than British reviewers; however, most recognized Lasdun's linguistic vigor and his skill in characterization, deployment of detail, and creation of ambiguity. *Three Evenings and Other Stories* includes seven texts. Only one, "Macrobiotic," is short (about eight pages), while most are approximately twenty pages long, and the title story is more than forty pages. All present complex personal experiences (and all are first-person narrations, or third-person narrations with a restricted point of view), although three stories look beyond the purely personal. "Trumpet Voluntary" is a dystopian satire on English social attitudes, set in the future, and "Spiders and Manatees," "Macrobiotic," and "The Volunteer" involve English characters' responses to aspects of life in the United States.

"Ate/Menos *or* The Miracle" is a story of mistaken identity and deception. The narrator is brought home by an aging actress, who thinks he is a famous director; they become drunk; they have sex; and he encounters her mentally retarded daughter, whom he cruelly teases about her name. As his deception is about to be revealed, he flees, leaving disturbance in his wake. The story is deeply ambiguous both in its overall meaning—is the narrator an agent of wickedness or of a certain truth? what has happened at the end of the story?—and in its constant allusions to religion and classical mythology. "The Coat," a story particularly admired by reviewers, involves Lasdun's abiding concern with

Dust jacket for the U.S. publication of Lasdun's 1992 collection of stories, many of which deal with complicated personal experiences (Richland County Public Library)

transience. A beautiful coat is passed on reluctantly and by chance from an older woman to her son's rather shallow girlfriend.

The next three stories deal with figures who are fascinated by the force of those who are different from them. In the future dystopia "Trumpet Voluntary," the unnamed narrator becomes a vassal to the aristocrats, who now, in the 2040s, run England. In "Spiders and Manatees," Victoria, an English teacher of classics working in the United States, is both repelled and fascinated by features of North American life. She finds psychic relief for her loneliness in the god-like and heroic bodies of young Americans, although the text ends in disillusion. This story anticipates *The Horned Man* in its picture of psychological dissociation from self and actions. "Macrobiotic" presents the uneasy musings of a young Englishman in New York as he tries to deal with his jealousy toward his lover's ostentatiously manly former companion.

"The Volunteer," too, shows a similar interest on the part of the narrator in someone utterly different from himself. Simon is a volunteer in a New York shelter for the homeless. There he encounters Tina D'Oliveira, a highly disturbed illegal immigrant. The story delicately presents the complexities of their relationship and ends violently as Simon realizes that Tina inhabits a spiritual "desolation" that is beyond his understanding. In "Three Evenings," the protagonist, Jonathan, also encounters his fascinating opposite. Katie Varish is older, successful, powerful, and dynamic, while he is drifting and unformed. In the course of the story Jonathan emancipates himself from Katie and develops independently. However, at the end of the text he is preparing to act deceitfully in accordance with her wishes. Like many of Lasdun's stories, "Three Evenings" is psychologically complex and ambiguous, and full of motifs of ripeness, excess, and transience.

Lasdun's volume of poetry *The Revenant* (1995) returns to many of the themes of the short stories and the earlier poetry. Transformation, transience, and the presence of the classical in the contemporary mark these poems, which had mixed reviews in the United States. *After Ovid: New Metamorphoses,* which Lasdun co-edited with Anglo-German poet Michael Hofmann, was published in 1994. This volume includes translations and reworkings of Ovid's poetry by Lasdun and Hofmann, but also by a host of distinguished contemporary poets. In the introduction to the volume, Lasdun and Hofmann argue for the Latin poet's modernity: Ovid's poems "offer a mythical key to most of the more extreme forms of human behavior and suffering." In the 1990s Lasdun extended into a new field of activity. He co-authored screenplays for two motion pictures directed by Jonathan Nossiter: *Sunday* (1997), the story material of which is reminiscent of "Ate/ Menos" from *Three Evenings,* and *Signs and Wonders* (2001). *Sunday* won the Dramatic Award at the Sundance Film Festival in 1997.

The Siege and Other Stories was published in 1999. The collection is made up entirely of stories from Lasdun's two previous volumes of short fiction. In the early years of the twenty-first century Lasdun's energies have gone into poetry and the novel, rather than into short fiction. A collection of poems, *Landscape with Chainsaw,* published in 2001, is remarkable for the degree of personal revelation the poems provide. "Returning the Gift," for example, is a short story in verse, which, like much of Lasdun's work after 1987, skillfully presents the complexities of being British in the United States. In 2002 Lasdun's novel *The Horned Man* was published, a well-received study of mental collapse and of gender and national uncertainty, which Lasdun himself has acknowledged started off as a short story, and which, indeed, includes within it one separate narrative (Lawrence Miller's relations with his stepfather's family) that could stand on its own as a short story.

Lasdun's short stories are examinations of transience and of fascination with what is different from oneself. They show characters negotiating difficult social, personal, and national boundaries, and point to the disturbing power of opulence and excess. Although Lasdun has recently turned his attention to other kinds of writing, they show affinities with the short fiction, and the stories themselves stand as important pieces of British short fiction in the 1980s and 1990s.

Interviews:

Kevin Connolly, "Film + Poetry=A Living" <http://www.eye.net/eye/issue/issue_10.23.97/plus/books.html>;

Euan Kerr, "From 'Unremarkable' to 'Terrifying'," MPR Books (30 April 2002) <http://www.mpr.org/books/titles/lasdun_thehornedman.shtml>.

Mary Lavin

(10 June 1912 – 25 March 1996)

Greg C. Winston
Husson College

See also the entry on Mary Lavin in *DLB 15: British Novelists, 1930–1959, Part I.*

BOOKS: *Tales from Bective Bridge,* with a preface by Edward John Moreton Drax Plunkett, Lord Dunsany (Boston: Little, Brown, 1942; London: Joseph, 1943);

The Long Ago and Other Stories (London: Joseph, 1944);

The House in Clewe Street (London: Joseph, 1945; Boston: Little, Brown, 1945);

The Becker Wives and Other Stories (London: Joseph, 1946; New York: New American Library, 1971);

At Sallygap and Other Stories (Boston: Little, Brown, 1947);

Mary O'Grady (London: Joseph, 1950; Boston: Little, Brown, 1950);

A Single Lady and Other Stories (London: Joseph, 1951);

The Patriot Son and Other Stories (London: Joseph, 1956);

A Likely Story (New York: Macmillan, 1957; Dublin: Dolmen Press, 1967);

Selected Stories (New York: Macmillan, 1959);

The Great Wave and Other Stories (London: Macmillan, 1961; New York: Macmillan, 1961);

The Stories of Mary Lavin, 3 volumes (London: Constable, 1964–1985);

In the Middle of the Fields and Other Stories (London: Constable, 1967; New York: Macmillan, 1969);

Happiness and Other Stories (London: Constable, 1969; Boston: Houghton Mifflin, 1970);

Collected Stories, with an introduction by V. S. Pritchett (Boston: Houghton Mifflin, 1971);

The Second Best Children in the World (London: Longmans Young Books, 1972; Boston: Houghton Mifflin, 1973);

A Memory and Other Stories (London: Constable, 1972; Boston: Houghton Mifflin, 1973);

The Shrine and Other Stories (London: Constable, 1977; Boston: Houghton Mifflin, 1977);

Selected Stories (New York & Harmondsworth, U.K.: Penguin, 1981);

Mary Lavin (frontispiece for Richard F. Peterson, Mary Lavin, *1978; Thomas Cooper Library, University of South Carolina)*

A Family Likeness and Other Stories (London: Constable, 1985);

In a Café (Dublin: Town House, 1995).

Mary Lavin once described the short story as "a powerful medium in which anything, anything, anything that is to be said can be said." In the short story, she asserted, "a writer distills the essence of his thought. I believe this because the short story ... is determined by the writer's own character. Both are one. Short-story writing—for me—is only looking closer than normal into the human heart." In more than four decades of writing, Lavin delved into her own heart for more than a hundred stories published in nineteen books and in many magazines, setting her among the most prolific and respected short-fiction writers on either side of the Atlantic.

Mary Josephine Lavin was born 10 June 1912 in East Walpole, Massachusetts, the only child of Nora and Thomas Lavin. The couple had been introduced four years earlier on a boat returning to their native Ireland. Thomas was well established in America, having spent some years already working as horse groom, chauffeur, and general caretaker for the family of Charles Bird. Nora, on the other hand, was only a brief visitor to Massachusetts, having just completed a stay with her granduncle, a parish priest in Waltham. Coming from a middle-class merchant family in Athenry, County Galway, Nora found America a coarse place and looked down upon its Irish community.

On shipboard Tom noticed Nora and managed to become partnered with her in a game of quoits. A correspondence developed following the crossing, and within a few years, despite her disregard for America, Nora returned to Massachusetts. The two were married in Waltham and moved to East Walpole to be near Tom's work. The marriage seemed to amplify the opposite personalities of the couple. Tom was lighthearted and sociable; Nora, more reserved and soberly strict, a distinction their daughter later portrayed through the characters of Mr. and Mrs. Delaney in the opening segment of her story "Lemonade."

> All Pappa's and Mama's friends had come to the house to say good bye, that is to say, all Pappa's friends. Mama didn't want them.
>
> "On our last night!" she sighed, when Pappa announced they were coming.
>
> "I know, I know," said Pappa, "only it wasn't me who asked them. They invited themselves—out of the goodness of their hearts!" he added.
>
> "—or maybe," cried Mama, "as a cure for the drought!"

From this conjunction of opposite natures sprang the thematic seeds of many of their daughter's best short stories in the decades to follow.

The excerpt also reflects the family's real-life move to Ireland in 1921. When Mary was nine years old, her mother took her to stay with her family in Athenry, County Galway. The sojourn stretched to eight months, at which time Nora wrote to Tom that she and Mary were remaining in Ireland. As Lavin proclaimed years later, her mother "loathed and detested" America and had no desire to return. Tom conceded to his wife's wishes, arranged to purchase a house in Dublin, and met Nora and Mary there within the year.

The time in Athenry was brief but influential. As Lavin later noted, "I have set a great number of my stories in the same place, the small town in the west of Ireland in which I spent only eight months." The young and perceptive only child absorbed the intricate details of her new place and its people. Spending much time in the shop run by her mother's family, Mary became especially aware of the economic and social tensions of her new country. The autobiographical story "Lemonade" concerns such issues, as Maudie, newly arrived in Ireland from America, ignores the village status quo by befriending the shunned, impoverished Sadie and her mournful mother.

When Tom joined Nora and Mary in Ireland the following year, they moved to Dublin, where Mary was enrolled in the Loreto Convent school. She excelled in the classroom, winning the Bishop's Medal for Christian doctrine, taking first place in English, and becoming captain of the debating team. Among her favorite literature of her school days were George Eliot's *The Mill on the Floss* (1860), Nathaniel Hawthorne's *The House of Seven Gables* (1851) and *Tanglewood Tales* (1853), as well as the poems of Henry Wadsworth Longfellow.

Lavin, who always took pride in her essay writing, around this time first tried her hand at stories. As she remarks in the preface to *Tales from Bective Bridge* (1942), "To my surprise, imaginative writing came easier to me, far easier than the composing of those school essays." In a November 1979 interview, Lavin nevertheless downplayed these earliest forays into fiction: "When I was about fourteen, fifteen or so, at school, I wrote a school-story for fun to amuse the class. And I illustrated it too but I took the writing no more seriously than the drawing. Both were terrible. The whole exercise was to show-off before the class."

By 1926 the Lavins relocated to Bective, County Meath, where Tom had been hired as manager of a hunting estate recently acquired by his American employer, Bird. The idyllic rural surroundings shaped some of Mary's fondest girlhood memories and later afforded the vivid rural landscapes found throughout her fiction. The narrator of "A Likely Story" offers the following description: "Do you know Bective? Like a bird in the nest, it presses close to the soft green mound of the river bank, its handful of houses no more significant by day than the sheep that dot the far fields."

In 1930 Lavin entered University College Dublin (UCD) where, following a slow start, she eventually shone as a student of literature, graduating with first honors. Many faculty members and fellow students believed at this point that Lavin was destined to be a writer because of the clarity and insight of her essays. Yet, she believed at this time that her soon-to-be husband, William Walsh, would become a writer and she "thought it would be very nice to be a writer's wife." Walsh became a lawyer while Mary continued in the UCD graduate program to complete an M.A. on the works of Jane Austen.

Tom Lavin had never been interested in his daughter's formal education; more than once (and to the dismay of Loreto school nuns) he had pulled Mary from classes to join him for a day out if the weather was fine. Thus, it was not altogether surprising as she neared completion of her master's thesis that her father asked her to join him for a holiday in America. She rushed to complete her typescript, entrusting the last of its retyping to a close friend. While her thesis director applauded the originality of her interpretation, he found its punctuation to be less than satisfactory. He was not sure whether to fail it on those grounds or pass it with high honors on the merit of its original critical contribution. Following some consultation, he elected to do the latter. Similarly, Edward John Moreton Drax Plunkett, Lord Dunsany, wrote in the preface to *Tales from Bective Bridge* that the only advice he felt he could ever offer Mary Lavin about writing would relate to her poor punctuation.

Lavin had also been a stellar student in French language and literature at Loreto Convent, so in 1938 she took a position as French teacher at her former school to support herself as she began to prepare for doctoral studies in literature at UCD. She planned to write her dissertation on Virginia Woolf, whose avantgarde modernist fiction, more than the work of any other writer, gave Lavin the sense that literature was real and relevant to the world. Lavin never completed the dissertation.

Instead, the project literally provided the space for Lavin to begin her own career as a writer of fiction. On the back of some dissertation draft pages she began by chance one day to draft her first story, "Miss Holland." The manuscript was accepted and published the same year (1938) by Seumas O'Sullivan, editor of *The Dublin Magazine*. Along with Dunsany, Lavin counted O'Sullivan an instrumental and encouraging figure in her decision to become a professional writer of fiction. At Dunsany's recommendation, her first American publications came with "The Green Grave and the Black Grave" in 1940 and "At Sallygap" in 1941, both published in the *Atlantic Monthly*. In subsequent decades Lavin also became a frequent contributor of stories to *The New Yorker*.

Front cover for the 1978 Dublin paperback edition of Lavin's first short-story collection (1942). Bective is a town in County Meath that was the scene of many of her happiest girlhood memories (Bruccoli Clark Layman Archives).

She married Walsh in 1942, and the couple soon split their time between Dublin, where Walsh had his legal practice, and Bective, where with Mary's inheritance following the death of her father in 1945, they purchased a property known as the Abbey Farm. The ensuing decade brought the couple three children: Valentine, Elizabeth, and Caroline. As Bonnie Kime Scott observed, "It is apparent that Mary Lavin's daughters have been a great source of daily satisfaction and stimulation as well as a rich resource for her writing."

The girls' births took place during the time of the publication of Lavin's first three collections of short stories and two novels, *The House in Clewe Street* (1945) and *Mary O'Grady* (1950). "Two bad novels," she called them decades later in an article in the *Irish University*

Review, wishing that "novels could be torn down like houses." Not all critics agreed with this stiff assessment, but Lavin nonetheless abandoned further efforts in the genre and concentrated the remainder of her career on the short story. As she once remarked in 1979, "With not much time to write, I tried to write with great intensity and the novel isn't an intense medium." To balance writing against the demands of motherhood, the emotional changes of marriage, widowhood, and remarriage, the short story seemed both a natural and logical solution.

Lavin's debut collection, *Tales from Bective Bridge,* draws its title from the locale where her father managed the Bird hunting estate starting in 1926. Many of its stories trace the quiet and often desperate lives of ordinary individuals caught in the grip of social regulations, economic limitations, or both. As Dunsany writes in the preface, "She tells the stories of quite ordinary lives, the stories of people who many might suppose have no story in all their experience." As if to underscore this observation, the lead story, "Lilacs," draws its thematic material from the more mundane details of small-town life.

"Lilacs" recounts the ambitions of two sisters, Stacy and Kate Mulloy, who inherit their parents' comfortable home and profitable manure business, yet long for a grander existence than the economy and society of the rural village have to offer. As the story commences, Kate and her father, Phelim, are at odds over the dunghill, which, even as it brings in a dependable income, thwarts the upward mobility to which the daughters, products of finishing schools and music lessons, constantly aspire. While Kate argues with her parents about the need to deal in dung, Stacy dreams of lilacs. But such flowery hopes run counter to the social fate of the Mulloy family, as demonstrated even through the simple detail that over time Phelim has begun calling his wife Ros instead of Rose.

With the subsequent deaths of both parents, followed immediately by Kate's marriage, each daughter in turn faces the decision to take over the business or make a change in her life. As do other stories in the collection, "Lilacs" defines the material conditions of 1940s Ireland and represents the interpersonal and intergenerational differences that accompanied life there just more than two decades after the founding of the Irish Free State. "But what will you live on, Miss Stacy?," the unanswered question that concludes the story, seems to interrogate not only the younger Mulloy daughter but also all of Ireland in its new postcolonial condition. Having gotten rid of accustomed ways of life and long-held power structures, what comes next? The rest of the collection, and indeed much of the rest of Lavin's early fiction, seems an attempt to answer this question in its various economic, social, and emotional dimensions. As Richard F. Peterson observes of Lavin's first collections, "Gradually emerging out of these early stories is the portrait of an Irish middle class peopled by lonely, sometimes bitter, characters trapped by their own natures and frustrated emotional needs. Within that portrait, Mary Lavin's characters act out their own individual failures or discover the terrible emptiness of their lives." "The Green Grave and the Black Grave," for instance, depicts the routine hardships and losses of a fishing village in the Irish Gaeltacht. Its focus on human risk at the hands of the natural environment in part forms an early-twentieth-century ethnography comparable to Tomás Ó Crohan's *The Islandman* (1929) or Robert O'Flaherty's motion picture *Man of Aran* (1934). Dunsany took issue with the story, noting its sentence-level repetition as an unnecessary imitation of John Millington Synge's drama *Riders to the Sea* (1904). Lavin defended this stylistic trait on the grounds of poetic experimentation, as "simply an attempt to create echoes of waves breaking on a shore." Synge's influence does seem readily apparent, though perhaps more in the sense of classical tragedy brought to a local setting.

By most critical accounts, Lavin is at her best when she remains closer to home and the world she knew to the minutest detail—namely, the middle-class shops and respectable houses of towns in the Irish Midlands. With the exception of "At Sallygap," which moves between Dublin and the mountains of County Wicklow, the stories generally take place in unnamed villages inspired by Bective. The people of those Midlands surroundings and the social tensions among them form the center of Lavin's fictional universe. As Zack Bowen observes, Lavin's "vision of reality is harsh and closely circumscribed by an acute awareness of social class and society's sanctions and rules. This is more than merely the theme of some of her stories; it is the donnée of her plots as well as the context of motive and constraint which condition the behavior of most of her characters."

In "Sarah," a servant girl's past reputation as much as her present actions seals a tragic fate; in "Love is for Lovers," a confirmed bachelor almost takes a chance at marriage before retreating into the comfort of his routine. Dunsany praised the latter story as exemplifying Lavin's talent for leading her readers away from their expectations for the "modern thriller" and toward new kinds of stories that rely on the everyday:

> The pivot of the story ["Love is For Lovers"], for instance, is where a fly thrown out of a cup of tea, "and celebrating his release a little too soon by sitting on a blade of grass rubbing his hands," is killed by a small

dog. It may seem too tiny a thing to notice, and the man's life, which turns in another direction from that moment, may seem tiny and unimportant too, to any who may not reflect how hard it is for any of us to say what is important and what is not.

"Brother Boniface" includes Lavin's first use of a pattern she developed in many stories: the extended flashback in a limited omniscient third-person narration. She deployed the same technique in "The Nun's Mother" and "The Great Wave." In "Brother Boniface," as a monk enters his last years, his responsibilities reduced to protecting the monastic flower garden from five resident cats, he meditates upon the lifetime that has brought him to this moment: his youthful stargazing and intimate glimpses into the glory of nature; his search for a way of life that will afford him a view of that glory; and his entry into monastic life with its social life and routine.

Lavin demonstrates the changes by skillful adjustments to sentence style throughout the story. The choppy, reductive feeling of the opening lines announces the slow tranquility of old age: "Brother Boniface sat in the sun. The sun shone full on the monastery walls, and brightened the gold coins of its ancient lichen." These lines yield to a more fluid sentence-level energy in the lengthy flashback to a restless childhood:

> At first when he went into the country lanes Barney was little better than a city man, exclaiming at the blatant beauties that paraded more brazenly in the hedgerows, the dowried hawthorn and the rambling honeysuckle. But after a time he grew in knowledge of the secrets and subtleties of nature, and he passed by the blossoming trees almost heedlessly and went into the deeps of the fields to seek out the secret scents that are released from the grass when the heavy cattle tread it down.

Despite such ruminations, the reader is left to wonder whether Boniface chose the monastery for sublime and vocational reasons or merely as an escape from the drudgery and routine "way of life that had been destined for him by his father and his mother." In this regard, the old monk could be said to bear more than a passing resemblance to the young Mulloy girls of "Lilacs" who wish to upgrade from an existence of manure heaps to a life of blossoms.

Four additional tales complete the collection, including "Say Could that Lad Be I?," based on Tom Lavin's childhood in Roscommon, and "Miss Holland," the story first written on the back of the dissertation manuscript five years earlier. From that decision one afternoon to try her hand at writing a short story Lavin had by the mid 1940s begun to consider herself first and foremost an imaginative writer. When *Tales*

Dust jacket for Lavin's 1969 collection of stories, many of which are set at the Abbey Farm, a property in Ireland that she and her husband bought in 1945 (Richland Public Library)

from Bective Bridge was awarded the James Tait Black Memorial Prize in 1943, Lavin knew she had found her calling and her form in the short story.

The title story from *The Long Ago and Other Stories* (1944) extends previous themes of small-town animosity, betrayal, and isolation, whether self-imposed or meted out as social penalty. As in "Sarah" and "Love is for Lovers," "The Long Ago" concerns an outcast and the contrast between her private longing and her public reality. Hallie, jilted in her youth, looks on as her friends Dolly and Ella attain the married life and motherhood that was so close to being her own as well. Marianne Koenig has remarked upon the fairy-tale pattern of the story, wherein "three young girls with similar sounding names" live out alternative histories. Any possibility of happily ever after dissolves, however, at the end of the story when, with only the best intentions, Hallie commits an unpardonable social gaffe when attempting to commiserate with the newly widowed Ella. By voicing her long-held desire that things will be once more as they were in their long-ago girlhood, Hallie not only breaches social etiquette but also the natural order. As harsh words and stares are exchanged and images of wedding rings lock Hallie out of the circle of friendship, the actions suggest her penance will be one of shame and loneliness.

Along with these recurring themes, Lavin also brings in specific characters from previous stories. For instance, Jasper Kane, the peripheral questioner at the end of "Lilacs," becomes a catalytic figure at the beginning of "The Long Ago" as the solicitor who encourages his apprentice to choose his daughter above Hallie. Such subtle nods to prior works serve to establish a network of linkage across stories and introduce a technique of tangential plot development and overlapping characterization that gradually increase as Lavin's fictional world grows.

At Sallygap and Other Stories (1947) features seven new stories alongside five from the debut collection. The title story—included in *Tales from Bective Bridge* but functioning more centrally in this one—interweaves mythic patterns with modern content. Mimicking the Celtic place-lore tradition, "At Sallygap" invokes a specific location and common topographic feature of the Irish landscape; on a symbolic level, it charts the emotional gulf that can exist between two people despite or resulting from years of marriage. Through such an interpersonal gap the main character steps into a recollection of his past and the decision that brought about his present domestic discord.

But before it concentrates on Manny Ryan—whose name plainly evinces a kind of Irish Everyman figure—the story commences with a telling bird's-eye description of Dublin from a mountaintop bus route. This landscape depiction hints that the psychological portrait to follow is not of a single man but of an entire city. In this way, Lavin seems to nod cleverly in the direction of one forefather of the Irish short story:

> Dublin was all exposed. The passengers told each other that you could see every inch of it. They could certainly see every church steeple and every tower. But, had they admitted as much, they would have said that the dark spires and steeples that rose up out of the blue pools of distance below looked little better than dark thistles rising up defiantly in a gentle pasture.

A generation after James Joyce's *Dubliners* (1914), Lavin's updated literary portrait of the Irish capital shows a state of general social paralysis still remains; the fundamental difference seems to be that the descendants of Joyce's fictional personages have begun to acknowledge their condition even as they stop just short of voicing it. In this way, the passage seems both an adoption of and an addendum to Joyce's thesis. The description appropriately resumes to underscore further the psychological inertia: "The sea that circled this indistinct city seemed as gray and motionless as the air."

Glimpsing the Dunlaoghaire mail boat prompts Manny to relate his own story of almost taking that boat away from Ireland to a bohemian, musical life in "gay Paree, as they call it over there." His possession of a faded band photograph suggests the routine nature of these reminiscences about lost glory days. Like Joyce's Eveline's, Manny's escape is halted at the quayside as the weight of social obligation bears down. This lost opportunity for a carefree existence is reenacted when Manny returns after nightfall to an unhappy marriage amid the shadowy, confining spaces of Dublin, utterly eclipsing his exultation and solitude in the sunny mountain surroundings. Lavin once noted her desire to transcend national boundaries with her writing: "Anything I wanted to achieve was in the traditions of world literature. I did not read the Irish writers until I had already dedicated myself to the short story." Nevertheless, "At Sallygap" shows her awareness of writing within the Irish short-story tradition of the twentieth century.

The dark emotional space between men and women in "At Sallygap" plays out in other studies of marriage from the second collection. If marriage seemed an inescapable prison in the first story, in "The Haymaking" it offers a young woman hope of escape to a country life. As a term referring either to courtship or agriculture, the title functions at first ambiguously then ironically when the attention of the long-time bachelor farmer remains fixed on his vast holdings rather than on his new wife. Fanny, the former teacher, perhaps should have known that Christopher Glebe, whose surname means land or soil, would have little interest in anything else.

"A Cup of Tea" portrays an equally disastrous marriage at a later phase when long silences and separate rooms have replaced volatility and direct confrontation. A mother's jealousy of her husband's close bond with their daughter Sophy becomes the primary source of tension in the house, a way of working out the unresolved issues between the couple. Having just returned from study at a university, Sophy's growing educational distance from her mother and increasing connection to her father leaves the mother isolated and troubled, searching for ways to connect. The situation literally reaches a boiling point when the mother accidentally scalds the milk for their tea, then proceeds to argue about it. As in other Lavin stories, such simple gestures speak volumes. Sophy's mother, whose name is never given, lacks a clear identity and the confidence that comes with it, a fact that has much to do with what comes to pass.

Koenig notes that "More than most short-story writers, Mary Lavin in her earlier stories both depends upon and exploits the envelope of silence which surrounds a story." One story that clearly demonstrates this dependence is "A Nun's Mother." Like "Brother Boniface," most of "A Nun's Mother" consists of an extended, interior meditation—in this case from the perspective of a parent watching her child choose a religious life. The limited third-person viewpoint establishes a keen tension between the mother's deep and fluctuating well of emotions and a reader's sympathy. As Mrs. Latimer strives to understand her daughter's decision to enter the convent, her thoughts move between the social prestige and the personal loss that accompany one another. As in many of Lavin's stories, the reader begins to have difficulty distinguishing sincere emotion from that motivated by class pressures and societal expectations. Thus, a fleeting but complex psychological vignette emerges by the end of the story.

Lavin's matrimonial themes recur in this story as well, as the mother looks back over years of relatively happy married life and regrets that her daughter will never know the same: "Angela was going to miss it all; the heavy weight of the hard male breast, the terror, the pain, the soft delirium seeping through. She clutched the hand strap tightly. Better not to remember those far-back years. She must forget them if she was to assume a role." Mrs. Latimer's thoughts of her daughter's future lead circuitously to reflections upon what her own life has meant. In quiet contrast to Sophy's mother in "A Cup of Tea," Mrs. Latimer values marriage but refrains from imposing her own life on Angela: "Even if she could have described the peace and beauty of marriage, perhaps she would not have done so. For why, after all, should she take the responsibility of interfering with a vocation."

While V. S. Pritchett, in the introduction to *Collected Stories* (1971), regards Lavin's first stories as dominated by "power-loving," "downtrodden," or "lonely" women, Scott offers a revised assessment: "Women characters are the most tyrannical and rigid enforcers of the social class distinctions. Prompted by anxieties about money, fears about public opinion, fatigue from hard work, ennui or lack of self-respect, women precipitate their own defeat and/or the torment of others." The women themselves are not so much to blame as the social codes they feel compelled to enforce or obey. In this regard, even some of the most hostile and conniving female characters can also be seen as ultimate victims.

The consequences for such women are usually painful and isolating, as Scott describes, "Often, in a structurally-important central incident, they unleash vituperative tongues to say things that they should have held back and may even have intended to keep inside. Consequently, they miss the emotional fulfillment found in the exchange of love, and also fail to know freedom, happiness and internal peace." Good examples of characters that demonstrate this theory are Kathleen Kedrigan in "Sarah," Annie Ryan in "At Sallygap," the mother in "A Cup of Tea," and the deceased mother and her unyielding daughter Kate in "The Will."

Lavin's short fiction of the 1950s exhibits new approaches to writing and reflects profound changes in her personal life, the death of Walsh in May 1954 having left her a young widow and single mother. While her first collections featured stories that enabled readers to experience emotional realities of characters' lives, her work now concentrated more on developing a sound structure and geometry behind the fiction. Of Lavin's second decade of writing, Peterson notes, "many stories that rely more on patterns of writing that impose the truth upon her characters and readers . . . stories with surprise endings and intrusive narrators are more typical of these collections."

A prime example of each of these devices occurs in the story "The Small Bequest," from the collection *A Single Lady and Other Stories* (1951). It is a cruel tale of social dysfunction and petty snobbishness. The first-person narrator of "The Small Bequest" is a female writer and the next-door neighbor of Adeline Tate and Emma Blodgett, two older women sharing a neo-Victorian existence of afternoon teas, knitting, and rose gardens. But the tranquility of their drawing room is disturbed by a constant underlying tension noticed only by the narrator and, by extension, the reader: Miss Blodgett, though not a blood relative, insists on calling Miss Tate by the familial title Aunt Adeline. This habit irritates the latter, who registers her displeasure with Miss Blodgett through a "little arrow of dissatisfaction" in glances detected only by the narrator.

In a final ironic gesture Miss Tate bequeaths £1,000 to Emma Blodgett by referring to Emma in her will as "my fond niece Emma." When the solicitors cannot locate an Emma among Miss Tate's fifty-four nieces, they conclude there is no such person; thus, Emma Blodgett is prevented from attaining the money she believes is rightfully hers. As blind to the gesture as she was to Miss Tate's glances, Miss Blodgett takes this act of naming as proof of her membership in the family instead of the posthumous passive-aggressive maneuver it truly is. She is left in an unresolved legal tangle and with little hope of ever claiming her legacy. The reader is left wondering whether she is better off not knowing the truth of her situation.

The title selection of *The Patriot Son and Other Stories* (1956) represents a rare foray for Lavin into Irish politics, though familial and communal relationships ultimately take precedence over abstract ideologies or sectarianism. While Bowen acknowledges "The Patriot Son" as "the only treatment of nationalism in the Lavin canon," he is quick to point out that "it's really about matriarchy and personal liberation." What the story proves most is the overall impossibility of separating inner psychology and interpersonal dynamics from outward political commitments. The story centers on Matty Conerty, whose life at the edge of manhood is controlled less by the ominous barracks of the Royal Irish Constabulary staring at his shop from across the road than by his domineering mother. But the young man finds a release for his frustration when Sean Monogon, a childhood friend and republican militia leader, first encourages Matty to take evening Gaelic classes and eventually to help fuel a republican arson attack on the barracks.

The tensions of gender and repressed sexuality become particularly striking themes throughout the story, commencing with the feminine personification of Ireland on the playbill for *The Colleen Bawn* that Sean brings to the Conerty shop. This nationalist poster introduces the sexually uninitiated Matty to the Dark Rosaleen or Ireland-as-woman, a potential target for all of his unrealized longing. In this regard, Lavin plays on legends of early Irish mythology reworked by such writers as William Butler Yeats, Lady Isabelle Augusta Gregory during the Irish Literary Revival: in the sovereignty myths, the would-be king asserted his claim to the land through union with the earth goddess.

When Matty literally awakens to the allure of the green fields and hills beyond the barracks, he sees the landscape for the first time in a highly eroticized light. Soon after, making his way toward the idyllic surroundings, Matty happens upon Sean in the middle of a reconnaissance mission for the unfolding plot to burn the constabulary barracks. Wading through a stream in his bare feet with trousers rolled, Sean looks "as slight as a girl." The curiously feminized description, in conjunction with Matty's thwarted attempts at courtship and marriage, completes a course of desire that finally brings him full circle to his mother's shop. Like Manny in "At Sallygap," Matty has no escape route. Nature offers a tempting but temporary release from his prison.

"My Vocation" delivers a completely different sort of experiment in narrative style and constitutes one of Lavin's most humorous writings. As Lavin biographer Leah Levenson declares, "It is Mary Lavin in a rollicking mood and is Irish to the core." The story looks back to the more serious "A Nun's Mother" of a decade before, only now offering a lighthearted account of a religious calling from the perspective of one called. A teenage girl is bent on becoming a nun until she learns the truth of what a nun's life might actually involve.

The story and dialect keenly portray Dublin's working-class north side in all its charm and attitude, from the jibes of the father and brother ("Do you hear that? Isn't that a good one?" and "We'll be alright if it isn't the Order of Mary Magdalen that one joins."), to the helpful if nosy Dorset Street neighbors. The simple title, reminiscent of a school essay, belies the complexity of a narrative that approaches the stream-of-consciousness writing of late modernism. "My Vocation" begins with a flourish that never ceases:

> I'm not married yet but I'm still in hopes. One thing is certain though: I was never cut out to be a nun in the first place. Anyway, I was only thirteen when I got the Call, and I think if we had been living out here in Crumlin at the time, in the new houses the Government gave us, I'd never have got it at all, because we hardly ever see nuns out here. And somehow, a person wouldn't take so much notice of them out here anyway.

With her combination of brash wit and wide-eyed naiveté, the narrator of "My Vocation" ranks among the most vibrant and down-to-earth female characters in all of Irish writing.

Lavin continued to perfect her young characters in her next project of short fiction. While often labeled juvenile fiction by publishers and critics, *A Likely Story* (1957) provides another interesting reworking of an Irish Revival theme, that of the Celtic *sidhe* (fairies) and the stolen child. Before heading in the direction of fairy tale, the story begins with a conversation between young Packy and his mother, a widow. Packy tells her if he were a man he would build her a new cottage:

> "Where would you build it, son? Up here on the hill, or down in the village? Would you have it thatched, or would you have it slated?"
>
> "Slated, of course," said Packy decisively, "unless you'd prefer tiles?"
>
> The widow looked at him in astonishment. Only the Council cottages had tiles.

Later, on first meeting the fairy, Packy takes him for a local gentleman, a foreigner, or a county councillor.

Lavin, herself a widow raising young children near the village of Bective, then clearly voices the extent of the single mother's concern for her child: "Hardly ever did he go out of the house that she didn't watch him out of sight, and hardly ever did he come home that she wasn't there again, waiting to get the first glimpse of him. And all the time between his going and his coming, her heart was in her mouth wondering if he was safe and sound." Soon Packy will be well out of her sight, however, when, from these hopes and fears of the human world the story shifts to an encounter with the *sìdhe* and a voyage underground.

A boy prone to retelling local stories of the fanciful or fantastic, Packy takes the trip of his young life with the little man he meets in the woods. The narrative setup for this encounter includes several of Packy's incredible accounts—of buried gold, of the *sìdhe*, and of changelings—to which his mother only offers her constant rejoinder, "A likely story." Thus, Packy's lively imagination is what makes him the most likely subject for the adventure about to unfold, a story he knows his mother will never believe.

From this point on Lavin's story depicts what Yeats's "The Stolen Child" and other literary versions of fairyland omit: the temptation and deception of the encounter and the adventure underground. In this case, the fairy exploits Packy's own desires for a nicer home by proffering improvements to the cottage in return for custody of Packy. As with so many traditional fairy tales, the psychological patterns are prominent as issues of childhood: growing up, security of home and parents, and the disruptive threat of outside forces all become apparent.

Guggenheim Fellowships in 1959 and 1960 plus winning the Katherine Mansfield Prize in 1961 enabled Lavin to concentrate more than ever on her fiction and, following a crisis of confidence that lasted several years after Walsh's death, helped prove to her again that her writing was appreciated and worthwhile. Not surprisingly, stories of widowhood, in all aspects of its struggles for emotional and economic survival, figure prominently during this period. In her short stories of the 1960s and 1970s, Lavin departed from the patterned structures that dominated her work in the preceding decade and, as Peterson observes, "returned to the impressionistic story that attempts to capture the emotional experience of her characters."

Predominant themes in *The Great Wave and Other Stories* (1961) are death, loss, and mourning. Bowen has noted in Lavin's writing her overall preoccupation with death and the effect of death upon the living. These stories address those concerns, while they also document a turning point in Lavin's work and personal life as well as in Ireland. By this time she and her daughters were dividing their time between the Abbey Farm and the Mews, a converted stables on Lad Lane in Dublin that had become a kind of literary salon and haven for aspiring young writers. The setting of these stories extends from the late nineteenth to the mid twentieth

Dust jacket for the 1973 U.S. edition of Lavin's 1972 collection that includes a novella about a man and a woman who have lived together so long that he takes her love for granted (Richland County Public Library)

century, exhibiting common human concerns and motifs against a backdrop of rapidly changing technological and social change. Some of them depict individuals coping with profound and sometimes surprising changes in their lives that are often deeply traumatic personal losses.

"The Great Wave" follows the making of a bishop, starting from his boyhood on a western island. As one of a few survivors of a natural catastrophe in his small fishing village, the boy identifies the miraculous quality of his life and finds his calling as a fisher of men. Biblical metaphors aside, Lavin based the story on a real-life episode at Boffin Island, where a devastating tidal wave all but wiped out the entire community of Cleggan. She noted in an interview that she had never read newspaper accounts of this tragedy—nor did she ever do research for her fiction writing—but only heard about the event from a friend, writer Michael McLaverty, who had visited with an old man who was among the handful to survive at Cleggan. Lavin was amazed to see how her story bore a striking similarity to the newspaper accounts she later discovered in the National Library in Dublin. To her, this coincidence was proof that imagination and fiction can lead one closer to truth.

The frame narrative, a study of religious vocation, invites comparison with the earlier works "Brother Boniface" and "The Nun's Mother." Like those stories, "The Great Wave" builds its structure on an extended flashback sequence compressed into just a few minutes of time in the narrative present. This compression creates a dynamic narrative as well as a sense of the eternal that seems appropriate to the mind-set of the bishop in the boat.

The next story, "The Mouse," transports the reader to seemingly gentler, more feminine surroundings, but these surroundings, too, are not without tragic victims and enduring consequences. The core episode of the story, young Leila's loss of her boyfriend to her best friend Mina, could be another sketch of hopeful love and intimate betrayal straight from *Tales from Bective Bridge* two decades before. What marks a new direction for Lavin's fiction is the calculated narrative layering, as three speakers in turn take the reader between generations and into the past.

An apparently simple story thereby becomes one of Lavin's most complex exercises in narrative and interpretation, challenging the reader to sift through three levels of narration prior to answering the final interpretive question directed at both daughter and reader—"Or can *you* make anything out of a story like that?" The open-ended question challenges every reader to consider the long-ago summer evening of Arthur (the boyfriend), Mina, and Leila, as well as his or her own experience.

"Lemonade" is among many clearly autobiographical stories Lavin composed at midcareer. It also takes a reflective look at America and Ireland, wealth and poverty, and parental love and regret. The tale focuses on the return of a mother and daughter from Massachusetts to Ireland. Like Nora Lavin, Mrs. Delaney in this tale evinces strong disapproval for the wild company kept by her husband in the Boston-Irish immigrant community. The title image is craftily woven throughout the story, gathering weight and acquiring new significance in each of the three segments. In America, spiked lemonade is served the evening before the departure of Maudie and her mother. Mr. Delaney, realizing he has forgotten to provide lemonade of the nonalcoholic variety for Maudie, tries to make up for this oversight with a promise to arrange for lemonade on shipboard. The cross he inscribes on the back of the boat tickets to symbolize this purchase foreshadows the crosses in the Franciscan cemetery where Mad Mary's son lies buried and where she mourns him with offerings of lemonade.

Immediately preceding "Lemonade," the name Maudie also occurs as that of a young widow in the story "In a Café," a reference to the meeting place for Maudie and the middle-aged widow Mary. Both women are coping with their personal losses and trying to rediscover their own individuality and capacity for future love. In this struggle they tread a peculiarly thin line between being each other's confidante or competitor. For Mary, potential love takes the form of the painter Johann van Stiegler, who frequents the small café; the exotic artist competes with the power of her husband's memory as Mary struggles in her decision about whether or not to pursue a deeper connection.

"The Yellow Beret" includes comparable portraits of grief and emotional turmoil; a father and mother discover a clue that their son is a university student by day and murderer by night. "Loving Memory" is about a widower's sorrowful obsession with his deceased young wife. As in "Lemonade," a parent's obsession over the dead siphons away love needed by living children.

In what seems a deliberately contrary wink at Joyce's placement of "The Dead" as the final story in *Dubliners*, *The Great Wave* concludes with a tale called "The Living." The gesture does not so much bow to Joyce's authority in the Irish short-story tradition as play cleverly upon it. The story itself, in which two boys look for an adventure and find an unexpectedly harsh dose of reality, parodies stories of childhood in *Dubliners* such as "An Encounter"; its ending, however, wherein the young narrator finds a dynamic life with home and family in the simple act of afternoon tea, seems quite the opposite of Joyce even as it echoes the famous final line of "The Dead": "And in the excitement, I forgot all about the living and the dead. For a long time."

In the Middle of the Fields and Other Stories (1967), a collection of six new short-fiction works, appeared while Lavin was serving the first of two years as writer in residence at the University of Connecticut. Even as such teaching opportunities and other foreign travel drew Lavin away from Ireland several times during the 1960s, the title and content of this volume firmly fix the collection at the Abbey Farm, to which Lavin and her daughters constantly returned.

In a clear reflection of Lavin's own experience, the title selection treats the emotional and financial challenges a widow faces in maintaining a busy farm on her own. The farm is both a protective compound and a lonely outpost of widowhood, as the descriptive ambiguity of the opening lines suggests, "Like a rock in the sea, she was islanded by fields, the heavy grass washing about the house, and the cattle wading in it as in water." "She" remains unnamed here, although a similar character is given the name Vera Traske both elsewhere in this collection and in enough subsequent stories for critic Koenig to dub them the "Vera stories." When she hires Bartley Crossen to cut grass in one of her fields, the main character is given a glimpse into Crossen's own experience of spousal loss.

Having heard Crossen's story of losing his young bride just days after the birth of their son, the widow naturally empathizes with his situation. But empathy soon converts to pity and annoyance when the remarried Crossen makes an unwelcome and rather pathetic advance toward her. As the story closes, she attempts to convince herself and Crossen that the memory of his first wife and true love was ultimately to blame for his embarrassing gaffe.

Also set amid the solitude of a Midlands farm, "The Cuckoo Spit" follows the relationship of Vera with Fergus, the young nephew of a neighbor. In this story Vera is the one who entertains the possibility of a second love with the younger man who has come to know and sympathize with her story. Still afraid to venture out after dark, she at last finds the courage to accompany Fergus through her own fields on a beautiful night when the young man offers his sympathetic words: "You must miss him very much. I suppose the more beautiful it is, the more lonely it must be for you." Her response is one of distancing and a decision to sever the connection developing between them. When even after a year apart romantic feelings toward the young man still linger, Vera closes the door on them for good. Much like "In the Middle of the Fields," this story depicts the tragic, self-imposed exile that is grieving.

During the 1970s Lavin achieved greater professional recognition and became more involved in the public life of writers' organizations. She won the Ella Lyman Cabot Award in 1972 and three years later received Ireland's most prestigious literary prize, the Gregory Medal. These awards came just on the heels of receiving an honorary doctorate from UCD, where thirty years earlier she had abandoned her doctoral studies to concentrate on imaginative writing. She also served one term as president of Irish PEN and two as president of the Irish Academy of Letters.

By far, Lavin's best-known work of short fiction is the title story from the 1969 collection *Happiness and Other Stories*. This much-anthologized anthem of Lavin's work, in its philosophical dialogue and insightful flashbacks, sums up many of the emotions of her life as widow and mother. Peterson has defined "Happiness" as "a counterpoint to Mary Lavin's compelling studies of the great loneliness of individuals trapped by their own emotional failures; and Vera is one of her rare

Dust jacket for the U.S. edition of Lavin's 1977 short-story collection, which includes the autobiographical story "Tom," about her father (Richland County Public Library)

characters to recognize that life, with all its tragic potential, also offers the chance for love, understanding, and happiness."

Vera is the main character, although the oldest of Vera's three daughters narrates the tale while another, Bea, becomes a perceptive reader of images and memories from across their mother's lifetime. The intimate mentor Father Hugh seems a clear fictional counterpart to Michael McDonald Scott, the former priest and longtime friend who became Lavin's second husband following his laicization in 1969. A good-natured debate as to what constitutes happiness forms the initial structure of the story: "'Take Father Hugh,' Mother's eyes flashed as she looked at him. 'According to him, sorrow is an ingredient of happiness—a necessary ingredient, if you please!' And when he tried to protest she put up her hand. 'There may be a freakish truth in the theory for some people. But not for me. And not, I hope, for my children.'"

From there, the story unfolds in a series of flashbacks about Vera's own parents and children each in various life struggles. Memories of a Continental holiday—during which the children worry about their mother's state of mind in her early widowhood—reflect similar travels by Lavin and her daughters following their loss of Walsh: "'Afterwards, it was nothing but foolishness the way I dragged you children after me all over Europe. As if any one place was going to be different from another, any better, any less desolate. But there was great satisfaction in bringing you places your father and I had planned to bring you— .'" Still, the mother and daughters find humor among the ruins as well—a humor that resides in the saving grace of language itself. Vera retells the story of four-year-old Linda in Italy who thought she had seen children's corpses and not pigs and goats hanging in the shops for Easter: "'Can't we go back, just once, and look again at the shop?' she whispered. 'The shop where they have the little children hanging up for Easter!' It was the young goats, of course, but I'd said 'kids,' I suppose. How we laughed."

Gardening, called by Scott "a common tranquiliser for Mary Lavin's characters" and one of the author's favorite pastimes, figures prominently in the story, specifically through floral imagery: daffodils represent Vera's strongest memory of her husband's hospitalization; an old tree peony in her garden refuge becomes an instrumental and symbolic prop in her final hours of life. Such imagery segues directly into the subsequent story, "The New Gardener," a concise but disturbing tale of paternal affection and a murderer at large. Three additional stories, "One Evening," "A Pure Accident," and "The Lost Child," round out the collection.

With regard to her early writing—what she later referred to as her "apprenticeship"— Lavin admitted in a question-and-answer section with Smith College students to an almost total lack of revision: "I do not think it entered into my head that I could, or should, try to make them better . . . for a while I disported myself turning out other stories. Fortunately, before too long I saw, by comparison with the work of writers I admired, that my imagination was running away with me." She gradually realized the need to revise in order for her imagination to become, as she put it, "fully disciplined." Janet Dunleavy's article "The Making of Mary Lavin's 'Happiness'" in the *Irish University Review* (Autumn 1979) describes how that story emerged from an outline scribbled on the pages of a *Vogue* magazine into a ninety-nine-page manuscript and finally a thirty-seven-page typescript on its way to publication. In all, the story went through "twenty-seven dated versions of heavily edited manuscript and typescript."

A look at the endings to two versions of the story "Assigh" demonstrates Lavin's abiding concern not only to get every word in the right place but also to emphasize different traits of a story against the changing backdrop of her career. The penultimate paragraph of the 1959 version, published in *Selected Stories,* reads:

At the door of the house she stood and looked back. The light of the day had not yet faded, but a few stars had made their way through the heavens. Their beauty stabbed her through and through. She used to want to share that beauty, first with Tod, and then, in a last hysterical longing, she'd wanted to share it with anyone—anyone—even the unborn. But now there would be no one with whom to share it, ever. Why did she have this terrible need? We try to make it a part of our life, she thought, and what are we but a part of it?

The version of the story included in *A Memory and Other Stories* (1972)—the title respelled "Asigh," more blatantly underscoring heartbreak and regret in the name of the rural townland—makes a key substitution for the ambiguous pronoun:

But now there would be no one with whom to share it, ever. Why did she have this terrible need? We try to make nature a part of our life, she thought, and what are we but a part of it?

In the revision "nature" replaces "it" and by extension the "need" or, prior to this, "beauty" that "it" represented as a quality to be shared or incorporated into human life. Bowen has noted how nature worship sometimes becomes a release, though rarely a solution, for Lavin's characters. In this minor emendation, Lavin makes a major point about her tragic protagonist in "Asigh."

The novelette "A Memory" follows longtime companions James and Myra, two scholars who almost cross the line and declare their love to each other. A prisoner of routine and work, James overlooks the potential for their relationship, drawing selfishly from it only to recharge his own strength, while Myra longs to be more to him than he will allow her to be. Lavin employs the image of an untended fire to represent how James takes his connection with Myra for granted: "Thinking of the solid phalanx of years that had been built up since that evening, James felt a glow of satisfaction, and for a moment he didn't realise that the fire he was supposed to be tending had got off to a good start, and part at least of his sense of well-being was coming from its warmth stealing over him."

Even as he warms himself at Myra's hearth, James remains stuck on the memory of Emmy, a former student now married and living in Asigh. Along with the place-name, the earlier story also echoes in Myra's comment that James has become "denatured," contrary to the protagonist of "Asigh," who reflected on how "we try to make nature a part of our life." This change foreshadows the ending of the story, in which James stumbles through the dark woods of Asigh toward a "green light" of evening sky he identifies with Emmy: "Ah, there was the green light! But how it had narrowed! It was only a thin line now. Still, James lurched towards it. The bushes had got dense again and he was throwing himself against them, as against a crashing wave, while they for their part seemed to thrust him back." Like F. Scott Fitzgerald's Gatsby looking out across the dark harbor to the green light of Daisy Buchanan's pier, James strives toward an impossible dream. The forces of nature vie against him to the bittersweet end.

The Shrine and Other Stories (1977) includes "Tom," a story first published four years earlier in *The New Yorker*. It is arguably Lavin's most autobiographical story, as evidenced by her rare use of first-person narrative. For its undisguised treatment of the parents' relationship and father's personality, "Tom" could well be taken as a nonfiction memoir or personal essay in the midst of the collection of short fiction. It recounts some of the information about Tom Lavin's childhood verified by Levenson, including the conflict with a Roscommon schoolmaster that forced Tom to leave school and home without even saying good-bye to his mother. The story moves backward and forward in time but culminates in a visit by father and daughter to the village and schoolhouse of Tom's youth.

Tom encounters some of the people he knew a half century earlier but hardly recognizes them in their old age. This journey creates a sort of antidote to the reverse emigration tale that has been a staple of Irish short fiction dating back at least to the 1903 George Moore story "Home Sickness." In Lavin's story, however, the returned exile has a desire to conceal rather than reveal his identity and celebrate his success. Although loath to admit it, he seems shaken by the experience. Like Oisin, the long-wandering warrior of Fenian legend, Tom seems ashamed and saddened by the mortal changes that seem to have occurred in his absence. His only escape from aging and sorrow is to deny his true identity.

"Senility" offers another study of the effects of aging on the individual and the family. In this case the point of view is that of Ada, an old woman moving in with her daughter and son-in-law. Along with the strain of adapting to this change, Ada must confront the humiliating problem of nightly incontinence, for which her daughter Laura shows little patience or sympathy.

Front cover for the 1995 Dublin paperback edition of Lavin's final work, her selection from five decades of her short stories (Bruccoli Clark Layman Archives)

Ada finds at least temporary escape in the beauty of her dreams of the past and young love:

> When Ada settled herself between the sheets and switched off the bedside light, she was, at once, in the domain of dreams or, it would be more correct to say, she was at the gateway to that domain, because there was always a moment when, if a dream threatened to be disagreeable or scary, she could, at will, hold back and refuse to enter. But tonight the prospect opened before her was full of wonder. She abandoned herself to it with joy. To begin with, she was young again. And more joyous still, she was again with Laura's father.

Nevertheless, the harsh, close-quartered reality of her waking hours always returns to bring the gentlest of dreams tumbling down. The definition of senility that emerges by the end of the story speaks to the effect of aging on more than just the individual.

The title story of *A Family Likeness and Other Stories* (1985), Lavin's penultimate collection, includes a sequel to "Senility." Several years later, Ada still lives with Laura and Richard, and now, her four-year-old granddaughter, Daphne. One fine April morning Laura and Ada decide to take the little girl on a walk in the nearby woods to look for primroses. But instead of flowers they find personal friction. Levenson notes how the story, along with "A Walk on the Cliff" from the same collection, was influenced by the author's own experience on both ends of tense mother-daughter relationships.

In a rather apt analogy for a writer who often sets her fiction in domestic spaces, in an interview with Catherine Murphy, Lavin likened writing to baking bread:

> Apart from the time consumed by having to rework stories, apart if you like from how well the dough is kneaded, all stories are better left aside for a period before considering them finished. Time seems to be a yeast without which a story cannot rise properly . . . For what it is worth that passage of time in my case always seems to be a decade. It makes me sad to think that therefore the last years of my experience may go unrecorded.

To date, whatever short fiction Lavin composed in her final decade remains unrecorded. Her final major task as a writer was the selection of sixteen previously published works for *In a Café* (1995). The stories of that volume strategically span the five decades of writing in the genre of which Lavin had become a master.

Less than a year after the publication of *In a Café*, Mary Lavin died in Dublin on 25 March 1996 at the age of eighty-three. In a tribute published in the *Guardian* newspaper the following day, William Trevor praised her contribution to the short story: "Lavin's stories eschew self-importance and that shrillness which is the bane of the form. They are subtle without making a palaver about it, beautifully told, no pat endings, no slickness; and as in life, nothing is resolved." From the 1940s to the 1990s, she published more than one hundred "beautifully told" stories in such a style. In a country especially renowned for short fiction, Lavin came to be known as one among the top practitioners of her craft.

Interview:

Catherine Murphy, "Mary Lavin: An Interview," *Irish University Review,* special Lavin issue (November 1979): 207–224;

References:

Zack Bowen, *Mary Lavin* (Lewisburg, Pa.: Bucknell University Press, 1975);

Maurice Harmon, ed., *Irish University Review,* special Lavin issue (Autumn 1979);

Marianne Koenig, "Mary Lavin: The Novels and the Stories," *Irish University Review,* 9 (1979): 244–261;

Leah Levenson, *The Four Seasons of Mary Lavin* (Dublin: Marino Books, 1998);

Thomas J. Murray, "Mary Lavin's World: Lovers and Strangers," *Eire-Ireland,* 7 (1972): 122–131;

Frank O'Connor, "The Girl at the Gaol Gate," *A Review of English Literature* (1 April 1960): 25–33; reprinted in *The Lonely Voice: A Study of the Short Story* (Cleveland & New York: World, 1963);

Richard F. Peterson, *Mary Lavin* (New York: Twayne, 1978);

Bonnie Kime Scott, "Mary Lavin and the Life of the Mind," *Irish University Review,* 9, no. 2 (1979): 262–278.

Papers:

Many of Mary Lavin's papers are housed in the Morris Library in the Special Collections Research Center at Southern Illinois University, Carbondale.

Toby Litt
(20 August 1968 –)

David Malcolm
University of Gdańsk

See also the Litt entry in *DLB 267: Twenty-First-Century British and Irish Novelists.*

BOOKS: *Adventures in Capitalism* (London: Secker & Warburg, 1996);
Beatniks: An English Road Movie (London: Secker & Warburg, 1997; New York: Marion Boyars, 2002);
Corpsing (London: Hamilton, 2000; New York: Marion Boyars, 2002);
deadkidsongs (London: Hamilton, 2001);
Exhibitionism (London & New York: Hamilton, 2002);
Finding Myself (London: Hamilton, 2003);
Ghost Story (London & New York: Hamilton, 2004).

OTHER: "Dada-Euro-Porn-Tale," in *The Erotic Review Bedside Companion,* edited by Rowan Pelling (London: Headline, 2000), pp. 188–193;
"A Small Matter for Your Attention," in *New Writing 9,* edited by John Fowles and A. L. Kennedy (London: Vintage/British Council, 2000), pp. 344–350;
Henry James, *The Outcry,* edited, with an introduction, by Litt (London: Penguin, 2001);
James, *Notes of a Son and a Brother: Forgotten Adolescent Memoirs,* introduction by Litt (London: Gibson Square, 2002);
"Seven," in *Thirteen: Images of Thirteen Women,* photography by Marc Atkins (London: Do-Not Press, 2002), pp. 13–15;
"Rare Books and Manuscripts," in *Diaspora City: The London New Writing Anthology,* introduction by Nick McDowell (London: Arcadia, 2003), pp. 1–19;
New Writing 13, edited by Litt and Ali Smith (London: Picador/British Council & Arts Council England, 2005).

SELECTED PERIODICAL PUBLICATIONS–UNCOLLECTED: "On Perversity," *Pretext,* 3 (Spring 2001): 56–66;
"Foxes," *Matter,* 3 (2003): 38–44.

Toby Litt (courtesy of the author)

Toby Litt is a controversial figure in contemporary British fiction. Since he made his publishing debut in 1996, he has garnered high praise from some critics and condemnation from others. In a review of *Adventures in Capitalism* (1996) in *The Independent on Sunday* (23 June 1996) Matt Seaton captured the ambivalence of much commentary on Litt's work: "At his best, Toby Litt seems to revive the spirit of Monty Python, mate it with a strain of magic realism, and let it roam about 1990s London. At his second-best he looks like an author in search of a subject." Such a mixed reception was echoed at a later stage in Litt's career by Wendy

Holden, writing about *Finding Myself* (2003) in the *New Statesman* (9 June 2003). Despite her negative observations about Litt's novel, Holden noted that she had always been "impressed by his writing, his flowing, precise sentences, his perception and imagination." Litt has published five novels, but his two short-story collections and his stories published in journals and anthologies form an important part of his work.

Born on 20 August 1968, Toby Litt grew up in Ampthill, Bedfordshire, a small, historic market town between London and Cambridge. His father, David Litt, was an antique dealer, and his mother was a research assistant. In a 2001 interview with Robert McCrum, Litt declared that his childhood and youth were not particularly literary. "I mostly watched television, to be honest," he said. "I started reading later on." Despite his parents' reading to him, he was easily bored by literature, but "films started to get me into books and then, once I started, I read odd things, like *The Glass Bead Game*. I was very much into science fiction, *Dune* and things like that." Educated at schools in Ampthill and Bedford, Litt went on to study English language and literature at Worcester College, Oxford University, from 1986 to 1989. There he wrote poetry, which, rather than fiction, remained his principal interest for many years. Indeed, in a 2004 interview with Paul Cunliffe, Litt argued that "poetry is a better form of expression than prose; prose tends towards oversimplification." After he graduated, Litt traveled in the United States for two and a half months and then moved to Glasgow, where he wrote a novel titled "The Lost Notebook of Babel," which has not been published. From 1990 to 1992 he taught English in Prague, during which time he worked on another unpublished novel, "The Prague Metro." In an interview with Richard Marshall in the on-line journal *3 A.M. Magazine* (October 2003), Litt said that he valued the anonymity of Prague: "I really wanted to be where people wouldn't know me or understand what I was saying on a bus."

Litt returned to England in 1992. Two years later he was accepted into the creative-writing program at the University of East Anglia, conducted by Malcolm Bradbury. Like another graduate of the course, Ian McEwan, Litt chose to write short stories while at East Anglia, and they drew Bradbury's attention and approval. One of his stories, "Moriarty," was published in *Harlequinned: New Writing* (1995), an anthology of works by students in the East Anglia writing program. Even more important was Bradbury's decision to include four of Litt's stories—"It Could Have Been Me and It Was," "Mr. Kipling," "Please Use a Basket," and "Cosmetic"—in *Class Work: The Best of Contemporary Short Fiction* (1995). Litt won the Curtis Brown Scholarship in 1995 for his work at East Anglia, and Secker and Warburg agreed to publish his first collection of short stories. *Adventures in Capitalism*, published in 1996, includes "Moriarty" and the four stories from *Class Work*.

As is usually the case with Litt's work, the reception of *Adventures in Capitalism* was mixed. In a review in *The Observer* (16 June 1996), Tobias Jones described the stories as "surreal journeys beneath the surface of our consumer lives." While noting that the stories were "full of up-to-the-minute themes," Jones insisted that "if their subjects seem trendy, they are told with great technical skill," and that the stories featured "shrewd observations." Jones compared Litt's writing to that of Will Self, but his final comment was ambivalent: "It is a very lively, if not always coherent, collection of short stories. They are not all good, but they are all surprising." In the *New Statesman* (30 August 1996) Mary Scott also compared Litt to Self, "who is brilliant, imaginative and under-endowed with human warmth." She found a "heavy dose of self-importance" in Litt's stories but noted that he was "acutely conscious of the current state of contemporary fiction," writing that the story "After Wagamama but Mostly Before" was "as deconstructed a postmodernist tale as you could possibly find." The review by Lucy O'Brien in *The Independent* (29 June 1996) was similarly ambivalent; O'Brien felt uneasy about whether Litt's satirical treatments of 1990s consumer culture did not themselves fall victim to the superficiality they criticized. Seaton, in his review in *The Independent on Sunday*, wrote that "There's no doubt that *Adventures in Capitalism* marks the arrival of a fresh satirical voice, full of brio. One just hopes that he'll settle down to something more serious."

Adventures in Capitalism comprises eighteen short stories divided into two groups, the first ten stories under the heading "Early Capitalism" and the remainder under "Late Capitalism." All but one story, "Trains," are either first-person narratives or include elements of first-person narration. In terms of genre, the texts are predominantly pieces of psychological or sociological fiction, usually with a satirical or socially critical purpose. Three stories have supernatural elements—"Moriarty," "Launderama," and "(Untitled)"—while "The Sunflower" draws its central motif from Kafkaesque fable. Most of "When I Met Michel Foucault" takes place in the world of the narrator's imagination. Technically, the stories vary from those that give an account of events in traditional linear fashion ("Fluffy Pink Bunny Rabbit," for example) to those that present events in a highly disrupted manner ("After Wagamama but Mostly Before").

The majority of the stories in the section "Early Capitalism" focus on the interaction of individuals with the institutions and artifacts of advanced industrial cap-

Front cover and signed title page for the 1997 paperback edition of Litt's 1996 collection of postmodern stories satirizing 1990s consumer culture (Bruccoli Clark Layman Archives)

italism in England in the 1990s. In "It Could Have Been Me and It Was," the narrator, having won the national lottery, decides to be completely guided in his life by the advice of advertising slogans. In "Mr. Kipling" the lonely narrator transforms, in his imagination, the brand name of a cake company into a person he knows and admires. Obsessed with a particular video system, the frame narrator of "Z-ward, BoJo, Kenneth and the BetamaxBoy" presents the conspiracy theory of another character who is convinced that a television personality is the source of evil in the world. The story is related through e-mails and the transcription of a video. In "Please Use a Basket" the narrator rebels against her reduction to an object by the company that employs her, only to join the equally conformist ranks of a radical socialist organization. The same destruction of the personal is evident in "Fluffy Pink Bunny Rabbit," in which an unemployed actor dresses up as a rabbit to collect money for a large national charity. His demeaning and absurd role in modern capitalist society is contrasted with the personal disaster of his wife's serious injury in an accident. The hopeful dreams of a horoscope are similarly contrasted with the actuality of an abandoned newborn baby in "'Polly.'" "IYouHeSheItWeYouThey & Why Gabriel?" recounts the beginning and end of a relationship between two celebrity models. The first eight parts are told using the eight different personal pronouns in the title. In the postscript, "Why Gabriel?," an unnamed speaker speculates on why celebrities such as Gabriel are of interest to people and thinks about the consumer ideal he embodies.

"Early Capitalism" includes three stories that differ from the rest in the section. In "The Sunflower" the narrator finds a flower growing out of his face. Here, too, Litt satirizes contemporary media culture: the narrator achieves his "proper apotheosis" as a newspaper celebrity. Despite the brand name of the title, "HMV" (the name of an English recording label and music-store chain) is the monologue of a gentleman who, in elaborate language, recounts a day in which he inadvertently walked around in public with his penis exposed. "Moriarty" is the story of two young girls' imaginary world, a compensation for the suburban domesticity that surrounds them. The story has a strong supernatural element; in the end, the reader cannot be sure the girls' dreams have not become reality.

The stories in the "Late Capitalism" section examine a variety of psychological states, some close to madness. "Trains" briefly describes a couple's becoming used to the noise of the trains outside their home, suggesting the individual's adaptation to his or her social environment. "Flies I" and "Flies II" present obsessive, isolated narrators, one fascinated by the behavior of flies, the other convinced that his neighbor is a murderer. In "(Untitled)" the narrator encounters a stranger who—echoing Kenneth's fantasy of total supervision in "Z-ward, BoJo, Kenneth and the Betamax-Boy"—gives her the details of her life in an uncanny fashion. Three stories show characters' minds shaped by consumer culture. "Enabled by money," the narrator of "Cosmetic" details a course of self-creation through radical plastic surgery, and that of "When I Met Michel Foucault" sets out his fantasies, drawn from commercial pornography, centered on the French philosopher. "After Wagamama but Mostly Before" does not involve madness but rather characters whose consciousnesses are permeated by Japanese and American movies and popular culture. At the center of the story is a love affair, but one that is recounted in a nonlinear way and with many motifs that draw attention to its fictionality. "Launderama" is a ghost story in which the successful contemporary narrator is haunted by the spirit of a beautiful, unattainable "early-to mid-sixties" girl who can step in and out of the machines in a launderette. The story suggests that the narrator's material and personal happiness is not complete.

Litt is a productive writer; in 1997 he published the novel *Beatniks: An English Road Movie*, which details the emotional entanglements of young people in the 1990s who are fascinated with the world of 1950s and 1960s beatnik culture. The reviewer in *Publishers Weekly* (4 November 2002) called the book "genuinely touching" and "a remarkable achievement." Litt had stories in three 1999 anthologies—"Story to be Translated from English into French and then Translated Back (without reference to the original)," in *The Time Out Book of Paris Short Stories;* "alphabed," in *Girlboy;* and "tourbusting," in *New Writing 8*–all of which were included in his 2002 collection *Exhibitionism*. Other stories by Litt appeared in *The Time Out Book of London Short Stories* and in *New Writing 9,* both published in 2000. For his second novel he chose the genre of crime fiction. *Corpsing* (2000) received positive reviews in *The Guardian* (5 February 2000) and *The Times* (30 September 2000). In *Library Journal* (1 November 2001), however, Bob Lunn declared that "This self-consciously hip debut . . . aspires to exude the style and wit of Bret Easton Ellis or Quentin Tarantino, but it fails to deliver." Litt also contributed to a 2000 anthology titled *All Hail the New Puritans,* edited by Nicolas Blincoe and Matt Thorne. The stories in this collection were specially commissioned, and all the authors were asked to adhere to the editors' "Pledge." This pledge, demanding narrative and linguistic simplicity and insisting that the stories be located in a "recognizable ethical reality," produced controversy in British literary circles because it constituted a rejection of postmodern technical complexity and relativism. Litt's contribution, "The New Puritans," was republished in *Exhibitionism*. In 2001 he published another novel, *deadkidsongs,* an examination of childhood cruelty set in the 1970s in a fictionalized version of his native Ampthill. The theme of the novel, according to Gerry Frehilly in the *New Statesman* (26 February 2001), is the "dark heart of boyhood."

Published in 2002, Litt's well-received second short-story collection, *Exhibitionism,* includes previously published stories as well as new ones. In *The Guardian Weekly* (20–26 February 2003) Alfred Hickling wrote, "Many people write about sex badly; few write about bad sex as well as Toby Litt." Hickling described *Exhibitionism* as "a post-coital chronicle of catastrophic copulations and ruined relationships with a bit of seedy S&M on the side. It can get a bit fatiguing . . . but Litt's energy never flags." In *The Observer* (24 February 2002) Zulfikar Abbany called one story, "Dreamgirls," "a brilliantly funny psycholanalytic affair" and described "Story to be Translated from English into French and then Translated Back (without reference to the original)" as "an intriguing account" of sexual power roles. He also admired "Litt's carefully placed emotional twists," summing up the collection as "a coherent body of work," the stories "standing together as they stand alone."

Like *Adventures in Capitalism, Exhibitionism* is divided into two sections on the contents page. Titled "Sex" and "And Other Subjects," each consists of eight stories. Texts from each section alternate throughout the collection, and some of the stories in "And Other Subjects" also deal with sexual matters (for example, "tourbusting," "Unhaunted," and "tourbusting 2"). "Sex" includes a mix of first-person and third-person narratives, as well as an instruction manual and a movie shooting script. "And Other Matters" features only one story, "The Audioguide," that is not told in the first person, and even that story is an interior monologue. In terms of genre, *Exhibitionism* shows more variety than *Adventures in Capitalism:* it includes not only sociological and psychological texts but also supernatural stories, a piece of pornography, a fable, a story with elements of Gothic fiction, and another that echoes science fiction. Many are satirical and humorous in intent.

All the stories in "Sex" deal with complex erotic situations. In "Dreamgirls" the narrator's sexual fantasies come alive, with disturbing consequences. "On the Etiquette of Eye-Contact During Oral Sex" is a parody of articles giving advice on social behavior. "Map-Making among the Middle-Classes" presents a traditional love triangle in a manner that draws attention to the fictionality of the story. In "Mimi (Both of Her) and Me (Hardly There at All)" the narrator cannot control his desire to observe two lesbians making love in the mausoleum of Radclyffe Hall, in London's Highgate Cemetery. As a result, and as a culmination of the Gothic motifs in the story, he is locked in the tomb at the end and waits in terror for death. Two texts focus directly on pornography. "'Legends of Porn' (Polly Morphous) Final Shooting Script" is a parody of a television program, full of self-importance, celebrating the achievements of a movie star. In this case, however, the star is a pornographic actress, and her great contribution is to have refreshed the genre with nonerotic motifs. Parody is also apparent in the title and content of the erotic, sadomasochistic "Story to be Translated from English into French and then Translated Back (with reference to the original)," which consists of the monologues of a man and a woman engaged in games of physical and mental cruelty with each other. "Alphabed" is also made up of brief monologues of a man and a woman, lovers who are involved in a boring and physically sordid relationship. Each monologue is marked by a letter of the alphabet, and Litt's instructions are that they be read "in any order other than the one printed." "The New Puritans," which closes the "Sex" section, also has allusions to pornography. A couple, engaged in mass production of pornographic videos, are themselves involved in another couple's perverse sexual relations and are finally, the end of the story implies, drawn into a sadistic intrigue echoing the videos they have been copying.

The stories in "And Other Subjects" are varied in character, setting, and genre, but all feature isolated, introspective, and ineffectual protagonist-narrators. In "A Higher Agency" an aspiring writer finds himself compelled to take a job as a dishwasher. The story ends in an improbable but comic shootout between his employers and his literary agents. "The Audioguide" is a return to the disturbed psychologies of some of the

Front cover for the 2003 paperback edition of Litt's 2002 collection of stories, many of which deal humorously with complex erotic situations (Bruccoli Clark Layman Archives)

stories in *Adventures in Capitalism*. In the form of a taped guided tour of a museum, it depicts a consciousness trapped within itself, filled with fears and longings. The stories "tourbusting" and "tourbusting 2" recount the sexual and emotional misadventures of a drummer in an American band. "Of the Third Kind" is a story of childhood maturation and misunderstanding between parent and child, while "Unhaunted" deals with the emotional failures and self-torment of a lonely lesbian. "My Cold War [February 1998]" is a parody of espionage fiction, in which a displaced narrator finds excitement and purpose. "The Waters," a story that is set in the future and has echoes of science fiction, also focuses on an unhappy, isolated narrator. The waters that fill the characters' apartments are metaphors of longing and emotional intensity.

Since the publication of *Exhibitionism*, Litt's career has continued to flourish. His novel *Finding Myself,* published in 2003, is a reworking of the characters and situations of "chick lit" (novels dealing with the lives of young urban women) and is directed particularly at the readers of such books, although, as James Franken pointed out in his review in *The London Review of Books* (7 August 2003), it includes strong metafictional elements. In 2003 Litt was named one of the Twenty Best Young British Novelists by the influential literary magazine *Granta*. He has continued to publish short stories, for instance in *Thirteen: Images of Thirteen Women* (2002), a collection of photographs by Marc Atkins; the literary annual *Matter* (2003); and *Diaspora City: The London New Writing Anthology* (2003). Litt's fifth novel, *Ghost Story*, was published in 2004. Described by Hugo Barnacle in the *New Statesman* (1 November 2004) as a "thoughtful, heavy-going novel of grief," it centers on the emotional complexities of two middle-class characters who buy a house on the coast of Kent.

Toby Litt is a prolific writer who since 1996 has made a successful career as a novelist and short-story writer. His work draws on many genres and frequently features metafictional elements. His short fiction, focusing on isolated individuals caught up in the complexities of consumer society or driven by erotic desire and unhappiness, is a central part of his work. Despite his five novels, Litt continues to return to the short story, and it is likely that he will play a role in the development of the genre in England in the twenty-first century.

Interviews:

James Eve, "Screen Test," *Times* (London), 19 February 2000, Metro section, p. 16;

Kevin Patrick Mahoney, "Toby Litt Interview," *Genre* (Summer 2000) <www.geocities.com/SoHo/Nook/1082/toby_litt_interview.html>;

Richard Marshall, "The New Bawdy," *3 A.M. Magazine* (October 2003) <www.3ammagazine.com/litarchives/2003/oct/interview_toby_litt.html>;

Robert McCrum, "I Wrote It to Be Honest about a Certain Kind of Violence. It's a Boy's Book," *Observer* (London), 11 February 2001, p. 17;

Paul Cunliffe, "Interview–Toby Litt," *Decode: Arts and Media Limited* (2004) <www.decodemedia.com/tiki-index.php?page=interviewToby+Litt>.

Reference:

Toby Litt <www.tobylitt.com>.

Shena Mackay

(6 June 1944 –)

Amy Lee
Hong Kong Baptist University

See also the Mackay entry in *DLB 231: British Novelists Since 1960, Fourth Series.*

BOOKS: *Dust Falls on Eugene Schlumburger/Toddler on the Run* (London: Deutsch, 1964);
Music Upstairs (London: Deutsch, 1965);
Toddler on the Run: A Novel (New York: Simon & Schuster, 1966);
Old Crow (London: Cape, 1967; New York: McGraw-Hill, 1968);
An Advent Calendar (London: Cape, 1971; Wakefield, R.I.: Moyer Bell, 1997);
Babies in Rhinestones and Other Stories (London: Heinemann, 1983);
A Bowl of Cherries (Brighton, U.K.: Harvester, 1984; Mt. Kisco, N.Y.: Moyer Bell, 1992);
Redhill Rococo (London: Heinemann, 1986);
Dreams of Dead Women's Handbags (London: Heinemann, 1987);
Dunedin (London: Heinemann, 1992; Wakefield, R.I.: Moyer Bell, 1993);
The Laughing Academy (London: Heinemann, 1993);
Dreams of Dead Women's Handbags: Collected Stories (Wakefield, R.I.: Moyer Bell / Emeryville, Cal.: Publishers Group West, 1994);
Death by Art Deco (London: Penguin, 1995);
The Orchard on Fire (London: Heinemann, 1995; Wakefield, R.I.: Moyer Bell, 1996; revised edition, London: Heinemann, 1996);
The Artist's Widow (London: Cape, 1998; Wakefield, R.I.: Moyer Bell, 1999);
The World's Smallest Unicorn and Other Stories (London: Cape, 1999; Wakefield, R.I.: Moyer Bell, 2000);
Heligoland (London: Cape, 2000).

PLAY PRODUCTION: *Nurse Macater*, London, National Theatre, 2 November 1969.

RECORDING: "Other People's Bathrobes," read by Mackay, BBC Radio Collection: Woman's Hour Short Stories, 1990.

Shena Mackay (photograph by Marjorie Carmichael; from dust jacket for The Artist's Widow, *1998; Bruccoli Clark Layman Archives)*

OTHER: "Slaves to the Mushroom," in *The Penguin Book of Modern Women's Short Stories,* edited by Susan Hill (London: Penguin, 1990);
Such Devoted Sisters: An Anthology of Stories, edited by Mackay (London: Virago, 1993);
"Cloud-Cuckoo-Land," in *The Secret Self: A Century of Short Stories by Women,* edited by Hermione Lee (London: Dent, 1995), pp. 501–517;
"Violets and Strawberries in the Snow," in *The Oxford Book of Scottish Short Stories,* edited by Douglas Dunn (Oxford: Oxford University Press, 1995), pp. 384–392;
Friendship, edited by Mackay (London: Dent, 1997).

Shena Mackay, who started her literary career in her teens, has written nine novels and five volumes of short stories, and has edited two short-story collections. In a chapter titled "Contemporary Fiction III: The Anglo-Scots" in *A History of Scottish Women's Writing* (1997), Flora Alexander describes Mackay as one of the notable "Anglo-Scots."Although born in Scotland, Mackay was brought up in Kent and London; and while she employs a principally Scottish cast of characters and situations, she also explores wider aspects of British society. She is well known for her deceptively quiet portrayal of banal domesticity, which disguises intense human frustration in the face of environmental and social constraints. Her characters are mostly ordinary people leading desperate lives, and her representations of their sufferings are made through meticulous attention to the conventional details of everyday life. Stylistically inventive, her stories draw attention to the unusual in ordinary circumstances.

Shena Mackay was born on 6 June 1944 in Edinburgh, Scotland, to Benjamin Carr Mackey and Morag (Carmichael) Mackey. She was educated at Tonbridge Girls' Grammar School in Kent and then Kidbrooke Comprehensive School in London. In her teens she discovered that the original spelling of her family name was "Mackay," and she has used it ever since. At sixteen, she left school and started working as well as writing. She has held a variety of jobs, including artist's model, librarian, herbalist, worker in a greeting-card factory, and sales assistant in an antique shop.

Mackay has professed a love of poetry and says that she was inspired to write after reading William Butler Yeats, W. H. Auden, and Louis MacNeice. She has found her own voice, however, in prose. In 1964 Mackay married Robin Francis Brown, and her first book, *Dust Falls on Eugene Schlumburger/Toddler on the Run*, two novellas in the same volume, was published. Written when she was still a teenager, the book brought Mackay almost instant recognition. The inventive linguistic style captures the feeling of loss and insecurity young people experience when surrounded by an incomprehensible reality. The notion of youthful helplessness in the face of a demanding world also permeates Mackay's first few novels–*Music Upstairs* (1965), *Old Crow* (1967), and *An Advent Calendar* (1971). These three books and the two novellas constitute the first stage of her creative career.

Although "Dust Falls on Eugene Schlumburger" and "Toddler on the Run" are not linked by any plot or character development, they share a similar concern with the lonely and alienated, especially youths. In the first story, the experience of Abigail and Eugene is a vivid portrayal of the sense of boredom and helplessness young people feel. Believing that adults do not understand them or care, teens are left to deal with life's problems alone. Abigail has no sense of self-awareness and can even break down in the middle of mocking people, one of her favorite pastimes. She clings to Eugene, who is equally disillusioned about life. When he is sentenced to two years in prison for dangerous driving, Abigail loses her orientation and falls apart. Eugene's profession of love is not enough for her. She wants him to escape from prison to prove his love. Eugene's death takes the last fragment of reality from Abigail's world. Consequently, when her parents want her to learn typing and find a job, she tamely submits because she feels she is already dead. Although the story of these young people, their disappointments, and their loss of innocence creates a bleak picture of life, a short and seemingly unimportant episode in the novella revives the possibility of hope. The characters Mr. Davis and Mrs. Mayhew find companionship in each other and seize the chance to enjoy themselves.

"Toddler on the Run" tells a similar story using different characters. Morris Todd is twenty-three years old, but he is only three feet nine inches tall and is constantly mistaken for a child. His stunted stature seems to reflect a similarly misshapen mind, for he commits petty crimes as a way of life. He always gets away with these crimes either because strangers do not realize that he is an adult or because people pity him for his deformity. But at the beginning of the story, he is involved accidentally in a case of murder and has to run for his life. In the course of his frantic escape, he meets Deirdre, a schoolgirl who spends all her time playing sports and is a social misfit. Even her parents fail to understand her needs and feelings: while she is dreaming away the time in her locked bedroom, they think that she is working hard for her General Certificate of Education. Morris and Deirdre have nothing in common except alienation from their social environments, but these two lonely people find a sense of sympathy for each other, something they had not experienced before. Circumstances separate them, and Morris continues his flight with the help of his girlfriend, Leda. Though Morris manages to evade the law, he leads a life of constant regret at being separated from his beloved Deidre.

The insensitivities of a society that ostracizes people such as Deirdre, Morris, and his friend Daniel, are seen in the subplot concerning Daniel and his wife, Elaine. Arriving home one day and finding the meal prepared by Elaine unsatisfactory, Daniel beats her so badly that she has to be hospitalized for a long time. The most shocking aspect about Daniel's battering his wife is not the act itself, however, but that he does not feel guilty at all and manages to distort the truth to suit his interests. Society has almost given him permission to twist things according to his desires simply because he dares to. The grim note on which "Toddler on the Run" ends continues Mackay's mourning for a generation of young people lost in an impersonal urban maze.

Music Upstairs, published after her early success with the double novella, was Mackay's first full-length novel. It tells the story of a young girl, Sidonie O'Neill, who goes through a difficult period of her life as she is facing challenges on different fronts. Temporarily jobless, she and her friend Joyce have to do their best to economize. At the same time, the uncertainty and occasional boredom of single life confuses Sidonie. So when Sidonie and Joyce move into a room in Earl's Court and their neighbors the Beacons let them share their larder, the girls find it too good to be true. Pam and Lennie Beacon turn out to be much more complicated, though, than the nice young couple they appear to be. After an initial suspicion of Lennie's intentions toward her, Sidonie is surprised to find that Pam too, has amorous designs on her. Confused and bored with life, Sidonie becomes the lover of each although she tries to keep her relationship with each a secret from the other. As jealousy increases and playing the innocent becomes increasingly difficult for her, Sidonie becomes the victim of Lennie's excessively neurotic behavior. News of her father's accident and death saves her; she moves home to live with her widowed mother.

In 1967, Mackay published *Old Crow,* a novel relating the frustrations of women's lives. The story is set in 1958 in an English village, conservative in both its emotional and moral beliefs. Coral Fairbrother becomes the butt of the vengeance of the village when she is discovered to be pregnant by a painter who was only a transient. The person most eager to condemn this moral transgression is not the patriarchal village authority but a malicious widow who is not content to be the only unhappy person in the village. In the name of cleansing the village of immorality, the parish council stages a witch-hunt that ends disastrously. Moyer Bell republished this early novel in June 2002 as part of a plan to make all Mackay's work available again. Thus, in the early 1990s her work for the first time became the focus of much attention outside Britain.

Mackay's third novel, *An Advent Calendar,* appeared in 1971. This narrative recounts the experience of a working-class family, their neighbors, and their immediate circle of friends and acquaintances during a twenty-five-day period just before Christmas. The journey toward the festive season starts with an absurd accident. John Wood is buying minced meat for his sick old uncle when one of the butcher's fingers is accidentally cut off and falls into the mincer. This ominous event starts John's nauseous descent toward Christmas. Before long he finds himself jobless, homeless, full of guilt, and treated coldly by his wife, Marguerite. Mar-

Dust jacket for Mackay's 1994 collection of three earlier short-story volumes—Babies in Rhinestones, Dreams of Dead Women's Handbags, *and* The Laughing Academy *(Richland County Public Library)*

guerite, meanwhile, finds her life totally boring and meaningless. The reappearance of her old love urges her to rethink her life and priorities. This pattern of disappointment is repeated in other relationships, but toward the end of the novel, when the last window of the cheap advent calendar is open, Christmas arrives and brings enlightenment and emotional fulfillment to these isolated people.

Mackay's early novels, written while she was still a young woman, have established her style as one of a careful and vivid depiction of the lives of young people in urban areas. Their loss of direction usually comes hand in hand with the claustrophobic, labyrinthine urban world they inhabit and has become a trademark of her writing, a style long mistaken for realism. This misconception has gradually been corrected because of the diversification of content and style in her later writing. These changes are particularly marked in the collections of her short stories. In 1981 she and her husband were divorced, and during this period she was busy bringing up her three daughters. The second stage of her writing career began some years later with the publication of *Babies in Rhinestones* (1983), a collection of short stories, some of which had already appeared in various magazines and journals or had been read on the BBC.

Mackay's short stories reveal qualities not previously evident in the novels. One of the most striking features of the stories is a surreal element half concealed behind the stable domestic environment but apt to invade its reality unexpectedly. This sense of the extraordinary embedded in the everyday is seen in both the titles of the stories and of the collections—*Babies in Rhinestones, Dreams of Dead Women's Handbags* (1987), and *The Laughing Academy* (1993). All suggest the bizarre lurking under the placid surface of ordinary life.

A Bowl of Cherries (1984) is the first novel Mackay published in which she fully developed the surreal imagery that appeared in some short stories of the previous collection. Mackay's next novel, *Redhill Rococo*, published in 1986, won the 1987 Fawcett Prize. The surreal imagery found in *A Bowl of Cherries* and in some of her short stories blossoms in this novel into a personal style, especially in her descriptions of the brutally humorous aspects of suburban life. The story is set in the outskirts of Surrey, an area accommodating quietly frustrated households. The narrative concerns the lifestyles of the Redhills and the Reigates, whose children attend the same school. In the end, Pearl and Helen discover a friendship out of a common problem. Through her use of black humor, Mackay uncovers the isolation and loneliness of life, whether that of genteel sophistication or that of bourgeois suburban squalor.

Dunedin (1992) won the Scottish Arts Council Book Award in 1992. This quasi-epic story unfolds across three generations and two continents, depicting seventy years of closely connected lives. Both the beginning and end of the novel are set between the years of 1909 and 1910, in which the seventy years have their origin. The sections set in New Zealand depict an affair between a Scottish Presbyterian minister, Jack Mackenzie, and a mixed-race laundress, Myrtile. The middle section of the novel is set in 1980s London. In this desolate world the descendants of Jack Mackenzie live out the lives set in motion years ago in Dunedin, New Zealand.

Dreams of Dead Women's Handbags: Collected Stories consists of thirty-one stories Mackay wrote over a period of twenty years. Among the thirty-one stories included, twenty-nine are reprinted stories from her three previous collections: *Babies in Rhinestones, Dreams of Dead Women's Handbags,* and *The Laughing Academy.* Like *Dunedin,* this book won a Scottish Arts Council Book Award of the year.

The stories in this collection show a wide spectrum of content and style. While most of the stories are observations of ordinary working-class life, its inherent boredom, loneliness, and frustration are seldom quite as one might expect. Small revolutions occur in the stories when ordinary people attempt something daring in order to escape their depressing daily routines, as in the story "Slaves to the Mushroom," in which Sylvia, a working woman who has to support her husband, steals mushrooms from her unknowing fellow workers to boost her own output. The banal working day is broken by interludes such as the sacking of fellow workers, one claiming to be HIV positive, and the loss and finding of her own knife. In "Cardboard City," teenage sisters Stella and Vanassa go to London on their own for a well-planned, exciting Christmas shopping spree, but the great malls and dazzling merchandise shock the sisters rather than make them happy.

Revolutions occur in the structure, language, and imagery of Mackay's works, even when the content is about the sheer ordinariness of life. Surprises often await both characters and readers as a story comes to an end, and often the journey leading toward that end is expressed in surreal language. In "Dreams of Dead Women's Handbags," the title story of an earlier collection and this one, a mystery writer is desperately trying to meet an approaching deadline. This irritation excites in her the memory of a murderous childhood experience. The fictional reality, the scene of her memory, and the plot she tries to construct for the coming novel are all merged together in Mackay's narrative. "Babies in Rhinestones" is the story of two lonely people, one the proprietor of an arts school and the other the proprietress of a dance school. These two neighbors discover in each other companionship and common interests that help improve the quality of their artistic and emotional lives.

In Mackay's stories ordinary life often appears as anything but ordinary. In "The Thirty-First of October" the celebration of Halloween induces an aging writer to plan the real-life murder of her neighbor's children. Only the timely ring of the doorbell signaling a visit and human companionship makes her put away the potential murder weapon. "The Most Beautiful Dress in the World" looks like a simple mother-daughter conflict, but the consequences of this conflict, together with the countless trivialities of running a household, put so much pressure on the housewife that she ends up murdering the gas-meter reader. Harriet's killing out of sheer frustration demonstrates a theme that runs throughout Mackay's stories and novel:

domesticity is never a safe and peaceful state. This story was adapted as a BBC 2 television movie in 1993.

Some stories go beyond the bounds of ordinary life in their titles, characters, and narrative developments. "Perpetual Spinach" tells the story of strange and cruel human desires. Although the pair of old pensioners in the story are pleasant neighbors, when they are the victims of a fatal accident, the only thing their young yuppie neighbors care about is buying the elderly couple's house. "Bananas" is the story of a neurotic woman and her thoughts of murder. Imogen Lemon is highly conscious of her name, and a chance encounter with an immigrant shopkeeper creates in her an uneasy feeling about him that haunts her. His image and behavior create such a disturbance for her that she goes on a holiday for fear of a nervous breakdown, only to come back and find him gone. "Electric-Blue Damsels" in turn recounts the unnatural infatuation of a man with a girl whose presence in his mind is symbolized by the blue devil, a kind of beautiful seahorse. After witnessing the girl's descent into becoming a third-rate singer, Maurice isolates himself from human companionship and builds in his own house a gigantic glass tank to accommodate beautiful seahorses, named the Electric Blue Damsels in memory of the once electrifying girl.

Mackay's repertoire includes people depressed by the realities of life. "Evening Surgery" presents the not uncommon story of an affair between two unhappy persons, a single mother who meets a married doctor at a party and goes on to meet him at his office in the evenings. When they are discovered, each returns to his/her painful and seemingly unchangeable life. "The Stained-Glass Door" portrays an equally unhappy marriage. One day the wife wakes up to discover the sudden departure of her husband together with the househelp next door and can do nothing but remain alone in the house. The harsh and disappointing reality, however, in Mackay's world, is often received and conquered by her characters' infinite flexibility and power to regenerate. The old Rowley couple in "Cloud-Cuckoo-Land" are typical do-gooders in the local community. Their eagerness to help, however, sometimes drives people away, including their own daughter. Old Rowley's world undergoes a radical change one day when, through borrowed glasses, he sees his flat and the community for what they are, and a transformation takes place. No longer do they seek out others to help; their daughter wants to come home to start a practice as a therapist and to have her baby. In "The Laughing Academy," Vincent McCloud, a once popular singer, feels that his life is coming to an unhappy end after the decline of his career. Angry with his incompetent agent and disillusioned about the business, he travels from town to town to get whatever work he can. Curiosity brings him to visit the grand house of his agent, where he meets the agent's neglected wife. These two disappointed people, once so unwanted and unvalued, are surprised to find in each other the confidence to face the future.

Though not always secure, life as depicted in Mackay's short stories often has something in store for its travelers. In "Curry at the Laburnums," Ivor and Roger trip Lal the porter over some curry takeout, giving him punctured lungs and a hospital stay. Fellow workers at the Chubleigh station make a collection and ask Ivor and Roger to take it to Lal's wife. Off his guard and not much troubled by his conscience, Roger takes the collection and enjoys a sumptuous meal at Lal's house, only to go home and fall terribly sick from food poisoning. He respects the silent revenge. Old scores have their own ways of being settled, too, in "Shinty." Old school friends Margaret and Suzy get together to congratulate their classmate of forty years ago, Veronica Sharples, who has become a famous writer and is doing a book launch in a local bookstore. While everyone is inside the bookstore, an IRA bomb goes off somewhere, and they are stuck inside. Old friends start to reminisce; old wounds are reopened; and Margaret pulls out a gun to demand that Veronica do the school physical training (PT) lesson again as a way to take revenge for her name-calling in the past.

The tone of stories ranges from the realistic to the bizarre. Another interesting feature about this collection is the frequent setting of Christmas, which helps unite stories vastly different in theme and context. Some characters are straightforward and ordinary, and other characters are living half in dream and half awake, but Christmas and the need to celebrate seem to be present always, even in the weirdest stories. Once again, this juxtaposition of the most comfortable daily life and the unexpected and accidental forms the core of Mackay's writing.

Mackay's 1995 novel, *The Orchard on Fire,* which was short-listed for the Booker Prize for that year, is arguably her best-known work. The vivid evocation of the early 1950s is something with which many readers have identified. The story is a poignant one of growth and friendship. Two girls meet each other in the paradise of their self-invented dreams, but reality intrudes and forces them to face the harshness of life and shed their protective naiveté. Ruby is the victim of her father's beatings; April has to repel the sexual advances of Mr. Greenridge. Nevertheless, the novel contrasts April's banal adult life of loneliness years later in a crowded city with the vivid hope of the remembered past.

Dust jacket for the 2000 U.S. edition of Mackay's 1999 collection of short stories, most of which make light of unusual personalities and circumstances (Richland County Public Library)

In 1999 Mackay brought out another collection of short stories. *The World's Smallest Unicorn* includes ten tales, most of which explore the lighthearted side of irregular personalities and circumstances. In a review titled "Tangled Tales" in *The Women's Review of Books* (May 2001), Barbara Croft writes that the stories are on the light side, with "little sense of movement," though the rendering of characters is "wonderfully human." Several eccentric characters are engaged in amusing activities. Uncle Bob in "The Index of Embarrassment" is determined to compile an index of embarrassing situations, and when his next-door neighbor dies suddenly without returning the ladder he borrowed, he sees a chance to enrich his collection. In "Crossing the Border," Flora, the niece of Looney the Clown, visits the Grimaldi House, a home for retired clowns, to interview her uncle for a biography. She is just one day too late and is left with a present from her uncle—a pair of clown's shoes. Determined to give her uncle his rightful funeral, Flora rents a baby elephant, which is decked with black funeral balloons, to lead the procession.

In "The World's Smallest Unicorn," Teddy, an expatriate returning from Hong Kong to London after years of being stationed in the Asian city, finds himself rootless, as he no longer feels at home in his own country. An advertisement about the world's smallest unicorn catches his attention as he wanders in the unfamiliar city, trying to find compensation in his new life for the loss of meaning in the old. The fake exoticness of the unicorn highlights the fake sense of success he enjoys as an expatriate who brings home nothing but leftover stationery from his company. "Trouser Ladies" documents the lives of two generations of women who have been treated differently by their societies. Catriona goes to visit Auntie Bee, whom she remembers as the stylish and fascinating trouser lady, her mother's best friend who was not welcomed by her father. Now an independent woman with a female partner, Catriona comes to appreciate the difficult conditions imposed on such women in the previous generation.

Mackay's stories sometimes favor description over plot. "A Silver Summer" tells of Tessa's finding and losing the boy of her dreams because of the jealous intervention of another boy. The thinness of plot is compensated for by the details devoted to Tessa, who suffers through the events of this summer for reasons other than her personal faults. "Death by Art Deco" is the title of the story Lily submits for a writing competition. Although she is not awarded a prize, one of the judges, Andrea Heysham, likes her style and invites her to be her personal assistant. Lily's long-dreamed-of ride to success turns out to be different from what she anticipates, for Andrea is losing her inspiration as a writer and is also having problems with her son. Finally, because of some misunderstandings over the son, Andrea fires Lily. Characters in Mackay's world often find themselves thwarted in the most ordinary endeavors. Communication becomes impossible either because the message was misinterpreted, or delivered at the wrong time and to the wrong place, or simply because people are not paying attention. Although presented in imaginative, colorful language, these characters' unusual encounters point to a deep-seated discontent with their lives. But the sharpness of observation translates these dreary disappointments of ordinary life into inventive situations and colorful images, making light of the real sorrows the characters, and perhaps even the readers, experience.

Mackay's latest novel, *The Artist's Widow*, was published in 1998 to critical acclaim. The story is set in the London art world and opens with the retrospective exhibition of a recently deceased artist, John Crane.

Family, friends, and other viewers are present at the gathering, putting their desires on display side by side with the works of the dead artist. Surrounded by their yearnings, lust, greed, pomposity, and selfishness, the artist's widow, Lyris, a painter in her own right, only wants to be left by herself so that she can do her own painting. The novel focuses on the deceptions of private and public life, especially those of the London art world. *The Artist's Widow* is a sharp satire with brisk and concise sketches of characters and events. No easy solutions are given to the problems characters face, and no ready consolation is given to the reader.

In recent years, Mackay has actively engaged in teaching creative writing in various universities. She was a visiting professor to the M.A. writing program at Middlesex University in 2001. She writes regularly for the BBC, which used her work in 1993 as the subject of a BBC2 Bookmark program on *Woman's Hour;* and she is a regular reviewer for the *Sunday Times*. She now lives in London.

Shena Mackay has been called "the best writer of fiction alive" by *The Mail* newspaper. The many editions of her short stories, her frequent BBC commissions to broadcast her stories, and the republication of her past works by American publisher Moyer Bell all bear witness to her reputation. One reason for her success is her wide range of subject matter and styles. She has also written a drama called *Nurse Macateer* for the National Theatre in London. Apart from literary prizes, she has received an Arts Council Bursary and a Society of Authors Traveling Scholarship and has been a judge for several major literary prizes. Evaluating the scene of Scottish writing today, Douglas Gifford and Dorothy McMillan in "Caught Between Worlds: The Fiction of Jane and Mary Findlater" in *A History of Scottish Women's Writing* see Mackay as using the modern context to criticize Scottish attitudes, and her latest novels offer social criticism.

Interview:

"Writing today is more of the visual kind," *Indian Express* (14 February 1998) <http://www.Expressindia.com/ie/daily/19980214/04550574.html%%%> [accessed 19 August 2002].

Biography:

Jules Smith, "Shena Mackay," British Council Contemporary Writers (12 March 2003) <www.contemporarywriters.com/authors>.

References:

Flora Alexander, "Contemporary Fiction III: The Anglo-Scots," in *A History of Scottish Women's Writing,* Douglas Gifford and Dorothy McMillan, eds. (Edinburgh: Edinburgh University Press, 1997), pp. 630–640;

Laurie Champion, "Shena Mackay," in *An Encyclopedia of British Women Writers,* Paul Schlueter and June Schlueter, eds. (New Brunswick, N.J. & London: Rutgers University Press, 1998), pp. 413–414;

Aileen Christianson and Alison Lumsden, eds., *Contemporary Scottish Women Writers* (Edinburgh: Edinburgh University Press, 2000), pp. 1–7;

Douglas Dunn, "Introduction," in *The Oxford Book of Scottish Short Stories,* edited by Dunn (Oxford: Oxford University Press, 1995);

Papers:

Collections of Shena Mackay's manuscripts and papers are held at the Duke University Library, British Studies Collection and in the Margaret Woodbridge Collection at Millersville University.

John MacKenna
(22 October 1952 –)

Lucy Collins
St. Martin's College, Carlisle

BOOKS: *The Occasional Optimist* (Athy: Winter Wood Books, 1976);
Castledermot and Kilkea: A Social History, with Notes on Ballytore, Graney, Moone and Mullaghmast (Athy: Winter Wood Books/South Leinster Literary Group, 1982);
The Lost Village: A Diary of Castledermot in 1925 (Athy: Stephen Scroop Press, 1985);
The Fallen and Other Stories (Belfast: Blackstaff Press, 1992);
Clare: A Novel (Belfast: Blackstaff Press, 1993);
A Year of Our Lives (London: Picador, 1995);
The Last Fine Summer (London: Picador, 1997);
A Haunted Heart (London: Picador, 1999);
Shackleton: An Irishman in Antarctica, by MacKenna and Jonathan Shackleton (Dublin: Lilliput Press / Madison: University of Wisconsin Press, 2002).

SELECTED PRODUCED SCRIPTS: *How the Heart Approaches What It Yearns,* radio, Radio Telefís Éireann, 9, 12 May 1988;
Secret Gardens of the Heart, radio, Radio Telefís Éireann, 1, 8, 15 January 1994;
The Children at the Bottom of the Garden, radio, Radio Telefís Éireann, 25 September 1997.

OTHER: Mary Leadbeater, *The Annals of Ballitore: 1766–1824,* edited, with an introduction, by MacKenna (Athy: Stephen Scroop Press, 1986);
Leadbeater, *Cottage Biography: Being a Collection of the Lives of the Irish Peasantry,* introduction by MacKenna (Athy: Stephen Scroop Press, 1987).

John MacKenna's reputation as a leading contemporary fiction writer in Ireland has been growing steadily after a long period in which he was relatively unknown. With the publication of his novel *The Last Fine Summer* (1997), which has been the subject of negotiations for a motion-picture adaptation, he gained the media attention hitherto denied him; yet, his short stories had been attracting attention since the publication of early works in the "New Irish Writing" pages of *The Irish Press* and in *The Second Blackstaff Book of Short Stories* (1991). For MacKenna, mastery of the short-story form has not been merely an apprenticeship for a more high-profile career as a novelist. Instead, he recognizes the precision of the story form and the fact that it provides a space within which to explore precarious emotional states and fleeting memories. His career has shown him to be a writer with a distinctive style: spare but musical, with attention to sensory detail. He also experiments with narrative voice and is accomplished in developing character within evocative geographical and historical contexts. These qualities set MacKenna apart from many of his contemporaries, both in Ireland and further afield.

Born on 22 October 1952 in Castledermot, County Kildare, to Jack MacKenna, a railway foreman, and Una Bray MacKenna, a teacher, John MacKenna presents the environment of his childhood vividly in his fiction. Typically, his work is set in a rural Irish community and explores the tensions that emerge in characters who are engaged in reflection and self-discovery in a socially restricted environment. In a profile in the *Kildare Nationalist* (25 February 2000) he is quoted as saying, "There is nothing that has happened in the world that hasn't happened in small towns—love, death, hate, murder, debauchery, betrayal. It doesn't take effort to bring it with you." The mingling of remembered past and present life in his works allows both memory and lived experience to be interwoven in exceptionally evocative ways.

MacKenna was educated at St. Clement's College in Limerick and later studied at University College, Dublin, where he took a degree in English and history in 1973 and a teaching diploma the following year. The interface between these subjects continues to be important in MacKenna's imaginative life, as his interest in the emotional subtleties of language is often colored by an awareness of the past and its role in shaping human passion and intellect. He has always been interested in social issues: his father, as he recalled in the *Kildare*

Nationalist, "ate, drank, and slept politics," and MacKenna himself was courted by the Labour Party as a potential candidate. He considered further study in law and journalism after graduation but instead decided to return to Kildare to teach in a local vocational school. It proved a rewarding job, and he stayed in it for seven years (1974–1980) before pursuing a career in the media. He published his first book, a poetry collection titled *The Occasional Optimist,* in 1976. The following year, MacKenna married Mary Cunningham, with whom he had two children: Lydia, born in 1981, and Ewan, born in 1984. The couple separated in 1992, and MacKenna married Caitriona Ni Fhlaithearta in 1999; he has a stepson from this marriage, Eoin, born in 1992.

From the beginning of his career MacKenna has gravitated toward documentary forms, which paradoxically allow him to work effectively in abstract ways by providing a vivid world within which to set his explorations of human emotion and behavior. His predilection for the documentary is also a result of his distinguished career as a radio producer for Radio Telefís Éireann (RTE), where he began work in 1980, first for 2FM and then for Radio 1, where his programs covered such diverse topics as current affairs, music, religion, and the arts. He worked as a radio producer for RTE until 2002. Among the programs he wrote, produced, and presented were *How the Heart Approaches What It Yearns* (1988), a two-part exploration of the life and music of Leonard Cohen, and *The Children at the Bottom of the Garden* (1997), a docudrama about how MacKenna learned from his dying mother that he had stillborn siblings who had been buried at the bottom of the family garden. The program on Cohen won a Jacob's Irish Radio Award. In 1985 MacKenna founded the Mend and Makedo Theatre Company in Athy, County Kildare. He has written several plays for the company and has acted in some of them as well.

MacKenna's documentary interest in place is also evident in *Castledermot and Kilkea: A Social History, with Notes on Ballytore, Graney, Moone and Mullaghmast,* published in 1982. At this time both his literary output and reputation grew; he received the prestigious Hennessy Literary Award in 1983, and his third book, *The Lost Village: A Diary of Castledermot in 1925,* was published two years later. In 1986 MacKenna received the Leitrim Guardian Award. By this time many of the key themes in his work had been established. Human-interest stories have always been important to him, and he has included autobiographical explorations in his broadcast material. This range of engagement gives a rich texture to his imaginative writing and encourages attention to a variety of ideas and forms; likewise, the shifting focus of the story-collection format suits his intense but flexible interests.

In the development of the short-story genre the importance of technique has become paramount, and MacKenna has attuned his artistic sensibility to the opportunities of this literary form. Attention, even intuition, is required of the reader in order to understand nuances of character and the fleeting glimpses of other lives and times. Memory often provides the center of gravity for MacKenna's characters as well as a means of achieving the kind of compression that the story form demands. The sense of pastness is restrained, though, by the visceral awareness of the present and by the acute and observant consciousness of his narrators. *The Fallen and Other Stories* (1992) was a landmark collection, refining established styles in MacKenna's writing and exploring themes of remembered eroticism, loss, and uncertainty. It received the 1993 Irish Times Award for a first book of fiction and made MacKenna newly visible as a fiction writer. In spite of the directness of much of the language, making him an heir to the spare precision of John McGahern, there is also a lyrical quality to the stories. MacKenna has a finely tuned ear as well as a capacity for vividly rendering visual elements, making the stories sensual and emotional as well as carefully and economically crafted.

The opening story in *The Fallen and Other Stories,* "The Unclouded Days"–which accounts for a third of the length of the collection–demonstrates many of the most telling features of MacKenna's fiction. It combines two narratives, both retrospective, one of an elderly man suffering from cancer and one of a widow; each relives the time they first met and became lovers in their youth. What makes this memory especially distinctive is that the widow was the daughter of traveling preachers (territory already explored by MacKenna in his nonfiction writing) who were driven from a rural community by an act of violent persecution. Narrative style is important from the start, but in oblique ways. "My son drove me home from Dublin tonight," the elderly man's narrative begins: "We talked for a while and then there was nothing to say." In those spaces where there is "nothing to say," the most raw and memorable discoveries are made by character and reader. First, though, the reader must learn to accommodate the shifts in perspective. A second voice is introduced into the text–"I never saw the point in wearing widow's weeds"–although the relationship between the two figures remains uncertain for some time. Gradually, the interweaving of narrative yields depth and clarity, the male narrator at first maintaining the larger part of the story before increasing intimacy allows the movement between voices to become swifter and more seamless. As in many of MacKenna's stories, the sense of place colludes in this intimacy; the two narrators became lovers in the natural world, but it could not shelter them from opposition and bigotry. The land informs the story in the way it shapes—and limits—the community inhabiting it, a community ambiguous in its attitude to outsiders and to the Catholic Church, which holds such sway over the emotions and actions of the town:

> I was lying out seventy or a hundred yards into the field to catch the last of the coppery rays. I must have been half asleep because it was nearly dark and I heard a banging in the yard and the sound of glass breaking. . . .
>
> I started shouting at them, for all I was worth.
>
> "What are you doing here, for Jesus' sake?"
>
> "Get outta here," someone said.
>
> I turned to the man nearest me, he was smashing a chair off the front wall.
>
> "Did the priest put you up to this?"
>
> A voice from behind me made me turn, it was Donnelly.
>
> "Fuck off outta that, ya little bollocks."
>
> "What are you doing here, Donnelly?" I shouted.
>
> "You learn to run with the hare and hunt with the hound, sonny. I always told ya that."

The weight of social opinion and the persistence of the divided community are also strong in the title story of the collection. "The Fallen" is set at the time of World War I. Frank Kinsella, one of the two central characters, suffers doubly when he leaves for the trenches, because many Irish who fought with the British were considered to have betrayed the nationalist cause: "There were other mouths that called me a traitor from the corners of the street, from black doorways, from the market crowds." Frank's lover, Mary, is another marginalized figure, since she replaces his wife, who has inexplicably left and returned to her own family. Mary's identity is formed and reinforced by her love for Frank and by the environment to which she belongs, while his identity is dismantled by the depravity of war and his isolation from a meaningful way of viewing the world. In MacKenna's short fiction, emotional development is often linked to experience, and this linkage is starkly presented in "The Fallen." The divided narrative accentuates the distance between Frank and Mary, first before they have properly met and then when he leaves to fight in the trenches. These narrative strands move almost imperceptibly from two disparate viewpoints to the letters that pass between the characters. Their ability to express experience deeply and directly confirms the enduring nature of their love and the importance of such expression for human survival:

> Later, lying in a trench, waiting for the whistle, I thought about all this and then I thought of her. I knew then I would write and tell her everything—but first about the horse, the wounded, the raving mad.
>
> His laburnum flowers fall, their golden rain scattering the grass. I get more letters from him now, full of the things he sees, the things he smells, the sounds of shells and guns and human voices. He tells me everything.

The natural world forms an important link between these two places. Mary's observation of the landscape, particularly the flowers, becomes a means not only of marking the passing seasons but also of affirming life and beauty in a community haunted by death. For the soldier, nature becomes a wasteland, affording neither comfort nor safety.

All of the stories in MacKenna's first collection are told in the shadow of death—either the decline that precedes the end or the effect of death on those left behind. Three stories scattered throughout the collection are titled "Absent Children," an interesting use of the plural for narratives that seem to depict the death of a single child from three differing perspectives. The narrative shifts that figure strongly in the collection are played out within a more fragmentary structure in "Absent Children." In the first of the stories a distance is maintained, with the child's accident revealed through an almost casual reference from a young man who is painting the house of the boy's aunt. The intimate revelation changes the atmosphere and disturbs the sexual tension between the two characters: "She stopped talking and we both sat there in the sunlit kitchen. She looked different to me. Not that she didn't look as well but this thing threw a different light on her. Hearing this little intimacy had done it. A week earlier I would have treasured any intimacy from her but now that I had heard one it had killed everything." The second narrator, a garbageman puzzling over the fact that a perfectly good child's bike has been left out with the trash, shows no such sensitivity. In the third narrative the focus is closer to the place of the tragedy: on the boy's mother, who believes the listening narrator to be incapable of understanding her grief. The narrator then remembers the death of another child, linking her own feelings with those of the bereaved mother. Plurality of grief is first clarified in this narrative: other experiences of loss are to be recalled and relived. The presence of death in MacKenna's fiction is at times overwhelming, both in the frequency of its occurrence and the breadth of its emotional effects. He refuses to fulfill the reader's expectations with easily understood tensions and resolutions; instead, life-changing events and resonant emotions are refracted through minor characters or seemingly inconsequential parallels.

Alongside this preoccupation with death MacKenna explores sexual expression with its attendant vulnerabilities and its impulse toward self-knowledge. His next foray into the short-story genre was the collection *A Year of Our Lives* (1995), which followed the publication of his novel *Clare* (1993), based on the life of the nineteenth-century English poet John Clare and again using the technique of split narration. *A Year of Our Lives* also shows advances in technique and sensibility. The stories are, in the words of Richard Francis (*TLS: The Times Literary Supplement,* 21 April 1995), "whispered in the reader's ear, and have a hushed, rapt quality about them." This sense of privacy, which shadowed MacKenna's earlier work, is still more evident in *A Year of Our Lives.* In "The Things We Say," sexuality becomes a mark of survival. Death has a strong imaginative grasp on the narrator but exemplifies the fleeting, intangible nature of memory and of feeling: "Even the window in the dead room was wide to the breeze from the sea.... Everything was white with light and her body seemed to be nothing more than a flimsy transfer on this cotton sheet. I had to look carefully to be sure she was really there." This scene is vividly recalled, not only because of the impact that the dead woman had once made on the narrator but also because it precedes a scene of sexual awakening for her in which the dead woman's husband asks to see her naked. This view of youthful sexuality as a counterpoint to decay and death is a preoccupation for MacKenna, who increasingly explores the sexual impulse against this backdrop.

In "In the Garden," the daughter of a Protestant clergyman uses sexual manipulation as a way of antagonizing her father. The incident occurs as a memory couched obliquely within the story of a broken marriage, with a frisson of betrayal. Imagery from the natural world plays an evocative symbolic role: the narrator works to clear an overgrown garden as a therapeutic way of dealing with the recurrence of emotional memory, but the garden is also resonant of the biblical themes of temptation, betrayal, and the first loss of trust. Sex in *A Year of Our Lives* is increasingly displaced: it occurs at times and places and between people not the primary focus of the stories. Seemingly disparate scenes contribute to the reader's understanding, not only of a particular narrative but also of MacKenna's larger themes and preoccupations.

In *A Year of Our Lives,* MacKenna explores the transgressive qualities of sex and of language. His representation of sex, relationships, and the body becomes

Front cover of John MacKenna's first collection of stories, published in 1992, which won the 1993 Irish Times Award for a first book of fiction (Bruccoli Clark Layman Archives)

gradually less lyrical throughout the collection. A strain of self-destructiveness is developed alongside a more immediate rendering of social dysfunction and the inability to relate to others. Language becomes more direct and explicit in some of the stories, especially those in which the characters manifest a voyeuristic attitude toward sex, such as "Street," in which a group of men gain gratification from following and watching a pair of young lovers. The exploitative attitude of these men reveals a community for whom feeling has become detached from experience. MacKenna again depicts, as in "The Unclouded Days" but in this case more starkly, the cost of the systematic repression of moral and sexual freedoms.

In narrative terms *A Year of Our Lives* mirrors the structure of *The Fallen and Other Stories* with a series of short narrative "epistles"–four in all, distributed throughout the collection. The series plays with sexual ambiguity; the narrator is a Catholic priest on a train journey to meet a bereaved friend. He recalls a youthful sexual encounter with this friend that is first presented as a homosexual experience and then as a heterosexual one. He remembers a chance encounter on a train years before and, finally, arrives at his destination with a letter—presumably a love letter—that he has written for the friend he is visiting. This series shows MacKenna's writing at its most oblique, demanding that the reader at once acknowledge and cancel out the preceding parts of the narrative. *A Year of Our Lives* is also linked to *The Fallen and Other Stories* by the inclusion of "Absent Child," which describes a living child, poignantly recaptured by the narrator, swinging through the air in play. The story exemplifies MacKenna's structural mode, with constant reminders of his earlier work; yet, even as he provides these reminders, he confirms the extent to which he has moved on as a writer.

MacKenna's novels *The Last Fine Summer*, published in 1997, and *A Haunted Heart* (1999) both return to themes and settings important to his writing. *The Last Fine Summer* introduces the memory of a dead lover alongside sexual ambiguity; loss and guilt are again the dominant emotions. *A Haunted Heart* moves back to territory painstakingly explored in the early diaries of Quaker life in Ireland, telling the story of a group of nonconformist Quakers through the eyes of one of their number, who has returned to Ireland many years later to die. (MacKenna himself was raised a Catholic but became a Quaker in 1982.) Religious devotion is combined with sexual obsession, or with obsession that borders on the sexual but is never made entirely explicit.

John MacKenna typically returns to characters who are on the edges of society, anxiously denying its rules and seeking their own way of life and mode of expression. Throughout his works he has attempted to capture his characters at what Michael Kerrigan (*TLS*, 13 August 1999) has called the "moments when they are . . . outside themselves, in those interstices when their 'real' lives are put on hold." This sense of being inside characters who are outside themselves continues to lend MacKenna's short fiction its intimate and disturbing quality.

Reference:

"A Sense of Place," *Kildare Nationalist*, 25 February 2000.

Julian Maclaren-Ross
(James McLaren Ross)
(7 July 1912 – 3 November 1964)

Paul Willetts

BOOKS: *The Stuff to Give the Troops: Twenty-five Tales of Army Life* (London: Cape, 1944);

Better Than a Kick in the Pants (London: Lawson & Dunn, 1945);

Bitten by the Tarantula: A Story of the South of France (London: Wingate, 1945);

The Nine Men of Soho (London: Wingate, 1946);

Of Love and Hunger (London: Wingate, 1947);

The Weeping and the Laughter: A Chapter of Autobiography (London: Hart-Davis, 1953);

The Funny Bone (London: Elek, 1956);

Until the Day She Dies: A Tale of Terror (London: Hamilton, 1960);

The Doomsday Book (London: Hamilton, 1961; New York: Obolensky, 1961);

My Name Is Love (Isle of Man: Times Press, 1964);

Memoirs of the Forties (London: Alan Ross, 1965).

Collections: *Collected Memoirs* (London: Black Spring Press, 2004);

Selected Stories (Stockport, U.K.: Dewi Lewis Publishing, 2004);

Bitten by the Tarantula and Other Writing (London: Black Spring Press, 2005).

TRANSLATIONS: Raymond Queneau, *Pierrot mon ami* (London: John Lehmann, 1950);

Georges Simenon, *Maigret and the Burglar's Wife* (London: Hamilton, 1955).

PRODUCED SCRIPTS: *Rogues and Vagabonds*, radio, BBC Home Service, 2 May 1946;

The Bowl of St. Giles, by Maclaren-Ross and Martin Jordan, radio, BBC Home Service, 1 August 1947;

The Two Fish Spivs and the King of the Goldfish Named Garth, radio, BBC Light Programme, 18 March 1948;

The Naked Heart, motion picture, Everest Pictures, 1950;

Four Days, motion picture, Vandyck Picture Corporation, 1951;

A Visit to the Villa Edouard Sept, radio, BBC Third Programme, 4 September 1956;

The Key Man, motion picture, Merton Park Studios, 1957;

Escapement (U.S. title: *The Electronic Monster*), motion picture, Merton Park Pictures, 1958;

The Strange Awakening, motion picture, Merton Park Studios, 1958;

You Have Been Warned, radio, BBC Light Programme, 19 February 1958;

Until the Day She Dies, radio, BBC Light Programme, 23 June 1958;

I Had to Go Sick, radio, BBC Light Programme, 14 July 1959;

Y-List, radio, BBC Light Programme, 2 April 1960;

The Doomsday Book, radio, BBC Light Programme, 4 April 1960;

Dream Man, radio, BBC Light Programme, 12 April 1960;

A Master of Suspense, radio, BBC Home Service, 5 May 1960;

They Put Me in Charge of a Squad, radio, BBC Home Service, 11 June 1960;

The Man in Aurora's Room, radio, BBC Home Service, 11 June 1960;

The Key Man, radio, BBC Home Service, 6 August 1960;

The Light Brown Hair, radio, BBC Home Service, 17 September 1960;

The Boy Who Could Have Been Chess Champion of the World, radio, BBC Home Service, 11 January 1961;

The High Priest of Buddha, radio, BBC Home Service, 15 March 1961;

Old Eighty Eight the Counterfeiter, radio, BBC Home Service, 27 April 1961;

The Intaglio, radio, BBC Home Service, 14 June 1961;

The Man with a Background of Flames, radio, BBC Home Service, 23 September 1961;

Julian Maclaren-Ross (©BBC Photo Library; from Paul Willetts, Fear and Loathing in Fitzrovia, *2003; North Carolina State University Library)*

The Girl in the Spotlight, radio, BBC Light Programme, 25 September 1961.

No other prominent twentieth-century English writer cultivated such a flamboyant persona or led such a bohemian existence as Julian Maclaren-Ross. Alongside Dylan Thomas, he is associated with the heavy-drinking world of Fitzrovia, which had, by the late 1930s, become the hub of artistic London. Fascinated by his chaotic way of life, at least a half dozen fellow writers—Anthony Powell and Olivia Manning, to name two—used him as the basis for characters in their novels. His tragicomic allure has, however, obscured both his achievements as a writer and the far-reaching, yet unacknowledged, influence of his work. Besides bringing him transient fame, his writing earned him the admiration of illustrious contemporaries, among them Evelyn Waugh, Graham Greene, and John Betjeman.

James McLaren Ross was born 7 July 1912 in South London, where his itinerant, shabby-genteel parents—John Lambden Ross, of Cuban and Scottish origin, and Gertrude (Pollock) Ross, of Anglo-Indian background—had lodgings. Living on a family trust fund, they resided in a series of seaside towns. In 1921 James and his parents immigrated to the French Riviera, a move prompted by the presence of other members of the family there as well as the chance to avoid paying income tax. Unlike most other British expatriate children, James ("Jimmy") was educated in French schools, enabling him to become bilingual. After his expulsion from a school in Paris, he rejoined his parents and embraced the café society that flourished in Nice. Under the influence of Oscar Wilde, he reinvented himself in the guise of an 1890s dandy, equipped with a malacca cane, a long cigarette holder, and the new name Julian.

Sensing that he would have to return to England if his literary goals were to be attained, he left France in 1933. He eventually moved to London, paying frequent visits to North Soho, dubbed Fitzrovia in honor of the reputation of Fitzroy Tavern, the most fashionable pub in the area. With his ambitions still unrealized, his attempts at placing a novel and a collection of short stories having failed, he courted and, in 1936, married Elizabeth Gott, a struggling actress. They then settled in Bognor, but the marriage soon collapsed.

Calling himself Maclaren-Ross, he persevered with his writing. In addition to writing innovative radio plays, two of which were purchased by the BBC, he produced more short stories. These included "The Hell of a Time" and "A Bit of a Smash in Madras," which utilize colonial India as a backdrop, even though Maclaren-Ross had never been there. One story focuses on a drinking spree in 1920s Madras; the other on a traffic accident with far-reaching ramifications. Narrated in the first person, their style is, like so much of

Maclaren-Ross's work, laconic and colloquial. This style owes something to American writers such as Dashiell Hammett and Ernest Hemingway; yet, it remains distinctively English, the use of authentic slang and obscenities enhancing its immediacy and its aura of verisimilitude. "A Bit of a Smash in Madras," for example, opens with the line, "Absolute fact, I knew damn-all about it," a line that immediately captures the reader's attention and conveys the personality of the narrator.

At the beginning of 1938, the allowance on which Maclaren-Ross had been living suddenly stopped. In search of a job that would yield material for his writing, he became a door-to-door salesman. Eventually dismissed, he found work as a gardener, but he was, before long, jobless again. World War II had, meanwhile, broken out, bringing with it the prospect of conscription into the military.

A turning point in his life was heralded by the sale of "A Bit of a Smash in Madras" to *Horizon*, the magazine edited by Cyril Connolly. Maclaren-Ross's story, its language toned down, appeared in the June 1940 issue. So convincing was the first-person narrator's tone that V. S. Pritchett, writing for *New Statesman and Nation* (24 September 1965), assumed that Maclaren-Ross was a veteran of the Raj. The story prompted Jonathan Cape to express interest in publishing a volume of Maclaren-Ross's work. Just as he was poised to establish himself as a writer, however, he was drafted into the army. Because of a knee problem that prevented him from marching, he was assigned to clerical duties.

By the following year he had started producing irreverent, sometimes brief, stories about the army, typically related by first-person narrators intent on pointing out official incompetence. Among the best-known of these were "I Had to Go Sick" and "Y-List," set in military hospitals where nobody appears to be in control. Writing in *Wartime and Aftermath* (1993), critic Bernard Bergonzi described "Y-List" as a story that "presents the military-medical bureaucracy as something out of Kafka rewritten by the Marx Brothers." Often autobiographical, such stories blended fiction and reportage. They soon became a feature of the many wartime literary magazines achieving high circulations, the popularity of Maclaren-Ross's stories marking him out as one of the leading representatives of the younger generation of English writers.

Despite his newfound literary success, he was disillusioned with the army and frustrated by his inability to make a tangible contribution to the war effort. Two and a half years after he joined the military, Maclaren-Ross deserted, but he was soon arrested. Spells in prison and in a psychiatric hospital ensued, culminating in his release from the army.

Now resident in London, he was hired as a screenwriter collaborating with Thomas on government-sponsored propaganda documentaries. He also became a celebrated figure in London bohemian circles. The abrupt transformation in his circumstances was reflected in his short-story output. Frequently beginning as barroom anecdotes, stories such as "Welsh Rabbit of Soap" portray the raffish milieu he inhabited. Maclaren-Ross often used narrators indistinguishable from himself, blurring the boundary between fact and fiction. Told from the point of view of a writer called "Julian" who is a regular in the Soho pubs, "Welsh Rabbit of Soap" depicts a whirlwind romance between the narrator and an ultimately elusive girl.

As with his short fiction about the army, his stories about civilian life were eagerly acquired by the editors of magazines and miscellanies. Not until the following summer, however, was his debut collection of short stories published. Titled *The Stuff to Give the Troops: Twenty-five Tales of Army Life* (1944), the collection included roughly half the army stories he had written; prominent examples are the farcical "They Put Me in Charge of a Squad" and the poignant "Are You Happy in Your Work," a vivid re-creation of his daily routine. Their wry humor and underlying melancholy elicited praise from Powell and Waugh.

When the movie company employing him went out of business early in 1944, Maclaren-Ross found himself in financial difficulties. Desperation compelled him to seek a temporary solution to his problems by selling *Better Than a Kick in the Pants* (1945), a collection of his civilian stories, to the novice firm of Lawson & Dunn. The book encompassed apprentice pieces such as "Five Finger Exercises," his risqué dramatization of a romance with an adolescent girl; late-1930s work such as "I'm Not Asking You to Buy," describing an incident when he was a door-to-door salesman; and recent stories such as "The Oxford Manner," his account of a disastrous holiday.

With the help of Greene, he also sold his nostalgic 1940 novella *Bitten by the Tarantula: A Story of the South of France* (1945). In its meandering depiction of the summer tenants of a remote prewar French chalet, it bears a strong resemblance to Connolly's novel *The Rock Pool* (1938). His new publisher advanced him additional money for a full-length novel and *The Nine Men of Soho* (1946), his next collection of stories; yet, his drinking and fondness for expensive hotels meant that his earnings were swiftly spent.

By the end of the war, Maclaren-Ross had, as John Lehmann observed in *The Listener* (7 October 1965), "already established a reputation, not only as a wit and a character, but as the author of some brilliant

THE
STUFF TO GIVE
THE TROOPS

Twenty-five Tales of Army Life

by

J. MACLAREN-ROSS

JONATHAN CAPE
THIRTY BEDFORD SQUARE
LONDON

Title page for Maclaren-Ross's 1944 first collection of short stories, some of which are humorous and others, melancholy (Western Illinois University Library)

short stories.... Everything seemed within his grasp, and he was tipped as one of the most promising young authors, likely to make his mark in films and on the air as well." His short-term need for cash deflecting him from the long-term aim of producing a novel, he wrote two radio plays for the BBC and four incisive essays about the cinema for *Penguin New Writing,* together with a memoir of poet Alun Lewis. In the meantime, *Better Than a Kick in the Pants* and then *Bitten by the Tarantula* were released. While his short-story collection made little impression, his novella sold well. Sales could have been even greater had André Deutsch, with whom Maclaren-Ross had fallen out, been capable of securing extra supplies of strictly rationed paper on which promptly to print a second edition.

Before Maclaren-Ross could find a new publisher, he had to submit the contracted novel to Deutsch. With that in mind, he reworked the material he had accumulated for a book, drawing on his days as a salesman. The result was *Of Love and Hunger* (1947), a bleakly comic novel about his impoverished alter ego's affair with a colleague's wife. Soon after he delivered the manuscript, Deutsch published *The Nine Men of Soho,* Maclaren-Ross's third collection of short fiction. Despite the title, the constituent stories were not solely about the Soho pub and club scene. They were also set in other places with which Maclaren-Ross was familiar, namely the Riviera of his youth, interwar Bognor, and 1930s London. To this varied collection, he added "My Father Was Born in Havana," a history of his colorful family. Reviewing the book for *The Tatler and Bystander* (25 December 1946), Elizabeth Bowen concluded that Maclaren-Ross was a "writer due for the first rank."

Within a short period of time, he was, nevertheless, again in financial difficulties. His situation forced him to work as a bit-part actor in BBC radio drama and to accept a commission from Lehmann to translate Raymond Queneau's *Pierrot mon ami* (1950). However, when *Of Love and Hunger* was published, it generated handsome sales, stimulated by the acclaim with which it was greeted, Powell's review in *Strand Magazine* (January 1947) placing it on a par with work by F. Scott Fitzgerald and Patrick Hamilton.

Faced by the latest of his recurrent financial crises, in mid 1947 Maclaren-Ross was rescued by Greene, who held a senior position at Eyre & Spottiswoode. From Greene, Maclaren-Ross obtained a generous advance for a thriller based on the crimes of a 1930s serial killer, but he rapidly lost confidence in the project. He had, in any case, run out of money before it could be finished, and necessity demanded that he review books for *The Times Literary Supplement (TLS).* Money, once again, was behind his decision to take on a commission for a screenplay of *Maria Chapdelaine,* a sentimental 1916 best-seller about a romance in the snowbound Canadian backwoods. So uncongenial did he find the subject, he recruited a friend to write the bulk of the script, ultimately retitled *The Naked Heart* (1950).

Maclaren-Ross entered the new decade with his career in stasis. Reviewing duties were juxtaposed with another screenwriting assignment, this time as a scriptwriter on a low-budget movie called *Four Days* (1951). A couple of months after this assignment was out of the way, his Queneau translation was published.

During 1951, Maclaren-Ross made money from a commission to write the script for what turned out to be an abortive movie version of Robert Louis Stevenson's *The Suicide Club* (1878). After that, he obtained an advance from Hamish Hamilton for a novel about Maclaren-Ross's frustrating experiences as a screenwriter, but he had trouble sculpting these into quasi-fictional form. His progress was hampered by a severe bout of writer's block, compounded by psychological problems arising from his reliance on amphetamines to help him work for protracted periods.

In pursuit of a way out of his current problems, he turned to nonfiction, abandoning his novel in favor of *The Weeping and the Laughter* (1953), a childhood memoir with which he hoped to revive his fortunes. Written in leisurely prose, its tender lyricism far removed from the spare, often vernacular, style associated with him, it focused on his eccentric family and peripatetic life from birth until the age of ten. Before its publication, he worked on screenplays for the new independent British television channel, as well as supplying reviews for *TLS* and *The Sunday Times*. Despite an enthusiastic critical reception, sales of his memoir were poor, the disappointment partially offset by the news that his champion, Powell, had been appointed literary editor of *Punch,* in which Maclaren-Ross published a string of parodies that provoked admiring comments from William Faulkner and P. G. Wodehouse.

Since 1949 he had been living with his latest girlfriend in a succession of bedsits and flats. She left him in late 1953. To make money, he wrote reviews for *Punch,* articles for various magazines, more television scripts, and a translation of Georges Simenon's *Maigret and the Burglar's Wife* (1955). On one of his periodic trips to London, he encountered George Orwell's widow, Sonia, for whom he developed an unrequited passion. Soon he was stalking her and planning to join her in London, the change of address financed by the sale of *The Funny Bone* (1956), his compilation of literary parodies as well as hitherto uncollected memoirs and stories. In stories such as "The Shoestring Budget" and "Old Ginger," scathing comedies about the movie business and the army, he once more drew on his experiences for material.

Back in London at the start of 1956, indebted not only to landlords and hoteliers but also the British tax authorities, he switched addresses with regularity. Before long, he was relying on friends for makeshift accommodation, his mental health simultaneously deteriorating to the point at which he became convinced that his personality had been hijacked by the fictional character of Mr. Hyde from *Dr Jekyll and Mr Hyde* (1886).

In the spring of 1956 Maclaren-Ross met Diana Bromley. Their ensuing romance, featuring bitter arguments, reconciliations, and occasional homelessness, distracted him from his obsession with Sonia Orwell, which had threatened to climax in murder. An erratic income was provided by journalism and scriptwriting

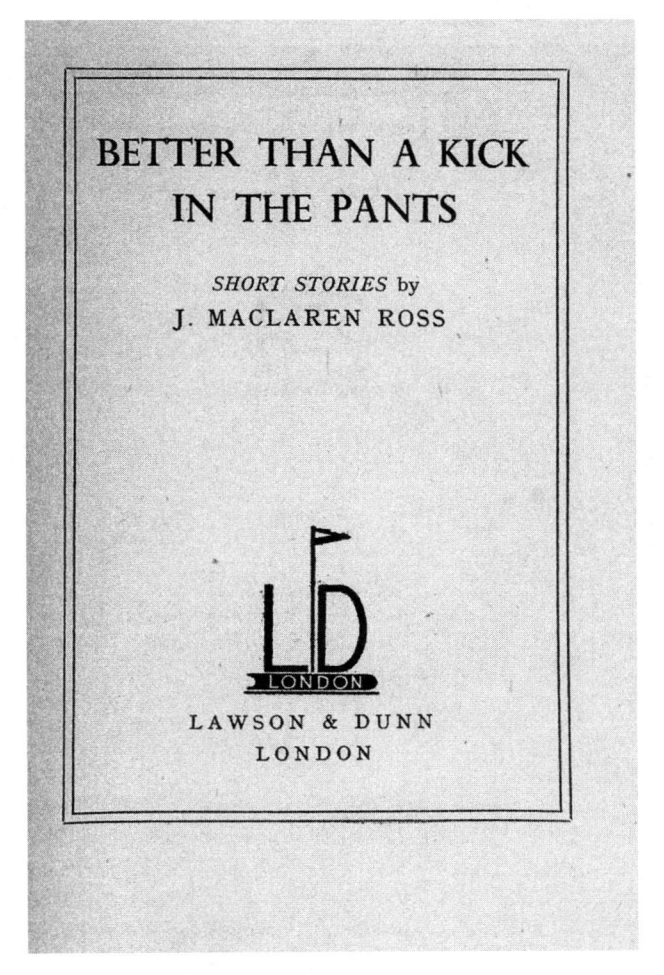

Title page for Maclaren-Ross's 1945 collection of stories about civilians, including one about his experiences as a door-to-door salesman, "I'm Not Asking You to Buy" (Carol M. Newman Library, Virginia Polytechnic Institute and State University)

commissions. Disenchanted with the movie business, Maclaren-Ross concentrated on supporting himself and Diana, whom he married just before the birth of their son, by writing popular, critically praised radio plays, in which he also acted and, in one instance, sang. His repeated failure to fulfill commissions, however, undermined his relationship with the BBC. He found an alternative source of income during the early 1960s when he relaunched his career as a novelist by making a radio play, *Until the Day She Dies* (1958), into the novel *Until the Day She Dies: A Tale of Terror* (1960). He went on to adapt two other radio thrillers as novels, *The Doomsday Book* (1961) and *My Name Is Love* (1964), which had been broadcast as *The Girl in the Spotlight* (1961).

After an unhappy four-month period in Brighton prefacing the breakup of his marriage, he resumed his routine in London, where he began writing essays and reviews for the *London Magazine*. He later persuaded its

Title page for Maclaren-Ross's 1956 compilation of literary parodies and memoirs (Auburn University Library)

editor to serialize his projected *Memoirs of the Forties* (1965), each installment concentrating on a particular person or aspect of his life during that decade. With less than half the manuscript completed, on 3 November 1964 he suffered a fatal heart attack. The book, nevertheless, was published posthumously to acclaim from Pritchett and other critics. In the wake of his premature death at the age of fifty-two, he also provided the model for characters in other people's fiction; the best known was X. Trapnel in Powell's *A Dance to the Music of Time* (1962).

Julian Maclaren-Ross left behind a significant body of work, interest in which is increasing. His *Memoirs of the Forties* is widely regarded as the definitive portrait of wartime Fitzrovia; his short stories are admired by leading contemporary writers such as Harold Pinter; and his novel *Of Love and Hunger* is among the books deemed worthy of inclusion in *The Readers' Companion to Twentieth-Century Writers* (1995), edited by Frank Kermode and Peter Parker. Through the demotic prose style that characterizes his work, Maclaren-Ross has exerted a pervasive influence over generations of English writers.

Interviews:

"J. Maclaren-Ross Talks to Eric Phillips," *Writer* (September 1961): 4–5;

"In The Shadow of Cain," *Writers' World*, BBC-TV, 5 October 1964.

Biography:

Paul Willetts, *Fear and Loathing in Fitzrovia: The Bizarre Life of Julian Maclaren-Ross* (Stockport, U.K.: Dewi Lewis, 2003).

References:

Bernard Bergonzi, *Wartime and Aftermath* (London: Oxford University Press, 1993), p. 42;

John Betjeman, letter to Julian Maclaren-Ross, 2 April 1953;

Frank Kermode and Peter Parker, *The Readers' Companion to Twentieth-Century Writers* (London: Fourth Estate, 1995);

Charles Eric Maine, *Escapement* (London: Hodder & Stoughton, 1956);

Evelyn Waugh, letter to Julian Maclaren-Ross, 4 July 1950.

Papers:

Julian Maclaren-Ross's papers are in the Harry Ransom Humanities Research Center, University of Texas at Austin; the Royal Literary Fund Collection; the BBC Written Archive; Northwestern University Library; the McFarlin Library, University of Tulsa; the Jonathan Cape Archive at the University of Reading; the Hamish Hamilton Archive at Bristol University; the Dan Davin Archive at the Andrew Turnbull Library; Emory University; Stanford University; the University of North Carolina at Chapel Hill; the library of Anthony Powell at the Chantry, Somerset, U.K.; and in the possession of Alex Maclaren-Ross, Maclaren-Ross's son, as well as Paul Willetts, Maclaren-Ross's biographer.

Bryan MacMahon

(29 September 1909 – 13 February 1998)

Mary Burke
University of Connecticut

BOOKS: *The Cobweb's Glory: A Comedy in Three Acts,* as Bryan Michael O'Connor (Listowel: Bookshop Publications, 1946; London: S. French, 1947);

Fledged and Flown: An Election Comedy in One Act, as O'Connor (Listowel: Bookshop Publications, 1946);

The Lion-Tamer and Other Stories (London: Macmillan, 1948; New York: Dutton, 1949);

Jack O'Moora and the King of Ireland's Son (New York: Dutton, 1950); republished as *Jackomoora and the King of Ireland's Son* (Dublin: Poolbeg, 1996);

Children of the Rainbow (London: Macmillan, 1952; New York: Dutton, 1952);

The Red Petticoat and Other Stories (London: Macmillan, 1955; New York: Dutton, 1955);

Brendan of Ireland, photographs by Wolfgang Suschitzky (London: Methuen, 1961; New York: Hastings House, 1967);

Seachtar Fear Seacht Lá (Dublin, 1966);

The Honey Spike (London: Bodley Head, 1967; New York: Dutton, 1967);

Patsy-O and His Wonderful Pets (New York: Dutton, 1970; Chalfont St. Giles, U.K.: R. Sadler, 1972);

Here's Ireland (London: Batsford, 1971; New York: Dutton, 1971; revised edition, Dublin: Butler Sims, 1982);

The End of the World and Other Stories (Dublin: Poolbeg, 1976);

The Sound of Hooves and Other Stories (London: Bodley Head, 1985);

Patsy-O (Swords: Poolbeg, 1989);

Mascot Patsy-O; Patsy-O and the Dolphin; and, The President and Patsy-O (Dublin: Poolbeg, 1992);

The Master (Dublin: Poolbeg, 1992);

Phoenix in the Flame (N.p., 1993);

The Storyman (Dublin: Poolbeg, 1994);

The Tallystick and Other Stories (Dublin: Poolbeg, 1994);

A Final Fling: Conversations between Men and Women (Dublin: Poolbeg, 1998);

Hero Town, edited by Maurice MacMahon (Dingle: Brandon, 2004);

Bryan MacMahon (photograph by Brendan Landy; from the dust jacket for The Master, *1992; Thomas Cooper Library, University of South Carolina)*

Streets of Listowel, by MacMahon and Seán McCarthy (Monavally: Comhairle Oiliuna, n.d.).

SELECTED PLAY PRODUCTIONS: *The Bugle in the Blood,* Dublin, Abbey Theatre, 14 March 1949;

The Golden Folk, Listowel, Listowel Drama Group, date unknown; revised as *The Song of the Anvil,* music by Seán Ó Riada, Dublin, Abbey Theatre, 1960;

The Honey Spike, Dublin, Abbey Theatre, 22 May 1961;

Seachtar Fear Seacht Lá, Dublin, Croke Park, 1966;

The Gap of Life, Dublin, Peacock Theatre, 1972.

SELECTED PRODUCED SCRIPTS: *I Was Born in a Market Place,* original story by MacMahon, radio, BBC, 26 December 1948;

The Balladmaker's Saturday Night, initially scripted by MacMahon, radio, Radio Éireann, 24 December 1951– ;

The Bicycle Man, television, Radio Telefís Éireann, 1966;

A Boy at the Train, television, Radio Telefís Éireann, 1966;

Children of Dreams, television, Radio Telefís Éireann, 1966;

The School on the Green, television, Radio Telefís Éireann, 1966.

OTHER: "The Master," "Countryman Comes to Dublin," "Canavawns," and "Corner Boys," in *Good-bye, Twilight: Songs of the Struggle in Ireland,* edited by Leslie H. Daiken (London: Lawrence & Wishart, 1936), pp. 44–49;

"Chestnut and Jet," in *Stories of Our Century by Catholic Authors,* edited by John G. Brunini and Francis X. Connolly (Philadelphia: Lippincott, 1949), pp. 244–249;

The Song of the Anvil, in *Seven Irish Plays, 1946–1964,* edited by Robert Hogan (Minneapolis: University of Minnesota Press, 1967), pp. 186–246;

"Place and People in Poetry," in *Irish Poets in English: The Thomas Davis Lectures on Anglo-Irish Poetry,* edited by Seán Lucy (Cork & Dublin: Mercier, 1973), pp. 60–74;

Peig Sayers, *Peig: The Autobiography of Peig Sayers of the Great Blasket Island,* translated by MacMahon, introduction by Eoin McKiernan (Dublin: Talbot, 1973; Syracuse: Syracuse University Press, 1974);

"Ballads and Balladmaking," in *Written on the Wind: Personal Memories of Irish Radio, 1926–76,* edited by Louis McRedmond (Dublin: Radio Telefís Éireann/Gill & Macmillan, 1976), pp. 107–122;

Doncha Ó Conchúir, *Treoir Guide: Corca Dhuibhne, a Muintir agus a Séadchomharthaí=Corca Dhuibhne, Its Peoples and Their Buildings,* translated by MacMahon (Kerry: Cló Dhuibhne, 1977);

"Peig Sayers and the Vernacular of the Storyteller," in *Literature and Folk Culture, Ireland and Newfoundland: Papers from the Ninth Annual Seminar of the Canadian Association for Irish Studies, at Memorial University of Newfoundland, February 11–15, 1976,* edited by Alison Feder and Bernice Schrank (St. John's, Newfoundland: Memorial University of Newfoundland, 1977), pp. 83–109;

Des O'Sullivan, *For Lovers & Rovers,* preface by MacMahon (Croydon, U.K.: Greenway Press, 1981);

Padraic Ó Conaire, "My Poet, Dark and Slender," translated by MacMahon, in *15 Short Stories,* translated by Con Houlihan and others (Dublin: Poolbeg, 1982), pp. 101–126;

Luaí Ó Murchú, *Journey Home,* foreword by MacMahon (Stillorgan: Sliabh Gullion, 1997).

SELECTED PERIODICAL PUBLICATIONS–UNCOLLECTED:

POETRY

"House Sinister," *Bell,* 1, no. 2 (1940): 87–89;

"Bright Little Braggart," *Bell,* 1, no. 5 (1941): 19–20.

DRAMA

The Death of Biddy Early: A Play in One Act and *Jack Furey: A Play in One Act, Journal of Irish Literature,* Listowel Writers Special Issue, 1, no. 2 (1972): 30–44, 45–62.

FICTION

"The Crape," *Bell,* 3, no. 3 (1941): 197–202;

"The Clarinet," *Bell,* 4, no. 2 (1942): 87–96;

"Sunday Morning," *Bell,* 6, no. 6 (1943): 473–478;

"The Plain People of England," as B. McM., *Bell,* 7, no. 2 (1943): 100–110;

"Yung Mari Li," *Bell,* 8, no. 2 (1944): 103–116;

"The Holy Kiss," *Bell,* 8, no. 5 (1944): 422–426;

"Sing, Milo, Sing!" *Bell,* 13, no. 4 (1947): 25–29;

"The World Is Lovely and the World Is Wide," *Bell,* 14, no. 3 (1947): 61–67;

"Chicken-Licken," *Bell,* 15, no. 5 (1948): 27–36;

"Sovereigns for Sale," *Catholic World,* 179 (July 1954): 274–280;

"Tinker Wedding," *Voice of St. Jude* (December 1959): 42–46.

NONFICTION

"A Country Bookshop," *Bell,* 1, no. 6 (1941): 7–18;

"I Made a Ballad," *Bell,* 5, no. 3 (1942): 165–173;

"Public Opinion," *Bell,* 6, no. 3 (1943): 248–250;

"The Small-Town Pub," as Danny Costello, *Bell,* 14, no. 2 (1947): 38–47;

"What the Tinker Woman Said to Me," *Envoy* (May 1950): 11–13;

"Pat McAuliffe of Listowel," *Typographica,* 6 (December 1962): 27–32;

"Footloose in the County Sligo," *Lamp* (March 1963): 12–13, 30–31;

"Thoughts on Sunday," *Furrow,* 15 (December 1964): 774–778;

"The Secret Gammon of the Woods Awaits You—Photo Feature," photographs by Maurice Fridberg, *Everyman,* 1 (1968): 89–103;

"A Portrait of Tinkers," *Natural History,* 80 (December 1971): 24–35, 104–109.

Bryan MacMahon was, by turns, a poet, short-story writer, novelist, folklorist, bookseller, scriptwriter, playwright, theater producer, teacher, lecturer, novelist, and balladeer. Best known for his affirming, compassionate, and much-anthologized stories celebrating the color and romance of Irish small-town life, MacMahon has repeatedly been described as among the most talented and accessible short-fiction writers of the generation after Frank O'Connor and Liam O'Flaherty. Popular in the United States in the 1940s and 1950s, he was a subtle and prolific writer, unusual among his mid-twentieth-century peers in not being overtly hostile to the Catholic Church. As Eileen Battersby has suggested in *The Irish Times* (14 February 1998), MacMahon was one of the great "people's writers" of twentieth-century Ireland.

MacMahon's hometown, Listowel, in County Kerry, fostered many celebrated twentieth-century Irish writers, from Maurice Walsh, whose short story "The Quiet Man" (1933) was adapted as a 1952 motion picture by John Ford, to George Fitzmaurice, the reclusive early Abbey Theatre dramatist whose revolutionary use of Kerry dialect MacMahon admired and studied. In *Here's Ireland* (1971; revised, 1982), a dense history of Ireland and its literary people and places, which MacMahon playfully and accurately introduces as a "prejudiced, wilful, discursive, amiable and cantankerous" guide to his native country, he implies that the uncommonly cultured atmosphere of the small town he was raised in shaped his development as a writer and a person:

> In Listowel we have a literary tradition nurtured by a rare bookseller called Dan Flavin who corresponded with Axel Munthe when the young Swedish doctor, then in Naples, had just written his first book, *Letters from a Mourning City.* Many years ago Dan sent to the Shakespeare Press in Paris for copies of the first edition of Joyce's *Ulysses:* a copy of the massive uncut book he thrust into my boyish hand and said: "Read that and don't let anyone see it."

MacMahon advised local writers that they had little need to search beyond Kerry for suitable subjects, telling them in a 1998 *Irish Times* article, "Beauty is not elsewhere. It's here beneath your boots." Thoroughly adept in the techniques of the modern short story, MacMahon affirms communality, love of place, and tolerance of one's neighbors, spouse, and family in his

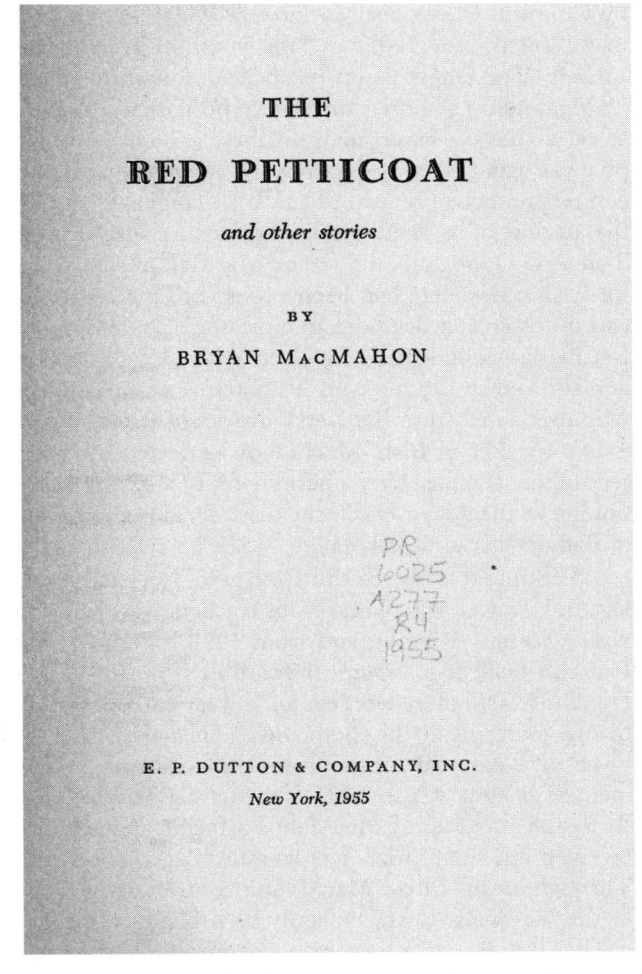

Title page for the American edition of MacMahon's second collection of short stories, some of which were originally published in magazines such as Sports Illustrated, Harper's Bazaar, *and* The Kenyon Review *(Thomas Cooper Library, University of South Carolina)*

writings, which may partially explain his great popularity with American readers. He lived, taught, and wrote in his hometown throughout his life.

Bryan Michael MacMahon was born on 29 September 1909 in Listowel to Joanna Caughlin MacMahon, a schoolteacher, and Patric Mary MacMahon, who served as the overseer of the town's market. The couple had three sons and one daughter. MacMahon's early memories were shaped by the enormous political turbulence shaking pre-Independence Ireland in the first two decades of the twentieth century. Despite the fact that he was only six and a half years old when the Easter Rising began on 24 April 1916, he recalled that he was completely conscious of the issues involved in the "rebellion of poets." As a boy he enthusiastically enrolled in Fianna Eireann, an organization cofounded by Countess Constance Markiewicz, which he referred to in *The Master* (1992) as "the youthful arm of the I.R.A." The emphasis on reconciliation and tolerance in MacMahon's short stories may be partially understood as having emerged from these memories. Such political agitation was inextricably entwined with the contemporaneous revival of the Irish language, and at the urging of a local Gaelic League idealist named Tomás O'Donoghue, the young MacMahon signed up for Irish classes. He had been exposed to the language to a much greater degree than most of his contemporaries: his father had been involved with Douglas Hyde and the Gaelic League, and his paternal grandmother, who originated from the Kerry district of Beale, was a native speaker of Irish. MacMahon perfected his mastery of the language over a period of fifty years by vacationing in the Kerry Gaeltacht (Irish-speaking districts) of Ballyferriter and Ballydavid.

Educated from 1921 to 1928 at St. Michael's College in Listowel, where one of his teachers was the local writer Seamus Wilmot, and from 1928 to 1930 at St. Patrick's College in Drumcondra, on the north side of Dublin, MacMahon worked for a year in the capital before returning to his hometown. He taught in Listowel at a national school from 1931 until his retirement as headmaster in 1975. Listowel playwright John B. Keane was one of MacMahon's former pupils and received his first prize for literature at the school. Throughout his career MacMahon contributed greatly to the life of his town, not only as a highly regarded teacher but also as a prominent member of and writer for the nationally acclaimed Listowel Drama Group, of which he was a founding member and an early producer. Listowel still hosts an internationally recognized annual writers' week of lectures and workshops, an institution MacMahon helped to found. The poet Patrick Kavanagh considered MacMahon's profession to be the worst a writer could have, but to MacMahon, whose own mother had also been a schoolteacher, the liberating arts of instruction and writing drew from the same internal source. In a 1974 interview with Gordon Henderson he stated, "One thing about teaching is that when you teach for six hours every day you are expending energy in communicating. You're drawing from the same reservoir of energy with which you write, which is pretty rough going." Doubtlessly, the persuasive didacticism of much of his output came naturally to one in his profession.

On 4 November 1936 MacMahon married Kathleen "Kitty" Ryan, with whom he had five sons, Patrick Gerald, James, Bryan, Maurice, and Eoin. The couple ran a bookshop on Church Street in Kitty's name from 1939 to 1948. Four poems by MacMahon were included in *Good-bye, Twilight: Songs of the Struggle in Ireland* (1936), a compilation of left-leaning Irish republican and nationalist poetry. His career as a short-story writer commenced, as with many Irish writers of his generation, with contributions to Sean O'Faolain's *The Bell* (1940–1954), an influential and iconoclastic literary and cultural journal. O'Faolain, himself a master short-story writer, coached MacMahon, and the younger author certainly benefited from this apprenticeship: with the exception of one piece returned by *The Bell* (which was later published elsewhere), MacMahon received no rejection slips throughout his writing career and never suffered from writer's block. His stories are generally suffused with a strong sense of place; it has been noted that the word *Ireland* occurs frequently in his narratives, a self-consciousness he ascribed to living in an island nation. In a contribution to the "Public Opinion" column of *The Bell* (June 1943) he suggests that small Irish towns would benefit from the establishment of exhibitions of folk customs and utensils. The story "Yung Mari Li" (1944) depicts the efforts of an Irish priest working in America to bring a Chinese woman to terms with her Irish Catholic ancestry.

In 1945 MacMahon was given the Bell Award for best short story of the year for the evocatively titled "The Good Dead in the Green Hills" (1945). His first collection, *The Lion-Tamer and Other Stories*, published in England in 1948 and the following year in the United States, included the award-winning story. The American edition was the subject of the cover review of the 5 February 1949 *Saturday Review of Literature*, making MacMahon eminent almost overnight in the United States and consolidating his position in the front rank of Irish writers. The laudatory review congratulated MacMahon on making characters, and not plots, his main concern: "He is artist enough to let them reveal themselves as much by implication as by what they do not say." *The Lion-Tamer* sold a thousand copies a week and went through four printings in two months. The collection consists of twenty-two stories that run mainly from seven to ten pages in length (as do the vast majority of MacMahon's stories). Seven of the stories were originally published in *The Bell* between 1942 and 1947.

The title story, "The Lion-Tamer," is a self-referential celebration of the magical art of weaving yarns: seeking conversation in a strange town, the narrator encounters a fantasist who shares a spellbinding tale of how he became the world's first Irish lion tamer. Throughout the stories in *The Lion-Tamer*, MacMahon is drawn to the chinks in the armor of the quotidian, countering the view that mid-twentieth-century Ireland was an oppressive, homogenous place. The stories are peopled by a varied community of neighbors, friends, itinerant musicians, show folks, the wounded in body, and the deformed in mind. "The Man Who Hated Movement" is an impeccable delineation of the everyday torments endured in secret by an obsessive personality. Typical of MacMahon's deft juxtaposition of the idealized and the realistic, "By the Sea" concerns a benevolent scoutmaster on an idyllic camping adventure and his reactions to the sudden death of a boy in his charge. In MacMahon's rural Ireland, the tragic and the wondrous, the monotonous and the quirky, and the extraordinary and the mundane are acknowledged to exist side by side. In "The Dancer's Aunt" the reaction of a small community, upon learning that a previously mocked local is an exquisite performer of Irish dance, yokes the provincial to the global: "Now at last we have beauty. Time, hear us protesting from our shabby valley. To us she is everything. Everything that is delicious to ear and eye. She is our Age of Innocence. She is Our Book of Kells, she is our Spring Song, she is our Un Carnet de Bal, she is our Venus of Milo."

As with James Joyce's *Dubliners* (1914), the significant action in MacMahon's stories is often an incident that on the surface seems of little importance, which he referred to in the 1974 interview as "a fleeting moment of epiphany which can open up transcendent issues and clarify snarled events." In the interview MacMahon's delineation of the wide-ranging sources and characteristics of the contemporary Irish story illuminates his own creative aims and influences:

> It came to us from Gogol, to Turgenev, to Chekhov–via the Garnetts in translation–through Daniel Corkery to a great extent, to Sean O'Faolain and Frank O'Connor, both of whom influenced me to a great extent in the pages of *The Bell*. George Moore is there too with *The Untilled Field,* and of course there is Joyce with the greatest short story ever written, "The Dead," although I reckon "The Adulterous Woman" by Camus a marvellous story too. There's a little dash of de Maupassant and other people in us, and maybe at second remove a Russian called Leskov and a Frenchman called Renard. I've been working on a couple of definitions of the short story. It's the interaction of characters in which we've grown interested, in a particular situation. I think I could get a better one if I groped for it: it's the interesting reactions of significant characters in significant situations. And if there is one standard that I'd judge a short story by, I would judge it by the quality of indelibility. You might read a thousand short stories and two or three of them–they may not be the best by critical standards–remain indelibly in your mind. You'll say, "I can't get these out of my head." They project, as it were, a fishing rod into the consciousness. These are important stories.

MacMahon's references to French and Russian literature are illuminating: according to Fintan O'Toole in "The Magic Glasses of George Fitzmaurice" (1994), Kerry writing is distinct in Irish literature because its stylistic points of contact stretch outside of Dublin, despite its ostensibly parochial concerns.

In the 1974 interview MacMahon also stressed the inspiration he received from the native Irish tradition of *seancaithe* (storytellers), "people who were full of folklore." One of his earliest literary productions–a song he composed as a child that lampooned certain locals, for which he received a shilling from a townswoman–was in this tradition of the celebration and recounting of incidents and personalities of local significance. Dr. Séamus Delargy, head of the influential Irish Folklore Commission, theorized that genuine history inhered in the lives of the anonymous majority, rather than the celebrated elite, an idea that greatly influenced his acquaintance MacMahon.

MacMahon's stories "Evening in Ireland" and "The Foxy Lad" were published in the August 1949 issue of the *Partisan Review* and later republished in his second collection, *The Red Petticoat and Other Stories* (1955). The latter story–retitled "The Foxy-Haired Lad" in the 1955 collection–is an account of a politician whose pompous oration is interrupted by a humble couple repeatedly asking for the return of the body of their son, who has been executed by the government. Despite his celebration of the traditional aspects of his native culture, MacMahon prided himself on his opposition to the dominant discourse of Irish life and clashed with the educational and clerical establishment throughout his teaching and writing career, particularly in regard to the appalling state of disrepair of Irish schools. The Kerry author sometimes gleefully boasted how a mildly anticlerical observation caused him to be denounced from the pulpit. Nonetheless, MacMahon's narratives were welcomed by Catholic publications: "Chestnut and Jet," a story from *The Lion-Tamer,* was included in the American anthology *Stories of Our Century by Catholic Authors* (1949), and his fiction was published by many Irish and American Catholic journals, such as *The Furrow, The Lamp,* and *The Sign*. His stories abound with individualistic noncompliance but often conclude with acceptance of the time-honored order. MacMahon's liberalism is tempered by respect for tradition, and his unflinching examination of the harsh ironies of sex, inequality, birth, and death is softened by a compassionate tone.

MacMahon abandoned the formal musical training of his youth to embrace Irish balladry, which he recorded by hauling around a huge portable wire recorder, one of the few of such devices then in use in Ireland. He also composed his own ballads on traditional themes and had them printed locally. On the basis of his song collection, MacMahon devised the popular Radio Éireann series *The Balladmaker's Saturday*

Dust jacket for MacMahon's 1994 collection of stories dealing with the heartaches of family life (Richland County Public Library)

Night in 1951, which has been credited with assisting in the twentieth-century revival of the ballad form.

MacMahon's ambitious first novel, *Children of the Rainbow* (1952), was chosen as a Book Find Club selection. It is set in Cloone, a thinly disguised version of the Convent Street district in Listowel, and depicts the intrinsic color, variety, and vigor of village life and dialect in the Ireland of earlier decades. The novel warns against increasing industrialization, with its concomitant loss of local identity, a subject explored in much of MacMahon's shorter fiction. In "The Fabulous Realism of Bryan MacMahon" (1994) Augustine Martin categorizes this repeated theme as the problematic "suppressed birth-pangs of modernity" and "ground bass of savage nostalgia" underlying MacMahon's celebration of the local, tribal, communal, and traditional. MacMahon's stories engage with, though never seek to dismantle, the oppositions of Irish life, and the opening lines of "The Cat and the Cornfield" (1953) explicate succinctly his oft-stated belief that narrative emerges from the coupling of "a male idea and a female idea": "In Ireland all you need to make a short story is two men with completed characters—say a parish priest and his sexton. There, at once, you have conflict."

The literary productions that emerged from MacMahon's formula earned him the respect of critics and readers alike. His successful 1955 collection, *The Red Petticoat*, was judged by *The Irish Book Lover* (July 1956) to be lyrical, masterful, and stylish. A story in the volume titled "Exile's Return," originally published as "The Return of Paddy Kinsella" in *Sports Illustrated* (6 December 1954), is a compassionate and subtly defiant tale of an angry cuckolded husband who is unexpectedly reconciled to his wife and her child by another man. *The Red Petticoat* also includes "The Windows of Wonder," a salute to the power of the inspiring schoolteacher and a story considered to be an exemplar of the genre. The majority of the twenty stories in the collection were originally published in periodicals such as *Harper's Bazaar*, *The Kenyon Review*, *Mademoiselle*, the *Partisan Review*, and *The Sign*. In defiance of the prevailing conditions of the time, when marriage and reproduction rates were historically low in economically depressed Ireland, stories such as "Wedding Eve," "The Broken Lyre," and "Evening in Ireland" celebrate matrimony, sexuality, and fecundity. Beneath the stern facade of Catholic Ireland, MacMahon detected a sense of mild subversiveness often invisible to his peers, as revealed by the skittish nuns of "The Nunnery Garden" and by the title story, "The Red Petticoat." MacMahon's appealing cast of characters includes a severely physically deformed young woman beguiled by the unexpected attentions of a stranger; an eccentric and untutored genius who fascinates a learned professor; and, in both "O, Lonely Moon!" and "Sunday Afternoon. Sunny," cantankerous fathers who are reconciled with long-estranged children.

MacMahon also wrote several successful plays for the stage and television. The Sean O'Casey–influenced *The Bugle in the Blood* (1949), *The Song of the Anvil* (produced, 1960; published, 1967), and *The Honey Spike* (produced, 1961; published, 1967) were all first acted at Dublin's Abbey Theatre. *The Song of the Anvil*, a mixture of fantasy, satire, and folklore with music composed by Seán Ó Riada, was the choice of the Abbey Theatre for the International Theatre Festival in 1960. *Seachtar Fear Seacht Lá* (Seven Men, Seven Days), a commemorative pageant created by MacMahon and commissioned by the Gaelic Athletic Association, was staged in 1966 at Croke Park, Dublin, as part of the fiftieth-anniversary celebration of the Easter Rising. The children's play *The Bicycle Man* (1966), celebrating O'Donoghue, the activist who had nurtured MacMahon's interest in the Irish language, was broadcast on national television that same year. The measured and subtly revolutionary portrayal of Irish Travelers (tinkers) in the lyrical and highly acclaimed *The Honey Spike* was rooted in the contemporaneous political mobilization of this minority group; MacMahon's vibrant 1967 novel of the same title was based on the play. He was on intimate terms with the Kerry Travelers, whose tribal identity fascinated him, and he was one of the few Irish writers from a settled background who could actually speak their language. "A Portrait of Tinkers," a landmark article by MacMahon, was published in *Natural History* in 1971.

In 1972 MacMahon was granted an LL.D. from the National University of Ireland in recognition of his services to Irish literature. His translation from Irish of *Peig: The Autobiography of Peig Sayers of the Great Blasket Island*, the transcribed memoir of his acquaintance Peig Sayers, was published the following year and has gone through several editions. *The End of the World and Other Stories* (1976) is chiefly an assemblage of previous stories from *The Lion-Tamer* and *The Red Petticoat* and other short works initially broadcast on Irish or British radio or originally published in Irish periodicals. One of the stories in the collection, "The Gap of Life," exults in the mystery of heterosexual love (a favorite theme) in its depiction of an elderly couple who momentarily defy death with the aid of an idealistic young intermediary.

Although MacMahon's early short-fiction style tended toward Romantic enthusiasm, his later collections were more sparingly written. *The Sound of Hooves and Other Stories* (1985)—which includes two stories from *The End of the World*, "A Woman's Hair" and "The Gap of Life"—consists of twelve psychologically insightful and well-written stories. "The Right to be Maudlin," the first-person narrative of a woman forced to return her adopted baby to its natural parents, is emotionally powerful. The *Dictionary of Irish Literature* (1996) praised the complexity of form in "The French Cradle," which uses the inventive framing device of a probing American ethnohistorian who uncovers the folk memory of a seventeenth-century event during her stay in Kerry. Although MacMahon's imagined Ireland is perhaps still disproportionately peopled by priests in these later stories, his writing reflects the concerns of the time, such as the dismal fate of the Irish smallholder in the European Economic Community and changing social attitudes to the Catholic Church, the clergy, sexuality, and birth outside marriage.

The anecdotal first volume of MacMahon's autobiography, *The Master* (1992), is an account of his philosophy of teaching and his affectionate relations with his pupils and the wider community. In the second volume, *The Storyman* (1994), which concentrates on his literary career, he stresses that his stories were always the result of his observation of those around him. Typical of the enduring aspects of MacMahon's style, the seventeen stories in *The Tallystick and Other Stories* (1994) vary in emotional register, ranging from illuminating encounters to revealing character sketches. A motley collection, it was assembled from a variety of projects. "Apples for Sale" was originally written in Irish; "The Telescope" had been broadcast by the British Broadcasting Corporation (BBC); and "The Gentry Bell," "The Time of the Whitethorn," and "Jack Furey" were originally one-act plays. The stories deal tenderly but unflinchingly with the secret but mundane heartaches of family life: infertility, hidden illiteracy, the incontinence of a child with Down's syndrome, a long-ago infidelity inadvertently revealed in the haze of senility, and the seasonal ebb and flow of hostility, affection, desire, and indifference in marriage relationships. The major international success of MacMahon's early career was not repeated in his later life, however: Poolbeg Press of Dublin published most of his later works.

A man of many parts and achievements, Bryan MacMahon was loquacious, practical, eager, vigorous, and diligent, and he enjoyed new people and experiences. He was a shareholder in the Abbey Theatre and a member of the Irish Academy of Letters and of Aosdána, a prestigious association of creative artists in Ireland. In addition, MacMahon introduced the concept of writers' workshops to the Irish literary scene from the University of Iowa, where he was a visiting lecturer in Irish literature and folklore in 1964. He was named Kerryman of the Year in 1987 and received the American Ireland Fund Literary Award in 1993. MacMahon died on 13 February 1998 at Beaumont Hospital in Dublin, after an illness of several months. His final story collection, *A Final Fling: Conversations between Men and Women* (1998), consists of austere studies of the intensity of human interaction. As the subtitle suggests, each of the nineteen stories records an exchange between a man and a woman, ranging from Adam and Eve in "First" to a sick priest and his feisty old housekeeper in "Egg-timer." As always, MacMahon's characters and tone range from the ingenuous and child-like to the pragmatic and worldly: a girl acts as matchmaker between her widowed father and her favorite teacher, while a no-nonsense woman suggests to a startled acquaintance that he should father the child she longs for.

A review of the second volume of MacMahon's autobiography, *The Storyman*, in *The Irish Times* (21 January 1995) referred to him as "one of our greatest national assets." In "The Fabulous Realism of Bryan MacMahon" Martin praises his "matchless skill as a storyteller, the lyrical energy of his prose style, his mastery of dialogue, his subtle and varied narrative technique." Despite the general acknowledgment of MacMahon's significance, a full-length consideration of his works has yet to be produced. His writing received much attention and popular approval in his heyday, and his stories continue to be anthologized and appreciated by the general reader. Nonetheless, his dramas are rarely revived in the national theater, and scholars of Irish literature often overlook his large published output; none of his works was included in the monumental five-volume *Field Day Anthology of Irish Writing* (1991-2002). The Listowel Writers' Week festival honored MacMahon's diverse achievements, however, by renaming their prestigious annual short-story competition after him in 2000. The writer who reveled in the local is now most respectfully remembered in his hometown.

Interview:

Gordon Henderson, "An Interview with Bryan MacMahon," *Journal of Irish Literature*, 3, no. 3 (1974): 3-23.

Bibliography:

Joanne L. Henderson, "Checklist of Four Kerry Writers: George Fitzmaurice, Maurice Walch, Bryan MacMahon, and John B. Keane," *Journal of Irish Literature,* Listowel Writers Special Issue, 1, no. 2 (1972): 101-119.

References:

Eileen Battersby, "The Master Teacher of Ireland," *Irish Times,* 14 February 1998; p. 8;

Patrick Kavanagh, "Diary," *Envoy* (January 1950): 81-86;

Augustine Martin, "The Fabulous Realism of Bryan MacMahon," in *The Listowel Literary Phenomenon: North Kerry Writers—A Critical Introduction,* edited by Gabriel Fitzmaurice (Inverin: Cló Iar-Chonnachta, 1994), pp. 83-95;

Fintan O'Toole, "The Magic Glasses of George Fitzmaurice," in *The Listowel Literary Phenomenon,* pp. 13-25.

Papers:

Bryan MacMahon's letters to collector Jack O'Reilly are in the John J. Burns Library of Rare Books and Special Collections at Boston College, and annotated typescripts of his Abbey Theatre plays are in the National Library of Ireland. MacMahon's son and literary executor, Maurice MacMahon, recorded his father's conversations for fifteen years before the author's death. A limited-edition recording of material from the collection was released in 1998. The original recordings remain with the MacMahon family.

E. A. Markham

(1 October 1939 –   )

Greg C. Winston
Husson College

BOOKS: *Lambchops,* as Paul St. Vincent (Leicester, U.K.: Omens, 1976);

Love, Politics and Food (Cambridge, Mass.: Von Hallet, 1982);

Human Rites: Selected Poems, 1970–1982 (London: Anvil, 1984);

Something Unusual (London: Ambit, 1986);

Living in Disguise (London: Anvil, 1986);

Lambchops in Papua New Guinea (Stafford, U.K.: Sowe's Ear, 1986);

Towards the End of a Century (London & Dover, N.H.: Anvil, 1989);

Letter from Ulster and the Hugo Poems (Todmorden: Littlewood Arc, 1993);

Ten Stories (Sheffield, PAVIC, U.K.: Sheffield Hallam University, 1994);

Misapprehensions (London: Anvil, 1995);

A Papua New Guinea Sojourn: More Pleasures of Exile (Manchester: Carcanet, 1998);

Marking Time (Leeds: Peepal Tree, 1999);

A Rough Climate (London: Anvil, 2002);

Taking the Drawing Room through Customs (Leeds: Peepal Tree, 2002);

Lambchops with Sally Goodman: The Selected Poems of Paul St. Vincent and Sally Goodman (Cambridge, U.K.: Salt, 2004);

Meet Me in Mozambique (Birmingham, U.K.: Tindal Street Press, 2005).

OTHER: *Merely a Matter of Colour,* edited by Markham and Arnold Kingston (Edgware, U.K.: "Q" Books, 1973);

Hinterland: Caribbean Poetry from the West Indies and Britain, edited by Markham (Newcastle upon Tyne, U.K.: Bloodaxe, 1989);

Hugo Versus Montserrat, edited by Markham and Howard A. Fergus (Londonderry: Linda Lee Books, 1989);

The Penguin Book of Caribbean Short Stories, edited, with an introduction, by Markham (London & New York: Penguin, 1996);

Plant Care: A Festschrift for Mimi Khalvati, edited by Markham (Sheffield, U.K.: Linda Lee Books, 2004);

Ten Hallam Poets, edited by Markham and others (Sheffield, U.K.: Mews Press, 2005).

In the late 1950s, as a teenager newly arrived from the West Indies, E. A. Markham fell in love with London's West End. Captivated by theater, especially the drama of Anton Chekhov and William Shakespeare, he set his sights early on becoming a playwright. While employed for several years in London's rag trade, he acquired knowledge of the working city that eventually complemented a university education. He came to know the Aldwych and the Royal Court Theatres as well as the writers, actors, directors, and critics who worked in them. All formed indelible impressions on him. As Markham says, "these were the heady days of theatre": the period of Samuel Beckett, of Eugène Ionesco and theater of the absurd, and of John Osborne's *Look Back in Anger* (1956). Markham began to write plays then, continued at the University of Wales, and, in the late 1960s, was a member of a writing workshop led by theater critic John Elsom. During the ensuing decades, these seeds of literary interest germinated and became diverse publications: several books of poems, a novel, a travelogue, short-story collections, and anthologies of verse and fiction. Although well known as a poet and anthologist, Markham's significant contributions—both critical and creative—to Caribbean short fiction make him a significant practitioner of the short story in English.

Edward Archibald Neighton Markham was born 1 October 1939 on the island of Montserrat in the British West Indies, the youngest child of Alexander and Linda Markham. The couple effectively separated a few years later when Alexander Markham moved to Montreal, where he attended McGill University divinity school, and like several relatives of earlier generations, became a Methodist minister. He headed a national consortium of churches based in Toronto, and although there was talk of the family joining him there, the plan never materialized. Markham's mother remained in Montserrat with the four children, three brothers and a sister who maintained only the loosest of ties with their father.

During Markham's first sixteen years, the family divided its time between Plymouth, the capital, and Harris', a small village in a region on the east of the island, where the family owned land and property. His maternal grandmother, Margaret Lee, known to all in Harris' as Miss Dovie, lived in a hilltop Big House that had been in the family for nearly a century, its original foundation constructed not long after the abolition of slavery in the British Empire. By Miss Dovie's time it had grown into a large estate that was a social and economic center of Harris'. Besides the twelve-room main house, the extensive grounds included an animal pound to house stray livestock (featured in the story "The Pig Was Mine"), vegetable and spice gardens, and fruit trees, all of which afforded the place a high degree of self-sufficiency. Many neighbors came to rely on the facilities of the house, often using the well-furnished kitchen to make cassava bread and other staples.

Although the house was abandoned and fell into disrepair following Miss Dovie's death in 1953 and the family's departure for England three years later, it remains a constant, centering presence in Markham's poetry and prose. Returning to Harris' years later, Markham noticed that many village houses contained wood and windows removed from the abandoned family home. This detail becomes an important motif in the story "Life before the Revolution," when the narrator returns to Montserrat and meets with a similar scene; rather than feeling downcast or bitter, he is "half-pleased" at seeing the memory and function of the old house endure through its pragmatic fragmentation. The ruin is also a key psychological space in such poems as "The Boy of the House," "Late Return," and "Nellie in the Bread Room." The last of these poems, in a grouping titled "The House in Montserrat," solemnly states that "the House eludes / both us and History."

As Markham recalls, family life at Miss Dovie's was a matriarchal affair. She ruled over the house and environs, despite a bad leg that often kept her bedridden. At night the grandchildren were often asked to read to her in her bedroom. More exciting to the youngest grandson was an adjacent drawing room with a large bookcase. In this room he first read and enjoyed such works as *Gulliver's Travels* (1726), *Pilgrim's Progress* (1678), and *Robinson Crusoe* (1719). Other volumes, such as Edward Gibbon's *Decline and Fall of the Roman Empire* (1776–1788), went unread but not unnoticed. The title of Markham's third collection of short stories, *Taking the Drawing Room through Customs* (2002), invokes that room and those early reading experiences as the beginnings of a literary education and career. As Markham now recalls, "We came to England to houses without drawing rooms. In the Caribbean, it was a metaphor for a thinking space, a relaxing space, a Dr. Johnson space to talk about things. That space in Harris', on a Sunday afternoon, extended the range of our interests; there was a range of reference there you wouldn't have even heard in school."

While books became more significant to him, the young Markham did not feel the influence of many people from beyond the family during the insular years at Harris'. He cites one notable exception in Teacher Morgan, a local schoolmaster and freethinker who regularly called at Miss Dovie's house. Teacher Morgan's atheistic intellect provided a diametric opposition to Miss Dovie's traditional Methodist Christianity. In frequent and typically animated visits (all the more so if they followed a stopover at the local rum shop), the schoolmaster imported a wide array of knowledge, including pedantic, provocative logic from beyond the pale of Miss Dovie's experience or interest. Teacher Morgan became the model for the character of Professor Croissant in the novel *Marking Time* (1999); he is also the basis for Markham's fictional character C. J. Harris. Among Teacher Morgan's favorite expressions was one suggesting that if someone is going to lie, he should at least do so intelligently. For a young boy beginning to take an interest in imagination and fictionalization, such advice took on a tenor all its own.

Although Markham left Montserrat shortly before his seventeenth birthday, life there had already shaped him to a great extent. As Howard Fergus observes, "half of the foundation of his artistic life was already laid in Montserrat, in his village, at the single grammar school for the privileged, by his family connection which guaranteed attendance at that school, in the landscape and in the culture." As with most Caribbean expatriates, the home island has remained at the core of Markham's identity. He regularly returns there, maintaining family and social ties; the island's history, culture, landscape, and climate figure prominently in much of his writing.

In 1956 when Markham moved with his mother and sister to England, his elder brothers were already there, doing jobs that belied their grammar school education, though studying in their spare time. Delaying school at his own volition, Markham spent the next three years working in various factories that manufactured women's belts and handbags. He did so, he says, more for the experience than for the money. His work, because of its location, exposed him to all the colorful life and artistic activity of the buzzing West End of London. Markham was participant and witness to one of the most significant periods of social and economic change in the city–a postwar building boom and a massive influx of new immigrants from Ireland and Eastern Europe (Hungary) as well as from Commonwealth nations and colonies around the globe, which were changing the look and feel of British life. For many, including the teenage Markham, theaters were at the core of this revitalization and process of reinvention. In addition to the dramatic playhouses, Markham took great interest in the lively music-hall scene, at one point even making his own record. He wrote his first novel ("mercifully lost," he says), but the theater remained, for the time being, his real passion.

In 1962 Markham enrolled at the University of Wales at Lampeter, earning a B.A. in English and philosophy in 1965. These two branches of study merged in his first play, *The Masterpiece,* performed at Lampeter by the university Drama Society in his final year there. He describes the play as "a bit of a Platonic game, idealism coming up against the reality of the body." This fundamental tension can be found in much of his subsequent work.

After Markham finished his university education, he found his way back to London and into Elsom's theater workshop at Shepherd's Bush, where plays were written and staged by a group of young and ambitious writers. The experience was enjoyable and enlightening, but as several of his own plays were rejected by the mainstream theaters, Markham began to recycle and reinvent his materials in new genres. Within a few years, by the start of the 1970s, he began to publish poems in magazines, many of which were speeches taken directly from the plays and developed into dramatic monologues somewhat reminiscent of poems by Robert Browning. In this way Markham gradually expanded his skills and amended his ambitions.

The initial phase of a teaching career followed from this writing. From 1968 to 1970 Markham was a lecturer in English and liberal studies at Kilburn Polytechnic in London. During this period he came to know the growing Caribbean artists' movement in Britain, guided by such writers as Edward Kamau Brathwaite, Andrew Salkey, and John La Rose. Markham spent some months performing on the road with a troupe of poets and actors, The Bluefoot Travellers, led by poet James Berry. In London's first black bookshops and at inaugural cultural events such as the Radical, Black and Third-World Book Fair, Markham began to meet other writers and artists intent on giving a voice to the West Indian experience in Britain. Such experiences have led Alison Donnell and Sarah Lawson to count Markham one of several key figures responsible for "charting the transition from Caribbean to Black British Writing" during the 1960s and 1970s.

Interest in drama kept Markham involved with Elsom's workshop. After a performance at Shepherd's

Front cover of Markham's 1986 story collection, which includes the story cycle "The Montserrat Connection," set on the British West Indian island of Markham's birth (Bruccoli Clark Layman Archives)

Bush, a visiting Jamaican named Noel Vaz was impressed with the "non-naturalistic style" of Markham's drama. Vaz, who was connected with the Creative Arts Centre in Jamaica, raised the idea of Markham's taking a West Indian theater troupe back to the islands. In 1970–1971 Markham traveled to St. Vincent, Montserrat, and Trinidad as director of the Caribbean Theatre Workshop, performing at University of the West Indies extramural centers and campuses and helping to establish satellite writing centers for the school. The repertoire for the tour included two of Markham's own unpublished plays, *The Private Life of the Public Man* and *Dropping Out Is Violence.*

Markham spent the next several years in continental Europe, first working with a building cooperative in the Alpes Maritimes region of France to restore old houses. He next taught English in Germany. Throughout this period he published poems and stories in many magazines, leading to a creative-writing fellowship at Hull College of Higher Education (where he met poet-librarian Philip Larkin) and a prestigious C. Day Lewis Fellowship at Brent, London. In 1983 Markham took a VSO-World Bank position as media coordinator for the Engan provincial government in the rural highlands of Papua New Guinea. He gives an account of the experience in the travelogue *A Papua New Guinea Sojourn: More Pleasures of Exile* (1998). From the titular nod toward the 1960 George Lamming memoir and through allusions to writers working across similar ethnic and cultural divisions—Joseph Conrad, Graham Greene, and V. S. Naipaul—the book developed a postcolonial perspective. Markham's West Indian and British background, along with the dual nature of his position, enabled him to raise provocative questions about residual imperialism in Papua New Guinea after independence. By the end of the account, the reader understands why Markham declined the World Bank's offer to extend his appointment.

Markham returned to the United Kingdom in 1985. In the late 1980s he served as writer-in-residence for the City of Ipswich and for the University of Ulster, Coleraine. In 1991 he became head and then professor of creative writing at Sheffield Hallam University in South Yorkshire. As Markham wrote in the introduction to *Hinterland* in 1989, "If I had an image for my life (and hence, one that informed my work) I suppose it would be 'Pioneer' . . . the resourceful traveller having something to offer the host society." In his extensive travels and diverse roles, Markham has made the pioneer image his reality. As Louis James asserts in *Caribbean Literature in English* (1999), "Markham reflects a centrifugal dynamic in Caribbean writing." This dynamic reflection clearly extends into the genre of the short story.

Markham branched into fiction relatively late in his career; his first short stories were not published until the mid 1970s. Stewart Brown notes in "E. A. Markham: *Towards the End of a Century* and *Hinterland: Carribbean Poetry from the West Indies and Britain*," a review in *Poetry Wales* (no. 2, 1990), "Markham's work has always resisted convenient critical pigeon-holes." Still, recurrent themes emerge in his fiction, ranging from black male identity, transatlantic migration, family dynamics, and island boyhood, to meditations on contemporary international travel, romantic relationships, and the pressures of being a writer. Constantly shifting settings—from Britain to Montserrat to continental Europe and back again—reflect the author's real-life travels and a willingness to invent literary places. An amalgam of styles supports this diversity of content. As James notes, "his first love, theatre, brings a multi-vocal quality to his writing which relates the Caribbean to the international scene." Thus, shifting perspectives and temporal structures shape many of Markham's stories. Objective third-person narration alternates with limited omniscient and first-person perspectives, sometimes within the frame of a single story. Occasionally, the effect resembles that of eavesdropping on conversations between familiars, with in-jokes and contextual meanings often tantalizingly suspended just beyond the reach of the reader.

Amid such overall fluidity of form, a consistency emerges, nonetheless, primarily at the levels of imagery and character. As in his poetry, domestic and natural images tend especially to dominate the Caribbean-based stories, tales of reminiscence that delve into early memories and associated images: white sheets spread to dry on the green lawn one warm afternoon decades before; tropical orchards, tended vegetable gardens, and cinnamon trees; and cassava breads and sugar cakes that connect youth to maturity, bright leeward islands to gray northern cities. Those who iron the linens and bake the cakes become a constant presence in the form of industrious servant girls, God-fearing grandmothers, and scandalously entertaining schoolmasters. Finally, he remembers the West Indian mother caught between her longing for lifestyle, social status, and possessions left behind and her hope that something better lies in store for her children in urban Britain.

Something Unusual, published in 1986, was Markham's first extended collection of stories. Its opening section, "Life-Swapping," features four stories centered on Philpot, one of several narrative personae Markham developed a decade earlier under the pseudonym Paul St. Vincent. In these stories, the aging Philpot appears worn down but not entirely devoid of hope, scheme, or dream. He retains a prideful but self-conscious fashion in "The White Suit"; looks back in wistful remembrance on multiple past lives and loves in "Wives of Forgetfulness"; and muses on potential destinations but improbable escapes in "The Albania Connection" and "A Continental Romance." The latter tale concludes with humor typical of many of Markham's stories and poems, as Philpot meets his femme fatale in the south of France: an apparent foul play gets locally interpreted as a quasi-sacrificial gesture, performed for the benefit of the tourist and wine-making trades while doing no significant harm to the production of literary fiction. As if propelled by the death of the character, the collection henceforth launches itself freely in multiple directions.

The first direction is across the Atlantic in "The Montserrat Connection," stories that form the heart of the book. Its tales link moments of stubborn childhood resolve to various grown-up calls for courage, whether in the face of romantic loss, institutional racism, or forgetfulness and mortality. As the subtitle suggests, Montserrat—by both its presence and its absence—is the focal point for the seven stories. Sometimes it forms a distant

Front cover for Markham's 2002 collection of stories that feature Caribbean-born Englishman Pewter Stapleton, the autobiographical protagonist of Markham's 1999 novel, Marking Time *(Bruccoli Clark Layman Archives)*

memory; other times, a distinct setting. As Fergus has noted of Markham's writing generally, "over all there is a brooding and abiding Montserratian consciousness." The statement perhaps most readily applies to this story sequence.

In "The Pig Was Mine," the first-person narrator relates a boyhood incident of bidding at auction for a stray pig held in his grandmother's animal pound. His theft of the family's church collection boxes to back the winning bid shocks and dismays his grandmother and all concerned. The often anthologized "Mammie's Form at the Post Office" revisits this sensitive theme of currency transfer, this time with the Royal Mail taking over the role of authority from the church. Deceivingly simple in its brevity and topic—a woman's unsuccessful attempt to send a postal money order to the West Indies—the story poses significant questions about race relations and postimperial consciousness in contemporary Britain.

Starting with confusion over the designations "HOME" and "ABROAD," and followed by a thoughtless bureaucratic conflation of such disparate Commonwealth locations as Bangladesh, Pakistan, and the West Indies, the story builds into a provocative and frustrating personal exchange between a customer and a postal clerk. Brown regards the story as a blend of "confusions, racism, and just plain crossed cultural wires. . . ." Miscommunication about basic geography and economics underlies the more serious problem of degrading someone perceived as cultural Other: "He was treating her like a child now." "Mammie's Form at the Post Office" also represents one of Markham's most effective prose portrayals of a female protagonist, providing a convincing glimpse into the interior urgencies and insecurities of a woman confronted by an insensitive male authority figure. As such, it invites reading on the overlapping levels of postcolonial, racial, and gender politics.

"Sugar-Cake Day" explores themes of aging and memory, as a migrant mother copes with the new pressures of living under the care of her adult children. Shortening autumn days in Britain parallel her diminishing lifetime, causing her thoughts to range across the distorted time span of her emigration from the West Indies: "–how much real time had passed? Fifteen years? Five?" The cluttered spaces and loud activity of the household–an amalgam of wrestling children and blaring television sets–add to her morbid sense of confinement, until at last the thought of making a sugar-cake opens into a liberating recollection of her youth. The limited omniscience of the narrative leads to an overall identification with the mother that contrasts with brief but telling glimpses into her children's calloused (if well-intentioned) approach to her situation.

"Diversions," the final segment of the collection, includes "Now What Was That All About?" among the most politically and sexually charged of Markham's stories. The central character, Sally, although her last name is not given, is Sally Goodman, a white Englishwoman whose fictional persona Markham devised in collaboration with a workshop of women writers in Germany in the 1970s. Tired of being the focus of constant and countless lecherous male stares in the park, Sally decides one day to call their collective bluff by inviting one of the complete strangers home with her. He is a stranger in the most literal sense, an immigrant of uncertain origin; Sally identifies him alternately as Turkish, Italian, and Greek but never ultimately resolves the question. It is not important. Much as Mammie was to the postal clerk, the man for Sally simply represents a cultural and racial Other. As he becomes her overnight prisoner and plaything in a sado-domestic mind game, Sally achieves a reversal of traditional gender power roles:

> She took him back to the bathroom, used her own toothbrush, and brought blood copiously from his mouth. When she kissed him, he whimpered.
>
> No hard feelings. She now made him understand that he was master of the house.

A kind of comic brutality yields eventually to a puzzling illusion of control as the story concludes when Sally encounters her own double in the park the next day.

Markham says his short fiction "grew up in total isolation of anyone I wanted to emulate. It grew out of poetic footnotes. Other writers were generally more of an influence on my ambition than on my style or form." He claims two such influences in Alice Munro and T. Coraghessan Boyle. In his introduction to *The Penguin Book of Caribbean Short Stories* (1996), Markham considers Boyle's work within the broader context of epic realism, features of which can be found in the "new wave" of Caribbean short fiction. Such characteristics include:

> non-linear structure (often fragmented and episodic; historical (or current affairs) frame of reference; political parody/satire; literary recycling and in-jokes, I'm afraid (captions, subheadings and the occasional footnote); research: familiarity with the esoteric (but undermined by being worn lightly, or presented as newspaper of encyclopedia inserts); surface sparkle; lack of solemnity–and, with an upbeat tone assuming the collusion of the reader.

Ten Stories (1994) includes several of these "new wave" formal features, even while it extends certain thematic preoccupations of the previous collection, including emigration, black male identity, and Caribbean domestic and natural landscapes.

"Miss Joyce and Bobcat" commences the collection in a West Indian village setting; the title characters, a haughty matriarch and an earthy handyman, involve themselves in a prolonged ritual dance of attraction and avoidance. Anything but simple romantic comedy or local color, the story offers a brief but poignant expression of island life through its profiling of class and gender relations. Like Mr. Watford in Paule Marshall's "Barbados," Miss Joyce is a returned emigrant whose years in England spent "lifting up racists off their hospital beds to clean them" have led her back home to a relatively comfortable retirement in the islands. But if Miss Joyce, like Mr. Watford, lives "profoundly alone," she is not "secure in loneliness."

Markham notes how the character of Bobcat has been misinterpreted by white editors, mainly by the inadvertent emendation of a single word from the opening of the story: "Bobcat, the brute, unaware of Miss Joyce, continued his desecration of Miss Joyce's lawn, digging a hole with an impressive-looking machine." The author originally intended the adjective "aware" (instead of "unaware"), as he puts it, to convey something of "an inner life" to Bobcat–something too often denied black male characters by white editors and readers. If "aware," then Bobcat hears Miss Joyce but makes a conscious decision to pretend he does not in order to proceed with his manipulative or flirtatious game. To regard Bobcat as "unaware"–either of Miss Joyce or the dynamic between the two of them–is to strip him of agency and humanity. This effect is just what the original editors of the story achieved; the misprint remains in subsequent printings.

"NJK Holt," two stories further along in the collection, enlarges this exploration of black male identity. The naming (or rather, unnaming) of the title character itself represents a problem of identity. His nickname is derived from that of a former Jamaican cricket star named J. K. Holt Jr., and, as the narrator notes, "even his name was not that original." As in the tradition of Caribbean calypso singers, the nickname reinvents identity but with a negating twist: "So when Holt opened up his shop in Ladbroke Grove in 1957, the boys decided to call him N. J. K. Holt–*Not* J. K. Holt, to distinguish him from the cricketer."

The style and direction of the story also express Holt's search for identity and economic opportunity as a mid-twentieth-century immigrant to Britain. A shifting narrative structure mirrors the changes; somewhat like the newly arrived West Indian in London, the form of the story must reinvent itself several times before taking firm root in its surroundings. Thus, Holt's own voice initiates the storytelling before gradually yielding to an omniscient voice that recounts the failures and successes from decades of immigrant experience. An unlucky business venture and unviable relationships are the milestones of this experience, shapes of a self made and remade over decades. Migrant existence becomes as temporary and protean as the fleeting identities of the taxi drivers at the end of the story, when Holt, hoping to meet his daughter (known herself by two names–Cristobel and Mandy), encounters a bearded stranger instead.

Ten Stories serves as the platform from which Markham introduces the fictitious Caribbean island of St. Caesare. In "A Short History of St. Caesare" a Montserratian writer living in Sweden invents a small island nation as a pretense for attending a United Nations conference on the sea. What begins as a cocktail-hour dare becomes an implemented hoax, as the narrator and his scholarly American girlfriend painstakingly research and "discover" their island, coloring it in as realistically as possible with a population, economics, history, and language. The joke extends in postmodern fashion beyond the text, as the opening pages of the collection include a map of Columbus's second voyage showing an undiscovered St. Caesare just east of Montserrat. As the story explains, "Columbus didn't name St. Caesare because he didn't *see* it. He couldn't see it because it was on the *Windward* side of Montserrat (also that's the rough side, another reason why he didn't take that route)."

Apart from the humor of its hoax, "A Short History of St. Caesare" provides a meditation on what making fiction means–in both a textual and a cultural sense.

Markham circa 2002 (photograph by Steven Earnshaw; from Taking the Drawing Room through Customs, *2002; Bruccoli Clark Layman Archives)*

Just as he did with the detached poetic personae Lambchops, Sally Goodman, and Philpot, Markham steps into the space he has created. As invented topography, St. Caesare is reminiscent of Lamming's fictionalized West Indies, the "virgin territories of San Cristobal" in the novel *Natives of My Person* (1972). Both afford their writers an opportunity to step outside history. Sometimes, however, such a step leads to an ironic turnabout, as the narrator of "A Short History" of St. Caesare discovers when he learns nearly two decades after his joke that a couple of dozen people claim to hail literally from the utopia. Unleashed by its author, the story takes on a life and momentum of its own.

Once introduced, Caribbean geography commands the remainder of the collection. A mother's and son's conflicting memories of the life left behind become the focus of "Life before the Revolution," perhaps the most autobiographical of Markham's stories. Following the death of the mother, the son returns to Montserrat to bring her body home for burial. While the real island name is used, Markham substitutes the fictitious village and town names of "Coderington" and "Barville" for Harris' and Plymouth. Walking amid the ruins of the family's former home and gardens at Coderington, the first-person narrator experiences an epiphany and confirmation of his mother's hold on the minute details and "secrets" of life before their 1956 embarkation for Britain.

The preoccupation with St. Caesare continues into the final story. "President Horace the Second, Howe" features an emboldened and quirky St. Caesarian launching a 1992 campaign for the White House. The tale ultimately says more about interpersonal than international political support, as the narrator and his family look after Horace from afar.

"O No, Not That One Again" tells of Markham's own development as a West Indian writer honing his skills in Britain, with a central character (known simply as the Professor) who feels compelled by fellow "Pioneers, St. Caesarians in exile," to use knowledge and secrets gained from First World experience "to extend the land-mass of St. Caesare." In a dialogue of transnational significations—Germans, Canadians, and Americans, *Gulliver's Travels,* and McDonald's fast food—in pioneer nicknames appropriated from notable European thinkers (Francis Bacon, John Calvin, and William Thomson, first Baron Kelvin), and in a final toast to Liverpool, the story exhibits the mixed unease, confidence, and sophistication of a West Indian life transplanted to international surroundings.

Taking the Drawing Room through Customs features twenty-two new and uncollected stories alongside eleven stories from the previous collections. Pewter Stapleton, protagonist of *Marking Time,* emerges as a central character and narrative voice. His relationship to an aging mother becomes a prominent theme, as do old friendships, "pioneering" international travel, politics, and cricket. The collection frequently skirts the thin boundary between fiction and nonfiction, story and essay; for instance, in "Our Man in KL," Stapleton refers to the title story of a new collection, "Taking the Drawing Room Through Customs." (In fact, there is no such story, though an essay of that title appears as a poetic footnote to *A Rough Climate* [2002].)

"A Short History of Employment in Britain" follows Pewter's mother through her one and only day of work at the belt and handbag factory that employed her son for several years and her struggle to accept the change in class status that comes with leaving the Caribbean for Britain. "Pascoe & Co." details the long friendship of three Caribbean emigrants and an institute of institutionalized racism that recalls "Mammie's Form at the Post Office" even while its victims, from a subsequent generation, respond quite differently. Philpot, Horace, Castine, and St. Caesare return in "Safe House for Philpot," extending the characters and landscapes of previous stories. Meanwhile, references to contemporary American politicians such as George Bush, Michael Dukakis, and Hillary Clinton give the stories both a contemporary humor and a more serious global outlook. Similarly, "World Cup, 2002," which begins as an account of a soccer game between Montserrat and Bhutan, the world's lowest-ranked teams, played simultaneously with the Brazil-Germany championship, becomes a meditation on much more than soccer. The story updates Markham's fictional project while echoing his pioneer's concerns of cross-cultural understanding and awareness.

Alongside his creative work, Markham has made significant critical contributions to the short story. James, in *Caribbean Literature in English,* describes Markham as "a tireless editor and publicist," words that apply to his editions of short fiction, drama, and poetry, and to his editorial roles for the magazines *Artrage* and *Ambit*. Markham describes his intention, as editor of *The Penguin Book of Caribbean Short Stories,* "to show that Caribbean writers have not been left behind . . . to show Caribbean people in touch with the form as well as the theme of the short story at the present time" (personal interview with Markham, August 2002). The introductory essay and range of selections themselves outline several distinct phases in the development of the Caribbean short story throughout the twentieth century; thus, it contributes to an ongoing discussion in Caribbean literary and cultural studies.

In a recent unpublished essay, Markham poses the question "Why do you write?" His response, in part, is

> Because I am curious about my own life in a way that I don't expect others to be, and writing about it seems a relatively harmless form of self-promotion. More respectably, I am fascinated by my inherited language (indeed, by the notion of language) and would like to add my inflections to its large meaning: I'm fascinated by the privilege—which seems to me in no way schizophrenic—of being a voice somewhat different from others and at the same time one that strangers can adopt as familiar; and I write because writing helps me to discover and reveal things about myself that I would prefer, in polite company, not to have revealed.

If the gift of the language is one reason for writing, elsewhere Markham has noted the importance of his writing as a type of personal legacy:

> Being a secular person who does not believe in religion or gods, any of those things, I still believe in a

sense of continuity, the notion of extending one's life. You do this in two ways if you are not religious, by having families or by making some sort of statement. I'm very happy at the notion that what will survive me is a shelf of books.

The contents of that shelf promise to provoke much critical discussion in the years to come. In a review of Markham's poetry, Brown notes the difficulty in categorizing his writing: "He's always seemed a maverick, determinedly dramatising that outsider's experience and measuring the world by its tangents and contradictions." The same might be said of his work in the short-story form. Gavin Ewart describes Markham as "a writer of great intelligence and vitality." Thus far, E. A. Markham's impact on British and Caribbean short fiction—from creative, scholarly, and editorial angles—suggests a vital, intelligent legacy well in the making.

References:

Stewart Brown, Introduction, in *Oxford Book of Caribbean Short Stories,* edited by Brown and John Wickham (Oxford: Oxford University Press, 1999);

Allison Donnell and Sarah Lawson, eds., *The Routledge Reader in Caribbean Literature* (New York: Routledge, 1996), pp. 295–297;

Howard Fergus, "E. A. Markham's Montserrat," in *A Festschrift for E. A. Markham,* edited by Freda Volans and Tracey O'Rourke (Sheffield: Linda Lee Books, 1999), pp. 38–50;

Bruno Gallo, "E. Archie Markham: A Poet of Many Voices," *Caribana,* 5 (1996): 71–116;

Polly Patullo, "Under the Volcano," *Guardian,* 31 August 2002.

Papers:

A collection of E. A. Markham's papers is at the Brynmore Jones Library at the University of Hull.

Adam Mars-Jones
(26 October 1954 –)

Brett Josef Grubisic
University of British Columbia

See also the Mars-Jones entry in *DLB 207: British Novelists Since 1960, Third Series.*

BOOKS: *Lantern Lecture and Other Stories* (London: Faber & Faber, 1981); republished as *Fabrications* (New York: Knopf, 1981);

The Darker Proof: Stories from a Crisis, by Mars-Jones and Edmund White (London: Faber & Faber, 1987; enlarged edition, New York: New American Library, 1988);

Monopolies of Loss (London: Faber & Faber, 1992; New York: Knopf, 1993);

The Waters of Thirst (London: Faber & Faber, 1993; New York: Knopf, 1994);

Blind Bitter Happiness (London: Chatto & Windus, 1997).

OTHER: *Mae West Is Dead: Recent Lesbian and Gay Fiction,* edited by Mars-Jones (London: Faber & Faber, 1983);

Venus Envy: On Masculinity and Its Discontents (London: Chatto & Windus, 1990);

Mafia!: An Anthology of New Fiction, introduction by Mars-Jones (Norwich: University of East Anglia, 1993).

SELECTED PERIODICAL PUBLICATION–
UNCOLLECTED: "Everything Is Different in Your House," *Granta,* 75 (Autumn 2001): 191–216.

Adam Mars-Jones writes for a living and for years has been a prolific contributor of occasional essays and movie and book reviews to influential American and British periodicals; his fiction, while appearing more sporadically, has assured him a secure place in contemporary literature. Moreover, described in *Washington Post Book World* (30 May 1988) as undertaking a "deeply original and unsentimental exploration of the effects of AIDS," and in the *Guardian* (25 July 1993) as "the Wilfred Owen of this new long-drawn and deadly trench warfare," Mars-Jones has become particularly renowned for his somber and understated observations of contemporary British middle-class white gay male culture and

Adam Mars-Jones (photograph by Jerry Bauer; from Monopolies of Loss, *1993; Bruccoli Clark Layman Archives)*

the AIDS pandemic that has become so much a part of its fabric.

Mars-Jones was born on 26 October 1954 in London and has remained close to it since; the city is the conventional backdrop for much of his fiction. He grew up in relative affluence with his parents William, a judge and an authoritarian father, and Sheila (Cobon), briefly an attorney, who was depressive and not infrequently ailing. Mars-Jones attended Westminster School and later Cambridge University, where he was awarded a B.A. (1976) and an M.A. (1978). His educational aspirations then led him to the United States to pursue a doctorate in American literature at the University of Virginia. Once there, in addition to being awarded a Hoyns Fellowship and the Benjamin C. Moomaw Prize for Oratory (1980), he also discovered the university's Creative Writing Program. In the introduction to *Mafia!: An Anthology of New Fiction* (1993), Mars-Jones recalls his three years in Virginia, ostensibly researching and writing a dissertation, as time well spent—auditing creative-writing courses and developing his craft: "my project was not learning how to write, exactly, but somehow finessing my way to self-belief, when my culture had taught me to prize only diffidence."

Mars-Jones returned to Britain with a manuscript, later published as *Lantern Lecture and Other Stories* (1981). The collection brought him acclaim; it was reviewed favorably in *TLS: The Times Literary Supplement* and *Washington Post Book World;* won the Somerset Maugham Award for 1982; and vaulted him to a visibility that led to his being chosen by *Granta* as one of Twenty Best Young Novelists (awarded to him once again in 1993). The three stories of *Lantern Lecture* (the titular one was excluded from the U.S. edition) showcase the formal and thematic variety of Mars-Jones's fiction as well as his not infrequently droll point of view.

"Hoosh-Mi: A Farrago of Scurrilous Untruths" (1977), for instance, is a playful, patently imaginary, and irreverent study of Queen Elizabeth's final weeks of life; she succumbs to hydrophobia, which was transmitted by her rabid dog. The story provides a relatively rare early example of British convention-flouting and self-reflexive postmodernist fiction; Chapter One is followed by Part Two, Book Three, Four and V, for instance; and the narrators of the story include Dr. John Bull, a speaker at the Republic Society's Annual Dinner (who lectures on "Royalty and the Unreal") and the unnamed operative in "Operation Pinprick," responsible for covering up the reasons for the queen's unseemly behavior during her Australian royal tour. While the story comes across as an elaborate, lengthy (seventy-seven-page), and clever joke, which affectionately, if at times pointedly, mocks the royal family and its value in English culture, Mars-Jones nonetheless incorporates a meditation on celebrity and the nature of a life led under constant public scrutiny.

"Bathpool Park" (1980) appropriates the life and trial of Donald Neilson ("The Black Panther"), the notorious British thief and kidnapper who was arrested in 1975. In a manner initially reminiscent of Truman Capote's *In Cold Blood* (1966), the ninety-five-page story traces details about Neilson's spree of domestic burglaries and supplies background to the botched kidnapping that resulted in the victim's accidental death. Mars-Jones re-creates the trial, complete with ersatz testimony and comic behind-the-scenes deliberation. The tone is decidedly ironic and gently mocking; while Mars-Jones's ostensible goal is observation of a criminal mind and the judicial system, his story is saturated with irreverence. In keeping with one of the preoccupations of "Hoosh-Mi," the narration's representation of the police and the press is less quasi-journalistic realism than a mannered presentation of players in a piece of complex social theater.

"Lantern Lecture" (1979), the briefest of the three stories, has an aptly episodic, slide-show-like structure and exhibits significant scenes from the life of Philip Scott Yorke. The protagonist grows up in threadbare Erddig Hall, a manor that "represents and monumentalizes" the Yorke family's crumbling foundation of coal money; in his adult years he lives there in a converted pantry and offers rambling tours of the family home, now maintained by the National Trust. "Lantern Lecture" is a strange but affecting portrait of extreme eccentricity. Isolated by his privilege and naturally inclined toward "puzzlement," he exists free to follow his caprices and compulsions within "one huge deranged machine perfectly corresponding to Philip's need for unlikely projects." He writes unperformed biblical dramas, drives a tour bus in Spain, gives magic-lantern lectures about his house and history, and otherwise "potters through the countryside on errands so small that no-one else would hear their call" before his slow fade into death.

Mars-Jones's later shift in focus and style is anticipated by his editing project, *Mae West Is Dead: Recent Lesbian and Gay Fiction* (1983). In the introduction, "Gay Fiction and the Reading Public," much of which muses on Nahan Aldyne's 1980 gay detective novel *Vermilion,* Mars-Jones surveys the recent growth and visibility of gay culture in Britain. He locates in it "an assortment of improvised moralities combining in various proportions reaction against, and imitation of, heterosexual precedents" and expresses concern about the political ramifications of particular formations or prevalent ideas within the gay urban "ghetto." In response to some of these pat and blinkered real-life assumptions (he highlights "The ghetto sets you free. Men are monoliths, women are mosaics. Politics are irrelevant," for instance), he promotes a model of literature (and a short-fiction anthology) that is politically engaged. Mars-Jones writes, "between one backlash and the next, with the appropriate fears and the appropriate confidence, this collection of lesbian and gay fiction sets itself as much against the expectations of subcultural commerce, as against the studied indifference of the dominant culture."

In the introduction to *Mae West Is Dead,* moreover, Mars-Jones speculates that his disquietude about the contemporary gay mainstream may soon be outdated. To him, AIDS, the "1982 epidemic of panic and sexual fear," is of such magnitude that earlier conditions and conflicts will lose their priority if not be rendered altogether irrelevant, both at a cultural and an individual level. He reiterates much the same point later in "Introduction: Monopolies of Loss" (1992): "Aids is a theme that won't let go of me, or else I won't let go of it. It isn't really a question of social responsibility. How often does a writer not have to go looking for a subject, but more or less have to barricade his door against it? There is a sweetness here not cancelled out by the bitterness of the subject itself." Without exception his subsequent fiction remains concentrated on gay male culture and the nuances and impact of mortal illnesses.

In contrast to the stories of *Lantern Lecture,* his later work reveals far less evidence of Mars-Jones's experimenting with form and playing with the conventions of literary representation. Instead, it is more traditionally realist and, despite its unapologetic sexual directness, proximate to the liberal humanist tradition. His next publication, the co-written *The Darker Proof: Stories from a Crisis* (1987), is composed of two stories by the preeminent American writer Edmund White and four by Mars-Jones.

The collection offers close inspections of the course of illness within a community; since AIDS is never named in the stories, illness takes on a more generic and thus universal function. Elegiac, yet documentary and on occasion pointedly political, the stories are literary meditations that play a necessary social and activist role. In retrospect, Mars-Jones explains in the introduction of *Monopolies of Loss* (1992): "Even when I thought that the problems of writings about Aids satisfactorily were insurmountable, for me at any rate, I still felt that it would be a good thing, even politically, if the trick could be managed. Fiction might create a psychological space in which the epidemic could be contemplated, with detachment rather than denial or apocalyptic fear."

Mars-Jones's four narratives in *The Darker Proof* capture the sheer discomfort of chronic illness while also commenting on what Susan Sontag calls the "trappings of metaphor" in *Illness as a Metaphor*—that is, the often deleterious cultural inscription of diseases and those afflicted by them. The narrator of "Slim" claims to have taken "that word" out of circulation; he has, he explains, heard it too often. In addition to providing a detailed portrait of the various tribulations and indignities of severe illnesses, the story gives an account of his prickly relationship with a medical volunteer, Buddy, whose services and companionship he appreciates far more than he lets on. In fact, Buddy's mystique, reflected in his determination to go on and on, is what helps draw the narrator away from complete apathy and surrender. "Over-overtired" from medication and the perpetual onslaught of the disease, the narrator's perspective veers between self-pity, determination, and gallows humor, and testifies to his frail heroism.

Gareth, the narrator of "An Executor," expresses frustration and sadness as he fulfills his executor's role and removes markedly "gay" personal effects from his friend's flat. His perspective makes a theme of the stigma of homosexuality (and a disease associated with it) within the heterosexual dominant culture, the failures of the body, and the stratified social significance of an individual's death. An intimate friend of Charles Hartly, recently dead after protracted infirmity, Gareth finds himself playing contradictory roles with Charles's family and friends. Though he was with Charles's family in a special ward of the hospital ("a unique horizontal mine of horror stories, all of them with morals") on Charles's last day, Gareth feels himself being shut out as the family refashions Charles in a way that makes him acceptable to their tastes. Gareth is installed at the center of the family group, but at the same time, the performance he is pressured to enact inhibits him from expressing himself or honoring the personality of the "true" Charles. Gareth himself expresses ambivalence about the role Charles has assigned to him; he respects the integrity of Charles's wish while maintaining critical distance from it.

A couple's weekend trip to Brighton, a resort frequented by gay men, is the setting for "A Small Spade." The story describes the halting and hesitant new romance between a twenty-four-year-old New Zealander, a hairdresser named Neil, and Bernard, a thirty-two-year-old professional. A detailed examination of the nuances of coupledom—the pleasures of gaining intimacy; how differences of temperament, class, and political belief are negotiated; emotions expressed; and problems handled and solved—"A Small Spade" also examines the peculiar stresses that come of a partnership between HIV-positive and HIV-negative men. Toward the end of their weekend, a small accident necessitates Neil's visit to a hospital; the experience foregrounds the illness's insistence and illustrates the singular reactions each man has in response to its existence. The obituary Mars-Jones wrote for his lover, New Zealand–born hairdresser Michael Jelicich (included in *Blind Bitter Happiness* [1997]), suggests the autobiographical component of the story.

The final narrative, "The Brake," describes the ongoing sexual evolution of Roger, a kind of gay English middle-class Everyman who came into adulthood in the late 1970s. As such, the story serves equally well as a gay urban chronicle. It gives a brief history of a hedonistic man with "a life-style that omitted almost nothing that was hostile to health." Roger's adult experiences privilege sexual expression. The opening sentence of the story, "Sex brought him a number of things, all of them more useful than pleasure," clearly establishes sexual consumerism as his modus vivendi. Much of "The Brake" charts Roger's varied experiences of sex and gay male culture in London and select American cities. The titular brake refers to Roger's mild heart attack, an event foreseen by his finger-wagging doctor some years earlier. The concluding pages of the story describe Roger's unexpectedly fearful response to the threat of death: not only does he give up his bad diet and smoking, but he also becomes abstinent; in place of his former recreational pastimes he develops interests in more-traditional areas, such as the care of his sister's children.

Mars-Jones published his first novel in 1993. *The Waters of Thirst* is narrated by a voice-over actor named William, who forms half of a London "odd couple" with Terry, an airline employee. The narration is retrospective, opening with William's thinking with satisfaction about Terry's reduced circumstances after the couple's recent breakup. William then recalls episodes from their relationship, which began in 1977, and covers scenes that inspect various elements of their union—from monogamy and pornography, on the one hand, to AIDS and chronic illness on the other. In spite of a plot that focuses increasingly on William's liver disease and his eventual stay in the AIDS ward of a hospital, the tone of the novel remains buoyant because it is lifted by William's wit, dry humor, and tart observations. Interweaving scenes of domesticity with broader social engagement (via dinner parties, especially), Mars-Jones ably captures many facets of coupledom.

Monopolies of Loss supplements the four stories already published in *The Darker Proof* with an additional five. Mars-Jones's use of AIDS as a theme (especially in conjunction with gay male culture) continues in this collection. In his introduction he calls the pandemic an intractable subject, one that invites the polarized responses of denial and paranoia. Concluding that the reality of the epidemic must lie somewhere in the middle, he places faith in the creative act: "writing about AIDS should be a way of finding a truer picture."

As represented by *Monopolies of Loss,* that "truer picture" is composed of complex and unfortunate narratives of loss that are nevertheless imbued with images of survival and flashes of wary contentment. Like "Slim," "Remission" describes in close detail the pains and dis-

Dust jacket for the 1981 U.S. edition of Mars-Jones's novellas "Hoosh-Mi: A Farrago of Scurrilous Untruths" and "Bathpool Park" (Richland County Public Library)

comforts of suffering a terminal disease. In it the narrator makes a tape-recorded journal, one a transcript of "the same old record of bodily disasters"; the other, named "remission," is designed to be a "hoard of positive moments" that can refresh him once the illness returns. Excerpts from the second tape, divided into labeled topics, make up the bulk of the story. He records his amorous relationships, quests for cures, and philosophical musings of the moment. With affection he also describes a trip, made during a fleeting period of health, to a swimming area. Appropriately, "Remission" ends with the narrator facing the return of sickness, his transcripts becoming fragmentary as he loses the ability to use his recording device properly.

"Bears in Mourning," "Baby Clutch," and "The Changes in Those Terrible Years" explore AIDS and its effects from various vantage points. Set within the gay "bear" subculture (populated by the hairy, masculine, and heavyset), "Bears in Mourning" relates the suicide

Dust jacket for the U.S. edition of Mars-Jones's 1992 collection of stories about AIDS (Bruccoli Clark Layman Archives)

of Victor, a man widely regarded as an icon by his community, after he tests positive for HIV. The narrator expresses qualified anger and resentment at both the relentlessness of AIDS and the cowardice of Victor, who had not yet become disabled by illness. Set in the familiar Mars-Jones medical milieu, "Baby Clutch" is told by a man whose lover is experiencing his first major hospital stay. Similar to *The Waters of Thirst,* it examines the vicissitudes of partnership, and in particular the nuances of coping with illness, compromise, and the stress of togetherness. The final story in *Monopolies of Loss* is about the ostensible philanthropy of a man who runs an ad hoc AIDS hospice in a building that he inherited from a deceased lover. He is in the business of caring, he says, but his professionalism and self-absorption call into question the quality of his empathy. He is accused at one point of having "grown fat on other people's misery," and his entitled sense of mission is clearly intended in the narrative to produce an ambivalent response.

Positioned as an interval between the two blocks of AIDS-related stories, "Summer Lightning" is eulogistic in form, narrated by a gay man befriended and influenced by his aunt, Olive, an older woman who embraced nudism after her husband left her. He describes their friendship, her admirable eccentricity, and how her own unconventional choices in life transformed his rather traditional and narrow-minded disposition. During their trip to a beach outside of Edinburgh, Olive dies suddenly while resting on the sand. Her nephew prepares a spontaneous and odd death ritual that celebrates her life in the most fitting way he can improvise.

In addition to contributing scores of movie and book reviews to a host of periodicals, including *TLS* and the *New York Times Book Review,* Mars-Jones published *Blind Bitter Happiness* in 1997. Like his short fiction, this collection of essays, reviews, and occasional pieces culled from the *Guardian,* the *Tatler,* the *London Review of Books,* and the *Independent* reflects a broad range of interests and concerns; yet, they are consistently focused on or filtered through gay male cultural debates and personalities. In addition to featuring profiles of popular gay celebrities such as Boy George, Gore Vidal, and Marc Almond, Mars-Jones inserts "Venus Envy," a lengthy critical interrogation of the political stances of Ian McEwan and Martin Amis, and "Blind Bitter Happiness," a portrait of his mother. In this latter affecting homage, he concludes, "She gave birth to Tim in 1953, Adam in 1954, and Matthew in 1957. I am the middle cough of her womb's coughing fit from the 1950s. I love my life, which isn't the same as saying that I expect happiness from it. One of Sheila's virtues as a mother was to have stopped telling us, quite early on, that everything was going to be all right." Adam Mars-Jones's most recent story, "Everything is Different in Your House" is set in Tamil Nadu, India, and is wittily narrated by a convalescing gay man satisfied to be immersed in an exotic, supportive milieu. His storytelling makes plain that everything is not all right, but it suggests that drops of happiness can be extracted from even the stoniest misery. Mars-Jones generally works within the realist British literary traditions. Yet, like his contemporary Alan Hollinghurst, Mars-Jones's frank representations of the politics and quotidian workings of a subcultural group place his writing outside that mainstream; as such it can be viewed in conjunction with the growth of minority writing such as that published by Hanif Kureishi, Salman Rushdie, Timothy Mo, and Zadie Smith.

References:

"Adam Mars-Jones" <http://www.contemporarywriters.com/authors>;

"Mars-Jones, Adam," in *Contemporary Authors,* New Revision Series, volume 134 (Detroit: Thomson Gale, 2005), p. 331.

Aidan Mathews
(16 January 1956 -   )

Patrick Lonergan
National University of Ireland, Galway

BOOKS: *Windfalls* (Dublin & Atlantic Highlands, N.J.: Dolmen, 1977);
Minding Ruth (Oldcastle, Ireland: Gallery, 1983);
Adventures in a Bathyscope (London: Secker & Warburg, 1988);
Exit/Entrance (Oldcastle, Ireland: Gallery, 1990);
Muesli at Midnight (London: Secker & Warburg, 1990; New York: Heinemann, 1991);
Lipstick on the Host (London: Secker & Warburg, 1992; New York: Harcourt Brace, 1993);
According to the Small Hours (London: Cape, 1998);
Communion, Abbey Theatre Playscript Series (London: Nick Hern, 2002).

PLAY PRODUCTIONS: *Antigone*, Dublin, Project Theatre, 12 February 1984;
The Diamond Body, Dublin, Project Theatre, 29 February 1984;
Exit/Entrance, Dublin, Peacock Theatre, 2 February 1988;
The House of Bernarda Alba (after Federico García Lorca), Dublin, Gate Theatre, September 1989;
Lipstick on the Host (adaptation), Dublin, Project Theatre, 22 February 1993;
"The Last Supper," *The Mysteries 2000*, Dublin, SFX Theatre, 1 November 1999;
Communion, Dublin, Peacock Theatre, 2 May 2002.

PRODUCED SCRIPTS: "Lipstick on the Host," radio, RTE, May 1999;
The House of Bernard Alba (adaptation), radio, RTE, November 2002.

OTHER: *Immediate Man: Cuimhni ar Chearbhall O Dalaigh*, edited by Mathews (Mountrath, Portlaoighise, Ireland: Dolmen, 1983);
"Charlie Chaplin's Wishbone," in *Irish Short Stories*, edited by Steve MacDonogh (Dingle: Mounteagle Press, 1998);
"Barber Surgeons," in *Arrows in Flight: Stories from a New Ireland* (Dublin: Townhouse, 2002).

Aidan Mathews (photograph © Tony Higgins; from Lipstick on the Host, *1993; Richland County Public Library)*

SELECTED PERIODICAL PUBLICATIONS–UNCOLLECTED: "Modern Irish Poetry: A Question of Covenants," *Crane Bag of Irish Studies*, 3, no. 1 (1978): 380–389;
"A God in Ruins Part 1, Notes on the Fall of the Artist," *Crane Bag of Irish Studies*, 5, no. 1 (1981): 777–782;
"Picture of Innocence," *Irish Times*, 4 May 2002, p. 81;

"Writing the Light: Ten Thoughts about Literature and Photography," *Source Magazine,* 17 (January 2003) <http://www.source.ie>.

Aidan Mathews is an Irish writer of poetry, fiction, and drama. He lives in Dublin, Ireland, and is a radio producer of drama and religious programs for Radio Telefís Éireann (RTE), the Irish state broadcaster. Having initially established his reputation with two collections of poetry, he has subsequently attracted praise for his short stories, plays, and novel. This virtuosity across several genres is one of Mathews's most notable characteristics.

His writings are characterized chiefly by a preoccupation with spirituality and religion, especially–but not exclusively–with Roman Catholicism. He is also known for formal inventiveness and wordplay. Recurring themes in his work include terminal illness, travel, birth, death, and marital discord. Mathews has also written frequently about the Holocaust, not only in *Minding Ruth* (1983) but also in the short stories "Fathers" and "Train Tracks." His work is particularly noted for the variety of narrative voices he employs. His short fiction is told from the perspective of children, middle-aged women, elderly priests, and animals; and his stories are set not only in Dublin, but also in Germany, France, the United States, Greece, Japan, and elsewhere.

Aidan Carl Mathews was born in Dublin on 16 January 1956, one of seven children. His father, Joseph, was a general surgeon and his mother, Norin Fitzgerald, worked in the home. He was educated at Gonzaga College, a private school run by Jesuits, between 1964 and 1973. The school is situated on Dublin's wealthy south side, where many of Mathews's stories are set. In 1973, he completed his secondary education and began attending University College Dublin, where he earned a bachelor of arts degree in English language and literature. The following year marked his first success as a poet, when he won the *Irish Times* poetry prize. He was a winner of the Literary and Historical Prize at University College Dublin in 1975 and was the auditor of its English Literature Society from 1975 until he graduated in 1976.

During this period, Mathews also traveled in Europe. His travel experiences were recounted directly in *Windfalls* (1977), and the variety of settings used in his work doubtless has its basis in these years. In 1975 Mathews spent a short time working as a porter at St. Michael's Hospital. The experiences he had in this post have affected much of his subsequent writing and are dealt with explicitly in "Heart Failure," "Infanticide," "Mortuaries," and "Still Birth," all of which were published in *Minding Ruth.*

His first book of poems, *Windfalls,* was published in 1977, having won the Patrick Kavanagh Award in manuscript form in 1976. Described by George O'Brien as being composed of poems that are marked by "the conflict between spirit and flesh," the book also includes work describing Mathews's experiences of traveling in Greece, France, and elsewhere.

In 1977 Mathews took up a post as teacher of English and religion at another Jesuit school, Belvedere College, alma mater of James Joyce (to whom Mathews is sometimes compared) and Austin Clarke. The following year he won the Macauley Fellowship in Literature given by the Irish Arts Council, and published "Modern Irish Poetry: A Question of Covenants" in the prestigious Irish journal the *Crane Bag.* It provoked a great deal of debate; Irish poet Gerard Dawe responded to it in detail in a subsequent 1979 issue of the journal.

Mathews attended Stanford University between 1980 and 1982, where he studied under theologian and anthropologist René Girard, earning an M.A. in English in 1982. On 19 June 1982 he married Trish Bourden. He received an M. Litt. in English from Trinity College Dublin in 1983 for his dissertation "Motives and Motifs in Northern Irish Poetry."

Mathews's attitude toward religion–so strong a feature of his work–was formed during this period. Having been educated by Jesuits at Gonzaga, the two years he spent at Belvedere were also a significant influence on his work. Priests appear throughout Mathews's writing, and undoubtedly he models many of his characters upon people he met at Gonzaga and Belvedere. Mathews has explained that, although he has always been a Christian, he had become quite disillusioned with Christianity by the end of the 1970s. As Helen Meany explains, however, his studies with Girard helped him "to reconcile his faith with his intellect." Meany quotes Mathews as saying that "In Girard and some of his peers I felt a marvellous reclarification had been undertaken. They opened the Hebrew bible and the gospels to fresh readings and readers. Girard offered me a reading of the atonement theories of Christianity that was rational and reasonable."

Mathews's reputation grew during his time at Stanford, where he won several prestigious awards. He received the Ina Coolbrith Poetry Prize in 1981 for his poems "Minding Ruth," "A Landing," and "Severances." In 1982 he received an Academy of American Poets Award for "Mongol," "Mother," "Descartes at Daybreak," and "The Wall."

These poems were collected in *Minding Ruth.* This collection shows the author's preoccupation with death, particularly the death of children, and is the first published example of Mathews's preoccupation with the

Holocaust. In his introduction to *Minding Ruth,* Irish academic, poet, and novelist Seamus Deane described the volume as "one of the scarce examples of the integrity of feeling and technique, the wholeness, that poetry always seeks."

After returning from Stanford, Mathews took a position as a radio producer for RTE. He edited *Immediate Man: Cuimhni ar Chearbhall O Dalaigh*–a tribute to a former Irish president–in 1983. Mathews's version of *Antigone* was produced in 1984, and his play *The Diamond Body,* about an androgyne on a Greek island, was produced in the Project, an independent Dublin theater, in the same year. It starred Olwen Fouéré, who has since become one of Ireland's most respected actors.

Adventures in a Bathyscope, Mathews's first collection of short stories, appeared in 1988. The book comprises fourteen stories told from various perspectives and set in many different countries. The majority of the stories, however, are set in Dublin. "Scholastics" and "The Figure on the Cross" describe the relationship of young Irish boys with different Catholic priests, echoing Joyce's story "The Sisters" in *Dubliners* (1914). Similarly, "Fathers" describes the relationship of a young boy with his father, though the Church is also an important part of the narrative.

The theme of marital discord is explored in three of the other Irish stories in the collection. In "The Strangest Feeling in Bernard's Bathroom," Bernard accidentally sees his elderly wife taking a bath and attempts to come to terms with the feelings this experience arouses in him. He considers discussing these feelings with a priest but finally decides against acting upon them. In "Things that Happen," a woman slices the tip of her finger off while washing dishes and criticizes her husband harshly for many offenses (of which the reader remains ignorant) as they drive to the hospital emergency room. In "In the Dark," a couple sits in a candlelit room during a power failure, awaiting the visit of their son.

Four stories from the collection are set in America, and three of these concern terminal illness or death. In "Nephritis," Jonathan informs many of his friends that he is dying, repeating to them all that his illness "begins with nephritis and it goes on from there." In "Daniel's Dialysis," a man being treated for kidney disease informs his sister that he wishes to cease his treatment so that he will die. When she organizes a gathering of his friends to say good-bye to him, he is so touched that he changes his mind, resuming the treatment. The story "Late at Night in the Stanford Library" is narrated by a young man who has developed a romantic interest in one of his fellow students. He spends several nights watching her studying at another table in Stanford Library. One night, the man believes that the woman has fallen asleep and watches her until morning–when he discovers that she has, in fact, died. Mathews's fourth American story, "Incident on the El Camino Road," describes the guilt experienced by a man who is unfaithful to his lover with a prostitute.

Front cover for the paperback edition of Mathews's first collection of short stories, published in 1988 (Bruccoli Clark Layman Archives)

"Proper Names" and "The Story of the German Parachutist Who Landed Forty-two Years Later" are both set in England. In "Proper Names," an Englishman, who is embarrassed by other men in a reputable gentlemen's club, forgets his name. In "The Story of the German Parachutist Who Landed Forty-two Years Later," a German soldier who had been involved in the Battle of Britain lands forty years later in the garden of a Norwich family. When the German attempts to seduce the daughter of the family, they decide to "undream" him.

The remaining two stories in the collection are also set outside of Ireland. In "The Little Merman" a

Dust jacket for the U.S. edition of Mathews's 1992 collection of stories, which includes a retelling of Jesus' entry into Jerusalem from the point of view of two donkeys and another story narrated by a flock of sheep (Richland County Public Library)

transsexual is murdered on a Greek island (a subject also considered in *The Diamond Body*); and "Nagasaki" describes a scene in a Catholic girls' school in Nagasaki shortly before an atomic bomb is detonated there in 1945.

This collection was well received. Christopher Wordsworth in "Certain Unquiet Spirits," written for the *Guardian* (5 February 1988), thought it "highly impressive for its style and quirky roving imagination" but also considered it "almost equally irritating for its modish metaphysics." This mixture of praise and criticism was typical of contemporary reviews of the collection. However, *Adventures in a Bathyscope* was short-listed for the inaugural Guinness Peat Aviation (GPA) award, and "Fathers" was anthologized by Seamus Deane in *The Field Day Anthology of Irish Writing* (1991).

In February 1988 Mathews's play *Exit/Entrance* was staged at the Peacock Theatre, Dublin. The production is notable for many reasons, among them that the play was one of the earlier successes of Irish director Ben Barnes, who was artistic director of the Abbey, Ireland's National Theatre, from 2000 to 2005. This two-act play presents Helen and Charles at two different periods in their lives together. In the first act of the play, titled *Exit,* Charles is aged seventy and Helen is sixty-five. The couple reminisces, discussing their honeymoon and other events in their married life. The second act of the play, *Entrance,* is set forty years earlier, before the couple were married, and shows them discussing their hopes for the future. The power of the play lies in the poignant contrast between the two scenes. *Exit/Entrance* was well received on its premiere and transferred to the Donmar Warehouse in Covent Garden in March 1988. It was published by Gallery Press in 1990 and dedicated to Arthur Lappin, who produced it at the Peacock.

In 1990 Mathews's only novel, *Muesli at Midnight,* was published. Describing two medical students cycling through Dublin with the skeleton of an archbishop to raise money for a cancer charity, the novel received unsympathetic reviews. Patricia Craig, writing in the *Independent* (London) for 24 June 1990, thought it a "virtually plotless novel which gains its effects from Irish logorrhoea overlaid with a kind of inter-continental chic," while John Walsh, writing for *The Sunday Times* (24 June 1990), called it "oddly inert." James Walton, writing for *The Sunday Times* (31 May 1992), considered it "disfigured" by "bad puns."

Mathews's second collection of stories, *Lipstick on the Host,* was published two years later. It comprises six stories, only two of which are set in Dublin. "Train Tracks" and "Elephant Bread and the Last Battle" describe the experiences of two young Irish boys who are visiting Germany and France, respectively. "Moonlight the Chambermaid," a novella, describes the relationship of an elderly Irish priest, Father Basil, with a young Dublin couple, Jane and Al. Jane, who is pregnant, asks Father Basil to baptize her child, but changes her mind when he tells her that years before he had been treated for depression after his return from Africa, where he had been a missionary. "All in a Day's Donkey-Work" narrates Jesus Christ's entry to Jerusalem from the perspective of two donkeys; similarly "Two Windows and a Watertank" is told from the perspective of a group of sheep.

The collection concludes with "Lipstick on the Host," a series of diary entries by Meggie, a middle-aged Irish schoolteacher, who is slowly developing a romantic relationship with Anthony, a gynecologist. The morning after they first sleep together, Anthony drives to Northern Ireland. After Meggie does not hear from him, she assumes that he no longer wishes to see her.

Then she discovers that he had in fact been killed in a car crash shortly after leaving her house. The story concludes with her decision not to attend his funeral.

The title of the collection and this story refers to an incident in which Meggie, who had attended a mass, accidentally brings home the wafer from the sacrament of Holy Communion. She performs the ceremony alone in her own home and realizes that her lipstick has stained the host. The unity of the lipstick and the host is a symbol for the communion of body and spirit, a theme that dominates Mathews's work.

While none of these stories is directly connected to another, many images and features recur in them. For example, a tortoise appears briefly in "Train Tracks" and plays an important part in "Moonlight the Chambermaid." Similarly, in "Moonlight the Chambermaid," a colleague arguing with Father Basil describes how he must comfort a parishioner who is dying of a terminal illness, and this revelation silences Father Basil. However, when Meggie in "Lipstick on the Host" is told the same news by a different priest, she glibly replies, "Give me her phone number . . . I'll pass on the message." Such internal jokes are a common feature of Mathews's fiction.

These stories received a far more positive response than *Muesli at Midnight*. Walton, in his 31 May 1992 article for *The Sunday Times*, stated that the collection "makes clear Mathews is not just an outstanding writer, he is also an outstanding religious writer." Maureen Freely, in "Dangerously Circling Round Secret Places" for *The Independent* (9 August 1992), wrote that "the language is beautiful, witty and charming despite its many tricks and allusions: I can't think of any other writer under 40 who can give his characters such a degree of emotional and spiritual complexity." The collection received the Cavour Prize in Italy for best foreign fiction in 1994, and Mathews adapted "Lipstick on the Host" for a stage production at Dublin's Project Theatre in 1993.

A third collection of poetry, *According to the Small Hours*, appeared in 1998. Peter Sirr, in "A Very Catholic Aesthetic" for *TLS: The Times Literary Supplement* (26 February 1999), described it as a "substantial volume, more than a hundred pages of densely imagined, elaborately wrought poems" and suggested that "in range, ambition and imaginative adventurousness, the book is a huge leap forward from the earlier work; the poems are always interesting, often breathtaking." In the same year, a new story, "Charlie Chaplin's Wishbone," was published in *Irish Short Stories*.

In 2002, Mathews's play *Communion* was presented at the Peacock Theatre, Dublin, and published in London. Commissioned by Barnes, who had directed *Exit/Entrance*, the play described the relationship of two brothers, one of whom is dying from terminal cancer. Karen Fricker, in a review for the *Guardian* (3 May 2002), wrote that "the first act is overly elongated by the onstage celebration of a Catholic mass, the second becomes a shared ritual between audience and performers . . . Mathews may have raised more problems than he can solve with this play, but his seriousness of intent and ambition are admirable." Ciaran Carty, in the *Sunday Tribune* (28 April 2002), called it a "movingly poetic baring of the soul." The play includes a scene in which a young woman dances before the dying man, a moment that recalls Mathews's short story "Daniel's Dialysis" from *Adventures in a Bathyscope*. In the same year, Mathews's short story "Barber Surgeons" was included in *Arrows in Flight: Stories from a New Ireland*, edited by Caroline Walsh.

Aidan Mathews continues to live in Dublin with his wife, Trish, an English teacher, and his daughters, Lucy and Laura. He writes regularly for Irish periodicals and is a noted commentator on religious affairs. While he has published less frequently since the mid 1990s, he is frequently cited as one of the more interesting contemporary Irish writers.

Interview:

Michael Cronin, "In Camera: Interview with Aidan Mathews," *Graph*, 8 (1990): 13–17.

References:

Seamus Deane, ed., *The Field Day Anthology of Irish Literature*, volume 3 (Derry: Field Day, 1991), p. 1436;

Richard Jones, "'Cognizant of the Past, While Trying to Invent the Future': Conversations with Aidan Mathews and Michael Scott," *Journal of Dramatic Theory and Criticism*, 13, no. 2 (Spring 1999): 79–92;

"Marianne McDonald: When Despair and History Rhyme: Colonialism and Greek Tragedy," *New Hibernia Review*, 1, no. 1 (Summer 1997): 57–70;

Helen Meany, "First Love, Last Rites," *Irish Times*, 1 May 2002, p. 14;

George O'Brien, "Aidan Carl Mathews: Three Snapshots and Two Commentaries," in *Irish Writing: Essays in Memory of Raymond J. Porter*, edited by James D. Brophy and Eamon Grennan (New Rochdale: Iona College Press, 1989), pp. 174–185.

Ian McEwan
(21 June 1948 –   )

James M. Lang
Assumption College

See also the McEwan entries in *DLB 14: British Novelists Since 1960* and *DLB 194: British Novelists Since 1960, Second Series.*

BOOKS: *First Love, Last Rites* (London: Cape, 1975; New York: Random House, 1975);

In Between the Sheets, and Other Stories (London: Cape, 1978; New York: Simon & Schuster, 1978);

The Cement Garden (London: Cape, 1978; New York: Simon & Schuster, 1978);

The Comfort of Strangers (London: Cape, 1981; New York: Simon & Schuster, 1981);

The Imitation Game: Three Plays for Television (London: Cape, 1981); republished as *The Imitation Game and Other Plays* (Boston: Houghton Mifflin, 1982);

Or Shall We Die? Words for an Oratorio Set to Music by Michael Berkeley (London: Cape, 1983);

The Ploughman's Lunch (London: Methuen, 1985); republished with *Or Shall We Die?* as *A Move Abroad* (London: Pan, 1989);

The Child in Time (London: Cape, 1987; Boston: Houghton Mifflin, 1987);

Soursweet (London: Faber & Faber, 1988);

The Innocent (London: Cape, 1990; New York: Doubleday, 1990);

Black Dogs (London: Cape, 1992; New York: Nan A. Talese, 1992);

The Daydreamer (London: Cape, 1994; New York: HarperCollins, 1994);

Enduring Love (London: Cape, 1997; New York: Nan A. Talese, 1998);

Amsterdam (London: Cape, 1998; New York: Nan A. Talese, 1999);

Atonement (London: Cape, 2001; New York: Nan A. Talese/Doubleday, 2002);

Saturday (London: Cape, 2005; New York: Nan A. Talese/Doubleday, 2005).

Collection: *The Short Stories* (London: Cape, 1995).

PLAY PRODUCTION: *Or Shall We Die?* London, Royal Festival Hall, 6 February 1983.

Ian McEwan (photograph by Jerry Bauer; from the dust jacket for In Between the Sheets, *1978; Richland County Public Library)*

PRODUCED SCRIPTS: *Conversations with a Cupboard Man,* radio, BBC, 1975;

Jack Flea's Birthday Celebration, television, BBC, 1975;

The Imitation Game, television, BBC, 1980;

The Last Day of Summer, television, BBC, 1983;

The Ploughman's Lunch, motion picture, Goldcrest Films/Greenpoint Films, 1983;

Soursweet, motion picture, Film Four International/First Film, 1988;

The Good Son, motion picture, 20th Century-Fox, 1993;

The Innocent, motion picture, Lakeheart/Miramax/Sievernich, 1993.

OTHER: Christophe Gallaz, *Rose Blanche,* text adapted by McEwan (London: Cape, 1985);

"Schoolboys," in *William Golding, the Man and His Books: A Tribute on His 75th Birthday,* edited by John Carey

(London: Faber & Faber, 1986; New York: Farrar, Straus & Giroux, 1987), pp. 157–160; republished as "Golding Portrays Young Boys Accurately," in *Readings on Lord of the Flies,* edited by Clarice Swisher (San Diego: Greenhaven Press, 1997), pp. 102–106;

Martin Parr, *Home and Abroad,* introduction by McEwan (London: Cape, 1993);

"Mother Tongue: A Memoir," in *On Modern British Fiction,* edited by Zachary Leader (Oxford & New York: Oxford University Press, 2002), pp. 34–44.

The short fiction of Ian McEwan, the bulk of which he wrote in the early years of his career as a professional writer, explores the multiple forms of depraved and socially unacceptable behavior—sadism, rape, bestiality, pedophilia, castration, and murder—of which seemingly normal human beings are capable. Most of the characters who commit these acts are alienated from the dominant culture in which they live, and they all narrate their tales in calm and rational tones, with the sort of attention to detail that one expects of sympathetic fictional narrators. McEwan's short fiction puts the reader in the difficult position of determining whether these characters are simply aberrations, monsters created by their heredity or their environment, or whether they represent the worst aspects of human nature. His stories are by turns shocking, prurient, innovative, and repulsive, but given the level of critical attention they have continued to receive throughout his long career, they undoubtedly constitute an important contribution to the short-fiction genre in the latter half of the twentieth century.

Ian Russell McEwan was born on 21 June 1948 in Aldershot, England, to David McEwan and Rose Lilian Violet Moore McEwan. His mother's first husband died during World War II; she subsequently married David McEwan, then a sergeant major in the British army. Ian's childhood was spent in the tracks of his father's assignments to empire outposts such as Singapore and Libya until he was sent to a boarding school in Suffolk.

McEwan entered the University of Sussex in Brighton in 1967 and graduated with a B.A. in English in 1970. He then enrolled in the M.A. program in English at the University of East Anglia, where he was permitted to submit some of his short fiction as part of the requirements for his degree. Under the tutelage of novelist Malcolm Bradbury, McEwan wrote more than two dozen short stories and earned his degree in 1971. Several of the stories written during that period were published in British and American periodicals, as well as in his first two books, both short-story collections: *First Love, Last Rites* (1975), which won the 1976 Somerset Maugham Award, and *In Between the Sheets, and Other Stories* (1978). The shocking nature and literary quality of these stories earned McEwan sufficient critical and popular attention to allow him to pursue writing as a full-time career, an occupation to which he has devoted himself exclusively ever since.

Jack Slay Jr. has described the publication of *First Love, Last Rites* as a "shock into literature," owing to the themes and subject matter of the eight stories in the collection, which include incest, rape, and murder. The stories shock at a second level by the neutral and nonjudgmental descriptions of violence. The narrators (six of the stories feature a first-person narrator) or main characters express no remorse for their actions and no sympathy for their victims; the stories do not seem to offer any moral or ethical judgments upon anyone or anything. At least one critic took special note of this element in McEwan's writing. Jonathan Raban, favorably reviewing *First Love, Last Rites* in *Encounter* (June 1975), noted that McEwan's writing was "constitutionally incapable of being appalled." Once a story has committed to depicting an act of murder or sexual perversion, McEwan follows it through to the end, leaving no detail unobserved. As David Malcolm has remarked of McEwan's short fiction, the main characters are usually "the alienated, the losers, the isolated and marginalized figures that are a central focus of much of English-language twentieth-century fiction in general." For McEwan's characters, isolation and alienation lead to a loss of sympathy and understanding of others, creating the conditions for the violence that predominates in his stories.

The first story in *First Love, Last Rites* is "Homemade," which opens with the fourteen-year-old narrator describing a seemingly innocent scene in which he is filling the bathtub for his younger sister. The story then shifts immediately into a chronicle of how the narrator's friend Raymond gradually initiated him into increasingly depraved kinds of behavior: smoking, drinking, shoplifting, and viewing pornographic movies. When the two make plans to visit a prostitute, the narrator, fearful that his lack of sexual experience will expose him as an innocent, decides to test his sexual powers first on his ten-year-old sister. On an evening on which his parents have left him at home to babysit her, he begins by playing her favorite games and describes his intentions in the neutral tones characteristic of McEwan's narrators: "She was happy. She was complete. . . . It was almost a shame I had it in mind to rape her." Rape her he does, predictably finding the sexual experience a disillusioning one: "I moved gently backwards and forwards, just a few times, and came in a miserable, played-out, barely pleasurable way." Afterwards, though, he notes with satisfaction that he "had

Dust jacket for McEwan's first short-story collection, published in 1975, which won the 1976 Somerset Maugham Award and created controversy because of the shocking nature of many of the stories (Chapel Hill Rare Books, catalogue 163, Spring 2005; Bruccoli Clark Layman Archives)

made it into the adult world finally." The story concludes on a mixed note: despite his pleasure at having been initiated into adult sexuality, the actual experience of intercourse has dissuaded him from visiting the prostitute the next day.

"Butterflies," the fifth story in *First Love, Last Rites*, bears strong similarities to "Homemade" in both subject matter and narrative tone. The first sentence promises a typical McEwan story: "I saw my first corpse Thursday." For several pages the narrator reports conversations with a neighbor, and eventually with the police, in which the reader learns that he witnessed the drowning death of a young girl in a canal. Gradually, the story of the narrator's encounter with the girl weaves itself into these recollections. Jane, a young neighborhood girl, had tagged along with the narrator on a walk. He expressed little interest in her initially: "I avoid talking to children, I find it hard to get the right tone with them." Without any overt signals or descriptions of his intention, he suddenly proposed to Jane that they walk along the edge of a dirty industrial canal, enticing her with the promise that they will see some beautiful butterflies further along. The girl followed, questioning him about his life and about the butterflies, until eventually he lured her under a noisy canal bridge. He exposed himself to her, persuaded her to touch him, and had an orgasm. Jane turned to run away but tripped and knocked herself unconscious. "'Silly girl,'" the narrator concludes, "'no butterflies.' Then I lifted her up gently, as gently as I could so as not to wake her, and eased her quietly into the canal." This story is typical of the collection in that small side helpings of violence and perversity accompany the main dish: as the narrator and the girl walk by the canal, they pass a group of boys who are preparing to roast a live cat over a fire.

The narrators of both "Homemade" and "Butterflies" are loners, but no story by McEwan depicts the theme of isolation more directly than "Conversations with a Cupboard Man," the sixth story in *First Love, Last Rites*. The narrator has been kept isolated from society, initially without his knowledge, but then, when offered freedom, he chooses to remain in isolation. Telling his story from within the cupboard to a listening social worker, he describes how his mother kept him in a state of suspended childhood, completely separate from the outside world. He never objected to this treatment for an obvious reason: "I didn't know any other life, I didn't think I was different." She fed him baby food, tried to construct a special high chair for him when he was fourteen, and kept him in a crib until he was seventeen. She loosened her hold upon him when she married another man, and the cupboard man found himself out in the world, forced to fend for himself for the first time. He took a job as a hotel dishwasher, where he was locked in a large oven by a sadistic chef on two occasions. After taking his violent revenge on the chef, he left the hotel and began stealing for a living, which eventually landed him in jail. He enjoyed the isolation of his cell so much that he asked the warden if he could stay indefinitely, but he was forced to leave. He abandoned his subsequent factory job for full-time life in his cupboard, where he remains at the conclusion of the story.

The cupboard man's trajectory is a familiar one in McEwan's short fiction: an initial state of isolation from society, which the character often does not choose, leads to voluntary behavior that alienates him from that society. The fourteen-year-old narrator of "Homemade" speaks contemptibly of the "thousands who each morning poured out of the terraced houses like our own to labour through the week" and separates himself from them with his drinking, smoking, stealing, and, eventually, the rape of his sister. The narrator of "Butterflies" suffers from the strange physical defect of having no chin, which frightens people: "it breeds distrust.... Women do not like my chin, they won't come near me." When he has his orgasm, he cements the connection between his isolation and his crime: "All the time I spent by myself came pumping out, all the hours walking alone and all the thoughts I had had, it all came out into my hand." Unable to establish meaningful human relations with anyone, he ends up expressing himself in his warped relationship with the girl he murders. In the cupboard man's case, that behavior—with the exception of his treatment of the chef, which one could argue is at least explicable as revenge—takes a relatively innocuous form, in his desire for isolation in small, enclosed spaces. In other stories the forms of behavior are more violent, perverse, or damaging.

The more violently shocking elements of McEwan's short fiction are somewhat muted in his 1978 collection, *In Between the Sheets*. The emphasis in these stories falls more upon the abnormal and the delusional. No doubt there is violence in these stories: the main character in "Pornography," a pornography bookseller who has passed along his venereal disease to two nurses, winds up on a makeshift operating table at the end of the story, about to undergo castration at their hands. But one finds in this collection far more examples of nonviolent behavior that still falls far outside the bounds of accepted social and cultural conventions. An Englishman in Los Angeles, in the midst of his narrative of exile, "Psychopolis," tells the story of a man whose lover asks him to urinate upon himself in the middle of a restaurant; after he has done so, she introduces him to her just-arrived parents. Themes of isolation and alienation recur in this collection as well, assuming an even more prominent place in the lives and motivations of the characters.

Without the signal given by the title, it might take the reader several pages to understand that the narrator of "Reflections of a Kept Ape," the second story in the collection, is indeed a primate. He tells the story of his relationship with Sally Klee, a writer of fiction, and offers his literary analysis of her work. But the obsessive focus of the primate is on the few days that he and Sally spent as physical lovers. The relationship was short-lived because the narrator's fur and semen caused her physical distress. Since then they have lived in uneasy coexistence, the ape longing for a reprise of their sexual relationship and brooding over the contents of a new novel she tries to keep hidden from him.

When he finally reads a few pages of the book while she is out, he is disappointed and contemplates leaving her. In the final paragraph of the story, the ape recollects a moment from his childhood in a zoo: "I am staring at my mother, who squats with her back to me, and then, for the first time in my life, I see past her shoulder as through a mist pale, spectral figures beyond the plate glass, pointing and mouthing silently." This memory serves as a metaphorical reminder of his isolation from the human contact he has come to crave, and at the close of the story he has come to understand that he and Sally will remain trapped forever in their separate but proximate realms.

The narrator of "Dead as They Come" describes an equally strange relationship between a human and nonhuman. A wealthy man, three times divorced, he claims to have neither time nor patience for the niceties of relationships with women: "I am a man in a hurry . . . I have no time for the analysis, the self-searching of frenzied relationships, the unspoken accusation, the silent defense." He expects the same distaste for communication from women: "I do not wish to be with women who have an urge to talk when we've finished our coupling. I want to lie still in peace and clarity . . . I prefer silent women who take their pleasure with apparent indifference." The narrator finds just such a woman in a store mannequin, the ideal partner for a man who, like the cupboard man, finds peace and comfort only in his solitude. He purchases her from the store, brings her to his home, and treats her as his wife. His relationship with her turns sour when he begins to suspect her of having an affair with his chauffeur, and at the end of the story, in a jealous rage, he rapes and murders her. Here again, the situation of exile from human society, whether voluntary or involuntary, serves as a major motivation for the actions or reflections the characters undertake in the stories.

Another element appearing in both *First Love, Last Rites* and *In Between the Sheets* and undoubtedly related to the themes of isolation and alienation is the banality of modern urban life. In a review of McEwan's first novel, *The Cement Garden* (1978), in *The New York Review of Books* (8 March 1979), Robert Towers looked back to McEwan's first story collection and described the setting in the stories as a "flat, rubble-strewn wasteland." This phrase accurately captures McEwan's depiction of the modern city. In "The Last Day of Summer," from *First Love, Last Rites,* the narrator remarks upon the final destination of the river that takes the lives of his friend and her surrogate daughter: "London is a terrible secret I try to keep from the river. It doesn't know about it yet while it's flowing past our house." When one compiles the descriptions of London and other cities in the two collections, it is no wonder that the narrator wants to

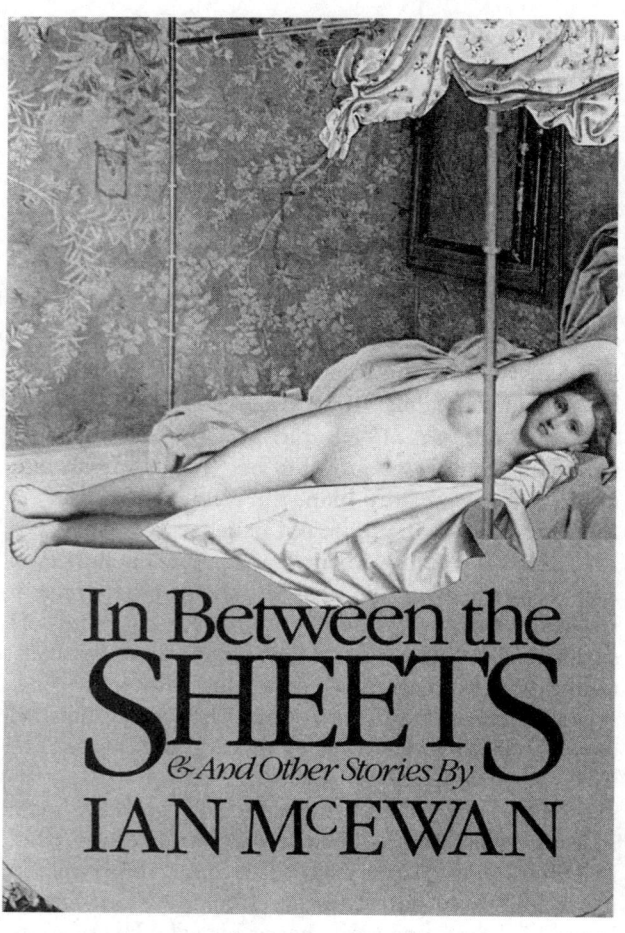

Dust jacket for McEwan's second short-story collection, published in 1978, which, like First Love, Last Rites, *explores the isolation and alienation of characters facing the banality of modern life (Richland County Public Library)*

keep the city a secret from the river. The narrator of "Homemade" describes watching long-distance runners pass through a "vast, dismal field, surrounded on all sides by factories, pylons, dull houses and garages." The molestation and murder in "Butterflies" occur beneath a bridge over a dirty brown canal running between rows of factories. In "Two Fragments: March 199–," a postapocalyptic story from *In Between the Sheets,* the narrator walks home from an encounter "down long avenues of rusted, broken cars." McEwan's stories take place almost entirely under the "uniform grey skies" the narrator mentions in "First Love, Last Rites," the title story of the first collection.

Clear connecting lines run between the settings, the themes of isolation and alienation, and the behavior of the characters. The stories depict contemporary urban existence as monotonous and conformist, a setting from which any individuals who do not fit in are cast out and exiled. These exiles, in turn, assert their individuality in any way that becomes available to them; murder or sexual perversity serves as a form of self-expression and as a rejection of the values of contemporary society. In this sense, these stories stand firmly in the tradition of twentieth-century literature of alienation and rebellion.

McEwan continued to explore these same themes in *The Cement Garden,* in which the backyard cement slab of the title serves as a metaphor for his perception of modern urban life. The publication of the novel in 1978 essentially marked the end of his career as a writer of short fiction. He has written in a variety of genres since then—including novels, plays, an oratorio, and motion-picture and television scripts—but he has published only a handful of short fiction. Critical acclaim for McEwan's novels has built steadily throughout his career, evident from the four nominations for the prestigious Booker Prize that he has received, for *The Comfort of Strangers* (1981), *Black Dogs* (1992), *Amsterdam* (1998), and *Atonement* (2001). *Amsterdam* won the prize in 1998.

In the mid 1980s McEwan's fiction moved into new territories. While traces of his interest in violence and abnormal psychological states remain, these subsequent works express much greater interest in broader questions of politics and history. With each subsequent novel, too, McEwan's narrators have become more readily understandable and sympathetic characters; they are often artists or writers, in relationships with spouses and children, and they pay attention to world history and politics in ways that the narrators and main characters from the short-story collections do not. In a 1987 interview with Amanda Smith in *Publishers Weekly,* McEwan noted that his 1982 marriage to Penny Allen, by which he acquired two stepdaughters, and the subsequent births of his two sons were at least partially responsible for this shift in focus: "Having children has been a major experience in my life in the past few years. It's extended me emotionally, personally, in ways that could never be guessed at. It's inevitable that that change would be reflected in my writing." After divorcing Allen in 1995, McEwan married Annalena McAfee in 1997.

The best evidence of the impact of family life on McEwan's writing comes from his return to the short-story genre with his 1994 collection of linked stories for children titled *The Daydreamer.* The protagonist in the title story is Peter Fortune, a ten-year-old English boy with a vivid imagination and a tendency to let his mind wander into elaborate daydreams, most of which involve his swapping bodies with other characters or objects: a cat, an adult, a baby, or a doll. The opening section, titled "Introducing Peter," sounds a familiar theme for McEwan's short fiction: "he liked being by himself. Not all the time, of course. Not even every day. But most he liked to go off somewhere for an hour—to his bedroom, or the park. He liked to be alone and think his thoughts." Again, the link is fairly direct; Peter's fondness for solitude leads to his daydreaming. But whereas in McEwan's earlier story collections, isolation and solitude lead to aberrant and often destructive behavior, in *The Daydreamer* those states produce a fertile and creative imagination that allows Peter to live more ethically and more happily.

"The Baby" opens with news that Peter's aunt and baby cousin will be coming to live in their house for a brief stay. Overwhelmed by the baby's presence, Peter initially resents him: "The baby had taken over the house. There was not a corner into which his yells, smells, and mad hyena laughter and grabbling little hands did not reach." His resentment turns to outrage when the baby swallows his best marble. McEwan describes Peter's transformation into the baby simply, without offering any explanation, either magical or pseudoscientific, as Peter sits and glowers at the baby from across the room: "The room began to brighten and turn floor-over-ceiling and grow larger and larger, until it was the size of an enormous hall in a palace." In the baby's body Peter sees the world anew, for both better and worse. He is amazed and delighted at the intense joy of tasting his mashed bananas but is frustrated and distressed at his inability to communicate his desires. When he has been transformed back into his own body, he comes to appreciate and understand the baby. At the close of the story Peter is holding and singing to the baby.

A similar dynamic structures other stories in *The Daydreamers,* in which Peter learns sympathy for a bully, for a cat, and for grown-ups. In this collection McEwan seems to have come full circle with the linked themes of his earlier stories, presenting a character who can live happily and successfully with a measure of solitude and with the help of his imagination. The stories do include occasional hints of menace. In "The Dolls" Peter daydreams that his sister's collection of dolls, led by a baby missing an arm and leg, come to life and pull off his own arm and leg as replacements for their leader's lost limbs. This story also helps readers to understand, when Peter's sister walks into her room just as the dolls are about to carry him away, that his transformations take place in his imagination. McEwan describes the moment from his sister's perspective: "She had come home from playing with her friend, she had walked into her bedroom, and there was her brother, lying on the spare bed, playing with her dolls, *all* her dolls, and he was moving them around and doing their voices." But if Peter's imagination takes him occasionally to a territory bordering the concerns and subject matter of McEwan's first two story collections, it never crosses fully into it.

Given the popular and critical success of Ian McEwan's novels, it seems likely that they will eclipse his short-story collections in appraisals of his work. Nevertheless, the stories remain an important means to the understanding of themes that have predominated in much of his other writing, and for this reason they will no doubt retain their appeal to readers of his works.

Interviews:

Christopher Ricks, "Adolescence and After—an Interview with Ian McEwan," *Listener* (12 April 1979): 526–527;

Amanda Smith, "*PW* Interviews," *Publishers Weekly,* 232 (11 September 1987): 68–69.

References:

David Malcolm, *Understanding Ian McEwan* (Columbia: University of South Carolina Press, 2002);

The Official Ian McEwan Website <www.ianmcewan.com> [accessed 9 August 2005];

Kiernan Ryan, *Ian McEwan* (Plymouth, U.K.: Northcote House/British Council, 1994);

Jack Slay Jr., *Ian McEwan* (New York: Twayne / London: Prentice Hall, 1996).

John McGahern
(12 November 1934 -   )

David Malcolm
University of Gdańsk

See also the McGahern entries in *DLB 14: British Novelists Since 1960* and *DLB 231: British Novelists Since 1960, Fourth Series.*

BOOKS: *The Barracks* (London: Faber & Faber, 1963; New York: Macmillan, 1964);

The Dark (London: Faber & Faber, 1965; New York: Knopf, 1966);

Nightlines (London: Faber & Faber, 1970; Boston: Little, Brown, 1971);

The Leavetaking (London: Faber & Faber, 1974; Boston: Little, Brown, 1975; revised edition, London: Faber & Faber, 1984);

Getting Through (London: Faber & Faber, 1978; New York: Harper & Row, 1980);

The Pornographer (London & Boston: Faber & Faber, 1979);

High Ground (London: Faber & Faber, 1985; New York: Viking, 1987);

Amongst Women (London & Boston: Faber & Faber, 1990);

The Power of Darkness (London & Boston: Faber & Faber, 1991);

The Collected Stories (London: Faber & Faber, 1992; New York: Knopf, 1993);

That They May Face the Rising Sun (London: Faber & Faber, 2002); republished as *By the Lake* (New York: Knopf, 2002).

PLAY PRODUCTION: *The Power of Darkness,* Dublin, Abbey Theatre, 16 October 1991.

PRODUCED SCRIPTS: *Sinclair,* BBC Radio 3, 1971;
Swallows, television, BBC, 1975;
The Rockingham Shoot, television, BBC, September 1987;
A Search for Happiness, television, 1989;
Amongst Women, television, BBC 2, July 1998.

OTHER: "The White Boat," in *New Writing 6,* edited by A. S. Byatt and Peter Porter (London: Vintage, in association with the British Council, 1997), pp. 342–372;

John Butler Yeats, *John Butler Yeats: Letters to His Son W. B. Yeats and Others, 1869–1922,* Joseph Hone Edition, abridged, with an introduction by McGahern (London: Faber & Faber, 1999; Syracuse, N.Y.: Syracuse University Press, 2000).

John McGahern (photograph by Jerry Bauer; from The Collected Stories, *1993; Richland County Public Library)*

SELECTED PERIODICAL PUBLICATIONS–
UNCOLLECTED: "The End or the Beginning of Love," *X: A Literary Magazine,* 2 (April 1961): 36–46;

"The Church and Its Spire," *Soho Square,* 6 (1993): 17–27;

"Creatures of the Earth," *Granta,* 49 (Winter 1994): 227–243;

"Love of the World," *Granta,* 59 (Autumn 1997): 219–250;

"Easter," *TLS: The Times Literary Supplement,* 30 April 1999, pp. 16–17, extract from *That They May Face the Rising Sun.*

John McGahern is one of the most highly regarded novelists and short-story writers of post-1945 Ireland. In her introduction to James Whyte's 2002 study of McGahern's work, Riana O'Dwyer describes McGahern as "the premier Irish novelist of the second half of the twentieth century." McGahern's short fiction is also widely praised. Contemporary novelist John Banville declared of McGahern in *The New York Review of Books* (6 December 1990): "he has . . . written some of the finest short stories to come out of modern Ireland." Liliane Louvel, in her introduction to a special edition of the *Journal of the Short Story in English* devoted to McGahern, suggests that "John McGahern's work has dominated the Irish literary landscape for almost forty years," and of his short fiction, she writes, "McGahern's short stories testify to a mastery of this problematic genre." The richness of McGahern's writing is attested to by the critical discussion that surrounds his work. His short stories and novels have been described as presenting a realistic picture of postwar Irish rural society and as setting out archetypal patterns that underlie much human existence. His fictions have been seen as "parables on the state of Ireland," yet also as explorations of individual psychological experience. McGahern has been discussed within an Irish tradition of William Butler Yeats, James Joyce, and Samuel Beckett, and also within a European tradition that includes Gustave Flaubert, Anton Chekhov, and Marcel Proust. He is seen as a traditional realist writer and also as one who explores the self-conscious and poetic possibilities of fiction. In Denis Sampson's words, moreover, McGahern's writing has "a large and loyal audience," and most of it is for many readers, as Alan Warner puts it, "compulsive reading."

McGahern has expressed his distaste for autobiographical fiction, but much of his writing refers to his experience as a child. He was born on 12 November 1934 in Dublin. His father was John McGahern, a sergeant in the Garda, the police force of the then Irish Free State. His mother was Susan (McManus) McGahern, a schoolteacher. McGahern has described his parents as "typical of a type of new class that came with independence." His father had fought against the British in the War of Independence and then joined the police force of the new state after 1922. McGahern describes people such as his father as former "gunmen" now in positions of authority. His mother was the first member of her family to receive a secondary education. She went even further and trained as a schoolteacher at Trinity College in Dublin. With his five sisters, McGahern lived with his mother in Ballinamore, County Leitrim, in the west of Ireland. His father lived apart from the family, approximately thirty miles away in Cootehall, County Roscommon, as the wives of Garda officers were not allowed to have jobs in the 1930s. In 1945 McGahern's mother died, a traumatic experience to which McGahern constantly returns in his fiction, and he moved to his father's Garda barracks. He attended the Presentation Brothers' secondary school in Carrick-on-Shannon.

"Ireland in the 1930s was essentially a nineteenth-century nation with nineteenth-century sights," McGahern said in an interview with Julia Carlson in 1990. He grew up in rural circumstances in what he has described in interviews as a conservative and patriarchal society. "I think the society I grew up in was very repressed, economically, sexually, extending out into all of life," he told Whyte in 2002. He talks, too, of the stultifying hypocrisy of the new rulers of an independent Ireland–civil servants, doctors, teachers, and policeman–and the "unhealthy emphasis on sexuality" coupled with sexual repression of the new state. He contrasts their way of life with the "sensible pagan lives" of "ordinary farming people." McGahern has also spoken of the marked segregation of men's and women's spheres of life in the world of his childhood and youth, and of the power of men over women in any areas in which they came into contact. In the Ireland of the 1930s and 1940s, McGahern feels that his own family occupied an uneasy position: "While the priest and the doctor were classed as being the top positions, we were in between the two worlds–not quite one or the other."

McGahern's background was not literary. His parents' homes contained few books, and McGahern came into contact with literature by being allowed to borrow books from the library of an eccentric Protestant family named Moloney, formerly wealthy and now fallen on hard times. (They are the basis for the Kirkwood family in stories in *High Ground* [1985].) At this time, McGahern read widely, unsystematically, and for pleasure. Another source of aesthetic pleasure (and more) for the young McGahern was the Catholic Church and its rituals. "The folk tradition," he says, "had died out except for the music. Some sense of the myths lingered on, but as a whisper. The sense of mystery, of luxury, of beauty or terror, all came from the Church, in its rituals and ceremonies." McGahern claims, "The church was my first book," and, despite ceasing to believe in the doctrines of the church at about the age of twenty, and despite his later conflict with the church, he has expressed his admiration, and even gratitude, for the beauty of church rituals and for its serious vision of the world.

McGahern was successful at school and attended St Patrick's Teacher Training College in Drumcondra, Dublin, from which he graduated in 1954. While he was "at university or thereabouts," his attitude toward literature changed, and he started to read less for pleasure and more for "the quality of the language" and for a focus on "the spiritual life." McGahern began his career as a schoolteacher in 1954 in Drogheda, County Louth, and also enrolled as a night student at University College Dublin. In 1955 he taught at St John the Baptist Boys School in Clontarf, Dublin, and began to move in Dublin literary circles. He completed his B.A. in 1957.

"I became a writer by accident," he told Louvel in 1993. "When I began to write, I had never met a writer." In the late 1950s McGahern worked on his first (and still unpublished) novel, "The End and the Beginning of Love," and published his first fiction, an extract from it (later rewritten and incorporated in *The Dark* [1965]), in *X: A Literary Magazine*. He also started work on his first published novel, *The Barracks* (1963). He was encouraged in this effort by both the Irish state and the literary world. In 1962 he won the Irish Arts Council's AE Memorial Award for extracts from *The Barracks*, one of which was also published.

The Barracks was published by Faber and Faber (indeed, this same London company has been the first to publish all McGahern's work). The novel establishes the main components of much of McGahern's fiction, which echo his own early life: complex family relationships, a rural Irish setting, death, the pointlessness of much of life, and the role of religion in such a world. Set in an isolated Garda barracks, it is presided over by the restless and embittered figure of Sergeant Reegan. Daily life in the barracks is presented in detail. The novel explores the complex relationship between Elizabeth Reegan and her husband, and her responses to her illness and inevitable death. Critics differ about the degree of bleakness in the novel, but most agree with Eileen Kennedy, who calls it "so extraordinary, its tone so distinctive, and its poise so remarkable that some feel it is his best."

On the basis of *The Barracks*, McGahern was awarded an Irish Arts Council Macauley Fellowship, which allowed him to take a year's leave of absence from teaching in 1964. He lived for a year in London where he met and married Finnish theatrical producer Anniki Laaksi. In 1965 *The Dark* was published. This novel charts the complex sexual and emotional experiences of a young Irishman growing up in rural Ireland in the 1950s. The novel has been compared to James Joyce's *A Portrait of the Artist as a Young Man* (1914–1915), although some critics see it as a grim and farcical reworking of Joyce's novel of rejection of and liberation from Ireland.

The Dark marked a turning point in McGahern's career. Copies were seized by Irish customs officials, and it was banned under the 1929 Censorship of Publications Act. McGahern was dismissed from his post as a schoolteacher, a move supported by the hierarchy of the Catholic Church, not only because of the explicit sexual experiences depicted in *The Dark,* but also because he had married a foreigner in a registry office. The banning of his second novel was a painful experience for McGahern. "In a way I was almost an official writer when *The Dark* was banned," he told Julia Carlson. Although he insists that "If you were a writer, you half expected it. . . . It was something that you lived with," he still felt "it was quite a social disgrace" for his family, and its consequences were enormous. McGahern could not work as a schoolteacher in Ireland, but left for London, where he found employment as a laborer on building sites and as a part-time teacher from 1965 to 1968. He also wrote book reviews and did some work for the BBC. His marriage with Laaksi came to an end at this time, and, as McGahern says, "I didn't manage to write for three or four years after the business" of the banning. However, McGahern was not without supporters in academic and literary circles in the United Kingdom and the United States. In 1968 he was appointed a research fellow at the University of Reading near London, a position he held until 1971. In 1968 he received a British Arts Council award. From 1969 to 1970 he was O'Connor Professor of Literature at Colgate University in New York State.

In 1970 Faber and Faber published McGahern's first volume of short stories, *Nightlines*. It was well received by critics. The anonymous reviewer in *TLS: The Times Literary Supplement* (27 November 1970) praised the convincing quality of the world depicted in the stories, the varied rhythms of the language employed in them, and the skill and complexity with which individual stories were organized. "My Love, My Umbrella" and "Why We're Here" won particular approval. In *The New York Times Book Review* (7 February 1971) David Pryce-Jones wrote a substantial appreciation of the collection. He admired the lack of sentimentality in the stories and McGahern's skill in choosing "something from the external world—the wheels of a train, an umbrella, the sea, the rain" and making it an integral part of a story. The reviewer emphasized McGahern's vision of Ireland as a place without a past and without a future, from which one can only escape, although he also points out that in "Peaches" McGahern shows how his "themes of desolation" recur in non-Irish settings. In *Newsweek* (8 February 1971) Peter Prescott praised the economy, richness, irony, and humor of the collection. *Nightlines* has also fared well in scholarly criticism; Sampson devoted a chapter to it in his monograph, and an extensive body of commentary was written on the collection and on individual short stories in books and journals in Britain, Ireland, and elsewhere.

Nightlines includes twelve short stories. They were written at various times during the 1960s and vary in length from four to five pages, as with "Why We're Here" and "Korea," to "Peaches," at approximately thirty pages. Stories also vary in narrational technique—from third-person omniscient ("Why We're Here") and third-person restricted ("Coming into His Kingdom" and "Peaches") to first-person ("Wheels," "Christmas," "Korea," and "Lavin"). First-person narration dominates, occurring in nine of the twelve stories and clearly indicating the focus of the collection on individual psychological portraiture. Seven of the stories depict childhood experience, and the remaining five have adult protagonists. Like all McGahern's fiction, the stories echo one another and also other parts of his output. These connections led Sampson to write of McGahern's use of "refrains" in these stories: "internal references, echoes, repetitions, and mirrorings of elements from other stories and novels."

The ordering of stories in *Nightlines* is important. The collection begins with two stories about adults: "Wheels" and "Why We're Here." Two stories about childhood follow: "Coming into His Kingdom" and "Christmas." The next two stories ("Hearts of Oak and Bellies of Brass" and "Strandhill, The Sea") depict adult experience, while the point of view in "Bomb Box" is that of an adolescent and in "Korea" is that of a young man. "Lavin" reverts to childhood experience, and the remaining three stories ("My Love, My Umbrella," "Peaches," and "The Recruiting Officer") focus on that of adults. The collection as a whole does not present a chronological progression, but rather an interweaving of experiences from different phases of life and an eventual circling back to adulthood. Time settings also reinforce this aspect of the collection. Although some stories take place in the 1950s and 1960s, others seem without a firm time setting. The same failures occur, whatever the period. The importance of circularity and repetition in McGahern's fiction has been discussed by several

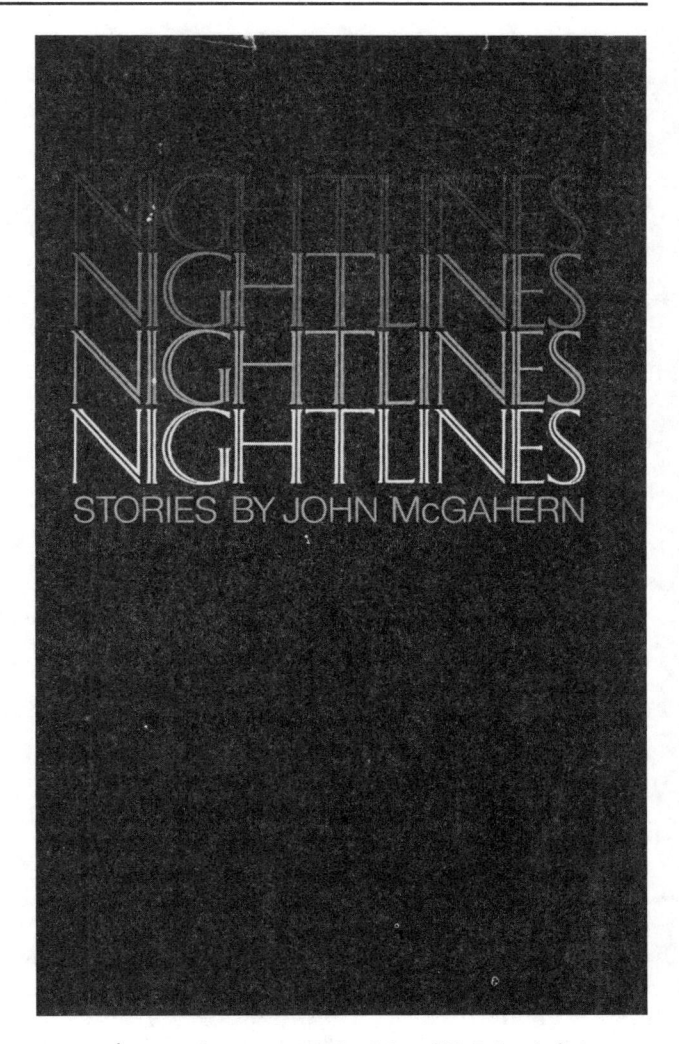

Title page for the 1971 U.S. edition of McGahern's first collection of stories, originally published in England in 1970 (Richland County Public Library)

critics, notably Bertrand Cardin. Indeed, Sampson goes so far as to compare McGahern's vision of time with a Buddhist one. Certainly, the return of the collection to a trapped and hopeless adult situation in its concluding story indicates a Joycean paralysis that is an important element in McGahern's view of the world.

This vision of the world is dark. Robert Hogan writes that "depression is the overriding feeling that one takes away from these accounts of death, futility, and disillusionment." None of the stories has the same title as the collection, but they are all, metaphorically, fishing lines sent down into dark waters to catch hidden and somber experiences and emotions. "Wheels" recounts the visit of a man to his family home, a recurrent event that is in McGahern's short stories. At the beginning of the text the unnamed protagonist travels to his father's farm in the Shannon valley. Two seemingly irrelevant encounters assume relevance in the light of later events. The protagonist overhears railway porters unsympathetically discussing a suicide attempt, and later, on the train, a workman from the London building sites swears by accident in front of a priest. The rest of the story is concerned with death, misery, and miscommunication. Once he arrives at his father's farm, the protagonist/narrator meets his stepmother, Rose, and later his father. At first, the father ignores the son and only speaks to him a considerable time after his arrival. The father resents that the son does not want his father to come to live with him in the city. Embedded in the text are the narrator's memories of his stepmother's unhappy relationship with his father, marked by disappointment and casual cruelty. The story ends with Rose's paring the corns on her husband's feet and the narrator's return to the city the following day. The narrator reflects on the circularity of human experience—the father has become a child again, dependent on wife and son; he, too, will go the same way—and on the disappointment of life, which promises much, but brings little but sadness. This story establishes the method, the mood, and the vision of subsequent stories. The "loose wheels rattling" of the porters' trolley at the beginning become the wheel of life and time that brings the father back to childishness and the narrator to a sense of life's disappointment. The failure of human relationships and a grim disillusion and cynicism pervade the text.

Matters are no better in the next story, "Why We're Here." In contrast with the title, the text emphasizes the purposelessness of life. It is largely made up of a dishonest and cynical conversation between Gillespie, who is stealing wood, and Mr. Boles, from whom he has stolen it. Crude physicality marks the world of this text: Gillespie breaks wind; his and Boles's dogs try to mount each other; Boles suffers from eczema. They cruelly mock an English former neighbor who has suffered from melancholy and is now apparently near death. Their conversation is full of coarse language. They mention, too, the smell of apples on the night air, but this odor comes from fruit that lies rotting on the ground because gathering it is not financially worthwhile. The conversation ends in banalities and more lies about woodcutting from Gillespie. Waste, mendacity, hopelessness, and barely concealed hostility between people are the themes of this story.

The two stories about childhood that follow also express a dark vision of the world. "Coming into His Kingdom" is an ironic title. The story about a boy's initiation into sexual experience is full of motifs of human cruelty, the coarse physicality of sex, and human life and death. In "Christmas" an orphan "homeboy" recounts his life on a farm to which authorities at the orphanage have sent him. His life is not unpleasant, but he spoils it by trying to manipulate a customer of his guardian. The gift he receives from the wealthy lady, a toy airplane, is "useless" to him in his life, and he offends both the lady and his guardian by his response to the gift. In the end he destroys the airplane and feels a liberation, having seen "the stupidity of human wishes." The story deals with human cynicism and coarseness. Characters make vulgar comments about the wealthy lady; a drunken policeman disrupts Christmas mass; and this disruption gives the narrator pleasure. Even nature is infected: a frozen lake is "a mirror fouled by white blotches."

Critic and novelist Walter Allen calls "Hearts of Oak, Bellies of Brass" "a picture of human dereliction." Once again, the noble-sounding title is ironic. A group of Irish workmen on a London building site talk and work. The tensions and hostilities of this group of migrant workers emerge forcefully. The narrator, who is one of them, although better educated than most, recalls his first days on the building site and describes the realities of such work. At the end of the story, a derelict methylated-spirits drinker appears, is struck by one of the workmen, sits in wet concrete, and is washed off. The language of the workmen is coarse; the work is hard and repetitive; and human beings are reduced to the status of animals. In addition, sex is degraded and joyless; the narrator is disillusioned and hopeless; and the environment is vile. In the background is the figure of Greenbaum, "old grey Jew out of Poland," whose presence in London suggests other examples of human viciousness and degradation. Stasis and futility mark the experiences set out in "Strandhill, the Sea." That the opening paragraph includes no finite verb suggests a lack of movement, while the conversations of a group of men in a guest house in a seaside resort (a middle-class version of the men in "Hearts of Oaks, Bellies of Brass") are marked by banality ("amazing the number of places in the world," one declares), vulgarity, and pretentiousness. They seem trapped by bad weather and lack of money in a paralysis that recalls that of the protagonists of Samuel Beckett's plays and prose fiction. The narrator does not use "I" until the fifth page of a story that is somewhat shorter than seven pages, thus underlining the drab oppression of his circumstances. He escapes from these conditions by stealing English 1950s comics for boys and by identifying himself with the heroes he finds in their pages.

The father figure, who is so important throughout McGahern's fiction, is central to "Bomb Box" and "Korea." The former is a comic story in which a Garda sergeant, as observed by his son, decides that he is terminally ill and melodramatically makes provisions for the future. The son clearly sees through the father's behavior in "Bomb Box," and a similar insight and judgment is the main event of "Korea," an altogether darker and more sinister story. A young man on the brink of adulthood realizes that his father wants him to immigrate to the United States so that he can be conscripted to fight in the Korean War and thus earn money for his father. If he is killed, his father will receive $10,000. The story begins with an excursion into Irish history that is unusual for the *Nightlines* collection. The narrator persuades his father to tell him about an execution he witnessed in 1919 during the war against the British. This request prompts the father to relate another memory, this one of the seedpods of furze bushes bursting like the buttons on the tunic of a boy who is one of those being executed. The father is disillusioned with postindependence Ireland: his small farm barely provides enough to live on; soon he will not be permitted to fish because it interferes with tourism from England. The hostility between father and son emerges slowly but clearly in the course of the story, especially when the son realizes his father's plan for him. However, the story ends on a complex note. In this last fishing expedition before the son goes off to university, the city, or England, the son feels close to the father. "I too had to prepare myself to murder," he says of himself, suggesting that he knows that his actions will destroy the older man's life and hopes. This complex story brings together in a striking manner Irish history, nature, and personal antagonisms.

In *Die Darstellung Irlands in der modernen irischen Short Story* (1981), Wolfgang F. W. Schmitz wrote that in the stories in *Nightlines*, sexuality is always marked by disappointment and failure. Such reactions are certainly true of the one childhood story and the two adult stories that follow "Korea": "Lavin," "My Love, My Umbrella," and "Peaches." The former is a reworking of Joyce's "An Encounter" from *Dubliners* (1914). It is a reminiscence of a boy's meetings with a pedophile called Lavin, whose lust has destroyed his life. The narrator also describes his own confused sexual feelings for his male friend. The story is full of explicit sexual language and descriptions of sexual acts; the boys also torture and kill a frog in a parody of sexual intercourse. Sexuality is seen as mysterious, cruel, dangerous, and unsatisfying. Mature sexual life is also full of tensions and failures in the next story, "My Love, My Umbrella," which recounts a brief love affair between two unnamed Dubliners. They make love under the man's umbrella because of the rain, "the constant weather of this city." The male narrator's attitude toward the woman is one of crude lust. He hopes for "a meal of each other's flesh"; intercourse with the woman reminds him of the artificial insemination of a cow. The narrator's present life is boring; any future married (and suburban) life with the woman repels him. He rejects her to find a brief freedom, only to discover that he has fallen into "the habit of her." But the woman refuses to restart the relationship, and the narrator is left contemplating the spilled seed of their liaisons, the wasted chance, and his failure to achieve any "quality" in their love, a failure that anticipates his "own future death."

A grim mood of failure and sexual tension is maintained in "Peaches," a story set in Francisco Franco's Spain. The point of view is that of a writer suffering from writer's block who has come to Spain with his wife (who is probably Finnish, since her father has died fighting the Russians), because "It was cheap and there was sea and sun and we thought it would be a good place to work." The collapse of their relationship is represented by the carcass of a shark that lies decaying on the nearby beach. The story does not suggest any way out of a hopeless personal and professional situation. Marital antagonisms are matched by the bitter legacy of the Spanish Civil War, and the two foreigners become caught up in Spanish politics when the local fascist magistrate shows he clearly has sexual designs on the wife. Her husband can only watch helplessly as he makes his power over the couple evident by crushing peaches down the front of the woman's dress in a partial sublimation of sexual abuse. At the end of the story, the couple plans to leave for London, but nothing suggests that life will be better there.

Sexual desire has led the narrator of "The Recruiting Officer" to abandon plans to become a Christian Brother, but this decision has itself led to disappointment. He has fled from freedom into a new entrapment. The narrator's paralysis is emphasized by the present tense of the narration: the story presents no future, no possibility of moving forward. Now "growing old" in a country school, he fills in his time waiting for the school day to end, watching a superior mistreat a pupil, and listening to a priest recruit the older boys in his class for the Christian Brothers. Despising the system he works within, he feels himself a hypocrite and a failure, and he drinks to kill the pain of this perception. A tinker comes to clean out and bury the excrement from the school lavatory, "the buried shit" embodying the narrator's feelings about his life, as the decaying shark embodies the moribund marriage in "Peaches."

Notwithstanding the grim mood of *Nightlines*, McGahern's life and career developed positively in the 1970s. In 1970 he bought a small farm in his native County Leitrim, which became his home in 1974. In 1971 a French translation of *Nightlines* was published, marking the start of McGahern's warm reception in France. Between 1972 and 1973, and again between 1976 and 1977, he returned to his post as professor of

JOHN McGAHERN

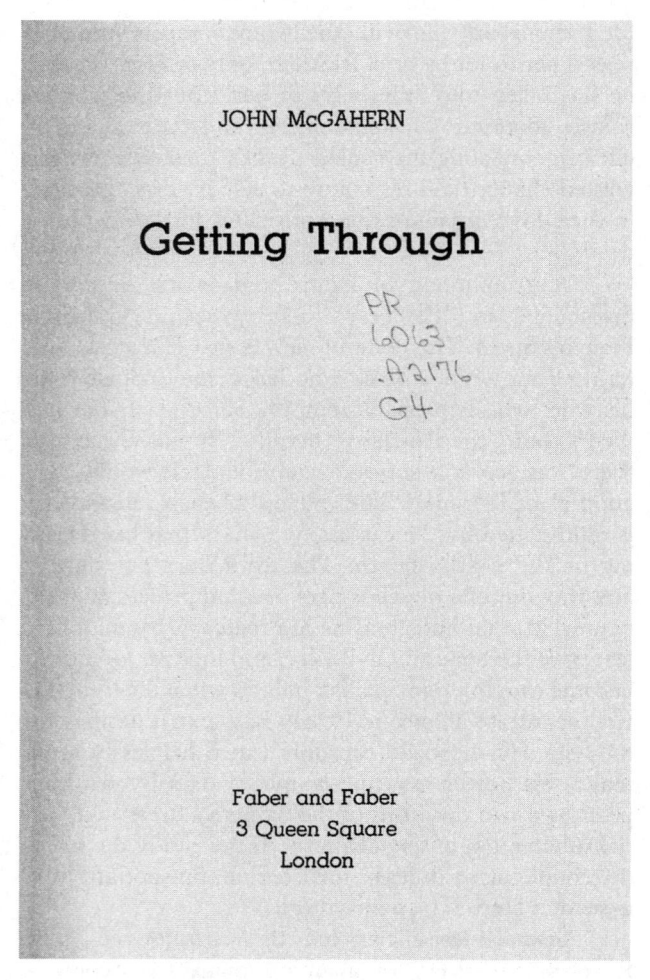

Getting Through

Faber and Faber
3 Queen Square
London

Title page for McGahern's 1978 collection of stories about various kinds of failure (Thomas Cooper Library, University of South Carolina)

literature at Colgate University. In 1973 he married an American, Madeline Green. Between 1974 and 1975 he was British Northern Arts Fellow at the University of Newcastle and the University of Durham in the north of England. In 1974 he published *The Leavetaking*, a novel that addresses several of the issues connected with the banning of *The Dark* and McGahern's departure from Ireland in 1965. *The Leavetaking* is narrated by an Irish schoolteacher on his last day at work, waiting for the evening when he knows he will be dismissed because he has married an American woman, who is not a Catholic, in a London registry office. His account of his day is interwoven with memories of his childhood, his mother's death, and, in the second part of the novel, his meeting and falling in love with the woman he marries. In language that is frequently poetic, the narrator speaks of his love and of the rapture of love in general. *The Leavetaking* had a mixed reception from critics. However, McGahern clearly thinks of it as an important part of his output, since in 1982 and 1983 he revised the second part of his "love story." The book was republished in 1984. McGahern's status as a major writer was recognized in Ireland when he was appointed writer-in-residence at University College Dublin, between 1977 and 1978.

In 1978 he published his second collection of short stories, *Getting Through*. According to the author, most of the stories, which vary in length from seven to twenty-six pages, were written during his residence in Newcastle and Durham. According to Sampson, "Swallows" dates from 1971. The U.S. edition of *Getting Through*, published in 1980, includes "Gold Watch," a story not included in the British edition. This story appeared in the 1985 collection *High Ground*. That a story could fit equally well into two volumes of short fiction is a sign of the persistence with which McGahern returns to the same locales and themes. In Sampson's opinion, McGahern's works "circle and converge on one another, and the reader is invited to contemplate the process of making within the context of an evolving life. Each new fiction casts light on earlier stories and novels." The stories in *Getting Through* have won praise from most commentators. In *Encounter* (June 1978) Tom Paulin wrote of the book as a "distinguished collection" and "a fine and interesting development from *Nightlines*." In *TLS* (16 June 1978) Michael Irwin called them "graceful, melancholy tales" and praised their careful choice of detail and the way in which individual incidents suggest wider patterns of experience. However, he also declared that he had read the collection "with rather more admiration than pleasure," since "for all its many merits *Getting Through* is a depressing work." Shaun O'Connell argued that the stories in the volume "stress reconciliation" rather than the "separation" of *Nightlines;* nonetheless, what O'Connell called "a mid-career summing up" on McGahern's part strikes many of the dark notes of his earlier fiction. The title of the collection suggests that all one can do in life is get through it as best one can, without much expectation of achievement or pleasure.

All the stories concern failure of some kind. With the exception of "Along the Edges," they reveal little hope of success for any of the protagonists. The stories themselves show no progression; all present adult experience at different ages. They are also timeless texts. Only two ("The Wine Breath" and "Sierra Leone") can be dated with any exactitude. The others are set largely in the 1960s or the 1970s, but without any precise dating. Only two ("Doorways" and "Sierra Leone") are narrated in the first person, although the others all have clear and restricted points of view. The first story, "The Beginning of an Idea," is unusual within McGahern's output in that it has a female protagonist. Eva Lindberg is a Scandinavian theater director who wishes to escape from her present successful career and less successful love life to write a novel based on a play inspired by an incident associated with Chekhov's death and by one of his short stories. She travels to Spain to do so. Despite rejecting distracting companionship on the way, she finds herself unable to write in the solitude of her Spanish retreat. Her life there is disrupted when she is duped by a seemingly friendly policeman and forced to have sexual intercourse with him and his superior. At the end of the story she is traveling further into the unknown, alone, with no writing done, perhaps toward death. The Chekhovian references throughout the text emphasize the theme of failure.

The protagonist of "A Slip-Up" is older than Lindberg, but he, too, is displaced and facing failure and death. Michael is an elderly Irishman living in London, having given up a small farm in Ireland to work as a janitor in a school. Now without any "function," he re-creates the farm in his imagination. He is deeply and publicly shamed, however, when his wife forgets that he is waiting for her outside the local supermarket and leaves him standing there, lost in a dream of the farm they gave up. But the lives of those who stay in Ireland are scarcely better. "All Sorts of Impossible Things" is set in a rural Irish community and presents several failures. James Sharkey, the schoolteacher, has failed in love and now wears a hat to cover the memento mori of his baldness. Tom Lennon, the agricultural instructor, has a heart problem and dies before he can pass the exam to be made permanent in his job. The greyhound with which they course hares does not win the championship for which the two friends have prepared her. The barman in the pub frequently steals his own liquor, perhaps killing his own sense of the futility of existence. "Life is a quare caper," Sharkey observes, in which only death and failure seem certainties, and "desire for all sorts of impossible things," such as joy and success, is best put aside. The character Sharkey appears again in "Faith, Hope and Charity." An Irish laborer dies in an accident on a London building site, partly through his own carelessness. Sharkey takes it upon himself to inform the dead man's family, who meet the fact of their son and brother's death with dignity. The community organizes a dance to cover the cost of bringing the body back from England. The story concludes with Sharkey and the postman observing the young men and women at the dance going into the dark countryside to make love. This concise story suggests a circle of life and death and powerfully presents both the futility of existence and the dignity of some human beings in the face of it. The story also highlights the positive strength of a traditional community and its ways.

Paulin (in *Encounter,* June 1978) argued that "a fusion of sex, death and hopelessness" runs through all McGahern's work and is marked in two stories of *Getting Through:* "The Stoat" and "Doorways." In the former, a student sardonically observes his widowed father's attempts to find a new wife and his horrified retreat from the lady he has chosen when she suffers a heart attack. The stoat of the title has pursued and killed a rabbit and becomes a metaphor for the elderly father in his search for a companion, the lady in her desperate attempts to please, and the mortality that makes everything pointless in the end. "Doorways," the first story in *Getting Through* to have a first-person narrator, is a familiar McGahern tale of a failed relationship. Life seems utterly futile, a point reinforced by the allusion to Ernest Hemingway's bleak "Hills Like White Elephants" ("We can have all this and more," the narrator reflects ironically). The best one can do is get through life, as do the two derelict street people whom the narrator observes each day occupying doorways in a Dublin street.

The next story, "The Wine Breath," also shows life as disappointing. An old, unnamed priest lives through one of his increasingly empty days: he has lost his beloved mother, his faith, and his traditional Catholic rituals (the Mass is now in English). He feels his own "absence," his ghost-like condition. Throughout the story, however, he has moments of ecstatic recall of scenes from the past. The memories are Proustian, stimulated by chance sensations: for example, the smell of crushed mint brings back a day of happiness with his mother. The most important of such sensations is the sight of beechwood shavings on a drab day that suddenly reminds him of the "white light" of a funeral in the snow thirty years earlier. This memory brings further memories of the dead man, Michael Bruen, whose vitality when alive contrasts with the gray limits of the priest's existence. At the end of the story, the title is echoed in the priest's vision of a young man, as he once was, bringing a bottle of wine to an evening meal, perhaps with a woman, but certainly entering a life quite different from the priest's present one. If "The Wine Breath" emphasizes the emptiness of the present moment, the next story, "Along the Edges," is an attempt to redeem the present and the actual. It is the most hopeful of the stories in *Getting Through*. Parable-like, in places densely metaphorical, it tells the story of nameless lovers. The first part, "Evening," details the collapse of a relationship; the second part, "Morning," shows the beginning of one that may grow positively. However, the experienced reader of McGahern's fiction realizes that the order of the two parts could easily be inverted to make the story more pessimistic.

Dust jacket for the 1987 U.S. edition of McGahern's 1985 collection of stories, which led some reviewers to compare him to Anton Chekhov (Richland County Public Library)

"Swallows" adds another character to McGahern's gallery of disaffected and disappointed middle-aged men. A Garda sergeant, intelligent and once a gifted musician, lives in a provincial backwater, his only companion a deaf housekeeper, his only society that of local "ignoramuses." The story depicts his meeting with a young state surveyor, a talented violinist, who has come to the sergeant's locality to measure the site of a road accident. What becomes apparent is that both the older man and the younger are damaged and unsatisfied. The younger one has chosen a safe job rather than a career in music. However, the younger man still plays, although on an amateur basis; the elder man's fiddle is dusty, and the bow is slack. Both are contrasted with Niccolò Paganini, the famous violinist, who risked all for his music. Schmitz suggested that the two men represent different Irelands, but Sampson points out that they are both driven by a sense of compromise and failure, and a fear of death. The swallows of the title are the harbingers of summer, and the moments of freedom and beauty that it includes, which both men look forward to and recall in the autumn rain.

This dark note also marks the last story of the collection, "Sierra Leone." A love affair starts between two unnamed Dubliners during the tension of the Cuban Missile Crisis of 1962. Once the fear of world destruction passes, however, the male narrator and his lover feel less excited by the affair. He appears to welcome the telegram that summons him back home, interrupting a weekend the lovers had planned together. At home he finds his father planning to disinherit his second wife, the narrator's stepmother. The breakdown of trust between husband and wife, and between father and son, when the narrator refuses to fit in with his father's plans, reflects the lovers' unease with each other. The affair, which was based on the deception of another lover, finishes, and the woman plans to go off with her other lover to Sierra Leone in Africa. The narrator's stepmother dies, her death suggesting that all the human travail of the story is finally of little moment.

The decade after the publication of *Getting Through* was a successful and productive one for McGahern. From 1978 to 1979 and from 1983 to 1984 he was once again a professor of literature at Colgate University. In 1979 he published his fourth novel, *The Pornographer*. This complex novel has been the subject of critical dispute. In *The New York Times Book Review* (2 December 1979) Alice Adams dismissed it as uninteresting and unappealing, and Jean Brihault described it as one of McGahern's unsatisfactory novels. Yet, John Updike called it "this vivid and involving novel," and its intricacies have been discussed by Seamus Deane, Kennedy, and O'Connell. Both O'Connell and Whyte saw it as a key text in McGahern's evolving attitude toward Ireland and traditional Irish communal ways. The novel brings together an old-fashioned and a modern Ireland, life, death, sex, and love in complex ways. James M. Cahalan sees the novel as a challenge to the Irish censors who had condemned McGahern for *The Dark*: in this novel, he argues, McGahern shows what real pornography is. The novel also relates to the rest of McGahern's oeuvre in its examination of the tension between sex and love, and in its consideration of the possibilities of redemption in a poisoned world at the end of which lies only death. McGahern's narrator finds these themes in his love of a young woman, but also in the courage and good sense of his dying aunt and his uncle, neither of whom has left his/her small community. Traditional and rural ways are not idealized in this novel, nor are the aunt and uncle, but they are seen in a positive way. This story develops the insight of "Faith, Hope and Charity" from *Getting Through* and anticipates the complex celebration of the traditional in "A Country Funeral" and *That They May Face the Rising Sun* (2002). French translations of his work were published throughout the 1980s and proved commercially and critically successful. In 1985 McGahern received an Irish American Foundation Award; in 1987 he was Visiting Professor of Creative Writing at the University of Victoria in Canada; from 1988 to 1989 he was writer-in-residence at Trinity College Dublin; and in 1989 he was named *Chevalier des Arts et Lettres* by the president of France.

In the decade after 1978, McGahern also began work (in 1980) on the novel that became *Amongst Women* (1990), and between 1982 and 1983 he rewrote the second part of *The Leavetaking,* republished in 1984. He also wrote and, in 1985, published his third collection of short stories, *High Ground*. Critics responded to this volume with respect and admiration. In *TLS* (13 September 1985), Patricia Craig wrote of the "authority and gravity" of McGahern's writing, while Pat Rogers in the *London Review of Books* (3 October 1985) compared these stories to the work of Chekhov, William Trevor, and William Faulkner. Joel Conarroe, in *The New York Times Book Review* (8 February 1987), also compared McGahern to Chekhov and argued that McGahern's prose in these stories demands the attention one normally gives to lyric poetry. Critics frequently comment on the depiction of social change in the stories of *High Ground,* seeing it as a new overt emphasis in McGahern's short fiction. This theme is an important focus in Nicola Bradbury's 1989 essay on the collection, as it is of Liz Heron's review in the *New Statesman* (13 September 1985), in which she wrote of the "elegiac mood of mourning in the wake of painful change" in *High Ground*. McGahern originally wanted to call the collection "Oldfashioned," emphasizing the concern with social and personal change.

High Ground includes ten stories. One, "Gold Watch," was published in the U.S. edition of *Getting Through*. Apart from "The Conversion of William Kirkwood" and "Bank Holiday," the other stories were published in journals such as *Encounter, The New Yorker,* and the *Irish Times*. They range in setting from a rural community during the early years of the Irish Free State to contemporary urban Ireland. Sampson writes that the whole collection deals with the search of single men for a place in a community. Certainly, the first two stories, "Parachutes" and "A Ballad," both first-person narrations, present deracinated and alienated young men. In the first, a typical McGahern protagonist/narrator is miserably trying to recover from a failed love affair. He wanders the streets of Dublin with an equally marginalized group of friends, their loud conversations and heavy drinking covering the emptiness of their lives. In a rich metaphor at the end of the story, life is compared to the thistledown that drifts through those same streets. The metaphor suggests the insubstantiality of the characters' lives, the possibility of fruitfulness that it includes, and also the connection of the modern city with its rural past. Alienation is also a major motif in "A Ballad," a story of sexual and social survival in a provincial Irish town. The central characters' unhappy isolation is matched by that of the Irish-speaking families transplanted by the attempts of the Irish government at social engineering.

The third story, "Oldfashioned," is also an examination of being out of place. The longest story in the volume, "Oldfashioned" is one of three stories—the others are "Eddie Mac" and "The Conversion of William Kirkwood"—in which McGahern takes up the subject of the Protestant landed gentry who continued to live in the independent Irish state after 1922. "Oldfashioned" has a broad historical and social perspective, only hinted at in McGahern's other fiction. It moves from the years immediately after independence to the 1950s to contemporary Ireland. Central figures in it are the Sinclairs, Anglo-Irish gentry who return to Ireland after World War II and become respected, if marginal, members of the local community. The limits of their integration into an independent Ireland become apparent when they offer to send the young son of a local Garda sergeant to become an officer in the British army. With an outrage that McGahern neither condemns nor approves, the father simply forbids this move. Colonel Sinclair dies alone, and the boy grows up to be a director of movies showing "the darker aspects of Irish life." He and his father remain distant from each other for the rest of their lives.

"Like All Other Men" is also a story about male alienation. A young man who has abandoned the priesthood picks up a young woman at a dance. They spend the night together, but he learns the next morning that she intends to become a nun. Like the main female characters in "Parachutes" and "A Ballad" (and also "Gold Watch"), this woman is no victim, but is determined to do what she wants. In this way she contrasts with many other abused and victimized female characters in McGahern's work. Other stories in the collection also emphasize the theme of estrangement, isolation, and absorption into a community. "Crossing the Line" depicts a young teacher beginning his first job, stepping into a local society fraught with the tensions of a teachers' strike in the past. The chains of the small town slowly begin to encase him as others start to determine his future for him. In "High Ground" the narrator, a young man freshly graduated from a university, is tempted by an older local politician to betray his admired former schoolteacher, now fallen into old age and drunkenness, by taking his mentor's job. The narrator, like the one in "Crossing the Line," is both a part of the local community and separate from it, on the brink of being sucked into it or of leaving, and the reader does not know what decision the young man will make. "Gold Watch" is one of McGahern's stories of bitter generational estrangement. The narrator is urban, middle-class, sexually liberated, and well off. Yet, the gains of his new life are shadowed by the breakdown of his relationship with his farmer father, who in an act of hatred and resentment destroys the modern watch his son gives him.

In two long and linked stories, "Eddie Mac" and "The Conversion of William Kirkwood," McGahern returns to the world of the Protestant Anglo-Irish gentry in an independent Ireland. The former covers about fourteen years in the lives of the main characters, Annie May Moran, a young servant girl of the Protestant Kirkwood family, and their herdsman, Eddie Mac. The Kirkwoods live in a large Georgian house on a run-down estate. Eddie Mac is a dynamic figure, but his days of glory in football, dancing, courting, and managing his cattle are increasingly in the past. Annie May, plain but loving, is used by Eddie Mac when no other women will have him. When she becomes pregnant, Eddie Mac steals some of the Kirkwoods' best cattle and escapes to England. McGahern expertly combines the personal with the social and historical in this story. Eddie Mac's decline parallels the Kirkwoods'; their isolation matches his and Annie May's. Eddie Mac, too, stands at odds with the community, satirically commenting on the singing of the Irish national anthem, looking forward to his escape into the industrial cities of England.

"Eddie Mac" carefully charts the differences between the Kirkwoods and the independent Catholic Ireland that surrounds them. However, "The Conversion of William Kirkwood," while continuing to show these contrasts, depicts the process whereby the "last of the Kirkwoods" becomes integrated into that other Ireland. This story takes up the Kirkwood family and Annie May thirteen years after Eddie Mac leaves Ireland for England. Annie May and her daughter, Lucy, live on in the Kirkwoods' big house, where the little girl is clearly the object of William Kirkwood's affection. They live in isolation from the surrounding community that has always found the Kirkwoods strange and amusing. Lucy has even assimilated some of the habits of voice and manner of her Protestant-gentry foster father. However, World War II ("The Emergency" in Irish terms) brings an end to William's isolation. He immediately joins the Irish Free State Army, is made an officer, and turns out to be good at being one, commanding his men's respect. This step into the community leads to others: his fellow farmers help him in the fields and he returns the favor; he converts to Catholicism; the teacher and the local Garda sergeant suggest he get married. As in other stories in *High Ground,* local society starts to determine the individual's life. William is fully integrated into the world around him by the end of the story, but at a cost. His future wife will force Annie May to leave; he has already lost Lucy's affections. Sampson calls it a "shocking tale of assimilation." However, *High Ground* ends on an optimistic note. Patrick McDonough, the protagonist of "Bank Holiday"—middle-aged and separated from his wife, a well-off, urbane, senior civil servant—has another chance at happiness with a divorced American woman visiting Dublin. Their summer days together in the city are idyllic and suggest that urban, modern Ireland is a place where joy and redemption may be found. The misery of "Parachutes" is rejected.

In 1990 McGahern's fifth novel, *Amongst Women,* was published. The novel relates parts of the life of Michael Moran, former guerilla leader in the war against the British, who has never felt at ease in the new independent Ireland. A frustrated and embittered man, he bullies and dominates his children, driving one son into exile in England. His attempts to browbeat his second wife, however, fail. Moran is a restless, part-heroic, part-tragic, part-monstrous presence at the center of a novel that has won widespread praise. Despite Fintan O'Toole's reservations (in the *Irish Times* of 15 September 1990) about its conservative technique, John Banville (in *The New York Review of Books* of 6 December 1990) struck a more representative note when he declared the book "an example of the novelist's art at its finest." "It will endure," he concluded. *Amongst Women* was nominated for the Booker Prize, and won the *Irish Times*/Aer Lingus Irish Fiction Prize, the *Sunday Independent*/Irish Life Arts Award, the Bank of Ireland Award, and the Hughes Award. In 1991 McGahern was awarded an honorary doctorate by Trinity College Dublin and again became a visiting professor at Colgate University. In the same year his play *The Power of Darkness,* a reworking of a play by Leo Tolstoy, was produced at the Abbey Theatre in Dublin to considerable controversy.

In 1992 McGahern's *The Collected Stories* was published. This volume gathers together all the short stories from the previous three volumes of short fiction. The book includes minor changes: "Bomb Box" from *Nightlines* is retitled "The Key"; "Gold Watch" is placed between "Swallows" and "Parachutes"; and "Sierra Leone" is moved to a later position between "High Ground" and "The Conversion of William Kirkwood." "The Stoat," from *Getting Through,* appears in this work as a first-person narration. However, such is the unified nature of McGahern's work that these changes do not detract. McGahern also adds two new stories, "The Creamery Manager," a brief study in weakness and failure that echoes an episode in *The Barracks,* and a long, thirty-five-page story, "The Country Funeral." This last text in the new volume, which Michael L. Storey, in *Studies in Short Fiction* (Winter 1994), called McGahern's "finest story," is an ambitious attempt to bring together modern urban Ireland and the traditional ways of rural society. Three brothers from Dublin travel to the funeral of their uncle in the rural community where he lived his whole life. They do not have fond memories of the uncle, especially the wheelchair-bound Fonsie. Each brother responds differently to the world of country traditions into which they enter, but Philly, who works abroad in the Saudi oil fields, is the one most moved by the old ways (which the narrator does not idealize). He even plans to buy the uncle's farm. *The Collected Stories* won praise from reviewers. D. J. Enright in the *London Review of Books* (8 October 1992) compared McGahern's work with that of Beckett and Proust. "Rarely," he insisted, "can anyone have depicted a small and constricted world in such detail and with such unfussy cogency." Writing in *The New York Review of Books* (8 April 1993), Banville, too, showed great respect for McGahern's short fiction. "This collection of half a life's work in the short story form," he argued, "would be a very considerable achievement even without the addition of the two new stories." Since the publication of *The Collected Stories,* McGahern has published two substantial short stories, "Creatures of the Earth" and "The White Boat." Both cover familiar topics: death, coming to terms with age, and the intersection of modern and traditional Ireland. "Creatures of the Earth" is unusual for the casual cruelty toward animals that it depicts and uses as a metaphor for the disruptions of modern urban life.

In 2002 McGahern published his sixth novel, *That They May Face the Rising Sun,* titled *By the Lake* in the United States. This careful, loving, but clear-eyed re-creation of life in a rural Irish community, which commentators identify as McGahern's County Leitrim, brings together all the major motifs and concerns of McGahern's novels and short stories. Indeed, it can be seen as an integrated string of short stories. Death, change, renewal, immigration, and the murderous politics of Ireland's war against the British Empire in the 1920s and of the present Northern Irish conflict are all fused into a novel that Paul Binding in the *Independent on Sunday* (27 January 2002) called "superb" and an "extraordinary and original achievement," and in which Hilary Mantel in *The New York Review of Books* (23 May 2002) perceived a "grave integrity." "By virtue

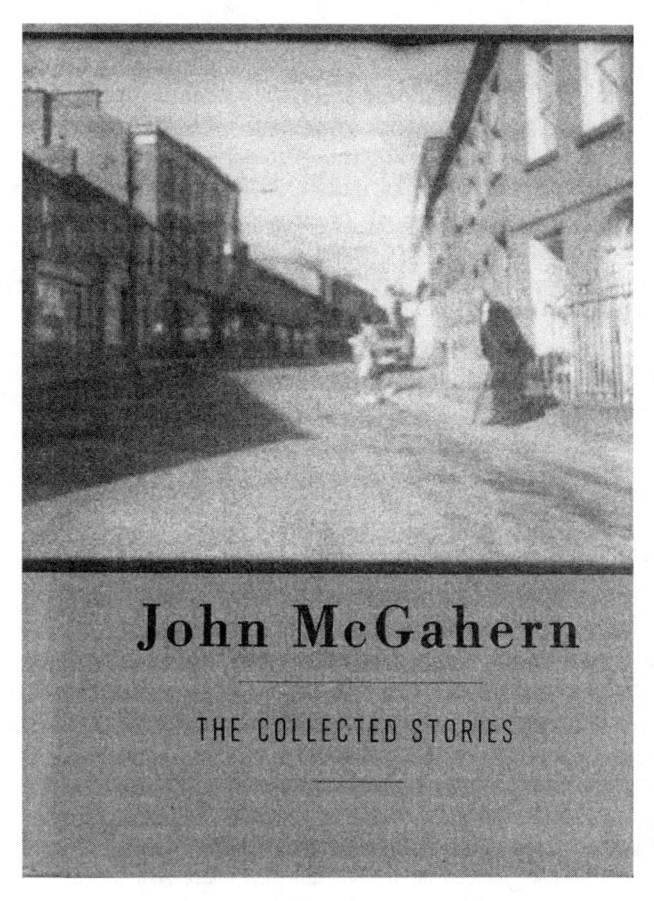

Dust jacket for the 1993 U.S. edition that includes McGahern's three previous story collections, along with two previously uncollected stories (Richland County Public Library)

of its simplicity the novel accretes power," she concluded.

In a career spanning forty years, McGahern has written some of the most highly regarded fiction in late-twentieth-century and early-twenty-first-century Ireland. He is a writer who addresses concerns that are universal in scope, yet he also documents in careful detail the particular experiences of Irish people at crucial points in twentieth-century Irish history. His vision is a dark one: failure, disappointment, isolation, and death are constant motifs in his work. Yet, as Roger Garfit and Bradbury have argued, he also provides moments of hope, fragmentary visions of joy and possibility, and depictions of relationships that do work and of communities that are flawed but humane. McGahern's work as a whole shows a striking continuity, and Banville described him (in *The New York Review of Books* of 8 April 1993) as "one of those rare artists . . . who do not 'develop.'" But of the short stories Banville wrote, "The best of these tales manage a magical blend of the specific and the general, and the result looks eerily like life itself, not in the drab sense of social realism, but in the distillation of moments of stillness and insight that are like those moments, rare and precious, when we seem to see ourselves most acutely and receptively alive." The substantial nature of McGahern's achievement led the editors of *The Antioch Review* (Fall 1993), commenting on *The Collected Stories,* to call him simply "the preeminent fiction writer working in Ireland today."

Interviews:

Patrick Goden, "Interview: John McGahern," *Scrivener: A Literary Magazine,* 5 (Summer 1984): 25–26;

Julia Carlson, "John McGahern," in her *Banned in Ireland: Censorship and the Irish Writer* (London: Routledge, 1990), pp. 53–67;

Denis Sampson, "A Conversation with John McGahern," *Canadian Journal of Irish Studies,* 17 (July 1991): 13–18;

Joe Jackson, "Tales from the Dark Side," *Hot Press* (14 November 1991): 18–20;

Liliane Louvel, Gilles Ménégaldo, and Claudine Verley, "John McGahern–17 November 1993," *La Licorne,* special McGahern issue, 32 (1995): 19–31;

Grace Heneghan, "Novel Experiences," *Garda Journal: The Journal of the International Police Association, Ireland Section* (November 1995): 34–38;

James Whyte, "An Interview with John McGahern," in his *History, Myth, and Ritual in the Fiction of John McGahern: Strategies of Transcendence* (Lewiston, N.Y., Queenstown, New Zealand & Lampeter, Wales: Edwin Mellen Press, 2002), pp. 227–235.

Bibliography:

James Whyte, "Bibliography," in his *History, Myth, and Ritual in the Fiction of John McGahern: Strategies of Transcendence* (Lewiston, N.Y., Queenstown, New Zealand & Lampeter, Wales: Edwin Mellen Press, 2002), pp. 241–261.

References:

Nicola Bradbury, "High Ground," in *Re-reading the Short Story,* edited by Clare Hanson (Basingstoke, U.K. & London: Macmillan, 1989), pp. 86–97;

Terence Brown, "John McGahern's *Nightlines:* Tone, Technique and Symbolism," in *The Irish Short Story,* edited by Patrick Rafroidi and Terence Brown (Gerrards Cross, U.K.: Colin Smythe / Atlantic Highlands, N.J.: Humanities Press, 1979), pp. 289–301;

James M. Cahalan, *The Irish Novel: A Critical History* (Dublin: Gill & Macmillan, 1988);

Seamus Deane, *A Short History of Irish Literature* (London: Hutchinson, 1986);

Roger Garfit, "Constants in Contemporary Irish Fiction," in *Two Decades of Irish Writing,* edited by Douglas Dunn (Cheadle, U.K.: Carcanet, 1975), pp. 207–241;

Robert Hogan, "Old Boys, Young Bucks, and New Women: The Contemporary Irish Short Story," in *The Irish Short Story: A Critical History,* edited by James F. Kilroy (Boston: Twayne, 1984), pp. 169–215;

Eileen Kennedy, "The Novels of John McGahern: The Road Away Becomes the Road Back," in *Contemporary Irish Writing,* edited by James D. Brophy and Raymond Porter (New Rochelle, N.Y.: Iona College Press / Boston: Twayne, 1982), pp. 115–126;

Jürgen Kramm, "John McGahern," in *Contemporary Irish Novelists,* edited by Rüdiger Imhof (Tübingen: Gunter Narr, 1990), pp. 175–191;

Liliane Louvel, "Introduction," *Journal of the Short Story in English,* special issue on the art of the Irish short story, featuring the short fiction of John McGahern, 34 (Spring 2000): 15–20;

Shaun O'Connell, "Door into the Light: John McGahern's Ireland," *Massachusetts Review,* 25, no. 2 (Summer 1984): 255–268;

Antoinette Quinn, "Varieties of Disenchantment: Narrative Technique in John McGahern's Short Stories," *Journal of the Short Story in English,* 13 (Autumn 1989): 77–89;

Denis Sampson, *Outstaring Nature's Eye: The Fiction of John McGahern* (Washington, D.C.: Catholic University of America Press, 1993);

John Updike, "An Old-Fashioned Novel," in his *Hugging the Shore: Essays and Criticism* (London: Deutsch, 1983), pp. 388–393;

Alan Warner, *A Guide to Anglo-Irish Literature* (Dublin: Gill & Macmillan / New York: St. Martin's Press, 1981);

James Whyte, *History, Myth, and Ritual in the Fiction of John McGahern: Strategies of Transcendence* (Lewiston, N.Y., Queenstown, New Zealand & Lampeter, Wales: Edwin Mellen Press, 2002).

Papers:

The James Hardiman Library of National University of Ireland Galway houses the literary archive of John McGahern. The archive consists of writings, personal papers, a novella and short stories, correspondence, and the manuscript of a novel, which although accepted for publication was subsequently withdrawn.

Naomi Mitchison

(1 November 1897 – 11 January 1999)

Moira Burgess

See also the Mitchison entries in *DLB 160: British Children's Writers, 1914–1960; DLB 191: British Novelists Between the Wars;* and *DLB 255: British Fantasy and Science-Fiction Writers, 1918–1960.*

BOOKS: *The Conquered* (London: Cape, 1923; New York: Harcourt, Brace, 1923);

When the Bough Breaks and Other Stories (London: Cape, 1924; New York: Harcourt, Brace, 1924);

Cloud Cuckoo Land (London: Cape, 1925; New York: Harcourt, Brace, 1926);

The Laburnum Branch: Poems (London: Cape, 1926; New York: Harcourt, Brace, 1926);

Anna Comnena (London: Gerald Howe, 1928);

Black Sparta: Greek Stories (London: Cape, 1928; New York: Harcourt, Brace, 1928);

Nix-Nought-Nothing: Four Plays for Children (London: Cape, 1928; New York: Harcourt, Brace, 1929);

Barbarian Stories (London: Cape, 1929; New York: Harcourt, Brace, 1929);

Comments on Birth Control (London: Faber & Faber, 1930);

The Hostages, and Other Stories for Boys and Girls (London: Cape, 1930; New York: Harcourt, Brace, 1931);

Boys and Girls and Gods (London: Watts, 1931);

The Corn King and the Spring Queen (London: Cape, 1931; New York: Harcourt, Brace, 1931); republished as *The Barbarian: The Corn King and the Spring Queen* (New York: Cameron, 1961);

Kate Crackernuts: A Fairy Play for Children (Oxford: Alden Press, 1931);

The Price of Freedom: A Play in Three Acts, by Mitchison and L. E. Gielgud (London: Cape, 1931);

The Powers of Light (London: Pharos, 1932);

The Delicate Fire: Short Stories and Poems (London: Cape, 1933; New York: Harcourt, Brace, 1933);

The Home and a Changing Civilisation (London: John Lane, 1934);

Naomi Mitchison's Vienna Diary (London: Gollancz, 1934; New York: Smith & Haas, 1934);

Beyond This Limit, illustrated by Wyndham Lewis (London: Cape, 1935);

Naomi Mitchison (Hulton/Getty)

We Have Been Warned: A Novel (London: Constable, 1935; New York: Vanguard, 1936);

The Fourth Pig (London: Constable, 1936);

An End and a Beginning, and Other Plays (London: Constable, 1937);

Socrates, by Mitchison and R. H. S. Crossman (London: Hogarth Press, 1937; New York: Stackpole, 1938);

The Moral Basis of Politics (London: Constable, 1938; Port Washington, N.Y.: Kennikat Press, 1971);

The Alban Goes Out, illustrated by Gertrude Hermes (Harrow: Raven Press, 1939);

As It Was in the Beginning: A Play in Three Acts, by Mitchison and Gielgud (London: Cape, 1939);

The Blood of the Martyrs (London: Constable, 1939; New York: McGraw-Hill, 1948);

Historical Plays for Schools (London: Constable, 1939);

The Kingdom of Heaven (London & Toronto: Heinemann, 1939);

The Bull Calves (London: Cape, 1947);

Men and Herring: A Documentary, by Mitchison and Denis Macintosh (Edinburgh: Serif Books, 1949);

The Big House (London: Faber & Faber, 1950);

Spindrift: A Play in Three Acts, by Mitchison and Macintosh (London: S. French, 1951);

Lobsters on the Agenda (London: Gollancz, 1952);

Travel Light (London: Faber & Faber, 1952; New York: Penguin/Virago, 1987);

Highlands and Islands (Glasgow: Unity, 1953);

Graeme and the Dragon (London: Faber & Faber, 1954);

The Swan's Road (London: Naldrett, 1954);

The Land the Ravens Found (London: Collins, 1955);

To the Chapel Perilous (London: Allen & Unwin, 1955);

Little Boxes (London: Faber & Faber, 1956);

Behold Your King: A Novel (London: Muller, 1957);

The Far Harbour: A Novel for Girls and Boys (London: Collins, 1957);

Five Men and a Swan (London: Allen & Unwin, 1957);

Other People's Worlds (London: Secker & Warburg, 1958);

Judy and Lakshmi (London: Collins, 1959);

A Fishing Village on the Clyde, by Mitchison and G. W. L. Paterson (London: Oxford University Press, 1960);

The Rib of the Green Umbrella (London: Collins, 1960);

The Young Alexander the Great (London: Parrish, 1960; New York: Roy, 1961);

Karensgaard: The Story of a Danish Farm (London: Collins, 1961);

Presenting Other People's Children (London: Hamlyn, 1961);

The Young Alfred the Great (London: Parrish, 1962; New York: Roy, 1963);

Memoirs of a Spacewoman (London: Gollancz, 1962; New York: Berkley, 1973);

The Fairy Who Couldn't Tell a Lie (London: Collins, 1963);

Alexander the Great (London: Longmans, 1964);

Henny and Crispies (Wellington, New Zealand: Department of Education, School Publications Branch, 1964);

Ketse and the Chief (London: Thomas Nelson, 1965; Camden, N.J.: Thomas Nelson, 1967);

A Mochudi Family (Wellington, New Zealand: Department of Education, School Publications Branch, 1965);

When We Become Men (London: Collins, 1965);

Friends and Enemies (London: Collins, 1966; New York: John Day, 1968);

Return to the Fairy Hill (London: Heinemann, 1966; New York: John Day, 1966);

The Big Surprise (London: Kaye & Ward, 1967);

Highland Holiday (Wellington, New Zealand: Department of Education, School Publications Branch, 1967);

African Heroes (London & Sydney: Bodley Head, 1968; New York: Farrar, Straus & Giroux, 1969);

Don't Look Back (London: Kaye & Ward, 1969);

The Family at Ditlabeng (London: Collins, 1969; New York: Farrar, Straus & Giroux, 1970);

The Africans (London: Blond, 1970);

Sun and Moon (London: Bodley Head, 1970; Nashville: Thomas Nelson, 1973);

Cleopatra's People (London: Heinemann, 1972);

The Danish Teapot (London: Kaye & Ward, 1973);

A Life for Africa: The Story of Bram Fischer (London: Merlin Press, 1973);

Small Talk—: Memories of an Edwardian Childhood (London: Bodley Head, 1973);

Sunrise Tomorrow: A Story of Botswana (London: Collins, 1973; New York: Farrar, Straus & Giroux, 1973);

Oil for the Highlands? (London: Fabian Society, 1974);

All Change Here: Girlhood and Marriage (London: Bodley Head, 1975);

Sittlichkeit (London: Birkbeck College, 1975);

Solution Three (London: Dobson, 1975; New York: Warner, 1975);

Snake! (London: Collins, 1976);

The Brave Nurse and Other Stories (Cape Town & New York: Oxford University Press, 1977);

The Cleansing of the Knife and Other Poems (Edinburgh: Canongate, 1978);

The Two Magicians, by Mitchison and Dick Mitchison (London: Dobson, 1978);

You May Well Ask: A Memoir, 1920–1940 (London: Gollancz, 1979);

Images of Africa (Edinburgh: Canongate, 1980);

The Vegetable War (London: Hamilton, 1980);

Mucking Around: Five Continents over Fifty Years (London: Gollancz, 1981);

Margaret Cole, 1893–1980, by Mitchison, John Parker, and John Saville, edited by Betty Vernon (London: Fabian Society, 1982);

What Do You Think Yourself? Scottish Short Stories (Edinburgh: Harris, 1982);

Not by Bread Alone: A Novel (London & New York: Boyars, 1983);

Among You Taking Notes—: The Wartime Diary of Naomi Mitchison, 1939–1945, edited by Dorothy Sheridan (London: Gollancz, 1985);

Naomi Mitchison (Edinburgh: Saltire Society, 1986);

Early in Orcadia (Glasgow: Drew, 1987);

A Girl Must Live: Stories and Poems (Glasgow: Drew, 1990);

The Oath-Takers (Nairn, Scotland: Balnain, 1991);

Sea-Green Ribbons (Nairn, Scotland: Balnain, 1991).

Collections: *Beyond This Limit: Selected Shorter Fiction of Naomi Mitchison,* edited by Isobel Murray (Edinburgh: Scottish Academic Press/Association for Scottish Literary Studies, 1986);

As It Was (Glasgow: Drew, 1988)—comprises *Small Talk* and *All Change Here;* republished as *Small Talk with All Change Here: An Autobiography, 1897–1918* (Argyll, Scotland: House of Lochar, 1999).

OTHER: "Elizabeth Garrett Anderson," in *Revaluations: Studies in Biography* (London: Oxford University Press/H. Milford, 1931; Brooklyn: Haskell House, 1976), pp. 155–195;

An Outline for Boys and Girls and Their Parents, edited by Mitchison (London: Gollancz, 1932);

"Archaeology and the Intellectual Worker," in *Twelve Studies in Soviet Russia,* edited by Margaret Cole (London: Gollancz, 1933), pp. 251–264;

"Rural Education," in *Re-educating Scotland,* edited by Mitchison, Robert Britton, and George Kilgour (Glasgow: Scoop Books, 1944), pp. 28–33;

Frederic Bartlett and others, *What the Human Race Is Up To,* edited, with a foreword and introductions, by Mitchison (London: Gollancz, 1962);

"Mithras, My Saviour," in *The Penguin Book of Scottish Short Stories,* edited by J. F. Hendry (Harmondsworth, U.K.: Penguin, 1970), pp. 196–200;

"Words," in *Dispatches from the Frontiers of the Female Mind,* edited by Jen Green and Sarah Lefanu (London: Women's Press, 1985), pp. 164–174;

"The Campaign Against Blonc," in *A Writers Ceilidh for Neil Gunn,* edited by Aonghas MacNeacail (Nairn, Scotland: Balnain, 1991), pp. 59–97.

SELECTED PERIODICAL PUBLICATIONS—UNCOLLECTED: "Disloyalty," *New Statesman and Nation,* 48 (28 August 1954): 229;

"The Profession of Science Fiction: Wonderful Deathless Ditties," *Foundation,* 21 (February 1981): 27–34; republished as "Wonderful Deathless Ditties," in *The Profession of Science Fiction: SF Writers on Their Craft and Ideas,* edited by Maxim Jakubowski and Edward James, foreword by Arthur C. Clarke (New York: St. Martin's Press, 1992), pp. 34–43;

"The Things from Space," *Chapman,* nos. 47–48 (Spring 1987): 131–133;

"The Box," *Chapman,* nos. 74–75 (Autumn–Winter 1993): 13–19.

The bibliography of Naomi Mitchison's writing published in book form comprises almost one hundred titles in the genres of fiction, poetry, drama, children's books, and nonfiction on many social and political topics. In spite of this prolific production, or perhaps because her work is so diverse and unpredictable in scope, Mitchison's popularity and critical status as a writer have fluctuated through the years. The historical novels and short stories with which she began her writing career in the 1920s and 1930s were enthusiastically received by both readers and critics, but her attempt at realist fiction in a contemporary setting proved less popular. On moving to Scotland just before World War II, she found that she was not only remote from the London literary scene but also apparently out of fashion as a writer, so that her fiction of the 1940s and 1950s—some historical, some realistic, and some tapping into fantasy and folklore—did not receive the attention it deserved. She continued to be relatively neglected in the 1960s and 1970s, when she extended the scope of her writing to include innovative science fiction and perceptive commentary, in both fiction and nonfiction, on developments in the newly independent nations of Africa. Mitchison's work began to be rediscovered during the 1980s, and she is now recognized as a significant figure not only in Scottish literature but also in an international context.

Mitchison was born Naomi Mary Margaret Haldane in Edinburgh on 1 November 1897, the younger child of physiologist John Scott Haldane and Louisa Kathleen Trotter Haldane. Naomi's father held a university post in Oxford, and she was brought up there in a household in which scientific and political discussion coexisted with the conventions and restrictions of English upper-middle-class life in the early twentieth century.

Haldane showed an early interest in and aptitude for science, particularly genetics and botany, but her education was not given a high priority by her family. While her elder brother, John "Jack" Burdon Sanderson Haldane, was educated at Eton and Oxford University before following a career in genetics, Naomi attended school (the Dragon School, Oxford, principally a boys' school) only until the onset of puberty, thereafter being educated by a governess. She enrolled as a home student at St. Anne's College of Oxford University but did not take a degree. Spells of illness during childhood, however, allowed time for wide reading and for the imaginative explorations that she later developed into her early works of fiction.

In February 1916, at the age of eighteen, Haldane married Gilbert Richard "Dick" Mitchison, who had been a friend and contemporary of her brother at Eton and Oxford. Mitchison was in the process of qualifying as a lawyer while serving as an officer in a cavalry regiment for the duration of World War I. The match was seen as highly suitable by both families, and the marriage was virtually an arranged one. The pressures of wartime, not least when Dick was seriously wounded in France, made for an unpromising start to married life. Nevertheless, the marriage endured until his death in 1970 and produced seven children, of whom five survived to adulthood. Naomi Mitchison published all her writing under her married name.

After the war Mitchison and her husband moved to London, where he built up a practice as a barrister. Mitchison was an enthusiastic hostess, and the couple developed a busy social life, uninhibited by their growing family. By the age of twenty-five Mitchison was the mother of three sons: Geoff, born in 1918, Denis (1919), and Murdoch (1922). At this time she began to write. She describes in her memoirs how her first book was partly written while walking one of her children in the park, with an open notebook laid on the perambulator. Her husband introduced her to classical history, and her first book, *The Conquered* (1923), is a novel set in Roman-occupied Gaul in the first century B.C. The epigraphs to each chapter indicate the relevance of the book to the troubled situation prevailing in Ireland at the time it was written; such comparison of past with present is a recurrent feature of Mitchison's writing. Her next novel, *Cloud Cuckoo Land* (1925), is set in Greece in the fifth century B.C.

In addition to her novels, Mitchison began to publish collections of short fiction, in some cases including thematically relevant poems. These early stories, with their settings in classical times or in the early years of European history, replicate to some extent the concerns of her novels written in the same period. *When the Bough Breaks and Other Stories* (1924) opens with "The Hostages," a popular and frequently reprinted story, echoing the question of the relationship between captor and captive that is considered in *The Conquered*. The three following stories in the collection, grouped together under the title "Vercingetorix and the Others," are similarly related to *The Conquered;* Vercingetorix, a Gallic chieftain whose rebellion was put down by Julius Caesar, is seen as a distant but admired heroic figure. "The Triumph of Faith" deals with the early days of Christianity, a period to which Mitchison later returned in her novel *The Blood of the Martyrs* (1939). The title story, "When the Bough Breaks," features a young female Viking as the heroine. The possibility of transcending the limitations of gender is another frequent theme in Mitchison's works.

As the 1920s progressed, Mitchison's personal life underwent several changes. Her fourth child and first daughter, Lois, was born in 1926. Two years later her eldest son, Geoff, contracted meningitis and died at the age of nine. Mitchison had another son, Avrion ("Av"), in 1928 and another daughter, Valentine ("Val"), in 1930. Meanwhile, she and her husband had embarked on a type of open marriage, allowing both of them to engage in other relationships.

Mitchison's next collection of short fiction, *Black Sparta: Greek Stories* (1928), includes thirteen stories set between 500 and 370 B.C., "the only time when democracy has really worked," she is quoted on the dust jacket as saying. The long story "The Epiphany of Poieessa," concerning a community of priestesses dedicated to serving the goddess Hera, is one of several in the volume to examine the role and position of women. Mitch-

Title page for Mitchison's first collection, published in 1924, which features stories set in the classical period and in the early years of European history (Thomas Cooper Library, University of South Carolina)

ison also investigates the situation of Sparta and raises the question of whether the Spartan state was well organized or overdisciplined, with underlying reference to the rise of fascism in Europe at the time the stories were written. Of the fifteen poems included in the volume, at least six appear to refer fairly directly to Mitchison's own experiences and emotions, an early sign of the move from historical to contemporary themes that was soon evident in her fiction.

Barbarian Stories (1929) shows a widening of scope, chronologically, geographically, and thematically. In a note on the dust jacket, Mitchison says of the stories, "Most deal with Gods, magic, war, and the processes of the mind, the wrangle between barbarian instincts and actions and whatever civilisation there may be from time to time." She adds, tongue in cheek, "The Author assures the Publishers that there is thought to be a moral or common idea, or what you will, running through them all, but she is not quite sure what it is."

Ten of the fifteen stories in *Barbarian Stories* are set in the period from the first century B.C. to the fifth century A.D., about which she had written previously, and two in the eleventh century, drawing on Russian and Scandinavian history. Other stories, however, venture much farther back in time, exploring the minds and culture of prehistoric people. The difficult task of interpreting such a distant period was one to which Mitchison returned nearly sixty years later in her novel *Early in Orcadia* (1987). In "The Barley Field," the opening story in *Barbarian Stories,* the central character is an Early Bronze Age farmer whose envy of his neighbor's fine field of barley leads him to destroy the crop. Is his downfall the result of spirits raised by the chief to avenge the destruction or of his own sense of guilt? Mitchison allows her character to believe the former but suggests the latter, just as she suggests a scientific reason for the superior crop of barley. The successful farmer muses that the gods must be pleased with him, "although perhaps also it had been useful to dig deep . . . a hand deeper than any of the others."

The most unexpected story in *Barbarian Stories* is "The Goat," set in 1935, a date still six years in the future at the time the book was published. In this future Britain, an act of Parliament is in force that prescribes an annual ritual to pacify the Have-Nots, the underclass: "The thing happens in turn at various of our larger and nastier industrial towns . . . all the owners have to meet, and one is chosen by lot to be legally and ritually killed . . . for the good of all." Mitchison brings together the idea of ritual sacrifice and her developing interest in politics, questioning the validity of both solutions. "The Goat" is her first science-fiction story; she returned to the genre some thirty years later.

The idea of ritual sacrifice is central to the epic novel Mitchison was writing at this time. Considered by some critics to be her masterpiece, *The Corn King and the Spring Queen* was published in 1931. For a setting Mitchison invented the country of Marob, situated in the region of the Black Sea. For the culture of Marob, based on fertility rituals and a god king, she drew heavily on Sir James George Frazer's seminal work of anthropology *The Golden Bough* (1890), which she had read at an early age in the full twelve-volume edition of 1906–1915.

At this time Mitchison had become involved with several social and political causes, supporting, for instance, a London clinic that advised working-class women on methods of birth control. In the general election of 1931 her husband, Dick, was nominated as the Labour Party candidate for a Birmingham constituency; although on this occasion he was not elected, his wife took part in the routine of canvassing and meetings. She also joined the party and in 1932 visited the Soviet Union as part of a Fabian Society fact-finding group.

The early 1930s can be seen as a time of change and experiment in Mitchison's fiction. Two collections of short fiction, *The Hostages, and Other Stories for Boys and Girls* (1930) and *Boys and Girls and Gods* (1931), were intended for children, though the former includes several stories from her earlier collections for adult readers. *The Delicate Fire: Short Stories and Poems* (1933) continues Mitchison's advance toward the use of contemporary themes. Though one section of the book consists of five linked stories set in Greece in the second century B.C., and the title story, "The Delicate Fire," depicts the poetess Sappho in old age, they are flanked by poems relating to Mitchison's own experience. The stories and poems in the final section engage directly with contemporary problems, such as censorship and industrial relations. In these years Mitchison also published two novellas, *The Powers of Light* (1932) and *Beyond This Limit* (1935). *The Powers of Light* is another exploration of the prehistoric mind and, more generally, of the situation of the outsider in a community, through the story of Fire Head, set apart because of her ability to make sparks by rubbing amber in her hair, and the Surprised One, who has the gift of drawing so that things "come real." These characters find refuge in a utopian community among rock walls covered with paintings similar to those in the caves of Lascaux; in this way Mitchison affirms the value of individuality and creativity.

Mitchison wrote *Beyond This Limit* in collaboration with the artist Wyndham Lewis, whose drawings illustrate the text. The central character, Phoebe Bathurst—who also appears in Mitchison's novel published in the same year, *We Have Been Warned,* and who may be in part a reflection of the author herself—is involved in a surreal journey that begins in the Left Bank quarter of

Illustration by artist and writer Wyndham Lewis for Mitchison's experimental 1935 novella Beyond This Limit, *which was republished in the 1986 collection* Beyond This Limit: Selected Shorter Fiction of Naomi Mitchison (from Isobel Murray, ed., Beyond This Limit, 1986; Collection of Moira Burgess)

Paris and proceeds, through swiftly changing scenes, dream-like encounters, and shape-shifting, to the Reading Room of the British Museum in London. The story, which ends abruptly with an elevator descending to Hades, remains one of Mitchison's most experimental and most interesting works of short fiction, written in a style to which she did not later return.

We Have Been Warned is set in contemporary Britain and Russia, drawing heavily on Mitchison's experiences as the wife of a parliamentary candidate in 1931 and on her trip to the Soviet Union in 1932. She had difficulty in getting the novel published, a situation unusual in her experience up to this time, because several publishers objected to her frank treatment of sexual matters. *We Have Been Warned* finally appeared in a somewhat revised form, additional alterations being made at the proof stage by the publisher without Mitchison's consent. It was not well received by critics or readers, who deplored her abandonment of the historical settings and themes of her earlier works. The experience damaged Mitchison's trust in publishers and critics, and she began to feel increasingly unappreciated as a writer and excluded from literary circles.

Mitchison's next collection of short stories, *The Fourth Pig* (1936), is a work of strong social commentary only slightly veiled by the use of the forms of fairy tale and myth. "Frogs and Panthers," for instance, brings the god Dionysos Bacchos, in the guise of a modern movie star, to an area of industrial England in the grip of unemployment. The children in "Hansel and Gretel" live in the slums of Birmingham and are enticed by the witch to her big house built of gold and silver and papered with banknotes. Mary Snow in "The Snow Maiden" is good at mathematics and headed for a university, but she chooses love and marriage instead and seems "to melt away, to fade right out somehow." Drawing on folklore and ballad, the long story "Mirk Mirk Night" describes a woman's escape from the deceptive pleasures of fairyland to the bleak but honest reality (as seen by Mitchison) of working-class life. "The Debateable Land" features Mitchison herself as a character in a narrative involving elements of several traditional tales.

In the title story, "The Fourth Pig," the approaching Wolf, gobbling up innocent animals, clearly represents the growing threat of fascism. Mitchison, who had lost many friends in World War I, had a horror of war, which she expressed not only in her writing but also in her work for pacifist and international causes through the years. *The Blood of the Martyrs,* the last novel she published before World War II, deals with Nero's persecution of the early Christian Church but draws a parallel with contemporary tyranny and oppression in Europe.

The approach of war brought about a great change in Mitchison's life. In 1937 she and her husband, Dick, bought Carradale House in the West Highlands of Scotland. A large house with a home farm and the remnants of an estate, it was at first intended for use on holidays but came to be seen as a safe base for the family if war broke out. In the event, Carradale became Mitchison's permanent home for the rest of her life. She rediscovered her Scottish roots, and much of her writing in the next two decades dealt with Scottish themes. She made close friendships in Carradale, particularly among the local fishermen, although cultural and social tensions also existed, since she adopted the role of Highland laird (or local landowner) while attempting to combine this role with ideas of utopian socialism.

In 1940 Mitchison gave birth to her last child, a daughter who survived only a few hours. Following this personal tragedy she became heavily involved in local concerns, both in the village of Carradale itself, where she was instrumental in obtaining a village hall and a new pier for the fishing fleet, and in the wider area of the Highlands. For nearly twenty years she was a member of the Argyll County Council and of the Highland Panel, an advisory body set up after World War II. In the general election of 1945 Dick was elected member of Parliament for Kettering, and Mitchison continued to be involved in socialist activities, but to this interest was now added an enthusiasm for Scottish nationalism, and she supported the Scottish Convention, an organization set up in 1943 to work for Scottish home rule.

Because of the pressures of work as she ran the house and farm at Carradale in wartime conditions, Mitchison published no book-length fiction between 1939 and 1947. Her new concern for Scotland is nevertheless reflected in a novel that she was occupied in writing during most of the war years, *The Bull Calves* (1947), set in eighteenth-century Perthshire, with her Haldane ancestors as leading characters. The novels published in the years following the war also have Scottish backgrounds. *The Big House* (1950), a children's novel with themes of relationship and community similar to those in Mitchison's adult fiction, is set in a village recognizable as Carradale. The events in *Lobsters on the Agenda* (1952) take place over the course of one week in a Highland village that owes something to Carradale and something to other areas visited by Mitchison on Highland Panel business. She also, however, maintained her interest in other places and periods. *Travel Light* (1952) is a fantasy with a female hero; *To the Chapel Perilous* (1955) is an Arthurian novel in which the events of the Grail story are observed by a group of modern journalists. *Behold Your King* (1957) is a novel about the crucifixion of Jesus.

Though Mitchison had published no novels during the war years, she had continued to write short stories and poems, some of which, together with later works, were collected as *Five Men and a Swan* (1957). The thirteen stories give evidence of her involvement with Scotland and also indicate that her move away from the classical settings and themes of her early works was complete. Of the five historical stories, the earliest, "Aud the Deep Minded," is set in Caithness and Orkney during the ninth and tenth centuries A.D., a period about which Mitchison also wrote in two books intended for younger readers, *The Swan's Road* (1954) and *The Land the Ravens Found* (1955). "A Story of St. Magnus" is set in twelfth-century Orkney, and "A Burgess of Irvine," "The Hunting of Ian Og," and "Occasion for Prayer" in seventeenth-century Scotland. The last two stories concern questions of vengeance and forgiveness following episodes of violence and rape during times of war; they attest further to Mitchison's utopian desire for peace and reconciliation.

The remaining stories in *Five Men and a Swan* are set in the contemporary West Highlands of Scotland and draw largely on Mitchison's experiences in Carradale. Social tensions in the village, a popular holiday resort as well as a fishing port, are reflected in "Round with the Boats," in which a fisherman, desperate for money after a bad season, dares to ask a regular summer visitor for a loan, only to find that their apparent friendship does not survive the request. For several years Mitchison was joint owner of a fishing boat with a Carradale fisherman, Denis Macintosh, with whom she co-authored *Men and Herring: A Documentary* (1949) and *Spindrift: A Play in Three Acts* (1951). Her knowledge of the economic troubles of the industry is further seen in "The Teeth," in which a skipper is driven to damage his own engine so that it looks like an "insurance job." Her concern for the status and treatment of the Scottish gypsies locally known as tinkers (now more often referred to as travelers) is evident in "The Way It Worked Out," in which "the fishermen's children and the crofters' children would have nothing to do with the wee tinkers" until a poaching adventure brings tinkers and fishermen closer together. "On an Island" illustrates the value of air ambulance service to the remote Highlands and islands, a topic also touched on in *The Far Harbour: A Novel for Girls and Boys* (1957). "In the 'Plane," "The Castle," and "In the Family" draw on Highland myth and superstition, a recurrent theme in Mitchison's works. In these stories, as elsewhere in her short fiction, supernatural events appear to occur in the context of everyday life, their reality half denied by the characters but half believed.

Mitchison had written the title story, "Five Men and a Swan," seventeen years earlier, in 1940, but it failed to appeal to magazine editors at that time. It opens in the cabin of a fishing boat with five fishermen yarning over their tea. The skipper tells of his encounter with a swan woman who appears in human form once a month at full moon and can be enticed to accompany a man by the theft of her swan skin. Mitchison uses the internationally known folk myth of the swan maiden but balances it delicately with her knowledge and observation of contemporary West Highland fishermen. The story, written in the darkest days of World War II, ends on a note of hope when the youngest fisherman, shipwrecked in war service, is rescued by the swan. "Five Men and a Swan" is considered Mitchison's finest work in the short-story genre.

In the early 1960s Mitchison's life entered another phase. Through a meeting with a young African named Linchwe, she became interested in his tribe, the Bakgatla, of which he was chief-designate, and in his country, then the British protectorate of Bechuanaland, which gained independence as Botswana in 1966. Mitchison visited the country in 1962, attended Linchwe's installation as chief in 1963, and began an

Dust jacket for Mitchison's 1982 collection of stories set in the West Highlands of Scotland, where she lived from the late 1930s until her death in 1999 (G. Ross Roy Collection of Scottish Literature, Thomas Cooper Library, University of South Carolina)

involvement with the Bakgatla that lasted for more than twenty years. She was adopted as honorary mother of both the chief and the tribe and worked hard to improve standards of health and education for the people. The novel *When We Become Men* (1965) and the memoir *Return to the Fairy Hill* (1966) arose from this involvement with Africa, which Mitchison continued to visit once or twice a year. She also wrote much nonfiction and many children's books with the aim of improving the understanding of African life.

Mitchison's use of fantasy and the supernatural had hitherto often verged on science fiction, to which her own interest in and knowledge of scientific topics had perhaps predisposed her. During the 1960s she began to write science fiction proper. Her first novel in the genre, *Memoirs of a Spacewoman* (1962), was an early example of feminist science fiction and is now regarded as a classic. The novel expresses Mitchison's abiding concern for female autonomy and peaceful communication.

Mitchison's husband, Dick, who had been created a life peer in 1964, died in 1970, but she continued to make her home in Carradale, with frequent trips to Africa and elsewhere. During the 1970s she published another science-fiction novel, *Solution Three* (1975), and three volumes of memoirs, *Small Talk—: Memories of an Edwardian Childhood* (1973), *All Change Here: Girlhood and Marriage* (1975), and *You May Well Ask: A Memoir, 1920–1940* (1979). While much of her writing of this period was intended for children, she also published a poetry collection, *The Cleansing of the Knife and Other Poems* (1978), and wrote much short fiction. Her science fiction and other types of stories were published in anthologies of original writing during the 1970s, although, as was often the case with Mitchison's stories, they were not collected in book form until much later.

In 1980 Mitchison published a short-story collection titled *Images of Africa*. In the foreword she explains her intention to build "bridges of understanding . . . not in terms of economics or politics, but in the deeper level of the imagination." The twelve stories are based on African myth and legend, some borrowing from traditional oral culture and others based on "actual happenings or imagined happenings of today." In "Above the Whirlwind" two children are swept up into a land, inhabited by cattle and ruled by a wise white bull, where violence is unknown. The children in "The Half-Person and the Scarlet Bird," abandoned by their parents in a time of famine, are first abducted by the evil half-person of the title and then saved by the bird, which embodies the spirit of his wife. In several of the stories African beliefs are juxtaposed with contemporary problems, and sometimes the old ways are seen to be best. In "The Hill Behind" a damaging drought can be relieved only if the king's daughter follows the traditional custom of meeting with the rain snake. In other stories the relation between past and present and real and supernatural is more ambiguous. The missionary in "The Coming of the New God" may damage the culture of the tribe or may help it in adapting to the inevitable advance of modernity. In "The Finger" a boy witness at a murder trial is almost prevented from giving evidence through sorcery, or it may be simply appendicitis. Mitchison allows the possibility of alternative interpretations, as she had done in "The Barley Field" fifty years earlier.

In the last story from *Images of Africa,* "To Deal with Witches," a Zambian village is afflicted by witchcraft, and several witch finders fail to help matters. The cure is finally brought about by a female witch finder, an attractive and powerful figure, an educated young woman who has discovered that she has the ability to deal with spirits. The tension between reality and the supernatural evident in some of Mitchison's Highland stories recurs in these African stories, and the character of the empowered woman may also relate on another level to Mitchison's self-imposed role as adviser and helper to the Bakgatla.

Stories Mitchison wrote during the 1970s as well as later works were included in her next collection, *What Do You Think Yourself? Scottish Short Stories* (1982). Most of the stories in this volume are set in the contemporary West Highlands, and while some are straightforwardly realistic—such as "The Return," in which a young man comes back to the town of his birth—the majority include an element of the supernatural. In the title story a farmer who has offended the tinkers finds himself attended by strange phenomena during a routine car journey. The phrase "What do you think yourself?" used as a title conveys his disbelief that such things can happen in the modern world, an attitude echoed in "The Warning," in which a policeman feels that his gift of second sight is in conflict with his official position. In "Call Me" the narrator finds an eerie, unexplained message in an old dollhouse. "The Sea Horse" is a treatment of the Scottish myth of the kelpie, or water horse. "The Hill Modipe" is set in Africa and at first glance seems out of place in a collection subtitled *Scottish Short Stories*. It is, however, a significant story, evidence of Mitchison's linking of Scottish superstition and folklore with the traditions she had found in Botswana. The central character is a Scottish botanist uneasy with the brutal ways of his Afrikaaner companions. He is saved, but they are destroyed by the snake spirit of the hill, which Mitchison links with the Scottish legend of the sea-serpent-like Loch Ness Monster.

The final story in *What Do You Think Yourself?*, "Remember Me," fuses Mitchison's skill as a science-fiction writer with her strong pacifism and her concern for the world in an age of nuclear threat. The narrator, an elderly woman living in the West Highlands, is speaking after a nuclear blast has devastated most of England. Her remote community has survived the first impact but is slowly being poisoned by radioactive fallout. It is a grim and all too plausible story in which no happy ending is supplied or foreseen.

Mitchison published a third science-fiction novel, *Not by Bread Alone*, in 1983. *Among You Taking Notes—: The Wartime Diary of Naomi Mitchison, 1939–1945* (1985), an extensive selection from the diary she kept during the war for the social-research organization Mass Observation, provided a further valuable biographical source to add to the memoirs she had published in the 1970s. During the 1980s a revival of critical interest in her writing led to the republication of several of her novels. A 1986 anthology, *Beyond This Limit: Selected Shorter Fiction of Naomi Mitchison*, includes Mitchison's

Dust jacket for Mitchison's last collection, published in 1990, which includes science fiction and stories set in Africa (G. Ross Roy Collection of Scottish Literature, Thomas Cooper Library, University of South Carolina)

two novellas from the 1930s, *Beyond This Limit* and *The Powers of Light*, as well as the short stories "The Wife of Aglaos," from *The Delicate Fire;* "Five Men and a Swan" and "The Hunting of Ian Og," from *Five Men and a Swan;* "The Hill Behind" and "The Coming of the New God," from *Images of Africa;* and "Remember Me," from *What Do You Think Yourself?* At the time the anthology was published, all of the original story collections were out of print, and the volume provided a much-needed introduction to Mitchison's shorter fiction, aiding the ongoing reassessment of her work.

Mitchison celebrated her ninetieth birthday in 1987. In spite of her advanced age, she published a novel that year, *Early in Orcadia*, in which she continued her explorations in prehistory by entering the minds of the earliest inhabitants of Orkney. Two more novels, *The Oath-Takers* and *Sea-Green Ribbons*, came out in 1991.

A Girl Must Live: Stories and Poems (1990) consists of works, some previously unpublished, from Mitchison's later years. The range of settings and themes is wide. The first half of the book includes the African stories "A Girl Must Live," "Nobody Likes a Refugee," and "If a Thing Can Be Done Once"; a comic Arthurian tale, "Death of a Peculiar Boar"; a further indictment of the mistreatment of tinkers, "A Matter of Behaviour"; and a haunting story of matriarchal religion in prehistoric times, "Telling to the Master." The second half of the collection is devoted to science-fiction stories, including several that had been published in the 1970s but not previously collected. "Mary and Joe" is an exploration of human cloning, with echoes of the story of the virgin birth of Christ. "Miss Omega Raven" is narrated by a raven possessed of both instinct and intelligence. "Out of the Deeps" foresees a postnuclear future when only dolphins remain to carry life on, and "Rat-World" is a vision of the world similarly abandoned to rats. These stories suggest that the human race has brought about its own destruction; as in "Remember Me," little hope for the future of humanity is expressed. There is a hint of optimism, however; the dolphins think that a few scattered humans may have survived and learned how to go forward in peace and cooperation.

Naomi Mitchison died in Carradale on 11 January 1999, at the age of 101. Many of her works were still out of print at the time of her death, and more remained uncollected or unpublished. The reevaluation that began in the last decades of her life has continued as critics have come to realize the range and significance of her writing, of which her short fiction can now be seen as an important part.

Interviews:

Isobel Murray, "Naomi Mitchison" (1984 interview), in *Scottish Writers Talking 2*, edited by Murray (East Linton, Scotland: Tuckwell, 2002), pp. 67–109;

Alison Henegan, "Naomi Mitchison Talking with Alison Henegan," in *Writing Lives: Conversations between Women Writers*, edited by Mary Chamberlain (London: Virago, 1988), pp. 169–180;

Raymond H. Thompson, "Interview with Naomi Mitchison" (15 April 1989), in his *Taliesin's Successors: Interviews with Authors of Modern Arthurian Literature*, Camelot Project, University of Rochester <www.lib.rochester.edu/camelot/intrvws/mitchisn.htm>.

Biographies:

Jill Benton, *Naomi Mitchison: A Century of Experiment in Life and Letters* (London: Pandora, 1990); republished as *Naomi Mitchison: A Biography* (London: Pandora, 1992);

Jenni Calder, *The Nine Lives of Naomi Mitchison* (London: Virago, 1997).

References:

Moira Burgess, *Naomi Mitchinson's Early in Orcadia, The Big House and Travel Light*, Scotnotes, no. 19 (Glasgow: Association for Scottish Literary Studies, 2004);

Jenni Calder, "More Than Merely Ourselves: Naomi Mitchison," in *A History of Scottish Women's Writing*, edited by Douglas Gifford and Dorothy McMillan (Edinburgh: Edinburgh University Press, 1997), pp. 444–455;

Beth Dickson, "From Personal to Global: The Fiction of Naomi Mitchison," *Chapman*, nos. 50–51 (Summer 1987): 34–40;

Gifford, "Forgiving the Past: Naomi Mitchison's *The Bull Calves*," in *Studies in Scottish Fiction: Twentieth Century*, edited by Joachim Schwend and Horst W. Drescher (Frankfurt & New York: Peter Lang, 1990), pp. 219–241;

Phyllis Lassner, "From Fascism in Britain to World War: Dystopic Warnings," in her *British Women Writers of World War II: Battlegrounds of Their Own* (Basingstoke: Macmillan / New York: St. Martin's Press, 1998), pp. 58–103;

Elizabeth Maslen, "Naomi Mitchison's Historical Fiction," in *Women Writers of the 1930s: Gender, Politics, and History*, edited by Maroula Joannou (Edinburgh: Edinburgh University Press, 1999), pp. 138–150;

Isobel Murray, "Human Relations: An Outline of Some Major Themes in Naomi Mitchison's Adult Fiction," in *Studies in Scottish Fiction: Twentieth Century*, pp. 243–256;

Gill Plain, "Constructing the Future through the Past: Naomi Mitchison's Brave New World," in her *Women's Fiction of the Second World War: Gender, Power and Resistance* (Edinburgh: Edinburgh University Press, 1996), pp. 139–165;

Alison Smith, "The Woman from the Big House: The Autobiographical Writings of Naomi Mitchison," *Chapman*, nos. 50–51 (Summer 1987): 10–17;

Kirsten Stirling, "The Roots of the Present: Naomi Mitchison, Agnes Mure Mackenzie and the Construction of History," in *The Polar Twins*, edited by Edward J. Cowan and Gifford (Edinburgh: John Donald, 1999), pp. 254–269.

Papers:

Naomi Mitchison's papers are in the National Library of Scotland, Edinburgh, and the Harry Ransom Humanities Research Center, University of Texas at Austin.

Michael Moorcock
(18 December 1939 –)

Mitchell R. Lewis
Elmira College

See also the Moorcock entries in *DLB 14: British Novelists Since 1960; DLB 231: British Novelists Since 1960, Fourth Series;* and *DLB 261: British Fantasy and Science-Fiction Writers Since 1960.*

BOOKS: *Caribbean Crisis,* by Moorcock and James Cawthorn, as Desmond Reid (London: Sexton Blake Library, 1962);

The Stealer of Souls and Other Stories (London: Spearman, 1963; New York: Lancer, 1967);

The Barbarians of Mars, as Edward P. Bradbury (London: Roberts & Vinter, 1965; New York: Ace, 1965); republished as *The Masters of the Pit,* as Moorcock (New York: Lancer, 1965; London: New English Library, 1971);

Blades of Mars, as Bradbury (London: Roberts & Vinter, 1965; New York: Lancer, 1966); republished as *The Lord of the Spiders,* as Moorcock (New York: Lancer, 1970; London: New English Library, 1971);

The Fireclown (London: Roberts & Vinter, 1965; New York: Paperback Library, 1967); republished as *The Blood-Red Game* (New York: Paperback Library, 1969; London: Sphere, 1970);

Stormbringer (London: Jenkins, 1965; New York: Lancer, 1967);

The Sundered Worlds (London: Roberts & Vinter, 1965; New York: Paperback Library, 1966); republished as *The Winds of Limbo* (New York: Paperback Library, 1969; London: Sphere, 1970);

Warriors of Mars, as Bradbury (London: Roberts & Vinter, 1965; New York: Lancer, 1966); republished as *The City of the Beast,* as Moorcock (New York: Lancer, 1970; London: New English Library, 1971);

The Deep Fix, as James Colvin (London: Roberts & Vinter, 1966);

Printer's Devil, as Bill Barclay (London: Roberts & Vinter, 1966); revised as *The Russian Intelligence,* as Moorcock (Manchester: Savoy, 1980);

Somewhere in the Night, as Barclay (London: Roberts & Vinter, 1966); revised as *The Chinese Agent,* as Moorcock (London: Hutchinson, 1970; New York: Macmillan, 1970);

The Twilight Man (London: Roberts & Vinter, 1966; New York: Berkley, 1970); republished as *The Shores of Death* (London: Sphere, 1970; New York: Dale, 1978; revised edition, New York: DAW, 1977);

The Jewel in the Skull (New York: Lancer, 1967; London: Mayflower, 1969);

The Wrecks of Time (New York: Ace, 1967); republished as *The Rituals of Infinity; or The New Adventures of Doctor Faustus* (London: Arrow, 1971; New York: DAW, 1978);

The Final Programme (New York: Avon, 1968; London: Allison & Busby, 1969; revised edition, London: Fontana, 1979);

Michael Moorcock (from the dust jacket for Mother London, *1988; Richland County Public Library)*

Sorcerer's Amulet (New York: Lancer, 1968); republished as *The Mad God's Amulet* (London: Mayflower, 1969; revised edition, New York: DAW, 1977);

The Sword of the Dawn (New York: Lancer, 1968; London: Mayflower, 1969; revised edition, New York: DAW, 1977);

Behold the Man (London: Allison & Busby, 1969; New York: Avon, 1970);

The Black Corridor, by Moorcock and Hilary Bailey (London: Mayflower, 1969; New York: Ace, 1969);

The Ice Schooner (New York: Berkley, 1969; London: Sphere, 1969; revised edition, New York: Dell, 1978; London: Harrap, 1985);

The Secret of the Runestaff (New York: Lancer, 1969); republished as *The Runestaff* (London: Mayflower, 1969; revised edition, New York: DAW, 1977);

The Time Dweller (London: Hart-Davis, 1969; New York: Berkley, 1971);

The Eternal Champion (St. Albans, U.K.: Mayflower, 1970); republished as *The Silver Warriors* (New York: Dell, 1970);

Phoenix in Obsidian (St. Albans, U.K.: Mayflower, 1970; New York: Dell, 1973);

The Singing Citadel (St. Albans, U.K.: Mayflower, 1970; New York: Berkley, 1970);

A Cure for Cancer (London: Allison & Busby, 1971; New York: Holt, Rinehart & Winston, 1971; revised edition, London: Fontana, 1979);

The King of the Swords (London: Mayflower, 1971; New York: Berkley, 1971);

The Knight of the Swords (London: Mayflower, 1971; New York: Berkley, 1971);

The Queen of the Swords (London: Mayflower, 1971; New York: Berkley, 1971);

The Sleeping Sorceress (London: New English Library, 1971; New York: Lancer, 1972); republished as *The Vanishing Tower* (London: New English Library, 1971; New York: DAW, 1977);

The Warlord of the Air (London: New English Library, 1971; New York: Ace, 1971);

Breakfast in the Ruins (London: New English Library, 1972; New York: Random House, 1974);

The English Assassin (London: Allison & Busby, 1972; New York: Harper & Row, 1972; revised edition, London: Fontana, 1979);

Elric of Melniboné (London: Hutchinson, 1972; New York: DAW, 1972); republished as *The Dreaming City* (New York: Lancer, 1972);

An Alien Heat (London: MacGibbon & Kee, 1972; New York: Harper & Row, 1972);

Count Brass (London: Mayflower, 1973; New York: Dell, 1976);

The Bull and the Spear (London: Allison & Busby, 1973; New York: Berkley, 1974);

The Champion of Garathorm (London: Mayflower, 1973; New York: Dell, 1976);

Elric: The Return to Melniboné (Brighton & Seattle: Unicorn Bookshop, 1973);

The Jade Man's Eyes (Brighton & Seattle: Unicorn Bookshop, 1973);

The Oak and the Ram (London: Allison & Busby, 1973; New York: Berkley, 1974);

The Hollow Lands (New York: Harper & Row, 1974; London: Hart-Davis, MacGibbon, 1975);

The Land Leviathan (London: Quartet, 1974; Garden City, N.Y.: Doubleday, 1974);

The Sword and the Stallion (London: Allison & Busby, 1974; New York: Berkley, 1974);

The Distant Suns, by Moorcock and Philip James (Llanfynydd, U.K.: Unicorn Bookshop, 1975);

The Quest for Tanelorn (London: Mayflower, 1975; New York: Dell, 1975);

The Lives and Times of Jerry Cornelius (London: Allison & Busby, 1976; New York: Dale, 1979);

The Adventures of Una Persson and Catherine Cornelius in the Twentieth Century (London: Quartet, 1976; New York: Dial, 1979);

The End of All Songs (New York: Harper & Row, 1976; London: Hart-Davis, MacGibbon, 1976);

Legends from the End of Time (New York: Harper & Row, 1976; London: W. H. Allen, 1976);

Moorcock's Book of Martyrs (London: Quartet, 1976); republished as *Dying for Tomorrow* (New York: DAW, 1978);

The Sailor on the Seas of Fate (London: Quartet, 1976; New York: DAW, 1976);

The Time of the Hawklords, by Moorcock and Michael Butterworth (London: Wyndham, 1976; New York: Warner, 1976);

The Bane of the Black Sword (New York: DAW, 1977; London: Panther, 1984);

The Condition of Muzak (London: Allison & Busby, 1977; Boston: Gregg Press, 1978);

The Cornelius Chronicles (1 volume, New York: Avon, 1977; 2 volumes, London: Fontana/Collins, 1988); republished as *The Cornelius Quartet* (London: Phoenix, 1993);

Sojan (Manchester: Savoy, 1977);

The Transformation of Miss Mavis Ming (London: W. H. Allen, 1977); republished as *A Messiah at the End of Time; or The Transformation of Miss Mavis Ming* (New York: DAW, 1978);

The Weird of the White Wolf (New York: DAW, 1977; London: Panther, 1984);

The Chronicles of Corum (New York: Berkley, 1978; London: Grafton, 1986); republished as *The Prince with the Silver Hand* (London: Millennium, 1993); republished as *Corum: The Prince with the Silver Hand* (Clarkston, Ga.: White Wolf, 1999);

Epic Pooh (Dagenham, U.K.: British Fantasy Society, 1978);

Gloriana, or The Unfulfill'd Queen (London: Allison & Busby, 1978; New York: Avon, 1979; revised edition, London: Phoenix, 1993);

The Golden Barge (Manchester: Savoy, 1979; New York: DAW, 1980);

The History of the Runestaff (St. Albans, U.K.: Granada, 1979); republished as *Hawkmoon* (London: Millennium, 1992; Clarkston, Ga.: White Wolf, 1995);

The Real Life Mr. Newman (Worcester, U.K.: Callow, 1979);

The Swords of Heaven, the Flowers of Hell, by Moorcock and Howard V. Chaykin (New York: HM/Simon & Schuster, 1979; London: Star, 1980);

The Great Rock 'n' Roll Swindle (London: Virgin, 1980);

My Experiences in the Third World War (Manchester: Savoy, 1980);

Byzantium Endures (London: Secker & Warburg, 1981; New York: Random House, 1981);

The Dancers at the End of Time (St. Albans, U.K.: Granada, 1982; Clarkston, Ga.: White Wolf, 1998);

The Entropy Tango (London: New English Library, 1981);

The Steel Tsar (London: Granada, 1981; New York: DAW, 1982);

The War Hound and the World's Pain (New York: Timescape, 1981; Sevenoaks, U.K.: New English Library, 1982);

Warrior of Mars (London: New English Library, 1981); republished as *Kane of Old Mars* (Clarkston, Ga.: White Wolf, 1998);

The Brothel in Rösenstrasse (London: New English Library, 1982; New York: Carroll & Graf, 1987);

The Nomad of Time (Garden City, N.Y.: Doubleday, 1982; London: Granada, 1984); republished as *A Nomad of the Time Streams* (London: Millennium, 1993; Clarkston, Ga.: White Wolf, 1995);

The Retreat from Liberty: The Erosion of Democracy in Today's Britain (London: Zomba, 1983);

Elric at the End of Time (Sevenoaks, U.K.: New English Library, 1984; New York: DAW, 1984);

The Elric Saga, 2 volumes (Garden City, N.Y.: Nelson Doubleday, 1984);

The Laughter of Carthage (London: Secker & Warburg, 1984; New York: Random House, 1984);

The Opium General and Other Stories (London: Harrap, 1984);

The Chronicles of Castle Brass (London: Granada, 1985); republished as *Count Brass* (London: Millennium, 1993; Clarkston, Ga.: White Wolf, 2000);

The City in the Autumn Stars (London: Grafton, 1986; New York: Ace, 1987);

The Cornelius Chronicles vol. II (New York: Avon, 1986);

The Crystal and the Amulet (Manchester: Savoy, 1986);

The Dragon in the Sword (New York: Ace, 1986; London: Grafton, 1987);

Letters from Hollywood, by Moorcock and Michael Foreman (London: Harrap, 1986);

The Cornelius Chronicles vol. III (New York: Avon, 1987);

Wizardry and Wild Romance: A Study of Epic Fantasy (London: Gollancz, 1987; Austin, Tex.: Monkey Brain, 2004);

Fantasy: The One Hundred Best Books, with James Cawthorn (London: Xanadu, 1988; New York: Carroll & Graf, 1988);

Mother London (London: Secker & Warburg, 1988; New York: Harmony, 1989);

Casablanca and Other Stories (London: Gollancz, 1989);

The Fortress of the Pearl (London: Gollancz, 1989; New York: Ace, 1989);

Tales from the End of Time (New York: Guild America, 1989); enlarged as *Legends from the End of Time* (Clarkston, Ga.: White Wolf, 1996);

The Revenge of the Rose (London: Grafton, 1991; New York: Ace, 1991);

The Eternal Champion (London: Millennium, 1992; Stone Mountain, Ga.: White Wolf, 1994);

Jerusalem Commands (London: Cape, 1992);

Hawkmoon (London: Millenium, 1992; Clarkston, Ga.: White Wolf, 1995);

Von Bek (London: Millenium, 1992; Stone Mountain, Ga.: White Wolf, 1995);

Earl Aubec and Other Stories (London: Millennium, 1993; Clarkston, Ga.: White Wolf, 1999);

A Cornelius Calendar (London: Phoenix, 1993);

Elric of Melniboné (London: Millennium, 1993); republished as *Elric: Song of the Black Sword* (Clarkston, Ga.: White Wolf, 1995);

Sailing to Utopia (London: Millenium, 1993; Clarkston, Ga.: White Wolf, 1997);

Behold the Man and Other Stories (London: Phoenix, 1994);

Blood: A Southern Fantasy (New York: Morrow, 1994; London: Millennium, 1995);

The Birds of the Moon (London: Jayde Design, 1995);

Fabulous Harbours (London: Millennium, 1995; New York: Avon, 1995);

Lunching with the Antichrist (Shingletown, Cal.: Ziesing, 1995);

The Adventure of the Dorset Street Lodger, as John H. Watson M.D. (London: Number Two Dorset Street, 1996);

The Roads Between the Worlds (Clarkston, Ga.: White Wolf, 1996);

The War Amongst the Angels (New York: Avon, 1996; London: Millennium, 1996);

Tales from the Texas Woods (Austin, Tex.: Mojo Press, 1997);

Elric: The Stealer of Souls (Clarkston, Ga.: White Wolf, 1998);

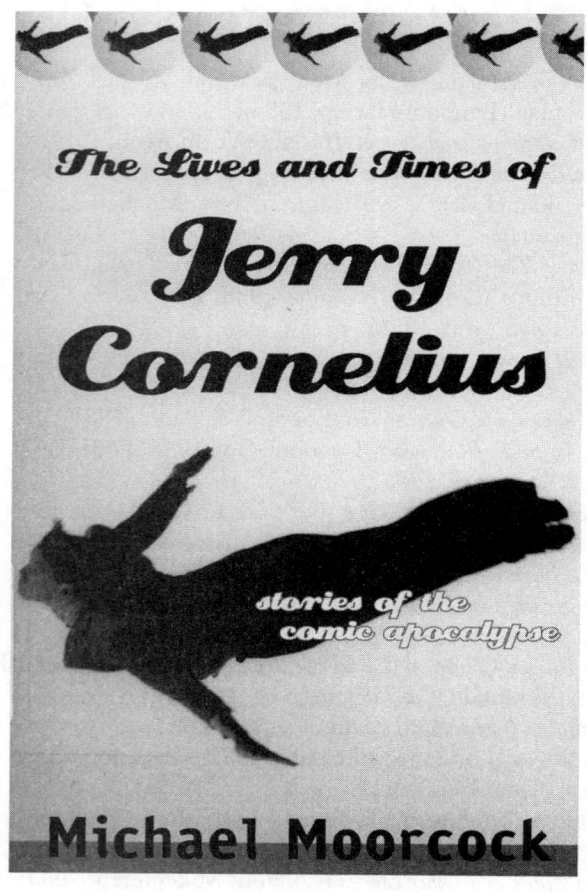

Front cover for the 2003 paperback edition of the 1976 collection of stories about a secret agent, ambivalent about his job, who is also the main character in four of Moorcock's novels and a novella (Richland County Public Library)

King of the City (London: Scribner, 2000; New York: Morrow, 2000);

Silverheart, by Moorcock and Storm Constantine (London: Simon & Schuster, 2000; Amherst, N.Y.: Pyr, 2005);

The Dreamthief's Daughter: A Tale of the Albino (New York: Warner, 2001; London: Earthlight, 2001);

London Bone (New York: Scribner, 2001; London: Simon & Schuster, 2001);

Firing the Cathedral (Harrogate, U.K.: PS Publishing, 2002);

The Mystery of the Texas Twister (Taylor, Ariz.: Coppervale, 2003);

The Skrayling Tree (New York: Warner, 2003);

New Worlds: An Anthology (New York: Thunder's Mouth Press, 2004);

Jerry Cornell's Comic Capers (Stafford, U.K.: Immanion Press, 2005);

The White Wolf's Son: The Albino Underground (New York: Warner, 2005).

PRODUCED SCRIPT: *The Land That Time Forgot,* motion picture, by Moorcock and James Cawthorn, American International Pictures/Amicus Productions, 1974.

OTHER: *The Best of New Worlds,* edited by Moorcock (London: Compact, 1965);

The Nature of the Catastrophe, edited by Moorcock and Langdon Jones (London: Hutchinson, 1971);

The New Nature of the Catastrophe, edited by Moorcock and Jones (London: Millenium, 1993);

Cities, edited by Paul Di Filippi, China Mieville, Moorcock, and Peter Crowther (New York: Four Walls Eight Windows, 2004).

Michael Moorcock is a prolific writer with a teeming imagination. Appealing to many different audiences, he has written works of historical fiction, heroic fantasy, science fiction, and mainstream literature. He has even written stories for comic books and composed song lyrics for rock bands. Typically, Moorcock's work crosses popular and mainstream genres, combining a populist sense of entertainment with a philosophical exploration of contemporary issues. His success in this regard is seen in the range of the recognition of his work, which includes a Nebula from the Science Fiction Writers of America as well as a nomination for the Booker Prize, Britain's premier award for serious fiction. This broad appeal to genre and mainstream audiences is what characterizes Moorcock's short stories.

Michael John Moorcock was born on 18 December 1939, in Mitcham, Surrey, a suburb of London. He had a difficult childhood. His earliest memories are of the Blitz in World War II, which significantly shaped his imagination. He also grew up without his father, Arthur Moorcock, who abandoned his family in 1945. Moorcock and his mother, June (Taylor) Moorcock, lived in suburban London until he left home in 1960; his mother continued to live there. Moorcock became rebellious, frequently challenging authority figures. For all his hardships, however, he developed an early interest in reading and writing. Self-educated, he was a voracious reader, and at age ten he was already producing homemade magazines. Encouraged by her son's interests, Moorcock's mother enrolled him at Pitman College, where he studied clerical education in the hope of pursuing a career in journalism. Four years later, after nearly being expelled, Moorcock left college to become an office junior. At fifteen he acquired an entry-level job at the management consultant firm of Harold Whitehead and Partners. At sixteen he went to work for Westworld Publications, and at seventeen he published his first short story, "Johnny Lonesome Comes to Town" (1956), a juvenile work of Western fiction that appeared first in *The Searchlight Book for Boys* (1956) and later in Moorcock's *Tales from the Texas Woods* (1997).

In 1956 Moorcock became editor of Whitehead's juvenile magazine, *Tarzan Adventures,* in which much of his early fiction appeared. His best-known works from this period are the Sojan stories, which cross science fiction and heroic fantasy. A wandering mercenary living on the planet of Zylor, Sojan inhabits a premodern, tribal world of basic technology, and the Sojan sequence chronicles a succession of episodic adventures, showing the influence of Edgar Rice Burroughs in its preference for action and fast pacing over theme and psychological subtlety. The sequence, however, does gesture toward some important subjects associated with Moorcock's later work, including the evils of organized religion, as well as the impending threat of apocalypse and chaos. The Sojan stories include "Sojan the Swordsman" (1957), "Revolt in Hatnor" (1957), "The Hordes Attack" (1957), "Sojan and the Hunters of Norj" (1958), "The Purple Galley" (1958), "The Sea Wolves" (1958), "Sojan at Sea" (1958), "The Sea of Demons" (1958), "Prisoners of Stone" (1958), "Sojan and the Plain of Mystery" (1958), "Sojan and the Sons of the Snake-God" (1958), and "Rens Karto of Bersnol" (1958), which was co-authored with Dick Ellingsworth. The Sojan stories were later collected in book form in *Sojan* (1977), to which was added "Mission to Asno." The same stories appeared again in *Elric at the End of Time* (1984). Several other early Moorcock stories in the Sojan vein also appeared in *Tarzan Adventures,* including "Dek of Noothar" (1957), which follows the adventures of the hero Dek as he quests for the mystic sword of life to make himself immune to illness and a more capable fighter; "The Seige of Noothar" (1957), which continues Dek's adventures, as he defeats a tyrant; and "Klan the Spoiler" (1958), in which the titular hero saves his sister Sherahl from his nemesis. The first two stories were co-authored with John Wisdom.

In 1958 Moorcock left *Tarzan Adventures* because the publisher wanted to emphasize comics over print and took a job at Amalgamated Press (later Fleetway Publications), where he wrote detective thrillers for the Sexton Blake Library, for which he was assistant editor, and comic strips featuring characters such as Tarzan, Robin Hood, and Billy the Kid. He also began to experiment with genre conventions, a project he continued throughout his career. In 1959 he published his first mature work, "Peace on Earth," co-authored with Barrington Bayley and later collected in *Earl Aubec and Other Stories* (1993). In this science-fiction story two immortal space travelers land their spaceship on an abandoned future Earth made uninhabitable by radiation. Discontented with their immortality and their lives of apathy and placidity, the travelers are on a quest for a more satisfying life. The story reaches its climax when the two travelers finally experience their own mortality, the resulting sense of impending death revitalizing their sense of the meaning of life. In its use of allegory and references to existential philosophy, the story marks a significant advance in Moorcock's storytelling.

In the early 1960s, after leaving Sexton Blake, Moorcock began freelance work for the British science-fiction pulp magazine *New Worlds*. He became a regular contributor to *New Worlds, Science Fantasy* and *Science Fiction Adventure*. Moorcock also started to develop a mythology involving three key elements that inform much of his subsequent work. The first is the Eternal Champion, a recurring character who made his first published appearance in the 1962 story "Eternal Champion," later rewritten as a novel (1970). The Champion is a heroic fantasy figure who, since the dawn of time, has participated in a cosmic battle between Law and Chaos, the second element of Moorcock's mythology. He may fight on either side of the battle, but ultimately he strives to balance the two, the success of which is determined by the mysterious Cosmic Balance. The battle itself is always raging, promising either some kind of apocalyptic end to the universe or a transition to a new age, and most of Moorcock's heroes are incarnations of the Eternal Champion. The last key element is the "multiverse," Moorcock's nonlinear fictional world of infinite, simultaneously existing, often interconnecting universes. The concept was first introduced in Moorcock's novel *The Sundered Worlds* (1965). In this world infinite variations on his characters and stories exist, all equally legitimate. For Moorcock, time is a field of infinite possibilities. His characters can travel through time in this endless universe, navigating what is variously known as the timestreams, the moonbeam roads, or the megaflow. For Moorcock the multiverse is a metaphor for the decentered postmodern world. One of the difficulties of reading Moorcock's interconnected stories is that in order to understand one fully, the reader has to know all. Matters are made more complicated by Moorcock's regularly revising his previously published stories.

In 1961 Moorcock's career took off with the publication of his short stories featuring Elric of Melniboné, a heroic fantasy character. On 25 October 1962 Moorcock married Hilary Denham Bailey, a writer, by whom he had three children: Sophie, Katherine, and Max. The couple divorced in April 1978.

The Elric stories take place in a premodern world typical of the sword-and-sorcery genre. Elric himself, however, is a more sophisticated character than the typical fantasy hero. Variously characterized as an antihero or a hero-villain, Elric is a brooding, melancholic outsider who seeks constantly for a purpose to life, but always remains skeptical, ironic, and cynical. The stories themselves usually chronicle Elric's efforts on behalf of various good

Front cover for the 1994 paperback edition of the 1992 collection of stories about the von Bek family, headed by the seventeenth-century German mercenary Ulrich von Bek, introduced in Moorcock's 1981 novel The War Hound and the World's Pain *(Richland County Public Library)*

causes, culminating with his participation in a war against Chaos, but they also explore the consequences of violence. This exploration is particularly evident in how Moorcock treats Elric's use of his sentient magic sword, Stormbringer. Physically weak because he is an albino, Elric requires the magical energy of his sword to give him strength. Without his sword, Elric would lose all vitality and eventually die. The sword, however, must kill to sustain its own vitality, and having the power to manipulate its bearer physically, it often causes Elric to kill the people closest to him, a quandary for him, because his health and well-being are dependent on the killing of others. For Elric the sword becomes the equivalent of a hated but inescapable addiction that ultimately leads not only to the deaths of his friends, family, lovers, and associates, but also to his own. This situation is unusual for a fantasy character because it raises ethical questions about the use of violence, for whatever end. It also differs from fantasy fiction because Moorcock makes no clear distinction between good and evil characters.

In the first Elric story, "The Dreaming City" (1961), Elric destroys Imrryr, the last city of his dying race, an act leading to his cohorts' destruction and inadvertently to the death of the woman he loves, all because he wants to take revenge against his cousin, who has usurped Elric's throne and proclaimed Elric a traitor. The story concludes with Elric all alone, filled with self-loathing, despising his sword and the power it gives him, but unable to relinquish it for fear of losing his life. "While the Gods Laugh" (1961) is an allegorical tale recounting the restless Elric's search for a book rumored to possess the key to absolute knowledge. In the end, Elric only discovers the remains of a book reduced to dust by time. In "The Stealer of Souls" (1962) Elric joins forces with survivors of Imrryr to defeat a sorcerer. His sword, however, overrides his intentions, again wreaking havoc on those near him. "Kings in Darkness" (1962) describes Elric's falling in love with Princess Zarozinia. For the first time, thanks to the help of special drugs and herbs, Elric fights without the aid of Stormbringer; the story ends with Elric's marriage to Zarozinia and his optimistic sense that he might be able to abandon his sword. Elric's hopes, however, are dashed in "The Flamebringers" (1962); he is forced to employ Stormbringer again and thus incurs the usual consequences as he saves human civilization from a barbarian warlord.

"Dead God's Homecoming" (1963), "Black Sword's Brother" (1963), "Sad Giant's Shield" (1964), and "Dead Lord's Passing" (1964)–later collected as *Stormbringer* (1965)–recount the final days of Elric and are linked by a narrative frame about the battle between Chaos and Law. Much of the plot concerns Elric's battle with sorcerer Jagreen Lern, who is bent on world domination and allied with the forces of Chaos. Elric eventually kills Lern, foils the plans of Chaos, and helps to usher in a new age for humanity characterized by a balance between Law and Chaos, but he has brought destruction on everyone around him, including his wife. Fittingly, the last story concludes with Stormbringer's taking Elric's life, thus fulfilling Elric's destiny. Subsequent Elric stories and novels flesh out the early life of Elric or take place between the times of previous stories, as in "The Singing Citadel" (1967), which recounts how Elric momentarily balances the forces of Chaos and Law by defeating Balo the Jester. The Elric stories can be found in *Elric of Melniboné* (1993) and *Elric: The Stealer of Souls* (1998).

In the 1960s, Moorcock also wrote many other fantasy as well as science-fiction short stories, most of which have been collected in *The Deep Fix* (1966), *The Time Dweller* (1969), *Moorcock's Book of Martyrs* (1976), and, in 1993, *Earl Aubec*. In "Going Home" (1962) neurotic spacemen from the artistically inclined planet

Veildo are disappointed when they return to Earth, their home planet, which their people left three centuries before. Discovering a bland, stagnant civilization, they gladly return to Veildo, feeling better off for their neuroses. "To Rescue Tanelorn" (1962) establishes the peaceful ideal city of Tanelorn as a counterpoint to the chaos of Elric's universe; it focuses on the hero Rackhir the Red Archer. Tanelorn becomes Moorcock's symbol for a balanced psychological state. "The Greater Conqueror" (1963), an historical fantasy, presents an archetypal struggle between Alexander the Great and his officer, Simon of Byzantium. The struggle is presented in the dualistic terms of Zoroastrian religion: Alexander embodies Ahriman and the powers of darkness, while Simon represents Ormuzd and the forces of light. The conflict becomes another opportunity for Moorcock to reflect on the eternal war between Chaos and Law.

In "Flux" (1963) representatives of the European Economic Community, seeking to control an unpredictable world, use a time machine to send Max File into the future to learn the secrets of time. File, however, becomes lost in time's nonlinear nature, visiting many time lines and eventually acquiring the power to create his own world. This story not only focuses on concepts related to Moorcock's "multiverse" but also presents his idea that human beings impose their own sense of time on the world. "Islands" (1963) explores a similar vein, presenting a psychologist who discovers that one of his patients literally lives in time-space dimensions of his own making. The psychologist insists that his discovery applies to all human beings, overturning John Donne's idea that "No man is an Island." In "The Time Dweller" (1964) a man on a depleted future Earth discovers how to manipulate time, becoming the first Time Dweller and mankind's salvation. "Master of Chaos" (1964) brings readers to the core of Moorcock's mythology, presenting the fantasy hero Earl Aubec in a cosmic struggle to wrest a new Order from Chaos. In "The Deep Fix" (1964) a psychologist in an overpopulated world succumbing to madness experiments on himself in order to construct a machine that manages insane people by inducing a dream state indistinguishable from the real world. Again Moorcock stresses the subjective nature of reality, but here he links it to a scientific-industrial-military complex concerned with managing an unruly global populace.

"Goodbye, Miranda" (1964) is a parable about obsessive love in which a ghost drives the woman he loves insane, causing her to kill her father and then herself. In "The Mountain" (1965) two male explorers, protected from a global nuclear catastrophe by peculiar weather patterns in an isolated spot of Sweden, follow the tracks of the last girl on Earth up a snow-covered mountain. One of the men dies because of his obsession with the girl, while the other turns his attention to his vast, impersonal environment, feeling insignificant in relationship to nature. Again Moorcock offers his reader a meditation on death and nothingness, expressed partly in the language of the sublime. "Escape from Evening" (1965) presents a dissatisfied inhabitant of a decadent moon colony who seeks to fulfill his yearning for the past but finds only a grim present. In "The Pleasure Garden of Felipe Sagittarius" (1965) Moorcock introduces the metatemporal investigator Mino Aquilanas. "The Golden Barge" (1965) is an allegorical tale in which its protagonist, Jephraim Tallow, sails up a river in pursuit of a mysterious golden barge, a kind of Holy Grail always out of reach, much like the absolute knowledge that Elric seeks in "While the Gods Laugh."

"The Lovebeast" (1966) depicts a world suffering from radiation sickness resulting from a series of nuclear tests in space. A moment of hope appears in this apocalyptic situation when the hearts of all mankind are filled with the selfless love of a strange alien entity. However, the so-called lovebeast cannot undo the radiation poisoning. The world is filled with love too late to make a difference. "The Real Life Mr. Newman" (1966) explores the nature of perception, reality, and time, as an astronaut returns from a mission to Mars only to find himself in a world of different psychic time zones. Moorcock again stresses the subjective nature of reality, but he raises unanswered ethical questions when the astronaut must deal with the senseless killing of innocent people by a German nihilist. "Wolf" (1966) is a disturbing story told by a sexual predator who claims that the woman he intends to kill has turned him into a sharp-toothed wolf. "Environment Problem" (1966) is a humorous reworking of the Faust theme in which an ambitious and ruthless young man sells his soul to Satan. In "The Ruins" (1966) a man without memory explores a ruined world while reflecting on the nature of time and identity. "Consuming Passion" (1966), another tale of dark obsession, concerns an arsonist who believes he is a god-like artist; he wreaks havoc on a city as he learns that he has the mental ability to create fires at will.

In 1964 Moorcock became editor of *New Worlds* and, along with J. G. Ballard and Brian Aldiss, established himself as a powerful voice in what became known as the New Wave, a 1960s science-fiction movement that attempted to infuse the tired conventions of the genre with experimental literary techniques, psychological subtlety, and philosophical reflection. Moorcock also published "Behold the Man" (1966), a significant work that won him a British Science Fiction Association Award and a Nebula from the Science Fiction Writers of America. Moorcock's most accomplished tale to date, it tells the story of a neurotic time-traveling psychologist, Karl Glogauer, who

Dust jacket for Moorcock's 1995 collection of further stories about the von Bek family; the title story concerns the English branch of the family, the Beggs (Richland County Public Library)

moves from the twentieth century to A.D. 28 in search of Jesus Christ and a religious life that cannot be sustained in the modern world. A follower of psychologist Carl Jung's Christian mysticism, Glogauer arrives in Palestine and, to his surprise, is mistaken for the Savior by John the Baptist. Spurred on by his own neuroticism, Karl accepts the role, eventually believing that he is Christ. Living out his dream of making mythological archetypes a reality, Karl is crucified, but on the cross he seems to recognize that his experience has all been a lie and his followers neurotics, political revolutionaries, or some combination of both. The story ends with Karl's corpse rotting and false stories already beginning to circulate about his resurrection. Exploring the nature of myth from a decidedly materialist perspective, Moorcock suggests that myth is rooted in psychological disorders and political realities. Moorcock unveils masochism, egotism, fear, neuroticism, and political ambition as behind myth.

In the mid 1960s Moorcock developed another influential character, Jerry Cornelius—the subject of four novels, a novella, and many short stories. A secret agent caught up in global political situations beyond his understanding or control, Cornelius is an antihero, a modern mythological figure intended to capture the ambiguities and tensions of the twentieth century. The Cornelius stories themselves are experimental, their fragmentary and elliptical nature reflecting the influences of French Surrealism and the early novels of William S. Burroughs. They also incorporate many quotations from nonfiction sources, usually newspapers. The overall organization emphasizes theme, imagery, and symbolism over linear narrative; Moorcock's express intention is to give the reader the role of interpreter. The Cornelius stories were Moorcock's first attempts to treat contemporary subjects in a contemporary manner, and they were his first stories to bring him serious literary attention.

The first three Cornelius stories were excerpts from the first Cornelius novel, *The Final Programme* (1968), the plot of which parallels events in the first two Elric stories. "Preliminary Data" (1965) presents a series of brief scenes between Jerry Cornelius and his friend Professor Hira. It juxtaposes the East and the West, Hindu mysticism and modern science, and raises questions about the nature of time and the possibility of drawing all information into a final equation. "Further Information" (1965) focuses on the all-purpose human, Cornelius Brunner, who is the result of a scientific experiment that merged Jerry Cornelius with Miss Brunner, the scientist behind the experiment. Cornelius Brunner is a creature of total knowledge, a kind of Nietzschean *Übermensch* (overman) beyond good and evil. He is Moorcock's symbol for the changes taking place in the 1960s. "Phase Three" (1966) presents background on Miss Brunner's scientific project to create the perfect human being for a world dying of entropy.

In "The Delhi Division" (1968) Cornelius attempts to assassinate an Indian political figure but has second thoughts when he finds his intended victim making love to a Pakistani woman. "The Tank Trapeze" (1968) alternates news accounts of the Soviet takeover of Prague with a story of Cornelius's operating as a hit man in Mandalay. In "The Peking Junction" (1969) Cornelius, posing as a U.S. Air Force officer, investigates the crash of an F111A in China and eventually assassinates an important Chinese general. The story reveals that Cornelius is a manifestation of the Eternal Champion and also focuses on the related theme of the battle between Chaos and Law. "The Dodgem Division" (1969) is a metafictional piece in which Moorcock justifies the literary techniques and subject matter of the Cornelius corpus. In the story Cornelius reflects on the state of contemporary British fiction and literary criticism, seeing the emergence of a "new fiction" that deals with the modern world in a manner suitable to its subject. What Cornelius says also describes the techniques and subject matter of the Cornelius stories themselves.

In the 1970s Moorcock continued his work on Jerry Cornelius, writing "Sea Wolves" (1970), "The Nature of the Catastrophe" (1970), "All the Dead Singers" (1971), "Voortrekker" (1971), "The Swastika Set-Up" (1972), "The Longford Cup" (1973), "A Dead Singer" (1974), "The Entropy Circuit" (1974), "The Minstrel Girl" (1977), and "The Kassandra Penninsula" (1978). These stories develop already established themes; Moorcock's technique is analogous to musical variation. "The Minstrel Girl" and "The Kassandra Penninsula" were later incorporated into the novel *The Entropy Tango* (1981), and the rest were gathered into the short-story collection *The Lives and Times of Jerry Cornelius* (1976), along with "The Delhi Division," "The Tank Trapeze," "The Peking Junction," and "The Dodgem Division." The Cornelius stories can be found in *The Nature of the Catastrophe* (1971) and *The New Nature of the Catastrophe* (1993), which also collect Cornelius stories by other hands, and in *The Cornelius Chronicles vol. II* (1986), *The Cornelius Chronicles vol. III* (1987), and *A Cornelius Calendar* (1993).

In the mid 1970s Moorcock started the End of Time series, about a race of eccentric, hedonistic immortals who have the power to resurrect themselves continuously and are living at a time when the universe is slowly winding down. Bored and jaded, they entertain themselves with fantastic illusions generated by the advanced technology of their "power rings," and they are often involved with travelers navigating the infinite timestreams of the multiverse. Because art has conquered nature, the immortals have absolute control over everything except the entropy of the universe. With the help of their power rings, which draw on the remaining energy in the universe, they even have the ability to create new worlds. Collected in *Tales from the End of Time* (1989), the stories are comic, but they address serious subjects, especially decadence, aestheticism, romanticism, ethics, time, and death.

In "Pale Roses" (1974) the unfulfilled End-of-Time immortal Werther de Goethe pines for the life of his ancient ancestors, who knew what morality was and experienced pain, death, love, and a range of human emotions. With the arrival of an orphaned girl named Catherine Gratitude, however, Werther begins to play the role of a protective father figure and, after a shocking episode with Catherine, manages to learn something about the meanings of love, sin, and death. In "White Stars" (1975) the inhabitants at the End of Time enliven the boredom of their lives with dueling, agreeing not to resurrect themselves if they lose a contest. Again the immortals have an opportunity to reflect on death and the meaning of life. In "Ancient Shadows" (1975) the Spartan culture of two recently arrived time travelers is contrasted with the decadence of the End of Time, a juxtaposition that evokes the conflict between Chaos and Law. Moorcock explores the relativity of value and, in spite of the tragic conclusion to the story, suggests that both cultures have a certain dignity. "The Murderer's Song" (1987) and "Elric at the End of Time" (1987) link the End of Time stories with the Jerry Cornelius cycle and the Elric mythos, respectively.

Additional stories from the 1970s include "Waiting for the End of Time" (1970), in which a highly evolved hermaphroditic human species waits helplessly for the destruction of its planet; "The Stone Thing" (1974), a self-conscious parody of Moorcock's heroic fantasy fiction; and "My Life" (1975), a piece commissioned by the editors of the anthology *You Always Remember the First Time* (1975). The selections in the anthology were supposed to be autobiographical essays about their authors' early experiences with sex, but Moorcock chose instead to write a tall tale on the assumption that the other contributors, like most people, would lie about their first sexual experiences. "The Last Enchantment" (1978), also known as "Jesting with Chaos," was written in the 1960s and was intended to be the second and final installment of the Elric saga; however, it was rejected by Moorcock's editor, who did not want the Elric series to conclude.

Moorcock married Jill Riches on 7 May 1978. They divorced in 1983, and he married Linda Mullens Steele on 23 September 1983.

In the 1980s Moorcock created the von Bek family and its various branches, including the English Beggs and Becks, as well as the Russian Bekovs. Introduced in Moorcock's novel *The War Hound and the World's Pain* (1981), the central figure is the virtually immortal Ulrich von Bek, a former seventeenth-century mercenary from Mirenburg, Wäldenstein, whose goals are to reconcile Satan with God and to pursue and defend the Holy Grail. Like Elric, Ulrich is an albino. The motto of his family is "Do You the Devil's Work." Ulrich also wields the powerful black sword of Elric. Like Moorcock's other characters, Ulrich (along with the rest of the Bek family) travels throughout the multiverse, usually in quest of the Holy Grail. The Bek stories typically have historical settings and blend adventure and philosophy.

In "Hanging the Fool" (1989), also known as "Wheel of Fortune," von Bek attempts to help his former wife, who is involved in a scheme to find a lost treasure, one that ultimately leads to her suicide and unanswerable questions. "The Cairene Purse" (1990) tells the story of Paul von Beck's search in Aswan, Egypt, for his missing sister, archeologist Beatrice von Beck, apparently linking the spontaneous occurrence of myth to madness and the alienation of the modern world. In "Lunching with the Antichrist" (1993), also known as "The Clapham Antichrist," Moorcock provides an historical overview of the English Beggs, focusing in particular on Edwin Begg, a prominent early-twentieth-century public figure whom the narrator interviews during a series of lunches. This story appears to address historical change, marking the end of traditional British culture and the beginning of a postmodern world. In "A Winter Admiral" (1994) Mrs. Marjorie Begg, a down-on-her-luck descendant of the Begg family, enjoys a redemptive moment of beauty at Crow Cottage on an unseasonably warm winter day.

"The Affair of the Seven Virgins" (1994) introduces what becomes an ongoing conflict between detective Sir Sexton Begg and Ulrich von Bek, one that mirrors the conflict between Law and Chaos. In "Crimson Eyes" (1994) Sir Sexton Begg, investigating a series of strange murders of business and political figures, discovers that the culprit is his arch-nemesis, Count Ulrich von Bek, who is attempting to retrieve the Holy Grail from the black market. The story juxtaposes the law-abiding nature of Sexton and the vigilantism of Ulrich. "The White Pirate" (1994) is a parodic reworking of the myth of the Wandering Jew, featuring Rose von Bek and her lover, Captain Horace Quelch. In "No Ordinary Christian" (1995) Ulrich von Bek avenges a murder in Egypt, while Poppy Begg marvels at the mysteries revealed to her at the ancient Egyptian temple that Ulrich now calls home. Originally published in 1974, but later revised for inclusion in the Bek cycle, "Dead Singers" (1995) is a story about the resurrection of Jimi Hendrix. Ambivalent about music, Hendrix prefers to remain in hiding with his roadie Mo Beck, who becomes increasingly confused about his idol. In Hendrix's surprising transformation and Mo's eventual drug-induced death, Moorcock seems to be writing an elegy for 1960s culture. "The Girl Who Killed Sylvia Blade" (1995) is another previously published piece revised for inclusion in the von Bek cycle of stories. Originally published in 1966, it is Moorcock's homage to hard-boiled detective fiction and features detective reporter Henry Beck. "The Birds of the Moon" (1995) is a touching story of how Tommy Bek and his family gain admittance to the mulitiverse after stumbling across the Holy Grail. The Beks are idealistic hippies from the 1960s, and the implication is that their unsatisfied utopian longings are fulfilled by the endless possibilities of the timestreams. "The Black Blade's Summoning" (1997) links the von Beks with the Elric mythos. Most of the von Bek stories can be found in *Von Bek* (1992), *Lunching with the Antichrist* (1995), and *Fabulous Harbours* (1995).

In the 1980s Moorcock also completed a sequence of four short stories about KGB secret agent Bekov titled "Some Reminiscences of the Third World War." Appearing most recently in *Earl Aubec* and inspired by Isaak Babel, the stories present a war-torn near-future Earth and are written from the perspective of Bekov, who assumes many aliases. They are similar to the Cornelius stories in that they depict an apocalyptic world divided by political intrigues and conflicts, the full context of which eludes the reader as well as the characters. Bekov, moreover, seems to be a combination of good and evil, an ambiguous hero similar to Cornelius and Elric. The stories touch on the end of rationalism, the euphoria of Armageddon, the uncertainties and ambiguities of politics, and the necessity for altruism and love. In "Casablanca" (1989), the first story chronologically, although the last written, Bekov assists the Algerian Secret Service department in its effort to bring a new monarch to the throne who might unite North Africa into a powerful political entity and Soviet ally. "Going to Canada" (1980) details Bekov's family history and its involvement in Russian politics, touching on his father's association with the Stalin regime and his own training with the KGB. The story concludes with an ominous outbreak of war between Russia and China that draws in Britain, the United States, and India, thus ushering in World War III. In "Leaving Pasadena" (1980) Bekov and his Chief go to Venezuela to await future orders, during which time they lead a dream-like existence of debauchery and despair, while the world at large deals with nuclear radiation. In "Crossing into Cambodia" (1979) Bekov assists the Vietnamese in repelling a Cambodian army, while all the nations of the world wage war against each other. The story ends on an apocalyptic note, as a nuclear bomb is detonated nearby, its mushroom cloud slowly filling the sky, providing a fitting emblem for the inevitable fate of humanity.

Moorcock also wrote several other short pieces in the 1980s, collected in *The Opium General and Other Stories* (1984) and *Casablanca and Other Stories* (1989). "The Opium General" (1984) is another tale of drug addiction and descent into madness, this time focused on the disillusionment of an addict's girlfriend. In "Last Call" (1987) the Eternal Champion is reluctantly resurrected at the End of Time to serve Chaos. "The Frozen Cardinal" (1987) depicts a scientific expedition exploring an uninhabited planet. Told as a series of letters by one of the explorers, the story moves toward the revelation of a buried, frozen Cardinal who, once set free, begins to sing an enchanting song. The rational scientific team, scornful of religion and superstition, finally succumbs to the spell of the Cardinal's song, but whether the expedition is experiencing a miracle or just hallucinating is uncertain. In "Mars" (1988) Moorcock presents another advanced but decadent civilization decaying from too much peace, this time an Earth civilization living underground on the planet Mars. Self-absorbed and feeble, the Martians have no desire other than to face their future with apathy. Two aliens from the future seem to herald the end of the Martian civilization, but they prove as feeble and decadent as the Martians. Again Moorcock presents a panoramic vision of history as the decline and fall of civilizations.

During the 1990s Moorcock continued his prolific short-story output, by mid decade moving with his American-born wife to Austin, Texas. Much of this work has been collected in *Tales from the Texas Woods* (1997) and *London Bone* (2001).

"The Museum of the Future" (1990) is an homage to H. G. Wells's *Time Machine* (1895), and "The Adventure of the Texan's Honour" (1995), also known as "The Adventure of the Dorset Street Lodger," presents a respectful pastiche of Arthur Conan Doyle's Sherlock Holmes stories, adding a New World twist involving two American characters. "The Enigma Windows" (1995) is a cyberpunk-influenced story of a dystopian future of vast ecological damage in which Jerry Cornelius, after waking from a long slumber, searches for his sister Catherine and his brother Frank. The story stresses the corporatization of the world and the subsequent dissolution of social responsibility. "Sir Milk-And-Blood" (1996) presents two Irish terrorists hiding after one of their bombs has prematurely detonated and killed innocent people. They wait for assistance from Monsieur Zodiac (Ulrich von Bek), who kills the men and takes from them the Holy Grail, which apparently fell into their possession after their recent attack. In "The Ghost Warriors" (1997) Moorcock, writing under the pseudonym of Warwick Colvin Jr., revisits juvenile Western fiction to tell a tale of a cowboy vigilante, the Masked Buckaroo, linking the story to the von Bek mythos, as Sir Sexton Begg and Ulrich von Bek make an appearance.

"Doves in the Circle" (1997) takes place in New York City, focusing on Houston Circle and its unusual history. "Cheering for the Rockets" (1998) is a Jerry Cornelius story that presents another apocalyptic world, which satirizes the imperialist foreign policy and escapist commodity culture of the United States. "Furniture" (1999) celebrates traditional English culture in its depiction of Mrs. Corren, who, thanks to her old-fashioned furniture, survives the terrorist bombing of her apartment building. "London Bone" (1999) is a timely satirical piece in which Moorcock criticizes the London tourism industry for turning its cultural heritage into commodities. The story is narrated by Raymond Gold, a Cockney "cultural speculator" who buys into a business selling pieces of ancient bone excavated in London. In "Through the Shaving Mirror" (2000) Moorcock presents a humorous discussion of the multiverse and the nature of time. "London Blood" (2000) is the story of the trials of a poor working-class London family; it focuses particularly on the mother, who protects her children from her abusive

Dust jacket for the 1997 American edition of Moorcock's 1995 collection of linked stories that is a sequel to Blood: A Southern Fantasy *(1994) and features stories about Jerry Cornelius and the von Beks (Richland County Public Library)*

husband. Told from the point of view of one of the children, the story is notable not only for its sophisticated narrative technique but also for the discrepancies that arise between the narrator's interpretations and the reader's observations.

At the beginning of the twenty-first century, Moorcock returned to his character Jerry Cornelius. He published a revised and expanded edition of *The Lives and Times of Jerry Cornelius* (2004), which collects "Cheering for the Rockets" and three other recent additions to the Cornelius mythos: "The Spencer Inheritance" (1997), "The Camus Connection" (1998), and "Firing the Cathedral" (2002).

Michael Moorcock's work has moved closer to mainstream fiction, a trend that became noticeable with the publication of the Booker Prize–nominated *Mother London* (1988). His work, however, is still grounded in the mythology that he first started developing in the 1960s. It still crosses many genres, including not only stories of heroic fantasy and science fiction but also Westerns and detective fiction. More importantly, Moorcock's work still has broad appeal, much as does the work of nineteenth-century novelist Charles Dickens, with whom Moorcock is often compared. From the heroic fantasy and New Wave science fiction of his early years to his work on London, Moorcock has remained committed to addressing a general audience, proving himself a role model for writers who want to bridge the divide between mainstream fiction and popular culture. His recent work, moreover, shows that he is still developing and honing his writing abilities, expanding his powers as a novelist and a short-story writer. As seen in *London Bone* and *The Lives and Times of Jerry Cornelius*, Moorcock continues to explore the possibilities for short fiction in the contemporary world. Having woven his many stories into a maze of postmodern textuality, he has accomplished much during his career, a career that seems far from over.

Interviews:

"The *Eildon Tree* Interview–Michael Moorcock," *Eildon Tree*, 1, no. 2 (1976): 4–8;

Paul Walker, *Speaking of Science Fiction: The Paul Walker Interviews* (Ordall, N.J.: Luna, 1978);

Ted Butler, "*Algol* Interview: Michael Moorcock," *Algol*, 15 (Winter 1978): 29–32;

Ian Covell, Interview with Michael Moorcock, *Science Fiction Review*, 8 (January 1979): 18–25;

Charles Platt, "Michael Moorcock," in his *Who Writes Science Fiction?* (Manchester: Savoy, 1980), pp. 233–242; republished as *Dream Makers: The Uncommon People Who Write Science Fiction* (New York: Berkley, 1980), pp. 97–104;

Moorcock and Colin Greenland, "Conversations," in *Death Is No Obstacle* (Manchester, U.K.: Savoy, 1992);

"The Locus Interview–Michael Moorcock: Movements and Myths," *Locus: The Newspaper of the Science Fiction Field*, 50, no. 3 (March 2003): 6–7, 71–73.

Bibliographies:

Andrew Harper and George McAuley, *Michael Moorcock: A Bibliography* (Kansas City, Mo.: T-K Graphics, 1976);

A. J. Callow, *The Chronicles of Moorcock* (London: Callow, 1978);

Richard Bilyeu, *The Tanelorn Archives: A Primary and Secondary Bibliography of the Works of Michael Moorcock, 1949–1979* (Neche, N.Dak.: Pandora's Books, 1981);

Brian Hinton, *Michael Moorcock, a Bibliography: Based on the Moorcock Deposit, Bodleian Library, Oxford* (Brighton, U.K.: J. L. Noyce, 1983).

References:

Michael Ashley, "Behold the Man Called Moorcock," *Science Fiction Monthly*, 2 (February 1975): 8–11;

Peter Caracciolo, "Michael Moorcock," in *Twentieth Century Science Fiction Writers*, second edition, edited by Curtis C. Smith (Chicago: St. James Press, 1986), pp. 519–522;

John Clute, "Michael Moorcock," in *Encyclopedia of Science Fiction*, edited by Clute and Peter Nicholls (New York: St. Martin's Griffin, 1995), pp. 822–825;

Clute, "The Repossession of Jerry Cornelius," introduction to *The Cornelius Chronicles*, volume 1 (New York: Avon, 1977);

John Dean, "'A Curious Note in the Wind': The New Literary Genre of Heroic Fantasy," *New Mexico Humanities Review*, 2 (Summer 1979): 34–41;

Michel Delville, "The Moorcock/Hawkwind Connection: Science Fiction and Rock 'n' Roll Culture," *Foundation: The Review of Science Fiction*, 62 (Winter 1994–1995): 64–69;

Nick Freeman, "British Barbarians at the Gates: Grant Allen, Michael Moorcock and Decadence," *Foundation: The International Review of Science Fiction*, 30 (Autumn 2001): 35–47;

David Glover, "Utopian Fantasy in the Late 1960s: Burroughs, Moorcock, Tolkien," in *Popular Fiction and Social Change*, edited by Christopher Pawling (New York: St. Martin's Press, 1984);

Colin Greenland, *The Entropy Exhibition: Michael Moorcock and the "New Wave" in British Science Fiction* (London: Routledge, 1983);

Michael Hoey, "Disguising Doom: A Study of the Linguistic Features of Audience Manipulation in Michael Moorcock's The Eternal Champion," in *Imagining Apocalypse: Studies in Cultural Crisis*, edited by David Seed (New York: Macmillan–St. Martin's Press, 2000), pp. 151–165;

Georges Letissier, "Pruning London Down to Her Marrow: Michael Moorcock's Attempt at a Strategy of the Implicit in London Bone," *Journal of the Short Story in English*, 40 (Spring 2003): 29–45;

Peter Nicholls, "Michael Moorcock," in *Science Fiction Writers*, edited by E. F. Bleiler (New York: Scribners, 1982), pp. 449–457;

Ralph Willett, "Moorcock's Achievement and Promise in the Jerry Cornelius Books," *Science-Fiction Studies*, 3 (1976): 75–79.

Papers:

Collections of Michael Moorcock's papers are housed at the Bodleian Library, Oxford University, and the Sterling Library, Texas A&M University.

Val Mulkerns

(14 February 1925 –)

Marti D. Lee
University of South Carolina

BOOKS: *A Time Outworn* (London: Chatto & Windus, 1951);
A Peacock Cry (London: Hodder & Stoughton, 1954);
Bettlekture Fur Liebende (Bern: Scherz Verlag, 1967);
Verrat Mich Nicht, Nina (Zurich: Benziger, 1969);
Es Ist Deine Schuld (Zurich: Benziger, 1974);
Antiquities: A Sequence of Short Stories (London: Deutsch, 1978);
An Idle Woman and Other Stories (Dublin: Poolbeg, 1980);
The Summerhouse (London: Murray, 1984);
Very Like a Whale (London: Murray, 1986);
A Friend of Don Juan (London: Murray, 1988).

OTHER: "The World Outside" [includes an extract from "A Peacock Cry"], in *44 Irish Stories: An Anthology of Irish Short Fiction from Yeats to Frank O'Connor,* edited by D. A. Garrity (Old Greenwich, Conn.: Devin Adair, 1955);
"Introduction," in *New Writings from the West,* edited by Mulkerns (Castlebar: Mayo County Council, 1988);
"The Aunts," in *Christmas in Ireland,* edited by Colin Morrison ([Dublin]: RTE in association with Mercier Press, 1989);
"Introduction," in *Hurrish,* by Emily Lawless (Belfast: Appletree, 1992);
Maurice Kennedy, *The Road to Vladivostok,* edited by Mulkerns and Professor Augustine Martin (Privately published, 2002).

SELECTED PERIODICAL PUBLICATIONS—
UNCOLLECTED: "Girls," *Bell,* 14, no. 4 (1947): 46–52;
"O'Casey Remembers," *Bell,* 18, no. 5 (October 1952): 290–293;
"The Unfortunate Cow," *Harper's Bazaar* (1953);
"Primavera," *Recorder,* 10, nos. 1–2 (1997): 169–177.

Val Mulkerns accurately depicts many of the issues facing Ireland, particularly Dublin, since the mid twentieth century. Her short stories and novels

Val Mulkerns (photograph by Pat Langan, Irish Times, *from* Antiquities, *1978)*

from the early 1950s to the late 1980s bring up Irish concerns in a subtle manner as she skillfully interweaves themes of the changing roles of women and of the nation with her realistic portraits of domestic characters. Mulkerns grew up in an Ireland that was newly free of British rule, but the lingering effects of that time and the Irish War of Independence (1918–1921) and subsequent Civil War (1922–1923) helped shape her personality and her literature. Mulkerns threads themes of patriotism and portraits of romantic nationalists into her works and often laments the increasing urbanization of the Irish countryside and the declining traditional beliefs and lifestyles. Although her fiction invokes nostalgia for the past, conversely it criticizes the unrealistic optimism of dreamers and presents the message that one must learn to live in the present.

Mulkerns's family tree includes both ardent nationalists and unionists. She based one short story on her father, Jimmy Mulkerns, who was actively involved in the 1916 Easter Rising and subsequently incarcerated at Frongoch in Wales. Although little is known about her mother, Esther O'Neill, her maternal great-grandmother was a Protestant, and her grandfather worked as a reporter for the *Freeman's Journal,* a well-known pro–Home Rule paper. With such a diverse political background, almost inevitably, political themes surface in many of Mulkerns's works.

Mulkerns cannot easily be labeled, however, and critics and academics have often neglected her for that reason. Although most writers in Ireland are classified as either feminists or nationalists (or, conversely, antifeminist, antinationalist), Mulkerns, with her subtle weaving of the two themes, resists such simplistic categories, and this lack of an easy label has caused her to be disregarded by both feminist and nationalist critics. Despite the lack of critical and academic articles on Mulkerns, she is generally recognized as one of the foremost Irish writers of the mid to late twentieth century and is often mentioned along with such figures as Frank O'Connor and Sean O'Faolain. She received the Allied Irish Banks Prize for Literature in 1984 for her novel *The Summerhouse* (1984), and she is a founding member of Aosdána, an affiliation of visual, performance, and literary artists whose members have made outstanding contributions to the arts in Ireland.

Mulkerns has made her home in and around Dublin for the majority of her life; born in the city on 14 February 1925 and appropriately christened Valentine, she currently lives in Dalkey, a small village in County Dublin. Educated at the Dominican College in Eccles Street, Mulkerns has worked in a variety of literary fields; her career has spanned more than half a century and has encompassed everything from editing magazines and short-story collections to writing editorials, radio spots, newspaper feature articles, theater reviews, introductions, short stories, and novels.

During her brief career in the civil service from 1945 to 1949, she published her first short story, "Girls," which first appeared in a 1947 edition of *The Bell*. It explores one night in the lives of three young women sharing a flat in Dublin and the inherent risks in their lives: the decision whether to enter into a new relationship haunts one, while another is apparently wrestling with her own latent homosexuality, and the third struggles with the age-old paradox of being outwardly popular yet inwardly lonely and depressed. Mulkerns successfully captures issues that will continue to confront all independent young people, especially females.

Mulkerns moved to London in 1949 where she worked as a teacher and freelance journalist until 1952. In 1951 she published her first novel, *A Time Outworn,* which was praised extensively by fellow novelists and critics such as C. P. Snow and O'Connor, who called it "the most interesting and significant to have come out of Ireland in 25 years." Such reviews by prominent literary figures helped to launch her publishing career. Through the story of a remarkably perceptive, yet otherwise average, schoolgirl, Mulkerns presents hauntingly beautiful descriptions of an Ireland that no longer exists. Framing the story of Maeve and her maturation are descriptions of Dublin, Howth, Eniskerry, Tipperary, and the Aran Isles interspersed with discussions of William Shakespeare, William Butler Yeats, James Joyce, and Lady Isabella Augusta Persse Gregory mixed with reflections on Catholicism, Celtic legends, and wandering bards that are analogous to the change in Ireland itself.

Mulkerns returned to Ireland in 1952 to become associate editor of the literary magazine *The Bell*. The magazine, founded in 1940 by O'Faolain and later edited by Peadar O'Donnell, was a liberal, socially conscious publication that not only showcased Ireland's finest professional and novice writers but also prided itself on being, as Mulkerns says, "a thorn in the side of the establishment." Mulkerns's affiliation with this journal reveals much about her political and literary influences and inclinations.

In 1953 Mulkerns married Maurice Kennedy, a civil servant and fellow writer, with whom she had three children, Maev, Conor, and Myles. She spent the ensuing years, 1953–1978, raising her children and writing regular pieces for radio, a weekly column for the *Evening Press,* children's novels (in German), and many articles and short stories for magazines. Many of the articles and short stories produced during this time, primarily for English and American periodicals, are now unavailable.

One such story, "The Unfortunate Cow," published in 1953 in *Harper's Bazaar,* abandons the modern young women that she wrote about in "Girls" in favor of an old man from rural Ireland who is forced to live with his married sister in her new Dublin home. After reading an obituary, Bartley Farrell proceeds to tell a story about a woman who once refused a young man and married a rich doctor's son instead. The young man in the story (by implication Bartley himself) tries to curse the girl by using a hair from her head, but she outsmarts him by sending a hair from a cow's tail. The comic twist is ruined by tragedy, however, when a young boy is trampled and badly injured by the cow gone mad. The intermingled comedy and tragedy along with the folksy tone of the story give it a flavor of classic Irish peasant tales.

Mulkerns's second novel, *A Peacock Cry*, published in 1954, deals with a popular novelist, Dara Joyce, whose arrogance is matched only by his mediocre and sensational writing. The commentary on the prevalence of great writers in Ireland, but the mistreatment of these writers by their own country, is obvious as the narrator muses on "the advanced absurdities of this fantastic country which had produced more writers to the acre than any country in Europe and had driven the best of them into exile, silence and cunning. . . ." As Mulkerns published this novel in 1954, two years after she began working for *The Bell*, her condemnation of "repressive literary censorship laws . . . presided over by the Roman Catholic Hierarchy, aided and abetted by Eamon de Valera" is unmistakable.

Mulkerns's short-story collection *Antiquities: A Sequence of Short Stories* (1978) is dedicated to O'Connor, who Mulkerns says taught her the "necessity for almost obsessive revision." Although the volume includes the standard disclaimer that the characters are fictitious and not related to any living person, Mulkerns admits that some of the stories are somewhat autobiographical, particularly "Special Category."

The subtitle of *Antiquities*, "A Sequence of Short Stories," is indicative of its structure. Rather than including disjointed or thematically related stories, the volume follows the lives of three generations of Irish women: Emily; her daughter, Sarah; and her mother, Fanny. The stories illustrate Emily's life from childhood in "A Bitch and a Dog Hanging" and "The Sisters," through her troubled marriage in "Four Green Fields," "France Is So Phoney," and "Summer," and through the necessity of caring for aging relatives in "Terminus." Mulkerns takes the reader back to the life of Emily's mother, Fanny, in "Special Category," which tells the story of how Emily's parents met when her father, whom Mulkerns calls "a Romantic revolutionary," is jailed after the 1916 Rising, and her mother, a starry-eyed nationalist, tries to bring comfort to a complete stranger by visiting him in prison. "A Cut Above the Rest" continues the story of Fanny and Red Mull's marriage, showing the impossibility of living on big dreams with little income. "The Torch" takes up the story of Sarah as a young woman living in Paris. "Loser" breaks away from the three women a bit as it tells the story of Emily's Uncle Dan, "The Gentleman," and his endless and fruitless quest to get along on his looks and charm.

Besides the intergenerational link of the stories in *Antiquities*, a thread of nationalism also runs through

Dust jacket for Mulkerns's 1978 collection of stories about three generations of women in an Irish family (Collection of Marti D. Lee)

all of them, from the most obvious in "Special Category" to Emily's presence at a tragic terrorist bombing in "Four Green Fields" to Sarah's attempt to distance herself from a blackmailing IRA acquaintance in "The Torch." A third commonality that runs through all of the stories in *Antiquities* is the metaphor of houses. Emily laments the passing of her nanny's old thatched cottage, which has given way to cold heartless tract houses in "A Bitch and a Dog Hanging." The many different houses are contrasted both overtly and subtly as they function as symbols of the various characters. The big house in which Aunt Harry lives is contrasted variously to the small humble home of Fanny, Red Mull, and Emily; the larger house left to Fanny by her father but sold to cover Dan's gambling debts; and the railway cottage in which Red Mull spent his childhood. The homes and the Dublin neighborhoods act as more than just settings to these stories: they become characters in their own rights as

Front cover for Mulkerns's 1980 collection of short stories about romantic and familial relationships in contemporary Irish society (Boston Public Library)

well. The generations of homes intertwine with the generations of women to make a statement about the loss of romanticism, hope for the future, and the everyday lives that people must lead in between. In a 1982 article James O'Brien states, "Emily looks backward to the idealism of her mother's era of the Easter Rising and forward to the personal freedom and prosperity of her daughter's era.... Emily discovers in retrospect how her personality was formed by the economically and culturally restricted Dublin of the 1930's and 1940's." Although not technically autobiographical, the similarities between the lives of Emily and Mulkerns, in location and era if nothing else, are inescapable.

Mulkerns's second volume of short stories, *An Idle Woman and Other Stories*, published in 1980, is less coherent as a series than *Antiquities*. In "The Saturday Interview: Caroline Walsh talks to the novelist and short-story writer" (*The Irish Times*, 11 June 1977, p. 14), Mulkerns calls *Antiquities* her "farewell to romantic patriotism" and includes little or no nationalist or political themes in the newer volume; instead, she focuses on social commentary and personal relationships. The settings also become less important; rather than treating Dublin and the countryside as characters, she presents settings as no more than scenery. The stories in this volume are thematically related, as all deal in some way with human, particularly family, relationships in contemporary Irish society. "An Idle Woman," "Humanae Vitae," "You Must Be Joking," "Still Life," and "The Open House" all explore the complexity of marriage. "Memory and Desire," probably Mulkerns's most frequently anthologized work, deals with the loneliness of divorce and homosexuality. "Away from It All" and "Phone You Sometime" delve into the tricky world of dating. "The Birthday Party" and "Home for Christmas" treat the relationships between family members, especially parents and children.

In "An Idle Woman," Mulkerns examines a married couple who have grown complacent; she also demonstrates the dangers inherent in being too "idle" as the productive businessman unintentionally ignores his wife, and she, in her boredom, has an affair with his friend. Similarly, "Still Life" looks at a husband and wife who have grown so familiar that they have stopped actually seeing each other; the wife's inattention to her art symbolizes the stagnation of their marriage, which has become a still life with no energy or action. In another story, "Away from It All," Mulkerns continues this theme but also works in a subtle political comment she reveals as a dating couple who have become too comfortable with each other until an innocuous incident on a beach opens the girl's eyes to her English lover's arrogance and his embarrassment regarding her Irish background.

Mulkerns also deals directly with typical Irish Catholic experiences. The story "Humanae Vitae" is called by the same name as the 1968 encyclical of Pope John Paul I, which reinforces the church's position on unlawful birth control but opens the way for the use of the rhythm method by practicing Catholics. Mulkerns explores this restriction, so prevalent in her predominantly Catholic nation, and the ramifications it has on marriages. In "A Summer in London," Mulkerns also delves into the paradox of the church's injunctions against contraception and abortion balanced against the growing sexual and economic independence of contemporary society.

Mulkerns departed from the short-story genre in 1984 and 1986 when she published two novels, *The Summerhouse* and *Very Like a Whale*, respectively. In these books, she steers away from political statements somewhat and returns to sorrow for the loss of tradition and beauty in Ireland mingled with the realization that one must live in the present. Reminiscent in many ways of *Antiquities*, *The Summerhouse*, dedicated to O'Faolain, tells the story of three generations of an Irish family anchored around the family's house in Ferrycarrig and the eccentric summerhouse built in the kitchen. The story wavers many times between pathos over the family's infighting and disintegration, and sorrow over the passing of the central home, with its elegant way of life. Finally, however, the message is that one cannot stay in Ferrycarrig and stagnate but must go out into the world and embrace change.

Very Like a Whale functions in a similar way but with respect to Dublin. Negative changes—such as drugs, poverty, and the increasing moral and physical decay—are taking over the city. The city becomes a metaphor for the family; yet, despite the bleak surroundings and the characters' inability to communicate, the novel ends on a hopeful note as young Ben dedicates his life to working within the changes to improve the lives of Dublin's citizens, particularly the children's. Readers can easily identify with the characters in *Very Like a Whale*, but its greater success lies in its overt social commentary.

Mulkerns returned to the short-story form in 1988 with the publication of a new anthology of short stories, *A Friend of Don Juan*. This volume includes several selections from *An Idle Woman* as well as new stories. The overall tone of the volume is grimmer than Mulkerns's previous efforts. The first story, "The Honda Ward," describes a young man, Jim, who has been in a serious accident on his Honda motorcycle. Accidents on these vehicles have become so common in Mulkerns's Dublin that the hospitals have nicknamed their trauma units "Honda Wards." She also interweaves a religious theme and criticism of the Catholic Church with the hospital chaplain, whose continual hounding to make his confession before it is too late terrorizes Jim. This criticism is furthered by the presence of a sympathetic and practical priest from Jim's school, who will be leaving the school next term for undisclosed reasons, although the inference is that he is being fired for suspected homosexuality. The complicated love/hate relationship between the boy and the church exemplifies the ambivalent feelings of many modern Irish people toward the church that has succored, supported, and yet dominated them for so long. Inclusion of "Humanae Vitae" as the next story in the anthology intensifies this theme. "The Birthday Party" demonstrates the problems of a condescendingly generous upper class with the story of a woman whose too determined philanthropy results in the tragic death of a young gypsy girl. This story brings to mind the condescending attitude of the Protestant Anglo-Irish to the Catholic Irish peasantry in pre-Republic Ireland.

Although Mulkerns returns to the Irish issues later in the volume, particularly with "A Summer in London" and "End of the Line" (which laments the passing of a beautiful old manor in Dublin that will soon be demolished to make way for a new condominium complex), she steers more toward universal issues of relationships with most of the other stories in this book. "Lord of the Back Seat," "The Zoological Gardens," "A Friend of Don Juan," and "Phone You Sometime" all explore the intricacies of dating and relationships. The title story, "A Friend of Don Juan," is a particularly poignant piece about a young man who has always lived in the shadow of his handsomer, richer, smarter friend, Dermot, until, finally, he takes

Title page for Mulkerns's 1988 story collection, which includes selections from An Idle Woman, *as well as previously uncollected stories (Gorgas Library, University of Alabama)*

a stand and refuses to help Dermot trick his girlfriend into sleeping with him.

During the late 1980s, when she was writing *A Friend of Don Juan,* Mulkerns worked as writer-in-residence for County Mayo Library and edited a volume of local poetry and short stories, *New Writings from the West* (1988). She also worked as an itinerant lecturer in the United States. After her husband's death in 1992, she worked with Professor Augustine Martin to co-edit *The Road to Vladivostok,* a collection of Kennedy's works.

During her career, Val Mulkerns has used literature to make social, political, and personal statements about Ireland, its people, its customs, its landscape, and its religion. She is currently working on her memoirs, "Friends with the Enemy," which, considering her close ties with many of the seminal literary figures of twentieth-century Ireland and her active involvement in so many of Ireland's issues and causes, should make for valuable and entertaining reading. Perhaps, with time, critics and academicians will recognize Mulkerns's contributions to contemporary Irish literature, and she will be accorded a more significant place in the canon.

References:

Virginia Mack, "Challenging the Authority of the Lonely Voice: Val Mulkerns and the Technique of Radical Ambiguity," in *New Voices in Irish Criticism,* edited by Karen Vandevelde, volume 3 (Dublin: Four Courts Press, 2002), pp. 94–101;

James O'Brien, "Three Irish Women Story Writers of the 1970s," in *Literature and the Changing Ireland,* edited by P. Connolly, Irish Literary Studies, volume 9 (Totowa, N.J.: Barnes & Noble, 1982), pp. 199–205;

Ulrike Paschel, *No Mean City?: The Image of Dublin in the Novels of Dermot Bolger, Roddy Doyle, and Val Mulkerns,* Aachen British and American Studies, no. 10 (Berlin: Peter Lang, 1998).

Papers:

The Special Collections division of the University of Delaware Library holds some personal and professional papers of Val Mulkerns.

Éilís Ní Dhuibhne

(22 February 1954 –)

Christopher Thomas Cairney
Istanbul Dogus University

BOOKS: *Blood and Water* (Dublin: Attic, 1988);
The Bray House (Dublin: Attic, 1990);
Long March, by Ní Dhuibhne and Michael Mullen (Dublin: Children's Poolbeg, 1990);
The Uncommon Cormorant (Dublin: Poolbeg, 1990);
Eating Women Is Not Recommended (Dublin: Attic, 1991);
Hugo and the Sunshine Girl (Dublin: Poolbeg, 1991);
The Hiring Fair, as Elizabeth O'Hara (Dublin: Poolbeg, 1992; Chester Springs, Pa.: Dufour, 1993);
Singles, as O'Hara (Dublin: Basement, 1994);
Blaeberry Sunday, as O'Hara (Dublin: Poolbeg, 1995);
Penny-Farthing Sally, as O'Hara (Dublin: Poolbeg, 1995);
The Inland Ice and Other Stories (Belfast: Blackstaff, 1997);
Milseog an tSamhraidh agus Dún na mBan Tí Thine (Dublin: Cois Life, 1998);
The Dancers Dancing (Belfast: Blackstaff, 1999);
Testi, intertesti, contesti: Seminario su "The Wife of Bath" di Éilís Ní Dhuibhne, edited by Gianfranca Balestra and Lesley-Anne Crowley (Milan: Vita e pensiero, 2000);
Dúnmharú sa Daingean (Dublin: Cois Life, 2000);
The Pale Gold of Alaska (Belfast: Blackstaff, 2000);
Midwife to the Fairies: New and Selected Stories (Dublin: Attic, 2003);
Cailíní beaga Ghleann na mBláth (Dublin: Cois Life, 2003);
The Sparkling Rain, as O'Hara (Dublin: Poolbeg, 2003).

PLAY PRODUCTION: *Dún na mBan Tí Thine,* Dublin, Peacock Theatre, 5 November 1994.

OTHER: *Viking Ale: Studies on the Folklore Contacts between the Northern and the Western Worlds,* edited by Ní Dhuibhne and Séamas Ó Catháin (Aberystwyth, Wales: Boethius, 1991);
Voices on the Wind: Women Poets of the Celtic Twilight, edited by Ní Dhuibhne (Dublin: New Island, 1995);
"It's a Miracle," in *Arrows in Flight: Short Stories from a New Ireland,* edited by Carolina Walsh (London & New York: Scribner/Townhouse, 2002); republished as *Dislocation: Stories from a New Ireland* (New York: Carroll & Graf, 2003).

Éilís Ní Dhuibhne (<kennysirishbookshop.ie>)

Éilís Ní Dhuibhne is a significant female voice in the traditionally male-dominated realm of Irish fiction. Known primarily as a writer of short fiction and as a novelist, she has also written poetry and drama and produced scholarly articles and scripts for Irish television. She has also written children's books, some under the pen name Elizabeth O'Hara. She has published works in Irish as well as in English. A significant aspect of her place in contemporary Irish fiction derives from the postmodern literary features in her works. She challenges the backward-looking nationalism of Irish bilingual writers of the past with her complex, forward-looking agenda, committed to feminism and a postmodern Irish literature that unself-consciously engages the reader in both Irish and English.

Ní Dhuibhne (whose surname translates as "Daughter of the Ill-Going One") was born in Walkinstown, Dublin, 22 February 1954, to Edward and Margaret O'Hara Deeney. She attended Scoil Chatríona in Dublin and also made trips into the Irish Gaeltacht, becoming fluent in Irish. After a formative decade at University College Dublin, during which time she learned several medieval languages and studied, thanks to a folklore scholarship, at the University of Copenhagen in Denmark, she was awarded a B.A. in 1974, an M.Phil. in 1976, and a Ph.D. in folklore and medieval literature at University College Dublin in 1982. She married Swedish-born Bo Almqvist, a professor of Irish folklore at University College Dublin from 1972 to 1996. They have two children, Ragnar and Olaf. After working as a civil servant in Dublin, as a folklore collector and as a lecturer, Ní Dhuibhne took a job as an assistant keeper at the National Library of Ireland, where her part-time work allowed time for writing and other commitments.

In 1974 Ní Dhuibhne, like many contemporary Irish writers, published her first story in the "New Irish Writing" page of the *Irish Press,* edited by David Marcus. In 1980 she was awarded a scholarship to Listowel Writers' Week in County Kerry, where she won the poetry award, and in the same year she also won the *Irish Independent* Story of the Month Award. In 1984 she spent two weeks at the Tyrone Guthrie Center, an experience that led to her first book of short fiction, *Blood and Water* (1988). She also participated in the National Women Writers' Workshop in 1986, and her short story "Fulfilment" (which eventually appeared in *Blood and Water*) was published in the anthology *Best Short Stories 1986,* published by Heinemann. In 1987 the Arts Council awarded her a bursary in literature. *Blood and Water* was published in Dublin by Attic Press, a well-known Irish feminist publisher, the following year.

Blood and Water, Ní Dhuibhne's first and shortest collection, is about women dealing with issues of personal identity and happiness in modern Irish society, a society portrayed as confused, struggling with a state of rapid change, and ultimately hostile to ordinary Irish citizens, especially women. Some of the stories appeared first in the *Irish Press,* the *Irish Times,* the *Sunday Independent, Image,* and *Panurge.* Alienation, a common theme in Irish fiction, is present in these stories, related to the usual conflicted oppositions of Ireland: urban/rural, past/present, Irish/English, woman/man, old/young. These opposites meet and struggle toward some kind of resolution, which is often not to be found. In "The Postmen's Strike," for instance, Ní Dhuibhne takes a satirical and sarcastic look at the conflict between traditional roles and expectations for women and the desire for freedom and a fresh start. The main character flees Ireland for Denmark, where she teaches Old Irish at the University of Copenhagen. Similar in tone to Ní Dhuibhne's 1990 novel *The Bray House,* "The Postmen's Strike" also passes satirical judgment on Scandinavia, literary and scientific conferences, and academia in general. The story is based on the author's experiences: Ní Dhuibhne studied Old Irish as an academic and also left Ireland to study in Copenhagen. The author further takes the opportunity in the same story to satirize Ireland for social policies that she derides as being particularly unfriendly to women. The effect is a comic version of typical themes in contemporary Irish fiction; in particular, one finds here what James M. Cahalan has described in *Double Visions: Women and Men in Modern and Contemporary Irish Fiction* (1999) as the conflict between the desire on the part of women for autonomy and their desire for relationships. A majority of Ní Dhuibhne's works are a description of the war between the sexes as told from women's point of view. Ní Dhuibhne lends many of her literary resources to a concerted self-irony, however, and is not entirely unsympathetic to the problems of Irish men.

"Midwife to the Fairies" also describes a woman's attempt to cope with the conflicts of modern Irish life. In this story, Ní Dhuibhne initiates her oft-used technique of mixing realism with a suggestion of the surreal, in this work by including elements from Irish folklore. In this way, "Midwife to the Fairies" is similar to "The Mermaid Legend" in *Eating Women Is Not Recommended* (1991) and is a forerunner of the dominant folklore motif used in *The Inland Ice and Other Stories* (1997). In "Midwife to the Fairies," Ní Dhuibhne specifically indicates that the italicized folktale text is translated from the original Irish of a manuscript in the folklore archive at University College Dublin. This assertion is partly a literary device; yet, it also points to Ní Dhuibhne's real-life work as an archivist and as a scholar of both Old Irish and Irish folklore.

In addition to her common use and updating of themes drawn from Irish folklore, Ní Dhuibhne also consistently writes about middle-class Dublin society, about people either on the way up socially or on the way down. The next story in *Blood and Water,* "Looking," deals with the suicidal impulse of an ostensibly happy woman, Margaret. She suffers from ennui, which Ní Dhuibhne presents as a suburban sickness, a boredom in the midst of ease that may be influenced by a confusion between Eros and Thanatos. In this story Ní Dhuibhne shows a typical propensity to talk about Dublin, suburbs such as Dun Laoghaire, and the seaside, a location made famous as the place where Stephen Dedalus contemplates the meaning of life in James Joyce's novel *Ulysses* (1922). Her veiled reference to Sylvia Plath's novel *The Bell Jar* (1963) reinforces the suggestion of suicide: "No bell-jar pinned her to barren patch of reality." The next story, "Kingston Ridge," begins to show what became Ní Dhuibhne's later style. She writes in the first person; plays with time, present and past; and addresses the reader directly. She also utilizes a mocking tone that verges on the cynical.

In "A Visit to Newgrange," the voice in the story is also mocking, reflecting the frustration that the main character, again a woman, feels about her relationship with a Germanic/Scandinavian foreigner, a stock situation in Ní Dhuibhne's fiction that carries a strong suggestion of autobiography. The protagonist thinks she wants marriage but, again, is placed by her circumstances in an almost impossible situation. Women being placed in difficult or impossible situations is a common theme in Ní Dhuibhne's fiction but also in contemporary Irish fiction in general, especially in fiction by women. As Shari A. Benstock notes concerning the Irish writer Jennifer Johnston, her "world is not masculine, not open, accessible, social, a world of action, but rather specifically feminine: closed, suffocated, lonely, and inward-turning." The same can be said for Ní Dhuibhne.

Irish writers such as Ní Dhuibhne and Johnston write about a male-dominated world, but Ní Dhuibhne's characters rarely show real growth. In "A Visit to Newgrange," however, the main character, a woman full of hate and intolerance, grows and learns to relate to others. Again, the story includes many autobiographical elements. The next story, "A Fairer House," has a strong element of magical realism, while "Roses Are Red," written in the first person as an open letter to a much-admired Swedish professional man, is a complex commentary on the kind of lies told by the bourgeois women of the city. Like "Looking," "Roses Are Red" includes a reference to Joyce, overt this time: "Are you not weary of ardent ways?," the narrator asks, an allusion to the poem that Stephen Dedalus writes in *A Portrait of the Artist As a Young Man* (1914–1915). "The Catechism Examination" discusses Catholic cruelty to children in an academic setting, a Joycean theme, while "The Duck-Billed Platypus"—which, unusually for Ní Dhuibhne, features a male protagonist—is a sardonic look at the predicament of liberal-arts graduates in the 1990s job market. The title short story, "Blood and Water," which is the foundation for Ní Dhuibhne's novel *The Dancers Dancing* (1999), examines a young woman's attempt to cope with the conflicts of modern Irish life. "Tandoori" is a story about the midlife crises of a bourgeois Dublin couple. Again there are references to academia (one central character possesses an M.A. in medieval history) and a sense of self-mocking autobiography and satire. One must read between the lines of the male character's narration to understand that the woman in the story leaves her husband and ends up working in an art gallery in London. "Fulfilment," the final story in the

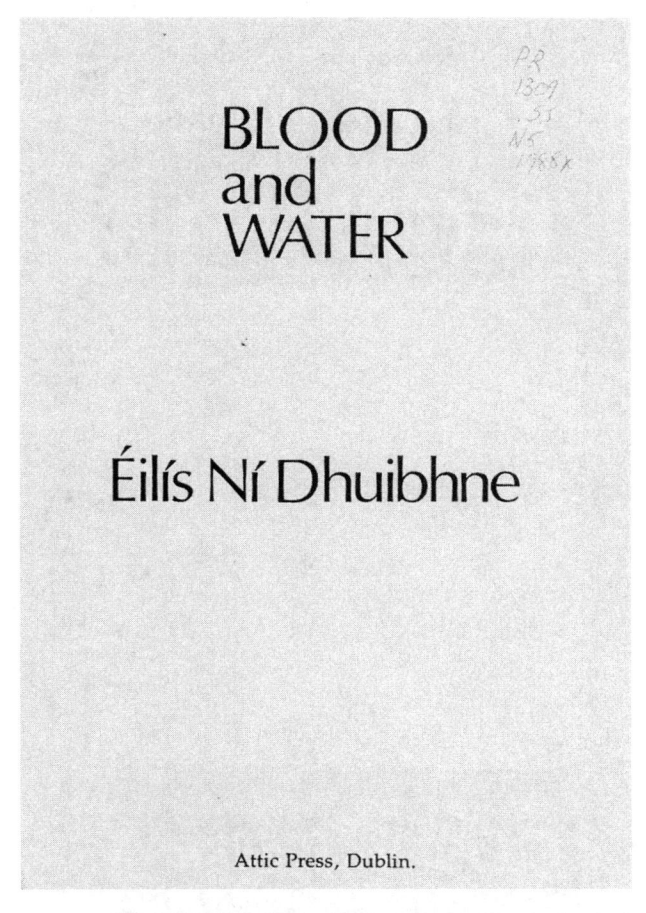

Title page for Ní Dhuibhne's first collection of stories, published by the feminist Attic Press in 1988 (Gorgas Library, University of Alabama)

collection, is a darkly ironic story of a woman striving for success in the economically difficult circumstances of Dublin in the 1980s. Though the story is one of Ní Dhuibhne's most anthologized, it is also one of her least typical.

In 1990 Ní Dhuibhne published her first novel, *The Bray House,* with Attic Press and a young-adult novel, *Long March,* co-authored with Michael Mullen. In the *Irish Times* (22 July 2000) John Kenny called *The Bray House* a "fascinating science fiction novel," while Gerry Smyth, in *The Novel and the Nation: Studies in the New Irish Fiction* (1997), identifies the novel as environmental fiction, calling it an ecological and political "dystopian narrative." Smyth finds in *The Bray House* a typically Irish preoccupation with the land, but "from the perspective of late twentieth-century eco-criticism." Bray is the name of a coastal community on the southern border of County Dublin. The novel examines the breakdown of community in Ireland. At the same time, it "explodes the myth of scientific rationalism," according to Smyth, and makes critical references to Sweden, Dublin, and academia. *The Bray House* was followed by a collection of short fiction, *Eating Women Is Not Recom-*

Front cover for Ní Dhuibhne's 1991 collection, which includes stories set in the fictional town of Wavesend in the Irish-speaking Donegal Gaeltacht, in County Donegal, Ireland

mended, in 1991. The same year, Ní Dhuibhne coedited with Séamas Ó Catháin, *Viking Ale,* in honor of Almqvist.

Eating Women Is Not Recommended, which includes the previously published stories "The Wife of Bath" and "The Bright Lights," explores the interaction of the dark and shocking events of people's lives and their mundane realities. The narration frequently digresses from events in the story to explore seemingly unrelated topics, as in the first story in the collection, "The Flowering": "Wolfe Tone passed by the house on his way to France. Drugged. Red Hugh passed by the house on his way to Dublin. Drunk. Lennie's great-great-great-grandmother saw the ship and waved. Hiya Wolfie! We're on your side! (Forget chronology. It doesn't reflect significance, usually)."

The flippant tone, with its comically ironic voice of complaint, looks back to Ní Dhuibhne's earlier, less mature work in *Blood and Water* and *The Bray House.* The stories reflect the author's desire to confront the past and to deal with murky issues of Irish identity and history. In this goal she is typical of contemporary Irish writers of both sexes, as Smyth points out; contemporary Irish fiction, he writes, "asks questions of what it is to be 'Irish.'" Smyth also notes that the contemporary Irish fiction writer is typically willing to "challenge established notions regarding the limits and possibilities of Irish Identity." Ní Dhuibhne challenges such notions particularly from an Irish woman's point of view.

Ní Dhuibhne is also typical of many modern Irish writers in that she makes use of Gaelic narrative styles and folk materials in her writing. For instance, she frequently addresses the reader directly, as in the informal narration of "The Flowering." According to Cahalan, this debt is one that modern Irish writers owe generally to a native oral tradition of Gaelic anecdotes and storytelling. Smyth finds Gaelic verbal and performative stylistic devices a special characteristic of Irish fiction because, as he puts it, "when prose-fiction did emerge as a form it was the short story—with its roots in the Gaelic story-telling tradition." The narrator is not separate from the world of the story, but is rather presented as part of it, and the story itself is seen as a performance in a specific context. This sense of the Gaelic short story as "half-oral" is echoed in Ní Dhuibhne's work in her informal addresses to the reader. As Cahalan notes, the Irish storytelling novel tends to be made up of a series of episodes or separate oral narratives. Such folk novels generally include earthy and often ribald qualities and act as bridges between the Irish and English languages. Ní Dhuibhne's novels and short stories exhibit these tendencies.

Ní Dhuibhne favors specific settings, for example Donegal, with its slow pace of life. The setting of the first, second, and final stories of *Eating Women Is Not Recommended,* as well as of the earlier short story "Blood and Water" and the novel *The Dancers Dancing,* is identified as Wavesend, an apparently fictitious location in the Donegal Gaeltacht that seems to be constructed from the author's personal reminiscences of the area.

Three stories from *Eating Women Is Not Recommended,* "The Flowering," "The Bright Lights," and "Night of the Fox," are about rural Donegal. They address the dichotomy between country and city as it applies to the issue of Irish identity and also to the issue of personal alienation in an urban setting, a key theme in Joyce's writings. "The Bright Lights," particularly, focuses on economic and social alienation, but all these stories examine the complex issue of modern Irish identities in times of social and economic dislocation. This concern can be seen in "See the Robbers Passing By," an ironically funny story dealing with the narrator's profound sense of alienation from home and family, an alienation that is evinced in details such as a contemptuous description of a grandmother's couch:

The sofa in Granny's sitting-room, the only room downstairs in the house apart from the kitchenette, is wine-coloured. The back and arms are shiny leatherette—ette, ette—and the cushion embossed velvet. It smells of people's bums, but it is a comfortable sofa to sit on, especially if you are alone.

In "The Bright Lights" the main character, a young Irish girl, talks about her aunt, Ingrid, but her narration reveals her sense of separation from her older relative. "Her smile," the girl relates, "had an unusual quality. It was a foreign smile, not innocent and sweet, or cute and sour, as Irish smiles were, but cool, elegant, inscrutable." Ingrid tells a joke, and the narrator reacts cautiously and suspiciously to her friendliness: "She laughed, excessively, I considered, for what seemed a rather feeble joke. But I laughed with her, for politeness' sake, and from admiration, not of her humor, but of her skill: I had never heard a grown woman tell a formal joke before. At wit and repartee the women I knew were excellent, but they did not know how to tell jokes. I felt close to Ingrid, for a minute." The last line is a commentary on Irish alienation that references many oppositions at once: urban/rural, past/present, Irish/English, woman/man, and old/young.

The stories show a conflict between the demands of the country and of the city that parallels conflicts between men and women. Ní Dhuibhne's main characters, usually women, typically suffer from alienation and have problems communicating with others. In "The Flowering" for instance, the main character reaches out for help but is ignored by her ignorant mother, a peasant woman: "Her mother, legs parted to catch the heat of the flames, looked at her—anxiously—shook her head and did not pursue the matter," the narrator notes. Ironically for the main character, the flowering of her sexuality and of her sense of independence, which arise from her learning to embroider, is negated by intrusive issues of gender and class that still constrain her. "Needlework" is another bitter story of remembrance, while "Sweet Sacrament Divine" carries a hard, cynical, and ironic tone, particularly with regard to the expectations of women in the sexual and social aspects of a relationship. This tone is found in the remaining stories in this collection, including the title story, "Eating Women Is Not Recommended," which appeared earlier in the *Irish Times*.

In 1991 Ní Dhuibhne published *Hugo and the Sunshine Girl*, a children's book. In 1993 she won a Bisto Merit Award for another children's book, *The Hiring Fair* (1992), published under her Elizabeth O'Hara pseudonym. A play in Irish, *Dún na mBan Tí Thine* (The Woman's Fort of Fire), was produced at the Peacock Theatre in November 1994 by the theater company An Amharclann de hIde, and in the same year she published *Singles,* a novel telling of a twenty-one-year-old woman, fresh from college in the 1970s, who thinks she must get married and wonders if her Danish lover or one of her teachers will become her husband.

In the same year that her play was performed at the Peacock, Ní Dhuibhne advocated more productions by female playwrights as her contribution to the "Don't Worry, Be Abbey" discussion at the Abbey Theatre on the occasion of its ninetieth birthday. The text was printed in the February 1995 issue of the magazine *Fortnight*. She won the Bisto Book of the Year Award in 1995 for her children's book *Blaeberry Sunday,* and edited the collection *Voices on the Wind: Women Poets of the Celtic Twilight*. In 1995 she also published *Penny-Farthing Sally,* a sequel to *The Hiring Fair* and *Blaeberry Sunday,* and was awarded the Readers' Association of Ireland Award—another award for children's books. In 1997 she received the Stuart Parker Award for Drama.

Ní Dhuibhne's collection *The Inland Ice and Other Stories,* published with the assistance of the Arts Council of Northern Ireland, is linked to her earlier work through her use of fantasy and myth. She combines folklore elements with realism to create a sense of magical realism in the stories. Having utilized folklore in the stories "Midwife to the Fairies" (from *Blood and Water*) and again in "The Mermaid Legend" (from *Eating Women Is Not Recommended*), Ní Dhuibhne ambitiously continues and expands the motif in *The Inland Ice and Other Stories.* Ní Dhuibhne reverses and reworks her sources in these stories; the collection is built around the folk theme she calls "The Search for the Lost Husband." Louise East, in the *Irish Times* (25 July 1997), called the stories in this collection "oddly unsettling," citing "a constant sense of uneasy nostalgia" combined with a "detached but authoritative narrative voice." The search for the lost husband is carried out in short installments inserted before, between, and after each of the thirteen stories, and the overall message of the collection is that emotions have the powerful ability to wreck lives and that people are too often powerless to stop this wreck from happening. Ní Dhuibhne, however, like Julia O'Faolain in a similar reworking of Irish legend, *No Country for Young Men* (1980), adds a feminist twist at the end of the text, effectively bringing her folktale up to date by creating a feminist mythology out of Irish material. Here the folktale involves a woman chasing after a man and accepting his arbitrary and self-serving rules for this pursuit. The woman in the folktale chases her man even to the underworld; when she finally catches him, however, she decides to leave him: "I am weary of ardent ways. Passion is so time consuming, and it makes me so unhappy." "I'm tired of all that fairytale stuff," she says to her surprised husband.

Cover for Ní Dhuibhne's 1997 collection in which the author interweaves stories set in modern times with a feminist retelling of an Irish folktale (Bruccoli Clark Layman Archives)

Some of the other stories in this collection include "Love, Hate and Friendship," another autobiographical, essayistic short story involving an academic conference; "Summer Pudding," which makes use of Irish language and magical realism; "Bill's New Wife," which documents gender role reversal and the "victory" of feminism; "Lili Marlene," a story with almost no dialogue; "Hot Earth," which like much of Ní Dhuibhne's fiction refers to Joyce's writing; and "Spool of Thread," which begins: "Fifty per cent of females practice endogamy. That leaves fifty per cent who are adventurous, liberated and verging on the foolhardy in their socio-sexual explorations." "Swiss Cheese" is another short story in the style of an essay. "My Pet" is an example of a story describing mundane events that are given interest by a surprise ending; another is "Estonia," which includes references to Sweden, Joyce, conferences, and infidelity. "The Inland Ice," the title story of the collection, is about a woman with a dying spouse who regrets hopelessly her meanness to him and resents deeply the alteration in her happiness. "The Woman with the Fish" is about insufferable academic people and the pointlessness of academic culture and also has autobiographical features. The female main character chases after a man who loves only himself, echoing the folk motif of the interpolated passages in the collection. The final story of the collection, "How Lovely the Slopes Are," again resembles an essay, this time on Sweden and academia, Ní Dhuibhne's two main autobiographical themes. One of the characters is "fired up so passionately by her thesis that she could hardly sleep at night. Her head was full of ideas about *Laxdaela Saga,* her main text."

The Inland Ice and Other Stories was followed by another Arts Council bursary in 1998 and by the publication that same year of *Dún na mBan Tí Thine* and another play by Ní Dhuibhne in Irish, *Milseog an tSamhraidh* (Summer Pudding). In 1998 Ní Dhuibhne also won an Oireachtas Award for drama in Irish. *Milseog an tSamhraidh* is based in part on her short story "Summer Pudding." The next year she published *The Dancers Dancing,* which moves from the postmodernism of *The Bray House* in the direction of what Des Traynor, in *Books Ireland* (October 1999), called the "mixing and merging of the realistic with something otherworldly." In *The Dancers Dancing* Ní Dhuibhne is still obsessed with the complexities of the Irish relationship to the rural and the mutual impact of the country and the city on Irish identity. The novel is a compassionate look at women growing up, an Irish woman's bildungsroman set at an Irish college in the County Donegal Gaeltacht. As Ní Dhuibhne does in much of her fiction, she explores issues relating to the use of Irish language and to cultural identity and makes substantial use of Irish in the text. Traynor specifically noted her "sardonic writing" and praised her "social observation." In 2000 *The Dancers Dancing* was short-listed for the Orange Prize, awarded annually to the best work of fiction by a woman published in the United Kingdom.

In 1999 Ní Dhuibhne contributed anonymously to the Dublin short-story collection *Ladies' Night at Finbar's Hotel,* edited by Dermot Bolger. In May of that year she also presented a paper titled "Where Has the Feminist Sentence Gone?" to a conference held at the Women's Education, Research and Resource Center (WERRC) at University College Dublin. In 2000 she was presented with the Butler Literature Award for Prose by the Irish American Cultural Institute and a second Oireachtas Award, this time for "major fiction," for her novel in Irish *Dúnmharú sa Daingean* (2000, Murder in a Fortress), a thriller set in the County Kerry Gaeltacht, an area known in Irish as *Corca Dhuibhne.*

The short-story collection *The Pale Gold of Alaska* (2000) includes nine stories that can be compared to essays: these stories concern Ní Dhuibhne's recurrent themes of adulterous couples and bourgeois ennui. Again, the tone of the collection is generally cynical; the content is autobiographical or academic; and the stories are set in either Dublin or Donegal. The collection was well received by the critical press: in *The Times* (18 October 2000) Christina Koning called it "beautifully written and full of humour," and Anne Fogarty in *The Irish Times* (30 September 2000) noted that "rather than rushing towards a predictable ending, these are indeed stories that take their time and surprise the reader with their unexpected tangents and detours. The emphasis throughout is on the intricacies of female desire and the division between outer appearances and the lived confusion of sexual relationships. . . . Moral and emotional dilemmas abound." Fogarty also cited Ní Dhuibhne's "willingness to experiment with the short story form" and called her work "spare, probing yet lyrical" and "innovative." The collection includes "The Pale Gold of Alaska," which can be described as an 1890s Irish woman's sexual fantasy of a love relationship with a tribal Native American. Other stories include "The Day Elvis Presley Died," "The Makers," "A Banana Boat," and "The Truth about Married Love," all studies in anxiety and loss. As with "The Pale Gold of Alaska," three of the four remaining stories in the collection—"At Sally Gap," "Oleander," and "Nomads Seek the Pavilions of Bliss on the Slopes of Middle Age"—are about characters who betray their lovers or spouses because they want more from life. Nevertheless, they remain unhappy and prone to anxiety and alienation. The story that concludes the volume, "Sex in the Context of Ireland," is narrated in the first person by Bella, a prostitute. Set in Dublin in the 1920s, it concerns the lives of prostitutes victimized by poverty and pimps, but also by the rapacious attentions of representatives of the Catholic Church.

Ní Dhuibhne is an active member of the Women's Studies Forum at University College Dublin and of the Folklore of Ireland Society. She has taught creative writing at People's College in Dublin and directs the advanced fiction-writing course at Listowel Writers' Week, with emphasis on the novel. Her story "Wuff Wuff Wuff!" is included as part of *Loose Horses: Stories from South Dublin*, a 2001 Internet project sponsored by the South Dublin County Council, and she conducts creative-writing workshops focusing on the writing of novels and short stories at the Irish Writers' Center in Dublin. Her dedication to feminism is apparent in many of her activities, including the lecture she delivered in March 2002 at the Women's Center at the University of South Florida, "Cathleen Ní Houlihan Fights Back: Irish Women Writers and the Nation in the Twentieth Century." That same year her story "It's a Miracle" was included in the anthology *Arrows in Flight: Short Stories from a New Ireland*. In 2003 *Midwife to the Fairies: New and Selected Stories,* an anthology of stories from her earlier collections (along with a previously uncollected story), was published, as well as another novel in Irish, *Cailíní beaga Ghleann na mBláth* (The Girls of the Flower Glen). She also contributed an essay to *Who Needs Irish? Reflections on the Importance of the Irish Language Today* (2004).

Despite the many awards she has received, Éilís Ní Dhuibhne is a writer whose reputation is still being made. In a 2001 interview with Nicola Warwick, she spoke of her intentions as a writer:

> I think I have what might seem to some people an inflated sense of the significance of what we call ordinary life. It doesn't seem at all ordinary to me. People's mundane experiences fascinate me. I want to describe them, perhaps in an attempt to understand how the world works. But there is an imperative to record: I feel like an historian of the emotional and psychological life of my time. I want to write it down, so people will know how it was.

While the plots of her stories may be predictable, they nevertheless have the ability to surprise the reader. Often the stories are about not the traditional Irish/English divide, but rather the clash of cultures between Europe or the United States, on the one hand, and an Ireland that seems essentially British. Many of her stories represent a form of Irish magical realism, and her narrators and characters show much honesty, cynicism, self-loathing, and alienation. Ní Dhuibhne is at her most cynical when writing of Dublin, and much more benign when writing about Donegal; but her texts always offer a distinctive flavor of life in Ireland.

Interview:

Nicola Warwick, "Éilís Ní Dhuibhne," *One Woman's Writing Retreat* (2001) <http://www.prairieden.com/front_porch/visiting_authors/dhuibhne.html>.

References:

Shari A. Benstock, "The Masculine World of Jennifer Johnston," in *Twentieth-Century Women Novelists,* edited by Thomas F. Staley (Totowa, N.J.: Barnes & Noble, 1982), pp. 191–217;

James M. Cahalan, *Double Visions: Women and Men in Modern and Contemporary Irish Fiction* (Syracuse, N.Y.: Syracuse University Press, 1999);

Cahalan, *The Irish Novel: A Critical History* (Boston: Twayne, 1988);

Gerry Smyth, *The Novel and the Nation: Studies in the New Irish Fiction* (London & Chicago: Pluto, 1997).

Edna O'Brien
(15 December 1930 -)

Robert Ellis Hosmer Jr.
Smith College

See also the O'Brien entries in *DLB 14: British Novelists Since 1960* and *DLB 231: British Novelists Since 1960, Fourth Series.*

BOOKS: *The Country Girls* (London: Hutchinson, 1960; New York: Knopf, 1960);

The Lonely Girl (London: Cape, 1962; New York: Random House, 1962); republished as *Girl with Green Eyes* (New York: Popular Library, 1962; Harmondsworth, U.K.: Penguin, 1964);

Girls in Their Married Bliss (London: Cape, 1964; New York: Simon & Schuster, 1968; revised, London: Cape, 1971);

August Is a Wicked Month (London: Cape, 1965; New York: Simon & Schuster, 1965);

Casualties of Peace (London: Cape, 1966; New York: Simon & Schuster, 1967);

The Love Object (London: Cape, 1968; New York: Knopf, 1969);

A Pagan Place: A Novel (London: Weidenfeld & Nicolson, 1970; New York: Knopf, 1970);

Zee & Co.: A Novel (London: Weidenfeld & Nicolson, 1971); revised as *X Y & Zee: A Novel* (New York: Lancer, 1971);

Night (London: Weidenfeld & Nicolson, 1972; New York: Knopf, 1973; revised edition, New York: Farrar, Straus & Giroux, 1987);

A Pagan Place: A Play (London: Faber & Faber, 1973);

A Scandalous Woman: Stories (London: Weidenfeld & Nicolson, 1974); republished as *A Scandalous Woman, and Other Stories* (New York: Harcourt Brace Jovanovich, 1974);

Mother Ireland (London: Weidenfeld & Nicolson, 1976; New York: Harcourt Brace Jovanovich, 1976);

Arabian Days, photographs by Gerard Klijn (London & New York: Quartet, 1977);

Johnny I Hardly Knew You: A Novel (London: Weidenfeld & Nicolson, 1977); republished as *I Hardly Knew You* (Garden City, N.Y.: Doubleday, 1978);

Edna O'Brien (photograph by Mark Gerson; from the dust jacket for A Scandalous Woman, and Other Stories, *1974; Richland County Public Library)*

Mrs. Reinhardt and Other Stories (London: Weidenfeld & Nicolson, 1978); revised as *A Rose in the Heart* (Garden City, N.Y.: Doubleday, 1979);

Virginia: A Play (London: Hogarth Press, 1981; San Diego: Harcourt Brace Jovanovich, 1981; revised, 1985);

The Dazzle (London: Hodder & Stoughton, 1981);

James and Nora: Portrait of Joyce's Marriage (Northridge, Cal.: Lord John Press, 1981);

A Christmas Treat (London: Hodder & Stoughton, 1982);

Returning: Tales (London: Weidenfeld & Nicolson, 1982);

The Rescue (London: Hodder & Stoughton, 1983);

A Fanatic Heart: Selected Stories of Edna O'Brien, foreword by Philip Roth (New York: Farrar, Straus & Giroux, 1984; London: Weidenfeld & Nicolson, 1985);

The Country Girls Trilogy and Epilogue (New York: Farrar, Straus & Giroux, 1986; London: Cape, 1987);

Tales for the Telling: Irish Folk & Fairy Stories (London: Pavilion/Joseph, 1986; New York: Atheneum, 1986);

Vanishing Ireland, photographs by Richard Fitzgerald (London: Cape, 1986; New York: C. N. Potter, 1987);

The High Road (London: Weidenfeld & Nicolson, 1988; New York: Farrar, Straus & Giroux, 1988);

On the Bone (Warwick: Greville Press, 1989);

Lantern Slides: Short Stories (London: Weidenfeld & Nicolson, 1990); republished as *Lantern Slides: Stories* (New York: Farrar, Straus & Giroux, 1990);

Time and Tide (London: Viking, 1992; New York: Farrar, Straus & Giroux, 1992);

House of Splendid Isolation (London: Weidenfeld & Nicolson, 1994; New York: Farrar, Straus & Giroux, 1994);

Down by the River (London: Weidenfeld & Nicolson, 1996; New York: Farrar, Straus & Giroux, 1997);

Love's Lesson (Alton, U.K.: Clarion, 1997);

James Joyce (London: Weidenfeld & Nicolson, 1999; New York: Viking/Penguin, 1999);

Wild Decembers (London: Weidenfeld & Nicolson, 1999; Boston: Houghton Mifflin, 2000);

In the Forest (London: Weidenfeld & Nicolson, 2002; Boston: Houghton Mifflin, 2002);

Triptych; and, Iphigenia, by O'Brien and Euripides (New York: Grove, 2003).

Collections: *Seven Novels and Other Short Stories,* introduction by O'Brien (London: Collins, 1978)—comprises *The Country Girls, Girl with Green Eyes, Girls in Their Married Bliss, August Is a Wicked Month, Casualties of Peace, The Love Object, A Pagan Place, Night,* and *A Scandalous Woman;*

An Edna O'Brien Reader (New York: Warner, 1994)—comprises *August Is a Wicked Month, Casualties of Peace,* and *Johnny I Hardly Knew You.*

PLAY PRODUCTIONS: *A Cheap Bunch of Nice Flowers,* London, New Arts Theatre, 20 November 1962;

A Pagan Place, London, Royal Court Theatre, 2 November 1972;

The Gathering, Dublin, Dublin Theatre Festival, 10 October 1974;

Virginia, Stratford, Ontario, Avon Theatre, 10 June 1980;

Flesh and Blood, Bath, Theatre Royal, 15 April 1985;

Madame Bovary, adapted from Gustave Flaubert's novel, Watford, The Palace, 29 January 1987;

Our Father, London, Almeida Theater, 18 November 1999;

Triptych, San Francisco, Magic Theatre, 2 December 2003;

Family Butchers, San Francisco, Magic Theatre, 24 September 2005.

PRODUCED SCRIPTS: *Girl with Green Eyes,* motion picture, Woodfall Film Productions, 1964;

I Was Happy Here, motion picture, by O'Brien and Desmond Davis, Partisan Productions/Rank Organisation, 1965;

The Keys of the Cafe, television, Associated Television, 1965;

Which of These Two Ladies Is He Married To? television, Rediffusion Television, 1967;

Nothing's Ever Over, television, Rediffusion Television, 1968;

Three into Two Won't Go, motion picture, Julian Blaustein Productions/Universal Pictures, 1969;

X, Y and Zee, motion picture, Columbia Pictures, 1972;

Mrs. Reinhardt, television, BBC, 1981;

Love, motion picture, by O'Brien, Nancy Dowd, Gael Greene, Joni Mitchell, Liv Ullmann, and Mai Zetterling, Coup Films, 1982;

The Country Girls, television, Channel 4 Television/London Film Productions, 1984.

RECORDINGS: *Portrait of a Mature Woman,* read by O'Brien, Center for Cassette Studies, 1973;

The Country Girls, abridged, read by O'Brien, Decca/Argo K206K 22, 1981;

The Country Girls, read by O'Brien, Chivers Audio Books 306, 1988;

The Lonely Girl, read by O'Brien, Chivers Audio Books 348, 1988;

Girls in Their Married Bliss, read by O'Brien, Chivers Audio Books 380, 1989;

The High Road, read by O'Brien, Sterling Audio Books 011, 1989.

OTHER: *Some Irish Loving: A Selection,* edited by O'Brien (London: Weidenfeld & Nicolson, 1979; New York: Harper & Row, 1979);

James Joyce, *Dubliners,* introduction by O'Brien (New York: New American Library, 1991);

Euripides, *Iphigenia,* adapted by O'Brien (London: Methuen, 2003).

SELECTED PERIODICAL PUBLICATIONS—
UNCOLLECTED:
FICTION
"Orphan on the Run," *Saturday Evening Post,* 228 (6 August 1955): 34–35, 87–90;

"Summer Encounter," *Saturday Evening Post,* 230 (21 December 1957): 22–23, 54–56;

"Four Eligible Bachelors in London," *Vogue,* 144 (15 September 1964): 140–143;

"My First Love," *Ladies' Home Journal,* 82 (June 1965): 60–61;

"Let the Rest of the World Go By," *Ladies' Home Journal,* 82 (July 1965): 48–49, 104;

"Ma," *New Yorker,* 48 (22 July 1972): 24–26;

"The Classroom," *New Yorker,* 51 (21 July 1975): 28–34;

"Green Georgette," *New Yorker,* 54 (23 October 1978): 38–44;

"Far Away in Australia," *New Yorker,* 54 (25 December 1978): 30–36;

"A Long Way from Home," *Redbook,* 165 (May 1985): 76, 148–153;

"A Day Out," *New Yorker,* 65 (24 April 1989): 39–44;

"No Place," *New Yorker,* 67 (17 June 1991): 35–40;

"The Cut," *New Yorker,* 67 (4 November 1991): 40–50;

"Wilderness," *New Yorker,* 68 (16 March 1992): 36–53;

"Sin," *New Yorker,* 70 (11 July 1994): 73–74;

"Blood," *Seventeen,* 57 (August 1998): 198–200;

"Forbidden," *New Yorker,* 76 (20 March 2000): 116–120;

"A Boy in the Forest," *New Yorker,* 77 (4 February 2002): 64–68.

NONFICTION

"From the Ground Up," *Writer,* 71 (October 1958): 13–15;

"Dear Mr. Joyce," *Audience,* 1 (July–August 1971): 75–77;

"Artist and His Country," *Vogue,* 158 (September 1971): 232–233, 312–317;

"A Reason of One's Own," *Times Saturday Review,* 30 September 1972, p. 28;

"Joyce & Nora," *Harper's,* 261 (September 1980): 60–73;

"Wherefore Feminism?" *Cosmopolitan,* 198 (February 1985): 236;

"Hers: Leaving Home," *New York Times,* 12 September 1985, sec. C, p. 2;

"Face to Face with Wrinkles and the Deeper Reality," *New York Times,* 19 September 1985, sec. C, p. 10;

"From Rome, a City of Flesh, Some Thoughts on the Perils of Promiscuity," *New York Times,* 26 September 1985, sec. C, p. 2;

"Why Haven't Women Created Fictional Characters to Rival an Emma Bovary?" *New York Times,* 3 October 1985, sec. C, p. 2;

"Why Irish Heroines Don't Have to Be Good Anymore," *New York Times Book Review,* 11 May 1986, p. 13;

"Samuel Beckett at Eighty," *World Press Review,* 33 (July 1986): 28–30;

"Lui–A View of Him," *New York Times Book Review,* 5 April 1987, p. 3;

"Nora: The Real Life of Ireland," *New York Times Book Review,* 19 June 1988, pp. 3, 33;

"Checking In: Edna O'Brien Withdraws to the Wyndham Hotel to Become a Lady of Leisure," *House & Garden,* 160 (September 1988): 64, 68;

"In the Sacred Company of Trees," *Independent,* 2 June 1990, p. 32;

"Going Solo," *Conde Nast Traveler,* 26 (March 1991): 130–135, 191–195;

"Love by the River Liffey," *Conde Nast Traveler,* 27 (January 1992): 124;

"Jazz," *New York Times Book Review,* 5 April 1992, p. 1;

"It's a Bad Time Out There for Emotion," *New York Times Book Review,* 14 February 1993, p. 1;

"Edna O'Brien on Ambition," *Independent Magazine,* 28 August 1993, pp. 18–19;

"Clinton's Chance to Ease Ulster Enmities," *Boston Globe,* 24 November 1993, p. 17;

"Ulster's Man of the Dark," *New York Times,* 1 February 1994, sec. A, p. 17;

"Among the Believers," *Washington Post,* 26 June 1994, sec. C, p. 1;

"Ritz: More Than Just a Word," *Conde Nast Traveler,* 30 (January 1995): 78–84, 185;

"Joyce's Odyssey: The Labors of Ulysses," *New Yorker,* 75 (7 June 1999): 82–91;

"Yeats in Love: The Poet in Search of his Muses," *New Yorker,* 75 (27 September 1999): 92–98.

With a professional literary career that began in the 1950s, Edna O'Brien stands today at the forefront of the ranks of distinguished, internationally recognized writers. Ireland has a rich history of great authors, but the males are ordinarily first thought of: Oscar Wilde, James Joyce, William Butler Yeats, and Samuel Beckett. O'Brien has become a member of this small group whose writing is distinctively Irish but somehow universal. Her achievement in several genres–the novel, poetry, drama, the essay, and biography–has earned her the admiration of peers and critics alike while enlisting substantial numbers of dedicated readers.

Josephine Edna O'Brien was born in the village of Tuamgraney, County Clare, located in the west of Ireland and destined to become the setting for some of her best fiction. The Records Office on Lombard Street in Dublin gives 15 December 1930 as her date of birth. Her parents, Michael O'Brien and Lena Cleary O'Brien, were an incendiary mismatch, their lives the reverse of the story of Irish immigrants who made their fortune in America: they returned home from Brooklyn with meager resources and married. O'Brien's father came from a family that had seen better days; he gambled and drank away a fortune made by relatives who had patented a cure-all elixir called "Fr John's Medicine." Her mother had a difficult life and was "a very sacrificial and wronged woman," as O'Brien told Nell Dunn in a 1965 interview. An artistic soul without outlet who was burdened with a ne'er-do-well husband, Lena was the prototype for many of the women in O'Brien's fiction. Likewise, perhaps, O'Brien's parents' marriage was the prototype for the marriages in her fiction. Her succinct characterization of the institution—"marriage is a mutual blackmail," she told a *Times* (London) interviewer in 1968—is based no doubt on more than her own single experience with marriage.

O'Brien was the couple's fifth and last child, born some time after the fourth had died and six years younger than her youngest surviving sibling. She has said that she felt much like an only child growing up, an only child with a fierce attachment to her mother and a lifelong sense of loneliness. In Tuamgraney, where life was "fervid, enclosed and catastrophic," as O'Brien notes in *Mother Ireland* (1976), she developed another fierce attachment, in this case to the written word. From an early age she knew she was going to become a writer, telling interviewer Molly McQuade, "I was never in doubt about what I wanted to do." O'Brien received encouragement from neither parent, growing up in a household where literature played no role. Her father read little more than the racing forms and blood-stock reports; her mother, prayer books and cookbooks. Indeed, her mother believed that literature was sinful. Despite this background and the town's lack of a library, O'Brien remembers reading three books, or at least parts of them, as a child: Margaret Mitchell's *Gone with the Wind* (1936), Daphne du Maurier's *Rebecca* (1938), and Richard Llewellyn's *How Green Was My Valley* (1939). The texts circulated as loose pages torn from the bindings, so that no one in the village was able to read the stories in proper narrative sequence. But this method of reading had a positive impact, for it stimulated O'Brien to fabricate the missing text, a good creative exercise for an aspiring writer.

Studying at the local national school in Scarriff from 1936 to 1941 and at the Convent of Mercy in Loughrea, County Galway, from 1941 to 1946, O'Brien found her writer's gifts nurtured. She discovered the great English essayists and William Shakespeare, and she absorbed the lyrical intensity, rhythmic cadences, and vivid imagery of Scripture and prayer texts read and recited in chapel. She distinguished herself as a student at the convent. Since many readers and critics assume exact correspondence between her life and her works, she has taken pains to point out that, unlike the main characters in *The Country Girls* (1960), she was never expelled for misbehavior.

O'Brien wanted to attend a university but lacked the funds. She went to Dublin instead, where she worked in a pharmacist's shop by day and attended lectures at a pharmaceutical college at night, preparing for certification as a registered pharmacist. One day at a bookstall she found a

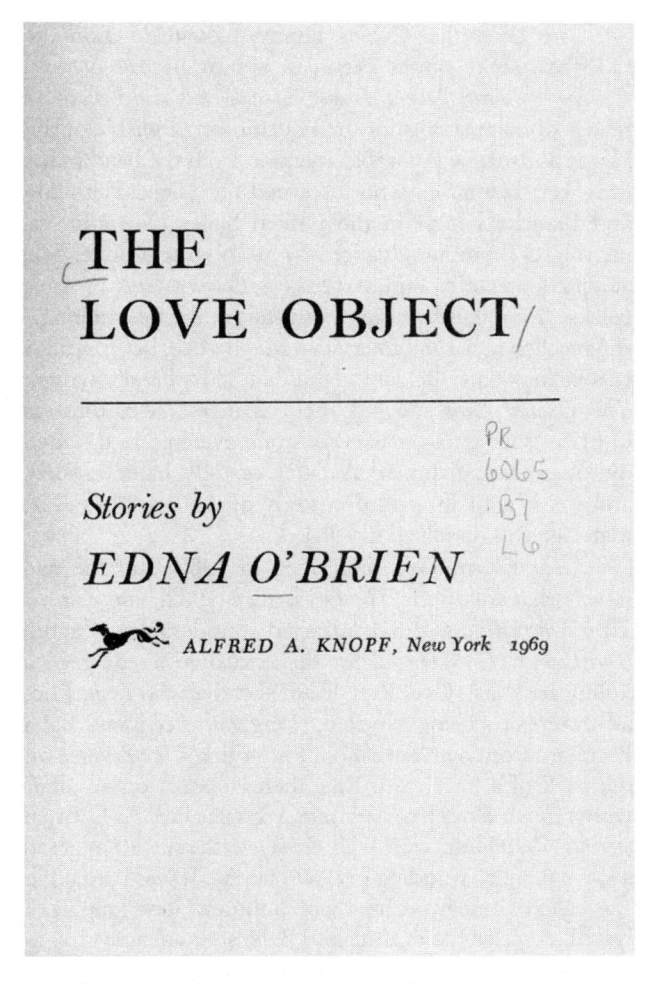

Title page for the American edition of O'Brien's first short-story collection, published in England in 1968, which centers on the theme of female desire (Thomas Cooper Library, University of South Carolina)

copy of *Introducing James Joyce: A Selection of Joyce's Prose* (1942), edited by T. S. Eliot. When she opened it to a section from *A Portrait of the Artist as a Young Man* (1916) and read the Christmas-dinner scene, she realized that her own experience would provide all the subject matter she needed for writing.

Publication of short nonfiction articles about nature in Dublin newspapers and the encouragement of Peadar O'Donnell, editor of the magazine *The Bell,* confirmed O'Brien in her decision to change her professional course. She met Ernest Gébler, a Czech-Irish writer, and eloped with the much older, divorced man in 1951, estranging herself from both family and the Catholic Church. O'Brien married Gébler because "he was the first non-Irishman I'd ever met," she told interviewer Christopher Hitchens in 1988. Although the marriage produced two sons—Carlo, born in 1954, and Sasha, born in 1956—it did not last.

In 1958 the Gébler family moved to London. O'Brien's short stories began to appear in *The Saturday Evening Post* and *Ladies' Home Journal,* and she became a reader of manuscripts for the Hutchinson publishing firm. Her reports drew favorable attention from the head of the firm, Iain Hamilton, who discerned her talent. Hamilton and Blanche Knopf in the United States joined forces, offering O'Brien an advance of £50 to write a novel. She accepted the offer and wrote *The Country Girls* in three weeks. "I wrote it so easily. I can still see the ink running," she recalled in a 1989 interview. Meanwhile, her marriage was falling apart; Gébler's claim that he had really written *The Country Girls* did not help matters. According to O'Brien, she simply walked out one evening, in the middle of preparing dinner. A bitter custody battle ensued, and she eventually gained custody of the two boys. The marriage was dissolved in 1964.

The Country Girls, published in 1960, and the two novels that followed, *The Lonely Girl* (1962) and *Girls in Their Married Bliss* (1964), attracted considerable attention. *The Country Girls* chronicles the sexual awakening of a young Irish girl, Caithleen "Kate" Brady, who begins her adventures by being expelled, along with her friend Baba Brennan, from convent school for writing a lewd verse on the back of a holy card. Kate then embarks on an affair with a much older married man, who jilts her. As O'Brien said in a 1995 interview with *Salon.com,* the novel "angered a lot of people, including my own family. It was banned; it was called a smear on Irish womanhood." The graphic, if lyrical, descriptions of Kate and Baba's sexual activities, as well as the depiction of a harshly repressive Catholic Church and the liberal use of profanity, created a scandal that ensured good book sales. As O'Brien told Julia Carlson in *Banned in Ireland: Censorship and the Irish Writer* (1990), the local priest in Tuamgraney seized the three copies of *The Country Girls* in the village and held a sacrificial burning, and a local woman suffered a seizure while reading the novel. *The Country Girls* was banned by the Irish Censorship Board, as were O'Brien's next six books.

The Lonely Girl (also published as *Girl with Green Eyes*) and *Girls in Their Married Bliss,* the second and third installments of the trilogy, follow the lives of Kate and Baba well into adulthood. Dealing with issues such as adultery, divorce, and sterilization, the novels only intensified public and critical response to O'Brien and her writing. The critical reaction demonstrated a sharp division that is provoked by her works to this day: some critics praised her for breaking taboos and transgressing boundaries in giving voice to the previously all-but-mute Irish female, while others expressed shock at her vivid, outspoken chronicle of female desire.

O'Brien's exile from Ireland was paradoxically painful and exhilarating; the imperative to escape led to expulsion into a wider world and released her creative powers. She felt that she had cut the cord between herself and Ireland, but she had to learn how mistaken she was in that sense, for her relationship to Mother Ireland remains central to all her fiction. The pain of separation from Ireland intensified the pain of separation from her biological mother. This double separation of maturation and exile created in O'Brien and her female protagonists a deep desire to restore primal unity. Her heroines embark on quests, taking roads that lead them to sundry locations—convents, pubs, village dances, Dublin, and London—in a poignant search for "life." Nuns and lovers become unconscious "replacements" for the lost mother. Yet, all these quests are doomed to fail. In Freudian myth O'Brien found what she called "the crux of female despair" in a 1984 interview with Philip Roth: "in the Greek myth and in Freud's exploration of it, the son's desire for his mother is admitted; the infant daughter also desires its mother but it is unthinkable, either in myth, in fantasy, or in fact, that the desire can be consummated." The next best thing, played out in O'Brien's stories, is the temporary unity her heroines achieve through sexual relations with men; the rituals preparatory and attendant to the act and the bittersweet aftermath are the stuff of much of her short fiction. As Anita Brookner noted, however, "no compensation for the loss of the mother is possible . . . all the men in the world could not replace the original closeness" (*Spectator,* 15 October 1988).

O'Brien's first short-story collection, *The Love Object* (1968), consists of eight stories, five previously published in *The New Yorker,* that emphasize female desire. The protagonists range from a seventeen-year-old farm girl to a thirty-year-old television presenter to a forty-seven-year-old housewife. Although the love objects are predominantly male, in "The Mouth of the Cave," lesbian fantasy is turned into debilitating disappointment. The title story, "The Love Object," features an archetypal O'Brien heroine, a woman filled with longing who is willing to invest her whole person in an unworthy man. In *The Washington Post* (9 February 1969) R. V. Cassill called this story "one of the most telling revelations . . . of what it means to be a woman." "Irish Revel," the first story by O'Brien to be published in *The New Yorker,* is the tale of a young girl who thinks herself invited to a party as a guest, only to find that she is expected to work. It is a bittersweet coming-of-age narrative; the ending, with "frost . . . everywhere," pays homage to Joyce's "The Dead," from *Dubliners* (1914). Some of the stories in *The Love Object* fall into the category of women's-magazine fiction. "Paradise" is a hothouse evocation of an affair on a Mediterranean island. This long story, about a woman learning to swim, lacks a solid foundation for the symbolic structure O'Brien seeks to design. Nonetheless, *The Love Object* marks out O'Brien's territory, the bleak landscape of female disappointment, and clearly distinguishes the characters who traverse it—women subjected to men and driven by desperate desire for them, and men used to the random exercise of authority.

A Scandalous Woman: Stories (1974) is a collection of nine stories; at the center of each is a sad, lost woman to whom the love of a man is essential. Men both create and destroy women at will, driving some into silent submission, some into endless childbearing, and others into madness. The women sacrifice themselves by both their own choice and that of others, while male privilege, sometimes in conjunction with the Catholic Church, makes the rules. Tess in "The Favourite" is kicked by her own father for attracting the "wrong" kind of man. Although she eventually marries well and lives comfortably, at midlife she wonders, "Is this how it is when one begins to be unhappy?" In "A Scandalous Woman," the title story, Eily, a vivacious village girl forced into a shotgun wedding with a bank clerk, suffers the opprobrium of family, village, and church. Bearing three children in four years, she slips into a madness "cured" only by shock treatments. The narrator, a village girl, ends the story by linking Eily's experience to her own and perhaps to that of all women when she muses, "I thought that ours was indeed a land of shame, a land of murder, and a land of strange, sacrificial women." Most of the women in *A Scandalous Woman* live in an obsessive state of romantic angst. The narrator of "Over" declares, "I suppose there is a sickness of heart as well as a sickness of mind and body." The epigraph of the collection, from Pierre-Ambroise-François Choderlos de Laclos's *Dangerous Liaisons* (1782)–"I assure you the world is not as amusing as we imagined"–reverberates throughout the stories. *A Scandalous Woman* is not a strong collection; some stories, such as "The Creature," "Honeymoon," "A Journey," "Sisters," and "Love Child," are mere sketches or have a forced, overfamiliar quality about them. Yet, the opening and closing stories, "A Scandalous Woman" and "The House of My Dreams," offer convincing proof of O'Brien's abilities.

O'Brien's third collection, *Mrs. Reinhardt and Other Stories* (1978), comprising twelve stories, was published in the United States as *A Rose in the Heart* (1979), with one change of story: "Mary" was replaced with "Starting" in the American edition. "Mary," a two-page letter from one woman to another about the goings-on in the house where she works, is a sketch at best; "Starting," a brief account of a middle-aged divorcée's rejection of an affair with a handsome, sensitive American, reworks familiar territory in an unconvincing manner. Likewise, "Clara," a long account of an outsider's stint in an Irish village, is weak and unsatisfying; the narrative voice, belonging to a forty-year-old man, does not ring true. "No. 10," with its repressed female protagonist in denial, feels both lightweight and contrived. Nearly all critics, however, have praised "A Rose in the Heart" (titled "A Rose in the Heart of New York" in the American edition), the most powerful story

Dust jacket for the American edition of O'Brien's 1974 collection of stories about women living in an obsessive state of romantic angst (Richland County Public Library)

in the collection and one of the best O'Brien has written. A paradigmatic O'Brien story of female consciousness and development, it confronts the consequences of the ruptured mother-daughter bond, established before birth, and reveals a paradoxical truth: for all the pain and stress following that rupture, woman's unfulfilled desire is directed unconsciously toward reestablishment of that primal bond. The married Irish woman's lot is a bad one, filled with abuse, torture (both physical and mental), and restriction to subservient roles. Desire, directed toward the male, always brings suffering since it is just a substitute for the primal connection with the mother. In the most straightforward statement of the dilemma so far in O'Brien's writing, the narrator of "A Rose in the Heart" notes that "the mother said that there was no such thing as love between the sexes. She reaffirmed that there was only one kind of love and that was a mother's love for her child." This realization does not make a woman's life any easier, however. The virtual anonymity of the two women at the center of "A Rose in the Heart" (the mother's name is given once, the daughter's not at all) extends its range into the general and perhaps even into the universal; add to that the easy alignment of mother with Mother Ireland, and the story becomes distinctly Joycean. As Julian Moynihan noted, "virtually epical in its treatment of the mother-daughter bond from birth to death, 'A Rose in the Heart' must be judged a classic of the new literature that bears the mark of the women's movement" (*New Republic*, 7–14 January 1985). Certainly, Mary Gordon's verdict still stands: "This is a story worthy of Joyce, but it could only have been written by a woman" (*Washington Post Book World*, 8 April 1979).

Three other stories in *Mrs. Reinhardt and Other Stories*, "Baby Blue," "Christmas Roses," and "Ways," demonstrate O'Brien's powers, but none eclipses "A Rose in the Heart." "Baby Blue," set in London, is the story of two women, radically different "types," locked in a battle for possession of a weak man. "Baby Blue" achieves extraordinary emotional intensity without sentimentality. "Christmas Roses" is a solid story about an older woman, still susceptible to the thrill of romance, brought to the brink of a fall; O'Brien's graceful resistance to cliché elevates the narrative considerably. "Ways" is the story of two women whose lives briefly intersect; the careful construction, technical precision, and emotional restraint in the story grant the reader an evocative glimpse into contemporary female experience.

O'Brien's literary production tapered off in the 1980s; she published stories and plays but no novels between *Johnny I Hardly Knew You* (1977) and *The High Road* (1988). She has attributed this decline in production to a long-term love affair with an unnamed, prominent politician. Her next story collection, *Returning: Tales* (1982), is stronger and more balanced than *Mrs. Reinhardt and Other Stories*. Even when, as in "Tough Men," "Savages," and "Courtship," O'Brien writes with less polish and substance, her insight and lyrical language make the stories worthwhile. Central to all nine stories is the figure of a child, deeply attached to mother and village, who grows up and goes away but in truth leaves neither mother nor village behind. The opening and closing stories, "The Connor Girls" and "Sister Imelda," are powerful evocations of female consciousness and experience. The former strikes the keynote for the volume: an adult woman returns to her native village, still filled with memories of childhood, and discovers the paradoxical truth that one can go home again, but it is no longer home. Her closing words underscore that bittersweet discovery: "I realized that by choosing his [her husband's] world I had said goodbye to my own and to those in it. By such choices we gradually become exiles; until at last we are quite alone." For O'Brien, as for Joyce, the metaphor of exile best expresses the human condition.

Most of the stories in *Returning* concern the alienation of the exile and amplify the primal fear in O'Brien's world, poignantly voiced by the narrator in "My Mother's Mother": "There was no one at home." Separation narratives dominate the volume; in "Sister Imelda," perhaps the best known of O'Brien's stories and the most frequently anthologized, the adult narrator recounts her convent schoolgirl days, culminating in her infatuation with the geometry nun, an experience so powerful that it prompts her to believe she has a vocation. Sister Imelda's eventual coolness—"we must not become attached," she tells her charge—sends the narrator to a university and on to another life; a chance encounter years later on a bus opens the floodgates of memory and desire. In technical terms, "Sister Imelda" demonstrates a delicate balancing of child and adult consciousness, reminiscent of Joyce's in "Araby," from *Dubliners;* unlike in "The Connor Girls," in which the abrupt and moralizing entrance of adult consciousness three-quarters of the way through spoils the story, in "Sister Imelda" the interplay of child and adult consciousness is highly nuanced. One of the lesser stories in *Returning,* "Ghosts," is not actually a story but three haunting character sketches; yet, it is memorable because of the narrator's closing statement about her subjects: "They live on; they are fixed in that far-off region called childhood, where nothing ever dies, not even oneself."

For *A Fanatic Heart: Selected Stories of Edna O'Brien* (1984), O'Brien chose to include all nine stories from *Returning,* selections from the three earlier collections, and four uncollected stories previously published in *The New Yorker*. These four stories, gathered as "Quartet (Uncollected Stories, 1979–1981)," neither deepen nor extend the range of O'Brien's short fiction. At the center of each is a middle-aged woman involved in an affair with a married man, desperately longing for his presence but acutely aware of the precarious, problematic nature of the relationship. With the possible exception of "The Call," in which the protagonist contemplates revenge in league with the wife, the "Quartet" stories, despite some of O'Brien's most evocative descriptive prose, emphasize the same predicament found in her other stories: a deeply neurotic woman is unable or willing to free herself from a narcissistic, manipulative man.

O'Brien's sixth collection, *Lantern Slides: Short Stories* (1990), published thirty years after *The Country Girls,* won the 1990 Los Angeles Times Book Prize. Most of the stories in the collection are distinguished by a deftness of touch, sureness of delineation, and lyricism of expression. None of the twelve stories charts new territory; half depict love affairs fractured or gone awry. Love and loss are the themes of all the stories. Central to each is a lone female figure, moving in her vulnerability, longing, and torment. In this collection, however, several of O'Brien's women are different, having achieved the self-knowledge that comes only through pain and suffering. As the deserted wife in the title story observes, "being 'of a certain age' is not the worst time in a woman's life." In "Epitaph" the female narrator chronicles the long, slow death of an affair; the remarriage of the title character in "The Widow" is foiled by a freak automobile accident. In "Storm" the recently jilted Eileen spends her holiday in a state of anxiety; in "Another Time" a former television announcer who long ago gave up her career for a man and family returns to a hotel near her childhood home to an unexpected encounter with the past. In "Long Distance" a woman, given the opportunity to resume an old affair, refuses, realizing that her refusal only deepens her love. Each of the stories swiftly and economically develops themes and situations familiar to readers of O'Brien's fiction.

Several stories in *Lantern Slides* transcend the limitations of time, space, and language. "Oft in the Stilly Night" is a study of female oppression and repression so severe that it leads to madness. O'Brien's use of cinematic technique makes the story vivid, and her conversational technique draws the reader into communion, if not complicity, with the characters. Ita McNamara, the pious sacristan of the village church, believes herself assaulted by both Christ and the devil. Taken to an asylum and later returning to assume the role of village madwoman, she becomes the object of spite and scorn. The story suggests the influence of Gustave Flaubert and Anton Chekhov, but ultimately Joyce figures most prominently, as the movement in the last line from the particular to the universal makes clear: "Perhaps your own village is much the same, perhaps everywhere is. . . ." Other stories in *Lantern Slides* demonstrate the degree to which O'Brien has polished her skills as storyteller. "Brother" is a horrifying interior monologue spoken, or perhaps only imagined, by a lunatic spinster, incestuously involved with her brother, who plots the murder of his intended wife. In "What a Sky," O'Brien charts new territory with her depiction of a woman whose sense of herself depends entirely on men and who is brought ultimately to the painful realization that her heart has turned to stone. In "Dramas," O'Brien enhances the lyrical grace of the narrative with a rarely exercised humor that softens the tragic lines of the tale.

The title story, "Lantern Slides," is O'Brien's greatest achievement in the collection. In this long paean to Joyce's own short-story masterpiece, "The Dead," O'Brien takes a swipe at the repressive provincialism of Dublin and the select of the city, gathered for a surprise birthday party. Archaeological images underscore the essential activity of the story: unearthing the buried feelings and ambitions of the party guests. The story explores the emotions of the celebrants as the narrative voice moves from one viewpoint to another, always returning to a young woman named Miss Lawless. The stories that link the party guests usually begin with love and end with disaster or humiliation: a tryst discovered, a miscarriage, or a desertion. As the story concludes, Miss Lawless, like the others, is caught up in the spell: "It was as if life were just beginning–tender, spectacular, all-embracing life–and she, like everyone, were jumping up to catch it. Catch it." "Lantern Slides" blends the haunting lyricism of Joyce and Yeats with the economy of Chekhov and the wicked insight of Flaubert.

Dust jacket for the American edition of O'Brien's 1984 selection of stories from her first four collections and four previously uncollected stories that were first published in The New Yorker *(Richland County Public Library)*

In her short-story writing O'Brien has demonstrated considerable talents but not a gift for tightly focused, dramatic plotting, which is more often found in her novels. With the passage of time her short fiction has not followed a course parallel to her novels. It is generally accepted that her novels can be grouped into early, middle, and later periods and that the general movement is through and away from the transparently autobiographical and into the political. Her three novels of the 1990s–*House of Splendid Isolation* (1994), *Down by the River* (1996), and *Wild Decembers* (1999)–are a political trilogy, each dealing with a different aspect of contemporary Irish politics (the Irish Republican

Army, the power of state and church to manipulate sexual lives and choices, and rural landownership). In her 2002 novel, *In the Forest,* based on a grisly triple murder committed by a psychotic young Irishman, she showed a deepening of her political concerns, wedding them to human concerns through echoes of biblical and Greek tragedy. In contrast, in her short fiction O'Brien has ignored the issues of the larger world and worked much the same ground from the outset, depicting the agonies of love and loss that attend women's experiences.

O'Brien has written more than seventy short stories, all of them documenting what Brookner called "the lovesickness [that] is really homesickness" (*Spectator,* 15 October 1988). Her stories dwell on the problem of trying to establish, solidify, and maintain a sense of self in a world of losses. As Tamsin Hargreaves has asserted, O'Brien's fiction is a series of "psychodramas in which the protagonists desperately attempt to replace the safety and wholeness, the sense of identity and meaning found with the mother." The tragedy of these "strange, throttled, sacrificial women" lies in the painful process of negotiating life and identity amid proliferating conflicts.

Praise for O'Brien by fellow writers such as Roth, Harold Pinter, Alice Munro, and Brookner, her most astute and perceptive critic, has placed her in literary company more distinguished than she could have imagined when she happened upon a copy of *Introducing James Joyce* in a Dublin bookstall. Her singular achievement is to have given voice to the silent Irish women of generations past in ways that other Irish writers, whether male (Joyce) or female (Maria Edgeworth, Elizabeth Bowen, and Molly Keane), had not. In giving voice to these women, O'Brien explores the territory of the female heart and soul in language so richly evocative as to justify Frank O'Connor's claim that "the nearest thing to lyric poetry is the short story."

O'Brien's auspicious literary debut with *The Country Girls* marked the beginning of a career that now encompasses a body of work including fifteen novels, six short-story collections, plays, television and motion-picture screenplays, poems, children's books, and nonfiction ranging from essays and reviews to a biography, *James Joyce* (1999). She always seems to have a novel and poems in progress and continues to write short stories, many published in *The New Yorker.* In all her work O'Brien continues to shock, puzzle, delight, and scandalize her readers as she ventures into new territory.

Like her own people, whom she described in a 1968 interview with Hunter Davies as "ferociously tenacious," Edna O'Brien has endured, never bowing to fashion or broken by a negative review or response. Today she is Ireland's best-known female writer, continuing to work at the craft that she described in a 1999 *Irish Times* interview as "struggling to make a living moment of both beauty and austerity."

Interviews:

Nell Dunn, "Edna," in her *Talking to Women* (London: MacGibbon & Kee, 1965), pp. 69–107;

Hunter Davies, "Writer in the Breaking: Edna O'Brien Talks to Hunter Davies," *Sunday Times Magazine* (London), 12 May 1968, pp. 44–49;

David Heycock, "Edna O'Brien Talks to David Heycock about Her New Novel, *A Pagan Place,*" *Listener,* 83 (7 May 1970): 616–617;

Ludovic Kennedy, "Three Loves of Childhood–Irish Thoughts by Edna O'Brien," *Listener,* 95 (3 June 1976): 701–702;

Janet McKerron, "A Day in the Life of Edna O'Brien: Janet McKerron Talks to Edna O'Brien," *Sunday Times Magazine,* 24 September 1978, p. 110;

Janet Watts, "In and Out of Grace: Janet Watts Listens to Edna O'Brien," *Observer,* 18 January 1981, p. 34;

Shusha Guppy, "The Art of Fiction LXXXII: Edna O'Brien," *Paris Review,* 26 (Summer 1984): 22–50; republished in *Writers at Work: The Paris Review Interviews, Seventh Series,* edited by George Plimpton (New York: Penguin, 1988), pp. 241–265; and in *Women Writers at Work: The Paris Review Interviews,* edited by Plimpton (New York: Viking, 1989), pp. 337–359;

Philip Roth, "A Conversation with Edna O'Brien: The Body Contains the Life Story," *New York Times Book Review,* 18 November 1984, pp. 38–40;

Howard Kissel, "Edna O'Brien: Give Me the Heart," *W* (22–29 March 1985): 6;

Maureen Howard, "Edna O'Brien: She's Earthy, Self-Possessed, and Not Afraid of Virginia Woolf," *Vogue,* 175 (April 1985): 196–199;

John Quinn, "Edna O'Brien," in *A Portrait of the Artist as a Young Girl,* edited by Quinn (London: Methuen, 1986), pp. 131–144;

Cal McCrystal, "Encountering Edna the Etherealised Woman," *Sunday Times Magazine,* 9 October 1988, sec. G, p. 8;

Marie Dawson, "In for a Deep End," *Guardian,* 12 October 1988, p. 20;

Christopher Hitchens, *Elle* (November 1988): 132, 134;

Richard B. Woodward, "Reveling in Heartbreak," *New York Times Magazine,* 12 March 1989, p. 42;

Julia Carlson, "Edna O'Brien: The Personal Experience of Censorship," in *Banned in Ireland: Censorship and the Irish Writer,* edited by Carlson (Athens: University of Georgia Press, 1990), pp. 69–79;

Molly McQuade, "Edna O'Brien," *Publishers Weekly,* 239 (18 May 1992): 48–49;

Mary Rourke, "Spellbinder," *Los Angeles Times,* 17 June 1992, sec. E, p. 1;

James Wolcott, "The Playgirl of the Western World," *Vanity Fair,* 55 (June 1992): 50–56;

David Streitfeld, "Edna O'Brien's Hard Edge of Heartbreak," *International Herald Tribune,* 31 July 1992, p. 16;

Coilin Owens, *Introducing Edna O'Brien,* videocassette, Howard County Poetry and Literature Society PA678-190, 1992;

James F. Clarity, "Casting a Cold Eye," *New York Times,* 30 August 1995, sec. C, pp. 1, 8;

"Lit Chat: Edna O'Brien," *Salon.com* (2 December 1995) <www.salon.com/02dec1995/departments/litchat.html>;

Sandra Manoogian Pearce, "An Interview with Edna O'Brien," *Canadian Journal of Irish Studies,* 22 (December 1996): 5–8;

Nicholas Wroe, "Country Matters," *Guardian Review,* 2 October 1999, pp. 6–7;

Eileen Battersby, "Life of O'Brien," *Irish Times,* 14 October 1999, p. 15;

Mary Kenny, "Women in Love: Edna O'Brien Talks to Mary Kenny," *Spectator* (4 May 2002): 14–16.

Bibliographies:

Kimball King, *Ten Modern Irish Playwrights: A Comprehensive Annotated Bibliography* (New York: Garland, 1979), pp. 95–105;

Douglas Skinner and Luke Greening, "Edna O'Brien Bibliography," *Canadian Journal of Irish Studies,* 22 (December 1996): 107–116.

References:

Donatella Abbate Badin, "The Mythical Context of Edna O'Brien's Short Stories," *Lingua e Letteratura,* nos. 24–25 (1995): 151–162;

James M. Cahalan, "Female and Male Perspectives on Growing Up Irish in Edna O'Brien, John McGahern, and Brian Moore," *Colby Quarterly,* 31 (March 1995): 55–73;

Canadian Journal of Irish Studies, special O'Brien issue, 22 (December 1996);

Mariana Cook, "Eight Portraits," *Yale Review,* 83 (1995): 28–36;

Grace Eckley, *Edna O'Brien* (Lewisburg, Pa.: Bucknell University Press, 1974);

Michael Patrick Gillespie, "(S)he Was Too Scrupulous Always: Edna O'Brien and the Comic Tradition," in *The Comic Tradition in Irish Women Writers,* edited by Theresa O'Connor (Gainesville: University Press of Florida, 1996), pp. 108–123;

Tamsin Hargreaves, "Women's Consciousness and Identity in Four Irish Women Novelists," in *Cultural Contexts and Literary Idioms in Contemporary Irish Literature,* edited by Michael Kenneally, Studies in Contemporary Irish Literature, no. 1 (Gerrards Cross, U.K.: Colin Smythe, 1988), pp. 290–305;

James Haule, "The Unfortunate Birth of Edna O'Brien," *Colby Library Quarterly,* 23 (December 1987): 216–224;

Benedict Kiely, "The Whores on the Half-Doors," in *Conor Cruise O'Brien Introduces Ireland,* edited by Owen Dudley Edwards (New York: McGraw-Hill, 1970), pp. 148–161;

Nancy Knowles, "Exiles to the Garden: Garden Imagery in Selections from Edna O'Brien's *A Fanatic Heart,*" *Notes on Modern Irish Literature,* 11 (1999): 4–12;

Frances M. Malpezzi, "Consuming Love: Edna O'Brien's 'A Rose in the Heart of New York,'" *Studies in Short Fiction,* 33 (Summer 1996): 355–360;

Eileen Morgan, "Mapping Out a Landscape of Female Suffering: Edna O'Brien's Demythologizing Novels," *Women's Studies: An Interdisciplinary Journal,* 29 (August 2000): 449–476;

Darcy O'Brien, "Edna O'Brien: A Kind of Irish Childhood," in *Twentieth-Century Women Novelists,* edited by Thomas F. Staley (London: Macmillan, 1982; Totowa, N.J.: Barnes & Noble, 1982), pp. 179–190;

Frank O'Connor, "The Art of Fiction: XIX," *Paris Review* (Autumn–Winter 1957): 42–64;

Kiera O'Hara, "Love Objects: Love and Obsession in the Stories of Edna O'Brien," *Studies in Short Fiction,* 30 (Summer 1993): 317–325;

Sandra Manoogian Pearce, "Edna O'Brien's 'Lantern Slides' and Joyce's 'The Dead': Shadows of a Bygone Era," *Studies in Short Fiction,* 32 (Summer 1995): 437–446;

Mary Salmon, "Edna O'Brien," in *Contemporary Irish Novelists,* edited by Rüdiger Imhof (Tübingen, Germany: G. Narr, 1990), pp. 143–158;

Jeanette Roberts Shumaker, "Sacrificial Women in Short Stories by Mary Lavin and Edna O'Brien," *Studies in Short Fiction,* 32 (Spring 1995): 185–197;

Lotus Snow, "'That Trenchant Childhood Route?' Quest in Edna O'Brien's Novels," *Eire-Ireland: A Journal of Irish Studies,* 14, no. 1 (1979): 74–83.

Máirtín Ó Cadhain

(January 1905 – 18 October 1970)

Pádraigín Riggs
University College, Cork

BOOKS: *Idir Shúgradh agus Dáiríre* (Dublin: An Gúm, 1939);

An Braon Broghach (Dublin: An Gúm, 1948);

Cré na Cille (Dublin: Sáirséal agus Dill, 1949);

Cois Caoláire (Dublin: Sáirséal agus Dill, 1953);

An tSraith ar Lár (Dublin: Sáirséal agus Dill, 1967);

Páipéir Bhána agus Páipéir Bhreaca (Dublin: An Clóchomhar, 1969);

An tSraith dhá Tógáil (Dublin: Sáirséal agus Dill, 1970);

An tSraith Tógtha (Dublin: Sáirséal agus Dill, 1977);

Athnuachan (Dublin: Coiscéim, 1995).

Edition in English: *The Road to Brightcity and Other Stories,* translated by Eoghan Ó Tuairisc (Dublin: Poolbeg Press, 1981)—includes one story from *Idir Shúgradh agus Dáiríre* and eight stories from *An Braon Broghach.*

OTHER: Charles Kickham, *Saile Ní Chaomhánaigh,* translated by Ó Cadhain (Dublin: An Gúm, 1932);

Saunders Lewis, *Bás nó Beatha?* translated by Ó Cadhain (Dublin: Sáirséal agus Dill, 1963);

Irish above Politics (Dublin: Preas Cúchulainn Teoranta, 1964);

Gluaiseacht na Gaeilge: Gluaiseacht ar Strae (Dublin: Misneach, 1970);

An Ghaeilge Bheo—Destined to Pass, edited by Seán Ó Laighin (Dublin: Coiscéim, 2002);

Barbed Wire, edited by Cathal Ó Háinle (Dublin: Coiscéim, 2002).

Máirtín Ó Cadhain (from Bosco Costigan, De Ghlaschloich an Oileáin, 1987; University of Virginia Library)

Máirtín Ó Cadhain's importance as a writer derives both from his unparalleled knowledge of the Irish language and from his innovative approach to the short story and the novel. He is considered by some as the most important prose writer of the twentieth century in the Irish language. By the end of the nineteenth century, because of a major language shift, Irish had become a predominantly oral language, spoken daily only by a small rural minority of the population of Ireland. Ó Cadhain, having been born in an Irish-speaking area of West Galway in the early years of the twentieth century, belonged to the last generation who were part of a monoglot Irish-speaking and a mainly English-speaking Ireland; his literary work is informed by this linguistic and cultural background. Both as an academic linguist and as a writer, he fully acknowledged the vital importance of the surviving spoken language—he was a deeply committed language activist to the end of his life—but he was acutely aware also of its deficiency as a modern literary medium. Consequently, his novels and short stories are written in a language that is based on his native dialect but that also draws extensively on earlier literary sources, both lexically and stylistically.

Between 1939 and his death in 1970, Ó Cadhain published five collections of short stories and one novel. He also wrote many essays and articles on literary subjects and on controversial issues related to the Irish language, some of which were subsequently edited and published in book form. In 1973, a collection of letters written by Ó Cadhain between 1939 and 1944 was published with a preface by the recipient of the letters, his friend Tomás Báiréad. A further collection of short stories was published seven years after Ó Cadhain's death, and in 1995 a previously unpublished novel appeared.

Born near Spiddle, about twelve miles west of Galway City, Máirtín was the eldest surviving child of the thirteen born to Bríd Ní Chonaola and Seán Ó Cadhain. The exact date of his birth is not known, but most likely he was born sometime in January 1905. Both of his parents were natives of the area, as were their forebears for several generations. Spiddle, then an extremely poor and isolated part of the country, was in the heart of the Connemara Gaeltacht (Irish speaking district), where, even as late as 1926, a substantial proportion of the local population were still Irish-speaking monoglots. Like most of his neighbors, Seán Ó Cadhain was a subsistence farmer, and the poverty and isolation that characterized the Connemara of Ó Cadhain's childhood and youth provide the background for his early stories.

Ó Cadhain grew up in an environment in which the native folk tradition, including an oral storytelling tradition, was still flourishing. His parents were both competent raconteurs, and his paternal uncle, Máirtín Beag ("little" Máirtín), was a renowned *seanchaí* (oral storyteller). A collection of this uncle's stories, transcribed by Máirtín, was published in *Bealoideas,* the journal of the Irish Folklore Commission, in 1935. Ó Cadhain's early exposure to folk narrative influenced him profoundly, a fact he acknowledged in a celebrated lecture delivered to the Merriman Winter School, an annual gathering of Irish scholars and literary enthusiasts, in 1969. He even admitted that his first attempts at writing were modeled on the traditional oral tale, though he rejected that model early in his writing career in favor of a more consciously literary one.

In 1911, at the age of six, Ó Cadhain was enrolled at the national school in Spiddle. Although he proved to be an exceptionally bright pupil, he was taken out of school once he reached the senior level, as his father needed him at home to help provide for the large family. The teacher and the schools inspector together persuaded the boy's father to allow Máirtín to return to school, however, and in 1923 he won a King's Scholarship. Unable to accept the scholarship because he was under the required age, he remained at the school as a monitor for a further year. He was awarded the scholarship again in 1924, and at the age of eighteen, he became a student teacher at St. Patrick's Teacher Training College in Dublin. Prior to this time, Ó Cadhain had never been to the capital city. He attended the college until July 1926 when, having completed his training course, he returned to his native Connemara to take up a temporary teaching appointment on Dinish Island.

The following September he moved to the Christian Brothers' school in Galway City and, while there, attended evening classes for primary schoolteachers at University College in Galway. In 1927 he was appointed principal of Camus primary school in Connemara, where he remained until 1932. By this time he had already begun writing, and his first attempt at a short story, "Siollántacht na Gaoithe" (The Soughing of the Wind), was published in an Irish-language paper, *An Stoc,* in two installments, in December 1926 and January 1927. The subject of this story is an old man who has recently lost his daughter, having previously lost his wife and only son. Distraught, he goes to visit the daughter's grave, where he falls asleep. On awakening he imagines that the young woman has appeared to him, and, in terror, he runs away, but as he leaves the graveyard, he falls and is killed. In this simple but poignant story, the old man's desolation is accentuated by his vain attempt to communicate with the dead woman.

Following the establishment of the Irish Free State, an Irish-language publishing scheme, An Gúm (The Scheme), was set up in 1926 under the auspices of the department of education in order to provide textbooks for schools as well as reading material for the public. Original material in the language was solicited on behalf of An Gúm from writers or potential writers, and translations into Irish from other languages, including English, were also sought. Ó Cadhain was one of the writers who responded to this call, attracted partly by the remuneration, which would help supplement his modest teacher's salary, and partly by the challenge of adapting his still fundamentally spoken Irish to the stylistic requirements of a novel. He began translating *Sally Kavanagh,* by the Irish novelist Charles Kickham. First published in 1869, this novel is a story of poverty, hardship, and injustice, and, though set in the rural Ireland of the nineteenth century, the social conditions it

Title page for Ó Cadhain's 1948 Irish-language short-story collection, whose title, translated as *The Dirty Drop*, refers to the first impure drop from the distillation of unlawful liquor (Ryan Library, Iona College, New Rochelle, New York)

depicted were not far removed from those experienced by Ó Cadhain in the Connemara of the early twentieth century. *Saile Ní Chaomhánaigh*, Ó Cadhain's translation, appeared in 1932. Though not his own original composition, it was his first published book, and the skills he acquired in the course of the translation proved extremely valuable to him as an apprentice writer.

In 1932 he left Camus to take up a new post in Carnmore, a village in the partly Irish-speaking area east of Galway City. By this time, Ó Cadhain was becoming politically active on behalf of the Irish-speaking population of the country, whom he considered to be deprived of their civil rights under the Free State. In 1934 he helped found an organization called Muintir na Gaeltachta (the People of the Gaeltacht), which was instrumental in obtaining from the government land in the fertile County Meath for several families from Connemara, thereby establishing what became the Gaeltacht of Rath Cairn, the only such community in the eastern part of the country. Ó Cadhain had become interested in the Irish Republican Army (IRA) when he was still a student teacher at St. Patrick's College. He was sworn into the organization while he was living at Camus, and about a year after his arrival at Carnmore, he became a captain of the local battalion. In 1936 the government banned the annual Wolfe Tone Republican Commemoration at Bodenstown, County Kildare. (This event commemorates eighteenth-century patriot Wolfe Tone, who is regarded as the father of Irish Republicanism.) Ó Cadhain was to have attended the event, but, along with the group who were to accompany him, he was arrested and detained overnight by the police in Galway. On the following day, he was dismissed from his teaching post on the order of the bishop; the grounds for his dismissal were his Republican connections. The local people objected to his removal from his post, refusing to accept the replacement teacher, and they organized a campaign to have him reinstated. Their campaign was not successful, and Ó Cadhain left Carnmore for Dublin.

On his arrival in Dublin, Ó Cadhain was without a permanent job. He continued to be active in the IRA, recruiting many new members for the organization, and he eked out a living by teaching evening classes for the Gaelic League, an Irish-language body. He was engaged in research also for an Irish-English Dictionary, to be published by An Gúm. He claimed that he started writing at this time because he had nothing else to do. He read voraciously during his early years in Dublin and described his first introduction to the work of Maksim Gor'ky as a seminal event in his subsequent writing career. He discovered a short story by Gor'ky in a French magazine that he bought in a secondhand bookstall and was immediately struck by the similarity between the peasants depicted by Gor'ky and the people of his own native Connemara. Ó Cadhain claimed to have been inspired to write stories about his own people as a result. Up to this time Ó Cadhain had spent his whole life, apart from his two years at St. Patrick's College, either in his native Connemara Gaeltacht or, briefly, in the partly English-speaking area east of Galway, and the stories included in his first collection, published in 1939 as *Idir Shúgradh agus Dáiríre* (Half in Jest, Wholly in Earnest), reflect this experience.

Idir Shúgradh agus Dáiríre is set in the author's native Connemara, and the characters all belong to what Ó Cadhain himself describes elsewhere as a "local organic community." The collection includes ten stories, many taking their titles from proverbs or traditional sayings. In some cases, the subject matter of the story is an ironic play on the words of the proverb or saying; this irony usually depends on a melodramatic turn of events. The first and title story of the collection, for example, tells of a row between two neighboring families as a result of which a man is killed. This row began because a child stole a ball from his friend, but by the time the father of one of the children has been killed and the father of the other has been arrested for his murder, the two children have resolved their differences and are playing together, oblivious to the tragedy they have caused. The word "súgradh," which means "in jest" in the popular expression used in the collection's title, also means "to play," hence the irony.

Although well received at the time of its publication, *Idir Shúgradh agus Dáiríre* is now regarded as juvenilia, depicting incidents in the life of a traditional community in an uncritical way, with an emphasis on the consequence of the incident rather than on its motives. It is not considered worthy of the critical attention given to Ó Cadhain's later work.

In September 1939 Ó Cadhain was arrested and imprisoned in Arbor Hill Prison in Dublin for membership in the IRA. He was released in December but was arrested again in the following April. This time he was interned in the Curragh, in County Kildare, and remained there until 1944. During the period of his internment, Ó Cadhain read widely and critically, and he began to write seriously. In his letters to his friend Báiréad, written between 1939 and 1944 and published in 1973 as *As an nGéibheann* (From Internment), he lists some of the authors whose work he has been reading, including Gor'ky, Ivan Turgenev, Leo Tolstoy, Anton Chekhov, Fyodor Dostoevsky, Nicolai Gogol, François Villon, Jean Racine, and Pierre Corneille. Ó Cadhain also mentions that he is reading the Bible, and his letters show that he has been studying Irish literature, both medieval and modern, assiduously. On the subject of his own writing, he says, in a letter to Báiréad dated April 1944, that he has written some short stories, and he describes himself as being more self-assured as a writer as a result of the time he spent in the internment camp. In May 1944 he sent Báiréad a package consisting of three copybooks that included six stories, and he refers to a further three stories that he had previously sent Báiréad. Ó Cadhain writes of submitting the stories to An Gúm for publication as a collection.

Ó Cadhain was released from the Curragh Internment Camp in July 1944. He was without work for some time when, along with a number of other former internees, he obtained work in the Phoenix Park in Dublin as part of a wartime scheme to accumulate reserves of turf. During this time he also resumed the work he had begun in 1936, collecting material for the Irish-English dictionary, until the project was terminated in 1946. In February 1945 he married Máirín Ní Rodaigh, a teacher, whom he had known since 1932.

He struggled to earn a living, doing translation for which he was paid according to the number of words. In 1947 he took up employment in the Translation Section of Leinster House, the Irish parliament, where he worked as part of a team translating the proceedings of Leinster House into Irish, in accordance with the requirements of the Irish constitution.

Three months after his release from the internment camp, in September 1944, Ó Cadhain entered into a contract with An Gúm for the publication of a collection of short stories, including those he had written while he was interned. According to the contract, the minister for education, or his representative, could alter the stories or even suppress them completely if he considered them to be unsuitable for publication. Two of the stories submitted by Ó Cadhain were rejected as unsuitable (the content and some descriptive phrases were considered unseemly), and the remainder, consisting of a collection of eleven stories titled *An Braon Broghach* (The Dirty Drop), was published in 1948. (The "dirty drop" refers to the first impure drops in the distillation process of poteen—that is, illicit liquor.)

Like *Idir Shúgradh agus Dáiríre*, *An Braon Broghach* is set in the author's native Connemara, but the stories in this collection are more critical in their depiction of traditional society, most of them dealing with women who are trapped in a conservative and unsympathetic system. The omniscient and slightly moralistic third-person narrator has been replaced by a narrative voice, which, though still mainly in the third person, is closely identifiable with that of the main protagonist, an individual who is helpless in the face of a thwarted life. The author's compassion for the individual is apparent, but the outcome of all the stories is pessimistic. "An Taoille Tuile" (translated as "Spring Tide" in *The Road to Brightcity and Other Stories*) and "An Bhearna Mhíl" (translated as "Harelip" in *The Road to Brightcity and Other Stories*) both take as their subject the situation of a recently married woman as she comes to terms with her new status. In "An Bóthar go dtí an Ghealchathair" (translated as "The Road to Brightcity," 1981) and "An Bhliain 1912" (translated as "The Year 1912," in *The Road to Brightcity and Other Stories*), the focus is on older women. Each of the stories takes place within the space of a single day.

Máiréad, in "An Taoille Tuile," has been married to Pádraig for three weeks, having recently returned from America, where she had spent ten years as a domestic servant earning her dowry. She and Pádraig are deeply in love, and this love has helped them overcome the threats to their union—threats posed by the disapproval of Pádraig's widowed mother, who would have preferred her only son to marry the neighbor's daughter, and threats posed by Máiréad's ten-year absence, with its many temptations, including an attractive proposal of marriage from a wealthy American. In the course of that day, the intense love between Mairéad and Pádraig is tested as the couple perform their first public duty together, gathering seaweed on the portion of shoreline that they share with their neighbor. As the challenges of the weather, the hostile terrain, the arduousness of the task, and the pressure to complete the harvest before the spring tide turns all combine gradually to defeat the young woman, Mairéad begins to question the wisdom of her decision to return to Ireland to marry Pádraig. Romance gives way to despair as she comes to realize that the life she dreamed of during her ten years in America was merely an illusion.

Nóra, in "An Bhearna Mhíl," has only been married since the previous evening, and her marriage has not yet been consummated. Hers is an arranged marriage, and, as was common in such cases, the couple did not know each other before the wedding. Although never stated explicitly in the story, clearly Nora has been close to Beairtlín, the hired laborer on her father's farm, and her feelings for this young man are contrasted, throughout the story, with the indifference she feels toward her new husband, in whose house the wedding has taken place. This house is Nóra's future home, and, as her new husband is at pains to point out, it is situated exactly twenty-six miles from Nóra's former home in the Irish-speaking area west of Galway. As she takes stock of her new situation, the young woman's thoughts focus on the house, its contents, and its surrounding landscape—a vista that, in contrast to her native place, is characterized by its monotony and predictability. Her gradual acceptance of her fate is sealed at the moment when she focuses her attention on her husband, who has fallen asleep at the fire, and she notices for the first time that the face of the man she has married, unlike that of her beloved Beairtlín, is not deformed by a harelip.

In "An Bóthar go dtí an Ghealchathair," Bríd makes her weekly journey, a nine-mile walk before dawn, to Galway, where she sells the small quantity of eggs and butter she produces on her small farm. This long and arduous trek has become a symbol of Bríd's life as a married woman. On arrival at the city, she experiences a brief sense of achievement in having successfully overcome her aversion to the early start, the inclement weather, the difficult road, and the loneliness of the journey with the many fears it provokes. She knows, however, that she will have to repeat this ordeal for the rest of her life until she is no longer physically able to walk. "An Bhliain 1912" has as its subject the Irish custom of the American Wake, the party held on the night before someone emigrates to America. The established association between the emigrant's departure and death is underlined in this story by the symbol of the trunk, which reminds the mother of Máirín, the young woman who is about to leave, of a coffin. The central theme is the mother's inability to communicate her love for her daughter before she bids her farewell, a situation made all the more poignant by the knowledge that the mother is unlikely ever to see her daughter again. The emphasis, in all these stories, is on the failure of communication between the main protagonist and the individuals closest to her; features of the external environment—the rising tide, the flat landscape, the interminable road—are used with considerable effect to convey the characters' unspoken emotions. Each of the women is depicted, ultimately, as an outsider, condemned to struggle alone against an implacable situation.

After the refusal by An Gúm to publish two of the stories in his original proposal, Ó Cadhain was unenthusiastic about submitting another manuscript to them. Fortunately for him, a new publisher emerged at this time who not only agreed to publish Ó Cadhain's next book but who became a source of much encouragement to him in his subsequent writing career. In 1942 an Irish-language magazine, *Comhar,* was established by *An Comhchaidreamh* (The Irish Linking Group), a group of Irish-speaking university students. This magazine had as one of its aims the publication of new material in the language, including poems, short stories, and literary criticism. Six years later, in 1948, a second magazine, *Feasta,* was established by the Gaelic League, and it, too, sought short stories in Irish. Ó Cadhain published stories in both magazines and became one of those writers who, collectively, represented a Golden Age of writing in Modern Irish. Seán Ó hÉigeartaigh, a student at Trinity College, Dublin, was one of the founders of *Comhar*. Aware of the need for a new Irish-language publishing company as an alternative to An Gúm, he established Sáirséal agus Dill in 1945. This company subsequently played a major role in the publication of literature in Irish. In 1949 Sáirséal agus Dill published Ó Cadhain's first novel, *Cré na Cille* (Graveyard Clay). Written during the three years following his release from the Curragh, it had won a major Irish literary prize in 1947. A highly original and controversial work, the book established Ó Cadhain as a major writer in the Irish language. Set in a graveyard in Connemara, *Cré na Cille* consists entirely of dialogue between the corpses who are interred there. Apparently based on the author's experience in the internment camp, even though the two main characters are female, the novel satirizes many aspects of contemporary life in Ireland. Essentially humorous, unlike Ó Cadhain's work to date, it represents a radically new approach to writing in Irish both structurally and linguistically. Two years after the publication of *Cré na Cille,* Ó Cadhain was awarded a literary prize for his second novel, *Athnuachan* (Renewal). For personal reasons, he did not wish that it be published until he had altered parts of it. It was eventually published in 1995, a quarter of a century after Ó Cadhain's death.

In 1953, Sáirséal agus Dill published Ó Cadhain's third collection of short stories. *Cois Caoláire* (By Caoláire) includes nine stories, two of which had previously been rejected by An Gúm, namely "Ciumhais an Chriathraigh" (The Edge of the Marsh) and "An Strainséara" (The Stranger). Like the stories in the collection of which they had originally been a part, both are set in Connemara, and each has a woman as its main protagonist. Muiréad in "Ciumhais an Chriathraigh" is unmarried and lives alone in an isolated, inhospitable location on the edge of the eponymous marsh. Her repressed sexual desire is aroused during a wedding she attends when a young man attempts to kiss her, not recognizing her in the darkness. As soon as he realizes who she is, he flees, but she takes pleasure in recalling the incident afterward, fantasizing about what might happen if the man ever came to visit her.

Ó Cadhain claimed that "An Strainséara" was based on the true story of a woman from Connemara who gave birth to twenty-three stillborn children. Nóra, the character in the story, has borne five children, all stillborn, and they are buried in the "claí tórann" (the boundary fence between two town-lands), an area of unconsecrated ground, which was used as a burial ground for children who had not been baptized. She and her husband have decided to invite her nephew to come to live with them in order to help on the farm; their intention is that when they die, he will inherit the place from them. Nóra, however, is unable to accept the presence of the young man, whom she regards as "the stranger," and as her aversion to him gradually turns into an obsession, she tries to blot him out of her consciousness completely by invoking her dead children, for whom she has invented names and an imaginary existence. She eventually dies, having become totally deranged; but just before her death, she imagines that she sees her children being rescued from limbo by the mother of God and taken, under her mantle, to heaven. When her husband finds her body, Nóra is clutching a picture of the Crucifixion.

In both of these stories, as in those in the 1948 collection, *An Braon Broghach,* the landscape is full of meaning, the "boundary fence" symbolizing Nora's liminal status, and the barren marsh symbolizing Muiréad's, for each of these women is a social outsider—Muiréad because she is unmarried and Nóra because, even though she is married and has borne children, none of her children was born alive. Another story in this collection, "Fios" (Knowing), first published in the magazine *Feasta* in 1948, is structurally similar to the novel *Cré na Cille* in that it consists almost entirely of dialogue. This story tells of three men who are engaged in a verbal contest, each one determined to elicit as much information as possible from the other two while revealing as little as possible himself. The issue under discussion is an incident involving two of their neighbors, about whom only one of the three knows the details. After several contributions, which alternate between evasiveness and provocation, one of the three announces that he knows what the other two want to know, and having established his ascendancy over his two companions, he walks away triumphantly, leaving them none the wiser. While the setting for this story is still the Connemara of Ó Cadhain's early work, the satirical tone is closer to that of the later, urban stories.

Front cover of Ó Cadhain's 1967 Irish-language short-story collection (The Corn Cut), some stories of which deal with urban settings and unlikely consequences from small events (Davis Library, University of North Carolina–Chapel Hill)

From 1953 to 1956, Ó Cadhain was a regular contributor to the national newspaper, *The Irish Times*. The subject matter of his articles included literature, politics, the Irish-language movement, the Gaelic language of Scotland, sport, education, travel, and general issues of the day. Some of these articles met with the disapproval of his superiors in the civil service, where he was still employed as translator, and Ó Cadhain became increasingly dissatisfied with his situation there. He could not return to teaching, as his Republican background made him unemployable within the primary-school system. Ó hÉigeartaigh, who was aware of Ó Cadhain's predicament, persuaded the authorities at Trinity College, Dublin, to offer him a position as lecturer, and, although he had no formal university degree (his teaching diploma was not considered to be one), he became a lecturer in Modern Irish at Trinity College in 1956.

Three years after his appointment to Trinity College, Ó Cadhain visited Kirghizia, in the U.S.S.R., to observe how the Soviets dealt with a minor culture. He was impressed with the level of literacy in the country but was disappointed with what he saw as the Russianization that was taking place there. He stated afterward that his visit to Kirghizia made him think—not of Karl Marx or Vladimir Lenin or even Dostoevsky, who, like Ó Cadhain himself, had spent a period as a political prisoner and had been interned in that place—but of the folktales of his childhood. His trip to the U.S.S.R. was, he said, like the trip to the Well of the World's End of those tales.

Ó Cadhain was a highly popular and influential university lecturer, and for the fourteen years following his appointment he devoted his energy to his academic duties and to the politics of the language movement. He became increasingly pessimistic about the status of Irish as a community language at this time, and he organized and participated in pressure groups on its behalf. In 1965 he was deeply disturbed emotionally by the death of his wife from cancer. He had been devoted to her, and she had been highly supportive of his writing career. Since his appointment to Trinity College he had published hardly any original literature, but in 1967 his fourth collection of short stories, *An tSraith ar Lár* (The Corn Cut), appeared, marking a radical change in his approach to his writing. He was awarded the prestigious Butler Prize for that book, by the Irish-American Cultural Foundation.

Two stories clearly exemplify the change in Ó Cadhain's writing, namely, "Cé Acu?" (Which?) and "An Eochair" (The Key). Both have an urban setting, though the city in question is not identified, and both deal with the preposterous consequences of an apparently insignificant incident. Although the language used is still basically that of the author's native dialect, the native speakers of that dialect would have considerable difficulty in understanding the style of the text. In "Cé Acu," a chain of increasingly bizarre events is triggered by the rumor that two buildings in the town have struck each other. Several explanations for the phenomenon are offered, each one representing a different interest group—the Church, the political parties, the commercial sector, and the various factions that comprise the complex fabric of urban society. The event, or alleged event, that triggered the pandemonium is unimportant, since it is merely a pretext for the different groups to voice their grievances with each other, and satire, directed at the Church and the political institutions in particular, underlies much of the narrative. Although fundamentally different in its setting and style from *Cré na Cille*, this relatively long story is similar in conception to Ó Cadhain's novel: the ultimate purpose, in both instances, is to expose the tensions and animosity that lie under the surface of normal social discourse. In locating the events of "Cé Acu?" in an urban environment, Ó Cadhain confronts a major challenge—generating a credible register of Irish appropriate to the requirements of the story. Referring to this story and to "An Eochair," he insisted that the Irish he attributed to the characters was correct, even though he admitted that no native speaker would speak in that way, because Irish had not fully evolved as an urban language.

"An Eochair" is a Kafkaesque satire, clearly based on the author's years in the civil service, in which the main character is simply referred to as "J" and his superior as "S" (signifying "junior" and "senior" respectively). The story tells of a minor functionary, a "keeper of papers," whose life turns into a nightmare as a result of a simple accident. He locks himself into a room, then breaks the key while attempting to unlock the door. All of his efforts to obtain help to escape are thwarted by the bureaucratic system, which decrees that only certain individuals can carry out certain tasks, and that everybody must observe rank. As his predicament becomes increasingly desperate, promises of help come from various sources, including all of the political parties, though no one succeeds in actually unlocking the door and releasing "J." Incarcerated for a whole weekend in a room without natural light or ventilation, deprived of food or drink and basic needs, because the only department that is officially authorized to tamper with a lock is off duty, he eventually dies, surrounded by the confidential files that it had been his duty to protect. Although the main target of Ó Cadhain's satire in this story is the civil-service bureaucracy, the Church and the political parties are also targets. "J"—the little man who, despite his efforts to operate by the rules, is

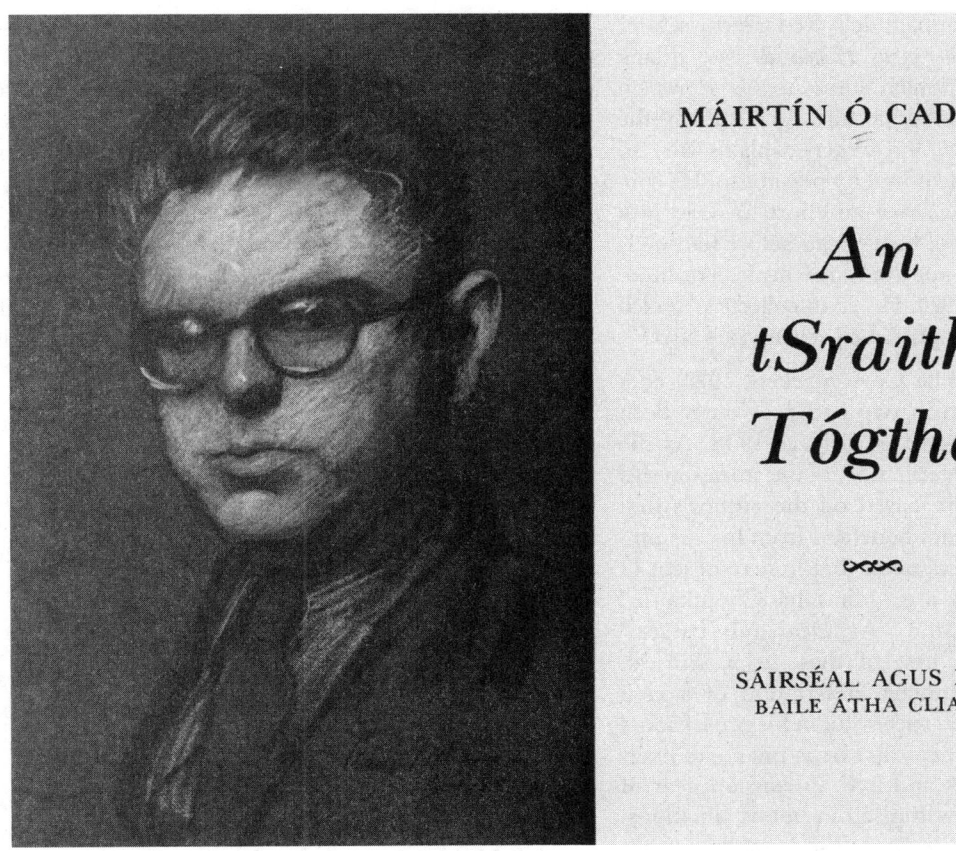

Frontispiece and title page for a 1977 edition of Ó Cadhain's 1970 short-story collection (translated as The Corn Stacked*), which includes his longest story, "Fuíoll Fuine" (After the End), in which the narrator, "N," tries to go home after hearing that his wife has died, but instead goes from pub to pub and encounters minor incidents that render him increasingly helpless (Boston College Library)*

finally broken by the system—has an affinity with the Máiréads and the Nóras of the early stories, who also try to live by the rules but find themselves struggling with an oppressive social system; ultimately, "Js'" fate is no happier than theirs.

Ó Cadhain was openly critical of Irish government policy regarding the language and, in particular, the Irish-speaking districts, the Gaeltacht. In 1969 he was instrumental in the establishment of a Civil Rights Movement, *Gluaiseacht Chearta Sibhialta na Gaeltachta*—modeled on the Civil Rights Movement in the North of Ireland—for the people of the Gaeltacht, whom he considered to be treated as second-class citizens by the state. In June of that year, he campaigned actively on behalf of Peadar Mac an Iomaire, a candidate for *Gluaiseacht Cearta Sibhialta na Gaeltachta* in the general election. Mac an Iomaire did not win a seat in government, but he received a substantial vote, and the campaign was highly successful as a consciousness-raising exercise; a separate local government authority for the Gaeltacht regions was subsequently established. During this time Ó Cadhain was still active as an academic. In 1967 he had been appointed lecturer in Modern Irish Literature and Culture at Queen's University, Belfast, and traveled to Belfast from Dublin once a week to deliver his lectures. In 1969 he was given a full professorship of Irish at Trinity College.

His fifth collection of short stories, *An tSraith dhá Tógáil* (The Corn Stacked), appeared in 1970. "Fuíoll Fuine" (After The End), the final story in the collection, is one of the longest stories Ó Cadhain wrote. Like "An Eochair," it is about a nameless civil servant, designated this time by the letter "N." On learning of his wife's death, "N" leaves his office, but, instead of going home, he sets out on what becomes an aimless odyssey from pub to pub. Unable to deal with the practical arrangements required for the funeral, he finds, like "J," that his attempts to help himself are thwarted by a series of minor mishaps, and he becomes progressively helpless, as the narrative becomes more and more nightmarish. Eventually, he encounters a sailor who, apparently, offers him passage to America. The conclusion is ambiguous, however, and the story is ultimately absurd.

Early in 1969 Ó Cadhain delivered a lecture, later published as *Páipéir Bhána agus Páipéir Bhreaca* (Blank Papers and Scribblings), which sums up his views on writing and literature. In this lecture, Ó Cadhain–the political activist, academic, and writer–explains why so much of his work is characterized by pessimism. He confesses that for a writer to make an effort to write in a medium that is in danger of being dead before himself is difficult. Ó Cadhain did not live to see his fear realized. He died on 18 October 1970. His sixth collection, which he had not yet edited, was published seven years later.

An tSraith Tógtha (The Corn Stacked, 1977) consists of ten stories, of which two had previously been published in magazines, one as early as 1948. As the publisher states in the preface, most of the stories in this posthumous collection are based on the author's first draft and therefore have not benefited from his customary rewriting. The two examples that best represent Ó Cadhain's mature phase are "Idir Dhá Chomhairle" (Between Two Minds) and "Ag Déanamh Páipéir" (Becoming Paper). The first of these is a satirical, though ultimately sympathetic, description of a civil servant, "F," who has been successful in his professional career but is so socially inept that he is unable to exercise his authority at work and lives in constant fear of making a laughingstock of himself in public situations. The story deals with his series of unsuccessful attempts to find a credible excuse for not attending a function organized by his colleagues. While "F" exhibits some of the frustration experienced by such characters as "J" in "An Eochair" and "N" in "Fuíoll Fuine," his plight is not as desperate as theirs, and the story concludes on a flippant note. "Ag Déanamh Paipéir" is another Kafkaesque fantasy about a clerk who eventually becomes the paper that is the focus of his work. While the story is ultimately pessimistic in its depiction of the individual who is systematically dehumanized by his occupation, the first-person narrative succeeds in mitigating that pessimism. Lacking any apparent thematic unity as a collection, *An tSraith Tógtha* evoked an unenthusiastic critical response following its publication.

Ó Cadhain's use of urban settings and themes was groundbreaking in literature in Irish, although his achievement was not confined merely to that aspect of his writing–for his early, rural, stories represent an innovative treatment of the established settings and themes of Irish fiction, reflecting the author's own expressed view that the function of modern literature is to reveal the mind, a part of the human being on which focusing the camera is impossible. Language, spoken or unspoken, he believed, was the source of that revelation. Consequently, Ó Cadhain took the spoken language of his own people and transformed it into a literary medium, both by expanding his inherited vocabulary through the introduction of elements from other dialects and from older literary sources and by developing a narrative technique that allowed him to experiment stylistically. In so doing, he demonstrated, more than any other writer of his time, the viability of Irish as a modern literary medium.

Letters:
As an nGéibheann (Dublin: Sáirséal agus Dill, 1973).

Bibliography:
Alan Titley, *Máirtín Ó Cadhain: Clár Saothair* (Dublin: An Clóchomhar, 1975).

Biography:
An tSr Bosco Costigan (i gcomhar le S. Ó Curraoin), *De Ghlaschloich an Oileáin* (Béal an Daingin, Ireland: Cló Iar-Chonnachta, 1987).

References:
Louis de Paor, *Faoin mBlaoisc Bheag Sin: An Aigneolaíocht i Scéalta Mháirtín Uí Chadhain* (Dublin: Coiscéim, 1991);

Gearóid Denvir, *Cadhan Aonair: Saothar Liteartha Uí Chadhain* (Dublin: An Clóchomhar, 1987);

Aindrias Ó Cathasaigh, *Ag Samhlú Troda* (Dublin: Coiscéim, 2002);

Gearóid Ó Crualaoich, "Domhan na Cille agus Domhan na Bréige," edited by Seán Ó Mórdha, *Scríobh*, 5 (Dublin: An Clóchomhar, 1981), pp. 80–86;

Breandán Ó Doibhlin, "Athléamh ar Cré na Cille," *Léachtaí Cholm Cille*, 5 (Maigh Nuad, 1974), pp. 40–53;

Eoghan Ó hAnluain, ed., *Léachtaí Uí Chadhain* (Dublin: An Clóchomhar, 1989);

Breandán Ó hEithir, "Cré na Cille," in *The Pleasures of Gaelic Literature*, edited by John Jordan (Dublin & Cork: Mercier, 1977), pp. 72–84.

Papers:
Máirtín Ó Cadhain's papers are held in the Library of Trinity College, Dublin, ref: TCD MS 10878-80.

Julia O'Faolain

(6 June 1932 -)

Peter Clandfield
Nipissing University

See also the O'Faolain entries in *DLB 14: British Novelists Since 1960* and *DLB 231: British Novelists Since 1960, Fourth Series.*

BOOKS: *We Might See Sights! and Other Stories* (London: Faber & Faber, 1968)–comprises "We Might See Sights!" "First Conjugation," "Melancholy Baby," "A Pot of Soothing Herbs," "Turkish Delight," "Her Trademark," "Chronic," "That Bastard Berto," "Dies Irae," "Death Duties," "An Afternoon on Elba," "Love in the Marble Foot," and "Mrs. Rossi";

Godded and Codded (London: Faber & Faber, 1970); republished as *Three Lovers* (New York: Coward, McCann & Geoghegan, 1971);

Man in the Cellar (London: Faber & Faber, 1974)–comprises "Man in the Cellar," "This is My Body," "It's a Long Way to Tipperary," "I Want Us to Be in Love," "The Knight," "A Travelled Man," and "Lots of Ghastlies";

Women in the Wall (London: Faber & Faber, 1975; New York: Viking, 1975);

Melancholy Baby and Other Stories (Dublin: Poolbeg Press, 1978)–includes "The Knight" and "It's a Long Way to Tipperary";

No Country for Young Men (London: John Lane, 1980; New York: Carroll & Graf, 1986);

The Obedient Wife (London: John Lane, 1982; New York: Carroll & Graf, 1986);

Daughters of Passion (Harmondsworth, U.K. & New York: Penguin, 1982)–comprises "Legend for a Painting," "The Nanny and the Antique Dealer," "Daughters of Passion," "Oh My Monsters!" "Mad Marga," "Why Should Not Old Men Be Mad?" "Will You Please Go Now," "Bought," and "Diego";

The Irish Signorina (Harmondsworth, U.K.: Viking, 1984; Bethesda, Md.: Adler & Adler, 1986);

The Judas Cloth (London: Sinclair-Stevenson, 1992);

Ercoli e il Guardiano Notturno (Rome: Editori Riuniti, 1999).

OTHER: *Two Memoirs of Florence: The Diaries of Buonaecorso Pitti and Gregorio Dati,* edited by Gene Brucker, translated by O'Faolain, as Julia Martines (New York: Harper & Row, 1967);

Piera Chiara, *A Man of Parts,* translated by O'Faolain, as Martines (Boston: Little, Brown, 1968; London: Barrie & Rockliff, 1969);

Not in God's Image, edited by O'Faolain and Lauro Martines (New York: Harper & Row, 1973; London: Temple Smith, 1973);

Preface to *The Heat of the Sun,* in *The Heat of the Sun and Other Stories* (London: Penguin, 1983), pp. 447–448;

"A Neo-Northerner," in *New Writing 3,* edited by Andrew Motion and Candice Rodd (London: Minerva, 1994), pp. 211–222;

"The Religious Wars of 1944," in *New Writing 4,* edited by A. S. Byatt and Alan Hollinghurst (London: Vintage, 1995), pp. 316–328;

"Man of Aran," in *New Writing 5,* edited by Christopher Hope and Peter Porter (London: Vintage, 1996), pp. 347–365;

"The Imagination as Battlefield," in *Arguing at the Crossroads: Essays on a Changing Ireland,* edited by Paul Brennan and Catherine de Sainte Phalle (Dublin: New Island Books, 1997), pp. 24–43;

"Morose Delectation," in *New Writing 9,* edited by John Fowles and A. L. Kennedy (London: Vintage, 2000), pp. 18–38;

"In a Small Circus," in *Sightlines,* edited by P. D. James and Harriet Harvey Wood (London: Vintage, 2001), pp. 181–195.

SELECTED PERIODICAL PUBLICATIONS–UNCOLLECTED: "Under the Rose," *New Yorker* (29 February 1994): 86–91;

Title page for Julia O'Faolain's first collection of short stories, published in 1968, which comprises six "Italian Stories" and seven "Irish Stories" (Perkins Library, Duke University)

Review of Patricia Craig, ed., *The Oxford Book of Modern Women's Short Stories*, TLS: The Times Literary Supplement (4 November 1994): 23.

Julia O'Faolain's literary careers are multiple: she has been a translator, anthologist, and reviewer as well as a novelist and short-story writer. The range of her activities has perhaps contributed to the underrecognition of her particular achievements with the short story. Reviewing *The Oxford Book of Modern Women's Short Stories*, edited by Patricia Craig, in *TLS: The Times Literary Supplement* in 1994, O'Faolain offers remarks that illuminate her own work in the genre. She suggests that "underdog crafts—irony and deviousness—have increasingly opened up literary space to the play of ambivalence." Such crafts are vigorously at work in O'Faolain's own allusive and multilayered prose. Yet, her writing aims beyond the exercise of craft for its own sake. It often examines subjects and situations—Irish history, Catholic politics, intercultural negotiations, and sexual relations—in which varieties of irony, ambivalence, and deviousness appear to be inherent. In this way, her work is rooted in forms of material reality. O'Faolain's concluding remarks on Craig's anthology are particularly suggestive with respect to her own practice: she praises both the humor and the playfulness that she finds in contemporary British women's writing and the "ability to catch the essence of several lives and compress whole histories into ritual moments" that she associates with contemporary North American stories. Her own writing exhibits both qualities and in so doing suggests the limited utility of generalizations about national cultural characteristics. O'Faolain's cosmopolitanism is something she shares with other leading Irish writers.

O'Faolain has not been particularly prolific in any one field or genre. She has published only three volumes of stories, and the most recent of these appeared in 1982. Her work is less well known than that of her more prolific contemporary Edna O'Brien, and it is not automatically included in anthologies where its presence might be expected: it goes unrepresented in Craig's Oxford volume, for example. After devoting much of the 1980s to writing novels, O'Faolain returned to the short story, publishing half a dozen substantial pieces in periodicals and anthologies. These stories incorporate the most characteristic features of her art: settings that range widely across space and time; deft and challenging shifts of perspective and register; unflinching, yet not compassionless, attention to intractable materialities and contradictions of bodies both human and politic. Critics have sometimes disliked O'Faolain's emphasis on corporealities, finding it overly insistent. They have also suggested that her style can become so striking as to be obtrusive, but O'Faolain's brilliant way with analogy and imagery has most often attracted particular praise.

O'Faolain was born 6 June 1932 in London, where her parents, Sean O'Faolain, a writer, and Eileen (Gould) O'Faolain, had lived since 1929. A year after her birth, the family returned to Ireland and settled near Dublin, where Julia grew up. Her birth in a foreign country may be cited as a foreshadowing of the multi-territoriality of her life and her writing, but the Ireland of her youth has been a substantial, if sometimes indirect, influence on her later careers.

In a 1984 interview that O'Faolain and her father conducted jointly with journalist and biographer Brenda Maddox, O'Faolain described her childhood: "In the early years I was closer to my mother than my father. She kept me home from school until I was eight and taught me herself. I was always aware that what the house produced was books." Eileen O'Faolain was independent-minded and intellectual and, according to Sean O'Faolain's biographer, Maurice Harmon, had helped to influence her husband's literary career. The O'Faolains were enthusiastic supporters of Irish Republicanism, Gaelicizing their surname (from Whelan) and speaking Gaelic at home. Their cosmopolitan leanings, however, put them, like other progressive thinkers, at odds with the conservative Catholic regime that imposed a climate of puritanism and introversion upon the Irish Free State in the decades following independence in 1921. In *Ireland: A Social and Cultural History, 1922-1985* (1985), Terence Brown describes the scope of the censorship that enforced this puritanism, reporting that during the 1930s, "some 1200 books . . . fell foul of the censors' displeasure." Brown also discusses in detail Sean O'Faolain's "remarkable periodical *The Bell* (founded in 1940 and edited by O'Faolain until 1946)," through which he attacked censorship and worked "to open Ireland's windows to the world beyond its shores. . . ."

In her 1997 essay "The Imagination as Battlefield," O'Faolain reflects on the effects of her father's activities on her day-to-day life: "we lived in a village where everyone knew everyone and where, during the 1940s, nobody had motorcars and everyone took the bus. On days when the passengers on our local number 59 turned their heads away and pretended not to see us, I knew that Sean had 'done it again.' He had attacked some pillar of the Establishment, 'let down the country in front of foreigners,' or, worse, criticized the church." As O'Faolain has noted, her own writing was never subjected to Irish censorship, the relaxation of which in the 1960s coincided with the start of her own career. Rather than directly attacking official censorship, she has been most interested in exposing indirect, unofficial–and thus perhaps more enduring–restrictions on thought and expression. O'Faolain suggests implicitly in "The Imagination as Battlefield" that realism, which she identifies as a dominant mode or ideal among Irish women writers, gains significance in an environment affected by censorship and other forms of repression. In her early experiences may lie the origins of her repeated fictional depiction of gossip, rumor, and censure as strong and debilitating social forces. O'Faolain's fiction also repeatedly challenges narrow or "Establishment" views of sexuality. Brown reports that censorship extended, in 1942, as far as "a book on the 'safe period' as a means to family planning written by an English Catholic gynaecologist," and the sustained attention of O'Faolain's work to the nuances, possibilities, and ramifications of women's, and men's, romantic and reproductive choices serves as an ongoing repudiation of all forms of sexual prescription.

After her early education at home, O'Faolain attended Sacred Heart School, The Hill, Monkstown. It was a convent school, but Sean O'Faolain said in the 1984 interview with Maddox that Julia herself was "never a Catholic." He also reported her disillusioned account of her first communion: "She said later, 'I knew it was a sell.'" Disappointing, ironic, and/or parodic communions recur in her fiction. Yet, vaunted events and rituals in other large realms–such as art, sex, and politics–are also treated with skepticism, and O'Faolain avoids strident or simplistic hostility to Catholicism at large even as she explores predicaments in which it can leave its adherents.

Entering University College Dublin in 1949 (and abandoning aspirations to be an actress), O'Faolain studied French and Italian. She completed a B.A. and an M.A. and went on to study at the Universita di Roma and at the Sorbonne in Paris. In Italy she met American historian Lauro Martines, whom she married in 1957. From then until 1961 they lived in Portland, Oregon, where O'Faolain taught French at Reed College and Italian at Portland State University. A son, Lucien Christopher, was born in 1958. They returned to Italy, where O'Faolain worked as an interpreter from 1962 to 1965. As Julia Martines, O'Faolain published, in 1967 and 1968, two translations of Italian works.

In the Maddox interview, O'Faolain said that on her father's advice, she took up fiction writing as a full-time career in the late 1960s. However, as early as 1957, in *The New Yorker,* she had published "Love in the Marble Foot," a story drawing on her time in Italy. It is one of six "Italian Stories" that join seven "Irish Stories" to constitute her first collection, *We Might See Sights!,* published by Faber and Faber in 1968. Some reviews belabored O'Faolain's family connections: "Miss O'Faolain springs fully armed from her father's head," wrote an anonymous critic for the *Observer* (16 June 1968). The two writers have similarities of theme and tone, which emerge, for example, in their satirical treatment of Dublin gossip. Sean O'Faolain offers, moreover, useful terms in which to describe his daughter's work. In the preface to his own collection *The Heat of the Sun* (1966), he distinguishes between the short story, which is limited in scope, and the tale, which "roves farther, has time and space for more complex characterization, more changes of mood, more incidents and scenes, even more plot." While several of the "Italian Stories" in *We Might See Sights!* are brief and localized, most of Julia O'Faolain's short fictions qualify as tales.

The title story of *We Might See Sights!* incorporates "complex characterization," "changes of mood," and range of incident. Its briskly surprising opening sentence sets the tone: "Under a furze bush one day–they were taking a pee–Madge broke with Rosie Fennel."

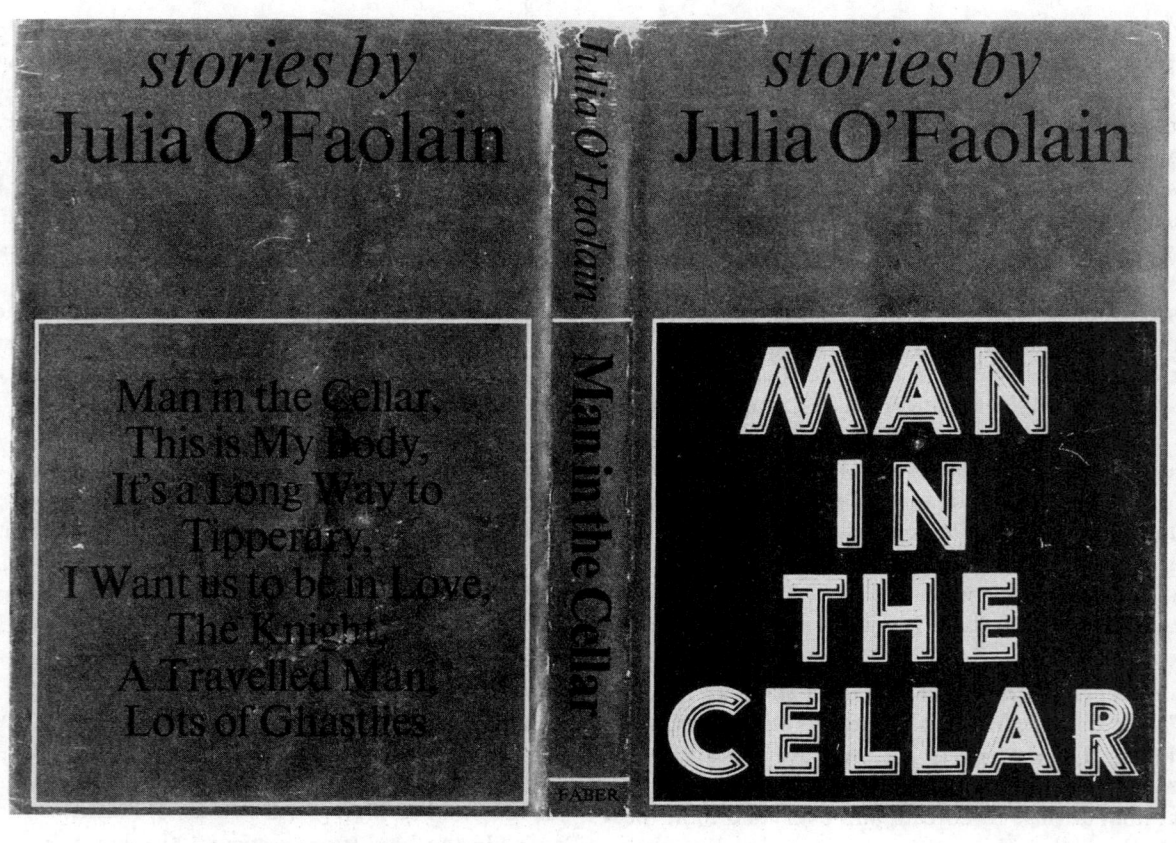

Dust jacket for O'Faolain's 1974 collection of feminist, frequently sexually explicit stories about dysfunctional relationships (Bruccoli Clark Layman Archives)

The clause between dashes can be read both as a challenge to the squeamish reader and as a matter-of-fact observation on the ordinary activities of the human, and more specifically, female, body. Madge is the thirteen-year-old daughter of a village doctor; Rosie is an anarchic, lice-haired urchin, whose company has been forbidden Madge by her class-conscious parents. Madge replaces Rosie's friendship with that of Bernie O'Toole, a girl closer to her own class, though not of it, as the story emphasizes by reporting Madge's condescending thoughts about the pub-keeping O'Toole family. Along with Bernie's younger brother, Pat, who has Down's syndrome, the two girls take an excursion one afternoon to the beach. The exclamation that provides the title is Bernie's part-anxious, part-hopeful comment on the possibility of their running across the sexual activities of Rosie Fennel's promiscuous sister, but Pat is the one who does so, with near-disastrous results. The title evokes the exploratory zest of youth, but the sights seen prove to be ones that might have been better left unseen.

Some reviewers felt that there were things that should have been left out of the volume: representative of a minority in critical opinion that has tended to see O'Faolain's writing as sensationalistic was the anonymous *TLS* review (23 January 1969), which called her style "free with adjectives and over-ready with an abstract noun for physical circumstances." The *Observer*'s review, despite its mythologization of O'Faolain's heritage, offered a more helpful description of her method: "A sharp eye is fixed on the point at which sentimentality meets or leads to brutal behaviour." In a similar vein, Mary Sullivan in *The Listener* (20 June 1968) suggested that "The stories have a pattern in common, a swoop into sourness and regret." These assessments apply especially well to several of the other "Irish Stories": "First Conjugation" (anthologized in William Trevor's 1989 *Oxford Book of Irish Short Stories*) is about the ironic complications of an Irish schoolgirl's crush on her glamorous Italian teacher; "Melancholy Baby" deals with the pathological effects of gossip, jealousy, and hypocrisy in an Irish village; "Chronic" casts a coldly humorous eye on Dublin masculinity, describing the commitment-fearing central character and his pub cronies as "puppies nuzzling the bitch-belly of the counter, each man grabbing the tit of his pint."

"Her Trademark," in partial contrast to these stories, foregrounds the imaginative compassion for which several critics have praised O'Faolain. The Captain, a

British army officer retired to genteel semipoverty in rural Ireland, is forced to find a job and becomes a guide for parties of fellow Catholics making pilgrimages to Lourdes. Many of them are women hoping for divine help in finding husbands, a purpose that complicates the Captain's life since he is himself both attractive and, as the story indicates tactfully, discreetly homosexual. Further complications bring the Captain together with a pilgrim, Maisie Lacey, and they find themselves spending a chaste but gossip-provoking night in a hotel bedroom and then agreeing—in what is perhaps the closest thing the volume provides to a happy ending—that a *mariage blanc* (marriage in name only) will suit them both. Sexual unorthodoxy, of various kinds and degrees, proves to be something of a trademark of other relatively positive endings in O'Faolain's work.

Detailed critical readings of individual stories by O'Faolain have been in short supply, but Ann Owens Weekes, in her chapter on O'Faolain in *Irish Women Writers: An Uncharted Tradition* (1990), offers an insightful assessment of the mythical and political resonances of the seemingly light sexual farce of "A Pot of Soothing Herbs," another of the most substantial pieces in *We Might See Sights!*. Weekes observes that "The protagonist of the story, Sheila, is depicted as attempting to understand both her own and her country's approach to sexuality, to experience," and goes on to demonstrate how the story shows this attempt being frustrated by the ways in which "the language of Irish myth effectively conceals experience."

The six Italian stories in *We Might See Sights!* are generally briefer than the Irish stories but not always lighter in subject matter. "Death Duties," in which an Irish woman married unhappily to an Italian has an affair and then an abortion, illustrates O'Faolain's unsettling way of handling serious material in a conversational tone. So does "That Bastard Berto," in which a young Italian man returns to the orphanage where he spent an unhappy part of his childhood. He wants to settle scores with the nun who abused him but finds himself still unable to express his real feelings when he encounters her. "Mrs. Rossi," about an Italian immigrant family in the United States, is more somber in tone but again illustrates O'Faolain's ability to cover wide spans of time convincingly in few pages. The title character, one of the many women in O'Faolain's fiction who find themselves living uneasily in a foreign country, has managed to endure abuse, loneliness, and bereavement but, the ending suggests, has lost her soul in the process.

O'Faolain's first novel appeared in 1970. Published in Britain as *Godded and Codded* and in the United States as *Three Lovers* (1971), it concerns the Parisian adventures of a middle-class Dublin girl studying at the Sorbonne. Several reviewers stressed that it was a first novel, for which allowances needed to be made, but they also praised its liveliness. Derek Mahon in *The Listener* (1 October 1970) found the protagonist's Algerian revolutionary lover unconvincing but noted O'Faolain's deftness with descriptions; J. A. Cuddon in *Books and Bookmen* (December 1970) mentioned O'Faolain's "delicate ear for the nuances of speech." O'Faolain's next book was a change of pace: *Not in God's Image*, co-edited by O'Faolain and her husband, Martines, and published in 1973, is an anthology of writings by and about European women from the Classical era to the nineteenth century; in the words of its foreword, "it aims at presenting a close-up picture of the lives of ordinary women from different social classes." The book was republished in 1979 by the British feminist publisher Virago.

O'Faolain's fiction certainly reads as feminist in its interests and sympathies. The title of her second collection of stories, *Man in the Cellar* (1974), could suggest an actively antimasculine agenda, and the title story does condemn specific forms of masculinism. Yet, the collection as a whole, like O'Faolain's work as a body, avoids programmatically attacking men as a group. The volume, as had its precursor, elicited mainly positive reviews for its thematic range and stylistic energy, with dissenting voices objecting to perceived extravagance. Lorna Sage in the *Observer* (21 July 1974) characterized the book as "concerned with monsters . . . , but the familiar domesticated kind we all know and sometimes are: predatory spouses, jealous decaying parents, bland narcissistic kids." Sage also pointed out O'Faolain's "power to engineer disturbing changes of perspective" and noted, as did the anonymous reviewer in the *TLS*, the range of her settings. The *TLS* review (16 August 1974) also praised O'Faolain's "brisk and joyful bawdiness" yet suggested that it leaves the collection, "like the husband in the title story, still fettered to the bedstead." James Brockway, in *Books and Bookmen* (February 1976), complained far more sharply about the sexual content of the book, asserting that "All the stories are overdone, both in their neurotic and modish insistence on the apparently constant itch of the clitoris, the penis's apparently constant will to tumescence . . . *and* in their use of language."

Less loftily, John Mellors in *The Listener* (26 September 1974) remarked on the way in which "O'Faolain's fraught stories reverberate after you have read them"; like other critics, he stressed the deftness with which the stories challenge the reader's initial impressions. Mellors judged the title story in particular to be "brilliantly disturbing." O'Faolain's longest "short" story at more than forty pages, "Man in the

Cellar" takes the somewhat awkward form of a series of letters that the central character, another of O'Faolain's expatriate protagonists, writes to explain her reasons for having imprisoned her Italian husband in the cellar of their home. She anatomizes both his physical and psychological abuse: he hits her, then blames her for provoking him, admonishing her, "Your looks are being ruined." The text comes close in places to lecturing but ends on an ambivalent note that, as O'Faolain's endings often do, complicates easy judgments.

If "Man in the Cellar" attacks the antifeminist legacies of Catholicism, fashionable psychological doctrines receive just as much disdain in two of the other stories of the volume, "I Want Us to Be in Love" and "A Travelled Man." The latter story is almost as long as the title piece and more varied in both subject matter and tone. A struggling young Italian scholar, Vanni, is patronized by a neurotic American academic couple, the Thornes, who take him to California; the story is notable as one of relatively few in which O'Faolain looks closely at American characters. The Thornes' combination of pseudoradicalism and self-indulgence is deftly summed up in their pampering of two poodle puppies named "Black Power" and "Brown [Latin-American] Power." The story also mocks, with relish, their sexual convolutions; yet, its most memorable material may be its observation, through the Italian eyes of Vanni, of more-routine details of the California milieu, such as its car-thralldom, which Vanni resists by taking a bus: "The only other passengers were three Black women wearing pastel livery and an old man asleep on the backseat. Still it was a bus and its rhythms were pleasantly familiar to Vanni who had been a passenger on public transport all his life." Such attention to quotidian details offsets and contextualizes—in a way that critics such as Brockway overlook—the more lurid passages in O'Faolain's fictions.

Irish settings and themes are also prominent in the volume. "The Knight" assesses the absurdities of Irish masculine rituals as practiced by the central character, Patrick Condon. Despite or because of having married an Englishwoman, Condon is fiercely hostile to the Anglo-Irish and the English, whom he thinks of as "Bloody snobs in their blazers with heraldic thingamybobs on the pockets." The story draws pointed attention, though, to resemblances between Irish Catholic and British Protestant machismo, showing both to be fueled by heavy drinking and crude bigotry. Condon himself senses these resemblances when he finds himself (in a pub) overhearing and beginning to sympathize with an Anglo-Irishman who proposes, like a crusading knight, to defend Western civilization against nonwhite people who "want what we've got." The story takes a turn, however, when the other man proves to be involved with Condon's wife, and the ending is violently funny and yet enigmatic. "It's a Long Way to Tipperary," the other mainly Irish story of the volume, also features an Irishman's problematic marriage to an Englishwoman but counterpoints the zestful brutality of "The Knight" with melancholic gentleness.

"Lots of Ghastlies," about a tense evening spent by a sophisticated young woman, Priss, with her parents, appears to revisit the territory of earlier O'Faolain pieces that contrast a conventionally middle-class generation with its livelier offspring, but in this case, the younger character's life is ghastlier. The most unusual story of the volume is "This is My Body," set in a convent in Gaul in A.D. 569. The title alludes clearly enough to Communion, but proves also to summarize the central character's reclamation of her physical being from the strictures of the church. O'Faolain's next novel, *Women in the Wall* (1975), revisits the setting and themes of "This is My Body." It drew praise particularly for its audacity: Sage in the *Observer* (6 April 1975) called it "a vivid, memorable book" and compared O'Faolain to Joyce Carol Oates as a writer "with a grudge against innocence."

Melancholy Baby, published in 1978 by Dublin's Poolbeg Press, collected the Irish stories from *We Might See Sights!* and *Man in the Cellar*. O'Faolain was meanwhile at work on the novel *No Country for Young Men,* published in Britain in 1980 but not in the United States until 1986. It moves back and forth between the Irish Civil War of the early 1920s and the modernizing Dublin of the late 1970s; in each setting, a naively well-meaning Irish American rushes into the complexities of Irish politics and comes to grief. For Val Warner in *Contemporary Novelists* (2001), *No Country for Young Men* is "O'Faolain's best novel . . . , enabling her to deploy all her skills of allusively connecting social, cultural, historical, and economic insights." On its eventual appearance in the United States, the book was especially successful with critics despite its sharply unsentimental treatment of romantic American notions about Ireland: Julian Moynahan in the *New York Times Book Review* (1 February 1987) praised its "bitter, comprehensive realism" and compared its intricacies to "those famous interlacings and knottings" of the Book of Kells. In Britain, *No Country for Young Men* was short-listed for the Booker Prize, though it received some ambivalent reviews. Hermione Lee in *The Observer* (1 June 1980) praised its "impressive range of subjects" but added that it "edges towards lecture-topics," while Patricia Craig in the *TLS* (13 June 1980) found the book overly ambitious: "Whole themes for novels are suggested and dealt with in a couple of paragraphs." This objection, though, could as easily be an objective description of

O'Faolain's allusive way of enlisting reader participation in the construction of meaning.

Material that could sustain whole novels is often found within the individual stories of O'Faolain's third collection, *Daughters of Passion,* published in 1982 as a Penguin paperback. Comprising pieces that appeared originally in various American and British periodicals between 1976 and 1981, the volume opens with a brief "Legend for a Painting," which extends O'Faolain's range into fantasy. Reimagining a traditional scenario, in a way somewhat reminiscent of Angela Carter's contemporaneous feminist revisions of fairy tales, the legend concerns a lady, a dragon, and a knight. The relationship between lady and dragon is an unusual one, while the knight is a simple-minded puritan: "he liked words that condemned words and this, as the lady could have told him, revealed inner contradictions likely to lead to trouble in the long run." They lead to trouble for the dragon, and also for the lady, who in an enigmatic ending, appears voluntarily to make herself the knight's prisoner.

New Statesman reviewer Harriet Gilbert (12 November 1982) saw "Legend for a Painting" as pattern setting for *Daughters of Passion* as a whole: "The dependence of women on men for their very identity, and the ways in which they abuse themselves in order to acquire that male-defined self, these are O'Faolain's themes." This description applies well to some of the pieces in the volume, notably "Oh My Monsters!" in which a woman tries and fails to leave her mentally ill and violent lover, and "Diego," in which the narrator, an avowed feminist, reveals in spite of herself her attraction to the charming-but-abusive title character. Gilbert's description also seems to apply to "The Nanny and the Antique Dealer," which follows the progress of Hanna, another O'Faolain heroine who seeks adventure in foreign territory: "A nanny, in a villa in Italy far from home and protective gossip, must attract assault. She wanted this." Yet, the story ultimately and unexpectedly celebrates the pleasures of the complicated encounters in which Hanna engages with the antique dealer; the piece becomes fantasy-like, but in a rather happier way than the opening story.

Gilbert summed up her assessment of *Daughters of Passion* somewhat cryptically with the claim that its "cumulative effect on the reader is one of frustrated irritation." Francis King in the *Spectator* (1 January 1983), on the other hand, praised the volume highly and singled out a different thematic thread for emphasis: "throughout this fine collection, people are metaphorically carrying bombs for others and so ensuring their own destruction." King alludes most clearly to the title story, "Daughters of Passion," in which Maggy, a young Irish woman writing a thesis on semiology, is

Front cover for O'Faolain's 1982 collection of stories about women who suffer because of their dependency on men (Bruccoli Clark Layman Archives)

drawn into nationalist extremism by a school friend, Dizzy, who is "of Anglo-Irish Protestant stock and [has] gone native in a programmed way." Maggy has always been skeptical of programs: her disappointing first Communion parallels O'Faolain's own (as described in the Maddox interview). The ease with which she nevertheless becomes irreversibly involved in violence suggests, in much the same way as does *No Country for Young Men,* how insidiously sectarianism can be perpetuated. In the wake of her actions, Maggy finds herself hunger-striking in a British prison, and her growing delirium, coupled with the efforts of her guards to persuade her to eat, brings her to a particularly memorable and enigmatic form of mock-communion.

Other stories in the volume also follow the basic plot King outlines, whereby an innocent is used and then betrayed by a better-placed individual. "Bought" concerns an eccentric artist who is made successful by a frivolous American patron but is gravely harmed in the process. The title character of "Mad Marga" is a gauche American woman (originally known as Peg) who leaves her native Iowa for Europe, where she tries to reinvent herself with the help of more-sophisticated friends, becomes disillusioned, but cannot return to ordinariness. The story gains power by depicting her plight through the eyes of one of the sophisticates who betrays her, and who is, even while doing so, unexpectedly moved by her vision of midwestern serenity. "Will You Please Go Now," which O'Faolain refers to in "The Imagination as Battlefield" as based on an incident from her own life, extends the use-and-betrayal pattern onto a global plane. At a political rally, Jenny, an English middle-class liberal, befriends Rao, an impoverished immigrant, and invites him to her family's home for what proves to be a disastrous Christmas dinner. The story is noteworthy for acknowledging both postcolonial inequities and the lack of simple remedies for them. Friendship and betrayal take on equally unsettling ramifications in the Irish context of "Why Should Not Old Men Be Mad?"

O'Faolain published two more full-length novels during the 1980s. *The Obedient Wife* (1982) concerns an Italian woman, Carla, who moves with her husband to Los Angeles, where she finds herself stranded with their son when their marriage falters and the husband returns to Italy. Sean O'Faolain opined in the Maddox interview that this is his daughter's best novel until its ending, which he faulted for what he saw as its deferral to traditional patriarchal values. Other commentators also viewed the book favorably on the whole. *The Irish Signorina* (1984), about a young Irish woman drawn to Italy and her recently deceased mother's romantic past there, had mixed reviews. While Shelley Cox in *Library Journal* (15 May 1986) called the book "the intelligent woman's alternative to the fake romance of Harlequin," Julia Whedon in the *New York Times Book Review* (20 July 1986) objected to what she saw as its "superfatted descriptions" and "surfeit of quotations and mythological references."

During the 1980s O'Faolain was occupied with what has proved to be both her longest novel and her most recent so far to be published in English, *The Judas Cloth* (1992). In a short interview with Barth Healey, which ran in the *New York Times Book Review* in 1987 alongside Moynahan's review of *No Country For Young Men,* O'Faolain criticized the rigorous orthodoxy of Pope John Paul II. The interview anticipates the themes of *The Judas Cloth,* which concerns Pope Pius IX, the nineteenth-century pontiff who decreed papal infallibility. David Gilmour in the *TLS* (25 September 1992), praising the book as "powerful, original and intelligent," noted its relevance to contemporary debates in Catholicism and quoted O'Faolain's publisher's description of her "as an ex-Catholic who 'still sees Irish Catholicism as the root of her writing.'"

Catholicism is certainly prominent among major subjects interlaced in O'Faolain's recent stories. In the Maddox interview, O'Faolain commented on the uneconomical nature of story writing as opposed to novel writing: "To me, a short story requires a lot of invention put into it and then you have to start again." Recently, she has returned to shorter forms, but with results that, even more than some of her earlier stories, read like compressed novels, ranging widely across time, space, and psychological terrain.

While O'Faolain has often been praised for her insights into women's lives in particular, many of these recent stories feature male central characters. "Under the Rose," published in the *New Yorker* in February 1994, details the shady and polymorphous sexual and professional histories of Dan Lydon—seducer, poet manqué, media personality, and rogue son of a dour Protestant parson. The title plays both on the Latin tag *sub rosa* for what is secret or covert and on the idea of Irish cultural and economic subordination to the English "rose." As the story progresses, it shifts perspective so that Lydon is seen through the eyes of a more sober compatriot, Declan Connors, who retains an ongoing interest in Lydon's doings despite, and increasingly because of, having been cuckolded by him. Lydon is, in fact, the biological father of Connors's son, Declan Jr., and the story ultimately emphasizes the sense of kinship that this fact produces: "Dan was a part of himself. Luminous alter ego? Partner in father- and grandfatherhood?" Connors reflects that his and Dan's shared grandchild may be a source of "pooled energy" for Ireland's future, and this liberalizing redefinition of paternity provides another of O'Faolain's unorthodox upbeat endings.

"Under the Rose" is reprinted in Susan Hill's *Second Penguin Book of Modern Women's Short Stories* (1997), whose note on O'Faolain mentions tantalizingly that the piece "is included in her new collection of stories, *The Corbies Communion.*" As of 2005, no such collection has been published. O'Faolain's work has, however, been featured in four of the annual anthologies of *New Writing* sponsored since 1992 by the British Council. *New Writing 3* (1994) includes "A Neo-Northerner," a mordantly comic saga of the rise and fall of an immigrant Italian café owner in London. A workaholic, he jokes with his relaxed English customers that he and they have "swopped characters." Problems arise when Doreen, his English-rose wife, becomes bored with his industriousness, and the story ends with pungent multiple ironies. Despite its knockabout qualities, the story alludes resonantly to sobering global and postcolonial realities (in a way that links it to "Will You Please Go Now"), relating the central character's migration to England to a much larger process: "the march of the hungry south upon the north."

"The Religious Wars of 1944," about ethnic and political tensions in an Irish community during World War II, appears in *New Writing 4* (1995). The most localized of O'Faolain's recent stories, it revisits her interest in the corrosiveness of gossip and ends with a particularly ironic and disturbing play on the motif of communion. "Man of Aran," O'Faolain's contribution to *New Writing 5* (1996), is as wide-ranging as any of her stories but perhaps more diffuse than some. This quality, however, may be apt, since the story evokes the bewildering fluidity of identities in the media-saturated contemporary Western world: the enigmatic narrator, another expatriate Irish woman, refers memorably to the cinema, for example, as "a thesaurus of codes and humours."

"Morose Delectation," published in *New Writing 9* (2000), and "In a Small Circus," published in the anthology *Sightlines* (2001), both address, among other things, contemporary problems of Catholic identity, and ones posed specifically by clerical celibacy. "Morose Delectation" uses the dilemmas of its narrator, a liberal French priest, both to voice criticism of rigid Catholic doctrine and to acknowledge that resistance to such doctrine brings problems of its own. "In a Small Circus" examines the legacy left to Sean Dunne, a hard-working market gardener trying to adapt to the economic expansiveness of contemporary Ireland, by Father Tim Cronin, a popular priest, family friend, and author of successful children's books (the source of his wealth). The story revisits and updates O'Faolain's concern with the corrosive effects of gossip and rumor, which it suggests may have mutated into particularly virulent contemporary strains. Cronin has died under accusations of sexual impropriety, and Dunne is uneasy about the legacy and, as it turns out, about the ambiguous nature of his own relationship with Cronin, whom the story nevertheless notably avoids judging. The story–like both "Morose Delectation" and, three decades before, "We Might See Sights!"–is startling and sobering in its refusal to evade the messier aspects of human physicality or to simplify the dangers of innocence.

O'Faolain is now based in London, after dividing her time for many years between there and Martines's teaching base in Los Angeles. In "The Imagination as Battlefield," nevertheless, she identifies herself strongly as Irish, referring to "the English and those of us who speak their language." That English is only one of her languages is reflected in the fact that her novel *Ercoli e il Guardiano Notturno* (1999; Hercules and the Night Watchman), was published in Italian. That it has yet to appear in English underscores the relative neglect of her work. Some recent critics imply that this neglect is partly justified: from the perspective of post-structuralist feminism, for example, Lorna Rooks-Hughes suggests that both O'Faolain and Edna O'Brien "problematize but also replicate the structures of the cultural misogyny they expose by their embrace of the defining structure of the family as the area of the feminine." This judgment may have some validity as regards O'Faolain's novels, but it is too broad to account for the range and the nuances of her stories. It serves, though, to illustrate the need for more specific critical attention to the stories themselves.

Warner in *Contemporary Novelists* writes that Julia O'Faolain's "style is so exciting that the reader may overlook that her characters tend to share a similar wide-ranging, ironic perception, imposed by the style." O'Faolain's stories extend this range even further than the novels, and, as many reviewers have suggested, they gain a particular and challenging energy from the tension between the exuberance of their style and the frequent sobriety of their subject matter. In "The Imagination as Battlefield" O'Faolain praises the "healthy irreverence in much writing coming out of [contemporary] Ireland." Her own writing has often received similar praise, but deserves more.

Interviews:

Brenda Maddox, "The Romantic and the Realist," *Sunday Times Magazine*, 1 April 1984, pp. 8–9;

Barth Healey, "Home Rule, Rome Rule," *New York Times Book Review*, 1 February 1987, p. 7.

References:

Terence Brown, *Ireland: A Social and Cultural History, 1922–1985* (London: Fontana, 1985);

Maurice Harmon, *Sean O'Faolain* (London: Constable, 1994);

Lorna Rooks-Hughes, "The Family and the Female Body in the Novels of Edna O'Brien and Julia O'Faolain," *Canadian Journal of Irish Studies*, 22, no. 2 (1996): 83–97;

Val Warner, "O'Faolain, Julia," in *Contemporary Novelists*, seventh edition, edited by Neil Schlager and Josh Lauer (Detroit & London: St. James, 2001), pp. 776–778;

Ann Owens Weekes, *Irish Women Writers: An Uncharted Tradition* (Lexington: University Press of Kentucky, 1990), pp. 174–190.

Ben Okri
(15 March 1959 -)

Wolfgang Görtschacher
University of Salzburg

See also the Okri entries in *DLB 157: Twentieth-Century Caribbean and Black African Writers, Third Series* and *DLB 231: British Novelists Since 1960, Fourth Series.*

BOOKS: *Flowers and Shadows* (London: Longman, 1980);
The Landscapes Within (Harlow: Longman, 1981);
Incidents at the Shrine: Short Stories (London: Heinemann, 1986; Boston: Faber & Faber, 1987);
Stars of the New Curfew (London: Secker & Warburg, 1988; New York: Viking, 1989);
The Famished Road (London: Cape, 1991; New York: Nan A. Talese, 1992);
An African Elegy (London: Cape, 1992);
Songs of Enchantment (London: Cape, 1993; New York: Nan A. Talese, 1993);
Astonishing the Gods (London: Phoenix House, 1995; Boston & Toronto: Little, Brown, 1995);
Birds of Heaven (London: Phoenix House, 1996);
Dangerous Love (London: Phoenix House, 1996);
A Way of Being Free (London: Phoenix House, 1997);
Infinite Riches (London: Phoenix House, 1998);
Mental Fight (London: Phoenix House, 1999);
The Awakening Age, music by Alan Bullard (Oxford: Oxford University Press, 2001);
Phoenix Rising (London: Phoenix House, 2001);
In Arcadia (London: Weidenfeld & Nicolson, 2002).

SELECTED PERIODICAL PUBLICATIONS—UNCOLLECTED: "In Another Country," *West Africa* (25 April 1981): 873-875;
"Fires Next Time Are Always Small Enough," *West Africa* (25 April 1983): 1020-1021;
"A Prayer for the Living," *New York Times,* 29 January 1993, p. A27; reprinted, *Toronto Star,* 27 February 1994, p. C1.

The short fiction of Ben Okri has received considerably less serious critical attention than his seven novels, the last of which, *In Arcadia,* was published in 2002. This critical bias in favor of his novels still holds true,

Ben Okri (© The Douglas Brothers; from the dust jacket for the U.S. edition of The Famished Road, *1992; Richland County Public Library)*

although in 1987 Okri received both the Commonwealth Writers' Prize for Africa and the *Paris Review* Aga Khan Prize for Fiction for *Incidents at the Shrine: Short Stories* (1986), his first collection.

Benjamin Okri was born in Minna, Nigeria, on 15 March 1959 to Silver Oghenegueke Loloje Okri, an Urhobo from near the town of Warri, on the Niger Delta, and Grace Okri, an Igbo from midwestern Nigeria. In 1961 Okri's father left for England to pursue a law degree at the Inner Temple in London. After the family had joined him some months later, the Okris settled in Peckham, in the Greater London borough of Southwark. From September 1964 Okri attended John Donne Primary School, a rough primary school in Southwark. After his father had been called to the bar in July 1965, Okri was horrified to discover that he had to return with his mother to Nigeria. "My mates told me," he recalled in a 1991 interview with Linda Grant, "that in Africa people lived in trees and lions walked about, so I told my Mum I was going to stay in south London with my comics." He went back to Nigeria, both a stranger and an innocent, at the age of six.

In 1967 Okri started attending the Children's Home School in Sapele. Months later, after Lieutenant Colonel Odumegwu Ojukwu had announced the secession of the autonomous state of Biafra, the Nigerian Civil War broke out. "My education took place simultaneously with my relations being killed," Okri recalled in a 1986 interview with Nicholas Shakespeare, "and friends who one day got up in class and went out to fight the war." Soon Okri was transferred to Christ's High School in Ibadan. His earliest reading included Greek, German, Roman, and African myths and folktales. In addition, his mother told him stories in which, he felt, the elements from these different cultures were intermingled. At the age of twelve Okri began writing essays and stories inspired by his reading and the music that he enjoyed, both of which shaped what he called his "aesthetic frames" in a 1986 interview with Jane Wilkinson that was published in 1992. In 1970 he started attending secondary school as a boarder at Urhobo College in Warri; he left in 1975 to move to Lagos, where his father had become a lawyer for the poor and the family, which included two other sons and a daughter, was living in the ghetto.

As he found himself constantly being withdrawn from good schools because the fees could not be paid, Okri continued with his education privately. His father had returned from London with a library of the modern and ancient classics of Western literature, everything from Jane Austen and Charles Dickens to Mark Twain, as well as the Greeks, the Romans, and the English essayists. Okri told Wilkinson that in his father's library he began to "discover the extraordinary quality of the imagination, of fiction."

Okri started his first novel in 1976, at age seventeen. In a 1991 interview with Clare Boylan he described how he began writing: "One day it was raining so hard that no one could get home. I was alone in the house so I took a piece of paper and first I drew a picture of all the things on the mantelpiece and then I wrote a poem. The picture was terrible and the poem was not too bad." Six months later he decided to write a short story, which, he told Boylan, "grew and grew and grew until it was a novel."

Armed with the manuscript of his novel, Okri left Nigeria for England in 1978 after he had been denied entrance to Nigerian universities. "I came to London because of Dickens and Shakespeare," Okri said in the interview with Boylan. "I had read all the classics in Nigeria. I had all the best dreams of artistic life. When I got here, it was to discover that Shakespeare had vanished, although there was still a lot of Dickens around." Okri lived with his uncle in New Cross, in the inner-London borough of Lewisham, while working as staff writer and librarian for *Afroscope,* a France-based current-affairs digest, and attending evening classes in Afro-Caribbean literature at Goldsmiths College in New Cross. Awarded a Nigerian government scholarship, Okri enrolled in 1980 as an undergraduate at the University of Essex, where he later obtained a B.A. in comparative literature.

Okri's first novel, *Flowers and Shadows,* was published in 1980, when he was twenty-one; his second novel, *The Landscapes Within,* came out the following year. As he told Boylan, "My first two novels were published and nobody paid any attention to my work at all. I did my hunger bit—living in the streets, living in tube stations." From 1983 to 1987 Okri served as poetry editor for the London-based weekly magazine *West Africa.* Although he enjoyed the job, he was depressed by the poems submitted to the journal, which were almost exclusively about human suffering. In the end he was fired because he was not publishing enough poetry. At the same time Okri started to work as a freelance broadcaster for the British Broadcasting Corporation (BBC) African Service, introducing the current-affairs and features program *Network Africa.* One year later he was awarded a bursary by the Arts Council of Great Britain that allowed him to continue work on his writing.

In the interview with Wilkinson, Okri stated that he felt he had "to go back to the basics." He had grown so distant from his first two novels that it seemed to him as if he were "just learning to write, as if I was writing for the first time." This change in his attitude to writing resulted in a change in his sense of both audience and language and required "a radical alteration of perception," which "consisted of an atomization of the way I looked at craft. I had to look at words with new eyes." While the short story is, in Okri's view, one of the most neglected genres in African literature, it is the closest to what he defines as the essence of fiction: "legends, myths, fables." To him the novel is a forest, but the short story is a seed, an atom that, he assumes, might contain "the secret of the universe." In *Dubliners* (1914) James Joyce provided a model, Okri believes, for both the construction of a short story and the demands it places on readers. As he told Shakespeare, one "can't read Joyce's *Dubliners* casually: you'd be bored stiff." In "The Joys of Storytelling III," from his essay collection titled *A Way of Being Free* (1997), Okri proclaims that writers face a "great challenge for our age," which is "to

Title page for Okri's first short-story collection (1986), which won the Commonwealth Writers' Prize for Africa and the Paris Review *Aga Khan Prize for Fiction in 1987 (James Branch Cabell Library, Virginia Commonwealth University)*

do for storytelling what Joyce did for language—to take it to the highest levels of enchantment and magic; to impact into story infinite richness and convergences."

Okri's 1986 collection of eight stories, *Incidents at the Shrine,* and *Stars of the New Curfew* (1988), which consists of six stories, marked a new phase in his artistic development. This phase can be characterized as an apprenticeship period for his later novels, the first result of which was to be *The Famished Road* (1991), the novel that won the 1991 Booker Prize. Five of the stories in *Incidents at the Shrine* are set in Lagos, two in London, and one in an unspecified location in rural Nigeria. In his review of the collection for *British Book News* (September 1986) Geoffrey Parker noted that the characters in six stories are "losers, struggling impotently against the tide of filth, injustice and violence in slum or war-

time life." Okri seeks in these stories, which are unified by the image of the shrine, to explore as many layers of reality as possible. The title story, Okri told Wilkinson, refers to "a new orientation, a return to origins, a different set of perceptions." Anderson, the protagonist, is an employee in the Department of Antiquities, situated in the capital. Although he draws his salary for knowing about the past, he knows hardly anything about the history of his own people. After being sacked, he flees home to his village, where he undergoes a hermetic rite. He has a meeting with the "Image-maker," an encounter with the "master Image" itself—"a hallucinatory warrior monolith decorated in its original splendour of precious stones and twinkling glass"—and a skirmish with the "image-eaters," spirit-like figures living on the village boundaries. Anderson, an urban official, can work vigorously in the city only if he retains spiritual contact with his village. "You must come home now and again," the Image-maker tells him; it "is where you derive power."

Two of the stories in *Incidents at the Shrine,* "Laughter beneath the Bridge" and "Crooked Prayer," are related by children who only half understand what they have witnessed. In the former, set at the outbreak of the Nigerian Civil War, this limited understanding is made clear to the reader right from the start, when the narrator likens the turmoil around him to "an insane feast" and remembers it "as a beautiful time. I don't know how." On a journey by truck in search of safety, he and his mother reach the final checkpoint, where, to identify passengers by ethnic origin, each is obliged to recite the paternoster in his or her mother tongue; meanwhile, a rape is going on behind some bushes. The mother is saved by saying the prayer in her husband's language, and the boy is similarly spared when he cries out the word for *shit* in his father's tongue. The most dramatic moment of the story occurs when the narrator recognizes some rubbish in a narrow stream for what it really is: "The stream was full of corpses that had swollen, huge massive bodies with enormous eyes and bloated cheeks." Alastair Niven is reminded of "those epiphanous moments in Joyce's *Dubliners* where children awake in a moment to the brutality and monstrousness of the adult world." In "Crooked Prayer" the narrator is an admiring nephew who functions as a go-between for his uncle Saba and a woman named Mary. Saba's relationship with her becomes more fixed when he moves in with her after she has given him the child his infertile wife has been unable to produce. Robert Fraser holds that both stories have affinities with Joyce "in their deliberate omissions, their ear for dialogue, their blending of sweet and sour."

"Disparities" and "A Hidden History," both set in London, are remarkable for their "exaggerated treatment of the unspeakable, an accumulation of nastiness that flirts with bathos," as John Melmoth remarked in his review of *Incidents at the Shrine* in *TLS: The Times Literary Supplement* (8 August 1986). In "Disparities," first published in *PEN New Fiction I* (1984), edited by Peter Ackroyd, the reader accompanies the first-person narrator, a tramp as critic, on a tour of London in decline. He encounters the squalid living conditions of a group of undergraduates and enters a reeking pub, peopled with the "very cream of leftovers, kicked-outs, eternal trendies, hoboes, weirdoes, addicts and pedlars." "A Hidden History," reminiscent of Okri's life in New Cross, is an experimental nightmare portrait of the labyrinthine realities of modern London. The first-person narrator, a "black . . . angel . . . , my wings heavy and black like all the sin," focuses on "immigrants from lands whose destinies had been altered by slavery."

For many of Okri's protagonists, life in Lagos is similarly lacking in comfort and glamour. In "Converging City," which Fraser calls "an experiment of relative velocities," the protagonist watches the trader Agodi's response to commercial disappointments: he grows a reddish beard, wears his hair in tiny braids, founds a new church, and goes into business as a true prophet. In "Masquerades" a night-soil worker compensates for the vileness of his job by creating a spotless slum penthouse, "a curious slum paradise," smelling of "perfumed soaps, clean sheets, new clothes, leather, and velvet materials," with blue walls hung with "several large photographs of him . . . , along with posters of London and Paris, Brazil with its Sango dancers, America with a saloon scene from the Wild West. . . . There was a Benin mask above the door; next to it was a picture of Jesus Christ." The nameless protagonist copes with the "inchoate nihilism," as Melmoth put it, that goes with his job ("When I look at people I see nothing—what doesn't turn to shit turns to dust") by obsessively dousing himself with "the smells of lavender and jasmine."

"The Dream-vendor's August," the longest and most complex story in *Incidents at the Shrine,* is set during the rainy season. Ajegunle Joe combats futility with occultism, selling quack cures by mail, along with pamphlets titled *How to Fight Witches and Wizards* and *How to Banish Poverty from Your Life,* and protecting himself from disaster with rings that belonged to Isaac Newton and King Solomon. Despite his lack of financial and personal success—he falls in love with a Ghanaian woman, but when they attempt to make love, he discovers that he is impotent—he finds happiness in disinterested serenity at the end: "Joe lay flat on his back and watched the clear sky."

In *Stars of the New Curfew* the influences are, according to Fraser, "fewer, far more intense, and largely African." Reviewing the collection in *The New York Times Book Review* (13 August 1989), Neil Bissoondath claimed that the stories "resonate well beyond their immediate settings, striking chords of recognition in anyone with more than a nodding acquaintance with underdeveloped countries." "In the Shadow of War," dating from 1983, deals with a child's experiences during the Nigerian Civil War and is reminiscent of "Laughter Beneath the Bridge," especially at the moment when the boy, Omovo, notices that "the dead animals on the river were in fact the corpses of grown men." Fraser reads "Worlds That Flourish" as "an allegory of invisibility and the need to flee from limiting notions of identity . . . a quest to the land of the dead in search of a lost self." The first-person narrator undergoes experiences similar to Anderson's in "Incidents at the Shrine." He is fired from his job and falsely imprisoned; upon his release, he escapes by car and, after swimming across a river, reaches the village of the dead, where he meets his dead wife. Running back along the road, he comes to consciousness "in the wreckage of the car. . . . The twisted wreck of metal seemed to have grown on me." He trudges back toward the gas station "with the hope of reaching [it] before I died."

Bissoondath found "In the City of Red Dust" to be "a relentless tale of exploitation and degradation . . . a frightening picture of urban life in Nigeria . . . , and one full of political commentary." The story, set in the eponymous city on the day of the military governor's fiftieth birthday, obeys all of the three classical unities of place, time, and action. Emokhai and Marjomi eke out an existence by "selling blood at Queen Mary's Memorial Hospital and by shifting the balances of people's pockets." After Dede, Marjomi's former girlfriend, avoids gang rape by a group of soldiers by cutting herself in the neck, she is rushed to a hospital. As they have the same blood type, Marjomi serves as the donor for a transfusion, the second tube of blood he has given that day.

The title story, "Stars of the New Curfew," the longest in the collection, is in Fraser's view "a satirical-cum-surrealist treatment of the theme of the 1970s oil boom." The first-person narrator is hired as a salesman to promote a phony panacea called POWER-DRUG. He sells it aboard a crowded *molue* (yellow public Nigerian bus) to the driver, but the driver loses control, and the *molue* splashes into a lagoon. Successive auctions structure the rest of the story. The first takes the form of a dream, in which bidders buy the stars in the sky by paying "either with huge sums of money, a special part of the human anatomy, or the decapitated heads of newly-dead children." In a flashback of the narrator's school days, two of his classmates bid for his services as

Title page for the 1989 U.S. edition of Okri's 1988 short-story collection, which has been described as an apprentice work for his Booker Prize–winning 1991 novel, The Famished Road *(Z. Smith Reynolds Library, Wake Forest University)*

a go-between with the prettiest girl in town. This flashback is followed by a nightmare auction, in which parts of the narrator's body are sold off. The climax is a nightmare contest staged by two millionaires, in which a crowd is tricked into fighting over fake currency after bags of it have been emptied overhead from a helicopter.

For Fraser, "When the Lights Return" is Okri's "reworking of the classical Orpheus-Eurydice myth," to which is added the motif of the quest. The protagonists are Ede, a minor pop musician and, in critic Ato Quayson's view, a male "chauvinist," and Ede's attractive girlfriend, Maria. After three weeks of ignoring her, Ede decides to walk to "her bungalow sinking in the depths of the Munshin ghetto," which Fraser regards as equivalent to Hades in Greek myth. Ede arrives to find Maria dying, attended by her herbalist, and he walks back home. After her death Ede wanders into a chaotic marketplace, where he is slain by market women, a scene reminiscent, as Fraser notes, of "Orpheus' dismemberment by enraged Thracian women."

The last story in *Stars of the New Curfew,* "What the Tapster Saw," is, according to Fraser, Okri's "transmutation" of Amos Tutuola's classic 1952 novel, *The Palm-Wine Drinkard and His Dead Palm-Wine Tapster in the Deads' Town.* The tapster's creeks and palm groves have been taken over by the Delta Oil Company. He undertakes a quest for his provisional decease "without the faintest idea of where he was going." With this quest "Okri seems to be suggesting," Fraser writes, "a series of initiations into realms that lie inside one another, like the successive skins of a Russian doll."

In 1991 Jonathan Cape published Okri's *The Famished Road,* winner of that year's Booker Prize and the first in a trilogy of novels centering on the same characters. That same year, Trinity College of Cambridge University named Okri the Trinity Fellow Commoner in the Creative Arts, an award that gave him the salary of an academic and allowed him to continue his writing. The Trinity judges were much influenced by the qualities of *Stars of the New Curfew* and had the opportunity of reading *The Famished Road* in proof form. In 1993 Cape published the second volume in the *Famished Road* sequence, titled *Songs of Enchantment;* the third volume, *Infinite Riches,* appeared five years later. In 1997 Okri was elected vice president of the English branch of International PEN and was made a fellow of the Royal Society of Literature. He was named a member of the Order of the British Empire (OBE) in 2001 and received an honorary doctorate from the University of Essex the following year.

In 2000 Ben Okri served as the chairman of the judges for the inaugural Caine Prize for African Writing, a prize that focuses on the short story or the narrative poem as a reflection of contemporary developments in the African storytelling tradition. When interviewed by Stella Orakwue at the prize ceremony, Okri told her that he viewed the short story as "the most rigorous form in all literature apart from the sonnet. It's much more difficult to write a good short story than to write a novel."

Interviews:
Nicholas Shakespeare, "Fantasies Born in the Ghetto," *Times,* 24 July 1986, p. 13;
Clare Boylan, "An Ear for the Inner Conversation," *Guardian,* 9 October 1991, p. 26;
Linda Grant, "The Lonely Road from Twilight to Hard Sun," *Observer,* 27 October 1991, p. G1;
Jane Wilkinson, "Ben Okri," in *Talking with African Writers: Interviews with African Poets, Playwrights & Novel-*

ists, edited by Wilkinson (London: J. Currey / Portsmouth, N.H.: Heinemann, 1992), pp. 76–89;

Delia Falconer, "Whisperings of the Gods: An Interview with Ben Okri," *Island,* 71 (Winter 1997): 43–51.

References:

Robert Bennett, "Ben Okri," in *Postcolonial African Writers: A Bio-Bibliographical Critical Sourcebook,* edited by Pushpa Naidu Parekh and Siga Fatima Jagne (Westport, Conn.: Greenwood Press, 1998), pp. 364–373;

Mariaconcetta Costantini, *Behind the Mask: A Study of Ben Okri's Fiction* (Rome: Carocci, 2002);

Robert Fraser, *Ben Okri: Towards the Invisible City* (Tavistock: Northcote House, 2002);

Douglas Killam and Ruth Rowe, eds., *The Companion to African Literatures* (Oxford: J. Currey / Bloomington: Indiana University Press, 2000), pp. 95, 120, 180–189;

Alastair Niven, "Achebe and Okri: Contrasts in the Response to Civil War," in *Short Fiction in the New Literatures in English: Proceedings of the Nice Conference of the European Association for Commonwealth Literature & Language Studies, March 1988,* edited by Jacqueline Bardolph (Nice: Faculté des Lettres et Sciences Humaines de Nice, 1989), pp. 277–283;

Ato Quayson, *Strategic Transformations in Nigerian Writing: Orality & History in the Work of Rev. Samuel Johnson, Amos Tutuola, Wole Soyinka & Ben Okri* (Oxford: J. Currey / Bloomington: Indiana University Press, 1997), pp. 101–120.

Frederic Raphael
(14 August 1931 –)

Mike W. Malm

See also the Raphael entry in *DLB 14: British Novelists Since 1960*.

BOOKS: *Obbligato* (London: Macmillan, 1956; New York: St. Martin's Press, 1956);

The Earlsdon Way (London: Cassell, 1958);

The Limits of Love (London: Cassell, 1960; Philadelphia: Lippincott, 1961);

The S-Man: A Grammar of Success, by Raphael and Tom Maschler, as Mark Caine (Harmondsworth, U.K.: Penguin, 1961);

A Wild Surmise (London: Cassell, 1961; Philadelphia: Lippincott, 1962);

The Graduate Wife (London: Cassell, 1962);

The Trouble with England (London: Cassell, 1962);

Lindmann (London: Cassell, 1963; New York: Holt, Rinehart & Winston, 1964);

Darling (London & Glasgow: Collins, 1965; New York: New American Library, 1965);

Two for the Road (London: Cape / New York: Holt, Rinehart & Winston, 1967);

Orchestra and Beginners (London: Cape, 1967; New York: Viking, 1968);

Like Men Betrayed (London: Cape, 1970; New York: Viking, 1971);

Who Were You With Last Night? (London: Cape, 1971);

April, June and November (London: Cape, 1972; Indianapolis: Bobbs-Merrill, 1976);

Richard's Things (London: Cape / Indianapolis: Bobbs-Merrill, 1973);

California Time (London: Cape, 1975; New York: Holt, Rinehart & Winston, 1976);

The Glittering Prizes (London: Allen Lane, 1976; New York: St. Martin's Press, 1977);

W. Somerset Maugham and His World (London: Thames & Hudson, 1976; New York: Scribners, 1977);

Cracks in the Ice: Views and Reviews (London: W. H. Allen, 1979);

Sleeps Six, and Other Stories (London: Cape, 1979);

Oxbridge Blues and Other Stories (London: Cape, 1980; Fayetteville: University of Arkansas Press, 1984);

Frederic Raphael (photograph by Nobby Clark; from Think of England, *1988; Richland County Public Library)*

The List of Books, by Raphael and Kenneth McLeish (London: Beazley / New York: Harmony, 1981);

Byron (London: Thames & Hudson / New York: Thames & Hudson, 1982);

Oxbridge Blues, and Other Plays for Television (London: British Broadcasting Corporation, 1984);

Heaven and Earth (London: Cape / New York: Beaufort Books, 1985);

Think of England (London: Cape, 1986; New York: Scribners, 1988);

After the War (London: Collins, 1988; New York: Viking, 1989);

The Necessity of Anti-Semitism (Southampton, U.K.: University of Southampton, 1989; enlarged, Manchester, U.K.: Carcanet, 1997; New York: St. Martin's Press, 1998);

Of Gods and Men, illustrated by Sarah Raphael (London: Folio Society, 1992);

A Double Life (London: Orion, 1993; North Haven, Conn.: Catbird Press, 2000);

France: The Four Seasons (London: Pavilion / New York: Cross River, 1994);

The Latin Lover and Other Stories (London: Orion, 1994);

Old Scores (London: Orion, 1995);

Coast to Coast (London: Orion, 1998; North Haven, Conn.: Catbird Press, 1999);

Popper (London: Phoenix, 1998; New York: Routledge, 1999);

All His Sons (London: Orion, 1999; North Haven, Conn.: Catbird Press, 2001);

Eyes Wide Open: A Memoir of Stanley Kubrick (New York: Ballantine, 1999; London: Orion, 1999);

Eyes Wide Shut: A Screenplay, by Raphael, Stanley Kubrick, and Arthur Schnitzler (New York: Warner, 1999; London: Penguin, 1999);

The Great Philosophers, series edited by Raphael and Ray Monk (London: Weidenfeld & Nicolson / New York: Routledge, 2000);

Personal Terms: The 1950s and 1960s (Manchester: Carcanet, 2001);

The Benefits of Doubt (Manchester: Carcanet, 2003);

A Spoilt Boy: A Memoir of Childhood (London: Orion, 2003);

Rough Copy: Personal Terms 2 (Manchester: Carcanet, 2004).

PLAY PRODUCTIONS: *Lady at the Wheel,* by Raphael and Lucienne Hill, London, 1958;

The Man on the Bridge, Hornchurch, Essex, England, 1961;

An Early Life, Leicester, England, 1979;

From the Greek, Cambridge, 1979;

Euripides, *Medea,* translated by Raphael and Kenneth McLeish, 2001;

Jean Anouilh, *Becket,* translated by Frederic Raphael and Stephen Raphael, Haymarket Theatre, London, 2004.

PRODUCED SCRIPTS: *The Executioners,* television, Independent Television Network, 1961;

A Well-Dressed Man, Independent Television Network, 1962;

Image of a Society, based on a novel by Roy Fuller, television, Independent Television Network, 1963;

The Trouble with England, television, Independent Television Network, 1964;

Nothing But the Best, based on a short story by Stanley Ellin, motion picture, Columbia, 1964;

Darling, motion picture, Embassy, 1965;

Two for the Road, motion picture, 20th Century-Fox, 1967;

Far from the Madding Crowd, based on a novel by Thomas Hardy, motion picture, M-G-M, 1967;

Daisy Miller, based on a novel by Hardy, motion picture, Paramount, 1974;

Rogue Male, based on a novel by Geoffrey Household, television, Independent Television Network, 1976;

Something's Wrong, television, Independent Television Network, 1978;

School Play, television, Independent Television Network, 1979;

The Daedalus Dimension, radio, BBC, 1979;

The Best of Friends, television, Independent Television Network, 1980;

Death in Trieste, radio, BBC, 1981;

Byron: A Personal Tour, television, Independent Television Network, 1981;

Oxbridge Blues, television, Independent Television Network, 1984;

The Thought of Lydia, radio, BBC, 1988;

After the War, television series, Independent Television Network, 1989;

The King's Whore, motion picture, ASC and others, 1990;

The Man in the Brooks Brothers Shirt, television, HBO, 1990;

The Empty Jew, radio, BBC, 1994;

"Armed Response," television, *Picture Windows,* HBO, 1995;

Eyes Wide Shut, based on a novella by Arthur Schnitzler, screenplay by Stanley Kubrick and Raphael, motion picture, Warner Bros., 1999;

Coast to Coast, Showtime (Paramount), 2004;

The Glittering Prizes, BBC Radio, 2005.

OTHER: *Bookmarks,* edited by Raphael (London: Cape, 1975);

The Hidden I: A Myth Revised, by Raphael, illustrated by Sarah Raphael (New York: Thames & Hudson, 1990);

Six Plays by Euripides, introduced by Raphael, J. Michael Walton, and Kenneth McLeish (London: Methuen Drama / Portsmouth, N.H.: Heinemann, 1997).

TRANSLATIONS: Catullus, *The Poems of Catullus,* translated by Raphael and Kenneth McLeish (London: Cape, 1978; Boston: Godine, 1979);

Aeschylus, *The Serpent Son: The Oresteia of Aeschylus,* translated by Raphael and McLeish (Cambridge & New York: Cambridge University Press, 1979);

Aeschylus, *The Complete Poems of Aeschylus,* translated by Raphael and McLeish (London: Methuen, 1991);

Aeschylus, *Plays—One,* translated by Raphael and McLeish (London: Methuen Drama, 1991);

Euripides, *Medea,* translated by Raphael and McLeish (London: Hern, 1994);

Euripides, *Ajax,* translated by Raphael and McLeish (Philadelphia: University of Pennsylvania Press, 1998);

Euripides, *Bacchae,* translated by Raphael and McLeish (London: Hern, 1998);

Petronius, *Satyrica* (London: Folio Society, 2004).

In the field of contemporary British fiction, Frederic Raphael is generally regarded as one of the most sophisticated stylists. He is praised for his brilliant and ironic writing that embraces both sociological analysis and sharp-edged satire. At the same time, though, Raphael's novels and short stories are sometimes criticized for their flashy dialogues and anecdotal plots.

Frederic Michael Raphael was born in Chicago, Illinois, on 14 August 1931 to Cedric Michael (an employee of Shell Oil Company), who was British, and Irene (Mauser) Raphael, an American. After his father took a new job and his family moved to London in 1938, Raphael attended Charterhouse School. In 1950 he went to St. John's College, Cambridge, where he studied classics and philosophy. He was particularly influenced by the philosophy of Ludwig Wittgenstein. He received his M.A. (Honors) in 1954, and in 1955 he married Sylvia Betty Glatt. The couple had three children, Paul Simon, Stephen Matthew Joshua, and Sarah Natasha. Raphael published his first novel, *Obbligato,* in 1956, and in the following years he not only established himself as a novelist but also earned a reputation as a sometimes controversial, but always witty and sophisticated, contributor to periodicals, especially when he wrote as a fiction critic for *The Sunday Times* (1962–1965). While releasing a considerable output of novels, reviews, and essays, Raphael also worked as a screenwriter and received several awards, among them the British Screen Writers Award (1965, 1966, and 1967), a British Academy Award (1965), and an Oscar for his screenplay for *Darling* (1965). In addition, Raphael adapted for the screen, texts written by Thomas Hardy, Henry James, and himself.

In his novels Raphael has covered a variety of plots and subjects ranging from common marriage problems to the more bizarre neuroses of diplomats. Mostly, but not exclusively, concerned with relationships in upper-middle-class milieus, Raphael's novels follow their protagonists to international settings and through eventful plots with cinematic dialogues. His characters are often haunted by past events, from which they try to escape, but with which they are finally confronted. This set of circumstances is true for such diverse texts as the widely acclaimed *Lindmann* (1963), in which one man becomes guilty of multiple deaths, and *Old Scores* (1995), in which a real-estate agent and a former resistance fighter are confronted with crimes they have committed and tried to forget. Precise historical backgrounds and realistic detail give factual depth to Raphael's novels. At the same time, Raphael is an ironic observer of human absurdities and ambitions. He has a generally acknowledged talent for humorous and clever dialogues full of puns and allusions. Some critics, however, have found that Raphael's novels often lack psychological depth because they concentrate on dialogues rather than on complex descriptions of their protagonists' inner motivations. For example, Peter Kemp remarked in *TLS: The Times Literary Supplement* (31 October 1980) that "Raphael writes more like a celebrity publicist than like the psychological anatomist he pretends to be."

Besides writing more than fifteen novels, Raphael has written many short stories. Most of them were published in periodicals, whereas others were written for radio broadcasts. Not until the later stage of his career, however, did they become available in collections. When Raphael's first collection appeared in 1979, he had not published a novel since *California Time* in 1975. During the time intervening he published a biographical study of W. Somerset Maugham, two translations of Greek and Roman classics, his collected reviews in *Cracks in the Ice* (1979), and some television works in *The Glittering Prizes* (1976). Whereas the latter was based on a television series, the stories in his first short-story collection, *Sleeps Six* (1979), were commissioned for radio by the BBC. The strongly condensed texts culminate in pointed dialogues and feature characters often caricatured as generic types, rather than individuals—"he," "she," the "economist," and the "intellectual," to name but a few. Raphael sometimes sacrifices psychology for verbal brilliance, but he is always ironic and satirical. The featured subjects are typical of both Raphael's short stories and his novels, and they range from marriage to the erotic escapades of young men. Sex and love loom large in the stories, as do competition and the eccentricities of the wealthy.

In "He'll See You Now," a successful young celebrity undergoes regular analysis by a prominent psychologist. When she breaks off her treatment because he fails to help her make a choice between two men, the psychologist surprises his former client by confessing his love for her. With their professional relationship ended, they are finally able to communicate on personal terms. The woman, however, agrees to sleep with her former doctor only if he acts as if he were still her analyst. "Similar Triangles" provides another ironic glance at the twists and paradoxes of relationships.

Two lovers, both married, end their affair when the woman's husband dies but relaunch their relationship as soon as she marries again. "Sleeps Six," the title story, is more complex and portrays the ambiguous friendship of a movie producer and his agent. The agent not only uses a visit to the producer's house to seduce a young girl and to receive a sexual favor from his friend's wife, but also neglects to invite the producer to his wedding. Raphael employs puns, parentheses, and sharp-edged dialogue to conduct pointed attacks on wealthy but hollow lifestyles. *Sleeps Six* was praised by critics for its stylish stories and realistic anatomies of relationships, but it was criticized for its abundant mannerisms and flashy dialogues. In *The Listener* (23 August 1979) John Mellors compared Raphael's characters to the protagonists of F. Scott Fitzgerald's novels, all "rich, randy, intelligent, unscrupulous and unhappy."

Raphael's next collection, *Oxbridge Blues and Other Stories* (1980), includes stories that expand, but do not transgress, the scope of earlier stories. Brief pastiche is replaced by more-complex narratives ranging from studies of middle-class marriages in trouble to an exercise in an Ernest Hemingway–like style. In "On the Black List," for example, a disillusioned American painter moves to France after his political attitudes put him on a blacklist. After he loses his professorship, his wife, and his children, he sets out to make a new start. In France he is warned that his servants are thieves. Nevertheless, he tries to build a personal relationship with his housekeeper. She allows him to paint her, but in the end she cheats him. The story features laconic descriptions of the painter's personal history and of a loose community of expatriates, while the plot is kept simple and realistic.

Other stories in the collection continue Raphael's preoccupation with relationship problems, as anticipated in *Sleeps Six* and his novels. The absurdities of class consciousness and ambition are satirized in the title story, "Oxbridge Blues," about brothers Victor and Philip. After graduating from Oxford, Victor works for the treasury and has little money for his family but a large amount of arrogance. Philip has only an average job but enjoys a seemingly harmonious family life. The story takes an unexpected turn when Philip becomes wealthy from writing best-selling crime novels. In the end, both brothers recognize the weaknesses of their marriages and swap wives. The story rests on the tension between class-conscious, but poor and jealous, Victor and Philip with his pragmatic attitude and nouveau riche lifestyle.

Ambition is also the main subject in "The Muse," in which a writer invents a sarcastic essayist as his nasty counterpart. The newspaper columns written by his creation gain him the attention of a neurotic critic with

Dust jacket for Raphael's 1980 story collection. He adapted the title story for British television in 1984 (Richland County Public Library).

whom he has a passionate affair before letting his alter ego "die." Raphael uses his talent for witty dialogues to caricature the London literary scene as a neurotic merry-go-round of ambition and aggressive rhetoric. "The Muse" verifies Blake Morrison's statement in the *Observer* (26 October 1980) that *Oxbridge Blues* is chiefly concerned with a cynical world of fierce competition. As Kemp remarked in *TLS* (31 October 1980), coming out on top and scoring points are the chief preoccupations of Raphael's characters.

In the years following the release of *Oxbridge Blues*, Raphael published another collection of works for television; a biographical study of Lord Byron; and a novel, *Heaven and Earth* (1985). Raphael's next collection of short stories, *Think of England* (1986), features more semi-autobiographical elements than his previous collections and shows an increasing awareness of the absurdities of show-business lives. Often built around anecdotal plots ranging from the gossipy to the maca-

Dust jacket for the U.S. edition of Raphael's 1986 story collection about people in show business (Richland County Public Library)

bre, the collection includes short pastiches as well as atmospheric studies. In "The Old Pro," the scriptwriting narrator—who is named "Freddie" and is obviously to be identified with Raphael—is a movie producer whose absurd ideas lead him from one failure to another. While writing a script that could be his last chance to stay in business, he finds his wife dead. Suddenly inspired with how to finish the script, he does so before informing the police of his wife's death. The story's antihero is a typical example of Raphael's parodies of ambitious, but incompetent, people. In "A Parting Guest" the same entertainment milieu is depicted as parasitic, while in "Ave atque vale" it appears as a loose sequence of relationships hovering on the verge of boredom.

In most of the stories, the protagonist "Freddie" is looking back on his encounters with the representatives of a self-centered business. The satirical overtones reveal Raphael's sharp eye for the jealousies and adulteries of his contemporaries, but they also betray his clinging to old rivalries and reputations sometimes dating back to his Cambridge days. The most complex story of the collection, "The Day Franco Came," is a satire about an arrogant Spanish mayor who prepares his small town for a visit by Francisco Franco. Mayor Don Antonio becomes the town's laughingstock when Franco does not appear, and Antonio's son is discovered having sex with the daughter of his housekeeper. The story carefully reconstructs the Franco era, adding local detail to a merciless look at the vanities of a small-town monarch.

After two more novels, Raphael published new short stories in *The Latin Lover* (1994). The collection is dominated by "semi-autobiographical anecdotes," as Anne Duchêne called them in *TLS* (14 October 1994), and includes many features well known to the readers of Raphael's stories. Apart from social satire and international settings ranging from the United States to Greece, characters from earlier stories, such as Raphael's wife Sylvia or movie producer Gino Amadei, appear again. Raphael's use of puns, rare words, and multiple alliterations is as vivid as ever, thereby sustaining his reputation as a clever mannerist. Among the more anecdotal stories of the collection is "Snowman," in which Raphael recounts his friendship with a movie producer whose wife demands snow for her birthday party in sunny California. In "Merce" a Hollywood lawyer discovers that his wife is selling counterfeit paintings and is then almost robbed by his own son, who is a gigolo. Sometimes the stories in this collection come dangerously close to the contents of a society column, but they are usually saved by Raphael's sense of irony.

In terms of plot and scope, the title story, "The Latin Lover," is more complex than the shorter pieces. A classics teacher with homosexual inclinations spends his holiday in Italy. Attracted to a beautiful male cook, he stays in a small town where he meets an American woman. Although she falls in love with him immediately, the teacher remains reluctant. A dinner intended to seduce him ends with his getting sick and the American woman so disappointed that she offers herself to the young cook. She is beaten up by the Italian and returns to her uneasy friend. In one respect this story is about unsatisfied desires and the attempt to satisfy them in a Mediterranean environment. In another respect, the text gains historical depth by its many allusions to classic love poets and art historian Johann Joachim Winckelmann. These multiple layers combine to create an historical continuity that turns the protagonists into timeless figures. As always, Raphael is much more interested in typical features than in individual character traits.

Raphael's next works after *The Latin Lover* testify to both his thematic scope and his productivity. He wrote a study of philosopher Karl Popper, translated Greek plays, and collaborated with director Stanley Kubrick on the script for *Eyes Wide Shut* (1999). In addition, he published two new novels. *Old Scores* is an entertainingly absurd, but at the same time historically charged, story about people who are haunted by past mistakes. The literary equivalent of a road movie, *Coast to Coast* (1998) reconstructs an elderly couple's journey into their past. The novel was followed by another collection of short stories, *All His Sons* (1999).

Among Raphael's collections, *All His Sons* is the broadest achievement in content and form. Although some of the featured stories deal with the same show-business people described in other stories, Raphael moves beyond the garish entertainment scenes ridiculed in earlier collections. "Lo and Behold!" is a chapter from the ghostwritten autobiography of Vladimir Nabokov's Lolita, Dolores Hayes. An experiment in form, the story includes a fake introductory letter and an editorial appendix with scholarly notes. Dolores's seemingly naive corrections of her life story as told by Humbert Humbert in *Lolita* (1955) are ironic in their constant denial of her seducer's erotic motives. The portrait of Dolores as an all-American girl implicitly criticizes the American Dream as an illusion.

"All His Sons," another story set in the United States, is about a Jewish family in New York: divorced patriarch Julius and his sons Sidney and Stanley. Julius is wealthy and employs a black servant whose son, Milton, also works for him. Milton's son, Moss, is generously supported by Julius, and when the old man suffers from his final illness, Moss attends him. When the brothers find Julius dead and Moss gone, they suspect Moss of killing their father but discover no proof for their theory. Instead, Julius's drawer reveals hints that Stanley might be the son of Julius's dead brother and Moss might be Julius's son. The plot of the story is important, but psychological detail reigns supreme. The two brothers experience a broad spectrum of feelings and doubts revealing their differences. The only thing the intellectual Stanley and the pragmatic Sidney have in common is their speculations about their family's love affairs.

In his portrait of two brothers who find the foundations of their family shaken, Raphael also presents an anatomy of Jewish upper-class society. Through many minor details he conveys the brothers' doubts and broader issues of identity. He achieves additional sociological depth by introducing Moss's family with their strong dependence on the well-to-do patriarch Julius. Raphael calls himself "the most marginal of Jews" and describes himself as agnostic. Yet, he treats subjects of Jewish identity and anti-Semitism in this and other short stories and in his journalistic writing. Typical of Raphael's stories, "All His Sons" presents Jewish identity as a social, rather than religious, construct.

Raphael's sociological approach in the collection was favorably remarked upon by reviewers, whereas his dialogue-driven writing was criticized as too cinematic. Throughout *All His Sons,* Raphael maintains a compact style that lends conciseness even to the semi-epic plot of "The Siren's Song," a story about the life of a fictitious shipping magnate named Jakobos. Once a young mate on a charter ship, he saves his and the captain's life when the ship sinks, but he leaves a group of Jewish refugees to die. Forty years later Jakobos is a rich man, but he is confronted with his past as an interviewer questions him about the shipwreck. Jakobos is later killed by his former captain, who is now his assistant. The story complements Raphael's novel *Lindmann,* which has been called his most significant work. Both the novel and the short story begin with the death, by shipwreck, of Jewish refugees. Lindmann seeks to escape from his guilt by assuming the identity of one of the dead Jews, while Jakobos ruthlessly pursues his ambitions. What distinguishes the novel from "The Siren's Song" is the latter's less ambiguous and morally charged finale.

Frederic Raphael's reputation has never rested on his short stories alone. His qualities as an anatomist of middle-class relationships are most obvious in his novels, and his best-known works are screenplays for movies such as *Eyes Wide Shut,* while his views on anti-Semitism play a prominent role in his essays. Raphael's short stories can be viewed as a microcosm of his work, however. They include elements of all his interests and stylistic abilities. Grounded in common experiences, especially the everyday vicissitudes of marriage, his short stories present intelligent, ambitious characters who vacillate between routine affairs and occasional breakups, on the one hand, and phases of domestic quiet, on the other. In Raphael's world of amorous attractions and erotic competition, however, the latter are rare and mostly transient.

References:

Frederick P. W. McDowell, "Raphael, Frederic," in *Contemporary Novelists,* edited by Susan Windisch Brown, sixth edition (New York: St. James Press, 1996), pp. 838–841;

McDowell, "The Varied Universe of Frederic Raphael's Fiction," *Critique: Studies in Modern Fiction,* 8, no. 1 (1965): 21–50;

David R. Slavitt, "Volubility, Exile, and Cunning: The Fiction of Frederic Raphael," *Hollins-Critic,* 36, no. 1 (1999): 1–16.

Kate Roberts
(13 February 1891 – 14 April 1985)

Harri Pritchard Jones
Yr Academi Gymreig (The Welsh Academy)

BOOKS: *Y Fam,* by Roberts and Betty Eynon Davies (London & Cardiff: Educational Publishing, 1920);

Y Canpunt: Comedi o Gwm Tawe, by Roberts, Davies, and Margaret Price (Newtown: Welsh Outlook Press, 1923);

O Gors y Bryniau: Naw Stori Fer (Wrexham: Hughes, 1925);

Deian a Loli: Stori am Blant (Cardiff: William Lewis, 1926);

Wel! Wel! Comedi, by Roberts, Davies, and Price (Newtown: Welsh Outlook Press, 1926);

Rhigolau Bywyd, a Storïau Eraill (Aberystwyth: Aberystwyth Press, 1929)—includes "Dydd o Haf," translated by Dafydd Jenkins as "A Summer Day," in *Welsh Short Stories,* revised edition, edited by George Ewart Evans (London: Faber & Faber, 1959), pp. 36–41; "Y Golled," translated by Walter Dowding as "The Loss," in *The Penguin Book of Welsh Short Stories,* edited by Alun Richards (Harmondsworth, U.K.: Penguin, 1976), pp. 94–101;

Laura Jones (Aberystwyth: Aberystwyth Press, 1930);

Traed Mewn Cyffion (Aberystwyth: Aberystwyth Press, 1936); translated by Idwal Walters and John Idris Jones as *Feet in Chains* (Cardiff: John Jones Cardiff, 1977; Chicago: Academy Chicago, 1978);

Ffair Gaeaf a Storïau Eraill (Denbigh: Gee Press, 1937);

Stryd y Glep (Denbigh: Gee Press, 1949);

Y Byw Sy'n Cysgu (Denbigh: Gee Press, 1956); translated by Wyn Griffith as *The Living Sleep* (Cardiff: John Jones Cardiff, 1976);

Te yn y Grug: Cyfrol o Storïau Byrion (Denbigh: Gee Press, 1959); translated by Griffith as *Tea in the Heather* (Ruthin: John Jones, 1968);

Y Lôn Wen: Darn o Hunangofiant (Denbigh: Gee Press, 1960);

Tywyll Heno: Stori Fer Hir (Denbigh: Gee Press, 1962);

Hyn o Fyd: Llyfr o Storïau (Denbigh: Gee Press, 1964)— includes "Cathod Mewn Ocsiwn," translated by Griffith as "Cats at an Auction," in *Twenty-Five*

Kate Roberts (from the dust jacket for the U.S. edition of Feet in Chains, *1978; Richland County Public Library)*

Welsh Stories, edited by Gwyn Jones and Islwyn Ffowc Elis (London: Oxford University Press, 1971), pp. 23–30;

Llên Doe a Heddiw, by Roberts and others (Denbigh: Gee Press, 1964);

Tegwch y Bore (Llandybie: Dryw, 1967);

Prynu Dol a Storïau Eraill (Denbigh: Gee Press, 1969);

Dau Lenor o Ochr Moeltryfan (Caernarfon: Caernarfonshire Library, 1970);

Gobaith a Storïau Eraill (Denbigh: Gee Press, 1972);

Yr Wylan Deg (Denbigh: Gee Press, 1976);

Erthyglau ac Ysgrifau Llenyddol, edited by David Jenkins (Swansea: C. Davies, 1978);

Haul a Drycin, a Storïau Eraill (Denbigh: Gee Press, 1981).

Collection: *Goreuon Storïau Kate Roberts,* edited, with an introduction, by Harri Pritchard Jones (Denbigh: Gee Press, 1997).

Editions in English: *A Summer Day and Other Stories,* translated by Dafydd Jenkins, Walter Dowding, and Wyn Griffith, foreword by Storm Jameson (Cardiff: Penmark Press, 1946);

Two Old Men and Other Stories, translated by Elan Closs Stephens and Griffith, introduction by John Gwilym Jones (Newtown: Gregynog Press, 1981);

The World of Kate Roberts: Selected Stories, 1925–1981, translated by Joseph P. Clancy (Philadelphia: Temple University Press, 1991);

Sun and Storm and Other Stories, translated by Carolyn Watcyn (Denbigh: Gee & Son, 2000).

Kate Roberts is generally regarded as the most distinguished Welsh-language prose writer of the twentieth century. Her career as a writer almost spanned that century, although she was born in the late nineteenth century and her roots were deep in the puritanical Wales of that period. At the time of her birth, the people of the nation were mainly Welsh-speaking and Nonconformist (that is, Protestant but dissenting from the doctrines and administration of the Church of England). Roberts grew up in a largely rural slate-quarrying district that employed and provided a frugal living for approximately thirteen thousand men and their families.

Katherine Roberts was born on 13 February 1891 in the village of Rhosgadfan, not far from Caernarfon, in northwestern Wales. Her father, Owen Roberts, was a quarryman and a widower with three children when he married a widow, Catrin, with a son from her first marriage. The couple had four children: Kate, the eldest, followed by Richard, Evan, and David. Richard died in 1953; Evan was seriously wounded in the Battle of the Somme in France in 1916 but lived until 1951; and David died in Malta in 1917 after being wounded in action.

When Kate was four and a half years old, the Roberts family moved to a house a few fields away. Her early years were confined to the close-knit community of the village. It had no church or tavern, as it had been built to service the slate industry and belonged to the local squire; there was, however, a Calvinistic Methodist chapel. The chapel was symbolic not only of the religious faith of many of its members but also of a degree of cultural autonomy in a period when the Welsh had almost no political institutions of their own. It was also a bastion against the great taboos of contemporary Welsh society: alcohol, publicly acknowledged sex, and prodigality.

Roberts went to the local primary school and in 1910 gained a scholarship to the Caernarfon Grammar School. Her going there meant a financial sacrifice for the family, as most girls of her age at that time would have gone into domestic service to earn money for the family. Taking a step that was unusual for women of her class and period, Roberts then attended the nearby University College of North Wales, in Bangor, where she studied Welsh and Welsh literature, together with Latin and history, and graduated in 1913. She also trained as a teacher, gaining a diploma in teaching and music.

Roberts started teaching shortly before the outbreak of World War I. Her first teaching post was a local one, at the primary school in Llanberis. She also worked for five months in 1914 as a peripatetic teacher in Caernarfonshire. In 1915 she moved to southern Wales, to the semiurban, industrial valleys of the coal, steel, and tin industries, where she continued to work as a teacher. This period was a time of industrial unrest and the rise of the socialist movement in the industrial areas of Wales. The first person to gain a seat for the Labour Party in the British Parliament had been elected in 1900 for the constituency of Merthyr Tydfil, located in one of these valleys.

In spite of her experience of the deprivation and exploitation of working people by landowners and industrialists, Roberts was not sympathetic to the miners. She contrasted them unfavorably with the quarrymen of the north, who proudly considered themselves artisans rather than laborers and insisted that they were selling their labor to the quarry owners rather than working for them. The quarrymen had held long strikes over this principle in 1896–1897 and 1900–1903, but they had been forced to yield eventually, after much suffering and conflict within the community. Their radicalism at that time was largely channeled through the Liberal Party, for which future British prime minister David Lloyd George was a noted advocate and a local member of Parliament.

Roberts's family, like most others in the quarrying area at that time, was constantly bereaved. Nearly every family had lost children, siblings, spouses, or sweethearts in various ways, through quarry accidents, poor obstetric care, tuberculosis, or World War I casualties. Second marriages and half siblings were common. One of Roberts's half brothers committed suicide in 1930, and there were many cases of cancer in the family. Family grief and loss are central themes in much of her work.

Title page for Roberts's first collection (From the Upland Marshes: Nine Short Stories), which depicts life in the close-knit society of the slate-quarrying districts of northwestern Wales, where she grew up (Sterling Memorial Library, Yale University)

In Roberts's *Y Lôn Wen: Darn o Hunangofiant* (1960, The White Road: Part of an Autobiography; the title refers to the road winding down the mountain from her home village to Caernarfon), she asserts that everything important to her had happened before 1917, but this was not the case. She continued teaching and living in south Wales until 1935, from 1929 to 1931 living in Cardiff. Many experiences after 1917 influenced her writing, but the wounding of her brother Evan at the Battle of the Somme in 1916 and the death of her brother David in 1917 triggered the process by which she became a writer. When asked by her friend and fellow author Saunders Lewis in a 1947 radio interview for the Welsh service of the BBC why she started writing, Roberts answered, "Marw fy mrawd ieuengaf yn rhyfel 1914–18, methu deall pethau a gorfod sgrifennu rhag mygu" (It was the death of my youngest brother in the war of 1914–18, and being unable to understand matters, and having to write rather than suffocate). The series of interviews was subsequently published as *Crefft y Stori Fer* (The Craft of the Short Story) in 1949.

Lewis, the principal founder of the Plaid Genedlaethol Cymru (Welsh Nationalist Party) in 1925, was a key figure in Roberts's life and especially in her career as a writer. They corresponded regularly from 1923 to 1983. Lewis's experience of life outside Wales—he was brought up in England and served in the British army in World War I—and his knowledge of French, Italian, and classical literature attracted her. Roberts relied on him for a wider perspective as a writer, and he, in turn, relied on her to acquaint him with the ethos and mores of northern Wales. Lewis romanticized the almost totally Welsh-speaking, rural, and slate-quarrying society of the north. He and Roberts knew each other when she lived in southern Wales and afterward corresponded to the end of their lives (both died in 1985). Roberts revealed many of her deeper thoughts to Lewis, and he constantly encouraged and advised her about her writing.

While teaching in Ystalyfera and Aberdare in Glamorgan, Roberts collaborated with her colleagues on three plays, now considered of little literary worth: *Y Fam* (1920, The Mother), a one-act play written with Betty Eynon Davies; *Y Canpunt: Comedi o Gwm Tawe* (1923, The Hundred Pounds: Comedy from the Tawe Valley), written with Davies and Margaret Price; and *Wel! Wel! Comedi* (1926, Well! Well! Comedy), by the same three authors. In 1932 Roberts also wrote a three-act comedy, "Ffarwel i Addysg" (Farewell Education), but it was never published.

In the 1920s Roberts started writing short stories and through them forged a distinctive attitude to life. These stories, her main literary output from 1925 to 1937, are Chekhovian, portraying proud but poverty-stricken characters in a tight-knit community clinging to the slopes of the Snowdonia Mountains, similar to the society in which she grew up. In a television interview with Gwyn Erfyl, broadcast in 1976 by HTV Wales and later published in *Kate Roberts: Ei Meddwl a'i Gwaith* (1983, Kate Roberts: Her Mind and Work), she insisted she had never wanted to leave the area where she was born and raised, saying that she dreamed about Cae Gors (Marsh Field), her family home, all the time. Wherever she went, she saw a train going up to Rhosgadfan, and she wanted to catch it and return to Cae Gors. In a 1974 monograph on Roberts, Derec Llwyd Morgan states that her writing from this first period, up to 1937, creates a world as authentically her own as is the Georgia of Carson McCullers. Morgan notes Roberts's mastery of idiom and syntax, stressing that her depiction of her native milieu is as accurate as that of any social historian.

Roberts grew up in an area associated with the Welsh medieval romances, the *Mabinogion,* and she studied these tales at University College. They belong to a tradition of oral storytelling that was still alive in Wales and Ireland in the early twentieth century. Roberts eschewed this tradition, however, in favor of a taut, economical style that gives her stories strength and subtle richness at the expense of drama and anecdote. This style was in opposition to the type of short stories popular in her youth, for example, those of O. Henry (William Sydney Porter). Her literary mentors and models were Dic Tryfan (Richard Hughes Williams), an earlier writer of short stories in Welsh from her area; Guy de Maupassant; Anton Chekhov; Thomas Hardy; August Strindberg; and Katherine Mansfield.

In her early stories Roberts's characters live like Sisyphus in the classical legend, condemned to push a great boulder up a hill but never able to reach the summit. They must always strive to keep things going but at the same time manage not to let the boulder roll back and crush them. They maintain a remarkable dignity, although their pride is tinged with conceit. They hold the Calvinist belief that they are a chosen people in some sense, in spite of the oppression of the alien, Anglican, and Anglophone squires and landowners who act as if they owned their tenants and quarrymen. In many ways the community is the principal character in most of Roberts's stories from the 1920s and 1930s. Her descriptions are objective, although they hide some of the worst features of the community, making it seem more heroic than it could possibly have been. The greatest defects in these stories are the absence of a sexual side to the characters' lives and their lack of any sense of injustice. They tend to live and accept things stoically; modesty is for them a cardinal virtue, and they eschew taboo subjects. Not only is sex absent from Roberts's short stories, which is understandable given the Victorian puritanism of the community she depicts, but so is religion. The chapel plays a prominent role, but it functions mainly as a cultural establishment where the community can congregate to hold youth and cultural events, mainly musical and literary. In a 1934 letter Roberts told Lewis that she felt much of chapel attendance was mere religiosity with a deeper layer of paganism.

Roberts's characters tend to be dutiful and devoted to the strict demands of traditional Welsh Nonconformist culture. There are hardly any reprobates. A rare exception is Wil Owen in the story "Pryfocio" (Provoking), originally published in the literary magazine *Y Llenor* (The Litterateur) in 1923 and included in Roberts's first collection, *O Gors y Bryniau: Naw Stori Fer* (1925, From the Upland Marshes: Nine Short Stories). Wil gets drunk every Saturday night and ends up in jail, while his wife, Catrin, ponders her fate, comparing it unfavorably with that of the other women of the village, who keep house and rear children while their quarrymen husbands dutifully provide the income. Despite this unfavorable picture of male behavior, Roberts's stories exhibit no hint of feminism, which is surprising since she pioneered the way to a university education for women from such a materially impoverished background. Her female characters are tied to the kitchen and the cradle, scouring the slate doorsteps that were the outward sign of cleanliness and respectability in Wales at that time and polishing their inexpensive furniture. Their only releases from this routine are the romance of courtship, the early days of marriage, children (when there is time for them), and the rare but significant luxuries they occasionally indulge in, against all the rules of their normal code of behavior.

In the title story from the collection *Rhigolau Bywyd, a Storïau Eraill* (1929, Life's Grooves, and Other Stories), the female protagonist, Beti, deals with the first day of retirement for her husband, Dafydd, who has had to give up working in the quarry because he is seventy. She looks back to the time of their early courtship and then to the years of routine and drudgery, punctuated by the rites of passage of their children and relatives but little affected by world events. Watching her husband filling his time by cutting a hedge, Beti realizes he will soon die. Her drudgery and addiction to duty are described in terms of churning milk to make butter, echoing a description of that process carried out by Roberts's own mother in *Y Lôn Wen:*

Rhoid y llaeth i gyd felly yn y corddwr i'w gorddi, a gwaith trwm oedd troi'r handlen am dri chwarter awr o amser nes iddo droi'n fenyn. Nid oedd wiw ychwanegu mwy o ddwr nag oedd yn angenrheidiol, er mwyn ei frysio (gwnâi rhai hynny) neu fe fyddai'r menyn yn wyn ac anodd ei drin. Wedyn, tri chwarter awr arall neu fwy i drin y menyn, er mwyn cael y dwr i gyd allan ohono, a'i gael yn bwysi solet i'w rhoi ar y lechen gron.

(All the milk was therefore poured into the churn to foam, and it was hard work, turning the handle for three quarters of an hour until it turned to butter. You dare not add more water than was necessary, in order to speed up the process [although some did do that], lest the butter become white and difficult to manage. Then another three quarters of an hour or more to treat the butter, to get all the water out of it, and make it into solid pounds to lay on the round slate.)

In the autobiography Roberts talks of her mother in a battle "bob master rhwng ei phleser a'i dyletswydd"

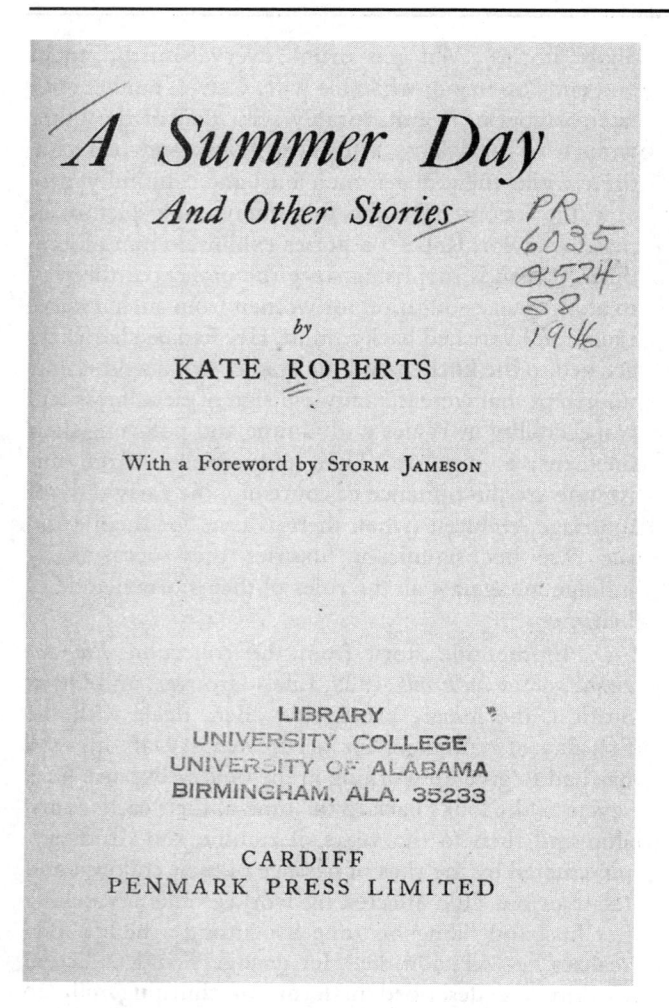

Title page for the first collection of Roberts's stories in English translation, published in 1946 (Mervyn H. Sterne Library, University of Alabama at Birmingham)

(always, between her pleasure and duty). She considered seeking pleasure a "pechod" (sin) and "yr oedd yn well ganddi aros gartref a darllen, a byw ar ei dychmygion ei hun"(preferred to stay home and read, and live on her own imaginations). Only rarely do pleasure and self-indulgence enter into Roberts's pictures of women's lives, although they do occasionally, and then with great significance. The theme of happiness ending with the loss of youth and the advent of family responsibilities is put in a more positive way in one of her earliest stories, "Y Golled" (translated as "The Loss," 1976), first published in 1926 and later included in *Rhigolau Bywyd*. In this story a husband and wife revisit a place where they had courted and realize what has been lost as their lives became one long struggle.

Roberts's early stories usually have a domestic setting and are usually told from a woman's point of view. The main exceptions are her attempts at portraying the life of people in southern Wales, as in "Diwrnod i'r Brenin" (A Day Out), a story about people making a day trip from the valleys to Cardiff that was first published in the literary magazine *Y Traethodydd* (The Essayist) in 1933 and later collected in *Ffair Gaeaf a Storïau Eraill* (1937, Winter Fair and Other Stories). "Buddugoliaeth Alaw Jim" (Alaw Jim's Victory), also from *Ffair Gaeaf*, is about a collier and his racing greyhound. Roberts was on surer ground describing her native community, as in the stories from *O Gors y Bryniau*. The plots of these stories are somewhat didactic and border on case histories at times, but in them Roberts shows her flair for language and significant detail. The society she depicts is hard, deprived, and lacking in social graces. Her writing, however, is graceful and elegant, and in this first collection she obviously showed a new talent that demanded to be watched. Nevertheless, the harsh realism of the stories elicited some negative criticism. In a 1925 review of the volume in *Y Llenor*, W. J. Gruffydd observed, "There is a tendency at times to believe that sometimes Miss Roberts depends on her memory rather than her imagination, that she is too prone to produce a photograph rather than paint a picture.... It is in Miss Roberts's lazy hours that she is tempted to reproduce rather than create."

Roberts's writing had a gentler side. Throughout her career, the softer, more attractive works she created were for and about children. The first of these was *Deian a Loli: Stori am Blant* (1927, Deian and Loli: Story for Children), which, while it reached an adult readership, did not succeed as a book for young readers. It has, though, like most of her books about children, a delightful lightness, a sense of wonderment, and a degree of mischief. Children are exempt from the strict rules of behavior that constrain the world of Roberts's adult characters.

Roberts returned to short stories about her native community with her 1929 collection, *Rhigolau Bywyd*. Her style was maturing, and she showed the lighter side of life in the quarrying district. This volume includes "Y Golled," but Roberts's mastery of the short-story genre is more evident in works such as "Rhwng Dau Damaid o Gyfleth" (Between Two Pieces of Toffee), in which an old man watches his daughter and granddaughter happily teasing out and twisting newly made treacle toffee. He recalls his first love and how the girl in question refused to marry him, as she felt marriage would end their happiness. Later, however, he married a similar girl, with whom he has been quite happy. The perspective then changes, and the reader sees the old man through the eyes of the women. At the end of the story the granddaughter feeds the old man some toffee, and "disgynnai rhaffan bychain, meinion, aur, oddi wrth y cyfleth ar ei farf" (thin, tiny twirls fall from the toffee onto his beard). The description is highly visual and a good example of what has been referred to as Roberts's power of discovering significant detail, as noted by novelist Storm Jameson in her foreword to a volume of Roberts's works in English translation, *A Summer Day, and Other Stories* (1946).

Laura Jones (1930), a novella, showed that Roberts was attempting to paint on a larger canvas than that of the short story. But, as Morgan notes, it "is not an exciting sequel" to *Deian a Loli*: "It is made up of letters to and by and about Laura in her new employment, and describes aspects of the sociocultural life of a Welsh village in the first decade of this [the twentieth] century. I dare say if it had been written by someone other than Kate Roberts it would have been forgotten long ago."

In 1928 Roberts married Morris T. Williams, a journalist almost ten years her junior who was part of a group working in Caernarfon in its 1920s heyday as the capital of Welsh publishing and journalism. Caernarfon is not a big city, but it is a real town and had a certain romantic air for people such as Roberts, living on the surrounding mountainsides looking down at it. For such people it was like an old Roman town, with shops, cafés, taverns, and a port with ships and sailors; it also offered a certain degree of anonymity. Many interesting young men of the same background as Roberts moved to Caernarfon after World War I to work as journalists and writers, including Williams and the poet Prosser Rhys, two debonair young men who challenged every Nonconformist taboo, following a life of pleasure, drinking, and prodigal living. They had style, wore bow ties, and were open, to some extent, about their homosexuality. Sigmund Freud was informed by the Welsh psychoanalyst Ernest Jones (later the author of the authoritative Freud biography) about Rhys's prizewinning ode at the 1924 Pontypool National Eisteddfod, the major annual festival of Welsh-language culture. The poem included descriptions of homosexual love and discussed psychoanalysis. Williams and Rhys had a long-lasting liaison.

Williams moved to Paris in 1924 to work as a compositor, and Rhys was supposed to follow but never made it. While there, Williams wrote a novel, "Troi a Throsi" (Twisting and Turning), in the style of James Joyce's *A Portrait of the Artist as a Young Man* (1916). It is an interesting and exciting work that was considered too risqué to be published in the 1920s. In the 6 January 1927 edition of the weekly newspaper *Baner ac Amserau Cymru* (Banner and Times of Wales), Rhys wrote in his column, "Led-led Cymru" (Wales-wide), that Williams's novel was "more like the work of D. H. Lawrence and James Joyce rather than the work of Hardy or Galsworthy, and recounting the thoughts in the mind of a Welshman between twenty and twenty-five years old in Wales and on the continent." Rhys assured his readers that the novel included "nothing to pollute anyone, but it does contain much that will frighten . . . literary critics." Three readers had considered the work on behalf of an anonymous publisher, and two of them were against publishing it. The third was Roberts, who was in favor of publication, but as she was in the minority, the work was turned down by the publisher.

Roberts had read Williams's novel shortly before she fell in love with the author. Although she had been attracted by the bohemian lifestyle of men such as Williams and Rhys, she was loath to recognize it openly; yet, when the question of marrying Williams arose in 1927, they considered living *tally* (without marrying), as it is called in Welsh. Roberts was determined not to marry in a chapel. Lewis persuaded her that marrying in an Anglican church rather than a chapel might be a different experience, something that she and Williams could tolerate.

Roberts was not disappointed in the wedding ceremony, but she was disappointed in her marriage. Williams maintained his homosexual relationship with Rhys, and he and Roberts had no children, although it is thought that she would have wished to do so. The complexities of his sexual orientation drove Williams to alcoholism and an early death in 1946. Yet, Roberts never acknowledged that her husband's sexual relationship with Rhys existed, and she grieved deeply when Williams died. After marrying, the couple first lived in Cardiff and then in Tonypandy, in the Rhondda Valley. Despite her unhappiness, she wrote (in Welsh) to Lewis on 8 December 1927:

> Ond yr wyf yn cwbl gredu bod Morris Williams a minnau yn gwneud y peth goreu er ein lles. Buom yn gyfeillion da er Machynlleth, a rhyw ddeufis yn ol syrthiasom i'r pwll hwnnw sy'n ddyfnach na chyfeillgarwch. . . . Gwn y geilw'r byd ni'n ffyliaid. . . . Mae gwahaniaeth mawr yn ein hoed–agos i ddeng mlynedd . . . a gwahaniaeth mawr mewn pethau eraill y gesyd y byd fawr bris arnynt. Ond . . . nid ydym ni o'r byd . . . os â'n bywyd yn gandryll arno ef y bydd hi waethaf am ei fod mor ifanc.

> (I am totally convinced that Morris Williams and I are doing the best for our happiness. We have been close friends since Machynlleth and about two months ago we fell into that pit that is deeper than friendship. . . . I know the world will think us fools. . . . There is a great discrepancy in our ages–nearly ten years . . . and a great difference in other matters the world puts great

emphasis on. But . . . we are not of the world . . . if our lives shatter, he will suffer the most, as he is so young.)

In a January 1929 letter to Lewis, Roberts refers to the old age of her parents and adds, in regard to Williams, "Yr wyf yn hapus wrth feddwl am fynd ato, oblegid gwn fod llawenydd yn fy aros, y llawenydd hwnnw a ddaw o garu a chael fy ngharu" (I am happy thinking about going to him, for I know that joy awaits me, the joy that comes from loving and being loved).

Roberts's hopes were not fulfilled. In 1935 she and her husband decided to return to the north and bought the Gee Press in Denbigh, in northeastern Wales. They moved together with Rhys, who was to edit *Baner ac Amserau Cymru*, published by their press. In addition to working on her own writing, Roberts played a part in running the press and contributing articles on various topics to the weekly paper. She was a convinced Welsh nationalist but almost never allowed any element of propaganda to taint her literary work. During the first two years in Denbigh, she published the last two works from the first period of her career: her first novel, *Traed Mewn Cyffion* (1936; translated as *Feet in Chains*, 1977), and her 1937 story collection, *Ffair Gaeaf*. Most of the stories had already appeared in periodicals.

Although Roberts was still dealing with her native region in *Traed Mewn Cyffion* and *Ffair Gaeaf*, her storytelling craft had developed. In well-wrought, balanced sentences she focuses readers' minds on the significant details of her characters' lives and enlarges the impact of her work by the use of suggestive ambiguity. She described this ambiguity in a written interview with J. E. Caerwyn Williams, published in *Ysgrifau Beirniadol III* (1967, Critical Essays III): "y gallu i agrwymu sy'n bwysig. Gellir gwneud hyn drwy beidio â dweud gormod, drwy sgwrs, trwy ddisgrifiadau cynnil . . . ond nid y cynildeb hwnnw nad yw'n dweud dim" (it is the ability to suggest that is important. This can be achieved by not saying too much, through dialogue, through sparing descriptions . . . but not so sparing that it says nothing). In her introduction to *A Summer Day,* Jameson also writes of the sensuous precision, economy, and overall achievement of Roberts's stories from 1937. "In the fewest words," Jameson declares,

> she evokes the weight of a hot sun pressing on the valley, throwing into relief the near hills, obliterating the more distant; and the silence, in which every movement is audible, of winter. . . . In these stories, not only the things seen, but things heard, touched, tasted, are evoked with an energy and purity which succeed because they are loyal first of all to the thing itself: the emotion springs from it, is not merely thrown round it. . . . It will be easy in a rapid reading to miss the truth about her characters: with her brief carefully considered strokes she gives them the density of life, commits them to time, lets it work on them, lets them construct themselves.

Lewis, discussing *Traed Mewn Cyffion* with Roberts when it was a work in progress, suggested in a letter that she should "dig into her own soul" to look into the minds and hearts of her characters, in addition to describing the life of the community. Roberts refused to follow his suggestion, but she later wrote Lewis to congratulate him on the psychological profundity of his novel *Monica* (1930), which is about the nemesis of a dissolute woman in a Swansea suburb. Roberts did not want to concentrate on examining individual souls but to chronicle the story of a whole community and to do so in loyalty to it; indeed, she wanted to celebrate it. In this aim she was following the Welsh Calvinist literary principles espoused by critics such as Bobi Jones, who demanded that authors write about what ought to be rather than what they see around them. Roberts certainly seems to have written this way at times and even admitted to presenting occasionally a rather rosy picture of her home community. As she writes in *Y Lôn Wen*, "[mae'n] amhosibl dweud y gwir. . . . Gadewais y pethau anhyfryd allan. Yr oedd yn fy hen ardal bethau cas, yr oedd yno bethau drwg, yr oedd yno bobl annymunol" ([it is] impossible to tell the truth. . . . I left out the unhappy bits. In my home-patch there were nasty things, there were bad things, there were unpleasant people). She did not always do so, however. In *Traed Mewn Cyffion* one character describes the local district, Arfon, as "rhyw hen le fel hyn . . . ym mhen draw'r byd, ymhell ar ôl yr oes, ac yn byta'r un peth bob dydd ar ôl ei gilydd" (an old place like this at the end of the earth . . . terribly old-fashioned, eating the same thing day after day).

The traditional Calvinist fear that enjoyment usually leads to sorrow is rife in Roberts's works from this early period in her career. The fear of accepting happiness when it is offered is seen in many of her characters, as is the battle against enjoying anything that could remotely be classed as a luxury. The psychological problems of many of her characters, as well as their innate dignity tainted with conceit, are well represented in Ffanni Rolant, in "Y Taliad Olaf" (The Final Payment), and Ffebi Williams, in "Y Cwilt" (The Quilt), both from *Ffair Gaeaf*. For all their poverty, these characters occasionally escape from their enslavement to it. Ffanni and Ffebi give in to prodigality once in a while by buying some luxury, such as a quilt or a fine tablecloth, or laying a table elegantly and serving a choice tea for a guest or even for themselves. In "Y

Frontispiece and title page for Roberts's 1960 account of her early life (The White Road: Part of an Autobiography), the title of which refers to the road winding down from her home village to the town of Caernarfon, where she attended grammar school (Widener Library, Harvard University)

Taliad Olaf," Ffanni and her husband have sold their smallholding and moved to a cottage. She goes to pay off her last account with the little local shop. There is a hint of the Last Judgment about this scene, with the shopkeeper dressed in priestly garb and the weighing scales prominently displayed in the shop. Ffanni has walked to the shop every Friday for years to make sure she pays any debt fully. She has been poor all her life, eking out a living from her husband's meager wages and from their smallholding. She admits she could have paid off her account in full on previous occasions but had, instead, given in to a yearning for finery and bought a choice tablecloth for the meal at harvest time. Her problem is explained thus: "yr oedd gan Ffanni Rolant chwaeth: peth damniol i'r sawl a fyn dalu ei ffordd. Fe wyddai hi beth oedd gwerth lliain a brethyn. Yr oedd yn bleser edrych arni'n eu bodio" (Ffanni Rolant had taste: a damnable thing for anyone who wishes to pay his way. She knew the worth of linen and tweed. It was a pleasure to see her fingering them).

In "Y Cwilt," Ffebi awakens to the day on which her and her husband's furniture is to be distrained by the bailiffs because of their debts. In stark contrast to this personal tragedy, her husband indulges her with breakfast in bed. The reader is also confronted with evidence of self-indulgence in the fine quilt Ffebi bought herself years ago. She recalls better days with her brother and her spouse in the area where she grew up. Everything is seen anew, and she feels sadness, loss, anger, and stubbornness, as well as momentary pleasure, as she appreciates the quilt she once bought. It is "Cwilt o wlanen wen dew ydoedd, a rhesi ar ei hyd— rhesi o bob lliwiau, glas a gwyrdd, melyn a choch, a'r rhesi, nid yn unionsyth, ond yn cwafrio. Yr oedd ei ridens yn drwchus ac yn brawf o drwch a gwead clòs y wlanen" (A thick white flannel quilt, with stripes— stripes in many colors, blue and green, yellow and red, and the stripes were not straight but quavered. The fringe was thick and proof of the thickness and close weave of the flannel). When she had first seen the quilt at a summer sale, Ffebi had noticed "gafaelai pob gwraig ynddo a'i fodio wrth fynd heibio a thaflu golwg hiraethlon arno wrth adael.... Daeth awydd ar Ffebi ei brynu, a pho fwyaf yr ystyriai ei thlodi, mwyaf yn y byd y cynyddai ei hawydd" (women fingering it as they went by, and looking longingly at it.... She had felt an urge to buy it, and the more she contemplated her poverty, the more her desire to buy it increased). As the bailiffs arrive to take her furniture, she wraps the quilt around herself defiantly.

Possession of such items as fine table linen also features in the much-acclaimed opening passage of *Traed Mewn Cyffion*. In this passage Roberts is at her best as a writer, though the novel deteriorates later. The main character, Jane Gruffydd, insists on preparing a memorable tea for people on the day of a preaching festival in order to show that she is no feckless peasant. She takes pride in the slimness of her waist and the excellence of her clothes and jewelry. The cleanliness of her home, the fine food she offers her guests, and the neatness of her glass plates are also celebrated. As in all her work, Roberts excels at describing the feel, smell, taste, and sound of things, in a manner reminiscent of Joyce. *Traed Mewn Cyffion* was dedicated to Rhys, with an enigmatic quotation from the Book of Job: "You prevail for ever against them, and they pass away; / You change their countenance, and send them away. / Their children come to honour, and they do not know it. / They are brought low, and it goes unnoticed."

In works such as "Y Taliad Olaf," "Y Cwilt," and *Traed Mewn Cyffion* the reader sees the internal struggle of Roberts's characters and what it is that keeps them going, especially the women: to keep at life, living respectably and modestly, without owing a penny to anyone when they die, and striving to hide any faults from each other. It is a hard life lived by people who are hard on themselves; a lonely and unfeeling life, with no emotional closeness and little room for play and fun or even for children at times. Children tend to be shooed out from under the adults' feet or upstairs as the parents come to the end of a hard day's work. In spite of her age when she married, Roberts might have hoped to have children. In the physical sense, she did not, but she created children in her stories, and only with them was she able to free herself from harsh, Nonconformist Welsh discipline and from a puritan hatred of being prodigal. Indeed, her most successful literary creations are children.

Whether because of unhappiness in her married life or the pressure of work or both, Roberts did not write creatively from 1937 to 1949. She then entered what was to be her second and final period as a writer. Following the death of her husband in 1946, she began to do what Lewis had advocated: she looked into her own soul. Rather than describe the lives of characters in the quarrying districts and grieve for them, she now had her characters grieve for themselves. In this way she also mourned her own losses. As her mother had also died a short time before Williams did, Roberts was left alone at age fifty-five to ponder her difficult life. In a 1963 interview for the Baptist magazine *Seren Gomer* (Gomer's Star) with the editor, Lewis Valentine, she recalled "hyn ddigwyddodd i mi yn 1946, pan syrthiodd fy myd yn deilchion o'm cwmpas. Y pryd hynny y dechreuais i edrych i mewn i mi fy hun" (what happened to me in 1946, when my world fell in fragments around me. It was at that time I started looking into myself).

Roberts's first work from this second period was *Stryd y Glep* (1949, Gossip Row), a long short story in diary form. It reveals a little of the cynicism that sometimes marred her writing from this point on, but it marked a turning point in her literary career. As R. Geraint Gruffydd notes,

> In this "long short story," she leaves for the present the main world of her literary activity to date, namely that of the cottagers of the slate-quarrying districts of Arfon with their assiduous battle against poverty and other external enemies, and turns, rather, to chronicle the internal battles of middle-class women in small towns not far from the north Wales coast. It is remarkable how she succeeded in taking possession of each of the two worlds.

Morgan agrees with this assessment. "The setting," he writes,

> is not Arfon or Glamorgan, it is a narrow street in a small town; the subject matter for her is novel; the characters have a new inner dimension. No longer do we have *Traed Mewn Cyffion*'s chronological story about people placed on a piece of earth told simply. Far from being simple and straightforward–though the book is that too ... this is not a "stream of consciousness" writing–*Stryd y Glep* is an allegory. The street itself is the world ... the parlour where Ffebi Beca lies is both salon and confessional, as everyone's house is sometimes.

Morgan goes on to argue that Ffebi and her neighbors embody the imperfections and good points of humanity. He insists that Roberts's "new world is also a literary model of the actual world."

Writing creative literature again, as well as editing and writing journalism, proved too taxing for Roberts. In 1956 she gave up the struggle to keep the Gee Press going and sold it. Running the press had been hard work, especially for the ten years after her husband died. From this time on, she dedicated herself to creative writing and had to depend on it to a large extent for her living. That same year, she published the novel *Y Byw Sy'n Cysgu* (translated as *The Living Sleep*, 1976), which depicts an abandoned woman living in suburbia. Her world is far away from Roberts's rural roots and is, in every sense, more urbane. The reader meets the bereft woman as she copes with having been abandoned; she also has to deal with solicitors, ministers, and her family, including her sister-in-law. There is a great deal of bitterness in the novel, as one would expect, but it won critical praise. For example, John Gwilym Jones notes that "*Y Byw Sy'n Cysgu* is a novel which, on the basis of its vision and expression, its instinct and its craft, belongs to the mind of its era, reflecting its unease, its insecurity and its apathetic irresponsibility, but which has in it also the eternal assiduity and basic energy which is a feature of humankind. After reading it we know ourselves and our fellow human beings more deeply."

Y Byw Sy'n Cysgu was followed by what is probably Roberts's finest work, *Te yn y Grug: Cyfrol o Storïau Byrion* (1959, Tea in the Heather: Volume of Short Stories; translated as *Tea in the Heather*, 1968), a cycle of stories about children. It was written in a completely different key from *Y Byw Sy'n Cysgu*. In the stories a respectable little girl, Begw, who is akin to Roberts herself as a child, befriends a quite different character, Winni Ffinni Hadog, a young teenager living on the edge of a village that is typically Nonconformist and respectable. Winni's father and mother are reprobates and drunkards who abuse her miserably. She, too, is unrespectable, erratic in behavior, loudmouthed, and badly dressed and groomed, but she is defiant and determined to succeed in her dreams, which include traveling to London and working for Queen Victoria. Winni is everything a child should not be in Roberts's world; yet, Roberts obviously enjoyed creating this character, and *Te yn y Grug* was her own favorite among her books.

When Begw manages to persuade her mother to invite Winni home for tea, the contrast between the two girls is stark. Later, Begw and a friend take a picnic up to the heather-clad mountainside on a fine, warm day. Winni turns up, steals the food, whips the girls, dances in a frenzy, and tells them of her woes and vain hopes for a better future. She is free of all the taboos that pervade Begw's (and Roberts's) world. In spite of everyone and everything, Winni faces up to life, has dreams, and fights to get her own way. She is Roberts's greatest creation and completely out of character with those of the community described in the author's early works. Yet, Winni represents a feature of that community, and Roberts was obviously attracted to the character. In a review of the 2002 reprint of the 1968

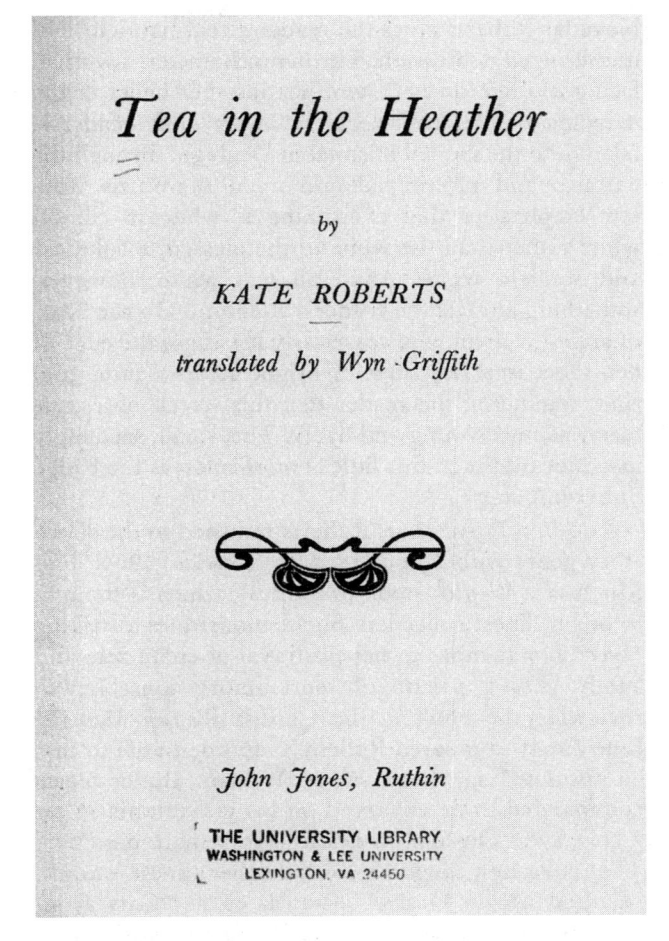

Title page for the 1968 translation of Roberts's 1959 collection, Te yn y Grug, *a cycle of stories about a little girl from a respectable family who befriends a free-spirited young teenage girl from a broken home (Washington and Lee University Library)*

translation, Dean Powell focused on Begw, rather than Winni. The collection, he wrote, is "Beautifully realised, never idealised," and

> it follows the life of Begw Gruffydd, the little girl who grows from the age of four to nine in the book. With her eye for detail and her ear for dialogue, Roberts's portrayal of childhood and childish concerns is charming and convincing. This is a time for friendships and rivalries, small luxuries and swift punishments, exciting excursions and tearful disappointments. And there is the sometimes hostile world of adults to contend with. (*Western Mail* [Cardiff], 25 May 2002)

Roberts's later works also exhibit much sadness, grief, and bereavement. She was an acknowledged master at presenting and describing loss, and she occasionally slipped into morbidity. In the widely praised *Tywyll Heno: Stori Fer Hir* (1962, Dark Tonight:

Novella) Roberts gives the reader a searing picture of middle-aged depression. The main character, a woman facing old age on her own, has lost her belief in the meaning of life; her world is empty. The reader is taken into the mental hospital in Denbigh, through the entrance and into the hall and one of the wards. Roberts emphasizes that everything is white: a clinical white rather than the white of the blessed, a colorless and soulless white. Amid all this white, however, something attracts the reader's attention. On the hand of an old woman who ceaselessly massages the edge of her sheet is a tiny spot of bright color—a little gold ring, reminding the reader that this wreck of a creature was once young and lively. This small, seemingly insignificant thing, this little spot of color, is the badge of her humanity.

After *Tywyll Heno,* Roberts returned to the short-story genre with *Hyn o Fyd: Llyfr o Storïau* (1964, This Much of a World: Book of Stories), which is thought to be her finest collection. She demonstrates a striking objectivity at times in her portrayal of characters and subtly uses a palette of sense impressions. Lewis, reviewing the book in the Cardiff *Western Mail* (11 June 1964), compared Roberts's attitude to life to that encapsulated in those words William Butler Yeats commanded to be engraved on his gravestone: "Cast a cold eye / On life, on death / Horseman, pass by!" The collection includes one of her finest stories, "Cathod Mewn Ocsiwn" (translated as "Cats at an Auction," 1971), which was also her own favorite. In it Roberts is once again the chronicler of unremitting grief. The story takes the form of an interior monologue as the female protagonist attends an auction of the goods of a deceased woman; the other women at the sale seem to her almost vulture-like in their attitude to the items being auctioned. Nostalgia pervades the main character as she recalls the supposed Eden of her youth and the early days of her marriage. Two aspects of this longing appear. The reader notes her sense of loss regarding her home, in the close-knit community of the slate-quarrying district. She also suffers a cruel sense of longing and loneliness stemming from the loss of her husband and her having to live in an anonymous suburb. In "Cathod Mewn Ocsiwn," Roberts demonstrates how people are unable to relate to each other without a community and its nexus of relationships and common rituals.

Roberts's next work was a long novel about the period from 1912 to 1917, set in the slate-quarrying district of her earlier fiction. *Tegwch y Bore* (1967, The Fairness of the Morn) was largely written in an earlier period, but it is in a different key from Roberts's earlier work. It is lighter in tone and almost romantic. Morgan compares the novel with the earlier *Traed Mewn Cyffion*. *Tegwch y Bore* has a similarly intelligent and rebellious female protagonist, and several other characters echo those in the earlier novel. Morgan also argues, however, that Roberts's attitude to home differs in the later work. Home is no longer "the axle of affairs" but, rather, "movement and exile have replaced stability and security." He also points out that *Tegwch y Bore* has a much broader range of settings and touches upon many theological and ethical topics that are foreign to *Traed Mewn Cyffion*. The later novel also lightly hints at Roberts's dislike of economic oppression and the madness of war. Nonetheless, *Tegwch y Bore* has never been as highly regarded as most of Roberts's other works, especially her short fiction. John Rowlands sums up this attitude. "Kate Roberts," he writes, "is at her best writing short works. . . . The truth is that it is not in her inventiveness in creating plots that her talent is shown at best, and the tendency is for her long novels to appear monotonous."

Four further collections of Roberts's short stories were published, some of the stories dating from an earlier period and most of them of declining literary value. She did, however, continue to work assiduously at her writing throughout most of the period from 1969, when she was seventy-eight, almost until her death in 1985. *Prynu Dol a Storïau Eraill* (1969, Buying a Doll and Other Stories), *Gobaith a Storïau Eraill* (1972, Hope and Other Stories), *Yr Wylan Deg* (1976, The Fair Seagull), and *Haul a Drycin, a Storïau Eraill* (1981, Sun and Storm, and Other Stories) were all published by the Gee Press in Denbigh.

In *Prynu Dol* there are two stories of interest, "Dwy Gwningen Fechan" (Two Small Rabbits) and "Y Daith" (The Journey). The former is about a boy who takes part in a recitation competition in which the set piece is about two rabbits, one of which is killed. This recitation is counterpointed with the protagonist's worries about his sick dog, which enable him to speak passionately about the rabbits and thus win the competition. His mother is delighted that he has beaten the other children, but the important figure for the boy is his grandmother, who has cured the dog of worms and restored him to full vigor. In "Y Daith" the reader is again made to face the ephemeral nature of things. Dafydd, the last of a family, is leaving home and going down south. The parents carry his tin trunk "fel petaent yn cario aberth at allor" (as if they were carrying a sacrifice to an altar). The father and son sit on each side of the trunk "eisteddai'r tad a'r mab un o bobtu'r tun fel petaent yn eistedd o bobtn arch" (as if sitting on each side of a coffin). This story marks a return to Roberts's familiar theme of change inevitably leading to loss.

Some critics choose the title story of *Yr Wylan Deg* for special mention. W. Cynwil Williams, who, as Roberts's minister, was close to her in her final years, sees the story as important. He spoke of it in his tribute to her at a memorial service in Capel Mawr, Denbigh, on 4 August 1985. "She was in hospital," he said, "having had her hip pinned after a fall. The one who had been used to standing up bravely was floored. Would some sweetness emanate from the lion's mouth this time? . . . It did. Within days it was a 'Fair Seagull' she could see from her single room. . . . She wrote the story in a few weeks time. . . . I suggested the bird was the Holy Spirit. . . . 'Perhaps you're right,' she said shyly." The danger, however, of sentimentality in stories such as "Yr Wylan Deg" has been noted by some critics. In *Enaid Clwyfus: Golwg ar Waith Kate Roberts* (1976, Wounded Life: A Look at the Works of Kate Roberts) John Emyr writes, "Sometimes, we notice the threat of too much softness in the form of self-pity. Kate Roberts's heroines also struggle against the wound of being too kind to themselves, but not always successfully." Emyr also includes her autobiography, *Y Lôn Wen,* in this category.

In her later years Roberts received many honors. In 1956 she was awarded a doctorate in literature by the University of Wales, and in 1961 she received the medal of the Honourable Society of Cymmrodorion, a Welsh cultural organization founded in London in 1751. The Welsh Arts Council awarded her the prize for prose writing in 1972, and in 1983 a national testimonial was gathered for her benefit. Roberts lived to a difficult old age, and the last letters between her and her lifetime mentor and admirer, Lewis, are sad and brave, as the two writers, both giants of twentieth-century Welsh literature, faced the problems attendant on aging. Roberts died on 14 April 1985 and Lewis on 1 September of the same year. Roberts was ninety-four at the time of her death.

Kate Roberts created the short story in Welsh. She moved narrative Welsh prose away from the anecdotal and forged a style and attitude to life and literature that eschewed propaganda. Her achievement is gradually being recognized in the English-speaking world and elsewhere, as is witnessed by Joseph P. Clancy's 1991 collection of her writing in translation, *The World of Kate Roberts: Selected Stories, 1925–1981*. Roberts's stature as a major figure in twentieth-century literature continues to grow.

Letters:

Dafydd Ifans, ed., *Annwyl Kate, Annwyl Saunders: Gohebiaeth, 1923–83* (Aberystwyth: National Library of Wales, 1992).

Interviews:

Saunders Lewis, ed., *Crefft y Stori Fer* (Aberystwyth: Welsh Book Club, 1949), pp. 9–21;

Lewis Valentine, *Seren Gomer,* 55, no. 4 (1962);

J. E. Caerwyn Williams, ed., *Ysgrifau Beirniadol III* (Denbigh: Gee Press, 1967), pp. 202–216;

Gwyn Erfyl, in *Kate Roberts: Ei Meddwl a'i Gwaith,* edited by Rhydwen Williams (Llandybie: C. Davies, 1983), pp. 30–37.

References:

John Emyr, *Enaid Clwyfus: Golwg ar Waith Kate Roberts* (Denbigh: Gee Press, 1976);

R. Geraint Gruffydd, "Nodyn ar 'Stryd y Glep,'" in *Kate Roberts: Ei Meddwl a'i Gwaith,* edited by Rhydwen Williams (Llandybie: C. Davies, 1983), pp. 66–71;

Bobi Jones, *Kate Roberts: Cyfrol Deyrnged* (Denbigh: Gee Press, 1969);

John Gwilym Jones, "Kate Roberts," in *Kate Roberts: Ei Meddwl a'i Gwaith,* pp. 108–113;

Derec Llwyd Morgan, *Kate Roberts* (Cardiff: University of Wales Press/Welsh Arts Council, 1974);

Morgan, ed., *Broa Bywyd Kate Roberts* (Cardiff: Welsh Arts Council, 1981);

John Rowlands, "Tywyll Heno," in *Kate Roberts: Ei Meddwl a'i Gwaith,* pp. 135–138.

Papers:

Kate Roberts's papers are in the National Library of Wales, Aberystwyth.

Dilys Rose
(7 February 1954 –)

Peter Clandfield
Nipissing University

BOOKS: *Madame Doubtfire's Dilemma* (Blackford, Perthshire, Scotland: Chapman, 1989);
Our Lady of the Pickpockets (London: Secker & Warburg, 1989);
Red Tides (London: Secker & Warburg, 1993);
When I Wear My Leopard Hat: Poems for Young Children (Edinburgh: Scottish Children's Press, 1997);
War Dolls (London: Headline/Review, 1998);
Pest Maiden (London: Headline/Review, 1999);
Lure (Edinburgh: Chapman, 2003);
Lord of Illusions, and Other Stories (Edinburgh: Luath, 2005).

Edition: *Selected Stories* (Edinburgh: Luath, 2005).

PLAY PRODUCTIONS: *Learning the Paso Doble,* Edinburgh, Traverse Theatre, spring 1999;
Fatal Attraction, music by Stephen Deazley, libretto by Rose, Edinburgh, North Edinburgh Arts Centre, 2003;
The Fires of Bride, music by Rory Boyle, libretto by Rose, Edinburgh, Queen's Hall, 2005.

PRODUCED SCRIPT: *Friendly Voices,* motion picture, screenplay by Rose and Jack Wyper, 1997.

OTHER: "Out of Touch: An Extract from a Work in Progress," in *The Canongate Prize for New Writing: Scotland into the New Era* (Edinburgh: Canongate, 2000), pp. 187–197;
Once upon Our Time: Portrait Miniatures by Moyna Flannigan, text by Rose (Edinburgh: National Galleries of Scotland, 2004).

Dilys Rose (from Madame Doubtfire's Dilemma, *1989; G. Ross Roy Collection of Scottish Literature, Thomas Cooper Library, University of South Carolina)*

Dilys Rose is a remarkably versatile writer. While short stories form the bulk of her output, she is also a notable poet and novelist. She writes for children as well as adults and has devoted considerable time to the teaching as well as the practice of writing. While some of her stories have been criticized as unresolved or diffuse, Rose's powers of concise observation and resonant understatement have been praised repeatedly by both reviewers and academic critics. "Although I have political beliefs," she told Rebecca E. Wilson in an interview published in 1990, "I don't feel the best way of getting them over in fiction is to preach about them." Feminist concerns and principles inform Rose's work but do not dominate it, and she writes insightfully and often sympathetically about men as well as about women. In a similar way, her Scottish nationality inflects her work without circumscribing it. She has written extensively about subjects close to home, such as the demands of quotidian life, the ambiguous benefits of consumer society, and the prospects of present-day Scotland. Just as notable, though, has been the variety of settings and narrative voices in each of her four collections, which feature travelers and expatriates whose migrations or displacements lead to self-discovery or self-loss. Rose's work draws attention to many kinds of distance that exist between individuals and between classes of people, but it also intimates that understandings and alliances can and should be pursued, however arduously or tentatively, across these distances.

Dilys Lindsay Rose was born on 7 February 1954 in Glasgow, where she grew up with her younger brother, Charles. Her father, Lindsay, was an art teacher and sculptor; her mother, Valentine, was a primary-school teacher and piano teacher. The family also included a widowed grandmother, whom Rose describes as its generous-spirited mainstay. "I started writing when I was sixteen," she told Wilson in the 1990 interview. "Then I came to university, studied English and lost all interest in writing. All we were doing was critical work.... So I suppose I didn't start writing seriously until about 1980." Rose graduated from Edinburgh University in 1974. She then traveled on several continents, supporting herself with temporary jobs, which ranged from working on a trawler to serving in cafes. She then settled in Edinburgh with another writer, Brian McCabe, and during the 1980s her poems and stories appeared in various, mostly Scottish, periodicals and anthologies. She and McCabe started a family with a daughter, Sophie, born in 1986 and another, Cleo, in 1989, the year in which Rose published both a volume of poetry, *Madame Doubtfire's Dilemma,* and her first collection of stories, *Our Lady of the Pickpockets.*

In *A History of Scottish Women's Writing* (1997), Douglas Gifford observes that the two collections share "strong ... imagery" and "wry, self-mocking feminism," and other critics have linked the economy and subtlety of Rose's fiction to her experience as a poet. The poems in *Madame Doubtfire's Dilemma* are brief. Some, such as "4 North American Totems," are built from what appear to be found fragments (place-names, road signs, advertisements) from Rose's travels. Others convey snapshot-like impressions of a specific scene; still others, though, have a strong narrative component. The title poem, one of several dramatic monologues in the book, voices the predicament of an antiques dealer who realizes that the untidiness of her shop is irritating a potential customer yet insists that it is small details—"the dust / Of decades dealing rag and bone"—and not the actual objects she sells that convey the authenticity of the past.

The twenty-three stories in *Our Lady of the Pickpockets* also demonstrate Rose's conciseness: the longest of them, "Before Oscar," is a twelve-page look at the fraught vacation of a couple made nostalgic for their younger selves by the trials of parenting. Tania Glyde, in *TLS: The Times Literary Supplement* (1 December 1989), began her detailed review with an observation that has become perhaps the most often recycled critical statement about Rose, quoted on the jackets of paperback editions of each of her first four books of fiction: "Dilys Rose can be compared to Katherine Mansfield in the way she takes hold of a life and exposes all of its vital elements in a few pages." Glyde also praised the variety of voices in the volume. The title story is told by an itinerant Mexican boy who dreams of being adopted by American tourists but must settle for pilfering from them; the piece shows the gulf in attitudes and aspirations between the privileged and the impoverished, a recurring theme for Rose. "Maya," the second story, uses the second-person *you* to implicate the reader in an account of transient relationships—and their unforeseen consequences—among self-absorbed European travelers in Latin America. The United States, too, provides an arena for the dramatization of cultural, gender, and class differences. "I Can Sing, Dance, Rollerskate" and "Landa Opportunity" both depict the indignities of temporary restaurant work, the former through the interior monologue of a woman searching for a job as a waitress in order to finance an abortion, the latter through the patter of a cook attempting to seduce a new waitress. "Little Black Lies" deals movingly with the life of a gay African American dancer who enters into a marriage of convenience with a British woman. "New York" uses Rose's skill with shifts of tone to describe a young Scottish woman's first day in the city, where an elderly local couple "find her terror of the streets just real cute" and are charmed by her accent—as, less innocuously, is a barman who becomes "forcefully friendly."

Ruth Pavey, in the *New Statesman and Society* (1 December 1989), sensed in the stories "a strong Scots flavour, even though they are far-flung." The collection finds breadth even in Scottish themes and places. In "Drifter," a young woman, "Fiona Fell of Maryhill, Glasgow," emulates earlier Scots in immigrating to the new world. Yet, having apparently arrived in a land of opportunity in western Canada, she finds it almost as disorienting as other Rose characters do less-fortunate places: "part of her couldn't quite acclimatise to the abundance of everything.... A hard dark seam ran through her." Among stories that take place in Scotland itself, "Snakes and Ladders" and "The New Café," set respectively on a decaying public housing estate and in a coffee shop colonized by a homeless woman, give mordantly comic accounts of intractable class differences, while "Repeat Please" voices the struggles with language and loneliness of a South Asian immigrant to the country. Counter-

Front cover for the 1994 paperback edition of Rose's first short-story collection, originally published in 1989 (Bruccoli Clark Layman Archives)

pointing the accounts of expatriate Scots, this piece demonstrates how the implicit relations among Rose's stories—which work across as well as within her collections—help to compensate for their brevity.

Another of the Scottish stories, "Child's Play," in which a young girl tells her doll about what turns out to have been a disastrous day at school, modulates from the whimsical through the satirical into the horrific as it reveals the accidental death of one of the girl's playmates in a game gone wrong and exposes the coldly class-conscious parenting that is shaping the girl's own life. While Gifford finds the story conventional and even derivative in its strong plotting, Glyde praised its avoidance of crude manipulation of the reader. Glyde suggested at the end of her review that "Rose could afford to harangue us more, to throw a few personal beliefs into what is already an intensely seen world."

Rose's personal circumstances continued to influence her work: "At the moment I'm so interested in fiction that poetry seems a little removed from me," she told Wilson in the 1990 interview, adding that her parental obligations were interfering with the concentration required for poetry. Her production of stories continued, and her second collection, *Red Tides,* was published in 1993. The book received a brief and hostile notice from Laurence O'Toole in the *New Statesman and Society* (6 August 1993) that inadvertently illuminated some of Rose's methods. "Rather than tell of things tumultuous and lyrical, she tells of all things small and grey. A stressed mother oversleeps, a singer with a sore throat buys a Fisherman's Friend!" O'Toole added that "There's no drama, nothing happens." This last remark is factually misleading. The opening story, "This Is Tomorrow," which features the stressed mother to whom O'Toole refers, describes the character's morning routine with a baby and a three-year-old: "She lifted the milk pan off the heat, stirred in the oats, turned down the gas, filled a beaker of juice for her daughter and gave her a book to look at while the porridge cooked, while she got the baby up, washed and dried its hot pink bottom, changed the nappy and dressed her in fresh clothes. . . ." The sentence continues, and its extravagant length and rhythmic vigor make it a happening in itself. The story goes on to outline the mother's fatigue-hampered efforts to find time for an extradomestic life. Tabitha Potts, in *TLS* (22 October 1993), praised Rose's attention to the everyday, suggesting that "the compression of her style is such that the reader rarely feels bogged down by too much detail."

Stories about the inevitable challenges of domesticity are prominent among the twenty-one pieces in *Red Tides*. The longest of these, "The Worst of It," describes a free-spirited American trawler captain and his increasingly disenchanted wife. It ends uncertainly with the man confronting danger at sea, and the final sentence has the kind of pointed open-endedness that frustrates some of Rose's critics but intrigues others: "in his mind is fog and deep water and there's no way of telling." "All the Little Loved Ones" (included in Peter Kravitz's 1997 *Picador Book of Contemporary Scottish Fiction*) is another story less about events than possibilities. A restless young mother finds herself tempted to become involved with a play-park acquaintance ("Pushing a swing, watching a little one arcing away and rushing back to your hands, it's natural to talk to another parent") and irresolutely contemplates the disaster that could ensue for both families. "Over Her Head," next in the volume, is told from the point of view of a grandmother who, weary of stresses imposed both by her family and by the therapy group she has joined in an effort to cope with her feelings, retreats to her cellar to eat sweets. "Jumping into Bed with Luis Fortuna" presents a more hopeful form of escapism, as a woman who has "got herself anchored:

house, job, man, kids" compensates by becoming infatuated with the romantic image of a popular novelist, then finds the unexpected results of the infatuation renewing her interest in her husband.

"The Fence" moves from a domestic scenario toward more-public matters. Two middle-class families on a country walk are led by their six-year-old daughters into a verbal class war with the family of the local aristocrat, Major Cunningham. The middle-class daughters are instantly antagonistic toward the Major's twin granddaughters, and the children's frank exchange of views ("If you kick us we'll CUT OFF YOUR FEET") at the gates of the Cunningham home elicits a more discreet but equally revealing comment from the landowner: "Vicious little monsters aren't they? Terribly nice to see you all." Beneath this dialogue the story hints at the survival of a seam of real territorial and political antagonism in Scotland. Social divisions are addressed from a variety of angles in other pieces. Critic Alison Lumsden, in a 2000 essay titled "Scottish Women's Short Stories," notes the acute sociogeographical commentary of "Street of the Three Terraces," in which "the trendy, yuppyish aspects of the reconstructed Leith and Scotland in general are set against the 'poof bashing' near Calton Hill." Potts praised Rose for her attention to "the way in which gender, race and class affect communication," singling out "Friendly Voices" for its juxtaposition of the interior monologues of a troubled housing-estate resident and the dedicated but reserved psychologist who visits to assess him. The man diagnoses the psychologist's loneliness and decides that "she could really dae wi a big hug," but his offering, clumsy though sincere, does not go over well. Like the work of Irvine Welsh, though more gently, the story asserts that the grimness of public-housing schemes in Scotland does not negate the humanity of their inhabitants but cannot be easily overcome by well-intentioned outsiders.

Potts qualified her praise of *Red Tides* by remarking—in direct contrast to Glyde's comment on the previous collection—that "Sometimes Rose's writing shows the strain of her polemical intentions." For Potts, "the two weakest stories in the collection" are "Hormones," which draws an insistent (though not utterly implausible) parallel between children and academics, and "Human Interest," in which an idealistic young photojournalist and her cynical colleagues encounter war-starved villagers with whom they decide they cannot share their food.

Noteworthy as a counterweight to such assertive stories, though, is "Glancing." A pensive Edinburgh woman waiting to meet city acquaintances in a pub on "an island off the scrag end of the country" is drawn reluctantly into a game of pool with a local man. While his interest in her is partly sexual, his behavior is respectful, and she leaves the pub refreshed by the game. The single-word title of the story epitomizes Rose's verbal economy: it describes both the visual activity that brings the two people into contact and the nature of that contact; it alludes to the physical principles of the game they play; and it names Rose's preferred method of evoking large and complex subjects.

Gifford notes the similar multivalence of the title *Red Tides* itself and discusses the story that provides the title (and concludes the volume) as a particularly fine example of "Rose's skilful circling around her stories' subjects." On a literal level the "red tides" are caused by algae, and the subjects are three resort-town waitresses who share beach space and casual sexual confessions. Gifford, however, finds "in this story of sea, and sand and boredom" a warning suggestion "that the red tides are moving, inexorably, towards storm—or the weathering down of change, age, and death." Gifford sees the tidal metaphor as covering the volume as a whole: "the overall impression is of ebbing and flowing, bleeding and enduring."

While writing, publishing, and parenting, Rose has also served as writing consultant or writer-in-residence at universities and public libraries in central Scotland and has edited four anthologies of her library students' fiction and poetry. Introducing one of these, *Hand Clap and Toe Tap: New Writing from Midlothian* (1996), she notes its "refreshing diversity of material," and many of its selections exhibit the kind of compression and deft understatement that characterize her own writing. *War Dolls*, her third collection, published in 1998, continues to display these qualities, though its stories tend to be slightly longer and sometimes larger-scaled than her previous work.

The title story updates its counterpart from *Our Lady of the Pickpockets*. The Mexican boy from the earlier story returns as an adult and an armed rebel. The narrative is presented as his monologue to an American documentary maker, in which he alternately lectures on the superficiality of first-world perspectives, reflects on the stages of his life, and menaces the mute visitor. The "war dolls," he explains, are crafted by the abandoned wife of the mysterious leader of the rebel group; "sometimes now," he muses, "I think Emilia's dolls is better than Angél's revolution." Yet, he also wonders, "If no war, what will Emilia sell?" The story leaves the situation, and the fate of the American visitor, unresolved. "Flowers of the Moon," again about a northerner encountering danger in the south, is, at slightly less than thirty pages, the longest of Rose's stories. Kay, a Scottish woman in early middle age, visits an old friend, Alison, long resident in Brazil. Kay meets both Alison's friendly sister-in-law, a member of a newly elected reformist administration, and an urbanely sinister member of the corrupt elite responsible for the social inequalities of the nation. Yet, the story

Front cover for Rose's 1993 collection of minutely observed stories about the challenges of domestic life (Thomas Cooper Library, University of South Carolina)

avoids creating an impression of one-sided judgment of social problems in Brazil by indicating that Alison is thriving in the country despite its problems.

TLS reviewer Margot Livesey (21 August 1998) found *War Dolls* "wonderfully far-ranging" yet "profoundly Scottish" and praised its attention to "those rare moments of sympathy that pass between individuals" even in unpromising circumstances. Livesey cited "Handholds" for its "sideways glimpses" into the life of a deaf girl and "The Four O'Clock Lady," in which a transsexual gains the sympathy of the woman he visits each week for laser hair removal. Livesey also remarked, however, that "Rose's method of revealing rather than explaining does at times lead to frustration" and passages of obscurity. A case in point might be "After the Gun," in which a man disfigured in a suicide attempt is drawn into conversation by an abrasively curious woman and thinks back to the moment before he shot himself: "he'd felt unaccountably happy, the way he does now. But it's different now. He's different now." Ending the story, these lines leave the nature of the difference to be at best guessed at. Other ambiguous endings, though, are effective. In "Beyond Vigilance" a Scottish couple on holiday in Spain grow anxious over the flirtatious friendship between their preadolescent daughter, Susie, and an older local man. At the end, having reluctantly allowed her to walk with him around the swimming pool at the hotel, they watch "Susie and the man in silhouette, hand in hand, edging along the high narrow wall." The man's intentions are probably chivalrous, but for the parents he augurs the inevitable limitations on their capacity to protect their child. A second story about a family vacation, "Verge," has an equally memorable final line. When his car breaks down some distance from the Devon cottage where he is staying with his wife and various members of his extended family, a middle-aged man is forced to hike perilously home with only a bottle of sherry for refreshment and has a belated and bedraggled reunion with his resentful wife and adoring granddaughter. "When he reaches the patio, he raises the empty bottle in greeting. It is the wrong gesture." Whether the wrongness is more tragic or comic is left to the reader's speculation.

Rose's willingness to imagine the concerns and ordeals of men as well as women strengthens rather than undermines her feminism, indicating that it provides not an ideological program but a confident basis for wide-ranging sympathies. In "Princess," Robert, a photographer struggling with his estranged wife over custody of their daughter, finds himself anxiously monitoring both his photographic and his physical interaction with the child: "could every gesture of affection between himself and his daughter now come under scrutiny . . . ?" Alongside its wry observations on his parenting tactics ("Roller skates and ice cream at the same time, he realised too late, were not a good idea"), the story also makes clear the depth of his need for his daughter's love. The final story in *War Dolls,* "Why Do the Hands Not Weep?," revisits the scenario of "Glancing": a lone woman in a remote pub is approached by a man. What he wants, however, is not sexual attention so much as sympathy for the recent accidental death of his son. Lumsden praises the piece for "reminding us that in Rose's stories things are not always what they seem and [that] Scotland, and what it is made of, cannot always be delimited by simple binary oppositions of gender and culture."

Pest Maiden (1999), Rose's first novel, offers further proof both of her ability to write convincingly about male protagonists and of her interest in the complexity of contemporary Scotland. It examines an ordinary Edinburgh man, Russell Fairley, whose upwardly mobile girlfriend, Arlene, abandons him in favor of a successful novelist, just as mysteriously multiplying problems hit the blood-processing plant where he works as a technician. The book meditates on the many metaphorical implications of blood and of its title: the latter alludes both to the troublesome Arlene and to the ancient plague-bringing figure that may be responsible for literal kinds of bad blood (and may even inhabit the cellar that houses the trendy restaurant Arlene runs). The book also has broader elements of comedy and satire, and reviewers disagreed on the relative merits of its components. Candia McWilliam, in the *Literary Review* (July 1999), relished Russell's campaign for vengeance against the novelist, whom he believes not only to have cuckolded him but also to have based a novel (titled *Eating Passion Fruit in Bed*) on the process. Praising the "tart look at the bogosities of writers" in the book, McWilliam suggested that Rose "is not—as she might prefer to be—a little-known Caledonian blossom but a commercial novelist at heart." McWilliam concluded that "The book is at its artistic best in passages of observation and listing that are the signs of a good poet." Margaret Walters, in the *TLS* (13 August 1999), also noted approvingly the attention to detail in the book and its poetic use of language but found the literary subplot tiresome and the blood imagery overdone. Walters dismissed the character who becomes perhaps the key figure in the second part of the novel, Muriel Gulf, a talkative, opinionated coworker of Russell's (another "pest maiden," in a way) who slyly seduces him. "Muriel," wrote Walters, "is half Filipina and half Scots, mainly, it seems, so that she can remark that 'mixed blood is nothing to do with who or what I am.'" Yet, at the end of the book, Muriel and Russell are journeying to investigate the Scottish side of her heritage; as a displaced person ambivalent about her own past and about national identities generally, Muriel both links the novel to Rose's earlier, briefer explorations of migration and extends her examination of the evolution of Scottishness.

Pest Maiden was nominated for the International IMPAC Dublin Literary Award in 2001, and it is one measure of Rose's growing reputation (at least in Europe) that the nomination came from the City Public Library of St. Petersburg, Russia. The scope of Rose's work has also grown. In 1997 she published *When I Wear My Leopard Hat: Poems for Young Children,* and in 1999 the Stellar Quines Theatre Company of Edinburgh produced her play *Learning the Paso Doble. Lure,* another collection of poetry, was published in 2003.

At the same time, she has published short fiction that takes up the use of the macabre in *Pest Maiden* to comment obliquely on the contemporary state of Scotland (and, by extension, of other relatively privileged, developed places). "Out of Touch: An Extract from a Work in Progress," which won a 1999 Canongate Prize for New Writing and was published in *The Canongate Prize for New Writing: Scotland into the New Era* (2000), presents a skeptical look at the "revived, renovated nation" that Scotland has become. The speaker, a scholar who has migrated to Scotland from an unnamed (but possibly Eastern European) country that seems to have undergone similar changes, moves from mild-toned commentary on the absurdities of packaged heritage to more-ominous reflections on the wolves, both literal and metaphorical, that lurk in the pasts of both nations. Like *Pest Maiden,* the piece speaks memorably of the survival of ancient dangers in the glossy present. In 2005 Luath Press of Edinburgh published Rose's fourth book of short fiction, *Lord of Illusions, and Other Stories,* along with *Selected Stories,* which was compiled from her three previous collections. Alfred Hickling, in *The Guardian* (26 March 2005), praised the "impressive range" of characters, settings, and themes in *Lord of Illusions, and Other Stories,* as well as Rose's knack for "swiftly establishing a mood." On the other hand, Hickling, mentioning that the short stories in the volume "are interspersed with even shorter character sketches," borrowed the title of one of the latter, "Bitsy," to suggest that the book as a whole is frustratingly fragmentary in its effects. As with other collections, however, the elliptical qualities of Rose's work also elicited critical praise: for Colin Waters in the *Glasgow Sunday Herald* (13 March 2005), "The terseness and apparent openness of these tiny portraits disguise a compositional skill that can only be cracked open after several reads." These "portraits" originated in Rose's collaboration with the Scottish artist Moyna Flannigan, whose miniature paintings of fictional people they were written to accompany. In the acknowledgements for *Lord of Illusions, and Other Stories,* Rose cites Flannigan's "visual inspiration" for several of the longer stories in the collection, including the title piece, which makes startling use of horse-racing imagery in its account of a jockey's uncertain pursuit of a former lover; "See You in Shangri-La," the monologue of a dying magician who confesses to his wife the trick that brought them together; and "I'm a Stranger Here Myself," another monologue, in which a Scottish visitor to an American "gambling haven in the desert" is moved by the strange luxury of his temporary environment to come out of the closet to a new acquaintance, whose uncertain identity (dancer or prostitute? transsexual or transvestite?) lends the piece the sort of ambiguity that appeals to some of Rose's critics while irritating others. Visual art in various forms also figures in other stories in the collection. "Salvage" charts the adventures of an abandoned painting; "Camille" is the narrative of a museum-employed misogynist who contrasts the supposed shortcomings of real women with the cool perfection of the Auguste Rodin sculpture he guards. In a rather different vein, "Pornographers at

Front cover for Rose's 1998 story collection. The title story is a sequel to the title story of Our Lady of the Pickpockets *(Thomas Cooper Library, University of South Carolina).*

Lunch" playfully juxtaposes erotic or pseudo-erotic dimensions of advertising and of gastronomy.

Waters detected a "refusal to name settings" directly in much of *Lord of Illusions, and Other Stories,* and suggested that this lack of specificity "is a way of avoiding the time-swallowing necessity of research." "Pornographers at Lunch," however, is set specifically in Barcelona, and other stories, like precursors in Rose's earlier collections, are grounded in particular places and times. "A Beautiful Restoration" finds a maid in a Polish hotel comparing the history-battered condition of her city to the "neglected architecture" of her own body and dreaming of the post-totalitarian restorations that independence and international influences may, or may not, bring. "Fern Heaven," located recognizably in a North American West Coast community affected by contemporary economic uncertainty, moves between the local and the mythic in its depiction of the domestic tensions of an underemployed couple, Sam and Lilah, who plan to use the Internet to generate and to sell stories "on the theme of betrayal" and choose, perhaps ominously, to name their Web site after their Old Testament near-namesakes. Illusory, temporary, or threatened paradises recur in the volume as a whole, as do contrasts between the promises of contemporary consumerism and the strictures imposed by intractable older realities.

Several stories in the volume take up Rose's interest in the development and redevelopment of contemporary Scotland. "Mazzard's Coop," also included in the anthology *Damage Land: New Scottish Gothic Fiction* (2001), deals with pagan magic at work in a decayed mining community soon to be replaced by "clusters of commuter homes in quaintly named cul-de-sacs"; Waters praised the "stanzalike paragraphs" of the story, "in which [Rose] unpacks her cultivated, rhythmic imagery." "The Multicultural Fashion Show," like several of Rose's earlier works, registers the demographic evolution of Scotland. Quietly, but firmly, it shows South Asian culture as an integral part of the nation. Old friends Elsie and Rawinda, "two small women in a growing world," go with their husbands, Johnny and Jamal, to watch their grandchildren in a fashion show. After a bomb threat, which "specially trained experts" investigate and identify as a hoax, the show goes ahead, and the friends endure it tensely, "in the hope that, if everyone is not blown to kingdom come," they will be able to enjoy "a jubilant dinner at the Taj." This story illustrates Rose's ability to use the present tense resonantly to dramatize contemporary uncertainties.

In the 1990 interview with Wilson, Dilys Rose remarked that she "would like Scotland to be a little more international." Both through the themes and through the reception of her work, she is contributing to this goal.

Interview:

Rebecca E. Wilson, "Dilys Rose," in *Sleeping with Monsters: Conversations with Scottish and Irish Women Poets,* edited by Wilson and Gillean Somerville-Arjat (Edinburgh: Polygon, 1990), pp. 208–215.

References:

Douglas Gifford, "Contemporary Fiction II," in *A History of Scottish Women's Writing,* edited by Gifford and Dorothy McMillan (Edinburgh: Edinburgh University Press, 1997);

Alison Lumsden, "Scottish Women's Short Stories: 'Repositories of Life Swiftly Apprehended,'" in *Contemporary Scottish Women Writers,* edited by Lumsden and Aileen Christianson (Edinburgh: Edinburgh University Press, 2000), pp. 156–169.

Clive Sinclair
(19 February 1948 –)

Cheryl Alexander Malcolm
University of Gdańsk

BOOKS: *Bibliosexuality* (London: Allison & Busby, 1973);

Hearts of Gold (London: Allison & Busby, 1979; New York: Schocken, 1982);

Bedbugs (London: Allison & Busby, 1982; Syracuse, N.Y.: Syracuse University Press, 2005);

The Brothers Singer (London: Allison & Busby, 1983; New York: Schocken, 1983);

Blood Libels (London: Allison & Busby, 1985; New York: Farrar, Straus & Giroux, 1986);

Diaspora Blues: A View of Israel (London: Heinemann, 1987);

Cosmetic Effects (London: Deutsch, 1989; New York: Viking, 1990);

For Good or Evil: Collected Stories (London: Penguin, 1991);

Augustus Rex (London: Deutsch, 1992; New York: Penguin, 1993);

The Lady with the Laptop and Other Stories (London: Picador, 1996);

Kidneys in the Mind: A Lecture (London: British Library, Centre for the Book, 1996);

A Soap Opera from Hell: Essays on the Facts of Life and the Facts of Death (London: Picador, 1998);

Meet the Wife (London: Picador, 2002).

OTHER: Esther Kreitman, *Deborah*, translated by Maurice Carr, introduction by Sinclair (London: Virago, 1983; New York: St. Martin's Press, 1983);

Isaac Bashevis Singer, *Enemies: A Love Story,* translated by Aliza Shevrin and Elizabeth Shub, introduction by Sinclair (London: Penguin, 1993);

Charles Neider, *The Grotto Berg: Two Novellas,* introduction by Sinclair (New York: Cooper Square, 2001).

The author of four collections of short stories, four novels, one biocritical study, one book of travel writing, and a collection of personal essays, Clive Sinclair is a versatile writer who is as comfortable writing

Clive Sinclair (photograph © Jerry Bauer; from the dust jacket for Cosmetic Effects, *1990; Richland County Public Library)*

in various genres as he is living in St. Albans, England, or Santa Cruz, California. Called "a cosmopolite" by Dennis Drabelle in the *Washington Post* (13 November 1983), Sinclair explains, in an essay "B'reshit" in the journal *Judaism* (Winter 2002), "Jews are at ease in San Francisco." Jewish identity and feelings of belonging are the major concerns in Sinclair's writing, but they rarely come easily to his characters or allow them to be comfortable for long. The tension as they strive for both, like the romantic tensions between men and women in his fiction, propels his narratives into surprising plot twists. Sinclair's explorations of these tensions have earned him much critical attention, praise, and many awards. He has been translated into eight languages, and most of his books have been published in both Britain and the United States.

Clive John Sinclair was named after his maternal grandfather, who, being a Yiddish speaker, bore a passport marked "illiterate" when he immigrated to Britain from Stachev in southwestern Poland. Joshua Jacobovitch, known as "Shia" (the Yiddish diminutive of Joshua), changed his name to Charles. Clive was an approximation of his anglicized name. Sinclair's middle name, John, is for his paternal grandmother, Shaindel from Grodno, whose name became Jane in England. The family name was Smolinsky, which his father abandoned at the outset of World War II when he joined the British army. Sinclair calls his name his "disguise" or *"nom de vivre."* He writes in his *Diaspora Blues: A View of Israel* (1987) that he is "stuck as Clive Sinclair" because, unlike his grandparents, his first language was English not Yiddish. His sense of being between cultures, feeling neither fully English nor Jewish, provides, according to David Brauner in his essay "Philip Roth and Clive Sinclair: Portraits of the Artist as a Jew(ish Other)" (2001), a "friction" to his work when his "almost pristine prose rubs against stories that properly belong in another language."

Sinclair was born on 19 February 1948 in London, to David and Betty (née Jacobs) Sinclair. His father was a company director, and his mother was a homemaker. His maternal grandfather died before he was born, but he grew up hearing stories about him from his grandmother, who said that the family had owned an orchard in Poland. At home, there were photographs of his paternal great-grandfather, Israel Zelinski, who immigrated to England in 1885. His parents met in London in the 1930s. Although they sent him to a heder at the orthodox synagogue in Raleigh Close in Hendon, Sinclair writes of his parents in *Diaspora Blues*: "They knew that my bar mitzvah was an important symbolic act, but that it was the dreaded eleven plus that would determine the course of my life." Relating how one day a group of boys ambushed him and another heder boy with stones and cries of "Down with the Jews!," Sinclair expresses no bitterness but only the fun he had when he pitched stones back. Whereas the heder teachers, Mrs. Freed and Miss Star, merely bored him, this first experience of anti-Semitism fueled his pride in being Jewish. While attending Orange Hill Grammar School for Boys in Burnt Oak, a suburb of northwest London, he felt a similar lack of enthusiasm for formal lessons. As a young boy, he read issues of *Buffalo Bill Wild West Annual* and supported the Wingate soccer team, the only Jewish one in the local league. Both provided an escape from an otherwise dull childhood in 1950s London.

While a freshman at the newly opened University of East Anglia, Sinclair saw an exhibition about Masada that inspired him to go to Israel. The Six-Day War of 1967 turned him, he says, into a Zionist. In 1969, after receiving his B.A. from the University of East Anglia, he went to the United States, where he studied and taught for a year at the University of California at Santa Cruz. Soon after returning to England, he went on the trip to Israel he had originally booked but had been unable to take in 1967. His first novel, *Bibliosexuality,* about the literary and sexual preoccupations of a young man, David Drollkind, was published in London in 1973 and earned him an advance of £150 but no royalties and few reviews, in spite of its provocative cover photograph of the author seated at a desk while a naked woman stretches on a couch as if posing for a centerfold. In the same year, he met Fran Redhouse, whom he later married. From 1973 to 1976, he worked in London as a copywriter for Young and Rubicam, writing advertisements for pimple cream, toothpaste, and Heinz soup. Although good at thinking up slogans, he was let go for what he calls his "lack of faith" in the whole enterprise. On 2 November 1979 he married Redhouse, and together they visited Poland and saw his maternal grandfather's birthplace.

Sinclair's first short-story collection, *Hearts of Gold,* came out that same year and won the Somerset Maugham Award from the Society of Authors. It features stories that had appeared in a variety of journals and anthologies, ranging from *Encounter* and *Transatlantic Review* to *Penthouse* and *The Year's Best Horror Stories.* Art Seidenbaum, in the *Los Angeles Times* (24 March 1982), called *Hearts of Gold* a "collection of comedic, kinky stories," some of which are "bloody good, others merely bloody." Seidenbaum was struck by its mix of "California craziness" with Jewish mysticism.

Hearts of Gold introduces Sinclair's detective character Joshua Smolinsky, who appears in three stories in the collection. "The Luftmensch" is ostensibly about a missing-person investigation. A ghostwriter, also called Smolinsky, wants to be released from his contract to a Yiddish writer but needs to find him first. Like Philip Roth's *The Ghost Writer,* published in the same year, "The Luftmensch" investigates serious issues of American Jewish identity and survivor guilt after the Holocaust. The second detective story, "The Texas State Steak-Eating Contest," is a reworking of

William Shakespeare's *Hamlet* (circa 1600–1601) in the contemporary United States with a Texas cattle baron in place of a king and a ranch instead of a castle. Smolinsky is hired by the son of Hammond Hammerhead I to uncover whether, as he suspects, his father's death was not an accident but murder. Shakespearean allusions lend an air of comedy to an otherwise negative portrait of life in the American heartland. In "Hearts of Gold," Smolinsky goes to Las Vegas in search of a woman's daughter. On the way he encounters varieties of sexual transgression and learns that "Princess" is different from the stereotype of the JAP, or Jewish American princess, that her name suggests.

Sinclair most radically challenges stereotypes of Jews in "The Evolution of the Jews," which is narrated by a giraffe. The story takes the form of a monologue in which the giraffe relates the history of his "lost tribe." In "Wingate Football Club," Sinclair dispels the stereotype of the intellectual Jewish male who is uninterested in sports with the story of a boy's passionate support for a local Jewish team. It is both a coming-of-age story and an account of how an Anglo-Jew, subjected to anti-Semitism, develops dual loyalties to Britain and Israel. In "The Creature on My Back," the protagonist seeks help for his paranoia from a psychoanalyst, who turns out to be a concentration-camp survivor and who gives him advice in the form of Yiddish sayings and folk wisdom. Sinclair writes of neuroses in "Le Docteur Enchaîné" and of totalitarian rule in "A Moment of Happiness." With the words "Call me Schlemiel," he begins "The Promised Land" with a play on the opening words of Herman Melville's *Moby-Dick* (1851), to correlate his protagonist's sexual misadventures in Israel with Ishmael's whaling voyage. The inference is that the Anglo-Jew is both an insider and an outsider in Israel. In "Titillatio," an aging professor of philosophy with a pronounced German accent is cured of his impotence after a fistfight with an American student who flirts with his English mistress. After having sex with her, he exposes their affair in a letter to her husband and feels "a free man." The power that women wield over men is also the subject of "Among School Children" with its allusions to Vladimir Nabokov's *Lolita* (1955), and of "Tante Rouge," in which the protagonist chooses to be an erotic writer rather than the sexual plaything of two French women. In "Uncle Vlad," the first story in *Hearts of Gold,* Sinclair reworks the conventions of the vampire story into a romantic tale of continental European family life and a young man's first experience of love. Whereas in other stories in the collection sex is often seen negatively, in "Uncle Vlad" the bite on the neck that turns Madeleine into a vampire is described in terms of her and the vampire's mutual passion and pleasure.

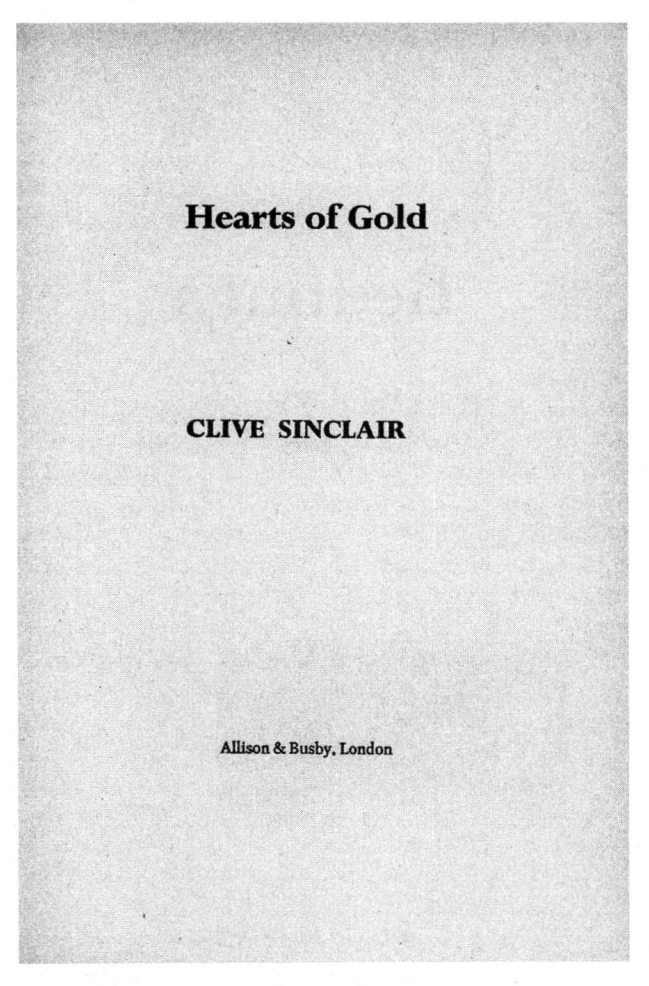

Title page for Sinclair's first collection of stories, published in 1979, in which he introduces his hard-boiled Jewish private detective, Joshua Smolinsky (Howard-Tilton Memorial Library, Tulane University)

From 1980 to 1981, Sinclair held a Bicentennial Arts fellowship from the British Council, which allowed him to travel again to the United States, where he worked as a visiting lecturer in literature at the University of California at Santa Cruz and wrote half of his next collection of short stories. During this time, his only son, Seth Benjamin, was born. In 1982 the collection, *Bedbugs,* was published. Smolinsky reappears, this time in two short stories—"The Incredible Case of the Stack o' Wheats Murders" and "Svoboda"—both featuring what Drabelle called his characteristic "Chandlerese-cum-Yiddish" speech. While the collection had a positive reception, those short stories focusing on Jews earned particular praise. Drabelle wrote that "there is an extra dimension of knowing playfulness, a sharper crackle of eroticism, when his

Title page for Sinclair's 1982 collection, which includes stories narrated by a Yiddish-speaking angel, the ghost of a Holocaust victim, and a disinterred skull (South Carolina State Library)

people are Chosen." The first short story in the collection, "Bedbugs," is an example of this quality. It is narrated by an Anglo-Jew who is asked to teach a summer course on British World War I poetry to a group of young German women. Scenes of sexual pleasure are interspersed with the narrator's thoughts of the Holocaust and his torment of being bitten each night by bedbugs. The setting of the next story, "Genesis," is California, and its first-person narrator is an angel. Although he says that angels follow no religion, his comic banter is sprinkled with Yiddish. "Tzimtzum"—narrated by a writer who, like Sinclair, is married to a teacher—is about a confrontation with neo-Nazis in Britain. "Somewhere over the Rainbow" concerns an artist and his voyeurism, which turns to love. Yet, as happens in many of Sinclair's stories, love ends violently. "America," with its anti-Semitic Polish narrator, may seem different from other stories in the collection, but Christopher is a characteristic Sinclair narrator in his preoccupation with sex and the ironic turns of life. "Tsatske," the shortest story in the collection, is narrated by a skull taken from a Warsaw cemetery to an American professor's study, where it is "married" to a shrunken head from Ecuador. The title, like the story, is full of ambiguities about the worth of artifacts and of suffering. The narrator says *tsatske* means a keepsake in Ecuador, but in Yiddish it can also mean an ineffectual or disappointing person. The title of the next story, "Kayn Aynhoreh," is a Yiddish exhortation to ward off evil. Narrated by Jonah Silkstone, the protagonist of Sinclair's novel *Cosmetic Effects* (1989), it is the most autobiographical story in the collection. "Ashkenazia" is about an imaginary country whose Yiddish-speaking inhabitants are wiped out by Adolf Hitler's "Operation Wawel." It is full of allusions to the Holocaust, and its narrator himself is one of the dead.

In 1983 Sinclair was chosen as one of the Twenty Best of Young British Novelists by the magazine *Granta*. He also received his doctorate from the University of East Anglia and published his first full-length nonfiction work, the biocritical study of Isaac Bashevis Singer and Israel Joshua Singer, *The Brothers Singer*, which also helped draw attention to the literary achievements of their sister, Esther (Singer) Kreitman. In the same year, Sinclair become literary editor for the only weekly Jewish newspaper in Britain, the *Jewish Chronicle*, a position that he held for the next four years. In 1984 he received a grant from the Arts Council in Britain that helped him to complete work on his second novel. *Blood Libels* was published in 1985 and mixes comedy and politics in its depiction of a Jewish man whose birth on the eve of the establishment of the state of modern-day Israel links his life to that of the nation. Peter Bricklebank wrote in the *Library Journal* (1 June 1986): "A victim of fate, Jake embodies the ambivalence of a Jew belonging neither to the old world nor to the new." Praised for its "good writing," the novel is seen as "sometimes stretched for wit."

In *Diaspora Blues*, Sinclair's "relation to England, his interest in Israel has provided him with a 'narrative' in which to situate himself," according to Bryan Cheyette in his essay "Philip Roth and Clive Sinclair: Representations of an 'Imaginary Homeland' in Postwar British and American-Jewish Literature" (1994). *Diaspora Blues* is a piece of travel writing but also reflects on Sinclair's family history of immigration to Britain from the Russian Pale. This search for a homeland beyond Britain is a recurring theme in Sinclair's writing, which, he told Cheyette in an interview in

1984, is an attempt "to write fiction that owes nothing to any English antecedents." Sinclair's travel writing has much in common with his short fiction, which, as Cheyette notes in his 1994 essay, continually locates his "'national' history as a Jew in Israel, America and Eastern Europe."

While a British Council guest writer-in-residence at Uppsala University in Sweden in 1988, Sinclair returned to novel writing. *Cosmetic Effects* was published in 1989 to mixed reviews. Kenneth Mintz, writing in the *Library Journal* (15 April 1990), called it "a bomb." In the novel, an Anglo-Jew bearing a close resemblance to Sinclair is turned into a human bomb when an Arab doctor fits him with a prosthetic arm containing an explosive. In 1991 Sinclair published *For Good or Evil: Collected Stories,* which includes all the stories in *Bedbugs* and *Hearts of Gold* and four additional stories. All take up themes typical of Sinclair's work. The shortest of the new stories, "The Last Jewish Joker," returns to the subject of a lost tribe that Sinclair explores in *Hearts of Gold* in "The Evolution of the Jews." Instead of a giraffe, the narrator in this story is a failed Jewish comedian whose last performance is a success when he suggests that dolphins might be the next lost tribe. He dies and is buried at sea while on a cruise to Haifa. "The Golem's Story" is narrated by a golem who foresees the Holocaust but cannot convince the rabbi who created him to flee to save his life or his daughter's. Years later, the golem tries but fails again to save a young Jewish woman, this time from Arab terrorists. The third new story, "Scriptophobia," is the first chapter of *Cosmetic Effects*. The last, "For Good or Evil," is narrated by the Tree of Knowledge in the Garden of Eden. In 1992, Sinclair published his fourth novel, *Augustus Rex*. Narrated by Beelzebub, this Faustian text brings the early-twentieth-century playwright August Strindberg back to life in the 1960s.

After his wife died in 1994, Sinclair traveled to Israel and Egypt with his son. The trip provided a form of solace and inspiration for new writing. From 1995 to 1996, he was a British Library Penguin Writer's Fellow. His third collection of short stories, *The Lady with the Laptop and Other Stories,* was published in 1996. It won the Macmillan Silver Pen Award for Fiction and was joint winner, with W. G. Sebald's *The Emigrants* (1996; originally published as *Die Ausgewanderten,* 1992), of the *Jewish Quarterly* prize for fiction in 1997. Cheyette, writing in his introduction to *Contemporary Jewish Writing in Britain and Ireland: An Anthology* (1998), calls Sinclair's return to short-story writing, a return to "his true métier."

The Lady with the Laptop and Other Stories is divided into two parts, with three short stories in each.

The first three stories, "Las Fiestas de Navidad," "The Lady with the Laptop," and "Smart-Alecks," feature Mexican, Egyptian, and Anglo-Jewish narrators. Although each has a distinctive voice, they share a feeling of moral superiority, if not outright antagonism, toward the English, which is expressed in a comic, but also at times self-deprecating, manner. Although not a continuation of "The Lady with the Laptop," "Smart-Alecks" includes some of the same characters, in particular one that closely resembles Sinclair, a man whose wife has recently died of cancer and who has a young teenager to raise on his own. The second section begins with another autobiographical story. "My CV" has an Anglo-Jewish narrator who is writing a thesis on English literature while working for an advertising agency. As his worries grow that he will lose his student grant because he is in undeclared employment, he imagines that he and his wife and child will be the victims of a modern-day pogrom. "The Iceman Cometh" and "In Praise of Impurity" have allusions to the story "Ashkenazia" from *Bedbugs*. Ashkenazia is the setting for both stories, which form one continuous narrative, although the narrator is an artist in the first story and a scientist in the second. What links the stories is the birth of a child who may or may not be the Messiah.

In 1998 Sinclair published *A Soap Opera from Hell: Essays on the Facts of Life and the Facts of Death*. Reflecting on the deaths of his parents, wife, and sister-in-law within three years of one another and his own experience of renal failure, dialysis, and a kidney transplant, its autobiographical essays address serious issues with self-effacement and comic irony. In 2002 Sinclair published *Meet the Wife*. Its two novellas, "Meet the Wife" and "The Naked and the Dead," weave classical allusions with historical fact, ranging from Homer's *Odyssey* and the legends of the Wild West to the death of Marshal Tito in the former Yugoslavia. Philip French in *The Guardian* (17 August 2002) called it "a funny, curiously touching book," and Alfred Hickling and Sarah Adams, also in *The Guardian* (23 August 2003), noted that Sinclair's "mature style shows no inclination to settle down and obey logic. His fabulous plots drift along in a dream-like trance, full of bizarre manifestations and unexpected metamorphoses." A new book, "Back in the Saddle Again," is scheduled for publication in 2006. Sinclair lives with his son in St. Albans in England.

As Brauner notes, "It has been the inevitable fate of every bright young male British Jewish novelist since the 1960s to be labeled 'the British (answer to) Philip Roth.'" Although this linkage has proved to be an epitaph for many writers, Brauner argues that Clive Sinclair has "survived the comparison." Like

Roth's work, Sinclair's irreverently comic treatment of Jewish characters and themes has drawn criticism as well as praise. Efraim Sicher, for example, in an essay in his *Beyond Marginality: Anglo-Jewish Literature after the Holocaust* (1985), calls Sinclair's writing "a rehash of *Portnoy's Complaint* in the worst taste." Nonetheless, Sinclair's comic and complex examinations of Anglo-Jewish identity, well represented by his short stories, are, according to Cheyette, important texts in late-twentieth-century British-Jewish fiction.

Interview:

Bryan Cheyette, "On the Edge of the Imagination: Interview with Clive Sinclair," *Jewish Quarterly*, 31, nos. 3–4 (1984): 26–29.

References:

David Brauner, "Philip Roth and Clive Sinclair: Portraits of the Artist as a Jew(ish Other)," in his *Post-War Jewish Fiction: Ambivalence, Self-Explanation and Transatlantic Connections* (Basingstoke, U.K. & New York: Palgrave, 2001), pp. 154–184;

Bryan Cheyette, Introduction, in *Contemporary Jewish Writing in Britain and Ireland: An Anthology,* edited by Cheyette (Lincoln: University of Nebraska, 1998), pp. xiii–lxxi;

Cheyette, "Philip Roth and Clive Sinclair: Representations of an 'Imaginary Homeland' in Postwar British and American-Jewish Literature," in *Forked Tongues?: Comparing Twentieth-Century British and American Literature,* edited by Ann Massa and Alistair Stead (London & New York: Longman, 1994), pp. 355–373;

Efraim Sicher, "The Poetry of Survival," in his *Beyond Marginality: Anglo-Jewish Literature after the Holocaust* (Albany: State University of New York Press, 1985), pp. 153–167.

Iain Crichton Smith
(Iain Mac A'Ghobhainn)
(1 January 1928 – 15 October 1998)

Fiona Wilson
Fordham University

See also the Smith entries in *DLB 40: Poets of Great Britain and Ireland Since 1960* and *DLB 139: British Short-Fiction Writers, 1945–1980*.

BOOKS: *The Long River* (Edinburgh: Macdonald, 1955);

New Poets, 1959, by Smith, Karen Gershon, and Christopher Levenson, edited by Edwin Muir (London: Eyre & Spottiswoode, 1959);

Burn is Aran, as Iain Mac A'Ghobhainn (Glasgow: Gairm, 1960);

Thistles and Roses (London: Eyre & Spottiswoode, 1961);

Deer on the High Hills (Edinburgh: Giles Gordon, 1962);

An Dubh is an Gorm, as Mac A'Ghobhainn (Aberdeen: Aberdeen University Press / Glasgow: Clo Chailleann, 1963);

Biobuill is Sanasan-Reice (Glasgow: Gairm, 1965);

The Law and the Grace (London: Eyre & Spottiswoode, 1965);

A'Chuirt, as Mac A'Ghobhainn (Glasgow: An Comunn Gaidhealach, 1966);

An Coileach, as Mac A'Ghobhainn (Glasgow: An Comunn Gaidhealach, 1966);

The Golden Lyric: An Essay on the Poetry of Hugh MacDiarmid (Preston: Akros, 1967);

At Helensburgh (Belfast: Queen's University of Belfast, 1968);

Consider the Lilies (London: Gollancz, 1968); republished as *The Alien Light* (Boston: Houghton Mifflin, 1969);

Three Regional Voices, by Smith, Michael Longley, and Barry Tebb (London: Poet & Printer, 1968);

From Bourgeois Land (London: Gollancz, 1969);

The Last Summer (London: Gollancz, 1969);

Iain am Measg nan Reultan, as Mac A'Ghobhainn (Glasgow: Gairm, 1970);

Maighstirean is Minstearan, as Mac A'Ghobhainn (Inverness: Club Leabhar, 1970);

Selected Poems (London: Gollancz, 1970);

Iain Crichton Smith (photograph by Carol Gow; from the dust jacket for Colin Nicholson, ed., Iain Crichton Smith: Critical Essays, *1992; Thomas Cooper Library, University of South Carolina)*

Survival without Error, and Other Stories (London: Gollancz, 1970);

My Last Duchess: A Novel (London: Gollancz, 1971);

Hamlet in Autumn (Loanhead: Macdonald, 1972);

Iain Crichton Smith, Norman MacCaig, George Mackay Brown, Penguin Modern Poets, no. 21 (Harmondsworth: Penguin, 1972);

Love Poems and Elegies (London: Gollancz, 1972);

An t-Adhar Ameireaganach: Is Sgeulachdan Eile, as Mac A'Ghobhainn (Inverness: Club Leabhar, 1973);

The Black and the Red, and Other Stories (London: Gollancz, 1973);

Rabhdan is Rudan, as Mac A'Ghobhainn (Glasgow: Gairm, 1973);

Eadar Fealla-dha is Glaschu: Orain Stòlda is Òrain Éibhinn, as Mac A'Ghobhainn (Glasgow: Department of Celtic, University of Glasgow, 1974);

Goodbye, Mr. Dixon (London: Gollancz, 1974);

Orpheus and Other Poems (Preston: Akros, 1974);

Poems for Donalda (Belfast: Ulsterman, 1974);

The Notebooks of Robinson Crusoe, and Other Poems (London: Gollancz, 1975);

The Permanent Island: Gaelic Poems (Loanhead: Macdonald, 1975);

An t-Aonaran, as Mac A'Ghobhainn (Glasgow: Department of Celtic, University of Glasgow, 1976);

Tormod's na Dolaichean; agus, Mairi's an t-Each Fiodh, as Mac A'Ghobhainn (Glasgow: Gairm, 1976);

The Village (Inverness: Club Leabhar, 1976);

The Hermit and Other Stories (London: Gollancz, 1977);

In the Middle (London: Gollancz, 1977);

Little Red Riding Hood; agus, An Dorus Iaruinn, as Mac A'Ghobhainn (Glasgow: Gairm, 1977);

An End to Autumn (London: Gollancz, 1978);

River, River: Poems for Children (Loanhead: Macdonald, 1978);

Na h-Ainmhidhean, as Mac A'Ghobhainn (Aberfeldy: Clo Chaillean, 1979);

On the Island (London: Gollancz, 1979);

Am Brudaraiche, as Mac A'Ghobhainn (Stornoway: Acair, 1980);

Murdo & Other Stories (London: Gollancz, 1981);

Selected Poems, 1955–1980, edited by Robin Fulton (Loanhead: Macdonald, 1981);

A Field Full of Folk: A Novel (London: Gollancz, 1982);

Na h-Eilthirich, as Mac A'Ghobhainn (Glasgow: Department of Celtic, University of Glasgow, 1983);

The Search (London: Gollancz, 1983);

The Exiles (Manchester: Carcanet / Dublin: Raven Arts Press, 1984);

Mr. Trill in Hades and Other Stories (London: Gollancz, 1984);

Selected Poems (Manchester: Carcanet, 1985);

The Tenement: A Novel (London: Gollancz, 1985);

A Life (Manchester & New York: Carcanet, 1986);

Towards the Human: Selected Essays (Edinburgh: Macdonald, 1986);

An t-Eilean agus an Cànan: Dà Ruith-Dhàn, as Mac A'Ghobhainn (Glasgow: Department of Celtic, University of Glasgow, 1987);

In the Middle of the Wood: A Novel (London: Gollancz, 1987);

George Douglas Brown's The House with the Green Shutters (Aberdeen: Association for Scottish Literary Studies, 1988);

Na Speuclairean Dubha, as Mac A'Ghobhainn (Glasgow: Gairm, 1989);

The Village and Other Poems (Manchester: Carcanet, 1989);

The Dream (London: Macmillan, 1990);

Selected Stories (Manchester: Carcanet, 1990);

Na Guthan, as Mac A'Ghobhainn (Glasgow: Gairm, 1991);

Turas Tro Shaoghal Falamh, as Mac A'Ghobhainn (Stornoway: Acair, 1991);

An Honourable Death (London: Macmillan, 1992);

Thoughts of Murdo (Nairn: Balnain, 1993);

An Rathad gu Somalia, as Mac A'Ghobhainn (Stornoway: Acair, 1994);

Ends and Beginnings (Manchester: Carcanet, 1994);

Robin Jenkins's The Cone-Gatherers (Aberdeen: Association for Scottish Literary Studies, 1995);

The Human Face (Manchester: Carcanet, 1996);

Seallaidhean Sùla, as Mac A'Ghobhainn (Stornoway: Acair, 1996);

Lazybed (Edinburgh: Traverse Theatre, 1997);

The Leaf and the Marble (Manchester: Carcanet, 1998);

Proiseact nan Ealan=The Gaelic Arts Agency, foreword by Brian Wilson (Stornoway: Gaelic Arts Agency, 1998);

A Country for Old Men; and, My Canadian Uncle (Manchester: Carcanet, 2000);

Murdo: The Life and Works, edited, with an introduction, by Stewart Conn (Edinburgh: Birlinn, 2001).

Collections: *Collected Poems* (Manchester: Carcanet, 1992);

Listen to the Voice: Selected Stories (Edinburgh: Canongate Press, 1993);

The Black Halo: The Complete English Stories, 1977–98, edited by Kevin MacNeil (Edinburgh: Birlinn, 2001);

The Red Door: The Complete English Short Stories, 1949–76, edited, with an introduction, by MacNeil (Edinburgh: Birlinn, 2001).

RECORDINGS: *Iain Crichton-Smith Reads a Selection of His Own Work,* Australian Broadcasting Corporation, 1980;

Iain Crichton Smith, read by Smith, with an interview by Michael Schmidt, Canto CPS004, 1985; rereleased as *Iain Crichton Smith: Selected Poems,* Canto, 2001.

OTHER: Duncan Ban MacIntyre, *Ben Dorain,* translated by Smith (Preston: Akros, 1969);

Sorley Maclean, *Poems to Eimhir,* translated by Smith (London: Gollancz / Newcastle upon Tyne: Northern House, 1971); republished, with origi-

nal Gaelic text, as *Eimhir* (Stornoway: Acair, 1999);
Angus Macintyre, *Angus Macintyre's Ceilidh Collection: Poems of Highland Life,* foreword by Smith (Glasgow: Famedram, 1975);
"Scottish Poetry in English," in *Scottish Writing and Writers,* edited by Norman Wilson (Edinburgh: Ramsay Head Press, 1977), pp. 29–37;
"Between Sea and Moor," in *As I Remember: Ten Scottish Authors Recall How Writing Began for Them,* edited by Maurice Lindsay (London: Hale, 1979), pp. 107–122;
Robin Jenkins, *The Cone Gatherers,* introduction by Smith (Edinburgh: P. Harris, 1980);
"MacDiarmid and Ideas, with Special Reference to 'On a Raised Beach,'" in *The Age of MacDiarmid: Essays on Hugh MacDiarmid and His Influence on Contemporary Scotland,* edited by P. H. Scott and A. C. Davis (Edinburgh: Mainstream, 1980), pp. 157–162;
"The Lyrics of Robert Burns," in *The Art of Robert Burns,* edited, with an introduction, by R. D. S. Jack and Andrew Noble (London: Vision Press / Totowa, N.J.: Barnes & Noble, 1982), pp. 22–35;
Scottish Highland Tales, edited by Smith (London: Ward Lock Educational, 1982);
"The Full Tide of Song: Poetry in Scott's Narrative Verse," in *Sir Walter Scott: The Long-Forgotten Melody,* edited by Alan Bold (Totowa, N.J.: Barnes & Noble, 1983), pp. 109–126;
Twelve More Modern Scottish Poets, edited by Smith and Charles King (London: Hodder & Stoughton, 1986);
Moments in the Glasshouse: Poetry & Prose by 5 New Scottish Writers, edited by Smith (Aberdeen: Thistle, 1987);
Scottish Short Stories 1987, introduction by Smith (London: Collins, 1987);
"Birds All Singing," in *Norman MacCaig: Critical Essays,* edited by Joy Hendry and Raymond Ross (Edinburgh: Edinburgh University Press, 1990), pp. 50–53;
A Hairst o' Words: New Writing from North-East Scotland, edited by Hellen Matthews, foreword by Smith (Aberdeen: Aberdeen University Press, 1991);
Fiona MacDonald, *Island Voices,* foreword by Smith (Edinburgh: Canongate Press, 1994);
"Structure in My Poetry," in *The Poet's Voice and Craft,* edited by C. B. McCully (Manchester: Carcanet, 1994), pp. 104–122.

SELECTED PERIODICAL PUBLICATIONS–UNCOLLECTED: "Iain Crichton Smith," *Aquarius,* no. 11 (1979): 74–77;
"A Terror and an Adventure," *Chapman,* nos. 100–101 (2002): 239–245.

Although best known as a poet, Iain Crichton Smith was also the author of a substantial body of short fiction. Smith's stories focus on the local—many of his stories are set on the Isle of Lewis, in the Outer Hebrides, where he grew up—but the concerns expressed in them are wide-ranging, including the effect of the modern world on traditional societies; the links between private repression and public cruelty; and, most consistently, the experience of the alienated individual—the hermit, misfit, or exile. Critics commonly identify Smith with the "second wave" of the Scottish literary renaissance, grouping him with such contemporaries as Edwin Morgan and Alasdair Gray. For Douglas Gifford, Smith's concern with moral and religious issues in Scotland connects him to prose writers such as Elspeth Davie, Muriel Spark, and Robin Jenkins. Maurice Lindsay, in contrast, pairs Smith with another northern writer of poetry and fiction, George Mackay Brown. What is indisputable is that many of Smith's English-language works were first developed in Gaelic, an aspect of his writing that also places it in relation to significant twentieth-century Gaelic literature.

Iain Crichton Smith was born to Highland parents, John Smith and Christina Campbell Smith, in Glasgow on 1 January 1928. Two years after his birth, the family returned to the Isle of Lewis, where John Smith soon died of tuberculosis. Iain and his two brothers were brought up by their devoutly Free Church Presbyterian mother in the crofter township of Bayble, an entirely Gaelic-speaking community. "English," Edwin Morgan points out in his memorial to the author in *ScotLit* (2000), "was his second language, first learned at school." Smith was a sickly child, plagued by bronchitis and asthma; his mother feared that he might contract the illness that had killed his father. Reading became his refuge, and English-language publications (which far outnumbered those in Gaelic) offered access to a variety of literature, from Percy Bysshe Shelley and John Keats to the detective stories in *Black Mask, The Phantom Detective,* and *The Spider* magazines. When he was eleven, World War II broke out. The war, Smith recalls in "Between Sea and Moor" (1979), seemed a distant event, relayed by radio. It did not occur to him immediately "that it would send out long searching tentacles from vast unimaginable distances to pick off one by one a number of the older boys of the village who drowned in oceans which they had never seen before except on a dusty globe in the village schoolroom." The outside world, he learned, might be far removed from the Isle of Lewis, but it was not without effect.

Dust jacket for Smith's third short-story collection, published in 1977, which explores paranoia, repression, and possessiveness in contemporary Scottish society (G. Ross Roy Collection of Scottish Literature, Thomas Cooper Library, University of South Carolina)

By his own account, Smith experienced island life as generally philistine, or, as he describes it in his verse autobiography, *A Life* (1986), "life without art—the minimum." Throughout his life he retained deeply ambivalent feelings about the Hebrides. In his works this ambivalence can appear as either a stultifying divisiveness or a fruitful tension. "When I think about Lewis now," Smith remarked in a 1979 interview, "when I try to feel it again in my bones and my flesh, what returns to me? The moor and the sea." This division between the rooted place of origin (moor) and the unfamiliar and undefined (sea) describes a crucial dynamic in his stories and poems. Together, moor and sea create the island, the "complex thing" at the heart of *A Life*, as it is at the heart of all of Smith's writing. Being an islander was for him the condition not only of the "Lewisman" but also of the artist, the Scot, and the human being. Place, Smith maintains, gives one a sense of identity.

The island offers itself as an orienting landmark, but it can also represent the refusal of difference, a crippling insistence on an isolation characterized by pride, selfishness, and paranoia.

Smith left Lewis for the first time when he attended the University of Aberdeen from 1945 to 1949, earning with honors a master's degree in English literature. The sudden immersion in modern, urban life in Aberdeen was at once thrilling and alienating. Smith later recalled his shock at the sight of a beggar in the street and his distressing sense of dislocation from Gaelic culture. Aberdeen, however, also expanded his intellectual horizons, and he began to write there. Smith was soon made aware that urban freedom is conditional; completion of his degree in 1949 marked the beginning of two years of compulsory military service as a sergeant in the Education Corps of the British army. The experience left him with a profound sense of the psychological violence inherent in all forms of group discipline. From 1950 to 1955 he worked as a schoolteacher in Clydebank and Dumbarton. In the posthumously published "A Terror and an Adventure" (2002) Smith describes this phase as one of confused longing and dislocation:

> Among the council houses of Dumbarton I was crying to the people I thought of as my ancestors, searching among mythology too for subject matter since I found Glasgow and Dumbarton opaque and poetically unmanageable. I could hardly bear the sheer ugliness of the area, and what appeared by that very ugliness to be a contempt for beauty. . . . I remember always running away from the ugliness to Helensburgh and the Lomond area: I was I think, thirsting for water and the sea.

In 1955 Smith returned to the Highlands to teach in Oban High School, a move that he came to see as important for him in a creative sense. His writing, he felt, "began to gain depth and lock itself to a certain extent with the real world." He remained in Oban for more than twenty years, and during this period he began to come to public attention, initially as a poet and then as a fiction writer. Although Smith had published several short works in Gaelic as Iain Mac A'Ghobhainn, his first volume of stories in English, *Survival without Error, and Other Stories,* did not come out until 1970. With their feeling for the vulnerable and ordinary, especially for the situation of the isolated individual, the stories in the collection explore situations and themes that appear over and over in Smith's later writing. The characters in the stories are haunted by an existential loneliness and by the suspicion that love is unlikely, cruelty routine, and alienation perhaps inevitable. Isolation can provoke a thrilling but deceptive sense of power in

Smith's characters. Just as often, however, it fosters a kind of helpless sorrow. The task, as one character says, is how to "learn to be alone." Most of the characters in these stories fail in this project, although sometimes an evanescent moment of bonding suggests possible redemption. In "Joseph," based on the biblical story of Joseph and his coat of many colors, isolation is the natural state of the artist, whose self-expression comes at the price of betraying the group, whether construed as family, society, or nation.

In "Close of Play" a schoolboy gambles his future on the outcome of a cricket match—an act that feels to him like freedom but that, seen more accurately, is full of despair. In "The Exiles," originally published in Gaelic as "An Duine Dubh," an elderly Highland woman, lonely, afraid, and living in public housing in the Lowlands, connects with a Pakistani traveling salesman. In "The Ships," Harry, a retired seaman in a dreary coastal town, nourishes himself on pathetically manufactured relationships and on his memories of World War II. He makes prank phone calls, attaches himself to complete strangers, and pretends to talk to his disappointed wife.

In "Je t'aime" language itself is the focus. An eleven-year-old schoolgirl's introduction to French sparks a vicious argument between her brutal father and her exhausted, battered mother. For the mother the study of a foreign language represents a possible escape route for the daughter: French, she says, will be "useful" and lead to "opportunities." For the father the issue is clear. Grace, he insists, should stick to Gaelic, "the language of her forefathers." "What does she want with French? She should stand up for Scotland." On one level, the argument is again about the "island" and the fear prompted by the least threat to control of local identity. As the story develops, however, it becomes apparent that, in different ways, both husband and wife are wounded by their ignorance of a language that would allow them to say "Je t'aime" (I love you). Beaten into subservience, the wife can conceive of language and of grace (a key word in Smith's early works, elsewhere associated with inspiration) only in a purely material way. The husband, in contrast, finds that the words force the memory of a miserable encounter, during military service, with a French prostitute, whose whispered "Je t'aime" after sex was clearly meant for someone else. Without release into language, this bruising narrative shows, such scenes of human desolation must be repeated over and over in the most cruel and intimate violence.

The ties between personal feeling and public behavior and between the individual and society that are presented in stories such as "The Ships" and "Je t'aime" are more explicitly depicted in other stories in *Survival without Error*. In "The Black and the White," for example, two old women in the Highlands externalize their inner hatred of each other through racist comments about the new black minister. "Home" complicates the picture of exile given in "Joseph." Whereas the latter story essentially justifies the exile's withdrawal of national loyalty, "Home" considers the ironic escape of two Scottish emigrants now most "at home" among the elite rulers of a British colony in Africa. In this case, the freedom of emigration becomes an opportunity to oppress others. Inner repression, especially sexual repression, is the key also to "Sweets to the Sweets" and "Murder without Pain." Both stories have a narrator who demonstrates how a hubristic sense of social superiority can be used to justify crime. In Smith's moral universe the freedom of the alienated individual does not come without responsibility. Characters in his stories who ignore this truth tend either to condone oppression or to become oppressors themselves.

The process by which individuals come to collaborate with oppression is the subject of the story most directly drawn from Smith's own experience, the title story, "Survival without Error." The narrator is a Scottish solicitor, or lawyer, assigned to defend two village louts accused of beating a drunk. The details of the case bring back memories of his experiences in the army as a national-service conscript. The main concern of the recruits was to avoid being singled out. Everyone was relieved when a scapegoat, Lecky, was selected to bear the corporal's rage, as well as the unacknowledged sadism of the soldiers as a group. Lecky's "crimes"—failing to keep step while marching and not polishing his boots properly—earned him additional punishments. Gradually, the soldiers began to collaborate in Lecky's mistreatment by ignoring and further isolating him. Indeed, the solicitor recalls his own intense pleasure in surrendering his individual identity to the group. This account of the seductiveness of fascism ends with the information that the plumber's mate subsequently committed suicide (an event based on an actual occurrence during Smith's own term of national service). The final pages of the story make clear that, although the solicitor recalls his army years in great detail, he does not recognize the real connections between past and present—between his collaboration in Lecky's victimization and his current unwillingness to confront his own role in the social forces that lead to bullying and violence.

The focus on power and helplessness seen in *Survival without Error* is also evident in Smith's next story collection, *The Black and the Red, and Other Stories* (1973), the title of which refers to his vision of human identity as riven by necessary, competing drives toward discipline (the "black") and freedom (the "red"). As in

Dust jacket for Smith's 1981 collection of brief stories about an eccentric character named Murdo, who pontificates on a variety of topics (G. Ross Roy Collection of Scottish Literature, Thomas Cooper Library, University of South Carolina)

Smith's previous works, these questions focus on the ambiguous situation of the exile or outsider. "An American Sky" explores the conflicting swirl of feelings—love, guilt, hatred, and longing—that can characterize the emigrant's ties to his or her native land. After his wife's death and his retirement as a newspaper editor, John Macleod decides to start life over with a trip to the Hebridean island of his birth, but his search for an innocent, unchanging Eden—a version of the past to which he can anchor the present—is frustrated at every turn. When he visits his old schoolteacher and confesses his betrayal of a friend during the Joseph McCarthy hearings, it becomes apparent that what he really seeks from the island is something it cannot give: absolution. Ultimately, Macleod, the new American, is forced to acknowledge the costs of his lack of attachment to the past.

Exile in another sense is the subject of the opening story in *The Black and the Red*, "The Dying," which describes in vivid detail the death of the narrator's mother: "So strange was it, so irretrievable, that he was shaken as if by an earthquake of pathos and pity." Exile is also the subject of "The Wedding," a story about the dislocating effects of what Smith sees as the decline of Gaelic culture. Young guests at a wedding in Glasgow mock the Hebrides and celebrate their escape from the parochial narrowness of the islands. Gaelic is avoided and only English spoken; when the father of the bride makes a fumbling, honest speech lamenting the passing of tradition, his words humiliate his daughter, "as if her wedding dress had been turned into a shroud." Once the talking and dancing is done, however, the guests become nostalgic for the songs of their childhood, and only the despised old man can provide what they want.

Just as "An American Sky," "The Dying," and "The Wedding" refer to autobiographical experience (the line "When did you get here?" in the first story is a motif in *A Life*), the title story, "The Black and the Red," appears to draw on aspects of Smith's university years. The story is narrated through letters that the protagonist sends to his mother. Kenneth comes to study in a city much like Aberdeen, armed with his best suit, a copy of Homer's works, and the tight, Free Church Presbyterian morality of his unyielding mother. He develops a friendship with George, a fellow boarder with a taste for jazz and atheism, a provocative sense of humor, and a girlfriend, Fiona. With her intense, liberated style and habit of thinking "like a man," Fiona fascinates Kenneth. Gradually, he is drawn away from George's empty hedonism (a false version, it turns out, of the "red") and toward Fiona's peace activism, a vote, as she puts it, "for life." Kenneth's task is to find his voice by rejecting monolithic attitudes in favor of a generous multiplicity. The island is rejected in favor of the cosmopolitan openness of the sea. Paradoxically, however, though "The Black and the Red" refuses what it characterizes as the life-denying temper of Scottish Presbyterianism, this intimate drama of the soul is obviously stamped by the religion it seeks to deny.

Each of these stories from *The Black and the Red* continues to develop strains in Smith's writing apparent in *Survival without Error*. The 1973 collection departs from the earlier one, however, in the inclusion of stories that swerve unexpectedly into the surreal and, sometimes, bizarre. Examples include "The Little People," an unusual story in which a fantasized microcosm takes on a life of its own; "The End," a vision of nuclear apocalypse; and "The Return," a strange, dream-like account of the narrator's return to his childhood home. "Through the Desert" is a two-page narrative describing the hallucinations of a protagonist crossing the desert, a kind of modern wasteland littered with insane slogans and uncannily animated machines. "Through the Desert" presents an inverted, nightmare version of Smith's earlier stories of cultural estrangement, such as "The Wedding." It also echoes the broad satire of another story in the collection, "The Professor and the Comics," in which an English professor wins the adoration of the media with his "radical" decision to abandon teaching the classics in favor of the comics—to replace the analysis of William Shakespeare's works with discussion of the British children's magazines *Beano* and *Dandy*. All of these stories, in different ways, decry the hollow stimulation of the modern.

The shift toward surrealism in *The Black and the Red* marks a deeper engagement in Smith's writing with the subconscious. "A Day in the Life of . . . " is about a middle-aged woman alone on vacation who wanders supermarkets, cinemas, and restaurants, trying to use her time in some fruitful way. Eventually, she finds herself in a theater in which an avant-garde play is being performed. "It was certainly not a conventional play. It began with sinister music on drums which went on and on, exerting a hypnotic dark rhythm." This music, "the music of dark Nazism," makes the woman feel "excited and disgusted," as she watches a ritualistic performance in which a dead German soldier is resurrected by a spastic girl. As she stumbles out of the theater, the woman is overcome with horror at the lack of purpose in her life: "I can't bear this total freedom any more. I can't, I can't. I don't know what to do. I cannot live like this." Unlike the title story, however, "A Day in the Life of . . ." withholds catharsis. In this instance, the protagonist's willingness to explore the limits of the "black and the red" appears to end symbolically in death or madness. The embrace of indeterminacy, taken to the limit, becomes a kind of schizophrenia. The narrative closes with the troubling image of the woman following the spastic girl into a dark wood.

In 1977 Smith married a former student, Donalda Logan, and retired from teaching to write full-time. That same year his third book of stories, *The Hermit and Other Stories,* was published. The concerns of his earlier works are further developed in this collection and are increasingly connected with his strong interest in psychology and modern philosophy. The tutelary gods of *The Hermit* (Sigmund Freud, Friedrich Nietzsche, and Søren Kierkegaard, all favorites of Smith) preside over stories of paranoia, repression, and murderous desire. The notion, hinted at in Smith's earlier works, that language is at the same time limited and made possible by Manichaean polarities, is examined from many angles. The stories emerge from the conflicting energies of male and female, black and white, native and foreign, self and other, and even the polarities of Cold War politics. For Smith the question, given such dualism, of how to "speak" or even how to be, is a moral issue. The answer suggested by the title story may not be easy or even palatable.

As in much of Smith's writing, "The Hermit" is narrated by a schoolteacher—someone, that is, who has spent his life instructing others on how to read and think. The retired headmaster and widower who tells the story is a troubling figure, morally implicated, as perhaps his readers are too, in the outcome of the narrative he tells. The story begins with the arrival in a small Highland village of a mysterious silent stranger, a hermit with bright blue eyes and a long black coat belted with rope, who takes up residence in the remnants of a disused Royal Air Force (RAF) base. Like a medieval anchorite, the hermit does not talk, which quickly provokes the villagers' curiosity, speculation, anger, and fear. Each of the villagers in some way resembles his or her version of who the hermit is. Far from the rural Arcadia of other literary versions of the Highlands, Smith's village is little more than a collection of alienated people all looking for ways to kill time and conceal their inner feelings and secrets. The real threat posed by the hermit, the narrator comes to see, is not embodied in anything he might be but in the danger that his mere presence will expose the hypocrisy that holds together the fiction of community. The narrator arranges for false charges of sexual molestation to be laid against the hermit; as a result, the intruder is expelled from the village, restoring an illusion of innocence to the community. The final lines of the story depict the narrator turning the pages of a Bible and reading "In the beginning was the Word." Although the headmaster's behavior is obviously reprehensible, the reader is also compromised by the act of reading a story suggesting that the narrator's actions may be justified.

Repression may be necessary, but its effects are no less guilt-inducing or even criminal. In "The Impulse" an "ordinary" husband and father is briefly compelled by a "Wanted" sign outside a police station to confess his guilt. The only problem is that, as he says, "I didn't know what sort of murder it was or who had murdered whom." That question also haunts "Timoshenko," about an old woman who, bullied and humiliated all her life by her brother, finally stabs him to death. In her mind her action resembles that of the Russian general Semyon Timoshenko in the defense of Stalingrad. In "Macbeth," as in "A Day in the Life of . . ." from *The Black and the Red,* life becomes art, and vice versa, when sexual jealousy prompts an actor to murder his rival on stage. Something similar is performed in "The Spy," which also explores the dynamics of possessive desire. The narrator is an aging psychiatrist who has married a much younger woman. The

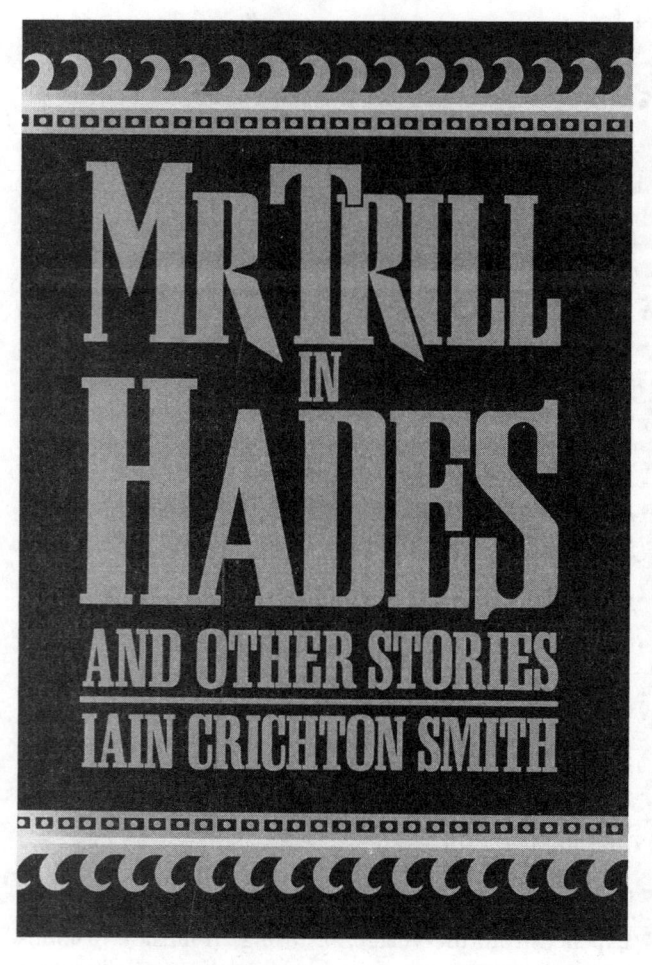

Dust jacket for Smith's last collection of stories, published in 1984, many of which depict the conflicts in the lives of schoolteachers (Richland County Public Library)

wife is an artist with an impressionistic, bohemian style quite at odds with the narrator's drier, more analytic character. When she develops a friendship with a charismatic painter named Rank, the psychiatrist is consumed with the paranoid fear that she is betraying him. When she—like his patients—was dependent on him, he felt in control of the narrative of their marriage. The psychiatrist's jealousy exposes the internal voyeur in him; he fears he is being betrayed by the circumstances that, in a way, he most desires. Again, Smith's focus is an unresolved dualism that pervades public ideology as much as private life. After his wife leaves him, the psychiatrist arranges to have her murdered by a psychopathic patient. As in stories such as "The Hermit" and "Survival without Error," the secret of order is revealed to be violence.

Perhaps the most unusual story in *The Hermit* is "The Brothers." Like "The Exorcism," the tale of a Highland student possessed by the spirit of Kierkegaard, "The Brothers" is a story of literary possession. In one sense, the ghost is Gaelic culture; in another, it is Smith's earlier story "Joseph," which is now reread and, in a self-conscious manner, rewritten. The narrative concerns a writer from the Highlands now living in Edinburgh. He freely concedes that he "left the Gaelic world wholly behind me, because I suppose I despised it." The haunting begins when his typewriter begins to convert the English-language version of the Joseph story he is writing into Gaelic. It also revises the point of Smith's original retelling of the story in "Joseph," transforming Joseph from existential artist into cultural traitor. This development provokes an impassioned defense from the narrator, in words that express at least some of Smith's feelings about place and belonging:

> Why should I allow this being, whatever it was, to tell me what I ought to do, how I ought to write? I was only doing what I thought I ought to be doing. Did I not have free will? What law stated that some ghost or other from another world should command my mind? The anger I felt was pure and ardent and innocent. If I wished to abandon my homeland, if that was what I was doing, why should I not do so? Indeed, in doing so was I not being an exception? Was I not in fact setting out to create a new being? That is, the exile who is able to speak from another land and in another language?

But the price that Smith's exile has paid has also been borne by the culture that denied his right to speak: in the form of Joseph's starving brothers, "the oppressed and inarticulate" of Gaeldom return to haunt the author. Release is obtained only when the narrator realizes that he cannot escape the "irrational gods" of the tribe and that he must confront and accept them. In this moment of epiphany, he realizes that his clothes have taken on the yellow color of the door, symbol of the exile's ideal condition. In the mystical interplay between the individual and the social and between English and Gaelic, the hypocritical "Word" of "The Hermit" is, temporarily at least, redeemed.

In the decade following the publication of *The Hermit*, Smith's works received important public recognition. Awards for his contributions to literature included the Queen's Jubilee Medal (1978); honorary doctorates from the University of Dundee (1983) and the University of Glasgow (1984); a fourth Scottish Arts Council Award (1977); the Scottish Arts Council Prize (1978); and, in 1980, elevation to the Order of the British Empire. The early 1980s were, however, a difficult period for Smith, who, in a crisis eerily predicted in "The Spy," suffered a nervous breakdown and was briefly hospitalized. The episode, Smith has said, became the direct source for his autobiographical novel *In the Middle of the Wood* (1987), the story of a writer who, in a bout of mania, becomes convinced that his wife is having an affair and that he is being spied on by enemies determined to destroy his talent. The writer is committed to a mental hospital, where he is finally cured and reunited with his wife, happy, as Smith has said of his own experience, to "rejoin the human race." According to the editors of *Scottish Literature in English and Scots* (2002), the close of the novel confirms the recognition that "it is the ordinary people of the world, the doctors, firemen and essentially human keepers of society who matter, and that no one can really live outside that community."

Smith's experience with mania led to other works besides *In the Middle of the Wood*. During the 1980s, in a series of quite brief stories, he began to develop the character of Murdo, a man who is either the village idiot or, as some critics have suggested, a holy fool. Certainly, the figure of Murdo, a kind of alter ego to the teacher-narrator in many of Smith's stories, was developed out of much earlier stories, such as "The Idiot and the Professor" and "On the Island," both from *Survival without Error*. In absurdist style Murdo pontificates on the meaning of the potato; writes a letter to Dante and "a Surrealist Tale"; applies for a bursary; and offers his opinions on tourists, the Caledonian MacBrayne ferry service, and the internal conflicts suffered by the bilingual writer. Collected in two volumes, *Murdo and Other Stories* (1981) and *Thoughts of Murdo* (1993), these odd, comic fragments provide a commentary on the body of Smith's fiction. Absurdity, sometimes of a rather dark variety, also pervades Smith's last volume of stories, *Mr. Trill in Hades and Other Stories* (1984). The figure of the faintly ridiculous but also cruel and punitive schoolteacher is a leitmotiv in the collection. In "The Ring" he is Frothy, in love with the unlovely science teacher. In "The Snowballs" he is Mr. Macrae, the enforcer of random and unjust punishment. In the title story he is a Latin teacher in the Greek underworld, disillusioned by what he learns from the ghosts of such figures as Agamemnon and Dido. Smith, however, never forgets the suffering human behind the mask of comedy. "What to Do about Ralph" sympathetically depicts the stresses on a teacher who is also the stepfather of his most challenging pupil. "The Play" describes how a young teacher finally finds a way to communicate with a class of teenage girls whose lives seem destined to end either in motherhood or on the factory line.

Selected Stories (1990) and *Listen to the Voice: Selected Stories* (1993) both largely consist of previously published works, although *Selected Stories* includes several original stories that originally appeared in literary journals and anthologies. Some of these stories reprise scenarios and characters from earlier works. The eccentric old couple in "Napoleon and I" recall the brother and sister in "Timoshenko," and the alarmingly jolly Canadian uncle in "By Their Fruits" is, apparently, a character first met as a child in "The Snowballs." Other stories in *Selected Stories* show Smith's interest in rendering themes that have always haunted him from new, sometimes experimental, perspectives. "Chagall's Return," for example, is another narrative about an exile's return, but in this case the story is mediated through the shapes, colors, and images of Marc Chagall's paintings. "The True Story of Sir Hector Macdonald" retells the history of a famous Victorian-era Highland soldier who killed himself in Paris when his homosexuality was revealed. In the closing lines Smith reveals that his own interest is less in the details of the historical account than in the fantasy that, shortly before his suicide, Macdonald might have passed Pablo

Front cover for Smith's second collection (1993) of stories about the humorous character who has been described as the author's alter ego (Thomas Cooper Library, University of South Carolina)

Picasso in the street on "a day in March at the beginning of the twentieth century." "The True Story of Sir Hector Macdonald" was later expanded by Smith into the novel *An Honourable Death* (1992).

Iain Crichton Smith's final years were spent in Taynuilt with his wife, Donalda. He died on 15 October 1998, an important, well-respected figure in Scottish literature. His fiction has sometimes been criticized as narrow in style and subject matter. For Lindsay, Smith is a writer of great intensity but ultimately flawed by his lack of scope. Morgan dismisses Smith's prose as inferior to his poetry, although he also acknowledges the "classic" status of some of the fiction. Gifford and others, however, have sought to claim Smith as one of Scotland's great fiction writers: "throughout Smith's fiction," Gifford states in *Scottish Literature in English and Scots,* "grace is found in humble places, eccentric characters, while the central protagonists winnow similar lonely gains from their too often fallen backgrounds." In Smith, he adds, "Scottish fiction can be seen changing, and moving towards hope."

Interviews:
John Horder, "Superego versus ID," *Scotsman,* 3 July 1965, p. 2;
Lorn Macintyre, "Poet in Bourgeois Land: Interview with Iain Crichton Smith," *Scottish International Review* (September 1971): 24;
Raymond Gardner, "Betwixt the Devil and the Deep Blue Sea," *Glasgow Herald,* 3 March 1979, p. 11;
"Iain Crichton Smith," in *Seven Poets,* edited by Christopher Carrell (Glasgow: Third Eye Centre / South Shields: E. Peterson, 1981), pp. 42–51;
Andrew Knight, "The Gael Prefers to Write in English," *Evening Express,* 14 November 1985, p. 10;
Steve Fraser, "An Hour with Iain Crichton Smith," *Gaudie,* 27 November 1985, p. 5;
Ronnie Black, "Urram do Sgriobhadair," *Scotsman,* 23 January 1988, p. ix.

Bibliography:
Grant F. Wilson, *A Bibligraphy of Iain Crichton Smith* (Aberdeen: Aberdeen University Press, 1990).

References:
Alan Bold, *Modern Scottish Literature* (London & New York: Longman, 1983), pp. 85–89;
Cairns Craig, ed., *The History of Scottish Literature,* volume 4 (Aberdeen: Aberdeen University Press, 1989), pp. 327–329;
Douglas Dunn, ed., *The Oxford Book of Scottish Short Stories* (Oxford & New York: Oxford University Press, 1995), pp. ix–xxix;
Douglas Gifford, Sarah Dunnigan, and Alan MacGillivray, eds., *Scottish Literature in English and Scots* (Edinburgh: Edinburgh University Press, 2002), pp. 890–898;
Peter Kravitz, ed., *The Picador Book of Contemporary Scottish Fiction* (London: Picador, 1997), pp. xi–xxxiii;
Maurice Lindsay, *History of Scottish Literature* (London: Hale, 1977), pp. 432–433;
Alisdair D. Macrae, "Remembering Iain Crichton Smith," *Dark Horse* (Autumn 1999): 52–58;
Edwin Morgan, "The Contribution of Iain Crichton Smith," *ScotLit,* 23 (Winter 2000): 1–6;
Colin Nicholson, ed., *Iain Crichton Smith: Critical Essays* (Edinburgh: Edinburgh University Press, 1992);
Alan Riach, "Iain Crichton Smith: An Appreciation," *PN Review,* 25 (March–April 1999): 6–8;
Trevor Royle, *The Macmillan Companion to Scottish Literature* (London: Macmillan, 1983), pp. 278–279;
Marshall Walker, *Scottish Literature since 1707* (London & New York: Longman, 1996), pp. 294–297;
Roderick Watson, *The Literature of Scotland* (Basingstoke: Macmillan, 1984), pp. 435–439.

Denton Welch
(29 March 1915 – 30 December 1948)

Jed Mayer
University of Canterbury

BOOKS: *Maiden Voyage* (London: Routledge, 1943; New York: Fischer, 1945);

In Youth Is Pleasure (London: Routledge, 1944; New York: Fischer, 1946);

Brave and Cruel and Other Stories (London: Hamilton, 1948);

A Voice through a Cloud (London: Lehmann, 1950; Austin: Humanities Research Center, University of Texas, 1966);

A Last Sheaf (London: Lehmann, 1951);

The Denton Welch Journals, edited, with an introduction, by Jocelyn Brooke (London: Hamilton, 1952); unexpurgated edition published as *The Journals of Denton Welch,* edited by Michael De-la-Noy (New York: Dutton, 1984; London: Allison & Busby, 1984);

I Left My Grandfather's House (London: Lion & Unicorn Press, 1958);

Dumb Instrument: Poems and Fragments, edited by Jean-Louis Chevalier (London: Enitharmon, 1976);

The Stories of Denton Welch, edited by Robert S. Phillips (New York: Dutton, 1985);

Fragments of a Life Story: The Collected Short Writings of Denton Welch, edited by De-la-Noy (London: Penguin, 1987).

In a writing career spanning merely eight years, Denton Welch earned a minor, though enduring, reputation as a writer of autobiographical fiction unflinching in its portrayal of an often painful and alienated existence. Remembered chiefly for his novels—particularly his final, unfinished, *A Voice through a Cloud* (1950), which records his recovery from the bicycling accident that shortened his life—Welch also produced a considerable body of short fiction in which he refined and crystallized the autobiographical methods developed in his longer works. While many of his best short works reveal Welch working toward a more recognizably classical sense of character and plot development, the hallmark of his style in both his novels and short stories remains his exact and sensual re-creation of remembered experiences. Comparing him to Marcel Proust, James Agate, writing in the *Daily Express* (15 May 1943), bestowed early and effusive praise on Welch for his "exquisite enumeration of nothing in particular, the

Denton Welch (from Robert S. Phillips, ed., The Stories of Denton Welch, *1985; Richland County Public Library)*

raising of the insignificant to the maximum of significance." This minimalist aspect of Welch's work was not calculated to appeal to a wide audience, particularly in the midst and aftermath of World War II, but the originality of his often idiosyncratic observations earned him a small but distinguished coterie of admirers that included W. H. Auden, Edith Sitwell, and Elizabeth Bowen. Despite such critical recognition, Welch's voice remains that of the outsider.

Welch's sense of himself as an outsider likely derived from the circumstances of his youth. Born on 29 March 1915 at the Victoria Nursing Home in Shanghai, Maurice Denton Welch spent the early years of his childhood in the prosperous, though isolated, community of expatriate entrepreneurs of which his father, partner in a firm of rubber-estate managers, was a prominent member. Arthur Welch, particularly as he is described in Denton's literary accounts of him, would seem to have had little patience with or affection for his third son. Denton was closest to his mother, Rosalind née Bassett. Their relationship was the only reassuring and stable element in a childhood spent traveling between China and England, with periodic visits to Canada, Korea, and Switzerland. This itinerant life was brought to a close when Welch began regular schooling at the age of nine. His transition to the rigid discipline and forced male camaraderie of English school life was made the more difficult by news of his mother's sudden death on 3 March 1927. By the time he followed his brothers in enrolling at Repton School, Derbyshire, at the age of fourteen, Welch had grown, if anything, more awkward and withdrawn from boys his own age. Difficult as his time at Repton was, the often sadistic behavior of the teachers and pupils provided him with an education in the perversities of human nature that decisively influenced his writing. These years came to serve as source material for many of his writings, as he looked back on his time in public school with an almost anthropological sense of detachment, and his work deftly captures the repressed erotic element of adolescent bullying, as well as the shadowy sadism present in even the most seemingly innocent of boyhood friendships.

Welch's schooling ended decisively when, at the age of sixteen, he failed to return to school after holidays. As described in his first novel, *Maiden Voyage* (1943), this impulsive escape proved short-lived, Welch having run out of pocket money after a visit to Salisbury Cathedral. As a statement of his unhappiness, however, his escape attempt was dramatic enough to get the attention of his father, who summoned his wayward son to Shanghai. The arrangement of incidents in *Maiden Voyage*, beginning with Welch's aborted escape attempt and continuing with his journey into a foreign world, conveys a sense of growing exultation as he begins to come to terms with his feelings of alienation. At first content simply to explore the ample open-air markets and junk shops of Shanghai, he begins to crave new experiences. In one of the more memorable scenes in the novel, the seventeen-year-old narrator dons a female acquaintance's clothing and makeup and goes for a late-night walk on the streets of Shanghai. This experiment in cross-dressing ends abruptly when he flees home after being accosted by a lusty sailor who mistakes him for a prostitute. Though *Maiden Voyage* includes detailed descriptions of Chinese culture, what is perhaps most striking about Welch's account of this period is its evenness of tone: China in the 1930s comes to seem hardly more exotic and threatening a place for its English protagonist than the school he fled, and the customs of the English expatriates come to seem as unfathomable as those of the Chinese.

Upon returning to England in 1933, Welch enrolled in Goldsmith School of Art in New Cross (now the School of Art and Design in Goldsmiths College, University of London). After some difficulty in adjusting during his first term, he found an inspiring creative outlet in painting and began to make lasting friendships among his bohemian colleagues. Just as he was beginning to find his artistic and social niche, however, on 7 June 1935 Welch was struck by a car while bicycling to his aunt's house. His final novel, *A Voice through a Cloud,* gives a harrowing account of the ordeal that followed, as the author came to terms with the spinal fracture and internal damage that drastically shortened his life. Welch's understated descriptions of his recovery powerfully convey the experience of physical pain and its emotional toll, and the novel is distinct among accounts of injury and illness for its precise rendering of the menace of hospitals and the often cruel treatment by doctors and nurses grown callous through continued exposure to pain and misery. After Welch recovered the use of his legs, he was at last transferred to Southcourt Nursing Home in Broadstairs, where he returned to painting under the encouragement of Jack Easton, a doctor with whom he became infatuated.

During his convalescence over the next several years, Welch also began his first experiments in autobiographical prose. It is perhaps no exaggeration to say that his accident was as much responsible for bringing that talent to fruition as it was for prematurely ending his career. Enforced convalescence turned Welch toward a recovery of lost time that occupied him for the rest of his life. While at Broadstairs he also made a visit to the artist Walter Sickert that later inspired his first published prose piece, "Sickert at St. Peter's," which was published in *Horizon* in August 1942. Welch's account of this meeting earned the admiration of, among others, Edith and Osbert Sitwell, and did much to launch his literary career. Ostensibly an essayistic treatment of a meeting with a then-renowned artist, the piece tells of the awkward event with the often painful candor and wicked humor characteristic of Welch's best autobiographical fiction.

In the years following his accident Welch experienced setbacks to his recovery and spent time at several other nursing homes before settling into a community of aesthetes and eccentrics in and around Tonbridge, England. Welch spent the rest of his life moving between various residences, accompanied first by his former landlady, Evelyn Sinclair, and later by his partner, Eric Oliver. In the early years of the war Welch began work on the manuscript that eventually became *Maiden Voyage*. With an enthusiastic dedication from Edith Sitwell, the book was published by Routledge in early 1943 to considerable acclaim. A novel about the interior life of a sensitive boy was an unlikely publishing risk for an English reading audience in the midst of World War II. As with Ronald Firbank a generation before, however, Welch's voice seemed to many a rare and exotic gift amid wartime deprivations. Reviewing *Maiden Voyage* in the *Tatler* (7 July 1943), Bowen celebrated Welch's concentration on tracts of experience thought insignificant in such times, observing that "one meets many books, these days, in which the ordinary imagination is applying itself to extraordinary events. In this book an extraordinary imagination is applying itself to ordinary events." Welch had his detractors, however, and even as devoted a supporter of his talent as Sitwell cautioned him privately, as he mentioned in a journal entry (20 April 1943), of the potential danger in what she called his "ingrowing toenail" ("Everything in, in, in"), emphasizing, "It is perfect in that book . . . but you must not do it again."

Despite his admiration for Sitwell, Welch's second novel, *In Youth Is Pleasure* (1944), differs little in style or voice from its predecessor, and many critics responded negatively to the book upon its publication in 1945. The element of defiance in continuing in the same autobiographical mode parallels Welch's increasing boldness in addressing homosexuality in his work. The publication history of what is generally considered to be his finest short story, "When I Was Thirteen," reflects the repressive moral climate of the time in which he wrote. Henry Treece, editor of the periodical *Kingdom Come*, received the manuscript in November 1943 but rejected it as "too amoral for publication," despite the fact that the story deals more with the homophobic suspicions of the narrator's older brother than with any sexual act committed by his timid sibling. When Cyril Connolly later accepted the story for *Horizon*, Welch wrote tauntingly to Treece that a less prudish

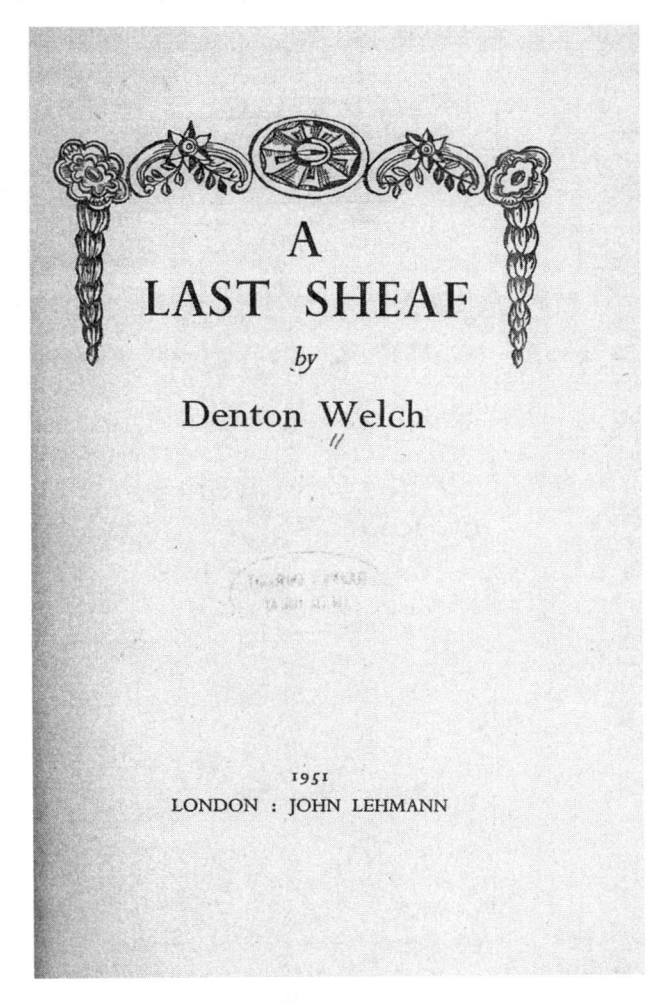

Title page for the volume of Welch's previously uncollected stories assembled by his companion, Eric Oliver (Mudd Library, Claremont College)

publisher had seen merit in the work. Treece wrote back to accuse Welch of flaunting his deviant sexuality at a time when every Englishman should be most concerned with the fate of his country, and Welch responded with a letter, dated 8 January 1944, clarifying his concerns as a writer: "I am conscious of the embarrassing qualities of my stories (so easy to guise effectively), but it would be dishonest of me to write in a more adroit and worldly-wise way. Perhaps it is wrong-headed of me to write of what I do, as I do, at this particular moment in the world's history, but it is certainly not mere frivolity or exhibitionism that prompts me." In a letter written to the Reverend Peter Gamble twelve days later, evidently still peeved at what he perceived as Treece's obstinacy, Welch further clarified what prompted him to write what he did as he did: "I am so tired of all this insistence on ordinariness, dullness, so-called normality (really the most unreal and

provides an unflattering portrait of the author during his recovery in a nursing home following his accident. Hardly a portrayal of innocent suffering, the narrator is depicted verbally abusing his nurses as well as the local townsfolk after going on a drinking binge in a local pub. Welch seems to have been at his best when he was most candid. This short story shows the author successfully bringing the insights of his childhood narratives to bear on the depiction of his adult life in a manner that anticipates *A Voice through a Cloud*, begun in the winter of 1944–1945. The grim mood of that work is reflected in two stories published during this period, "Narcissus Bay" and "The Coffin on the Hill" (both collected in *Brave and Cruel and Other Stories*). Memories of childhood bring intimations of mortality in these short stories. In his book *Decadence: A Philosophical Inquiry* (1948), C. E. M. Joad invokes "Narcissus Bay" as representative of a literary decadence that would uphold any occurrence, regardless of its significance or propriety, as inherently valuable and worthy of transcription. In terms of plot, the work seems to bear out Joad's accusation of the author's apparent lack of purpose, though Welch was never one to strive for artificial dramatic effects. Insofar as its primary theme would seem to be human cruelty and its essential meaninglessness, however, the structure of the story (or lack thereof) is entirely appropriate to its subject. Recalling events that may have occurred when the six-year-old Welch and his mother vacationed in the Chinese province of Wei-hai Wei, the narrator describes seeing a woman, bloodied and beaten, coming down a hill in the company of two official-looking men and their two bound and battered prisoners. When he relates the incident to his companions, he is not believed. Nonetheless, it has an impact on those who hear it, as is symbolized by several small but significant acts of cruelty that take place afterward. "The Coffin on the Hill" also takes place during Welch's childhood in China and depicts his first sight of a corpse, seen rotting in an exposed casket in a graveyard near where the boy is picnicking with his family. As they return home on their riverboat, the boy ceremoniously throws his childhood doll into the river, watching as it fades into the distance riding on the wake. The act suggests a burial at sea and symbolizes an end of innocence for the boy.

Title page for the 1987 anthology of Welch's stories, which the editor arranged in chronological order according to the events in Welch's life that inspired them (James Branch Cabell Library, Virginia Commonwealth University)

bizarre thing of all). . . . It is extraordinary to think of the great wastes of unmentionableness in all our minds." In bringing heretofore unrepresented dimensions of human thought and experience into the realm of literature, Welch may be seen as writing in the tradition of such high-modernist innovators in fiction as James Joyce and Dorothy Richardson. Unlike these stylistic innovators, however, Welch conveys the errant thoughts and sensual impressions of a singular sensibility with unadorned directness.

Other stories from the mid to late 1940s show Welch coming to terms with the more recent past, as he extended his autobiographical range to address adult themes and situations. "Leaves from a Young Person's Notebook," in *Brave and Cruel and Other Stories* (1948)

The winter of 1947 was an exceptionally harsh one in Britain, and Welch's health deteriorated. The fevers resulting from the kidney infections that he contracted as a result of his accident grew more frequent. In the early 1940s Welch experienced periods of robust health, enough for him to go hiking and bicycling again, but those days rapidly came to an end. Having temporarily abandoned work on his final novel, Welch now concentrated on writing the several short stories that completed his only authorized collection, *Brave and Cruel and Other Stories,* contracted by the publisher Hamish Hamilton earlier in the year. Between bouts of fever and blinding headaches, Welch composed some of the finest stories of his career. The title story of the collection suggests a possible new direction for him in its depiction of the circle of country ladies and eccentrics who befriended the author during his time in Kent. The tale is told with a wit and ironic detachment distinct in Welch's oeuvre, the more surprising considering the author's poor state of health. In the later months of 1948 he was able to see the proofs of his short-story collection through the press, but he did not live to finish his final novel. Welch died on 30 December 1948 because of kidney damage, asthma, and various other ailments resulting from the 1935 collision.

Days after Welch's funeral, in January 1949 (but with a 1948 imprint), *Brave and Cruel* was published to mixed reviews, though Harold Nicolson remarked in the *Observer* (12 March 1950) that the collection "showed increasing power. And this, his last book, proves that, by his death, the meagre world of contemporary letters has suffered a tragic loss." After the celebrated *A Voice through a Cloud* was published by John Lehmann in 1950, some of Welch's uncollected stories were brought together under the guidance of Oliver in the volume *A Last Sheaf* (1951). Although this book includes two of Welch's less successful attempts at writing more-commercial fiction, "The Hateful Word" and "The Diamond Badge," it also collects several of his best stories. Most valuable are those stories that show Welch addressing later periods of his life, as in "A Picture in the Snow" and "Memories of a Vanished Period." In these short stories, he re-creates his eccentric acquaintances in a manner similar to "Brave and Cruel" and extends his range while still remaining within the autobiographical mode that had fostered his finest work.

Welch admirer and publisher Lehmann perceptively observes in his memoir, *I Am My Brother* (1960), that had Welch lived, he would have most likely developed "into the most disconcerting diarist of our day." The many previously unpublished or uncollected short works that have been brought to print reinforce Lehmann's prediction. *Fragments of a Life Story: The Collected Short Writings of Denton Welch* (1987), for example, edited by Michael De-la-Noy, presents all of Welch's known shorter works chronologically according to the autobiographical events described. De-la-Noy also edited the first full, unexpurgated edition of *The Journals of Denton Welch* (1984). Reviewing this edition for *TLS: The Times Literary Supplement* (21 December 1984), Alan Hollinghurst noted the continuity of Welch's writing and observed that the journal entries, like the epiphanies that make up his stories and novels, "reflect life's tendency to anti-climax and fragmentation (and also, one suspects, a challenge to the heterosexual criteria of fiction)."

These elements of Denton Welch's style have brought his work to a wider audience, though his peculiar sensibility will most likely continue to inspire the admiration of a devoted few. He remains the unacknowledged laureate of the unnoticed, the quiet voice of the outsider in English letters.

Biographies:

Noël Adeney, *No Coward Soul* (London: Hogarth Press, 1956);

Robert S. Phillips, *Denton Welch* (New York: Twayne, 1974);

Michael De-la-Noy, *Denton Welch: The Making of a Writer* (Harmondsworth, U.K. & New York: Viking, 1984);

James Methuen-Campbell, *Denton Welch: Writer and Artist* (Carlton-in-Coverdale, U.K.: Tartarus, 2002).

References:

Cyril Connolly, "Denton Welch," in *Previous Convictions* (London: Hamilton, 1963), pp. 328–330;

C. E. M. Joad, *Decadence: A Philosophical Inquiry* (London: Faber & Faber, 1948), pp. 289–292;

John Updike, "Promising," *New Yorker,* 42 (29 October 1966): 236–241;

Richard Whittington-Egan, "A New Assessment of Denton Welch," *Contemporary Review,* 246 (June 1985): 319–325; 247 (September 1985): 149–154; 248 (January 1986): 32–36; 249 (July 1986): 41–44; 249 (September 1986): 146–152.

Papers:

Most of Denton Welch's papers and manuscripts are housed at the Harry Ransom Humanities Research Center, University of Texas at Austin.

Fay Weldon
(22 September 1931 –   )

Michael Meyer
University of Koblenz-Landau

See also the Weldon entries in *DLB 14: British Novelists Since 1960* and *DLB 194: British Novelists Since 1960, Second Series*.

BOOKS: *The Fat Woman's Joke* (London: MacGibbon & Kee, 1967); republished as *. . . And the Wife Ran Away* (New York: McKay, 1968);
Down among the Women (London: Heinemann, 1971; New York: St. Martin's Press, 1972);
Words of Advice (London & New York: S. French, 1974);
Female Friends (New York: St. Martin's Press, 1974; London: Heinemann, 1975);
Remember Me (London: Hodder & Stoughton, 1976; New York: Random House, 1976);
Words of Advice (New York: Random House, 1977); republished as *Little Sisters* (London: Hodder & Stoughton, 1978);
Praxis (London: Hodder & Stoughton, 1978; New York: Summit, 1978);
Puffball (London: Hodder & Stoughton, 1980; New York: Summit, 1980);
Action Replay: A Play (London & New York: S. French, 1980);
Watching Me, Watching You (London: Hodder & Stoughton, 1981; New York: Summit, 1981);
The President's Child (London: Hodder & Stoughton, 1982; Garden City, N.Y.: Doubleday, 1983);
The Life and Loves of a She-Devil (London: Hodder & Stoughton, 1983; New York: Pantheon, 1984);
Letters to Alice: On First Reading Jane Austen (London: Joseph/Rainbird, 1984; New York: Taplinger, 1985);
I Love My Love: A Play (London & New York: S. French, 1984);
Polaris and Other Stories (London: Hodder & Stoughton, 1985; New York: Penguin, 1989);
Rebecca West (London & New York: Viking, 1985);
The Shrapnel Academy (London: Hodder & Stoughton, 1986; New York: Viking, 1987);
The Hearts and Lives of Men (London: Heinemann, 1987; New York: Viking, 1988);

Fay Weldon (photograph by Isolde Ohlbaum; from Rhode Island Blues, *2000; Richland County Public Library)*

The Rules of Life (London: Hutchinson, 1987; New York: Harper & Row, 1987);
The Heart of the Country (London: Hutchinson, 1987; New York: Viking, 1988);
Wolf the Mechanical Dog (London: Collins, 1988);
Leader of the Band (London: Hodder & Stoughton, 1988; New York: Viking, 1989);
Party Puddle (London: Collins, 1989);
Sacred Cows: A Portrait of BRITAIN, post-RUSHDIE, pre-UTOPIAN (London: Chatto & Windus, 1989);
The Cloning of Joanna May (London: Collins, 1989; New York: Viking, 1990);

Darcy's Utopia (London: Collins, 1990; New York: Viking, 1991);

Moon over Minneapolis, or, Why She Couldn't Stay (London: Collins, 1991; New York: Penguin, 1992);

Growing Rich (London & New York: HarperCollins, 1992);

Life Force (London: HarperCollins, 1992; New York: Viking, 1992);

A Question of Timing (London: Colophon, 1992);

Affliction (London: HarperCollins, 1993); republished as *Trouble* (New York: Viking, 1993);

Wicked Women: A Collection of Short Stories (London: Flamingo, 1995; New York: Atlantic Monthly Press, 1997);

Splitting (London: Flamingo, 1995; New York: Atlantic Monthly Press, 1995);

Worst Fears (London: Flamingo, 1996; New York: Atlantic Monthly Press, 1996);

Nobody Likes Me! (London: Bodley Head, 1997);

Big Women (London: Flamingo, 1997); republished as *Big Girls Don't Cry* (New York: Atlantic Monthly Press, 1997);

A Hard Time to Be a Father: A Collection of Short Stories (London: Flamingo, 1998; New York: Atlantic Monthly Press, 1998);

The Reading Group: A Play (London & New York: S. French, 1999);

Godless in Eden: A Book of Essays (London: Flamingo, 1999);

Rhode Island Blues (London: Flamingo, 2000; New York: Atlantic Monthly Press, 2000);

The Bulgari Connection (London: Flamingo, 2001; New York: Atlantic Monthly Press, 2001);

Auto da Fay (London: Flamingo, 2002; New York: Grove, 2003);

Nothing to Wear and Nowhere to Hide: Stories (London: Flamingo, 2002);

Flood Warning: A Play (London: S. French, 2003);

Mantrapped (London: Flamingo, 2003; New York: Grove, 2004);

She May Not Leave (London: Fourth Estate, 2005).

Collection: *Angel, All Innocence, and Other Stories* (London: Bloomsbury, 1995).

PLAY PRODUCTIONS: *Permanence*, in *Mixed Doubles: An Entertainment on Marriage*, London, Comedy Theatre, 9 April 1969;

Words of Advice, Richmond (England), Orange Tree Theatre, 1 March 1974;

Friends, Richmond, Orange Tree Theatre, April 1975;

Moving House, Farnham, Redgrave Theatre, 9 June 1976;

Mr. Director, Richmond, Orange Tree Theatre, 24 March 1978; revised, 1994;

Action Replay, Birmingham Repertory Studio Theatre, 22 February 1979;

I Love My Love, Exeter, Northcott Theatre, 18 February 1981;

After the Prize, New York, Phoenix Theatre, November 1981; produced as *Woodworm*, Melbourne, Australia, Playbox Theatre, March 1983;

Jane Eyre, adapted by Weldon, Birmingham Repertory Studio Theatre, 1986;

The Hole in the Top of the World, Richmond, Orange Tree Theatre, 1987;

Someone Like You, Cambridge Theatre Workshop Tour, 1989; London, Strand Theatre, March 1990;

Tess of the d'Urbervilles, adapted by Weldon, West Yorkshire Playhouse, 1992;

The Four Alice Bakers, Birmingham Repertory Theatre, 1999;

Madame Bovary, adapted by Weldon from the novel by Gustave Flaubert, Liverpool, Liverpool Playhouse, 28 October 2003.

PRODUCED SCRIPTS: *The Fat Woman's Tale*, television, Granada, 1966;

Wife in a Blond Wig, television, BBC, 1966;

Office Party, television, Thames TV, 1970;

"On Trial," television, *Upstairs, Downstairs*, London Weekend Television, 1971;

Hands, television, BBC, 1972;

Spider, radio, BBC 3, 1972;

Housebreaker, radio, BBC 3, 1973;

Mr. Fox and Mr. First, radio, BBC 3, 1974;

The Doctor's Wife, radio, BBC 4, 1975;

Poor Baby, television, Anglia TV, 1975;

The Terrible Tale of Timothy Bagshott, television, BBC, 1975;

Aunt Tatty, adaptation of the Elizabeth Bowen short story, television, BBC, 1975;

Married Love, television, BBC, 1977;

Polaris, radio, ABC, 1977;

Pride and Prejudice, adaptation of the Jane Austen novel, television, BBC, 1979;

"Weekend," radio, *Just before Midnight*, BBC 4, 1979;

All the Bells of Paradise, radio, BBC 4, 1979;

"Watching Me, Watching You," television, *Leap in the Dark*, BBC, 1980;

Life for Christine, television, Granada, 1980;

I Love My Love, radio, BBC 4, 1981; ABC, 1983;

Little Miss Perkins, television, London Weekend Television, 1982;

Loving Women, television, Granada, 1983;

Redundant, or, The Wife's Revenge, television, BBC, 1983;

On First Reading Jane Austen, television, BBC, 1985;

The Heart of the Country, television, BBC, 1986;

A Dangerous Kind of Love, television, BBC, 1986;

Face at the Window, television, Thames TV, 1986;
The Life and Loves of a She-Devil, television, BBC, 1986;
Heart of the Country, television, BBC, 1987;
Growing Rich, television, Anglia TV, 1992;
The Cloning of Joanna May, television, Granada, 1992;
The Hole in the Top of the World, radio, BBC 4, 1993;
A Hard Time to Be a Father, radio, BBC 4, 1995;
Everyone Needs an Ancestor, radio, BBC 4, 1995;
Heat Haze, radio, BBC 4, 1995;
Web Central, radio, BBC 4, 1995;
Blood Relations, television, BBC, 1996;
I, Boadicea, radio, BBC 4, 2002.

SELECTED PERIODICAL PUBLICATIONS–UNCOLLECTED: "Towards a Humorous View of the Universe," *Women's Studies: An Interdisciplinary Journal,* 15 (1988): 309–311;

"Will No One Rid Us of These Turbulent Priests?" *Times Saturday Review* (London), 20 February 1993, pp. 4–6;

"Mind at the End of Its Tether," *Guardian,* 11 January 1997, p. 21.

According to Fay Weldon's frank, humorous, and vivid autobiography, *Auto da Fay* (2002), she has experienced or witnessed almost everything she has written about: the war of the sexes, disintegrating families, and women's struggle for survival in poverty. The autobiographer shares sympathy, irony, pragmatism, and a strong sense of justice with many of her fictional narrators. Weldon's story of her own life and her stories of other women's lives reveal the same pattern of incredible coincidences, repetitions, and the sudden intrusion of chaos into life. Her fictional narratives are often based on the "downside" of Weldon's life and loves, she admits in *Auto da Fay,* but always transform and transcend the autobiographical. Many writers on the mother's side of her family lived bohemian lives, whereas the traders and professionals on her father's side preferred bourgeois lives. The husbands seem to have been less concerned with practical and financial than with erotic affairs. Weldon laconically remarks in her autobiography that the "tendency to marry faithless men comes running down the female side of the family, the tendency to faithlessness runs in the male."

Weldon was born Franklin Birkinshaw on 22 September 1931 in Alvechurch, Worcestershire. The daughter of Frank Thornton Birkinshaw, a medical doctor, and Margaret Jepson Birkinshaw, a writer, she was baptized "Franklin" because her parents wanted a boy after their first daughter. In 1936, the family of four moved to New Zealand, where the immigrants were considered to be outsiders and had a hard time getting established. Her father's debts and affairs soon led to the separation of the couple. According to *Auto da Fay,* Weldon contemplated suicide because "One of the terrors of divorce is the knowledge that the safe place, home, has become the source of danger and betrayal: and there is nowhere, psychically or physically, to which to return." Her mother raised the daughters on her own, moved back to England when Birkinshaw was fourteen years of age, and managed to survive with the help of odd jobs and relatives. Birkinshaw's attendance at a convent school and her life with her sister, mother, and grandmother led to her appreciation of female solidarity. In 1949, she enrolled at the University of St. Andrews on a scholarship and gained her M.A. in economics and psychology. She declined to marry the father of her first son, Nicholas (born in 1955), being in love with another man. Birkinshaw earned money and also received her mother's support, as did her sister, who was married to an unreliable artist. Birkinshaw tried to escape financial anxiety by marrying a schoolteacher, who was twenty years her senior and denied her need for pleasure and work. The frustrated, isolated housewife left him and worked as a propaganda writer for the British Foreign Office; as a journalist, writing the "Reader's Advice" column and doing market research for the *Daily Mirror;* and as a successful copywriter with advertising agencies. In 1960, she married the artist and antique dealer Ronald Weldon, with whom she had three sons (Daniel in 1963, Thomas in 1970, and Samuel in 1977); she divorced Weldon thirty years later when he became involved with his longtime psychoanalyst. She subsequently married Nicholas Fox in 1995 and still pursues her career as a popular and immensely prolific writer. In 2000, she was made a Commander of the British Empire.

By the time Weldon published her first collection of short stories, *Watching Me, Watching You* (1981), she had already acquired fame as a playwright, radio and television scriptwriter, and above all as a novelist. She had received many awards, including the Society of Film and Television Arts Award for best series for the "On Trial" episode of the television series *Upstairs, Downstairs* in 1971; the Giles Cooper Award for best radio play for *Polaris* (produced 1977) in 1978; and the Booker McConnell Prize nomination of the National Book League in 1979 for her novel *Praxis* (1978). Many of her approximately eighty short stories were first published in magazines such as *Cosmopolitan, Elle, Vanity Fair, Woman, The New Statesman, The New Yorker, The Observer,* and *The Times.* Some were originally written as radio or television plays.

Weldon's first short stories display features similar to those of her subsequent ones in terms of form, content, and function. Like her novels, which Agate Nesaule Krouse characterizes as dark "feminist comedies" in her essay "Feminism and Art in Fay Weldon's

Novels" (1978), the stories are terrible and funny at the same time and often take a positive turn toward the end in spite of all the previous abuse and suffering of the characters. Her stories are sometimes Gothic and usually satiric. Her Gothic tales evoke the terror of the haunted house, which symbolizes the pervasive victimization of women in patriarchal society. The satiric exaggeration and censure of her fiction foregrounds the grotesque nature of human folly and social reality. Weldon prefers intrusive third-person narrators, who display an attitude of sympathy and irony, which she relates to her own share of suffering and flaws and to her opinion that "*people* are more to be pitied than to be despised," as she told John Haffenden in a 1985 interview. She also developed a particular version of first-person narratives that are akin to dramatic monologues, which express processes of women's insight into their own situations in the presence of a silent psychotherapist. In her interview with Haffenden she described her direct, succinct, and witty style as "a matter of economy, of how to get down rapidly and exactly, with precision, what you wish to say," an approach that is influenced by her work as a copywriter. Weldon's stories cover the full range of women's experience and are designed to be read as parables of their lives. She revealed to Haffenden that her entertaining cautionary tales are meant to expose male lies and female delusions and thus begin social reform by changing views of reality.

"Watching Me, Watching You," the satiric and Gothic title story of Weldon's first collection, establishes one of her characteristic cyclical plots: a selfish, cruel, and dominating husband twice replaces his loving wife with a younger, more beautiful, and more adoring woman, who in turn blames his previous wife for his shortcomings. His former wives suffer from jealousy, loneliness, and penury but finally achieve insight into and distance from their past. The former rivalry between the lovers is replaced by a feminist solidarity among the single women. The alter ego of the omniscient and intrusive narrator is a ghost with a feminist bias in the roles of an observer who is specifically sensitive to human emotions and imminent conflicts, a warning presence who causes incidents that may be read as ominous prefigurations of doom, and a judge with a sense of justice and sympathy for the victims of domestic abuse. Another ghost haunts the house, the spirit of a previous female inhabitant who was betrayed and hung herself. Her shadow on the wall warns the present tenant of her potential fate. Whereas the husband prefers to ignore the writing on the wall, his wife is ill at ease but can only fully realize in retrospect what the ghost had anticipated: "What I sensed was my self now, looking back; me now watching me then, myself remembering me with sorrow for what I was and need never have

Cover for the first U.S. edition, published in 1989, of Weldon's 1985 collection of stories featuring exploitative husbands and vindictive wives (Richland County Public Library)

been." The title story maintains that the insight of one woman can be generalized and that the cycle of blind love and disillusionment can be broken by growing insight and mutual help among sisters.

Weldon herself feels ambivalent about ghosts; she believes in their objective existence but also explains them as psychic phenomena. The uncertainty about the existence of a ghost in imagination or reality in her stories often creates a sense of satiric disenchantment, according to Barbara Puschmann-Nalenz in her essay "'Cloudy Symbols of a (not so) High Romance': Feminine and Feminist Fantasy in the Fiction of Fay Weldon" (1996). Whatever their nature, the ghosts express the collective female memory of anxiety, victimization, and revenge. In "Angel, All Innocence," the ghost of an abused mother haunts the young, beautiful, and pregnant Angel, prefiguring her own beatings and betrayal by her egoistic and sadistic husband but also motivating her to leave him. The title of the story "Man with No

Eyes" characterizes an intrusive and frightening ghost as well as the tyrannical husband, who claims reason but represses, exploits, and terrifies his wife as much as his alter ego, the devouring ghost. In "Breakages," a husband's most cherished objects break in his absence, and it is open to question whether a ghost or his scorned and neglected wife, who denies any evil intention and mends all things, is to be held responsible.

Among the satirical parables in this collection, "Weekend" stands out because it succinctly captures the repressive patriarchal view women share to their own detriment. Martha, housewife, mother, and employee, pays the bills and likewise pays a price for mistaking her husband's kind words and concern about domestic issues as a sign of thoughtfulness rather than a strategy to dominate her and use her as a servant. Martha internalizes her husband's point of view, which accompanies each of her thoughts, represented by his comments in brackets. Her everyday drudgery, continuous haste, and psychological pressure are summarized in catalogues of activities and incomplete sentences, which convey her inability to reflect upon her situation because of the sheer amount of work. The ritual journey to the cottage in the country at the weekend does not mean relaxation and an escape from routine for Martha but rather augments her chores. She not only has to shoulder the burden of two households but is also compelled to ensure the convenience of her husband's friends. On top of that, she is humiliated by the degrading comparison with the sexy, young girlfriend of her husband's recently divorced friend, who represents her husband's fantasy and potential future apart from his family, as Wolfgang Riedel argues in his essay "Fay Weldons 'Weekend'–eine Geschichte von der subversiven Ironie des Glücks" (1993, Fay Weldon's "Weekend": A Story about the Subversive Irony of Happiness). Martha is torn between her attempts to fulfill the impossible demands of being both the perfect housewife, who serves everybody's needs but her own, and the attractive lady. In spite of her efforts she is rewarded with nothing but scorn and condescension. Finally, the tension between her exertions and her humiliation makes the exhausted mother break down crying when her daughter Jenny gets her first period and will become "wife, mother, friend," which may remind Martha of her own hopes and delusions.

Because of her own experience, Weldon repeatedly questions the individual and social function of psychotherapy in her stories. Her second husband, who talked about personal problems with his analyst rather than with his partner, compelled her to undergo therapy, which she described to Haffenden as "dreadfully painful and very interesting," a way to acquire self-knowledge and to take responsibility for one's actions.

In *Auto da Fay,* Weldon realizes that she tried "to change herself to suit a patriarchal society, when she would be better employed changing society to suit herself."

"Threnody," also from *Watching Me, Watching You,* is the first of Weldon's short stories that resembles a dramatic monologue, in which a woman half reluctantly, often upon the instigation of her husband, talks to a female analyst, Mrs. Jacobs, who is usually silent except for rare expressions of surprise and questions, which are implicit in the client's reactions. The reader is asked to play the psychotherapist in order to discover the silences, delusions, and repressions in the stories, which also relieve the clients and lead to their limited insights into their own selves. Some of those clients stress their reason and control over their lives, ignoring problems; others explain their deviant behavior or emotions as a normal reaction to abusive relationships, which the reader understands as social rather than individual issues. "Threnody" delineates a woman's intermittent periods of psychoanalysis between 1976 and 1980. The client denies suffering from depression but desires self-knowledge and wishes to speak about things that, if uttered at home, would disrupt her family. Her name, Threnody, which her mother mistook for a happy melody, is telling because her story is a lament about the series of mishaps and abuses–rape, repression, abandonment, and futile attempts at escape–for which she takes all the blame and considers suicide. She exemplifies the female victim who takes over the guilt from the men who abused her and is bound to punish herself, thus upholding the repressive patriarchal society that led to her victimization.

Weldon's first collection and her second, *Polaris and Other Stories* (1985), met with much critical acclaim on account of their witty satire, succinct style, and vivid, well-crafted plots. The stories in *Polaris* deal with two episodes in postwar gender relationships: the war of the sexes, in which women rival women for men and side with men; and the transformation of gender relationships by the empowerment and liberation of women, who rebel against their subordination to men.

Two first-person monologues reveal women's unconscious and deliberate resistance to men. "Delights of France or Horrors of the Road" captures the contradiction inherent in the perspective of a fifty-year-old wife who is devoted to her husband in spite of her deep anxiety. She is sent to the psychoanalyst on the suspicion of hysterical paralysis because her legs simply collapse for no medical reason when she tries to get into her husband's car. She has assimilated her husband's view of himself as the perfect driver and connoisseur, whose "admirable" skills, however, only meet with aggression and derision by the French during their "delightful" holidays. To the unbiased reader, her narration characterizes her husband as an arrogant, condescending, shortsighted, pedantic, and irresponsible narcissist, who always blames others for his faults. The Valium she took in order to calm her nerves against the horror of her husband's driving apparently did not provide sufficient protection, so her body had to prevent her from further harm by refusing to ride in his car. Ironically, her involuntary paralysis renders her even more dependent on his help (and transport), which she reads as another proof of his love for her.

In "The Sad Life of the Rich," an aging, ruthless beauty confesses her sins but defies God and therefore the patriarchal order because she claims that she had to deceive in order to enjoy herself and get what she wanted. She has learned not to speak the truth, to distrust others, and to rely only on herself after being shuttled in and out of an orphanage during the war, neglected by her unmarried mother, who was afraid of social censure, and her father, a careless American soldier. Her truthfulness in words and unconventional love affairs met with resentment, so she took to deception and theft in order to make up for her disadvantages. A shadow of conscience is cast over her life, however, because she pays for getting ahead with feeling worse.

The most sardonic among the satires in this volume is a story about gynecologists in Newcastle, Australia, "And Then Turn Out the Light." The cynical narrator blames these doctors not only for their frequent sexual harassment of their patients but also for destroying women's identities and opportunities as mothers by performing premature hysterectomies in order to support their luxurious lifestyles. Other stories in the volume show means of escape for victimized women. In "In the Great War" women fight women instead of men: an omniscient, ironic narrator describes Enid, who wants to avoid in her own life her plain mother's defeat by an attractive rival but in turn only duplicates the pattern by displacing her professor's wife. The wife manages to place her vindictive children with her young rival and to retrieve her former husband when Enid is pregnant. Enid, whose abandonment and disillusionment is punishment for her guilt in nearly destroying a family, becomes "a propagandist in the new cold war against men."

The title story, "Polaris," was first published in *Best Radio Plays of 1978: The Giles Cooper Award Winners* (1979). Men and women live in separate worlds, the all-male crew of a nuclear submarine and their wives on a navy base in Scotland. Both communities are regarded with suspicion by others. The navy officers, whom a female detachment of the peace movement supposes are trigger-happy warmongers, enjoy cooking and sociable gourmet dinners under the sea. Their wives are deemed helpless by male villagers, who offer unasked-for advice. The

Cover for the U.S. edition of Weldon's 1992 collection, which includes stories about professional women whose careers conflict with the demands of families and relationships (Richland County Public Library)

wives are self-reliant, however, and organize their lives with a little help from the "spare man," Tony, who takes care of their practical and sexual needs during the absence of their husbands. Conflicts mar the encounters of the couples until they compromise, are reconciled with each other, and look forward to the birth of their babies.

In "Redundant, or The Wife's Revenge," entropy rules life in an outrageous story, which is told to the "little light relief" of its readers. An omniscient, intrusive, and ironic narrator tells a burlesque farce of wild hetero- and homosexual affairs, which primarily serve the husbands' pleasures but also their wives' revenge. The aging Alan Sussman changed his name and had a facelift after he left his family and was made redundant by his company and his young bisexual lover. His wife, Esther, tracks him down in the hospital and hurts him by mocking his pains, singing the praises of her new lover, and slapping his face. In the end, however, Alan is reconciled to his wife, who still loves him, and the other lovers pair off in new but happy combinations.

By the time Weldon's collection *Moon over Minneapolis, or, Why She Couldn't Stay* appeared in 1991, she had achieved greater fame through her novels *The Life and Loves of a She-Devil* (1983), which was turned into a controversial television series and a Hollywood movie, and *The Heart of the Country* (1987), which received the Los Angeles Times Book Award for Fiction in 1989. In addition, the University of St. Andrews awarded her an honorary doctorate in 1989. Her new stories were hailed as refreshingly unsentimental, intelligent, and subversive, conveying a serious and at times bitter message with caustic humor.

Some of these stories reflect topical developments: Weldon accords more space than in earlier stories to energetic professional women who achieve success in their jobs but have to live with the discontent of their neglected private lives, and records an unprecedented generational conflict between liberated mothers and their more traditional daughters. In "Subject to Diary," a forty-year-old female yuppie, who submitted her whole life to a strictly controlled time schedule in order to achieve success and luxury, intends to have her third abortion, albeit with hesitation as this pregnancy is her last chance at motherhood. She is finally moved to cancel her appointment by an uncooperative and critical young receptionist and mother at the abortion clinic. In "A Gentle Tonic Effect," a vain, callous, and aggressive professional woman defiantly displays a lack of moral concerns in private and public life but suffers from the return of the repressed in the form of nightmares, which express her subconscious guilt over the neglect of her son and the promotion of one of her company's pharmaceutical products, which causes monstrous birth defects. Two stories, "I Do What I Can and I Am What I Am" and "Au Pair," deal with the quarrel between liberated mothers and their innocent daughters, who defy their feminist mothers' sexual and professional preferences in favor of romances with more-experienced men and more-traditional career choices.

The stories in *Moon over Minneapolis* explore a wider variety of resolutions for conflicts in relationships than before. Sharon in "Sharon Loves Daron" attempts suicide and rejects the help of nurses in order to attract the attention of a rather indifferent boy. In "Un Crime Maternel" a mother of two, who killed her husband and his lover with poisoned mushrooms, is submitted to a psychiatric test. She argues that it is not her but the law that is mad if it does not acquit her, because she did not commit a crime of passion but a "maternal crime" in order to prevent a divorce and protect her children's interest. Other stories present harmonious resolutions to difficult situations, as in "Who Goes There?," in which a young second wife hates the family her husband left for her but finally consents to take care of his children over Christmas. In "The Search for Mother Christmas" a mother, who raised four children on her own and is glad they have left home, takes in the two daughters of her reckless son and his careless wife rather than giving them up to the heartless care offered by the state.

Almost half of the stories in Weldon's third collection are first-person narratives, which, in addition to those that depict talking cures under the eyes of the ever-silent psychotherapist Mrs. Jacobs, present talkative narrators who are eager to relate their embarrassing secrets to whoever may come along, as Lee A. Jacobus notes in his "The Monologic Narrator in Fay Weldon's Short Fiction" (1994). "The Year of the Green Pudding" is based on a mistake Weldon made in a Christmas pudding recipe she published in a popular magazine. Her oversensitive fictional protagonist is extremely afraid to do anything that harms others, and after her mistake with a recipe she resigns from her job and even falls out of love because of her free-floating anxiety. In "Down the Clinical Disco," a slightly paranoid woman tells a stranger in a bar how female and male inmates had to show "proper" gendered behavior in order to be released from the psychiatric ward. In the ward she met the love of her life; both of them were released but still feel compelled to simulate stereotypical behavior in public in order to hide their deviant transvestite urges and comply with rigid social norms. Whereas Mrs. Jacob's clients feel rather self-assured on the surface but inhibited from revealing their secret selves, the extroverted speakers who confide in random acquaintances suffer from serious social-psychological pressure and are in desperate need of attention and recognition by others.

Whereas most reviews appreciated the vengeful moral satires of *Wicked Women: A Collection of Short Stories* (1995), Alev Adil, in *TLS: The Times Literary Supplement* (12 August 1995), questioned whether Weldon's stories were feminist or conservative: while the author debunks weak men and accords justice to female victims, she also condemns the wicked and "cunning young sirens." These stories register the contemporary increase of competitive individualism across all ages and both sexes for lovers, jobs, and social status. Weldon also pays attention to the weakening of the strict binary segregation of the sexes in terms of deviant social behavior, sexual predilection, and physical sex by masculine women, feminized men, lesbians, homosexuals, and transsexuals.

The first section, "Tales of Wicked Women," indicates that such women only succeed at times because they do not play by the rules. In "The End of the Line" a selfish young journalist holds an idiosyncratic view of karma: you get what you deserve. She still lives in her parents' home in order to save money and uses sex as an instrument to advance her career and to improve her social situation. Like a trickster, she ruthlessly and without any moral concerns manipulates and provokes people. Although her ploys fail in the end, another opportunity immediately offers itself in the form of a rich man, to whose compassion she appeals. Weldon's mothers are as clever and as versatile as their daughters. In "Not Even a Blood Relation" a legacy hunter marries a duke and after his death outwits her arrogant and envious daughters. She wards off their claim to their father's inheritance by giving birth to a son, who was conceived by artificial insemination using her dead husband's frozen semen.

In a second section, "Tales of Wicked Men," such men are shown to be losers in a moral sense and are unable to cope with changes. "Love among the Artists" reveals that the traditional dominant patriarch still remains hidden under politically and artistically progressive ideas. In "Leda and the Swan," a jealous boy grows up to become an envious husband, who tries to impede his young wife's career in sports. She swims from victory to victory, however, in defiance of his attempts at restraining her successful exertions. In "Wasted Lives" a left-wing movie executive, who is married but lives apart from his English family, is shocked by the dissolution of families under socialism in Eastern Europe. During his sojourn in the East, however, he jilts his pregnant lover, who has already lost one child to state care.

Several stories explore strained relationships between parents and children. The narrator of "In the Great War (II)" argues that a mother should kill her children before she commits suicide in order to save them from living out her life sentence. Other stories show resilient children who are able to face hardship. In "Knock-Knock," a clever, witty, and strong boy belies his mother's worries about his suffering from a possible divorce, and in "Santa Claus's New Clothes," a boy rebels against his manipulative stepmothers. In "Heat Haze" a daughter sacrifices herself for her gay father but suffers from her self-renunciation, and in "The Pardoner" another daughter holds her father responsible for each of her failures and makes him pay enormous sums of money for therapy because of his alleged abuse of her in childhood.

The scientific dystopia "Web Central," which maintains that the postfeminist future does not eliminate class conflict, is unique among Weldon's short stories. A privileged 132-year-old woman, who has had cosmetic surgery and medication in order to make her look twenty-five years old forever, lives in an antiseptic female cyber-world, which seems to protect her from the dirty, physical life of the lower classes outside, who have a low life expectancy because of HIV. The lower classes manage to take over the control of the cyber-

Dust jacket for the U.S. edition of Weldon's 1995 collection of satirical stories, which includes the sections "Tales of Wicked Women," "Tales of Wicked Men," and "Tales of Wicked Children" (Richland County Public Library)

world of the rich and eliminate them by turning around the process of aging until the inmates experience their birth in reverse and lose consciousness.

The volume *Angel, All Innocence, and Other Stories* (1995) is a selection of previously collected stories. *A Hard Time to Be a Father: A Collection of Short Stories* (1998), which includes four texts from Weldon's earlier anthologies, met with mixed reviews. Critiques of the repetitiveness and superficiality of her moral statements and her characterization of men in particular alternate with praise for her wit, vengeful justice, and the timeless truths and appeal of her writing. The disillusioned protagonist of the story "Move Out: Move On" summarizes her own changing relationships and women's experience in history, but her comment also characterizes the stories in this volume: "Things change, but don't necessarily get any better." The breaking of rules has become the norm. Repeated affairs by both men and women destroy friendships,

Title page for Weldon's 1998 collection of stories, in which female protagonists are driven to seek revenge after disappointments in love (Thomas Cooper Library, University of South Carolina)

marriages, and the bond between parents and children. The major difference between people lies less in the act of than in the reaction to betrayal. Characters hardly show any remorse as perpetrators but are vengeful as victims of betrayal, such as the beautiful woman who steals her old pal's husband ("Come on, Everybody"); the mother of two who is hurt when she finds her husband in bed with her best friend but who "savaged someone else's nest" on her own ("Move Out: Move On"); and the beautiful art critic who seduces a married artist merely to test her power of attraction and to humiliate his wife, who commits suicide ("Inspector Remorse"). The victims of betrayal do not wallow in self-pity but turn to revenge and new beginnings with or without men. In "Stasi" a movie star is suspected of having suffocated the therapist who invited her husband's verbal and sexual betrayal, and a jilted wife drives her rival away by continuously interfering with her husband's young love in "New Year's Day." In "Once in Love in Oslo" another wife warns her former rival of her husband's new affair and moves on to affairs of her own. The apparent loss of moral norms cannot simply be blamed on the younger generation, because often parents no longer serve as a model to their children. In "My Mother Said" the guidelines for life that an anxious mother passes on to her daughter are so contradictory as to be useless, and in "A Libation of Blood" mothers as well as their daughters exhibit deviant behavior.

In the final stories of the book, Weldon castigates the national health system in Great Britain. The geriatric comedy "Noisy into the Night" depicts the resumption of the ancient quarrel between a divorced husband and his former wife, who end up in hospital beds next to each other in the story "Terminal Mixed." The old feminist still upbraids her former husband for his patriarchal behavior and complains about disadvantages of the neglectful medical treatment and the burial of women. The situation appears equally bleak for each of them, however. The title story, "A Hard Time to Be a Father," is a mock-heroic, grotesque tour de force that ridicules the bureaucracy and chaos of public health. The situation is as unpleasant for the staff as for the patients because the hospital serves as a deficient refuge that attracts the homeless and the derelict. The feminized, innocent Candide Newman, who faints at the mere mention of the word *baby* and suffers from a stomachache, experiences the nightmare of a public hospital, which frustrates his pleas for medical treatment. The staff ignore the hypochondriac man as well as the snoring rugby player with an open fracture. Yet, when Candide's wife goes into labor, the staff responds quickly and everything turns out well. The grotesque events and the improbable happy ending exaggerate the shortcomings of public health and suggest the desirable forms of service.

Fay Weldon's witty stories cover the whole range of postwar developments in gender relationships, from the prefeminist domination of male chauvinism to the feminist negation of men in favor of women's solidarity and the postfeminist rise of confident and successful women. Her lucid insight, satiric exaggeration, and ironic comments highlight the strength, cleverness, versatility, and resourcefulness of women without neglecting their shortcomings and their complicity in their sufferings at the hands of men. For all her denunciation of the patriarchal system, Weldon never releases her individual characters from being responsible for their actions in the face of difficult moral decisions.

Interviews:

Melvin Maddocks, "Mothers and Masochists," *Time,* 101 (26 February 1973): 91;

John Heilpern, "Facts of Female Life," *London Observer Magazine,* 18 February 1979, pp. 36–37;

Angela Neustatter, "Earth Mother Truths," *Guardian,* 20 February 1979, p. 24;

Elisabeth Dunn, "Among the Women," *London Telegraph Sunday Magazine,* 16 December 1979, pp. 55, 58, 61, 64;

Pauline Peters, "The Fay behind Puffball," *Sunday Times* (London), 17 February 1980, p. 36;

Michelene Wandor, ed., *On Gender and Writing* (London & Boston: Pandora, 1983), pp. 160–165;

John Haffenden, *Novelists in Interview* (London & New York: Methuen, 1985), pp. 305–320;

Brenda Polan, "Reading between the Power Lines," *Guardian,* 14 August 1985, p. 18;

Libby Purves, "Weldon Takes the High Wire," *Times* (London), 2 September 1987, p. 15;

"Gentle Rebel Who She-Devils the Hardback Heavies," *Sunday Times* (London), 6 September 1987, p. 10;

Don Swaim, "Interview with Fay Weldon," *Wired for Books* (1988) <wiredforbooks.org/fayweldon/>;

Cliff Terry, "Interview," *Chicago Tribune,* 18 March 1990, p. 4;

Angela Lambert, "Not Such a She-Devil," *Independent on Sunday* (London), 5 May 1991, pp. 13–14;

Valerie Grove, "Ups and Downs among the Women," *Times Saturday Review* (London), 25 January 1992, pp. 10–11;

Hunter Davies, "Fay Weldon, a Sexy Rich Granny Having Fun," *Independent* (London), 2 February 1993, p. 13;

Mickey Pearlman, "Fay Weldon," in her *Listen to Their Voices: Twenty Interviews with Women Who Write* (New York: Norton, 1993), pp. 79–90;

Mina Kumar, "Interview: Fay Weldon," *Belles Lettres,* 10, no. 2 (1995): 16–18;

Joanna Zylinska, "Nature, Science and Witchcraft: An Interview with Fay Weldon," *Critical Survey,* 12, no. 3 (2000): 108–122.

References:

Flora Alexander, *Contemporary Women Novelists* (London: Edward Arnold, 1989), pp. 51–55;

Robyn Alexander, "Fay Weldon's Use of Form and the 'Female Voice,'" *Inter Action,* 4 (1996): 13–20;

Regina Barreca, ed., *Fay Weldon's Wicked Fictions* (Hanover, N.H.: University Press of New England, 1994);

Liz Bird and Joe Eliot, "The Lives and Loves of a She Devil (Fay Weldon–Ted Whitehead)," in *British Television Drama in the 1980s,* edited by George W. Brandt (Cambridge & New York: Cambridge University Press, 1993), pp. 214–233;

Wendy Brandmark, *Fay Weldon* (London: Book Trust in Conjunction with the British Council, 1988);

Finuala Dowling, *Fay Weldon's Fiction* (Madison, N.J.: Fairleigh Dickinson University Press, 1998);

Lana Faulks, *Fay Weldon* (New York: Twayne, 1998);

Liz Fekete, "Fay Weldon: Radical Heretic or Social Puritan?" *Race and Class,* 31, no. 2 (1989): 73–78;

Anne-Marie Herbert, "Rewriting the Feminine Script: Fay Weldon's Wicked Laughter," *Critical Matrix: The Princeton Journal of Women, Gender and Culture,* 7, no. 1 (1993): 21–40;

Lee A. Jacobus, "The Monologic Narrator in Fay Weldon's Short Fiction," in *Fay Weldon's Wicked Fictions,* edited by Barreca, pp. 163–171;

Olga Kenyon, "Fay Weldon and the Radicalising of Language," in her *Women Novelists Today: A Survey of English Writing in the Seventies and Eighties* (Brighton, U.K.: Harvester, 1988), pp. 104–128;

Agate Nesaule Krouse, "Feminism and Art in Fay Weldon's Novels," *Critique: Studies in Modern Fiction,* 20, no. 2 (1978): 5–20;

Barbara Puschmann-Nalenz, "'Cloudy Symbols of a (not so) High Romance': Feminine and Feminist Fantasy in the Fiction of Fay Weldon," *Anglistik und Englischunterricht,* 59 (1996): 163–179;

Bernhard Reitz, "'Miseries Are Political, Not Personal': Fay Weldon's Women and the Quest for Self Realization," in *Lineages of the Novel: Essays in Honour of Raimund Borgmeier,* edited by Reitz and Eckart Voigts-Virchow (Trier, Germany: Wissenschaftlicher, 2000), pp. 213–229;

Wolfgang Riedel, "Fay Weldons 'Weekend'–eine Geschichte von der subversiven Ironie des Glücks," *Anglistik und Englischunterricht,* 50 (1993): 55–65;

Lorna Sage, *Women in the House of Fiction: Post-War Women Novelists* (Basingstoke, U.K.: Macmillan, 1992), pp. 153–160;

Patricia Waugh, "Contemporary Women Writers: Challenging Postmodern Aesthetics," in her *Feminine Fictions: Revisiting the Postmodern* (London & New York: Routledge, 1989), pp. 168–217;

Alan Wilde, "'Bold, but Not Too Bold': Fay Weldon and the Limits of Poststructuralist Criticism," *Contemporary Literature,* 29, no. 3 (1988): 403–419;

Pauline Young, "Selling the Emperor's New Clothes: Fay Weldon as Contemporary Folklorist," *Folklore in Use,* 2, no. 1 (1994): 103–113.

Arnold Wesker
(24 May 1932 -)

Kevin De Ornellas
Queen's University, Belfast

See also the Wesker entries in *DLB 13: British Dramatists Since World War II; Concise Dictionary of British Literary Biography, Volume 8: Contemporary Writers, 1960 to Present;* and *DLB 310: British and Irish Dramatists Since World War II, Fourth Series.*

BOOKS: *Roots* (Harmondsworth, U.K.: Penguin, 1959);

I'm Talking about Jerusalem (Harmondsworth, U.K. & Baltimore, Md.: Penguin, 1960);

The Wesker Trilogy (London: Cape, 1960; New York: Random House, 1961)—comprises *Chicken Soup with Barley, Roots,* and *I'm Talking about Jerusalem;*

Labour and the Arts (Oxford: Gemini, 1960);

The Modern Playwright, or, O, Mother, Is It Worth It? (London: Gemini, 1960);

Chicken Soup with Barley (London: M. Evans, 1961);

The Kitchen (London: Cape, 1961; New York: Random House, 1961);

Chips with Everything (London: Cape, 1962; New York: Random House, 1962);

Their Very Own and Golden City (London: Cape, 1966);

The Four Seasons (London: Cape, 1966);

The Friends (London: Cape, 1970);

Fears of Fragmentation (London: Cape, 1970);

Six Sundays in January (London: Cape, 1971);

The Old Ones (London: Cape, 1973; revised edition, edited by Michael Marland, London & Glasgow: Blackie, 1974);

Say Goodbye, You May Never See Them Again: Scenes from Two East-End Backgrounds, text by Wesker, illustrations by John Allin (London: Cape, 1974);

Love Letters on Blue Paper: Three Stories (London: Cape, 1974; New York: Harper & Row, 1975);

The Journalists (London: Writers and Readers Publishing Cooperative, 1975);

The Plays of Arnold Wesker (New York: Harper & Row, 1976);

Words as Definitions of Experience (London: Writers and Readers Publishing Cooperative, 1976);

Arnold Wesker (photograph by Christopher Jackson/Getty Images)

Journey into Journalism: A Very Personal Account in Four Parts (London: Writers and Readers Publishing Cooperative, 1977);

Fatlips: A Story for Children (London: Writers and Readers Publishing Cooperative, 1978; New York: Harper & Row, 1978);

Said the Old Man to the Young Man: Three Stories (London: Cape, 1978);

The Journalists: A Triptych (London: Cape, 1979)—comprises *The Journalists*, "A Journal of the Writing of *The Journalists*," and *Journey into Journalism*;

Chips with Everything, The Friends, The Old Ones, Love Letters on Blue Paper [play] (Harmondsworth, U.K.: Penguin, 1980);

The Journalists, The Wedding Feast, The Merchant (Harmondsworth, U.K.: Penguin, 1980);

Love Letters on Blue Paper and Other Stories (Harmondsworth, U.K. & New York: Penguin, 1980);

Caritas (London: Cape, 1981);

The Merchant, edited by Glenda Leeming (London: Methuen, 1983);

Distinctions (London: Cape, 1985);

One-Woman Plays (Harmondsworth, U.K: Penguin, 1989)— comprises *Yardsale, Whatever Happened to Betty Lemon, Four Portraits of Mothers, The Mistress,* and *Annie Wobbler*;

Lady Othello and Other Plays (Harmondsworth, U.K.: Penguin, 1990)—comprises *One More Ride on the Merry Go Round, Caritas, When God Wanted a Son, Lady Othello,* and *Bluey*;

As Much As I Dare: An Autobiography (London: Century, 1994);

Wild Spring and Other Plays (Harmondsworth, U.K.: Penguin, 1994)—comprises *Badenheim 1939, Beorhtel's Hill, Three Women Talking, Letter to a Daughter, Blood Libel,* and *Wild Spring*;

The Birth of Shylock and the Death of Zero Mostel: Diary of a Play 1973 to 1980 (London: Quartet, 1997; New York: Fromm International, 1999);

Break My Heart (Cardiff: Drama Association of Wales, 1997);

The King's Daughters: Twelve Erotic Stories (London: Quartet, 1998).

PLAY PRODUCTIONS: *Chicken Soup with Barley,* Coventry, Belgrade Theatre, 7 July 1958; London, Royal Court Theatre, 14 July 1958;

Roots, Coventry, Belgrade Theatre, 25 May 1959; London, Royal Court Theatre, 30 June 1959 (transferred 30 July 1959 to Duke of York's Theatre); New York, Mayfair Theatre, 6 March 1961;

The Kitchen, short version, London, Royal Court Theatre, 13 September 1959; full production, Coventry, Belgrade Theatre, 19 June 1961; London, Royal Court Theatre, 27 June 1961; New York, New Theatre Workshop, 9 May 1966; New York, New 81st St. Theatre, 13 June 1966; revised version, Madison, University of Wisconsin, October 1990;

I'm Talking about Jerusalem, Coventry, Belgrade Theatre, 28 March 1960; London, Royal Court Theatre, 27 July 1960;

Chips with Everything, London, Royal Court Theatre, 27 April 1962; New York, Plymouth Theatre, 1 October 1963;

The Nottingham Captain, libretto by Wesker, Wellingborough, Centre 42 Festival, 11 September 1962;

Their Very Own and Golden City, Brussels, Belgium National Theatre, 13 August 1965; London, Royal Court Theatre, 19 May 1966;

The Four Seasons, Coventry, Belgrade Theatre, 24 August 1965; London, Saville Theatre, 21 September 1965; New York, Theatre Four, 14 March 1968; revised, Mold, Theatr Clywd, 4 November 2002;

The Friends, Stockholm, Stadsteater, 24 January 1970; London, Roundhouse, 19 May 1970;

The Old Ones, London, Royal Court Theatre, 8 August 1972; revised, Munich, Kammerspiele Theatre, February 1973; New York, Theatre at the Lambs Club, 6 December 1974;

The Wedding Feast, based on Fyodor Dostoevsky's "An Unpleasant Predicament," Stockholm, Stadsteater, 8 May 1974; revised, Leeds, Leeds Playhouse, 20 January 1977; revised again, Granville, Ohio, Dennison University, 1995;

The Journalists, professional reading, Highgate, Jackson's Lane Community Centre, 13 July 1975; amateur production, Coventry, Criterion Theatre, 27 March 1977; workshop production, Los Angeles, 1979; professional production, Wilhelmshaven, West Germany, 10 October 1981; London, Questors Theatre, 1996;

The Merchant, based on William Shakespeare's *The Merchant of Venice,* Stockholm, Royal Dramaten Theater, 8 October 1976; Philadelphia, Forrest Theatre, 2 September 1977; Washington, D.C., Kennedy Center, 29 September 1977; New York, Plymouth Theatre, 16 November 1977; Birmingham, Birmingham Repertory Theatre, 12 October 1978; revised as *Shylock,* dramatized reading, London, Riverside Studios, 16 October 1989;

Love Letters on Blue Paper, Syracuse, New York, Syracuse Stage, 14 October 1977; London, Cottesloe Theatre (National Theatre), 15 February 1978;

Caritas, London, Cottesloe Theatre (National Theatre), 7 October 1981; opera version, with music by Robert Saxton, Wakefield, Wakefield Opera House, 21 November 1991;

Four Portraits, Tokyo, Mitzukoshi Royal Theatre, 2 July 1982; Edinburgh, Edinburgh Festival, 20 August 1984; London, Man in the Moon Theatre, 20 October 1987;

Annie Wobbler, Birmingham, Birmingham Repertory Theatre Studio, 5 July 1983; London, New End Theatre, 26 July 1983; London, Fortune Theatre,

13 November 1984; New York, Westbeth Theatre Centre, 16 October 1986;

Sullied Hand, Edinburgh, Edinburgh Festival, Theatre at The Netherbow, 10 August 1984;

One More Ride on the Merry Go Round, Leicester, Phoenix Theatre, 25 April 1985;

Yardsale, Edinburgh, Fourth RSC/W. H. Smith Festival, 12 August 1985; performed with *Whatever Happened to Betty Lemon,* London, Hammersmith Lyric Studio, 17 February 1987;

Whatever Happened to Betty Lemon, Paris, Théâtre du Rond-Point, 12 November 1986; performed with *Yardsale,* London, Hammersmith Lyric Studio, 17 February 1987;

When God Wanted a Son, professional reading, Highgate, Jackson's Lane Community Centre, 19 February 1989; full production, London, New End Theatre, 6 February 1997;

Beorhtel's Hill, book by Wesker, music by Ian Stewart, Basildon, Towngate Theatre, 6 June 1989;

The Mistress, Arezzo, Festival of One Act Plays, 18 November 1991; performed with *Break, My Heart,* Cardiff, Sherman Theatre, 4 June 1997;

Three Women Talking [later retitled *Men Die, Women Survive*], Chicago, Northlight Theatre, 15 January 1992;

Letter to a Daughter, Seoul, Sanwoolim Theatre Company, 20 March 1992;

Wild Spring, Tokyo, Bungaku-za Theatre Company, 14 October 1994;

Blood Libel, text by Wesker, music by Derek Barnes, Norwich, Norwich Playhouse, 1 February 1996;

The Confession, reading, London, Lyric Hammersmith Studio, 12 April 1997;

Break, My Heart, performed with *The Mistress,* Cardiff, Sherman Theatre, 4 June 1997; performed with *The Four Seasons,* London, Blue Elephant Theatre, 10 March 2003;

Denial, Bristol, Bristol Old Vic, 16 May 2000;

The Kitchen [musical version], text by Wesker, music by Barnes and Barrington Pheloung, lyrics by Nigel Forde, Tokyo, 16 July 2000;

Groupie, Naples, Festival di Todi, 21 July 2002;

Letter to Myself, Hay-on-Wye, Hay Community Centre, 30 May 2004.

PRODUCED SCRIPTS: *Menace,* television, BBC, December 1963;

The Trilogy, television and radio, BBC, 1964;

Love Letters on Blue Paper, television, BBC, 2 March 1975;

The Kitchen, television, BBC, 1976;

Chips with Everything, television, BBC, 1977;

Annie, Anna, Annabella [Annie Wobbler], radio, Suddeutscher Rundfunk (Germany), 3 February 1983;

Caritas, radio, BBC Radio 3, 1983;

Yardsale, radio, BBC Radio 3, 6 October 1984;

Bluey, radio, Cologne Radio, 16 May 1985; BBC Radio 3, 11 December 1985;

Letter to a Daughter, television, Norwegian television, September 1992;

Roots, television, BBC2, 1992;

Break, My Heart, television, HTV, 1997.

SELECTED PERIODICAL PUBLICATION–UNCOLLECTED: "The Smaller Picture," *Guardian,* 15 March 2003 <http://books.guardian.co.uk/review/story/0,12084,913643,00.html>.

In early 2003, at a time of speculation as to whether or not British forces should assist American intervention in Iraq, Arnold Wesker submitted a comment, supporting direct action, to *The Sunday Times News Review.* Below his credit, he was referred to as a "left-wing playwright." This description of Wesker and the article itself indicate several things about this writer's status: that Wesker is still prepared to engage with the media to address contemporary issues; that the press still pigeonhole him as a sort of socialist, one-man pressure group; and that Wesker is known as a dramatist, not as a writer of prose fiction. Critics regularly ignore his short fiction; the Harry Ransom Humanities Research Center of the University of Texas at Austin, which owns his archive, lists Wesker's fictional prose in one sentence; and, unlike his plays, his prose narratives are all out of print and often difficult to obtain. Yet, Wesker has, throughout his career, published short fiction that is both interesting in its own right and also related to some of the major concerns of his better-known dramatic works.

In 2003 Wesker wrote, "Experience rather than political belief has driven me as a writer." This statement accounts for many of the subjects of Wesker's prose fiction as well as for those of his drama. Wesker was born on 24 May 1932 into a family of Jewish immigrants. They had settled in Stepney, a district in London's East End. Both his father, Joseph Wesker, and his mother, Leah (Perlmutter) Wesker, were of Eastern European origin—the former from Russia; the latter from Hungary. The Weskers were not particularly religious, but that did not dilute their cultural Jewishness. Wesker grew up in a working-class milieu. His nostalgia for his youth in East London is exemplified in an illustrated book of memories that he compiled in collaboration with artist John Allin, *Say Goodbye, You May Never See Them Again: Scenes from Two East-End Backgrounds* (1974). Joseph Wesker was a tailor with plenty

Wesker, backstage at the Belgrade Theatre in Coventry in 1959 at a performance of his second play, Roots; *with him are (clockwise) his mother, Leah whom he is hugging; his wife, Dusty; and actresses Joan Plowright and Mary Ure (courtesy of the author; from* As Much As I Dare: An Autobiography, *1994; Gorgas Library, University of Alabama)*

of work, but his wife was often obliged to supplement the family income by menial jobs such as cooking assistant. The range of experiences that Arnold acquired was broadened by four years spent in western England and in Wales. He was evacuated from London in 1939 and was allowed to return in 1943. As was typical for a youth from a lower-income family of this period, Wesker left school at the age of fifteen. He embarked on several professional false starts: carpentry, antique reproduction, bookselling, plumbing, rural laboring, and kitchen portering. He worked in places as diverse as Norfolk and Paris. More-substantial periods of employment gave material for his dramas and short prose: he worked as a pastry cook in an upscale restaurant in the West End of London, and he spent more than twenty months as an airman in the Royal Air Force (RAF).

By the mid 1950s, Wesker was tired of this unfixed way of life. Encouraged by his new partner, Doreen "Dusty" Bicker, he decided to pursue a writing career that he initially assumed would be preceded by formal education. Attempts at acquiring a formal education faltered at the London School of Film Technique, where he disliked technical training. As a result, Wesker is largely an autodidact. He began to write plays and in the 1950s enjoyed success as part of a young generation of playwrights—including John Arden, Shelagh Delaney, John Osborne, and Harold Pinter—who revitalized the British theater. The first staging of Wesker's first play, *Chicken Soup with Barley,* took place in Coventry in July 1958. He also married Dusty in 1958, and the couple eventually had three children, two boys and a girl (born in 1959, 1961, and 1962). *Chicken Soup with Barley* and its two sequels, *Roots* and *I'm Talking about Jerusalem,* had been staged in London by 1960 and were published in 1960 as *The Wesker Trilogy.* Many of the themes of these plays—the experience of Jews in Britain, the complexities of working-class life, and the difficulties of political commitment—return in his later short fiction.

Despite financial and social success, the 1960s proved to be a disappointing decade for Wesker. His two major works from this decade, *Their Very Own and Golden City* (performed, 1965; published, 1966) and *The Four Seasons* (performed, 1965; published, 1966) were, in terms of audience attendance, theatrical failures. But what most grieved Wesker were political rather than fiscal reversals. Between 1961 and 1970, he worked with the British Trades Union Congress to further the aims of its Resolution 42. The aim was to make the arts accessible to underprivileged members of the workforce. But Centre 42, the society that was founded to further the policies of the resolution, and that Wesker chaired for a decade, was continually underfunded and undersubscribed. It was finally declared to be an unserviceable failure in 1970. With a sense of the limitations of the ability of theater to penetrate everyday working-class life, Wesker began to publish prose narratives. Between 1971 and 1978, Wesker's three major short-story collections were presented to the public.

Of the five works gathered together in Wesker's 1971 collection, *Six Sundays in January,* only two are actually prose fiction. (Two of the other pieces are theatrical, and one is a diary.) Both of the stories, "Pools" and "Six Sundays in January," had been printed several years before in Jewish periodicals with limited circulation. But by publishing the stories in a book, Wesker insisted on the importance of these works within his better-known output. "Pools" is set in the area of Stepney, where Wesker was born and raised. The main family in the tale are Jewish by identity rather than spiritual practice—as were Wesker's own. The main character, a lonely widow, Mrs. Hyams, is treated with immense respect by Wesker. Her dreams about winning a huge sum of money on the soccer pools are not dismissed as self-indulgent cravings but are seen as a manifestation of a lonely conviction. Unlike her penny-pinching employers in a Brick Lane factory, the widow is generous and community spirited. Her desire to win money through gambling on predicting soccer results (the "Pools" of the title) is not selfish; she wishes to spend most of any possible winnings on others. The family unity and happiness of her dreams is contrasted with the indifference of her son toward his mother. Mrs. Hyams does not win the pools, and at the end of the story she begins to see herself as "nothing," just as her son and gentile Britain see her. Wesker's story insists that socially marginalized persons such as Mrs. Hyams are not "nothing." Rather, they are benevolently inclined, but their hopes for family unity and communal respect are frustrated by the apathy and tiredness that modern life exerts on citizens who are hardworking by necessity.

Wesker had hoped that "Pools" would be shot as a full-length motion picture. He sent the manuscript to a professedly interested director, Jack Clayton. Clayton, Wesker alleges in his autobiography, *As Much As I Dare* (1994), held on to the manuscript for a long time, eventually sending it back only after threats from a legally trained relative of Wesker. Wesker had already been disgruntled by editors' treatment of the story. He had to wait for more than three years before the *Jewish Quarterly* eventually published it. "Pools," then, marks the beginning of Wesker's continuing battle against what he perceives to be the discourtesy of directors, producers, and publishers.

"Pools" had originally been published in the mid 1950s, whereas "Six Sundays in January" dates from the latter half of the 1960s. The main character of "Six Sundays in January" is a Jewish woman from Stepney who has moved into married life in Hampstead, North London. Her trajectory from working-class hardship to middle-class affluence mirrors Wesker's own path in the 1960s. The impossibility of the title—there cannot be more than five Sundays in any one month—is significant. Sundays, for Marcia Needham, are a time of leisure; on these days, despite the demands of her three children, she has time to think. There are too many Sundays, and, consequently, there is too much time to think. Marcia is not satisfied by the material luxuries acquired through marriage to her almost anonymous husband, Buddy, and she receives no sexual fulfillment from the marriage. Margaret Drabble, in one of the few substantial critical notices of Wesker's fiction, refers to Marcia's "private disillusion." Marcia is, in short, lonely in her large bourgeois house, with a husband whose affection has been eroded by tiredness caused by family and work commitments. Emphasizing the lack of love within the wider family, Marcia has only a cool relationship with her mother, who is still appalled at "Marcia marrying a gentile." The elderly Mrs. Newman is the first of many embittered former Communists in Wesker's prose. Her Jewish identity, which is eternal (unlike the vanished ideals of Marxism), is now her only real link to a familial present—she eats only kosher food, for instance. Friendship, too, provides little relief for Marcia in this story. An attempt to revive acquaintance with a former girlfriend leads to nothing; indeed, the friend commits suicide, thus depriving Marcia of her last link to the East London of her youth. At the end of the story she is left attempting to find solace in her children, a solace that will presumably be as transient as Marcia's relationship with her mother.

All three of the works in Wesker's 1974 collection, *Love Letters on Blue Paper,* are prose narratives. (Wesker later adapted the title story as a stage play.) To describe the middle piece, "A Time of Dying," as "fiction," however, is difficult. This piece is given the subtitle "A Sort of Story." Wesker made no attempt to conceal that he was writing about the demise of his own elderly relatives: he gave all of them their historical names; the first-person "I" is Wesker himself; and his wife, Dusty, is present as she would be in any conventional Wesker autobiography. Nothing qualifies this work as fiction except its ending at a point of self-conscious optimism, a point that contrasts vividly with the unchecked bleakness of every other point.

The story describes how several elderly aunts are nursed by Wesker's family as they die slowly. The narrator states that he is "surrounded by dying": this phrase neatly encapsulates the air of decline and withering that characterizes the late stages of his relatives' lives. The dying women had all been East End socialists in their youths, but are now disillusioned. One aunt, Sarah, according to one of her sisters, "never recovered from the Khrushchev revelations [about past tactics of the Soviet regime]." For Wesker, no explanation of why the aunts no longer believe in the leftist principles of their youth is satisfactory. Instead, flawed health and intellectual fragmentation parallel the collapse of their effective opposition to the excesses of capitalism. When Sarah dies, Wesker confronts death grimly. Taking his time to assess the deceased woman, he "stared and stared at the face." So straightforward and relentless is this narrative about dying that the reader, too, must confront the grimness of death scenes, the inevitability of which is matched by the conspicuous lack of dignity endured by the sufferer. At the denouement of the piece, Wesker concentrates on his father-in-law, Poppy Bicker. Poppy has been ill, but the last lines focus on his recovery. Regaining some vigor, "he's started to ride a bike again." This energetic, happy ending contrasts with the focus on mortality.

Personal experiences of the author are also reflected in the first story from *Love Letters on Blue Paper*. The main character of "The Man Who Became Afraid" has been, like Wesker, a socialist activist. Unlike Wesker, however, Brewster has given up all socialist ideals. Sheridan Brewster's wan personality is depicted through a portrait of a broken, middle-aged, middle-class male. Ideological disappointment is mirrored by matrimonial misery. Sheridan's marriage to a spoiled American, Mildred, is summed up in the sentence "It was a mistake." Various efforts by Sheridan to achieve physical closeness are rebuffed by his unloving wife. Lonely and failing, Sheridan is possessed by a fear of the seemingly ceaseless violence of the world. The focus of the text is on environmental destruction. Words such as "waste" and "pollution" transcend the personal malaise of Sheridan, bringing attention to broader concerns. The dangers for the world are understood by Sheridan, but, enervated and disengaged, he has no energy to protest even modestly against what is seen as the reckless trend of laissez-faire mercantile expansion.

The themes of marital breakdown, political failure, and human mortality coalesce in the title story of *Love Letters on Blue Paper*. The first-person narrator is, again, clearly modeled on Wesker himself: opinions expressed by the narrator closely parallel opinions articulated by Wesker in his large corpus of criticism, journalism, and cultural commentary. Maurice, as many bourgeois figures in the stories, has been transported from proletarian roots. He is obliged to return to a one-time political mentor because of the older man's illness. With typical plainness of expression, Victor, a trade-union leader, tells Maurice, "I'm dying, lad." Again, a character's slow, physical decline parallels an admission that hopes for a socialist England have been vanquished. The cancer-stricken Victor laments that left-wingers "Can't win now, Maurice, capitalism's built up a resistance to criticism." The main criticism of the story, however, is aimed at a more specific target than capitalism. Some old union officials appear for a visit to the ailing Victor. Much to the annoyance of his hard-talking wife, Sonia, their company tires him. She accuses the visiting union members of being "selfish men who used you [Victor], built their careers on you and then left you." In one letter Sonia sees Victor as merely an indulgent failure, a being "filled with pity and shit." The letters are written on blue notepaper, but not all can be described as "love letters." By the end of the story, Victor dies. Two last letters addressed to him by Sonia are given to Maurice. These express a positive, but still unsentimental, appreciation of her life with her trade union official husband. The word "love" is repeatedly used to describe her feelings for him, now that all the rancorous urges have been exorcised through the earlier letters. Taken as a whole, this 1974 collection questions whether or not ideological or personal relationships can ever be successful.

In 1978 Wesker published two books of fiction. One was a new trio of stories for adults, *Said the Old Man to the Young Man*. The other was a large-print, ninety-page children's novella, *Fatlips*. The latter is, on the surface, an innocuous yarn about an eleven-year-old boy, Joel Amersham, who, for a short time, is given the power to fly by Fatlips, an odd but well-wishing magician. Wesker's political beliefs are just as apparent in this novella as they are in his adult-oriented work. One episode, in which the protagonist's parents confront a bully's family, embodies Wesker's socialist principles. Joel's father, a former trade-union representative, argues against the exploitation of the weak by the strong, while the bully's father believes in the law of the jungle. Also, in the ugly and despised character of Fatlips himself, Wesker again insists on the value of marginalized individuals.

Wesker's collection of adult stories from 1978, *Said the Old Man to the Young Man*, retains many continuities from the earlier works: as with *Love Letters on Blue Paper*, Wesker includes three stories in the book, and thematic preoccupations such as death and decline, marital disaffection, the loss of proletarian roots, and political defeat are foregrounded. These stories, how-

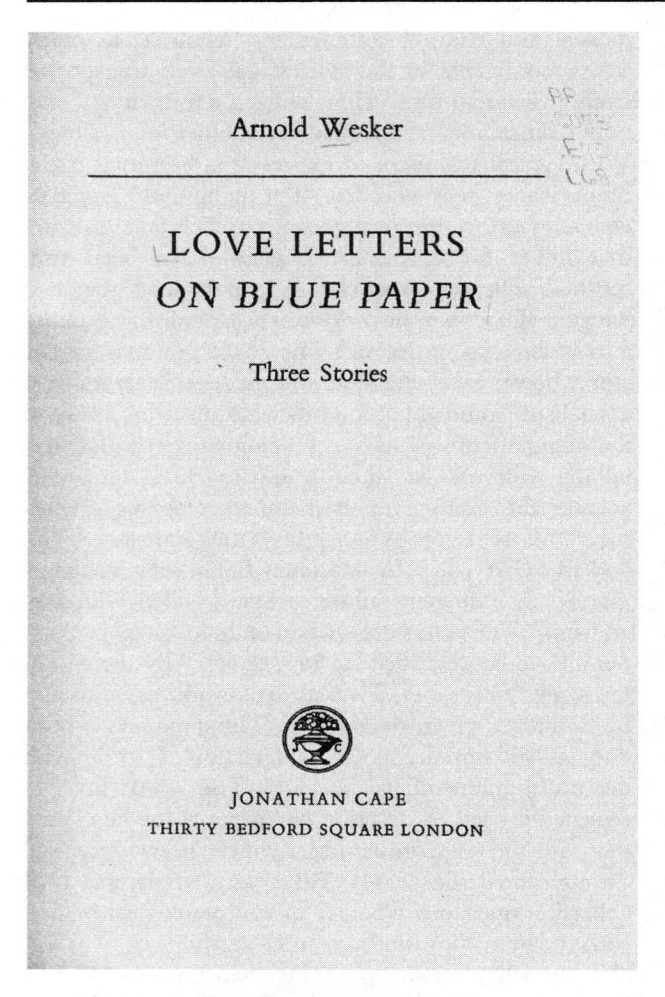

Title page for Wesker's 1974 collection. He adapted the title story into a stage play in 1977 (Thomas Cooper Library, University of South Carolina).

ever, reveal evidence of progression. In the middle story, the title piece, the targets for Wesker's disfavor are exposed more subtly than in the earlier work. In "Said the Old Man to the Young Man," two mentalities are attacked: one is the belief that workers can flourish within a capitalist system; the other is anti-Semitism. These targets are familiar ones in the Wesker canon, but in this story they are cast into relief through delicate characterization. The "Young Man" of the title, Amos, has no interest in whether average workers thrive under capitalism. His belief is that the free market quite properly rewards the few who deserve to be rewarded. Wesker's contempt for this character's attitude toward art is apparent. Art, for Amos, is a "commodity," a set of consumer goods. Wesker's more nuanced characterization is seen in the construction of Amos's gentile girlfriend, Miranda. Her views seem, at first, more sympathetic to lower-income workers' withdrawal of their labor; Miranda supports the principle of striking, alleging that "the simplest Marxist lesson has filtered through." This "lesson" is that "a worker's capital is his labour." Miranda goes on to assert that any worker, as much as any businessman, is "also in possession of capital to be invested . . . that labour has an existence of its own and he wants it to earn a profit." For Wesker, this thinking erroneously places the rights-seeking worker within the limited aspirations feasible within the confines of capitalism. Miranda's thoughts collude with, rather than oppose, libertarian economics. More subtly than Amos's overt conservatism, her comments differentiate her generation from the impassioned socialism that was actively agitated for by Amos's older relatives in the East End during the 1930s.

During the mid 1970s, Wesker was preoccupied with the Shakespearean character Shylock. Efforts to have his *The Merchant* (1976)—a reassessment of the sources William Shakespeare used for *The Merchant of Venice* (1600)—staged in an uncompromised manner are accounted for in Wesker's retrospective compilation of documents, *The Birth of Shylock and the Death of Zero Mostel: Diary of a Play 1973 to 1980* (1997). In delineating the birth of Shylock, Wesker demonstrates his entrenched belief that this Shakespearean character is an anti-Semitic creation. Prior to "Said the Old Man to the Young Man," all of Wesker's stories had, to a greater or lesser extent, focused on the problems Jews face in Britain, where the Jewish minority culture is often seen as marginal and even alien. The author's bitterness at the ignoring of British anti-Semitism is as apparent in "Said the Old Man to the Young Man" as it is in *The Merchant*. The "Old Man" is Martin, an unattractive eighty-two-year-old. Unlike his great-nephew, Amos, whose capitalistic traits are anathema to Martin, the old man is doctrinaire in both Jewishness and socialism. He speaks for Wesker in one regard—he denounces the historical negative way Western society views the Jewish way of life. Demanding toward his relations, irascible, and obstreperous, Martin has few appealing qualities. But, like previous Wesker characters, he is valued as he has opinions that are not held attentively, if at all, by England's youth. The angry invective of this story is new in Wesker's prose fiction, but the insistence that value can be found in the thoughts of even the most jaded and jading individual continues the moral vein of his earlier work.

Like Amos, the young Jewish male in "The Man Who Would Never Write like Balzac" has a naive girlfriend who remains unnamed. Wesker castigates this female character for ignorance. Her "main attraction" for the protagonist, a weak poet, Constantine, is "her enthusiasm for the arts, which she expressed with a coy bewilderment that he mistook for perceptive awe." The character is seen as bereft of the insight necessary for cultural appreciation. An impatience with women is also apparent in the construction of Constantine's mother, Mrs. Lander. An insignificant spat with her husband spirals into a more serious row. Constantine himself is a weak figure: he reveres but cannot emulate great writers such as Honoré de Balzac, Franz Kafka, George Bernard Shaw, and Virginia Woolf.

In terms of both length (one hundred pages) and thematic scope, "The Visit," the final story in *Said the Old Man to the Young Man*, is Wesker's most notable prose story. Familiar topics of emotional vagaries in marriage and loss of political will are addressed with more-elaborate changes of pace and tone. The temptations of adultery are recounted with extended care. In the story, two couples spend some leisure time together. The Danish husband and wife, Karl-Olaf and Janika (whose marriage is in trouble), entertain Raphael and Maddeau (whose partnership seems to be flourishing) at their country home in their adopted land, England. Some years previously, the then twenty-something Danes had been taught and mentored by the academic Maurice. During one midmorning coffee session, Raphael, who normally countenances only "high" art, enjoys, with the others, a recording of songs written and performed by The Beatles. "Now time has passed," he concedes, "and the silly adulation is over I find . . . they've—um—aged well. Pleasingly." This nostalgia-induced tolerance of Beatle appreciation exactly mirrors Wesker's comments in "A Diary for Stockholm" (one of the nonfiction pieces in *Six Sundays in January*). Music, in this story, including the music of the distinguished collector, singer, and writer of workers' songs, Ewan MacColl, becomes important in the rehearsal of anxieties about both nuptial and political crises.

The principal characters engage in sexual games. Maddeau dances in a provocative manner; Karl-Olaf recalls masturbating at the thought of Maddeau; Raphael, in front of the other two adults, slowly caresses Janika's breasts, visibly arousing her; Janika, languishing at the edge of total estrangement from Karl-Olaf, rejects her husband's sexual advances, but does, eventually, engage in an intense kissing session with Raphael. The partner swapping is completed as Karl-Olaf boasts about passionately kissing Maddeau. Like any belief in marital fidelity, Raphael's faith in ideological purity is tested by several factors; one of them is observance of the changed environment of the countryside. Around the young Danes' dwelling is "no building," but "no clump of trees" either. The land has been stripped of trees in order to further agriculture. Brutality wrought by man on nature is aligned with larger species' exploitation of their prey. The ruthless competitiveness of natural creatures disturbs the left-wing ideals of Raphael. The younger man, Karl-Olaf, seems, to some extent, to have already shifted to the political right. He strives to give credence to his professional study of economic documentation, arguing that "the real history of nations" can be found in textual remains of trading deals. Trade, for him, is a "natural" activity. Raphael, clinging to a long-held criticism of the free market, refuses to accept that human endeavor must reflect natural competitiveness. But so dominant is rival-crushing capitalism that even Raphael has to accept that it seems inevitable, just as virulent exploitation in nature is unchangeable. The two male characters quarrel over a wide range of political and social issues, and Raphael's thinking matures during the visit. He has, like all other socialist characters in Wesker's stories, tested his ideology against the writings of such disparate theorists as Karl Marx, William Morris, and John Ruskin. But exposure (through translations by Karl-Olaf) to contemporary Chinese poetry moderates his sense of righteousness in political thought. The poetry, which seems to derive from anti-Maoist dissidents, simply insists that positive virtues and blameless victimhood are not restricted to enlightened communists and uninformed workers. Thinkers in the center, or even on the Right, can be socially aware.

In the quarter of a century following the publication of *Fatlips* and *Said the Old Man to the Young Man*, Wesker produced one more collection of short fiction. *The King's Daughters: Twelve Erotic Stories*, published in 1998, was poorly received by reviewers. Wesker began working on the book in the late 1970s. Despite its long gestation, the book appeared in a badly printed edition, full of typographical errors, published by Quartet Books. The concept of the book was gleaned from European folk legends and from fairy tales by the Brothers Grimm. A king, Melania, has ruled the kingdom of Melandia for many years. He has, at various times, married a dozen different women, all of whom have taught him some particular skill. Each wife has borne Melania a daughter. The sexual awakening of each daughter forms the narrative of each story. All twelve stories are told by the king's chronicler, Coaxandria, who has somehow acquired omniscient knowledge of the daughters' most intimate conduct. Each is a sort of mini bildungsroman in which a daughter comes of age by taking part in bizarre sex acts.

Unlike other Wesker stories, these tales show no evidence of substantial political thought; *The King's Daughters* is, Wesker has admitted in interviews, escapist, erotic fantasy. Coaxandria, the narrator, tells the reader at the beginning of the book that as well as editing and relating the stories, he will "interpret and summarize" their significance. But he does not interpret the tales. He merely recounts the daughters' experiences with as much sexual detail as is feasible. Coaxandria has planned to make the tales appear politically or morally significant but instead revels in the sensuality, ignoring social issues. The king himself retires from rule altogether at the end of the book. No comment is made on the absolute monarchy that has been exercised in Melandia. *The King's Daughters,* instead, dramatizes a deliberate turning away from politics. This rejection of serious political discourse is an anomaly in Wesker's writing.

During the 1980s, the 1990s, and in the early twenty-first century, Arnold Wesker has continued to write drama and nonfictional prose prolifically. The drama tends to be more acclaimed than the nonfiction. He complains against political apathy and withdrawal, against mercantile apathy in general, and against what he sees as the profusion of injustice and tyranny throughout the world. However, he retains hope and ambition. According to Wesker's agent, Nicky Lund, Wesker began to write the novel provisionally titled "Honey" on 19 May 2003: it will be Wesker's first published novel. Wesker lives in the Welsh village of Blaendigeddi; Dusty Wesker lives many miles away at Hove.

Despite the enduring success of *Chips with Everything* (1962) and *The Kitchen* (1959), Arnold Wesker insists, "I still feel my masterpiece has yet to be written." Wesker's plays are by far the best-known part of his work, but since the 1970s he has also produced a substantial body of short fiction that addresses the major concerns central to his drama and nonfiction. It forms an integral part of his oeuvre.

References:

Reade W. Dornan, *Arnold Wesker Revisited* (New York: Twayne, 1994);

Margaret Drabble, "Arnold Wesker," in *Arnold Wesker: A Casebook,* edited by Dornan (London & New York: Garland, 1999), pp. 75–88;

Ronald Hayman, *Arnold Wesker,* third edition (London: Heinemann, 1979);

John O'Mahony, "Piques and Troughs: Profile on [and interview with] Arnold Wesker," *Guardian,* 25 May 2002 <www.guardian.co.uk/saturday_review/story/0,3605,721464,00.html>;Wesker, comp. <www.arnoldwesker.com>.

Papers:

Arnold Wesker's papers are in the Harry Ransom Humanities Research Center, University of Texas at Austin <www.hrc.utexas.edu/research/fa/wesker.html>.

Checklist of Further Readings

Allen, Walter. *The Short Story in English.* Oxford: Clarendon Press / New York: Oxford University Press, 1981.

Baldwin, Dean. "The Tardy Evolution of the British Short Story," *Studies in Short Fiction,* 30 (Winter 1993): 23-33.

Baldwin and Gregory L. Morris. *The Short Story in English–Britain and North America: An Annotated Bibliography.* Metuchen, N.J.: Scarecrow Press / Pasadena, Cal.: Salem Press, 1994.

Bayley, John. *The Short Story: Henry James to Elizabeth Bowen.* New York: St. Martin's Press, 1988.

Beachcroft, T. O. *The Modest Art: A Survey of the Short Story in English.* London & New York: Oxford University Press, 1968.

Carlson, Julia, ed. *Banned in Ireland: Censorship and the Irish Writer.* Athens: University of Georgia Press, 1990.

Carter, Angela, ed. *Wayward Girls and Wicked Women: An Anthology of Stories.* London: Virago, 1986.

Fallon, Erin, and others, eds. *A Reader's Companion to the Short Story in English.* Westport, Conn.: Greenwood Press, 2001.

Forkner, Ben, and Philippe Séjourné. "An Interview with V. S. Pritchett," *Journal of the Short Story in English,* 6 (Spring 1986): 11-38.

Gullason, Thomas A. "The Short Story: An Underrated Art," *Studies in Short Fiction,* 2 (Fall 1964): 13-31.

Gullason. "The Short Story: Revision and Renewal," *Studies in Short Fiction,* 19 (Summer 1982): 221-230.

Hanson, Clare. *Short Stories and Short Fictions, 1880-1980.* London: Macmillan, 1985.

Hanson, ed. *Re-reading the Short Story.* Basingstoke, U.K.: Macmillan, 1989.

Head, Dominic. *The Modernist Short Story: A Study in Theory and Practice.* Cambridge & New York: Cambridge University Press, 1992.

Kilroy, James F., ed. *The Irish Short Story: A Critical History.* Boston: Twayne, 1984.

Klaus, Gustav H. "The Other Short Story: Working-Class Tales of the 1920s," *Journal of the Short Story in English,* 7 (Autumn 1986): 29-42.

Lee, Hermione, ed. *The Secret Self: Short Stories by Women.* London: Dent, 1985.

May, Charles E. "The Nature of Knowledge in Short Fiction," *Studies in Short Fiction,* 21 (Fall 1984): 327-338.

May. "Prolegomenon to a Generic Study of the Short Story," *Studies in Short Fiction,* 33 (Fall 1996): 461-473.

May. *The Short Story: The Reality of Artifice.* New York: Twayne, 1995.

Monod, Sylvère. "Quatre Auteurs en quête d'un genre," *Journal of the Short Story in English,* 2 (January 1984): 11-29.

Moosmüller, Birgit. *Die experimentelle englische Kurzgeschichte der Gegenwart.* Munich: W. Fink, 1993.

O'Faolain, Sean. *The Short Story,* second edition. Cork: Mercier Press, 1972.

Rafroidi, Patrick, and Terence Brown, eds. *The Irish Short Story.* Gerrards Cross, U.K.: C. Smythe / Atlantic Highlands, N.J.: Humanities Press, 1979.

Reid, Ian. *The Short Story.* Critical Idiom, no. 37. London: Eyre Methuen / New York: Barnes & Noble, 1977.

Schmitz, Wolfgang F. W. *Die Darstellung Irlands in der modernen irischen Short Story: Eine Bestandsaufnahme zur thematisch-inhaltlichen Ausrichtung irischer Short-Story-Autoren in den sechziger und siebziger Jahren.* Europäische Hochschulschriften, no. 95. Frankfurt am Main & Bern: Peter Lang, 1981.

Séjourné, Philippe. "Graham Greene on the Short Story," *Journal of the Short Story in English,* 4 (Spring 1985): 11–24.

Séjourné. "La Nouvelle à la recherche d'un troisième souffle," *Journal of the Short Story in English,* 1 (1983): 7–16.

Shaw, Valerie. *The Short Story: A Critical Introduction.* London & New York: Longman, 1983.

Trussler, Michael. "Suspended Narratives: The Short Story and Temporality," *Studies in Short Fiction,* 33 (Fall 1996): 557–577.

Vannatta, Dennis, ed. *The English Short Story, 1945–1980: A Critical History.* Boston: Twayne, 1985.

Watson, Noelle, ed. *Reference Guide to Short Fiction.* Detroit: St. James Press, 1994.

Contributors

Moira Burgess
Mary Burke . . . . *University of Connecticut*
Christopher Thomas Cairney . . . . *Istanbul Dogus University*
Pilar Sánchez Calle . . . . *University of Jaén, Spain*
Moira E. Casey . . . . *Miami University of Ohio at Middletown*
Pradyumna S. Chauhan . . . . *Arcadia University*
Peter Clandfield . . . . *Nipissing University*
Sabine Coelsch-Foisner . . . . *University of Salzburg*
Lucy Collins . . . . *St. Martin's College, Carlisle*
Kevin De Ornellas . . . . *Queen's University, Belfast*
Andrzej Gasiorek . . . . *University of Birmingham*
Irene Gilsenin-Nordin . . . . *Dalarna University, Sweden*
Wolfgang Görtschacher . . . . *University of Salzburg*
Brett Josef Grubisic . . . . *University of British Columbia*
Ralf Hertel . . . . *Free University Berlin*
Robert Ellis Hosmer Jr. . . . . *Smith College*
Günther Jarfe . . . . *University of Passau*
Harri Pritchard Jones . . . . *Yr Academi Gymreig (The Welsh Academy)*
James M. Lang . . . . *Assumption College*
Amy Lee . . . . *Hong Kong Baptist University*
Marti D. Lee . . . . *University of South Carolina*
Mitchell R. Lewis . . . . *Elmira College*
Patrick Lonergan . . . . *National University of Ireland, Galway*
Graeme Macdonald . . . . *University of Warwick*
Cheryl Alexander Malcolm . . . . *University of Gdańsk*
David Malcolm . . . . *University of Gdańsk*
Mike W. Malm
Bridget Matthews-Kane . . . . *University of Massachusetts, Amherst*
Jed Mayer . . . . *University of Canterbury*
Jude R. Meche . . . . *Missouri Southern State University*
Michael Meyer . . . . *University of Koblenz-Landau*
Gavin Miller . . . . *University of Glasgow*
Rosina Neginsky . . . . *University of Illinois at Springfield*
Shawn O'Hare . . . . *Carson-Newman College*
Pietra Palazzolo . . . . *University of Essex*

Contributors

Pádraigín Riggs	*University College, Cork*
G. H. Timmermans	*University of Macau*
Janine Utell	*Widener University*
Paul Willetts	
Fiona Wilson	*Fordham University*
Greg C. Winston	*Husson College*

Cumulative Index

Dictionary of Literary Biography, Volumes 1-319
Dictionary of Literary Biography Yearbook, 1980-2002
Dictionary of Literary Biography Documentary Series, Volumes 1-19
Concise Dictionary of American Literary Biography, Volumes 1-7
Concise Dictionary of British Literary Biography, Volumes 1-8
Concise Dictionary of World Literary Biography, Volumes 1-4

Cumulative Index

DLB before number: *Dictionary of Literary Biography,* Volumes 1-319
Y before number: *Dictionary of Literary Biography Yearbook,* 1980-2002
DS before number: *Dictionary of Literary Biography Documentary Series,* Volumes 1-19
CDALB before number: *Concise Dictionary of American Literary Biography,* Volumes 1-7
CDBLB before number: *Concise Dictionary of British Literary Biography,* Volumes 1-8
CDWLB before number: *Concise Dictionary of World Literary Biography,* Volumes 1-4

A

Aakjær, Jeppe 1866-1930 .... DLB-214
Aarestrup, Emil 1800-1856 .... DLB-300
Abbey, Edward 1927-1989 .... DLB-256, 275
Abbey, Edwin Austin 1852-1911 .... DLB-188
Abbey, Maj. J. R. 1894-1969 .... DLB-201
Abbey Press DLB-49
The Abbey Theatre and Irish Drama, 1900-1945 .... DLB-10
Abbot, Willis J. 1863-1934 .... DLB-29
Abbott, Edwin A. 1838-1926 .... DLB-178
Abbott, Jacob 1803-1879 .... DLB-1, 42, 243
Abbott, Lee K. 1947- DLB-130
Abbott, Lyman 1835-1922 .... DLB-79
Abbott, Robert S. 1868-1940 .... DLB-29, 91
'Abd al-Hamid al-Katib circa 689-750 .... DLB-311
Abe Kōbō 1924-1993 .... DLB-182
Abelaira, Augusto 1926- DLB-287
Abelard, Peter circa 1079-1142? DLB-115, 208
Abelard-Schuman DLB-46
Abell, Arunah S. 1806-1888 .... DLB-43
Abell, Kjeld 1901-1961 .... DLB-214
Abercrombie, Lascelles 1881-1938 .... DLB-19
The Friends of the Dymock Poets Y-00
Aberdeen University Press Limited DLB-106
Abish, Walter 1931- DLB-130, 227
Ablesimov, Aleksandr Onisimovich 1742-1783 .... DLB-150
Abraham à Sancta Clara 1644-1709 ..... DLB-168
Abrahams, Peter 1919- DLB-117, 225; CDWLB-3
Abramov, Fedor Aleksandrovich 1920-1983 .... DLB-302
Abrams, M. H. 1912- DLB-67
Abramson, Jesse 1904-1979 .... DLB-241
Abrogans circa 790-800 .... DLB-148
Abschatz, Hans Aßmann von 1646-1699 .... DLB-168
Abse, Dannie 1923- DLB-27, 245
Abu al-'Atahiyah 748-825? DLB-311

Abu Nuwas circa 757-814 or 815 .... DLB-311
Abu Tammam circa 805-845 .... DLB-311
Abutsu-ni 1221-1283 .... DLB-203
Academy Chicago Publishers DLB-46
Accius circa 170 B.C.-circa 80 B.C. DLB-211
"An account of the death of the Chevalier de La Barre," Voltaire DLB-314
Accrocca, Elio Filippo 1923-1996 .... DLB-128
Ace Books DLB-46
Achebe, Chinua 1930- DLB-117; CDWLB-3
Achtenberg, Herbert 1938- DLB-124
Ackerman, Diane 1948- DLB-120
Ackroyd, Peter 1949- DLB-155, 231
Acorn, Milton 1923-1986 .... DLB-53
Acosta, José de 1540-1600 .... DLB-318
Acosta, Oscar Zeta 1935?-1974? DLB-82
Acosta Torres, José 1925- DLB-209
Actors Theatre of Louisville DLB-7
Adair, Gilbert 1944- DLB-194
Adair, James 1709?-1783? DLB-30
Aðalsteinn Kristmundsson (see Steinn Steinarr)
Adam, Graeme Mercer 1839-1912 .... DLB-99
Adam, Robert Borthwick, II 1863-1940 .... DLB-187
Adame, Leonard 1947- DLB-82
Adameşteanu, Gabriel 1942- DLB-232
Adamic, Louis 1898-1951 .... DLB-9
Adamovich, Georgii 1894-1972 .... DLB-317
Adams, Abigail 1744-1818 .... DLB-183, 200
Adams, Alice 1926-1999 .... DLB-234; Y-86
Adams, Bertha Leith (Mrs. Leith Adams, Mrs. R. S. de Courcy Laffan) 1837?-1912 .... DLB-240
Adams, Brooks 1848-1927 .... DLB-47
Adams, Charles Francis, Jr. 1835-1915 .... DLB-47
Adams, Douglas 1952-2001 .... DLB-261; Y-83
Adams, Franklin P. 1881-1960 .... DLB-29
Adams, Hannah 1755-1832 .... DLB-200
Adams, Henry 1838-1918 ...... DLB-12, 47, 189
Adams, Herbert Baxter 1850-1901 ...... DLB-47
Adams, James Truslow 1878-1949 .... DLB-17; DS-17

Adams, John 1735-1826 .... DLB-31, 183
Adams, John Quincy 1767-1848 .... DLB-37
Adams, Léonie 1899-1988 .... DLB-48
Adams, Levi 1802-1832 .... DLB-99
Adams, Richard 1920- DLB-261
Adams, Samuel 1722-1803 .... DLB-31, 43
Adams, Sarah Fuller Flower 1805-1848 .... DLB-199
Adams, Thomas 1582/1583-1652 .... DLB-151
Adams, William Taylor 1822-1897 .... DLB-42
J. S. and C. Adams [publishing house] DLB-49
Adamson, Harold 1906-1980 .... DLB-265
Adamson, Sir John 1867-1950 .... DLB-98
Adamson, Robert 1943- DLB-289
Adcock, Arthur St. John 1864-1930 .... DLB-135
Adcock, Betty 1938- DLB-105
"Certain Gifts" DLB-105
Tribute to James Dickey Y-97
Adcock, Fleur 1934- DLB-40
Addams, Jane 1860-1935 .... DLB-303
Addison, Joseph 1672-1719 .... DLB-101; CDBLB-2
Ade, George 1866-1944 .... DLB-11, 25
Adeler, Max (see Clark, Charles Heber)
Adlard, Mark 1932- DLB-261
Adler, Richard 1921- DLB-265
Adonias Filho (Adonias Aguiar Filho) 1915-1990 .... DLB-145, 307
Adorno, Theodor W. 1903-1969 .... DLB-242
Adoum, Jorge Enrique 1926- DLB-283
Advance Publishing Company DLB-49
Ady, Endre 1877-1919 ...... DLB-215; CDWLB-4
AE 1867-1935 .... DLB-19; CDBLB-5
Ælfric circa 955-circa 1010 .... DLB-146
Aeschines circa 390 B.C.-circa 320 B.C. DLB-176
Aeschylus 525-524 B.C.-456-455 B.C. DLB-176; CDWLB-1
Aesthetic Papers DLB-1
Aesthetics
Eighteenth-Century Aesthetic Theories DLB-31

Cumulative Index

African Literature
  Letter from Khartoum Y-90
African American
  Afro-American Literary Critics:
    An Introduction DLB-33
  The Black Aesthetic: Background DS-8
  The Black Arts Movement,
    by Larry Neal DLB-38
  Black Theaters and Theater Organizations
    in America, 1961-1982:
    A Research List DLB-38
  Black Theatre: A Forum [excerpts] ... DLB-38
  Callaloo [journal] Y-87
  Community and Commentators:
    Black Theatre and Its Critics DLB-38
  The Emergence of Black
    Women Writers DS-8
  The Hatch-Billops Collection DLB-76
  A Look at the Contemporary Black
    Theatre Movement DLB-38
  The Moorland-Spingarn Research
    Center DLB-76
  "The Negro as a Writer," by
    G. M. McClellan DLB-50
  "Negro Poets and Their Poetry," by
    Wallace Thurman DLB-50
  Olaudah Equiano and Unfinished Journeys:
    The Slave-Narrative Tradition and
    Twentieth-Century Continuities, by
    Paul Edwards and Pauline T.
    Wangman DLB-117
  PHYLON (Fourth Quarter, 1950),
    The Negro in Literature:
    The Current Scene DLB-76
  The Schomburg Center for Research
    in Black Culture DLB-76
  Three Documents [poets], by John
    Edward Bruce DLB-50
After Dinner Opera Company Y-92
Agassiz, Elizabeth Cary 1822-1907 ...... DLB-189
Agassiz, Louis 1807-1873 .... DLB-1, 235
Agee, James
  1909-1955 .... DLB-2, 26, 152; CDALB-1
  The Agee Legacy: A Conference at
    the University of Tennessee
    at Knoxville Y-89
Aguilera Malta, Demetrio 1909-1981 .... DLB-145
Aguirre, Isidora 1919- DLB-305
Agustini, Delmira 1886-1914 .... DLB-290
Ahlin, Lars 1915-1997 .... DLB-257
Ai 1947- DLB-120
Aichinger, Ilse 1921- DLB-85, 299
Aickman, Robert 1914-1981 .... DLB-261
Aidoo, Ama Ata 1942- DLB-117; CDWLB-3
Aiken, Conrad
  1889-1973 .... DLB-9, 45, 102; CDALB-5
Aiken, Joan 1924-2004 .... DLB-161
Aikin, Lucy 1781-1864 .... DLB-144, 163
Ainsworth, William Harrison
  1805-1882 .... DLB-21
Aïssé, Charlotte-Elizabeth 1694?-1733 ... DLB-313
Aistis, Jonas 1904-1973 ..... DLB-220; CDWLB-4

Aitken, George A. 1860-1917 .... DLB-149
Robert Aitken [publishing house] DLB-49
Aitmatov, Chingiz 1928- DLB-302
Akenside, Mark 1721-1770 .... DLB-109
Akhmatova, Anna Andreevna
  1889-1966 .... DLB-295
Akins, Zoë 1886-1958 .... DLB-26
Aksakov, Ivan Sergeevich 1823-1826 ..... DLB-277
Aksakov, Sergei Timofeevich
  1791-1859 .... DLB-198
Aksyonov, Vassily 1932- DLB-302
Akunin, Boris (Grigorii Shalvovich
  Chkhartishvili) 1956- DLB-285
Akutagawa Ryūnsuke 1892-1927 .... DLB-180
Alabaster, William 1568-1640 .... DLB-132
Alain de Lille circa 1116-1202/1203 ..... DLB-208
Alain-Fournier 1886-1914 .... DLB-65
Alanus de Insulis (see Alain de Lille)
Alarcón, Francisco X. 1954- DLB-122
Alarcón, Justo S. 1930- DLB-209
Alba, Nanina 1915-1968 .... DLB-41
Albee, Edward 1928- ... DLB-7, 266; CDALB-1
Albert, Octavia 1853-ca. 1889 .... DLB-221
Albert the Great circa 1200-1280 ...... DLB-115
Alberti, Rafael 1902-1999 .... DLB-108
Albertinus, Aegidius circa 1560-1620 .... DLB-164
Alcaeus born circa 620 B.C. DLB-176
Alcoforado, Mariana, the Portuguese Nun
  1640-1723 .... DLB-287
Alcott, Amos Bronson
  1799-1888 .... DLB-1, 223; DS-5
Alcott, Louisa May 1832-1888
  ... DLB-1, 42, 79, 223, 239; DS-14; CDALB-3
Alcott, William Andrus 1798-1859 .... DLB-1, 243
Alcuin circa 732-804 .... DLB-148
Aldana, Francisco de 1537-1578 .... DLB-318
Aldanov, Mark (Mark Landau)
  1886-1957 .... DLB-317
Alden, Henry Mills 1836-1919 .... DLB-79
Alden, Isabella 1841-1930 .... DLB-42
John B. Alden [publishing house] DLB-49
Alden, Beardsley, and Company DLB-49
Aldington, Richard
  1892-1962 .... DLB-20, 36, 100, 149
Aldis, Dorothy 1896-1966 .... DLB-22
Aldis, H. G. 1863-1919 .... DLB-184
Aldiss, Brian W. 1925- DLB-14, 261, 271
Aldrich, Thomas Bailey
  1836-1907 .... DLB-42, 71, 74, 79
Alegría, Ciro 1909-1967 .... DLB-113
Alegría, Claribel 1924- DLB-145, 283
Aleixandre, Vicente 1898-1984 .... DLB-108
Aleksandravičius, Jonas (see Aistis, Jonas)
Aleksandrov, Aleksandr Andreevich
  (see Durova, Nadezhda Andreevna)
Alekseeva, Marina Anatol'evna
  (see Marinina, Aleksandra)
d'Alembert, Jean Le Rond 1717-1783 .... DLB-313

Alencar, José de 1829-1877 .... DLB-307
Aleramo, Sibilla (Rena Pierangeli Faccio)
  1876-1960 .... DLB-114, 264
Aleshkovsky, Petr Markovich 1957- ... DLB-285
Aleshkovsky, Yuz 1929- DLB-317
Alexander, Cecil Frances 1818-1895 .... DLB-199
Alexander, Charles 1868-1923 .... DLB-91
Charles Wesley Alexander
  [publishing house] DLB-49
Alexander, James 1691-1756 .... DLB-24
Alexander, Lloyd 1924- DLB-52
Alexander, Sir William, Earl of Stirling
  1577?-1640 .... DLB-121
Alexie, Sherman 1966- DLB-175, 206, 278
Alexis, Willibald 1798-1871 .... DLB-133
Alf laylah wa laylah
  ninth century onward DLB-311
Alfred, King 849-899 .... DLB-146
Alger, Horatio, Jr. 1832-1899 .... DLB-42
Algonquin Books of Chapel Hill DLB-46
Algren, Nelson
  1909-1981 .... DLB-9; Y-81, 82; CDALB-1
  Nelson Algren: An International
    Symposium Y-00
'Ali ibn Abi Talib circa 600-661 .... DLB-311
Aljamiado Literature DLB-286
Allan, Andrew 1907-1974 .... DLB-88
Allan, Ted 1916-1995 .... DLB-68
Allbeury, Ted 1917- DLB-87
Alldritt, Keith 1935- DLB-14
Allen, Dick 1939- DLB-282
Allen, Ethan 1738-1789 .... DLB-31
Allen, Frederick Lewis 1890-1954 ...... DLB-137
Allen, Gay Wilson 1903-1995 ..... DLB-103; Y-95
Allen, George 1808-1876 .... DLB-59
Allen, Grant 1848-1899 .... DLB-70, 92, 178
Allen, Henry W. 1912-1991 .... Y-85
Allen, Hervey 1889-1949 .... DLB-9, 45, 316
Allen, James 1739-1808 .... DLB-31
Allen, James Lane 1849-1925 .... DLB-71
Allen, Jay Presson 1922- DLB-26
John Allen and Company DLB-49
Allen, Paula Gunn 1939- DLB-175
Allen, Samuel W. 1917- DLB-41
Allen, Woody 1935- DLB-44
George Allen [publishing house] DLB-106
George Allen and Unwin Limited DLB-112
Allende, Isabel 1942- DLB-145; CDWLB-3
Alline, Henry 1748-1784 .... DLB-99
Allingham, Margery 1904-1966 .... DLB-77
  The Margery Allingham Society Y-98
Allingham, William 1824-1889 .... DLB-35
W. L. Allison [publishing house] DLB-49
The *Alliterative Morte Arthure and the Stanzaic
  Morte Arthur* circa 1350-1400 .... DLB-146
Allott, Kenneth 1912-1973 .... DLB-20

Allston, Washington 1779-1843 .... DLB-1, 235
Almeida, Manuel Antônio de 1831-1861 .... DLB-307
John Almon [publishing house] DLB-154
Alonzo, Dámaso 1898-1990 .... DLB-108
Alsop, George 1636-post 1673 .... DLB-24
Alsop, Richard 1761-1815 .... DLB-37
Henry Altemus and Company DLB-49
Altenberg, Peter 1885-1919 .... DLB-81
Althusser, Louis 1918-1990 .... DLB-242
Altolaguirre, Manuel 1905-1959 .... DLB-108
Aluko, T. M. 1918- DLB-117
Alurista 1947- DLB-82
Alvarez, A. 1929- DLB-14, 40
Alvarez, Julia 1950- DLB-282
Alvaro, Corrado 1895-1956 .... DLB-264
Alver, Betti 1906-1989 ..... DLB-220; CDWLB-4
Amadi, Elechi 1934- DLB-117
Amado, Jorge 1912-2001 .... DLB-113
Amalrik, Andrei 1938-1980 .... DLB-302
Ambler, Eric 1909-1998 .... DLB-77
The Library of America DLB-46
The Library of America: An Assessment After Two Decades Y-02
America: or, A Poem on the Settlement of the British Colonies, by Timothy Dwight DLB-37
American Bible Society Department of Library, Archives, and Institutional Research Y-97
American Conservatory Theatre DLB-7
American Culture American Proletarian Culture: The Twenties and Thirties DS-11
Studies in American Jewish Literature Y-02
The American Library in Paris Y-93
American Literature The Literary Scene and Situation and ... (Who Besides Oprah) Really Runs American Literature? Y-99
Who Owns American Literature, by Henry Taylor Y-94
Who Runs American Literature? Y-94
American News Company DLB-49
A Century of Poetry, a Lifetime of Collecting: J. M. Edelstein's Collection of Twentieth-Century American Poetry Y-02
The American Poets' Corner: The First Three Years (1983-1986) Y-86
American Publishing Company DLB-49
American Spectator [Editorial] Rationale From the Initial Issue of the American Spectator (November 1932) DLB-137
American Stationers' Company DLB-49
The American Studies Association of Norway Y-00
American Sunday-School Union DLB-49
American Temperance Union DLB-49

American Tract Society DLB-49
The American Trust for the British Library .. Y-96
American Writers' Congress 25-27 April 1935 .... DLB-303
American Writers Congress The American Writers Congress (9-12 October 1981) Y-81
The American Writers Congress: A Report on Continuing Business Y-81
Ames, Fisher 1758-1808 .... DLB-37
Ames, Mary Clemmer 1831-1884 .... DLB-23
Ames, William 1576-1633 .... DLB-281
Amfiteatrov, Aleksandr 1862-1938 ...... DLB-317
Amiel, Henri-Frédéric 1821-1881 .... DLB-217
Amini, Johari M. 1935- DLB-41
Amis, Kingsley 1922-1995 ...... DLB-15, 27, 100, 139, Y-96; CDBLB-7
Amis, Martin 1949- DLB-14, 194
Ammianus Marcellinus circa A.D. 330-A.D. 395 .... DLB-211
Ammons, A. R. 1926-2001 .... DLB-5, 165
Amory, Thomas 1691?-1788 .... DLB-39
Anania, Michael 1939- DLB-193
Anaya, Rudolfo A. 1937- DLB-82, 206, 278
Ancrene Riwle circa 1200-1225 .... DLB-146
Andersch, Alfred 1914-1980 .... DLB-69
Andersen, Benny 1929- DLB-214
Andersen, Hans Christian 1805-1875 .... DLB-300
Anderson, Alexander 1775-1870 .... DLB-188
Anderson, David 1929- DLB-241
Anderson, Frederick Irving 1877-1947 .... DLB-202
Anderson, Margaret 1886-1973 .... DLB-4, 91
Anderson, Maxwell 1888-1959 .... DLB-7, 228
Anderson, Patrick 1915-1979 .... DLB-68
Anderson, Paul Y. 1893-1938 .... DLB-29
Anderson, Poul 1926-2001 .... DLB-8
Tribute to Isaac Asimov Y-92
Anderson, Robert 1750-1830 .... DLB-142
Anderson, Robert 1917- DLB-7
Anderson, Sherwood 1876-1941 ..... DLB-4, 9, 86; DS-1; CDALB-4
Andrade, Jorge (Aluísio Jorge Andrade Franco) 1922-1984 .... DLB-307
Andrade, Mario de 1893-1945 .... DLB-307
Andrade, Oswald de (José Oswald de Sousa Andrade) 1890-1954 .... DLB-307
Andreae, Johann Valentin 1586-1654 .... DLB-164
Andreas Capellanus fl. circa 1185 .... DLB-208
Andreas-Salomé, Lou 1861-1937 .... DLB-66
Andreev, Leonid Nikolaevich 1871-1919 .... DLB-295
Andres, Stefan 1906-1970 .... DLB-69
Andresen, Sophia de Mello Breyner 1919- DLB-287
Andreu, Blanca 1959- DLB-134
Andrewes, Lancelot 1555-1626 ..... DLB-151, 172
Andrews, Charles M. 1863-1943 .... DLB-17

Andrews, Miles Peter ?-1814 .... DLB-89
Andrews, Stephen Pearl 1812-1886 ...... DLB-250
Andrian, Leopold von 1875-1951 .... DLB-81
Andrić, Ivo 1892-1975 ...... DLB-147; CDWLB-4
Andrieux, Louis (see Aragon, Louis)
Andrus, Silas, and Son DLB-49
Andrzejewski, Jerzy 1909-1983 .... DLB-215
Angell, James Burrill 1829-1916 .... DLB-64
Angell, Roger 1920- DLB-171, 185
Angelou, Maya 1928- DLB-38; CDALB-7
Tribute to Julian Mayfield Y-84
Anger, Jane fl. 1589 .... DLB-136
Angers, Félicité (see Conan, Laure)
The Anglo-Saxon Chronicle circa 890-1154 .... DLB-146
Angus and Robertson (UK) Limited DLB-112
Anhalt, Edward 1914-2000 .... DLB-26
Anissimov, Myriam 1943- DLB-299
Anker, Nini Roll 1873-1942 .... DLB-297
Annenkov, Pavel Vasil'evich 1813?-1887 .... DLB-277
Annensky, Innokentii Fedorovich 1855-1909 .... DLB-295
Henry F. Anners [publishing house] DLB-49
Annolied between 1077 and 1081 .... DLB-148
Anscombe, G. E. M. 1919-2001 .... DLB-262
Anselm of Canterbury 1033-1109 .... DLB-115
Anstey, F. 1856-1934 .... DLB-141, 178
'Antarah ('Antar ibn Shaddad al-'Absi) ?-early seventh century? DLB-311
Anthologizing New Formalism DLB-282
Anthony, Michael 1932- DLB-125
Anthony, Piers 1934- DLB-8
Anthony, Susanna 1726-1791 .... DLB-200
Antin, David 1932- DLB-169
Antin, Mary 1881-1949 .... DLB-221; Y-84
Anton Ulrich, Duke of Brunswick-Lüneburg 1633-1714 .... DLB-168
Antschel, Paul (see Celan, Paul)
Antunes, António Lobo 1942- DLB-287
Anyidoho, Kofi 1947- DLB-157
Anzaldúa, Gloria 1942- DLB-122
Anzengruber, Ludwig 1839-1889 .... DLB-129
Apess, William 1798-1839 .... DLB-175, 243
Apodaca, Rudy S. 1939- DLB-82
Apollinaire, Guillaume 1880-1918 .... DLB-258
Apollonius Rhodius third century B.C. DLB-176
Apple, Max 1941- DLB-130
Appelfeld, Aharon 1932- DLB-299
D. Appleton and Company DLB-49
Appleton-Century-Crofts DLB-46
Applewhite, James 1935- DLB-105
Tribute to James Dickey Y-97
Apple-wood Books DLB-46
April, Jean-Pierre 1948- DLB-251

Cumulative Index

Apukhtin, Aleksei Nikolaevich
  1840-1893 ....DLB-277
Apuleius circa A.D. 125-post A.D. 164
  .... DLB-211; CDWLB-1
Aquin, Hubert 1929-1977 .... DLB-53
Aquinas, Thomas 1224/1225-1274 ...... DLB-115
Aragon, Louis 1897-1982 .... DLB-72, 258
Aragon, Vernacular Translations in the
  Crowns of Castile and 1352-1515 ... DLB-286
Aralica, Ivan 1930- DLB-181
Aratus of Soli
  circa 315 B.C.-circa 239 B.C. DLB-176
Arbasino, Alberto 1930- DLB-196
Arbor House Publishing Company DLB-46
Arbuthnot, John 1667-1735............ DLB-101
Arcadia House DLB-46
Arce, Julio G. (see Ulica, Jorge)
Archer, William 1856-1924 .... DLB-10
Archilochhus
  mid seventh century B.C.E..........DLB-176
The Archpoet circa 1130?-? DLB-148
Archpriest Avvakum (Petrovich)
  1620?-1682..................... DLB-150
Arden, John 1930- DLB-13, 245
Arden of Faversham DLB-62
Ardis Publishers Y-89
Ardizzone, Edward 1900-1979 .... DLB-160
Arellano, Juan Estevan 1947- DLB-122
The Arena Publishing Company DLB-49
Arena Stage......................... DLB-7
Arenas, Reinaldo 1943-1990........... DLB-145
Arendt, Hannah 1906-1975 .... DLB-242
Arensberg, Ann 1937- Y-82
Arghezi, Tudor 1880-1967....DLB-220; CDWLB-4
Arguedas, José María 1911-1969 .... DLB-113
Argüelles, Hugo 1932-2003 .... DLB-305
Argueta, Manlio 1936- DLB-145
'Arib al-Ma'muniyah 797-890 .... DLB-311
Arias, Ron 1941- DLB-82
Arishima Takeo 1878-1923............. DLB-180
Aristophanes circa 446 B.C.-circa 386 B.C.
  .... DLB-176; CDWLB-1
Aristotle 384 B.C.-322 B.C.
  .... DLB-176; CDWLB-1
Ariyoshi Sawako 1931-1984 .... DLB-182
Arland, Marcel 1899-1986 .... DLB-72
Arlen, Michael 1895-1956 ....DLB-36, 77, 162
Arlt, Roberto 1900-1942.............. DLB-305
Armah, Ayi Kwei 1939- ...DLB-117; CDWLB-3
Armantrout, Rae 1947- DLB-193
Der arme Hartmann ?-after 1150 ...... DLB-148
Armed Services Editions................ DLB-46
Armitage, G. E. (Robert Edric) 1956- .. DLB-267
Armstrong, Martin Donisthorpe
  1882-1974..................... DLB-197
Armstrong, Richard 1903-1986 .... DLB-160
Armstrong, Terence Ian Fytton (see Gawsworth, John)

Arnauld, Antoine 1612-1694 .... DLB-268
Arndt, Ernst Moritz 1769-1860......... DLB-90
Arnim, Achim von 1781-1831........... DLB-90
Arnim, Bettina von 1785-1859 .... DLB-90
Arnim, Elizabeth von (Countess Mary Annette
  Beauchamp Russell) 1866-1941 .... DLB-197
Arno Press DLB-46
Arnold, Edwin 1832-1904 .... DLB-35
Arnold, Edwin L. 1857-1935............DLB-178
Arnold, Matthew
  1822-1888 .... DLB-32, 57; CDBLB-4
  Preface to *Poems* (1853)............ DLB-32
Arnold, Thomas 1795-1842 .... DLB-55
Edward Arnold [publishing house]...... DLB-112
Arnott, Peter 1962- DLB-233
Arnow, Harriette Simpson 1908-1986 ..... DLB-6
Arp, Bill (see Smith, Charles Henry)
Arpino, Giovanni 1927-1987.............DLB-177
Arrebo, Anders 1587-1637 .... DLB-300
Arreola, Juan José 1918-2001 .... DLB-113
Arrian circa 89-circa 155............. DLB-176
J. W. Arrowsmith [publishing house] DLB-106
Arrufat, Antón 1935- DLB-305
Art
  John Dos Passos: Artist Y-99
  The First Post-Impressionist
  Exhibition......................DS-5
  The Omega Workshops DS-10
  The Second Post-Impressionist
  Exhibition....................DS-5
Artaud, Antonin 1896-1948 .... DLB-258
Artel, Jorge 1909-1994 .... DLB-283
Arthur, Timothy Shay
  1809-1885 ....DLB-3, 42, 79, 250; DS-13
Artmann, H. C. 1921-2000............. DLB-85
Artsybashev, Mikhail Petrovich
  1878-1927.................... DLB-295
Arvin, Newton 1900-1963 .... DLB-103
Asch, Nathan 1902-1964 .... DLB-4, 28
  Nathan Asch Remembers Ford Madox
  Ford, Sam Roth, and Hart Crane Y-02
Ascham, Roger 1515/1516-1568........ DLB-236
Aseev, Nikolai Nikolaevich
  1889-1963 .... DLB-295
Ash, John 1948- DLB-40
Ashbery, John 1927- DLB-5, 165; Y-81
Ashbridge, Elizabeth 1713-1755 .... DLB-200
Ashburnham, Bertram Lord
  1797-1878 .... DLB-184
Ashendene Press................... DLB-112
Asher, Sandy 1942- Y-83
Ashton, Winifred (see Dane, Clemence)
Asimov, Isaac 1920-1992 ....DLB-8; Y-92
  Tribute to John Ciardi................ Y-86
Askew, Anne circa 1521-1546 .... DLB-136
Aspazija 1865-1943........ DLB-220; CDWLB-4
Asselin, Olivar 1874-1937 .... DLB-92

The Association of American Publishers Y-99
The Association for Documentary Editing.... Y-00
The Association for the Study of
  Literature and Environment (ASLE) Y-99
Astell, Mary 1666-1731................ DLB-252
Astley, Thea 1925- DLB-289
Astley, William (see Warung, Price)
Asturias, Miguel Ángel
  1899-1974.........DLB-113, 290; CDWLB-3
Atava, S. (see Terpigorev, Sergei Nikolaevich)
Atheneum Publishers DLB-46
Atherton, Gertrude 1857-1948 .....DLB-9, 78, 186
Athlone Press DLB-112
Atkins, Josiah circa 1755-1781......... DLB-31
Atkins, Russell 1926- DLB-41
Atkinson, Kate 1951- DLB-267
Atkinson, Louisa 1834-1872 .... DLB-230
The Atlantic Monthly Press DLB-46
Attaway, William 1911-1986 .... DLB-76
Atwood, Margaret 1939- DLB-53, 251
Aubert, Alvin 1930- DLB-41
Aubert de Gaspé, Phillipe-Ignace-François
  1814-1841 .... DLB-99
Aubert de Gaspé, Phillipe-Joseph
  1786-1871..................... DLB-99
Aubin, Napoléon 1812-1890............ DLB-99
Aubin, Penelope
  1685-circa 1731 .... DLB-39
  Preface to *The Life of Charlotta
  du Pont* (1723)................. DLB-39
Aubrey-Fletcher, Henry Lancelot (see Wade, Henry)
Auchincloss, Louis 1917- DLB-2, 244; Y-80
Auden, W. H.
  1907-1973 .... DLB-10, 20; CDBLB-6
Audio Art in America: A Personal Memoir ... Y-85
Audubon, John James 1785-1851 ...... DLB-248
Audubon, John Woodhouse
  1812-1862 .... DLB-183
Auerbach, Berthold 1812-1882 .... DLB-133
Auernheimer, Raoul 1876-1948 .... DLB-81
Augier, Emile 1820-1889 .... DLB-192
Augustine 354-430 .... DLB-115
Aulnoy, Marie-Catherine Le Jumel
  de Barneville, comtesse d'
  1650/1651-1705.................DLB-268
Aulus Gellius
  circa A.D. 125-circa A.D. 180?........ DLB-211
Austen, Jane 1775-1817 ...... DLB-116; CDBLB-3
Auster, Paul 1947- DLB-227
Austin, Alfred 1835-1913 .... DLB-35
Austin, J. L. 1911-1960............... DLB-262
Austin, Jane Goodwin 1831-1894....... DLB-202
Austin, John 1790-1859............... DLB-262
Austin, Mary Hunter
  1868-1934 ....DLB-9, 78, 206, 221, 275
Austin, William 1778-1841 .... DLB-74
Australie (Emily Manning)
  1845-1890 .... DLB-230

378

Authors and Newspapers Association DLB-46
Authors' Publishing Company. DLB-49
Avallone, Michael 1924-1999. . . . . . DLB-306; Y-99
  Tribute to John D. MacDonald. Y-86
  Tribute to Kenneth Millar. Y-83
  Tribute to Raymond Chandler Y-88
Avalon Books. DLB-46
Avancini, Nicolaus 1611-1686 . . . . DLB-164
Avendaño, Fausto 1941- DLB-82
Averroës 1126-1198. . . . . DLB-115
Avery, Gillian 1926- DLB-161
Avicenna 980-1037. . . . . DLB-115
Ávila Jiménez, Antonio 1898-1965. . . . . . . DLB-283
Avison, Margaret 1918-1987 . . . . DLB-53
Avon Books DLB-46
Avyžius, Jonas 1922-1999 . . . . .DLB-220
Awdry, Wilbert Vere 1911-1997 . . . . DLB-160
Awoonor, Kofi 1935- DLB-117
Ayckbourn, Alan 1939- DLB-13, 245
Ayer, A. J. 1910-1989. . . . . .DLB-262
Aymé, Marcel 1902-1967. . . . . .DLB-72
Aytoun, Sir Robert 1570-1638 . . . . .DLB-121
Aytoun, William Edmondstoune
 1813-1865 . . . . DLB-32, 159
Azevedo, Aluísio 1857-1913 . . . . .DLB-307
Azevedo, Manuel Antônio Álvares de
 1831-1852 . . . . DLB-307

B

B.V. (see Thomson, James)
Babbitt, Irving 1865-1933 . . . . DLB-63
Babbitt, Natalie 1932- DLB-52
John Babcock [publishing house] DLB-49
Babel, Isaak Emmanuilovich
 1894-1940 . . . . DLB-272
Babits, Mihály 1883-1941 . . . DLB-215; CDWLB-4
Babrius circa 150-200. . . . . .DLB-176
Babson, Marian 1929- DLB-276
Baca, Jimmy Santiago 1952- DLB-122
Bacchelli, Riccardo 1891-1985. . . . . DLB-264
Bache, Benjamin Franklin 1769-1798 . . . . . DLB-43
Bachelard, Gaston 1884-1962 . . . . .DLB-296
Bacheller, Irving 1859-1950. . . . . .DLB-202
Bachmann, Ingeborg 1926-1973. . . . . DLB-85
Bačinskaitė-Bučienė, Salomėja (see Nėris, Salomėja)
Bacon, Delia 1811-1859 . . . . DLB-1, 243
Bacon, Francis
 1561-1626 . . . . DLB-151, 236, 252; CDBLB-1
Bacon, Sir Nicholas circa 1510-1579 . . . . . DLB-132
Bacon, Roger circa 1214/1220-1292 . . . . . DLB-115
Bacon, Thomas circa 1700-1768. . . . . DLB-31
Bacovia, George
 1881-1957 . . . . DLB-220; CDWLB-4
Richard G. Badger and Company DLB-49
Bagaduce Music Lending Library Y-00

Bage, Robert 1728-1801. . . . . .DLB-39
Bagehot, Walter 1826-1877 . . . . DLB-55
Baggesen, Jens 1764-1826 . . . . DLB-300
Bagley, Desmond 1923-1983. . . . . .DLB-87
Bagley, Sarah G. 1806-1848? DLB-239
Bagnold, Enid 1889-1981 . . DLB-13, 160, 191, 245
Bagryana, Elisaveta
 1893-1991 . . . . DLB-147; CDWLB-4
Bahr, Hermann 1863-1934 . . . . .DLB-81, 118
Bailey, Abigail Abbot
 1746-1815 . . . . DLB-200
Bailey, Alfred Goldsworthy 1905-1997 . . . . DLB-68
Bailey, H. C. 1878-1961. . . . . DLB-77
Bailey, Jacob 1731-1808. . . . . .DLB-99
Bailey, Paul 1937- DLB-14, 271
Bailey, Philip James 1816-1902 . . . . .DLB-32
Francis Bailey [publishing house] DLB-49
Baillargeon, Pierre 1916-1967 . . . . DLB-88
Baillie, Hugh 1890-1966 . . . . DLB-29
Baillie, Joanna 1762-1851 . . . . DLB-93
Bailyn, Bernard 1922- DLB-17
Bain, Alexander
 English Composition and Rhetoric (1866)
 [excerpt] DLB-57
Bainbridge, Beryl 1933- DLB-14, 231
Baird, Irene 1901-1981 . . . . DLB-68
Baker, Augustine 1575-1641 . . . . .DLB-151
Baker, Carlos 1909-1987 . . . . DLB-103
Baker, David 1954- DLB-120
Baker, George Pierce 1866-1935 . . . . .DLB-266
Baker, Herschel C. 1914-1990 . . . . .DLB-111
Baker, Houston A., Jr. 1943- DLB-67
Baker, Howard
 Tribute to Caroline Gordon Y-81
 Tribute to Katherine Anne Porter Y-80
Baker, Nicholson 1957- DLB-227; Y-00
 Review of Nicholson Baker's *Double Fold:
  Libraries and the Assault on Paper* Y-00
Baker, Samuel White 1821-1893 . . . . .DLB-166
Baker, Thomas 1656-1740 . . . . DLB-213
Walter H. Baker Company
 ("Baker's Plays"). DLB-49
The Baker and Taylor Company DLB-49
Bakhtin, Mikhail Mikhailovich
 1895-1975 . . . . DLB-242
Bakunin, Mikhail Aleksandrovich
 1814-1876 . . . . DLB-277
Balaban, John 1943- DLB-120
Bald, Wambly 1902-1990 . . . . DLB-4
Balde, Jacob 1604-1668 . . . . DLB-164
Balderston, John 1889-1954. . . . . DLB-26
Baldwin, James 1924-1987
 . . . . . DLB-2, 7, 33, 249, 278; Y-87; CDALB-1
Baldwin, Joseph Glover
 1815-1864 . . . . .DLB-3, 11, 248
Baldwin, Louisa (Mrs. Alfred Baldwin)
 1845-1925 . . . . DLB-240
Baldwin, William circa 1515-1563. . . . . . . DLB-132

Richard and Anne Baldwin
 [publishing house] DLB-170
Bale, John 1495-1563. . . . . .DLB-132
Balestrini, Nanni 1935- DLB-128, 196
Balfour, Sir Andrew 1630-1694 . . . . .DLB-213
Balfour, Arthur James 1848-1930 . . . . DLB-190
Balfour, Sir James 1600-1657 . . . . .DLB-213
Ballantine Books .DLB-46
Ballantyne, R. M. 1825-1894 . . . . .DLB-163
Ballard, J. G. 1930- DLB-14, 207, 261, 319
Ballard, Martha Moore 1735-1812. . . . . . . DLB-200
Ballerini, Luigi 1940- DLB-128
Ballou, Maturin Murray (Lieutenant Murray)
 1820-1895 . . . . DLB-79, 189
Robert O. Ballou [publishing house] DLB-46
Bal'mont, Konstantin Dmitrievich
 1867-1942 . . . . DLB-295
Balzac, Guez de 1597?-1654 . . . . .DLB-268
Balzac, Honoré de 1799-1855 . . . . .DLB-119
Bambara, Toni Cade
 1939-1995 . . . . .DLB-38, 218; CDALB-7
Bamford, Samuel 1788-1872 . . . . .DLB-190
A. L. Bancroft and Company DLB-49
Bancroft, George 1800-1891 . . . DLB-1, 30, 59, 243
Bancroft, Hubert Howe 1832-1918 . . . DLB-47, 140
Bandeira, Manuel 1886-1968. . . . . .DLB-307
Bandelier, Adolph F. 1840-1914 . . . . DLB-186
Bang, Herman 1857-1912 . . . . .DLB-300
Bangs, John Kendrick 1862-1922 . . . . . DLB-11, 79
Banim, John 1798-1842 . . . . DLB-116, 158, 159
Banim, Michael 1796-1874 . . . . .DLB-158, 159
Banks, Iain (M.) 1954- DLB-194, 261
Banks, John circa 1653-1706 . . . . DLB-80
Banks, Russell 1940- DLB-130, 278
Bannerman, Helen 1862-1946 . . . . .DLB-141
Bantam Books DLB-46
Banti, Anna 1895-1985 . . . . .DLB-177
Banville, John 1945- DLB-14, 271
Banville, Théodore de 1823-1891 . . . . DLB-217
Baraka, Amiri
 1934- DLB-5, 7, 16, 38; DS-8; CDALB-1
Barańczak, Stanisław 1946- DLB-232
Baranskaia, Natal'ia Vladimirovna
 1908- DLB-302
Baratynsky, Evgenii Abramovich
 1800-1844 . . . . DLB-205
Barba-Jacob, Porfirio 1883-1942 . . . . DLB-283
Barbauld, Anna Laetitia
 1743-1825 . . . . .DLB-107, 109, 142, 158
Barbeau, Marius 1883-1969. . . . . DLB-92
Barber, John Warner 1798-1885 . . . . .DLB-30
Bàrberi Squarotti, Giorgio 1929- DLB-128
Barbey d'Aurevilly, Jules-Amédée
 1808-1889 . . . . DLB-119
Barbier, Auguste 1805-1882 . . . . .DLB-217
Barbilian, Dan (see Barbu, Ion)
Barbour, John circa 1316-1395 . . . . .DLB-146

Cumulative Index

Barbour, Ralph Henry 1870-1944 . . . . DLB-22
Barbu, Ion 1895-1961 . . . . . . DLB-220; CDWLB-4
Barbusse, Henri 1873-1935 . . . . DLB-65
Barclay, Alexander circa 1475-1552 . . . . . DLB-132
E. E. Barclay and Company DLB-49
C. W. Bardeen [publishing house] DLB-49
Barham, Richard Harris 1788-1845 . . . . . DLB-159
Barich, Bill 1943- DLB-185
Baring, Maurice 1874-1945 . . . . DLB-34
Baring-Gould, Sabine 1834-1924 . . . DLB-156, 190
Barker, A. L. 1918-2002 . . . . DLB-14, 139
Barker, Clive 1952- DLB-261
Barker, Dudley (see Black, Lionel)
Barker, George 1913-1991 . . . . DLB-20
Barker, Harley Granville 1877-1946 . . . . . . DLB-10
Barker, Howard 1946- DLB-13, 233
Barker, James Nelson 1784-1858 . . . . DLB-37
Barker, Jane 1652-1727 . . . . DLB-39, 131
Barker, Lady Mary Anne 1831-1911 . . . . . DLB-166
Barker, Pat 1943- DLB-271
Barker, William circa 1520-after 1576 . . . DLB-132
Arthur Barker Limited DLB-112
Barkov, Ivan Semenovich 1732-1768 . . . . DLB-150
Barks, Coleman 1937- DLB-5
Barlach, Ernst 1870-1938 . . . . DLB-56, 118
Barlow, Joel 1754-1812 . . . . DLB-37
The Prospect of Peace (1778) DLB-37
Barnard, John 1681-1770 . . . . DLB-24
Barnard, Marjorie (M. Barnard Eldershaw)
  1897-1987 . . . . DLB-260
Barnard, Robert 1936- DLB-276
Barne, Kitty (Mary Catherine Barne)
  1883-1957 . . . . DLB-160
Barnes, Barnabe 1571-1609 . . . . DLB-132
Barnes, Djuna 1892-1982 . . . . DLB-4, 9, 45; DS-15
Barnes, Jim 1933- DLB-175
Barnes, Julian 1946- DLB-194; Y-93
  Notes for a Checklist of Publications Y-01
Barnes, Margaret Ayer 1886-1967 . . . . DLB-9
Barnes, Peter 1931- DLB-13, 233
Barnes, William 1801-1886 . . . . DLB-32
A. S. Barnes and Company DLB-49
Barnes and Noble Books DLB-46
Barnet, Miguel 1940- DLB-145
Barney, Natalie 1876-1972 . . . . DLB-4; DS-15
Barnfield, Richard 1574-1627 . . . . .DLB-172
Richard W. Baron [publishing house] DLB-46
Barr, Amelia Edith Huddleston
  1831-1919 . . . . DLB-202, 221
Barr, Robert 1850-1912 . . . . DLB-70, 92
Barral, Carlos 1928-1989 . . . . DLB-134
Barrax, Gerald William 1933- DLB-41, 120
Barrès, Maurice 1862-1923 . . . . DLB-123
Barreno, Maria Isabel (see The Three Marias:
  A Landmark Case in Portuguese
  Literary History)

Barrett, Eaton Stannard 1786-1820 . . . . . . DLB-116
Barrie, J. M.
  1860-1937 . . . . . . DLB-10, 141, 156; CDBLB-5
Barrie and Jenkins DLB-112
Barrio, Raymond 1921- DLB-82
Barrios, Gregg 1945- DLB-122
Barry, Philip 1896-1949 . . . . DLB-7, 228
Barry, Robertine (see Françoise)
Barry, Sebastian 1955- DLB-245
Barse and Hopkins DLB-46
Barstow, Stan 1928- DLB-14, 139, 207
  Tribute to John Braine Y-86
Barth, John 1930- DLB-2, 227
Barthelme, Donald
  1931-1989 . . . . .DLB-2, 234; Y-80, 89
Barthelme, Frederick 1943- DLB-244; Y-85
Barthes, Roland 1915-1980 . . . . DLB-296
Bartholomew, Frank 1898-1985 . . . . DLB-127
Bartlett, John 1820-1905 . . . . DLB-1, 235
Bartol, Cyrus Augustus 1813-1900 . . . . DLB-1, 235
Barton, Bernard 1784-1849 . . . . DLB-96
Barton, John ca. 1610-1675 . . . . DLB-236
Barton, Thomas Pennant 1803-1869 . . . . DLB-140
Bartram, John 1699-1777 . . . . DLB-31
Bartram, William 1739-1823 . . . . DLB-37
Barykova, Anna Pavlovna 1839-1893 . . . .DLB-277
Bashshar ibn Burd circa 714-circa 784 . . . DLB-311
Basic Books DLB-46
Basille, Theodore (see Becon, Thomas)
Bass, Rick 1958- DLB-212, 275
Bass, T. J. 1932- Y-81
Bassani, Giorgio 1916-2000 . . . . DLB-128, 177, 299
Basse, William circa 1583-1653 . . . . DLB-121
Bassett, John Spencer 1867-1928 . . . . DLB-17
Bassler, Thomas Joseph (see Bass, T. J.)
Bate, Walter Jackson 1918-1999 . . . . . .DLB-67, 103
Bateman, Stephen circa 1510-1584 . . . . . . DLB-136
Christopher Bateman
  [publishing house] DLB-170
Bates, H. E. 1905-1974 . . . . DLB-162, 191
Bates, Katharine Lee 1859-1929 . . . . DLB-71
Batiushkov, Konstantin Nikolaevich
  1787-1855 . . . . DLB-205
B. T. Batsford [publishing house] DLB-106
Batteux, Charles 1713-1780 . . . . DLB-313
Battiscombe, Georgina 1905- DLB-155
The Battle of Maldon circa 1000 . . . . DLB-146
Baudelaire, Charles 1821-1867 . . . . DLB-217
Baudrillard, Jean 1929- DLB-296
Bauer, Bruno 1809-1882 . . . . DLB-133
Bauer, Wolfgang 1941- DLB-124
Baum, L. Frank 1856-1919 . . . . DLB-22
Baum, Vicki 1888-1960 . . . . DLB-85
Baumbach, Jonathan 1933- Y-80
Bausch, Richard 1945- DLB-130

Tribute to James Dickey Y-97
Tribute to Peter Taylor Y-94
Bausch, Robert 1945- DLB-218
Bawden, Nina 1925- DLB-14, 161, 207
Bax, Clifford 1886-1962 . . . . .DLB-10, 100
Baxter, Charles 1947- DLB-130
Bayer, Eleanor (see Perry, Eleanor)
Bayer, Konrad 1932-1964 . . . . DLB-85
Bayle, Pierre 1647-1706 . . . . .DLB-268, 313
Bayley, Barrington J. 1937- DLB-261
Baynes, Pauline 1922- DLB-160
Baynton, Barbara 1857-1929 . . . . DLB-230
Bazin, Hervé (Jean Pierre Marie Hervé-Bazin)
  1911-1996 . . . . DLB-83
The BBC Four Samuel Johnson Prize
  for Non-fiction Y-02
Beach, Sylvia
  1887-1962 . . . . DLB-4; DS-15
Beacon Press DLB-49
Beadle and Adams DLB-49
Beagle, Peter S. 1939- Y-80
Beal, M. F. 1937- Y-81
Beale, Howard K. 1899-1959 . . . . .DLB-17
Beard, Charles A. 1874-1948 . . . . .DLB-17
Beat Generation (Beats)
  As I See It, by Carolyn Cassady DLB-16
  A Beat Chronology: The First Twenty-five
    Years, 1944-1969 . . . . DLB-16
  The Commercialization of the Image
    of Revolt, by Kenneth Rexroth . . . DLB-16
  Four Essays on the Beat Generation . . DLB-16
  in New York City DLB-237
  in the West DLB-237
  Outlaw Days DLB-16
  Periodicals of DLB-16
Beattie, Ann 1947- DLB-218, 278; Y-82
Beattie, James 1735-1803 . . . . DLB-109
Beatty, Chester 1875-1968 . . . . DLB-201
Beauchemin, Nérée 1850-1931 . . . . DLB-92
Beauchemin, Yves 1941- DLB-60
Beaugrand, Honoré 1848-1906 . . . . DLB-99
Beaulieu, Victor-Lévy 1945- DLB-53
Beaumarchais, Pierre-Augustin Caron de
  1732-1799 . . . . DLB-313
Beaumer, Mme de ?-1766 . . . . DLB-313
Beaumont, Francis circa 1584-1616
  and Fletcher, John
  1579-1625 . . . . DLB-58; CDBLB-1
Beaumont, Sir John 1583?-1627 . . . . . . DLB-121
Beaumont, Joseph 1616-1699 . . . . DLB-126
Beauvoir, Simone de 1908-1986 . . . . .DLB-72; Y-86
  Personal Tribute to Simone de Beauvoir . . . Y-86
Beaver, Bruce 1928- DLB-289
Becher, Ulrich 1910-1990 . . . . DLB-69
Becker, Carl 1873-1945 . . . . .DLB-17
Becker, Jurek 1937-1997 . . . . .DLB-75, 299
Becker, Jurgen 1932- DLB-75

Beckett, Mary 1926- DLB-319	Robert Bell [publishing house]..........DLB-49	Bennett, James Gordon, Jr. 1841-1918.....DLB-23
Beckett, Samuel 1906-1989 ......DLB-13, 15, 233, 319; Y-90; CDBLB-7	Bellamy, Edward 1850-1898............DLB-12	Bennett, John 1865-1956...............DLB-42
Beckford, William 1760-1844.......DLB-39, 213	Bellamy, Joseph 1719-1790.............DLB-31	Bennett, Louise 1919- DLB-117; CDWLB-3
Beckham, Barry 1944- DLB-33	John Bellamy [publishing house] DLB-170	Benni, Stefano 1947- DLB-196
Bećković, Matija 1939- DLB-181	*La Belle Assemblée* 1806-1837............DLB-110	Benoist, Françoise-Albine Puzin de La Martinière 1731-1809...........DLB-313
Becon, Thomas circa 1512-1567 ....DLB-136	Bellezza, Dario 1944-1996.............DLB-128	Benoit, Jacques 1941- DLB-60
Becque, Henry 1837-1899 ....DLB-192	Belli, Carlos Germán 1927- DLB-290	Benson, A. C. 1862-1925................DLB-98
Beddoes, Thomas 1760-1808...........DLB-158	Belli, Gioconda 1948- DLB-290	Benson, E. F. 1867-1940..........DLB-135, 153
Beddoes, Thomas Lovell 1803-1849 ......DLB-96	Belloc, Hilaire 1870-1953 .... DLB-19, 100, 141, 174	The E. F. Benson Society Y-98
Bede circa 673-735...................DLB-146	Belloc, Madame (see Parkes, Bessie Rayner)	The Tilling Society Y-98
Bedford-Jones, H. 1887-1949 ....DLB-251	Bellonci, Maria 1902-1986.............DLB-196	Benson, Jackson J. 1930- DLB-111
Bedregal, Yolanda 1913-1999 ....DLB-283	Bellow, Saul 1915-2005 .... DLB-2, 28, 299; Y-82; DS-3; CDALB-1	Benson, Robert Hugh 1871-1914.........DLB-153
Beebe, William 1877-1962 ....DLB-275	Tribute to Isaac Bashevis Singer Y-91	Benson, Stella 1892-1933............DLB-36, 162
Beecher, Catharine Esther 1800-1878 ....DLB-1, 243	Belmont Productions DLB-46	Bent, James Theodore 1852-1897 ....DLB-174
Beecher, Henry Ward 1813-1887.................DLB-3, 43, 250	Belov, Vasilii Ivanovich 1932- DLB-302	Bent, Mabel Virginia Anna ?-? DLB-174
Beer, George L. 1872-1920 ....DLB-47	Bels, Alberts 1938- DLB-232	Bentham, Jeremy 1748-1832 ... DLB-107, 158, 252
Beer, Johann 1655-1700................DLB-168	Belševica, Vizma 1931- DLB-232; CDWLB-4	Bentley, E. C. 1875-1956 ....DLB-70
Beer, Patricia 1919-1999 ....DLB-40	Bely, Andrei 1880-1934.............DLB-295	Bentley, Phyllis 1894-1977.............DLB-191
Beerbohm, Max 1872-1956 ....DLB-34, 100	Bemelmans, Ludwig 1898-1962.........DLB-22	Bentley, Richard 1662-1742............DLB-252
Beer-Hofmann, Richard 1866-1945.......DLB-81	Bemis, Samuel Flagg 1891-1973 ....DLB-17	Richard Bentley [publishing house]......DLB-106
Beers, Henry A. 1847-1926 ....DLB-71	William Bemrose [publishing house].....DLB-106	Benton, Robert 1932- DLB-44
S. O. Beeton [publishing house]........DLB-106	Ben no Naishi 1228?-1271?............DLB-203	Benziger Brothers DLB-49
Begley, Louis 1933- DLB-299	Benchley, Robert 1889-1945 ....DLB-11	*Beowulf* circa 900-1000 or 790-825 ....DLB-146; CDBLB-1
Bégon, Elisabeth 1696-1755 ....DLB-99	Bencúr, Matej (see Kukučin, Martin)	Berberova, Nina 1901-1993............DLB-317
Behan, Brendan 1923-1964 ....DLB-13, 233; CDBLB-7	Benedetti, Mario 1920- DLB-113	Berent, Wacław 1873-1940 ....DLB-215
Behn, Aphra 1640?-1689........DLB-39, 80, 131	Benedict, Pinckney 1964- DLB-244	Beresford, Anne 1929- DLB-40
Behn, Harry 1898-1973 ....DLB-61	Benedict, Ruth 1887-1948 ....DLB-246	Beresford, John Davys 1873-1947 .... DLB-162, 178, 197
Behrman, S. N. 1893-1973 .... DLB-7, 44	Benedictus, David 1938- DLB-14	"Experiment in the Novel" (1929) [excerpt] DLB-36
Beklemishev, Iurii Solomonvich (see Krymov, Iurii Solomonovich)	Benedikt Gröndal 1826-1907...........DLB-293	Beresford-Howe, Constance 1922- DLB-88
Belaney, Archibald Stansfeld (see Grey Owl)	Benedikt, Michael 1935- DLB-5	R. G. Berford Company DLB-49
Belasco, David 1853-1931 ....DLB-7	Benediktov, Vladimir Grigor'evich 1807-1873.....................DLB-205	Berg, Elizabeth 1948- DLB-292
Clarke Belford and Company DLB-49	Benét, Stephen Vincent 1898-1943 .... DLB-4, 48, 102, 249	Berg, Stephen 1934- DLB-5
Belgian Luxembourg American Studies Association Y-01	Stephen Vincent Benét Centenary Y-97	Bergengruen, Werner 1892-1964 ....DLB-56
Belinsky, Vissarion Grigor'evich 1811-1848 ....DLB-198	Benét, William Rose 1886-1950 ....DLB-45	Berger, John 1926- DLB-14, 207, 319
Belitt, Ben 1911-2003...................DLB-5	Benford, Gregory 1941- Y-82	Berger, Meyer 1898-1959 ....DLB-29
Belknap, Jeremy 1744-1798 ....DLB-30, 37	Benítez, Sandra 1941- DLB-292	Berger, Thomas 1924- DLB-2; Y-80
Bell, Adrian 1901-1980 ....DLB-191	Benjamin, Park 1809-1864..... DLB-3, 59, 73, 250	A Statement by Thomas Berger Y-80
Bell, Clive 1881-1964................. DS-10	Benjamin, Peter (see Cunningham, Peter)	Bergman, Hjalmar 1883-1931 ....DLB-259
Bell, Daniel 1919- DLB-246	Benjamin, S. G. W. 1837-1914...........DLB-189	Bergman, Ingmar 1918- DLB-257
Bell, Gertrude Margaret Lowthian 1868-1926 ....DLB-174	Benjamin, Walter 1892-1940 ....DLB-242	Berkeley, Anthony 1893-1971 ....DLB-77
Bell, James Madison 1826-1902..........DLB-50	Benlowes, Edward 1602-1676 ....DLB-126	Berkeley, George 1685-1753 .... DLB-31, 101, 252
Bell, Madison Smartt 1957- DLB-218, 278	Benn, Gottfried 1886-1956 ....DLB-56	The Berkley Publishing Corporation......DLB-46
Tribute to Andrew Nelson Lytle........ Y-95	Benn Brothers Limited................DLB-106	Berkman, Alexander 1870-1936.........DLB-303
Tribute to Peter Taylor............... Y-94	Bennett, Alan 1934- DLB-310	Berlin, Irving 1888-1989 ....DLB-265
Bell, Marvin 1937- DLB-5	Bennett, Arnold 1867-1931 ....DLB-10, 34, 98, 135; CDBLB-5	Berlin, Lucia 1936- DLB-130
Bell, Millicent 1919- DLB-111	The Arnold Bennett Society Y-98	Berman, Marshall 1940- DLB-246
Bell, Quentin 1910-1996 ....DLB-155	Bennett, Charles 1899-1995............DLB-44	Berman, Sabina 1955- DLB-305
Bell, Vanessa 1879-1961 .... DS-10	Bennett, Emerson 1822-1905...........DLB-202	Bernal, Vicente J. 1888-1915 ....DLB-82
George Bell and Sons................DLB-106	Bennett, Gwendolyn 1902-1981 ....DLB-51	Bernanos, Georges 1888-1948 ....DLB-72
	Bennett, Hal 1930- DLB-33	Bernard, Catherine 1663?-1712 ....DLB-268
	Bennett, James Gordon 1795-1872.......DLB-43	Bernard, Harry 1898-1979..............DLB-92

Bernard, John 1756-1828 . . . . DLB-37	Bibliography	Remarks at the Opening of "The Biographical Part of Literature" Exhibition, by William R. Cagle. Y-98
Bernard of Chartres circa 1060-1124? . . . DLB-115	Bibliographical and Textual Scholarship Since World War II Y-89	
Bernard of Clairvaux 1090-1153 . . . . DLB-208	Center for Bibliographical Studies and Research at the University of California, Riverside Y-91	Survey of Literary Biographies Y-00
Bernard, Richard 1568-1641/1642 . . . . . . DLB-281		A Transit of Poets and Others: American Biography in 1982. . . . . Y-82
Bernard Silvestris fl. circa 1130-1160 . . . . DLB-208	The Great Bibliographers Series Y-93	The Year in Literary Biography Y-83–01
Bernardin de Saint-Pierre 1737-1814 . . . . . DLB-313	Primary Bibliography: A Retrospective . . . Y-95	
Bernari, Carlo 1909-1992 . . . . .DLB-177	Bichsel, Peter 1935- DLB-75	Biography, The Practice of: An Interview with B. L. Reid. Y-83
Bernhard, Thomas 1931-1989 . . . . DLB-85, 124; CDWLB-2	Bickerstaff, Isaac John 1733-circa 1808 . . . . DLB-89	An Interview with David Herbert Donald . . Y-87
	Drexel Biddle [publishing house] DLB-49	An Interview with Humphrey Carpenter. . . .Y-84
Berniéres, Louis de 1954- DLB-271	Bidermann, Jacob 1577 or 1578-1639 . . . . DLB-164	An Interview with Joan Mellen Y-94
Bernstein, Charles 1950- DLB-169		An Interview with John Caldwell Guilds Y-92
Berriault, Gina 1926-1999 . . . . DLB-130	Bidwell, Walter Hilliard 1798-1881 . . . . . . DLB-79	An Interview with William Manchester. . . Y-85
Berrigan, Daniel 1921- DLB-5	Biehl, Charlotta Dorothea 1731-1788 . . . . DLB-300	John Bioren [publishing house]. DLB-49
Berrigan, Ted 1934-1983 . . . . . . DLB-5, 169	Bienek, Horst 1930-1990 . . . . DLB-75	Bioy Casares, Adolfo 1914-1999 . . . . DLB-113
Berry, Wendell 1934- DLB-5, 6, 234, 275	Bierbaum, Otto Julius 1865-1910 . . . . DLB-66	Bird, Isabella Lucy 1831-1904 . . . . DLB-166
Berryman, John 1914-1972 . . . . DLB-48; CDALB-1	Bierce, Ambrose 1842-1914? DLB-11, 12, 23, 71, 74, 186; CDALB-3	Bird, Robert Montgomery 1806-1854 . . . DLB-202
Bersianik, Louky 1930- DLB-60	Bigelow, William F. 1879-1966. . . . . DLB-91	Bird, William 1888-1963 . . . . DLB-4; DS-15
Berssenbrugge, Mei-mei 1947- DLB-312	Biggers, Earl Derr 1884-1933 . . . . DLB-306	The Cost of the Cantos: William Bird to Ezra Pound Y-01
Thomas Berthelet [publishing house] DLB-170	Biggle, Lloyd, Jr. 1923-2002 . . . . DLB-8	
Berto, Giuseppe 1914-1978. . . . . .DLB-177	Bigiaretti, Libero 1905-1993 . . . . .DLB-177	Birken, Sigmund von 1626-1681 . . . . DLB-164
Bertocci, Peter Anthony 1910-1989 . . . . . .DLB-279	Bigland, Eileen 1898-1970. . . . . DLB-195	Birney, Earle 1904-1995 . . . . DLB-88
Bertolucci, Attilio 1911-2000. . . . . DLB-128	Biglow, Hosea (see Lowell, James Russell)	Birrell, Augustine 1850-1933 . . . . DLB-98
Berton, Pierre 1920-2004 . . . . DLB-68	Bigongiari, Piero 1914-1997 . . . . DLB-128	Bisher, Furman 1918- DLB-171
Bertrand, Louis "Aloysius" 1807-1841 . . . DLB-217	Bilac, Olavo 1865-1918 . . . . DLB-307	Bishop, Elizabeth 1911-1979. . . . . DLB-5, 169; CDALB-6
Besant, Sir Walter 1836-1901 . . . . . . DLB-135, 190	Bilenchi, Romano 1909-1989 . . . . DLB-264	
Bessa-Luís, Agustina 1922- DLB-287	Billinger, Richard 1890-1965 . . . . DLB-124	The Elizabeth Bishop Society. Y-01
Bessette, Gerard 1920- DLB-53	Billings, Hammatt 1818-1874 . . . . DLB-188	Bishop, John Peale 1892-1944 . . . . . . DLB-4, 9, 45
Bessie, Alvah 1904-1985. . . . . DLB-26	Billings, John Shaw 1898-1975 . . . . DLB-137	Bismarck, Otto von 1815-1898. . . . . DLB-129
Bester, Alfred 1913-1987. . . . . DLB-8	Billings, Josh (see Shaw, Henry Wheeler)	Bisset, Robert 1759-1805 . . . . DLB-142
Besterman, Theodore 1904-1976 . . . . DLB-201	Binchy, Maeve 1940- DLB-319	Bissett, Bill 1939- DLB-53
Beston, Henry (Henry Beston Sheahan) 1888-1968 .DLB-275	Binding, Rudolf G. 1867-1938 . . . . DLB-66	Bitov, Andrei Georgievich 1937- DLB-302
	Bingay, Malcolm 1884-1953. . . . . DLB-241	Bitzius, Albert (see Gotthelf, Jeremias)
Best-Seller Lists An Assessment Y-84	Bingham, Caleb 1757-1817 . . . . DLB-42	Bjørnboe, Jens 1920-1976 . . . . DLB-297
What's Really Wrong With Bestseller Lists Y-84	Bingham, George Barry 1906-1988 . . . . . DLB-127	Bjørnvig, Thorkild 1918- DLB-214
	Bingham, Sallie 1937- DLB-234	Black, David (D. M.) 1941- DLB-40
Bestuzhev, Aleksandr Aleksandrovich (Marlinsky) 1797-1837 . . . . DLB-198	William Bingley [publishing house] DLB-154	Black, Gavin (Oswald Morris Wynd) 1913-1998 .DLB-276
Bestuzhev, Nikolai Aleksandrovich 1791-1855. . . . . DLB-198	Binyon, Laurence 1869-1943 . . . . DLB-19	
	Biographia Brittanica DLB-142	Black, Lionel (Dudley Barker) 1910-1980 .DLB-276
Betham-Edwards, Matilda Barbara (see Edwards, Matilda Barbara Betham-)	Biography Biographical Documents Y-84, 85	
Betjeman, John 1906-1984 . . . . DLB-20; Y-84; CDBLB-7		Black, Winifred 1863-1936. . . . . DLB-25
	A Celebration of Literary Biography Y-98	Walter J. Black [publishing house] DLB-46
Betocchi, Carlo 1899-1986 . . . . DLB-128	Conference on Modern Biography Y-85	Blackamore, Arthur 1679-? DLB-24, 39
Bettarini, Mariella 1942- DLB-128	The Cult of Biography Excerpts from the Second Folio Debate: "Biographies are generally a disease of English Literature" Y-86	Blackburn, Alexander L. 1929- Y-85
Betts, Doris 1932- DLB-218; Y-82		Blackburn, John 1923-1993 . . . . DLB-261
Beveridge, Albert J. 1862-1927 . . . . DLB-17		Blackburn, Paul 1926-1971 . . . . .DLB-16; Y-81
Beverley, Robert circa 1673-1722 . . . . . DLB-24, 30	New Approaches to Biography: Challenges from Critical Theory, USC Conference on Literary Studies, 1990 . . . . Y-90	Blackburn, Thomas 1916-1977 . . . . DLB-27
Bevilacqua, Alberto 1934- DLB-196		Blacker, Terence 1948- DLB-271
Bevington, Louisa Sarah 1845-1895 . . . . . DLB-199		Blackmore, R. D. 1825-1900 . . . . DLB-18
Beyle, Marie-Henri (see Stendhal)	"The New Biography," by Virginia Woolf, New York Herald Tribune, 30 October 1927 . . . . DLB-149	Blackmore, Sir Richard 1654-1729 . . . . . . DLB-131
Białoszewski, Miron 1922-1983 . . . . DLB-232		Blackmur, R. P. 1904-1965. . . . . DLB-63
Bianco, Margery Williams 1881-1944 . . . DLB-160	"The Practice of Biography," in The English Sense of Humour and Other Essays, by Harold Nicolson DLB-149	Blackwell, Alice Stone 1857-1950 . . . . . . DLB-303
Bibaud, Adèle 1854-1941 . . . . DLB-92		Basil Blackwell, Publisher DLB-106
Bibaud, Michel 1782-1857. . . . . DLB-99	"Principles of Biography," in Elizabethan and Other Essays, by Sidney Lee . . DLB-149	Blackwood, Algernon Henry 1869-1951 . . . . DLB-153, 156, 178

Blackwood, Caroline 1931-1996 . . . . . DLB-14, 207

William Blackwood and Sons, Ltd. DLB-154

Blackwood's Edinburgh Magazine 1817-1980 . . . . DLB-110

Blades, William 1824-1890 . . . . DLB-184

Blaga, Lucian 1895-1961 . . . . DLB-220

Blagden, Isabella 1817?-1873 . . . . DLB-199

Blair, Eric Arthur (see Orwell, George)

Blair, Francis Preston 1791-1876 . . . . DLB-43

Blair, Hugh
Lectures on Rhetoric and Belles Lettres (1783), [excerpts] DLB-31

Blair, James circa 1655-1743 . . . . DLB-24

Blair, John Durburrow 1759-1823 . . . . DLB-37

Blais, Marie-Claire 1939- DLB-53

Blaise, Clark 1940- DLB-53

Blake, George 1893-1961 . . . . DLB-191

Blake, Lillie Devereux 1833-1913 . . . . DLB-202, 221

Blake, Nicholas (C. Day Lewis) 1904-1972 . . . . DLB-77

Blake, William 1757-1827 . . . . DLB-93, 154, 163; CDBLB-3

The Blakiston Company DLB-49

Blanchard, Stephen 1950- DLB-267

Blanchot, Maurice 1907-2003 . . . . DLB-72, 296

Blanckenburg, Christian Friedrich von 1744-1796 . . . . DLB-94

Blandiana, Ana 1942- DLB-232; CDWLB-4

Blanshard, Brand 1892-1987 . . . . DLB-279

Blaser, Robin 1925- DLB-165

Blaumanis, Rudolfs 1863-1908 . . . . DLB-220

Bleasdale, Alan 1946- DLB-245

Bledsoe, Albert Taylor 1809-1877 . . . . DLB-3, 79, 248

Bleecker, Ann Eliza 1752-1783 . . . . DLB-200

Blelock and Company DLB-49

Blennerhassett, Margaret Agnew 1773-1842 . . . . DLB-99

Geoffrey Bles [publishing house] DLB-112

Blessington, Marguerite, Countess of 1789-1849 . . . . DLB-166

Blew, Mary Clearman 1939- DLB-256

Blicher, Steen Steensen 1782-1848 . . . . DLB-300

The Blickling Homilies circa 971 . . . . DLB-146

Blind, Mathilde 1841-1896 . . . . DLB-199

Blish, James 1921-1975 . . . . DLB-8

E. Bliss and E. White [publishing house] DLB-49

Bliven, Bruce 1889-1977 . . . . DLB-137

Blixen, Karen 1885-1962 . . . . DLB-214

Bloch, Ernst 1885-1977 . . . . DLB-296

Bloch, Robert 1917-1994 . . . . DLB-44
Tribute to John D. MacDonald Y-86

Block, Lawrence 1938- DLB-226

Block, Rudolph (see Lessing, Bruno)

Blok, Aleksandr Aleksandrovich 1880-1921 . . . . DLB-295

Blondal, Patricia 1926-1959 . . . . DLB-88

Bloom, Harold 1930- DLB-67

Bloomer, Amelia 1818-1894 . . . . DLB-79

Bloomfield, Robert 1766-1823 . . . . DLB-93

Bloomsbury Group DS-10

The *Dreadnought* Hoax DS-10

Bloor, Ella Reeve 1862-1951 . . . . DLB-303

Blotner, Joseph 1923- DLB-111

Blount, Thomas 1618?-1679 . . . . DLB-236

Bloy, Léon 1846-1917 . . . . DLB-123

Blume, Judy 1938- DLB-52
Tribute to Theodor Seuss Geisel Y-91

Blunck, Hans Friedrich 1888-1961 . . . . DLB-66

Blunden, Edmund 1896-1974 . . . DLB-20, 100, 155

Blundeville, Thomas 1522?-1606 . . . . DLB-236

Blunt, Lady Anne Isabella Noel 1837-1917 . . . . DLB-174

Blunt, Wilfrid Scawen 1840-1922 . . . . DLB-19, 174

Bly, Nellie (see Cochrane, Elizabeth)

Bly, Robert 1926- DLB-5

Blyton, Enid 1897-1968 . . . . DLB-160

Boaden, James 1762-1839 . . . . DLB-89

Boal, Augusto 1931- DLB-307

Boas, Frederick S. 1862-1957 . . . . DLB-149

The Bobbs-Merrill Company DLB-46, 291

The Bobbs-Merrill Archive at the Lilly Library, Indiana University Y-90

Boborykin, Petr Dmitrievich 1836-1921 . . . . DLB-238

Bobrov, Semen Sergeevich 1763?-1810 . . . . DLB-150

Bobrowski, Johannes 1917-1965 . . . . DLB-75

Bocage, Manuel Maria Barbosa du 1765-1805 . . . . DLB-287

Bodenheim, Maxwell 1892-1954 . . . . DLB-9, 45

Bodenstedt, Friedrich von 1819-1892 . . . . DLB-129

Bodini, Vittorio 1914-1970 . . . . DLB-128

Bodkin, M. McDonnell 1850-1933 . . . . DLB-70

Bodley, Sir Thomas 1545-1613 . . . . DLB-213

Bodley Head DLB-112

Bodmer, Johann Jakob 1698-1783 . . . . DLB-97

Bodmershof, Imma von 1895-1982 . . . . DLB-85

Bodsworth, Fred 1918- DLB-68

Böðvar Guðmundsson 1939- DLB-293

Boehm, Sydney 1908-1990 . . . . DLB-44

Boer, Charles 1939- DLB-5

Boethius circa 480-circa 524 . . . . DLB-115

Boethius of Dacia circa 1240-? DLB-115

Bogan, Louise 1897-1970 . . . . DLB-45, 169

Bogarde, Dirk 1921-1999 . . . . DLB-14

Bogdanov, Aleksandr Aleksandrovich 1873-1928 . . . . DLB-295

Bogdanovich, Ippolit Fedorovich circa 1743-1803 . . . . DLB-150

David Bogue [publishing house] DLB-106

Bohjalian, Chris 1960- DLB-292

Böhme, Jakob 1575-1624 . . . . DLB-164

H. G. Bohn [publishing house] DLB-106

Bohse, August 1661-1742 . . . . DLB-168

Boie, Heinrich Christian 1744-1806 . . . . . . DLB-94

Boileau-Despréaux, Nicolas 1636-1711 . . . DLB-268

Bojunga, Lygia 1932- DLB-307

Bok, Edward W. 1863-1930 . . . . . . DLB-91; DS-16

Boland, Eavan 1944- DLB-40

Boldrewood, Rolf (Thomas Alexander Browne) 1826?-1915 . . . . DLB-230

Bolingbroke, Henry St. John, Viscount 1678-1751 . . . . DLB-101

Böll, Heinrich 1917-1985 . . . . DLB-69; Y-85; CDWLB-2

Bolling, Robert 1738-1775 . . . . DLB-31

Bolotov, Andrei Timofeevich 1738-1833 . . . . DLB-150

Bolt, Carol 1941- DLB-60

Bolt, Robert 1924-1995 . . . . DLB-13, 233

Bolton, Herbert E. 1870-1953 . . . . DLB-17

Bonaventura DLB-90

Bonaventure circa 1217-1274 . . . . DLB-115

Bonaviri, Giuseppe 1924- DLB-177

Bond, Edward 1934- DLB-13, 310

Bond, Michael 1926- DLB-161

Bondarev, Iurii Vasil'evich 1924- DLB-302

Albert and Charles Boni [publishing house] DLB-46

Boni and Liveright DLB-46

Bonnefoy, Yves 1923- DLB-258

Bonner, Marita 1899-1971 . . . . DLB-228

Bonner, Paul Hyde 1893-1968 . . . . DS-17

Bonner, Sherwood (see McDowell, Katharine Sherwood Bonner)

Robert Bonner's Sons DLB-49

Bonnin, Gertrude Simmons (see Zitkala-Ša)

Bonsanti, Alessandro 1904-1984 . . . . DLB-177

Bontempelli, Massimo 1878-1960 . . . . DLB-264

Bontemps, Arna 1902-1973 . . . . DLB-48, 51

The Book Buyer (1867-1880, 1884-1918, 1935-1938) DS-13

The Book League of America DLB-46

Book Reviewing
The American Book Review: A Sketch . . Y-92

Book Reviewing and the Literary Scene Y-96, 97

Book Reviewing in America Y-87–94

Book Reviewing in America and the Literary Scene Y-95

Book Reviewing in Texas Y-94

Book Reviews in Glossy Magazines Y-95

Do They or Don't They? Writers Reading Book Reviews Y-01

The Most Powerful Book Review in America [*New York Times Book Review*] Y-82

Some Surprises and Universal Truths . . . Y-92

The Year in Book Reviewing and the Literary Situation Y-98

Book Supply Company DLB-49

Cumulative Index

The Book Trade History Group Y-93
The Booker Prize Y-96–98
   Address by Anthony Thwaite, Chairman of the Booker Prize Judges Comments from Former Booker Prize Winners Y-86
Boorde, Andrew circa 1490-1549 .... DLB-136
Boorstin, Daniel J. 1914- DLB-17
   Tribute to Archibald MacLeish Y-82
   Tribute to Charles Scribner Jr. Y-95
Booth, Franklin 1874-1948 .... DLB-188
Booth, Mary L. 1831-1889 .... DLB-79
Booth, Philip 1925- Y-82
Booth, Wayne C. 1921- DLB-67
Booth, William 1829-1912 .... DLB-190
Bor, Josef 1906-1979 .... DLB-299
Borchardt, Rudolf 1877-1945 .... DLB-66
Borchert, Wolfgang 1921-1947 ..... DLB-69, 124
Bording, Anders 1619-1677 .... DLB-300
Borel, Pétrus 1809-1859 .... DLB-119
Borgen, Johan 1902-1979 .... DLB-297
Borges, Jorge Luis 1899-1986 ...DLB-113, 283; Y-86; CDWLB-3
   The Poetry of Jorge Luis Borges Y-86
   A Personal Tribute. Y-86
Borgese, Giuseppe Antonio 1882-1952 ... DLB-264
Börne, Ludwig 1786-1837 .... DLB-90
Bornstein, Miriam 1950- DLB-209
Borowski, Tadeusz 1922-1951 .... DLB-215; CDWLB-4
Borrow, George 1803-1881 ..... DLB-21, 55, 166
Bosanquet, Bernard 1848-1923 .... DLB-262
Boscán, Juan circa 1490-1542 .... DLB-318
Bosch, Juan 1909-2001 .... DLB-145
Bosco, Henri 1888-1976 .... DLB-72
Bosco, Monique 1927- DLB-53
Bosman, Herman Charles 1905-1951.... DLB-225
Bossuet, Jacques-Bénigne 1627-1704 ...... DLB-268
Bostic, Joe 1908-1988 .... DLB-241
Boston, Lucy M. 1892-1990 .... DLB-161
Boston Quarterly Review DLB-1
Boston University
   Editorial Institute at Boston University ... Y-00
   Special Collections at Boston University .. Y-99
Boswell, James 1740-1795 .... DLB-104, 142; CDBLB-2
Boswell, Robert 1953- DLB-234
Bosworth, David. Y-82
   Excerpt from "Excerpts from a Report of the Commission," in The Death of Descartes Y-82
Bote, Hermann circa 1460-circa 1520 ....DLB-179
Botev, Khristo 1847-1876 .... DLB-147
Botkin, Vasilii Petrovich 1811-1869 .....DLB-277
Botta, Anne C. Lynch 1815-1891 ..... DLB-3, 250
Botto, Ján (see Krasko, Ivan)
Bottome, Phyllis 1882-1963 .... DLB-197

Bottomley, Gordon 1874-1948 .... DLB-10
Bottoms, David 1949- DLB-120; Y-83
   Tribute to James Dickey Y-97
Bottrall, Ronald 1906-1959............ DLB-20
Bouchardy, Joseph 1810-1870.......... DLB-192
Boucher, Anthony 1911-1968 .... DLB-8
Boucher, Jonathan 1738-1804 .... DLB-31
Boucher de Boucherville, Georges 1814-1894 .... DLB-99
Boudreau, Daniel (see Coste, Donat)
Bouhours, Dominique 1628-1702 ....DLB-268
Bourassa, Napoléon 1827-1916......... DLB-99
Bourget, Paul 1852-1935 .... DLB-123
Bourinot, John George 1837-1902 .... DLB-99
Bourjaily, Vance 1922- DLB-2, 143
Bourne, Edward Gaylord 1860-1908..... DLB-47
Bourne, Randolph 1886-1918........... DLB-63
Bousoño, Carlos 1923- DLB-108
Bousquet, Joë 1897-1950 .... DLB-72
Bova, Ben 1932- Y-81
Bovard, Oliver K. 1872-1945 .... DLB-25
Bove, Emmanuel 1898-1945............ DLB-72
Bowen, Elizabeth 1899-1973 .... DLB-15, 162; CDBLB-7
Bowen, Francis 1811-1890 .... DLB-1, 59, 235
Bowen, John 1924- DLB-13
Bowen, Marjorie 1886-1952 .... DLB-153
Bowen-Merrill Company DLB-49
Bowering, George 1935- DLB-53
Bowers, Bathsheba 1671-1718.......... DLB-200
Bowers, Claude G. 1878-1958 .... DLB-17
Bowers, Edgar 1924-2000 .... DLB-5
Bowers, Fredson Thayer 1905-1991 .... DLB-140; Y-91
   The Editorial Style of Fredson Bowers ... Y-91
   Fredson Bowers and Studies in Bibliography Y-91
   Fredson Bowers and the Cambridge Beaumont and Fletcher Y-91
   Fredson Bowers as Critic of Renaissance Dramatic Literature Y-91
   Fredson Bowers as Music Critic. Y-91
   Fredson Bowers, Master Teacher Y-91
   An Interview [on Nabokov] Y-80
   Working with Fredson Bowers Y-91
Bowles, Paul 1910-1999 ......DLB-5, 6, 218; Y-99
Bowles, Samuel, III 1826-1878 .... DLB-43
Bowles, William Lisle 1762-1850 .... DLB-93
Bowman, Louise Morey 1882-1944 ..... DLB-68
Bowne, Borden Parker 1847-1919 ......DLB-270
Boyd, James 1888-1944 .... DLB-9; DS-16
Boyd, John 1912-2002 .... DLB-310
Boyd, John 1919- DLB-8
Boyd, Martin 1893-1972 .... DLB-260
Boyd, Thomas 1898-1935 .... DLB-9, 316; DS-16
Boyd, William 1952- DLB-231

Boye, Karin 1900-1941................ DLB-259
Boyesen, Hjalmar Hjorth 1848-1895 ....DLB-12, 71; DS-13
Boylan, Clare 1948- DLB-267
Boyle, Kay 1902-1992   DLB-4, 9, 48, 86; DS-15; Y-93
Boyle, Roger, Earl of Orrery 1621-1679 ... DLB-80
Boyle, T. Coraghessan 1948- DLB-218, 278; Y-86
Božić, Mirko 1919- DLB-181
Brackenbury, Alison 1953- DLB-40
Brackenridge, Hugh Henry 1748-1816.................... DLB-11, 37
   The Rising Glory of America DLB-37
Brackett, Charles 1892-1969 .... DLB-26
Brackett, Leigh 1915-1978 .... DLB-8, 26
John Bradburn [publishing house] DLB-49
Bradbury, Malcolm 1932-2000........DLB-14, 207
Bradbury, Ray 1920- DLB-2, 8; CDALB-6
Bradbury and Evans................. DLB-106
Braddon, Mary Elizabeth 1835-1915 ....DLB-18, 70, 156
Bradford, Andrew 1686-1742 .... DLB-43, 73
Bradford, Gamaliel 1863-1932 ....DLB-17
Bradford, John 1749-1830 .... DLB-43
Bradford, Roark 1896-1948 .... DLB-86
Bradford, William 1590-1657 .... DLB-24, 30
Bradford, William, III 1719-1791 ..... DLB-43, 73
Bradlaugh, Charles 1833-1891 .... DLB-57
Bradley, David 1950- DLB-33
Bradley, F. H. 1846-1924 .... DLB-262
Bradley, Katherine Harris (see Field, Michael)
Bradley, Marion Zimmer 1930-1999 .... DLB-8
Bradley, William Aspenwall 1878-1939 .... DLB-4
Ira Bradley and Company DLB-49
J. W. Bradley and Company DLB-49
Bradshaw, Henry 1831-1886 .... DLB-184
Bradstreet, Anne 1612 or 1613-1672 .... DLB-24; CDALB-2
Bradūnas, Kazys 1917- DLB-220
Bradwardine, Thomas circa 1295-1349 .. DLB-115
Brady, Frank 1924-1986............. DLB-111
Frederic A. Brady [publishing house] DLB-49
Braga, Rubem 1913-1990 .... DLB-307
Bragg, Melvyn 1939- DLB-14, 271
Brahe, Tycho 1546-1601 .... DLB-300
Charles H. Brainard [publishing house] ... DLB-49
Braine, John 1922-1986 .... DLB-15; Y-86; CDBLB-7
Braithwait, Richard 1588-1673 .... DLB-151
Braithwaite, William Stanley 1878-1962. .... DLB-50, 54
Bräker, Ulrich 1735-1798 .... DLB-94
Bramah, Ernest 1868-1942............. DLB-70
Branagan, Thomas 1774-1843 .... DLB-37
Brancati, Vitaliano 1907-1954.......... DLB-264
Branch, William Blackwell 1927- DLB-76

Brand, Christianna 1907-1988 . . . . DLB-276

Brand, Max (see Faust, Frederick Schiller)

Brandão, Raul 1867-1930 . . . . DLB-287

Branden Press DLB-46

Brandes, Georg 1842-1927 . . . . DLB-300

Branner, H.C. 1903-1966 . . . . DLB-214

Brant, Sebastian 1457-1521 . . . . DLB-179

Brassey, Lady Annie (Allnutt)
1839-1887 . . . . DLB-166

Brathwaite, Edward Kamau
1930- DLB-125; CDWLB-3

Brault, Jacques 1933- DLB-53

Braun, Matt 1932- DLB-212

Braun, Volker 1939- DLB-75, 124

Brautigan, Richard
1935-1984 . . . . DLB-2, 5, 206; Y-80, 84

Braxton, Joanne M. 1950- DLB-41

Bray, Anne Eliza 1790-1883 . . . . DLB-116

Bray, Thomas 1656-1730 . . . . DLB-24

Brazdžionis, Bernardas 1907-2002 . . . . . . DLB-220

George Braziller [publishing house] DLB-46

The Bread Loaf Writers' Conference 1983 . . . Y-84

Breasted, James Henry 1865-1935 . . . . DLB-47

Brecht, Bertolt
1898-1956 . . . . DLB-56, 124; CDWLB-2

Bredel, Willi 1901-1964 . . . . DLB-56

Bregendahl, Marie 1867-1940 . . . . DLB-214

Breitinger, Johann Jakob 1701-1776 . . . . . . DLB-97

Brekke, Paal 1923-1993 . . . . DLB-297

Bremser, Bonnie 1939- DLB-16

Bremser, Ray 1934-1998 . . . . DLB-16

Brennan, Christopher 1870-1932 . . . . DLB-230

Brentano, Bernard von 1901-1964 . . . . . . DLB-56

Brentano, Clemens 1778-1842 . . . . DLB-90

Brentano, Franz 1838-1917 . . . . DLB-296

Brentano's DLB-49

Brenton, Howard 1942- DLB-13

Breslin, Jimmy 1929-1996 . . . . DLB-185

Breton, André 1896-1966 . . . . DLB-65, 258

Breton, Nicholas circa 1555-circa 1626 . . . DLB-136

The Breton Lays
1300-early fifteenth century DLB-146

Brett, Simon 1945- DLB-276

Brewer, Gil 1922-1983 . . . . DLB-306

Brewer, Luther A. 1858-1933 . . . . DLB-187

Brewer, Warren and Putnam DLB-46

Brewster, Elizabeth 1922- DLB-60

Breytenbach, Breyten 1939- DLB-225

Bridge, Ann (Lady Mary Dolling Sanders
O'Malley) 1889-1974 . . . . DLB-191

Bridge, Horatio 1806-1893 . . . . DLB-183

Bridgers, Sue Ellen 1942- DLB-52

Bridges, Robert
1844-1930 . . . . DLB-19, 98; CDBLB-5

The Bridgewater Library DLB-213

Bridie, James 1888-1951 . . . . DLB-10

Brieux, Eugene 1858-1932 . . . . DLB-192

Brigadere, Anna
1861-1933 . . . . DLB-220; CDWLB-4

Briggs, Charles Frederick
1804-1877 . . . . DLB-3, 250

Brighouse, Harold 1882-1958 . . . . DLB-10

Bright, Mary Chavelita Dunne
(see Egerton, George)

Brightman, Edgar Sheffield 1884-1953 . . . DLB-270

B. J. Brimmer Company DLB-46

Brines, Francisco 1932- DLB-134

Brink, André 1935- DLB-225

Brinley, George, Jr. 1817-1875 . . . . DLB-140

Brinnin, John Malcolm 1916-1998 . . . . DLB-48

Brisbane, Albert 1809-1890 . . . . DLB-3, 250

Brisbane, Arthur 1864-1936 . . . . DLB-25

British Academy DLB-112

The British Critic 1793-1843 . . . . DLB-110

British Library
The American Trust for the
British Library Y-96

The British Library and the Regular
Readers' Group Y-91

Building the New British Library
at St Pancras Y-94

British Literary Prizes DLB-207; Y-98

British Literature
The "Angry Young Men" DLB-15

Author-Printers, 1476-1599 . . . . DLB-167

The Comic Tradition Continued DLB-15

Documents on Sixteenth-Century
Literature DLB-167, 172

Eikon Basilike 1649 . . . . DLB-151

Letter from London Y-96

A Mirror for Magistrates DLB-167

"Modern English Prose" (1876),
by George Saintsbury DLB-57

Sex, Class, Politics, and Religion [in the
British Novel, 1930-1959] DLB-15

Victorians on Rhetoric and Prose
Style DLB-57

The Year in British Fiction Y-99–01

"You've Never Had It So Good," Gusted
by "Winds of Change": British
Fiction in the 1950s, 1960s,
and After DLB-14

British Literature, Old and Middle English
Anglo-Norman Literature in the
Development of Middle English
Literature DLB-146

The *Alliterative Morte Arthure and the
Stanzaic Morte Arthur*
circa 1350-1400 . . . . DLB-146

Ancrene Riwle circa 1200-1225 . . . . . . DLB-146

The *Anglo-Saxon Chronicle* circa
890-1154 . . . . DLB-146

The Battle of Maldon circa 1000 . . . . . . DLB-146

Beowulf circa 900-1000 or
790-825 . . . . DLB-146; CDBLB-1

The Blickling Homilies circa 971 . . . . . DLB-146

The Breton Lays
1300-early fifteenth century DLB-146

The Castle of Perserverance
circa 1400-1425 . . . . DLB-146

The Celtic Background to Medieval
English Literature DLB-146

The Chester Plays circa 1505-1532;
revisions until 1575 . . . . DLB-146

Cursor Mundi circa 1300 . . . . DLB-146

The English Language: 410
to 1500 . . . . DLB-146

The Germanic Epic and Old English
Heroic Poetry: *Widsith, Waldere,*
and *The Fight at Finnsburg* DLB-146

Judith circa 930 . . . . DLB-146

The Matter of England 1240-1400 . . . DLB-146

The Matter of Rome early twelfth to
late fifteenth centuries DLB-146

Middle English Literature:
An Introduction DLB-146

The Middle English Lyric DLB-146

Morality Plays: *Mankind* circa 1450-1500
and *Everyman* circa 1500 . . . . DLB-146

N-Town Plays circa 1468 to early
sixteenth century DLB-146

Old English Literature:
An Introduction DLB-146

Old English Riddles
eighth to tenth centuries DLB-146

The Owl and the Nightingale
circa 1189-1199 . . . . DLB-146

The Paston Letters 1422-1509 . . . . DLB-146

The Seafarer circa 970 . . . . DLB-146

The *South English Legendary* circa
thirteenth to fifteenth centuries DLB-146

*The British Review and London Critical
Journal* 1811-1825 . . . . DLB-110

Brito, Aristeo 1942- DLB-122

Brittain, Vera 1893-1970 . . . . DLB-191

Briusov, Valerii Iakovlevich
1873-1924 . . . . DLB-295

Brizeux, Auguste 1803-1858 . . . . DLB-217

Broadway Publishing Company DLB-46

Broch, Hermann
1886-1951 . . . . DLB-85, 124; CDWLB-2

Brochu, André 1942- DLB-53

Brock, Edwin 1927-1997 . . . . DLB-40

Brockes, Barthold Heinrich 1680-1747 . . . DLB-168

Brod, Max 1884-1968 . . . . DLB-81

Brodber, Erna 1940- DLB-157

Brodhead, John R. 1814-1873 . . . . DLB-30

Brodkey, Harold 1930-1996 . . . . DLB-130

Brodsky, Joseph (Iosif Aleksandrovich
Brodsky) 1940-1996 . . . . DLB-285; Y-87

Nobel Lecture 1987 . . . . Y-87

Brodsky, Michael 1948- DLB-244

Broeg, Bob 1918- DLB-171

Brøgger, Suzanne 1944- DLB-214

Brome, Richard circa 1590-1652 . . . . DLB-58

Brome, Vincent 1910-2004 . . . . DLB-155

Bromfield, Louis 1896-1956 . . . . DLB-4, 9, 86

Bromige, David 1933- DLB-193

Broner, E. M. 1930- DLB-28
    Tribute to Bernard Malamud.......... Y-86
Bronk, William 1918-1999 .... DLB-165
Bronnen, Arnolt 1895-1959 .... DLB-124
Brontë, Anne 1820-1849........... DLB-21, 199
Brontë, Charlotte
    1816-1855...... DLB-21, 159, 199; CDBLB-4
Brontë, Emily
    1818-1848....... DLB-21, 32, 199; CDBLB-4
The Brontë Society..................... Y-98
Brook, Stephen 1947- DLB-204
Brook Farm 1841-1847........ DLB-1; 223; DS-5
Brooke, Frances 1724-1789 .... DLB-39, 99
Brooke, Henry 1703?-1783 .... DLB-39
Brooke, L. Leslie 1862-1940.............. DLB-141
Brooke, Margaret, Ranee of Sarawak
    1849-1936 .... DLB-174
Brooke, Rupert
    1887-1915.......... DLB-19, 216; CDBLB-6
    The Friends of the Dymock Poets Y-00
Brooker, Bertram 1888-1955 .... DLB-88
Brooke-Rose, Christine 1923- DLB-14, 231
Brookner, Anita 1928- DLB-194; Y-87
Brooks, Charles Timothy 1813-1883 .. DLB-1, 243
Brooks, Cleanth 1906-1994 .... DLB-63; Y-94
    Tribute to Katherine Anne Porter Y-80
    Tribute to Walker Percy Y-90
Brooks, Gwendolyn
    1917-2000........ DLB-5, 76, 165; CDALB-1
    Tribute to Julian Mayfield Y-84
Brooks, Jeremy 1926-1994 .... DLB-14
Brooks, Mel 1926- DLB-26
Brooks, Noah 1830-1903 .... DLB-42; DS-13
Brooks, Richard 1912-1992 .... DLB-44
Brooks, Van Wyck 1886-1963 ... DLB-45, 63, 103
Brophy, Brigid 1929-1995 .... DLB-14, 70, 271
Brophy, John 1899-1965................ DLB-191
Brorson, Hans Adolph 1694-1764 ...... DLB-300
Brossard, Chandler 1922-1993 .... DLB-16
Brossard, Nicole 1943- DLB-53
Broster, Dorothy Kathleen 1877-1950.... DLB-160
Brother Antoninus (see Everson, William)
Brotherton, Lord 1856-1930............ DLB-184
Brougham, John 1810-1880 .... DLB-11
Brougham and Vaux, Henry Peter
    Brougham, Baron 1778-1868 ... DLB-110, 158
Broughton, James 1913-1999 .... DLB-5
Broughton, Rhoda 1840-1920 .... DLB-18
Broun, Heywood 1888-1939 .... DLB-29, 171
Browder, Earl 1891-1973 .... DLB-303
Brown, Alice 1856-1948 .... DLB-78
Brown, Bob 1886-1959........ DLB-4, 45; DS-15
Brown, Cecil 1943- DLB-33
Brown, Charles Brockden
    1771-1810.........DLB-37, 59, 73; CDALB-2
Brown, Christy 1932-1981 .... DLB-14

Brown, Dee 1908-2002.................. Y-80
Brown, Frank London 1927-1962........ DLB-76
Brown, Fredric 1906-1972 .... DLB-8
Brown, George Mackay
    1921-1996 .... DLB-14, 27, 139, 271
Brown, Harry 1917-1986 .... DLB-26
Brown, Ian 1945- DLB-310
Brown, Larry 1951- DLB-234, 292
Brown, Lew 1893-1958 .... DLB-265
Brown, Marcia 1918- DLB-61
Brown, Margaret Wise 1910-1952 .... DLB-22
Brown, Morna Doris (see Ferrars, Elizabeth)
Brown, Oliver Madox 1855-1874........ DLB-21
Brown, Sterling 1901-1989 ...... DLB-48, 51, 63
Brown, T. E. 1830-1897................ DLB-35
Brown, Thomas Alexander (see Boldrewood, Rolf)
Brown, Warren 1894-1978............ DLB-241
Brown, William Hill 1765-1793 .... DLB-37
Brown, William Wells
    1815-1884 .... DLB-3, 50, 183, 248
Brown University
    The Festival of Vanguard Narrative Y-93
Browne, Charles Farrar 1834-1867........ DLB-11
Browne, Frances 1816-1879 .... DLB-199
Browne, Francis Fisher 1843-1913 .... DLB-79
Browne, Howard 1908-1999 .... DLB-226
Browne, J. Ross 1821-1875 .... DLB-202
Browne, Michael Dennis 1940- DLB-40
Browne, Sir Thomas 1605-1682........ DLB-151
Browne, William, of Tavistock
    1590-1645 .... DLB-121
Browne, Wynyard 1911-1964 ...... DLB-13, 233
Browne and Nolan DLB-106
Brownell, W. C. 1851-1928 .... DLB-71
Browning, Elizabeth Barrett
    1806-1861 .... DLB-32, 199; CDBLB-4
Browning, Robert
    1812-1889 .... DLB-32, 163; CDBLB-4
    Essay on Chatterton DLB-32
    Introductory Essay: *Letters of Percy
    Bysshe Shelley* (1852) DLB-32
    "The Novel in [Robert Browning's]
    'The Ring and the Book'" (1912),
    by Henry James................ DLB-32
Brownjohn, Allan 1931- DLB-40
    Tribute to John Betjeman.............. Y-84
Brownson, Orestes Augustus
    1803-1876..........DLB-1, 59, 73, 243; DS-5
Bruccoli, Matthew J. 1931- DLB-103
    Joseph [Heller] and George [V. Higgins] ... Y-99
    Response [to Busch on Fitzgerald] Y-96
    Tribute to Albert Erskine............. Y-93
    Tribute to Charles E. Feinberg.......... Y-88
    Working with Fredson Bowers Y-91
Bruce, Charles 1906-1971............... DLB-68
Bruce, John Edward 1856-1924
    Three Documents [African American
    poets].................... DLB-50

Bruce, Leo 1903-1979................. DLB-77
Bruce, Mary Grant 1878-1958 .... DLB-230
Bruce, Philip Alexander 1856-1933 ...... DLB-47
Bruce-Novoa, Juan 1944- DLB-82
Bruckman, Clyde 1894-1955 .... DLB-26
Bruckner, Ferdinand 1891-1958........ DLB-118
Brundage, John Herbert (see Herbert, John)
Brunner, John 1934-1995 .... DLB-261
    Tribute to Theodore Sturgeon.......... Y-85
Brutus, Dennis
    1924- DLB-117, 225; CDWLB-3
Bryan, C. D. B. 1936- DLB-185
Bryan, William Jennings 1860-1925..... DLB-303
Bryant, Arthur 1899-1985 .... DLB-149
Bryant, William Cullen 1794-1878
    .... DLB-3, 43, 59, 189, 250; CDALB-2
Bryce, James 1838-1922 .... DLB-166, 190
Bryce Echenique, Alfredo
    1939- DLB-145; CDWLB-3
Bryden, Bill 1942- DLB-233
Brydges, Sir Samuel Egerton
    1762-1837................. DLB-107, 142
Bryskett, Lodowick 1546?-1612........ DLB-167
Buchan, John 1875-1940..........DLB-34, 70, 156
Buchanan, George 1506-1582 .... DLB-132
Buchanan, Robert 1841-1901........ DLB-18, 35
    "The Fleshly School of Poetry and
    Other Phenomena of the Day"
    (1872) DLB-35
    "The Fleshly School of Poetry:
    Mr. D. G. Rossetti" (1871),
    by Thomas Maitland........... DLB-35
Buchler, Justus 1914-1991 .... DLB-279
Buchman, Sidney 1902-1975 .... DLB-26
Buchner, Augustus 1591-1661 .... DLB-164
Büchner, Georg
    1813-1837............DLB-133; CDWLB-2
Bucholtz, Andreas Heinrich 1607-1671.... DLB-168
Buck, Pearl S. 1892-1973 .. DLB-9, 102; CDALB-7
Bucke, Charles 1781-1846 .... DLB-110
Bucke, Richard Maurice 1837-1902 ...... DLB-99
Buckingham, Edwin 1810-1833 .... DLB-73
Buckingham, Joseph Tinker 1779-1861 ... DLB-73
Buckler, Ernest 1908-1984 .... DLB-68
Buckley, Vincent 1925-1988............ DLB-289
Buckley, William F., Jr. 1925- DLB-137; Y-80
    Publisher's Statement From the
    Initial Issue of *National Review*
    (19 November 1955).......... DLB-137
Buckminster, Joseph Stevens
    1784-1812 .... DLB-37
Buckner, Robert 1906-1989 .... DLB-26
Budd, Thomas ?-1698 .... DLB-24
Budrys, A. J. 1931- DLB-8
Buechner, Frederick 1926- Y-80
Buell, John 1927- DLB-53
Buenaventura, Enrique 1925-2003...... DLB-305
Bufalino, Gesualdo 1920-1996 .... DLB-196

Buffon, Georges-Louis Leclerc de
 1707-1788 ....DLB-313
 "Le Discours sur le style" DLB-314
Job Buffum [publishing house] DLB-49
Bugnet, Georges 1879-1981 ....DLB-92
al-Buhturi 821-897 ....DLB-311
Buies, Arthur 1840-1901 ....DLB-99
Bukiet, Melvin Jules 1953- DLB-299
Bukowski, Charles 1920-1994 .... DLB-5, 130, 169
Bulatović, Miodrag
 1930-1991 ....DLB-181; CDWLB-4
Bulgakov, Mikhail Afanas'evich
 1891-1940 ....DLB-272
Bulgarin, Faddei Venediktovich
 1789-1859 ....DLB-198
Bulger, Bozeman 1877-1932 ....DLB-171
Bull, Olaf 1883-1933 ....DLB-297
Bullein, William
 between 1520 and 1530-1576 ....DLB-167
Bullins, Ed 1935- DLB-7, 38, 249
Bulosan, Carlos 1911-1956 ....DLB-312
Bulwer, John 1606-1656 ....DLB-236
Bulwer-Lytton, Edward (also Edward
 Bulwer) 1803-1873 ....DLB-21
 "On Art in Fiction "(1838) DLB-21
Bumpus, Jerry 1937- Y-81
Bunce and Brother....................DLB-49
Bunin, Ivan 1870-1953 ....DLB-317
Bunner, H. C. 1855-1896 .... DLB-78, 79
Bunting, Basil 1900-1985................DLB-20
Buntline, Ned (Edward Zane Carroll
 Judson) 1821-1886 ....DLB-186
Bunyan, John 1628-1688 ..... DLB-39; CDBLB-2
 The Author's Apology for
  His Book....................DLB-39
Burch, Robert 1925- DLB-52
Burciaga, José Antonio 1940- DLB-82
Burdekin, Katharine (Murray Constantine)
 1896-1963 ....DLB-255
Bürger, Gottfried August 1747-1794 ....DLB-94
Burgess, Anthony (John Anthony Burgess Wilson)
 1917-1993 ......DLB-14, 194, 261; CDBLB-8
 The Anthony Burgess Archive at
  the Harry Ransom Humanities
  Research Center Y-98
 Anthony Burgess's 99 Novels:
  An Opinion Poll Y-84
Burgess, Gelett 1866-1951 ....DLB-11
Burgess, John W. 1844-1931 ....DLB-47
Burgess, Thornton W. 1874-1965 ....DLB-22
Burgess, Stringer and Company DLB-49
Burgos, Julia de 1914-1953 ....DLB-290
Burick, Si 1909-1986 ....DLB-171
Burk, John Daly circa 1772-1808 ....DLB-37
Burk, Ronnie 1955- DLB-209
Burke, Edmund 1729?-1797........DLB-104, 252
Burke, James Lee 1936- DLB-226
Burke, Johnny 1908-1964 ....DLB-265

Burke, Kenneth 1897-1993..........DLB-45, 63
Burke, Thomas 1886-1945 ....DLB-197
Burley, Dan 1907-1962 ....DLB-241
Burley, W. J. 1914- DLB-276
Burlingame, Edward Livermore
 1848-1922 ....DLB-79
Burliuk, David 1882-1967 ....DLB-317
Burman, Carina 1960- DLB-257
Burnet, Gilbert 1643-1715 ....DLB-101
Burnett, Frances Hodgson
 1849-1924 ....DLB-42, 141; DS-13, 14
Burnett, W. R. 1899-1982 ....DLB-9, 226
Burnett, Whit 1899-1973 ....DLB-137
Burney, Fanny 1752-1840 ....DLB-39
 Dedication, The Wanderer (1814) DLB-39
 Preface to Evelina (1778) DLB-39
Burns, Alan 1929- DLB-14, 194
Burns, Joanne 1945- DLB-289
Burns, John Horne 1916-1953.............Y-85
Burns, Robert 1759-1796 .....DLB-109; CDBLB-3
Burns and Oates DLB-106
Burnshaw, Stanley 1906- DLB-48; Y-97
 James Dickey and Stanley Burnshaw
  Correspondence Y-02
 Review of Stanley Burnshaw: The
  Collected Poems and Selected
  Prose........................ Y-02
 Tribute to Robert Penn Warren Y-89
Burr, C. Chauncey 1815?-1883 ....DLB-79
Burr, Esther Edwards 1732-1758 ....DLB-200
Burroughs, Edgar Rice 1875-1950 ....DLB-8
 The Burroughs Bibliophiles Y-98
Burroughs, John 1837-1921 ....DLB-64, 275
Burroughs, Margaret T. G. 1917- DLB-41
Burroughs, William S., Jr. 1947-1981......DLB-16
Burroughs, William Seward 1914-1997
 .... DLB-2, 8, 16, 152, 237; Y-81, 97
Burroway, Janet 1936- DLB-6
Burt, Maxwell Struthers
 1882-1954 ....DLB-86; DS-16
A. L. Burt and Company...............DLB-49
Burton, Hester 1913-2000 ....DLB-161
Burton, Isabel Arundell 1831-1896 ......DLB-166
Burton, Miles (see Rhode, John)
Burton, Richard Francis
 1821-1890 ....DLB-55, 166, 184
Burton, Robert 1577-1640 ....DLB-151
Burton, Virginia Lee 1909-1968 ....DLB-22
Burton, William Evans 1804-1860........DLB-73
Burwell, Adam Hood 1790-1849 ....DLB-99
Bury, Lady Charlotte 1775-1861 ....DLB-116
Busch, Frederick 1941- DLB-6, 218
 Excerpts from Frederick Busch's USC
  Remarks [on F. Scott Fitzgerald] ... Y-96
 Tribute to James Laughlin Y-97
 Tribute to Raymond Carver.......... Y-88
Busch, Niven 1903-1991 ....DLB-44

Bushnell, Horace
 1802-1876 ....DS-13
Business & Literature
 The Claims of Business and Literature:
  An Undergraduate Essay by
  Maxwell Perkins................. Y-01
Bussières, Arthur de 1877-1913 ....DLB-92
Butler, Charles circa 1560-1647........DLB-236
Butler, Guy 1918- DLB-225
Butler, Joseph 1692-1752 ....DLB-252
Butler, Josephine Elizabeth
 1828-1906 ....DLB-190
Butler, Juan 1942-1981 ....DLB-53
Butler, Judith 1956- DLB-246
Butler, Octavia E. 1947- DLB-33
Butler, Pierce 1884-1953 ....DLB-187
Butler, Robert Olen 1945- DLB-173
Butler, Samuel 1613-1680 ....DLB-101, 126
Butler, Samuel
 1835-1902 .... DLB-18, 57, 174; CDBLB-5
Butler, William Francis 1838-1910 ......DLB-166
E. H. Butler and Company DLB-49
Butor, Michel 1926- DLB-83
Nathaniel Butter [publishing house]......DLB-170
Butterworth, Hezekiah 1839-1905........DLB-42
Buttitta, Ignazio 1899-1997 ....DLB-114
Butts, Mary 1890-1937 ....DLB-240
Buzo, Alex 1944- DLB-289
Buzzati, Dino 1906-1972 ....DLB-177
Byars, Betsy 1928- DLB-52
Byatt, A. S. 1936- DLB-14, 194, 319
Byles, Mather 1707-1788................DLB-24
Henry Bynneman [publishing house] DLB-170
Bynner, Witter 1881-1968...............DLB-54
Byrd, William circa 1543-1623 .... DLB-172
Byrd, William, II 1674-1744........DLB-24, 140
Byrne, John Keyes (see Leonard, Hugh)
Byron, George Gordon, Lord
 1788-1824 ....DLB-96, 110; CDBLB-3
 The Byron Society of America Y-00
Byron, Robert 1905-1941 ....DLB-195
Byzantine Novel, The Spanish..........DLB-318

C

Caballero Bonald, José Manuel
 1926- DLB-108
Cabañero, Eladio 1930- DLB-134
Cabell, James Branch 1879-1958 ....DLB-9, 78
Cabeza de Baca, Manuel 1853-1915 .....DLB-122
Cabeza de Baca Gilbert, Fabiola
 1898-1993 ....DLB-122
Cable, George Washington
 1844-1925 .... DLB-12, 74; DS-13
Cable, Mildred 1878-1952 ....DLB-195
Cabral, Manuel del 1907-1999..........DLB-283
Cabral de Melo Neto, João
 1920-1999 ....DLB-307
Cabrera, Lydia 1900-1991 ....DLB-145

Cumulative Index

Cabrera Infante, Guillermo
1929- DLB-113; CDWLB-3
Cabrujas, José Ignacio 1937-1995 .... DLB-305
Cadell [publishing house] DLB-154
Cady, Edwin H. 1917- DLB-103
Caedmon fl. 658-680 .... DLB-146
Caedmon School circa 660-899 .... DLB-146
Caesar, Irving 1895-1996 .... DLB-265
Cafés, Brasseries, and Bistros DS-15
Cage, John 1912-1992................ DLB-193
Cahan, Abraham 1860-1951....... DLB-9, 25, 28
Cahn, Sammy 1913-1993.............. DLB-265
Cain, George 1943- DLB-33
Cain, James M. 1892-1977 .... DLB-226
Cain, Paul (Peter Ruric, George Sims)
1902-1966 .... DLB-306
Caird, Edward 1835-1908 .... DLB-262
Caird, Mona 1854-1932................ DLB-197
Čaks, Aleksandrs
1901-1950 .... DLB-220; CDWLB-4
Caldecott, Randolph 1846-1886........ DLB-163
John Calder Limited
[Publishing house] DLB-112
Calderón de la Barca, Fanny
1804-1882 .... DLB-183
Caldwell, Ben 1937- DLB-38
Caldwell, Erskine 1903-1987 .... DLB-9, 86
H. M. Caldwell Company DLB-49
Caldwell, Taylor 1900-1985................ DS-17
Calhoun, John C. 1782-1850 .... DLB-3, 248
Călinescu, George 1899-1965.......... DLB-220
Calisher, Hortense 1911- DLB-2, 218
Calkins, Mary Whiton 1863-1930 ....DLB-270
Callaghan, Mary Rose 1944- DLB-207
Callaghan, Morley 1903-1990 .... DLB-68; DS-15
Callahan, S. Alice 1868-1894 ....DLB-175, 221
Callaloo [journal] Y-87
Callimachus circa 305 B.C.-240 B.C. DLB-176
Calmer, Edgar 1907-1986 .... DLB-4
Calverley, C. S. 1831-1884............ DLB-35
Calvert, George Henry
1803-1889 .... DLB-1, 64, 248
Calverton, V. F. (George Goetz)
1900-1940..................... DLB-303
Calvino, Italo 1923-1985 .... DLB-196
Cambridge, Ada 1844-1926 .... DLB-230
Cambridge Press..................... DLB-49
Cambridge Songs (Carmina Cantabrigensia)
circa 1050..................... DLB-148
Cambridge University
Cambridge and the Apostles DS-5
Cambridge University Press............DLB-170
Camden, William 1551-1623 ....DLB-172
Camden House: An Interview with
James Hardin....................... Y-92
Cameron, Eleanor 1912-2000 .... DLB-52
Cameron, George Frederick
1854-1885 .... DLB-99

Cameron, Lucy Lyttelton 1781-1858 .... DLB-163
Cameron, Peter 1959- DLB-234
Cameron, William Bleasdell 1862-1951 ... DLB-99
Camm, John 1718-1778................ DLB-31
Camões, Luís de 1524-1580 .... DLB-287
Camon, Ferdinando 1935- DLB-196
Camp, Walter 1859-1925.............. DLB-241
Campana, Dino 1885-1932............ DLB-114
Campbell, Bebe Moore 1950- DLB-227
Campbell, David 1915-1979 .... DLB-260
Campbell, Gabrielle Margaret Vere
(see Shearing, Joseph, and Bowen, Marjorie)
Campbell, James Dykes 1838-1895 ..... DLB-144
Campbell, James Edwin 1867-1896....... DLB-50
Campbell, John 1653-1728 .... DLB-43
Campbell, John W., Jr. 1910-1971 ...... DLB-8
Campbell, Ramsey 1946- DLB-261
Campbell, Robert 1927-2000 .... DLB-306
Campbell, Roy 1901-1957 .... DLB-20, 225
Campbell, Thomas 1777-1844 ...... DLB-93, 144
Campbell, William Edward (see March, William)
Campbell, William Wilfred 1858-1918 ... DLB-92
Campion, Edmund 1539-1581 .... DLB-167
Campion, Thomas
1567-1620.......... DLB-58, 172; CDBLB-1
Campo, Rafael 1964- DLB-282
Campton, David 1924- DLB-245
Camus, Albert 1913-1960 .... DLB-72
Camus, Jean-Pierre 1584-1652 ....DLB-268
The Canadian Publishers' Records Database .. Y-96
Canby, Henry Seidel 1878-1961........ DLB-91
Cancioneros DLB-286
Candelaria, Cordelia 1943- DLB-82
Candelaria, Nash 1928- DLB-82
Candide, Voltaire DLB-314
Canetti, Elias
1905-1994 ....DLB-85, 124; CDWLB-2
Canham, Erwin Dain 1904-1982 ...... DLB-127
Canitz, Friedrich Rudolph Ludwig von
1654-1699 .... DLB-168
Cankar, Ivan 1876-1918 .....DLB-147; CDWLB-4
Cannan, Gilbert 1884-1955 ....DLB-10, 197
Cannan, Joanna 1896-1961 .... DLB-191
Cannell, Kathleen 1891-1974 .... DLB-4
Cannell, Skipwith 1887-1957............ DLB-45
Canning, George 1770-1827 .... DLB-158
Cannon, Jimmy 1910-1973 ....DLB-171
Cano, Daniel 1947- DLB-209
Old Dogs / New Tricks? New
Technologies, the Canon, and the
Structure of the Profession Y-02
Cantú, Norma Elia 1947- DLB-209
Cantwell, Robert 1908-1978............ DLB-9
Jonathan Cape and Harrison Smith
[publishing house] DLB-46
Jonathan Cape Limited................ DLB-112

Čapek, Karel 1890-1938.....DLB-215; CDWLB-4
Capen, Joseph 1658-1725 .... DLB-24
Capes, Bernard 1854-1918............. DLB-156
Capote, Truman 1924-1984
........DLB-2, 185, 227; Y-80, 84; CDALB-1
Capps, Benjamin 1922- DLB-256
Caproni, Giorgio 1912-1990........... DLB-128
Caragiale, Mateiu Ioan 1885-1936 ...... DLB-220
Carballido, Emilio 1925- DLB-305
Cardarelli, Vincenzo 1887-1959 .... DLB-114
Cardenal, Ernesto 1925- DLB-290
Cárdenas, Reyes 1948- DLB-122
Cardinal, Marie 1929-2001 .... DLB-83
Cardoza y Aragón, Luis 1901-1992 ..... DLB-290
Carew, Jan 1920- DLB-157
Carew, Thomas 1594 or 1595-1640 .... DLB-126
Carey, Henry circa 1687-1689-1743 ..... DLB-84
Carey, Mathew 1760-1839 ....DLB-37, 73
M. Carey and Company DLB-49
Carey, Peter 1943- DLB-289
Carey and Hart DLB-49
Carlell, Lodowick 1602-1675 .... DLB-58
Carleton, William 1794-1869 .... DLB-159
G. W. Carleton [publishing house]....... DLB-49
Carlile, Richard 1790-1843.........DLB-110, 158
Carlson, Ron 1947- DLB-244
Carlyle, Jane Welsh 1801-1866 .... DLB-55
Carlyle, Thomas
1795-1881.......... DLB-55, 144; CDBLB-3
"The Hero as Man of Letters:
Johnson, Rousseau, Burns"
(1841) [excerpt] DLB-57
The Hero as Poet. Dante; Shakspeare
(1841) DLB-32
Carman, Bliss 1861-1929.............. DLB-92
Carmina Burana circa 1230............. DLB-138
Carnap, Rudolf 1891-1970 ....DLB-270
Carnero, Guillermo 1947- DLB-108
Carossa, Hans 1878-1956 .... DLB-66
Carpenter, Humphrey
1946-2005 ....DLB-155; Y-84, 99
Carpenter, Stephen Cullen ?-1820? DLB-73
Carpentier, Alejo
1904-1980 ....DLB-113; CDWLB-3
Carr, Emily 1871-1945................ DLB-68
Carr, John Dickson 1906-1977 .... DLB-306
Carr, Marina 1964- DLB-245
Carr, Virginia Spencer 1929- DLB-111; Y-00
Carrera Andrade, Jorge 1903-1978...... DLB-283
Carrier, Roch 1937- DLB-53
Carrillo, Adolfo 1855-1926............. DLB-122
Carroll, Gladys Hasty 1904-1999......... DLB-9
Carroll, John 1735-1815 .... DLB-37
Carroll, John 1809-1884 .... DLB-99
Carroll, Lewis
1832-1898 ......DLB-18, 163, 178; CDBLB-4
The Lewis Carroll Centenary Y-98

The Lewis Carroll Society
of North America Y-00
Carroll, Paul 1927-1996 .... DLB-16
Carroll, Paul Vincent 1900-1968 .... DLB-10
Carroll and Graf Publishers DLB-46
Carruth, Hayden 1921- DLB-5, 165
    Tribute to James Dickey Y-97
    Tribute to Raymond Carver Y-88
Carryl, Charles E. 1841-1920 .... DLB-42
Carson, Anne 1950- DLB-193
Carson, Rachel 1907-1964 .... DLB-275
Carswell, Catherine 1879-1946 .... DLB-36
Cartagena, Alfonso de ca. 1384-1456 .... DLB-286
Cartagena, Teresa de 1425?-? DLB-286
Cărtărescu, Mirea 1956- DLB-232
Carter, Angela
    1940-1992 .... DLB-14, 207, 261, 319
Carter, Elizabeth 1717-1806 .... DLB-109
Carter, Henry (see Leslie, Frank)
Carter, Hodding, Jr. 1907-1972 .... DLB-127
Carter, Jared 1939- DLB-282
Carter, John 1905-1975 .... DLB-201
Carter, Landon 1710-1778 .... DLB-31
Carter, Lin 1930-1988 .... Y-81
Carter, Martin 1927-1997 .... DLB-117; CDWLB-3
Carter, Robert, and Brothers DLB-49
Carter and Hendee DLB-49
Cartwright, Jim 1958- DLB-245
Cartwright, John 1740-1824 .... DLB-158
Cartwright, William circa 1611-1643 ..... DLB-126
Caruthers, William Alexander
    1802-1846 .... DLB-3, 248
Carver, Jonathan 1710-1780 .... DLB-31
Carver, Raymond 1938-1988 .. DLB-130; Y-83,88
    First Strauss "Livings" Awarded to Cynthia
    Ozick and Raymond Carver
    An Interview with Raymond Carver ... Y-83
Carvic, Heron 1917?-1980 .... DLB-276
Cary, Alice 1820-1871 .... DLB-202
Cary, Joyce 1888-1957 .... DLB-15, 100; CDBLB-6
Cary, Patrick 1623?-1657 .... DLB-131
Casal, Julián del 1863-1893 .... DLB-283
Case, John 1540-1600 .... DLB-281
Casey, Gavin 1907-1964 .... DLB-260
Casey, Juanita 1925- DLB-14
Casey, Michael 1947- DLB-5
Cassady, Carolyn 1923- DLB-16
    "As I See It" DLB-16
Cassady, Neal 1926-1968 .... DLB-16, 237
Cassell and Company DLB-106
Cassell Publishing Company DLB-49
Cassill, R. V. 1919-2002 .... DLB-6, 218; Y-02
    Tribute to James Dickey Y-97
Cassity, Turner 1929- DLB-105; Y-02
Cassius Dio circa 155/164-post 229 ...... DLB-176

Cassola, Carlo 1917-1987 .... DLB-177
Castellano, Olivia 1944- DLB-122
Castellanos, Rosario
    1925-1974 .... DLB-113, 290; CDWLB-3
Castelo Branco, Camilo 1825-1890 ...... DLB-287
Castile, Protest Poetry in DLB-286
Castile and Aragon, Vernacular Translations
    in Crowns of 1352-1515 .... DLB-286
Castillejo, Cristóbal de 1490?-1550 ..... DLB-318
Castillo, Ana 1953- DLB-122, 227
Castillo, Rafael C. 1950- DLB-209
The Castle of Perserverance
    circa 1400-1425 .... DLB-146
Castlemon, Harry (see Fosdick, Charles Austin)
Castro, Consuelo de 1946- DLB-307
Castro Alves, Antônio de 1847-1871 ..... DLB-307
Čašule, Kole 1921- DLB-181
Caswall, Edward 1814-1878 .... DLB-32
Catacalos, Rosemary 1944- DLB-122
Cather, Willa 1873-1947
    .... DLB-9, 54, 78, 256; DS-1; CDALB-3
    The Willa Cather Pioneer Memorial
    and Education Foundation Y-00
Catherine II (Ekaterina Alekseevna), "The Great,"
    Empress of Russia 1729-1796 ...... DLB-150
Catherwood, Mary Hartwell 1847-1902 ... DLB-78
Catledge, Turner 1901-1983 .... DLB-127
Catlin, George 1796-1872 .... DLB-186, 189
Cato the Elder 234 B.C.-149 B.C. DLB-211
Cattafi, Bartolo 1922-1979 .... DLB-128
Catton, Bruce 1899-1978 .... DLB-17
Catullus circa 84 B.C.-54 B.C.
    .... DLB-211; CDWLB-1
Causley, Charles 1917-2003 .... DLB-27
Caute, David 1936- DLB-14, 231
Cavendish, Duchess of Newcastle,
    Margaret Lucas
    1623?-1673 .... DLB-131, 252, 281
Cawein, Madison 1865-1914 .... DLB-54
William Caxton [publishing house] DLB-170
The Caxton Printers, Limited DLB-46
Caylor, O. P. 1849-1897 .... DLB-241
Caylus, Marthe-Marguerite de
    1671-1729 .... DLB-313
Cayrol, Jean 1911-2005 .... DLB-83
Cecil, Lord David 1902-1986 .... DLB-155
Cela, Camilo José 1916-2002 .... Y-89
    Nobel Lecture 1989 .... Y-89
Celan, Paul 1920-1970 ...... DLB-69; CDWLB-2
Celati, Gianni 1937- DLB-196
Celaya, Gabriel 1911-1991 .... DLB-108
Céline, Louis-Ferdinand 1894-1961 ...... DLB-72
Celtis, Conrad 1459-1508 .... DLB-179
Cendrars, Blaise 1887-1961 .... DLB-258
    The Steinbeck Centennial Y-02
Censorship
    The Island Trees Case: A Symposium on
    School Library Censorship Y-82

Center for Bibliographical Studies and
    Research at the University of
    California, Riverside Y-91
Center for Book Research Y-84
The Center for the Book in the Library
    of Congress Y-93
    A New Voice: The Center for the
    Book's First Five Years Y-83
Centlivre, Susanna 1669?-1723 .... DLB-84
The Centre for Writing, Publishing and
    Printing History at the University
    of Reading Y-00
The Century Company DLB-49
A Century of Poetry, a Lifetime of Collecting:
    J. M. Edelstein's Collection of
    Twentieth-Century American Poetry ... Y-02
Cernuda, Luis 1902-1963 .... DLB-134
Cerruto, Oscar 1912-1981 .... DLB-283
Cervantes, Lorna Dee 1954- DLB-82
de Céspedes, Alba 1911-1997 .... DLB-264
Cetina, Gutierre de 1514-17?-1556 ...... DLB-318
Ch., T. (see Marchenko, Anastasiia Iakovlevna)
Cha, Theresa Hak Kyung 1951-1982 .... DLB-312
Chaadaev, Petr Iakovlevich
    1794-1856 .... DLB-198
Chabon, Michael 1963- DLB-278
Chacel, Rosa 1898-1994 .... DLB-134
Chacón, Eusebio 1869-1948 .... DLB-82
Chacón, Felipe Maximiliano 1873-? DLB-82
Chadwick, Henry 1824-1908 .... DLB-241
Chadwyck-Healey's Full-Text Literary Databases:
    Editing Commercial Databases of
    Primary Literary Texts Y-95
Challans, Eileen Mary (see Renault, Mary)
Chalmers, George 1742-1825 .... DLB-30
Chaloner, Sir Thomas 1520-1565 .... DLB-167
Chamberlain, Samuel S. 1851-1916 ...... DLB-25
Chamberland, Paul 1939- DLB-60
Chamberlin, William Henry 1897-1969 .... DLB-29
Chambers, Charles Haddon 1860-1921 ... DLB-10
Chambers, María Cristina (see Mena, María Cristina)
Chambers, Robert W. 1865-1933 .... DLB-202
W. and R. Chambers
    [publishing house] DLB-106
Chambers, Whittaker 1901-1961 .... DLB-303
Chamfort, Sébastien-Roch Nicolas de
    1740?-1794 .... DLB-313
Chamisso, Adelbert von 1781-1838 .... DLB-90
Champfleury 1821-1889 .... DLB-119
Chan, Jeffery Paul 1942- DLB-312
Chandler, Harry 1864-1944 .... DLB-29
Chandler, Norman 1899-1973 .... DLB-127
Chandler, Otis 1927- DLB-127
Chandler, Raymond
    1888-1959 .... DLB-226, 253; DS-6; CDALB-5
    Raymond Chandler Centenary Y-88
Chang, Diana 1934- DLB-312
Channing, Edward 1856-1931 .... DLB-17

Cumulative Index

Channing, Edward Tyrrell
    1790-1856 .... DLB-1, 59, 235
Channing, William Ellery
    1780-1842 .... DLB-1, 59, 235
Channing, William Ellery, II
    1817-1901 .... DLB-1, 223
Channing, William Henry
    1810-1884 .... DLB-1, 59, 243
Chapelain, Jean 1595-1674 .... DLB-268
Chaplin, Charlie 1889-1977 .... DLB-44
Chapman, George
    1559 or 1560-1634 .... DLB-62, 121
Chapman, Olive Murray 1892-1977 ..... DLB-195
Chapman, R. W. 1881-1960 .... DLB-201
Chapman, William 1850-1917 .... DLB-99
John Chapman [publishing house] DLB-106
Chapman and Hall [publishing house] ... DLB-106
Chappell, Fred 1936- DLB-6, 105
    "A Detail in a Poem" DLB-105
    Tribute to Peter Taylor Y-94
Chappell, William 1582-1649 .... DLB-236
Char, René 1907-1988 .... DLB-258
Charbonneau, Jean 1875-1960 .... DLB-92
Charbonneau, Robert 1911-1967 .... DLB-68
Charles, Gerda 1914-1996 .... DLB-14
William Charles [publishing house] DLB-49
Charles d'Orléans 1394-1465 .... DLB-208
Charley (see Mann, Charles)
Charrière, Isabelle de 1740-1805 ...... DLB-313
Charskaia, Lidiia 1875-1937 .... DLB-295
Charteris, Leslie 1907-1993 .... DLB-77
Chartier, Alain circa 1385-1430 ...... DLB-208
Charyn, Jerome 1937- Y-83
Chase, Borden 1900-1971 .... DLB-26
Chase, Edna Woolman 1877-1957 .... DLB-91
Chase, James Hadley (René Raymond)
    1906-1985 .... DLB-276
Chase, Mary Coyle 1907-1981 .... DLB-228
Chase-Riboud, Barbara 1936- DLB-33
Chateaubriand, François-René de
    1768-1848 .... DLB-119
Châtelet, Gabrielle-Emilie Du
    1706-1749 .... DLB-313
Chatterton, Thomas 1752-1770 .... DLB-109
    Essay on Chatterton (1842), by
        Robert Browning DLB-32
Chatto and Windus DLB-106
Chatwin, Bruce 1940-1989 .... DLB-194, 204
Chaucer, Geoffrey
    1340?-1400 .... DLB-146; CDBLB-1
    New Chaucer Society Y-00
Chaudhuri, Amit 1962- DLB-267
Chauncy, Charles 1705-1787 .... DLB-24
Chauveau, Pierre-Joseph-Olivier
    1820-1890 .... DLB-99
Chávez, Denise 1948- DLB-122
Chávez, Fray Angélico 1910-1996 .... DLB-82
Chayefsky, Paddy 1923-1981 ..... DLB-7, 44; Y-81

Cheesman, Evelyn 1881-1969 .... DLB-195
Cheever, Ezekiel 1615-1708 .... DLB-24
Cheever, George Barrell 1807-1890 ..... DLB-59
Cheever, John 1912-1982
    .... DLB-2, 102, 227; Y-80, 82; CDALB-1
Cheever, Susan 1943- Y-82
Cheke, Sir John 1514-1557 .... DLB-132
Chekhov, Anton Pavlovich 1860-1904 ... DLB-277
Chelsea House DLB-46
Chênedollé, Charles de 1769-1833 ..... DLB-217
Cheney, Brainard
    Tribute to Caroline Gordon Y-81
Cheney, Ednah Dow 1824-1904 ..... DLB-1, 223
Cheney, Harriet Vaughan 1796-1889 ..... DLB-99
Chénier, Marie-Joseph 1764-1811 ...... DLB-192
Cherny, Sasha 1880-1932 .... DLB-317
Chernyshevsky, Nikolai Gavrilovich
    1828-1889 .... DLB-238
Cherry, Kelly 1940 .... Y-83
Cherryh, C. J. 1942- Y-80
Chesebro', Caroline 1825-1873 .... DLB-202
Chesney, Sir George Tomkyns
    1830-1895 .... DLB-190
Chesnut, Mary Boykin 1823-1886 ...... DLB-239
Chesnutt, Charles Waddell
    1858-1932 .... DLB-12, 50, 78
Chesson, Mrs. Nora (see Hopper, Nora)
Chester, Alfred 1928-1971 .... DLB-130
Chester, George Randolph 1869-1924 ... DLB-78
The Chester Plays circa 1505-1532;
    revisions until 1575 .... DLB-146
Chesterfield, Philip Dormer Stanhope,
    Fourth Earl of 1694-1773 .... DLB-104
Chesterton, G. K. 1874-1936
    ... DLB-10, 19, 34, 70, 98, 149, 178; CDBLB-6
    "The Ethics of Elfland" (1908) DLB-178
Chettle, Henry
    circa 1560-circa 1607 .... DLB-136
Cheuse, Alan 1940- DLB-244
Chew, Ada Nield 1870-1945 .... DLB-135
Cheyney, Edward P. 1861-1947 .... DLB-47
Chiang Yee 1903-1977 .... DLB-312
Chiara, Piero 1913-1986 .... DLB-177
Chicanos
    Chicano History DLB-82
    Chicano Language DLB-82
    Chicano Literature: A Bibliography .. DLB-209
    A Contemporary Flourescence of Chicano
        Literature Y-84
    Literatura Chicanesca: The View From
        Without DLB-82
Child, Francis James 1825-1896 ... DLB-1, 64, 235
Child, Lydia Maria 1802-1880 ..... DLB-1, 74, 243
Child, Philip 1898-1978 .... DLB-68
Childers, Erskine 1870-1922 .... DLB-70
Children's Literature
    Afterword: Propaganda, Namby-Pamby,
        and Some Books of Distinction ... DLB-52
    Children's Book Awards and Prizes ... DLB-61

Children's Book Illustration in the
    Twentieth Century DLB-61
Children's Illustrators, 1800-1880 ... DLB-163
The Harry Potter Phenomenon Y-99
    Pony Stories, Omnibus
        Essay on DLB-160
The Reality of One Woman's Dream:
    The de Grummond Children's
    Literature Collection Y-99
School Stories, 1914-1960 .... DLB-160
The Year in Children's
    Books Y-92–96, 98–01
The Year in Children's Literature Y-97
Childress, Alice 1916-1994 .... DLB-7, 38, 249
Childress, Mark 1957- DLB-292
Childs, George W. 1829-1894 .... DLB-23
Chilton Book Company DLB-46
Chin, Frank 1940- DLB-206, 312
Chin, Justin 1969- DLB-312
Chin, Marilyn 1955- DLB-312
Chinweizu 1943- DLB-157
Chinnov, Igor' 1909-1996 .... DLB-317
Chitham, Edward 1932- DLB-155
Chittenden, Hiram Martin 1858-1917 ... DLB-47
Chivers, Thomas Holley 1809-1858 .. DLB-3, 248
Chkhartishvili, Grigorii Shalvovich
    (see Akunin, Boris)
Chocano, José Santos 1875-1934 ...... DLB-290
Cholmondeley, Mary 1859-1925 .... DLB-197
Chomsky, Noam 1928- DLB-246
Chopin, Kate 1850-1904 ... DLB-12, 78; CDALB-3
Chopin, René 1885-1953 .... DLB-92
Choquette, Adrienne 1915-1973 .... DLB-68
Choquette, Robert 1905-1991 .... DLB-68
Choyce, Lesley 1951- DLB-251
Chrétien de Troyes
    circa 1140-circa 1190 .... DLB-208
Christensen, Inger 1935- DLB-214
Christensen, Lars Saabye 1953- DLB-297
The Christian Examiner DLB-1
The Christian Publishing Company DLB-49
Christie, Agatha
    1890-1976 .... DLB-13, 77, 245; CDBLB-6
Christine de Pizan
    circa 1365-circa 1431 .... DLB-208
Christopher, John (Sam Youd) 1922- .. DLB-255
Christus und die Samariterin circa 950 ..... DLB-148
Christy, Howard Chandler 1873-1952 ... DLB-188
Chu, Louis 1915-1970 .... DLB-312
Chukovskaia, Lidiia 1907-1996 .... DLB-302
Chulkov, Mikhail Dmitrievich
    1743?-1792 .... DLB-150
Church, Benjamin 1734-1778 .... DLB-31
Church, Francis Pharcellus 1839-1906 ... DLB-79
Church, Peggy Pond 1903-1986 .... DLB-212
Church, Richard 1893-1972 .... DLB-191
Church, William Conant 1836-1917 ..... DLB-79

Churchill, Caryl 1938- DLB-13, 310
Churchill, Charles 1731-1764.......... DLB-109
Churchill, Winston 1871-1947.......... DLB-202
Churchill, Sir Winston
 1874-1965 .... DLB-100; DS-16; CDBLB-5
Churchyard, Thomas 1520?-1604....... DLB-132
E. Churton and Company............ DLB-106
Chute, Marchette 1909-1994........... DLB-103
Ciardi, John 1916-1986 .... DLB-5; Y-86
Cibber, Colley 1671-1757................DLB-84
Cicero 106 B.C.-43 B.C. DLB-211, CDWLB-1
Cima, Annalisa 1941- DLB-128
Čingo, Živko 1935-1987 ....DLB-181
Cioran, E. M. 1911-1995................DLB-220
Čipkus, Alfonsas (see Nyka-Niliūnas, Alfonsas)
Cirese, Eugenio 1884-1955 ....DLB-114
Cīrulis, Jānis (see Bels, Alberts)
Cisneros, Antonio 1942- DLB-290
Cisneros, Sandra 1954- DLB-122, 152
City Lights Books DLB-46
Civil War (1861–1865)
 Battles and Leaders of the Civil War ... DLB-47
 Official Records of the Rebellion DLB-47
 Recording the Civil War............ DLB-47
Cixous, Hélène 1937- DLB-83, 242
Claire d'Albe, Sophie Cottin............DLB-314
Clampitt, Amy 1920-1994 ....DLB-105
 Tribute to Alfred A. Knopf........... Y-84
Clancy, Tom 1947- DLB-227
Clapper, Raymond 1892-1944...........DLB-29
Clare, John 1793-1864 ....DLB-55, 96
Clarendon, Edward Hyde, Earl of
 1609-1674 .... DLB-101
Clark, Alfred Alexander Gordon
 (see Hare, Cyril)
Clark, Ann Nolan 1896-1995 ....DLB-52
Clark, C. E. Frazer, Jr. 1925-2001 .. DLB-187; Y-01
 C. E. Frazer Clark Jr. and
  Hawthorne Bibliography DLB-269
 The Publications of C. E. Frazer
  Clark Jr..................... DLB-269
Clark, Catherine Anthony 1892-1977 .....DLB-68
Clark, Charles Heber 1841-1915.........DLB-11
Clark, Davis Wasgatt 1812-1871 ....DLB-79
Clark, Douglas 1919-1993 ....DLB-276
Clark, Eleanor 1913-1996 ....DLB-6
Clark, J. P. 1935- DLB-117; CDWLB-3
Clark, Lewis Gaylord
 1808-1873 .... DLB-3, 64, 73, 250
Clark, Mary Higgins 1929- DLB-306
Clark, Walter Van Tilburg
 1909-1971 ....DLB-9, 206
Clark, William 1770-1838 ....DLB-183, 186
Clark, William Andrews, Jr.
 1877-1934 .... DLB-187
C. M. Clark Publishing Company........DLB-46
Clarke, Sir Arthur C. 1917- DLB-261

Tribute to Theodore Sturgeon Y-85
Clarke, Austin 1896-1974........... DLB-10, 20
Clarke, Austin C. 1934- DLB-53, 125
Clarke, Gillian 1937- DLB-40
Clarke, James Freeman
 1810-1888 .... DLB-1, 59, 235; DS-5
Clarke, John circa 1596-1658.......... DLB-281
Clarke, Lindsay 1939- DLB-231
Clarke, Marcus 1846-1881 ....DLB-230
Clarke, Pauline 1921- DLB-161
Clarke, Rebecca Sophia 1833-1906 ....DLB-42
Clarke, Samuel 1675-1729 ....DLB-252
Robert Clarke and Company DLB-49
Clarkson, Thomas 1760-1846 ....DLB-158
Claudel, Paul 1868-1955 .... DLB-192, 258
Claudius, Matthias 1740-1815 ....DLB-97
Clausen, Andy 1943- DLB-16
Claussen, Sophus 1865-1931 ....DLB-300
Clawson, John L. 1865-1933 ....DLB-187
Claxton, Remsen and Haffelfinger DLB-49
Clay, Cassius Marcellus 1810-1903........DLB-43
Clayton, Richard (see Haggard, William)
Cleage, Pearl 1948- DLB-228
Cleary, Beverly 1916- DLB-52
Cleary, Kate McPhelim 1863-1905 ......DLB-221
Cleaver, Vera 1919-1992 and
 Cleaver, Bill 1920-1981.............DLB-52
Cleeve, Brian 1921-2003 ....DLB-276
Cleland, John 1710-1789 ....DLB-39
Clemens, Samuel Langhorne (Mark Twain)
 1835-1910 .... DLB-11, 12, 23, 64, 74,
  186, 189; CDALB-3
 Comments From Authors and Scholars on
  their First Reading of Huck Finn..... Y-85
 Huck at 100: How Old Is
  Huckleberry Finn? Y-85
 Mark Twain on Perpetual Copyright Y-92
 A New Edition of Huck Finn Y-85
Clement, Hal 1922-2003 ....DLB-8
Clemo, Jack 1916-1994 ....DLB-27
Clephane, Elizabeth Cecilia 1830-1869 ...DLB-199
Cleveland, John 1613-1658 ....DLB-126
Cliff, Michelle 1946- DLB-157; CDWLB-3
Clifford, Lady Anne 1590-1676.......... DLB-151
Clifford, James L. 1901-1978 ....DLB-103
Clifford, Lucy 1853?-1929..... DLB-135, 141, 197
Clift, Charmian 1923-1969 ....DLB-260
Clifton, Lucille 1936- DLB-5, 41
Clines, Francis X. 1938- DLB-185
Clive, Caroline (V) 1801-1873..........DLB-199
Edward J. Clode [publishing house]....... DLB-46
Clough, Arthur Hugh 1819-1861 ....DLB-32
Cloutier, Cécile 1930- DLB-60
Clouts, Sidney 1926-1982 ....DLB-225
Clutton-Brock, Arthur 1868-1924 ....DLB-98

Coates, Robert M.
 1897-1973 .... DLB-4, 9, 102; DS-15
Coatsworth, Elizabeth 1893-1986 ....DLB-22
Cobb, Charles E., Jr. 1943- DLB-41
Cobb, Frank I. 1869-1923 ....DLB-25
Cobb, Irvin S. 1876-1944.......... DLB-11, 25, 86
Cobbe, Frances Power 1822-1904 ....DLB-190
Cobbett, William 1763-1835 .... DLB-43, 107, 158
Cobbledick, Gordon 1898-1969 ....DLB-171
Cochran, Thomas C. 1902-1999 ....DLB-17
Cochrane, Elizabeth 1867-1922 ......DLB-25, 189
Cockerell, Sir Sydney 1867-1962 ....DLB-201
Cockerill, John A. 1845-1896 ....DLB-23
Cocteau, Jean 1889-1963........... DLB-65, 258
Coderre, Emile (see Jean Narrache)
Cody, Liza 1944- DLB-276
Coe, Jonathan 1961- DLB-231
Coetzee, J. M. 1940- DLB-225
Coffee, Lenore J. 1900?-1984 ....DLB-44
Coffin, Robert P. Tristram 1892-1955..... DLB-45
Coghill, Mrs. Harry (see Walker, Anna Louisa)
Cogswell, Fred 1917- DLB-60
Cogswell, Mason Fitch 1761-1830 ....DLB-37
Cohan, George M. 1878-1942 ....DLB-249
Cohen, Arthur A. 1928-1986...........DLB-28
Cohen, Leonard 1934- DLB-53
Cohen, Matt 1942- DLB-53
Cohen, Morris Raphael 1880-1947 ......DLB-270
Colasanti, Marina 1937- DLB-307
Colbeck, Norman 1903-1987...........DLB-201
Colden, Cadwallader
 1688-1776 .... DLB-24, 30, 270
Colden, Jane 1724-1766 ....DLB-200
Cole, Barry 1936- DLB-14
Cole, George Watson 1850-1939 ....DLB-140
Colegate, Isabel 1931- DLB-14, 231
Coleman, Emily Holmes 1899-1974 ....DLB-4
Coleman, Wanda 1946- DLB-130
Coleridge, Hartley 1796-1849 ....DLB-96
Coleridge, Mary 1861-1907..........DLB-19, 98
Coleridge, Samuel Taylor
 1772-1834 .... DLB-93, 107; CDBLB-3
Coleridge, Sara 1802-1852..............DLB-199
Colet, John 1467-1519 ....DLB-132
Colette 1873-1954 ....DLB-65
Colette, Sidonie Gabrielle (see Colette)
Colinas, Antonio 1946- DLB-134
Coll, Joseph Clement 1881-1921 ....DLB-188
A Century of Poetry, a Lifetime of Collecting:
 J. M. Edelstein's Collection of
 Twentieth-Century American Poetry Y-02
Collier, John 1901-1980............ DLB-77, 255
Collier, John Payne 1789-1883 ....DLB-184
Collier, Mary 1690-1762 ....DLB-95
Collier, Robert J. 1876-1918...........DLB-91
P. F. Collier [publishing house] DLB-49

Cumulative Index

Collin and Small DLB-49	Condorcet, Marie-Jean-Antoine-Nicolas Caritat, marquis de 1743-1794 .... DLB-313	Coolbrith, Ina 1841-1928 .... DLB-54, 186
Collingwood, R. G. 1889-1943 .... DLB-262	"The Tenth Stage" DLB-314	Cooley, Peter 1940- DLB-105
Collingwood, W. G. 1854-1932 .... DLB-149	Congreve, William	"Into the Mirror" DLB-105
Collins, An floruit circa 1653 .... DLB-131	1670-1729 .... DLB-39, 84; CDBLB-2	Coolidge, Clark 1939- DLB-193
Collins, Anthony 1676-1729 .... DLB-252	Preface to *Incognita* (1692) DLB-39	Coolidge, Susan (see Woolsey, Sarah Chauncy)
Collins, Merle 1950- DLB-157	W. B. Conkey Company DLB-49	George Coolidge [publishing house] DLB-49
Collins, Michael 1964- DLB-267	Conlon, Evelyn 1952- DLB-319	Cooper, Anna Julia 1858-1964 .... DLB-221
Collins, Michael (see Lynds, Dennis)	Conn, Stewart 1936- DLB-233	Cooper, Edith Emma 1862-1913 .... DLB-240
Collins, Mortimer 1827-1876 .... DLB-21, 35	Connell, Evan S., Jr. 1924- DLB-2; Y-81	Cooper, Giles 1918-1966 .... DLB-13
Collins, Tom (see Furphy, Joseph)	Connelly, Marc 1890-1980 .... DLB-7; Y-80	Cooper, J. California 19??- DLB-212
Collins, Wilkie 1824-1889 ...... DLB-18, 70, 159; CDBLB-4	Connolly, Cyril 1903-1974 .... DLB-98	Cooper, James Fenimore 1789-1851 .... DLB-3, 183, 250; CDALB-2
"The Unknown Public" (1858) [excerpt] DLB-57	Connolly, James B. 1868-1957 .... DLB-78	The Bicentennial of James Fenimore Cooper: An International Celebration Y-89
The Wilkie Collins Society Y-98	Connor, Ralph (Charles William Gordon) 1860-1937 .... DLB-92	The James Fenimore Cooper Society Y-01
Collins, William 1721-1759 .... DLB-109	Connor, Tony 1930- DLB-40	Cooper, Kent 1880-1965 .... DLB-29
Isaac Collins [publishing house] DLB-49	Conquest, Robert 1917- DLB-27	Cooper, Susan 1935- DLB-161, 261
William Collins, Sons and Company DLB-154	Conrad, Joseph 1857-1924 .... DLB-10, 34, 98, 156; CDBLB-5	Cooper, Susan Fenimore 1813-1894 ..... DLB-239
Collis, Maurice 1889-1973 .... DLB-195	John Conrad and Company DLB-49	William Cooper [publishing house] DLB-170
Collyer, Mary 1716?-1763? DLB-39	Conroy, Jack 1899-1990 .... Y-81	J. Coote [publishing house] DLB-154
Colman, Benjamin 1673-1747 .... DLB-24	A Tribute [to Nelson Algren] Y-81	Coover, Robert 1932- DLB-2, 227; Y-81
Colman, George, the Elder 1732-1794 .... DLB-89	Conroy, Pat 1945- DLB-6	Tribute to Donald Barthelme Y-89
Colman, George, the Younger 1762-1836 .... DLB-89	Considine, Bob 1906-1975 .... DLB-241	Tribute to Theodor Seuss Geisel Y-91
S. Colman [publishing house] DLB-49	Consolo, Vincenzo 1933- DLB-196	Copeland and Day DLB-49
Colombo, John Robert 1936- DLB-53	Constable, Henry 1562-1613 .... DLB-136	Ćopić, Branko 1915-1984 .... DLB-181
Colonial Literature DLB-307	Archibald Constable and Company DLB-154	Copland, Robert 1470?-1548 .... DLB-136
Colquhoun, Patrick 1745-1820 .... DLB-158	Constable and Company Limited DLB-112	Coppard, A. E. 1878-1957 .... DLB-162
Colter, Cyrus 1910-2002 .... DLB-33	Constant, Benjamin 1767-1830 .... DLB-119	Coppée, François 1842-1908 .... DLB-217
Colum, Padraic 1881-1972 .... DLB-19	Constant de Rebecque, Henri-Benjamin de (see Constant, Benjamin)	Coppel, Alfred 1921-2004 .... Y-83
The Columbia History of the American Novel A Symposium on Y-92	Constantine, David 1944- DLB-40	Tribute to Jessamyn West Y-84
Columbus, Christopher 1451-1506 ..... DLB-318	Constantine, Murray (see Burdekin, Katharine)	Coppola, Francis Ford 1939- DLB-44
Columella fl. first century A.D. DLB-211	Constantin-Weyer, Maurice 1881-1964 ... DLB-92	Copway, George (Kah-ge-ga-gah-bowh) 1818-1869 .... DLB-175, 183
Colvin, Sir Sidney 1845-1927 .... DLB-149	*Contempo* (magazine) Contempo Caravan: Kites in a Windstorm Y-85	Copyright The Development of the Author's Copyright in Britain DLB-154
Colwin, Laurie 1944-1992 .... DLB-218; Y-80	The Continental Publishing Company DLB-49	The Digital Millennium Copyright Act: Expanding Copyright Protection in Cyberspace and Beyond Y-98
Comden, Betty 1915- and Green, Adolph 1918-2002 ...... DLB-44, 265	A Conversation between William Riggan and Janette Turner Hospital Y-02	Editorial: The Extension of Copyright ... Y-02
Comi, Girolamo 1890-1968 .... DLB-114	Conversations with Editors Y-95	Mark Twain on Perpetual Copyright Y-92
Comisso, Giovanni 1895-1969 .... DLB-264	Conway, Anne 1631-1679 .... DLB-252	Public Domain and the Violation of Texts Y-97
Commager, Henry Steele 1902-1998 ..... DLB-17	Conway, Moncure Daniel 1832-1907 .... DLB-1, 223	The Question of American Copyright in the Nineteenth Century Preface, by George Haven Putnam The Evolution of Copyright, by Brander Matthews Summary of Copyright Legislation in the United States, by R. R. Bowker Analysis of the Provisions of the Copyright Law of 1891, by George Haven Putnam The Contest for International Copyright, by George Haven Putnam Cheap Books and Good Books, by Brander Matthews DLB-49
Commynes, Philippe de circa 1447-1511 .... DLB-208	Cook, Ebenezer circa 1667-circa 1732 ..... DLB-24	
Compton, D. G. 1930- DLB-261	Cook, Edward Tyas 1857-1919 .... DLB-149	
Compton-Burnett, Ivy 1884?-1969 .... DLB-36	Cook, Eliza 1818-1889 .... DLB-199	
Conan, Laure (Félicité Angers) 1845-1924 .... DLB-99	Cook, George Cram 1873-1924 .... DLB-266	
Concord, Massachusetts Concord History and Life DLB-223	Cook, Michael 1933-1994 .... DLB-53	
Concord: Literary History of a Town DLB-223	David C. Cook Publishing Company DLB-49	
The Old Manse, by Hawthorne DLB-223	Cooke, George Willis 1848-1923 .... DLB-71	
The Thoreauvian Pilgrimage: The Structure of an American Cult .. DLB-223	Cooke, John Esten 1830-1886 .... DLB-3, 248	
	Cooke, Philip Pendleton 1816-1850 .... DLB-3, 59, 248	Writers and Their Copyright Holders: the WATCH Project Y-94
Concrete Poetry DLB-307	Cooke, Rose Terry 1827-1892 .... DLB-12, 74	
Conde, Carmen 1901-1996 .... DLB-108	Increase Cooke and Company DLB-49	Corazzini, Sergio 1886-1907 .... DLB-114
Condillac, Etienne Bonnot de 1714-1780 .... DLB-313	Cook-Lynn, Elizabeth 1930- DLB-175	Corbett, Richard 1582-1635 .... DLB-121

Corbière, Tristan 1845-1875 . . . . DLB-217	Cotton, John 1584-1652. . . . . DLB-24	Cranch, Christopher Pearse 1813-1892 . . . . DLB-1, 42, 243; DS-5
Corcoran, Barbara 1911- DLB-52	Cotton, Sir Robert Bruce 1571-1631 . . . . . DLB-213	Crane, Hart 1899-1932 . . . . . DLB-4, 48; CDALB-4
Cordelli, Franco 1943- DLB-196	Coulter, John 1888-1980 . . . . DLB-68	Nathan Asch Remembers Ford Madox
Corelli, Marie 1855-1924. . . . . DLB-34, 156	Cournos, John 1881-1966 . . . . DLB-54	Ford, Sam Roth, and Hart Crane Y-02
Corle, Edwin 1906-1956 . . . . Y-85	Courteline, Georges 1858-1929 . . . . DLB-192	Crane, R. S. 1886-1967 . . . . DLB-63
Corman, Cid 1924-2004 . . . . DLB-5, 193	Cousins, Margaret 1905-1996 . . . . DLB-137	Crane, Stephen
Cormier, Robert 1925-2000 . . . . DLB-52; CDALB-6	Cousins, Norman 1915-1990 . . . . DLB-137	1871-1900 . . . . DLB-12, 54, 78; CDALB-3
Tribute to Theodor Seuss Geisel. Y-91	Couvreur, Jessie (see Tasma)	Stephen Crane: A Revaluation, Virginia
Corn, Alfred 1943- DLB-120, 282; Y-80	Coventry, Francis 1725-1754 . . . . DLB-39	Tech Conference, 1989 . . . . Y-89
Corneille, Pierre 1606-1684. . . . . DLB-268	Dedication, *The History of Pompey*	The Stephen Crane Society. Y-98, 01
Cornford, Frances 1886-1960 . . . . DLB-240	*the Little* (1751). DLB-39	Crane, Walter 1845-1915 . . . . DLB-163
Cornish, Sam 1935- DLB-41	Coverdale, Miles 1487 or 1488-1569. . . . . DLB-167	Cranmer, Thomas 1489-1556 . . . . . . DLB-132, 213
Cornish, William	N. Coverly [publishing house] DLB-49	Crapsey, Adelaide 1878-1914. . . . . DLB-54
circa 1465-circa 1524. . . . . DLB-132	Covici-Friede DLB-46	Crashaw, Richard 1612/1613-1649 . . . . . . DLB-126
Cornwall, Barry (see Procter, Bryan Waller)	Cowan, Peter 1914-2002 . . . . DLB-260	Craven, Avery 1885-1980 . . . . DLB-17
Cornwallis, Sir William, the Younger	Coward, Noel	Crawford, Charles 1752-circa 1815 . . . . . . DLB-31
circa 1579-1614 . . . . DLB-151	1899-1973 . . . . DLB-10, 245; CDBLB-6	Crawford, F. Marion 1854-1909 . . . . DLB-71
Cornwell, David John Moore (see le Carré, John)	Coward, McCann and Geoghegan DLB-46	Crawford, Isabel Valancy 1850-1887 . . . . . DLB-92
Cornwell, Patricia 1956- DLB-306	Cowles, Gardner 1861-1946 . . . . DLB-29	Crawley, Alan 1887-1975 . . . . DLB-68
Coronel Urtecho, José 1906-1994 . . . . . . DLB-290	Cowles, Gardner "Mike", Jr.	Crayon, Geoffrey (see Irving, Washington)
Corpi, Lucha 1945- DLB-82	1903-1985 . . . . DLB-127, 137	Crayon, Porte (see Strother, David Hunter)
Corrington, John William	Cowley, Abraham 1618-1667 . . . . . . DLB-131, 151	Creamer, Robert W. 1922- DLB-171
1932-1988 . . . . DLB-6, 244	Cowley, Hannah 1743-1809 . . . . DLB-89	Creasey, John 1908-1973 . . . . DLB-77
Corriveau, Monique 1927-1976 . . . . DLB-251	Cowley, Malcolm	Creative Age Press. DLB-46
Corrothers, James D. 1869-1917 . . . . DLB-50	1898-1989 . . . . DLB-4, 48; DS-15; Y-81, 89	Creative Nonfiction Y-02
Corso, Gregory 1930-2001 . . . . . . DLB-5, 16, 237	Cowper, Richard (John Middleton Murry Jr.)	Crébillon, Claude-Prosper Jolyot de *fils*
Cortázar, Julio 1914-1984 . . . DLB-113; CDWLB-3	1926-2002 . . . . DLB-261	1707-1777 . . . . DLB-313
Cortéz, Carlos 1923-2005 . . . . DLB-209	Cowper, William 1731-1800 . . . . . . DLB-104, 109	Crébillon, Claude-Prosper Jolyot de *père*
Cortez, Jayne 1936- DLB-41	Cox, A. B. (see Berkeley, Anthony)	1674-1762 . . . . DLB-313
Corvinus, Gottlieb Siegmund	Cox, James McMahon 1903-1974 . . . . . . DLB-127	William Creech [publishing house] DLB-154
1677-1746. . . . . DLB-168	Cox, James Middleton 1870-1957 . . . . . . DLB-127	Thomas Creede [publishing house] DLB-170
Corvo, Baron (see Rolfe, Frederick William)	Cox, Leonard circa 1495-circa 1550 . . . . . DLB-281	Creel, George 1876-1953 . . . . DLB-25
Cory, Annie Sophie (see Cross, Victoria)	Cox, Palmer 1840-1924 . . . . DLB-42	Creeley, Robert 1926-2005
Cory, Desmond (Shaun Lloyd McCarthy)	Coxe, Louis 1918-1993 . . . . DLB-5	. . . . DLB-5, 16, 169; DS-17
1928- DLB-276	Coxe, Tench 1755-1824 . . . . DLB-37	Creelman, James
Cory, William Johnson 1823-1892 . . . . DLB-35	Cozzens, Frederick S. 1818-1869 . . . . DLB-202	1859-1915 . . . . DLB-23
Coryate, Thomas 1577?-1617 . . . . . . DLB-151, 172	Cozzens, James Gould 1903-1978	Cregan, David 1931- DLB-13
Ćosić, Dobrica 1921- DLB-181; CDWLB-4	. . . . DLB-9, 294; Y-84; DS-2; CDALB-1	Creighton, Donald 1902-1979 . . . . DLB-88
Cosin, John 1595-1672. . . . . DLB-151, 213	Cozzens's *Michael Scarlett* Y-97	Crémazie, Octave 1827-1879 . . . . DLB-99
Cosmopolitan Book Corporation DLB-46	Ernest Hemingway's Reaction to	Crémer, Victoriano 1909?- DLB-108
Cossa, Roberto 1934- DLB-305	James Gould Cozzens Y-98	Crescas, Hasdai circa 1340-1412? DLB-115
Costa, Maria Velho da (see The Three Marias:	James Gould Cozzens–A View	Crespo, Angel 1926-1995 . . . . DLB-134
A Landmark Case in Portuguese	from Afar Y-97	Cresset Press DLB-112
Literary History)	James Gould Cozzens: How to	Cresswell, Helen 1934- DLB-161
Costain, Thomas B. 1885-1965 . . . . DLB-9	Read Him Y-97	Crèvecoeur, Michel Guillaume Jean de
Coste, Donat (Daniel Boudreau)	James Gould Cozzens Symposium and	1735-1813 . . . . DLB-37
1912-1957 . . . . DLB-88	Exhibition at the University of	Crewe, Candida 1964- DLB-207
Costello, Louisa Stuart 1799-1870 . . . . . . DLB-166	South Carolina, Columbia Y-00	Crews, Harry 1935- DLB-6, 143, 185
Cota-Cárdenas, Margarita 1941- DLB-122	*Mens Rea* (or Something) Y-97	Crichton, Michael (John Lange, Jeffrey Hudson,
Côté, Denis 1954- DLB-251	Novels for Grown-Ups Y-97	Michael Douglas) 1942- DLB-292; Y-81
Cotten, Bruce 1873-1954 . . . . DLB-187	Crabbe, George 1754-1832 . . . . DLB-93	Crispin, Edmund (Robert Bruce Montgomery)
Cotter, Joseph Seamon, Jr. 1895-1919 . . . . . DLB-50	Crace, Jim 1946- DLB-231	1921-1978 . . . . DLB-87
Cotter, Joseph Seamon, Sr. 1861-1949. . . . . DLB-50	Crackanthorpe, Hubert 1870-1896 . . . . . . DLB-135	Cristofer, Michael 1946- DLB-7
Cottin, Sophie 1770-1807 . . . . DLB-313	Craddock, Charles Egbert (see Murfree, Mary N.)	Criticism
Claire d'Albe DLB-314	Cradock, Thomas 1718-1770 . . . . DLB-31	Afro-American Literary Critics:
Joseph Cottle [publishing house] DLB-154	Craig, Daniel H. 1811-1895. . . . . DLB-43	An Introduction DLB-33
Cotton, Charles 1630-1687 . . . . DLB-131	Craik, Dinah Maria 1826-1887 . . . . . . DLB-35, 163	The Consolidation of Opinion: Critical
	Cramer, Richard Ben 1950- DLB-185	Responses to the Modernists DLB-36

Cumulative Index

"Criticism in Relation to Novels"
(1863), by G. H. Lewes DLB-21

The Limits of Pluralism DLB-67

Modern Critical Terms, Schools, and
Movements DLB-67

"Panic Among the Philistines":
A Postscript, An Interview
with Bryan Griffin Y-81

The Recovery of Literature: Criticism
in the 1990s: A Symposium Y-91

The Stealthy School of Criticism (1871),
by Dante Gabriel Rossetti DLB-35

Crnjanski, Miloš
1893-1977 .... DLB-147; CDWLB-4

Crocker, Hannah Mather 1752-1829 .... DLB-200

Crockett, David (Davy)
1786-1836 .... DLB-3, 11, 183, 248

Croft-Cooke, Rupert (see Bruce, Leo)

Crofts, Freeman Wills 1879-1957 .... DLB-77

Croker, John Wilson 1780-1857 .... DLB-110

Croly, George 1780-1860 .... DLB-159

Croly, Herbert 1869-1930 .... DLB-91

Croly, Jane Cunningham 1829-1901 ..... DLB-23

Crompton, Richmal 1890-1969 .... DLB-160

Cronin, A. J. 1896-1981 .... DLB-191

Cros, Charles 1842-1888 .... DLB-217

Crosby, Caresse 1892-1970 and
Crosby, Harry 1898-1929 and ... DLB-4; DS-15

Crosby, Harry 1898-1929 .... DLB-48

Crosland, Camilla Toulmin (Mrs. Newton
Crosland) 1812-1895 .... DLB-240

Cross, Amanda (Carolyn G. Heilbrun)
1926-2003 .... DLB-306

Cross, Gillian 1945- DLB-161

Cross, Victoria 1868-1952 .... DLB-135, 197

Crossley-Holland, Kevin 1941- DLB-40, 161

Crothers, Rachel 1870-1958 .... DLB-7, 266

Thomas Y. Crowell Company DLB-49

Crowley, John 1942- Y-82

Crowley, Mart 1935- DLB-7, 266

Crown Publishers DLB-46

Crowne, John 1641-1712 .... DLB-80

Crowninshield, Edward Augustus
1817-1859 .... DLB-140

Crowninshield, Frank 1872-1947 .... DLB-91

Croy, Homer 1883-1965 .... DLB-4

Crumley, James 1939- DLB-226; Y-84

Cruse, Mary Anne 1825?-1910 .... DLB-239

Cruz, Migdalia 1958- DLB-249

Cruz, Sor Juana Inés de la 1651-1695 .... DLB-305

Cruz, Victor Hernández 1949- DLB-41

Cruz e Sousa, João 1861-1898 .... DLB-307

Csokor, Franz Theodor 1885-1969 ...... DLB-81

Csoóri, Sándor 1930- DLB-232; CDWLB-4

Cuadra, Pablo Antonio 1912-2002 ...... DLB-290

Cuala Press DLB-112

Cudworth, Ralph 1617-1688 .... DLB-252

Cueva, Juan de la 1543-1612 .... DLB-318

Cugoano, Quobna Ottabah 1797-? Y-02

Cullen, Countee
1903-1946 .... DLB-4, 48, 51; CDALB-4

Culler, Jonathan D. 1944- DLB-67, 246

Cullinan, Elizabeth 1933- DLB-234

Culverwel, Nathaniel 1619?-1651? DLB-252

Cumberland, Richard 1732-1811 .... DLB-89

Cummings, Constance Gordon
1837-1924 .... DLB-174

Cummings, E. E.
1894-1962 .... DLB-4, 48; CDALB-5

The E. E. Cummings Society Y-01

Cummings, Ray 1887-1957 .... DLB-8

Cummings and Hilliard DLB-49

Cummins, Maria Susanna 1827-1866 .... DLB-42

Cumpián, Carlos 1953- DLB-209

Cunard, Nancy 1896-1965 .... DLB-240

Joseph Cundall [publishing house] DLB-106

Cuney, Waring 1906-1976 .... DLB-51

Cuney-Hare, Maude 1874-1936 .... DLB-52

Cunha, Euclides da 1866-1909 .... DLB-307

Cunningham, Allan
1784-1842 .... DLB-116, 144

Cunningham, J. V. 1911-1985 .... DLB-5

Cunningham, Michael 1952- DLB-292

Cunningham, Peter (Peter Lauder, Peter
Benjamin) 1947- DLB-267

Peter F. Cunningham
[publishing house] DLB-49

Cunqueiro, Alvaro 1911-1981 .... DLB-134

Cuomo, George 1929- Y-80

Cupples, Upham and Company DLB-49

Cupples and Leon DLB-46

Cuppy, Will 1884-1949 .... DLB-11

Curiel, Barbara Brinson 1956- DLB-209

Edmund Curll [publishing house] DLB-154

Currie, James 1756-1805 .... DLB-142

Currie, Mary Montgomerie Lamb Singleton,
Lady Currie (see Fane, Violet)

Cursor Mundi circa 1300 .... DLB-146

Curti, Merle E. 1897-1996 .... DLB-17

Curtis, Anthony 1926- DLB-155

Curtis, Cyrus H. K. 1850-1933 .... DLB-91

Curtis, George William
1824-1892 .... DLB-1, 43, 223

Curzon, Robert 1810-1873 .... DLB-166

Curzon, Sarah Anne 1833-1898 .... DLB-99

Cusack, Dymphna 1902-1981 .... DLB-260

Cushing, Eliza Lanesford
1794-1886 .... DLB-99

Cushing, Harvey 1869-1939 .... DLB-187

Custance, Olive (Lady Alfred Douglas)
1874-1944 .... DLB-240

Cynewulf circa 770-840 .... DLB-146

Cyrano de Bergerac, Savinien de
1619-1655 .... DLB-268

Czepko, Daniel 1605-1660 .... DLB-164

Czerniawski, Adam 1934- DLB-232

D

Dabit, Eugène 1898-1936 .... DLB-65

Daborne, Robert circa 1580-1628 ...... DLB-58

Dąbrowska, Maria
1889-1965 .... DLB-215; CDWLB-4

Dacey, Philip 1939- DLB-105

"Eyes Across Centuries:
Contemporary Poetry and 'That
Vision Thing,'" DLB-105

Dach, Simon 1605-1659 .... DLB-164

Dacier, Anne Le Fèvre 1647-1720 ..... DLB-313

Dagerman, Stig 1923-1954 .... DLB-259

Daggett, Rollin M. 1831-1901 .... DLB-79

D'Aguiar, Fred 1960- DLB-157

Dahl, Roald 1916-1990 .... DLB-139, 255

Tribute to Alfred A. Knopf Y-84

Dahlberg, Edward 1900-1977 .... DLB-48

Dahn, Felix 1834-1912 .... DLB-129

The Daily Worker DLB-303

Dal', Vladimir Ivanovich (Kazak Vladimir
Lugansky) 1801-1872 .... DLB-198

Dale, Peter 1938- DLB-40

Daley, Arthur 1904-1974 .... DLB-171

Dall, Caroline Healey 1822-1912 ..... DLB-1, 235

Dallas, E. S. 1828-1879 .... DLB-55

The Gay Science [excerpt](1866) DLB-21

The Dallas Theater Center DLB-7

D'Alton, Louis 1900-1951 .... DLB-10

Dalton, Roque 1935-1975 .... DLB-283

Daly, Carroll John 1889-1958 .... DLB-226

Daly, T. A. 1871-1948 .... DLB-11

Damon, S. Foster 1893-1971 .... DLB-45

William S. Damrell [publishing house] ... DLB-49

Dana, Charles A. 1819-1897 ...... DLB-3, 23, 250

Dana, Richard Henry, Jr.
1815-1882 .... DLB-1, 183, 235

Dandridge, Ray Garfield 1882-1930 ..... DLB-51

Dane, Clemence 1887-1965 .... DLB-10, 197

Danforth, John 1660-1730 .... DLB-24

Danforth, Samuel, I 1626-1674 .... DLB-24

Danforth, Samuel, II 1666-1727 .... DLB-24

Dangerous Acquaintances, Pierre-Ambroise-François
Choderlos de Laclos DLB-314

Daniel, John M. 1825-1865 .... DLB-43

Daniel, Samuel 1562 or 1563-1619 ...... DLB-62

Daniel Press DLB-106

Daniel', Iulii 1925-1988 .... DLB-302

Daniells, Roy 1902-1979 .... DLB-68

Daniels, Jim 1956- DLB-120

Daniels, Jonathan 1902-1981 .... DLB-127

Daniels, Josephus 1862-1948 .... DLB-29

Daniels, Sarah 1957- DLB-245

Danilevsky, Grigorii Petrovich
1829-1890 .... DLB-238

Dannay, Frederic 1905-1982 .... DLB-137

Danner, Margaret Esse 1915- DLB-41
John Danter [publishing house] DLB-170
Dantin, Louis (Eugene Seers)
    1865-1945 ....DLB-92
Danto, Arthur C. 1924- DLB-279
Danzig, Allison 1898-1987............DLB-171
D'Arcy, Ella circa 1857-1937 ....DLB-135
Darío, Rubén 1867-1916 ....DLB-290
Dark, Eleanor 1901-1985..............DLB-260
Darke, Nick 1948- DLB-233
Darley, Felix Octavious Carr
    1822-1888 ....DLB-188
Darley, George 1795-1846.............DLB-96
Darmesteter, Madame James
    (see Robinson, A. Mary F.)
Darrow, Clarence 1857-1938 ....DLB-303
Darwin, Charles 1809-1882......... DLB-57, 166
Darwin, Erasmus 1731-1802 ....DLB-93
Daryush, Elizabeth 1887-1977 ....DLB-20
Dashkova, Ekaterina Romanovna
    (née Vorontsova) 1743-1810 ....DLB-150
Dashwood, Edmée Elizabeth Monica de la Pasture
    (see Delafield, E. M.)
Daudet, Alphonse 1840-1897..........DLB-123
d'Aulaire, Edgar Parin 1898-1986 and
    d'Aulaire, Ingri 1904-1980 ....DLB-22
Davenant, Sir William 1606-1668 ....DLB-58, 126
Davenport, Guy 1927-2005 ....DLB-130
    Tribute to John Gardner.............. Y-82
Davenport, Marcia 1903-1996............ DS-17
Davenport, Robert circa 17th century DLB-58
Daves, Delmer 1904-1977 ....DLB-26
Davey, Frank 1940- DLB-53
Davidson, Avram 1923-1993............DLB-8
Davidson, Donald 1893-1968 ....DLB-45
Davidson, Donald 1917-2003 ....DLB-279
Davidson, John 1857-1909............DLB-19
Davidson, Lionel 1922-   DLB-14, 276
Davidson, Robyn 1950- DLB-204
Davidson, Sara 1943- DLB-185
Davið Stefánsson frá Fagraskógi
    1895-1964 ....DLB-293
Davie, Donald 1922-1995 ....DLB-27
Davie, Elspeth 1919-1995 ....DLB-139
Davies, Sir John 1569-1626 ....DLB-172
Davies, John, of Hereford 1565?-1618....DLB-121
Davies, Rhys 1901-1978..........DLB-139, 191
Davies, Robertson 1913-1995 ....DLB-68
Davies, Samuel 1723-1761 ....DLB-31
Davies, Thomas 1712?-1785........DLB-142, 154
Davies, W. H. 1871-1940............ DLB-19, 174
Peter Davies Limited DLB-112
Davin, Nicholas Flood 1840?-1901 ....DLB-99
Daviot, Gordon 1896?-1952 ....DLB-10
    (see also Tey, Josephine)
Davis, Arthur Hoey (see Rudd, Steele)

Davis, Benjamin J. 1903-1964 ....DLB-303
Davis, Charles A. (Major J. Downing)
    1795-1867 ....DLB-11
Davis, Clyde Brion 1894-1962 ....DLB-9
Davis, Dick 1945- DLB-40, 282
Davis, Frank Marshall 1905-1987 ....DLB-51
Davis, H. L. 1894-1960 ....DLB-9, 206
Davis, John 1774-1854 ....DLB-37
Davis, Lydia 1947- DLB-130
Davis, Margaret Thomson 1926- DLB-14
Davis, Ossie 1917-2005 .... DLB-7, 38, 249
Davis, Owen 1874-1956 ....DLB-249
Davis, Paxton 1925-1994 .... Y-89
Davis, Rebecca Harding
    1831-1910 .... DLB-74, 239
Davis, Richard Harding 1864-1916
    .... DLB-12, 23, 78, 79, 189; DS-13
Davis, Samuel Cole 1764-1809 ....DLB-37
Davis, Samuel Post 1850-1918.........DLB-202
Davison, Frank Dalby 1893-1970 ....DLB-260
Davison, Peter 1928- DLB-5
Davydov, Denis Vasil'evich
    1784-1839 ....DLB-205
Davys, Mary 1674-1732 ....DLB-39
    Preface to The Works of Mrs. Davys
    (1725) DLB-39
DAW Books.........................DLB-46
Dawe, Bruce 1930- DLB-289
Dawson, Ernest 1882-1947 .... DLB-140; Y-02
Dawson, Fielding 1930- DLB-130
Dawson, Sarah Morgan 1842-1909 .....DLB-239
Dawson, William 1704-1752 ....DLB-31
Day, Angel fl. 1583-1599 .... DLB-167, 236
Day, Benjamin Henry 1810-1889 ....DLB-43
Day, Clarence 1874-1935 ....DLB-11
Day, Dorothy 1897-1980 ....DLB-29
Day, Frank Parker 1881-1950 ....DLB-92
Day, John circa 1574-circa 1640 ....DLB-62
Day, Thomas 1748-1789 ....DLB-39
John Day [publishing house] DLB-170
The John Day Company DLB-46
Mahlon Day [publishing house].........DLB-49
Day Lewis, C. (see Blake, Nicholas)
Dazai Osamu 1909-1948 ....DLB-182
Deacon, William Arthur 1890-1977.......DLB-68
Deal, Borden 1922-1985 ....DLB-6
de Angeli, Marguerite 1889-1987.........DLB-22
De Angelis, Milo 1951- DLB-128
Debord, Guy 1931-1994 ....DLB-296
De Bow, J. D. B. 1820-1867....... DLB-3, 79, 248
Debs, Eugene V. 1855-1926 ....DLB-303
de Bruyn, Günter 1926- DLB-75
de Camp, L. Sprague 1907-2000 ....DLB-8
De Carlo, Andrea 1952- DLB-196
De Casas, Celso A. 1944- DLB-209
Dechert, Robert 1895-1975 ....DLB-187

Declaration of the Rights of Man and of
    the Citizen.....................DLB-314
Declaration of the Rights of Woman, Olympe
    de Gouges DLB-314
Dedications, Inscriptions, and
    Annotations.................. Y-01–02
Dee, John 1527-1608 or 1609....... DLB-136, 213
Deeping, George Warwick 1877-1950 ....DLB-153
Deffand, Marie de Vichy-Chamrond,
    marquise Du 1696-1780 ....DLB-313
Defoe, Daniel
    1660-1731 .... DLB-39, 95, 101; CDBLB-2
    Preface to Colonel Jack (1722).........DLB-39
    Preface to The Farther Adventures of
        Robinson Crusoe (1719) DLB-39
    Preface to Moll Flanders (1722) DLB-39
    Preface to Robinson Crusoe (1719) DLB-39
    Preface to Roxana (1724) DLB-39
de Fontaine, Felix Gregory 1834-1896.....DLB-43
De Forest, John William
    1826-1906................... DLB-12, 189
DeFrees, Madeline 1919- DLB-105
    "The Poet's Kaleidoscope: The
    Element of Surprise in the
    Making of the Poem" DLB-105
DeGolyer, Everette Lee 1886-1956 ......DLB-187
de Graff, Robert 1895-1981............... Y-81
de Graft, Joe 1924-1978 ....DLB-117
De Heinrico circa 980?.................DLB-148
Deighton, Len 1929- DLB-87; CDBLB-8
DeJong, Meindert 1906-1991............DLB-52
Dekker, Thomas
    circa 1572-1632...... DLB-62, 172; CDBLB-1
Delacorte, George T., Jr. 1894-1991 ......DLB-91
Delafield, E. M. 1890-1943 ....DLB-34
Delahaye, Guy (Guillaume Lahaise)
    1888-1969 ....DLB-92
de la Mare, Walter 1873-1956
    .... DLB-19, 153, 162, 255; CDBLB-6
Deland, Margaret 1857-1945 ....DLB-78
Delaney, Shelagh 1939- DLB-13; CDBLB-8
Delano, Amasa 1763-1823 ....DLB-183
Delany, Martin Robinson 1812-1885 .....DLB-50
Delany, Samuel R. 1942- DLB-8, 33
de la Roche, Mazo 1879-1961 ....DLB-68
Delavigne, Jean François Casimir
    1793-1843 ....DLB-192
Delbanco, Nicholas 1942- DLB-6, 234
Delblanc, Sven 1931-1992 ....DLB-257
Del Castillo, Ramón 1949- DLB-209
Deledda, Grazia 1871-1936 ....DLB-264
De León, Nephtal 1945- DLB-82
Deleuze, Gilles 1925-1995 ....DLB-296
Delfini, Antonio 1907-1963 ....DLB-264
Delgado, Abelardo Barrientos 1931- DLB-82
Del Giudice, Daniele 1949- DLB-196
De Libero, Libero 1906-1981 ....DLB-114
Delicado, Francisco
    circa 1475-circa 1540?.............DLB-318

DeLillo, Don 1936- DLB-6, 173	Desbordes-Valmore, Marceline 1786-1859..................... DLB-217	Díaz del Castillo, Bernal circa 1496-1584 .... DLB-318
de Lint, Charles 1951- DLB-251	Descartes, René 1596-1650 ....DLB-268	Dibble, L. Grace 1902-1998 .... DLB-204
de Lisser H. G. 1878-1944 .... DLB-117	Deschamps, Emile 1791-1871 .... DLB-217	Dibdin, Thomas Frognall 1776-1847..................... DLB-184
Dell, Floyd 1887-1969................. DLB-9	Deschamps, Eustache 1340?-1404 ...... DLB-208	Di Cicco, Pier Giorgio 1949- DLB-60
Dell Publishing Company.............. DLB-46	Desbiens, Jean-Paul 1927- DLB-53	Dick, Philip K. 1928-1982 .... DLB-8
delle Grazie, Marie Eugene 1864-1931.... DLB-81	des Forêts, Louis-Rene 1918-2001 .... DLB-83	Dick and Fitzgerald................... DLB-49
Deloney, Thomas died 1600 .... DLB-167	Desiato, Luca 1941- DLB-196	Dickens, Charles 1812-1870
Deloria, Ella C. 1889-1971 ....DLB-175	Desjardins, Marie-Catherine (see Villedieu, Madame de)	.... DLB-21, 55, 70, 159, 166; DS-5; CDBLB-4
Deloria, Vine, Jr. 1933- DLB-175	Desnica, Vladan 1905-1967 .... DLB-181	Dickey, Eric Jerome 1961- DLB-292
del Rey, Lester 1915-1993 .... DLB-8	Desnos, Robert 1900-1945 .... DLB-258	Dickey, James 1923-1997 .... DLB-5, 193; Y-82, 93, 96, 97; DS-7, 19; CDALB-6
Del Vecchio, John M. 1947- DS-9	DesRochers, Alfred 1901-1978 .... DLB-68	James Dickey and Stanley Burnshaw Correspondence Y-02
Del'vig, Anton Antonovich 1798-1831 ... DLB-205	Desrosiers, Léo-Paul 1896-1967 .... DLB-68	James Dickey at Seventy–A Tribute Y-93
de Man, Paul 1919-1983............... DLB-67	Dessaulles, Louis-Antoine 1819-1895..... DLB-99	James Dickey, American Poet Y-96
DeMarinis, Rick 1934- DLB-218	Dessì, Giuseppe 1909-1977.............DLB-177	The James Dickey Society Y-99
Demby, William 1922- DLB-33	Destouches, Louis-Ferdinand (see Céline, Louis-Ferdinand)	The Life of James Dickey: A Lecture to the Friends of the Emory Libraries, by Henry Hart Y-98
De Mille, James 1833-1880......... DLB-99, 251	DeSylva, Buddy 1895-1950 .... DLB-265	Tribute to Archibald MacLeish Y-82
de Mille, William 1878-1955........... DLB-266	De Tabley, Lord 1835-1895............ DLB-35	Tribute to Malcolm Cowley Y-89
Deming, Philander 1829-1915 .... DLB-74	Deutsch, Babette 1895-1982........... DLB-45	Tribute to Truman Capote Y-84
Deml, Jakub 1878-1961................ DLB-215	Deutsch, Niklaus Manuel (see Manuel, Niklaus)	Tributes [to Dickey].................. Y-97
Demorest, William Jennings 1822-1895 ... DLB-79	André Deutsch Limited DLB-112	Dickey, William 1928-1994 .... DLB-5
De Morgan, William 1839-1917 .... DLB-153	Devanny, Jean 1894-1962............. DLB-260	Dickinson, Emily 1830-1886 .... DLB-1, 243; CDALB-3
Demosthenes 384 B.C.-322 B.C. DLB-176	Deveaux, Alexis 1948- DLB-38	Dickinson, John 1732-1808............. DLB-31
Henry Denham [publishing house].......DLB-170	De Vere, Aubrey 1814-1902............ DLB-35	Dickinson, Jonathan 1688-1747 .... DLB-24
Denham, Sir John 1615-1669 .... DLB-58, 126	Devereux, second Earl of Essex, Robert 1565-1601 .... DLB-136	Dickinson, Patric 1914-1994........... DLB-27
Denison, Merrill 1893-1975 .... DLB-92	The Devin-Adair Company DLB-46	Dickinson, Peter 1927- DLB-87, 161, 276
T. S. Denison and Company DLB-49	De Vinne, Theodore Low 1828-1914..................... DLB-187	John Dicks [publishing house] DLB-106
Dennery, Adolphe Philippe 1811-1899... DLB-192	Devlin, Anne 1951- DLB-245	Dickson, Gordon R. 1923-2001 .... DLB-8
Dennie, Joseph 1768-1812......DLB-37, 43, 59, 73	DeVoto, Bernard 1897-1955.......... DLB-9, 256	Dictionary of Literary Biography Annual Awards for Dictionary of Literary Biography Editors and Contributors Y-98–02
Dennis, C. J. 1876-1938 .... DLB-260	De Vries, Peter 1910-1993 ....DLB-6; Y-82	
Dennis, John 1658-1734 .... DLB-101	Tribute to Albert Erskine.............. Y-93	
Dennis, Nigel 1912-1989 .... DLB-13, 15, 233	Dewart, Edward Hartley 1828-1903 ..... DLB-99	Dictionary of Literary Biography Yearbook Awards Y-92–93, 97–02
Denslow, W. W. 1856-1915........... DLB-188	Dewdney, Christopher 1951- DLB-60	
Dent, J. M., and Sons DLB-112	Dewdney, Selwyn 1909-1979 .... DLB-68	The Dictionary of National Biography DLB-144
Dent, Lester 1904-1959 .... DLB-306	Dewey, John 1859-1952 ....DLB-246, 270	Diderot, Denis 1713-1784 .... DLB-313
Dent, Tom 1932-1998 .... DLB-38	Dewey, Orville 1794-1882 .... DLB-243	"The Encyclopedia"................ DLB-314
Denton, Daniel circa 1626-1703 .... DLB-24	Dewey, Thomas B. 1915-1981 .... DLB-226	Didion, Joan 1934- DLB-2, 173, 185; Y-81, 86; CDALB-6
DePaola, Tomie 1934- DLB-61	DeWitt, Robert M., Publisher DLB-49	
De Quille, Dan 1829-1898 .... DLB-186	DeWolfe, Fiske and Company DLB-49	Di Donato, Pietro 1911-1992 .... DLB-9
De Quincey, Thomas 1785-1859......... DLB-110, 144; CDBLB-3	Dexter, Colin 1930- DLB-87	Die Fürstliche Bibliothek Corvey........... Y-96
"Rhetoric" (1828; revised, 1859) [excerpt]..................... DLB-57	de Young, M. H. 1849-1925........... DLB-25	Diego, Gerardo 1896-1987 .... DLB-134
	Dhlomo, H. I. E. 1903-1956........DLB-157, 225	Dietz, Howard 1896-1983 .... DLB-265
"Style" (1840; revised, 1859) [excerpt]..................... DLB-57	Dhu al-Rummah (Abu al-Harith Ghaylan ibn 'Uqbah) circa 696-circa 735 .... DLB-311	Digby, Everard 1550?-1605 .... DLB-281
Derby, George Horatio 1823-1861....... DLB-11	Dhuoda circa 803-after 843 .... DLB-148	Digges, Thomas circa 1546-1595 .... DLB-136
J. C. Derby and Company DLB-49	The Dial 1840-1844................... DLB-223	The Digital Millennium Copyright Act: Expanding Copyright Protection in Cyberspace and Beyond Y-98
Derby and Miller DLB-49	The Dial Press DLB-46	
De Ricci, Seymour 1881-1942 .... DLB-201	"Dialogue entre un prêtre et un moribond," Marquis de Sade DLB-314	Diktonius, Elmer 1896-1961........... DLB-259
Derleth, August 1909-1971 .... DLB-9; DS-17		Dillard, Annie 1945- DLB-275, 278; Y-80
Derrida, Jacques 1930-2004 .... DLB-242	Diamond, I. A. L. 1920-1988 .... DLB-26	
The Derrydale Press.................. DLB-46	Dias Gomes, Alfredo 1922-1999........ DLB-307	Dillard, R. H. W. 1937- DLB-5, 244
Derzhavin, Gavriil Romanovich 1743-1816..................... DLB-150		
Desai, Anita 1937- DLB-271		
Desaulniers, Gonzalve 1863-1934........ DLB-92		

Charles T. Dillingham Company DLB-49	Doderer, Heimito von 1896-1966 . . . . .DLB-85	Doubrovsky, Serge 1928- DLB-299
G. W. Dillingham Company DLB-49	B. W. Dodge and Company DLB-46	Dougall, Lily 1858-1923 . . . . .DLB-92
Edward and Charles Dilly [publishing house] DLB-154	Dodge, Mary Abigail 1833-1896 . . . . .DLB-221	Doughty, Charles M. 1843-1926 . . . . .DLB-19, 57, 174
Dilthey, Wilhelm 1833-1911 . . . . .DLB-129	Dodge, Mary Mapes 1831?-1905 . . . . DLB-42, 79; DS-13	Douglas, Lady Alfred (see Custance, Olive)
Dimitrova, Blaga 1922- . . .DLB-181; CDWLB-4	Dodge Publishing Company DLB-49	Douglas, Ellen (Josephine Ayres Haxton) 1921- DLB-292
Dimov, Dimitr 1909-1966 . . . . .DLB-181	Dodgson, Charles Lutwidge (see Carroll, Lewis)	Douglas, Gavin 1476-1522 . . . . .DLB-132
Dimsdale, Thomas J. 1831?-1866 . . . . . . .DLB-186	Dodsley, Robert 1703-1764 . . . . .DLB-95	Douglas, Keith 1920-1944 . . . . .DLB-27
Dinescu, Mircea 1950- DLB-232	R. Dodsley [publishing house] DLB-154	Douglas, Norman 1868-1952 . . . . . . .DLB-34, 195
Dinesen, Isak (see Blixen, Karen)	Dodson, Owen 1914-1983 . . . . .DLB-76	Douglass, Frederick 1817-1895
Dingelstedt, Franz von 1814-1881 . . . . . . .DLB-133	Dodwell, Christina 1951- DLB-204	. . . . DLB-1, 43, 50, 79, 243; CDALB-2
Dinis, Júlio (Joaquim Guilherme Gomes Coelho) 1839-1871 . . . . .DLB-287	Doesticks, Q. K. Philander, P. B. (see Thomson, Mortimer)	Frederick Douglass Creative Arts Center Y-01
Dintenfass, Mark 1941- Y-84	Doheny, Carrie Estelle 1875-1958 . . . . . . .DLB-140	Douglass, William circa 1691-1752 . . . . . . .DLB-24
Diogenes, Jr. (see Brougham, John)	Doherty, John 1798?-1854 . . . . .DLB-190	Dourado, Autran 1926- DLB-145, 307
Diogenes Laertius circa 200 . . . . .DLB-176	Doig, Ivan 1939- DLB-206	Dove, Arthur G. 1880-1946 . . . . .DLB-188
DiPrima, Diane 1934- DLB-5, 16	Doinaş, Ştefan Augustin 1922- DLB-232	Dove, Rita 1952- DLB-120; CDALB-7
Disch, Thomas M. 1940- DLB-8, 282	Domínguez, Sylvia Maida 1935- DLB-122	Dover Publications DLB-46
"Le Discours sur le style," Georges-Louis Leclerc de Buffon DLB-314	Donaghy, Michael 1954- DLB-282	Doves Press DLB-112
Diski, Jenny 1947- DLB-271	Patrick Donahoe [publishing house] DLB-49	Dovlatov, Sergei Donatovich 1941-1990 .DLB-285
Disney, Walt 1901-1966 . . . . .DLB-22	Donald, David H. 1920- DLB-17; Y-87	Dowden, Edward 1843-1913 . . . . . . .DLB-35, 149
Disraeli, Benjamin 1804-1881 . . . . .DLB-21, 55	Donaldson, Scott 1928- DLB-111	Dowell, Coleman 1925-1985 . . . . .DLB-130
D'Israeli, Isaac 1766-1848 . . . . .DLB-107	Doni, Rodolfo 1919- DLB-177	Dowland, John 1563-1626 . . . . .DLB-172
DLB Award for Distinguished Literary Criticism Y-02	Donleavy, J. P. 1926- DLB-6, 173	Downes, Gwladys 1915- DLB-88
Ditlevsen, Tove 1917-1976 . . . . .DLB-214	Donnadieu, Marguerite (see Duras, Marguerite)	Downing, J., Major (see Davis, Charles A.)
Ditzen, Rudolf (see Fallada, Hans)	Donne, John 1572-1631 . . . . .DLB-121, 151; CDBLB-1	Downing, Major Jack (see Smith, Seba)
Dix, Dorothea Lynde 1802-1887 . . . . . .DLB-1, 235	Donnelly, Ignatius 1831-1901 . . . . .DLB-12	Dowriche, Anne before 1560-after 1613 . . . . .DLB-172
Dix, Dorothy (see Gilmer, Elizabeth Meriwether)	R. R. Donnelley and Sons Company DLB-49	Dowson, Ernest 1867-1900 . . . . .DLB-19, 135
Dix, Edwards and Company DLB-49	Donoghue, Emma 1969- DLB-267	William Doxey [publishing house] DLB-49
Dix, Gertrude circa 1874-? DLB-197	Donohue and Henneberry DLB-49	Doyle, Sir Arthur Conan 1859-1930 . . . DLB-18, 70, 156, 178; CDBLB-5
Dixie, Florence Douglas 1857-1905 . . . . . .DLB-174	Donoso, José 1924-1996 . . . .DLB-113; CDWLB-3	The Priory Scholars of New York Y-99
Dixon, Ella Hepworth 1855 or 1857-1932 . . . . .DLB-197	M. Doolady [publishing house] DLB-49	Doyle, Kirby 1932- DLB-16
Dixon, Paige (see Corcoran, Barbara)	Dooley, Ebon (see Ebon)	Doyle, Roddy 1958- DLB-194
Dixon, Richard Watson 1833-1900 . . . . . . .DLB-19	Doolittle, Hilda 1886-1961 . . . . .DLB-4, 45; DS-15	Drabble, Margaret 1939- DLB-14, 155, 231; CDBLB-8
Dixon, Stephen 1936- DLB-130	Doplicher, Fabio 1938- DLB-128	Tribute to Graham Greene Y-91
DLB Award for Distinguished Literary Criticism Y-02	Dor, Milo 1923- DLB-85	Drach, Albert 1902-1995 . . . . .DLB-85
Dmitriev, Andrei Viktorovich 1956- . . .DLB-285	George H. Doran Company DLB-46	Drachmann, Holger 1846-1908 . . . . .DLB-300
Dmitriev, Ivan Ivanovich 1760-1837 . . . . .DLB-150	Dorcey, Mary 1950- DLB-319	Dracula (Documentary) DLB-304
Dobell, Bertram 1842-1914 . . . . .DLB-184	Dorgelès, Roland 1886-1973 . . . . .DLB-65	Dragojević, Danijel 1934- DLB-181
Dobell, Sydney 1824-1874 . . . . .DLB-32	Dorn, Edward 1929-1999 . . . . .DLB-5	Dragún, Osvaldo 1929-1999 . . . . .DLB-305
Dobie, J. Frank 1888-1964 . . . . .DLB-212	Dorr, Rheta Childe 1866-1948 . . . . .DLB-25	Drake, Samuel Gardner 1798-1875 . . . . . .DLB-187
Dobles Yzaguirre, Julieta 1943- DLB-283	Dorris, Michael 1945-1997 . . . . .DLB-175	Drama (See Theater)
Döblin, Alfred 1878-1957 . . . . .DLB-66; CDWLB-2	Dorset and Middlesex, Charles Sackville, Lord Buckhurst, Earl of 1643-1706 . . . .DLB-131	The Dramatic Publishing Company DLB-49
Dobroliubov, Nikolai Aleksandrovich 1836-1861 .DLB-277	Dorsey, Candas Jane 1952- DLB-251	Dramatists Play Service DLB-46
Dobson, Austin 1840-1921 . . . . .DLB-35, 144	Dorst, Tankred 1925- DLB-75, 124	Drant, Thomas early 1540s?-1578 . . . . .DLB-167
Dobson, Rosemary 1920- DLB-260	Dos Passos, John 1896-1970 . . . . .DLB-4, 9, 316; DS-1, 15; CDALB-5	Draper, John W. 1811-1882 . . . . .DLB-30
Doctorow, E. L. 1931- DLB-2, 28, 173; Y-80; CDALB-6	John Dos Passos: A Centennial Commemoration Y-96	Draper, Lyman C. 1815-1891 . . . . .DLB-30
Dodd, Susan M. 1946- DLB-244	John Dos Passos: Artist Y-99	Drayton, Michael 1563-1631 . . . . .DLB-121
Dodd, William E. 1869-1940 . . . . .DLB-17	John Dos Passos Newsletter Y-00	Dreiser, Theodore 1871-1945 . . . . DLB-9, 12, 102, 137; DS-1; CDALB-3
Anne Dodd [publishing house] DLB-154	U.S.A. (Documentary) DLB-274	The International Theodore Dreiser Society Y-01
Dodd, Mead and Company DLB-49	Dostoevsky, Fyodor 1821-1881 . . . . .DLB-238	
	Doubleday and Company DLB-49	

Notes from the Underground
  of *Sister Carrie* Y-01
Dresser, Davis 1904-1977 .... DLB-226
Drew, Elizabeth A.
  "A Note on Technique" [excerpt]
  (1926) DLB-36
Drewitz, Ingeborg 1923-1986 .... DLB-75
Drieu La Rochelle, Pierre 1893-1945 ..... DLB-72
Drinker, Elizabeth 1735-1807 .... DLB-200
Drinkwater, John 1882-1937 ...... DLB-10, 19, 149
  The Friends of the Dymock Poets Y-00
Droste-Hülshoff, Annette von
  1797-1848 .... DLB-133; CDWLB-2
The Drue Heinz Literature Prize
  Excerpt from "Excerpts from a Report
  of the Commission," in David
  Bosworth's *The Death of Descartes*
  An Interview with David Bosworth Y-82
Drummond, William, of Hawthornden
  1585-1649 .... DLB-121, 213
Drummond, William Henry 1854-1907 ... DLB-92
Drummond de Andrade, Carlos
  1902-1987 .... DLB-307
Druzhinin, Aleksandr Vasil'evich
  1824-1864 .... DLB-238
Druzhnikov, Yuri 1933- DLB-317
Dryden, Charles 1860?-1931 .... DLB-171
Dryden, John
  1631-1700 ...... DLB-80, 101, 131; CDBLB-2
Držić, Marin
  circa 1508-1567 .... DLB-147; CDWLB-4
Duane, William 1760-1835 .... DLB-43
Dubé, Marcel 1930- DLB-53
Dubé, Rodolphe (see Hertel, François)
Dubie, Norman 1945- DLB-120
Dubin, Al 1891-1945 .... DLB-265
Du Boccage, Anne-Marie 1710-1802 ..... DLB-313
Dubois, Silvia 1788 or 1789?-1889 ...... DLB-239
Du Bois, W. E. B.
  1868-1963 .... DLB-47, 50, 91, 246; CDALB-3
Du Bois, William Pène 1916-1993 .... DLB-61
Dubrovina, Ekaterina Oskarovna
  1846-1913 .... DLB-238
Dubus, Andre 1936-1999 .... DLB-130
  Tribute to Michael M. Rea Y-97
Dubus, Andre, III 1959- DLB-292
Ducange, Victor 1783-1833 .... DLB-192
Du Chaillu, Paul Belloni 1831?-1903 ..... DLB-189
Ducharme, Réjean 1941- DLB-60
Dučić, Jovan 1871-1943 ..... DLB-147; CDWLB-4
Duck, Stephen 1705?-1756 .... DLB-95
Gerald Duckworth and Company
  Limited DLB-112
Duclaux, Madame Mary (see Robinson, A. Mary F.)
Dudek, Louis 1918-2001 .... DLB-88
Dudintsev, Vladimir Dmitrievich
  1918-1998 .... DLB-302
Dudley-Smith, Trevor (see Hall, Adam)
Duell, Sloan and Pearce DLB-46
Duerer, Albrecht 1471-1528 .... DLB-179

Duff Gordon, Lucie 1821-1869 .... DLB-166
Dufferin, Helen Lady, Countess of Gifford
  1807-1867 .... DLB-199
Duffield and Green DLB-46
Duffy, Maureen 1933- DLB-14, 310
Dufief, Nicholas Gouin 1776-1834 ...... DLB-187
Dufresne, John 1948- DLB-292
Dugan, Alan 1923-2003 .... DLB-5
Dugard, William 1606-1662 .... DLB-170, 281
William Dugard [publishing house] DLB-170
Dugas, Marcel 1883-1947 .... DLB-92
William Dugdale [publishing house] DLB-106
Duhamel, Georges 1884-1966 .... DLB-65
Dujardin, Edouard 1861-1949 .... DLB-123
Dukes, Ashley 1885-1959 .... DLB-10
Dumas, Alexandre *fils* 1824-1895 .... DLB-192
Dumas, Alexandre *père* 1802-1870 ..... DLB-119, 192
Dumas, Henry 1934-1968 .... DLB-41
du Maurier, Daphne 1907-1989 .... DLB-191
Du Maurier, George 1834-1896 ..... DLB-153, 178
Dummett, Michael 1925- DLB-262
Dunbar, Paul Laurence
  1872-1906 .... DLB-50, 54, 78; CDALB-3
  Introduction to *Lyrics of Lowly Life* (1896),
  by William Dean Howells DLB-50
Dunbar, William
  circa 1460-circa 1522 .... DLB-132, 146
Duncan, Dave 1933- DLB-251
Duncan, David James 1952- DLB-256
Duncan, Norman 1871-1916 .... DLB-92
Duncan, Quince 1940- DLB-145
Duncan, Robert 1919-1988 .... DLB-5, 16, 193
Duncan, Ronald 1914-1982 .... DLB-13
Duncan, Sara Jeannette 1861-1922 .... DLB-92
Dunigan, Edward, and Brother DLB-49
Dunlap, John 1747-1812 .... DLB-43
Dunlap, William 1766-1839 ...... DLB-30, 37, 59
Dunlop, William "Tiger" 1792-1848 ...... DLB-99
Dunmore, Helen 1952- DLB-267
Dunn, Douglas 1942- DLB-40
Dunn, Harvey Thomas 1884-1952 ..... DLB-188
Dunn, Stephen 1939- DLB-105
  "The Good, The Not So Good" DLB-105
Dunne, Dominick 1925- DLB-306
Dunne, Finley Peter 1867-1936 .... DLB-11, 23
Dunne, John Gregory 1932- Y-80
Dunne, Philip 1908-1992 .... DLB-26
Dunning, Ralph Cheever 1878-1930 ...... DLB-4
Dunning, William A. 1857-1922 .... DLB-17
Duns Scotus, John circa 1266-1308 ..... DLB-115
Dunsany, Lord (Edward John Moreton
  Drax Plunkett, Baron Dunsany)
  1878-1957 .... DLB-10, 77, 153, 156, 255
Dunton, W. Herbert 1878-1936 .... DLB-188
John Dunton [publishing house] DLB-170
Dupin, Amantine-Aurore-Lucile (see Sand, George)

Du Pont de Nemours, Pierre Samuel
  1739-1817 .... DLB-313
Dupuy, Eliza Ann 1814-1880 .... DLB-248
Durack, Mary 1913-1994 .... DLB-260
Durand, Lucile (see Bersianik, Louky)
Duranti, Francesca 1935- DLB-196
Duranty, Walter 1884-1957 .... DLB-29
Duras, Marguerite (Marguerite Donnadieu)
  1914-1996 .... DLB-83
Durfey, Thomas 1653-1723 .... DLB-80
Durova, Nadezhda Andreevna
  (Aleksandr Andreevich Aleksandrov)
  1783-1866 .... DLB-198
Durrell, Lawrence 1912-1990
  .... DLB-15, 27, 204; Y-90; CDBLB-7
William Durrell [publishing house] DLB-49
Dürrenmatt, Friedrich
  1921-1990 .... DLB-69, 124; CDWLB-2
Duston, Hannah 1657-1737 .... DLB-200
Dutt, Toru 1856-1877 .... DLB-240
E. P. Dutton and Company DLB-49
Duun, Olav 1876-1939 .... DLB-297
Duvoisin, Roger 1904-1980 .... DLB-61
Duyckinck, Evert Augustus
  1816-1878 .... DLB-3, 64, 250
Duyckinck, George L.
  1823-1863 .... DLB-3, 250
Duyckinck and Company DLB-49
Dwight, John Sullivan 1813-1893 ..... DLB-1, 235
Dwight, Timothy 1752-1817 .... DLB-37
  America: or, A Poem on the Settlement
  of the British Colonies, by
  Timothy Dwight DLB-37
Dybek, Stuart 1942- DLB-130
  Tribute to Michael M. Rea Y-97
Dyer, Charles 1928- DLB-13
Dyer, Sir Edward 1543-1607 .... DLB-136
Dyer, George 1755-1841 .... DLB-93
Dyer, John 1699-1757 .... DLB-95
Dyk, Viktor 1877-1931 .... DLB-215
Dylan, Bob 1941- DLB-16

E

Eager, Edward 1911-1964 .... DLB-22
Eagleton, Terry 1943- DLB-242
Eames, Wilberforce
  1855-1937 .... DLB-140
Earle, Alice Morse
  1853-1911 .... DLB-221
Earle, John 1600 or 1601-1665 .... DLB-151
James H. Earle and Company DLB-49
East Europe
  Independence and Destruction,
  1918-1941 .... DLB-220
  Social Theory and Ethnography:
  Language and Ethnicity in
  Western versus Eastern Man ... DLB-220
Eastlake, William 1917-1997 .... DLB-6, 206
Eastman, Carol ?- DLB-44

Eastman, Charles A. (Ohiyesa)
1858-1939 .... DLB-175

Eastman, Max 1883-1969 .... DLB-91

Eaton, Daniel Isaac 1753-1814 .... DLB-158

Eaton, Edith Maude 1865-1914 ..... DLB-221, 312

Eaton, Winnifred 1875-1954 .... DLB-221, 312

Eberhart, Richard 1904-2005 ... DLB-48; CDALB-1

   Tribute to Robert Penn Warren Y-89

Ebner, Jeannie 1918-2004 .... DLB-85

Ebner-Eschenbach, Marie von
1830-1916 .... DLB-81

Ebon 1942- DLB-41

E-Books' Second Act in Libraries Y-02

Ecbasis Captivi circa 1045 .... DLB-148

Ecco Press DLB-46

Eckhart, Meister circa 1260-circa 1328 ... DLB-115

The Eclectic Review 1805-1868 .... DLB-110

Eco, Umberto 1932- DLB-196, 242

Eddison, E. R. 1882-1945 .... DLB-255

Edel, Leon 1907-1997 .... DLB-103

Edelfeldt, Inger 1956- DLB-257

J. M. Edelstein's Collection of Twentieth-
Century American Poetry (A Century of Poetry,
a Lifetime of Collecting) Y-02

Edes, Benjamin 1732-1803 .... DLB-43

Edgar, David 1948- DLB-13, 233

   Viewpoint: Politics and
   Performance DLB-13

Edgerton, Clyde 1944- DLB-278

Edgeworth, Maria
1768-1849 .... DLB-116, 159, 163

The Edinburgh Review 1802-1929 .... DLB-110

Edinburgh University Press DLB-112

Editing
   Conversations with Editors Y-95
   Editorial Statements DLB-137
   The Editorial Style of Fredson Bowers ... Y-91
   Editorial: The Extension of Copyright ... Y-02
   We See the Editor at Work Y-97
   Whose *Ulysses*? The Function of Editing .. Y-97

The Editor Publishing Company DLB-49

Editorial Institute at Boston University Y-00

Edmonds, Helen Woods Ferguson
(see Kavan, Anna)

Edmonds, Randolph 1900-1983 .... DLB-51

Edmonds, Walter D. 1903-1998 .... DLB-9

Edric, Robert (see Armitage, G. E.)

Edschmid, Kasimir 1890-1966 .... DLB-56

Edson, Margaret 1961- DLB-266

Edson, Russell 1935- DLB-244

Edwards, Amelia Anne Blandford
1831-1892 .... DLB-174

Edwards, Dic 1953- DLB-245

Edwards, Edward 1812-1886 .... DLB-184

Edwards, Jonathan 1703-1758 .... DLB-24, 270

Edwards, Jonathan, Jr. 1745-1801 .... DLB-37

Edwards, Junius 1929- DLB-33

Edwards, Matilda Barbara Betham
1836-1919 .... DLB-174

Edwards, Richard 1524-1566 .... DLB-62

Edwards, Sarah Pierpont 1710-1758 ...... DLB-200

James Edwards [publishing house] DLB-154

Effinger, George Alec 1947- DLB-8

Egerton, George 1859-1945 .... DLB-135

Eggleston, Edward 1837-1902 .... DLB-12

Eggleston, Wilfred 1901-1986 .... DLB-92

Eglītis, Anšlavs 1906-1993 .... DLB-220

Eguren, José María 1874-1942 .... DLB-290

Ehrenreich, Barbara 1941- DLB-246

Ehrenstein, Albert 1886-1950 .... DLB-81

Ehrhart, W. D. 1948- DS-9

Ehrlich, Gretel 1946- DLB-212, 275

Eich, Günter 1907-1972 .... DLB-69, 124

Eichendorff, Joseph Freiherr von
1788-1857 .... DLB-90

Eifukumon'in 1271-1342 .... DLB-203

Eigner, Larry 1926-1996 .... DLB-5, 193

Eikon Basilike 1649 .... DLB-151

Eilhart von Oberge
circa 1140-circa 1195 .... DLB-148

Einar Benediktsson 1864-1940 .... DLB-293

Einar Kárason 1955- DLB-293

Einar Már Guðmundsson 1954- DLB-293

Einhard circa 770-840 .... DLB-148

Eiseley, Loren 1907-1977 .... DLB-275, DS-17

Eisenberg, Deborah 1945- DLB-244

Eisenreich, Herbert 1925-1986 .... DLB-85

Eisner, Kurt 1867-1919 .... DLB-66

Ekelöf, Gunnar 1907-1968 .... DLB-259

Eklund, Gordon 1945- Y-83

Ekman, Kerstin 1933- DLB-257

Ekwensi, Cyprian 1921- ... DLB-117; CDWLB-3

Elaw, Zilpha circa 1790-? DLB-239

George Eld [publishing house] DLB-170

Elder, Lonne, III 1931- DLB-7, 38, 44

Paul Elder and Company DLB-49

Eldershaw, Flora (M. Barnard Eldershaw)
1897-1956 .... DLB-260

Eldershaw, M. Barnard (see Barnard, Marjorie and
Eldershaw, Flora)

The Electronic Text Center and the Electronic
Archive of Early American Fiction at the
University of Virginia Library Y-98

Eliade, Mircea 1907-1986 .... DLB-220; CDWLB-4

Elie, Robert 1915-1973 .... DLB-88

Elin Pelin 1877-1949 .... DLB-147; CDWLB-4

Eliot, George
1819-1880 .... DLB-21, 35, 55; CDBLB-4

   The George Eliot Fellowship Y-99

Eliot, John 1604-1690 .... DLB-24

Eliot, T. S. 1888-1965
.... DLB-7, 10, 45, 63, 245; CDALB-5

   T. S. Eliot Centennial: The Return
   of the Old Possum Y-88

   The T. S. Eliot Society: Celebration and
   Scholarship, 1980-1999 .... Y-99

Eliot's Court Press DLB-170

Elizabeth I 1533-1603 .... DLB-136

Elizabeth von Nassau-Saarbrücken
after 1393-1456 .... DLB-179

Elizondo, Salvador 1932- DLB-145

Elizondo, Sergio 1930- DLB-82

Elkin, Stanley
1930-1995 .... DLB-2, 28, 218, 278; Y-80

Elles, Dora Amy (see Wentworth, Patricia)

Ellet, Elizabeth F. 1818?-1877 .... DLB-30

Elliot, Ebenezer 1781-1849 .... DLB-96, 190

Elliot, Frances Minto (Dickinson)
1820-1898 .... DLB-166

Elliott, Charlotte 1789-1871 .... DLB-199

Elliott, George 1923- DLB-68

Elliott, George P. 1918-1980 .... DLB-244

Elliott, Janice 1931-1995 .... DLB-14

Elliott, Sarah Barnwell 1848-1928 .... DLB-221

Elliott, Sumner Locke 1917-1991 .... DLB-289

Elliott, Thomes and Talbot DLB-49

Elliott, William, III 1788-1863 .... DLB-3, 248

Ellin, Stanley 1916-1986 .... DLB-306

Ellis, Alice Thomas (Anna Margaret Haycraft)
1932- DLB-194

Ellis, Bret Easton 1964- DLB-292

Ellis, Edward S. 1840-1916 .... DLB-42

Frederick Staridge Ellis
[publishing house] DLB-106

Ellis, George E.
   "The New Controversy Concerning
   Miracles DS-5

The George H. Ellis Company DLB-49

Ellis, Havelock 1859-1939 .... DLB-190

Ellison, Harlan 1934- DLB-8

   Tribute to Isaac Asimov Y-92

Ellison, Ralph
1914-1994 ... DLB-2, 76, 227; Y-94; CDALB-1

Ellmann, Richard 1918-1987 ...... DLB-103; Y-87

Ellroy, James 1948- DLB-226; Y-91

   Tribute to John D. MacDonald Y-86

   Tribute to Raymond Chandler Y-88

Eluard, Paul 1895-1952 .... DLB-258

Elyot, Thomas 1490?-1546 .... DLB-136

Emanuel, James Andrew 1921- DLB-41

Emecheta, Buchi 1944- ... DLB-117; CDWLB-3

Emerson, Ralph Waldo
1803-1882 ...... DLB-1, 59, 73, 183, 223, 270;
DS-5; CDALB-2

   Ralph Waldo Emerson in 1982 .... Y-82

   The Ralph Waldo Emerson Society Y-99

Emerson, William 1769-1811 .... DLB-37

Emerson, William R. 1923-1997 .... Y-97

Emin, Fedor Aleksandrovich
circa 1735-1770 .... DLB-150

Emmanuel, Pierre 1916-1984 .... DLB-258

Empedocles fifth century B.C. DLB-176

Empson, William 1906-1984 .... DLB-20

Enchi Fumiko 1905-1986 .... DLB-182

"The Encyclopedia," Denis Diderot DLB-314

Ende, Michael 1929-1995 .... DLB-75

Endō Shūsaku 1923-1996 .... DLB-182

Engel, Marian 1933-1985 .... DLB-53

Engel'gardt, Sof'ia Vladimirovna
   1828-1894 .... DLB-277

Engels, Friedrich 1820-1895 .... DLB-129

Engle, Paul 1908-1991 .... DLB-48

   Tribute to Robert Penn Warren Y-89

English, Thomas Dunn 1819-1902 ...... DLB-202

Ennius 239 B.C.-169 B.C. DLB-211

Enquist, Per Olov 1934- DLB-257

Enright, Anne 1962- DLB-267

Enright, D. J. 1920-2002 .... DLB-27

Enright, Elizabeth 1909-1968 .... DLB-22

Epic, The Sixteenth-Century Spanish DLB-318

Epictetus circa 55-circa 125-130 .... DLB-176

Epicurus 342/341 B.C.-271/270 B.C. DLB-176

d'Epinay, Louise (Louise-Florence-Pétronille Tardieu
   d'Esclavelles, marquise d'Epinay)
   1726-1783 .... DLB-313

Epps, Bernard 1936- DLB-53

Epshtein, Mikhail Naumovich 1950- .. DLB-285

Epstein, Julius 1909-2000 and
   Epstein, Philip 1909-1952 .... DLB-26

Epstein, Leslie 1938- DLB-299

Editors, Conversations with Y-95

Equiano, Olaudah
   circa 1745-1797 .... DLB-37, 50; CDWLB-3

   Olaudah Equiano and Unfinished
   Journeys: The Slave-Narrative
   Tradition and Twentieth-Century
   Continuities DLB-117

Eragny Press DLB-112

Erasmus, Desiderius 1467-1536 .... DLB-136

Erba, Luciano 1922- DLB-128

Erdman, Nikolai Robertovich
   1900-1970 .... DLB-272

Erdrich, Louise
   1954- DLB-152, 175, 206; CDALB-7

Erenburg, Il'ia Grigor'evich 1891-1967 .. DLB-272

Erichsen-Brown, Gwethalyn Graham
   (see Graham, Gwethalyn)

Eriugena, John Scottus circa 810-877 .... DLB-115

Ernst, Paul 1866-1933 .... DLB-66, 118

Erofeev, Venedikt Vasil'evich
   1938-1990 .... DLB-285

Erofeev, Viktor Vladimirovich 1947- .. DLB-285

Ershov, Petr Pavlovich 1815-1869 ...... DLB-205

Erskine, Albert 1911-1993 .... Y-93

   At Home with Albert Erskine Y-00

Erskine, John 1879-1951 .... DLB-9, 102

Erskine, Mrs. Steuart ?-1948 .... DLB-195

Ertel', Aleksandr Ivanovich
   1855-1908 .... DLB-238

Ervine, St. John Greer 1883-1971 .... DLB-10

Eschenburg, Johann Joachim
   1743-1820 .... DLB-97

Escofet, Cristina 1945- DLB-305

Escoto, Julio 1944- DLB-145

Esdaile, Arundell 1880-1956 .... DLB-201

Esenin, Sergei Aleksandrovich
   1895-1925 .... DLB-295

Eshleman, Clayton 1935- DLB-5

Espaillat, Rhina P. 1932- DLB-282

Espanca, Florbela 1894-1930 .... DLB-287

Espriu, Salvador 1913-1985 .... DLB-134

Ess Ess Publishing Company DLB-49

Essex House Press DLB-112

Esson, Louis 1878-1943 .... DLB-260

Essop, Ahmed 1931- DLB-225

Esterházy, Péter 1950- DLB-232; CDWLB-4

Estes, Eleanor 1906-1988 .... DLB-22

Estes and Lauriat DLB-49

Estleman, Loren D. 1952- DLB-226

Eszterhas, Joe 1944- DLB-185

Etherege, George 1636-circa 1692 ...... DLB-80

Ethridge, Mark, Sr. 1896-1981 .... DLB-127

Ets, Marie Hall 1893-1984 .... DLB-22

Etter, David 1928- DLB-105

Ettner, Johann Christoph
   1654-1724 .... DLB-168

Eudora Welty Remembered in
   Two Exhibits Y-02

Eugene Gant's Projected Works Y-01

Eupolemius fl. circa 1095 .... DLB-148

Euripides circa 484 B.C.-407/406 B.C.
   .... DLB-176; CDWLB-1

Evans, Augusta Jane 1835-1909 .... DLB-239

Evans, Caradoc 1878-1945 .... DLB-162

Evans, Charles 1850-1935 .... DLB-187

Evans, Donald 1884-1921 .... DLB-54

Evans, George Henry 1805-1856 .... DLB-43

Evans, Hubert 1892-1986 .... DLB-92

Evans, Mari 1923- DLB-41

Evans, Mary Ann (see Eliot, George)

Evans, Nathaniel 1742-1767 .... DLB-31

Evans, Sebastian 1830-1909 .... DLB-35

Evans, Ray 1915- DLB-265

M. Evans and Company DLB-46

Evaristi, Marcella 1953- DLB-233

Everett, Alexander Hill 1790-1847 ..... DLB-59

Everett, Edward 1794-1865 ...... DLB-1, 59, 235

Everson, R. G. 1903- DLB-88

Everson, William 1912-1994 ..... DLB-5, 16, 212

Evreinov, Nikolai 1879-1953 .... DLB-317

Ewald, Johannes 1743-1781 .... DLB-300

Ewart, Gavin 1916-1995 .... DLB-40

Ewing, Juliana Horatia
   1841-1885 .... DLB-21, 163

The Examiner 1808-1881 .... DLB-110

Exley, Frederick 1929-1992 .... DLB-143; Y-81

Editorial: The Extension of Copyright Y-02

von Eyb, Albrecht 1420-1475 .... DLB-179

Eyre and Spottiswoode DLB-106

Ezera, Regīna 1930- DLB-232

Ezzo ?-after 1065 .... DLB-148

F

Faber, Frederick William 1814-1863 ..... DLB-32

Faber and Faber Limited DLB-112

Faccio, Rena (see Aleramo, Sibilla)

Facsimiles
   The Uses of Facsimile: A Symposium Y-90

Fadeev, Aleksandr Aleksandrovich
   1901-1956 .... DLB-272

Fagundo, Ana María 1938- DLB-134

Fainzil'berg, Il'ia Arnol'dovich
   (see Il'f, Il'ia and Petrov, Evgenii)

Fair, Ronald L. 1932- DLB-33

Fairfax, Beatrice (see Manning, Marie)

Fairlie, Gerard 1899-1983 .... DLB-77

Faldbakken, Knut 1941- DLB-297

Falkberget, Johan (Johan Petter Lillebakken)
   1879-1967 .... DLB-297

Fallada, Hans 1893-1947 .... DLB-56

Fancher, Betsy 1928- Y-83

Fane, Violet 1843-1905 .... DLB-35

Fanfrolico Press DLB-112

Fanning, Katherine 1927- DLB-127

Fanon, Frantz 1925-1961 .... DLB-296

Fanshawe, Sir Richard 1608-1666 ...... DLB-126

Fantasy Press Publishers DLB-46

Fante, John 1909-1983 .... DLB-130; Y-83

Al-Farabi circa 870-950 .... DLB-115

Farabough, Laura 1949- DLB-228

Farah, Nuruddin 1945- DLB-125; CDWLB-3

Farber, Norma 1909-1984 .... DLB-61

A Farewell to Arms (Documentary) DLB-308

Fargue, Léon-Paul 1876-1947 .... DLB-258

Farigoule, Louis (see Romains, Jules)

Farjeon, Eleanor 1881-1965 .... DLB-160

Farley, Harriet 1812-1907 .... DLB-239

Farley, Walter 1920-1989 .... DLB-22

Farmborough, Florence 1887-1978 ...... DLB-204

Farmer, Penelope 1939- DLB-161

Farmer, Philip José 1918- DLB-8

Farnaby, Thomas 1575?-1647 .... DLB-236

Farningham, Marianne (see Hearn, Mary Anne)

Farquhar, George circa 1677-1707 ...... DLB-84

Farquharson, Martha (see Finley, Martha)

Farrar, Frederic William 1831-1903 ..... DLB-163

Farrar, Straus and Giroux DLB-46

Farrar and Rinehart DLB-46

Farrell, J. G. 1935-1979 .... DLB-14, 271

Farrell, James T. 1904-1979 ... DLB-4, 9, 86; DS-2

Fast, Howard 1914-2003 .... DLB-9

Faulkner, William 1897-1962 . . . .
  DLB-9, 11, 44, 102, 316; DS-2; Y-86; CDALB-5
  Faulkner and Yoknapatawpha
    Conference, Oxford, Mississippi Y-97
  Faulkner Centennial Addresses Y-97
  "Faulkner 100–Celebrating the Work,"
    University of South Carolina,
    Columbia Y-97
  Impressions of William Faulkner Y-97
  William Faulkner and the People-to-People
    Program Y-86
  William Faulkner Centenary
    Celebrations Y-97
  The William Faulkner Society Y-99
George Faulkner [publishing house] DLB-154
Faulks, Sebastian 1953- DLB-207
Fauset, Jessie Redmon 1882-1961 . . . . DLB-51
Faust, Frederick Schiller (Max Brand)
  1892-1944 . . . . DLB-256
Faust, Irvin
  1924- DLB-2, 28, 218, 278; Y-80, 00
  I Wake Up Screaming [Response to
    Ken Auletta] Y-97
  Tribute to Bernard Malamud Y-86
  Tribute to Isaac Bashevis Singer Y-91
  Tribute to Meyer Levin Y-81
Fawcett, Edgar 1847-1904 . . . . DLB-202
Fawcett, Millicent Garrett 1847-1929 . . . . . DLB-190
Fawcett Books DLB-46
Fay, Theodore Sedgwick 1807-1898 . . . . . DLB-202
Fearing, Kenneth 1902-1961 . . . . DLB-9
Federal Writers' Project DLB-46
Federman, Raymond 1928- Y-80
Fedin, Konstantin Aleksandrovich
  1892-1977 . . . . DLB-272
Fedorov, Innokentii Vasil'evich
  (see Omulevsky, Innokentii Vasil'evich)
Feiffer, Jules 1929- DLB-7, 44
Feinberg, Charles E. 1899-1988 . . . . DLB-187; Y-88
Feind, Barthold 1678-1721 . . . . DLB-168
Feinstein, Elaine 1930- DLB-14, 40
Feirstein, Frederick 1940- DLB-282
Feiss, Paul Louis 1875-1952 . . . . DLB-187
Feldman, Irving 1928- DLB-169
Felipe, Carlos 1911-1975 . . . . DLB-305
Felipe, León 1884-1968 . . . . DLB-108
Fell, Frederick, Publishers DLB-46
Fellowship of Southern Writers Y-98
Felltham, Owen 1602?-1668 . . . . DLB-126, 151
Felman, Shoshana 1942- DLB-246
Fels, Ludwig 1946- DLB-75
Felton, Cornelius Conway
  1807-1862 . . . . DLB-1, 235
Fel'zen, Iurii (Nikolai Berngardovich Freidenshtein)
  1894?-1943 . . . . DLB-317
Mothe-Fénelon, François de Salignac de la
  1651-1715 . . . . DLB-268
Fenn, Harry 1837-1911 . . . . DLB-188
Fennario, David 1947- DLB-60

Fenner, Dudley 1558?-1587? DLB-236
Fenno, Jenny 1765?-1803 . . . . DLB-200
Fenno, John 1751-1798 . . . . DLB-43
R. F. Fenno and Company DLB-49
Fenoglio, Beppe 1922-1963 . . . . DLB-177
Fenton, Geoffrey 1539?-1608 . . . . DLB-136
Fenton, James 1949- DLB-40
  The Hemingway/Fenton
    Correspondence Y-02
Ferber, Edna 1885-1968 . . . . DLB-9, 28, 86, 266
Ferdinand, Vallery, III (see Salaam, Kalamu ya)
Ferguson, Sir Samuel 1810-1886 . . . . DLB-32
Ferguson, William Scott 1875-1954 . . . . . . DLB-47
Fergusson, Robert 1750-1774 . . . . DLB-109
Ferland, Albert 1872-1943 . . . . DLB-92
Ferlinghetti, Lawrence
  1919- DLB-5, 16; CDALB-1
  Tribute to Kenneth Rexroth Y-82
Fermor, Patrick Leigh 1915- DLB-204
Fern, Fanny (see Parton, Sara Payson Willis)
Ferrars, Elizabeth (Morna Doris Brown)
  1907-1995 . . . . DLB-87
Ferré, Rosario 1942- DLB-145
Ferreira, Vergílio 1916-1996 . . . . DLB-287
E. Ferret and Company DLB-49
Ferrier, Susan 1782-1854 . . . . DLB-116
Ferril, Thomas Hornsby 1896-1988 . . . . . DLB-206
Ferrini, Vincent 1913- DLB-48
Ferron, Jacques 1921-1985 . . . . DLB-60
Ferron, Madeleine 1922- DLB-53
Ferrucci, Franco 1936- DLB-196
Fet, Afanasii Afanas'evich
  1820?-1892 . . . . DLB-277
Fetridge and Company DLB-49
Feuchtersleben, Ernst Freiherr von
  1806-1849 . . . . DLB-133
Feuchtwanger, Lion 1884-1958 . . . . DLB-66
Feuerbach, Ludwig 1804-1872 . . . . DLB-133
Feuillet, Octave 1821-1890 . . . . DLB-192
Feydeau, Georges 1862-1921 . . . . DLB-192
Fibiger, Mathilde 1830-1872 . . . . DLB-300
Fichte, Johann Gottlieb 1762-1814 . . . . . . DLB-90
Ficke, Arthur Davison 1883-1945 . . . . DLB-54
Fiction
  American Fiction and the 1930s DLB-9
  Fiction Best-Sellers, 1910-1945 . . . . DLB-9
  Postmodern Holocaust Fiction DLB-299
  The Year in Fiction Y-84, 86, 89, 94–99
  The Year in Fiction: A Biased View Y-83
  The Year in U.S. Fiction Y-00, 01
  The Year's Work in Fiction: A Survey . . . Y-82
Fiedler, Leslie A. 1917-2003 . . . . DLB-28, 67
  Tribute to Bernard Malamud Y-86
  Tribute to James Dickey Y-97
Field, Barron 1789-1846 . . . . DLB-230
Field, Edward 1924- DLB-105

Field, Eugene 1850-1895 . . DLB-23, 42, 140; DS-13
Field, John 1545?-1588 . . . . DLB-167
Field, Joseph M. 1810-1856 . . . . DLB-248
Field, Marshall, III 1893-1956 . . . . DLB-127
Field, Marshall, IV 1916-1965 . . . . DLB-127
Field, Marshall, V 1941- DLB-127
Field, Michael (Katherine Harris Bradley)
  1846-1914 . . . . DLB-240
  "The Poetry File" DLB-105
Field, Nathan 1587-1619 or 1620 . . . . DLB-58
Field, Rachel 1894-1942 . . . . DLB-9, 22
Fielding, Helen 1958- DLB-231
Fielding, Henry
  1707-1754 . . . . DLB-39, 84, 101; CDBLB-2
  "Defense of Amelia" (1752) DLB-39
  The History of the Adventures of Joseph Andrews
    [excerpt] (1742) DLB-39
  Letter to [Samuel] Richardson on Clarissa
    (1748) DLB-39
  Preface to Joseph Andrews (1742) DLB-39
  Preface to Sarah Fielding's Familiar
    Letters (1747) [excerpt] DLB-39
  Preface to Sarah Fielding's The
    Adventures of David Simple (1744) . . . DLB-39
  Review of Clarissa (1748) DLB-39
  Tom Jones (1749) [excerpt] DLB-39
Fielding, Sarah 1710-1768 . . . . DLB-39
  Preface to The Cry (1754) DLB-39
Fields, Annie Adams 1834-1915 . . . . DLB-221
Fields, Dorothy 1905-1974 . . . . DLB-265
Fields, James T. 1817-1881 . . . . DLB-1, 235
Fields, Julia 1938- DLB-41
Fields, Osgood and Company DLB-49
Fields, W. C. 1880-1946 . . . . DLB-44
Fierstein, Harvey 1954- DLB-266
Figes, Eva 1932- DLB-14, 271
Figuera, Angela 1902-1984 . . . . DLB-108
Filmer, Sir Robert 1586-1653 . . . . DLB-151
Filson, John circa 1753-1788 . . . . DLB-37
Finch, Anne, Countess of Winchilsea
  1661-1720 . . . . DLB-95
Finch, Annie 1956- DLB-282
Finch, Robert 1900- DLB-88
Findley, Timothy 1930-2002 . . . . DLB-53
Finlay, Ian Hamilton 1925- DLB-40
Finley, Martha 1828-1909 . . . . DLB-42
Finn, Elizabeth Anne (McCaul)
  1825-1921 . . . . DLB-166
Finnegan, Seamus 1949- DLB-245
Finney, Jack 1911-1995 . . . . DLB-8
Finney, Walter Braden (see Finney, Jack)
Firbank, Ronald 1886-1926 . . . . DLB-36
Firmin, Giles 1615-1697 . . . . DLB-24
First Edition Library/Collectors'
  Reprints, Inc. Y-91
Fischart, Johann
  1546 or 1547-1590 or 1591 . . . . DLB-179

Fischer, Karoline Auguste Fernandine 1764-1842 . . . . DLB-94	Fleming, May Agnes 1840-1880 . . . . DLB-99	Force, Peter 1790-1868 . . . . DLB-30
Fischer, Tibor 1959- DLB-231	Fleming, Paul 1609-1640 . . . . DLB-164	Forché, Carolyn 1950- DLB-5, 193
Fish, Stanley 1938- DLB-67	Fleming, Peter 1907-1971 . . . . DLB-195	Ford, Charles Henri 1913-2002 . . . . DLB-4, 48
Fishacre, Richard 1205-1248 . . . . DLB-115	Fletcher, Giles, the Elder 1546-1611 . . . . . DLB-136	Ford, Corey 1902-1969 . . . . DLB-11
Fisher, Clay (see Allen, Henry W.)	Fletcher, Giles, the Younger 1585 or 1586-1623 . . . . DLB-121	Ford, Ford Madox 1873-1939 . . . . DLB-34, 98, 162; CDBLB-6
Fisher, Dorothy Canfield 1879-1958 . . . DLB-9, 102	Fletcher, J. S. 1863-1935 . . . . DLB-70	Nathan Asch Remembers Ford Madox Ford, Sam Roth, and Hart Crane Y-02
Fisher, Leonard Everett 1924- DLB-61	Fletcher, John 1579-1625 . . . . DLB-58	J. B. Ford and Company DLB-49
Fisher, Roy 1930- DLB-40	Fletcher, John Gould 1886-1950 . . . . . . DLB-4, 45	Ford, Jesse Hill 1928-1996 . . . . DLB-6
Fisher, Rudolph 1897-1934 . . . . DLB-51, 102	Fletcher, Phineas 1582-1650 . . . . DLB-121	Ford, John 1586-? DLB-58; CDBLB-1
Fisher, Steve 1913-1980 . . . . DLB-226	Flieg, Helmut (see Heym, Stefan)	Ford, R. A. D. 1915-1998 . . . . DLB-88
Fisher, Sydney George 1856-1927 . . . . DLB-47	Flint, F. S. 1885-1960 . . . . DLB-19	Ford, Richard 1944- DLB-227
Fisher, Vardis 1895-1968 . . . . DLB-9, 206	Flint, Timothy 1780-1840 . . . . DLB-73, 186	Ford, Worthington C. 1858-1941 . . . . DLB-47
Fiske, John 1608-1677 . . . . DLB-24	Fløgstad, Kjartan 1944- DLB-297	Fords, Howard, and Hulbert DLB-49
Fiske, John 1842-1901 . . . . DLB-47, 64	Florensky, Pavel Aleksandrovich 1882-1937 . . . . DLB-295	Foreman, Carl 1914-1984 . . . . DLB-26
Fitch, Thomas circa 1700-1774 . . . . DLB-31	Flores, Juan de fl. 1470-1500 . . . . DLB-286	Forester, C. S. 1899-1966 . . . . DLB-191
Fitch, William Clyde 1865-1909 . . . . DLB-7	Flores-Williams, Jason 1969- DLB-209	The C. S. Forester Society Y-00
FitzGerald, Edward 1809-1883 . . . . DLB-32	Florio, John 1553?-1625 . . . . DLB-172	Forester, Frank (see Herbert, Henry William)
Fitzgerald, F. Scott 1896-1940 . . . . DLB-4, 9, 86; Y-81, 92; DS-1, 15, 16; CDALB-4	Fludd, Robert 1574-1637 . . . . DLB-281	Formalism, New
	Flynn, Elizabeth Gurley 1890-1964 . . . . . DLB-303	Anthologizing New Formalism DLB-282
F. Scott Fitzgerald: A Descriptive Bibliography, Supplement (2001) Y-01	Fo, Dario 1926- Y-97	The Little Magazines of the New Formalism DLB-282
F. Scott Fitzgerald Centenary Celebrations Y-96	Nobel Lecture 1997: Contra Jogulatores Obloquentes Y-97	The New Narrative Poetry DLB-282
F. Scott Fitzgerald Inducted into the American Poets' Corner at St. John the Divine; Ezra Pound Banned Y-99	Foden, Giles 1967- DLB-267	Presses of the New Formalism and the New Narrative DLB-282
	Fofanov, Konstantin Mikhailovich 1862-1911 . . . . DLB-277	The Prosody of the New Formalism . DLB-282
"F. Scott Fitzgerald: St. Paul's Native Son and Distinguished American Writer": University of Minnesota Conference, 29-31 October 1982 . . . . Y-82	Foix, J. V. 1893-1987 . . . . DLB-134	Younger Women Poets of the New Formalism DLB-282
	Foley, Martha 1897-1977 . . . . DLB-137	Forman, Harry Buxton 1842-1917 . . . . . . DLB-184
	Folger, Henry Clay 1857-1930 . . . . DLB-140	Fornés, María Irene 1930- DLB-7
First International F. Scott Fitzgerald Conference Y-92	Folio Society DLB-112	Forrest, Leon 1937-1997 . . . . DLB-33
	Follain, Jean 1903-1971 . . . . DLB-258	Forsh, Ol'ga Dmitrievna 1873-1961 . . . . . . DLB-272
The Great Gatsby (Documentary) DLB-219	Follen, Charles 1796-1840 . . . . DLB-235	Forster, E. M. 1879-1970 . . DLB-34, 98, 162, 178, 195; DS-10; CDBLB-6 "Fantasy," from Aspects of the Novel (1927) DLB-178
Tender Is the Night (Documentary) . . . DLB-273	Follen, Eliza Lee (Cabot) 1787-1860 . . . DLB-1, 235	
Fitzgerald, Penelope 1916-2000 . . . . . DLB-14, 194	Follett, Ken 1949- DLB-87; Y-81	
Fitzgerald, Robert 1910-1985 . . . . Y-80	Follett Publishing Company DLB-46	
FitzGerald, Robert D. 1902-1987 . . . . DLB-260	John West Folsom [publishing house] DLB-49	Forster, Georg 1754-1794 . . . . DLB-94
Fitzgerald, Thomas 1819-1891 . . . . DLB-23	Folz, Hans between 1435 and 1440-1513 . . . . DLB-179	Forster, John 1812-1876 . . . . DLB-144
Fitzgerald, Zelda Sayre 1900-1948 . . . . Y-84		Forster, Margaret 1938- DLB-155, 271
Fitzhugh, Louise 1928-1974 . . . . DLB-52	Fonseca, Manuel da 1911-1993 . . . . DLB-287	Forsyth, Frederick 1938- DLB-87
Fitzhugh, William circa 1651-1701 . . . . DLB-24	Fonseca, Rubem 1925- DLB-307	Forsyth, William "Literary Style" (1857) [excerpt] DLB-57
Flagg, James Montgomery 1877-1960 . . . . DLB-188	Fontane, Theodor 1819-1898 . . . . DLB-129; CDWLB-2	
Flanagan, Thomas 1923-2002 . . . . Y-80		Forten, Charlotte L. 1837-1914 . . . . . . DLB-50, 239
Flanner, Hildegarde 1899-1987 . . . . DLB-48	Fontenelle, Bernard Le Bovier de 1657-1757 . . . . DLB-268, 313	Pages from Her Diary DLB-50
Flanner, Janet 1892-1978 . . . . DLB-4; DS-15		Fortini, Franco 1917-1994 . . . . DLB-128
Flannery, Peter 1951- DLB-233	Fontes, Montserrat 1940- DLB-209	Fortune, Mary ca. 1833-ca. 1910 . . . . DLB-230
Flaubert, Gustave 1821-1880 . . . . DLB-119, 301	Fonvisin, Denis Ivanovich 1744 or 1745-1792 . . . . DLB-150	Fortune, T. Thomas 1856-1928 . . . . DLB-23
Flavin, Martin 1883-1967 . . . . DLB-9		Fosdick, Charles Austin 1842-1915 . . . . . . DLB-42
Fleck, Konrad (fl. circa 1220) DLB-138	Foote, Horton 1916- DLB-26, 266	Fosse, Jon 1959- DLB-297
Flecker, James Elroy 1884-1915 . . . . . . DLB-10, 19	Foote, Mary Hallock 1847-1938 . . . . DLB-186, 188, 202, 221	Foster, David 1944- DLB-289
Fleeson, Doris 1901-1970 . . . . DLB-29		Foster, Genevieve 1893-1979 . . . . DLB-61
Fleißer, Marieluise 1901-1974 . . . . DLB-56, 124	Foote, Samuel 1721-1777 . . . . DLB-89	Foster, Hannah Webster 1758-1840 . . . . DLB-37, 200
Fleischer, Nat 1887-1972 . . . . DLB-241	Foote, Shelby 1916-2005 . . . . DLB-2, 17	
Fleming, Abraham 1552?-1607 . . . . DLB-236	Forbes, Calvin 1945- DLB-41	Foster, John 1648-1681 . . . . DLB-24
Fleming, Ian 1908-1964 . . DLB-87, 201; CDBLB-7	Forbes, Ester 1891-1967 . . . . DLB-22	Foster, Michael 1904-1956 . . . . DLB-9
Fleming, Joan 1908-1980 . . . . DLB-276	Forbes, Rosita 1893?-1967 . . . . DLB-195	Foster, Myles Birket 1825-1899 . . . . DLB-184
	Forbes and Company DLB-49	

Foster, William Z. 1881-1961 ....DLB-303
Foucault, Michel 1926-1984............DLB-242
Robert and Andrew Foulis
 [publishing house]...............DLB-154
Fouqué, Caroline de la Motte 1774-1831....DLB-90
Fouqué, Friedrich de la Motte
 1777-1843......................DLB-90
Four Seas Company..................DLB-46
Four Winds Press...................DLB-46
Fournier, Henri Alban (see Alain-Fournier)
Fowler, Christopher 1953- DLB-267
Fowler, Connie May 1958- DLB-292
Fowler and Wells Company DLB-49
Fowles, John
 1926- DLB-14, 139, 207; CDBLB-8
Fox, John 1939- DLB-245
Fox, John, Jr. 1862 or 1863-1919....DLB-9; DS-13
Fox, Paula 1923- DLB-52
Fox, Richard Kyle 1846-1922 ....DLB-79
Fox, William Price 1926- DLB-2; Y-81
 Remembering Joe Heller............... Y-99
Richard K. Fox [publishing house]........DLB-49
Foxe, John 1517-1587................DLB-132
Fraenkel, Michael 1896-1957............DLB-4
Frame, Ronald 1953- DLB-319
France, Anatole 1844-1924 ....DLB-123
France, Richard 1938- DLB-7
Francis, Convers 1795-1863..........DLB-1, 235
Francis, Dick 1920- DLB-87; CDBLB-8
Francis, Sir Frank 1901-1988 ....DLB-201
Francis, Jeffrey, Lord 1773-1850 ....DLB-107
C. S. Francis [publishing house]..........DLB-49
Franck, Sebastian 1499-1542 ....DLB-179
Francke, Kuno 1855-1930 ....DLB-71
Françoise (Robertine Barry) 1863-1910....DLB-92
François, Louise von 1817-1893.........DLB-129
Frank, Bruno 1887-1945................DLB-118
Frank, Leonhard 1882-1961 ....DLB-56, 118
Frank, Melvin 1913-1988...............DLB-26
Frank, Waldo 1889-1967............DLB-9, 63
Franken, Rose 1895?-1988 ......DLB-228, Y-84
Franklin, Benjamin
 1706-1790.....DLB-24, 43, 73, 183; CDALB-2
Franklin, James 1697-1735...........DLB-43
Franklin, John 1786-1847..............DLB-99
Franklin, Miles 1879-1954............DLB-230
Franklin Library....................DLB-46
Frantz, Ralph Jules 1902-1979 ....DLB-4
Franzos, Karl Emil 1848-1904 ....DLB-129
Fraser, Antonia 1932- DLB-276
Fraser, G. S. 1915-1980...............DLB-27
Fraser, Kathleen 1935- DLB-169
Frattini, Alberto 1922-................DLB-128
Frau Ava ?-1127...................DLB-148
Fraunce, Abraham 1558?-1592 or 1593...DLB-236

Frayn, Michael 1933- DLB-13, 14, 194, 245
Frazier, Charles 1950- DLB-292
Fréchette, Louis-Honoré 1839-1908.......DLB-99
Frederic, Harold 1856-1898....DLB-12, 23; DS-13
Freed, Arthur 1894-1973 ....DLB-265
Freeling, Nicolas 1927-2003 ....DLB-87
 Tribute to Georges Simenon.......... Y-89
Freeman, Douglas Southall
 1886-1953 .... DLB-17; DS-17
Freeman, Joseph 1897-1965 ....DLB-303
Freeman, Judith 1946- DLB-256
Freeman, Legh Richmond 1842-1915 .....DLB-23
Freeman, Mary E. Wilkins
 1852-1930 ....DLB-12, 78, 221
Freeman, R. Austin 1862-1943 ....DLB-70
Freidank circa 1170-circa 1233..........DLB-138
Freiligrath, Ferdinand 1810-1876 ....DLB-133
Fremlin, Celia 1914- DLB-276
Frémont, Jessie Benton 1834-1902.......DLB-183
Frémont, John Charles
 1813-1890.................DLB-183, 186
French, Alice 1850-1934 .... DLB-74; DS-13
French, David 1939- DLB-53
French, Evangeline 1869-1960...........DLB-195
French, Francesca 1871-1960 ....DLB-195
James French [publishing house] DLB-49
Samuel French [publishing house].......DLB-49
Samuel French, Limited DLB-106
French Literature
 Georges-Louis Leclerc de Buffon, "Le Discours
  sur le style"..................DLB-314
 Marie-Jean-Antoine-Nicolas Caritat, marquis de
  Condorcet, "The Tenth Stage"...DLB-314
 Sophie Cottin, *Claire d'Albe* DLB-314
 Declaration of the Rights of Man and of
  the Citizen DLB-314
 Denis Diderot, "The Encyclopedia" ..DLB-314
 Epic and Beast Epic..............DLB-208
 French Arthurian Literature DLB-208
 Olympe de Gouges, *Declaration of the Rights
  of Woman*...................DLB-314
 Françoise d'Issembourg de Graffigny, *Letters from
  a Peruvian Woman*...............DLB-314
 Claude-Adrien Helvétius, *The Spirit of
  Laws*......................DLB-314
 Paul Henri Thiry, baron d'Holbach (writing as
  Jean-Baptiste de Mirabaud), *The System
  of Nature* DLB-314
 Pierre-Ambroise-François Choderlos de Laclos,
  Dangerous Acquaintances.........DLB-314
 Lyric Poetry DLB-268
 Louis-Sébastien Mercier, *Le Tableau
  de Paris* DLB-314
 Charles-Louis de Secondat, baron de
  Montesquieu, *The Spirit of Laws*...DLB-314
 Other Poets....................DLB-217
 Poetry in Nineteenth-Century France:
  Cultural Background and Critical
  Commentary DLB-217

Roman de la Rose: Guillaume de Lorris
 1200 to 1205-circa 1230, Jean de
 Meun 1235/1240-circa 1305.....DLB-208
Jean-Jacques Rousseau, *The Social
 Contract* DLB-314
Marquis de Sade, "Dialogue entre un prêtre et
 un moribond"................DLB-314
Saints' Lives DLB-208
Troubadours, *Trobairitz,* and
 Trouvères....................DLB-208
Anne-Robert-Jacques Turgot, baron de l'Aulne,
 "Memorandum on Local
 Government" DLB-314
Voltaire, "An account of the death of the cheva-
 lier de La Barre"...............DLB-314
Voltaire, *Candide* DLB-314
Voltaire, *Philosophical Dictionary*.......DLB-314
French Theater
 Medieval French Drama DLB-208
 Parisian Theater, Fall 1984: Toward
  a New Baroque................. Y-85
Freneau, Philip 1752-1832 .... DLB-37, 43
 The Rising Glory of America DLB-37
Freni, Melo 1934- DLB-128
Fréron, Elie Catherine 1718-1776........DLB-313
Freshfield, Douglas W. 1845-1934 ...... DLB-174
Freud, Sigmund 1856-1939 ....DLB-296
Freytag, Gustav 1816-1895 ....DLB-129
Fríða Á. Sigurðardóttir 1940- DLB-293
Fridegård, Jan 1897-1968 ....DLB-259
Fried, Erich 1921-1988 ....DLB-85
Friedan, Betty 1921- DLB-246
Friedman, Bruce Jay 1930- DLB-2, 28, 244
Friedman, Carl 1952- DLB-299
Friedman, Kinky 1944- DLB-292
Friedrich von Hausen circa 1171-1190....DLB-138
Friel, Brian 1929- DLB-13, 319
Friend, Krebs 1895?-1967?.............DLB-4
Fries, Fritz Rudolf 1935- DLB-75
Frisch, Max
 1911-1991 ....DLB-69, 124; CDWLB-2
Frischlin, Nicodemus 1547-1590 ....DLB-179
Frischmuth, Barbara 1941- DLB-85
Fritz, Jean 1915- DLB-52
Froissart, Jean circa 1337-circa 1404......DLB-208
Fromm, Erich 1900-1980...............DLB-296
Fromentin, Eugene 1820-1876 ....DLB-123
Frontinus circa A.D. 35-A.D. 103/104 .....DLB-211
Frost, A. B. 1851-1928 ....DLB-188; DS-13
Frost, Robert
 1874-1963 ....DLB-54; DS-7; CDALB-4
 The Friends of the Dymock Poets Y-00
Frostenson, Katarina 1953- DLB-257
Frothingham, Octavius Brooks
 1822-1895 ....DLB-1, 243
Froude, James Anthony
 1818-1894 .... DLB-18, 57, 144
Fruitlands 1843-1844..........DLB-1, 223; DS-5
Fry, Christopher 1907-2005............DLB-13

Cumulative Index

Tribute to John Betjeman............Y-84
Fry, Roger 1866-1934.................DS-10
Fry, Stephen 1957-..............DLB-207
Frye, Northrop 1912-1991.......DLB-67, 68, 246
Fuchs, Daniel 1909-1993.....DLB-9, 26, 28; Y-93
   Tribute to Isaac Bashevis Singer........Y-91
Fuentes, Carlos 1928-......DLB-113; CDWLB-3
Fuertes, Gloria 1918-1998..........DLB-108
Fugard, Athol 1932-............DLB-225
The Fugitives and the Agrarians:
   The First Exhibition................Y-85
Fujiwara no Shunzei 1114-1204........DLB-203
Fujiwara no Tameaki 1230s?-1290s?....DLB-203
Fujiwara no Tameie 1198-1275.........DLB-203
Fujiwara no Teika 1162-1241..........DLB-203
Fuks, Ladislav 1923-1994............DLB-299
Fulbecke, William 1560-1603?........DLB-172
Fuller, Charles 1939-..........DLB-38, 266
Fuller, Henry Blake 1857-1929.........DLB-12
Fuller, John 1937-..............DLB-40
Fuller, Margaret (see Fuller, Sarah)
Fuller, Roy 1912-1991............DLB-15, 20
   Tribute to Christopher Isherwood.......Y-86
Fuller, Samuel 1912-1997............DLB-26
Fuller, Sarah 1810-1850.........DLB-1, 59, 73, 183, 223, 239; DS-5; CDALB-2
Fuller, Thomas 1608-1661............DLB-151
Fullerton, Hugh 1873-1945...........DLB-171
Fullwood, William fl. 1568...........DLB-236
Fulton, Alice 1952-..............DLB-193
Fulton, Len 1934-..............Y-86
Fulton, Robin 1937-..............DLB-40
Furbank, P. N. 1920-..............DLB-155
Furetière, Antoine 1619-1688.........DLB-268
Furman, Laura 1945-..............Y-86
Furmanov, Dmitrii Andreevich
   1891-1926....................DLB-272
Furness, Horace Howard 1833-1912....DLB-64
Furness, William Henry
   1802-1896..................DLB-1, 235
Furnivall, Frederick James 1825-1910....DLB-184
Furphy, Joseph (Tom Collins)
   1843-1912....................DLB-230
Furthman, Jules 1888-1966............DLB-26
   Shakespeare and Montaigne: A
   Symposium by Jules Furthman......Y-02
Furui Yoshikichi 1937-............DLB-182
Fushimi, Emperor 1265-1317..........DLB-203
Futabatei Shimei (Hasegawa Tatsunosuke)
   1864-1909....................DLB-180
Fyleman, Rose 1877-1957............DLB-160

G

Gaarder, Jostein 1952-............DLB-297
Gadallah, Leslie 1939-............DLB-251
Gadamer, Hans-Georg 1900-2002......DLB-296

Gadda, Carlo Emilio 1893-1973.......DLB-177
Gaddis, William 1922-1998........DLB-2, 278
   William Gaddis: A Tribute..........Y-99
Gág, Wanda 1893-1946..............DLB-22
Gagarin, Ivan Sergeevich 1814-1882....DLB-198
Gagnon, Madeleine 1938-............DLB-60
Gaiman, Neil 1960-..............DLB-261
Gaine, Hugh 1726-1807............DLB-43
Hugh Gaine [publishing house].......DLB-49
Gaines, Ernest J.
   1933-.....DLB-2, 33, 152; Y-80; CDALB-6
Gaiser, Gerd 1908-1976............DLB-69
Gaitskill, Mary 1954-..............DLB-244
Galarza, Ernesto 1905-1984..........DLB-122
Galaxy Science Fiction Novels..........DLB-46
Galbraith, Robert (or Caubraith)
   circa 1483-1544................DLB-281
Gale, Zona 1874-1938..........DLB-9, 228, 78
Galen of Pergamon 129-after 210.......DLB-176
Gales, Winifred Marshall 1761-1839....DLB-200
Galich, Aleksandr 1918-1977.........DLB-317
Medieval Galician-Portuguese Poetry....DLB-287
Gall, Louise von 1815-1855..........DLB-133
Gallagher, Tess 1943-.......DLB-120, 212, 244
Gallagher, Wes 1911-1997...........DLB-127
Gallagher, William Davis 1808-1894.....DLB-73
Gallant, Mavis 1922-..............DLB-53
Gallegos, María Magdalena 1935-......DLB-209
Gallico, Paul 1897-1976............DLB-9, 171
Gallop, Jane 1952-..............DLB-246
Galloway, Grace Growden 1727-1782....DLB-200
Galloway, Janice 1956-............DLB-319
Gallup, Donald 1913-2000...........DLB-187
Galsworthy, John 1867-1933
   .....DLB-10, 34, 98, 162; DS-16; CDBLB-5
Galt, John 1779-1839.........DLB-99, 116, 159
Galton, Sir Francis 1822-1911.........DLB-166
Galvin, Brendan 1938-..............DLB-5
Gambaro, Griselda 1928-............DLB-305
Gambit......................DLB-46
Gamboa, Reymundo 1948-...........DLB-122
Gammer Gurton's Needle..........DLB-62
Gan, Elena Andreevna (Zeneida R-va)
   1814-1842....................DLB-198
Gandlevsky, Sergei Markovich
   1952-........................DLB-285
Gannett, Frank E. 1876-1957.........DLB-29
Gant, Eugene: Projected Works........Y-01
Gao Xingjian 1940-..............Y-00
   Nobel Lecture 2000: "The Case for
   Literature"....................Y-00
Gaos, Vicente 1919-1980............DLB-134
García, Andrew 1854?-1943..........DLB-209
García, Cristina 1958-............DLB-292
García, Lionel G. 1935-............DLB-82
García, Richard 1941-............DLB-209

García, Santiago 1928-............DLB-305
García Márquez, Gabriel
   1928-........DLB-113; Y-82; CDWLB-3
   The Magical World of Macondo.......Y-82
   Nobel Lecture 1982: The Solitude of
   Latin America.................Y-82
   A Tribute to Gabriel García Márquez....Y-82
García Marruz, Fina 1923-..........DLB-283
García-Camarillo, Cecilio 1943-......DLB-209
Garcilaso de la Vega circa 1503-1536....DLB-318
Garcilaso de la Vega, Inca 1539-1616....DLB-318
Gardam, Jane 1928-........DLB-14, 161, 231
Gardell, Jonas 1963-..............DLB-257
Garden, Alexander circa 1685-1756.....DLB-31
Gardiner, John Rolfe 1936-..........DLB-244
Gardiner, Margaret Power Farmer
   (see Blessington, Marguerite, Countess of)
Gardner, John
   1933-1982........DLB-2; Y-82; CDALB-7
Garfield, Leon 1921-1996............DLB-161
Garis, Howard R. 1873-1962..........DLB-22
Garland, Hamlin 1860-1940...DLB-12, 71, 78, 186
   The Hamlin Garland Society..........Y-01
Garneau, François-Xavier 1809-1866....DLB-99
Garneau, Hector de Saint-Denys
   1912-1943....................DLB-88
Garneau, Michel 1939-.............DLB-53
Garner, Alan 1934-............DLB-161, 261
Garner, Hugh 1913-1979............DLB-68
Garnett, David 1892-1981...........DLB-34
Garnett, Eve 1900-1991............DLB-160
Garnett, Richard 1835-1906..........DLB-184
Garrard, Lewis H. 1829-1887.........DLB-186
Garraty, John A. 1920-............DLB-17
Garrett, Almeida (João Baptista da Silva
   Leitão de Almeida Garrett)
   1799-1854....................DLB-287
Garrett, George
   1929-..........DLB-2, 5, 130, 152; Y-83
   Literary Prizes.................Y-00
   My Summer Reading Orgy: Reading
   for Fun and Games: One Reader's
   Report on the Summer of 2001......Y-01
   A Summing Up at Century's End......Y-99
   Tribute to James Dickey...........Y-97
   Tribute to Michael M. Rea..........Y-97
   Tribute to Paxton Davis............Y-94
   Tribute to Peter Taylor.............Y-94
   Tribute to William Goyen...........Y-83
   A Writer Talking: A Collage..........Y-00
Garrett, John Work 1872-1942........DLB-187
Garrick, David 1717-1779........DLB-84, 213
Garrison, William Lloyd
   1805-1879........DLB-1, 43, 235; CDALB-2
Garro, Elena 1920-1998............DLB-145
Garshin, Vsevolod Mikhailovich
   1855-1888....................DLB-277
Garth, Samuel 1661-1719............DLB-95

Garve, Andrew 1908-2001	DLB-87
Gary, Romain 1914-1980	DLB-83, 299
Gascoigne, George 1539?-1577	DLB-136
Gascoyne, David 1916-2001	DLB-20
Gash, Jonathan (John Grant) 1933-	DLB-276
Gaskell, Elizabeth Cleghorn 1810-1865	DLB-21, 144, 159; CDBLB-4
The Gaskell Society	Y-98
Gaskell, Jane 1941-	DLB-261
Gaspey, Thomas 1788-1871	DLB-116
Gass, William H. 1924-	DLB-2, 227
Gates, Doris 1901-1987	DLB-22
Gates, Henry Louis, Jr. 1950-	DLB-67
Gates, Lewis E. 1860-1924	DLB-71
Gatto, Alfonso 1909-1976	DLB-114
Gault, William Campbell 1910-1995	DLB-226
Tribute to Kenneth Millar	Y-83
Gaunt, Mary 1861-1942	DLB-174, 230
Gautier, Théophile 1811-1872	DLB-119
Gautreaux, Tim 1947-	DLB-292
Gauvreau, Claude 1925-1971	DLB-88
The *Gawain*-Poet fl. circa 1350-1400	DLB-146
Gawsworth, John (Terence Ian Fytton Armstrong) 1912-1970	DLB-255
Gay, Ebenezer 1696-1787	DLB-24
Gay, John 1685-1732	DLB-84, 95
Gayarré, Charles E. A. 1805-1895	DLB-30
Charles Gaylord [publishing house]	DLB-49
Gaylord, Edward King 1873-1974	DLB-127
Gaylord, Edward Lewis 1919-2003	DLB-127
Gazdanov, Gaito 1903-1971	DLB-317
Gébler, Carlo 1954-	DLB-271
Geda, Sigitas 1943-	DLB-232
Geddes, Gary 1940-	DLB-60
Geddes, Virgil 1897-1989	DLB-4
Gedeon (Georgii Andreevich Krinovsky) circa 1730-1763	DLB-150
Gee, Maggie 1948-	DLB-207
Gee, Shirley 1932-	DLB-245
Geibel, Emanuel 1815-1884	DLB-129
Geiogamah, Hanay 1945-	DLB-175
Geis, Bernard, Associates	DLB-46
Geisel, Theodor Seuss 1904-1991	DLB-61; Y-91
Gelb, Arthur 1924-	DLB-103
Gelb, Barbara 1926-	DLB-103
Gelber, Jack 1932-	DLB-7, 228
Gélinas, Gratien 1909-1999	DLB-88
Gellert, Christian Füerchtegott 1715-1769	DLB-97
Gellhorn, Martha 1908-1998	Y-82, 98
Gems, Pam 1925-	DLB-13
Genet, Jean 1910-1986	DLB-72; Y-86
Genette, Gérard 1930-	DLB-242
Genevoix, Maurice 1890-1980	DLB-65
Genis, Aleksandr Aleksandrovich 1953-	DLB-285
Genlis, Stéphanie-Félicité Ducrest, comtesse de 1746-1830	DLB-313
Genovese, Eugene D. 1930-	DLB-17
Gent, Peter 1942-	Y-82
Geoffrey of Monmouth circa 1100-1155	DLB-146
George, Elizabeth 1949-	DLB-306
George, Henry 1839-1897	DLB-23
George, Jean Craighead 1919-	DLB-52
George, W. L. 1882-1926	DLB-197
George III, King of Great Britain and Ireland 1738-1820	DLB-213
Georgslied 896?	DLB-148
Gerber, Merrill Joan 1938-	DLB-218
Gerhardie, William 1895-1977	DLB-36
Gerhardt, Paul 1607-1676	DLB-164
Gérin, Winifred 1901-1981	DLB-155
Gérin-Lajoie, Antoine 1824-1882	DLB-99
German Literature A Call to Letters and an Invitation to the Electric Chair	DLB-75
The Conversion of an Unpolitical Man	DLB-66
The German Radio Play	DLB-124
The German Transformation from the Baroque to the Enlightenment	DLB-97
Germanophilism	DLB-66
A Letter from a New Germany	Y-90
The Making of a People	DLB-66
The Novel of Impressionism	DLB-66
Pattern and Paradigm: History as Design	DLB-75
Premisses	DLB-66
The 'Twenties and Berlin	DLB-66
Wolfram von Eschenbach's *Parzival*: Prologue and Book 3	DLB-138
Writers and Politics: 1871-1918	DLB-66
German Literature, Middle Ages *Abrogans* circa 790-800	DLB-148
Annolied between 1077 and 1081	DLB-148
The Arthurian Tradition and Its European Context	DLB-138
Cambridge Songs (*Carmina Cantabrigensia*) circa 1050	DLB-148
Christus und die Samariterin circa 950	DLB-148
De Heinrico circa 980?	DLB-148
Ecbasis Captivi circa 1045	DLB-148
Georgslied 896?	DLB-148
German Literature and Culture from Charlemagne to the Early Courtly Period	DLB-148; CDWLB-2
The Germanic Epic and Old English Heroic Poetry: *Widsith, Waldere,* and *The Fight at Finnsburg*	DLB-146
Graf Rudolf between circa 1170 and circa 1185	DLB-148
Heliand circa 850	DLB-148
Das Hildebrandslied circa 820	DLB-148; CDWLB-2
Kaiserchronik circa 1147	DLB-148
The Legends of the Saints and a Medieval Christian Worldview	DLB-148
Ludus de Antichristo circa 1160	DLB-148
Ludwigslied 881 or 882	DLB-148
Muspilli circa 790-circa 850	DLB-148
Old German Genesis and *Old German Exodus* circa 1050-circa 1130	DLB-148
Old High German Charms and Blessings	DLB-148; CDWLB-2
The *Old High German Isidor* circa 790-800	DLB-148
Petruslied circa 854?	DLB-148
Physiologus circa 1070-circa 1150	DLB-148
Ruodlieb circa 1050-1075	DLB-148
"*Spielmannsepen*" (circa 1152 circa 1500)	DLB-148
The Strasbourg Oaths 842	DLB-148
Tatian circa 830	DLB-148
Waltharius circa 825	DLB-148
Wessobrunner Gebet circa 787-815	DLB-148
German Theater German Drama 800-1280	DLB-138
German Drama from Naturalism to Fascism: 1889-1933	DLB-118
Gernsback, Hugo 1884-1967	DLB-8, 137
Gerould, Katharine Fullerton 1879-1944	DLB-78
Samuel Gerrish [publishing house]	DLB-49
Gerrold, David 1944-	DLB-8
Gersão, Teolinda 1940-	DLB-287
Gershon, Karen 1923-1993	DLB-299
Gershwin, Ira 1896-1983	DLB-265
The Ira Gershwin Centenary	Y-96
Gerson, Jean 1363-1429	DLB-208
Gersonides 1288-1344	DLB-115
Gerstäcker, Friedrich 1816-1872	DLB-129
Gertsen, Aleksandr Ivanovich (see Herzen, Alexander)
Gerstenberg, Heinrich Wilhelm von 1737-1823	DLB-97
Gervinus, Georg Gottfried 1805-1871	DLB-133
Gery, John 1953-	DLB-282
Geßner, Solomon 1730-1788	DLB-97
Geston, Mark S. 1946-	DLB-8
Al-Ghazali 1058-1111	DLB-115
Gibbings, Robert 1889-1958	DLB-195
Gibbon, Edward 1737-1794	DLB-104
Gibbon, John Murray 1875-1952	DLB-92
Gibbon, Lewis Grassic (see Mitchell, James Leslie)
Gibbons, Floyd 1887-1939	DLB-25
Gibbons, Kaye 1960-	DLB-292
Gibbons, Reginald 1947-	DLB-120
Gibbons, William eighteenth century	DLB-73

Cumulative Index

Gibson, Charles Dana 1867-1944 .... DLB-188; DS-13
Gibson, Graeme 1934- DLB-53
Gibson, Margaret 1944- DLB-120
Gibson, Margaret Dunlop 1843-1920 .... DLB-174
Gibson, Wilfrid 1878-1962 .... DLB-19
   The Friends of the Dymock Poets Y-00
Gibson, William 1914- DLB-7
Gibson, William 1948- DLB-251
Gide, André 1869-1951 .... DLB-65
Giguère, Diane 1937- DLB-53
Giguère, Roland 1929- DLB-60
Gil de Biedma, Jaime 1929-1990 .... DLB-108
Gil-Albert, Juan 1906-1994 .... DLB-134
Gilbert, Anthony 1899-1973 .... DLB-77
Gilbert, Elizabeth 1969- DLB-292
Gilbert, Sir Humphrey 1537-1583 .... DLB-136
Gilbert, Michael 1912- DLB-87
Gilbert, Sandra M. 1936- DLB-120, 246
Gilchrist, Alexander 1828-1861 .... DLB-144
Gilchrist, Ellen 1935- DLB-130
Gilder, Jeannette L. 1849-1916 .... DLB-79
Gilder, Richard Watson 1844-1909 .... DLB-64, 79
Gildersleeve, Basil 1831-1924 .... DLB-71
Giles, Henry 1809-1882 .... DLB-64
Giles of Rome circa 1243-1316 .... DLB-115
Gilfillan, George 1813-1878 .... DLB-144
Gill, Eric 1882-1940 .... DLB-98
Gill, Sarah Prince 1728-1771 .... DLB-200
William F. Gill Company DLB-49
Gillespie, A. Lincoln, Jr. 1895-1950 .... DLB-4
Gillespie, Haven 1883-1975 .... DLB-265
Gilliam, Florence fl. twentieth century DLB-4
Gilliatt, Penelope 1932-1993 .... DLB-14
Gillott, Jacky 1939-1980 .... DLB-14
Gilman, Caroline H. 1794-1888 .... DLB-3, 73
Gilman, Charlotte Perkins 1860-1935 .... DLB-221
   The Charlotte Perkins Gilman Society Y-99
W. and J. Gilman [publishing house] DLB-49
Gilmer, Elizabeth Meriwether 1861-1951 .... DLB-29
Gilmer, Francis Walker 1790-1826 .... DLB-37
Gilmore, Mary 1865-1962 .... DLB-260
Gilroy, Frank D. 1925- DLB-7
Gimferrer, Pere (Pedro) 1945- DLB-134
Ginger, Aleksandr S. 1897-1965 .... DLB-317
Gingrich, Arnold 1903-1976 .... DLB-137
   Prospectus From the Initial Issue of *Esquire* (Autumn 1933) DLB-137
   "With the Editorial Ken," Prospectus From the Initial Issue of *Ken* (7 April 1938) DLB-137
Ginsberg, Allen 1926-1997 .... DLB-5, 16, 169, 237; CDALB-1
Ginzburg, Evgeniia 1904-1977 .... DLB-302

Ginzburg, Lidiia Iakovlevna 1902-1990 .... DLB-302
Ginzburg, Natalia 1916-1991 .... DLB-177
Ginzkey, Franz Karl 1871-1963 .... DLB-81
Gioia, Dana 1950- DLB-120, 282
Giono, Jean 1895-1970 .... DLB-72
Giotti, Virgilio 1885-1957 .... DLB-114
Giovanni, Nikki 1943- DLB-5, 41; CDALB-7
Giovannitti, Arturo 1884-1959 .... DLB-303
Gipson, Lawrence Henry 1880-1971 .... DLB-17
Girard, Rodolphe 1879-1956 .... DLB-92
Giraudoux, Jean 1882-1944 .... DLB-65
Girondo, Oliverio 1891-1967 .... DLB-283
Gissing, George 1857-1903 .... DLB-18, 135, 184
   The Place of Realism in Fiction (1895) DLB-18
Giudici, Giovanni 1924- DLB-128
Giuliani, Alfredo 1924- DLB-128
Gjellerup, Karl 1857-1919 .... DLB-300
Glackens, William J. 1870-1938 .... DLB-188
Gladilin, Anatolii Tikhonovich 1935- DLB-302
Gladkov, Fedor Vasil'evich 1883-1958 .... DLB-272
Gladstone, William Ewart 1809-1898 .... DLB-57, 184
Glaeser, Ernst 1902-1963 .... DLB-69
Glancy, Diane 1941- DLB-175
Glanvill, Joseph 1636-1680 .... DLB-252
Glanville, Brian 1931- DLB-15, 139
Glapthorne, Henry 1610-1643? DLB-58
Glasgow, Ellen 1873-1945 .... DLB-9, 12
   The Ellen Glasgow Society Y-01
Glasier, Katharine Bruce 1867-1950 .... DLB-190
Glaspell, Susan 1876-1948 .... DLB-7, 9, 78, 228
Glass, Montague 1877-1934 .... DLB-11
Glassco, John 1909-1981 .... DLB-68
Glauser, Friedrich 1896-1938 .... DLB-56
Glavin, Anthony 1946- DLB-319
F. Gleason's Publishing Hall DLB-49
Gleim, Johann Wilhelm Ludwig 1719-1803 .... DLB-97
Glendinning, Robin 1938- DLB-310
Glendinning, Victoria 1937- DLB-155
Glidden, Frederick Dilley (Luke Short) 1908-1975 .... DLB-256
Glinka, Fedor Nikolaevich 1786-1880 .... DLB-205
Glover, Keith 1966- DLB-249
Glover, Richard 1712-1785 .... DLB-95
Glover, Sue 1943- DLB-310
Glück, Louise 1943- DLB-5
Glyn, Elinor 1864-1943 .... DLB-153
Gnedich, Nikolai Ivanovich 1784-1833 .... DLB-205
Gobineau, Joseph-Arthur de 1816-1882 .... DLB-123
Godber, John 1956- DLB-233
Godbout, Jacques 1933- DLB-53
Goddard, Morrill 1865-1937 .... DLB-25

Goddard, William 1740-1817 .... DLB-43
Godden, Rumer 1907-1998 .... DLB-161
Godey, Louis A. 1804-1878 .... DLB-73
Godey and McMichael DLB-49
Godfrey, Dave 1938- DLB-60
Godfrey, Thomas 1736-1763 .... DLB-31
Godine, David R., Publisher DLB-46
Godkin, E. L. 1831-1902 .... DLB-79
Godolphin, Sidney 1610-1643 .... DLB-126
Godwin, Gail 1937- DLB-6, 234
M. J. Godwin and Company DLB-154
Godwin, Mary Jane Clairmont 1766-1841 .... DLB-163
Godwin, Parke 1816-1904 .... DLB-3, 64, 250
Godwin, William 1756-1836 .... DLB-39, 104, 142, 158, 163, 262; CDBLB-3
   Preface to *St. Leon* (1799) DLB-39
Goering, Reinhard 1887-1936 .... DLB-118
Goes, Albrecht 1908- DLB-69
Goethe, Johann Wolfgang von 1749-1832 .... DLB-94; CDWLB-2
Goetz, Curt 1888-1960 .... DLB-124
Goffe, Thomas circa 1592-1629 .... DLB-58
Goffstein, M. B. 1940- DLB-61
Gogarty, Oliver St. John 1878-1957 .... DLB-15, 19
Gogol, Nikolai Vasil'evich 1809-1852 .... DLB-198
Goines, Donald 1937-1974 .... DLB-33
Gold, Herbert 1924- DLB-2; Y-81
   Tribute to William Saroyan Y-81
Gold, Michael 1893-1967 .... DLB-9, 28
Goldbarth, Albert 1948- DLB-120
Goldberg, Dick 1947- DLB-7
Golden Cockerel Press DLB-112
Golding, Arthur 1536-1606 .... DLB-136
Golding, Louis 1895-1958 .... DLB-195
Golding, William 1911-1993 .... DLB-15, 100, 255; Y-83; CDBLB-7
   Nobel Lecture 1993 .... Y-83
   The Stature of William Golding Y-83
Goldman, Emma 1869-1940 .... DLB-221
Goldman, William 1931- DLB-44
Goldring, Douglas 1887-1960 .... DLB-197
Goldschmidt, Meir Aron 1819-1887 .... DLB-300
Goldsmith, Oliver 1730?-1774 .... DLB-39, 89, 104, 109, 142; CDBLB-2
Goldsmith, Oliver 1794-1861 .... DLB-99
Goldsmith Publishing Company DLB-46
Goldstein, Richard 1944- DLB-185
Gollancz, Sir Israel 1864-1930 .... DLB-201
Victor Gollancz Limited DLB-112
Gomberville, Marin Le Roy, sieur de 1600?-1674 .... DLB-268
Gombrowicz, Witold 1904-1969 .... DLB-215; CDWLB-4
Gomez, Madeleine-Angélique Poisson de 1684-1770 .... DLB-313

Gómez de Ciudad Real, Alvar (Alvar Gómez de Guadalajara) 1488-1538 . . . . DLB-318	Tribute to Raymond Chandler Y-88	Graham, W. S. 1918-1986 . . . . DLB-20
Gómez-Quiñones, Juan 1942- DLB-122	Gorey, Edward 1925-2000 . . . . DLB-61	William H. Graham [publishing house] DLB-49
Laurence James Gomme [publishing house] DLB-46	Gorgias of Leontini circa 485 B.C.-376 B.C. DLB-176	Graham, Winston 1910-2003 . . . . DLB-77
Gompers, Samuel 1850-1924 . . . . DLB-303	Gor'ky, Maksim 1868-1936 . . . . DLB-295	Grahame, Kenneth 1859-1932 . . . DLB-34, 141, 178
Gonçalves Dias, Antônio 1823-1864 . . . . . DLB-307	Gorodetsky, Sergei Mitrofanovich 1884-1967 . . . . DLB-295	Grainger, Martin Allerdale 1874-1941 . . . . . DLB-92
Goncharov, Ivan Aleksandrovich 1812-1891 . . . . DLB-238	Gorostiza, José 1901-1979 . . . . DLB-290	Gramatky, Hardie 1907-1979 . . . . DLB-22
Goncourt, Edmond de 1822-1896 . . . . DLB-123	Görres, Joseph 1776-1848 . . . . DLB-90	Gramcko, Ida 1924-1994 . . . . DLB-290
Goncourt, Jules de 1830-1870 . . . . DLB-123	Gosse, Edmund 1849-1928 . . . . . DLB-57, 144, 184	Gramsci, Antonio 1891-1937 . . . . DLB-296
Gonzales, Rodolfo "Corky" 1928- DLB-122	Gosson, Stephen 1554-1624 . . . . DLB-172	Granada, Fray Luis de 1504-1588 . . . . DLB-318
Gonzales-Berry, Erlinda 1942- DLB-209	*The Schoole of Abuse* (1579) DLB-172	Grand, Sarah 1854-1943 . . . . DLB-135, 197
"Chicano Language" DLB-82	Gotanda, Philip Kan 1951- DLB-266	Grandbois, Alain 1900-1975 . . . . DLB-92
González, Angel 1925- DLB-108	Gotlieb, Phyllis 1926- DLB-88, 251	Grandson, Oton de circa 1345-1397 . . . . . DLB-208
Gonzalez, Genaro 1949- DLB-122	Go-Toba 1180-1239 . . . . DLB-203	Grange, John circa 1556-? DLB-136
Gonzalez, N. V. M. 1915-1999 . . . . DLB-312	Gottfried von Straßburg died before 1230 . . . . DLB-138; CDWLB-2	Granger, Thomas 1578-1627 . . . . DLB-281
González, Otto-Raúl 1921- DLB-290	Gotthelf, Jeremias 1797-1854 . . . . DLB-133	Granich, Irwin (see Gold, Michael)
Gonzalez, Ray 1952- DLB-122	Gottschalk circa 804/808-869 . . . . DLB-148	Granin, Daniil 1918- DLB-302
González de Mireles, Jovita 1899-1983 . . . . DLB-122	Gottsched, Johann Christoph 1700-1766 . . . . DLB-97	Granovsky, Timofei Nikolaevich 1813-1855 . . . . DLB-198
González Martínez, Enrique 1871-1952 . . . DLB-290	Götz, Johann Nikolaus 1721-1781 . . . . DLB-97	Grant, Anne MacVicar 1755-1838 . . . . DLB-200
González-T., César A. 1931- DLB-82	Goudge, Elizabeth 1900-1984 . . . . DLB-191	Grant, Duncan 1885-1978 . . . . DS-10
Goodis, David 1917-1967 . . . . DLB-226	Gouges, Olympe de 1748-1793 . . . . DLB-313	Grant, George 1918-1988 . . . . DLB-88
Goodison, Lorna 1947- DLB-157	*Declaration of the Rights of Woman* DLB-314	Grant, George Monro 1835-1902 . . . . DLB-99
Goodman, Allegra 1967- DLB-244	Gough, John B. 1817-1886 . . . . DLB-243	Grant, Harry J. 1881-1963 . . . . DLB-29
Goodman, Nelson 1906-1998 . . . . DLB-279	Gould, Wallace 1882-1940 . . . . DLB-54	Grant, James Edward 1905-1966 . . . . DLB-26
Goodman, Paul 1911-1972 . . . . DLB-130, 246	Govoni, Corrado 1884-1965 . . . . DLB-114	Grant, John (see Gash, Jonathan)
The Goodman Theatre DLB-7	Govrin, Michal 1950- DLB-299	War of the Words (and Pictures): The Creation of a Graphic Novel Y-02
Goodrich, Frances 1891-1984 and Hackett, Albert 1900-1995 . . . . DLB-26	Gower, John circa 1330-1408 . . . . DLB-146	Grass, Günter 1927- . . . DLB-75, 124; CDWLB-2
Goodrich, Samuel Griswold 1793-1860 . . . . DLB-1, 42, 73, 243	Goyen, William 1915-1983 . . . . . DLB-2, 218; Y-83	Nobel Lecture 1999: "To Be Continued . . ." Y-99
S. G. Goodrich [publishing house] DLB-49	Goytisolo, José Augustín 1928- DLB-134	Tribute to Helen Wolff Y-94
C. E. Goodspeed and Company DLB-49	Gozzano, Guido 1883-1916 . . . . DLB-114	Grasty, Charles H. 1863-1924 . . . . DLB-25
Goodwin, Stephen 1943- Y-82	Grabbe, Christian Dietrich 1801-1836 . . . . DLB-133	Grau, Shirley Ann 1929- DLB-2, 218
Googe, Barnabe 1540-1594 . . . . DLB-132	Gracq, Julien (Louis Poirier) 1910- DLB-83	Graves, John 1920- Y-83
Gookin, Daniel 1612-1687 . . . . DLB-24	Grady, Henry W. 1850-1889 . . . . DLB-23	Graves, Richard 1715-1804 . . . . DLB-39
Goran, Lester 1928- DLB-244	Graf, Oskar Maria 1894-1967 . . . . DLB-56	Graves, Robert 1895-1985 . . . DLB-20, 100, 191; DS-18; Y-85; CDBLB-6
Gordimer, Nadine 1923- DLB-225; Y-91	*Graf Rudolf* between circa 1170 and circa 1185 . . . . DLB-148	The St. John's College Robert Graves Trust Y-96
Nobel Lecture 1991 . . . . Y-91	Graff, Gerald 1937- DLB-246	Gray, Alasdair 1934- DLB-194, 261, 319
Gordon, Adam Lindsay 1833-1870 . . . . . . DLB-230	Graffigny, Françoise d'Issembourg de 1695-1758 . . . . DLB-313	Gray, Asa 1810-1888 . . . . DLB-1, 235
Gordon, Caroline 1895-1981 . . . . . . DLB-4, 9, 102; DS-17; Y-81	*Letters from a Peruvian Woman* DLB-314	Gray, David 1838-1861 . . . . DLB-32
Gordon, Charles F. (see OyamO)	Richard Grafton [publishing house] DLB-170	Gray, Simon 1936- DLB-13
Gordon, Charles William (see Connor, Ralph)	Grafton, Sue 1940- DLB-226	Gray, Thomas 1716-1771 . . . . . DLB-109; CDBLB-2
Gordon, Giles 1940- DLB-14, 139, 207	Graham, Frank 1893-1965 . . . . DLB-241	Grayson, Richard 1951- DLB-234
Gordon, Helen Cameron, Lady Russell 1867-1949 . . . . DLB-195	Graham, George Rex 1813-1894 . . . . DLB-73	Grayson, William J. 1788-1863 . . . . DLB-3, 64, 248
Gordon, Lyndall 1941- DLB-155	Graham, Gwethalyn (Gwethalyn Graham Erichsen-Brown) 1913-1965 . . . . DLB-88	The Great Bibliographers Series Y-93
Gordon, Mack 1904-1959 . . . . DLB-265	Graham, Jorie 1951- DLB-120	*The Great Gatsby* (Documentary) DLB-219
Gordon, Mary 1949- DLB-6; Y-81	Graham, Katharine 1917-2001 . . . . DLB-127	"The Greatness of Southern Literature": League of the South Institute for the Study of Southern Culture and History Y-02
Gordone, Charles 1925-1995 . . . . DLB-7	Graham, Lorenz 1902-1989 . . . . DLB-76	
Gore, Catherine 1800-1861 . . . . DLB-116	Graham, Philip 1915-1963 . . . . DLB-127	Grech, Nikolai Ivanovich 1787-1867 . . . . . DLB-198
Gore-Booth, Eva 1870-1926 . . . . DLB-240	Graham, R. B. Cunninghame 1852-1936 . . . . DLB-98, 135, 174	Greeley, Horace 1811-1872 . . . DLB-3, 43, 189, 250
Gores, Joe 1931- DLB-226; Y-02	Graham, Shirley 1896-1977 . . . . DLB-76	Green, Adolph 1915-2002 . . . . DLB-44, 265
Tribute to Kenneth Millar Y-83	Graham, Stephen 1884-1975 . . . . DLB-195	Green, Anna Katharine 1846-1935 . . . . DLB-202, 221

Green, Duff 1791-1875 .... DLB-43
Green, Elizabeth Shippen 1871-1954 .... DLB-188
Green, Gerald 1922- DLB-28
Green, Henry 1905-1973 .... DLB-15
Green, Jonas 1712-1767 .... DLB-31
Green, Joseph 1706-1780 .... DLB-31
Green, Julien 1900-1998 .... DLB-4, 72
Green, Paul 1894-1981 .... DLB-7, 9, 249; Y-81
Green, T. H. 1836-1882 .... DLB-190, 262
Green, Terence M. 1947- DLB-251
T. and S. Green [publishing house] DLB-49
Green Tiger Press....................... DLB-46
Timothy Green [publishing house]........ DLB-49
Greenaway, Kate 1846-1901............. DLB-141
Greenberg: Publisher DLB-46
Greene, Asa 1789-1838 .... DLB-11
Greene, Belle da Costa 1883-1950 ...... DLB-187
Greene, Graham 1904-1991
    .... DLB-13, 15, 77, 100, 162, 201, 204;
    Y-85, 91; CDBLB-7
    Tribute to Christopher Isherwood....... Y-86
Greene, Robert 1558-1592 .... DLB-62, 167
Greene, Robert Bernard (Bob), Jr.
    1947- DLB-185
Benjamin H Greene [publishing house] ... DLB-49
Greenfield, George 1917-2000............ Y-91, 00
    Derek Robinson's Review of George
    Greenfield's *Rich Dust*................ Y-02
Greenhow, Robert 1800-1854 .... DLB-30
Greenlee, William B. 1872-1953........ DLB-187
Greenough, Horatio 1805-1852 ..... DLB-1, 235
Greenwell, Dora 1821-1882 .... DLB-35, 199
Greenwillow Books DLB-46
Greenwood, Grace (see Lippincott, Sara Jane Clarke)
Greenwood, Walter 1903-1974...... DLB-10, 191
Greer, Ben 1948- DLB-6
Greflinger, Georg 1620?-1677.......... DLB-164
Greg, W. R. 1809-1881 .... DLB-55
Greg, W. W. 1875-1959 .... DLB-201
Gregg, Josiah 1806-1850 .... DLB-183, 186
Gregg Press........................... DLB-46
Gregory, Horace 1898-1982............. DLB-48
Gregory, Isabella Augusta Persse, Lady
    1852-1932 .... DLB-10
Gregory of Rimini circa 1300-1358 ..... DLB-115
Gregynog Press....................... DLB-112
Greiff, León de 1895-1976 .... DLB-283
Greiffenberg, Catharina Regina von
    1633-1694 .... DLB-168
Greig, Noël 1944- DLB-245
Grekova, Irina (Elena Sergeevna Venttsel')
    1907-2002........................ DLB-302
Grenfell, Wilfred Thomason
    1865-1940 .... DLB-92
Gress, Elsa 1919-1988................. DLB-214
Greve, Felix Paul (see Grove, Frederick Philip)

Greville, Fulke, First Lord Brooke
    1554-1628 .... DLB-62, 172
Grey, Sir George, K.C.B. 1812-1898 .... DLB-184
Grey, Lady Jane 1537-1554 .... DLB-132
Grey, Zane 1872-1939 .... DLB-9, 212
    Zane Grey's West Society Y-00
Grey Owl (Archibald Stansfeld Belaney)
    1888-1938 .... DLB-92; DS-17
Grey Walls Press DLB-112
Griboedov, Aleksandr Sergeevich
    1795?-1829 .... DLB-205
Grice, Paul 1913-1988 ....DLB-279
Grier, Eldon 1917- DLB-88
Grieve, C. M. (see MacDiarmid, Hugh)
Griffin, Bartholomew fl. 1596...........DLB-172
Griffin, Bryan
    "Panic Among the Philistines":
    A Postscript, An Interview
    with Bryan Griffin................. Y-81
Griffin, Gerald 1803-1840 .... DLB-159
The Griffin Poetry Prize.................. Y-00
Griffith, Elizabeth 1727?-1793 .... DLB-39, 89
    Preface to *The Delicate Distress* (1769) .. DLB-39
Griffith, George 1857-1906............. DLB-178
Ralph Griffiths [publishing house] DLB-154
Griffiths, Trevor 1935- DLB-13, 245
S. C. Griggs and Company DLB-49
Griggs, Sutton Elbert 1872-1930........ DLB-50
Grignon, Claude-Henri 1894-1976 ...... DLB-68
Grigor'ev, Apollon Aleksandrovich
    1822-1864 ....DLB-277
Grigorovich, Dmitrii Vasil'evich
    1822-1899 .... DLB-238
Grigson, Geoffrey 1905-1985........... DLB-27
Grillparzer, Franz
    1791-1872............. DLB-133; CDWLB-2
Grimald, Nicholas
    circa 1519-circa 1562 .... DLB-136
Grimké, Angelina Weld 1880-1958 ... DLB-50, 54
Grimké, Sarah Moore 1792-1873 ...... DLB-239
Grimm, Frédéric Melchior 1723-1807.... DLB-313
Grimm, Hans 1875-1959 .... DLB-66
Grimm, Jacob 1785-1863 .... DLB-90
Grimm, Wilhelm
    1786-1859............. DLB-90; CDWLB-2
Grimmelshausen, Johann Jacob Christoffel von
    1621 or 1622-1676 ..... DLB-168; CDWLB-2
Grimshaw, Beatrice Ethel 1871-1953 .....DLB-174
Grímur Thomsen 1820-1896 .... DLB-293
Grin, Aleksandr Stepanovich
    1880-1932 ....DLB-272
Grindal, Edmund 1519 or 1520-1583.... DLB-132
Gripe, Maria (Kristina) 1923- DLB-257
Griswold, Rufus Wilmot
    1815-1857................. DLB-3, 59, 250
Gronlund, Laurence 1846-1899 .... DLB-303
Grosart, Alexander Balloch 1827-1899 ... DLB-184
Grosholz, Emily 1950- DLB-282

Gross, Milt 1895-1953 .... DLB-11
Grosset and Dunlap DLB-49
Grosseteste, Robert circa 1160-1253..... DLB-115
Grossman, Allen 1932- DLB-193
Grossman, David 1954- DLB-299
Grossman, Vasilii Semenovich
    1905-1964 ....DLB-272
Grossman Publishers DLB-46
Grosvenor, Gilbert H. 1875-1966........ DLB-91
Groth, Klaus 1819-1899 .... DLB-129
Groulx, Lionel 1878-1967 .... DLB-68
Grove, Frederick Philip (Felix Paul Greve)
    1879-1948........................ DLB-92
Grove Press DLB-46
Groys, Boris Efimovich 1947- DLB-285
Grubb, Davis 1919-1980 .... DLB-6
Gruelle, Johnny 1880-1938............. DLB-22
von Grumbach, Argula
    1492-after 1563? DLB-179
Grundtvig, N. F. S. 1783-1872 .... DLB-300
Grymeston, Elizabeth
    before 1563-before 1604 .... DLB-136
Grynberg, Henryk 1936- DLB-299
Gryphius, Andreas
    1616-1664 ....DLB-164; CDWLB-2
Gryphius, Christian 1649-1706......... DLB-168
Guare, John 1938- DLB-7, 249
Guarnieri, Gianfrancesco 1934- DLB-307
Guberman, Igor Mironovich 1936- ... DLB-285
Guðbergur Bergsson 1932- DLB-293
Guðmundur Böðvarsson 1904-1974..... DLB-293
Guðmundur Gíslason Hagalín
    1898-1985 .... DLB-293
Guðmundur Magnússon (see Jón Trausti)
Guerra, Tonino 1920- DLB-128
Guest, Barbara 1920- DLB-5, 193
Guevara, Fray Antonio de 1480?-1545 .. DLB-318
Guèvremont, Germaine 1893-1968 ...... DLB-68
Guglielminetti, Amalia 1881-1941 ..... DLB-264
Guidacci, Margherita 1921-1992 ...... DLB-128
Guillén, Jorge 1893-1984 .... DLB-108
Guillén, Nicolás 1902-1989 .... DLB-283
Guilloux, Louis 1899-1980............. DLB-72
Guilpin, Everard
    circa 1572-after 1608? DLB-136
Guiney, Louise Imogen 1861-1920 ...... DLB-54
Guiterman, Arthur 1871-1943 .... DLB-11
Gul', Roman 1896-1986...............DLB-317
Gumilev, Nikolai Stepanovich
    1886-1921 .... DLB-295
Günderrode, Caroline von
    1780-1806....................... DLB-90
Gundulić, Ivan 1589-1638 ...DLB-147; CDWLB-4
Gunesekera, Romesh 1954- DLB-267
Gunn, Bill 1934-1989 .... DLB-38
Gunn, James E. 1923- DLB-8
Gunn, Neil M. 1891-1973.............. DLB-15

Gunn, Thom 1929- DLB-27; CDBLB-8	Hake, Edward fl. 1566-1604 ....DLB-136	Halstead, Murat 1829-1908.............DLB-23
Gunnar Gunnarsson 1889-1975........DLB-293	Hake, Thomas Gordon 1809-1895.......DLB-32	Hamann, Johann Georg 1730-1788.......DLB-97
Gunnars, Kristjana 1948- DLB-60	Hakluyt, Richard 1552?-1616...........DLB-136	Hamburger, Michael 1924- DLB-27
Günther, Johann Christian 1695-1723....DLB-168	Halas, František 1901-1949 ....DLB-215	Hamilton, Alexander 1712-1756.........DLB-31
Gurik, Robert 1932- DLB-60	Halbe, Max 1865-1944 ....DLB-118	Hamilton, Alexander 1755?-1804 ....DLB-37
Gurney, A. R. 1930- DLB-266	Halberstam, David 1934- DLB-241	Hamilton, Cicely 1872-1952 ....DLB-10, 197
Gurney, Ivor 1890-1937................. Y-02	Haldane, Charlotte 1894-1969..........DLB-191	Hamilton, Edmond 1904-1977............DLB-8
The Ivor Gurney Society Y-98	Haldane, J. B. S. 1892-1964............DLB-160	Hamilton, Elizabeth 1758-1816 .....DLB-116, 158
Guro, Elena Genrikhovna 1877-1913.....DLB-295	Haldeman, Joe 1943- DLB-8	Hamilton, Gail (see Corcoran, Barbara)
Gustafson, Ralph 1909-1995 ....DLB-88	Haldeman-Julius Company DLB-46	Hamilton, Gail (see Dodge, Mary Abigail)
Gustafsson, Lars 1936- DLB-257	Hale, E. J., and Son DLB-49	Hamish Hamilton Limited.............DLB-112
Gütersloh, Albert Paris 1887-1973 ....DLB-81	Hale, Edward Everett 1822-1909 ....DLB-1, 42, 74, 235	Hamilton, Hugo 1953- DLB-267
Guterson, David 1956- DLB-292	Hale, Janet Campbell 1946- DLB-175	Hamilton, Ian 1938-2001...........DLB-40, 155
Guthrie, A. B., Jr. 1901-1991........DLB-6, 212	Hale, Kathleen 1898-2000 ....DLB-160	Hamilton, Janet 1795-1873............DLB-199
Guthrie, Ramon 1896-1973 ....DLB-4	Hale, Leo Thomas (see Ebon)	Hamilton, Mary Agnes 1884-1962 ......DLB-197
Guthrie, Thomas Anstey (see Anstey, FC)	Hale, Lucretia Peabody 1820-1900 ....DLB-42	Hamilton, Patrick 1904-1962........DLB-10, 191
Guthrie, Woody 1912-1967............DLB-303	Hale, Nancy 1908-1988........ DLB-86; DS-17; Y-80, 88	Hamilton, Virginia 1936-2002... DLB-33, 52; Y-01
The Guthrie Theater DLB-7	Hale, Sarah Josepha (Buell) 1788-1879 ....DLB-1, 42, 73, 243	Hamilton, Sir William 1788-1856 ....DLB-262
Gutiérrez Nájera, Manuel 1859-1895.....DLB-290	Hale, Susan 1833-1910 ....DLB-221	Hamilton-Paterson, James 1941- DLB-267
Guttormur J. Guttormsson 1878-1966....DLB-293	Hales, John 1584-1656.................DLB-151	Hammerstein, Oscar, 2nd 1895-1960 ... DLB-265
Gutzkow, Karl 1811-1878 ....DLB-133	Halévy, Ludovic 1834-1908 ....DLB-192	Hammett, Dashiell 1894-1961........DLB-226; DS-6; CDALB-5
Guy, Ray 1939- DLB-60	Haley, Alex 1921-1992 ....DLB-38; CDALB-7	An Appeal in *TAC*................. Y-91
Guy, Rosa 1925- DLB-33	Haliburton, Thomas Chandler 1796-1865 ....DLB-11, 99	*The Glass Key* and Other Dashiell Hammett Mysteries Y-96
Guyot, Arnold 1807-1884 .... DS-13	Hall, Adam (Trevor Dudley-Smith) 1920-1995 ....DLB-276	Knopf to Hammett: The Editoral Correspondence................. Y-00
Gwynn, R. S. 1948- DLB-282	Hall, Anna Maria 1800-1881...........DLB-159	*The Maltese Falcon* (Documentary) DLB-280
Gwynne, Erskine 1898-1948 ....DLB-4	Hall, Donald 1928- DLB-5	Hammon, Jupiter 1711-died between 1790 and 1806..................DLB-31, 50
Gyles, John 1680-1755 ....DLB-99	Hall, Edward 1497-1547...............DLB-132	Hammond, John ?-1663.................DLB-24
Gyllembourg, Thomasine 1773-1856.....DLB-300	Hall, Halsey 1898-1977 ....DLB-241	Hamner, Earl 1923- DLB-6
Gyllensten, Lars 1921- DLB-257	Hall, James 1793-1868 .... DLB-73, 74	Hampson, John 1901-1955 ....DLB-191
Gyrðir Elíasson 1961- DLB-293	Hall, Joseph 1574-1656 ....DLB-121, 151	Hampton, Christopher 1946- DLB-13
Gysin, Brion 1916-1986................DLB-16	Hall, Radclyffe 1880-1943.............DLB-191	Hamsun, Knut 1859-1952 ....DLB-297
	Hall, Rodney 1935- DLB-289	Handel-Mazzetti, Enrica von 1871-1955 ...DLB-81
H	Hall, Sarah Ewing 1761-1830...........DLB-200	Handke, Peter 1942- DLB-85, 124
H.D. (see Doolittle, Hilda)	Hall, Stuart 1932- DLB-242	Handlin, Oscar 1915- DLB-17
Habermas, Jürgen 1929- DLB-242	Samuel Hall [publishing house] DLB-49	Hankin, St. John 1869-1909.............DLB-10
Habington, William 1605-1654 ....DLB-126	al-Hallaj 857-922 ....DLB-311	Hanley, Clifford 1922- DLB-14
Hacker, Marilyn 1942- DLB-120, 282	Hallam, Arthur Henry 1811-1833........DLB-32	Hanley, James 1901-1985 ....DLB-191
Hackett, Albert 1900-1995............DLB-26	On Some of the Characteristics of Modern Poetry and On the Lyrical Poems of Alfred Tennyson (1831) DLB-32	Hannah, Barry 1942- DLB-6, 234
Hacks, Peter 1928- DLB-124		Hannay, James 1827-1873 ....DLB-21
Hadas, Rachel 1948- DLB-120, 282		Hannes Hafstein 1861-1922............DLB-293
Hadden, Briton 1898-1929 ....DLB-91		Hano, Arnold 1922- DLB-241
Hagedorn, Friedrich von 1708-1754......DLB-168	Halldór Laxness (Halldór Guðjónsson) 1902-1998 ....DLB-293	Hanrahan, Barbara 1939-1991 ....DLB-289
Hagedorn, Jessica Tarahata 1949- DLB-312		Hansberry, Lorraine 1930-1965............ DLB-7, 38; CDALB-1
Hagelstange, Rudolf 1912-1984..........DLB-69	Halleck, Fitz-Greene 1790-1867 ....DLB-3, 250	
Hagerup, Inger 1905-1985 ....DLB-297	Haller, Albrecht von 1708-1777..........DLB-168	Hansen, Joseph 1923-2004 ....DLB-226
Haggard, H. Rider 1856-1925 ....DLB-70, 156, 174, 178	Halliday, Brett (see Dresser, Davis)	Hansen, Martin A. 1909-1955..........DLB-214
Haggard, William (Richard Clayton) 1907-1993 .... DLB-276; Y-93	Halliwell-Phillipps, James Orchard 1820-1889 ....DLB-184	Hansen, Thorkild 1927-1989 ....DLB-214
Hagy, Alyson 1960- DLB-244	Hallmann, Johann Christian 1640-1704 or 1716? DLB-168	Hanson, Elizabeth 1684-1737...........DLB-200
Hahn-Hahn, Ida Gräfin von 1805-1880...DLB-133		Hapgood, Norman 1868-1937..........DLB-91
Haig-Brown, Roderick 1908-1976 ....DLB-88	Hallmark Editions DLB-46	Happel, Eberhard Werner 1647-1690 ....DLB-168
Haight, Gordon S. 1901-1985 ....DLB-103	Halper, Albert 1904-1984 ....DLB-9	Harbach, Otto 1873-1963 ....DLB-265
Hailey, Arthur 1920-2004 ....DLB-88; Y-82	Halperin, John William 1941- DLB-111	*The Harbinger* 1845-1849 ....DLB-1, 223
Haines, John 1924- DLB-5, 212		

Cumulative Index

Harburg, E. Y. "Yip" 1896-1981 .... DLB-265
Harcourt Brace Jovanovich DLB-46
Hardenberg, Friedrich von (see Novalis)
Harding, Walter 1917-1996 .... DLB-111
Hardwick, Elizabeth 1916- DLB-6
Hardy, Alexandre 1572?-1632 .... DLB-268
Hardy, Frank 1917-1994............. DLB-260
Hardy, Thomas
    1840-1928 ...... DLB-18, 19, 135; CDBLB-5
    "Candour in English Fiction" (1890)....DLB-18
Hare, Cyril 1900-1958 .... DLB-77
Hare, David 1947- DLB-13, 310
Hare, R. M. 1919-2002................ DLB-262
Hargrove, Marion 1919-2003.......... DLB-11
Häring, Georg Wilhelm Heinrich
    (see Alexis, Willibald)
Harington, Donald 1935- DLB-152
Harington, Sir John 1560-1612....... DLB-136
Harjo, Joy 1951- DLB-120, 175
Harkness, Margaret (John Law)
    1854-1923 .... DLB-197
Harley, Edward, second Earl of Oxford
    1689-1741................... DLB-213
Harley, Robert, first Earl of Oxford
    1661-1724................... DLB-213
Harlow, Robert 1923- DLB-60
Harman, Thomas fl. 1566-1573.........DLB-136
Harness, Charles L. 1915- DLB-8
Harnett, Cynthia 1893-1981.......... DLB-161
Harnick, Sheldon 1924- DLB-265
    Tribute to Ira Gershwin............... Y-96
    Tribute to Lorenz Hart Y-95
Harper, Edith Alice Mary (see Wickham, Anna)
Harper, Fletcher 1806-1877 .... DLB-79
Harper, Frances Ellen Watkins
    1825-1911................. DLB-50, 221
Harper, Michael S. 1938- DLB-41
Harper and Brothers.................. DLB-49
Harpur, Charles 1813-1868 .... DLB-230
Harraden, Beatrice 1864-1943 .... DLB-153
George G. Harrap and Company
    Limited..................... DLB-112
Harriot, Thomas 1560-1621.......... DLB-136
Harris, Alexander 1805-1874 .... DLB-230
Harris, Benjamin ?-circa 1720........ DLB-42, 43
Harris, Christie 1907-2002 .... DLB-88
Harris, Errol E. 1908- DLB-279
Harris, Frank 1856-1931............DLB-156, 197
Harris, George Washington
    1814-1869................. DLB-3, 11, 248
Harris, Joanne 1964- DLB-271
Harris, Joel Chandler
    1848-1908 ....DLB-11, 23, 42, 78, 91
    The Joel Chandler Harris Association Y-99
Harris, Mark 1922- DLB-2; Y-80
    Tribute to Frederick A. Pottle Y-87
Harris, William Torrey 1835-1909.......DLB-270

Harris, Wilson 1921- DLB-117; CDWLB-3
Harrison, Mrs. Burton
    (see Harrison, Constance Cary)
Harrison, Charles Yale 1898-1954 .... DLB-68
Harrison, Constance Cary 1843-1920 ... DLB-221
Harrison, Frederic 1831-1923........DLB-57, 190
    "On Style in English Prose" (1898) ... DLB-57
Harrison, Harry 1925- DLB-8
James P. Harrison Company DLB-49
Harrison, Jim 1937- Y-82
Harrison, M. John 1945- DLB-261
Harrison, Mary St. Leger Kingsley
    (see Malet, Lucas)
Harrison, Paul Carter 1936- DLB-38
Harrison, Susan Frances 1859-1935 ...... DLB-99
Harrison, Tony 1937- DLB-40, 245
Harrison, William 1535-1593.......... DLB-136
Harrison, William 1933- DLB-234
Harrisse, Henry 1829-1910 .... DLB-47
The Harry Ransom Humanities Research Center
    at the University of Texas at Austin..... Y-00
Harryman, Carla 1952- DLB-193
Harsdörffer, Georg Philipp 1607-1658 ... DLB-164
Harsent, David 1942- DLB-40
Hart, Albert Bushnell 1854-1943 .... DLB-17
Hart, Anne 1768-1834 .... DLB-200
Hart, Elizabeth 1771-1833............ DLB-200
Hart, Julia Catherine 1796-1867 .... DLB-99
Hart, Lorenz 1895-1943 .... DLB-265
    Larry Hart: Still an Influence........... Y-95
    Lorenz Hart: An American Lyricist...... Y-95
    The Lorenz Hart Centenary Y-95
Hart, Moss 1904-1961 ....DLB-7, 266
Hart, Oliver 1723-1795................ DLB-31
Rupert Hart-Davis Limited............ DLB-112
Harte, Bret 1836-1902
    ....DLB-12, 64, 74, 79, 186; CDALB-3
Harte, Edward Holmead 1922- DLB-127
Harte, Houston Harriman 1927- DLB-127
Harte, Jack 1944- DLB-319
Hartlaub, Felix 1913-1945 .... DLB-56
Hartleben, Otto Erich 1864-1905....... DLB-118
Hartley, David 1705-1757 .... DLB-252
Hartley, L. P. 1895-1972............ DLB-15, 139
Hartley, Marsden 1877-1943............ DLB-54
Hartling, Peter 1933- DLB-75
Hartman, Geoffrey H. 1929- DLB-67
Hartmann, Sadakichi 1867-1944......... DLB-54
Hartmann von Aue
    circa 1160-circa 1205 ... DLB-138; CDWLB-2
Hartshorne, Charles 1897-2000 ....DLB-270
Haruf, Kent 1943- DLB-292
Harvey, Gabriel 1550?-1631 ... DLB-167, 213, 281
Harvey, Jack (see Rankin, Ian)
Harvey, Jean-Charles 1891-1967 .... DLB-88
Harvill Press Limited DLB-112

Harwood, Gwen 1920-1995........... DLB-289
Harwood, Lee 1939- DLB-40
Harwood, Ronald 1934- DLB-13
al-Hasan al-Basri 642-728............. DLB-311
Hašek, Jaroslav 1883-1923...DLB-215; CDWLB-4
Haskins, Charles Homer 1870-1937...... DLB-47
Haslam, Gerald 1937- DLB-212
Hass, Robert 1941- DLB-105, 206
Hasselstrom, Linda M. 1943- DLB-256
Hastings, Michael 1938- DLB-233
Hatar, Győző 1914- DLB-215
The Hatch-Billops Collection DLB-76
Hathaway, William 1944- DLB-120
Hatherly, Ana 1929- DLB-287
Hauch, Carsten 1790-1872 .... DLB-300
Hauff, Wilhelm 1802-1827 .... DLB-90
Hauge, Olav H. 1908-1994 .... DLB-297
Haugen, Paal-Helge 1945- DLB-297
Haugwitz, August Adolph von
    1647-1706................... DLB-168
Hauptmann, Carl 1858-1921 .... DLB-66, 118
Hauptmann, Gerhart
    1862-1946 ....DLB-66, 118; CDWLB-2
Hauser, Marianne 1910- Y-83
Havel, Václav 1936- DLB-232; CDWLB-4
Haven, Alice B. Neal 1827-1863........ DLB-250
Havergal, Frances Ridley 1836-1879 .... DLB-199
Hawes, Stephen 1475?-before 1529 ..... DLB-132
Hawker, Robert Stephen 1803-1875...... DLB-32
Hawkes, John
    1925-1998 .... DLB-2, 7, 227; Y-80, Y-98
    John Hawkes: A Tribute Y-98
    Tribute to Donald Barthelme.......... Y-89
Hawkesworth, John 1720-1773 .... DLB-142
Hawkins, Sir Anthony Hope (see Hope, Anthony)
Hawkins, Sir John 1719-1789 ....DLB-104, 142
Hawkins, Walter Everette 1883-?........ DLB-50
Hawthorne, Nathaniel 1804-1864
    ....DLB-1, 74, 183, 223, 269; DS-5; CDALB-2
    The Nathaniel Hawthorne Society....... Y-00
    The Old Manse DLB-223
Hawthorne, Sophia Peabody
    1809-1871.................. DLB-183, 239
Hay, John 1835-1905 ....DLB-12, 47, 189
Hay, John 1915- DLB-275
Hayashi Fumiko 1903-1951 .... DLB-180
Haycox, Ernest 1899-1950............ DLB-206
Haycraft, Anna Margaret (see Ellis, Alice Thomas)
Hayden, Robert
    1913-1980 .... DLB-5, 76; CDALB-1
Haydon, Benjamin Robert 1786-1846 ... DLB-110
Hayes, John Michael 1919- DLB-26
Hayley, William 1745-1820 .... DLB-93, 142
Haym, Rudolf 1821-1901............. DLB-129
Hayman, Robert 1575-1629 .... DLB-99
Hayman, Ronald 1932- DLB-155

Hayne, Paul Hamilton 1830-1886 .... DLB-3, 64, 79, 248

Hays, Mary 1760-1843 .... DLB-142, 158

Hayslip, Le Ly 1949- DLB-312

Hayward, John 1905-1965 .... DLB-201

Haywood, Eliza 1693?-1756 .... DLB-39

    Dedication of *Lasselia* [excerpt] (1723) DLB-39

    Preface to *The Disguis'd Prince* [excerpt] (1723) DLB-39

    The Tea-Table [excerpt] DLB-39

Haywood, William D. 1869-1928 .... DLB-303

Willis P. Hazard [publishing house] DLB-49

Hazlitt, William 1778-1830 .... DLB-110, 158

Hazzard, Shirley 1931- DLB-289; Y-82

Head, Bessie 1937-1986 .... DLB-117, 225; CDWLB-3

Headley, Joel T. 1813-1897 .... DLB-30, 183; DS-13

Heaney, Seamus 1939- DLB-40; Y-95; CDBLB-8

    Nobel Lecture 1994: Crediting Poetry Y-95

Heard, Nathan C. 1936- DLB-33

Hearn, Lafcadio 1850-1904 .... DLB-12, 78, 189

Hearn, Mary Anne (Marianne Farningham, Eva Hope) 1834-1909 .... DLB-240

Hearne, John 1926- DLB-117

Hearne, Samuel 1745-1792 .... DLB-99

Hearne, Thomas 1678?-1735 .... DLB-213

Hearst, William Randolph 1863-1951 .... DLB-25

Hearst, William Randolph, Jr. 1908-1993 .... DLB-127

Heartman, Charles Frederick 1883-1953 .... DLB-187

Heath, Catherine 1924- DLB-14

Heath, James Ewell 1792-1862 .... DLB-248

Heath, Roy A. K. 1926- DLB-117

Heath-Stubbs, John 1918- DLB-27

Heavysege, Charles 1816-1876 .... DLB-99

Hebbel, Friedrich 1813-1863 .... DLB-129; CDWLB-2

Hebel, Johann Peter 1760-1826 .... DLB-90

Heber, Richard 1774-1833 .... DLB-184

Hébert, Anne 1916-2000 .... DLB-68

Hébert, Jacques 1923- DLB-53

Hebreo, León circa 1460-1520 .... DLB-318

Hecht, Anthony 1923- DLB-5, 169

Hecht, Ben 1894-1964 .... DLB-7, 9, 25, 26, 28, 86

Hecker, Isaac Thomas 1819-1888 .... DLB-1, 243

Hedge, Frederic Henry 1805-1890 .... DLB-1, 59, 243; DS-5

Hefner, Hugh M. 1926- DLB-137

Hegel, Georg Wilhelm Friedrich 1770-1831 .... DLB-90

Heiberg, Johan Ludvig 1791-1860 .... DLB-300

Heiberg, Johanne Luise 1812-1890 .... DLB-300

Heide, Robert 1939- DLB-249

Heidegger, Martin 1889-1976 .... DLB-296

Heidish, Marcy 1947- Y-82

Heißenbüttel, Helmut 1921-1996 .... DLB-75

Heike monogatari DLB-203

Hein, Christoph 1944- DLB-124; CDWLB-2

Hein, Piet 1905-1996 .... DLB-214

Heine, Heinrich 1797-1856 .... DLB-90; CDWLB-2

Heinemann, Larry 1944- DS-9

William Heinemann Limited DLB-112

Heinesen, William 1900-1991 .... DLB-214

Heinlein, Robert A. 1907-1988 .... DLB-8

Heinrich, Willi 1920- DLB-75

Heinrich Julius of Brunswick| 1564-1613 .... DLB-164

Heinrich von dem Türlîn fl. circa 1230 .... DLB-138

Heinrich von Melk fl. after 1160 .... DLB-148

Heinrich von Veldeke circa 1145-circa 1190 .... DLB-138

Heinse, Wilhelm 1746-1803 .... DLB-94

Heinz, W. C. 1915- DLB-171

Heiskell, John 1872-1972 .... DLB-127

Hejinian, Lyn 1941- DLB-165

Helder, Herberto 1930- DLB-287

Heliand circa 850 .... DLB-148

Heller, Joseph 1923-1999 .... DLB-2, 28, 227; Y-80, 99, 02

    Excerpts from Joseph Heller's USC Address, "The Literature of Despair" Y-96

    Remembering Joe Heller, by William Price Fox Y-99

    A Tribute to Joseph Heller Y-99

Heller, Michael 1937- DLB-165

Hellman, Lillian 1906-1984 .... DLB-7, 228; Y-84

Hellwig, Johann 1609-1674 .... DLB-164

Helprin, Mark 1947- Y-85; CDALB-7

Helvétius, Claude-Adrien 1715-1771 .... DLB-313

    The Spirit of Laws DLB-314

Helwig, David 1938- DLB-60

Hemans, Felicia 1793-1835 .... DLB-96

Hemenway, Abby Maria 1828-1890 .... DLB-243

Hemingway, Ernest 1899-1961 .... DLB-4, 9, 102, 210, 316; Y-81, 87, 99; DS-1, 15, 16; CDALB-4

    A Centennial Celebration Y-99

    Come to Papa Y-99

    The Ernest Hemingway Collection at the John F. Kennedy Library Y-99

    Ernest Hemingway Declines to Introduce *War and Peace* Y-01

    Ernest Hemingway's Reaction to James Gould Cozzens Y-98

    Ernest Hemingway's Toronto Journalism Revisited: With Three Previously Unrecorded Stories Y-92

    Falsifying Hemingway Y-96

    A Farewell to Arms (Documentary) DLB-308

    Hemingway Centenary Celebration at the JFK Library Y-99

    The Hemingway/Fenton Correspondence Y-02

    Hemingway in the JFK Y-99

    The Hemingway Letters Project Finds an Editor Y-02

    Hemingway Salesmen's Dummies Y-00

    Hemingway: Twenty-Five Years Later Y-85

    A Literary Archaeologist Digs On: A Brief Interview with Michael Reynolds Y-99

    Not Immediately Discernible... but Eventually Quite Clear: The *First Light* and *Final Years* of Hemingway's Centenary Y-99

    Packaging Papa: *The Garden of Eden* Y-86

    Second International Hemingway Colloquium: Cuba Y-98

Hémon, Louis 1880-1913 .... DLB-92

Hempel, Amy 1951- DLB-218

Hempel, Carl G. 1905-1997 .... DLB-279

Hemphill, Paul 1936- Y-87

Hénault, Gilles 1920-1996 .... DLB-88

Henchman, Daniel 1689-1761 .... DLB-24

Henderson, Alice Corbin 1881-1949 .... DLB-54

Henderson, Archibald 1877-1963 .... DLB-103

Henderson, David 1942- DLB-41

Henderson, George Wylie 1904-1965 .... DLB-51

Henderson, Zenna 1917-1983 .... DLB-8

Henighan, Tom 1934- DLB-251

Henisch, Peter 1943- DLB-85

Henley, Beth 1952- Y-86

Henley, William Ernest 1849-1903 .... DLB-19

Henniker, Florence 1855-1923 .... DLB-135

Henning, Rachel 1826-1914 .... DLB-230

Henningsen, Agnes 1868-1962 .... DLB-214

Henry, Alexander 1739-1824 .... DLB-99

Henry, Buck 1930- DLB-26

Henry, Marguerite 1902-1997 .... DLB-22

Henry, O. (see Porter, William Sydney)

Henry, Robert Selph 1889-1970 .... DLB-17

Henry, Will (see Allen, Henry W.)

Henry VIII of England 1491-1547 .... DLB-132

Henry of Ghent circa 1217-1229 - 1293 .... DLB-115

Henryson, Robert 1420s or 1430s-circa 1505 .... DLB-146

Henschke, Alfred (see Klabund)

Hensher, Philip 1965- DLB-267

Hensley, Sophie Almon 1866-1946 .... DLB-99

Henson, Lance 1944- DLB-175

Henty, G. A. 1832-1902 .... DLB-18, 141

    The Henty Society Y-98

Hentz, Caroline Lee 1800-1856 .... DLB-3, 248

Heraclitus fl. circa 500 B.C. DLB-176

Herbert, Agnes circa 1880-1960 .... DLB-174

Herbert, Alan Patrick 1890-1971 .... DLB-10, 191

Herbert, Edward, Lord, of Cherbury 1582-1648 .... DLB-121, 151, 252

Herbert, Frank 1920-1986 .... DLB-8; CDALB-7

Cumulative Index

Herbert, George 1593-1633 . . DLB-126; CDBLB-1
Herbert, Henry William 1807-1858 . . . . DLB-3, 73
Herbert, John 1926-2001 . . . . DLB-53
Herbert, Mary Sidney, Countess of Pembroke (see Sidney, Mary)
Herbert, Xavier 1901-1984. . . . . DLB-260
Herbert, Zbigniew 1924-1998 . . . . DLB-232; CDWLB-4
Herbst, Josephine 1892-1969 . . . . DLB-9
Herburger, Gunter 1932- DLB-75, 124
Herculano, Alexandre 1810-1877 . . . . . . DLB-287
Hercules, Frank E. M. 1917-1996 . . . . DLB-33
Herder, Johann Gottfried 1744-1803 . . . . . DLB-97
B. Herder Book Company DLB-49
Heredia, José-María de 1842-1905 . . . . . DLB-217
Herford, Charles Harold 1853-1931 . . . . DLB-149
Hergesheimer, Joseph 1880-1954 . . . . . DLB-9, 102
Heritage Press. DLB-46
Hermann the Lame 1013-1054. . . . . DLB-148
Hermes, Johann Timotheu 1738-1821 . . . . DLB-97
Hermlin, Stephan 1915-1997 . . . . DLB-69
Hernández, Alfonso C. 1938- DLB-122
Hernández, Inés 1947- DLB-122
Hernández, Miguel 1910-1942 . . . . DLB-134
Hernton, Calvin C. 1932- DLB-38
Herodotus circa 484 B.C.-circa 420 B.C. DLB-176; CDWLB-1
Heron, Robert 1764-1807 . . . . DLB-142
Herr, Michael 1940- DLB-185
Herrera, Darío 1870-1914. . . . . DLB-290
Herrera, Fernando de 1534?-1597 . . . . . DLB-318
Herrera, Juan Felipe 1948- DLB-122
E. R. Herrick and Company DLB-49
Herrick, Robert 1591-1674 . . . . DLB-126
Herrick, Robert 1868-1938. . . . . . . .DLB-9, 12, 78
Herrick, William 1915-2004 . . . . Y-83
Herrmann, John 1900-1959 . . . . DLB-4
Hersey, John 1914-1993. . . .DLB-6, 185, 278, 299; CDALB-7
Hertel, François 1905-1985. . . . . DLB-68
Hervé-Bazin, Jean Pierre Marie (see Bazin, Hervé)
Hervey, John, Lord 1696-1743 . . . . DLB-101
Herwig, Georg 1817-1875 . . . . DLB-133
Herzen, Alexander (Aleksandr Ivanovich Gersten) 1812-1870 . . . . .DLB-277
Herzog, Emile Salomon Wilhelm (see Maurois, André)
Hesiod eighth century B.C.. . . . . .DLB-176
Hesse, Hermann 1877-1962 . . . . DLB-66; CDWLB-2
Hessus, Eobanus 1488-1540. . . . . .DLB-179
Heureka! (see Kertész, Imre and Nobel Prize in Literature: 2002) Y-02
Hewat, Alexander circa 1743-circa 1824. . . DLB-30
Hewett, Dorothy 1923-2002. . . . . DLB-289
Hewitt, John 1907-1987. . . . . DLB-27
Hewlett, Maurice 1861-1923 . . . . . . DLB-34, 156

Heyen, William 1940- DLB-5
Heyer, Georgette 1902-1974. . . . . . . .DLB-77, 191
Heym, Stefan 1913-2001 . . . . DLB-69
Heyse, Paul 1830-1914. . . . . DLB-129
Heytesbury, William circa 1310-1372 or 1373 . . . . DLB-115
Heyward, Dorothy 1890-1961 . . . . .DLB-7, 249
Heyward, DuBose 1885-1940 . . .DLB-7, 9, 45, 249
Heywood, John 1497?-1580? DLB-136
Heywood, Thomas 1573 or 1574-1641. . . . DLB-62
Hiaasen, Carl 1953- DLB-292
Hibberd, Jack 1940- DLB-289
Hibbs, Ben 1901-1975. . . . . DLB-137
"The Saturday Evening Post reaffirms a policy," Ben Hibb's Statement in *The Saturday Evening Post* (16 May 1942). DLB-137
Hichens, Robert S. 1864-1950 . . . . DLB-153
Hickey, Emily 1845-1924 . . . . DLB-199
Hickman, William Albert 1877-1957. . . . . DLB-92
Hicks, Granville 1901-1982 . . . . DLB-246
Hidalgo, José Luis 1919-1947 . . . . DLB-108
Hiebert, Paul 1892-1987. . . . . DLB-68
Hieng, Andrej 1925- DLB-181
Hierro, José 1922-2002. . . . . DLB-108
Higgins, Aidan 1927- DLB-14
Higgins, Colin 1941-1988. . . . . DLB-26
Higgins, George V. 1939-1999 . . . . .DLB-2; Y-81, 98–99
  Afterword [in response to Cozzen's *Mens Rea* (or Something)]. Y-97
  At End of Day: The Last George V. Higgins Novel Y-99
  The Books of George V. Higgins: A Checklist of Editions and Printings Y-00
  George V. Higgins in Class Y-02
  Tribute to Alfred A. Knopf Y-84
  Tributes to George V. Higgins Y-99
  "What You Lose on the Swings You Make Up on the Merry-Go-Round" . . . Y-99
Higginson, Thomas Wentworth 1823-1911 . . . . DLB-1, 64, 243
Highsmith, Patricia 1921-1995 . . . . DLB-306
Highwater, Jamake 1942?- DLB-52; Y-85
Hijuelos, Oscar 1951- DLB-145
Hildegard von Bingen 1098-1179 . . . . . . DLB-148
Das Hildesbrandslied circa 820. . . . . DLB-148; CDWLB-2
Hildesheimer, Wolfgang 1916-1991 . . DLB-69, 124
Hildreth, Richard 1807-1865 . . DLB-1, 30, 59, 235
Hill, Aaron 1685-1750 . . . . DLB-84
Hill, Geoffrey 1932- DLB-40; CDBLB-8
George M. Hill Company DLB-49
Hill, "Sir" John 1714?-1775 . . . . DLB-39
Lawrence Hill and Company, Publishers. DLB-46
Hill, Joe 1879-1915 . . . . DLB-303

Hill, Leslie 1880-1960. . . . . DLB-51
Hill, Reginald 1936- DLB-276
Hill, Susan 1942- DLB-14, 139
Hill, Walter 1942- DLB-44
Hill and Wang DLB-46
Hillberry, Conrad 1928- DLB-120
Hillerman, Tony 1925- DLB-206, 306
Hilliard, Gray and Company DLB-49
Hills, Lee 1906-2000. . . . . .DLB-127
Hillyer, Robert 1895-1961 . . . . DLB-54
Hilsenrath, Edgar 1926- DLB-299
Hilton, James 1900-1954 . . . . .DLB-34, 77
Hilton, Walter died 1396 . . . . DLB-146
Hilton and Company DLB-49
Himes, Chester 1909-1984. . . .DLB-2, 76, 143, 226
Joseph Hindmarsh [publishing house] DLB-170
Hine, Daryl 1936- DLB-60
Hingley, Ronald 1920- DLB-155
Hinojosa-Smith, Rolando 1929- DLB-82
Hinton, S. E. 1948- CDALB-7
Hippel, Theodor Gottlieb von 1741-1796. . . . . DLB-97
Hippius, Zinaida Nikolaevna 1869-1945 . . . . DLB-295
Hippocrates of Cos fl. circa 425 B.C.. . . . . .DLB-176; CDWLB-1
Hirabayashi Taiko 1905-1972 . . . . DLB-180
Hirsch, E. D., Jr. 1928- DLB-67
Hirsch, Edward 1950- DLB-120
"Historical Novel," The Holocaust DLB-299
Hoagland, Edward 1932- DLB-6
Hoagland, Everett H., III 1942- DLB-41
Hoban, Russell 1925- DLB-52; Y-90
Hobbes, Thomas 1588-1679 . . . DLB-151, 252, 281
Hobby, Oveta 1905-1995. . . . . .DLB-127
Hobby, William 1878-1964 . . . . .DLB-127
Hobsbaum, Philip 1932- DLB-40
Hobsbawm, Eric (Francis Newton) 1917- DLB-296
Hobson, Laura Z. 1900-1986 . . . . DLB-28
Hobson, Sarah 1947- DLB-204
Hoby, Thomas 1530-1566 . . . . DLB-132
Hoccleve, Thomas circa 1368-circa 1437 . . . . DLB-146
Hoch, Edward D. 1930- DLB-306
Hochhuth, Rolf 1931- DLB-124
Hochman, Sandra 1936- DLB-5
Hocken, Thomas Morland 1836-1910 . . . DLB-184
Hocking, William Ernest 1873-1966. . . . .DLB-270
Hodder and Stoughton, Limited. DLB-106
Hodgins, Jack 1938- DLB-60
Hodgman, Helen 1945- DLB-14
Hodgskin, Thomas 1787-1869 . . . . DLB-158
Hodgson, Ralph 1871-1962 . . . . DLB-19
Hodgson, William Hope 1877-1918. . . . . .DLB-70, 153, 156, 178

Hoe, Robert, III 1839-1909 . . . . .DLB-187	Holloway, John 1920- DLB-27	Hope, Laurence (Adela Florence Cory Nicolson) 1865-1904 . . . . .DLB-240
Hoeg, Peter 1957- DLB-214	Holloway House Publishing Company DLB-46	Hopkins, Ellice 1836-1904. . . . . .DLB-190
Hoel, Sigurd 1890-1960. . . . . .DLB-297	Holme, Constance 1880-1955 . . . . .DLB-34	Hopkins, Gerard Manley 1844-1889 . . . . .DLB-35, 57; CDBLB-5
Hoem, Edvard 1949- DLB-297	Holmes, Abraham S. 1821?-1908 . . . . .DLB-99	Hopkins, John ?-1570. . . . . .DLB-132
Hoffenstein, Samuel 1890-1947 . . . . .DLB-11	Holmes, John Clellon 1926-1988. . . . . DLB-16, 237	Hopkins, John H., and Son DLB-46
Hoffman, Alice 1952- DLB-292	"Four Essays on the Beat Generation" DLB-16	Hopkins, Lemuel 1750-1801 . . . . .DLB-37
Hoffman, Charles Fenno 1806-1884 . . .DLB-3, 250	Holmes, Mary Jane 1825-1907 . . . . .DLB-202, 221	Hopkins, Pauline Elizabeth 1859-1930 . . . .DLB-50
Hoffman, Daniel 1923- DLB-5	Holmes, Oliver Wendell 1809-1894 . . . . . . .DLB-1, 189, 235; CDALB-2	Hopkins, Samuel 1721-1803 . . . . .DLB-31
Tribute to Robert Graves Y-85	Holmes, Richard 1945- DLB-155	Hopkinson, Francis 1737-1791 . . . . .DLB-31
Hoffmann, E. T. A. 1776-1822 . . . . .DLB-90; CDWLB-2	Holmes, Thomas James 1874-1959 . . . . . .DLB-187	Hopkinson, Nalo 1960- DLB-251
Hoffman, Frank B. 1888-1958 . . . . .DLB-188	The Holocaust "Historical Novel". DLB-299	Hopper, Nora (Mrs. Nora Chesson) 1871-1906 .DLB-240
Hoffman, William 1925- DLB-234	Holocaust Fiction, Postmodern DLB-299	Hoppin, Augustus 1828-1896 . . . . .DLB-188
Tribute to Paxton Davis Y-94	Holocaust Novel, The "Second-Generation" DLB-299	Hora, Josef 1891-1945 . . . . . . .DLB-215; CDWLB-4
Hoffmanswaldau, Christian Hoffman von 1616-1679 . . . . .DLB-168	Holroyd, Michael 1935- DLB-155; Y-99	Horace 65 B.C.-8 B.C. DLB-211; CDWLB-1
Hofmann, Michael 1957- DLB-40	Holst, Hermann E. von 1841-1904 . . . . . . .DLB-47	Horgan, Paul 1903-1995 . . . . .DLB-102, 212; Y-85
Hofmannsthal, Hugo von 1874-1929 . . . . .DLB-81, 118; CDWLB-2	Holt, John 1721-1784 . . . . .DLB-43	Tribute to Alfred A. Knopf Y-84
Hofmo, Gunvor 1921-1995 . . . . .DLB-297	Henry Holt and Company DLB-49, 284	Horizon Press DLB-46
Hofstadter, Richard 1916-1970 . . . . . DLB-17, 246	Holt, Rinehart and Winston DLB-46	Horkheimer, Max 1895-1973. . . . . .DLB-296
Hogan, Desmond 1950- DLB-14, 319	Holtby, Winifred 1898-1935 . . . . .DLB-191	Hornby, C. H. St. John 1867-1946. . . . . . .DLB-201
Hogan, Linda 1947- DLB-175	Holthusen, Hans Egon 1913-1997 . . . . . . .DLB-69	Hornby, Nick 1957- DLB-207
Hogan and Thompson. DLB-49	Hölty, Ludwig Christoph Heinrich 1748-1776. . . . . .DLB-94	Horne, Frank 1899-1974 . . . . .DLB-51
Hogarth Press DLB-112; DS-10	Holub, Miroslav 1923-1998 . . . . .DLB-232; CDWLB-4	Horne, Richard Henry (Hengist) 1802 or 1803-1884 . . . . .DLB-32
Hogg, James 1770-1835 . . . . .DLB-93, 116, 159	Holz, Arno 1863-1929 . . . . .DLB-118	Horne, Thomas 1608-1654 . . . . .DLB-281
Hohberg, Wolfgang Helmhard Freiherr von 1612-1688 . . . . .DLB-168	Home, Henry, Lord Kames (see Kames, Henry Home, Lord)	Horney, Karen 1885-1952. . . . . .DLB-246
von Hohenheim, Philippus Aureolus Theophrastus Bombastus (see Paracelsus)	Home, John 1722-1808 . . . . .DLB-84	Hornung, E. W. 1866-1921. . . . . .DLB-70
Hohl, Ludwig 1904-1980. . . . . .DLB-56	Home, William Douglas 1912-1992 . . . . . .DLB-13	Horovitz, Israel 1939- DLB-7
Højholt, Per 1928- DLB-214	Home Publishing Company DLB-49	Horta, Maria Teresa (see The Three Marias: A Landmark Case in Portuguese Literary History)
Holan, Vladimir 1905-1980. . . . . .DLB-215	Homer circa eighth-seventh centuries B.C. DLB-176; CDWLB-1	Horton, George Moses 1797?-1883? DLB-50
d'Holbach, Paul Henri Thiry, baron 1723-1789 . . . . .DLB-313	Homer, Winslow 1836-1910 . . . . .DLB-188	George Moses Horton Society Y-99
The System of Nature (as Jean-Baptiste de Mirabaud). DLB-314	Homes, Geoffrey (see Mainwaring, Daniel)	Horváth, Ödön von 1901-1938. . . . . .DLB-85, 124
Holberg, Ludvig 1684-1754 . . . . .DLB-300	Honan, Park 1928- DLB-111	Horwood, Harold 1923- DLB-60
Holbrook, David 1923- DLB-14, 40	Hone, William 1780-1842 . . . . .DLB-110, 158	E. and E. Hosford [publishing house] DLB-49
Holcroft, Thomas 1745-1809 . . . . .DLB-39, 89, 158	Hongo, Garrett Kaoru 1951- DLB-120, 312	Hoskens, Jane Fenn 1693-1770?. DLB-200
Preface to Alwyn (1780) DLB-39	Honig, Edwin 1919- DLB-5	Hoskyns, John circa 1566-1638 . . . . . .DLB-121, 281
Holden, Jonathan 1941- DLB-105	Hood, Hugh 1928-2000. . . . . .DLB-53	Hosokawa Yūsai 1535-1610 . . . . .DLB-203
"Contemporary Verse Story-telling" . . .DLB-105	Hood, Mary 1946- DLB-234	Hospers, John 1918- DLB-279
Holden, Molly 1927-1981 . . . . .DLB-40	Hood, Thomas 1799-1845 . . . . .DLB-96	Hostovský, Egon 1908-1973 . . . . .DLB-215
Hölderlin, Friedrich 1770-1843 . . . . .DLB-90; CDWLB-2	Hook, Sidney 1902-1989 . . . . .DLB-279	Hotchkiss and Company. DLB-49
Holdstock, Robert 1948- DLB-261	Hook, Theodore 1788-1841. . . . . .DLB-116	Hough, Emerson 1857-1923 . . . . .DLB-9, 212
Holiday House. DLB-46	Hooker, Jeremy 1941- DLB-40	Houghton, Stanley 1881-1913 . . . . .DLB-10
Holinshed, Raphael died 1580. . . . . .DLB-167	Hooker, Richard 1554-1600 . . . . .DLB-132	Houghton Mifflin Company DLB-49
Holland, J. G. 1819-1881 . . . . DS-13	Hooker, Thomas 1586-1647 . . . . .DLB-24	Hours at Home DS-13
Holland, Norman N. 1927- DLB-67	hooks, bell 1952- DLB-246	Household, Geoffrey 1900-1988 . . . . .DLB-87
Hollander, John 1929- DLB-5	Hooper, Johnson Jones 1815-1862 . . . . .DLB-3, 11, 248	Housman, A. E. 1859-1936 . . . .DLB-19; CDBLB-5
Holley, Marietta 1836-1926 . . . . .DLB-11	Hope, A. D. 1907-2000 . . . . .DLB-289	Housman, Laurence 1865-1959. . . . . .DLB-10
Hollinghurst, Alan 1954- DLB-207	Hope, Anthony 1863-1933 . . . . .DLB-153, 156	Houston, Pam 1962- DLB-244
Hollingsworth, Margaret 1940- DLB-60	Hope, Christopher 1944- DLB-225	Houwald, Ernst von 1778-1845 . . . . .DLB-90
Hollo, Anselm 1934- DLB-40	Hope, Eva (see Hearn, Mary Anne)	Hovey, Richard 1864-1900 . . . . .DLB-54
Holloway, Emory 1885-1977. . . . . .DLB-103		Howard, Donald R. 1927-1987 . . . . .DLB-111
		Howard, Maureen 1930- Y-83

Cumulative Index

Howard, Richard 1929- DLB-5
Howard, Roy W. 1883-1964 .... DLB-29
Howard, Sidney 1891-1939 .... DLB-7, 26, 249
Howard, Thomas, second Earl of Arundel
  1585-1646 .... DLB-213
Howe, E. W. 1853-1937 .... DLB-12, 25
Howe, Henry 1816-1893 .... DLB-30
Howe, Irving 1920-1993 .... DLB-67
Howe, Joseph 1804-1873 .... DLB-99
Howe, Julia Ward 1819-1910 .... DLB-1, 189, 235
Howe, Percival Presland 1886-1944 ..... DLB-149
Howe, Susan 1937- DLB-120
Howell, Clark, Sr. 1863-1936 .... DLB-25
Howell, Evan P. 1839-1905 .... DLB-23
Howell, James 1594?-1666 .... DLB-151
Howell, Soskin and Company DLB-46
Howell, Warren Richardson
  1912-1984 .... DLB-140
Howells, William Dean 1837-1920
  .... DLB-12, 64, 74, 79, 189; CDALB-3
  Introduction to Paul Laurence
  Dunbar's *Lyrics of Lowly Life*
  (1896) DLB-50
  The William Dean Howells Society Y-01
Howitt, Mary 1799-1888 .... DLB-110, 199
Howitt, William 1792-1879 .... DLB-110
Hoyem, Andrew 1935- DLB-5
Hoyers, Anna Ovena 1584-1655 ...... DLB-164
Hoyle, Fred 1915-2001 .... DLB-261
Hoyos, Angela de 1940- DLB-82
Henry Hoyt [publishing house] DLB-49
Hoyt, Palmer 1897-1979 .... DLB-127
Hrabal, Bohumil 1914-1997 .... DLB-232
Hrabanus Maurus 776?-856 .... DLB-148
Hronský, Josef Cíger 1896-1960 .... DLB-215
Hrotsvit of Gandersheim
  circa 935-circa 1000 .... DLB-148
Hubbard, Elbert 1856-1915 .... DLB-91
Hubbard, Kin 1868-1930 .... DLB-11
Hubbard, William circa 1621-1704 .... DLB-24
Huber, Therese 1764-1829 .... DLB-90
Huch, Friedrich 1873-1913 .... DLB-66
Huch, Ricarda 1864-1947 .... DLB-66
Huddle, David 1942- DLB-130
Hudgins, Andrew 1951- DLB-120, 282
Hudson, Henry Norman 1814-1886 ...... DLB-64
Hudson, Stephen 1868?-1944 .... DLB-197
Hudson, W. H. 1841-1922 ...... DLB-98, 153, 174
Hudson and Goodwin DLB-49
Huebsch, B. W., oral history Y-99
B. W. Huebsch [publishing house] DLB-46
Hueffer, Oliver Madox 1876-1931 ...... DLB-197
Huet, Pierre Daniel
  Preface to *The History of Romances*
  (1715) DLB-39
Hugh of St. Victor circa 1096-1141 ..... DLB-208
Hughes, David 1930- DLB-14

Hughes, Dusty 1947- DLB-233
Hughes, Hatcher 1881-1945 .... DLB-249
Hughes, John 1677-1720 .... DLB-84
Hughes, Langston 1902-1967 ..... DLB-4, 7, 48,
  51, 86, 228, 315; DS-15; CDALB-5
Hughes, Richard 1900-1976 .... DLB-15, 161
Hughes, Ted 1930-1998 .... DLB-40, 161
Hughes, Thomas 1822-1896 .... DLB-18, 163
Hugo, Richard 1923-1982 .... DLB-5, 206
Hugo, Victor 1802-1885 ...... DLB-119, 192, 217
Hugo Awards and Nebula Awards DLB-8
Huidobro, Vicente 1893-1948 .... DLB-283
Hull, Richard 1896-1973 .... DLB-77
Hulda (Unnur Benediktsdóttir Bjarklind)
  1881-1946 .... DLB-293
Hulme, T. E. 1883-1917 .... DLB-19
Hulton, Anne ?-1779? DLB-200
Humanism, Sixteenth-Century
  Spanish DLB-318
Humboldt, Alexander von 1769-1859 .... DLB-90
Humboldt, Wilhelm von 1767-1835 ..... DLB-90
Hume, David 1711-1776 .... DLB-104, 252
Hume, Fergus 1859-1932 .... DLB-70
Hume, Sophia 1702-1774 .... DLB-200
Hume-Rothery, Mary Catherine
  1824-1885 .... DLB-240
Humishuma
  (see Mourning Dove)
Hummer, T. R. 1950- DLB-120
Humor
  American Humor: A Historical
  Survey DLB-11
  American Humor Studies Association Y-99
  The Comic Tradition Continued
  [in the British Novel] DLB-15
  Humorous Book Illustration DLB-11
  International Society for Humor Studies .. Y-99
  Newspaper Syndication of American
  Humor DLB-11
  Selected Humorous Magazines
  (1820-1950) DLB-11
Bruce Humphries [publishing house] DLB-46
Humphrey, Duke of Gloucester
  1391-1447 .... DLB-213
Humphrey, William
  1924-1997 .... DLB-6, 212, 234, 278
Humphreys, David 1752-1818 .... DLB-37
Humphreys, Emyr 1919- DLB-15
Humphreys, Josephine 1945- DLB-292
Hunayn ibn Ishaq 809-873 or 877 ..... DLB-311
Huncke, Herbert 1915-1996 .... DLB-16
Huneker, James Gibbons
  1857-1921 .... DLB-71
Hunold, Christian Friedrich
  1681-1721 .... DLB-168
Hunt, Irene 1907- DLB-52
Hunt, Leigh 1784-1859 .... DLB-96, 110, 144
Hunt, Violet 1862-1942 .... DLB-162, 197
Hunt, William Gibbes 1791-1833 .... DLB-73

Hunter, Evan (Ed McBain)
  1926-2005 .... DLB-306; Y-82
  Tribute to John D. MacDonald Y-86
Hunter, Jim 1939- DLB-14
Hunter, Kristin 1931- DLB-33
  Tribute to Julian Mayfield Y-84
Hunter, Mollie 1922- DLB-161
Hunter, N. C. 1908-1971 .... DLB-10
Hunter-Duvar, John 1821-1899 .... DLB-99
Huntington, Henry E. 1850-1927 ...... DLB-140
  The Henry E. Huntington Library Y-92
Huntington, Susan Mansfield
  1791-1823 .... DLB-200
Hurd and Houghton DLB-49
Hurst, Fannie 1889-1968 .... DLB-86
Hurst and Blackett DLB-106
Hurst and Company DLB-49
Hurston, Zora Neale
  1901?-1960 .... DLB-51, 86; CDALB-7
Husserl, Edmund 1859-1938 .... DLB-296
Husson, Jules-François-Félix (see Champfleury)
Huston, John 1906-1987 .... DLB-26
Hutcheson, Francis 1694-1746 ..... DLB-31, 252
Hutchinson, Ron 1947- DLB-245
Hutchinson, R. C. 1907-1975 .... DLB-191
Hutchinson, Thomas 1711-1780 ..... DLB-30, 31
Hutchinson and Company
  (Publishers) Limited DLB-112
Huth, Angela 1938- DLB-271
Hutton, Richard Holt
  1826-1897 .... DLB-57
von Hutten, Ulrich 1488-1523 .... DLB-179
Huxley, Aldous 1894-1963
  ...... DLB-36, 100, 162, 195, 255; CDBLB-6
Huxley, Elspeth Josceline
  1907-1997 .... DLB-77, 204
Huxley, T. H. 1825-1895 .... DLB-57
Huyghue, Douglas Smith 1816-1891 ..... DLB-99
Huysmans, Joris-Karl 1848-1907 .... DLB-123
Hwang, David Henry
  1957- DLB-212, 228, 312
Hyde, Donald 1909-1966 .... DLB-187
Hyde, Mary 1912-2003 .... DLB-187
Hyman, Trina Schart 1939- DLB-61

I

Iavorsky, Stefan 1658-1722 .... DLB-150
Iazykov, Nikolai Mikhailovich
  1803-1846 .... DLB-205
Ibáñez, Armando P. 1949- DLB-209
Ibáñez, Sara de 1909-1971 .... DLB-290
Ibarbourou, Juana de 1892-1979 ...... DLB-290
Ibn Abi Tahir Tayfur 820-893 .... DLB-311
Ibn Qutaybah 828-889 .... DLB-311
Ibn al-Rumi 836-896 .... DLB-311
Ibn Sa'd 784-845 .... DLB-311
Ibrahim al-Mawsili 742 or 743-803 or 804 DLB-311

Ibn Bajja circa 1077-1138	DLB-115	
Ibn Gabirol, Solomon circa 1021-circa 1058	DLB-115	
Ibn al-Muqaffa' circa 723-759	DLB-311	
Ibn al-Mu'tazz 861-908	DLB-311	
Ibuse Masuji 1898-1993	DLB-180	
Ichijō Kanera (see Ichijō Kaneyoshi)		
Ichijō Kaneyoshi (Ichijō Kanera) 1402-1481	DLB-203	
Iffland, August Wilhelm 1759-1814	DLB-94	
Iggulden, John 1917-	DLB-289	
Ignatieff, Michael 1947-	DLB-267	
Ignatow, David 1914-1997	DLB-5	
Ike, Chukwuemeka 1931-	DLB-157	
Ikkyū Sōjun 1394-1481	DLB-203	
Iles, Francis (see Berkeley, Anthony)		
Il'f, Il'ia (Il'ia Arnol'dovich Fainzil'berg) 1897-1937	DLB-272	
Illich, Ivan 1926-2002	DLB-242	
Illustration		
Children's Book Illustration in the Twentieth Century	DLB-61	
Children's Illustrators, 1800-1880	DLB-163	
Early American Book Illustration	DLB-49	
The Iconography of Science-Fiction Art	DLB-8	
The Illustration of Early German Literary Manuscripts, circa 1150-circa 1300	DLB-148	
Minor Illustrators, 1880-1914	DLB-141	
Illyés, Gyula 1902-1983	DLB-215; CDWLB-4	
Imbs, Bravig 1904-1946	DLB-4; DS-15	
Imbuga, Francis D. 1947-	DLB-157	
Immermann, Karl 1796-1840	DLB-133	
Imru' al-Qays circa 526-circa 565	DLB-311	
Inchbald, Elizabeth 1753-1821	DLB-39, 89	
Indiana University Press	Y-02	
Ingamells, Rex 1913-1955	DLB-260	
Inge, William 1913-1973	DLB-7, 249; CDALB-1	
Ingelow, Jean 1820-1897	DLB-35, 163	
Ingemann, B. S. 1789-1862	DLB-300	
Ingersoll, Ralph 1900-1985	DLB-127	
The Ingersoll Prizes	Y-84	
Ingoldsby, Thomas (see Barham, Richard Harris)		
Ingraham, Joseph Holt 1809-1860	DLB-3, 248	
Inman, John 1805-1850	DLB-73	
Innerhofer, Franz 1944-	DLB-85	
Innes, Michael (J. I. M. Stewart) 1906-1994	DLB-276	
Innis, Harold Adams 1894-1952	DLB-88	
Innis, Mary Quayle 1899-1972	DLB-88	
Inō Sōgi 1421-1502	DLB-203	
Inoue Yasushi 1907-1991	DLB-182	
"The Greatness of Southern Literature": League of the South Institute for the Study of Southern Culture and History	Y-02	
International Publishers Company	DLB-46	
Internet (publishing and commerce)		
Author Websites	Y-97	
The Book Trade and the Internet	Y-00	
E-Books Turn the Corner	Y-98	
The E-Researcher: Possibilities and Pitfalls	Y-00	
Interviews on E-publishing	Y-00	
John Updike on the Internet	Y-97	
LitCheck Website	Y-01	
Virtual Books and Enemies of Books	Y-00	
Interviews		
Adoff, Arnold	Y-01	
Aldridge, John W.	Y-91	
Anastas, Benjamin	Y-98	
Baker, Nicholson	Y-00	
Bank, Melissa	Y-98	
Bass, T. J.	Y-80	
Bernstein, Harriet	Y-82	
Betts, Doris	Y-82	
Bosworth, David	Y-82	
Bottoms, David	Y-83	
Bowers, Fredson	Y-80	
Burnshaw, Stanley	Y-97	
Carpenter, Humphrey	Y-84, 99	
Carr, Virginia Spencer	Y-00	
Carver, Raymond	Y-83	
Cherry, Kelly	Y-83	
Conroy, Jack	Y-81	
Coppel, Alfred	Y-83	
Cowley, Malcolm	Y-81	
Davis, Paxton	Y-89	
Devito, Carlo	Y-94	
De Vries, Peter	Y-82	
Dickey, James	Y-82	
Donald, David Herbert	Y-87	
Editors, Conversations with	Y-95	
Ellroy, James	Y-91	
Fancher, Betsy	Y-83	
Faust, Irvin	Y-00	
Fulton, Len	Y-86	
Furst, Alan	Y-01	
Garrett, George	Y-83	
Gelfman, Jane	Y-93	
Goldwater, Walter	Y-93	
Gores, Joe	Y-02	
Greenfield, George	Y-91	
Griffin, Bryan	Y-81	
Groom, Winston	Y-01	
Guilds, John Caldwell	Y-92	
Hamilton, Virginia	Y-01	
Hardin, James	Y-92	
Harris, Mark	Y-80	
Harrison, Jim	Y-82	
Hazzard, Shirley	Y-82	
Herrick, William	Y-01	
Higgins, George V.	Y-98	
Hoban, Russell	Y-90	
Holroyd, Michael	Y-99	
Horowitz, Glen	Y-90	
Iggulden, John	Y-01	
Jakes, John	Y-83	
Jenkinson, Edward B.	Y-82	
Jenks, Tom	Y-86	
Kaplan, Justin	Y-86	
King, Florence	Y-85	
Klopfer, Donald S.	Y-97	
Krug, Judith	Y-82	
Lamm, Donald	Y-95	
Laughlin, James	Y-96	
Lawrence, Starling	Y-95	
Lindsay, Jack	Y-84	
Mailer, Norman	Y-97	
Manchester, William	Y-85	
Max, D. T.	Y-94	
McCormack, Thomas	Y-98	
McNamara, Katherine	Y-97	
Mellen, Joan	Y-94	
Menaker, Daniel	Y-97	
Mooneyham, Lamarr	Y-82	
Murray, Les	Y-01	
Nosworth, David	Y-82	
O'Connor, Patrick	Y-84, 99	
Ozick, Cynthia	Y-83	
Penner, Jonathan	Y-83	
Pennington, Lee	Y-82	
Penzler, Otto	Y-96	
Plimpton, George	Y-99	
Potok, Chaim	Y-84	
Powell, Padgett	Y-01	
Prescott, Peter S.	Y-86	
Rabe, David	Y-91	
Rechy, John	Y-82	
Reid, B. L.	Y-83	
Reynolds, Michael	Y-95, 99	
Robinson, Derek	Y-02	
Rollyson, Carl	Y-97	
Rosset, Barney	Y-02	
Schlafly, Phyllis	Y-82	
Schroeder, Patricia	Y-99	
Schulberg, Budd	Y-81, 01	
Scribner, Charles, III	Y-94	
Sipper, Ralph	Y-94	
Smith, Cork	Y-95	
Staley, Thomas F.	Y-00	
Styron, William	Y-80	
Talese, Nan	Y-94	

Thornton, John	Y-94
Toth, Susan Allen	Y-86
Tyler, Anne	Y-82
Vaughan, Samuel	Y-97
Von Ogtrop, Kristin	Y-92
Wallenstein, Barry	Y-92
Weintraub, Stanley	Y-82
Williams, J. Chamberlain	Y-84
Into the Past: William Jovanovich's Reflections in Publishing	Y-02
Ireland, David 1927-	DLB-289
The National Library of Ireland's New James Joyce Manuscripts	Y-02
Irigaray, Luce 1930-	DLB-296
Irving, John 1942-	DLB-6, 278; Y-82
Irving, Washington 1783-1859	DLB-3, 11, 30, 59, 73, 74, 183, 186, 250; CDALB-2
Irwin, Grace 1907-	DLB-68
Irwin, Will 1873-1948	DLB-25
Isaksson, Ulla 1916-2000	DLB-257
Iser, Wolfgang 1926-	DLB-242
Isherwood, Christopher 1904-1986	DLB-15, 195; Y-86
The Christopher Isherwood Archive, The Huntington Library	Y-99
Ishiguro, Kazuo 1954-	DLB-194
Ishikawa Jun 1899-1987	DLB-182
Iskander, Fazil' Abdulevich 1929-	DLB-302
The Island Trees Case: A Symposium on School Library Censorship An Interview with Judith Krug An Interview with Phyllis Schlafly An Interview with Edward B. Jenkinson An Interview with Lamarr Mooneyham An Interview with Harriet Bernstein	Y-82
Islas, Arturo 1938-1991	DLB-122
Issit, Debbie 1966-	DLB-233
Ivanišević, Drago 1907-1981	DLB-181
Ivanov, Georgii 1894-1954	DLB-317
Ivanov, Viacheslav Ivanovich 1866-1949	DLB-295
Ivanov, Vsevolod Viacheslavovich 1895-1963	DLB-272
Ivask, Yuri 1907-1986	DLB-317
Ivaska, Astrīde 1926-	DLB-232
M. J. Ivers and Company	DLB-49
Iwaniuk, Wacław 1915-2001	DLB-215
Iwano Hōmei 1873-1920	DLB-180
Iwaszkiewicz, Jarosław 1894-1980	DLB-215
Iyayi, Festus 1947-	DLB-157
Izumi Kyōka 1873-1939	DLB-180

J

Jackmon, Marvin E. (see Marvin X)	
Jacks, L. P. 1860-1955	DLB-135
Jackson, Angela 1951-	DLB-41
Jackson, Charles 1903-1968	DLB-234
Jackson, Helen Hunt 1830-1885	DLB-42, 47, 186, 189
Jackson, Holbrook 1874-1948	DLB-98
Jackson, Laura Riding 1901-1991	DLB-48
Jackson, Shirley 1916-1965	DLB-6, 234; CDALB-1
Jacob, Max 1876-1944	DLB-258
Jacob, Naomi 1884?-1964	DLB-191
Jacob, Piers Anthony Dillingham (see Anthony, Piers)	
Jacob, Violet 1863-1946	DLB-240
Jacobi, Friedrich Heinrich 1743-1819	DLB-94
Jacobi, Johann Georg 1740-1814	DLB-97
George W. Jacobs and Company	DLB-49
Jacobs, Harriet 1813-1897	DLB-239
Jacobs, Joseph 1854-1916	DLB-141
Jacobs, W. W. 1863-1943	DLB-135
The W. W. Jacobs Appreciation Society	Y-98
Jacobsen, J. P. 1847-1885	DLB-300
Jacobsen, Jørgen-Frantz 1900-1938	DLB-214
Jacobsen, Josephine 1908-	DLB-244
Jacobsen, Rolf 1907-1994	DLB-297
Jacobson, Dan 1929-	DLB-14, 207, 225, 319
Jacobson, Howard 1942-	DLB-207
Jacques de Vitry circa 1160/1170-1240	DLB-208
Jæger, Frank 1926-1977	DLB-214
Ja'far al-Sadiq circa 702-765	DLB-311
William Jaggard [publishing house]	DLB-170
Jahier, Piero 1884-1966	DLB-114, 264
al-Jahiz circa 776-868 or 869	DLB-311
Jahnn, Hans Henny 1894-1959	DLB-56, 124
Jaimes, Freyre, Ricardo 1866?-1933	DLB-283
Jakes, John 1932-	DLB-278; Y-83
Tribute to John Gardner	Y-82
Tribute to John D. MacDonald	Y-86
Jakobína Johnson (Jakobína Sigurbjarnardóttir) 1883-1977	DLB-293
Jakobson, Roman 1896-1982	DLB-242
James, Alice 1848-1892	DLB-221
James, C. L. R. 1901-1989	DLB-125
James, George P. R. 1801-1860	DLB-116
James, Henry 1843-1916	DLB-12, 71, 74, 189; DS-13; CDALB-3
"The Future of the Novel" (1899)	DLB-18
"The Novel in [Robert Browning's] 'The Ring and the Book'" (1912)	DLB-32
James, John circa 1633-1729	DLB-24
James, M. R. 1862-1936	DLB-156, 201
James, Naomi 1949-	DLB-204
James, P. D. (Phyllis Dorothy James White) 1920-	DLB-87, 276; DS-17; CDBLB-8
Tribute to Charles Scribner Jr.	Y-95
James, Thomas 1572?-1629	DLB-213
U. P. James [publishing house]	DLB-49
James, Will 1892-1942	DS-16
James, William 1842-1910	DLB-270
James VI of Scotland, I of England 1566-1625	DLB-151, 172
Ane Schort Treatise Conteining Some Revlis and Cautelis to Be Obseruit and Eschewit in Scottis Poesi (1584)	DLB-172
Jameson, Anna 1794-1860	DLB-99, 166
Jameson, Fredric 1934-	DLB-67
Jameson, J. Franklin 1859-1937	DLB-17
Jameson, Storm 1891-1986	DLB-36
Jančar, Drago 1948-	DLB-181
Janés, Clara 1940-	DLB-134
Janevski, Slavko 1920-2000	DLB-181; CDWLB-4
Janowitz, Tama 1957-	DLB-292
Jansson, Tove 1914-2001	DLB-257
Janvier, Thomas 1849-1913	DLB-202
Japan	
"The Development of Meiji Japan"	DLB-180
"Encounter with the West"	DLB-180
Japanese Literature	
Letter from Japan	Y-94, 98
Medieval Travel Diaries	DLB-203
Surveys: 1987-1995	DLB-182
Jaramillo, Cleofas M. 1878-1956	DLB-122
Jaramillo Levi, Enrique 1944-	DLB-290
Jarir after 650-circa 730	DLB-311
Jarman, Mark 1952-	DLB-120, 282
Jarrell, Randall 1914-1965	DLB-48, 52; CDALB-1
Jarrold and Sons	DLB-106
Jarry, Alfred 1873-1907	DLB-192, 258
Jarves, James Jackson 1818-1888	DLB-189
Jasmin, Claude 1930-	DLB-60
Jaunsudrabiņš, Jānis 1877-1962	DLB-220
Jay, John 1745-1829	DLB-31
Jean de Garlande (see John of Garland)	
Jefferies, Richard 1848-1887	DLB-98, 141
The Richard Jefferies Society	Y-98
Jeffers, Lance 1919-1985	DLB-41
Jeffers, Robinson 1887-1962	DLB-45, 212; CDALB-4
Jefferson, Thomas 1743-1826	DLB-31, 183; CDALB-2
Jégé 1866-1940	DLB-215
Jelinek, Elfriede 1946-	DLB-85
Jellicoe, Ann 1927-	DLB-13, 233
Jemison, Mary circa 1742-1833	DLB-239
Jen, Gish 1955-	DLB-312
Jenkins, Dan 1929-	DLB-241
Jenkins, Elizabeth 1905-	DLB-155
Jenkins, Robin 1912-2005	DLB-14, 271
Jenkins, William Fitzgerald (see Leinster, Murray)	
Herbert Jenkins Limited	DLB-112
Jennings, Elizabeth 1926-	DLB-27
Jens, Walter 1923-	DLB-69
Jensen, Axel 1932-2003	DLB-297
Jensen, Johannes V. 1873-1950	DLB-214
Jensen, Merrill 1905-1980	DLB-17

Jensen, Thit 1876-1957 .... DLB-214	Johnson, James Weldon 1871-1938 .... DLB-51; CDALB-4	Jones, Glyn 1905-1995 .... DLB-15
Jephson, Robert 1736-1803 .... DLB-89	Johnson, John H. 1918- DLB-137	Jones, Gwyn 1907- DLB-15, 139
Jerome, Jerome K. 1859-1927 .... DLB-10, 34, 135	"Backstage," Statement From the Initial Issue of *Ebony* (November 1945 .... DLB-137	Jones, Henry Arthur 1851-1929 .... DLB-10
The Jerome K. Jerome Society Y-98		Jones, Hugh circa 1692-1760 .... DLB-24
Jerome, Judson 1927-1991 .... DLB-105		Jones, James 1921-1977 .... DLB-2, 143; DS-17
"Reflections: After a Tornado" DLB-105	Johnson, Joseph [publishing house] DLB-154	James Jones Papers in the Handy Writers' Colony Collection at the University of Illinois at Springfield Y-98
Jerrold, Douglas 1803-1857 .... DLB-158, 159	Johnson, Linton Kwesi 1952- DLB-157	
Jersild, Per Christian 1935- DLB-257	Johnson, Lionel 1867-1902 .... DLB-19	
Jesse, F. Tennyson 1888-1958 .... DLB-77	Johnson, Nunnally 1897-1977 .... DLB-26	
Jewel, John 1522-1571 .... DLB-236	Johnson, Owen 1878-1952 .... Y-87	The James Jones Society Y-92
John P. Jewett and Company DLB-49	Johnson, Pamela Hansford 1912-1981 .... DLB-15	Jones, Jenkin Lloyd 1911-2004 .... DLB-127
Jewett, Sarah Orne 1849-1909 .... DLB-12, 74, 221	Johnson, Pauline 1861-1913 .... DLB-92	Jones, John Beauchamp 1810-1866 .... DLB-202
The Jewish Publication Society DLB-49	Johnson, Ronald 1935-1998 .... DLB-169	Jones, Joseph, Major (see Thompson, William Tappan)
Studies in American Jewish Literature Y-02	Johnson, Samuel 1696-1772 .... DLB-24; CDBLB-2	Jones, LeRoi (see Baraka, Amiri)
Jewitt, John Rodgers 1783-1821 .... DLB-99	Johnson, Samuel 1709-1784 .... DLB-39, 95, 104, 142, 213	Jones, Lewis 1897-1939 .... DLB-15
Jewsbury, Geraldine 1812-1880 .... DLB-21		Jones, Madison 1925- DLB-152
Jewsbury, Maria Jane 1800-1833 .... DLB-199	*Rambler*, no. 4 (1750) [excerpt] DLB-39	Jones, Marie 1951- DLB-233
Jhabvala, Ruth Prawer 1927- DLB-139, 194	The BBC Four Samuel Johnson Prize for Non-fiction Y-02	Jones, Preston 1936-1979 .... DLB-7
Jiménez, Juan Ramón 1881-1958 .... DLB-134		Jones, Rodney 1950- DLB-120
Jin, Ha 1956- DLB-244, 292	Johnson, Samuel 1822-1882 .... DLB-1, 243	Jones, Thom 1945- DLB-244
Joans, Ted 1928-2003 .... DLB-16, 41	Johnson, Susanna 1730-1810 .... DLB-200	Jones, Sir William 1746-1794 .... DLB-109
Jóha 1525-1602 .... DLB-203	Johnson, Terry 1955- DLB-233	Jones, William Alfred 1817-1900 .... DLB-59
Jóhann Sigurjónsson 1880-1919 .... DLB-293	Johnson, Uwe 1934-1984 .... DLB-75; CDWLB-2	Jones's Publishing House DLB-49
Jóhannes úr Kötlum 1899-1972 .... DLB-293	Benjamin Johnson [publishing house] DLB-49	Jong, Erica 1942- DLB-2, 5, 28, 152
Johannis de Garlandia (see John of Garland)	Benjamin, Jacob, and Robert Johnson [publishing house] DLB-49	Jonke, Gert F. 1946- DLB-85
John, Errol 1924-1988 .... DLB-233		Jonson, Ben 1572?-1637 .... DLB-62, 121; CDBLB-1
John, Eugenie (see Marlitt, E.)	Johnston, Annie Fellows 1863-1931 .... DLB-42	
John of Dumbleton circa 1310-circa 1349 .... DLB-115	Johnston, Basil H. 1929- DLB-60	Jonsson, Tor 1916-1951 .... DLB-297
	Johnston, David Claypole 1798?-1865 .... DLB-188	Jordan, June 1936- DLB-38
John of Garland (Jean de Garlande, Johannis de Garlandia) circa 1195-circa 1272 .... DLB-208	Johnston, Denis 1901-1984 .... DLB-10	Jorgensen, Johannes 1866-1956 .... DLB-300
	Johnston, Ellen 1835-1873 .... DLB-199	Joseph, Jenny 1932- DLB-40
	Johnston, George 1912-1970 .... DLB-260	Joseph and George Y-99
The John Reed Clubs DLB-303	Johnston, George 1913-1970 .... DLB-88	Michael Joseph Limited DLB-112
Johns, Captain W. E. 1893-1968 .... DLB-160	Johnston, Sir Harry 1858-1927 .... DLB-174	Josephson, Matthew 1899-1978 .... DLB-4
Johnson, Mrs. A. E. ca. 1858-1922 .... DLB-221	Johnston, Jennifer 1930- DLB-14	Josephus, Flavius 37-100 .... DLB-176
Johnson, Amelia (see Johnson, Mrs. A. E.)	Johnston, Mary 1870-1936 .... DLB-9	Josephy, Alvin M., Jr. Tribute to Alfred A. Knopf Y-84
Johnson, B. S. 1933-1973 .... DLB-14, 40	Johnston, Richard Malcolm 1822-1898 .... DLB-74	
Johnson, Charles 1679-1748 .... DLB-84	Johnstone, Charles 1719?-1800? DLB-39	Josiah Allen's Wife (see Holley, Marietta)
Johnson, Charles 1948- DLB-33, 278	Johst, Hanns 1890-1978 .... DLB-124	Josipovici, Gabriel 1940- DLB-14, 319
Johnson, Charles S. 1893-1956 .... DLB-51, 91	Jökull Jakobsson 1933-1978 .... DLB-293	Josselyn, John ?-1675 .... DLB-24
Johnson, Colin (Mudrooroo) 1938- DLB-289	Jolas, Eugene 1894-1952 .... DLB-4, 45	Joudry, Patricia 1921-2000 .... DLB-88
Johnson, Denis 1949- DLB-120	Jón Stefán Sveinsson or Svensson (see Nonni)	Jouve, Pierre Jean 1887-1976 .... DLB-258
Johnson, Diane 1934- Y-80	Jón Trausti (Guðmundur Magnússon) 1873-1918 .... DLB-293	Jovanovich, William 1920-2001 .... Y-01
Johnson, Dorothy M. 1905–1984 .... DLB-206		Into the Past: William Jovanovich's Reflections on Publishing Y-02
Johnson, E. Pauline (Tekahionwake) 1861-1913 .... DLB-175	Jón úr Vör (Jón Jónsson) 1917-2000 .... DLB-293	
	Jónas Hallgrímsson 1807-1845 .... DLB-293	[Response to Ken Auletta] Y-97
Johnson, Edgar 1901-1995 .... DLB-103	Jones, Alice C. 1853-1933 .... DLB-92	*The Temper of the West*: William Jovanovich Y-02
Johnson, Edward 1598-1672 .... DLB-24	Jones, Charles C., Jr. 1831-1893 .... DLB-30	
Johnson, Eyvind 1900-1976 .... DLB-259	Jones, D. G. 1929- DLB-53	Tribute to Charles Scribner Jr. Y-95
Johnson, Fenton 1888-1958 .... DLB-45, 50	Jones, David 1895-1974 .... DLB-20, 100; CDBLB-7	Jovine, Francesco 1902-1950 .... DLB-264
Johnson, Georgia Douglas 1877?-1966 .... DLB-51, 249		Jovine, Giuseppe 1922- DLB-128
	Jones, Diana Wynne 1934- DLB-161	Joyaux, Philippe (see Sollers, Philippe)
Johnson, Gerald W. 1890-1980 .... DLB-29	Jones, Ebenezer 1820-1860 .... DLB-32	Joyce, Adrien (see Eastman, Carol)
Johnson, Greg 1953- DLB-234	Jones, Ernest 1819-1868 .... DLB-32	Joyce, James 1882-1941 .... DLB-10, 19, 36, 162, 247; CDBLB-6
Johnson, Helene 1907-1995 .... DLB-51	Jones, Gayl 1949- DLB-33, 278	
Jacob Johnson and Company DLB-49	Jones, George 1800-1870 .... DLB-183	Danis Rose and the Rendering of *Ulysses* Y-97

James Joyce Centenary: Dublin, 1982 . . . . Y-82	Kames, Henry Home, Lord 1696-1782 . . . . DLB-31, 104	Kaverin, Veniamin Aleksandrovich (Veniamin Aleksandrovich Zil'ber) 1902-1989 . . . . DLB-272
James Joyce Conference Y-85	Kamo no Chōmei (Kamo no Nagaakira) 1153 or 1155-1216 . . . . DLB-203	Kawabata Yasunari 1899-1972 . . . . DLB-180
A Joyce (Con)Text: Danis Rose and the Remaking of *Ulysses* Y-97	Kamo no Nagaakira (see Kamo no Chōmei)	Kay, Guy Gavriel 1954- DLB-251
The National Library of Ireland's New James Joyce Manuscripts Y-02	Kampmann, Christian 1939-1988 . . . . DLB-214	Kaye-Smith, Sheila 1887-1956 . . . . DLB-36
The New *Ulysses* Y-84	Kandel, Lenore 1932- DLB-16	Kazakov, Iurii Pavlovich 1927-1982 . . . . . DLB-302
Public Domain and the Violation of Texts Y-97	Kane, Sarah 1971-1999 . . . . DLB-310	Kazin, Alfred 1915-1998 . . . . DLB-67
The Quinn Draft of James Joyce's Circe Manuscript Y-00	Kaneko, Lonny 1939- DLB-312	Keane, John B. 1928-2002 . . . . DLB-13
Stephen Joyce's Letter to the Editor of *The Irish Times* Y-97	Kang, Younghill 1903-1972 . . . . DLB-312	Keary, Annie 1825-1879 . . . . DLB-163
Ulysses, Reader's Edition: First Reactions . . Y-97	Kanin, Garson 1912-1999 . . . . DLB-7	Keary, Eliza 1827-1918 . . . . DLB-240
We See the Editor at Work Y-97	A Tribute (to Marc Connelly) Y-80	Keating, H. R. F. 1926- DLB-87
Whose *Ulysses?* The Function of Editing . . Y-97	Kaniuk, Yoram 1930- DLB-299	Keatley, Charlotte 1960- DLB-245
Jozsef, Attila 1905-1937 . . . . . DLB-215; CDWLB-4	Kant, Hermann 1926- DLB-75	Keats, Ezra Jack 1916-1983 . . . . DLB-61
San Juan de la Cruz 1542-1591 . . . . DLB-318	Kant, Immanuel 1724-1804 . . . . DLB-94	Keats, John 1795-1821 . . . DLB-96, 110; CDBLB-3
Juarroz, Roberto 1925-1995 . . . . DLB-283	Kantemir, Antiokh Dmitrievich 1708-1744 . . . . DLB-150	Keble, John 1792-1866 . . . . DLB-32, 55
Orange Judd Publishing Company DLB-49	Kantor, MacKinlay 1904-1977 . . . . DLB-9, 102	Keckley, Elizabeth 1818?-1907 . . . . DLB-239
Judd, Sylvester 1813-1853 . . . . DLB-1, 243	Kanze Kōjirō Nobumitsu 1435-1516 . . . . DLB-203	Keeble, John 1944- Y-83
Judith circa 930 . . . . DLB-146	Kanze Motokiyo (see Zeimi)	Keeffe, Barrie 1945- DLB-13, 245
Juel-Hansen, Erna 1845-1922 . . . . DLB-300	Kaplan, Fred 1937- DLB-111	Keeley, James 1867-1934 . . . . DLB-25
Julian of Norwich 1342-circa 1420 . . . . . DLB-1146	Kaplan, Johanna 1942- DLB-28	W. B. Keen, Cooke and Company DLB-49
Julius Caesar 100 B.C.-44 B.C. DLB-211; CDWLB-1	Kaplan, Justin 1925- DLB-111; Y-86	The Mystery of Carolyn Keene Y-02
June, Jennie (see Croly, Jane Cunningham)	Kaplinski, Jaan 1941- DLB-232	Kefala, Antigone 1935- DLB-289
Jung, Carl Gustav 1875-1961 . . . . DLB-296	Kapnist, Vasilii Vasilevich 1758?-1823 . . . DLB-150	Keillor, Garrison 1942- Y-87
Jung, Franz 1888-1963 . . . . DLB-118	Karadžić, Vuk Stefanović 1787-1864 . . . . DLB-147; CDWLB-4	Keith, Marian (Mary Esther MacGregor) 1874?-1961 . . . . DLB-92
Jünger, Ernst 1895-1998 . . . . . DLB-56; CDWLB-2	Karamzin, Nikolai Mikhailovich 1766-1826 . . . . DLB-150	Keller, Gary D. 1943- DLB-82
Der jüngere Titurel circa 1275 . . . . DLB-138	Karinthy, Frigyes 1887-1938 . . . . DLB-215	Keller, Gottfried 1819-1890 . . . . DLB-129; CDWLB-2
Jung-Stilling, Johann Heinrich 1740-1817 . . . . DLB-94	Karmel, Ilona 1925-2000 . . . . DLB-299	Keller, Helen 1880-1968 . . . . DLB-303
Junqueiro, Abílio Manuel Guerra 1850-1923 . . . . DLB-287	Karsch, Anna Louisa 1722-1791 . . . . DLB-97	Kelley, Edith Summers 1884-1956 . . . . DLB-9
Justice, Donald 1925- Y-83	Kasack, Hermann 1896-1966 . . . . DLB-69	Kelley, Emma Dunham ?-? DLB-221
Juvenal circa A.D. 60-circa A.D. 130 . . . . DLB-211; CDWLB-1	Kasai Zenzō 1887-1927 . . . . DLB-180	Kelley, Florence 1859-1932 . . . . DLB-303
The Juvenile Library (see M. J. Godwin and Company)	Kaschnitz, Marie Luise 1901-1974 . . . . DLB-69	Kelley, William Melvin 1937- DLB-33
	Kassák, Lajos 1887-1967 . . . . DLB-215	Kellogg, Ansel Nash 1832-1886 . . . . DLB-23
K	Kaštelan, Jure 1919-1990 . . . . DLB-147	Kellogg, Steven 1941- DLB-61
	Kästner, Erich 1899-1974 . . . . DLB-56	Kelly, George E. 1887-1974 . . . . DLB-7, 249
Kacew, Romain (see Gary, Romain)	Kataev, Evgenii Petrovich (see Il'f, Il'ia and Petrov, Evgenii)	Kelly, Hugh 1739-1777 . . . . DLB-89
Kafka, Franz 1883-1924 . . . . . DLB-81; CDWLB-2	Kataev, Valentin Petrovich 1897-1986 . . . . DLB-272	Kelly, Piet and Company DLB-49
Kahn, Gus 1886-1941 . . . . DLB-265	Katenin, Pavel Aleksandrovich 1792-1853 . . . . DLB-205	Kelly, Robert 1935- DLB-5, 130, 165
Kahn, Roger 1927- DLB-171	Kattan, Naim 1928- DLB-53	Kelman, James 1946- DLB-194, 319
Kaikō Takeshi 1939-1989 . . . . DLB-182	Katz, Steve 1935- Y-83	Kelmscott Press DLB-112
Káinn (Kristján Níels Jónsson/Kristjan Niels Julius) 1860-1936 . . . . DLB-293	Ka-Tzetnik 135633 (Yehiel Dinur) 1909-2001 . . . . DLB-299	Kelton, Elmer 1926- DLB-256
Kaiser, Georg 1878-1945 . . . . DLB-124; CDWLB-2	Kauffman, Janet 1945- DLB-218; Y-86	Kemble, E. W. 1861-1933 . . . . DLB-188
Kaiserchronik circa 1147 . . . . DLB-148	Kauffmann, Samuel 1898-1971 . . . . DLB-127	Kemble, Fanny 1809-1893 . . . . DLB-32
Kaleb, Vjekoslav 1905- DLB-181	Kaufman, Bob 1925-1986 . . . . DLB-16, 41	Kemelman, Harry 1908-1996 . . . . DLB-28
Kalechofsky, Roberta 1931- DLB-28	Kaufman, George S. 1889-1961 . . . . DLB-7	Kempe, Margery circa 1373-1438 . . . . DLB-146
Kaler, James Otis 1848-1912 . . . . DLB-12, 42	Kaufmann, Walter 1921-1980 . . . . DLB-279	Kempinski, Tom 1938- DLB-310
Kalmar, Bert 1884-1947 . . . . DLB-265	Kavan, Anna (Helen Woods Ferguson Edmonds) 1901-1968 . . . . DLB-255	Kempner, Friederike 1836-1904 . . . . DLB-129
Kamensky, Vasilii Vasil'evich 1884-1961 . . . . DLB-295	Kavanagh, P. J. 1931- DLB-40	Kempowski, Walter 1929- DLB-75
	Kavanagh, Patrick 1904-1967 . . . . DLB-15, 20	Kenan, Randall 1963- DLB-292
		Claude Kendall [publishing company] DLB-46
		Kendall, Henry 1839-1882 . . . . DLB-230
		Kendall, May 1861-1943 . . . . DLB-240
		Kendell, George 1809-1867 . . . . DLB-43

Keneally, Thomas 1935- DLB-289, 299
Kenedy, P. J., and Sons DLB-49
Kenkō circa 1283-circa 1352 ....DLB-203
Kenna, Peter 1930-1987...............DLB-289
Kennan, George 1845-1924............DLB-189
Kennedy, A. L. 1965- DLB-271
Kennedy, Adrienne 1931- DLB-38
Kennedy, John Pendleton 1795-1870...DLB-3, 248
Kennedy, Leo 1907-2000 ....DLB-88
Kennedy, Margaret 1896-1967 ....DLB-36
Kennedy, Patrick 1801-1873 ....DLB-159
Kennedy, Richard S. 1920- DLB-111; Y-02
Kennedy, William 1928- DLB-143; Y-85
Kennedy, X. J. 1929- DLB-5
   Tribute to John Ciardi Y-86
Kennelly, Brendan 1936- DLB-40
Kenner, Hugh 1923-2003 ....DLB-67
   Tribute to Cleanth Brooks Y-80
Mitchell Kennerley [publishing house].....DLB-46
Kenny, Maurice 1929- DLB-175
Kent, Frank R. 1877-1958 ....DLB-29
Kenyon, Jane 1947-1995 ....DLB-120
Kenzheev, Bakhyt Shkurullaevich
   1950- DLB-285
Keough, Hugh Edmund 1864-1912......DLB-171
Keppler and Schwartzmann............DLB-49
Ker, John, third Duke of Roxburghe
   1740-1804 ....DLB-213
Ker, N. R. 1908-1982................DLB-201
Keralio-Robert, Louise-Félicité de
   1758-1822 ....DLB-313
Kerlan, Irvin 1912-1963...............DLB-187
Kermode, Frank 1919- DLB-242
Kern, Jerome 1885-1945 ....DLB-187
Kernaghan, Eileen 1939- DLB-251
Kerner, Justinus 1786-1862 ....DLB-90
Kerouac, Jack
   1922-1969...DLB-2, 16, 237; DS-3; CDALB-1
   Auction of Jack Kerouac's
      On the Road Scroll Y-01
   The Jack Kerouac Revival.............Y-95
   "Re-meeting of Old Friends":
      The Jack Kerouac Conference Y-82
   Statement of Correction to "The Jack
      Kerouac Revival" Y-96
Kerouac, Jan 1952-1996...............DLB-16
Charles H. Kerr and Company DLB-49
Kerr, Orpheus C. (see Newell, Robert Henry)
Kersh, Gerald 1911-1968..............DLB-255
Kertész, Imre DLB-299; Y-02
Kesey, Ken
   1935-2001......DLB-2, 16, 206; CDALB-6
Kessel, Joseph 1898-1979..............DLB-72
Kessel, Martin 1901-1990 ....DLB-56
Kesten, Hermann 1900-1996...........DLB-56
Keun, Irmgard 1905-1982 ....DLB-69
Key, Ellen 1849-1926.................DLB-259

Key and Biddle DLB-49
Keynes, Sir Geoffrey 1887-1982........DLB-201
Keynes, John Maynard 1883-1946 ....DS-10
Keyserling, Eduard von 1855-1918.......DLB-66
al-Khalil ibn Ahmad circa 718-791......DLB-311
Khan, Ismith 1925-2002 ....DLB-125
al-Khansa' fl. late sixth-mid
   seventh centuries DLB-311
Kharitonov, Evgenii Vladimirovich
   1941-1981....................DLB-285
Kharitonov, Mark Sergeevich 1937- DLB-285
Khaytov, Nikolay 1919- DLB-181
Khemnitser, Ivan Ivanovich
   1745-1784 ....DLB-150
Kheraskov, Mikhail Matveevich
   1733-1807 ....DLB-150
Khlebnikov, Velimir 1885-1922 ....DLB-295
Khodasevich, Vladislav 1886-1939 ......DLB-317
Khomiakov, Aleksei Stepanovich
   1804-1860 ....DLB-205
Khristov, Boris 1945- DLB-181
Khvoshchinskaia, Nadezhda Dmitrievna
   1824-1889 ....DLB-238
Khvostov, Dmitrii Ivanovich
   1757-1835.....................DLB-150
Kibirov, Timur Iur'evich (Timur
   Iur'evich Zapoev) 1955- DLB-285
Kidd, Adam 1802?-1831 ....DLB-99
William Kidd [publishing house].......DLB-106
Kidde, Harald 1878-1918..............DLB-300
Kidder, Tracy 1945- DLB-185
Kiely, Benedict 1919- DLB-15, 319
Kieran, John 1892-1981 ....DLB-171
Kierkegaard, Søren 1813-1855.........DLB-300
Kies, Marietta 1853-1899..............DLB-270
Kiley, Jed 1889-1962 ....DLB-4
Kilgore, Bernard 1908-1967............DLB-127
Kilian, Crawford 1941- DLB-251
Killens, John Oliver 1916-1987 ....DLB-33
   Tribute to Julian Mayfield............Y-84
Killigrew, Anne 1660-1685 ....DLB-131
Killigrew, Thomas 1612-1683 ....DLB-58
Kilmer, Joyce 1886-1918 ....DLB-45
Kilroy, Thomas 1934- DLB-233
Kilwardby, Robert circa 1215-1279 .....DLB-115
Kilworth, Garry 1941- DLB-261
Kim, Anatolii Andreevich 1939- DLB-285
Kimball, Richard Burleigh 1816-1892 ....DLB-202
Kincaid, Jamaica 1949-
   ......DLB-157, 227; CDALB-7; CDWLB-3
Kinck, Hans Ernst 1865-1926 ....DLB-297
King, Charles 1844-1933..............DLB-186
King, Clarence 1842-1901 ....DLB-12
King, Florence 1936- Y-85
King, Francis 1923- DLB-15, 139
King, Grace 1852-1932 ....DLB-12, 78

King, Harriet Hamilton 1840-1920 ......DLB-199
King, Henry 1592-1669...............DLB-126
Solomon King [publishing house] DLB-49
King, Stephen 1947- DLB-143; Y-80
King, Susan Petigru 1824-1875 ....DLB-239
King, Thomas 1943- DLB-175
King, Woodie, Jr. 1937- DLB-38
Kinglake, Alexander William
   1809-1891 ....DLB-55, 166
Kingo, Thomas 1634-1703.............DLB-300
Kingsbury, Donald 1929- DLB-251
Kingsley, Charles
   1819-1875 ....DLB-21, 32, 163, 178, 190
Kingsley, Henry 1830-1876..........DLB-21, 230
Kingsley, Mary Henrietta 1862-1900.....DLB-174
Kingsley, Sidney 1906-1995..............DLB-7
Kingsmill, Hugh 1889-1949............DLB-149
Kingsolver, Barbara
   1955- DLB-206; CDALB-7
Kingston, Maxine Hong
   1940- ..DLB-173, 212, 312; Y-80; CDALB-7
Kingston, William Henry Giles
   1814-1880 ....DLB-163
Kinnan, Mary Lewis 1763-1848.........DLB-200
Kinnell, Galway 1927- DLB-5; Y-87
Kinsella, Thomas 1928- DLB-27
Kipling, Rudyard 1865-1936
   ....DLB-19, 34, 141, 156; CDBLB-5
Kipphardt, Heinar 1922-1982 ....DLB-124
Kirby, William 1817-1906 ....DLB-99
Kircher, Athanasius 1602-1680 ....DLB-164
Kireevsky, Ivan Vasil'evich 1806-1856 ...DLB-198
Kireevsky, Petr Vasil'evich 1808-1856 ...DLB-205
Kirk, Hans 1898-1962................DLB-214
Kirk, John Foster 1824-1904 ....DLB-79
Kirkconnell, Watson 1895-1977 ....DLB-68
Kirkland, Caroline M.
   1801-1864 ....DLB-3, 73, 74, 250; DS-13
Kirkland, Joseph 1830-1893.............DLB-12
Francis Kirkman [publishing house] DLB-170
Kirkpatrick, Clayton 1915-2004 ....DLB-127
Kirkup, James 1918- DLB-27
Kirouac, Conrad (see Marie-Victorin, Frère)
Kirsch, Sarah 1935- DLB-75
Kirst, Hans Hellmut 1914-1989.........DLB-69
Kiš, Danilo 1935-1989......DLB-181; CDWLB-4
Kita Morio 1927- DLB-182
Kitcat, Mabel Greenhow 1859-1922 ....DLB-135
Kitchin, C. H. B. 1895-1967 ....DLB-77
Kittredge, William 1932- DLB-212, 244
Kiukhel'beker, Vil'gel'm Karlovich
   1797-1846.....................DLB-205
Kizer, Carolyn 1925- DLB-5, 169
Kjaerstad, Jan 1953- DLB-297
Klabund 1890-1928 ....DLB-66
Klaj, Johann 1616-1656 ....DLB-164
Klappert, Peter 1942- DLB-5

Cumulative Index

Klass, Philip (see Tenn, William)
Klein, A. M. 1909-1972 .... DLB-68
Kleist, Ewald von 1715-1759 .... DLB-97
Kleist, Heinrich von
   1777-1811 .... DLB-90; CDWLB-2
Klíma, Ivan 1931- DLB-232; CDWLB-4
Klimentev, Andrei Platonovic
   (see Platonov, Andrei Platonovich)
Klinger, Friedrich Maximilian
   1752-1831 .... DLB-94
Kliuev, Nikolai Alekseevich 1884-1937 . . DLB-295
Kliushnikov, Viktor Petrovich
   1841-1892 .... DLB-238
Klopfer, Donald S.
   Impressions of William Faulkner Y-97
   Oral History Interview with Donald
     S. Klopfer..................... Y-97
   Tribute to Alfred A. Knopf Y-84
Klopstock, Friedrich Gottlieb
   1724-1803 .... DLB-97
Klopstock, Meta 1728-1758 .... DLB-97
Kluge, Alexander 1932- DLB-75
Kluge, P. F. 1942- Y-02
Knapp, Joseph Palmer 1864-1951 .... DLB-91
Knapp, Samuel Lorenzo 1783-1838 ...... DLB-59
J. J. and P. Knapton [publishing house] . . DLB-154
Kniazhnin, Iakov Borisovich
   1740-1791 .... DLB-150
Knickerbocker, Diedrich (see Irving, Washington)
Knigge, Adolph Franz Friedrich Ludwig,
   Freiherr von 1752-1796 .... DLB-94
Charles Knight and Company DLB-106
Knight, Damon 1922-2002 .... DLB-8
Knight, Etheridge 1931-1992 .... DLB-41
Knight, John S. 1894-1981 .... DLB-29
Knight, Sarah Kemble 1666-1727 .... DLB-24, 200
Knight-Bruce, G. W. H. 1852-1896 ......DLB-174
Knister, Raymond 1899-1932 .... DLB-68
Knoblock, Edward 1874-1945 .... DLB-10
Knopf, Alfred A. 1892-1984 .... Y-84
   Knopf to Hammett: The Editoral
     Correspondence Y-00
Alfred A. Knopf [publishing house] DLB-46
Knorr von Rosenroth, Christian
   1636-1689 .... DLB-168
Knowles, John 1926-2001 ...... DLB-6; CDALB-6
Knox, Frank 1874-1944 .... DLB-29
Knox, John circa 1514-1572 .... DLB-132
Knox, John Armoy 1850-1906 .... DLB-23
Knox, Lucy 1845-1884 .... DLB-240
Knox, Ronald Arbuthnott 1888-1957 ..... DLB-77
Knox, Thomas Wallace 1835-1896 ..... DLB-189
Knudsen, Jakob 1858-1917 .... DLB-300
Knut, Dovid 1900-1955 .... DLB-317
Kobayashi Takiji 1903-1933 .... DLB-180
Kober, Arthur 1900-1975 .... DLB-11
Kobiakova, Aleksandra Petrovna
   1823-1892 .... DLB-238

Kocbek, Edvard 1904-1981 . . .DLB-147; CDWLB-4
Koch, C. J. 1932- DLB-289
Koch, Howard 1902-1995 .... DLB-26
Koch, Kenneth 1925-2002 .... DLB-5
Kōda Rohan 1867-1947 .... DLB-180
Koehler, Ted 1894-1973 .... DLB-265
Koenigsberg, Moses 1879-1945 .... DLB-25
Koeppen, Wolfgang 1906-1996 .... DLB-69
Koertge, Ronald 1940- DLB-105
Koestler, Arthur 1905-1983 ...... Y-83; CDBLB-7
Kohn, John S. Van E. 1906-1976 .... DLB-187
Kokhanovskaia
   (see Sokhanskaia, Nadezhda Stepanova)
Kokoschka, Oskar 1886-1980 .... DLB-124
Kolb, Annette 1870-1967 .... DLB-66
Kolbenheyer, Erwin Guido
   1878-1962 .... DLB-66, 124
Kolleritsch, Alfred 1931- DLB-85
Kolodny, Annette 1941- DLB-67
Kol'tsov, Aleksei Vasil'evich
   1809-1842 .... DLB-205
Komarov, Matvei circa 1730-1812 ..... DLB-150
Komroff, Manuel 1890-1974............ DLB-4
Komunyakaa, Yusef 1947- DLB-120
Kondoleon, Harry 1955-1994 .... DLB-266
Koneski, Blaže 1921-1993. . . DLB-181; CDWLB-4
Konigsburg, E. L. 1930- DLB-52
Konparu Zenchiku 1405-1468? DLB-203
Konrád, György 1933- DLB-232; CDWLB-4
Konrad von Würzburg
   circa 1230-1287 .... DLB-138
Konstantinov, Aleko 1863-1897 .... DLB-147
Konwicki, Tadeusz 1926- DLB-232
Koontz, Dean 1945- DLB-292
Kooser, Ted 1939- DLB-105
Kopit, Arthur 1937- DLB-7
Kops, Bernard 1926?- DLB-13
Kornbluth, C. M. 1923-1958 .... DLB-8
Körner, Theodor 1791-1813............ DLB-90
Kornfeld, Paul 1889-1942.............. DLB-118
Korolenko, Vladimir Galaktionovich
   1853-1921 ....DLB-277
Kosinski, Jerzy 1933-1991 ......DLB-2, 299; Y-82
Kosmač, Ciril 1910-1980 .... DLB-181
Kosovel, Srečko 1904-1926 .... DLB-147
Kostrov, Ermil Ivanovich 1755-1796..... DLB-150
Kotzebue, August von 1761-1819 .... DLB-94
Kotzwinkle, William 1938- DLB-173
Kovačić, Ante 1854-1889 .... DLB-147
Kovalevskaia, Sof'ia Vasil'evna
   1850-1891 ....DLB-277
Kovič, Kajetan 1931- DLB-181
Kozlov, Ivan Ivanovich 1779-1840 ..... DLB-205
Kracauer, Siegfried 1889-1966 .... DLB-296
Kraf, Elaine 1946- Y-81
Kramer, Jane 1938- DLB-185

Kramer, Larry 1935- DLB-249
Kramer, Mark 1944- DLB-185
Kranjčević, Silvije Strahimir 1865-1908 . . .DLB-147
Krasko, Ivan 1876-1958 .... DLB-215
Krasna, Norman 1909-1984........... DLB-26
Kraus, Hans Peter 1907-1988 ....DLB-187
Kraus, Karl 1874-1936 .... DLB-118
Krause, Herbert 1905-1976............ DLB-256
Krauss, Ruth 1911-1993.............. DLB-52
Kreisel, Henry 1922-1991.............. DLB-88
Krestovsky V.
   (see Khvoshchinskaia, Nadezhda Dmitrievna)
Krestovsky, Vsevolod Vladimirovich
   1839-1895 .... DLB-238
Kreuder, Ernst 1903-1972.............. DLB-69
Krėvė-Mickevičius, Vincas 1882-1954 . . . DLB-220
Kreymborg, Alfred 1883-1966 .... DLB-4, 54
Krieger, Murray 1923-2000 .... DLB-67
Krim, Seymour 1922-1989 .... DLB-16
Kripke, Saul 1940- DLB-279
Kristensen, Tom 1893-1974 .... DLB-214
Kristeva, Julia 1941- DLB-242
Kristján Níels Jónsson/Kristjan Niels Julius
   (see Káinn)
Kritzer, Hyman W. 1918-2002............. Y-02
Krivulin, Viktor Borisovich 1944-2001 . . DLB-285
Krleža, Miroslav
   1893-1981 ....DLB-147; CDWLB-4
Krock, Arthur 1886-1974 .... DLB-29
Kroetsch, Robert 1927- DLB-53
Kropotkin, Petr Alekseevich 1842-1921 . . .DLB-277
Kross, Jaan 1920- DLB-232
Kruchenykh, Aleksei Eliseevich
   1886-1968 .... DLB-295
Krúdy, Gyula 1878-1933 .... DLB-215
Krutch, Joseph Wood
   1893-1970.................DLB-63, 206, 275
Krylov, Ivan Andreevich 1769-1844..... DLB-150
Krymov, Iurii Solomonovich
   (Iurii Solomonovich Beklemishev)
   1908-1941 ....DLB-272
Kubin, Alfred 1877-1959............... DLB-81
Kubrick, Stanley 1928-1999 .... DLB-26
Kudrun circa 1230-1240 .... DLB-138
Kuffstein, Hans Ludwig von 1582-1656. . DLB-164
Kuhlmann, Quirinus 1651-1689........ DLB-168
Kuhn, Thomas S. 1922-1996 ....DLB-279
Kuhnau, Johann 1660-1722 .... DLB-168
Kukol'nik, Nestor Vasil'evich
   1809-1868 .... DLB-205
Kukučín, Martin
   1860-1928 ....DLB-215; CDWLB-4
Kumin, Maxine 1925- DLB-5
Kuncewicz, Maria 1895-1989 .... DLB-215
Kundera, Milan 1929- DLB-232; CDWLB-4
Kunene, Mazisi 1930- DLB-117
Kunikida Doppo 1869-1908........... DLB-180

Kunitz, Stanley 1905- DLB-48	La Fontaine, Jean de 1621-1695. . . . . .DLB-268	Lane, Patrick 1939- DLB-53
Kunjufu, Johari M. (see Amini, Johari M.)	Laforge, Jules 1860-1887 . . . . .DLB-217	Lane, Pinkie Gordon 1923- DLB-41
Kunnert, Gunter 1929- DLB-75	Lagerkvist, Pär 1891-1974 . . . . .DLB-259	John Lane Company DLB-49
Kunze, Reiner 1933- DLB-75	Lagerlöf, Selma 1858-1940 . . . . .DLB-259	Laney, Al 1896-1988 . . . . DLB-4, 171
Kuo, Helena 1911-1999. . . . . .DLB-312	Lagorio, Gina 1922- DLB-196	Lang, Andrew 1844-1912 . . . . . .DLB-98, 141, 184
Kupferberg, Tuli 1923- DLB-16	La Guma, Alex 1925-1985 . . . . .DLB-117, 225; CDWLB-3	Langer, Susanne K. 1895-1985 . . . . .DLB-270
Kuprin, Aleksandr Ivanovich 1870-1938 . . . . .DLB-295	Lahaise, Guillaume (see Delahaye, Guy)	Langevin, André 1927- DLB-60
Kuraev, Mikhail Nikolaevich 1939- DLB-285	La Harpe, Jean-François de 1739-1803. . . . .DLB-313	Langford, David 1953- DLB-261
Kurahashi Yumiko 1935- DLB-182	Lahontan, Louis-Armand de Lom d'Arce, Baron de 1666-1715?. DLB-99	Langgässer, Elisabeth 1899-1950. . . . . . . .DLB-69
Kureishi, Hanif 1954- DLB-194, 245	Laing, Kojo 1946- DLB-157	Langhorne, John 1735-1779 . . . . .DLB-109
Kürnberger, Ferdinand 1821-1879. . . . . . .DLB-129	Laird, Carobeth 1895-1983 . . . . Y-82	Langland, William circa 1330-circa 1400. .DLB-146
Kurz, Isolde 1853-1944 . . . . .DLB-66	Laird and Lee DLB-49	Langton, Anna 1804-1893 . . . . .DLB-99
Kusenberg, Kurt 1904-1983. . . . . .DLB-69	Lake, Paul 1951- DLB-282	Lanham, Edwin 1904-1979 . . . . .DLB-4
Kushchevsky, Ivan Afanas'evich 1847-1876. . . . . .DLB-238	Lalić, Ivan V. 1931-1996 . . . . .DLB-181	Lanier, Sidney 1842-1881 . . . . . . .DLB-64; DS-13
Kushner, Tony 1956- DLB-228	Lalić, Mihailo 1914-1992 . . . . .DLB-181	Lanyer, Aemilia 1569-1645 . . . . .DLB-121
Kuttner, Henry 1915-1958. . . . . .DLB-8	Lalonde, Michèle 1937- DLB-60	Lapointe, Gatien 1931-1983 . . . . .DLB-88
Kuzmin, Mikhail Alekseevich 1872-1936 . . . . .DLB-295	Lamantia, Philip 1927- DLB-16	Lapointe, Paul-Marie 1929- DLB-88
Kuznetsov, Anatoli 1929-1979 . . . . .DLB-299, 302	Lamartine, Alphonse de 1790-1869 . . . . .DLB-217	Larcom, Lucy 1824-1893. . . . . .DLB-221, 243
Kyd, Thomas 1558-1594. . . . . .DLB-62	Lamb, Lady Caroline 1785-1828 . . . . .DLB-116	Lardner, John 1912-1960. . . . . DLB-171
Kyffin, Maurice circa 1560?-1598 . . . . . .DLB-136	Lamb, Charles 1775-1834 . . . . . .DLB-93, 107, 163; CDBLB-3	Lardner, Ring 1885-1933 . . . . . .DLB-11, 25, 86, 171; DS-16; CDALB-4
Kyger, Joanne 1934- DLB-16	Lamb, Mary 1764-1874 . . . . .DLB-163	Lardner 100: Ring Lardner Centennial Symposium. Y-85
Kyne, Peter B. 1880-1957 . . . . .DLB-78	Lambert, Angela 1940- DLB-271	Lardner, Ring, Jr. 1915-2000 . . . . . . .DLB-26, Y-00
Kyōgoku Tamekane 1254-1332. . . . . .DLB-203	Lambert, Anne-Thérèse de (Anne-Thérèse de Marguenat de Courcelles, marquise de Lambert) 1647-1733. . . . . .DLB-313	Larkin, Philip 1922-1985 . . . . . .DLB-27; CDBLB-8
Kyrklund, Willy 1921- DLB-257	Lambert, Betty 1933-1983 . . . . .DLB-60	The Philip Larkin Society Y-99
L	La Mettrie, Julien Offroy de 1709-1751 . . . . .DLB-313	La Roche, Sophie von 1730-1807. . . . . . . .DLB-94
L. E. L. (see Landon, Letitia Elizabeth)	Lamm, Donald Goodbye, Gutenberg? A Lecture at the New York Public Library, 18 April 1995 . . . . Y-95	La Rochefoucauld, François duc de 1613-1680 . . . . .DLB-268
Laberge, Albert 1871-1960. . . . . .DLB-68		La Rocque, Gilbert 1943-1984. . . . . .DLB-60
Laberge, Marie 1950- DLB-60	Lamming, George 1927- DLB-125; CDWLB-3	Laroque de Roquebrune, Robert (see Roquebrune, Robert de)
Labiche, Eugène 1815-1888 . . . . .DLB-192	La Mothe Le Vayer, François de 1588-1672 . . . . .DLB-268	Larrick, Nancy 1910-2004 . . . . .DLB-61
Labrunie, Gerard (see Nerval, Gerard de)	L'Amour, Louis 1908-1988 . . . . . . .DLB-206; Y-80	Lars, Claudia 1899-1974 . . . . .DLB-283
La Bruyère, Jean de 1645-1696 . . . . .DLB-268	Lampman, Archibald 1861-1899 . . . . .DLB-92	Larsen, Nella 1893-1964 . . . . .DLB-51
La Calprenède 1609?-1663 . . . . .DLB-268	Lamson, Wolffe and Company DLB-49	Larsen, Thøger 1875-1928 . . . . .DLB-300
Lacan, Jacques 1901-1981 . . . . .DLB-296	Lancer Books. DLB-46	Larson, Clinton F. 1919-1994 . . . . .DLB-256
La Capria, Raffaele 1922- DLB-196	Lanchester, John 1962- DLB-267	La Sale, Antoine de circa 1386-1460/1467 . . . . .DLB-208
La Chaussée, Pierre-Claude Nivelle de 1692-1754 . . . . .DLB-313	Lander, Peter (see Cunningham, Peter)	Las Casas, Fray Bartolomé de 1474-1566 . . . . .DLB-318
Laclos, Pierre-Ambroise-François Choderlos de 1741-1803 . . . . .DLB-313	Landesman, Jay 1919- and Landesman, Fran 1927- DLB-16	Lasch, Christopher 1932-1994. . . . . .DLB-246
Dangerous Acquaintances DLB-314	Landolfi, Tommaso 1908-1979 . . . . .DLB-177	Lasdun, James 1958- DLB-319
Lacombe, Patrice (see Trullier-Lacombe, Joseph Patrice)	Landon, Letitia Elizabeth 1802-1838 . . . . . .DLB-96	Lasker-Schüler, Else 1869-1945 . . . . . .DLB-66, 124
Lacretelle, Jacques de 1888-1985 . . . . .DLB-65	Landor, Walter Savage 1775-1864 . . . .DLB-93, 107	Lasnier, Rina 1915-1997 . . . . .DLB-88
Lacy, Ed 1911-1968. . . . . .DLB-226	Landry, Napoléon-P. 1884-1956 . . . . .DLB-92	Lassalle, Ferdinand 1825-1864. . . . . .DLB-129
Lacy, Sam 1903- DLB-171	Landvik, Lorna 1954- DLB-292	Late-Medieval Castilian Theater DLB-286
Ladd, Joseph Brown 1764-1786 . . . . .DLB-37	Lane, Charles 1800-1870 . . . . . . .DLB-1, 223; DS-5	Latham, Robert 1912-1995 . . . . .DLB-201
La Farge, Oliver 1901-1963. . . . . .DLB-9	Lane, F. C. 1885-1984 . . . . .DLB-241	Lathan, Emma (Mary Jane Latsis [1927-1997] and Martha Henissart [1929-]) DLB-306
Lafayette, Marie-Madeleine, comtesse de 1634-1693 . . . . .DLB-268	Lane, Laurence W. 1890-1967 . . . . .DLB-91	Lathrop, Dorothy P. 1891-1980 . . . . .DLB-22
Laffan, Mrs. R. S. de Courcy (see Adams, Bertha Leith)	Lane, M. Travis 1934- DLB-60	Lathrop, George Parsons 1851-1898 . . . . . .DLB-71
Lafferty, R. A. 1914-2002 . . . . .DLB-8		Lathrop, John, Jr. 1772-1820 . . . . .DLB-37
La Flesche, Francis 1857-1932 . . . . .DLB-175		Latimer, Hugh 1492?-1555 . . . . .DLB-136
		Latimore, Jewel Christine McLawler (see Amini, Johari M.)
		Latin Literature, The Uniqueness of DLB-211

Cumulative Index

La Tour du Pin, Patrice de 1911-1975 ... DLB-258
Latymer, William 1498-1583 .... DLB-132
Laube, Heinrich 1806-1884 .... DLB-133
Laud, William 1573-1645 .... DLB-213
Laughlin, James 1914-1997 ...... DLB-48; Y-96, 97
    A Tribute [to Henry Miller] Y-80
    Tribute to Albert Erskine Y-93
    Tribute to Kenneth Rexroth Y-82
    Tribute to Malcolm Cowley Y-89
Laumer, Keith 1925-1993 .... DLB-8
Lauremberg, Johann 1590-1658 .... DLB-164
Laurence, Margaret 1926-1987 .... DLB-53
Laurentius von Schnüffis 1633-1702 ..... DLB-168
Laurents, Arthur 1918- DLB-26
Laurie, Annie (see Black, Winifred)
Laut, Agnes Christiana 1871-1936 .... DLB-92
Lauterbach, Ann 1942- DLB-193
Lautréamont, Isidore Lucien Ducasse,
    Comte de 1846-1870 .... DLB-217
Lavater, Johann Kaspar 1741-1801 .... DLB-97
Lavin, Mary 1912-1996 .... DLB-15, 319
Law, John (see Harkness, Margaret)
Lawes, Henry 1596-1662 .... DLB-126
Lawler, Ray 1922- DLB-289
Lawless, Anthony (see MacDonald, Philip)
Lawless, Emily (The Hon. Emily Lawless)
    1845-1913 .... DLB-240
Lawrence, D. H. 1885-1930
    ..... DLB-10, 19, 36, 98, 162, 195; CDBLB-6
    The D. H. Lawrence Society of
    North America Y-00
Lawrence, David 1888-1973 .... DLB-29
Lawrence, Jerome 1915-2004 .... DLB-228
Lawrence, Seymour 1926-1994 .... Y-94
    Tribute to Richard Yates Y-92
Lawrence, T. E. 1888-1935 .... DLB-195
    The T. E. Lawrence Society Y-98
Lawson, George 1598-1678 .... DLB-213
Lawson, Henry 1867-1922 .... DLB-230
Lawson, John ?-1711 .... DLB-24
Lawson, John Howard 1894-1977 ...... DLB-228
Lawson, Louisa Albury 1848-1920 ...... DLB-230
Lawson, Robert 1892-1957 .... DLB-22
Lawson, Victor F. 1850-1925 .... DLB-25
Layard, Austen Henry 1817-1894 ...... DLB-166
Layton, Irving 1912- DLB-88
LaZamon fl. circa 1200 .... DLB-146
Lazarević, Laza K. 1851-1890 .... DLB-147
Lazarus, George 1904-1997 .... DLB-201
Lazhechnikov, Ivan Ivanovich
    1792-1869 .... DLB-198
Lea, Henry Charles 1825-1909 .... DLB-47
Lea, Sydney 1942- DLB-120, 282
Lea, Tom 1907-2001 .... DLB-6
Leacock, John 1729-1802 .... DLB-31
Leacock, Stephen 1869-1944 .... DLB-92

Lead, Jane Ward 1623-1704 .... DLB-131
Leadenhall Press DLB-106
"The Greatness of Southern Literature":
    League of the South Institute for the
    Study of Southern Culture and History
    .... Y-02
Leakey, Caroline Woolmer 1827-1881 .... DLB-230
Leapor, Mary 1722-1746 .... DLB-109
Lear, Edward 1812-1888 ...... DLB-32, 163, 166
Leary, Timothy 1920-1996 .... DLB-16
W. A. Leary and Company DLB-49
Léautaud, Paul 1872-1956 .... DLB-65
Leavis, F. R. 1895-1978 .... DLB-242
Leavitt, David 1961- DLB-130
Leavitt and Allen DLB-49
Le Blond, Mrs. Aubrey 1861-1934 ...... DLB-174
le Carré, John (David John Moore Cornwell)
    1931- DLB-87; CDBLB-8
    Tribute to Graham Greene Y-91
    Tribute to George Greenfield Y-00
Lécavelé, Roland (see Dorgeles, Roland)
Lechlitner, Ruth 1901- DLB-48
Leclerc, Félix 1914-1988 .... DLB-60
Le Clézio, J. M. G. 1940- DLB-83
Leder, Rudolf (see Hermlin, Stephan)
Lederer, Charles 1910-1976 .... DLB-26
Ledwidge, Francis 1887-1917 .... DLB-20
Lee, Chang-rae 1965- DLB-312
Lee, Cherylene 1953- DLB-312
Lee, Dennis 1939- DLB-53
Lee, Don L. (see Madhubuti, Haki R.)
Lee, George W. 1894-1976 .... DLB-51
Lee, Gus 1946- DLB-312
Lee, Harper 1926- DLB-6; CDALB-1
Lee, Harriet 1757-1851 and
    Lee, Sophia 1750-1824 .... DLB-39
Lee, Laurie 1914-1997 .... DLB-27
Lee, Leslie 1935- DLB-266
Lee, Li-Young 1957- DLB-165, 312
Lee, Manfred B. 1905-1971 .... DLB-137
Lee, Nathaniel circa 1645-1692 .... DLB-80
Lee, Robert E. 1918-1994 .... DLB-228
Lee, Sir Sidney 1859-1926 .... DLB-149, 184
    "Principles of Biography," in
    Elizabethan and Other Essays DLB-149
Lee, Tanith 1947- DLB-261
Lee, Vernon
    1856-1935 .... DLB-57, 153, 156, 174, 178
Lee and Shepard DLB-49
Le Fanu, Joseph Sheridan
    1814-1873 .... DLB-21, 70, 159, 178
Leffland, Ella 1931- Y-84
le Fort, Gertrud von 1876-1971 .... DLB-66
Le Gallienne, Richard 1866-1947 .... DLB-4
Legaré, Hugh Swinton
    1797-1843 .... DLB-3, 59, 73, 248
Legaré, James Mathewes 1823-1859 ... DLB-3, 248

Léger, Antoine-J. 1880-1950 .... DLB-88
Leggett, William 1801-1839 .... DLB-250
Le Guin, Ursula K.
    1929- DLB-8, 52, 256, 275; CDALB-6
Lehman, Ernest 1920- DLB-44
Lehmann, John 1907-1989 .... DLB-27, 100
John Lehmann Limited DLB-112
Lehmann, Rosamond 1901-1990 .... DLB-15
Lehmann, Wilhelm 1882-1968 .... DLB-56
Leiber, Fritz 1910-1992 .... DLB-8
Leibniz, Gottfried Wilhelm 1646-1716 ... DLB-168
Leicester University Press DLB-112
Leigh, Carolyn 1926-1983 .... DLB-265
Leigh, W. R. 1866-1955 .... DLB-188
Leinster, Murray 1896-1975 .... DLB-8
Leiser, Bill 1898-1965 .... DLB-241
Leisewitz, Johann Anton 1752-1806 ..... DLB-94
Leitch, Maurice 1933- DLB-14
Leithauser, Brad 1943- DLB-120, 282
Leland, Charles G. 1824-1903 .... DLB-11
Leland, John 1503?-1552 .... DLB-136
Lemay, Pamphile 1837-1918 .... DLB-99
Lemelin, Roger 1919-1992 .... DLB-88
Lemercier, Louis-Jean-Népomucène
    1771-1840 .... DLB-192
Le Moine, James MacPherson 1825-1912 . DLB-99
Lemon, Mark 1809-1870 .... DLB-163
Le Moyne, Jean 1913-1996 .... DLB-88
Lemperly, Paul 1858-1939 .... DLB-187
Leñero, Vicente 1933- DLB-305
L'Engle, Madeleine 1918- DLB-52
Lennart, Isobel 1915-1971 .... DLB-44
Lennox, Charlotte 1729 or 1730-1804 .... DLB-39
Lenox, James 1800-1880 .... DLB-140
Lenski, Lois 1893-1974 .... DLB-22
Lentricchia, Frank 1940- DLB-246
Lenz, Hermann 1913-1998 .... DLB-69
Lenz, J. M. R. 1751-1792 .... DLB-94
Lenz, Siegfried 1926- DLB-75
León, Fray Luis de 1527-1591 .... DLB-318
Leonard, Elmore 1925- DLB-173, 226
Leonard, Hugh 1926- DLB-13
Leonard, William Ellery 1876-1944 ..... DLB-54
Leong, Russell C. 1950- DLB-312
Leonov, Leonid Maksimovich
    1899-1994 .... DLB-272
Leonowens, Anna 1834-1914 .... DLB-99, 166
Leont'ev, Konstantin Nikolaevich
    1831-1891 .... DLB-277
Leopold, Aldo 1887-1948 .... DLB-275
LePan, Douglas 1914-1998 .... DLB-88
Lepik, Kalju 1920-1999 .... DLB-232
Leprohon, Rosanna Eleanor 1829-1879 ... DLB-99
Le Queux, William 1864-1927 .... DLB-70
Lermontov, Mikhail Iur'evich
    1814-1841 .... DLB-205

Lerner, Alan Jay 1918-1986 . . . . DLB-265	Lewis, Alfred H. 1857-1914 . . . . DLB-25, 186	Lilly, J. K., Jr. 1893-1966 . . . . DLB-140
Lerner, Max 1902-1992 . . . . DLB-29	Lewis, Alun 1915-1944 . . . . DLB-20, 162	Lilly, Wait and Company DLB-49
Lernet-Holenia, Alexander 1897-1976 . . . . . DLB-85	Lewis, C. Day (see Day Lewis, C.)	Lily, William circa 1468-1522 . . . . DLB-132
Le Rossignol, James 1866-1969 . . . . DLB-92	Lewis, C. I. 1883-1964 . . . . DLB-270	Lim, Shirley Geok-lin 1944- DLB-312
Lesage, Alain-René 1668-1747 . . . . DLB-313	Lewis, C. S. 1898-1963	Lima, Jorge de 1893-1953 . . . . DLB-307
Lescarbot, Marc circa 1570-1642 . . . . DLB-99	. . . . DLB-15, 100, 160, 255; CDBLB-7	Lima Barreto, Afonso Henriques de
LeSeur, William Dawson 1840-1917 . . . . . . DLB-92	The New York C. S. Lewis Society Y-99	1881-1922 . . . . DLB-307
LeSieg, Theo. (see Geisel, Theodor Seuss)	Lewis, Charles B. 1842-1924 . . . . DLB-11	Limited Editions Club DLB-46
Leskov, Nikolai Semenovich	Lewis, David 1941-2001 . . . . DLB-279	Limón, Graciela 1938- DLB-209
1831-1895 . . . . DLB-238	Lewis, Henry Clay 1825-1850 . . . . DLB-3, 248	Limonov, Eduard 1943- DLB-317
Leslie, Doris before 1902-1982 . . . . DLB-191	Lewis, Janet 1899-1999 . . . . Y-87	Lincoln and Edmands DLB-49
Leslie, Eliza 1787-1858 . . . . DLB-202	Tribute to Katherine Anne Porter Y-80	Lind, Jakov 1927- DLB-299
Leslie, Frank (Henry Carter)	Lewis, Matthew Gregory	Linda Vilhjálmsdóttir 1958- DLB-293
1821-1880 . . . . DLB-43, 79	1775-1818 . . . . DLB-39, 158, 178	Lindesay, Ethel Forence
Frank Leslie [publishing house] DLB-49	Lewis, Meriwether 1774-1809 . . . . . . DLB-183, 186	(see Richardson, Henry Handel)
Leśmian, Bolesław 1878-1937 . . . . DLB-215	Lewis, Norman 1908-2003 . . . . DLB-204	Lindgren, Astrid 1907-2002 . . . . DLB-257
Lesperance, John 1835?-1891 . . . . DLB-99	Lewis, R. W. B. 1917-2002 . . . . DLB-111	Lindgren, Torgny 1938- DLB-257
Lespinasse, Julie de 1732-1776 . . . . DLB-313	Lewis, Richard circa 1700-1734 . . . . DLB-24	Lindsay, Alexander William, Twenty-fifth
Lessing, Bruno 1870-1940 . . . . DLB-28	Lewis, Saunders 1893-1985 . . . . DLB-310	Earl of Crawford 1812-1880 . . . . DLB-184
Lessing, Doris	Lewis, Sinclair	Lindsay, Sir David circa 1485-1555 . . . . . . DLB-132
1919- DLB-15, 139; Y-85; CDBLB-8	1885-1951 . . . . . . DLB-9, 102; DS-1; CDALB-4	Lindsay, David 1878-1945 . . . . DLB-255
Lessing, Gotthold Ephraim	Sinclair Lewis Centennial Conference Y-85	Lindsay, Jack 1900-1990 . . . . Y-84
1729-1781 . . . . DLB-97; CDWLB-2	The Sinclair Lewis Society Y-99	Lindsay, Lady (Caroline Blanche
The Lessing Society Y-00	Lewis, Wilmarth Sheldon 1895-1979 . . . . . DLB-140	Elizabeth Fitzroy Lindsay)
Le Sueur, Meridel 1900-1996 . . . . DLB-303	Lewis, Wyndham 1882-1957 . . . . DLB-15	1844-1912 . . . . DLB-199
Lettau, Reinhard 1929-1996 . . . . DLB-75	Time and Western Man	Lindsay, Norman 1879-1969 . . . . DLB-260
Letters from a Peruvian Woman, Françoise d'Issembourg	[excerpt] (1927) DLB-36	Lindsay, Vachel
de Graffigny DLB-314	Lewisohn, Ludwig 1882-1955 . . . DLB-4, 9, 28, 102	1879-1931 . . . . DLB-54; CDALB-3
The Hemingway Letters Project Finds	Leyendecker, J. C. 1874-1951 . . . . DLB-188	Linebarger, Paul Myron Anthony
an Editor Y-02	Leyner, Mark 1956- DLB-292	(see Smith, Cordwainer)
Lever, Charles 1806-1872 . . . . DLB-21	Lezama Lima, José 1910-1976 . . . . . . DLB-113, 283	Link, Arthur S. 1920-1998 . . . . DLB-17
Lever, Ralph ca. 1527-1585 . . . . DLB-236	Lézardière, Marie-Charlotte-Pauline Robert de	Linn, Ed 1922-2000 . . . . DLB-241
Leverson, Ada 1862-1933 . . . . DLB-153	1754-1835 . . . . DLB-313	Linn, John Blair 1777-1804 . . . . DLB-37
Levertov, Denise	L'Heureux, John 1934- DLB-244	Lins, Osman 1924-1978 . . . . DLB-145, 307
1923-1997 . . . . DLB-5, 165; CDALB-7	Libbey, Laura Jean 1862-1924 . . . . DLB-221	Linton, Eliza Lynn 1822-1898 . . . . DLB-18
Levi, Peter 1931-2000 . . . . DLB-40	Libedinsky, Iurii Nikolaevich	Linton, William James 1812-1897 . . . . DLB-32
Levi, Primo 1919-1987 . . . . DLB-177, 299	1898-1959 . . . . DLB-272	Barnaby Bernard Lintot
Levien, Sonya 1888-1960 . . . . DLB-44	The Liberator DLB-303	[publishing house] DLB-170
Levin, Meyer 1905-1981 . . . . DLB-9, 28; Y-81	Library History Group Y-01	Lion Books DLB-46
Levin, Phillis 1954- DLB-282	E-Books' Second Act in Libraries Y-02	Lionni, Leo 1910-1999 . . . . DLB-61
Lévinas, Emmanuel 1906-1995 . . . . DLB-296	The Library of America DLB-46	Lippard, George 1822-1854 . . . . DLB-202
Levine, Norman 1923- DLB-88	The Library of America: An Assessment	Lippincott, Sara Jane Clarke
Levine, Philip 1928- DLB-5	After Two Decades Y-02	1823-1904 . . . . DLB-43
Levis, Larry 1946- DLB-120	Licensing Act of 1737 . . . . DLB-84	J. B. Lippincott Company DLB-49
Lévi-Strauss, Claude 1908- DLB-242	Leonard Lichfield I [publishing house] . . . DLB-170	Lippmann, Walter 1889-1974 . . . . DLB-29
Levitov, Aleksandr Ivanovich	Lichtenberg, Georg Christoph	Lipton, Lawrence 1898-1975 . . . . DLB-16
1835?-1877 . . . . DLB-277	1742-1799 . . . . DLB-94	Lisboa, Irene 1892-1958 . . . . DLB-287
Levy, Amy 1861-1889 . . . . DLB-156, 240	The Liddle Collection Y-97	Liscow, Christian Ludwig
Levy, Benn Wolfe 1900-1973 . . . . . . DLB-13; Y-81	Lidman, Sara 1923-2004 . . . . DLB-257	1701-1760 . . . . DLB-97
Levy, Deborah 1959- DLB-310	Lieb, Fred 1888-1980 . . . . DLB-171	Lish, Gordon 1934- DLB-130
Lewald, Fanny 1811-1889 . . . . DLB-129	Liebling, A. J. 1904-1963 . . . . DLB-4, 171	Tribute to Donald Barthelme Y-89
Lewes, George Henry 1817-1878 . . . . . DLB-55, 144	Lieutenant Murray (see Ballou, Maturin Murray)	Tribute to James Dickey Y-97
"Criticism in Relation to Novels"	Lighthall, William Douw 1857-1954 . . . . . . DLB-92	Lisle, Charles-Marie-René Leconte de
(1863) DLB-21	Lihn, Enrique 1929-1988 . . . . DLB-283	1818-1894 . . . . DLB-217
The Principles of Success in Literature	Lilar, Françoise (see Mallet-Joris, Françoise)	Lispector, Clarice
(1865) [excerpt] DLB-57	Lili'uokalani, Queen 1838-1917 . . . . DLB-221	1925?-1977 . . . . DLB-113, 307; CDWLB-3
Lewis, Agnes Smith 1843-1926 . . . . DLB-174	Lillo, George 1691-1739 . . . . DLB-84	LitCheck Website Y-01
		Literary Awards and Honors Y-81–02

Cumulative Index   DLB 319

Booker Prize. Y-86, 96–98
The Drue Heinz Literature Prize Y-82
The Elmer Holmes Bobst Awards
    in Arts and Letters Y-87
The Griffin Poetry Prize Y-00
Literary Prizes [British] DLB-15, 207
National Book Critics Circle
    Awards. Y-00–01
The National Jewish
    Book Awards Y-85
Nobel Prize. Y-80–02
Winning an Edgar Y-98

The Literary Chronicle and Weekly Review
    1819-1828 . . . . DLB-110
Literary Periodicals:
    Callaloo Y-87
    Expatriates in Paris DS-15
    New Literary Periodicals:
        A Report for 1987 . . . . Y-87
        A Report for 1988 . . . . Y-88
        A Report for 1989 . . . . Y-89
        A Report for 1990 . . . . Y-90
        A Report for 1991 . . . . Y-91
        A Report for 1992 . . . . Y-92
        A Report for 1993 . . . . Y-93
Literary Research Archives
    The Anthony Burgess Archive at
        the Harry Ransom Humanities
        Research Center Y-98
    Archives of Charles Scribner's Sons. DS-17
    Berg Collection of English and
        American Literature of the
        New York Public Library Y-83
    The Bobbs-Merrill Archive at the
        Lilly Library, Indiana University Y-90
    Die Fürstliche Bibliothek Corvey Y-96
    Guide to the Archives of Publishers,
        Journals, and Literary Agents in
        North American Libraries Y-93
    The Henry E. Huntington Library Y-92
    The Humanities Research Center,
        University of Texas. Y-82
    The John Carter Brown Library Y-85
    Kent State Special Collections Y-86
    The Lilly Library Y-84
    The Modern Literary Manuscripts
        Collection in the Special
        Collections of the Washington
        University Libraries. Y-87
    A Publisher's Archives: G. P. Putnam Y-92
    Special Collections at Boston
        University Y-99
    The University of Virginia Libraries Y-91
    The William Charvat American Fiction
        Collection at the Ohio State
        University Libraries. Y-92
Literary Societies Y-98–02
    The Margery Allingham Society Y-98
    The American Studies Association
        of Norway Y-00
    The Arnold Bennett Society Y-98

The Association for the Study of
    Literature and Environment
    (ASLE) Y-99
Belgian Luxembourg American Studies
    Association Y-01
The E. F. Benson Society Y-98
The Elizabeth Bishop Society Y-01
The [Edgar Rice] Burroughs
    Bibliophiles Y-98
The Byron Society of America Y-00
The Lewis Carroll Society
    of North America Y-00
The Willa Cather Pioneer Memorial
    and Education Foundation Y-00
New Chaucer Society. Y-00
The Wilkie Collins Society Y-98
The James Fenimore Cooper Society Y-01
The Stephen Crane Society Y-98, 01
The E. E. Cummings Society. Y-01
The James Dickey Society Y-99
John Dos Passos Newsletter Y-00
The Priory Scholars [Sir Arthur Conan
    Doyle] of New York Y-99
The International Theodore Dreiser
    Society Y-01
The Friends of the Dymock Poets Y-00
The George Eliot Fellowship Y-99
The T. S. Eliot Society: Celebration and
    Scholarship, 1980-1999 . . . . Y-99
The Ralph Waldo Emerson Society Y-99
The William Faulkner Society Y-99
The C. S. Forester Society Y-00
The Hamlin Garland Society Y-01
The [Elizabeth] Gaskell Society Y-98
The Charlotte Perkins Gilman Society . . Y-99
The Ellen Glasgow Society Y-01
Zane Grey's West Society Y-00
The Ivor Gurney Society Y-98
The Joel Chandler Harris Association Y-99
The Nathaniel Hawthorne Society. Y-00
The [George Alfred] Henty Society Y-98
George Moses Horton Society Y-99
The William Dean Howells Society Y-01
WW2 HMSO Paperbacks Society Y-98
American Humor Studies Association Y-99
International Society for Humor Studies . . . Y-99
The W. W. Jacobs Appreciation Society . . Y-98
The Richard Jefferies Society Y-98
The Jerome K. Jerome Society Y-98
The D. H. Lawrence Society of
    North America Y-00
The T. E. Lawrence Society Y-98
The [Gotthold] Lessing Society Y-00
The New York C. S. Lewis Society Y-99
The Sinclair Lewis Society Y-99
The Jack London Research Center Y-00
The Jack London Society. Y-99

The Cormac McCarthy Society. Y-99
The Melville Society Y-01
The Arthur Miller Society Y-01
The Milton Society of America Y-00
International Marianne Moore Society . . . Y-98
International Nabokov Society. Y-99
The Vladimir Nabokov Society Y-01
The Flannery O'Connor Society Y-99
The Wilfred Owen Association Y-98
Penguin Collectors' Society Y-98
The [E. A.] Poe Studies Association Y-99
The Katherine Anne Porter Society Y-01
The Beatrix Potter Society Y-98
The Ezra Pound Society Y-01
The Powys Society. Y-98
Proust Society of America Y-00
The Dorothy L. Sayers Society Y-98
The Bernard Shaw Society. Y-99
The Society for the Study of
    Southern Literature Y-00
The Wallace Stevens Society Y-99
The Harriet Beecher Stowe Center Y-00
The R. S. Surtees Society Y-98
The Thoreau Society Y-99
The Tilling [E. F. Benson] Society Y-98
The Trollope Societies Y-00
H. G. Wells Society Y-98
The Western Literature Association Y-99
The William Carlos Williams Society Y-99
The Henry Williamson Society Y-98
The [Nero] Wolfe Pack Y-99
The Thomas Wolfe Society Y-99
Worldwide Wodehouse Societies Y-98
The W. B. Yeats Society of N.Y. Y-99
The Charlotte M. Yonge Fellowship Y-98
Literary Theory
    The Year in Literary Theory Y-92–Y-93
Literature at Nurse, or Circulating Morals (1885),
    by George Moore. DLB-18
Litt, Toby 1968- DLB-267, 319
Littell, Eliakim 1797-1870 . . . . DLB-79
Littell, Robert S. 1831-1896 . . . . DLB-79
Little, Brown and Company. DLB-49
Little Magazines and Newspapers DS-15
    Selected English-Language Little
        Magazines and Newspapers
        [France, 1920-1939] DLB-4
The Little Magazines of the
    New Formalism DLB-282
The Little Review 1914-1929 . . . . DS-15
Littlewood, Joan 1914-2002 . . . . DLB-13
Liu, Aimee E. 1953- DLB-312
Lively, Penelope 1933- DLB-14, 161, 207
Liverpool University Press. DLB-112
The Lives of the Poets (1753). DLB-142
Livesay, Dorothy 1909-1996 . . . . DLB-68

424

Livesay, Florence Randal 1874-1953......DLB-92
Livings, Henry 1929-1998..............DLB-13
Livingston, Anne Howe 1763-1841...DLB-37, 200
Livingston, Jay 1915-2001..............DLB-265
Livingston, Myra Cohn 1926-1996.......DLB-61
Livingston, William 1723-1790..........DLB-31
Livingstone, David 1813-1873..........DLB-166
Livingstone, Douglas 1932-1996........DLB-225
Livshits, Benedikt Konstantinovich
 1886-1938 or 1939...............DLB-295
Livy 59 B.C.-A.D. 17........DLB-211; CDWLB-1
Liyong, Taban lo (see Taban lo Liyong)
Lizárraga, Sylvia S. 1925-..............DLB-82
Llewellyn, Richard 1906-1983..........DLB-15
Lloréns Torres, Luis 1876-1944.........DLB-290
Edward Lloyd [publishing house].......DLB-106
Lobato, José Bento Monteiro
 1882-1948......................DLB-307
Lobel, Arnold 1933-....................DLB-61
Lochhead, Liz 1947-...................DLB-310
Lochridge, Betsy Hopkins (see Fancher, Betsy)
Locke, Alain 1886-1954.................DLB-51
Locke, David Ross 1833-1888........DLB-11, 23
Locke, John 1632-1704.....DLB-31, 101, 213, 252
Locke, Richard Adams 1800-1871........DLB-43
Locker-Lampson, Frederick
 1821-1895...................DLB-35, 184
Lockhart, John Gibson
 1794-1854............... DLB-110, 116 144
Lockridge, Francis 1896-1963..........DLB-306
Lockridge, Richard 1898-1982..........DLB-306
Lockridge, Ross, Jr. 1914-1948....DLB-143; Y-80
Locrine and Selimus....................DLB-62
Lodge, David 1935-.................DLB-14, 194
Lodge, George Cabot 1873-1909.........DLB-54
Lodge, Henry Cabot 1850-1924..........DLB-47
Lodge, Thomas 1558-1625..............DLB-172
 Defence of Poetry (1579) [excerpt]......DLB-172
Loeb, Harold 1891-1974...........DLB-4; DS-15
Loeb, William 1905-1981...............DLB-127
Loesser, Frank 1910-1969..............DLB-265
Lofting, Hugh 1886-1947...............DLB-160
Logan, Deborah Norris 1761-1839......DLB-200
Logan, James 1674-1751............DLB-24, 140
Logan, John 1923-1987..................DLB-5
Logan, Martha Daniell 1704?-1779......DLB-200
Logan, William 1950-..................DLB-120
Logau, Friedrich von 1605-1655........DLB-164
Logue, Christopher 1926-...............DLB-27
Lohenstein, Daniel Casper von
 1635-1683......................DLB-168
Lo-Johansson, Ivar 1901-1990..........DLB-259
Lokert, George (or Lockhart)
 circa 1485-1547.................DLB-281
Lomonosov, Mikhail Vasil'evich
 1711-1765......................DLB-150

London, Jack
 1876-1916.....DLB-8, 12, 78, 212; CDALB-3
 The Jack London Research Center......Y-00
 The Jack London Society.............Y-99
The London Magazine 1820-1829.........DLB-110
Long, David 1948-...................DLB-244
Long, H., and Brother..................DLB-49
Long, Haniel 1888-1956.................DLB-45
Long, Ray 1878-1935..................DLB-137
Longfellow, Henry Wadsworth
 1807-1882........DLB-1, 59, 235; CDALB-2
Longfellow, Samuel 1819-1892...........DLB-1
Longford, Elizabeth 1906-2002.........DLB-155
 Tribute to Alfred A. Knopf............Y-84
Longinus circa first century............DLB-176
Longley, Michael 1939-.................DLB-40
T. Longman [publishing house].........DLB-154
Longmans, Green and Company.........DLB-49
Longmore, George 1793?-1867...........DLB-99
Longstreet, Augustus Baldwin
 1790-1870...............DLB-3, 11, 74, 248
D. Longworth [publishing house].........DLB-49
Lønn, Øystein 1936-..................DLB-297
Lonsdale, Frederick 1881-1954..........DLB-10
Loos, Anita 1893-1981.....DLB-11, 26, 228; Y-81
Lopate, Phillip 1943-...................Y-80
Lope de Rueda 1510?-1565?............DLB-318
Lopes, Fernão 1380/1390?-1460?........DLB-287
Lopez, Barry 1945-.............DLB-256, 275
López, Diana (see Isabella, Ríos)
López, Josefina 1969-.................DLB-209
López de Mendoza, Íñigo
 (see Santillana, Marqués de)
López Velarde, Ramón 1888-1921......DLB-290
Loranger, Jean-Aubert 1896-1942........DLB-92
Lorca, Federico García 1898-1936......DLB-108
Lord, John Keast 1818-1872.............DLB-99
Lorde, Audre 1934-1992................DLB-41
Lorimer, George Horace 1867-1937......DLB-91
A. K. Loring [publishing house].........DLB-49
Loring and Mussey.....................DLB-46
Lorris, Guillaume de (see *Roman de la Rose*)
Lossing, Benson J. 1813-1891...........DLB-30
Lothar, Ernst 1890-1974................DLB-81
D. Lothrop and Company...............DLB-49
Lothrop, Harriet M. 1844-1924..........DLB-42
Loti, Pierre 1850-1923.................DLB-123
Lotichius Secundus, Petrus 1528-1560...DLB-179
Lott, Emmeline fl. nineteenth century....DLB-166
Louisiana State University Press.........Y-97
Lounsbury, Thomas R. 1838-1915.......DLB-71
Louÿs, Pierre 1870-1925...............DLB-123
Løveid, Cecile 1951-..................DLB-297
Lovejoy, Arthur O. 1873-1962..........DLB-270
Lovelace, Earl 1935-.......DLB-125; CDWLB-3

Lovelace, Richard 1618-1657..........DLB-131
John W. Lovell Company..............DLB-49
Lovell, Coryell and Company...........DLB-49
Lover, Samuel 1797-1868..........DLB-159, 190
Lovesey, Peter 1936-..................DLB-87
 Tribute to Georges Simenon..........Y-89
Lovinescu, Eugen
 1881-1943............DLB-220; CDWLB-4
Lovingood, Sut
 (see Harris, George Washington)
Low, Samuel 1765-?...................DLB-37
Lowell, Amy 1874-1925............DLB-54, 140
Lowell, James Russell 1819-1891
 ......DLB-1, 11, 64, 79, 189, 235; CDALB-2
Lowell, Robert
 1917-1977............DLB-5, 169; CDALB-7
Lowenfels, Walter 1897-1976............DLB-4
Lowndes, Marie Belloc 1868-1947........DLB-70
Lowndes, William Thomas 1798-1843...DLB-184
Humphrey Lownes [publishing house]...DLB-170
Lowry, Lois 1937-....................DLB-52
Lowry, Malcolm 1909-1957....DLB-15; CDBLB-7
Lowther, Pat 1935-1975................DLB-53
Loy, Mina 1882-1966................DLB-4, 54
Loynaz, Dulce María 1902-1997........DLB-283
Lozeau, Albert 1878-1924...............DLB-92
Lubbock, Percy 1879-1965.............DLB-149
Lucan A.D. 39-A.D. 65................DLB-211
Lucas, E. V. 1868-1938........DLB-98, 149, 153
Fielding Lucas Jr. [publishing house]......DLB-49
Luce, Clare Booth 1903-1987..........DLB-228
Luce, Henry R. 1898-1967..............DLB-91
John W. Luce and Company............DLB-46
Lucena, Juan de ca. 1430-1501.........DLB-286
Lucian circa 120-180..................DLB-176
Lucie-Smith, Edward 1933-.............DLB-40
Lucilius circa 180 B.C.-102/101 B.C......DLB-211
Lucini, Gian Pietro 1867-1914..........DLB-114
Luco Cruchaga, Germán 1894-1936.....DLB-305
Lucretius circa 94 B.C.-circa 49 B.C.
 ....DLB-211; CDWLB-1
Luder, Peter circa 1415-1472...........DLB-179
Ludlam, Charles 1943-1987............DLB-266
Ludlum, Robert 1927-2001..............Y-82
Ludus de Antichristo circa 1160..........DLB-148
Ludvigson, Susan 1942-...............DLB-120
Ludwig, Jack 1922-...................DLB-60
Ludwig, Otto 1813-1865...............DLB-129
Ludwigslied 881 or 882.................DLB-148
Luera, Yolanda 1953-.................DLB-122
Luft, Lya 1938-.......................DLB-145
Lugansky, Kazak Vladimir
 (see Dal', Vladimir Ivanovich)
Lugn, Kristina 1948-..................DLB-257
Lugones, Leopoldo 1874-1938..........DLB-283
Luhan, Mabel Dodge 1879-1962........DLB-303

Cumulative Index

Lukács, Georg (see Lukács, György)
Lukács, György 1885-1971 .... DLB-215, 242; CDWLB-4
Luke, Peter 1919-1995 .... DLB-13
Lummis, Charles F. 1859-1928 .... DLB-186
Lundkvist, Artur 1906-1991 .... DLB-259
Lunts, Lev Natanovich 1901-1924 ...... DLB-272
F. M. Lupton Company DLB-49
Lupus of Ferrières circa 805-circa 862 ... DLB-148
Lurie, Alison 1926- DLB-2
Lussu, Emilio 1890-1975 .... DLB-264
Lustig, Arnošt 1926- DLB-232, 299
Luther, Martin 1483-1546 .... DLB-179; CDWLB-2
Luzi, Mario 1914-2005 .... DLB-128
L'vov, Nikolai Aleksandrovich 1751-1803 .... DLB-150
Lyall, Gavin 1932-2003 .... DLB-87
Lydgate, John circa 1370-1450 .... DLB-146
Lyly, John circa 1554-1606 .... DLB-62, 167
Lynch, Martin 1950- DLB-310
Lynch, Patricia 1898-1972 .... DLB-160
Lynch, Richard fl. 1596-1601 .... DLB-172
Lynd, Robert 1879-1949 .... DLB-98
Lynds, Dennis (Michael Collins) 1924- DLB-306
    Tribute to John D. MacDonald Y-86
    Tribute to Kenneth Millar Y-83
    Why I Write Mysteries: Night and Day .. Y-85
Lyon, Matthew 1749-1822 .... DLB-43
Lyotard, Jean-François 1924-1998 ...... DLB-242
Lyricists
    Additional Lyricists: 1920-1960 ..... DLB-265
Lysias circa 459 B.C.-circa 380 B.C. DLB-176
Lytle, Andrew 1902-1995 .... DLB-6; Y-95
    Tribute to Caroline Gordon Y-81
    Tribute to Katherine Anne Porter Y-80
Lytton, Edward (see Bulwer-Lytton, Edward)
Lytton, Edward Robert Bulwer 1831-1891 .... DLB-32

M

Maass, Joachim 1901-1972 .... DLB-69
Mabie, Hamilton Wright 1845-1916 ..... DLB-71
Mac A'Ghobhainn, Iain (see Smith, Iain Crichton)
MacArthur, Charles 1895-1956 ..... DLB-7, 25, 44
Macaulay, Catherine 1731-1791 .... DLB-104
Macaulay, David 1945- DLB-61
Macaulay, Rose 1881-1958 .... DLB-36
Macaulay, Thomas Babington 1800-1859 .... DLB-32, 55; CDBLB-4
Macaulay Company DLB-46
MacBeth, George 1932-1992 .... DLB-40
Macbeth, Madge 1880-1965 .... DLB-92
MacCaig, Norman 1910-1996 .... DLB-27

MacDiarmid, Hugh 1892-1978 .... DLB-20; CDBLB-7
MacDonald, Cynthia 1928- DLB-105
MacDonald, George 1824-1905 .... DLB-18, 163, 178
MacDonald, John D. 1916-1986 .... DLB-8, 306; Y-86
MacDonald, Philip 1899?-1980 .... DLB-77
Macdonald, Ross (see Millar, Kenneth)
Macdonald, Sharman 1951- DLB-245
MacDonald, Wilson 1880-1967 .... DLB-92
Macdonald and Company (Publishers) .. DLB-112
MacEwen, Gwendolyn 1941-1987 ... DLB-53, 251
Macfadden, Bernarr 1868-1955 ...... DLB-25, 91
MacGregor, John 1825-1892 .... DLB-166
MacGregor, Mary Esther (see Keith, Marian)
Macherey, Pierre 1938- DLB-296
Machado, Antonio 1875-1939 .... DLB-108
Machado, Manuel 1874-1947 .... DLB-108
Machado de Assis, Joaquim Maria 1839-1908 .... DLB-307
Machar, Agnes Maule 1837-1927 .... DLB-92
Machaut, Guillaume de circa 1300-1377 .... DLB-208
Machen, Arthur Llewelyn Jones 1863-1947 .... DLB-36, 156, 178
MacIlmaine, Roland fl. 1574 .... DLB-281
MacInnes, Colin 1914-1976 .... DLB-14
MacInnes, Helen 1907-1985 .... DLB-87
Mac Intyre, Tom 1931- DLB-245
Mačiulis, Jonas (see Maironis, Jonas)
Mack, Maynard 1909-2001 .... DLB-111
Mackall, Leonard L. 1879-1937 .... DLB-140
MacKay, Isabel Ecclestone 1875-1928 .... DLB-92
Mackay, Shena 1944- DLB-231, 319
MacKaye, Percy 1875-1956 .... DLB-54
Macken, Walter 1915-1967 .... DLB-13
MacKenna, John 1952- DLB-319
Mackenzie, Alexander 1763-1820 ...... DLB-99
Mackenzie, Alexander Slidell 1803-1848 .... DLB-183
Mackenzie, Compton 1883-1972 .... DLB-34, 100
Mackenzie, Henry 1745-1831 .... DLB-39
    The Lounger, no. 20 (1785) DLB-39
Mackenzie, Kenneth (Seaforth Mackenzie) 1913-1955 .... DLB-260
Mackenzie, William 1758-1828 .... DLB-187
Mackey, Nathaniel 1947- DLB-169
Mackey, William Wellington 1937- DLB-38
Mackintosh, Elizabeth (see Tey, Josephine)
Mackintosh, Sir James 1765-1832 .... DLB-158
Macklin, Charles 1699-1797 .... DLB-89
Maclaren, Ian (see Watson, John)
Maclaren-Ross, Julian 1912-1964 .... DLB-319
MacLaverty, Bernard 1942- DLB-267
MacLean, Alistair 1922-1987 .... DLB-276
MacLean, Katherine Anne 1925- DLB-8

Maclean, Norman 1902-1990 .... DLB-206
MacLeish, Archibald 1892-1982 .... DLB-4, 7, 45; Y-82; DS-15; CDALB-7
MacLennan, Hugh 1907-1990 .... DLB-68
MacLeod, Alistair 1936- DLB-60
Macleod, Fiona (see Sharp, William)
Macleod, Norman 1906-1985 .... DLB-4
Mac Low, Jackson 1922-2004 .... DLB-193
MacMahon, Bryan 1909-1998 .... DLB-319
Macmillan and Company DLB-106
The Macmillan Company DLB-49
Macmillan's English Men of Letters, First Series (1878-1892) DLB-144
MacNamara, Brinsley 1890-1963 .... DLB-10
MacNeice, Louis 1907-1963 .... DLB-10, 20
Macphail, Andrew 1864-1938 .... DLB-92
Macpherson, James 1736-1796 .... DLB-109
Macpherson, Jay 1931- DLB-53
Macpherson, Jeanie 1884-1946 .... DLB-44
Macrae Smith Company DLB-46
MacRaye, Lucy Betty (see Webling, Lucy)
John Macrone [publishing house] DLB-106
MacShane, Frank 1927-1999 .... DLB-111
Macy-Masius DLB-46
Madden, David 1933- DLB-6
Madden, Sir Frederic 1801-1873 ...... DLB-184
Maddow, Ben 1909-1992 .... DLB-44
Maddux, Rachel 1912-1983 .... DLB-234; Y-93
Madgett, Naomi Long 1923- DLB-76
Madhubuti, Haki R. 1942- DLB-5, 41; DS-8
Madison, James 1751-1836 .... DLB-37
Madsen, Svend Åge 1939- DLB-214
Madrigal, Alfonso Fernández de (El Tostado) ca. 1405-1455 .... DLB-286
Maeterlinck, Maurice 1862-1949 ...... DLB-192
Mafūz, Najīb 1911- Y-88
    Nobel Lecture 1988 .... Y-88
The Little Magazines of the New Formalism DLB-282
Magee, David 1905-1977 .... DLB-187
Maginn, William 1794-1842 .... DLB-110, 159
Magoffin, Susan Shelby 1827-1855 ...... DLB-239
Mahan, Alfred Thayer 1840-1914 .... DLB-47
Maheux-Forcier, Louise 1929- DLB-60
Mahin, John Lee 1902-1984 .... DLB-44
Mahon, Derek 1941- DLB-40
Maiakovsky, Vladimir Vladimirovich 1893-1930 .... DLB-295
Maikov, Apollon Nikolaevich 1821-1897 .... DLB-277
Maikov, Vasilii Ivanovich 1728-1778 .... DLB-150
Mailer, Norman 1923- DLB-2, 16, 28, 185, 278; Y-80, 83, 97; DS-3; CDALB-6
    Tribute to Isaac Bashevis Singer Y-91
    Tribute to Meyer Levin Y-81
Maillart, Ella 1903-1997 .... DLB-195

Maillet, Adrienne 1885-1963 . . . . .DLB-68

Maillet, Antonine 1929- DLB-60

Maillu, David G. 1939- DLB-157

Maimonides, Moses 1138-1204 . . . . .DLB-115

Main Selections of the Book-of-the-Month
    Club, 1926-1945 . . . . .DLB-9

Mainwaring, Daniel 1902-1977 . . . . .DLB-44

Mair, Charles 1838-1927 . . . . .DLB-99

Mair, John circa 1467-1550 . . . . .DLB-281

Maironis, Jonas 1862-1932 . .DLB-220; CDWLB-4

Mais, Roger 1905-1955 . . . . . DLB-125; CDWLB-3

Maitland, Sara 1950- DLB-271

Major, Andre 1942- DLB-60

Major, Charles 1856-1913 . . . . .DLB-202

Major, Clarence 1936- DLB-33

Major, Kevin 1949- DLB-60

Major Books DLB-46

Makanin, Vladimir Semenovich
    1937- DLB-285

Makarenko, Anton Semenovich
    1888-1939 .DLB-272

Makemie, Francis circa 1658-1708 . . . . . . .DLB-24

The Making of Americans Contract Y-98

Makovsky, Sergei 1877-1962 . . . . .DLB-317

Maksimov, Vladimir Emel'ianovich
    1930-1995 .DLB-302

Maksimović, Desanka
    1898-1993 . . . . DLB-147; CDWLB-4

Malamud, Bernard 1914-1986
    . . . . .DLB-2, 28, 152; Y-80, 86; CDALB-1

    Bernard Malamud Archive at the
        Harry Ransom Humanities
        Research Center Y-00

Mălăncioiu, Ileana 1940- DLB-232

Malaparte, Curzio
    (Kurt Erich Suckert) 1898-1957 . . . . . .DLB-264

Malerba, Luigi 1927- DLB-196

Malet, Lucas 1852-1931 . . . . .DLB-153

Mallarmé, Stéphane 1842-1898 . . . . .DLB-217

Malleson, Lucy Beatrice (see Gilbert, Anthony)

Mallet-Joris, Françoise (Françoise Lilar)
    1930- DLB-83

Mallock, W. H. 1849-1923 . . . . .DLB-18, 57

    "Every Man His Own Poet; or,
        The Inspired Singer's Recipe
        Book" (1877) DLB-35

    "Le Style c'est l'homme" (1892) DLB-57

    Memoirs of Life and Literature (1920),
        [excerpt] DLB-57

Malone, Dumas 1892-1986 . . . . .DLB-17

Malone, Edmond 1741-1812 . . . . .DLB-142

Malory, Sir Thomas
    circa 1400-1410 - 1471 . . . DLB-146; CDBLB-1

Malouf, David 1934- DLB-289

Malpede, Karen 1945- DLB-249

Malraux, André 1901-1976 . . . . .DLB-72

The Maltese Falcon (Documentary) DLB-280

Malthus, Thomas Robert
    1766-1834 . . . . DLB-107, 158

Maltz, Albert 1908-1985 . . . . .DLB-102

Malzberg, Barry N. 1939- DLB-8

Mamet, David 1947- DLB-7

Mamin, Dmitrii Narkisovich
    1852-1912 .DLB-238

Manaka, Matsemela 1956- DLB-157

Manchester University Press DLB-112

Mandel, Eli 1922-1992 . . . . .DLB-53

Mandel'shtam, Nadezhda Iakovlevna
    1899-1980 .DLB-302

Mandel'shtam, Osip Emil'evich
    1891-1938 .DLB-295

Mandeville, Bernard 1670-1733 . . . . .DLB-101

Mandeville, Sir John
    mid fourteenth century DLB-146

Mandiargues, André Pieyre de
    1909-1991 . . . . .DLB-83

Manea, Norman 1936- DLB-232

Manfred, Frederick 1912-1994 . . . .DLB-6, 212, 227

Manfredi, Gianfranco 1948- DLB-196

Mangan, Sherry 1904-1961 . . . . .DLB-4

Manganelli, Giorgio 1922-1990 . . . . .DLB-196

Manilius fl. first century A.D. DLB-211

Mankiewicz, Herman 1897-1953 . . . . .DLB-26

Mankiewicz, Joseph L. 1909-1993 . . . . . . .DLB-44

Mankowitz, Wolf 1924-1998 . . . . .DLB-15

Manley, Delarivière 1672?-1724 . . . . . . .DLB-39, 80

    Preface to *The Secret History, of Queen
        Zarah, and the Zarazians* (1705) DLB-39

Mann, Abby 1927- DLB-44

Mann, Charles 1929-1998 . . . . Y-98

Mann, Emily 1952- DLB-266

Mann, Heinrich 1871-1950 . . . . .DLB-66, 118

Mann, Horace 1796-1859 . . . . .DLB-1, 235

Mann, Klaus 1906-1949 . . . . .DLB-56

Mann, Mary Peabody 1806-1887 . . . . . . .DLB-239

Mann, Thomas 1875-1955 . . . .DLB-66; CDWLB-2

Mann, William D'Alton 1839-1920 . . . . . .DLB-137

Mannin, Ethel 1900-1984 . . . . .DLB-191, 195

Manning, Emily (see Australie)

Manning, Frederic 1882-1935 . . . . .DLB-260

Manning, Laurence 1899-1972 . . . . .DLB-251

Manning, Marie 1873?-1945 . . . . .DLB-29

Manning and Loring DLB-49

Mannyng, Robert fl.
    1303-1338 .DLB-146

Mano, D. Keith 1942- DLB-6

Manor Books .DLB-46

Manrique, Gómez 1412?-1490 . . . . .DLB-286

Manrique, Jorge ca. 1440-1479 . . . . .DLB-286

Mansfield, Katherine 1888-1923 . . . . .DLB-162

Mantel, Hilary 1952- DLB-271

Manuel, Niklaus circa 1484-1530 . . . . . . .DLB-179

Manzini, Gianna 1896-1974 . . . . .DLB-177

Mapanje, Jack 1944- DLB-157

Maraini, Dacia 1936- DLB-196

Maraise, Marie-Catherine-Renée Darcel de
    1737-1822 .DLB-314

Maramzin, Vladimir Rafailovich
    1934- DLB-302

March, William (William Edward Campbell)
    1893-1954 . . . . DLB-9, 86, 316

Marchand, Leslie A. 1900-1999 . . . . .DLB-103

Marchant, Bessie 1862-1941 . . . . .DLB-160

Marchant, Tony 1959- DLB-245

Marchenko, Anastasiia Iakovlevna
    1830-1880 .DLB-238

Marchessault, Jovette 1938- DLB-60

Marcinkevičius, Justinas 1930- DLB-232

Marcos, Plínio (Plínio Marcos de Barros)
    1935-1999 .DLB-307

Marcus, Frank 1928- DLB-13

Marcuse, Herbert 1898-1979 . . . . .DLB-242

Marden, Orison Swett 1850-1924 . . . . . . .DLB-137

Marechera, Dambudzo 1952-1987 . . . . . . .DLB-157

Marek, Richard, Books DLB-46

Mares, E. A. 1938- DLB-122

Margulies, Donald 1954- DLB-228

Mariana, Juan de 1535 or 1536-1624 . . . .DLB-318

Mariani, Paul 1940- DLB-111

Marie de France fl. 1160-1178 . . . . .DLB-208

Marie-Victorin, Frère (Conrad Kirouac)
    1885-1944 . . . . .DLB-92

Marin, Biagio 1891-1985 . . . . .DLB-128

Marinetti, Filippo Tommaso
    1876-1944 . . . . DLB-114, 264

Marinina, Aleksandra (Marina Anatol'evna
    Alekseeva) 1957- DLB-285

Marinković, Ranko
    1913-2001 . . . . DLB-147; CDWLB-4

Marion, Frances 1886-1973 . . . . .DLB-44

Marius, Richard C. 1933-1999 . . . . Y-85

Marivaux, Pierre Carlet de Chamblain de
    1688-1763 .DLB-314

Markevich, Boleslav Mikhailovich
    1822-1884 .DLB-238

Markfield, Wallace 1926-2002 . . . . . . .DLB-2, 28

Markham, E. A. 1939- DLB-319

Markham, Edwin 1852-1940 . . . . . .DLB-54, 186

Markish, David 1938- DLB-317

Markle, Fletcher 1921-1991 . . . . . . .DLB-68; Y-91

Marlatt, Daphne 1942- DLB-60

Marlitt, E. 1825-1887 . . . . .DLB-129

Marlowe, Christopher
    1564-1593 . . . . .DLB-62; CDBLB-1

Marlyn, John 1912-1985 . . . . .DLB-88

Marmion, Shakerley 1603-1639 . . . . .DLB-58

Marmontel, Jean-François 1723-1799 . . . . .DLB-314

Der Marner before 1230-circa 1287 . . . . . .DLB-138

Marnham, Patrick 1943- DLB-204

The Marprelate Tracts 1588-1589 . . . . .DLB-132

Marquand, John P. 1893-1960 . . . . . . .DLB-9, 102

Marques, Helena 1935- DLB-287

Marqués, René 1919-1979 . . . . .DLB-113, 305

Cumulative Index

Marquis, Don 1878-1937 .... DLB-11, 25
Marriott, Anne 1913-1997 .... DLB-68
Marryat, Frederick 1792-1848 ...... DLB-21, 163
Marsh, Capen, Lyon and Webb......... DLB-49
Marsh, George Perkins
  1801-1882 .... DLB-1, 64, 243
Marsh, James 1794-1842............. DLB-1, 59
Marsh, Narcissus 1638-1713 .... DLB-213
Marsh, Ngaio 1899-1982 .... DLB-77
Marshall, Alan 1902-1984............. DLB-260
Marshall, Edison 1894-1967 .... DLB-102
Marshall, Edward 1932- DLB-16
Marshall, Emma 1828-1899 .... DLB-163
Marshall, James 1942-1992............ DLB-61
Marshall, Joyce 1913- DLB-88
Marshall, Paule 1929- DLB-33, 157, 227
Marshall, Tom 1938-1993 .... DLB-60
Marsilius of Padua
  circa 1275-circa 1342 .... DLB-115
Mars-Jones, Adam 1954- DLB-207, 319
Marson, Una 1905-1965............... DLB-157
Marston, John 1576-1634 ....DLB-58, 172
Marston, Philip Bourke 1850-1887....... DLB-35
Martens, Kurt 1870-1945 .... DLB-66
Martí, José 1853-1895................ DLB-290
Martial circa A.D. 40-circa A.D. 103
  .... DLB-211; CDWLB-1
William S. Martien [publishing house] DLB-49
Martin, Abe (see Hubbard, Kin)
Martin, Catherine ca. 1847-1937........ DLB-230
Martin, Charles 1942- DLB-120, 282
Martin, Claire 1914- DLB-60
Martin, David 1915-1997 .... DLB-260
Martin, Jay 1935- DLB-111
Martin, Johann (see Laurentius von Schnüffis)
Martin, Thomas 1696-1771............ DLB-213
Martin, Violet Florence (see Ross, Martin)
Martin du Gard, Roger 1881-1958....... DLB-65
Martineau, Harriet
  1802-1876.....DLB-21, 55, 159, 163, 166, 190
Martínez, Demetria 1960- DLB-209
Martínez de Toledo, Alfonso
  1398?-1468.................... DLB-286
Martínez, Eliud 1935- DLB-122
Martínez, Max 1943- DLB-82
Martínez, Rubén 1962- DLB-209
Martinson, Harry 1904-1978 .... DLB-259
Martinson, Moa 1890-1964 .... DLB-259
Martone, Michael 1955- DLB-218
Martyn, Edward 1859-1923 .... DLB-10
Marvell, Andrew
  1621-1678.............. DLB-131; CDBLB-2
Marvin X 1944- DLB-38
Marx, Karl 1818-1883 .... DLB-129
Marzials, Theo 1850-1920 .... DLB-35

Masefield, John 1878-1967
  .... DLB-10, 19, 153, 160; CDBLB-5
Masham, Damaris Cudworth, Lady
  1659-1708..................... DLB-252
Masino, Paola 1908-1989 .... DLB-264
Mason, A. E. W. 1865-1948 .... DLB-70
Mason, Bobbie Ann
  1940- DLB-173; Y-87; CDALB-7
Mason, F. van Wyck (Geoffrey Coffin, Frank W.
  Mason, Ward Weaver) 1901-1978 ... DLB-306
Mason, William 1725-1797 .... DLB-142
Mason Brothers DLB-49
The Massachusetts Quarterly Review
  1847-1850 .... DLB-1
The Masses....................... DLB-303
Massey, Gerald 1828-1907 .... DLB-32
Massey, Linton R. 1900-1974 .... DLB-187
Massie, Allan 1938- DLB-271
Massinger, Philip 1583-1640 .... DLB-58
Masson, David 1822-1907 .... DLB-144
Masters, Edgar Lee
  1868-1950 .... DLB-54; CDALB-3
Masters, Hilary 1928- DLB-244
Mastronardi, Lucio 1930-1979 ....DLB-177
Mat' Maria (Elizaveta Kuz'mina-Karavdeva
  Skobtsova, née Pilenko) 1891-1945 .... DLB-317
Matevski, Mateja 1929- ... DLB-181; CDWLB-4
Mather, Cotton
  1663-1728....... DLB-24, 30, 140; CDALB-2
Mather, Increase 1639-1723 .... DLB-24
Mather, Richard 1596-1669 .... DLB-24
Matheson, Annie 1853-1924............ DLB-240
Matheson, Richard 1926- DLB-8, 44
Matheus, John F. 1887-1986 .... DLB-51
Mathews, Aidan 1956- DLB-319
Mathews, Cornelius 1817?-1889... DLB-3, 64, 250
Elkin Mathews [publishing house] DLB-112
Mathews, John Joseph 1894-1979........DLB-175
Mathias, Roland 1915- DLB-27
Mathis, June 1892-1927 .... DLB-44
Mathis, Sharon Bell 1937- DLB-33
Matković, Marijan 1915-1985 .... DLB-181
Matoš, Antun Gustav 1873-1914 .... DLB-147
Matos Paoli, Francisco 1915-2000 ...... DLB-290
Matsumoto Seichō 1909-1992 .... DLB-182
The Matter of England 1240-1400 ...... DLB-146
The Matter of Rome early twelfth to late
  fifteenth century................ DLB-146
Matthew of Vendôme
  circa 1130-circa 1200 .... DLB-208
Matthews, Brander 1852-1929 ..DLB-71, 78; DS-13
Matthews, Jack 1925- DLB-6
Matthews, Victoria Earle 1861-1907 .... DLB-221
Matthews, William 1942-1997 .... DLB-5
Matthías Jochumsson 1835-1920 .... DLB-293
Matthías Johannessen 1930- DLB-293
Matthiessen, F. O. 1902-1950........... DLB-63

Matthiessen, Peter 1927- DLB-6, 173, 275
Maturin, Charles Robert 1780-1824......DLB-178
Maugham, W. Somerset 1874-1965
  .... DLB-10, 36, 77, 100, 162, 195; CDBLB-6
Maupassant, Guy de 1850-1893 .... DLB-123
Maupertuis, Pierre-Louis Moreau de
  1698-1759 .... DLB-314
Maupin, Armistead 1944- DLB-278
Mauriac, Claude 1914-1996............ DLB-83
Mauriac, François 1885-1970 .... DLB-65
Maurice, Frederick Denison 1805-1872 ... DLB-55
Maurois, André 1885-1967............. DLB-65
Maury, James 1718-1769................ DLB-31
Mavor, Elizabeth 1927- DLB-14
Mavor, Osborne Henry (see Bridie, James)
Maxwell, Gavin 1914-1969 .... DLB-204
Maxwell, William
  1908-2000 ....DLB-218, 278; Y-80
  Tribute to Nancy Hale............... Y-88
H. Maxwell [publishing house]......... DLB-49
John Maxwell [publishing house] DLB-106
May, Elaine 1932- DLB-44
May, Karl 1842-1912 .... DLB-129
May, Thomas 1595/1596-1650 .... DLB-58
Mayer, Bernadette 1945- DLB-165
Mayer, Mercer 1943- DLB-61
Mayer, O. B. 1818-1891............ DLB-3, 248
Mayes, Herbert R. 1900-1987 ....DLB-137
Mayes, Wendell 1919-1992 .... DLB-26
Mayfield, Julian 1928-1984..........DLB-33; Y-84
Mayhew, Henry 1812-1887 ......DLB-18, 55, 190
Mayhew, Jonathan 1720-1766........... DLB-31
Mayne, Ethel Colburn 1865-1941 ....DLB-197
Mayne, Jasper 1604-1672 .... DLB-126
Mayne, Seymour 1944- DLB-60
Mayor, Flora Macdonald 1872-1932 ..... DLB-36
Mayröcker, Friederike 1924- DLB-85
Mazrui, Ali A. 1933- DLB-125
Mažuranić, Ivan 1814-1890 ....DLB-147
Mazursky, Paul 1930- DLB-44
McAlmon, Robert 1896-1956... DLB-4, 45; DS-15
  "A Night at Bricktop's" Y-01
McArthur, Peter 1866-1924 .... DLB-92
McAuley, James 1917-1976 .... DLB-260
Robert M. McBride and Company DLB-46
McCabe, Patrick 1955- DLB-194
McCafferty, Owen 1961- DLB-310
McCaffrey, Anne 1926- DLB-8
McCann, Colum 1965- DLB-267
McCarthy, Cormac 1933- DLB-6, 143, 256
  The Cormac McCarthy Society......... Y-99
McCarthy, Mary 1912-1989.........DLB-2; Y-81
McCarthy, Shaun Lloyd (see Cory, Desmond)
McCay, Winsor 1871-1934 .... DLB-22
McClane, Albert Jules 1922-1991........DLB-171

McClatchy, C. K. 1858-1936 . . . . DLB-25	McGinniss, Joe 1942- DLB-185	Mda, Zakes 1948- DLB-225
McClellan, George Marion 1860-1934 . . . . DLB-50	McGirt, James E. 1874-1930 . . . . DLB-50	Mead, George Herbert 1863-1931 . . . . DLB-270
"The Negro as a Writer" DLB-50	McGlashan and Gill DLB-106	Mead, L. T. 1844-1914 . . . . DLB-141
McCloskey, Robert 1914-2003 . . . . DLB-22	McGough, Roger 1937- DLB-40	Mead, Matthew 1924- DLB-40
McCloy, Helen 1904-1992 . . . . DLB-306	McGrath, John 1935- DLB-233	Mead, Taylor circa 1931- DLB-16
McClung, Nellie Letitia 1873-1951 . . . . . . DLB-92	McGrath, Patrick 1950- DLB-231	Meany, Tom 1903-1964 . . . . DLB-171
McClure, James 1939- DLB-276	McGraw-Hill DLB-46	Mechthild von Magdeburg
McClure, Joanna 1930- DLB-16	McGuane, Thomas 1939- DLB-2, 212; Y-80	circa 1207-circa 1282 . . . . DLB-138
McClure, Michael 1932- DLB-16	Tribute to Seymour Lawrence Y-94	Medieval Galician-Portuguese Poetry DLB-287
McClure, Phillips and Company DLB-46	McGuckian, Medbh 1950- DLB-40	Medill, Joseph 1823-1899 . . . . DLB-43
McClure, S. S. 1857-1949 . . . . DLB-91	McGuffey, William Holmes 1800-1873 . . . . DLB-42	Medoff, Mark 1940- DLB-7
A. C. McClurg and Company DLB-49	McGuinness, Frank 1953- DLB-245	Meek, Alexander Beaufort
McCluskey, John A., Jr. 1944- DLB-33	McHenry, James 1785-1845 . . . . DLB-202	1814-1865 . . . . DLB-3, 248
McCollum, Michael A. 1946- Y-87	McIlvanney, William 1936- DLB-14, 207	Meeke, Mary ?-1816 . . . . DLB-116
McConnell, William C. 1917- DLB-88	McIlwraith, Jean Newton 1859-1938 . . . . . DLB-92	Mei, Lev Aleksandrovich 1822-1862 . . . . . DLB-277
McCord, David 1897-1997 . . . . DLB-61	McInerney, Jay 1955- DLB-292	Meinke, Peter 1932- DLB-5
McCord, Louisa S. 1810-1879 . . . . DLB-248	McInerny, Ralph 1929- DLB-306	Meireles, Cecília 1901-1964 . . . . DLB-307
McCorkle, Jill 1958- DLB-234; Y-87	McIntosh, Maria Jane 1803-1878 . . . . DLB-239, 248	Mejía, Pedro 1497-1551 . . . . DLB-318
McCorkle, Samuel Eusebius 1746-1811 . . . . DLB-37	McIntyre, James 1827-1906 . . . . DLB-99	Mejia Vallejo, Manuel 1923- DLB-113
McCormick, Anne O'Hare 1880-1954 . . . . DLB-29	McIntyre, O. O. 1884-1938 . . . . DLB-25	Melanchthon, Philipp 1497-1560 . . . . DLB-179
McCormick, Kenneth Dale 1906-1997 . . . . . . Y-97	McKay, Claude 1889-1948 . . . . DLB-4, 45, 51, 117	Melançon, Robert 1947- DLB-60
McCormick, Robert R. 1880-1955 . . . . . . DLB-29	The David McKay Company DLB-49	Mell, Max 1882-1971 . . . . DLB-81, 124
McCourt, Edward 1907-1972 . . . . DLB-88	McKean, William V. 1820-1903 . . . . DLB-23	Mellow, James R. 1926-1997 . . . . DLB-111
McCoy, Horace 1897-1955 . . . . DLB-9	McKenna, Stephen 1888-1967 . . . . DLB-197	Mel'nikov, Pavel Ivanovich 1818-1883 . . . DLB-238
McCrae, Hugh 1876-1958 . . . . DLB-260	The McKenzie Trust Y-96	Meltzer, David 1937- DLB-16
McCrae, John 1872-1918 . . . . DLB-92	McKerrow, R. B. 1872-1940 . . . . DLB-201	Meltzer, Milton 1915- DLB-61
McCrumb, Sharyn 1948- DLB-306	McKinley, Robin 1952- DLB-52	Melville, Elizabeth, Lady Culross
McCullagh, Joseph B. 1842-1896 . . . . DLB-23	McKnight, Reginald 1956- DLB-234	circa 1585-1640 . . . . DLB-172
McCullers, Carson	McLachlan, Alexander 1818-1896 . . . . DLB-99	Melville, Herman
1917-1967 . . . . . DLB-2, 7, 173, 228; CDALB-1	McLaren, Floris Clark 1904-1978 . . . . DLB-68	1819-1891 . . . . DLB-3, 74, 250; CDALB-2
McCulloch, Thomas 1776-1843 . . . . DLB-99	McLaverty, Michael 1907-1992 . . . . DLB-15	The Melville Society Y-01
McCunn, Ruthanne Lum 1946- DLB-312	McLean, Duncan 1964- DLB-267	Melville, James
McDermott, Alice 1953- DLB-292	McLean, John R. 1848-1916 . . . . DLB-23	(Roy Peter Martin) 1931- DLB-276
McDonald, Forrest 1927- DLB-17	McLean, William L. 1852-1931 . . . . DLB-25	"Memorandum on Local Government," Anne-
McDonald, Walter 1934- DLB-105, DS-9	McLennan, William 1856-1904 . . . . DLB-92	Robert-Jacques Turgot, bacon de
"Getting Started: Accepting the	McLoughlin Brothers DLB-49	l'Aulne DLB-314
Regions You Own–or Which	McLuhan, Marshall 1911-1980 . . . . DLB-88	Mena, Juan de 1411-1456 . . . . DLB-286
Own You" DLB-105	McMaster, John Bach 1852-1932 . . . . DLB-47	Mena, María Cristina 1893-1965 . . . . DLB-209, 221
Tribute to James Dickey Y-97	McMillan, Terri 1951- DLB-292	Menander 342-341 B.C.-circa 292-291 B.C.
McDougall, Colin 1917-1984 . . . . DLB-68	McMurtry, Larry 1936-	. . . . DLB-176; CDWLB-1
McDowell, Katharine Sherwood Bonner	. . . . . . DLB-2, 143, 256; Y-80, 87; CDALB-6	Menantes (see Hunold, Christian Friedrich)
1849-1883 . . . . DLB-202, 239	McNally, Terrence 1939- DLB-7, 249	Mencke, Johann Burckhard 1674-1732 . . . DLB-168
Obolensky McDowell	McNeil, Florence 1937- DLB-60	Mencken, H. L. 1880-1956
[publishing house] DLB-46	McNeile, Herman Cyril 1888-1937 . . . . . . DLB-77	. . . . DLB-11, 29, 63, 137, 222; CDALB-4
McEwan, Ian 1948- DLB-14, 194, 319	McNickle, D'Arcy 1904-1977 . . . . DLB-175, 212	"Berlin, February, 1917" Y-00
McFadden, David 1940- DLB-60	McPhee, John 1931- DLB-185, 275	From the Initial Issue of American Mercury
McFall, Frances Elizabeth Clarke	McPherson, James Alan 1943- DLB-38, 244	(January 1924) DLB-137
(see Grand, Sarah)	McPherson, Sandra 1943- Y-86	Mencken and Nietzsche: An
McFarland, Ron 1942- DLB-256	McTaggart, J. M. E. 1866-1925 . . . . DLB-262	Unpublished Excerpt from H. L.
McFarlane, Leslie 1902-1977 . . . . DLB-88	McWhirter, George 1939- DLB-60	Mencken's My Life as Author and
McFee, William 1881-1966 . . . . DLB-153	McWilliam, Candia 1955- DLB-267	Editor Y-93
McGahern, John 1934- DLB-14, 231, 319	McWilliams, Carey 1905-1980 . . . . DLB-137	Mendelssohn, Moses 1729-1786 . . . . DLB-97
McGee, Thomas D'Arcy 1825-1868 . . . . . . DLB-99	"The Nation's Future," Carey	Mendes, Catulle 1841-1909 . . . . DLB-217
McGeehan, W. O. 1879-1933 . . . . . . DLB-25, 171	McWilliams's Editorial Policy	Méndez M., Miguel 1930- DLB-82
McGill, Ralph 1898-1969 . . . . DLB-29	in Nation DLB-137	Mendoza, Diego Hurtado de
McGinley, Phyllis 1905-1978 . . . . DLB-11, 48		1504-1575 . . . . DLB-318
		The Mercantile Library of New York Y-96
		Mercer, Cecil William (see Yates, Dornford)
		Mercer, David 1928-1980 . . . . DLB-13, 310

Mercer, John 1704-1768 . . . . DLB-31	Micheaux, Oscar 1884-1951. . . . . DLB-50	Miller, Webb 1892-1940 . . . . DLB-29
Mercer, Johnny 1909-1976 . . . . DLB-265	Michel of Northgate, Dan circa 1265-circa 1340 . . . . DLB-146	James Miller [publishing house] DLB-49
Mercier, Louis-Sébastien 1740-1814 . . . . . DLB-314		Millett, Kate 1934- DLB-246
Le Tableau de Paris. DLB-314	Micheline, Jack 1929-1998 . . . . DLB-16	Millhauser, Steven 1943- DLB-2
Meredith, George 1828-1909 . . . . DLB-18, 35, 57, 159; CDBLB-4	Michener, James A. 1907?-1997 . . . . DLB-6	Millican, Arthenia J. Bates 1920- DLB-38
	Micklejohn, George circa 1717-1818 . . . . . . DLB-31	Milligan, Alice 1866-1953. . . . . DLB-240
Meredith, Louisa Anne 1812-1895 . . DLB-166, 230	Middle Hill Press DLB-106	Mills, Magnus 1954- DLB-267
Meredith, Owen (see Lytton, Edward Robert Bulwer)	Middleton, Christopher 1926- DLB-40	Mills and Boon. DLB-112
	Middleton, Richard 1882-1911. . . . . DLB-156	Milman, Henry Hart 1796-1868. . . . . DLB-96
Meredith, William 1919- DLB-5	Middleton, Stanley 1919- DLB-14	Milne, A. A. 1882-1956 . . . . . DLB-10, 77, 100, 160
Meres, Francis Palladis Tamia, Wits Treasurie (1598) [excerpt] DLB-172	Middleton, Thomas 1580-1627 . . . . DLB-58	Milner, Ron 1938- DLB-38
	Miegel, Agnes 1879-1964 . . . . DLB-56	William Milner [publishing house] DLB-106
Merezhkovsky, Dmitrii Sergeevich 1865-1941 . . . . DLB-295	Mieželaitis, Eduardas 1919-1997 . . . . DLB-220	Milnes, Richard Monckton (Lord Houghton) 1809-1885 . . . . DLB-32, 184
	Miguéis, José Rodrigues 1901-1980 . . . . . DLB-287	
Mergerle, Johann Ulrich (see Abraham ä Sancta Clara)	Mihailović, Dragoslav 1930- DLB-181	Milton, John 1608-1674. . . . . DLB-131, 151, 281; CDBLB-2
Mérimée, Prosper 1803-1870 . . . . . . DLB-119, 192	Mihalić, Slavko 1928- DLB-181	The Milton Society of America Y-00
Merivale, John Herman 1779-1844 . . . . . . DLB-96	Mikhailov, A. (see Sheller, Aleksandr Konstantinovich)	Miłosz, Czesław 1911-2004 . . . . .DLB-215; CDWLB-4
Meriwether, Louise 1923- DLB-33		
Merleau-Ponty, Maurice 1908-1961 . . . . . DLB-296	Mikhailov, Mikhail Larionovich 1829-1865 . . . . DLB-238	Minakami Tsutomu 1919- DLB-182
Merlin Press DLB-112	Mikhailovsky, Nikolai Konstantinovich 1842-1904 . . . . .DLB-277	Minamoto no Sanetomo 1192-1219 . . . . . DLB-203
Merriam, Eve 1916-1992 . . . . DLB-61		Minco, Marga 1920- DLB-299
The Merriam Company DLB-49	Miles, Josephine 1911-1985 . . . . DLB-48	The Minerva Press. DLB-154
Merril, Judith 1923-1997. . . . . DLB-251	Miles, Susan (Ursula Wyllie Roberts) 1888-1975. . . . . DLB-240	Minnesang circa 1150-1280. . . . . DLB-138
Tribute to Theodore Sturgeon Y-85		The Music of Minnesang DLB-138
Merrill, James 1926-1995 . . . . . . .DLB-5, 165; Y-85	Miliković, Branko 1934-1961 . . . . DLB-181	Minns, Susan 1839-1938 . . . . DLB-140
Merrill and Baker DLB-49	Milius, John 1944- DLB-44	Minsky, Nikolai 1855-1937 . . . . .DLB-317
The Mershon Company. DLB-49	Mill, James 1773-1836. . . . . DLB-107, 158, 262	Minton, Balch and Company DLB-46
Merton, Thomas 1915-1968 . . . . DLB-48; Y-81	Mill, John Stuart 1806-1873. . . . . . DLB-55, 190, 262; CDBLB-4	Mirbeau, Octave 1848-1917 . . . . DLB-123, 192
Merwin, W. S. 1927- DLB-5, 169		Mirikitani, Janice 1941- DLB-312
Julian Messner [publishing house] DLB-46	Thoughts on Poetry and Its Varieties (1833) DLB-32	Mirk, John died after 1414? DLB-146
Mészöly, Miklós 1921- DLB-232		Miró, Ricardo 1883-1940 . . . . DLB-290
J. Metcalf [publishing house]. DLB-49	Andrew Millar [publishing house] DLB-154	Miron, Gaston 1928-1996 . . . . DLB-60
Metcalf, John 1938- DLB-60	Millar, Kenneth 1915-1983 . . . . .DLB-2, 226; Y-83; DS-6	A Mirror for Magistrates. DLB-167
The Methodist Book Concern DLB-49	Millay, Edna St. Vincent 1892-1950 . . . . DLB-45, 249; CDALB-4	Mirsky, D. S. 1890-1939. . . . . .DLB-317
Methuen and Company DLB-112		Mishima Yukio 1925-1970 . . . . DLB-182
Meun, Jean de (see Roman de la Rose)	Millen, Sarah Gertrude 1888-1968 . . . . . . DLB-225	Mistral, Gabriela 1889-1957 . . . . DLB-283
Mew, Charlotte 1869-1928 . . . . DLB-19, 135	Miller, Andrew 1960- DLB-267	Mitchel, Jonathan 1624-1668 . . . . DLB-24
Mewshaw, Michael 1943- Y-80	Miller, Arthur 1915-2005 . . DLB-7, 266; CDALB-1	Mitchell, Adrian 1932- DLB-40
Tribute to Albert Erskine. Y-93	The Arthur Miller Society Y-01	Mitchell, Donald Grant 1822-1908 . . . . DLB-1, 243; DS-13
Meyer, Conrad Ferdinand 1825-1898 . . . DLB-129	Miller, Caroline 1903-1992. . . . . DLB-9	
Meyer, E. Y. 1946- DLB-75	Miller, Eugene Ethelbert 1950- DLB-41	Mitchell, Gladys 1901-1983 . . . . DLB-77
Meyer, Eugene 1875-1959 . . . . DLB-29	Tribute to Julian Mayfield Y-84	Mitchell, James Leslie 1901-1935 . . . . DLB-15
Meyer, Michael 1921-2000 . . . . DLB-155	Miller, Heather Ross 1939- DLB-120	Mitchell, John (see Slater, Patrick)
Meyers, Jeffrey 1939- DLB-111	Miller, Henry 1891-1980 . . . . DLB-4, 9; Y-80; CDALB-5	Mitchell, John Ames 1845-1918 . . . . DLB-79
Meynell, Alice 1847-1922 . . . . . DLB-19, 98		Mitchell, Joseph 1908-1996 . . . . . . .DLB-185; Y-96
Meynell, Viola 1885-1956 . . . . DLB-153	Miller, Hugh 1802-1856. . . . . DLB-190	Mitchell, Julian 1935- DLB-14
Meyrink, Gustav 1868-1932. . . . . DLB-81	Miller, J. Hillis 1928- DLB-67	Mitchell, Ken 1940- DLB-60
Mézières, Philipe de circa 1327-1405. . . . . DLB-208	Miller, Jason 1939- DLB-7	Mitchell, Langdon 1862-1935. . . . . DLB-7
Michael, Ib 1945- DLB-214	Miller, Joaquin 1839-1913 . . . . DLB-186	Mitchell, Loften 1919-2001. . . . . DLB-38
Michael, Livi 1960- DLB-267	Miller, May 1899-1995. . . . . DLB-41	Mitchell, Margaret 1900-1949 . . DLB-9; CDALB-7
Michaëlis, Karen 1872-1950 . . . . DLB-214	Miller, Paul 1906-1991 . . . . DLB-127	Mitchell, S. Weir 1829-1914 . . . . DLB-202
Michaels, Anne 1958- DLB-299	Miller, Perry 1905-1963 . . . . .DLB-17, 63	Mitchell, W. J. T. 1942- DLB-246
Michaels, Leonard 1933-2003 . . . . DLB-130	Miller, Sue 1943- DLB-143	Mitchell, W. O. 1914-1998. . . . . DLB-88
Michaux, Henri 1899-1984 . . . . DLB-258	Miller, Vassar 1924-1998 . . . . DLB-105	Mitchison, Naomi Margaret (Haldane) 1897-1999. . . . . .DLB-160, 191, 255, 319
	Miller, Walter M., Jr. 1923-1996 . . . . DLB-8	

Mitford, Mary Russell 1787-1855 .... DLB-110, 116	Montherlant, Henry de 1896-1972 .... DLB-72	More, Sir Thomas 1477/1478-1535 .... DLB-136, 281
Mitford, Nancy 1904-1973 .... DLB-191	*The Monthly Review* 1749-1844 .... DLB-110	Morejón, Nancy 1944- DLB-283
Mittelholzer, Edgar 1909-1965 .... DLB-117; CDWLB-3	Monti, Ricardo 1944- DLB-305	Morellet, André 1727-1819 .... DLB-314
Mitterer, Erika 1906-2001 .... DLB-85	Montigny, Louvigny de 1876-1955 .... DLB-92	Morency, Pierre 1942- DLB-60
Mitterer, Felix 1948- DLB-124	Montoya, José 1932- DLB-122	Moreno, Dorinda 1939- DLB-122
Mitternacht, Johann Sebastian 1613-1679 .... DLB-168	Moodie, John Wedderburn Dunbar 1797-1869 .... DLB-99	Moretti, Marino 1885-1979 .... DLB-114, 264
Miyamoto Yuriko 1899-1951 .... DLB-180	Moodie, Susanna 1803-1885 .... DLB-99	Morgan, Berry 1919-2002 .... DLB-6
Mizener, Arthur 1907-1988 .... DLB-103	Moody, Joshua circa 1633-1697 .... DLB-24	Morgan, Charles 1894-1958 .... DLB-34, 100
Mo, Timothy 1950- DLB-194	Moody, William Vaughn 1869-1910 .... DLB-7, 54	Morgan, Edmund S. 1916- DLB-17
Moberg, Vilhelm 1898-1973 .... DLB-259	Moorcock, Michael 1939- DLB-14, 231, 261, 319	Morgan, Edwin 1920- DLB-27
Modern Age Books DLB-46	Moore, Alan 1953- DLB-261	Morgan, John Pierpont 1837-1913 .... DLB-140
Modern Language Association of America The Modern Language Association of America Celebrates Its Centennial .. Y-84	Moore, Brian 1921-1999 .... DLB-251	Morgan, John Pierpont, Jr. 1867-1943 .... DLB-140
	Moore, Catherine L. 1911-1987 .... DLB-8	Morgan, Robert 1944- DLB-120, 292
The Modern Library DLB-46	Moore, Clement Clarke 1779-1863 .... DLB-42	Morgan, Sydney Owenson, Lady 1776?-1859 .... DLB-116, 158
Modiano, Patrick 1945- DLB-83, 299	Moore, Dora Mavor 1888-1979 .... DLB-92	
Moffat, Yard and Company DLB-46	Moore, G. E. 1873-1958 .... DLB-262	Morgner, Irmtraud 1933-1990 .... DLB-75
Moffet, Thomas 1553-1604 .... DLB-136	Moore, George 1852-1933 .... DLB-10, 18, 57, 135	Morhof, Daniel Georg 1639-1691 .... DLB-164
Mofolo, Thomas 1876-1948 .... DLB-225	*Literature at Nurse, or Circulating Morals* (1885) DLB-18	Mori, Kyoko 1957- DLB-312
Mohr, Nicholasa 1938- DLB-145		Mori Ōgai 1862-1922 .... DLB-180
Moix, Ana María 1947- DLB-134	Moore, Lorrie 1957- DLB-234	Mori, Toshio 1910-1980 .... DLB-312
Molesworth, Louisa 1839-1921 .... DLB-135	Moore, Marianne 1887-1972 .... DLB-45; DS-7; CDALB-5	Móricz, Zsigmond 1879-1942 .... DLB-215
Molière (Jean-Baptiste Poquelin) 1622-1673 .... DLB-268	International Marianne Moore Society ... Y-98	Morier, James Justinian 1782 or 1783?-1849 .... DLB-116
Møller, Poul Martin 1794-1838 .... DLB-300	Moore, Mavor 1919- DLB-88	Mörike, Eduard 1804-1875 .... DLB-133
Möllhausen, Balduin 1825-1905 .... DLB-129	Moore, Richard 1927- DLB-105	Morin, Paul 1889-1963 .... DLB-92
Molnár, Ferenc 1878-1952 ... DLB-215; CDWLB-4	"The No Self, the Little Self, and the Poets" DLB-105	Morison, Richard 1514?-1556 .... DLB-136
Molnár, Miklós (see Mészöly, Miklós)		Morison, Samuel Eliot 1887-1976 .... DLB-17
Momaday, N. Scott 1934- DLB-143, 175, 256; CDALB-7	Moore, T. Sturge 1870-1944 .... DLB-19	Morison, Stanley 1889-1967 .... DLB-201
	Moore, Thomas 1779-1852 .... DLB-96, 144	Moritz, Karl Philipp 1756-1793 .... DLB-94
Monkhouse, Allan 1858-1936 .... DLB-10	Moore, Ward 1903-1978 .... DLB-8	*Moriz von Craûn* circa 1220-1230 .... DLB-138
Monro, Harold 1879-1932 .... DLB-19	Moore, Wilstach, Keys and Company DLB-49	Morley, Christopher 1890-1957 .... DLB-9
Monroe, Harriet 1860-1936 .... DLB-54, 91	Moorehead, Alan 1901-1983 .... DLB-204	Morley, John 1838-1923 .... DLB-57, 144, 190
Monsarrat, Nicholas 1910-1979 .... DLB-15	Moorhouse, Frank 1938- DLB-289	Moro, César 1903-1956 .... DLB-290
Montagu, Lady Mary Wortley 1689-1762 .... DLB-95, 101	Moorhouse, Geoffrey 1931- DLB-204	Morris, George Pope 1802-1864 .... DLB-73
	Moorish Novel of the Sixteenth Century, The DLB-318	Morris, James Humphrey (see Morris, Jan)
Montague, C. E. 1867-1928 .... DLB-197		Morris, Jan 1926- DLB-204
Montague, John 1929- DLB-40	The Moorland-Spingarn Research Center DLB-76	Morris, Lewis 1833-1907 .... DLB-35
Montale, Eugenio 1896-1981 .... DLB-114		Morris, Margaret 1737-1816 .... DLB-200
Montalvo, Garci Rodríguez de ca. 1450?-before 1505 .... DLB-286	Moorman, Mary C. 1905-1994 .... DLB-155	Morris, Mary McGarry 1943- DLB-292
	Mora, Pat 1942- DLB-209	Morris, Richard B. 1904-1989 .... DLB-17
Montalvo, José 1946-1994 .... DLB-209	Moraes, Vinicius de 1913-1980 .... DLB-307	Morris, William 1834-1896 .... DLB-18, 35, 57, 156, 178, 184; CDBLB-4
Montemayor, Jorge de 1521?-1561? DLB-318	Moraga, Cherríe 1952- DLB-82, 249	
Monterroso, Augusto 1921-2003 .... DLB-145	Morales, Alejandro 1944- DLB-82	Morris, Willie 1934-1999 .... Y-80
Montesquieu, Charles-Louis de Secondat, baron de 1689-1755 .... DLB-314	Morales, Mario Roberto 1947- DLB-145	Tribute to Irwin Shaw Y-84
	Morales, Rafael 1919- DLB-108	Tribute to James Dickey Y-97
The Spirit of Laws DLB-314	Morality Plays: *Mankind* circa 1450-1500 and *Everyman* circa 1500 .... DLB-146	Morris, Wright 1910-1998 .... DLB-2, 206, 218; Y-81
Montesquiou, Robert de 1855-1921 ..... DLB-217		
Montgomerie, Alexander circa 1550?-1598 .... DLB-167	Morand, Paul (1888-1976) DLB-65	Morrison, Arthur 1863-1945 .... DLB-70, 135, 197
	Morante, Elsa 1912-1985 .... DLB-177	Morrison, Charles Clayton 1874-1966 .... DLB-91
Montgomery, James 1771-1854 ...... DLB-93, 158	Morata, Olympia Fulvia 1526-1555 ...... DLB-179	Morrison, John 1904-1998 .... DLB-260
Montgomery, John 1919- DLB-16	Moravia, Alberto 1907-1990 .... DLB-177	Morrison, Toni 1931- DLB-6, 33, 143; Y-81, 93; CDALB-6
Montgomery, Lucy Maud 1874-1942 .... DLB-92; DS-14	Mordaunt, Elinor 1872-1942 .... DLB-174	
	Mordovtsev, Daniil Lukich 1830-1905 ... DLB-238	Nobel Lecture 1993 .... Y-93
Montgomery, Marion 1925- DLB-6	More, Hannah 1745-1833 .... DLB-107, 109, 116, 158	Morrissy, Mary 1957- DLB-267
Montgomery, Robert Bruce (see Crispin, Edmund)		
	More, Henry 1614-1687 .... DLB-126, 252	William Morrow and Company DLB-46

Morse, James Herbert 1841-1923 . . . . DLB-71	Mudford, William 1782-1848 . . . . DLB-159	Murger, Henry 1822-1861 . . . . DLB-119
Morse, Jedidiah 1761-1826 . . . . DLB-37	Mudrooroo (see Johnson, Colin)	Murger, Louis-Henri (see Murger, Henry)
Morse, John T., Jr. 1840-1937 . . . . DLB-47	Mueller, Lisel 1924- DLB-105	Murnane, Gerald 1939- DLB-289
Morselli, Guido 1912-1973 . . . . .DLB-177	Muhajir, El (see Marvin X)	Murner, Thomas 1475-1537 . . . . .DLB-179
Morte Arthure, the *Alliterative* and the *Stanzaic* circa 1350-1400 . . . . DLB-146	Muhajir, Nazzam Al Fitnah (see Marvin X)	Muro, Amado 1915-1971 . . . . DLB-82
	Muhammad the Prophet circa 570-632 . . . DLB-311	Murphy, Arthur 1727-1805 . . . . DLB-89, 142
Mortimer, Favell Lee 1802-1878 . . . . DLB-163	Mühlbach, Luise 1814-1873 . . . . DLB-133	Murphy, Beatrice M. 1908-1992 . . . . DLB-76
Mortimer, John 1923- DLB-13, 245, 271; CDBLB-8	Muir, Edwin 1887-1959 . . . . .DLB-20, 100, 191	Murphy, Dervla 1931- DLB-204
Morton, Carlos 1942- DLB-122	Muir, Helen 1937- DLB-14	Murphy, Emily 1868-1933 . . . . DLB-99
Morton, H. V. 1892-1979 . . . . DLB-195	Muir, John 1838-1914 . . . . .DLB-186, 275	Murphy, Jack 1923-1980 . . . . DLB-241
John P. Morton and Company DLB-49	Muir, Percy 1894-1979 . . . . DLB-201	John Murphy and Company DLB-49
Morton, Nathaniel 1613-1685 . . . . DLB-24	Mujū Ichien 1226-1312 . . . . DLB-203	Murphy, John H., III 1916- DLB-127
Morton, Sarah Wentworth 1759-1846 . . . . DLB-37	Mukherjee, Bharati 1940- DLB-60, 218	Murphy, Richard 1927-1993 . . . . DLB-40
Morton, Thomas circa 1579-circa 1647 . . . DLB-24	Mulcaster, Richard 1531 or 1532-1611 . . DLB-167	Murphy, Tom 1935- DLB-310
Moscherosch, Johann Michael 1601-1669 . . . . DLB-164	Muldoon, Paul 1951- DLB-40	Murray, Albert L. 1916- DLB-38
	Mulisch, Harry 1927- DLB-299	Murray, Gilbert 1866-1957 . . . . DLB-10
Humphrey Moseley [publishing house] DLB-170	Mulkerns, Val 1925- DLB-319	Murray, Jim 1919-1998 . . . . DLB-241
	Müller, Friedrich (see Müller, Maler)	John Murray [publishing house] DLB-154
Möser, Justus 1720-1794 . . . . DLB-97	Müller, Heiner 1929-1995 . . . . DLB-124	Murray, Judith Sargent 1751-1820 . . . .DLB-37, 200
Mosley, Nicholas 1923- DLB-14, 207	Müller, Maler 1749-1825 . . . . DLB-94	Murray, Les 1938- DLB-289
Mosley, Walter 1952- DLB-306	Muller, Marcia 1944- DLB-226	Murray, Pauli 1910-1985 . . . . DLB-41
Moss, Arthur 1889-1969 . . . . DLB-4	Müller, Wilhelm 1794-1827 . . . . DLB-90	Murry, John Middleton 1889-1957 . . . . . DLB-149
Moss, Howard 1922-1987 . . . . DLB-5	Mumford, Lewis 1895-1990 . . . . DLB-63	"The Break-Up of the Novel" (1922) DLB-36
Moss, Thylias 1954- DLB-120	Munby, A. N. L. 1913-1974 . . . . DLB-201	
Motion, Andrew 1952- DLB-40	Munby, Arthur Joseph 1828-1910 . . . . . . DLB-35	Murry, John Middleton, Jr. (see Cowper, Richard)
Motley, John Lothrop 1814-1877 . . . . DLB-1, 30, 59, 235	Munday, Anthony 1560-1633 . . . . . . .DLB-62, 172	Musäus, Johann Karl August 1735-1787 . . . DLB-97
	Mundt, Clara (see Mühlbach, Luise)	Muschg, Adolf 1934- DLB-75
Motley, Willard 1909-1965 . . . DLB-76, 143	Mundt, Theodore 1808-1861 . . . . DLB-133	Musil, Robert 1880-1942 . . . . .DLB-81, 124; CDWLB-2
Mott, Lucretia 1793-1880 . . . . DLB-239	Munford, Robert circa 1737-1783 . . . . DLB-31	
Benjamin Motte Jr. [publishing house] DLB-154	Mungoshi, Charles 1947- DLB-157	*Muspilli* circa 790-circa 850 . . . . DLB-148
	Munk, Kaj 1898-1944 . . . . DLB-214	Musset, Alfred de 1810-1857 . . . . . . .DLB-192, 217
Motteux, Peter Anthony 1663-1718 . . . . . . DLB-80	Munonye, John 1929- DLB-117	Benjamin B. Mussey and Company DLB-49
Mottram, R. H. 1883-1971 . . . . DLB-36	Munro, Alice 1931- DLB-53	
Mount, Ferdinand 1939- DLB-231	George Munro [publishing house] DLB-49	Muste, A. J. 1885-1967 . . . . DLB-303
Mouré, Erin 1955- DLB-60	Munro, H. H. 1870-1916 . . . . DLB-34, 162; CDBLB-5	Mutafchieva, Vera 1929- DLB-181
Mourning Dove (Humishuma) between 1882 and 1888?-1936 . . . . .DLB-175, 221		Mutis, Alvaro 1923- DLB-283
	Munro, Neil 1864-1930 . . . . DLB-156	Mwangi, Meja 1948- DLB-125
Movies Fiction into Film, 1928-1975: A List of Movies Based on the Works of Authors in British Novelists, 1930-1959 . . . . DLB-15	Norman L. Munro [publishing house] DLB-49	Myers, Frederic W. H. 1843-1901 . . . . DLB-190
	Munroe, Kirk 1850-1930 . . . . DLB-42	
	Munroe and Francis DLB-49	Myers, Gustavus 1872-1942 . . . . DLB-47
	James Munroe and Company DLB-49	Myers, L. H. 1881-1944 . . . . DLB-15
Movies from Books, 1920-1974 . . . . DLB-9	Joel Munsell [publishing house] DLB-49	Myers, Walter Dean 1937- DLB-33
Mowat, Farley 1921- DLB-68	Munsey, Frank A. 1854-1925 . . . . DLB-25, 91	Myerson, Julie 1960- DLB-267
A. R. Mowbray and Company, Limited DLB-106	Frank A. Munsey and Company DLB-49	Mykle, Agnar 1915-1994 . . . . DLB-297
	Mura, David 1952- DLB-312	Mykolaitis-Putinas, Vincas 1893-1967 . . . . DLB-220
Mowrer, Edgar Ansel 1892-1977 . . . . DLB-29	Murakami Haruki 1949- DLB-182	
Mowrer, Paul Scott 1887-1971 . . . . DLB-29	Muratov, Pavel 1881-1950 . . . . DLB-317	Myles, Eileen 1949- DLB-193
Edward Moxon [publishing house] DLB-106	Murayama, Milton 1923- DLB-312	Myrdal, Jan 1927- DLB-257
Joseph Moxon [publishing house] DLB-170	Murav'ev, Mikhail Nikitich 1757-1807 . . . DLB-150	Mystery 1985: The Year of the Mystery: A Symposium Y-85
Moyes, Patricia 1923-2000 . . . . .DLB-276	Murdoch, Iris 1919-1999 . . . . DLB-14, 194, 233; CDBLB-8	
Mphahlele, Es'kia (Ezekiel) 1919- DLB-125, 225; CDWLB-3		Comments from Other Writers Y-85
	Murdock, James From *Sketches of Modern Philosophy* DS-5	The Second Annual New York Festival of Mystery Y-00
Mrożek, Sławomir 1930- . . DLB-232; CDWLB-4		
Mtshali, Oswald Mbuyiseni 1940- DLB-125, 225	Murdoch, Rupert 1931- DLB-127	Why I Read Mysteries Y-85
	Murfree, Mary N. 1850-1922 . . . . .DLB-12, 74	Why I Write Mysteries: Night and Day, by Michael Collins Y-85
al-Mubarrad 826-898 or 899 . . . . DLB-311		
Mucedorus DLB-62		

N

Na Prous Boneta circa 1296-1328 . . . . DLB-208

Nabl, Franz 1883-1974 . . . . DLB-81

Nabakov, Véra 1902-1991 . . . . Y-91

Nabokov, Vladimir 1899-1977 . . . . . . DLB-2, 244, 278, 317; Y-80, 91; DS-3; CDALB-1

   International Nabokov Society Y-99

   An Interview [On Nabokov], by Fredson Bowers Y-80

   Nabokov Festival at Cornell Y-83

   The Vladimir Nabokov Archive in the Berg Collection of the New York Public Library: An Overview Y-91

   The Vladimir Nabokov Society Y-01

Nádaši, Ladislav (see Jégé)

Naden, Constance 1858-1889 . . . . DLB-199

Nadezhdin, Nikolai Ivanovich 1804-1856 . . . . DLB-198

Nadson, Semen Iakovlevich 1862-1887 . . . DLB-277

Naevius circa 265 B.C.-201 B.C. DLB-211

Nafis and Cornish DLB-49

Nagai Kafū 1879-1959 . . . . DLB-180

Nagel, Ernest 1901-1985 . . . . DLB-279

Nagibin, Iurii Markovich 1920-1994 . . . . . DLB-302

Nagrodskaia, Evdokiia Apollonovna 1866-1930 . . . . DLB-295

Naipaul, Shiva 1945-1985 . . . . DLB-157; Y-85

Naipaul, V. S. 1932- DLB-125, 204, 207; Y-85, Y-01; CDBLB-8; CDWLB-3

   Nobel Lecture 2001: "Two Worlds" Y-01

Nakagami Kenji 1946-1992 . . . . DLB-182

Nakano-in Masatada no Musume (see Nijō, Lady)

Nałkowska, Zofia 1884-1954 . . . . DLB-215

Namora, Fernando 1919-1989 . . . . DLB-287

Joseph Nancrede [publishing house] DLB-49

Naranjo, Carmen 1930- DLB-145

Narbikova, Valeriia Spartakovna 1958- DLB-285

Narezhny, Vasilii Trofimovich 1780-1825 . . . . DLB-198

Narrache, Jean (Emile Coderre) 1893-1970 . . . . DLB-92

Nasby, Petroleum Vesuvius (see Locke, David Ross)

Eveleigh Nash [publishing house] DLB-112

Nash, Ogden 1902-1971 . . . . DLB-11

Nashe, Thomas 1567-1601? DLB-167

Nason, Jerry 1910-1986 . . . . DLB-241

Nasr, Seyyed Hossein 1933- DLB-279

Nast, Condé 1873-1942 . . . . DLB-91

Nast, Thomas 1840-1902 . . . . DLB-188

Nastasijević, Momčilo 1894-1938 . . . . DLB-147

Nathan, George Jean 1882-1958 . . . . DLB-137

Nathan, Robert 1894-1985 . . . . DLB-9

Nation, Carry A. 1846-1911 . . . . DLB-303

National Book Critics Circle Awards Y-00–01

The National Jewish Book Awards Y-85

Natsume Sōseki 1867-1916 . . . . DLB-180

Naughton, Bill 1910-1992 . . . . DLB-13

Nava, Michael 1954- DLB-306

Navarro, Joe 1953- DLB-209

Naylor, Gloria 1950- DLB-173

Nazor, Vladimir 1876-1949 . . . . DLB-147

Ndebele, Njabulo 1948- DLB-157, 225

Neagoe, Peter 1881-1960 . . . . DLB-4

Neal, John 1793-1876 . . . . DLB-1, 59, 243

Neal, Joseph C. 1807-1847 . . . . DLB-11

Neal, Larry 1937-1981 . . . . DLB-38

The Neale Publishing Company DLB-49

Nearing, Scott 1883-1983 . . . . DLB-303

Nebel, Frederick 1903-1967 . . . . DLB-226

Nebrija, Antonio de 1442 or 1444-1522 . . DLB-286

Nedreaas, Torborg 1906-1987 . . . . DLB-297

F. Tennyson Neely [publishing house] DLB-49

Negoițescu, Ion 1921-1993 . . . . DLB-220

Negri, Ada 1870-1945 . . . . DLB-114

Neihardt, John G. 1881-1973 . . . . . DLB-9, 54, 256

Neidhart von Reuental circa 1185-circa 1240 . . . . DLB-138

Neilson, John Shaw 1872-1942 . . . . DLB-230

Nekrasov, Nikolai Alekseevich 1821-1877 . . . . DLB-277

Nekrasov, Viktor Platonovich 1911-1987 . . . . DLB-302

Neledinsky-Meletsky, Iurii Aleksandrovich 1752-1828 . . . . DLB-150

Nelligan, Emile 1879-1941 . . . . DLB-92

Nelson, Alice Moore Dunbar 1875-1935 . . . DLB-50

Nelson, Antonya 1961- DLB-244

Nelson, Kent 1943- DLB-234

Nelson, Richard K. 1941- DLB-275

Nelson, Thomas, and Sons [U.K.] DLB-106

Nelson, Thomas, and Sons [U.S.] DLB-49

Nelson, William 1908-1978 . . . . DLB-103

Nelson, William Rockhill 1841-1915 . . . . . DLB-23

Nemerov, Howard 1920-1991 . . . . . DLB-5, 6; Y-83

Németh, László 1901-1975 . . . . DLB-215

Nepos circa 100 B.C.-post 27 B.C. DLB-211

Nėris, Salomėja 1904-1945 . . DLB-220; CDWLB-4

Neruda, Pablo 1904-1973 . . . . DLB-283

Nerval, Gérard de 1808-1855 . . . . DLB-217

Nervo, Amado 1870-1919 . . . . DLB-290

Nesbit, E. 1858-1924 . . . . DLB-141, 153, 178

Ness, Evaline 1911-1986 . . . . DLB-61

Nestroy, Johann 1801-1862 . . . . DLB-133

Nettleship, R. L. 1846-1892 . . . . DLB-262

Neugeboren, Jay 1938- DLB-28

Neukirch, Benjamin 1655-1729 . . . . DLB-168

Neumann, Alfred 1895-1952 . . . . DLB-56

Neumann, Ferenc (see Molnár, Ferenc)

Neumark, Georg 1621-1681 . . . . DLB-164

Neumeister, Erdmann 1671-1756 . . . . DLB-168

Nevins, Allan 1890-1971 . . . . DLB-17; DS-17

Nevinson, Henry Woodd 1856-1941 . . . . DLB-135

The New American Library DLB-46

New Directions Publishing Corporation . . . DLB-46

The New Monthly Magazine 1814-1884 . . . . . DLB-110

New York Times Book Review Y-82

John Newbery [publishing house] DLB-154

Newbolt, Henry 1862-1938 . . . . DLB-19

Newbound, Bernard Slade (see Slade, Bernard)

Newby, Eric 1919- DLB-204

Newby, P. H. 1918-1997 . . . . DLB-15

Thomas Cautley Newby [publishing house] DLB-106

Newcomb, Charles King 1820-1894 . . . DLB-1, 223

Newell, Peter 1862-1924 . . . . DLB-42

Newell, Robert Henry 1836-1901 . . . . DLB-11

Newhouse, Samuel I. 1895-1979 . . . . DLB-127

Newman, Cecil Earl 1903-1976 . . . . DLB-127

Newman, David 1937- DLB-44

Newman, Frances 1883-1928 . . . . Y-80

Newman, Francis William 1805-1897 . . . . DLB-190

Newman, G. F. 1946- DLB-310

Newman, John Henry 1801-1890 . . . . DLB-18, 32, 55

Mark Newman [publishing house] DLB-49

Newmarch, Rosa Harriet 1857-1940 . . . . . DLB-240

George Newnes Limited DLB-112

Newsome, Effie Lee 1885-1979 . . . . DLB-76

Newton, A. Edward 1864-1940 . . . . DLB-140

Newton, Sir Isaac 1642-1727 . . . . DLB-252

Nexø, Martin Andersen 1869-1954 . . . . . DLB-214

Nezval, Vítěslav 1900-1958 . . . . DLB-215; CDWLB-4

Ngugi wa Thiong'o 1938- DLB-125; CDWLB-3

Niatum, Duane 1938- DLB-175

The *Nibelungenlied* and the *Klage* circa 1200 . . . . DLB-138

Nichol, B. P. 1944-1988 . . . . DLB-53

Nicholas of Cusa 1401-1464 . . . . DLB-115

Nichols, Ann 1891?-1966 . . . . DLB-249

Nichols, Beverly 1898-1983 . . . . DLB-191

Nichols, Dudley 1895-1960 . . . . DLB-26

Nichols, Grace 1950- DLB-157

Nichols, John 1940- Y-82

Nichols, Mary Sargeant (Neal) Gove 1810-1884 . . . . DLB-1, 243

Nichols, Peter 1927- DLB-13, 245

Nichols, Roy F. 1896-1973 . . . . DLB-17

Nichols, Ruth 1948- DLB-60

Nicholson, Edward Williams Byron 1849-1912 . . . . DLB-184

Nicholson, Geoff 1953- DLB-271

Nicholson, Norman 1914-1987 . . . . DLB-27

Nicholson, William 1872-1949 . . . . DLB-141

Ní Chuilleanáin, Eiléan 1942- DLB-40

Nicol, Eric 1919- DLB-68

Cumulative Index

Nicolai, Friedrich 1733-1811 . . . . DLB-97
Nicolas de Clamanges circa 1363-1437 . . . DLB-208
Nicolay, John G. 1832-1901 and
    Hay, John 1838-1905 . . . . DLB-47
Nicole, Pierre 1625-1695 . . . . DLB-268
Nicolson, Adela Florence Cory (see Hope, Laurence)
Nicolson, Harold 1886-1968 . . . . . . DLB-100, 149
    "The Practice of Biography," in
      *The English Sense of Humour and
      Other Essays* DLB-149
Nicolson, Nigel 1917-2004 . . . . DLB-155
Ní Dhuibhne, Éilís 1954- DLB-319
Niebuhr, Reinhold 1892-1971 . . . . . . DLB-17; DS-17
Niedecker, Lorine 1903-1970 . . . . DLB-48
Nieman, Lucius W. 1857-1935 . . . . DLB-25
Nietzsche, Friedrich
    1844-1900 . . . . DLB-129; CDWLB-2
    Mencken and Nietzsche: An Unpublished
      Excerpt from H. L. Mencken's *My Life
      as Author and Editor* Y-93
Nievo, Stanislao 1928- DLB-196
Niggli, Josefina 1910-1983 . . . . Y-80
Nightingale, Florence 1820-1910 . . . . DLB-166
Nijō, Lady (Nakano-in Masatada no Musume)
    1258-after 1306 . . . . DLB-203
Nijō Yoshimoto 1320-1388 . . . . DLB-203
Nikitin, Ivan Savvich 1824-1861 . . . . DLB-277
Nikitin, Nikolai Nikolaevich 1895-1963 . . DLB-272
Nikolev, Nikolai Petrovich 1758-1815 . . . DLB-150
Niles, Hezekiah 1777-1839 . . . . DLB-43
Nims, John Frederick 1913-1999 . . . . DLB-5
    Tribute to Nancy Hale Y-88
Nin, Anaïs 1903-1977 . . . . DLB-2, 4, 152
Nína Björk Árnadóttir 1941-2000 . . . . DLB-293
Niño, Raúl 1961- DLB-209
Nissenson, Hugh 1933- DLB-28
Niven, Frederick John 1878-1944 . . . . DLB-92
Niven, Larry 1938- DLB-8
Nixon, Howard M. 1909-1983 . . . . DLB-201
Nizan, Paul 1905-1940 . . . . DLB-72
Njegoš, Petar II Petrović
    1813-1851 . . . . DLB-147; CDWLB-4
Nkosi, Lewis 1936- DLB-157, 225
Noah, Mordecai M. 1785-1851 . . . . DLB-250
Noailles, Anna de 1876-1933 . . . . DLB-258
Nobel Peace Prize
    The Nobel Prize and Literary Politics Y-88
    Elie Wiesel Y-86
Nobel Prize in Literature
    Joseph Brodsky Y-87
    Camilo José Cela Y-89
    Dario Fo Y-97
    Gabriel García Márquez Y-82
    William Golding Y-83
    Nadine Gordimer Y-91
    Günter Grass Y-99
    Seamus Heaney Y-95

Imre Kertész Y-02
Najīb Mahfūz Y-88
Toni Morrison Y-93
V. S. Naipaul Y-01
Kenzaburō Ōe Y-94
Octavio Paz Y-90
José Saramago Y-98
Jaroslav Seifert Y-84
Claude Simon Y-85
Wole Soyinka Y-86
Wisława Szymborska Y-96
Derek Walcott Y-92
Gao Xingjian Y-00
Nobre, António 1867-1900 . . . . DLB-287
Nodier, Charles 1780-1844 . . . . DLB-119
Noël, Marie (Marie Mélanie Rouget)
    1883-1967 . . . . DLB-258
Noel, Roden 1834-1894 . . . . DLB-35
Nogami Yaeko 1885-1985 . . . . DLB-180
Nogo, Rajko Petrov 1945- DLB-181
Nolan, William F. 1928- DLB-8
    Tribute to Raymond Chandler Y-88
Noland, C. F. M. 1810?-1858 . . . . DLB-11
Noma Hiroshi 1915-1991 . . . . DLB-182
Nonesuch Press DLB-112
Creative Nonfiction Y-02
Nonni (Jón Stefán Sveinsson or Svensson)
    1857-1944 . . . . DLB-293
Noon, Jeff 1957- DLB-267
Noonan, Robert Phillipe (see Tressell, Robert)
Noonday Press DLB-46
Noone, John 1936- DLB-14
Nora, Eugenio de 1923- DLB-134
Nordan, Lewis 1939- DLB-234
Nordbrandt, Henrik 1945- DLB-214
Nordhoff, Charles 1887-1947 . . . . DLB-9
Norén, Lars 1944- DLB-257
Norfolk, Lawrence 1963- DLB-267
Norman, Charles 1904-1996 . . . . DLB-111
Norman, Marsha 1947- DLB-266; Y-84
Norris, Charles G. 1881-1945 . . . . DLB-9
Norris, Frank
    1870-1902 . . . . . . DLB-12, 71, 186; CDALB-3
Norris, Helen 1916- DLB-292
Norris, John 1657-1712 . . . . DLB-252
Norris, Leslie 1921- DLB-27, 256
Norse, Harold 1916- DLB-16
Norte, Marisela 1955- DLB-209
North, Marianne 1830-1890 . . . . DLB-174
North Point Press DLB-46
Nortje, Arthur 1942-1970 . . . . DLB-125, 225
Norton, Alice Mary (see Norton, Andre)
Norton, Andre 1912-2005 . . . . DLB-8, 52
Norton, Andrews 1786-1853 . . . DLB-1, 235; DS-5
Norton, Caroline 1808-1877 . . . DLB-21, 159, 199

Norton, Charles Eliot
    1827-1908 . . . . DLB-1, 64, 235
Norton, John 1606-1663 . . . . DLB-24
Norton, Mary 1903-1992 . . . . DLB-160
Norton, Thomas 1532-1584 . . . . DLB-62
W. W. Norton and Company DLB-46
Norwood, Robert 1874-1932 . . . . DLB-92
Nosaka Akiyuki 1930- DLB-182
Nossack, Hans Erich 1901-1977 . . . . DLB-69
Notker Balbulus circa 840-912 . . . . DLB-148
Notker III of Saint Gall
    circa 950-1022 . . . . DLB-148
Notker von Zweifalten ?-1095 . . . . DLB-148
Nourse, Alan E. 1928-1992 . . . . DLB-8
Novak, Slobodan 1924- DLB-181
Novak, Vjenceslav 1859-1905 . . . . DLB-147
Novakovich, Josip 1956- DLB-244
Novalis 1772-1801 . . . . DLB-90; CDWLB-2
Novaro, Mario 1868-1944 . . . . DLB-114
Novás Calvo, Lino 1903-1983 . . . . DLB-145
Novelists
    Library Journal Statements and
      Questionnaires from First Novelists Y-87
Novels
    The Columbia History of the American Novel
      A Symposium on Y-92
    The Great Modern Library Scam Y-98
    Novels for Grown-Ups Y-97
    The Proletarian Novel DLB-9
    Novel, The "Second-Generation" Holocaust
      . . . . DLB-299
    The Year in the Novel Y-87-88, Y-90-93
Novels, British
    "The Break-Up of the Novel" (1922),
      by John Middleton Murry DLB-36
    The Consolidation of Opinion: Critical
      Responses to the Modernists DLB-36
    "Criticism in Relation to Novels"
      (1863), by G. H. Lewes DLB-21
    "Experiment in the Novel" (1929)
      [excerpt], by John D. Beresford . . . DLB-36
    "The Future of the Novel" (1899), by
      Henry James DLB-18
    The Gay Science (1866), by E. S. Dallas
      [excerpt] DLB-21
    A Haughty and Proud Generation
      (1922), by Ford Madox Hueffer . . DLB-36
    Literary Effects of World War II DLB-15
    "Modern Novelists –Great and Small"
      (1855), by Margaret Oliphant DLB-21
    The Modernists (1932),
      by Joseph Warren Beach DLB-36
    A Note on Technique (1926), by
      Elizabeth A. Drew [excerpts] DLB-36
    Novel-Reading: *The Works of Charles
      Dickens; The Works of W. Makepeace
      Thackeray* (1879),
      by Anthony Trollope DLB-21
    Novels with a Purpose (1864), by
      Justin M'Carthy DLB-21
    "On Art in Fiction" (1838),
      by Edward Bulwer DLB-21

The Present State of the English Novel
  (1892), by George Saintsbury.....DLB-18
Representative Men and Women:
  A Historical Perspective on
  the British Novel, 1930-1960.....DLB-15
"The Revolt" (1937), by Mary Colum
  [excerpts]...................DLB-36
"Sensation Novels" (1863), by
  H. L. Manse..................DLB-21
Sex, Class, Politics, and Religion [in
  the British Novel, 1930-1959].....DLB-15
Time and Western Man (1927),
  by Wyndham Lewis [excerpts]....DLB-36
Noventa, Giacomo 1898-1960..........DLB-114
Novikov, Nikolai Ivanovich
  1744-1818.....................DLB-150
Novomeský, Laco 1904-1976...........DLB-215
Nowlan, Alden 1933-1983.............DLB-53
Noyes, Alfred 1880-1958.............DLB-20
Noyes, Crosby S. 1825-1908..........DLB-23
Noyes, Nicholas 1647-1717...........DLB-24
Noyes, Theodore W. 1858-1946........DLB-29
Nozick, Robert 1938-2002............DLB-279
N-Town Plays circa 1468 to early
  sixteenth century..............DLB-146
Nugent, Frank 1908-1965.............DLB-44
Nunez, Sigrid 1951-..................DLB-312
Nušić, Branislav
  1864-1938............DLB-147; CDWLB-4
David Nutt [publishing house]..........DLB-106
Nwapa, Flora
  1931-1993............DLB-125; CDWLB-3
Nye, Edgar Wilson (Bill)
  1850-1896.................DLB-11, 23, 186
Nye, Naomi Shihab 1952-..............DLB-120
Nye, Robert 1939-..................DLB-14, 271
Nyka-Niliūnas, Alfonsas 1919-........DLB-220

O

Oakes, Urian circa 1631-1681...........DLB-24
Oakes Smith, Elizabeth
  1806-1893................DLB-1, 239, 243
Oakley, Violet 1874-1961..............DLB-188
Oates, Joyce Carol 1938-
  ....DLB-2, 5, 130; Y-81; CDALB-6
  Tribute to Michael M. Rea............Y-97
Ōba Minako 1930-....................DLB-182
Ober, Frederick Albion 1849-1913......DLB-189
Ober, William 1920-1993................Y-93
Oberholtzer, Ellis Paxson 1868-1936....DLB-47
The Obituary as Literary Form..........Y-02
Obradović, Dositej 1740?-1811..........DLB-147
O'Brien, Charlotte Grace 1845-1909.....DLB-240
O'Brien, Edna 1932- DLB-14, 231, 319; CDBLB-8
O'Brien, Fitz-James 1828-1862..........DLB-74
O'Brien, Flann (see O'Nolan, Brian)
O'Brien, Kate 1897-1974................DLB-15
O'Brien, Tim
  1946-.....DLB-152; Y-80; DS-9; CDALB-7

Ó Cadhain, Máirtín 1905-1970.........DLB-319
O'Casey, Sean 1880-1964.....DLB-10; CDBLB-6
Occom, Samson 1723-1792..............DLB-175
Occomy, Marita Bonner 1899-1971......DLB-51
Ochs, Adolph S. 1858-1935.............DLB-25
Ochs-Oakes, George Washington
  1861-1931....................DLB-137
O'Connor, Flannery 1925-1964
  ....DLB-2, 152; Y-80; DS-12; CDALB-1
  The Flannery O'Connor Society........Y-99
O'Connor, Frank 1903-1966.............DLB-162
O'Connor, Joseph 1963-..................DLB-267
Octopus Publishing Group...............DLB-112
Oda Sakunosuke 1913-1947..............DLB-182
Odell, Jonathan 1737-1818..............DLB-31, 99
O'Dell, Scott 1903-1989................DLB-52
Odets, Clifford 1906-1963..............DLB-7, 26
Odhams Press Limited..................DLB-112
Odio, Eunice 1922-1974................DLB-283
Odoevsky, Aleksandr Ivanovich
  1802-1839....................DLB-205
Odoevsky, Vladimir Fedorovich
  1804 or 1803-1869..............DLB-198
Odoevtseva, Irina 1895-1990...........DLB-317
O'Donnell, Peter 1920-..................DLB-87
O'Donovan, Michael (see O'Connor, Frank)
O'Dowd, Bernard 1866-1953.............DLB-230
Ōe, Kenzaburō 1935-..........DLB-182; Y-94
  Nobel Lecture 1994: Japan, the
    Ambiguous, and Myself...........Y-94
Oehlenschläger, Adam 1779-1850........DLB-300
O'Faolain, Julia 1932-.........DLB-14, 231, 319
O'Faolain, Sean 1900-1991.............DLB-15, 162
Off-Loop Theatres.....................DLB-7
Offord, Carl Ruthven 1910-1990........DLB-76
O'Flaherty, Liam 1896-1984...DLB-36, 162; Y-84
Ogarev, Nikolai Platonovich 1813-1877..DLB-277
J. S. Ogilvie and Company..............DLB-49
Ogilvy, Eliza 1822-1912................DLB-199
Ogot, Grace 1930-......................DLB-125
O'Grady, Desmond 1935-.................DLB-40
Ogunyemi, Wale 1939-..................DLB-157
O'Hagan, Howard 1902-1982.............DLB-68
O'Hara, Frank 1926-1966..........DLB-5, 16, 193
O'Hara, John
  1905-1970.........DLB-9, 86; DS-2; CDALB-5
  John O'Hara's Pottsville Journalism......Y-88
O'Hare, Kate Richards 1876-1948.......DLB-303
O'Hegarty, P. S. 1879-1955............DLB-201
Ohio State University
  The William Charvat American Fiction
    Collection at the Ohio State
    University Libraries..............Y-92
Okada, John 1923-1971.................DLB-312
Okara, Gabriel 1921-........DLB-125; CDWLB-3
O'Keeffe, John 1747-1833..............DLB-89
Nicholas Okes [publishing house]......DLB-170

Okigbo, Christopher
  1930-1967............DLB-125; CDWLB-3
Okot p'Bitek 1931-1982.....DLB-125; CDWLB-3
Okpewho, Isidore 1941-................DLB-157
Okri, Ben 1959-..........DLB-157, 231, 319
Ólafur Jóhann Sigurðsson 1918-1988....DLB-293
Old Dogs / New Tricks? New Technologies,
  the Canon, and the Structure of
  the Profession...................Y-02
Old Franklin Publishing House.........DLB-49
Old German Genesis and *Old German Exodus*
  circa 1050-circa 1130............DLB-148
The *Old High German Isidor*
  circa 790-800....................DLB-148
Older, Fremont 1856-1935..............DLB-25
Oldham, John 1653-1683................DLB-131
Oldman, C. B. 1894-1969...............DLB-201
Olds, Sharon 1942-....................DLB-120
Olearius, Adam 1599-1671..............DLB-164
O'Leary, Ellen 1831-1889..............DLB-240
O'Leary, Juan E. 1879-1969............DLB-290
Olesha, Iurii Karlovich 1899-1960.....DLB-272
Oliphant, Laurence 1829?-1888.....DLB-18, 166
Oliphant, Margaret 1828-1897...DLB-18, 159, 190
  "Modern Novelists–Great and Small"
    (1855).......................DLB-21
Oliveira, Carlos de 1921-1981.........DLB-287
Oliver, Chad 1928-1993.................DLB-8
Oliver, Mary 1935-....................DLB-5, 193
Ollier, Claude 1922-....................DLB-83
Olsen, Tillie 1912/1913-
  ....DLB-28, 206; Y-80; CDALB-7
Olson, Charles 1910-1970..........DLB-5, 16, 193
Olson, Elder 1909-1992................DLB-48, 63
Olson, Sigurd F. 1899-1982............DLB-275
The Omega Workshops..................DS-10
Omotoso, Kole 1943-..................DLB-125
Omulevsky, Innokentii Vasil'evich
  1836 [or 1837]-1883..............DLB-238
Ondaatje, Michael 1943-................DLB-60
O'Neill, Eugene 1888-1953.....DLB-7; CDALB-5
  Eugene O'Neill Memorial Theater
    Center.........................DLB-7
  Eugene O'Neill's Letters: A Review......Y-88
Onetti, Juan Carlos
  1909-1994............DLB-113; CDWLB-3
Onions, George Oliver 1872-1961.......DLB-153
Onofri, Arturo 1885-1928..............DLB-114
O'Nolan, Brian 1911-1966..............DLB-231
Oodgeroo of the Tribe Noonuccal
  (Kath Walker) 1920-1993..........DLB-289
Opie, Amelia 1769-1853............DLB-116, 159
Opitz, Martin 1597-1639...............DLB-164
Oppen, George 1908-1984...............DLB-5, 165
Oppenheim, E. Phillips 1866-1946......DLB-70
Oppenheim, James 1882-1932............DLB-28
Oppenheimer, Joel 1930-1988..........DLB-5, 193
Optic, Oliver (see Adams, William Taylor)

Orczy, Emma, Baroness 1865-1947 ...... DLB-70
Oregon Shakespeare Festival Y-00
Origo, Iris 1902-1988 .... DLB-155
O'Riordan, Kate 1960- DLB-267
Orlovitz, Gil 1918-1973 .... DLB-2, 5
Orlovsky, Peter 1933- DLB-16
Ormond, John 1923- DLB-27
Ornitz, Samuel 1890-1957 ...... DLB-28, 44
O'Rourke, P. J. 1947- DLB-185
Orozco, Olga 1920-1999............... DLB-283
Orten, Jiří 1919-1941 .... DLB-215
Ortese, Anna Maria 1914- DLB-177
Ortiz, Simon J. 1941- DLB-120, 175, 256
Ortnit and *Wolfdietrich* circa 1225-1250.... DLB-138
Orton, Joe 1933-1967 .... DLB-13, 310; CDBLB-8
Orwell, George (Eric Arthur Blair)
  1903-1950 .. DLB-15, 98, 195, 255; CDBLB-7
  The Orwell Year Y-84
  (Re-)Publishing Orwell................ Y-86
Ory, Carlos Edmundo de 1923- DLB-134
Osbey, Brenda Marie 1957- DLB-120
Osbon, B. S. 1827-1912................. DLB-43
Osborn, Sarah 1714-1796 .... DLB-200
Osborne, John 1929-1994..... DLB-13; CDBLB-7
Osgood, Frances Sargent 1811-1850..... DLB-250
Osgood, Herbert L. 1855-1918........... DLB-47
James R. Osgood and Company DLB-49
Osgood, McIlvaine and Company DLB-112
O'Shaughnessy, Arthur 1844-1881....... DLB-35
Patrick O'Shea [publishing house] DLB-49
Osipov, Nikolai Petrovich 1751-1799 .... DLB-150
Oskison, John Milton 1879-1947........DLB-175
Osler, Sir William 1849-1919 .... DLB-184
Osofisan, Femi 1946- DLB-125; CDWLB-3
Ostenso, Martha 1900-1963............. DLB-92
Ostrauskas, Kostas 1926- DLB-232
Ostriker, Alicia 1937- DLB-120
Ostrovsky, Aleksandr Nikolaevich
  1823-1886 ....DLB-277
Ostrovsky, Nikolai Alekseevich
  1904-1936 .... DLB-272
Osundare, Niyi 1947- DLB-157; CDWLB-3
Oswald, Eleazer 1755-1795 .... DLB-43
Oswald von Wolkenstein
  1376 or 1377-1445 ....DLB-179
Otero, Blas de 1916-1979 .... DLB-134
Otero, Miguel Antonio 1859-1944 ...... DLB-82
Otero, Nina 1881-1965................. DLB-209
Otero Silva, Miguel 1908-1985 .... DLB-145
Otfried von Weißenburg
  circa 800-circa 875? DLB-148
Otis, Broaders and Company DLB-49
Otis, James (see Kaler, James Otis)
Otis, James, Jr. 1725-1783 .... DLB-31
Otsup, Nikolai 1894-1958................ DLB-317
Ottaway, James 1911-2000.............. DLB-127

Ottendorfer, Oswald 1826-1900......... DLB-23
Ottieri, Ottiero 1924-2002 ....DLB-177
Otto-Peters, Louise 1819-1895 .... DLB-129
Otway, Thomas 1652-1685 .... DLB-80
Ouellette, Fernand 1930- DLB-60
Ouida 1839-1908 .... DLB-18, 156
Outing Publishing Company DLB-46
Overbury, Sir Thomas
  circa 1581-1613 .... DLB-151
The Overlook Press DLB-46
Ovid 43 B.C.-A.D. 17 .... DLB-211; CDWLB-1
Oviedo, Gonzalo Fernández de
  1478-1557 .... DLB-318
Owen, Guy 1925-1981 .... DLB-5
Owen, John 1564-1622................. DLB-121
John Owen [publishing house] DLB-49
Peter Owen Limited DLB-112
Owen, Robert 1771-1858 ....DLB-107, 158
Owen, Wilfred
  1893-1918 .... DLB-20; DS-18; CDBLB-6
  A Centenary Celebration............. Y-93
  The Wilfred Owen Association Y-98
The Owl and the Nightingale
  circa 1189-1199 .... DLB-146
Owsley, Frank L. 1890-1956 .... DLB-17
Oxford, Seventeenth Earl of, Edward
  de Vere 1550-1604................DLB-172
OyamO (Charles F. Gordon)
  1943- DLB-266
Ozerov, Vladislav Aleksandrovich
  1769-1816...................... DLB-150
Ozick, Cynthia 1928- ...DLB-28, 152, 299; Y-82
  First Strauss "Livings" Awarded
    to Cynthia Ozick and
    Raymond Carver
  An Interview with Cynthia Ozick Y-83
  Tribute to Michael M. Rea Y-97

P

Pace, Richard 1482?-1536 .... DLB-167
Pacey, Desmond 1917-1975 .... DLB-88
Pacheco, José Emilio 1939- DLB-290
Pack, Robert 1929- DLB-5
Padell Publishing Company DLB-46
Padgett, Ron 1942- DLB-5
Padilla, Ernesto Chávez 1944- DLB-122
L. C. Page and Company.............. DLB-49
Page, Louise 1955- DLB-233
Page, P. K. 1916- DLB-68
Page, Thomas Nelson
  1853-1922 ....DLB-12, 78; DS-13
Page, Walter Hines 1855-1918....... DLB-71, 91
Paget, Francis Edward 1806-1882 ...... DLB-163
Paget, Violet (see Lee, Vernon)
Pagliarani, Elio 1927- DLB-128
Pain, Barry 1864-1928 ....DLB-135, 197
Pain, Philip ?-circa 1666 .... DLB-24
Paine, Robert Treat, Jr. 1773-1811 .... DLB-37

Paine, Thomas
  1737-1809 .... DLB-31, 43, 73, 158; CDALB-2
Painter, George D. 1914- DLB-155
Painter, William 1540?-1594 .... DLB-136
Palazzeschi, Aldo 1885-1974....... DLB-114, 264
Palei, Marina Anatol'evna 1955- DLB-285
Palencia, Alfonso de 1424-1492 .... DLB-286
Palés Matos, Luis 1898-1959 .... DLB-290
Paley, Grace 1922- DLB-28, 218
Paley, William 1743-1805.............. DLB-252
Palfrey, John Gorham
  1796-1881................. DLB-1, 30, 235
Palgrave, Francis Turner 1824-1897...... DLB-35
Palmer, Joe H. 1904-1952...............DLB-171
Palmer, Michael 1943- DLB-169
Palmer, Nettie 1885-1964............. DLB-260
Palmer, Vance 1885-1959.............. DLB-260
Paltock, Robert 1697-1767 .... DLB-39
Paludan, Jacob 1896-1975............. DLB-214
Paludin-Müller, Frederik 1809-1876..... DLB-300
Pan Books Limited DLB-112
Panaev, Ivan Ivanovich 1812-1862...... DLB-198
Panaeva, Avdot'ia Iakovlevna
  1820-1893 .... DLB-238
Panama, Norman 1914-2003 and
  Frank, Melvin 1913-1988........... DLB-26
Pancake, Breece D'J 1952-1979......... DLB-130
Panduro, Leif 1923-1977 .... DLB-214
Panero, Leopoldo 1909-1962 .... DLB-108
Pangborn, Edgar 1909-1976 .... DLB-8
Panizzi, Sir Anthony 1797-1879......... DLB-184
Panneton, Philippe (see Ringuet)
Panova, Vera Fedorovna 1905-1973..... DLB-302
Panshin, Alexei 1940- DLB-8
Pansy (see Alden, Isabella)
Pantheon Books DLB-46
Papadat-Bengescu, Hortensia
  1876-1955...................... DLB-220
Papantonio, Michael 1907-1976 ....DLB-187
Paperback Library DLB-46
Paperback Science Fiction............. DLB-8
Papini, Giovanni 1881-1956........... DLB-264
Paquet, Alfons 1881-1944.............. DLB-66
Paracelsus 1493-1541 ....DLB-179
Paradis, Suzanne 1936- DLB-53
Páral, Vladimír, 1932- DLB-232
Pardoe, Julia 1804-1862 .... DLB-166
Paredes, Américo 1915-1999 .... DLB-209
Pareja Diezcanseco, Alfredo 1908-1993 .. DLB-145
Parents' Magazine Press DLB-46
Paretsky, Sara 1947- DLB-306
Parfit, Derek 1942- DLB-262
Parise, Goffredo 1929-1986 ....DLB-177
Parish, Mitchell 1900-1993............ DLB-265
Parizeau, Alice 1930-1990............. DLB-60
Park, Ruth 1923?- DLB-260

Parke, John 1754-1789	DLB-31
Parker, Dan 1893-1967	DLB-241
Parker, Dorothy 1893-1967	DLB-11, 45, 86
Parker, Gilbert 1860-1932	DLB-99
Parker, James 1714-1770	DLB-43
Parker, John [publishing house]	DLB-106
Parker, Matthew 1504-1575	DLB-213
Parker, Robert B. 1932-	DLB-306
Parker, Stewart 1941-1988	DLB-245
Parker, Theodore 1810-1860	DLB-1, 235; DS-5
Parker, William Riley 1906-1968	DLB-103
J. H. Parker [publishing house]	DLB-106
Parkes, Bessie Rayner (Madame Belloc) 1829-1925	DLB-240
Parkman, Francis 1823-1893	DLB-1, 30, 183, 186, 235
Parks, Gordon 1912-	DLB-33
Parks, Tim 1954-	DLB-231
Parks, William 1698-1750	DLB-43
William Parks [publishing house]	DLB-49
Parley, Peter (see Goodrich, Samuel Griswold)
Parmenides late sixth-fifth century B.C.	DLB-176
Parnell, Thomas 1679-1718	DLB-95
Parnicki, Teodor 1908-1988	DLB-215
Parnok, Sofiia Iakovlevna (Parnokh) 1885-1933	DLB-295
Parr, Catherine 1513?-1548	DLB-136
Parra, Nicanor 1914-	DLB-283
Parrington, Vernon L. 1871-1929	DLB-17, 63
Parrish, Maxfield 1870-1966	DLB-188
Parronchi, Alessandro 1914-	DLB-128
Parshchikov, Aleksei Maksimovich (Raiderman) 1954-	DLB-285
Partisan Review	DLB-303
Parton, James 1822-1891	DLB-30
Parton, Sara Payson Willis 1811-1872	DLB-43, 74, 239
S. W. Partridge and Company	DLB-106
Parun, Vesna 1922-	DLB-181; CDWLB-4
Pascal, Blaise 1623-1662	DLB-268
Pasinetti, Pier Maria 1913-	DLB-177
Tribute to Albert Erskine	Y-93
Pasolini, Pier Paolo 1922-1975	DLB-128, 177
Pastan, Linda 1932-	DLB-5
Pasternak, Boris 1890-1960	DLB-302
Paston, George (Emily Morse Symonds) 1860-1936	DLB-149, 197
The Paston Letters 1422-1509	DLB-146
Pastoral Novel of the Sixteenth Century, The	DLB-318
Pastorius, Francis Daniel 1651-circa 1720	DLB-24
Patchen, Kenneth 1911-1972	DLB-16, 48
Pater, Walter 1839-1894	DLB-57, 156; CDBLB-4
Aesthetic Poetry (1873)	DLB-35
"Style" (1888) [excerpt]	DLB-57
Paterson, A. B. "Banjo" 1864-1941	DLB-230
Paterson, Katherine 1932-	DLB-52
Patmore, Coventry 1823-1896	DLB-35, 98
Paton, Alan 1903-1988	DLB-225; DS-17
Paton, Joseph Noel 1821-1901	DLB-35
Paton Walsh, Jill 1937-	DLB-161
Patrick, Edwin Hill ("Ted") 1901-1964	DLB-137
Patrick, John 1906-1995	DLB-7
Pattee, Fred Lewis 1863-1950	DLB-71
Patterson, Alicia 1906-1963	DLB-127
Patterson, Eleanor Medill 1881-1948	DLB-29
Patterson, Eugene 1923-	DLB-127
Patterson, Joseph Medill 1879-1946	DLB-29
Pattillo, Henry 1726-1801	DLB-37
Paul, Elliot 1891-1958	DLB-4; DS-15
Paul, Jean (see Richter, Johann Paul Friedrich)
Paul, Kegan, Trench, Trubner and Company Limited	DLB-106
Peter Paul Book Company	DLB-49
Stanley Paul and Company Limited	DLB-112
Paulding, James Kirke 1778-1860	DLB-3, 59, 74, 250
Paulin, Tom 1949-	DLB-40
Pauper, Peter, Press	DLB-46
Paustovsky, Konstantin Georgievich 1892-1968	DLB-272
Pavese, Cesare 1908-1950	DLB-128, 177
Pavić, Milorad 1929-	DLB-181; CDWLB-4
Pavlov, Konstantin 1933-	DLB-181
Pavlov, Nikolai Filippovich 1803-1864	DLB-198
Pavlova, Karolina Karlovna 1807-1893	DLB-205
Pavlović, Miodrag 1928-	DLB-181; CDWLB-4
Pavlovsky, Eduardo 1933-	DLB-305
Paxton, John 1911-1985	DLB-44
Payn, James 1830-1898	DLB-18
Payne, John 1842-1916	DLB-35
Payne, John Howard 1791-1852	DLB-37
Payson and Clarke	DLB-46
Paz, Octavio 1914-1998	DLB-290; Y-90, 98
Nobel Lecture 1990	Y-90
Pazzi, Roberto 1946-	DLB-196
Pea, Enrico 1881-1958	DLB-264
Peabody, Elizabeth Palmer 1804-1894	DLB-1, 223
Preface to *Record of a School: Exemplifying the General Principles of Spiritual Culture*	DS-5
Elizabeth Palmer Peabody [publishing house]	DLB-49
Peabody, Josephine Preston 1874-1922	DLB-249
Peabody, Oliver William Bourn 1799-1848	DLB-59
Peace, Roger 1899-1968	DLB-127
Peacham, Henry 1578-1644?	DLB-151
Peacham, Henry, the Elder 1547-1634	DLB-172, 236
Peachtree Publishers, Limited	DLB-46
Peacock, Molly 1947-	DLB-120
Peacock, Thomas Love 1785-1866	DLB-96, 116
Pead, Deuel ?-1727	DLB-24
Peake, Mervyn 1911-1968	DLB-15, 160, 255
Peale, Rembrandt 1778-1860	DLB-183
Pear Tree Press	DLB-112
Pearce, Philippa 1920-	DLB-161
H. B. Pearson [publishing house]	DLB-49
Pearson, Hesketh 1887-1964	DLB-149
Peattie, Donald Culross 1898-1964	DLB-275
Pechersky, Andrei (see Mel'nikov, Pavel Ivanovich)
Peck, George W. 1840-1916	DLB-23, 42
H. C. Peck and Theo. Bliss [publishing house]	DLB-49
Peck, Harry Thurston 1856-1914	DLB-71, 91
Peden, William 1913-1999	DLB-234
Tribute to William Goyen	Y-83
Peele, George 1556-1596	DLB-62, 167
Pegler, Westbrook 1894-1969	DLB-171
Péguy, Charles 1873-1914	DLB-258
Peirce, Charles Sanders 1839-1914	DLB-270
Pekić, Borislav 1930-1992	DLB-181; CDWLB-4
Pelecanos, George P. 1957-	DLB-306
Pelevin, Viktor Olegovich 1962-	DLB-285
Pellegrini and Cudahy	DLB-46
Pelletier, Aimé (see Vac, Bertrand)
Pelletier, Francine 1959-	DLB-251
Pellicer, Carlos 1897?-1977	DLB-290
Pemberton, Sir Max 1863-1950	DLB-70
de la Peña, Terri 1947-	DLB-209
Penfield, Edward 1866-1925	DLB-188
Penguin Books [U.K.]	DLB-112
Fifty Penguin Years	Y-85
Penguin Collectors' Society	Y-98
Penguin Books [U.S.]	DLB-46
Penn, William 1644-1718	DLB-24
Penn Publishing Company	DLB-49
Penna, Sandro 1906-1977	DLB-114
Pennell, Joseph 1857-1926	DLB-188
Penner, Jonathan 1940-	Y-83
Pennington, Lee 1939-	Y-82
Penton, Brian 1904-1951	DLB-260
Pepper, Stephen C. 1891-1972	DLB-270
Pepys, Samuel 1633-1703	DLB-101, 213; CDBLB-2
Percy, Thomas 1729-1811	DLB-104
Percy, Walker 1916-1990	DLB-2; Y-80, 90
Tribute to Caroline Gordon	Y-81
Percy, William 1575-1648	DLB-172
Perec, Georges 1936-1982	DLB-83, 299
Perelman, Bob 1947-	DLB-193
Perelman, S. J. 1904-1979	DLB-11, 44
Pérez de Guzmán, Fernán ca. 1377-ca. 1460	DLB-286

Perez, Raymundo "Tigre"
1946- DLB-122
Peri Rossi, Cristina 1941- DLB-145, 290
Perkins, Eugene 1932- DLB-41
Perkins, Maxwell
  The Claims of Business and Literature:
    An Undergraduate Essay Y-01
Perkins, William 1558-1602 .... DLB-281
Perkoff, Stuart Z. 1930-1974........... DLB-16
Perley, Moses Henry 1804-1862 .... DLB-99
Permabooks DLB-46
Perovsky, Aleksei Alekseevich
  (Antonii Pogorel'sky) 1787-1836..... DLB-198
Perrault, Charles 1628-1703 .... DLB-268
Perri, Henry 1561-1617 .... DLB-236
Perrin, Alice 1867-1934................ DLB-156
Perry, Anne 1938- DLB-276
Perry, Bliss 1860-1954 .... DLB-71
Perry, Eleanor 1915-1981............... DLB-44
Perry, Henry (see Perri, Henry)
Perry, Matthew 1794-1858 .... DLB-183
Perry, Sampson 1747-1823 .... DLB-158
Perse, Saint-John 1887-1975 .... DLB-258
Persius A.D. 34-A.D. 62 .... DLB-211
Perutz, Leo 1882-1957 .... DLB-81
Pesetsky, Bette 1932- DLB-130
Pessanha, Camilo 1867-1926 .... DLB-287
Pessoa, Fernando 1888-1935 .... DLB-287
Pestalozzi, Johann Heinrich 1746-1827 .... DLB-94
Peter, Laurence J. 1919-1990 .... DLB-53
Peter of Spain circa 1205-1277 .... DLB-115
Peterkin, Julia 1880-1961 .... DLB-9
Peters, Ellis (Edith Pargeter)
  1913-1995.....................DLB-276
Peters, Lenrie 1932- DLB-117
Peters, Robert 1924- DLB-105
  "Foreword to *Ludwig of Bavaria*" DLB-105
Petersham, Maud 1889-1971 and
  Petersham, Miska 1888-1960........ DLB-22
Peterson, Charles Jacobs 1819-1887 ...... DLB-79
Peterson, Len 1917- DLB-88
Peterson, Levi S. 1933- DLB-206
Peterson, Louis 1922-1998 .... DLB-76
Peterson, T. B., and Brothers DLB-49
Petitclair, Pierre 1813-1860............ DLB-99
Petrescu, Camil 1894-1957 .... DLB-220
Petronius circa A.D. 20-A.D. 66
  .... DLB-211; CDWLB-1
Petrov, Aleksandar 1938- DLB-181
Petrov, Evgenii (Evgenii Petrovich Kataev)
  1903-1942 .... DLB-272
Petrov, Gavriil 1730-1801.............. DLB-150
Petrov, Valeri 1920- DLB-181
Petrov, Vasilii Petrovich 1736-1799 ..... DLB-150
Petrović, Rastko
  1898-1949 .... DLB-147; CDWLB-4

Petrushevskaia, Liudmila Stefanovna
  1938- DLB-285
Petruslied circa 854? DLB-148
Petry, Ann 1908-1997................. DLB-76
Pettie, George circa 1548-1589......... DLB-136
Pétur Gunnarsson 1947- DLB-293
Peyton, K. M. 1929- DLB-161
Pfaffe Konrad fl. circa 1172 .... DLB-148
Pfaffe Lamprecht fl. circa 1150......... DLB-148
Pfeiffer, Emily 1827-1890 .... DLB-199
Pforzheimer, Carl H. 1879-1957 .... DLB-140
Phaedrus circa 18 B.C.-circa A.D. 50 .... DLB-211
Phaer, Thomas 1510?-1560 .... DLB-167
Phaidon Press Limited DLB-112
Pharr, Robert Deane 1916-1992........ DLB-33
Phelps, Elizabeth Stuart 1815-1852..... DLB-202
Phelps, Elizabeth Stuart 1844-1911... DLB-74, 221
Philander von der Linde
  (see Mencke, Johann Burckhard)
Philby, H. St. John B. 1885-1960 .... DLB-195
Philip, Marlene Nourbese 1947- DLB-157
Philippe, Charles-Louis 1874-1909 ...... DLB-65
Philips, John 1676-1708................ DLB-95
Philips, Katherine 1632-1664 .... DLB-131
Phillipps, Sir Thomas 1792-1872....... DLB-184
Phillips, Caryl 1958- DLB-157
Phillips, David Graham
  1867-1911............... DLB-9, 12, 303
Phillips, Jayne Anne 1952- DLB-292; Y-80
  Tribute to Seymour Lawrence.......... Y-94
Phillips, Robert 1938- DLB-105
  "Finding, Losing, Reclaiming: A Note
    on My Poems" DLB-105
  Tribute to William Goyen............. Y-83
Phillips, Stephen 1864-1915 .... DLB-10
Phillips, Ulrich B. 1877-1934........... DLB-17
Phillips, Wendell 1811-1884 .... DLB-235
Phillips, Willard 1784-1873 .... DLB-59
Phillips, William 1907-2002 .... DLB-137
Phillips, Sampson and Company DLB-49
Phillpotts, Adelaide Eden (Adelaide Ross)
  1896-1993 .... DLB-191
Phillpotts, Eden 1862-1960...DLB-10, 70, 135, 153
Philo circa 20-15 B.C.-circa A.D. 50 ....DLB-176
Philosophical Dictionary, Voltaire DLB-314
Philosophical Library DLB-46
Philosophy
  Eighteenth-Century Philosophical
    Background................... DLB-31
  Philosophic Thought in Boston DLB-235
  Translators of the Twelfth Century:
    Literary Issues Raised and
    Impact Created DLB-115
Elihu Phinney [publishing house]........ DLB-49
Phoenix, John (see Derby, George Horatio)
PHYLON (Fourth Quarter, 1950),
  The Negro in Literature:
  The Current Scene................. DLB-76

Physiologus circa 1070-circa 1150 .... DLB-148
Piccolo, Lucio 1903-1969 .... DLB-114
Pickard, Tom 1946- DLB-40
William Pickering [publishing house].... DLB-106
Pickthall, Marjorie 1883-1922 .... DLB-92
Picoult, Jodi 1966- DLB-292
Pictorial Printing Company DLB-49
Piel, Gerard 1915-2004................DLB-137
  "An Announcement to Our Readers,"
    Gerard Piel's Statement in *Scientific
    American* (April 1948)..........DLB-137
Pielmeier, John 1949- DLB-266
Piercy, Marge 1936- DLB-120, 227
Pierro, Albino 1916-1995 .... DLB-128
Pignotti, Lamberto 1926- DLB-128
Pike, Albert 1809-1891................ DLB-74
Pike, Zebulon Montgomery 1779-1813... DLB-183
Pillat, Ion 1891-1945 .... DLB-220
Pil'niak, Boris Andreevich (Boris Andreevich
  Vogau) 1894-1938.................DLB-272
Pilon, Jean-Guy 1930- DLB-60
Pinar, Florencia fl. ca. late
  fifteenth century................. DLB-286
Pinckney, Eliza Lucas 1722-1793 .... DLB-200
Pinckney, Josephine 1895-1957 .... DLB-6
Pindar circa 518 B.C.-circa 438 B.C.
  .... DLB-176; CDWLB-1
Pindar, Peter (see Wolcot, John)
Pineda, Cecile 1942- DLB-209
Pinero, Arthur Wing 1855-1934......... DLB-10
Piñero, Miguel 1946-1988 .... DLB-266
Pinget, Robert 1919-1997 .... DLB-83
Pinkney, Edward Coote 1802-1828 ..... DLB-248
Pinnacle Books DLB-46
Piñon, Nélida 1935- DLB-145, 307
Pinsky, Robert 1940- Y-82
  Reappointed Poet Laureate Y-98
Pinter, Harold 1930- ... DLB-13, 310; CDBLB-8
  Writing for the Theatre DLB-13
Pinto, Fernão Mendes 1509/1511?-1583... DLB-287
Piontek, Heinz 1925- DLB-75
Piozzi, Hester Lynch [Thrale]
  1741-1821....................DLB-104, 142
Piper, H. Beam 1904-1964.............. DLB-8
Piper, Watty....................... DLB-22
Pirandello, Luigi 1867-1936 .... DLB-264
Pirckheimer, Caritas 1467-1532 ....DLB-179
Pirckheimer, Willibald 1470-1530 ....DLB-179
Pires, José Cardoso 1925-1998 .... DLB-287
Pisar, Samuel 1929- Y-83
Pisarev, Dmitrii Ivanovich 1840-1868 ....DLB-277
Pisemsky, Aleksei Feofilaktovich
  1821-1881 .... DLB-238
Pitkin, Timothy 1766-1847............. DLB-30
Pitter, Ruth 1897-1992 .... DLB-20
Pix, Mary 1666-1709 .... DLB-80

Pixerécourt, René Charles Guilbert de 1773-1844 .... DLB-192

Pizarnik, Alejandra 1936-1972 .... DLB-283

Plá, Josefina 1909-1999 .... DLB-290

Plaatje, Sol T. 1876-1932 .... DLB-125, 225

Plante, David 1940- Y-83

Platen, August von 1796-1835 .... DLB-90

Plantinga, Alvin 1932- DLB-279

Plath, Sylvia 1932-1963 .... DLB-5, 6, 152; CDALB-1

Plato circa 428 B.C.-348-347 B.C. DLB-176; CDWLB-1

Plato, Ann 1824-? DLB-239

Platon 1737-1812 .... DLB-150

Platonov, Andrei Platonovich (Andrei Platonovich Klimentev) 1899-1951 .... DLB-272

Platt, Charles 1945- DLB-261

Platt and Munk Company DLB-46

Plautus circa 254 B.C.-184 B.C. DLB-211; CDWLB-1

Playboy Press DLB-46

John Playford [publishing house] DLB-170

Der Pleier fl. circa 1250 .... DLB-138

Pleijel, Agneta 1940- DLB-257

Plenzdorf, Ulrich 1934- DLB-75

Pleshcheev, Aleksei Nikolaevich 1825?-1893 .... DLB-277

Plessen, Elizabeth 1944- DLB-75

Pletnev, Petr Aleksandrovich 1792-1865 .... DLB-205

Pliekšāne, Elza Rozenberga (see Aspazija)

Pliekšāns, Jānis (see Rainis, Jānis)

Plievier, Theodor 1892-1955 .... DLB-69

Plimpton, George 1927-2003 .. DLB-185, 241; Y-99

Pliny the Elder A.D. 23/24-A.D. 79 .... DLB-211

Pliny the Younger circa A.D. 61-A.D. 112 .... DLB-211

Plomer, William 1903-1973 .... DLB-20, 162, 191, 225

Plotinus 204-270 .... DLB-176; CDWLB-1

Plowright, Teresa 1952- DLB-251

Plume, Thomas 1630-1704 .... DLB-213

Plumly, Stanley 1939- DLB-5, 193

Plumpp, Sterling D. 1940- DLB-41

Plunkett, James 1920-2003 .... DLB-14

Plutarch circa 46-circa 120 .... DLB-176; CDWLB-1

Plymell, Charles 1935- DLB-16

Pocket Books DLB-46

Podestá, José J. 1858-1937 .... DLB-305

Poe, Edgar Allan 1809-1849 .... DLB-3, 59, 73, 74, 248; CDALB-2

The Poe Studies Association Y-99

Poe, James 1921-1980 .... DLB-44

The Poet Laureate of the United States Y-86

Statements from Former Consultants in Poetry Y-86

Poetry

Aesthetic Poetry (1873) DLB-35

A Century of Poetry, a Lifetime of Collecting: J. M. Edelstein's Collection of Twentieth-Century American Poetry Y-02

"Certain Gifts," by Betty Adcock DLB-105

Concrete Poetry DLB-307

Contempo Caravan: Kites in a Windstorm Y-85

"Contemporary Verse Story-telling," by Jonathan Holden DLB-105

"A Detail in a Poem," by Fred Chappell DLB-105

"The English Renaissance of Art" (1908), by Oscar Wilde DLB-35

"Every Man His Own Poet; or, The Inspired Singer's Recipe Book" (1877), by H. W. Mallock DLB-35

"Eyes Across Centuries: Contemporary Poetry and 'That Vision Thing,'" by Philip Dacey DLB-105

A Field Guide to Recent Schools of American Poetry Y-86

"Finding, Losing, Reclaiming: A Note on My Poems, by Robert Phillips" DLB-105

"The Fleshly School of Poetry and Other Phenomena of the Day" (1872) ... DLB-35

"The Fleshly School of Poetry: Mr. D. G. Rossetti" (1871) DLB-35

The G. Ross Roy Scottish Poetry Collection at the University of South Carolina .. Y-89

"Getting Started: Accepting the Regions You Own—or Which Own You," by Walter McDonald DLB-105

"The Good, The Not So Good," by Stephen Dunn DLB-105

The Griffin Poetry Prize Y-00

The Hero as Poet. Dante; Shakspeare (1841), by Thomas Carlyle DLB-32

"Images and 'Images,'" by Charles Simic DLB-105

"Into the Mirror," by Peter Cooley ... DLB-105

"Knots into Webs: Some Autobiographical Sources," by Dabney Stuart DLB-105

"L'Envoi" (1882), by Oscar Wilde DLB-35

"Living in Ruin," by Gerald Stern ... DLB-105

Looking for the Golden Mountain: Poetry Reviewing Y-89

Lyric Poetry (French) DLB-268

Medieval Galician-Portuguese Poetry DLB-287

"The No Self, the Little Self, and the Poets," by Richard Moore DLB-105

On Some of the Characteristics of Modern Poetry and On the Lyrical Poems of Alfred Tennyson (1831) DLB-32

The Pitt Poetry Series: Poetry Publishing Today Y-85

"The Poetry File," by Edward Field DLB-105

Poetry in Nineteenth-Century France: Cultural Background and Critical Commentary DLB-217

The Poetry of Jorge Luis Borges Y-86

"The Poet's Kaleidoscope: The Element of Surprise in the Making of the Poem" by Madeline DeFrees DLB-105

The Pre-Raphaelite Controversy DLB-35

Protest Poetry in Castile DLB-286

"Reflections: After a Tornado," by Judson Jerome DLB-105

Statements from Former Consultants in Poetry Y-86

Statements on the Art of Poetry DLB-54

The Study of Poetry (1880), by Matthew Arnold DLB-35

A Survey of Poetry Anthologies, 1879-1960 .... DLB-54

Thoughts on Poetry and Its Varieties (1833), by John Stuart Mill DLB-32

Under the Microscope (1872), by A. C. Swinburne DLB-35

The Unterberg Poetry Center of the 92nd Street Y Y-98

Victorian Poetry: Five Critical Views DLBV-35

Year in Poetry Y-83–92, 94–01

Year's Work in American Poetry Y-82

Poets

The Lives of the Poets (1753) DLB-142

Minor Poets of the Earlier Seventeenth Century DLB-121

Other British Poets Who Fell in the Great War DLB-216

Other Poets [French] DLB-217

Second-Generation Minor Poets of the Seventeenth Century DLB-126

Third-Generation Minor Poets of the Seventeenth Century DLB-131

Pogodin, Mikhail Petrovich 1800-1875 ... DLB-198

Pogorel'sky, Antonii (see Perovsky, Aleksei Alekseevich)

Pohl, Frederik 1919- DLB-8

Tribute to Isaac Asimov Y-92

Tribute to Theodore Sturgeon Y-85

Poirier, Louis (see Gracq, Julien)

Poláček, Karel 1892-1945 ... DLB-215; CDWLB-4

Polanyi, Michael 1891-1976 .... DLB-100

Pole, Reginald 1500-1558 .... DLB-132

Polevoi, Nikolai Alekseevich 1796-1846 .. DLB-198

Polezhaev, Aleksandr Ivanovich 1804-1838 .... DLB-205

Poliakoff, Stephen 1952- DLB-13

Polidori, John William 1795-1821 .... DLB-116

Polite, Carlene Hatcher 1932- DLB-33

Pollard, Alfred W. 1859-1944 .... DLB-201

Pollard, Edward A. 1832-1872 .... DLB-30

Pollard, Graham 1903-1976 .... DLB-201

Pollard, Percival 1869-1911 .... DLB-71

Pollard and Moss DLB-49

Cumulative Index

Pollock, Sharon 1936- DLB-60
Polonsky, Abraham 1910-1999......... DLB-26
Polonsky, Iakov Petrovich 1819-1898 ....DLB-277
Polotsky, Simeon 1629-1680 .... DLB-150
Polybius circa 200 B.C.-118 B.C. DLB-176
Pomialovsky, Nikolai Gerasimovich
  1835-1863 .... DLB-238
Pomilio, Mario 1921-1990 ....DLB-177
Pompéia, Raul (Raul d'Avila Pompéia)
  1863-1895 .... DLB-307
Ponce, Mary Helen 1938- DLB-122
Ponce-Montoya, Juanita 1949- DLB-122
Ponet, John 1516?-1556 .... DLB-132
Ponge, Francis 1899-1988........ DLB-258; Y-02
Poniatowska, Elena
  1933- DLB-113; CDWLB-3
Ponsard, François 1814-1867 .... DLB-192
William Ponsonby [publishing house] DLB-170
Pontiggia, Giuseppe 1934- DLB-196
Pontoppidan, Henrik 1857-1943 .... DLB-300
Pony Stories, Omnibus Essay on DLB-160
Poole, Ernest 1880-1950............... DLB-9
Poole, Sophia 1804-1891 .... DLB-166
Poore, Benjamin Perley 1820-1887....... DLB-23
Popa, Vasko 1922-1991 .... DLB-181; CDWLB-4
Pope, Abbie Hanscom 1858-1894....... DLB-140
Pope, Alexander
  1688-1744...... DLB-95, 101, 213; CDBLB-2
Poplavsky, Boris 1903-1935 .... DLB-317
Popov, Aleksandr Serafimovich
  (see Serafimovich, Aleksandr Serafimovich)
Popov, Evgenii Anatol'evich 1946- DLB-285
Popov, Mikhail Ivanovich
  1742-circa 1790................ DLB-150
Popović, Aleksandar 1929-1996 .... DLB-181
Popper, Karl 1902-1994 .... DLB-262
Popular Culture Association/
  American Culture Association Y-99
Popular Library DLB-46
Poquelin, Jean-Baptiste (see Molière)
Porete, Marguerite ?-1310............ DLB-208
Porlock, Martin (see MacDonald, Philip)
Porpoise Press...................... DLB-112
Porta, Antonio 1935-1989 .... DLB-128
Porter, Anna Maria 1780-1832 ..... DLB-116, 159
Porter, Cole 1891-1964.............. DLB-265
Porter, David 1780-1843.............. DLB-183
Porter, Eleanor H. 1868-1920........... DLB-9
Porter, Gene Stratton (see Stratton-Porter, Gene)
Porter, Hal 1911-1984 .... DLB-260
Porter, Henry circa sixteenth century..... DLB-62
Porter, Jane 1776-1850 .... DLB-116, 159
Porter, Katherine Anne 1890-1980
  ......DLB-4, 9, 102; Y-80; DS-12; CDALB-7
  The Katherine Anne Porter Society...... Y-01
Porter, Peter 1929- DLB-40, 289

Porter, William Sydney (O. Henry)
  1862-1910 ....DLB-12, 78, 79; CDALB-3
Porter, William T. 1809-1858 .... DLB-3, 43, 250
Porter and Coates................... DLB-49
Portillo Trambley, Estela 1927-1998..... DLB-209
Portis, Charles 1933- DLB-6
Medieval Galician-Portuguese Poetry.... DLB-287
Posey, Alexander 1873-1908...........DLB-175
Postans, Marianne circa 1810-1865 ..... DLB-166
Postgate, Raymond 1896-1971 ....DLB-276
Postl, Carl (see Sealsfield, Carl)
Postmodern Holocaust Fiction DLB-299
Poston, Ted 1906-1974................ DLB-51
Potekhin, Aleksei Antipovich
  1829-1908 .... DLB-238
Potok, Chaim 1929-2002 .... DLB-28, 152
  A Conversation with Chaim Potok Y-84
  Tribute to Bernard Malamud Y-86
Potter, Beatrix 1866-1943............ DLB-141
  The Beatrix Potter Society............. Y-98
Potter, David M. 1910-1971 .... DLB-17
Potter, Dennis 1935-1994 .... DLB-233
John E. Potter and Company DLB-49
Pottle, Frederick A. 1897-1987 .....DLB-103; Y-87
Poulin, Jacques 1937- DLB-60
Pound, Ezra 1885-1972
  .... DLB-4, 45, 63; DS-15; CDALB-4
  The Cost of the Cantos: William Bird
    to Ezra Pound Y-01
  The Ezra Pound Society Y-01
Poverman, C. E. 1944- DLB-234
Povey, Meic 1950- DLB-310
Povich, Shirley 1905-1998 ....DLB-171
Powell, Anthony 1905-2000 ... DLB-15; CDBLB-7
  The Anthony Powell Society: Powell and
    the First Biennial Conference Y-01
Powell, Dawn 1897-1965
  Dawn Powell, Where Have You Been
    All Our Lives?................... Y-97
Powell, John Wesley 1834-1902 .... DLB-186
Powell, Padgett 1952- DLB-234
Powers, J. F. 1917-1999............... DLB-130
Powers, Jimmy 1903-1995 .... DLB-241
Pownall, David 1938- DLB-14
Powys, John Cowper 1872-1963..... DLB-15, 255
Powys, Llewelyn 1884-1939 .... DLB-98
Powys, T. F. 1875-1953 .... DLB-36, 162
  The Powys Society................... Y-98
Poynter, Nelson 1903-1978............ DLB-127
Prado, Adélia 1935- DLB-307
Prado, Pedro 1886-1952.............. DLB-283
Prados, Emilio 1899-1962 .... DLB-134
Praed, Mrs. Caroline (see Praed, Rosa)
Praed, Rosa (Mrs. Caroline Praed)
  1851-1935 .... DLB-230
Praed, Winthrop Mackworth 1802-1839 .. DLB-96
Praeger Publishers DLB-46

Praetorius, Johannes 1630-1680 .... DLB-168
Pratolini, Vasco 1913-1991.............DLB-177
Pratt, E. J. 1882-1964 .... DLB-92
Pratt, Samuel Jackson 1749-1814 .... DLB-39
Preciado Martin, Patricia 1939- DLB-209
Préfontaine, Yves 1937- DLB-53
Prelutsky, Jack 1940- DLB-61
Prentice, George D. 1802-1870.......... DLB-43
Prentice-Hall....................... DLB-46
Prescott, Orville 1906-1996 .... Y-96
Prescott, William Hickling
  1796-1859.............. DLB-1, 30, 59, 235
Prešeren, Francè
  1800-1849 ....DLB-147; CDWLB-4
Presses (See also Publishing)
  Small Presses in Great Britain and
    Ireland, 1960-1985 .... DLB-40
  Small Presses I: Jargon Society.......... Y-84
  Small Presses II: The Spirit That Moves
    Us Press Y-85
  Small Presses III: Pushcart Press Y-87
Preston, Margaret Junkin
  1820-1897 .... DLB-239, 248
Preston, May Wilson 1873-1949 .... DLB-188
Preston, Thomas 1537-1598............ DLB-62
Prévert, Jacques 1900-1977 .... DLB-258
Prévost d'Exiles, Antoine François
  1697-1763..................... DLB-314
Price, Anthony 1928- DLB-276
Price, Reynolds 1933- DLB-2, 218, 278
Price, Richard 1723-1791 .... DLB-158
Price, Richard 1949- Y-81
Prichard, Katharine Susannah
  1883-1969 .... DLB-260
Prideaux, John 1578-1650............. DLB-236
Priest, Christopher 1943- DLB-14, 207, 261
Priestley, J. B. 1894-1984
  .... DLB-10, 34, 77, 100, 139; Y-84; CDBLB-6
Priestley, Joseph 1733-1804 .... DLB-252
Prigov, Dmitrii Aleksandrovich 1940- . DLB-285
Prime, Benjamin Young 1733-1791....... DLB-31
Primrose, Diana floruit circa 1630 ...... DLB-126
Prince, F. T. 1912-2003 .... DLB-20
Prince, Nancy Gardner
  1799-circa 1856 .... DLB-239
Prince, Thomas 1687-1758 .... DLB-24, 140
Pringle, Thomas 1789-1834 .... DLB-225
Printz, Wolfgang Casper 1641-1717 .... DLB-168
Prior, Matthew 1664-1721 .... DLB-95
Prisco, Michele 1920-2003 ....DLB-177
Prishvin, Mikhail Mikhailovich
  1873-1954......................DLB-272
Pritchard, William H. 1932- DLB-111
Pritchett, V. S. 1900-1997.......... DLB-15, 139
Probyn, May 1856 or 1857-1909 .... DLB-199
Procter, Adelaide Anne 1825-1864... DLB-32, 199
Procter, Bryan Waller 1787-1874 ... DLB-96, 144
Proctor, Robert 1868-1903............ DLB-184

Prokopovich, Feofan 1681?-1736........DLB-150
Prokosch, Frederic 1906-1989..........DLB-48
Pronzini, Bill 1943- DLB-226
Propertius circa 50 B.C.-post 16 B.C.
    ....DLB-211; CDWLB-1
Propper, Dan 1937- DLB-16
Prose, Francine 1947- DLB-234
Protagoras circa 490 B.C.-420 B.C........DLB-176
Protest Poetry in Castile
    ca. 1445-ca. 1506.................DLB-286
Proud, Robert 1728-1813..............DLB-30
Proust, Marcel 1871-1922.............DLB-65
    Marcel Proust at 129 and the Proust
        Society of America Y-00
    Marcel Proust's *Remembrance of Things Past*:
        The Rediscovered Galley Proofs Y-00
Prutkov, Koz'ma Petrovich
    1803-1863......................DLB-277
Prynne, J. H. 1936- DLB-40
Przybyszewski, Stanislaw 1868-1927......DLB-66
Pseudo-Dionysius the Areopagite floruit
    circa 500 ....DLB-115
Public Lending Right in America
    PLR and the Meaning of Literary
        Property Y-83
    Statement by Sen. Charles
        McC. Mathias, Jr. PLR........... Y-83
    Statements on PLR by American Writers ... Y-83
Public Lending Right in the United Kingdom
    The First Year in the United Kingdom ... Y-83
Publishers [listed by individual names]
Publishers, Conversations with:
    An Interview with Charles Scribner III .. Y-94
    An Interview with Donald Lamm........ Y-95
    An Interview with James Laughlin Y-96
    An Interview with Patrick O'Connor Y-84
Publishing
    The Art and Mystery of Publishing:
        Interviews...................... Y-97
    Book Publishing Accounting: Some Basic
        Concepts....................... Y-98
    1873 Publishers' Catalogues DLB-49
    The Literary Scene 2002: Publishing, Book
        Reviewing, and Literary Journalism .. Y-02
    Main Trends in Twentieth-Century
        Book Clubs....................DLB-46
    Overview of U.S. Book Publishing,
        1910-1945......................DLB-9
    The Pitt Poetry Series: Poetry Publishing
        Today......................... Y-85
    Publishing Fiction at LSU Press Y-87
    The Publishing Industry in 1998:
        Sturm-und-drang.com................ Y-98
    The Publishing Industry in 1999 .... Y-99
    Publishers and Agents: The Columbia
        Connection.................... Y-87
    Responses to Ken Auletta Y-97
    Southern Writers Between the Wars....DLB-9
    The State of Publishing............... Y-97
    Trends in Twentieth-Century
        Mass Market Publishing........DLB-46

The Year in Book Publishing Y-86
Pückler-Muskau, Hermann von
    1785-1871........................DLB-133
Pufendorf, Samuel von 1632-1694.......DLB-168
Pugh, Edwin William 1874-1930........DLB-135
Pugin, A. Welby 1812-1852..............DLB-55
Puig, Manuel 1932-1990 .... DLB-113; CDWLB-3
Puisieux, Madeleine d'Arsant de
    1720-1798......................DLB-314
Pulgar, Hernando del (Fernando del Pulgar)
    ca. 1436-ca. 1492..................DLB-286
Pulitzer, Joseph 1847-1911 ....DLB-23
Pulitzer, Joseph, Jr. 1885-1955..........DLB-29
Pulitzer Prizes for the Novel, 1917-1945 ....DLB-9
Pulliam, Eugene 1889-1975 ....DLB-127
Purcell, Deirdre 1945- DLB-267
Purchas, Samuel 1577?-1626 ....DLB-151
Purdy, Al 1918-2000 ....DLB-88
Purdy, James 1923- DLB-2, 218
Purdy, Ken W. 1913-1972..............DLB-137
Pusey, Edward Bouverie 1800-1882 ......DLB-55
Pushkin, Aleksandr Sergeevich
    1799-1837......................DLB-205
Pushkin, Vasilii L'vovich
    1766-1830......................DLB-205
Putnam, George Palmer
    1814-1872 .... DLB-3, 79, 250, 254
G. P. Putnam [publishing house] DLB-254
G. P. Putnam's Sons [U.K.] DLB-106
G. P. Putnam's Sons [U.S.] DLB-49
    A Publisher's Archives: G. P. Putnam ... Y-92
Putnam, Hilary 1926- DLB-279
Putnam, Samuel 1892-1950........DLB-4; DS-15
Puttenham, George 1529?-1590.........DLB-281
Puzo, Mario 1920-1999 ....DLB-6
Pyle, Ernie 1900-1945 ....DLB-29
Pyle, Howard
    1853-1911........DLB-42, 188; DS-13
Pyle, Robert Michael 1947- DLB-275
Pym, Barbara 1913-1980...... DLB-14, 207; Y-87
Pynchon, Thomas 1937- DLB-2, 173
Pyramid Books DLB-46
Pyrnelle, Louise-Clarke 1850-1907 ......DLB-42
Pythagoras circa 570 B.C.-? DLB-176

Q

Qays ibn al-Mulawwah circa 680-710 ....DLB-311
Quad, M. (see Lewis, Charles B.)
Quaritch, Bernard 1819-1899 ....DLB-184
Quarles, Francis 1592-1644 ....DLB-126
The Quarterly Review 1809-1967..........DLB-110
Quasimodo, Salvatore 1901-1968 ....DLB-114
Queen, Ellery (see Dannay, Frederic, and
    Manfred B. Lee)
Queen, Frank 1822-1882................DLB-241
The Queen City Publishing House DLB-49
Queirós, Eça de 1845-1900 ....DLB-287

Queneau, Raymond 1903-1976......DLB-72, 258
Quennell, Peter 1905-1993 ....DLB-155, 195
Quental, Antero de
    1842-1891......................DLB-287
Quesada, José Luis 1948- DLB-290
Quesnel, Joseph 1746-1809 ....DLB-99
Quiller-Couch, Sir Arthur Thomas
    1863-1944 .... DLB-135, 153, 190
Quin, Ann 1936-1973 ....DLB-14, 231
Quinault, Philippe 1635-1688...........DLB-268
Quincy, Samuel, of Georgia
    fl. eighteenth century...............DLB-31
Quincy, Samuel, of Massachusetts
    1734-1789......................DLB-31
Quindlen, Anna 1952- DLB-292
Quine, W. V. 1908-2000 ....DLB-279
Quinn, Anthony 1915-2001.............DLB-122
Quinn, John 1870-1924 ....DLB-187
Quiñónez, Naomi 1951- DLB-209
Quintana, Leroy V. 1944- DLB-82
Quintana, Miguel de 1671-1748
    A Forerunner of Chicano
        Literature DLB-122
Quintilian
    circa A.D. 40-circa A.D. 96 ....DLB-211
Quintus Curtius Rufus
    fl. A.D. 35.....................DLB-211
Harlin Quist Books DLB-46
Quoirez, Françoise (see Sagan, Françoise)

R

Raabe, Wilhelm 1831-1910............DLB-129
Raban, Jonathan 1942- DLB-204
Rabe, David 1940- DLB-7, 228; Y-91
Rabi'ah al-'Adawiyyah circa 720-801.....DLB-311
Raboni, Giovanni 1932- DLB-128
Rachilde 1860-1953 ....DLB-123, 192
Racin, Kočo 1908-1943 ....DLB-147
Racine, Jean 1639-1699................DLB-268
Rackham, Arthur 1867-1939 ....DLB-141
Raczymow, Henri 1948- DLB-299
Radauskas, Henrikas
    1910-1970 .... DLB-220; CDWLB-4
Radcliffe, Ann 1764-1823........... DLB-39, 178
Raddall, Thomas 1903-1994 ....DLB-68
Radford, Dollie 1858-1920 ....DLB-240
Radichkov, Yordan 1929-2004 ....DLB-181
Radiguet, Raymond 1903-1923..........DLB-65
Radishchev, Aleksandr Nikolaevich
    1749-1802......................DLB-150
Radnóti, Miklós
    1909-1944 .... DLB-215; CDWLB-4
Radrigán, Juan 1937- DLB-305
Radványi, Netty Reiling (see Seghers, Anna)
Rahv, Philip 1908-1973 ....DLB-137
Raich, Semen Egorovich 1792-1855......DLB-205
Raičković, Stevan 1928- DLB-181

Cumulative Index

Raiderman (see Parshchikov, Aleksei Maksimovich)
Raimund, Ferdinand Jakob 1790-1836 .... DLB-90
Raine, Craig 1944- DLB-40
Raine, Kathleen 1908-2003............. DLB-20
Rainis, Jānis 1865-1929..... DLB-220; CDWLB-4
Rainolde, Richard
    circa 1530-1606 .... DLB-136, 236
Rainolds, John 1549-1607.............. DLB-281
Rakić, Milan 1876-1938 .....DLB-147; CDWLB-4
Rakosi, Carl 1903-2004 .... DLB-193
Ralegh, Sir Walter
    1554?-1618............ DLB-172; CDBLB-1
Raleigh, Walter
    Style (1897) [excerpt]............... DLB-57
Ralin, Radoy 1923-2004............... DLB-181
Ralph, Julian 1853-1903 .... DLB-23
Ramat, Silvio 1939- DLB-128
Ramée, Marie Louise de la (see Ouida)
Ramírez, Sergío 1942- DLB-145
Ramke, Bin 1947- DLB-120
Ramler, Karl Wilhelm 1725-1798 .... DLB-97
Ramon Ribeyro, Julio 1929-1994....... DLB-145
Ramos, Graciliano 1892-1953 .... DLB-307
Ramos, Manuel 1948- DLB-209
Ramos Sucre, José Antonio 1890-1930... DLB-290
Ramous, Mario 1924- DLB-128
Rampersad, Arnold 1941- DLB-111
Ramsay, Allan 1684 or 1685-1758 .... DLB-95
Ramsay, David 1749-1815 .... DLB-30
Ramsay, Martha Laurens 1759-1811 .... DLB-200
Ramsey, Frank P. 1903-1930 .... DLB-262
Ranch, Hieronimus Justesen
    1539-1607..................... DLB-300
Ranck, Katherine Quintana 1942- DLB-122
Rand, Avery and Company DLB-49
Rand, Ayn 1905-1982....DLB-227, 279; CDALB-7
Rand McNally and Company DLB-49
Randall, David Anton 1905-1975 ...... DLB-140
Randall, Dudley 1914-2000 .... DLB-41
Randall, Henry S. 1811-1876 .... DLB-30
Randall, James G. 1881-1953 .... DLB-17
    The Randall Jarrell Symposium: A Small
    Collection of Randall Jarrells........ Y-86
    Excerpts From Papers Delivered at the
    Randall Jarrel Symposium.......... Y-86
Randall, John Herman, Jr. 1899-1980 ...DLB-279
Randolph, A. Philip 1889-1979......... DLB-91
Anson D. F. Randolph
    [publishing house] DLB-49
Randolph, Thomas 1605-1635...... DLB-58, 126
Random House.................... DLB-46
Rankin, Ian (Jack Harvey) 1960- DLB-267
Henry Ranlet [publishing house] DLB-49
Ransom, Harry 1908-1976 .... DLB-187
Ransom, John Crowe
    1888-1974.......... DLB-45, 63; CDALB-7
Ransome, Arthur 1884-1967 .... DLB-160

Raphael, Frederic 1931- DLB-14, 319
Raphaelson, Samson 1896-1983......... DLB-44
Rare Book Dealers
    Bertram Rota and His Bookshop........ Y-91
    An Interview with Glenn Horowitz Y-90
    An Interview with Otto Penzler......... Y-96
    An Interview with Ralph Sipper........ Y-94
    New York City Bookshops in the
    1930s and 1940s: The Recollections
    of Walter Goldwater.............. Y-93
Rare Books
    Research in the American Antiquarian
    Book Trade................... Y-97
    Two Hundred Years of Rare Books and
    Literary Collections at the
    University of South Carolina Y-00
Rascón Banda, Víctor Hugo 1948- DLB-305
Rashi circa 1040-1105................ DLB-208
Raskin, Ellen 1928-1984.............. DLB-52
Rasputin, Valentin Grigor'evich
    1937- DLB-302
Rastell, John 1475?-1536..........DLB-136, 170
Rattigan, Terence
    1911-1977.............. DLB-13; CDBLB-7
Raven, Simon 1927-2001 ....DLB-271
Ravenhill, Mark 1966- DLB-310
Ravnkilde, Adda 1862-1883.......... DLB-300
Rawicz, Piotr 1919-1982.............. DLB-299
Rawlings, Marjorie Kinnan 1896-1953
    .... DLB-9, 22, 102; DS-17; CDALB-7
Rawlinson, Richard 1690-1755......... DLB-213
Rawlinson, Thomas 1681-1725 .... DLB-213
Rawls, John 1921-2002................DLB-279
Raworth, Tom 1938- DLB-40
Ray, David 1932- DLB-5
Ray, Gordon Norton 1915-1986 ... DLB-103, 140
Ray, Henrietta Cordelia 1849-1916 ...... DLB-50
Raymond, Ernest 1888-1974 .... DLB-191
Raymond, Henry J. 1820-1869........ DLB-43, 79
Raymond, René (see Chase, James Hadley)
Razaf, Andy 1895-1973................ DLB-265
al-Razi 865?-925? DLB-311
Rea, Michael 1927-1996 .... Y-97
    Michael M. Rea and the Rea Award for
    the Short Story Y-97
Reach, Angus 1821-1856 .... DLB-70
Read, Herbert 1893-1968......... DLB-20, 149
Read, Martha Meredith
    fl. nineteenth century............. DLB-200
Read, Opie 1852-1939 .... DLB-23
Read, Piers Paul 1941- DLB-14
Reade, Charles 1814-1884 .... DLB-21
Reader's Digest Condensed Books....... DLB-46
Readers Ulysses Symposium Y-97
Reading, Peter 1946- DLB-40
Reading Series in New York City.......... Y-96
Reaney, James 1926- DLB-68
Rebhun, Paul 1500?-1546..........DLB-179

Rèbora, Clemente 1885-1957 .... DLB-114
Rebreanu, Liviu 1885-1944 .... DLB-220
Rechy, John 1934- DLB-122, 278; Y-82
Redding, J. Saunders 1906-1988.......DLB-63, 76
J. S. Redfield [publishing house] DLB-49
Redgrove, Peter 1932-2003 .... DLB-40
Redmon, Anne 1943- Y-86
Redmond, Eugene B. 1937- DLB-41
Redol, Alves 1911-1969 .... DLB-287
James Redpath [publishing house] DLB-49
Reed, Henry 1808-1854............... DLB-59
Reed, Henry 1914-1986 .... DLB-27
Reed, Ishmael
    1938- DLB-2, 5, 33, 169, 227; DS-8
Reed, Rex 1938- DLB-185
Reed, Sampson 1800-1880 .... DLB-1, 235
Reed, Talbot Baines 1852-1893 .... DLB-141
Reedy, William Marion 1862-1920 ...... DLB-91
Reese, Lizette Woodworth 1856-1935 .... DLB-54
Reese, Thomas 1742-1796 .... DLB-37
Reeve, Clara 1729-1807 .... DLB-39
    Preface to *The Old English Baron*
    (1778)...................... DLB-39
    The Progress of Romance (1785)
    [excerpt]..................... DLB-39
Reeves, James 1909-1978 .... DLB-161
Reeves, John 1926- DLB-88
Reeves-Stevens, Garfield 1953- DLB-251
Régio, José (José Maria dos Reis Pereira)
    1901-1969 .... DLB-287
Henry Regnery Company DLB-46
Rêgo, José Lins do 1901-1957 .... DLB-307
Rehberg, Hans 1901-1963 .... DLB-124
Rehfisch, Hans José 1891-1960 .... DLB-124
Reich, Ebbe Kløvedal 1940- DLB-214
Reid, Alastair 1926- DLB-27
Reid, B. L. 1918-1990................. DLB-111
Reid, Christopher 1949- DLB-40
Reid, Forrest 1875-1947 .... DLB-153
Reid, Helen Rogers 1882-1970 .... DLB-29
Reid, James fl. eighteenth century DLB-31
Reid, Mayne 1818-1883 .... DLB-21, 163
Reid, Thomas 1710-1796 .... DLB-31, 252
Reid, V. S. (Vic) 1913-1987 .... DLB-125
Reid, Whitelaw 1837-1912 .... DLB-23
Reilly and Lee Publishing Company DLB-46
Reimann, Brigitte 1933-1973 .... DLB-75
Reinmar der Alte circa 1165-circa 1205 .. DLB-138
Reinmar von Zweter
    circa 1200-circa 1250 .... DLB-138
Reisch, Walter 1903-1983 .... DLB-44
Reizei Family DLB-203
Religion
    A Crisis of Culture: The Changing
    Role of Religion in the
    New Republic DLB-37

Remarque, Erich Maria 1898-1970 .... DLB-56; CDWLB-2
Remington, Frederic 1861-1909 .... DLB-12, 186, 188
Remizov, Aleksei Mikhailovich 1877-1957 .... DLB-295
Renaud, Jacques 1943- DLB-60
Renault, Mary 1905-1983 .... Y-83
Rendell, Ruth (Barbara Vine) 1930- DLB-87, 276
Rensselaer, Maria van Cortlandt van 1645-1689 .... DLB-200
Repplier, Agnes 1855-1950 .... DLB-221
Reshetnikov, Fedor Mikhailovich 1841-1871 .... DLB-238
Restif (Rétif) de La Bretonne, Nicolas-Edme 1734-1806 .... DLB-314
Rettenbacher, Simon 1634-1706 .... DLB-168
Retz, Jean-François-Paul de Gondi, cardinal de 1613-1679 .... DLB-268
Reuchlin, Johannes 1455-1522 .... DLB-179
Reuter, Christian 1665-after 1712 .... DLB-168
Fleming H. Revell Company DLB-49
Reverdy, Pierre 1889-1960 .... DLB-258
Reuter, Fritz 1810-1874 .... DLB-129
Reuter, Gabriele 1859-1941 .... DLB-66
Reventlow, Franziska Gräfin zu 1871-1918 .... DLB-66
Review of Reviews Office DLB-112
Rexroth, Kenneth 1905-1982 ...... DLB-16, 48, 165, 212; Y-82; CDALB-1
   The Commercialization of the Image of Revolt DLB-16
Rey, H. A. 1898-1977 .... DLB-22
Reyes, Carlos José 1941- DLB-305
Reynal and Hitchcock DLB-46
Reynolds, G. W. M. 1814-1879 .... DLB-21
Reynolds, John Hamilton 1794-1852 .... DLB-96
Reynolds, Sir Joshua 1723-1792 .... DLB-104
Reynolds, Mack 1917-1983 .... DLB-8
Reznikoff, Charles 1894-1976 .... DLB-28, 45
Rhetoric
   Continental European Rhetoricians, 1400-1600, and Their Influence in Reaissance England DLB-236
   A Finding Guide to Key Works on Microfilm DLB-236
   Glossary of Terms and Definitions of Rhetoic and Logic DLB-236
Rhett, Robert Barnwell 1800-1876 .... DLB-43
Rhode, John 1884-1964 .... DLB-77
Rhodes, Eugene Manlove 1869-1934 .... DLB-256
Rhodes, James Ford 1848-1927 .... DLB-47
Rhodes, Richard 1937- DLB-185
Rhys, Jean 1890-1979 .... DLB-36, 117, 162; CDBLB-7; CDWLB-3
Ribeiro, Bernadim fl. ca. 1475/1482-1526/1544 .... DLB-287
Ricardo, David 1772-1823 .... DLB-107, 158

Ricardou, Jean 1932- DLB-83
Riccoboni, Marie-Jeanne (Marie-Jeanne de Heurles Laboras de Mézières Riccoboni) 1713-1792 .... DLB-314
Rice, Anne (A. N. Roquelare, Anne Rampling) 1941- DLB-292
Rice, Christopher 1978- DLB-292
Rice, Elmer 1892-1967 .... DLB-4, 7
Rice, Grantland 1880-1954 .... DLB-29, 171
Rich, Adrienne 1929- DLB-5, 67; CDALB-7
Richard, Mark 1955- DLB-234
Richard de Fournival 1201-1259 or 1260 .... DLB-208
Richards, David Adams 1950- DLB-53
Richards, George circa 1760-1814 .... DLB-37
Richards, I. A. 1893-1979 .... DLB-27
Richards, Laura E. 1850-1943 .... DLB-42
Richards, William Carey 1818-1892 ...... DLB-73
Grant Richards [publishing house] DLB-112
Richardson, Charles F. 1851-1913 .... DLB-71
Richardson, Dorothy M. 1873-1957 ...... DLB-36
   The Novels of Dorothy Richardson (1918), by May Sinclair DLB-36
Richardson, Henry Handel (Ethel Florence Lindesay Robertson) 1870-1946 .... DLB-197, 230
Richardson, Jack 1935- DLB-7
Richardson, John 1796-1852 .... DLB-99
Richardson, Samuel 1689-1761 .... DLB-39, 154; CDBLB-2
   Introductory Letters from the Second Edition of *Pamela* (1741) DLB-39
   Postscript to [the Third Edition of] *Clarissa* (1751) DLB-39
   Preface to the First Edition of *Pamela* (1740) DLB-39
   Preface to the Third Edition of *Clarissa* (1751) [excerpt] DLB-39
   Preface to Volume 1 of *Clarissa* (1747) DLB-39
   Preface to Volume 3 of *Clarissa* (1748) DLB-39
Richardson, Willis 1889-1977 .... DLB-51
Riche, Barnabe 1542-1617 .... DLB-136
Richepin, Jean 1849-1926 .... DLB-192
Richler, Mordecai 1931-2001 .... DLB-53
Richter, Conrad 1890-1968 .... DLB-9, 212
Richter, Hans Werner 1908-1993 .... DLB-69
Richter, Johann Paul Friedrich 1763-1825 .... DLB-94; CDWLB-2
Joseph Rickerby [publishing house] DLB-106
Rickword, Edgell 1898-1982 .... DLB-20
Riddell, Charlotte 1832-1906 .... DLB-156
Riddell, John (see Ford, Corey)
Ridge, John Rollin 1827-1867 .... DLB-175
Ridge, Lola 1873-1941 .... DLB-54
Ridge, William Pett 1859-1930 .... DLB-135
Riding, Laura (see Jackson, Laura Riding)
Ridler, Anne 1912-2001 .... DLB-27

Ridruego, Dionisio 1912-1975 .... DLB-108
Riel, Louis 1844-1885 .... DLB-99
Riemer, Johannes 1648-1714 .... DLB-168
Rifbjerg, Klaus 1931- DLB-214
Riffaterre, Michael 1924- DLB-67
A Conversation between William Riggan and Janette Turner Hospital Y-02
Riggs, Lynn 1899-1954 .... DLB-175
Riis, Jacob 1849-1914 .... DLB-23
John C. Riker [publishing house] DLB-49
Riley, James 1777-1840 .... DLB-183
Riley, John 1938-1978 .... DLB-40
Rilke, Rainer Maria 1875-1926 .... DLB-81; CDWLB-2
Rimanelli, Giose 1926- DLB-177
Rimbaud, Jean-Nicolas-Arthur 1854-1891 .... DLB-217
Rinehart and Company DLB-46
Ringuet 1895-1960 .... DLB-68
Ringwood, Gwen Pharis 1910-1984 .... DLB-88
Rinser, Luise 1911-2002 .... DLB-69
Ríos, Alberto 1952- DLB-122
Ríos, Isabella 1948- DLB-82
Ripley, Arthur 1895-1961 .... DLB-44
Ripley, George 1802-1880 ..... DLB-1, 64, 73, 235
The Rising Glory of America: Three Poems DLB-37
The Rising Glory of America: Written in 1771 (1786), by Hugh Henry Brackenridge and Philip Freneau DLB-37
Riskin, Robert 1897-1955 .... DLB-26
Risse, Heinz 1898-1989 .... DLB-69
Rist, Johann 1607-1667 .... DLB-164
Ristikivi, Karl 1912-1977 .... DLB-220
Ritchie, Anna Mowatt 1819-1870 ..... DLB-3, 250
Ritchie, Anne Thackeray 1837-1919 ...... DLB-18
Ritchie, Thomas 1778-1854 .... DLB-43
The Ritz Paris Hemingway Award Y-85
   Mario Varga Llosa's Acceptance Speech .. Y-85
Rivard, Adjutor 1868-1945 .... DLB-92
Rive, Richard 1931-1989 .... DLB-125, 225
Rivera, José 1955- DLB-249
Rivera, Marina 1942- DLB-122
Rivera, Tomás 1935-1984 .... DLB-82
Rivers, Conrad Kent 1933-1968 .... DLB-41
Riverside Press DLB-49
Rivington, James circa 1724-1802 .... DLB-43
Charles Rivington [publishing house] DLB-154
Rivkin, Allen 1903-1990 .... DLB-26
Roa Bastos, Augusto 1917-2005 .... DLB-113
Robbe-Grillet, Alain 1922- DLB-83
Robbins, Tom 1936- Y-80
Roberts, Charles G. D. 1860-1943 .... DLB-92
Roberts, Dorothy 1906-1993 .... DLB-88
Roberts, Elizabeth Madox 1881-1941 .... DLB-9, 54, 102

Cumulative Index

Roberts, John (see Swynnerton, Thomas)
Roberts, Kate 1891-1985 .... DLB-319
Roberts, Keith 1935-2000 .... DLB-261
Roberts, Kenneth 1885-1957 .... DLB-9
Roberts, Michèle 1949- DLB-231
Roberts, Theodore Goodridge
    1877-1953 .... DLB-92
Roberts, Ursula Wyllie (see Miles, Susan)
Roberts, William 1767-1849 .... DLB-142
James Roberts [publishing house] DLB-154
Roberts Brothers DLB-49
A. M. Robertson and Company DLB-49
Robertson, Ethel Florence Lindesay
    (see Richardson, Henry Handel)
Robertson, William 1721-1793 .... DLB-104
Robin, Leo 1895-1984 .... DLB-265
Robins, Elizabeth 1862-1952 .... DLB-197
Robinson, A. Mary F. (Madame James
    Darmesteter, Madame Mary
    Duclaux) 1857-1944 .... DLB-240
Robinson, Casey 1903-1979 .... DLB-44
Robinson, Derek 1932- Y-02
Robinson, Edwin Arlington
    1869-1935 .... DLB-54; CDALB-3
    Review by Derek Robinson of George
    Greenfield's *Rich Dust* Y-02
Robinson, Henry Crabb 1775-1867 ...... DLB-107
Robinson, James Harvey 1863-1936 ..... DLB-47
Robinson, Lennox 1886-1958 .... DLB-10
Robinson, Mabel Louise 1874-1962 ..... DLB-22
Robinson, Marilynne 1943- DLB-206
Robinson, Mary 1758-1800 .... DLB-158
Robinson, Richard circa 1545-1607 .... DLB-167
Robinson, Therese 1797-1870 .... DLB-59, 133
Robison, Mary 1949- DLB-130
Roblès, Emmanuel 1914-1995 .... DLB-83
Roccatagliata Ceccardi, Ceccardo
    1871-1919 .... DLB-114
Rocha, Adolfo Correira da (see Torga, Miguel)
Roche, Billy 1949- DLB-233
Rochester, John Wilmot, Earl of
    1647-1680 .... DLB-131
Rochon, Esther 1948- DLB-251
Rock, Howard 1911-1976 .... DLB-127
Rockwell, Norman Perceval 1894-1978 .. DLB-188
Rodgers, Carolyn M. 1945- DLB-41
Rodgers, W. R. 1909-1969 .... DLB-20
Rodney, Lester 1911- DLB-241
Rodrigues, Nelson 1912-1980 .... DLB-307
Rodríguez, Claudio 1934-1999 .... DLB-134
Rodríguez, Joe D. 1943- DLB-209
Rodríguez, Luis J. 1954- DLB-209
Rodriguez, Richard 1944- DLB-82, 256
Rodríguez Julia, Edgardo 1946- DLB-145
Roe, E. P. 1838-1888 .... DLB-202
Roethke, Theodore
    1908-1963 .... DLB-5, 206; CDALB-1

Rogers, Jane 1952- DLB-194
Rogers, Pattiann 1940- DLB-105
Rogers, Samuel 1763-1855 .... DLB-93
Rogers, Will 1879-1935 .... DLB-11
Rohmer, Sax 1883-1959 .... DLB-70
Roiphe, Anne 1935- Y-80
Rojas, Arnold R. 1896-1988 .... DLB-82
Rojas, Fernando de ca. 1475-1541 ..... DLB-286
Roland de la Platière, Marie-Jeanne
    (Madame Roland) 1754-1793 .... DLB-314
Rolfe, Edwin (Solomon Fishman)
    1909-1954 .... DLB-303
Rolfe, Frederick William
    1860-1913 .... DLB-34, 156
Rolland, Romain 1866-1944 .... DLB-65
Rolle, Richard circa 1290-1300 - 1349 ... DLB-146
Rölvaag, O. E. 1876-1931 .... DLB-9, 212
Romains, Jules 1885-1972 .... DLB-65
A. Roman and Company DLB-49
Roman de la Rose: Guillaume de Lorris
    1200/1205-circa 1230, Jean de
    Meun 1235-1240-circa 1305 .... DLB-208
Romano, Lalla 1906-2001 .... DLB-177
Romano, Octavio 1923- DLB-122
Rome, Harold 1908-1993 .... DLB-265
Romero, Leo 1950- DLB-122
Romero, Lin 1947- DLB-122
Romero, Orlando 1945- DLB-82
Rook, Clarence 1863-1915 .... DLB-135
Roosevelt, Theodore
    1858-1919 .... DLB-47, 186, 275
Root, Waverley 1903-1982 .... DLB-4
Root, William Pitt 1941- DLB-120
Roquebrune, Robert de 1889-1978 ...... DLB-68
Rorty, Richard 1931- DLB-246, 279
Rosa, João Guimarāres 1908-1967 ..... DLB-113, 307
Rosales, Luis 1910-1992 .... DLB-134
Roscoe, William 1753-1831 .... DLB-163
Rose, Dilys 1954- DLB-319
Rose, Reginald 1920-2002 .... DLB-26
Rose, Wendy 1948- DLB-175
Rosegger, Peter 1843-1918 .... DLB-129
Rosei, Peter 1946- DLB-85
Rosen, Norma 1925- DLB-28
Rosenbach, A. S. W. 1876-1952 .... DLB-140
Rosenbaum, Ron 1946- DLB-185
Rosenbaum, Thane 1960- DLB-299
Rosenberg, Isaac 1890-1918 .... DLB-20, 216
Rosenfeld, Isaac 1918-1956 .... DLB-28
Rosenthal, Harold 1914-1999 .... DLB-241
    Jimmy, Red, and Others: Harold
    Rosenthal Remembers the Stars of
    the Press Box Y-01
Rosenthal, M. L. 1917-1996 .... DLB-5
Rosenwald, Lessing J. 1891-1979 ...... DLB-187
Ross, Alexander 1591-1654 .... DLB-151
Ross, Harold 1892-1951 .... DLB-137

Ross, Jerry 1926-1955 .... DLB-265
Ross, Leonard Q. (see Rosten, Leo)
Ross, Lillian 1927- DLB-185
Ross, Martin 1862-1915 .... DLB-135
Ross, Sinclair 1908-1996 .... DLB-88
Ross, W. W. E. 1894-1966 .... DLB-88
Rosselli, Amelia 1930-1996 .... DLB-128
Rossen, Robert 1908-1966 .... DLB-26
Rosset, Barney 1922- Y-02
Rossetti, Christina 1830-1894 ... DLB-35, 163, 240
Rossetti, Dante Gabriel
    1828-1882 .... DLB-35; CDBLB-4
    The Stealthy School of
    Criticism (1871) DLB-35
Rossner, Judith 1935- DLB-6
Rostand, Edmond 1868-1918 .... DLB-192
Rosten, Leo 1908-1997 .... DLB-11
Rostenberg, Leona 1908-2005 .... DLB-140
Rostopchina, Evdokiia Petrovna
    1811-1858 .... DLB-205
Rostovsky, Dimitrii 1651-1709 .... DLB-150
Rota, Bertram 1903-1966 .... DLB-201
    Bertram Rota and His Bookshop Y-91
Roth, Gerhard 1942- DLB-85, 124
Roth, Henry 1906?-1995 .... DLB-28
Roth, Joseph 1894-1939 .... DLB-85
Roth, Philip
    1933- DLB-2, 28, 173; Y-82; CDALB-6
Rothenberg, Jerome 1931- DLB-5, 193
Rothschild Family DLB-184
Rotimi, Ola 1938- DLB-125
Rotrou, Jean 1609-1650 .... DLB-268
Rousseau, Jean-Jacques 1712-1778 ..... DLB-314
    The Social Contract DLB-314
Routhier, Adolphe-Basile 1839-1920 ... DLB-99
Routier, Simone 1901-1987 .... DLB-88
George Routledge and Sons DLB-106
Roversi, Roberto 1923- DLB-128
Rowe, Elizabeth Singer 1674-1737 .... DLB-39, 95
Rowe, Nicholas 1674-1718 .... DLB-84
Rowlands, Ian 1964- DLB-310
Rowlands, Samuel circa 1570-1630 ..... DLB-121
Rowlandson, Mary
    circa 1637-circa 1711 .... DLB-24, 200
Rowley, William circa 1585-1626 ...... DLB-58
Rowling, J. K.
    The Harry Potter Phenomenon Y-99
Rowse, A. L. 1903-1997 .... DLB-155
Rowson, Susanna Haswell
    circa 1762-1824 .... DLB-37, 200
Roy, Camille 1870-1943 .... DLB-92
The G. Ross Roy Scottish Poetry Collection
    at the University of South Carolina ... Y-89
Roy, Gabrielle 1909-1983 .... DLB-68
Roy, Jules 1907-2000 .... DLB-83
The Royal Court Theatre and the English
    Stage Company DLB-13

The Royal Court Theatre and the New Drama ... DLB-10	Russell, Willy 1947- ... DLB-233	Saenz, Jaime 1921-1986 ... DLB-145, 283
The Royal Shakespeare Company at the Swan ... Y-88	B. B. Russell and Company ... DLB-49	Saffin, John circa 1626-1710 ... DLB-24
Royall, Anne Newport 1769-1854 ... DLB-43, 248	R. H. Russell and Son ... DLB-49	Sagan, Françoise 1935- ... DLB-83
Royce, Josiah 1855-1916 ... DLB-270	Rutebeuf fl.1249-1277 ... DLB-208	Sage, Robert 1899-1962 ... DLB-4
The Roycroft Printing Shop ... DLB-49	Rutherford, Mark 1831-1913 ... DLB-18	Sagel, Jim 1947- ... DLB-82
Royde-Smith, Naomi 1875-1964 ... DLB-191	Ruxton, George Frederick 1821-1848 ... DLB-186	Sagendorph, Robb Hansell 1900-1970 ... DLB-137
Royster, Vermont 1914-1996 ... DLB-127	R-va, Zeneida (see Gan, Elena Andreevna)	Sahagún, Carlos 1938- ... DLB-108
Richard Royston [publishing house] ... DLB-170	Ryan, James 1952- ... DLB-267	Sahkomaapii, Piitai (see Highwater, Jamake)
Rozanov, Vasilii Vasil'evich 1856-1919 ... DLB-295	Ryan, Michael 1946- ... Y-82	Sahl, Hans 1902-1993 ... DLB-69
Różewicz, Tadeusz 1921- ... DLB-232	Ryan, Oscar 1904- ... DLB-68	Said, Edward W. 1935- ... DLB-67
Ruark, Gibbons 1941- ... DLB-120	Rybakov, Anatolii Naumovich 1911-1994 ... DLB-302	Saigyō 1118-1190 ... DLB-203
Ruban, Vasilii Grigorevich 1742-1795 ... DLB-150	Ryder, Jack 1871-1936 ... DLB-241	Saijo, Albert 1926- ... DLB-312
Rubens, Bernice 1928-2004 ... DLB-14, 207	Ryga, George 1932-1987 ... DLB-60	Saiko, George 1892-1962 ... DLB-85
Rubião, Murilo 1916-1991 ... DLB-307	Rylands, Enriqueta Augustina Tennant 1843-1908 ... DLB-184	Sainte-Beuve, Charles-Augustin 1804-1869 ... DLB-217
Rubina, Dina Il'inichna 1953- ... DLB-285	Rylands, John 1801-1888 ... DLB-184	Saint-Exupéry, Antoine de 1900-1944 ... DLB-72
Rubinshtein, Lev Semenovich 1947- ... DLB-285	Ryle, Gilbert 1900-1976 ... DLB-262	St. John, J. Allen 1872-1957 ... DLB-188
Rudd and Carleton ... DLB-49	Ryleev, Kondratii Fedorovich 1795-1826 ... DLB-205	St John, Madeleine 1942- ... DLB-267
Rudd, Steele (Arthur Hoey Davis) ... DLB-230	Rymer, Thomas 1643?-1713 ... DLB-101	St. Johns, Adela Rogers 1894-1988 ... DLB-29
Rudkin, David 1936- ... DLB-13	Ryskind, Morrie 1895-1985 ... DLB-26	St. Omer, Garth 1931- ... DLB-117
Rudnick, Paul 1957- ... DLB-266	Rzhevsky, Aleksei Andreevich 1737-1804 ... DLB-150	Saint Pierre, Michel de 1916-1987 ... DLB-83
Rudnicki, Adolf 1909-1990 ... DLB-299		Saintsbury, George 1845-1933 ... DLB-57, 149
Rudolf von Ems circa 1200-circa 1254 ... DLB-138	**S**	"Modern English Prose" (1876) ... DLB-57
Ruffin, Josephine St. Pierre 1842-1924 ... DLB-79	The Saalfield Publishing Company ... DLB-46	The Present State of the English Novel (1892), ... DLB-18
Rufo, Juan Gutiérrez 1547?-1620? ... DLB-318	Saba, Umberto 1883-1957 ... DLB-114	Saint-Simon, Louis de Rouvroy, duc de 1675-1755 ... DLB-314
Ruganda, John 1941- ... DLB-157	Sábato, Ernesto 1911- ... DLB-145; CDWLB-3	St. Dominic's Press ... DLB-112
Ruggles, Henry Joseph 1813-1906 ... DLB-64	Saberhagen, Fred 1930- ... DLB-8	The St. John's College Robert Graves Trust ... Y-96
Ruiz de Burton, María Amparo 1832-1895 ... DLB-209, 221	Sabin, Joseph 1821-1881 ... DLB-187	St. Martin's Press ... DLB-46
Rukeyser, Muriel 1913-1980 ... DLB-48	Sabino, Fernando (Fernando Tavares Sabino) 1923-2004 ... DLB-307	*St. Nicholas* 1873-1881 ... DS-13
Rule, Jane 1931- ... DLB-60	Sacer, Gottfried Wilhelm 1635-1699 ... DLB-168	Saiokuken Sōchō 1448-1532 ... DLB-203
Rulfo, Juan 1918-1986 ... DLB-113; CDWLB-3	Sachs, Hans 1494-1576 ... DLB-179; CDWLB-2	Saki (see Munro, H. H.)
Rumaker, Michael 1932- ... DLB-16	Sá-Carneiro, Mário de 1890-1916 ... DLB-287	Salaam, Kalamu ya 1947- ... DLB-38
Rumens, Carol 1944- ... DLB-40	Sack, John 1930-2004 ... DLB-185	Šalamun, Tomaž 1941- ... DLB-181; CDWLB-4
Rummo, Paul-Eerik 1942- ... DLB-232	Sackler, Howard 1929-1982 ... DLB-7	Salas, Floyd 1931- ... DLB-82
Runyon, Damon 1880-1946 ... DLB-11, 86, 171	Sackville, Lady Margaret 1881-1963 ... DLB-240	Sálaz-Marquez, Rubén 1935- ... DLB-122
Ruodlieb circa 1050-1075 ... DLB-148	Sackville, Thomas 1536-1608 and Norton, Thomas 1532-1584 ... DLB-62	Salcedo, Hugo 1964- ... DLB-305
Rush, Benjamin 1746-1813 ... DLB-37	Sackville, Thomas 1536-1608 ... DLB-132	Salemson, Harold J. 1910-1988 ... DLB-4
Rush, Rebecca 1779-? ... DLB-200	Sackville-West, Edward 1901-1965 ... DLB-191	Salesbury, William 1520?-1584? ... DLB-281
Rushdie, Salman 1947- ... DLB-194	Sackville-West, Vita 1892-1962 ... DLB-34, 195	Salinas, Luis Omar 1937- ... DLB-82
Rusk, Ralph L. 1888-1962 ... DLB-103	Sá de Miranda, Francisco de 1481-1588? ... DLB-287	Salinas, Pedro 1891-1951 ... DLB-134
Ruskin, John 1819-1900 ... DLB-55, 163, 190; CDBLB-4	Sade, Marquis de (Donatien-Alphonse-François, comte de Sade) 1740-1814 ... DLB-314	Salinger, J. D. 1919- ... DLB-2, 102, 173; CDALB-1
Russ, Joanna 1937- ... DLB-8	"Dialogue entre un prêtre et un moribond" ... DLB-314	Salkey, Andrew 1928-1995 ... DLB-125
Russell, Benjamin 1761-1845 ... DLB-43	Sadlier, Mary Anne 1820-1903 ... DLB-99	Sallust circa 86 B.C.-35 B.C. ... DLB-211; CDWLB-1
Russell, Bertrand 1872-1970 ... DLB-100, 262	D. and J. Sadlier and Company ... DLB-49	Salt, Waldo 1914-1987 ... DLB-44
Russell, Charles Edward 1860-1941 ... DLB-25	Sadoff, Ira 1945- ... DLB-120	Salter, James 1925- ... DLB-130
Russell, Charles M. 1864-1926 ... DLB-188	Sadoveanu, Mihail 1880-1961 ... DLB-220	Salter, Mary Jo 1954- ... DLB-120
Russell, Eric Frank 1905-1978 ... DLB-255	Sadur, Nina Nikolaevna 1950- ... DLB-285	Saltus, Edgar 1855-1921 ... DLB-202
Russell, Fred 1906-2003 ... DLB-241	Sáenz, Benjamin Alire 1954- ... DLB-209	Saltykov, Mikhail Evgrafovich 1826-1889 ... DLB-238
Russell, George William (see AE)		Salustri, Carlo Alberto (see Trilussa)
Russell, Countess Mary Annette Beauchamp (see Arnim, Elizabeth von)		Salverson, Laura Goodman 1890-1970 ... DLB-92
		Samain, Albert 1858-1900 ... DLB-217

Cumulative Index

Sampson, Richard Henry (see Hull, Richard)
Samuels, Ernest 1903-1996 . . . . DLB-111
Sanborn, Franklin Benjamin
    1831-1917 . . . . DLB-1, 223
Sánchez, Florencio 1875-1910 . . . . DLB-305
Sánchez, Luis Rafael 1936- DLB-145, 305
Sánchez, Philomeno "Phil" 1917- DLB-122
Sánchez, Ricardo 1941-1995 . . . . DLB-82
Sánchez, Saúl 1943- DLB-209
Sanchez, Sonia 1934- DLB-41; DS-8
Sánchez de Arévalo, Rodrigo
    1404-1470 . . . . DLB-286
Sánchez de Badajoz, Diego ?-1552? DLB-318
Sand, George 1804-1876 . . . . DLB-119, 192
Sandburg, Carl
    1878-1967 . . . . DLB-17, 54; CDALB-3
Sandel, Cora (Sara Fabricius)
    1880-1974 . . . . DLB-297
Sandemose, Aksel 1899-1965 . . . . DLB-297
Sanders, Edward 1939- DLB-16, 244
Sanderson, Robert 1587-1663 . . . . DLB-281
Sandoz, Mari 1896-1966 . . . . DLB-9, 212
Sandwell, B. K. 1876-1954 . . . . DLB-92
Sandy, Stephen 1934- DLB-165
Sandys, George 1578-1644 . . . . DLB-24, 121
Sangster, Charles 1822-1893 . . . . DLB-99
Sanguineti, Edoardo 1930- DLB-128
Sanjōnishi Sanetaka 1455-1537 . . . . DLB-203
San Pedro, Diego de fl. ca. 1492 . . . . DLB-286
Sansay, Leonora ?-after 1823 . . . . DLB-200
Sansom, William 1912-1976 . . . . DLB-139
Sant'Anna, Affonso Romano de
    1937- DLB-307
Santayana, George
    1863-1952 . . . . . . DLB-54, 71, 246, 270; DS-13
Santiago, Danny 1911-1988 . . . . DLB-122
Santillana, Marqués de (Íñigo López de Mendoza)
    1398-1458 . . . . DLB-286
Santmyer, Helen Hooven 1895-1986 . . . . Y-84
Santos, Bienvenido 1911-1996 . . . . DLB-312
Sanvitale, Francesca 1928- DLB-196
Sapidus, Joannes 1490-1561 . . . . DLB-179
Sapir, Edward 1884-1939 . . . . DLB-92
Sapper (see McNeile, Herman Cyril)
Sappho circa 620 B.C.-circa 550 B.C.
    . . . . DLB-176; CDWLB-1
Saramago, José 1922- DLB-287; Y-98
    Nobel Lecture 1998: How Characters
    Became the Masters and the Author
    Their Apprentice Y-98
Sarban (John W. Wall) 1910-1989 . . . . . DLB-255
Sardou, Victorien 1831-1908 . . . . DLB-192
Sarduy, Severo 1937-1993 . . . . DLB-113
Sargent, Pamela 1948- DLB-8
Saro-Wiwa, Ken 1941- DLB-157
Saroyan, Aram
    Rites of Passage [on William Saroyan] Y-83

Saroyan, William
    1908-1981 . . . . . DLB-7, 9, 86; Y-81; CDALB-7
Sarraute, Nathalie 1900-1999 . . . . DLB-83
Sarrazin, Albertine 1937-1967 . . . . DLB-83
Sarris, Greg 1952- DLB-175
Sarton, May 1912-1995 . . . . DLB-48; Y-81
Sartre, Jean-Paul 1905-1980 . . . . DLB-72, 296
Sassoon, Siegfried
    1886-1967 . . . . DLB-20, 191; DS-18
    A Centenary Essay Y-86
    Tributes from Vivien F. Clarke and
    Michael Thorpe Y-86
Sata Ineko 1904-1998 . . . . DLB-180
Saturday Review Press DLB-46
Saunders, James 1925-2004 . . . . DLB-13
Saunders, John Monk 1897-1940 . . . . DLB-26
Saunders, Margaret Marshall
    1861-1947 . . . . DLB-92
Saunders and Otley DLB-106
Saussure, Ferdinand de 1857-1913 . . . . . . DLB-242
Savage, James 1784-1873 . . . . DLB-30
Savage, Marmion W. 1803?-1872 . . . . DLB-21
Savage, Richard 1697?-1743 . . . . DLB-95
Savard, Félix-Antoine 1896-1982 . . . . DLB-68
Savery, Henry 1791-1842 . . . . DLB-230
Saville, (Leonard) Malcolm 1901-1982 . . . DLB-160
Savinio, Alberto 1891-1952 . . . . DLB-264
Sawyer, Robert J. 1960- DLB-251
Sawyer, Ruth 1880-1970 . . . . DLB-22
Sayers, Dorothy L.
    1893-1957 . . . . . DLB-10, 36, 77, 100; CDBLB-6
    The Dorothy L. Sayers Society Y-98
Sayle, Charles Edward 1864-1924 . . . . . . DLB-184
Sayles, John Thomas 1950- DLB-44
Sbarbaro, Camillo 1888-1967 . . . . DLB-114
Scalapino, Leslie 1947- DLB-193
Scannell, Vernon 1922- DLB-27
Scarry, Richard 1919-1994 . . . . DLB-61
Schack, Hans Egede 1820-1859 . . . . DLB-300
Schaefer, Jack 1907-1991 . . . . DLB-212
Schaeffer, Albrecht 1885-1950 . . . . DLB-66
Schaeffer, Susan Fromberg 1941- . . DLB-28, 299
Schaff, Philip 1819-1893 . . . . DS-13
Schaper, Edzard 1908-1984 . . . . DLB-69
Scharf, J. Thomas 1843-1898 . . . . DLB-47
Schede, Paul Melissus 1539-1602 . . . . DLB-179
Scheffel, Joseph Viktor von 1826-1886 . . . DLB-129
Scheffler, Johann 1624-1677 . . . . DLB-164
Schelling, Friedrich Wilhelm Joseph von
    1775-1854 . . . . DLB-90
Scherer, Wilhelm 1841-1886 . . . . DLB-129
Scherfig, Hans 1905-1979 . . . . DLB-214
Schickele, René 1883-1940 . . . . DLB-66
Schiff, Dorothy 1903-1989 . . . . DLB-127
Schiller, Friedrich
    1759-1805 . . . . DLB-94; CDWLB-2

Schirmer, David 1623-1687 . . . . DLB-164
Schlaf, Johannes 1862-1941 . . . . DLB-118
Schlegel, August Wilhelm 1767-1845 . . . . . DLB-94
Schlegel, Dorothea 1763-1839 . . . . DLB-90
Schlegel, Friedrich 1772-1829 . . . . DLB-90
Schleiermacher, Friedrich 1768-1834 . . . . . DLB-90
Schlesinger, Arthur M., Jr. 1917- DLB-17
Schlumberger, Jean 1877-1968 . . . . DLB-65
Schmid, Eduard Hermann Wilhelm
    (see Edschmid, Kasimir)
Schmidt, Arno 1914-1979 . . . . DLB-69
Schmidt, Johann Kaspar (see Stirner, Max)
Schmidt, Michael 1947- DLB-40
Schmidtbonn, Wilhelm August
    1876-1952 . . . . DLB-118
Schmitz, Aron Hector (see Svevo, Italo)
Schmitz, James H. 1911-1981 . . . . DLB-8
Schnabel, Johann Gottfried 1692-1760 . . . DLB-168
Schnackenberg, Gjertrud 1953- DLB-120
Schnitzler, Arthur
    1862-1931 . . . . DLB-81, 118; CDWLB-2
Schnurre, Wolfdietrich 1920-1989 . . . . DLB-69
Schocken Books DLB-46
Scholartis Press DLB-112
Scholderer, Victor 1880-1971 . . . . DLB-201
The Schomburg Center for Research
    in Black Culture DLB-76
Schönbeck, Virgilio (see Giotti, Virgilio)
Schönherr, Karl 1867-1943 . . . . DLB-118
Schoolcraft, Jane Johnston 1800-1841 . . . . DLB-175
School Stories, 1914-1960 . . . . DLB-160
Schopenhauer, Arthur 1788-1860 . . . . DLB-90
Schopenhauer, Johanna 1766-1838 . . . . . . DLB-90
Schorer, Mark 1908-1977 . . . . DLB-103
Schottelius, Justus Georg 1612-1676 . . . . DLB-164
Schouler, James 1839-1920 . . . . DLB-47
Schoultz, Solveig von 1907-1996 . . . . DLB-259
Schrader, Paul 1946- DLB-44
Schreiner, Olive
    1855-1920 . . . . DLB-18, 156, 190, 225
Schroeder, Andreas 1946- DLB-53
Schubart, Christian Friedrich Daniel
    1739-1791 . . . . DLB-97
Schubert, Gotthilf Heinrich 1780-1860 . . . DLB-90
Schücking, Levin 1814-1883 . . . . DLB-133
Schulberg, Budd 1914- DLB-6, 26, 28; Y-81
    Excerpts from USC Presentation
    [on F. Scott Fitzgerald] Y-96
F. J. Schulte and Company DLB-49
Schulz, Bruno 1892-1942 . . . DLB-215; CDWLB-4
Schulze, Hans (see Praetorius, Johannes)
Schupp, Johann Balthasar 1610-1661 . . . . DLB-164
Schurz, Carl 1829-1906 . . . . DLB-23
Schuyler, George S. 1895-1977 . . . . . . DLB-29, 51
Schuyler, James 1923-1991 . . . . DLB-5, 169
Schwartz, Delmore 1913-1966 . . . . DLB-28, 48

Schwartz, Jonathan 1938- Y-82
Schwartz, Lynne Sharon 1939- DLB-218
Schwarz, Sibylle 1621-1638 ....DLB-164
Schwarz-Bart, Andre 1928- DLB-299
Schwerner, Armand 1927-1999 ....DLB-165
Schwob, Marcel 1867-1905 ....DLB-123
Sciascia, Leonardo 1921-1989 ....DLB-177
Science Fiction and Fantasy
  Documents in British Fantasy and
    Science Fiction DLB-178
  Hugo Awards and Nebula Awards DLB-8
  The Iconography of Science-Fiction
    Art DLB-8
  The New Wave DLB-8
  Paperback Science Fiction DLB-8
  Science Fantasy DLB-8
  Science-Fiction Fandom and
    Conventions DLB-8
  Science-Fiction Fanzines: The Time
    Binders DLB-8
  Science-Fiction Films DLB-8
  Science Fiction Writers of America
    and the Nebula Award DLB-8
  Selected Science-Fiction Magazines and
    Anthologies DLB-8
  A World Chronology of Important Science
    Fiction Works (1818-1979) DLB-8
  The Year in Science Fiction
    and Fantasy Y-00, 01
Scot, Reginald circa 1538-1599 ....DLB-136
Scotellaro, Rocco 1923-1953 ....DLB-128
Scott, Alicia Anne (Lady John Scott)
  1810-1900 ....DLB-240
Scott, Catharine Amy Dawson
  1865-1934 ....DLB-240
Scott, Dennis 1939-1991 ....DLB-125
Scott, Dixon 1881-1915 ....DLB-98
Scott, Duncan Campbell 1862-1947 ....DLB-92
Scott, Evelyn 1893-1963 ....DLB-9, 48
Scott, F. R. 1899-1985 ....DLB-88
Scott, Frederick George 1861-1944 ....DLB-92
Scott, Geoffrey 1884-1929 ....DLB-149
Scott, Harvey W. 1838-1910 ....DLB-23
Scott, Lady Jane (see Scott, Alicia Anne)
Scott, Paul 1920-1978 ....DLB-14, 207
Scott, Sarah 1723-1795 ....DLB-39
Scott, Tom 1918-1995 ....DLB-27
Scott, Sir Walter 1771-1832
  ....DLB-93, 107, 116, 144, 159; CDBLB-3
Scott, William Bell 1811-1890 ....DLB-32
Walter Scott Publishing Company
  Limited DLB-112
William R. Scott [publishing house] DLB-46
Scott-Heron, Gil 1949- DLB-41
Scribe, Eugene 1791-1861 ....DLB-192
Scribner, Arthur Hawley 1859-1932 ....DS-13, 16
Scribner, Charles 1854-1930 ....DS-13, 16
Scribner, Charles, Jr. 1921-1995 ....Y-95

Reminiscences DS-17
Charles Scribner's Sons DLB-49; DS-13, 16, 17
  Archives of Charles Scribner's Sons DS-17
Scribner's Magazine DS-13
Scribner's Monthly DS-13
Scripps, E. W. 1854-1926 ....DLB-25
Scudder, Horace Elisha 1838-1902 ....DLB-42, 71
Scudder, Vida Dutton 1861-1954 ....DLB-71
Scudéry, Madeleine de 1607-1701 ....DLB-268
Scupham, Peter 1933- DLB-40
Seabrook, William 1886-1945 ....DLB-4
Seabury, Samuel 1729-1796 ....DLB-31
Seacole, Mary Jane Grant 1805-1881 ....DLB-166
The Seafarer circa 970 ....DLB-146
Sealsfield, Charles (Carl Postl)
  1793-1864 ....DLB-133, 186
Searle, John R. 1932- DLB-279
Sears, Edward I. 1819?-1876 ....DLB-79
Sears Publishing Company DLB-46
Seaton, George 1911-1979 ....DLB-44
Seaton, William Winston 1785-1866 ....DLB-43
Martin Secker [publishing house] DLB-112
Martin Secker, and Warburg Limited DLB-112
The "Second Generation" Holocaust
  Novel DLB-299
Sedgwick, Arthur George 1844-1915 ....DLB-64
Sedgwick, Catharine Maria
  1789-1867 ....DLB-1, 74, 183, 239, 243
Sedgwick, Ellery 1872-1960 ....DLB-91
Sedgwick, Eve Kosofsky 1950- DLB-246
Sedley, Sir Charles 1639-1701 ....DLB-131
Seeberg, Peter 1925-1999 ....DLB-214
Seeger, Alan 1888-1916 ....DLB-45
Seers, Eugene (see Dantin, Louis)
Segal, Erich 1937- Y-86
Segal, Lore 1928- DLB-299
Šegedin, Petar 1909-1998 ....DLB-181
Seghers, Anna 1900-1983 ....DLB-69; CDWLB-2
Seid, Ruth (see Sinclair, Jo)
Seidel, Frederick Lewis 1936- Y-84
Seidel, Ina 1885-1974 ....DLB-56
Seifert, Jaroslav
  1901-1986 ....DLB-215; Y-84; CDWLB-4
  Jaroslav Seifert Through the Eyes of
    the English-Speaking Reader Y-84
  Three Poems by Jaroslav Seifert Y-84
Seifullina, Lidiia Nikolaevna 1889-1954 ....DLB-272
Seigenthaler, John 1927- DLB-127
Seizin Press DLB-112
Séjour, Victor 1817-1874 ....DLB-50
Séjour Marcou et Ferrand, Juan Victor
  (see Séjour, Victor)
Sekowski, Józef-Julian, Baron Brambeus
  (see Senkovsky, Osip Ivanovich)
Selby, Bettina 1934- DLB-204
Selby, Hubert Jr. 1928-2004 ....DLB-2, 227

Selden, George 1929-1989 ....DLB-52
Selden, John 1584-1654 ....DLB-213
Selenić, Slobodan 1933-1995 ....DLB-181
Self, Edwin F. 1920- DLB-137
Self, Will 1961- DLB-207
Seligman, Edwin R. A. 1861-1939 ....DLB-47
Selimović, Meša
  1910-1982 ....DLB-181; CDWLB-4
Sellars, Wilfrid 1912-1989 ....DLB-279
Sellings, Arthur (Arthur Gordon Ley)
  1911-1968 ....DLB-261
Selous, Frederick Courteney 1851-1917 ....DLB-174
Seltzer, Chester E. (see Muro, Amado)
Thomas Seltzer [publishing house] DLB-46
Selvon, Sam 1923-1994 ....DLB-125; CDWLB-3
Semel, Nava 1954- DLB-299
Semmes, Raphael 1809-1877 ....DLB-189
Senancour, Etienne de 1770-1846 ....DLB-119
Sena, Jorge de 1919-1978 ....DLB-287
Sendak, Maurice 1928- DLB-61
Seneca the Elder
  circa 54 B.C.-circa A.D. 40 ....DLB-211
Seneca the Younger
  circa 1 B.C.-A.D. 65 ....DLB-211; CDWLB-1
Senécal, Eva 1905-1988 ....DLB-92
Sengstacke, John 1912-1997 ....DLB-127
Senior, Olive 1941- DLB-157
Senkovsky, Osip Ivanovich
  (Józef-Julian Sekowski, Baron Brambeus)
  1800-1858 ....DLB-198
Šenoa, August 1838-1881 ....DLB-147; CDWLB-4
Sentimental Fiction of the Sixteenth
  Century DLB-318
Sepamla, Sipho 1932- DLB-157, 225
Serafimovich, Aleksandr Serafimovich
  (Aleksandr Serafimovich Popov)
  1863-1949 ....DLB-272
Serao, Matilde 1856-1927 ....DLB-264
Seredy, Kate 1899-1975 ....DLB-22
Sereni, Vittorio 1913-1983 ....DLB-128
William Seres [publishing house] DLB-170
Sergeev-Tsensky, Sergei Nikolaevich (Sergei
  Nikolaevich Sergeev) 1875-1958 ....DLB-272
Serling, Rod 1924-1975 ....DLB-26
Sernine, Daniel 1955- DLB-251
Serote, Mongane Wally 1944- DLB-125, 225
Serraillier, Ian 1912-1994 ....DLB-161
Serrano, Nina 1934- DLB-122
Service, Robert 1874-1958 ....DLB-92
Sessler, Charles 1854-1935 ....DLB-187
Seth, Vikram 1952- DLB-120, 271
Seton, Elizabeth Ann 1774-1821 ....DLB-200
Seton, Ernest Thompson
  1860-1942 ....DLB-92; DS-13
Seton, John circa 1509-1567 ....DLB-281
Setouchi Harumi 1922- DLB-182
Settle, Mary Lee 1918- DLB-6
Seume, Johann Gottfried 1763-1810 ....DLB-94

Seuse, Heinrich 1295?-1366 . . . . DLB-179	The Bernard Shaw Society Y-99	Sherrod, Blackie 1919- DLB-241
Seuss, Dr. (see Geisel, Theodor Seuss)	"Stage Censorship: The Rejected Statement" (1911) [excerpts] DLB-10	Sherry, Norman 1935- DLB-155
Severianin, Igor' 1887-1941 . . . . DLB-295	Shaw, Henry Wheeler 1818-1885 . . . . DLB-11	Tribute to Graham Greene Y-91
Severin, Timothy 1940- DLB-204	Shaw, Irwin 1913-1984 . . . . . DLB-6, 102; Y-84; CDALB-1	Sherry, Richard 1506-1551 or 1555 . . . . . DLB-236
Sévigné, Marie de Rabutin Chantal, Madame de 1626-1696 . . . . DLB-268	Shaw, Joseph T. 1874-1952. . . . . DLB-137	Sherwood, Mary Martha 1775-1851 . . . . . DLB-163
Sewall, Joseph 1688-1769 . . . . DLB-24	"As I Was Saying," Joseph T. Shaw's Editorial Rationale in *Black Mask* (January 1927) DLB-137	Sherwood, Robert E. 1896-1955 . . . DLB-7, 26, 249
Sewall, Richard B. 1908-2003 . . . . DLB-111		Shevyrev, Stepan Petrovich 1806-1864 . . . . DLB-205
Sewall, Samuel 1652-1730 . . . . DLB-24	Shaw, Mary 1854-1929 . . . . DLB-228	Shiel, M. P. 1865-1947 . . . . DLB-153
Sewell, Anna 1820-1878 . . . . DLB-163	Shaw, Robert 1927-1978 . . . . DLB-13, 14	Shiels, George 1886-1949 . . . . DLB-10
Sexton, Anne 1928-1974 . . . DLB-5, 169; CDALB-1	Shaw, Robert B. 1947- DLB-120	Shiga Naoya 1883-1971 . . . . DLB-180
Seymour-Smith, Martin 1928-1998 . . . . . . DLB-155	Shawn, Wallace 1943- DLB-266	Shiina Rinzō 1911-1973 . . . . DLB-182
Sgorlon, Carlo 1930- DLB-196	Shawn, William 1907-1992 . . . . DLB-137	Shikishi Naishinnō 1153?-1201 . . . . DLB-203
Shaara, Michael 1929-1988 . . . . Y-83	Frank Shay [publishing house] DLB-46	Shillaber, Benjamin Penhallow 1814-1890 . . . . DLB-1, 11, 235
Shabel'skaia, Aleksandra Stanislavovna 1845-1921 . . . . DLB-238	Shchedrin, N. (see Saltykov, Mikhail Evgrafovich)	Shimao Toshio 1917-1986 . . . . DLB-182
Shadwell, Thomas 1641?-1692 . . . . DLB-80	Shcherbakova, Galina Nikolaevna 1932- DLB-285	Shimazaki Tōson 1872-1943 . . . . DLB-180
Shaffer, Anthony 1926-2001 . . . . DLB-13	Shcherbina, Nikolai Fedorovich 1821-1869 . . . . DLB-277	Shimose, Pedro 1940- DLB-283
Shaffer, Peter 1926- DLB-13, 233; CDBLB-8		Shine, Ted 1931- DLB-38
Muhammad ibn Idris al-Shafi'i 767-820 . . DLB-311	Shea, John Gilmary 1824-1892 . . . . DLB-30	Shinkei 1406-1475 . . . . DLB-203
Shaftesbury, Anthony Ashley Cooper, Third Earl of 1671-1713 . . . . DLB-101	Sheaffer, Louis 1912-1993 . . . . DLB-103	Ship, Reuben 1915-1975 . . . . DLB-88
	Sheahan, Henry Beston (see Beston, Henry)	Shirer, William L. 1904-1993 . . . . DLB-4
Shaginian, Marietta Sergeevna 1888-1982 . . . . DLB-272	Shearing, Joseph 1886-1952 . . . . DLB-70	Shirinsky-Shikhmatov, Sergii Aleksandrovich 1783-1837 . . . . DLB-150
Shairp, Mordaunt 1887-1939 . . . . DLB-10	Shebbeare, John 1709-1788 . . . . DLB-39	Shirley, James 1596-1666 . . . . DLB-58
Shakespeare, Nicholas 1957- DLB-231	Sheckley, Robert 1928- DLB-8	Shishkov, Aleksandr Semenovich 1753-1841 . . . . DLB-150
Shakespeare, William 1564-1616 . . . . . . DLB-62, 172, 263; CDBLB-1	Shedd, William G. T. 1820-1894 . . . . DLB-64	
	Sheed, Wilfrid 1930- DLB-6	Shmelev, I. S. 1873-1950 . . . . DLB-317
The New Variorum Shakespeare Y-85	Sheed and Ward [U.S.] DLB-46	Shockley, Ann Allen 1927- DLB-33
Shakespeare and Montaigne: A Symposium by Jules Furthman Y-02	Sheed and Ward Limited [U.K.] DLB-112	Sholokhov, Mikhail Aleksandrovich 1905-1984 . . . . DLB-272
$6,166,000 for a *Book!* Observations on *The Shakespeare First Folio: The History of the Book* Y-01	Sheldon, Alice B. (see Tiptree, James, Jr.)	
	Sheldon, Edward 1886-1946 . . . . DLB-7	Shōno Junzō 1921- DLB-182
	Sheldon and Company DLB-49	Shore, Arabella 1820?-1901 . . . . DLB-199
Taylor-Made Shakespeare? Or Is "Shall I Die?" the Long-Lost Text of Bottom's Dream? Y-85	Sheller, Aleksandr Konstantinovich 1838-1900 . . . . DLB-238	Shore, Louisa 1824-1895 . . . . DLB-199
		Short, Luke (see Glidden, Frederick Dilley)
The Shakespeare Globe Trust Y-93	Shelley, Mary Wollstonecraft 1797-1851 . . . . DLB-110, 116, 159, 178; CDBLB-3	Peter Short [publishing house] DLB-170
Shakespeare Head Press DLB-112		Shorter, Dora Sigerson 1866-1918 . . . . . DLB-240
Shakhova, Elisaveta Nikitichna 1822-1899 . . . . DLB-277	Preface to *Frankenstein; or, The Modern Prometheus* (1818) DLB-178	Shorthouse, Joseph Henry 1834-1903 . . . . DLB-18
	Shelley, Percy Bysshe 1792-1822 . . . . . . DLB-96, 110, 158; CDBLB-3	Short Stories
Shakhovskoi, Aleksandr Aleksandrovich 1777-1846 . . . . DLB-150		Michael M. Rea and the Rea Award for the Short Story Y-97
Shalamov, Varlam Tikhonovich 1907-1982 . . . . DLB-302	Shelnutt, Eve 1941- DLB-130	The Year in Short Stories Y-87
	Shenshin (see Fet, Afanasii Afanas'evich)	The Year in the Short Story Y-88, 90–93
al-Shanfara fl. sixth century DLB-311	Shenstone, William 1714-1763 . . . . DLB-95	Shōtetsu 1381-1459 . . . . DLB-203
Shange, Ntozake 1948- DLB-38, 249	Shepard, Clark and Brown DLB-49	Showalter, Elaine 1941- DLB-67
Shapcott, Thomas W. 1935- DLB-289	Shepard, Ernest Howard 1879-1976 . . . . . DLB-160	Shreve, Anita 1946- DLB-292
Shapir, Ol'ga Andreevna 1850-1916 . . . . . DLB-295	Shepard, Sam 1943- DLB-7, 212	Shteiger, Anatolii 1907-1944 . . . . DLB-317
Shapiro, Karl 1913-2000 . . . . DLB-48	Shepard, Thomas I, 1604 or 1605-1649 . . . DLB-24	Shukshin, Vasilii Makarovich 1929-1974 . . . . DLB-302
Sharon Publications DLB-46	Shepard, Thomas, II, 1635-1677 . . . . DLB-24	
Sharov, Vladimir Aleksandrovich 1952- DLB-285	Shepherd, Luke fl. 1547-1554 . . . . DLB-136	Shulevitz, Uri 1935- DLB-61
	Sherburne, Edward 1616-1702 . . . . DLB-131	Shulman, Max 1919-1988 . . . . DLB-11
Sharp, Margery 1905-1991 . . . . DLB-161	Sheridan, Frances 1724-1766 . . . . DLB-39, 84	Shute, Henry A. 1856-1943 . . . . DLB-9
Sharp, William 1855-1905 . . . . DLB-156	Sheridan, Richard Brinsley 1751-1816 . . . . DLB-89; CDBLB-2	Shute, Nevil (Nevil Shute Norway) 1899-1960 . . . . DLB-255
Sharpe, Tom 1928- DLB-14, 231		
Shaw, Albert 1857-1947 . . . . DLB-91	Sherman, Francis 1871-1926 . . . . DLB-92	Shuttle, Penelope 1947- DLB-14, 40
Shaw, George Bernard 1856-1950 . . . . . . DLB-10, 57, 190, CDBLB-6	Sherman, Martin 1938- DLB-228	Shvarts, Evgenii L'vovich 1896-1958 . . . . . DLB-272
	Sherriff, R. C. 1896-1975 . . . . . . DLB-10, 191, 233	Sibawayhi circa 750-circa 795 . . . . DLB-311

Sibbes, Richard 1577-1635 ....DLB-151	Simon and Schuster DLB-46	Slade, Bernard 1930- DLB-53
Sibiriak, D. (see Mamin, Dmitrii Narkisovich)	Simonov, Konstantin Mikhailovich 1915-1979 ....DLB-302	Slamnig, Ivan 1930- DLB-181
Siddal, Elizabeth Eleanor 1829-1862 .....DLB-199	Simons, Katherine Drayton Mayrant 1890-1969 .... Y-83	Slančeková, Bożena (see Timrava)
Sidgwick, Ethel 1877-1970 ....DLB-197		Slataper, Scipio 1888-1915..............DLB-264
Sidgwick, Henry 1838-1900............DLB-262	Simović, Ljubomir 1935- DLB-181	Slater, Patrick 1880-1951................DLB-68
Sidgwick and Jackson Limited DLB-112	Simpkin and Marshall [publishing house]................DLB-154	Slaveykov, Pencho 1866-1912..........DLB-147
Sidney, Margaret (see Lothrop, Harriet M.)	Simpson, Helen 1897-1940..............DLB-77	Slaviček, Milivoj 1929- DLB-181
Sidney, Mary 1561-1621 ....DLB-167	Simpson, Louis 1923- DLB-5	Slavitt, David 1935- DLB-5, 6
Sidney, Sir Philip 1554-1586 ....DLB-167; CDBLB-1	Simpson, N. F. 1919- DLB-13	Sleigh, Burrows Willcocks Arthur 1821-1869 ....DLB-99
An Apologie for Poetrie (the Olney edition, 1595, of *Defence of Poesie*) DLB-167	Sims, George 1923-1999 ....DLB-87; Y-99	Sleptsov, Vasilii Alekseevich 1836-1878...DLB-277
	Sims, George Robert 1847-1922...DLB-35, 70, 135	Slesinger, Tess 1905-1945 ....DLB-102
Sidney's Press DLB-49	Sinán, Rogelio 1902-1994 ....DLB-145, 290	Slessor, Kenneth 1901-1971 ....DLB-260
Sierra, Rubén 1946- DLB-122	Sinclair, Andrew 1935- DLB-14	Slick, Sam (see Haliburton, Thomas Chandler)
Sierra Club Books DLB-49	Sinclair, Bertrand William 1881-1972 .....DLB-92	Sloan, John 1871-1951................DLB-188
Siger of Brabant circa 1240-circa 1284....DLB-115	Sinclair, Catherine 1800-1864 ....DLB-163	Sloane, William, Associates DLB-46
Sigourney, Lydia Huntley 1791-1865 ...... DLB-1, 42, 73, 183, 239, 243	Sinclair, Clive 1948- DLB-319	Slonimsky, Mikhail Leonidovich 1897-1972 ....DLB-272
Silkin, Jon 1930-1997..................DLB-27	Sinclair, Jo 1913-1995 ....DLB-28	Sluchevsky, Konstantin Konstantinovich 1837-1904 .... DLB-277
Silko, Leslie Marmon 1948- DLB-143, 175, 256, 275	Sinclair, Lister 1921- DLB-88	Small, Maynard and Company DLB-49
	Sinclair, May 1863-1946 ....DLB-36, 135	Smart, Christopher 1722-1771 ....DLB-109
Silliman, Benjamin 1779-1864 ....DLB-183	The Novels of Dorothy Richardson (1918)......................DLB-36	Smart, David A. 1892-1957 ....DLB-137
Silliman, Ron 1946- DLB-169	Sinclair, Upton 1878-1968 ......DLB-9; CDALB-5	Smart, Elizabeth 1913-1986 ....DLB-88
Silliphant, Stirling 1918-1996............DLB-26	Upton Sinclair [publishing house] DLB-46	Smart, J. J. C. 1920- DLB-262
Sillitoe, Alan 1928- DLB-14, 139; CDBLB-8	Singer, Isaac Bashevis 1904-1991 .... DLB-6, 28, 52, 278; Y-91; CDALB-1	Smedley, Menella Bute 1820?-1877 ......DLB-199
Tribute to J. B. Priestly Y-84		William Smellie [publishing house] DLB-154
Silman, Roberta 1934- DLB-28	Singer, Mark 1950- DLB-185	Smiles, Samuel 1812-1904 ....DLB-55
Silone, Ignazio (Secondino Tranquilli) 1900-1978 ....DLB-264	Singmaster, Elsie 1879-1958..............DLB-9	Smiley, Jane 1949- DLB-227, 234
	Siniavsky, Andrei (Abram Tertz) 1925-1997 ....DLB-302	Smith, A. J. M. 1902-1980 ....DLB-88
Silva, Beverly 1930- DLB-122	Sinisgalli, Leonardo 1908-1981 ....DLB-114	Smith, Adam 1723-1790...........DLB-104, 252
Silva, Clara 1905-1976 ....DLB-290	Siodmak, Curt 1902-2000 ....DLB-44	Smith, Adam (George Jerome Waldo Goodman) 1930- DLB-185
Silva, José Asunció 1865-1896 ....DLB-283	Sîrbu, Ion D. 1919-1989 ....DLB-232	
Silverberg, Robert 1935- DLB-8	Siringo, Charles A. 1855-1928..........DLB-186	Smith, Alexander 1829-1867 ....DLB-32, 55
Silverman, Kaja 1947- DLB-246	Sissman, L. E. 1928-1976 ....DLB-5	"On the Writing of Essays" (1862)....DLB-57
Silverman, Kenneth 1936- DLB-111	Sisson, C. H. 1914-2003 ....DLB-27	Smith, Amanda 1837-1915..............DLB-221
Simak, Clifford D. 1904-1988 ....DLB-8	Sitwell, Edith 1887-1964....... DLB-20; CDBLB-7	Smith, Betty 1896-1972 .... Y-82
Simcoe, Elizabeth 1762-1850 ....DLB-99	Sitwell, Osbert 1892-1969 .... DLB-100, 195	Smith, Carol Sturm 1938- Y-81
Simcox, Edith Jemima 1844-1901 ....DLB-190	Sixteenth-Century Spanish Epic, The DLB-318	Smith, Charles Henry 1826-1903 ....DLB-11
Simcox, George Augustus 1841-1905 .....DLB-35	Skácel, Jan 1922-1989 ....DLB-232	Smith, Charlotte 1749-1806 .... DLB-39, 109
Sime, Jessie Georgina 1868-1958 ....DLB-92	Skalbe, Kārlis 1879-1945 ....DLB-220	Smith, Chet 1899-1973 ....DLB-171
Simenon, Georges 1903-1989 ...... DLB-72; Y-89	Skármeta, Antonio 1940- DLB-145; CDWLB-3	Smith, Cordwainer 1913-1966............DLB-8
Simic, Charles 1938- DLB-105		Smith, Dave 1942- DLB-5
"Images and 'Images'".............DLB-105	Skavronsky, A. (see Danilevsky, Grigorii Petrovich)	Tribute to James Dickey Y-97
Simionescu, Mircea Horia 1928- DLB-232	Skeat, Walter W. 1835-1912 ....DLB-184	Tribute to John Gardner.............. Y-82
Simmel, Georg 1858-1918 ....DLB-296	William Skeffington [publishing house] ...DLB-106	Smith, Dodie 1896-1990 ....DLB-10
Simmel, Johannes Mario 1924- DLB-69	Skelton, John 1463-1529 ....DLB-136	Smith, Doris Buchanan 1934-2002 .....DLB-52
Valentine Simmes [publishing house] DLB-170	Skelton, Robin 1925-1997 .... DLB-27, 53	Smith, E. E. 1890-1965 ....DLB-8
Simmons, Ernest J. 1903-1972 ....DLB-103	Škéma, Antanas 1910-1961 ....DLB-220	Smith, Elihu Hubbard 1771-1798.........DLB-37
Simmons, Herbert Alfred 1930- DLB-33	Skinner, Constance Lindsay 1877-1939 ....DLB-92	Smith, Elizabeth Oakes (Prince) (see Oakes Smith, Elizabeth)
Simmons, James 1933- DLB-40		
Simms, William Gilmore 1806-1870 .... DLB-3, 30, 59, 73, 248	Skinner, John Stuart 1788-1851 ....DLB-73	Smith, Eunice 1757-1823 ....DLB-200
	Skipsey, Joseph 1832-1903..............DLB-35	Smith, F. Hopkinson 1838-1915 .... DS-13
Simms and M'Intyre DLB-106	Skou-Hansen, Tage 1925- DLB-214	Smith, George D. 1870-1920 ....DLB-140
Simon, Claude 1913-2005 .... DLB-83; Y-85	Skrzynecki, Peter 1945- DLB-289	Smith, George O. 1911-1981 ....DLB-8
Nobel Lecture Y-85	Škvorecký, Josef 1924- DLB-232; CDWLB-4	Smith, Goldwin 1823-1910 ....DLB-99
Simon, Neil 1927- DLB-7, 266		

Smith, H. Allen 1907-1976 .... DLB-11, 29
Smith, Harry B. 1860-1936............ DLB-187
Smith, Hazel Brannon 1914-1994....... DLB-127
Smith, Henry circa 1560-circa 1591 ..... DLB-136
Smith, Horatio (Horace)
  1779-1849.................... DLB-96, 116
Smith, Iain Crichton (Iain Mac A'Ghobhainn)
  1928-1998 .... DLB-40, 139, 319
Smith, J. Allen 1860-1924.............. DLB-47
Smith, James 1775-1839 .... DLB-96
Smith, Jessie Willcox 1863-1935........ DLB-188
Smith, John 1580-1631 .... DLB-24, 30
Smith, John 1618-1652 .... DLB-252
Smith, Josiah 1704-1781 .... DLB-24
Smith, Ken 1938- DLB-40
Smith, Lee 1944- DLB-143; Y-83
Smith, Logan Pearsall 1865-1946 .... DLB-98
Smith, Margaret Bayard 1778-1844 ..... DLB-248
Smith, Mark 1935- Y-82
Smith, Michael 1698-circa 1771 .... DLB-31
Smith, Pauline 1882-1959.............. DLB-225
Smith, Red 1905-1982 ....DLB-29, 171
Smith, Roswell 1829-1892 .... DLB-79
Smith, Samuel Harrison 1772-1845....... DLB-43
Smith, Samuel Stanhope 1751-1819 ...... DLB-37
Smith, Sarah (see Stretton, Hesba)
Smith, Sarah Pogson 1774-1870 .... DLB-200
Smith, Seba 1792-1868 .... DLB-1, 11, 243
Smith, Stevie 1902-1971 .... DLB-20
Smith, Sydney 1771-1845 .... DLB-107
Smith, Sydney Goodsir 1915-1975 .... DLB-27
Smith, Sir Thomas 1513-1577........... DLB-132
Smith, W. Gordon 1928-1996 .... DLB-310
Smith, Wendell 1914-1972 ....DLB-171
Smith, William fl. 1595-1597 .... DLB-136
Smith, William 1727-1803 .... DLB-31
  A General Idea of the College of Mirania
   (1753) [excerpts]................ DLB-31
Smith, William 1728-1793.............. DLB-30
Smith, William Gardner 1927-1974....... DLB-76
Smith, William Henry 1808-1872........ DLB-159
Smith, William Jay 1918- DLB-5
Smith, Elder and Company DLB-154
Harrison Smith and Robert Haas
  [publishing house] DLB-46
J. Stilman Smith and Company DLB-49
W. B. Smith and Company DLB-49
W. H. Smith and Son DLB-106
Leonard Smithers [publishing house] DLB-112
Smollett, Tobias
  1721-1771 .... DLB-39, 104; CDBLB-2
  Dedication to *Ferdinand Count Fathom*
    (1753)..................... DLB-39
  Preface to *Ferdinand Count Fathom*
    (1753)..................... DLB-39
  Preface to *Roderick Random* (1748) DLB-39

Smythe, Francis Sydney 1900-1949 ..... DLB-195
Snelling, William Joseph 1804-1848..... DLB-202
Snellings, Rolland (see Touré, Askia Muhammad)
Snodgrass, W. D. 1926- DLB-5
Snorri Hjartarson 1906-1986 .... DLB-293
Snow, C. P.
  1905-1980 .... DLB-15, 77; DS-17; CDBLB-7
Snyder, Gary
  1930- DLB-5, 16, 165, 212, 237, 275
Sobiloff, Hy 1912-1970 .... DLB-48
The Social Contract, Jean-Jacques
  Rousseau DLB-314
The Society for Textual Scholarship and
  TEXT.......................... Y-87
The Society for the History of Authorship,
  Reading and Publishing Y-92
Söderberg, Hjalmar 1869-1941......... DLB-259
Södergran, Edith 1892-1923 .... DLB-259
Soffici, Ardengo 1879-1964......... DLB-114, 264
Sofola, 'Zulu 1938- DLB-157
Sokhanskaia, Nadezhda Stepanovna
  (Kokhanovskaia) 1823?-1884.........DLB-277
Sokolov, Sasha (Aleksandr Vsevolodovich
  Sokolov) 1943- DLB-285
Solano, Solita 1888-1975................ DLB-4
Soldati, Mario 1906-1999 ....DLB-177
Soledad (see Zamudio, Adela)
Šoljan, Antun 1932-1993 .... DLB-181
Sollers, Philippe (Philippe Joyaux)
  1936- DLB-83
Sollogub, Vladimir Aleksandrovich
  1813-1882 .... DLB-198
Sollors, Werner 1943- DBL-246
Solmi, Sergio 1899-1981.............. DLB-114
Sologub, Fedor 1863-1927 .... DLB-295
Solomon, Carl 1928- DLB-16
Solórzano, Carlos 1922- DLB-305
Soloukhin, Vladimir Alekseevich
  1924-1997..................... DLB-302
Solov'ev, Sergei Mikhailovich
  1885-1942 .... DLB-295
Solov'ev, Vladimir Sergeevich
  1853-1900 .... DLB-295
Solstad, Dag 1941- DLB-297
Solway, David 1941- DLB-53
Solzhenitsyn, Aleksandr
  1918- DLB-302
  Solzhenitsyn and America Y-85
Some Basic Notes on Three Modern Genres:
  Interview, Blurb, and Obituary Y-02
Somerville, Edith Œnone 1858-1949 .... DLB-135
Somov, Orest Mikhailovich 1793-1833... DLB-198
Sønderby, Knud 1909-1966 .... DLB-214
Sone, Monica 1919- DLB-312
Song, Cathy 1955- DLB-169, 312
Sonnevi, Göran 1939- DLB-257
Sono Ayako 1931- DLB-182
Sontag, Susan 1933-2004 .... DLB-2, 67

Sophocles 497/496 B.C.-406/405 B.C.
  ....DLB-176; CDWLB-1
Šopov, Aco 1923-1982 .... DLB-181
Sorel, Charles ca.1600-1674 ....DLB-268
Sørensen, Villy 1929- DLB-214
Sorensen, Virginia 1912-1991.......... DLB-206
Sorge, Reinhard Johannes 1892-1916.... DLB-118
Sorokin, Vladimir Georgievich
  1955- DLB-285
Sorrentino, Gilbert 1929- DLB-5, 173; Y-80
Sosa, Roberto 1930- DLB-290
Sotheby, James 1682-1742 .... DLB-213
Sotheby, John 1740-1807 .... DLB-213
Sotheby, Samuel 1771-1842 .... DLB-213
Sotheby, Samuel Leigh 1805-1861 ...... DLB-213
Sotheby, William 1757-1833 .... DLB-93, 213
Soto, Gary 1952- DLB-82
Soueif, Ahdaf 1950- DLB-267
Souster, Raymond 1921- DLB-88
The *South English Legendary* circa
  thirteenth-fifteenth centuries DLB-146
Southerland, Ellease 1943- DLB-33
Southern, Terry 1924-1995 .... DLB-2
Southern Illinois University Press Y-95
Southern Literature
  Fellowship of Southern Writers Y-98
  The Fugitives and the Agrarians:
    The First Exhibition Y-85
  "The Greatness of Southern Literature":
    League of the South Institute for the
    Study of Southern Culture and
    History Y-02
  The Society for the Study of
    Southern Literature Y-00
  Southern Writers Between the Wars ... DLB-9
Southerne, Thomas 1659-1746.......... DLB-80
Southey, Caroline Anne Bowles
  1786-1854..................... DLB-116
Southey, Robert 1774-1843...... DLB-93, 107, 142
Southwell, Robert 1561?-1595 .... DLB-167
Southworth, E. D. E. N. 1819-1899 ..... DLB-239
Sowande, Bode 1948- DLB-157
Tace Sowle [publishing house] DLB-170
Soyfer, Jura 1912-1939 .... DLB-124
Soyinka, Wole
  1934- DLB-125; Y-86, Y-87; CDWLB-3
  Nobel Lecture 1986: This Past Must
    Address Its Present Y-86
Spacks, Barry 1931- DLB-105
Spalding, Frances 1950- DLB-155
Spanish Byzantine Novel, The DLB-318
Spanish Travel Writers of the
  Late Middle Ages................. DLB-286
Spark, Muriel 1918- ... DLB-15, 139; CDBLB-7
Michael Sparke [publishing house] DLB-170
Sparks, Jared 1789-1866 .... DLB-1, 30, 235
Sparshott, Francis 1926- DLB-60
Späth, Gerold 1939- DLB-75

Spatola, Adriano 1941-1988...........DLB-128

Spaziani, Maria Luisa 1924-...........DLB-128

Specimens of Foreign Standard Literature 1838-1842......................DLB-1

The Spectator 1828-.................DLB-110

Spedding, James 1808-1881............DLB-144

Spee von Langenfeld, Friedrich 1591-1635.....................DLB-164

Speght, Rachel 1597-after 1630.........DLB-126

Speke, John Hanning 1827-1864........DLB-166

Spellman, A. B. 1935-................DLB-41

Spence, Catherine Helen 1825-1910.....DLB-230

Spence, Thomas 1750-1814............DLB-158

Spencer, Anne 1882-1975............DLB-51, 54

Spencer, Charles, third Earl of Sunderland 1674-1722.....................DLB-213

Spencer, Elizabeth 1921-..........DLB-6, 218

Spencer, George John, Second Earl Spencer 1758-1834.....................DLB-184

Spencer, Herbert 1820-1903........DLB-57, 262

"The Philosophy of Style" (1852).....DLB-57

Spencer, Scott 1945-....................Y-86

Spender, J. A. 1862-1942..............DLB-98

Spender, Stephen 1909-1995..DLB-20; CDBLB-7

Spener, Philipp Jakob 1635-1705........DLB-164

Spenser, Edmund circa 1552-1599.........DLB-167; CDBLB-1

Envoy from *The Shepheardes Calender*....DLB-167

"The Generall Argument of the Whole Booke," from *The Shepheardes Calender*.........DLB-167

"A Letter of the Authors Expounding His Whole Intention in the Course of this Worke: Which for that It Giueth Great Light to the Reader, for the Better Vnderstanding Is Hereunto Annexed," from *The Faerie Queene* (1590)....DLB-167

"To His Booke," from *The Shepheardes Calender* (1579)...DLB-167

"To the Most Excellent and Learned Both Orator and Poete, Mayster Gabriell Haruey, His Verie Special and Singular Good Frend E. K. Commendeth the Good Lyking of This His Labour, and the Patronage of the New Poete," from *The Shepheardes Calender*.........DLB-167

Sperr, Martin 1944-.................DLB-124

Spewack, Bella Cowen 1899-1990.......DLB-266

Spewack, Samuel 1899-1971...........DLB-266

Spicer, Jack 1925-1965..........DLB-5, 16, 193

Spiegelman, Art 1948-...............DLB-299

Spielberg, Peter 1929-..................Y-81

Spielhagen, Friedrich 1829-1911........DLB-129

"Spielmannsepen" (circa 1152-circa 1500)...DLB-148

Spier, Peter 1927-...................DLB-61

Spillane, Mickey 1918-...............DLB-226

Spink, J. G. Taylor 1888-1962..........DLB-241

Spinrad, Norman 1940-................DLB-8

Tribute to Isaac Asimov..............Y-92

Spires, Elizabeth 1952-..............DLB-120

The Spirit of Laws, Claude-Adrien Helvétius....................DLB-314

The Spirit of Laws, Charles-Louis de Secondat, baron de Montesquieu.................DLB-314

Spitteler, Carl 1845-1924.............DLB-129

Spivak, Lawrence E. 1900-1994........DLB-137

Spofford, Harriet Prescott 1835-1921..................DLB-74, 221

Sports
Jimmy, Red, and Others: Harold Rosenthal Remembers the Stars of the Press Box.................Y-01

The Literature of Boxing in England through Arthur Conan Doyle.......Y-01

Notable Twentieth-Century Books about Sports.................DLB-241

Sprigge, Timothy L. S. 1932-.........DLB-262

Spring, Howard 1889-1965...........DLB-191

Springs, Elliott White 1896-1959........DLB-316

Squibob (see Derby, George Horatio)

Squier, E. G. 1821-1888..............DLB-189

Staal-Delaunay, Marguerite-Jeanne Cordier de 1684-1750.....................DLB-314

Stableford, Brian 1948-..............DLB-261

Stacpoole, H. de Vere 1863-1951........DLB-153

Staël, Germaine de 1766-1817......DLB-119, 192

Staël-Holstein, Anne-Louise Germaine de (see Staël, Germaine de)

Staffeldt, Schack 1769-1826...........DLB-300

Stafford, Jean 1915-1979............DLB-2, 173

Stafford, William 1914-1993..........DLB-5, 206

Stallings, Laurence 1894-1968.....DLB-7, 44, 316

Stallworthy, Jon 1935-................DLB-40

Stampp, Kenneth M. 1912-............DLB-17

Stănescu, Nichita 1933-1983...........DLB-232

Stanev, Emiliyan 1907-1979...........DLB-181

Stanford, Ann 1916-1987...............DLB-5

Stangerup, Henrik 1937-1998..........DLB-214

Stanihurst, Richard 1547-1618.........DLB-281

Stanitsky, N. (see Panaeva, Avdot'ia Iakovlevna)

Stankevich, Nikolai Vladimirovich 1813-1840.....................DLB-198

Stanković, Borisav ("Bora") 1876-1927...........DLB-147; CDWLB-4

Stanley, Henry M. 1841-1904....DLB-189; DS-13

Stanley, Thomas 1625-1678...........DLB-131

Stannard, Martin 1947-..............DLB-155

William Stansby [publishing house].....DLB-170

Stanton, Elizabeth Cady 1815-1902......DLB-79

Stanton, Frank L. 1857-1927..........DLB-25

Stanton, Maura 1946-................DLB-120

Stapledon, Olaf 1886-1950.........DLB-15, 255

Star Spangled Banner Office...........DLB-49

Stark, Freya 1893-1993...............DLB-195

Starkey, Thomas circa 1499-1538.......DLB-132

Starkie, Walter 1894-1976............DLB-195

Starkweather, David 1935-.............DLB-7

Starrett, Vincent 1886-1974...........DLB-187

Stationers' Company of London, The....DLB-170

Statius circa A.D. 45-A.D. 96..........DLB-211

Stead, Christina 1902-1983............DLB-260

Stead, Robert J. C. 1880-1959..........DLB-92

Steadman, Mark 1930-.................DLB-6

Stearns, Harold E. 1891-1943........DLB-4; DS-15

Stebnitsky, M. (see Leskov, Nikolai Semenovich)

Stedman, Edmund Clarence 1833-1908...DLB-64

Steegmuller, Francis 1906-1994.........DLB-111

Steel, Flora Annie 1847-1929.......DLB-153, 156

Steele, Max 1922-.....................Y-80

Steele, Richard 1672-1729..........DLB-84, 101; CDBLB-2

Steele, Timothy 1948-...............DLB-120

Steele, Wilbur Daniel 1886-1970........DLB-86

Wallace Markfield's "Steeplechase".........Y-02

Steere, Richard circa 1643-1721.........DLB-24

Stefán frá Hvítadal (Stefán Sigurðsson) 1887-1933.....................DLB-293

Stefán Guðmundsson (see Stephan G. Stephansson)

Stefán Hörður Grímsson 1919 or 1920-2002.................DLB-293

Steffens, Lincoln 1866-1936...........DLB-303

Stefanovski, Goran 1952-.............DLB-181

Stegner, Wallace 1909-1993..........DLB-9, 206, 275; Y-93

Stehr, Hermann 1864-1940............DLB-66

Steig, William 1907-2003..............DLB-61

Stein, Gertrude 1874-1946 ......DLB-4, 54, 86, 228; DS-15; CDALB-4

Stein, Leo 1872-1947..................DLB-4

Stein and Day Publishers...............DLB-46

Steinbeck, John 1902-1968 ....DLB-7, 9, 212, 275, 309; DS-2; CDALB-5

John Steinbeck Research Center, San Jose State University..........Y-85

The Steinbeck Centennial.............Y-02

Steinem, Gloria 1934-................DLB-246

Steiner, George 1929-............DLB-67, 299

Steinhoewel, Heinrich 1411/1412-1479...DLB-179

Steinn Steinarr (Aðalsteinn Kristmundsson) 1908-1958.....................DLB-293

Steinunn Sigurðardóttir 1950-........DLB-293

Steloff, Ida Frances 1887-1989.........DLB-187

Stendhal 1783-1842.................DLB-119

Stephan G. Stephansson (Stefán Guðmundsson) 1853-1927.....................DLB-293

Stephen, Leslie 1832-1904......DLB-57, 144, 190

Stephen Family (Bloomsbury Group)......DS-10

Stephens, A. G. 1865-1933.............DLB-230

Stephens, Alexander H. 1812-1883........DLB-47

Stephens, Alice Barber 1858-1932.......DLB-188

Stephens, Ann 1810-1886........DLB-3, 73, 250

Stephens, Charles Asbury 1844?-1931....DLB-42

Stephens, James 1882?-1950....DLB-19, 153, 162

Stephens, John Lloyd 1805-1852....DLB-183, 250

Stephens, Michael 1946- DLB-234	Stoddard, Elizabeth 1823-1902. . . . . DLB-202	Strauß, David Friedrich 1808-1874. . . . . . DLB-133
Stephensen, P. R. 1901-1965 . . . . DLB-260	Stoddard, Richard Henry 1825-1903 . . . . DLB-3, 64, 250; DS-13	The Strawberry Hill Press DLB-154
Sterling, George 1869-1926 . . . . DLB-54	Stoddard, Solomon 1643-1729 . . . . DLB-24	Strawson, P. F. 1919- DLB-262
Sterling, James 1701-1763 . . . . DLB-24	Stoker, Bram 1847-1912. . . . . . . DLB-36, 70, 178; CDBLB-5	Streatfeild, Noel 1895-1986 . . . . DLB-160
Sterling, John 1806-1844. . . . . DLB-116	On Writing *Dracula*, from the Introduction to *Dracula* (1897). . . . DLB-178	Street, Cecil John Charles (see Rhode, John)
Stern, Gerald 1925- DLB-105	*Dracula* (Documentary). DLB-304	Street, G. S. 1867-1936 . . . . DLB-135
"Living in Ruin". DLB-105	Frederick A. Stokes Company DLB-49	Street and Smith DLB-49
Stern, Gladys B. 1890-1973. . . . . DLB-197	Stokes, Thomas L. 1898-1958 . . . . DLB-29	Streeter, Edward 1891-1976 . . . . DLB-11
Stern, Madeleine B. 1912- DLB-111, 140	Stokesbury, Leon 1945- DLB-120	Streeter, Thomas Winthrop 1883-1965 . . DLB-140
Stern, Richard 1928- DLB-218; Y-87	Stolberg, Christian Graf zu 1748-1821 . . . . DLB-94	Stretton, Hesba 1832-1911 . . . . DLB-163, 190
Stern, Stewart 1922- DLB-26	Stolberg, Friedrich Leopold Graf zu 1750-1819. . . . . DLB-94	Stribling, T. S. 1881-1965 . . . . DLB-9
Sterne, Laurence 1713-1768 . . . DLB-39; CDBLB-2	Stone, Lucy 1818-1893 . . . . DLB-79, 239	Der Stricker circa 1190-circa 1250 . . . . . . DLB-138
Sternheim, Carl 1878-1942 . . . . DLB-56, 118	Stone, Melville 1848-1929 . . . . DLB-25	Strickland, Samuel 1804-1867. . . . . DLB-99
Sternhold, Thomas ?-1549 . . . . DLB-132	Stone, Robert 1937- DLB-152	Strindberg, August 1849-1912 . . . . DLB-259
Steuart, David 1747-1824 . . . . DLB-213	Stone, Ruth 1915- DLB-105	Stringer, Arthur 1874-1950. . . . . DLB-92
Stevens, Henry 1819-1886 . . . . DLB-140	Stone, Samuel 1602-1663 . . . . DLB-24	Stringer and Townsend DLB-49
Stevens, Wallace 1879-1955 . . . DLB-54; CDALB-5	Stone, William Leete 1792-1844 . . . . DLB-202	Strittmatter, Erwin 1912-1994 . . . . DLB-69
The Wallace Stevens Society Y-99	Herbert S. Stone and Company DLB-49	Strniša, Gregor 1930-1987 . . . . DLB-181
Stevenson, Anne 1933- DLB-40	Stone and Kimball DLB-49	Strode, William 1630-1645 . . . . DLB-126
Stevenson, D. E. 1892-1973 . . . . DLB-191	Stoppard, Tom 1937- DLB-13, 233; Y-85; CDBLB-8	Strong, L. A. G. 1896-1958 . . . . DLB-191
Stevenson, Lionel 1902-1973 . . . . DLB-155	Playwrights and Professors DLB-13	Strother, David Hunter (Porte Crayon) 1816-1888 . . . . DLB-3, 248
Stevenson, Robert Louis 1850-1894 . . . . DLB-18, 57, 141, 156, 174; DS-13; CDBLB-5	Storey, Anthony 1928- DLB-14	Strouse, Jean 1945- DLB-111
"On Style in Literature: Its Technical Elements" (1885) . . . DLB-57	Storey, David 1933- DLB-13, 14, 207, 245	Strugatsky, Arkadii Natanovich 1925- DLB-302
Stewart, Donald Ogden 1894-1980 . . . . DLB-4, 11, 26; DS-15	Storm, Theodor 1817-1888. . . . . DLB-129; CDWLB-2	Strugatsky, Boris Natanovich 1933- . . . DLB-302
Stewart, Douglas 1913-1985 . . . . DLB-260	Storni, Alfonsina 1892-1938 . . . . DLB-283	Stuart, Dabney 1937- DLB-105
Stewart, Dugald 1753-1828 . . . . DLB-31	Story, Thomas circa 1670-1742 . . . . DLB-31	"Knots into Webs: Some Autobiographical Sources" DLB-105
Stewart, George, Jr. 1848-1906. . . . . DLB-99	Story, William Wetmore 1819-1895. . . DLB-1, 235	Stuart, Jesse 1906-1984. . . . . . DLB-9, 48, 102; Y-84
Stewart, George R. 1895-1980 . . . . DLB-8	Storytelling: A Contemporary Renaissance . . . Y-84	Lyle Stuart [publishing house] DLB-46
Stewart, Harold 1916-1995 . . . . DLB-260	Stoughton, William 1631-1701 . . . . DLB-24	Stuart, Ruth McEnery 1849?-1917 . . . . . . DLB-202
Stewart, J. I. M. (see Innes, Michael)	Stout, Rex 1886-1975 . . . . DLB-306	Stub, Ambrosius 1705-1758 . . . . DLB-300
Stewart, Maria W. 1803?-1879 . . . . DLB-239	Stow, John 1525-1605. . . . . DLB-132	Stubbs, Harry Clement (see Clement, Hal)
Stewart, Randall 1896-1964 . . . . DLB-103	Stow, Randolph 1935- DLB-260	Stubenberg, Johann Wilhelm von 1619-1663 . . . . DLB-164
Stewart, Sean 1965- DLB-251	Stowe, Harriet Beecher 1811-1896 . . . . . DLB-1,12, 42, 74, 189, 239, 243; CDALB-3	Stuckenberg, Viggo 1763-1905 . . . . DLB-300
Stewart and Kidd Company DLB-46	The Harriet Beecher Stowe Center Y-00	Studebaker, William V. 1947- DLB-256
Sthen, Hans Christensen 1544-1610 . . . . . DLB-300	Stowe, Leland 1899-1994 . . . . DLB-29	Studies in American Jewish Literature Y-02
Stickney, Trumbull 1874-1904 . . . . DLB-54	Stoyanov, Dimitr Ivanov (see Elin Pelin)	Studio DLB-112
Stieler, Caspar 1632-1707 . . . . DLB-164	Strabo 64/63 B.C.-circa A.D. 25 . . . . DLB-176	Stump, Al 1916-1995 . . . . DLB-241
Stifter, Adalbert 1805-1868 . . . . DLB-133; CDWLB-2	Strachey, Lytton 1880-1932 . . . . . DLB-149; DS-10	Sturgeon, Theodore 1918-1985 . . . . DLB-8; Y-85
Stiles, Ezra 1727-1795 . . . . DLB-31	Preface to *Eminent Victorians*. DLB-149	Sturges, Preston 1898-1959 . . . . DLB-26
Still, James 1906-2001. . . . . DLB-9; Y-01	William Strahan [publishing house] DLB-154	Styron, William 1925- DLB-2, 143, 299; Y-80; CDALB-6
Stirling, S. M. 1953- DLB-251	Strahan and Company DLB-106	Tribute to James Dickey Y-97
Stirner, Max 1806-1856 . . . . DLB-129	Strand, Mark 1934- DLB-5	Suard, Jean-Baptiste-Antoine 1732-1817. DLB-314
Stith, William 1707-1755 . . . . DLB-31	The Strasbourg Oaths 842 . . . . DLB-148	Suárez, Clementina 1902-1991 . . . . DLB-290
Stivens, Dal 1911-1997 . . . . DLB-260	Stratemeyer, Edward 1862-1930 . . . . DLB-42	Suárez, Mario 1925- DLB-82
Elliot Stock [publishing house] DLB-106	Strati, Saverio 1924- DLB-177	Suassuna, Ariano 1927- DLB-307
Stockton, Annis Boudinot 1736-1801 . . . . DLB-200	Stratton and Barnard DLB-49	Such, Peter 1939- DLB-60
Stockton, Frank R. 1834-1902 . . . . DLB-42, 74; DS-13	Stratton-Porter, Gene 1863-1924 . . . . DLB-221; DS-14	Suckling, Sir John 1609-1641? DLB-58, 126
Stockton, J. Roy 1892-1972 . . . . DLB-241	Straub, Peter 1943- Y-84	Suckow, Ruth 1892-1960 . . . . DLB-9, 102
Ashbel Stoddard [publishing house] DLB-49	Strauß, Botho 1944- DLB-124	Sudermann, Hermann 1857-1928 . . . . DLB-118
Stoddard, Charles Warren 1843-1909 . . . DLB-186		

Sue, Eugène 1804-1857 . . . . DLB-119	Swope, Herbert Bayard 1882-1958 . . . . DLB-25	Talev, Dimitr 1898-1966 . . . . DLB-181
Sue, Marie-Joseph (see Sue, Eugène)	Swords, James ?-1844 . . . . DLB-73	Taliaferro, H. E. 1811-1875 . . . . DLB-202
Suetonius circa A.D. 69-post A.D. 122 . . . . . DLB-211	Swords, Thomas 1763-1843 . . . . DLB-73	Tallent, Elizabeth 1954- DLB-130
Suggs, Simon (see Hooper, Johnson Jones)	T. and J. Swords and Company DLB-49	TallMountain, Mary 1918-1994 . . . . DLB-193
Sui Sin Far (see Eaton, Edith Maude)	Swynnerton, Thomas (John Roberts) circa 1500-1554 . . . . DLB-281	Talvj 1797-1870 . . . . DLB-59, 133
Suits, Gustav 1883-1956 . . . . DLB-220; CDWLB-4	Sykes, Ella C. ?-1939 . . . . DLB-174	Tamási, Áron 1897-1966 . . . . DLB-215
Sukenick, Ronald 1932-2004 . . . . . . DLB-173; Y-81	Sylvester, Josuah 1562 or 1563-1618 . . . . . DLB-121	Tammsaare, A. H. 1878-1940 . . . . DLB-220; CDWLB-4
An Author's Response Y-82	Symonds, Emily Morse (see Paston, George)	Tan, Amy 1952- DLB-173, 312; CDALB-7
Sukhovo-Kobylin, Aleksandr Vasil'evich 1817-1903 . . . . DLB-277	Symonds, John Addington 1840-1893 . . . . DLB-57, 144	Tandori, Dezső 1938- DLB-232
Suknaski, Andrew 1942- DLB-53	"Personal Style" (1890) DLB-57	Tanner, Thomas 1673/1674-1735 . . . . DLB-213
Sullivan, Alan 1868-1947 . . . . DLB-92	Symons, A. J. A. 1900-1941 . . . . DLB-149	Tanizaki Jun'ichirō 1886-1965 . . . . DLB-180
Sullivan, C. Gardner 1886-1965 . . . . DLB-26	Symons, Arthur 1865-1945 . . . . . . DLB-19, 57, 149	Tapahonso, Luci 1953- DLB-175
Sullivan, Frank 1892-1976 . . . . DLB-11	Symons, Julian 1912-1994 . . . . . DLB-87, 155; Y-92	The Mark Taper Forum DLB-7
Sulte, Benjamin 1841-1923 . . . . DLB-99	Julian Symons at Eighty Y-92	Taradash, Daniel 1913-2003 . . . . DLB-44
Sulzberger, Arthur Hays 1891-1968 . . . . . DLB-127	Symons, Scott 1933- DLB-53	Tarasov-Rodionov, Aleksandr Ignat'evich 1885-1938 . . . . DLB-272
Sulzberger, Arthur Ochs 1926- DLB-127	Synge, John Millington 1871-1909 . . . . DLB-10, 19; CDBLB-5	Tarbell, Ida M. 1857-1944 . . . . DLB-47
Sulzer, Johann Georg 1720-1779 . . . . DLB-97	Synge Summer School: J. M. Synge and the Irish Theater, Rathdrum, County Wiclow, Ireland Y-93	Tardivel, Jules-Paul 1851-1905 . . . . DLB-99
Sumarokov, Aleksandr Petrovich 1717-1777 . . . . DLB-150		Targan, Barry 1932- DLB-130
Summers, Hollis 1916-1987 . . . . DLB-6	Syrett, Netta 1865-1943 . . . . DLB-135, 197	Tribute to John Gardner Y-82
Sumner, Charles 1811-1874 . . . . DLB-235	The System of Nature, Paul Henri Thiry, baron d'Holbach (as Jean-Baptiste de Mirabaud) DLB-314	Tarkington, Booth 1869-1946 . . . . DLB-9, 102
Sumner, William Graham 1840-1910 . . . . DLB-270		Tashlin, Frank 1913-1972 . . . . DLB-44
Henry A. Sumner [publishing house] DLB-49		Tasma (Jessie Couvreur) 1848-1897 . . . . . DLB-230
Sundman, Per Olof 1922-1992 . . . . DLB-257	Szabó, Lőrinc 1900-1957 . . . . DLB-215	Tate, Allen 1899-1979 . . . . . . DLB-4, 45, 63; DS-17
Supervielle, Jules 1884-1960 . . . . DLB-258	Szabó, Magda 1917- DLB-215	Tate, James 1943- DLB-5, 169
Surtees, Robert Smith 1803-1864 . . . . DLB-21	Szymborska, Wisława 1923- DLB-232, Y-96; CDWLB-4	Tate, Nahum circa 1652-1715 . . . . DLB-80
The R. S. Surtees Society Y-98	Nobel Lecture 1996: The Poet and the World Y-96	Tatian circa 830 . . . . DLB-148
Sutcliffe, Matthew 1550?-1629 . . . . DLB-281		Taufer, Veno 1933- DLB-181
Sutcliffe, William 1971- DLB-271	**T**	Tauler, Johannes circa 1300-1361 . . . . DLB-179
Sutherland, Efua Theodora 1924-1996 . . . DLB-117		Tavares, Salette 1922-1994 . . . . DLB-287
Sutherland, John 1919-1956 . . . . DLB-68	Taban lo Liyong 1939?- DLB-125	Tavčar, Ivan 1851-1923 . . . . DLB-147
Sutro, Alfred 1863-1933 . . . . DLB-10	al-Tabari 839-923 . . . . DLB-311	Taverner, Richard ca. 1505-1575 . . . . DLB-236
Svava Jakobsdóttir 1930- DLB-293	Tablada, José Juan 1871-1945 . . . . DLB-290	Taylor, Ann 1782-1866 . . . . DLB-163
Svendsen, Hanne Marie 1933- DLB-214	Le Tableau de Paris, Louis-Sébastien Mercier DLB-314	Taylor, Bayard 1825-1878 . . . . DLB-3, 189, 250
Svevo, Italo (Ettore Schmitz) 1861-1928 . . . . DLB-264		Taylor, Bert Leston 1866-1921 . . . . DLB-25
Swados, Harvey 1920-1972 . . . . DLB-2	Tabori, George 1914- DLB-245	Taylor, Charles H. 1846-1921 . . . . DLB-25
Swain, Charles 1801-1874 . . . . DLB-32	Tabucchi, Antonio 1943- DLB-196	Taylor, Edward circa 1642-1729 . . . . DLB-24
Swallow Press DLB-46	Taché, Joseph-Charles 1820-1894 . . . . DLB-99	Taylor, Elizabeth 1912-1975 . . . . DLB-139
Swan Sonnenschein Limited DLB-106	Tachihara Masaaki 1926-1980 . . . . DLB-182	Taylor, Sir Henry 1800-1886 . . . . DLB-32
Swanberg, W. A. 1907-1992 . . . . DLB-103	Tacitus circa A.D. 55-circa A.D. 117 . . . . DLB-211; CDWLB-1	Taylor, Henry 1942- DLB-5
Swedish Literature The Literature of the Modern Breakthrough DLB-259		Who Owns American Literature Y-94
	Tadijanović, Dragutin 1905- DLB-181	Taylor, Jane 1783-1824 . . . . DLB-163
Swenson, May 1919-1989 . . . . DLB-5	Tafdrup, Pia 1952- DLB-214	Taylor, Jeremy circa 1613-1667 . . . . DLB-151
Swerling, Jo 1897-1964 . . . . DLB-44	Tafolla, Carmen 1951- DLB-82	Taylor, John 1577 or 1578 - 1653 . . . . DLB-121
Swift, Graham 1949- DLB-194	Taggard, Genevieve 1894-1948 . . . . DLB-45	Taylor, Mildred D. 1943- DLB-52
Swift, Jonathan 1667-1745 . . . . DLB-39, 95, 101; CDBLB-2	Taggart, John 1942- DLB-193	Taylor, Peter 1917-1994 . . . DLB-218, 278; Y-81, 94
	Tagger, Theodor (see Bruckner, Ferdinand)	Taylor, Susie King 1848-1912 . . . . DLB-221
Swinburne, A. C. 1837-1909 . . . . DLB-35, 57; CDBLB-4	Taiheiki late fourteenth century DLB-203	Taylor, William Howland 1901-1966 . . . DLB-241
	Tait, J. Selwin, and Sons DLB-49	William Taylor and Company DLB-49
Under the Microscope (1872) DLB-35	Tait's Edinburgh Magazine 1832-1861 . . . . . . DLB-110	Teale, Edwin Way 1899-1980 . . . . DLB-275
Swineshead, Richard floruit circa 1350 . . . DLB-115	The Takarazaka Revue Company Y-91	Teasdale, Sara 1884-1933 . . . . DLB-45
Swinnerton, Frank 1884-1982 . . . . DLB-34	Talander (see Bohse, August)	Teffi, Nadezhda 1872-1952 . . . . DLB-317
Swisshelm, Jane Grey 1815-1884 . . . . DLB-43	Talese, Gay 1932- DLB-185	Teillier, Jorge 1935-1996 . . . . DLB-283
	Tribute to Irwin Shaw Y-84	Telles, Lygia Fagundes 1924- DLB-113, 307

The Temper of the West: William Jovanovich.... Y-02
Temple, Sir William 1555?-1627 .... DLB-281
Temple, Sir William 1628-1699 .... DLB-101
Temple, William F. 1914-1989 .... DLB-255
Temrizov, A. (see Marchenko, Anastasia Iakovlevna)
Tench, Watkin ca. 1758-1833 .... DLB-230
Tencin, Alexandrine-Claude Guérin de
   1682-1749 .... DLB-314
Tender Is the Night (Documentary) DLB-273
Tendriakov, Vladimir Fedorovich
   1923-1984 .... DLB-302
Tenn, William 1919- DLB-8
Tennant, Emma 1937- DLB-14
Tenney, Tabitha Gilman 1762-1837 ... DLB-37, 200
Tennyson, Alfred 1809-1892 .. DLB-32; CDBLB-4
   On Some of the Characteristics of
     Modern Poetry and On the Lyrical
     Poems of Alfred Tennyson
     (1831) DLB-32
Tennyson, Frederick 1807-1898 .... DLB-32
Tenorio, Arthur 1924- DLB-209
"The Tenth Stage," Marie-Jean-Antoine-Nicolas
   Caritat, marquis de Condorcet DLB-314
Tepl, Johannes von
   circa 1350-1414/1415 .... DLB-179
Tepliakov, Viktor Grigor'evich
   1804-1842 .... DLB-205
Terence circa 184 B.C.-159 B.C. or after
   .... DLB-211; CDWLB-1
St. Teresa de Ávila 1515-1582 .... DLB-318
Terhune, Albert Payson 1872-1942 ...... DLB-9
Terhune, Mary Virginia 1830-1922 ...... DS-13
Terpigorev, Sergei Nikolaevich (S. Atava)
   1841-1895 .... DLB-277
Terry, Megan 1932- DLB-7, 249
Terson, Peter 1932- DLB-13
Tesich, Steve 1943-1996 .... Y-83
Tessa, Delio 1886-1939 .... DLB-114
Testori, Giovanni 1923-1993
   .... DLB-128, 177
Texas
   The Year in Texas Literature Y-98
Tey, Josephine 1896?-1952 .... DLB-77
Thacher, James 1754-1844 .... DLB-37
Thacher, John Boyd 1847-1909 .... DLB-187
Thackeray, William Makepeace
   1811-1863 ... DLB-21, 55, 159, 163; CDBLB-4
Thames and Hudson Limited DLB-112
Thanet, Octave (see French, Alice)
Thaxter, Celia Laighton
   1835-1894 .... DLB-239
Thayer, Caroline Matilda Warren
   1785-1844 .... DLB-200
Thayer, Douglas H. 1929- DLB-256
Theater
   Black Theatre: A Forum [excerpts] ... DLB-38
   Community and Commentators:
     Black Theatre and Its Critics DLB-38
   German Drama from Naturalism
     to Fascism: 1889-1933 .... DLB-118

A Look at the Contemporary Black
   Theatre Movement DLB-38
The Lord Chamberlain's Office and
   Stage Censorship in England DLB-10
New Forces at Work in the American
   Theatre: 1915-1925 .... DLB-7
Off Broadway and Off-Off Broadway .. DLB-7
Oregon Shakespeare Festival Y-00
Plays, Playwrights, and Playgoers DLB-84
Playwrights on the Theater DLB-80
Playwrights and Professors DLB-13
Producing *Dear Bunny, Dear Volodya:*
   The Friendship and the Feud Y-97
Viewpoint: Politics and Performance,
   by David Edgar DLB-13
Writing for the Theatre,
   by Harold Pinter DLB-13
The Year in Drama Y-82-85, 87-98
The Year in U.S. Drama Y-00
Theater, English and Irish
   Anti-Theatrical Tracts DLB-263
   The Chester Plays circa 1505-1532;
     revisions until 1575 .... DLB-146
   Dangerous Years: London Theater,
     1939-1945 .... DLB-10
   A Defense of Actors DLB-263
   The Development of Lighting in the
     Staging of Drama, 1900-1945 .... DLB-10
   Education DLB-263
   The End of English Stage Censorship,
     1945-1968 .... DLB-13
   Epigrams and Satires DLB-263
   Eyewitnesses and Historians DLB-263
   Fringe and Alternative Theater in
     Great Britain DLB-13
   The Great War and the Theater,
     1914-1918 [Great Britain] DLB-10
   Licensing Act of 1737 .... DLB-84
   Morality Plays: *Mankind* circa 1450-1500
     and *Everyman* circa 1500 ...... DLB-146
   The New Variorum Shakespeare Y-85
   N-Town Plays circa 1468 to early
     sixteenth century DLB-146
   Politics and the Theater DLB-263
   Practical Matters DLB-263
   Prologues, Epilogues, Epistles to
     Readers, and Excerpts from
     Plays DLB-263
   The Publication of English
     Renaissance Plays DLB-62
   Regulations for the Theater DLB-263
   Sources for the Study of Tudor and
     Stuart Drama DLB-62
   Stage Censorship: "The Rejected
     Statement" (1911), by Bernard
     Shaw [excerpts] DLB-10
   Synge Summer School: J. M. Synge and
     the Irish Theater, Rathdrum,
     County Wiclow, Ireland Y-93
   The Theater in Shakespeare's Time .. DLB-62
   The Theatre Guild DLB-7

   The Townely Plays fifteenth and
     sixteenth centuries DLB-146
   The Year in British Drama Y-99-01
   The Year in Drama: London Y-90
   The Year in London Theatre Y-92
   A Yorkshire Tragedy DLB-58
Theaters
   The Abbey Theatre and Irish Drama,
     1900-1945 .... DLB-10
   Actors Theatre of Louisville DLB-7
   American Conservatory Theatre DLB-7
   Arena Stage DLB-7
   Black Theaters and Theater
     Organizations in America,
     1961-1982: A Research List DLB-38
   The Dallas Theater Center DLB-7
   Eugene O'Neill Memorial Theater
     Center DLB-7
   The Goodman Theatre DLB-7
   The Guthrie Theater DLB-7
   The Mark Taper Forum DLB-7
   The National Theatre and the Royal
     Shakespeare Company: The
     National Companies DLB-13
   Off-Loop Theatres DLB-7
   The Royal Court Theatre and the
     English Stage Company DLB-13
   The Royal Court Theatre and the
     New Drama DLB-10
   The Takarazaka Revue Company Y-91
Thegan and the Astronomer
   fl. circa 850 .... DLB-148
Thelwall, John 1764-1834 .... DLB-93, 158
Theocritus circa 300 B.C.-260 B.C. DLB-176
Theodorescu, Ion N. (see Arghezi, Tudor)
Theodulf circa 760-circa 821 .... DLB-148
Theophrastus circa 371 B.C.-287 B.C. ...DLB-176
Thériault, Yves 1915-1983 .... DLB-88
Thério, Adrien 1925- DLB-53
Theroux, Paul 1941- DLB-2, 218; CDALB-7
Thesiger, Wilfred 1910-2003 .... DLB-204
They All Came to Paris DS-15
Thibaudeau, Colleen 1925- DLB-88
Thiele, Colin 1920- DLB-289
Thielen, Benedict 1903-1965 .... DLB-102
Thiong'o Ngugi wa (see Ngugi wa Thiong'o)
Thiroux d'Arconville, Marie-Geneviève
   1720-1805 .... DLB-314
This Quarter 1925-1927, 1929-1932 .... DS-15
Thoma, Ludwig 1867-1921 .... DLB-66
Thoma, Richard 1902-1974 .... DLB-4
Thomas, Audrey 1935- DLB-60
Thomas, D. M.
   1935- ...DLB-40, 207, 299; Y-82; CDBLB-8
   The Plagiarism Controversy Y-82
Thomas, Dylan
   1914-1953 ...... DLB-13, 20, 139; CDBLB-7
   The Dylan Thomas Celebration Y-99
Thomas, Ed 1961- DLB-310

Thomas, Edward 1878-1917 .... DLB-19, 98, 156, 216
   The Friends of the Dymock Poets....... Y-00
Thomas, Frederick William 1806-1866 ...DLB-202
Thomas, Gwyn 1913-1981 .... DLB-15, 245
Thomas, Isaiah 1750-1831 .... DLB-43, 73, 187
Thomas, Johann 1624-1679 .... DLB-168
Thomas, John 1900-1932 .... DLB-4
Thomas, Joyce Carol 1938- DLB-33
Thomas, Lewis 1913-1993 .... DLB-275
Thomas, Lorenzo 1944- DLB-41
Thomas, Norman 1884-1968 .... DLB-303
Thomas, R. S. 1915-2000 ...... DLB-27; CDBLB-8
Isaiah Thomas [publishing house] DLB-49
Thomasîn von Zerclære circa 1186-circa 1259 .... DLB-138
Thomason, George 1602?-1666 .... DLB-213
Thomasius, Christian 1655-1728 .... DLB-168
Thompson, Daniel Pierce 1795-1868 ..... DLB-202
Thompson, David 1770-1857 .... DLB-99
Thompson, Dorothy 1893-1961 .... DLB-29
Thompson, E. P. 1924-1993 .... DLB-242
Thompson, Flora 1876-1947 .... DLB-240
Thompson, Francis 1859-1907 .... DLB-19; CDBLB-5
Thompson, George Selden (see Selden, George)
Thompson, Henry Yates 1838-1928 ..... DLB-184
Thompson, Hunter S. 1939-2005 .... DLB-185
Thompson, Jim 1906-1977 .... DLB-226
Thompson, John 1938-1976 .... DLB-60
Thompson, John R. 1823-1873 .... DLB-3, 73, 248
Thompson, Lawrance 1906-1973 .... DLB-103
Thompson, Maurice 1844-1901 ...... DLB-71, 74
Thompson, Ruth Plumly 1891-1976 ...... DLB-22
Thompson, Thomas Phillips 1843-1933 ... DLB-99
Thompson, William 1775-1833 .... DLB-158
Thompson, William Tappan 1812-1882 .... DLB-3, 11, 248
Thomson, Cockburn "Modern Style" (1857) [excerpt] DLB-57
Thomson, Edward William 1849-1924 .... DLB-92
Thomson, James 1700-1748 .... DLB-95
Thomson, James 1834-1882 .... DLB-35
Thomson, Joseph 1858-1895 .... DLB-174
Thomson, Mortimer 1831-1875 .... DLB-11
Thomson, Rupert 1955- DLB-267
Thon, Melanie Rae 1957- DLB-244
Thor Vilhjálmsson 1925- DLB-293
Þórarinn Eldjárn 1949- DLB-293
Þórbergur Þórðarson 1888-1974 .... DLB-293
Thoreau, Henry David 1817-1862 ... DLB-1, 183, 223, 270, 298; DS-5; CDALB-2
   The Thoreau Society Y-99
   The Thoreauvian Pilgrimage: The Structure of an American Cult ...DLB-223
Thorne, William 1568?-1630 .... DLB-281

Thornton, John F. [Repsonse to Ken Auletta] Y-97
Thorpe, Adam 1956- DLB-231
Thorpe, Thomas Bangs 1815-1878 .... DLB-3, 11, 248
Thorup, Kirsten 1942- DLB-214
Thotl, Birgitte 1610-1662 .... DLB-300
Thrale, Hester Lynch (see Piozzi, Hester Lynch [Thrale])
The Three Marias: A Landmark Case in Portuguese Literary History (Maria Isabel Barreno, 1939- ; Maria Teresa Horta, 1937- ; Maria Velho da Costa, 1938-) DLB-287
Thubron, Colin 1939- DLB-204, 231
Thucydides circa 455 B.C.-circa 395 B.C. DLB-176
Thulstrup, Thure de 1848-1930 .... DLB-188
Thümmel, Moritz August von 1738-1817 .... DLB-97
Thurber, James 1894-1961 ..... DLB-4, 11, 22, 102; CDALB-5
Thurman, Wallace 1902-1934 .... DLB-51
   "Negro Poets and Their Poetry" DLB-50
Thwaite, Anthony 1930- DLB-40
   The Booker Prize, Address Y-86
Thwaites, Reuben Gold 1853-1913 .... DLB-47
Tibullus circa 54 B.C.-circa 19 B.C. DLB-211
Ticknor, George 1791-1871 ....DLB-1, 59, 140, 235
Ticknor and Fields................. DLB-49
Ticknor and Fields (revived) DLB-46
Tieck, Ludwig 1773-1853..... DLB-90; CDWLB-2
Tietjens, Eunice 1884-1944 .... DLB-54
Tikkanen, Märta 1935- DLB-257
Tilghman, Christopher circa 1948 .... DLB-244
Tilney, Edmund circa 1536-1610 .... DLB-136
Charles Tilt [publishing house] DLB-106
J. E. Tilton and Company DLB-49
Time-Life Books DLB-46
Times Books DLB-46
Timothy, Peter circa 1725-1782 .... DLB-43
Timrava 1867-1951 .... DLB-215
Timrod, Henry 1828-1867 .... DLB-3, 248
Tindal, Henrietta 1818?-1879 .... DLB-199
Tinker, Chauncey Brewster 1876-1963 .... DLB-140
Tinsley Brothers DLB-106
Tiptree, James, Jr. 1915-1987 .... DLB-8
Tišma, Aleksandar 1924-2003 .... DLB-181
Titus, Edward William 1870-1952 .... DLB-4; DS-15
Tiutchev, Fedor Ivanovich 1803-1873 .... DLB-205
Tlali, Miriam 1933- DLB-157, 225
Todd, Barbara Euphan 1890-1976....... DLB-160
Todorov, Tzvetan 1939- DLB-242
Tofte, Robert 1561 or 1562-1619 or 1620........ DLB-172
Tóibín, Colm 1955- DLB-271
Toklas, Alice B. 1877-1967 .... DLB-4; DS-15

Tokuda Shūsei 1872-1943 ....DLB-180
Toland, John 1670-1722................DLB-252
Tolkien, J. R. R. 1892-1973 ......DLB-15, 160, 255; CDBLB-6
Toller, Ernst 1893-1939................DLB-124
Tollet, Elizabeth 1694-1754 .... DLB-95
Tolson, Melvin B. 1898-1966 .... DLB-48, 76
Tolstaya, Tatyana 1951- DLB-285
Tolstoy, Aleksei Konstantinovich 1817-1875........................DLB-238
Tolstoy, Aleksei Nikolaevich 1883-1945 .. DLB-272
Tolstoy, Leo 1828-1910................ DLB-238
Tomalin, Claire 1933- DLB-155
Tómas Guðmundsson 1901-1983 ....DLB-293
Tomasi di Lampedusa, Giuseppe 1896-1957 .... DLB-177
Tomlinson, Charles 1927- DLB-40
Tomlinson, H. M. 1873-1958 ... DLB-36, 100, 195
Abel Tompkins [publishing house] DLB-49
Tompson, Benjamin 1642-1714 .... DLB-24
Tomson, Graham R. (see Watson, Rosamund Marriott)
Ton'a 1289-1372 .... DLB-203
Tondelli, Pier Vittorio 1955-1991 .... DLB-196
Tonks, Rosemary 1932- DLB-14, 207
Tonna, Charlotte Elizabeth 1790-1846 ... DLB-163
Jacob Tonson the Elder [publishing house] DLB-170
Toole, John Kennedy 1937-1969 .... Y-81
Toomer, Jean 1894-1967 ....DLB-45, 51; CDALB-4
Topsoe, Vilhelm 1840-1881 .... DLB-300
Tor Books DLB-46
Torberg, Friedrich 1908-1979 .... DLB-85
Torga, Miguel (Adolfo Correira da Rocha) 1907-1995 .... DLB-287
Torre, Francisco de la ?-? DLB-318
Torrence, Ridgely 1874-1950....... DLB-54, 249
Torres-Metzger, Joseph V. 1933- DLB-122
Torres Naharro, Bartolomé de 1485?-1523? DLB-318
El Tostado (see Madrigal, Alfonso Fernández de)
Toth, Susan Allen 1940- Y-86
Richard Tottell [publishing house]....... DLB-170
   "The Printer to the Reader," (1557) DLB-167
Tough-Guy Literature.................. DLB-9
Touré, Askia Muhammad 1938- DLB-41
Tourgée, Albion W. 1838-1905......... DLB-79
Tournemir, Elizaveta Sailhas de (see Tur, Evgeniia)
Tourneur, Cyril circa 1580-1626........DLB-58
Tournier, Michel 1924- DLB-83
Frank Tousey [publishing house]........ DLB-49
Tower Publications DLB-46
Towne, Benjamin circa 1740-1793 ...... DLB-43
Towne, Robert 1936- DLB-44

Cumulative Index

The Townely Plays fifteenth and sixteenth centuries...DLB-146

Townsend, Sue 1946- ...DLB-271

Townshend, Aurelian by 1583-circa 1651...DLB-121

Toy, Barbara 1908-2001...DLB-204

Tozzi, Federigo 1883-1920...DLB-264

Tracy, Honor 1913-1989...DLB-15

Traherne, Thomas 1637?-1674...DLB-131

Traill, Catharine Parr 1802-1899...DLB-99

Train, Arthur 1875-1945...DLB-86; DS-16

Tranquilli, Secondino (see Silone, Ignazio)

The Transatlantic Publishing Company...DLB-49

The Transatlantic Review 1924-1925...DS-15

The Transcendental Club 1836-1840...DLB-1; DLB-223

Transcendentalism...DLB-1; DLB-223; DS-5

   "A Response from America," by John A. Heraud...DS-5

   Publications and Social Movements...DLB-1

   The Rise of Transcendentalism, 1815-1860...DS-5

   Transcendentalists, American...DS-5

   "What Is Transcendentalism? By a Thinking Man," by James Kinnard Jr...DS-5

transition 1927-1938...DS-15

Translations (Vernacular) in the Crowns of Castile and Aragon 1352-1515...DLB-286

Tranströmer, Tomas 1931-...DLB-257

Tranter, John 1943-...DLB-289

Travel Writing

   American Travel Writing, 1776-1864 (checklist)...DLB-183

   British Travel Writing, 1940-1997 (checklist)...DLB-204

   Travel Writers of the Late Middle Ages...DLB-286

   (1876-1909)...DLB-174

   (1837-1875)...DLB-166

   (1910-1939)...DLB-195

Traven, B. 1882?/1890?-1969?...DLB-9, 56

Travers, Ben 1886-1980...DLB-10, 233

Travers, P. L. (Pamela Lyndon) 1899-1996...DLB-160

Trediakovsky, Vasilii Kirillovich 1703-1769...DLB-150

Treece, Henry 1911-1966...DLB-160

Treitel, Jonathan 1959-...DLB-267

Trejo, Ernesto 1950-1991...DLB-122

Trelawny, Edward John 1792-1881...DLB-110, 116, 144

Tremain, Rose 1943-...DLB-14, 271

Tremblay, Michel 1942-...DLB-60

Trent, William P. 1862-1939...DLB-47, 71

Trescot, William Henry 1822-1898...DLB-30

Tressell, Robert (Robert Phillipe Noonan) 1870-1911...DLB-197

Trevelyan, Sir George Otto 1838-1928...DLB-144

Trevisa, John circa 1342-circa 1402...DLB-146

Trevisan, Dalton 1925-...DLB-307

Trevor, William 1928-...DLB-14, 139

Triana, José 1931-...DLB-305

Trierer Floyris circa 1170-1180...DLB-138

Trifonov, Iurii Valentinovich 1925-1981...DLB-302

Trillin, Calvin 1935-...DLB-185

Trilling, Lionel 1905-1975...DLB-28, 63

Trilussa 1871-1950...DLB-114

Trimmer, Sarah 1741-1810...DLB-158

Triolet, Elsa 1896-1970...DLB-72

Tripp, John 1927-...DLB-40

Trocchi, Alexander 1925-1984...DLB-15

Troisi, Dante 1920-1989...DLB-196

Trollope, Anthony 1815-1882...DLB-21, 57, 159; CDBLB-4

   Novel-Reading: *The Works of Charles Dickens; The Works of W. Makepeace Thackeray* (1879)...DLB-21

   The Trollope Societies...Y-00

Trollope, Frances 1779-1863...DLB-21, 166

Trollope, Joanna 1943-...DLB-207

Troop, Elizabeth 1931-...DLB-14

Tropicália...DLB-307

Trotter, Catharine 1679-1749...DLB-84, 252

Trotti, Lamar 1898-1952...DLB-44

Trottier, Pierre 1925-...DLB-60

Trotzig, Birgitta 1929-...DLB-257

Troupe, Quincy Thomas, Jr. 1943-...DLB-41

John F. Trow and Company...DLB-49

Trowbridge, John Townsend 1827-1916...DLB-202

Trudel, Jean-Louis 1967-...DLB-251

Truillier-Lacombe, Joseph-Patrice 1807-1863...DLB-99

Trumbo, Dalton 1905-1976...DLB-26

Trumbull, Benjamin 1735-1820...DLB-30

Trumbull, John 1750-1831...DLB-31

Trumbull, John 1756-1843...DLB-183

Truth, Sojourner 1797?-1883...DLB-239

Tscherning, Andreas 1611-1659...DLB-164

Tsubouchi Shōyō 1859-1935...DLB-180

Tsvetaeva, Marina Ivanovna 1892-1941...DLB-295

Tuchman, Barbara W. Tribute to Alfred A. Knopf...Y-84

Tucholsky, Kurt 1890-1935...DLB-56

Tucker, Charlotte Maria 1821-1893...DLB-163, 190

Tucker, George 1775-1861...DLB-3, 30, 248

Tucker, James 1808?-1866?...DLB-230

Tucker, Nathaniel Beverley 1784-1851...DLB-3, 248

Tucker, St. George 1752-1827...DLB-37

Tuckerman, Frederick Goddard 1821-1873...DLB-243

Tuckerman, Henry Theodore 1813-1871...DLB-64

Tumas, Juozas (see Vaizgantas)

Tunis, John R. 1889-1975...DLB-22, 171

Tunstall, Cuthbert 1474-1559...DLB-132

Tunström, Göran 1937-2000...DLB-257

Tuohy, Frank 1925-...DLB-14, 139

Tupper, Martin F. 1810-1889...DLB-32

Tur, Evgeniia 1815-1892...DLB-238

Turbyfill, Mark 1896-1991...DLB-45

Turco, Lewis 1934-...Y-84

   Tribute to John Ciardi...Y-86

Turgenev, Aleksandr Ivanovich 1784-1845...DLB-198

Turgenev, Ivan Sergeevich 1818-1883...DLB-238

Turgot, baron de l'Aulne, Anne-Robert-Jacques 1727-1781...DLB-314

   "Memorandum on Local Government"...DLB-314

Turnbull, Alexander H. 1868-1918...DLB-184

Turnbull, Andrew 1921-1970...DLB-103

Turnbull, Gael 1928-...DLB-40

Turner, Arlin 1909-1980...DLB-103

Turner, Charles (Tennyson) 1808-1879...DLB-32

Turner, Ethel 1872-1958...DLB-230

Turner, Frederick 1943-...DLB-40

Turner, Frederick Jackson 1861-1932...DLB-17, 186

A Conversation between William Riggan and Janette Turner Hospital...Y-02

Turner, Joseph Addison 1826-1868...DLB-79

Turpin, Waters Edward 1910-1968...DLB-51

Turrini, Peter 1944-...DLB-124

Tutuola, Amos 1920-1997...DLB-125; CDWLB-3

Twain, Mark (see Clemens, Samuel Langhorne)

Tweedie, Ethel Brilliana circa 1860-1940...DLB-174

A Century of Poetry, a Lifetime of Collecting: J. M. Edelstein's Collection of Twentieth-Century American Poetry...YB-02

Twombly, Wells 1935-1977...DLB-241

Twysden, Sir Roger 1597-1672...DLB-213

Ty-Casper, Linda 1931-...DLB-312

Tyler, Anne 1941-...DLB-6, 143; Y-82; CDALB-7

Tyler, Mary Palmer 1775-1866...DLB-200

Tyler, Moses Coit 1835-1900...DLB-47, 64

Tyler, Royall 1757-1826...DLB-37

Tylor, Edward Burnett 1832-1917...DLB-57

Tynan, Katharine 1861-1931...DLB-153, 240

Tyndale, William circa 1494-1536...DLB-132

Tyree, Omar 1969-...DLB-292

U

Uchida, Yoshiko 1921-1992...DLB-312; CDALB-7

Udall, Nicholas 1504-1556...DLB-62

Ugrêsić, Dubravka 1949-...DLB-181

Uhland, Ludwig 1787-1862...DLB-90

Uhse, Bodo 1904-1963 . . . . .DLB-69	Untermeyer, Louis 1885-1977 . . . . .DLB-303	Valerius Maximus fl. circa A.D. 31 . . . . . .DLB-211
Ujević, Augustin "Tin" 1891-1955 . . . . .DLB-147	T. Fisher Unwin [publishing house] DLB-106	Valéry, Paul 1871-1945 . . . . .DLB-258
Ulenhart, Niclas fl. circa 1600 . . . . .DLB-164	Upchurch, Boyd B. (see Boyd, John)	Valesio, Paolo 1939- DLB-196
Ulfeldt, Leonora Christina 1621-1698 . . . .DLB-300	Updike, John 1932- DLB-2, 5, 143, 218, 227; Y-80, 82; DS-3; CDALB-6	Valgardson, W. D. 1939- DLB-60
Ulibarrí, Sabine R. 1919-2003 . . . . .DLB-82	John Updike on the Internet Y-97	Valle, Luz 1899-1971 . . . . .DLB-290
Ulica, Jorge 1870-1926 . . . . .DLB-82	Tribute to Alfred A. Knopf Y-84	Valle, Víctor Manuel 1950- DLB-122
Ulitskaya, Liudmila Evgen'evna 1943- DLB-285	Tribute to John Ciardi Y-86	Valle-Inclán, Ramón del 1866-1936 . . . . . .DLB-134
Ulivi, Ferruccio 1912- DLB-196	Upīts, Andrejs 1877-1970 . . . . .DLB-220	Vallejo, Armando 1949- DLB-122
Ulizio, B. George 1889-1969 . . . . .DLB-140	Uppdal, Kristofer 1878-1961 . . . . .DLB-297	Vallejo, César Abraham 1892-1938 . . . . . .DLB-290
Ulrich von Liechtenstein circa 1200-circa 1275 . . . . .DLB-138	Upton, Bertha 1849-1912 . . . . .DLB-141	Vallès, Jules 1832-1885 . . . . .DLB-123
	Upton, Charles 1948- DLB-16	Vallette, Marguerite Eymery (see Rachilde)
Ulrich von Zatzikhoven before 1194-after 1214 . . . . .DLB-138	Upton, Florence K. 1873-1922 . . . . .DLB-141	Valverde, José María 1926-1996 . . . . .DLB-108
'Umar ibn Abi Rabi'ah 644-712 or 721 . . .DLB-311	Upward, Allen 1863-1926 . . . . .DLB-36	Vampilov, Aleksandr Valentinovich (A. Sanin) 1937-1972 . . . . .DLB-302
Unaipon, David 1872-1967 . . . . .DLB-230	Urban, Milo 1904-1982 . . . . .DLB-215	Van Allsburg, Chris 1949- DLB-61
Unamuno, Miguel de 1864-1936 . . . . .DLB-108	Ureña de Henríquez, Salomé 1850-1897 . .DLB-283	Van Anda, Carr 1864-1945 . . . . .DLB-25
Under, Marie 1883-1980 . . .DLB-220; CDWLB-4	Urfé, Honoré d' 1567-1625 . . . . .DLB-268	Vanbrugh, Sir John 1664-1726 . . . . .DLB-80
Underhill, Evelyn 1875-1941 . . . . .DLB-240	Urista, Alberto Baltazar (see Alurista)	Vance, Jack 1916?- DLB-8
Undset, Sigrid 1882-1949 . . . . .DLB-297	Urquhart, Fred 1912-1995 . . . . .DLB-139	Vančura, Vladislav 1891-1942 . . . . .DLB-215; CDWLB-4
Ungaretti, Giuseppe 1888-1970 . . . . .DLB-114	Urrea, Luis Alberto 1955- DLB-209	
Unger, Friederike Helene 1741-1813 . . . . .DLB-94	Urzidil, Johannes 1896-1970 . . . . .DLB-85	van der Post, Laurens 1906-1996 . . . . . . .DLB-204
	U.S.A. (Documentary) DLB-274	Van Dine, S. S. (see Wright, Williard Huntington)
United States Book Company DLB-49	Usigli, Rodolfo 1905-1979 . . . . .DLB-305	Van Doren, Mark 1894-1972 . . . . .DLB-45
Universal Publishing and Distributing Corporation DLB-46	Usk, Thomas died 1388 . . . . .DLB-146	van Druten, John 1901-1957 . . . . .DLB-10
	Uslar Pietri, Arturo 1906-2001 . . . . .DLB-113	Van Duyn, Mona 1921-2004 . . . . .DLB-5
University of Colorado Special Collections at the University of Colorado at Boulder Y-98	Uspensky, Gleb Ivanovich 1843-1902 . . . . .DLB-277	Tribute to James Dickey Y-97
		Van Dyke, Henry 1852-1933 . . . . .DLB-71; DS-13
Indiana University Press Y-02	Ussher, James 1581-1656 . . . . .DLB-213	Van Dyke, Henry 1928- DLB-33
The University of Iowa Writers' Workshop Golden Jubilee Y-86	Ustinov, Peter 1921-2004 . . . . .DLB-13	Van Dyke, John C. 1856-1932 . . . . .DLB-186
	Uttley, Alison 1884-1976 . . . . .DLB-160	Vane, Sutton 1888-1963 . . . . .DLB-10
University of Missouri Press Y-01	Uz, Johann Peter 1720-1796 . . . . .DLB-97	Van Gieson, Judith 1941- DLB-306
University of South Carolina The G. Ross Roy Scottish Poetry Collection Y-89	**V**	Vanguard Press DLB-46
		van Gulik, Robert Hans 1910-1967 . . . . .DS-17
	Vadianus, Joachim 1484-1551 . . . . .DLB-179	van Itallie, Jean-Claude 1936- DLB-7
Two Hundred Years of Rare Books and Literary Collections at the University of South Carolina Y-00	Vac, Bertrand (Aimé Pelletier) 1914- DLB-88	Van Loan, Charles E. 1876-1919 . . . . .DLB-171
	Vācietis, Ojārs 1933-1983 . . . . .DLB-232	Vann, Robert L. 1879-1940 . . . . .DLB-29
	Vaculík, Ludvík 1926- DLB-232	Van Rensselaer, Mariana Griswold 1851-1934 . . . . .DLB-47
The University of South Carolina Press Y-94	Vaičiulaitis, Antanas 1906-1992 . . . . .DLB-220	
University of Virginia The Book Arts Press at the University of Virginia Y-96	Vaičiūnaite, Judita 1937- DLB-232	Van Rensselaer, Mrs. Schuyler (see Van Rensselaer, Mariana Griswold)
	Vail, Laurence 1891-1968 . . . . .DLB-4	
	Vail, Petr L'vovich 1949- DLB-285	Van Vechten, Carl 1880-1964 . . . . . . .DLB-4, 9, 51
The Electronic Text Center and the Electronic Archive of Early American Fiction at the University of Virginia Library Y-98	Vailland, Roger 1907-1965 . . . . .DLB-83	van Vogt, A. E. 1912-2000 . . . . .DLB-8, 251
	Vaižgantas 1869-1933 . . . . .DLB-220	Varela, Blanca 1926- DLB-290
	Vajda, Ernest 1887-1954 . . . . .DLB-44	Vargas Llosa, Mario 1936- DLB-145; CDWLB-3
	Valdés, Alfonso de circa 1490?-1532 . . . . .DLB-318	
University of Virginia Libraries Y-91	Valdés, Gina 1943- DLB-122	Acceptance Speech for the Ritz Paris Hemingway Award Y-85
University of Wales Press DLB-112	Valdes, Juan de 1508-1541 . . . . .DLB-318	
University Press of Florida Y-00	Valdez, Luis Miguel 1940- DLB-122	Varley, John 1947- Y-81
University Press of Kansas Y-98	Valduga, Patrizia 1953- DLB-128	Varnhagen von Ense, Karl August 1785-1858 . . . . .DLB-90
University Press of Mississippi Y-99	Vale Press DLB-112	
Unnur Benediktsdóttir Bjarklind (see Hulda)	Valente, José Ángel 1929-2000 . . . . .DLB-108	Varnhagen von Ense, Rahel 1771-1833 . . . . .DLB-90
Uno Chiyo 1897-1996 . . . . .DLB-180	Valenzuela, Luisa 1938- . . .DLB-113; CDWLB-3	
Unruh, Fritz von 1885-1970 . . . . .DLB-56, 118	Valera, Diego de 1412-1488 . . . . .DLB-286	Varro 116 B.C.-27 B.C. DLB-211
Unsworth, Barry 1930- DLB-194	Valeri, Diego 1887-1976 . . . . .DLB-128	Vasilenko, Svetlana Vladimirovna 1956- DLB-285
Unt, Mati 1944- DLB-232	Valerius Flaccus fl. circa A.D. 92 . . . . .DLB-211	
The Unterberg Poetry Center of the 92nd Street Y Y-98		Vasiliu, George (see Bacovia, George)
		Vásquez, Richard 1928- DLB-209

Cumulative Index DLB 319

Vásquez Montalbán, Manuel 1939- ... DLB-134
Vassa, Gustavus (see Equiano, Olaudah)
Vassalli, Sebastiano 1941- ... DLB-128, 196
Vaugelas, Claude Favre de 1585-1650 ... DLB-268
Vaughan, Henry 1621-1695 ... DLB-131
Vaughan, Thomas 1621-1666 ... DLB-131
Vaughn, Robert 1592?-1667 ... DLB-213
Vaux, Thomas, Lord 1509-1556 ... DLB-132
Vazov, Ivan 1850-1921 ... DLB-147; CDWLB-4
Véa, Alfredo, Jr. 1950- ... DLB-209
Veblen, Thorstein 1857-1929 ... DLB-246
Vedel, Anders Sørensen 1542-1616 ... DLB-300
Vega, Janine Pommy 1942- ... DLB-16
Veiller, Anthony 1903-1965 ... DLB-44
Velásquez-Trevino, Gloria 1949- ... DLB-122
Veley, Margaret 1843-1887 ... DLB-199
Velleius Paterculus circa 20 B.C.-circa A.D. 30 ... DLB-211
Veloz Maggiolo, Marcio 1936- ... DLB-145
Vel'tman, Aleksandr Fomich 1800-1870 ... DLB-198
Venegas, Daniel ?-? ... DLB-82
Venevitinov, Dmitrii Vladimirovich 1805-1827 ... DLB-205
Verbitskaia, Anastasiia Alekseevna 1861-1928 ... DLB-295
Verde, Cesário 1855-1886 ... DLB-287
Vergil, Polydore circa 1470-1555 ... DLB-132
Veríssimo, Erico 1905-1975 ... DLB-145, 307
Verlaine, Paul 1844-1896 ... DLB-217
Vernacular Translations in the Crowns of Castile and Aragon 1352-1515 ... DLB-286
Verne, Jules 1828-1905 ... DLB-123
Verplanck, Gulian C. 1786-1870 ... DLB-59
Vertinsky, Aleksandr 1889-1957 ... DLB-317
Very, Jones 1813-1880 ... DLB-1, 243; DS-5
Vesaas, Halldis Moren 1907-1995 ... DLB-297
Vesaas, Tarjei 1897-1970 ... DLB-297
Vian, Boris 1920-1959 ... DLB-72
Viazemsky, Petr Andreevich 1792-1878 ... DLB-205
Vicars, Thomas 1591-1638 ... DLB-236
Vicente, Gil 1465-1536/1540? ... DLB-287, 318
Vickers, Roy 1888?-1965 ... DLB-77
Vickery, Sukey 1779-1821 ... DLB-200
Victoria 1819-1901 ... DLB-55
Victoria Press ... DLB-106
La vida de Lazarillo de Tormes ... DLB-318
Vidal, Gore 1925- ... DLB-6, 152; CDALB-7
Vidal, Mary Theresa 1815-1873 ... DLB-230
Vidmer, Richards 1898-1978 ... DLB-241
Viebig, Clara 1860-1952 ... DLB-66
Vieira, António, S. J. (Antonio Vieyra) 1608-1697 ... DLB-307
Viereck, George Sylvester 1884-1962 ... DLB-54
Viereck, Peter 1916- ... DLB-5

Vietnam War (ended 1975) Resources for the Study of Vietnam War Literature ... DLB-9
Viets, Roger 1738-1811 ... DLB-99
Vigil-Piñon, Evangelina 1949- ... DLB-122
Vigneault, Gilles 1928- ... DLB-60
Vigny, Alfred de 1797-1863 ... DLB-119, 192, 217
Vigolo, Giorgio 1894-1983 ... DLB-114
Vik, Bjorg 1935- ... DLB-297
The Viking Press ... DLB-46
Vilde, Eduard 1865-1933 ... DLB-220
Vilinskaia, Mariia Aleksandrovna (see Vovchok, Marko)
Villa, José García 1908-1997 ... DLB-312
Villanueva, Alma Luz 1944- ... DLB-122
Villanueva, Tino 1941- ... DLB-82
Villard, Henry 1835-1900 ... DLB-23
Villard, Oswald Garrison 1872-1949 ... DLB-25, 91
Villarreal, Edit 1944- ... DLB-209
Villarreal, José Antonio 1924- ... DLB-82
Villaseñor, Victor 1940- ... DLB-209
Villedieu, Madame de (Marie-Catherine Desjardins) 1640?-1683 ... DLB-268
Villegas, Antonio de ?-? ... DLB-318
Villegas de Magnón, Leonor 1876-1955 ... DLB-122
Villehardouin, Geoffroi de circa 1150-1215 ... DLB-208
Villemaire, Yolande 1949- ... DLB-60
Villena, Enrique de ca. 1382/84-1432 ... DLB-286
Villena, Luis Antonio de 1951- ... DLB-134
Villiers, George, Second Duke of Buckingham 1628-1687 ... DLB-80
Villiers de l'Isle-Adam, Jean-Marie Mathias Philippe-Auguste, Comte de 1838-1889 ... DLB-123, 192
Villon, François 1431-circa 1463? ... DLB-208
Vine Press ... DLB-112
Viorst, Judith 1931- ... DLB-52
Vipont, Elfrida (Elfrida Vipont Foulds, Charles Vipont) 1902-1992 ... DLB-160
Viramontes, Helena María 1954- ... DLB-122
Virgil 70 B.C.-19 B.C. ... DLB-211; CDWLB-1
Vischer, Friedrich Theodor 1807-1887 ... DLB-133
Vitier, Cintio 1921- ... DLB-283
Vitruvius circa 85 B.C.-circa 15 B.C. ... DLB-211
Vitry, Philippe de 1291-1361 ... DLB-208
Vittorini, Elio 1908-1966 ... DLB-264
Vivanco, Luis Felipe 1907-1975 ... DLB-108
Vives, Juan Luis 1493-1540 ... DLB-318
Vivian, E. Charles (Charles Henry Cannell, Charles Henry Vivian, Jack Mann, Barry Lynd) 1882-1947 ... DLB-255
Viviani, Cesare 1947- ... DLB-128
Vivien, Renée 1877-1909 ... DLB-217
Vizenor, Gerald 1934- ... DLB-175, 227

Vizetelly and Company ... DLB-106
Vladimov, Georgii 1931-2003 ... DLB-302
Voaden, Herman 1903-1991 ... DLB-88
Voß, Johann Heinrich 1751-1826 ... DLB-90
Vogau, Boris Andreevich (see Pil'niak, Boris Andreevich)
Voigt, Ellen Bryant 1943- ... DLB-120
Voinovich, Vladimir Nikolaevich 1932- ... DLB-302
Vojnović, Ivo 1857-1929 ... DLB-147; CDWLB-4
Vold, Jan Erik 1939- ... DLB-297
Volkoff, Vladimir 1932- ... DLB-83
P. F. Volland Company ... DLB-46
Vollbehr, Otto H. F. 1872?-1945 or 1946 ... DLB-187
Vologdin (see Zasodimsky, Pavel Vladimirovich)
Voloshin, Maksimilian Aleksandrovich 1877-1932 ... DLB-295
Volponi, Paolo 1924-1994 ... DLB-177
Voltaire (François-Marie Arouet) 1694-1778 ... DLB-314
"An account of the death of the chevalier de La Barre" ... DLB-314
Candide ... DLB-314
Philosophical Dictionary ... DLB-314
Vonarburg, Élisabeth 1947- ... DLB-251
von der Grün, Max 1926- ... DLB-75
Vonnegut, Kurt 1922- ... DLB-2, 8, 152; Y-80; DS-3; CDALB-6
Tribute to Isaac Asimov ... Y-92
Tribute to Richard Brautigan ... Y-84
Voranc, Prežihov 1893-1950 ... DLB-147
Voronsky, Aleksandr Konstantinovich 1884-1937 ... DLB-272
Vorse, Mary Heaton 1874-1966 ... DLB-303
Vovchok, Marko 1833-1907 ... DLB-238
Voynich, E. L. 1864-1960 ... DLB-197
Vroman, Mary Elizabeth circa 1924-1967 ... DLB-33

W

Wace, Robert ("Maistre") circa 1100-circa 1175 ... DLB-146
Wackenroder, Wilhelm Heinrich 1773-1798 ... DLB-90
Wackernagel, Wilhelm 1806-1869 ... DLB-133
Waddell, Helen 1889-1965 ... DLB-240
Waddington, Miriam 1917-2004 ... DLB-68
Wade, Henry 1887-1969 ... DLB-77
Wagenknecht, Edward 1900-2004 ... DLB-103
Wägner, Elin 1882-1949 ... DLB-259
Wagner, Heinrich Leopold 1747-1779 ... DLB-94
Wagner, Henry R. 1862-1957 ... DLB-140
Wagner, Richard 1813-1883 ... DLB-129
Wagoner, David 1926- ... DLB-5, 256
Wah, Fred 1939- ... DLB-60
Waiblinger, Wilhelm 1804-1830 ... DLB-90

458

Cumulative Index

Wain, John
    1925-1994 ... DLB-15, 27, 139, 155; CDBLB-8
    Tribute to J. B. Priestly Y-84

Wainwright, Jeffrey 1944- DLB-40

Waite, Peirce and Company DLB-49

Wakeman, Stephen H. 1859-1924 .... DLB-187

Wakoski, Diane 1937- DLB-5

Walahfrid Strabo circa 808-849 .... DLB-148

Henry Z. Walck [publishing house] DLB-46

Walcott, Derek
    1930- DLB-117; Y-81, 92; CDWLB-3

    Nobel Lecture 1992: The Antilles:
    Fragments of Epic Memory Y-92

Robert Waldegrave [publishing house] ... DLB-170

Waldis, Burkhard circa 1490-1556? DLB-178

Waldman, Anne 1945- DLB-16

Waldrop, Rosmarie 1935- DLB-169

Walker, Alice 1900-1982 .... DLB-201

Walker, Alice
    1944- DLB-6, 33, 143; CDALB-6

Walker, Annie Louisa (Mrs. Harry Coghill)
    circa 1836-1907 .... DLB-240

Walker, George F. 1947- DLB-60

Walker, John Brisben 1847-1931 .... DLB-79

Walker, Joseph A. 1935- DLB-38

Walker, Kath (see Oodgeroo of the Tribe Noonuccal)

Walker, Margaret 1915-1998 .... DLB-76, 152

Walker, Obadiah 1616-1699 .... DLB-281

Walker, Ted 1934- DLB-40

Walker, Evans and Cogswell Company ... DLB-49

Wall, John F. (see Sarban)

Wallace, Alfred Russel 1823-1913 .... DLB-190

Wallace, Dewitt 1889-1981 .... DLB-137

Wallace, Edgar 1875-1932 .... DLB-70

Wallace, Lew 1827-1905 .... DLB-202

Wallace, Lila Acheson 1889-1984 .... DLB-137

    "A Word of Thanks," From the Initial
    Issue of *Reader's Digest*
    (February 1922) DLB-137

Wallace, Naomi 1960- DLB-249

Wallace Markfield's "Steeplechase" Y-02

Wallace-Crabbe, Chris 1934- DLB-289

Wallant, Edward Lewis
    1926-1962 .... DLB-2, 28, 143, 299

Waller, Edmund 1606-1687 .... DLB-126

Walpole, Horace 1717-1797 ..... DLB-39, 104, 213

    Preface to the First Edition of
    The Castle of Otranto (1764) DLB-39, 178

    Preface to the Second Edition of
    The Castle of Otranto (1765) DLB-39, 178

Walpole, Hugh 1884-1941 .... DLB-34

Walrond, Eric 1898-1966 .... DLB-51

Walser, Martin 1927- DLB-75, 124

Walser, Robert 1878-1956 .... DLB-66

Walsh, Ernest 1895-1926 .... DLB-4, 45

Walsh, Robert 1784-1859 .... DLB-59

Walters, Henry 1848-1931 .... DLB-140

Waltharius circa 825 .... DLB-148

Walther von der Vogelweide
    circa 1170-circa 1230 .... DLB-138

Walton, Izaak
    1593-1683 .... DLB-151, 213; CDBLB-1

Wambaugh, Joseph 1937- DLB-6; Y-83

Wand, Alfred Rudolph 1828-1891 ...... DLB-188

Wandor, Michelene 1940- DLB-310

Waniek, Marilyn Nelson 1946- DLB-120

Wanley, Humphrey 1672-1726 .... DLB-213

War of the Words (and Pictures):
    The Creation of a Graphic Novel Y-02

Warburton, William 1698-1779 .... DLB-104

Ward, Aileen 1919- DLB-111

Ward, Artemus (see Browne, Charles Farrar)

Ward, Arthur Henry Sarsfield (see Rohmer, Sax)

Ward, Douglas Turner 1930- DLB-7, 38

Ward, Mrs. Humphry 1851-1920 .... DLB-18

Ward, James 1843-1925 .... DLB-262

Ward, Lynd 1905-1985 .... DLB-22

Ward, Lock and Company DLB-106

Ward, Nathaniel circa 1578-1652 .... DLB-24

Ward, Theodore 1902-1983 .... DLB-76

Wardle, Ralph 1909-1988 .... DLB-103

Ware, Henry, Jr. 1794-1843 .... DLB-235

Ware, William 1797-1852 .... DLB-1, 235

Warfield, Catherine Ann 1816-1877 ..... DLB-248

Waring, Anna Letitia 1823-1910 .... DLB-240

Frederick Warne and Company [U.K.] DLB-106

Frederick Warne and Company [U.S.] DLB-49

Warner, Anne 1869-1913 .... DLB-202

Warner, Charles Dudley 1829-1900 ..... DLB-64

Warner, Marina 1946- DLB-194

Warner, Rex 1905-1986 .... DLB-15

Warner, Susan 1819-1885 .... DLB-3, 42, 239, 250

Warner, Sylvia Townsend
    1893-1978 .... DLB-34, 139

Warner, William 1558-1609 .... DLB-172

Warner Books DLB-46

Warr, Bertram 1917-1943 .... DLB-88

Warren, John Byrne Leicester
    (see De Tabley, Lord)

Warren, Lella 1899-1982 .... Y-83

Warren, Mercy Otis 1728-1814 ...... DLB-31, 200

Warren, Robert Penn 1905-1989 ..... DLB-2, 48, 152; Y-80, 89; CDALB-6

    Tribute to Katherine Anne Porter Y-80

Warren, Samuel 1807-1877 .... DLB-190

Die Wartburgkrieg circa 1230-circa 1280 ... DLB-138

Warton, Joseph 1722-1800 .... DLB-104, 109

Warton, Thomas 1728-1790 .... DLB-104, 109

Warung, Price (William Astley)
    1855-1911 .... DLB-230

Washington, George 1732-1799 .... DLB-31

Washington, Ned 1901-1976 .... DLB-265

Wassermann, Jakob 1873-1934 .... DLB-66

Wasserstein, Wendy 1950- DLB-228

Wassmo, Herbjorg 1942- DLB-297

Wasson, David Atwood 1823-1887 .... DLB-1, 223

Watanna, Onoto (see Eaton, Winnifred)

Waten, Judah 1911?-1985 .... DLB-289

Waterhouse, Keith 1929- DLB-13, 15

Waterman, Andrew 1940- DLB-40

Waters, Frank 1902-1995 .... DLB-212; Y-86

Waters, Michael 1949- DLB-120

Watkins, Tobias 1780-1855 .... DLB-73

Watkins, Vernon 1906-1967 .... DLB-20

Watmough, David 1926- DLB-53

Watson, Colin 1920-1983 .... DLB-276

Watson, Ian 1943- DLB-261

Watson, James Wreford (see Wreford, James)

Watson, John 1850-1907 .... DLB-156

Watson, Rosamund Marriott
    (Graham R. Tomson) 1860-1911 .... DLB-240

Watson, Sheila 1909-1998 .... DLB-60

Watson, Thomas 1545?-1592 .... DLB-132

Watson, Wilfred 1911-1998 .... DLB-60

W. J. Watt and Company DLB-46

Watten, Barrett 1948- DLB-193

Watterson, Henry 1840-1921 .... DLB-25

Watts, Alan 1915-1973 .... DLB-16

Watts, Isaac 1674-1748 .... DLB-95

Franklin Watts [publishing house] DLB-46

Waugh, Alec 1898-1981 .... DLB-191

Waugh, Auberon 1939-2000 ... DLB-14, 194; Y-00

Waugh, Evelyn 1903-1966
    .... DLB-15, 162, 195; CDBLB-6

Way and Williams DLB-49

Wayman, Tom 1945- DLB-53

Weatherly, Tom 1942- DLB-41

Weaver, Gordon 1937- DLB-130

Weaver, Robert 1921- DLB-88

Webb, Beatrice 1858-1943 .... DLB-190

Webb, Francis 1925-1973 .... DLB-260

Webb, Frank J. fl. 1857 .... DLB-50

Webb, James Watson 1802-1884 .... DLB-43

Webb, Mary 1881-1927 .... DLB-34

Webb, Phyllis 1927- DLB-53

Webb, Sidney 1859-1947 .... DLB-190

Webb, Walter Prescott 1888-1963 .... DLB-17

Webbe, William ?-1591 .... DLB-132

Webber, Charles Wilkins
    1819-1856? DLB-202

Weber, Max 1864-1920 .... DLB-296

Webling, Lucy (Lucy Betty MacRaye)
    1877-1952 .... DLB-240

Webling, Peggy (Arthur Weston)
    1871-1949 .... DLB-240

Webster, Augusta 1837-1894 .... DLB-35, 240

Webster, John
    1579 or 1580-1634? DLB-58; CDBLB-1

    The Melbourne Manuscript Y-86

Webster, Noah
    1758-1843 .... DLB-1, 37, 42, 43, 73, 243

459

Cumulative Index

Webster, Paul Francis 1907-1984 .... DLB-265
Charles L. Webster and Company....... DLB-49
Weckherlin, Georg Rodolf 1584-1653 ... DLB-164
Wedekind, Frank
 1864-1918........... DLB-118; CDWLB-2
Weeks, Edward Augustus, Jr.
 1898-1989 .... DLB-137
Weeks, Stephen B. 1865-1918 .... DLB-187
Weems, Mason Locke 1759-1825...DLB-30, 37, 42
Weerth, Georg 1822-1856 .... DLB-129
Weidenfeld and Nicolson............ DLB-112
Weidman, Jerome 1913-1998 .... DLB-28
Weigl, Bruce 1949- DLB-120
Weil, Jiří 1900-1959 .... DLB-299
Weinbaum, Stanley Grauman
 1902-1935 .... DLB-8
Weiner, Andrew 1949- DLB-251
Weintraub, Stanley 1929- DLB-111; Y82
Weise, Christian 1642-1708 .... DLB-168
Weisenborn, Gunther 1902-1969.... DLB-69, 124
Weiss, John 1818-1879 .... DLB-1, 243
Weiss, Paul 1901-2002 ....DLB-279
Weiss, Peter 1916-1982 .... DLB-69, 124
Weiss, Theodore 1916-2003............. DLB-5
Weiß, Ernst 1882-1940................ DLB-81
Weiße, Christian Felix 1726-1804........ DLB-97
Weitling, Wilhelm 1808-1871......... DLB-129
Welch, Denton 1915-1948 .... DLB-319
Welch, James 1940- DLB-175, 256
Welch, Lew 1926-1971? DLB-16
Weldon, Fay 1931- DLB-14, 194, 319; CDBLB-8
Wellek, René 1903-1995 .... DLB-63
Wells, Carolyn 1862-1942 .... DLB-11
Wells, Charles Jeremiah
 circa 1800-1879.................... DLB-32
Wells, Gabriel 1862-1946............. DLB-140
Wells, H. G. 1866-1946
 ....DLB-34, 70, 156, 178; CDBLB-6
 H. G. Wells Society Y-98
 Preface to *The Scientific Romances of
  H. G. Wells* (1933) DLB-178
Wells, Helena 1758?-1824 .... DLB-200
Wells, Rebecca 1952- DLB-292
Wells, Robert 1947- DLB-40
Wells-Barnett, Ida B. 1862-1931..... DLB-23, 221
Welsh, Irvine 1958- DLB-271
Welty, Eudora 1909-2001 ...... DLB-2, 102, 143;
 Y-87, 01; DS-12; CDALB-1
 Eudora Welty: Eye of the Storyteller..... Y-87
 Eudora Welty Newsletter................. Y-99
 Eudora Welty's Funeral Y-01
 Eudora Welty's Ninetieth Birthday Y-99
 Eudora Welty Remembered in
  Two Exhibits................. Y-02
Wendell, Barrett 1855-1921 .... DLB-71
Wentworth, Patricia 1878-1961 .... DLB-77

Wentworth, William Charles
 1790-1872.................... DLB-230
Werder, Diederich von dem 1584-1657 .. DLB-164
Werfel, Franz 1890-1945 .... DLB-81, 124
Werner, Zacharias 1768-1823........... DLB-94
The Werner Company................ DLB-49
Wersba, Barbara 1932- DLB-52
Wescott, Glenway
 1901-1987............DLB-4, 9, 102; DS-15
Wesker, Arnold
 1932- DLB-13, 310, 319; CDBLB-8
Wesley, Charles 1707-1788 .... DLB-95
Wesley, John 1703-1791 .... DLB-104
Wesley, Mary 1912-2002 .... DLB-231
Wesley, Richard 1945- DLB-38
Wessel, Johan Herman 1742-1785 ..... DLB-300
A. Wessels and Company DLB-46
Wessobrunner Gebet circa 787-815 .... DLB-148
West, Anthony 1914-1988 .... DLB-15
 Tribute to Liam O'Flaherty Y-84
West, Cheryl L. 1957- DLB-266
West, Cornel 1953- DLB-246
West, Dorothy 1907-1998............. DLB-76
West, Jessamyn 1902-1984..........DLB-6; Y-84
West, Mae 1892-1980................. DLB-44
West, Michael Lee 1953- DLB-292
West, Michelle Sagara 1963- DLB-251
West, Morris 1916-1999............. DLB-289
West, Nathanael
 1903-1940 .... DLB-4, 9, 28; CDALB-5
West, Paul 1930- DLB-14
West, Rebecca 1892-1983..........DLB-36; Y-83
West, Richard 1941- DLB-185
West and Johnson DLB-49
Westcott, Edward Noyes 1846-1898 .... DLB-202
The Western Literature Association......... Y-99
The Western Messenger
 1835-1841 .... DLB-1; DLB-223
Western Publishing Company DLB-46
Western Writers of America Y-99
The Westminster Review 1824-1914 .... DLB-110
Weston, Arthur (see Webling, Peggy)
Weston, Elizabeth Jane circa 1582-1612...DLB-172
Wetherald, Agnes Ethelwyn 1857-1940 ... DLB-99
Wetherell, Elizabeth (see Warner, Susan)
Wetherell, W. D. 1948- DLB-234
Wetzel, Friedrich Gottlob 1779-1819 ..... DLB-90
Weyman, Stanley J. 1855-1928 .... DLB-141, 156
Wezel, Johann Karl 1747-1819 .... DLB-94
Whalen, Philip 1923-2002 .... DLB-16
Whalley, George 1915-1983............ DLB-88
Wharton, Edith 1862-1937.........DLB-4, 9, 12,
 78, 189; DS-13; CDALB-3
Wharton, William 1925- Y-80
Whately, Mary Louisa 1824-1889 ...... DLB-166
Whately, Richard 1787-1863........... DLB-190

Elements of Rhetoric (1828;
 revised, 1846) [excerpt] DLB-57
Wheatley, Dennis 1897-1977 ....DLB-77, 255
Wheatley, Phillis
 circa 1754-1784....... DLB-31, 50; CDALB-2
Wheeler, Anna Doyle 1785-1848? DLB-158
Wheeler, Charles Stearns 1816-1843 .. DLB-1, 223
Wheeler, Monroe 1900-1988 .... DLB-4
Wheelock, John Hall 1886-1978......... DLB-45
 From John Hall Wheelock's
  Oral Memoir................... Y-01
Wheelwright, J. B. 1897-1940........... DLB-45
Wheelwright, John circa 1592-1679 ...... DLB-24
Whetstone, George 1550-1587......... DLB-136
Whetstone, Colonel Pete (see Noland, C. F. M.)
Whewell, William 1794-1866 .... DLB-262
Whichcote, Benjamin 1609?-1683 ...... DLB-252
Whicher, Stephen E. 1915-1961 .... DLB-111
Whipple, Edwin Percy 1819-1886 ..... DLB-1, 64
Whitaker, Alexander 1585-1617........ DLB-24
Whitaker, Daniel K. 1801-1881 .... DLB-73
Whitcher, Frances Miriam
 1812-1852 .... DLB-11, 202
White, Andrew 1579-1656 .... DLB-24
White, Andrew Dickson 1832-1918...... DLB-47
White, E. B. 1899-1985 ... DLB-11, 22; CDALB-7
White, Edgar B. 1947- DLB-38
White, Edmund 1940- DLB-227
White, Ethel Lina 1887-1944 .... DLB-77
White, Hayden V. 1928- DLB-246
White, Henry Kirke 1785-1806 .... DLB-96
White, Horace 1834-1916 .... DLB-23
White, James 1928-1999............. DLB-261
White, Patrick 1912-1990............. DLB-260
White, Phyllis Dorothy James (see James, P. D.)
White, Richard Grant 1821-1885........ DLB-64
White, T. H. 1906-1964.......... DLB-160, 255
White, Walter 1893-1955............. DLB-51
Wilcox, James 1949- DLB-292
William White and Company DLB-49
White, William Allen 1868-1944 ...... DLB-9, 25
White, William Anthony Parker
 (see Boucher, Anthony)
White, William Hale (see Rutherford, Mark)
Whitchurch, Victor L. 1868-1933....... DLB-70
Whitehead, Alfred North
 1861-1947 ....DLB-100, 262
Whitehead, E. A. (Ted Whitehead)
 1933- DLB-310
Whitehead, James 1936- Y-81
Whitehead, William 1715-1785...... DLB-84, 109
Whitfield, James Monroe 1822-1871 ..... DLB-50
Whitfield, Raoul 1898-1945 .... DLB-226
Whitgift, John circa 1533-1604 .... DLB-132
Whiting, John 1917-1963 .... DLB-13
Whiting, Samuel 1597-1679 .... DLB-24
Whitlock, Brand 1869-1934............ DLB-12

460

Whitman, Albery Allson 1851-1901 ......DLB-50
Whitman, Alden 1913-1990................ Y-91
Whitman, Sarah Helen (Power)
 1803-1878 ....DLB-1, 243
Whitman, Walt
 1819-1892 ....DLB-3, 64, 224, 250; CDALB-2
Albert Whitman and Company..........DLB-46
Whitman Publishing Company..........DLB-46
Whitney, Geoffrey
 1548 or 1552?-1601................DLB-136
Whitney, Isabella fl. 1566-1573 ....DLB-136
Whitney, John Hay 1904-1982 ....DLB-127
Whittemore, Reed 1919-1995 ....DLB-5
Whittier, John Greenleaf
 1807-1892 ....DLB-1, 243; CDALB-2
Whittlesey House DLB-46
Wickham, Anna (Edith Alice Mary Harper)
 1884-1947 ....DLB-240
Wickram, Georg circa 1505-circa 1561 ...DLB-179
Wicomb, Zoë 1948- DLB-225
Wideman, John Edgar 1941- DLB-33, 143
Widener, Harry Elkins 1885-1912........DLB-140
Wiebe, Rudy 1934- DLB-60
Wiechert, Ernst 1887-1950...............DLB-56
Wied, Gustav 1858-1914................DLB-300
Wied, Martina 1882-1957 ....DLB-85
Wiehe, Evelyn May Clowes (see Mordaunt, Elinor)
Wieland, Christoph Martin 1733-1813 ....DLB-97
Wienbarg, Ludolf 1802-1872...........DLB-133
Wieners, John 1934- DLB-16
Wier, Ester 1910-2000...................DLB-52
Wiesel, Elie
 1928- DLB-83, 299; Y-86, 87; CDALB-7
 Nobel Lecture 1986: Hope, Despair and
  Memory Y-86
Wiggin, Kate Douglas 1856-1923 ....DLB-42
Wigglesworth, Michael 1631-1705.........DLB-24
Wilberforce, William 1759-1833 ....DLB-158
Wilbrandt, Adolf 1837-1911.............DLB-129
Wilbur, Richard 1921- ...DLB-5, 169; CDALB-7
 Tribute to Robert Penn Warren Y-89
Wilcox, James 1949- DLB-292
Wild, Peter 1940- DLB-5
Wilde, Lady Jane Francesca Elgee
 1821?-1896 ....DLB-199
Wilde, Oscar 1854-1900
 . DLB-10, 19, 34, 57, 141, 156, 190; CDBLB-5
 "The Critic as Artist" (1891).........DLB-57
 "The Decay of Lying" (1889) DLB-18
 "The English Renaissance of
  Art" (1908) DLB-35
 "L'Envoi" (1882)..................DLB-35
 Oscar Wilde Conference at Hofstra
  University..................... Y-00
Wilde, Richard Henry 1789-1847 ......DLB-3, 59
W. A. Wilde Company DLB-49
Wilder, Billy 1906-2002..................DLB-26
Wilder, Laura Ingalls 1867-1957 .....DLB-22, 256
Wilder, Thornton
 1897-1975........DLB-4, 7, 9, 228; CDALB-7
 Thornton Wilder Centenary at Yale..... Y-97

Wildgans, Anton 1881-1932 ....DLB-118
Wiley, Bell Irvin 1906-1980.............DLB-17
John Wiley and Sons DLB-49
Wilhelm, Kate 1928- DLB-8
Wilkes, Charles 1798-1877..............DLB-183
Wilkes, George 1817-1885 ....DLB-79
Wilkins, John 1614-1672 ....DLB-236
Wilkinson, Anne 1910-1961 ....DLB-88
Wilkinson, Christopher 1941- DLB-310
Wilkinson, Eliza Yonge
 1757-circa 1813 ....DLB-200
Wilkinson, Sylvia 1940- Y-86
Wilkinson, William Cleaver 1833-1920 ...DLB-71
Willard, Barbara 1909-1994 ....DLB-161
Willard, Emma 1787-1870 ....DLB-239
Willard, Frances E. 1839-1898 ....DLB-221
Willard, Nancy 1936- DLB-5, 52
Willard, Samuel 1640-1707 ....DLB-24
L. Willard [publishing house] DLB-49
Willeford, Charles 1919-1988 ....DLB-226
William of Auvergne 1190-1249 ....DLB-115
William of Conches
 circa 1090-circa 1154..............DLB-115
William of Ockham circa 1285-1347 .....DLB-115
William of Sherwood
 1200/1205-1266/1271 ....DLB-115
The William Charvat American Fiction
 Collection at the Ohio State
 University Libraries Y-92
Williams, Ben Ames 1889-1953.........DLB-102
Williams, C. K. 1936- DLB-5
Williams, Chancellor 1905-1992 ....DLB-76
Williams, Charles 1886-1945... DLB-100, 153, 255
Williams, Denis 1923-1998 ....DLB-117
Williams, Emlyn 1905-1987..........DLB-10, 77
Williams, Garth 1912-1996 ....DLB-22
Williams, George Washington
 1849-1891 ....DLB-47
Williams, Heathcote 1941- DLB-13
Williams, Helen Maria 1761-1827 ......DLB-158
Williams, Hugo 1942- DLB-40
Williams, Isaac 1802-1865..............DLB-32
Williams, Joan 1928- DLB-6
Williams, Joe 1889-1972 ....DLB-241
Williams, John A. 1925- DLB-2, 33
Williams, John E. 1922-1994 ....DLB-6
Williams, Jonathan 1929- DLB-5
Williams, Miller 1930- DLB-105
Williams, Nigel 1948- DLB-231
Williams, Raymond
 1921-1988 ....DLB-14, 231, 242
Williams, Roger circa 1603-1683 ....DLB-24
Williams, Rowland 1817-1870 ....DLB-184
Williams, Samm-Art 1946- DLB-38
Williams, Sherley Anne 1944-1999 ......DLB-41
Williams, T. Harry 1909-1979 ....DLB-17
Williams, Tennessee
 1911-1983 .....DLB-7; Y-83; DS-4; CDALB-1
Williams, Terry Tempest 1955- ... DLB-206, 275

Williams, Ursula Moray 1911- DLB-160
Williams, Valentine 1883-1946 ....DLB-77
Williams, William Appleman 1921-1990... DLB-17
Williams, William Carlos
 1883-1963 ......DLB-4, 16, 54, 86; CDALB-4
 The William Carlos Williams Society.... Y-99
Williams, Wirt 1921-1986................DLB-6
A. Williams and Company DLB-49
Williams Brothers DLB-49
Williamson, David 1942- DLB-289
Williamson, Henry 1895-1977..........DLB-191
 The Henry Williamson Society Y-98
Williamson, Jack 1908- DLB-8
Willingham, Calder Baynard, Jr.
 1922-1995 ....DLB-2, 44
Williram of Ebersberg circa 1020-1085 ...DLB-148
Willis, John circa 1572-1625 ....DLB-281
Willis, Nathaniel Parker 1806-1867
 ....DLB-3, 59, 73, 74, 183, 250; DS-13
Willis, Ted 1918-1992 ....DLB-310
Willkomm, Ernst 1810-1886 ....DLB-133
Wills, Garry 1934- DLB-246
 Tribute to Kenneth Dale McCormick..... Y-97
Willson, Meredith 1902-1984 ....DLB-265
Willumsen, Dorrit 1940- DLB-214
Wilmer, Clive 1945- DLB-40
Wilson, A. N. 1950- DLB-14, 155, 194
Wilson, Angus 1913-1991 ......DLB-15, 139, 155
Wilson, Arthur 1595-1652 ....DLB-58
Wilson, August 1945- DLB-228
Wilson, Augusta Jane Evans 1835-1909 ...DLB-42
Wilson, Colin 1931- DLB-14, 194
 Tribute to J. B. Priestly Y-84
Wilson, Edmund 1895-1972 ....DLB-63
Wilson, Ethel 1888-1980 ....DLB-68
Wilson, F. P. 1889-1963 ....DLB-201
Wilson, Harriet E.
 1827/1828?-1863?.........DLB-50, 239, 243
Wilson, Harry Leon 1867-1939..........DLB-9
Wilson, John 1588-1667 ....DLB-24
Wilson, John 1785-1854................DLB-110
Wilson, John Anthony Burgess
 (see Burgess, Anthony)
Wilson, John Dover 1881-1969.........DLB-201
Wilson, Lanford 1937- DLB-7
Wilson, Margaret 1882-1973 ....DLB-9
Wilson, Michael 1914-1978 ....DLB-44
Wilson, Mona 1872-1954 ....DLB-149
Wilson, Robert Charles 1953- DLB-251
Wilson, Robert McLiam 1964- DLB-267
Wilson, Robley 1930- DLB-218
Wilson, Romer 1891-1930...............DLB-191
Wilson, Thomas 1524-1581 ....DLB-132, 236
Wilson, Woodrow 1856-1924............DLB-47
Effingham Wilson [publishing house] DLB-154
Wimpfeling, Jakob 1450-1528 ....DLB-179
Wimsatt, William K., Jr. 1907-1975 ....DLB-63

Cumulative Index

Winchell, Walter 1897-1972 . . . . DLB-29
J. Winchester [publishing house] DLB-49
Winckelmann, Johann Joachim
   1717-1768 . . . . DLB-97
Winckler, Paul 1630-1686 . . . . DLB-164
Wind, Herbert Warren 1916-2005 . . . . DLB-171
John Windet [publishing house] DLB-170
Windham, Donald 1920- DLB-6
Wing, Donald Goddard 1904-1972 . . . . . DLB-187
Wing, John M. 1844-1917 . . . . DLB-187
Allan Wingate [publishing house] DLB-112
Winnemucca, Sarah 1844-1921 . . . . DLB-175
Winnifrith, Tom 1938- DLB-155
Winsloe, Christa 1888-1944 . . . . DLB-124
Winslow, Anna Green 1759-1780 . . . . DLB-200
Winsor, Justin 1831-1897 . . . . DLB-47
John C. Winston Company DLB-49
Winters, Yvor 1900-1968 . . . . DLB-48
Winterson, Jeanette 1959- DLB-207, 261
Winther, Christian 1796-1876 . . . . DLB-300
Winthrop, John 1588-1649 . . . . DLB-24, 30
Winthrop, John, Jr. 1606-1676 . . . . DLB-24
Winthrop, Margaret Tyndal
   1591-1647 . . . . DLB-200
Winthrop, Theodore
   1828-1861 . . . . DLB-202
Wirt, William 1772-1834 . . . . DLB-37
Wise, John 1652-1725 . . . . DLB-24
Wise, Thomas James 1859-1937 . . . . DLB-184
Wiseman, Adele 1928-1992 . . . . DLB-88
Wishart and Company DLB-112
Wisner, George 1812-1849 . . . . DLB-43
Wister, Owen 1860-1938 . . . . DLB-9, 78, 186
Wister, Sarah 1761-1804 . . . . DLB-200
Wither, George 1588-1667 . . . . DLB-121
Witherspoon, John 1723-1794 . . . . DLB-31
   The Works of the Rev. John Witherspoon
   (1800-1801) [excerpts] DLB-31
Withrow, William Henry 1839-1908 . . . . . DLB-99
Witkacy (see Witkiewicz, Stanisław Ignacy)
Witkiewicz, Stanisław Ignacy
   1885-1939 . . . . DLB-215; CDWLB-4
Wittenwiler, Heinrich before 1387-
   circa 1414? DLB-179
Wittgenstein, Ludwig 1889-1951 . . . . DLB-262
Wittig, Monique 1935- DLB-83
Wodehouse, P. G.
   1881-1975 . . . . DLB-34, 162; CDBLB-6
   Worldwide Wodehouse Societies Y-98
Wohmann, Gabriele 1932- DLB-75
Woiwode, Larry 1941- DLB-6
   Tribute to John Gardner Y-82
Wolcot, John 1738-1819 . . . . DLB-109
Wolcott, Roger 1679-1767 . . . . DLB-24
Wolf, Christa 1929- DLB-75; CDWLB-2
Wolf, Friedrich 1888-1953 . . . . DLB-124

Wolfe, Gene 1931- DLB-8
Wolfe, Thomas 1900-1938 . . . .
   DLB-9, 102, 229; Y-85; DS-2, DS-16; CDALB-5
   "All the Faults of Youth and Inexperience":
     A Reader's Report on
     Thomas Wolfe's *O Lost* Y-01
   Emendations for *Look Homeward, Angel*. . . . Y-00
   Eugene Gant's Projected Works Y-01
   Fire at the Old Kentucky Home
     [Thomas Wolfe Memorial] Y-98
   Thomas Wolfe Centennial
     Celebration in Asheville Y-00
   The Thomas Wolfe Collection at
     the University of North Carolina
     at Chapel Hill Y-97
   The Thomas Wolfe Society Y-97, 99
Wolfe, Tom 1931- DLB-152, 185
John Wolfe [publishing house] DLB-170
Reyner (Reginald) Wolfe
   [publishing house] DLB-170
Wolfenstein, Martha 1869-1906 . . . . DLB-221
Wolff, David (see Maddow, Ben)
Wolff, Egon 1926- DLB-305
Wolff, Helen 1906-1994 . . . . Y-94
Wolff, Tobias 1945- DLB-130
   Tribute to Michael M. Rea Y-97
   Tribute to Raymond Carver Y-88
Wolfram von Eschenbach
   circa 1170-after 1220 . . . DLB-138; CDWLB-2
   Wolfram von Eschenbach's *Parzival*:
     Prologue and Book 3 . . . . DLB-138
Wolker, Jiří 1900-1924 . . . . DLB-215
Wollstonecraft, Mary 1759-1797
   . . . . DLB-39, 104, 158, 252; CDBLB-3
Women
   Women's Work, Women's Sphere:
     Selected Comments from Women
     Writers DLB-200
Women Writers in Sixteenth-Century
   Spain DLB-318
Wondratschek, Wolf 1943- DLB-75
Wong, Elizabeth 1958- DLB-266
Wong, Nellie 1934- DLB-312
Wong, Shawn 1949- DLB-312
Wood, Anthony à 1632-1695 . . . . DLB-213
Wood, Benjamin 1820-1900 . . . . DLB-23
Wood, Charles 1932-1980 . . . . DLB-13
   The Charles Wood Affair:
     A Playwright Revived Y-83
Wood, Mrs. Henry 1814-1887 . . . . DLB-18
Wood, Joanna E. 1867-1927 . . . . DLB-92
Wood, Sally Sayward Barrell Keating
   1759-1855 . . . . DLB-200
Wood, William fl. seventeenth century . . . DLB-24
Samuel Wood [publishing house] DLB-49
Woodberry, George Edward
   1855-1930 . . . . DLB-71, 103
Woodbridge, Benjamin 1622-1684 . . . . . . DLB-24
Woodbridge, Frederick J. E. 1867-1940 . . . DLB-270
Woodcock, George 1912-1995 . . . . DLB-88
Woodhull, Victoria C. 1838-1927 . . . . DLB-79

Woodmason, Charles circa 1720-? DLB-31
Woodress, James Leslie, Jr. 1916- DLB-111
Woods, Margaret L. 1855-1945 . . . . DLB-240
Woodson, Carter G. 1875-1950 . . . . DLB-17
Woodward, C. Vann 1908-1999 . . . . DLB-17
Woodward, Stanley 1895-1965 . . . . DLB-171
Woodworth, Samuel 1785-1842 . . . . DLB-250
Wooler, Thomas 1785 or 1786-1853 . . . . DLB-158
Woolf, David (see Maddow, Ben)
Woolf, Douglas 1922-1992 . . . . DLB-244
Woolf, Leonard 1880-1969 . . . . . . DLB-100; DS-10
Woolf, Virginia 1882-1941
   . . . . DLB-36, 100, 162; DS-10; CDBLB-6
   "The New Biography," *New York Herald
   Tribune,* 30 October 1927 . . . . DLB-149
Woollcott, Alexander 1887-1943 . . . . DLB-29
Woolman, John 1720-1772 . . . . DLB-31
Woolner, Thomas 1825-1892 . . . . DLB-35
Woolrich, Cornell 1903-1968 . . . . DLB-226
Woolsey, Sarah Chauncy 1835-1905 . . . . . DLB-42
Woolson, Constance Fenimore
   1840-1894 . . . . DLB-12, 74, 189, 221
Worcester, Joseph Emerson
   1784-1865 . . . . DLB-1, 235
Wynkyn de Worde [publishing house] . . . DLB-170
Wordsworth, Christopher 1807-1885 . . . . DLB-166
Wordsworth, Dorothy 1771-1855 . . . . DLB-107
Wordsworth, Elizabeth
   1840-1932 . . . . DLB-98
Wordsworth, William
   1770-1850 . . . . DLB-93, 107; CDBLB-3
Workman, Fanny Bullock
   1859-1925 . . . . DLB-189
World Literature Today: A Journal for the
   New Millennium Y-01
World Publishing Company DLB-46
World War I (1914-1918) DS-18
   The Great War Exhibit and Symposium
     at the University of South Carolina . . Y-97
   The Liddle Collection and First World
     War Research Y-97
   Other British Poets Who Fell
     in the Great War DLB-216
   The Seventy-Fifth Anniversary of
     the Armistice: The Wilfred Owen
     Centenary and the Great War Exhibit
     at the University of Virginia Y-93
World War II (1939–1945)
   Literary Effects of World War II DLB-15
   World War II Writers Symposium
     at the University of South Carolina,
     12–14 April 1995 . . . . Y-95
   WW2 HMSO Paperbacks Society Y-98
R. Worthington and Company DLB-49
Wotton, Sir Henry 1568-1639 . . . . DLB-121
Wouk, Herman 1915- Y-82; CDALB-7
   Tribute to James Dickey Y-97
Wreford, James 1915-1990 . . . . DLB-88
Wren, Sir Christopher 1632-1723 . . . . DLB-213
Wren, Percival Christopher 1885-1941 . . . DLB-153
Wrenn, John Henry 1841-1911 . . . . DLB-140

Wright, C. D. 1949- ... DLB-120	Yates, J. Michael 1938- ... DLB-60	Zech, Paul 1881-1946 ... DLB-56
Wright, Charles 1935- ... DLB-165; Y-82	Yates, Richard 1926-1992 ... DLB-2, 234; Y-81, 92	Zeidner, Lisa 1955- ... DLB-120
Wright, Charles Stevenson 1932- ... DLB-33	Yau, John 1950- ... DLB-234, 312	Zeidonis, Imants 1933- ... DLB-232
Wright, Chauncey 1830-1875 ... DLB-270	Yavorov, Peyo 1878-1914 ... DLB-147	Zeimi (Kanze Motokiyo) 1363-1443 ... DLB-203
Wright, Frances 1795-1852 ... DLB-73	Yearsley, Ann 1753-1806 ... DLB-109	Zelazny, Roger 1937-1995 ... DLB-8
Wright, Harold Bell 1872-1944 ... DLB-9	Yeats, William Butler 1865-1939 ... DLB-10, 19, 98, 156; CDBLB-5	Zenger, John Peter 1697-1746 ... DLB-24, 43
Wright, James 1927-1980 ... DLB-5, 169; CDALB-7	The W. B. Yeats Society of N.Y. ... Y-99	Zepheria ... DLB-172
Wright, Jay 1935- ... DLB-41	Yellen, Jack 1892-1991 ... DLB-265	Zernova, Ruf' 1919-2004 ... DLB-317
Wright, Judith 1915-2000 ... DLB-260	Yep, Laurence 1948- ... DLB-52, 312	Zesen, Philipp von 1619-1689 ... DLB-164
Wright, Louis B. 1899-1984 ... DLB-17	Yerby, Frank 1916-1991 ... DLB-76	Zhadovskaia, Iuliia Valerianovna 1824-1883 ... DLB-277
Wright, Richard 1908-1960 ... DLB-76, 102; DS-2; CDALB-5	Yezierska, Anzia 1880-1970 ... DLB-28, 221	Zhukova, Mar'ia Semenovna 1805-1855 ... DLB-277
Wright, Richard B. 1937- ... DLB-53	Yolen, Jane 1939- ... DLB-52	Zhukovsky, Vasilii Andreevich 1783-1852 ... DLB-205
Wright, S. Fowler 1874-1965 ... DLB-255	Yonge, Charlotte Mary 1823-1901 ... DLB-18, 163	Zhvanetsky, Mikhail Mikhailovich 1934- ... DLB-285
Wright, Sarah Elizabeth 1928- ... DLB-33	The Charlotte M. Yonge Fellowship ... Y-98	G. B. Zieber and Company ... DLB-49
Wright, T. H. "Style" (1877) [excerpt] ... DLB-57	The York Cycle circa 1376-circa 1569 ... DLB-146	Ziedonis, Imants 1933- ... CDWLB-4
Wright, Willard Huntington (S. S. Van Dine) 1887-1939 ... DLB-306; DS-16	A Yorkshire Tragedy ... DLB-58	Zieroth, Dale 1946- ... DLB-60
Wrightson, Patricia 1921- ... DLB-289	Thomas Yoseloff [publishing house] ... DLB-46	Zigler und Kliphausen, Heinrich Anshelm von 1663-1697 ... DLB-168
Wrigley, Robert 1951- ... DLB-256	Youd, Sam (see Christopher, John)	Zil'ber, Veniamin Aleksandrovich (see Kaverin, Veniamin Aleksandrovich)
Writers' Forum ... Y-85	Young, A. S. "Doc" 1919-1996 ... DLB-241	Zimmer, Paul 1934- ... DLB-5
Writing A Writing Life ... Y-02	Young, Al 1939- ... DLB-33	Zinberg, Len (see Lacy, Ed)
On Learning to Write ... Y-88	Young, Arthur 1741-1820 ... DLB-158	Zincgref, Julius Wilhelm 1591-1635 ... DLB-164
The Profession of Authorship: Scribblers for Bread ... Y-89	Young, Dick 1917 or 1918-1987 ... DLB-171	Zindel, Paul 1936- ... DLB-7, 52; CDALB-7
A Writer Talking: A Collage ... Y-00	Young, Edward 1683-1765 ... DLB-95	Zinnes, Harriet 1919- ... DLB-193
Wroth, Lawrence C. 1884-1970 ... DLB-187	Young, Frank A. "Fay" 1884-1957 ... DLB-241	Zinov'ev, Aleksandr Aleksandrovich 1922- ... DLB-302
Wroth, Lady Mary 1587-1653 ... DLB-121	Young, Francis Brett 1884-1954 ... DLB-191	Zinov'eva-Annibal, Lidiia Dmitrievna 1865 or 1866-1907 ... DLB-295
Wurlitzer, Rudolph 1937- ... DLB-173	Young, Gavin 1928- ... DLB-204	Zinzendorf, Nikolaus Ludwig von 1700-1760 ... DLB-168
Wyatt, Sir Thomas circa 1503-1542 ... DLB-132	Young, Stark 1881-1963 ... DLB-9, 102; DS-16	Zitkala-Ša 1876-1938 ... DLB-175
Wycherley, William 1641-1715 ... DLB-80; CDBLB-2	Young, Waldeman 1880-1938 ... DLB-26	Zīverts, Mārtiņš 1903-1990 ... DLB-220
Wyclif, John circa 1335-1384 ... DLB-146	William Young [publishing house] ... DLB-49	Zlatovratsky, Nikolai Nikolaevich 1845-1911 ... DLB-238
Wyeth, N. C. 1882-1945 ... DLB-188; DS-16	Young Bear, Ray A. 1950- ... DLB-175	Zola, Emile 1840-1902 ... DLB-123
Wyle, Niklas von circa 1415-1479 ... DLB-179	Yourcenar, Marguerite 1903-1987 ... DLB-72; Y-88	Zolla, Elémire 1926- ... DLB-196
Wylie, Elinor 1885-1928 ... DLB-9, 45	Yovkov, Yordan 1880-1937 ... DLB-147; CDWLB-4	Zolotow, Charlotte 1915- ... DLB-52
Wylie, Philip 1902-1971 ... DLB-9	Yushkevich, Semen 1868-1927 ... DLB-317	Zoshchenko, Mikhail Mikhailovich 1895-1958 ... DLB-272
Wyllie, John Cook 1908-1968 ... DLB-140	**Z**	Zschokke, Heinrich 1771-1848 ... DLB-94
Wyman, Lillie Buffum Chace 1847-1929 ... DLB-202	Zachariä, Friedrich Wilhelm 1726-1777 ... DLB-97	Zubly, John Joachim 1724-1781 ... DLB-31
Wymark, Olwen 1934- ... DLB-233	Zagajewski, Adam 1945- ... DLB-232	Zu-Bolton, Ahmos, II 1936- ... DLB-41
Wynd, Oswald Morris (see Black, Gavin)	Zagoskin, Mikhail Nikolaevich 1789-1852 ... DLB-198	Zuckmayer, Carl 1896-1977 ... DLB-56, 124
Wyndham, John (John Wyndham Parkes Lucas Beynon Harris) 1903-1969 ... DLB-255	Zaitsev, Boris 1881-1972 ... DLB-317	Zukofsky, Louis 1904-1978 ... DLB-5, 165
Wynne-Tyson, Esmé 1898-1972 ... DLB-191	Zajc, Dane 1929- ... DLB-181	Zupan, Vitomil 1914-1987 ... DLB-181
X	Zālīte, Māra 1952- ... DLB-232	Župančič, Oton 1878-1949 ... DLB-147; CDWLB-4
Xenophon circa 430 B.C.-circa 356 B.C. ... DLB-176	Zalygin, Sergei Pavlovich 1913-2000 ... DLB-302	zur Mühlen, Hermynia 1883-1951 ... DLB-56
Y	Zamiatin, Evgenii Ivanovich 1884-1937 ... DLB-272	Zweig, Arnold 1887-1968 ... DLB-66
Yamamoto, Hisaye 1921- ... DLB-312	Zamora, Bernice 1938- ... DLB-82	Zweig, Stefan 1881-1942 ... DLB-81, 118
Yamanaka, Lois-Ann 1961- ... DLB-312	Zamudio, Adela (Soledad) 1854-1928 ... DLB-283	Zwinger, Ann 1925- ... DLB-275
Yamashita, Karen Tei 1951- ... DLB-312	Zand, Herbert 1923-1970 ... DLB-85	Zwingli, Huldrych 1484-1531 ... DLB-179
Yamauchi, Wakako 1924- ... DLB-312	Zangwill, Israel 1864-1926 ... DLB-10, 135, 197	**Ø**
Yasuoka Shōtarō 1920- ... DLB-182	Zanzotto, Andrea 1921- ... DLB-128	Øverland, Arnulf 1889-1968 ... DLB-297
Yates, Dornford 1885-1960 ... DLB-77, 153	Zapata Olivella, Manuel 1920- ... DLB-113	
	Zapoev, Timur Iur'evich (see Kibirov, Timur Iur'evich)	
	Zasodimsky, Pavel Vladimirovich 1843-1912 ... DLB-238	
	Zebra Books ... DLB-46	
	Zebrowski, George 1945- ... DLB-8	

ISBN 0-7876-8137-7

PR
829
.B67

2006